MICROSOFT® OFFICE

Word 2003

Comprehensive Concepts
and Techniques

D1309998

Gary B. Shelly
Thomas J. Cashman
Misty E. Vermaat

THOMSON
COURSE TECHNOLOGY

THOMSON COURSE TECHNOLOGY
25 THOMSON PLACE
BOSTON MA 02210

SHELLY
CASHMAN
SERIES®

Australia • Canada • Denmark • Japan • Mexico • New Zealand • Philippines • Puerto Rico • Singapore • South Africa
Spain • United Kingdom • United States

THOMSON
COURSE TECHNOLOGY

Microsoft Office Word 2003:
Comprehensive Concepts and Techniques, CourseCard Edition

Gary B. Shelly
Thomas J. Cashman
Misty E. Vermaat

Managing Editor:
Alexandra Arnold

Senior Aquisitions Editor:
Dana Merk

Product Manager:
Reed Cotter

Editorial Assistant:
Selena Coppock

Print Buyer:
Laura Burns

Series Consulting Editor:
Jim Quasney

Director of Production:
Patty Stephen

Production Editor:
Aimee Poirier

Production Assistant:
Jill Klaffky

Development Editor:
Ginny Harvey

Copy Editor:
Lyn Markowicz

Proofreader:
Kim Kosmatka

Interior Designer:
Becky Herrington

Cover Designer:
Richard Herrera

Illustrators:
Richard Herrera
Andrew Bartel

Compositors:
Andrew Bartel
Jeanne Black
GEX Publishing Services

Indexer:
Cristina Haley

Printer:
Banta Menasha

ISBN-13: 978-1-4188-4357-1
ISBN-10: 1-4188-4357-1

MICROSOFT° OFFICE

Word 2003

Comprehensive Concepts and Techniques

COURSECARD EDITION

Contents

Preface	viii
To the Student	xiv

Project One

Creating and Editing a Word Document

Objectives	**WD 4**
What Is Microsoft Office Word 2003?	**WD 4**
Project One — Grand Prix Announcement	**WD 5**
Starting and Customizing Word	**WD 6**
The Word Window	**WD 10**
Document Window	WD 10
Menu Bar and Toolbars	WD 12
Resetting Menus and Toolbars	WD 15
Speech Recognition	**WD 16**
Entering Text	**WD 16**
Typing Text	WD 17
Entering Blank Lines in a Document	WD 20
Displaying Formatting Marks	WD 20
Entering More Text	WD 22
Using Wordwrap	WD 22
Entering Text that Scrolls the Document Window	WD 23
Checking Spelling and Grammar as You Type	WD 25
Saving a Document	**WD 28**
Formatting Paragraphs and Characters	
in a Document	**WD 31**
Selecting and Formatting Paragraphs and Characters	WD 33
Selecting Multiple Paragraphs	WD 33
Changing the Font Size of Text	WD 34
Changing the Font of Text	WD 36
Right-Align a Paragraph	WD 36
Center a Paragraph	WD 38
Undoing, Redoing, and Repeating Commands or Actions	WD 39
Selecting a Line and Formatting It	WD 40
Italicizing Text	WD 41
Underlining Text	WD 42
Scrolling	WD 43
Selecting a Group of Words	WD 43
Bolding Text	WD 44
Inserting Clip Art in a Word Document	**WD 45**
Inserting Clip Art	WD 46
Resizing a Graphic	WD 49
Saving an Existing Document with the Same	
File Name	**WD 51**
Printing a Document	**WD 53**
Quitting Word	**WD 54**
Starting Word and Opening a Document	**WD 55**

Correcting Errors	**WD 56**
Types of Changes Made to Documents	WD 56
Inserting Text in an Existing Document	WD 57
Deleting Text from an Existing Document	WD 58
Closing the Entire Document	WD 59
Word Help System	**WD 60**
Using the Type a Question for Help Box	WD 60
Quitting Word	WD 62
Project Summary	**WD 62**
What You Should Know	**WD 63**
Learn It Online	**WD 64**
Apply Your Knowledge	**WD 65**
In the Lab	**WD 67**
Cases and Places	**WD 71**

Project Two

Creating a Research Paper

Objectives	**WD 74**
Introduction	**WD 74**
Project Two — Biometrics Research Paper	**WD 74**
MLA Documentation Style	WD 76
Starting and Customizing Word	WD 76
Displaying Formatting Marks	WD 77
Changing the Margins	**WD 77**
Adjusting Line Spacing	**WD 79**
Using a Header to Number Pages	**WD 81**
Headers and Footers	WD 81
Entering Text Using Click and Type	WD 82
Entering a Page Number into the Header	WD 83
Typing the Body of a Research Paper	**WD 84**
Applying Formatting Using Shortcut Keys	WD 85
Saving the Research Paper	WD 87
Indenting Paragraphs	WD 87
Using Word's AutoCorrect Feature	WD 89
Adding Footnotes	WD 93
Modifying a Style	WD 95
Using Word Count	WD 100
Automatic Page Breaks	WD 101
Recounting Words in a Document	WD 102
Creating an Alphabetical Works Cited Page	**WD 102**
Manual Page Breaks	WD 103
Centering the Title of the Works Cited Page	WD 104
Creating a Hanging Indent	WD 104
Inserting Arrows, Faces, and Other Symbols Automatically	WD 106
Creating a Hyperlink	WD 107
Sorting Paragraphs	WD 109

Proofing and Revising the Research Paper **WD 110**
Going to a Specific Location in a Document WD 110
Moving Text WD 112
Smart Tags WD 115
Finding and Replacing Text WD 116
Finding Text WD 117
Finding and Inserting a Synonym WD 118
Checking Spelling and Grammar at Once WD 119
Saving Again and Printing the Document WD 120
Working with Main and Custom Dictionaries WD 121
Navigating to a Hyperlink **WD 122**
E-Mailing a Copy of the Research Paper **WD 123**
Using the Research Task Pane **WD 124**
Project Summary **WD 126**
What You Should Know **WD 127**
Learn It Online **WD 128**
Apply Your Knowledge **WD 129**
In the Lab **WD 130**
Cases and Places **WD 135**

Project Three

Creating a Resume Using a Wizard and a Cover Letter with a Table

Objectives **WD 138**
Introduction **WD 138**
Project Three — Resume and Cover Letter **WD 139**
Starting and Customizing Word WD 140
Displaying Formatting Marks WD 141
Using Word's Resume Wizard to Create a Resume **WD 141**
Personalizing the Resume **WD 150**
Tables WD 150
Styles WD 151
Selecting and Replacing Text WD 152
Entering a Line Break WD 154
AutoFormat As You Type WD 155
Viewing and Printing the Resume in Print Preview WD 158
Saving the Resume WD 159
Creating a Letterhead **WD 160**
Opening a New Document Window WD 160
Changing Color of Text WD 161
Inserting and Resizing a Graphic WD 162
Setting Tab Stops Using the Tabs Dialog Box WD 163
Collecting and Pasting WD 165
Adding a Bottom Border to a Paragraph WD 172
Clearing Formatting WD 173
Creating a Cover Letter **WD 175**
Components of a Business Letter WD 175
Saving the Cover Letter with a New File Name WD 175
Setting Tab Stops Using the Ruler WD 176
Inserting the Current Date in a Document WD 177
Creating an AutoText Entry WD 178
Entering a Nonbreaking Space WD 180
Inserting an AutoText Entry WD 181
Creating a Table with the Insert Table Button WD 182
Entering Data in a Word Table WD 183
Resizing Table Columns WD 185
Changing the Table Alignment WD 186
Bulleting a List WD 187
Saving Again and Printing the Cover Letter WD 189

Addressing and Printing Envelopes and Mailing Labels **WD 190**
Smart Tags **WD 191**
Document Summary **WD 193**
Project Summary **WD 195**
What You Should Know **WD 195**
Learn It Online **WD 197**
Apply Your Knowledge **WD 198**
In the Lab **WD 199**
Cases and Places **WD 201**

Web Feature

Creating Web Pages Using Word

Objectives **WD 203**
Introduction **WD 203**
Saving a Word Document as a Web Page **WD 205**
Formatting and Previewing a Web Page **WD 206**
Formatting the E-Mail Address as a Hyperlink WD 206
Applying a Theme to the Web Page WD 207
Viewing the Web Page in Your Default Browser WD 208
Creating and Modifying a Frames Page **WD 209**
Web Feature Summary **WD 215**
What You Should Know **WD 215**
In the Lab **WD 216**

Project Four

Creating a Document with a Table, Chart, and Watermark

Objectives **WD 218**
Introduction **WD 218**
Project Four — Sales Proposal **WD 218**
Starting and Customizing Word WD 220
Displaying Formatting Marks WD 220
Zooming Page Width WD 220
Creating a Title Page **WD 221**
Formatting and Entering Characters WD 221
Adding a Border and Shading to a Paragraph WD 221
Formatting Characters Using the Font Dialog Box WD 226
Inserting Clip Art from the Web in a Word Document WD 229
Centering the Title Page Contents Vertically on the Page WD 232
Saving the Title Page WD 234
Inserting an Existing Document into an Open Document **WD 235**
Inserting a Section Break WD 235
Inserting a Word Document into an Open Document WD 238
Saving the Active Document with a New File Name WD 240
Printing Specific Pages in a Document WD 240
Deleting a Page Break WD 244
Cutting Text WD 245
Creating Headers and Footers **WD 246**
Creating a Header Different from a Previous Section Header WD 246
Creating a Footer Different from a Previous Section Footer WD 249
Formatting and Charting a Table **WD 250**
Adding and Deleting Table Rows and Columns WD 250
Summing Table Contents WD 254
Formatting a Table WD 255
Formatting Nonadjacent Characters WD 257
Charting a Word Table WD 258

Changing the Chart in Graph WD 260
Formatting the Chart Object in Word WD 264
Working with Formats, Styles, and Bulleted Lists **WD 265**
Finding a Format WD 265
Creating and Applying a Character Style WD 267
Customizing Bullets in a List WD 270
Drawing a Table **WD 271**
Drawing an Empty Table WD 272
Single-Space the Table Contents WD 275
Entering Data into the Table WD 275
Formatting the Table WD 276
Creating a Watermark **WD 280**
Checking Spelling, Saving Again, and Printing the Sales
Proposal WD 282
Revealing Formatting **WD 282**
Project Summary **WD 284**
What You Should Know **WD 285**
Learn It Online **WD 286**
Apply Your Knowledge **WD 287**
In the Lab **WD 289**
Cases and Places **WD 295**

Project Five

Generating Form Letters, Mailing Labels, and Directories

Objectives **WD 298**
Introduction **WD 298**
**Project Five — Form Letters, Mailing Labels,
and Directories** **WD 300**
Starting and Customizing Word WD 300
Displaying Formatting Marks WD 301
Zooming Page Width WD 301
Identifying the Main Document for Form Letters **WD 301**
Identifying the Main Document WD 301
**Working with AutoShapes and the Drawing
Canvas** **WD 304**
Adding an AutoShape in a Drawing Canvas WD 304
Formatting an AutoShape WD 307
Resizing and Formatting the Drawing Canvas WD 309
Creating a Folder WD 313
Creating a Data Source **WD 314**
Editing Records in the Data Source WD 321
**Composing the Main Document for the Form
Letters** **WD 321**
Modifying a Field WD 322
Inserting Merge Fields in the Main Document WD 323
Using an IF Field to Conditionally Print Text
in a Form Letter WD 326
Creating an Outline Numbered List WD 329
Applying a Paragraph Style WD 332
Saving the Document Again WD 334
Displaying Field Codes WD 335
Printing Field Codes WD 336
Merging the Documents and Printing the Letters WD 338
Selecting Data Records to Merge and Print WD 339
Sorting Data Records to Merge and Print WD 342
Viewing Merged Data WD 343
Renaming a Folder WD 344
Addressing and Printing Mailing Labels **WD 345**
Saving the Mailing Labels WD 350
Addressing and Printing Envelopes WD 350

Merging All Data Records to a Directory **WD 352**
Saving the Directory WD 362
Closing All Open Word Documents WD 362
Project Summary **WD 363**
What You Should Know **WD 363**
Learn It Online **WD 365**
Apply Your Knowledge **WD 366**
In the Lab **WD 367**
Cases and Places **WD 375**

Project Six

Creating a Professional Newsletter

Objectives **WD 378**
Introduction **WD 378**
Project Six — Clever Clicks Newsletter **WD 378**
Desktop Publishing Terminology WD 380
Starting and Customizing Word WD 380
Displaying Formatting Marks WD 381
Zooming Page Width WD 381
Changing All Margin Settings WD 381
Creating the Nameplate **WD 382**
Inserting a WordArt Drawing Object WD 382
Formatting a WordArt Drawing Object WD 384
Changing the WordArt Shape WD 386
Adding Ruling Lines WD 388
Inserting Symbols WD 389
Inserting and Formatting a Floating Graphic WD 392
Saving the Newsletter WD 398
**Formatting the First Page of the Body
of the Newsletter** **WD 398**
Formatting a Document into Multiple Columns WD 398
Justifying a Paragraph WD 401
Inserting the Remainder of the Feature Article WD 401
Formatting a Letter as a Drop Cap WD 403
Inserting a Column Break WD 404
Inserting Text from a File, Viewing the Document,
and Modifying the Inserted Text WD 406
Adding a Vertical Rule between Columns WD 409
Creating a Pull-Quote **WD 410**
Inserting a Text Box WD 411
Formatting the Second Page of the Newsletter **WD 415**
Changing Column Formatting WD 415
Using the Paste Special Command to Link Text WD 418
Balancing Columns WD 419
Creating a Diagram WD 421
Using the Format Painter Button WD 427
Copying, Pasting, and Positioning a Diagram WD 429
**Enhancing the Newsletter with Color
and a Page Border** **WD 431**
Adding a Page Border WD 433
Enhancing a Document for Online Viewing **WD 436**
Highlighting Text WD 436
Animating Text WD 437
Changing a Document's Background WD 438
Splitting the Window and Arranging Open Windows WD 441
Viewing a Document in Reading Layout WD 443
Project Summary **WD 445**
What You Should Know **WD 445**
Learn It Online **WD 447**
Apply Your Knowledge **WD 448**
In the Lab **WD 450**
Cases and Places **WD 455**

Collaboration Feature

Using Word's Collaboration Tools

Objectives	WD 457
Introduction	WD 457
Creating an Outline	WD 458
Reviewing a Document	WD 461
E-Mailing a Document for Review	WD 461
Inserting, Viewing, and Editing Comments	WD 463
Tracking Changes	WD 466
Reviewing Tracked Changes and Comments	WD 468
Changing Review Settings	WD 472
Comparing and Merging Documents	WD 473
Sending an Outline to PowerPoint	WD 475
Collaboration Feature Summary	WD 478
What You Should Know	WD 478
In the Lab	WD 479

Project Seven

Creating an Online Form

Objectives	WD 482
Introduction	WD 482
Project Seven — Online Form	WD 483
Starting and Customizing Word	WD 484
Displaying Formatting Marks	WD 485
Zooming Page Width	WD 485
Designing an Online Form	WD 485
Creating an Online Form	WD 486
Creating a Template	WD 487
Formatting Graphics	WD 490
Entering Form Instructions	WD 494
Inserting a Table into a Form	WD 495
Inserting a Text Form Field that Accepts Any Text	WD 497
Inserting a Drop-Down Form Field	WD 500
Inserting a Text Form Field that Requires a Number	WD 504
Inserting a Check Box	WD 505
Inserting a Text Form Field that Displays the Current Date	WD 509
Formatting Form Fields	WD 511
Using the Format Painter Button	WD 512
Adding Help Text to Form Fields	WD 514
Removing Form Field Shading	WD 517
Inserting and Formatting a Rectangle Drawing Object	WD 518
Protecting a Form	WD 528
Working with an Online Form	WD 530
Saving Data on the Form	WD 533
Working with Templates	WD 538
Project Summary	WD 540
What You Should Know	WD 541
Learn It Online	WD 542
Apply Your Knowledge	WD 543
In the Lab	WD 545
Cases and Places	WD 550

Project Eight

Working With Macros and Visual Basic for Applications (VBA)

Objectives	WD 554
Introduction	WD 554
Project Eight — Online Form Revised	WD 554
Starting and Customizing Word	WD 557
Opening a Word Template	WD 557
Saving the Document with a New File Name	WD 558
Unprotecting a Document	WD 558
Setting a Security Level in Word	WD 559
Displaying Formatting Marks	WD 561
Zooming Page Width	WD 561
Modifying a Form	WD 561
Formatting Text	WD 561
Cropping Graphics	WD 563
Cropping a Graphic	WD 564
Creating a New Style with a Shortcut Key	WD 568
Filling a Drawing Object with a Preset Effect	WD 572
Adding a 3-D Effect to a Drawing Object	WD 574
Using a Macro to Automate a Task	WD 576
Recording and Executing a Macro	WD 576
Customizing Toolbars and Menus	WD 582
Recording an Automatic Macro	WD 587
Editing a Recorded Macro	WD 592
Viewing a Macro's VBA Code	WD 592
Adding Comments to a Procedure	WD 594
Modifying Existing Code in a Procedure	WD 596
Entering Code Statements	WD 597
Creating a Macro from Scratch Using VBA	WD 598
Modifying Form Field Options	WD 598
Inserting a New Procedure	WD 600
Planning and Writing a VBA Procedure	WD 601
Running a Macro When a User Exits a Form Field	WD 603
Copying, Renaming, and Deleting Macros	WD 604
Adding an Activex Control to a Form	WD 605
Inserting an ActiveX Control	WD 606
Setting Properties of an ActiveX Control	WD 608
Writing a Procedure for the ActiveX Control	WD 610
More About Visual Basic for Applications	WD 614
Protecting a Form	WD 614
Testing the Online Form	WD 615
Digital Signatures	WD 617
Attaching a Digital Signature to a File	WD 617
Project Summary	WD 620
What You Should Know	WD 621
Learn It Online	WD 622
Apply Your Knowledge	WD 623
In the Lab	WD 625
Cases and Places	WD 630

Project Nine

Working with a Master Document, an Index, a Table of Contents, and XML

Objectives	WD 634
Introduction	WD 634
Project Nine — Reference Document	WD 634
Starting and Customizing Word	WD 636
Displaying Formatting Marks	WD 637
Zooming Page Width	WD 637
Opening a Document and Saving It with a New File Name	WD 637
Saving Multiple Versions of a Document	WD 638
Preparing a Document To Be Included in a Longer Document	WD 640
Inserting and Formatting a Graphic	WD 640
Adding a Caption	WD 645

Creating a Cross-Reference WD 647
Marking Index Entries WD 649
Hyphenating a Document WD 652
Controlling Widows and Orphans WD 653
Sorting a List WD 655
Working with a Master Document **WD 657**
Creating an Outline WD 657
Inserting a Subdocument in a Master Document WD 660
Creating a Subdocument in a Master Document WD 664
Entering Text and Graphics as Part of the Master Document WD 667
Creating a Table of Figures WD 670
Building an Index WD 672
Creating a Table of Contents WD 673
Adding Bookmarks WD 675
Creating Alternating Headers and Footers WD 677
Setting a Gutter Margin WD 679
Opening a Master Document WD 681
Using the Document Map WD 683
Updating an Index WD 684
Summarize a Document WD 685
Using Readability Statistics WD 687
Go To a Bookmark WD 688
Customizing Document Properties WD 689
Password-Protecting a File WD 691
Working with XML **WD 693**
Working with an XML Schema WD 693
Managing Elements in an XML Document WD 696
Setting Editing Restrictions WD 703
Project Summary **WD 706**
What You Should Know **WD 706**
Learn It Online **WD 708**
Apply Your Knowledge **WD 709**
In the Lab **WD 710**
Cases and Places **WD 717**

Integration Feature

Linking an Excel Worksheet and Charting Its Data in Word

Objectives **WD 721**
Introduction **WD 721**
Starting Word and Opening a Document WD 723
Saving the Document with a New File Name WD 723
Linking an Excel Worksheet **WD 724**
Creating a Chart from an Excel Worksheet **WD 726**
Editing a Linked Worksheet **WD 732**
Integration Feature Summary **WD 734**
What You Should Know **WD 734**
In the Lab **WD 735**

Appendix A

Microsoft Word Help System

Using the Microsoft Word Help System **APP 1**
Navigating the Word Help System **APP 2**
Other Help Commands on the Help Menu **APP 8**
Use Help **APP 10**

Appendix B

Speech and Handwriting Recognition and Speech Playback

Introduction **APP 11**
Speech Recognition **APP 15**
Handwriting Recognition **APP 19**
Speech Playback **APP 22**

Appendix C

Publishing Office Web Pages to a Web Server

Using Web Folders to Publish Office Web Pages APP 24
Using FTP to Publish Office Web Pages APP 24

Appendix D

Changing Screen Resolution and Resetting the Word Toolbars and Menus

Changing Screen Resolution **APP 25**
Resetting the Word Toolbars and Menus **APP 27**

Appendix E

Microsoft Office Specialist Certification

What Is Microsoft Office Specialist Certification? **APP 31**
Why Should You Be Certified? **APP 31**
The Microsoft Office Specialist Certification Exams **APP 32**
How to Prepare for the Microsoft Office Specialist Certification Exams **APP 32**
How to Find an Authorized Testing Center **APP 32**
Shelly Cashman Series Microsoft Office Specialist Center **APP 32**
Microsoft Office Specialist Certification Maps for Microsoft Office Word 2003 **APP 33**

Index **IND 38**

Quick Reference Summary **QR 45**

Word 2003 CourseCard

Preface

The Shelly Cashman Series® offers the finest textbooks in computer education. We are proud of the fact that our series of Microsoft Office 4.3, Microsoft Office 95, Microsoft Office 97, Microsoft Office 2000, and Microsoft Office XP textbooks have been the most widely used books in education. With each new edition of our Office books, we have made significant improvements based on the software and comments made by the instructors and students. The *Microsoft Office 2003* books continue with the innovation, quality, and reliability that you have come to expect from the Shelly Cashman Series.

In this *Microsoft Office Word 2003* 2003 book, you will find an educationally sound, highly visual, and easy-to-follow pedagogy that combines a vastly improved step-by-step approach with corresponding screens. All projects and exercises in this book are designed to take full advantage of the Word 2003 enhancements. The project material is developed to ensure that students will see the importance of learning Word for future course-work. The popular Other Ways and More About features offer in-depth knowledge of Word 2003, and the new Q&A feature offers students a way to solidify important word processing concepts. The Learn It Online page presents a wealth of additional exercises to ensure your students have all the reinforcement they need.

Objectives of This Textbook

Microsoft Office Word 2003: Comprehensive Concepts and Techniques, CourseCard Edition is intended for a full-semester course that presents Microsoft Office Word 2003. No experience with a computer is assumed, and no mathematics beyond the high school freshman level is required. The objectives of this book are:

- To teach the fundamentals of Word 2003
- To emphasize the word processing document development cycle
- To expose students to practical examples of the computer as a useful tool
- To acquaint students with the proper procedures to create word processing documents
- To develop an exercise-oriented approach that allows learning by doing
- To introduce students to new input technologies
- To encourage independent study and help those who are working alone
- To assist students preparing to take the Microsoft Office Specialist examinations for both the Microsoft Office Word 2003 specialist-level and expert-level certification

Approved by Microsoft as Courseware for Microsoft Office Specialist Certification

Microsoft Office Word 2003: Comprehensive Concepts and Techniques, CourseCard Edition has been approved by Microsoft as courseware for Microsoft Office Specialist certification. After completing the first six projects in this book, students will be prepared to take the specialist-level examination for Microsoft Office Word 2003. After completing the book, students will be prepared to take the expert-level examination for Microsoft Office Word 2003.

By passing the certification exam for a Microsoft software application, students demonstrate their proficiency in that application to employers. This exam is offered at participating centers, corporations, and employment agencies. See Appendix E for additional information about obtaining Microsoft Office Specialist certification and for a table that includes the Microsoft Office Word 2003 skill sets and corresponding page numbers where a skill is discussed in the book, or visit the Web site microsoft.com/officespecialist.

The Shelly Cashman Series Microsoft Office Specialist Center (Figure 1) has links to valuable information on the certification program. The Web page (scsite.com/winoff2003/cert) includes links to general information on certification, choosing an application for certification, preparing for the certification exam, and taking and passing the certification exams.

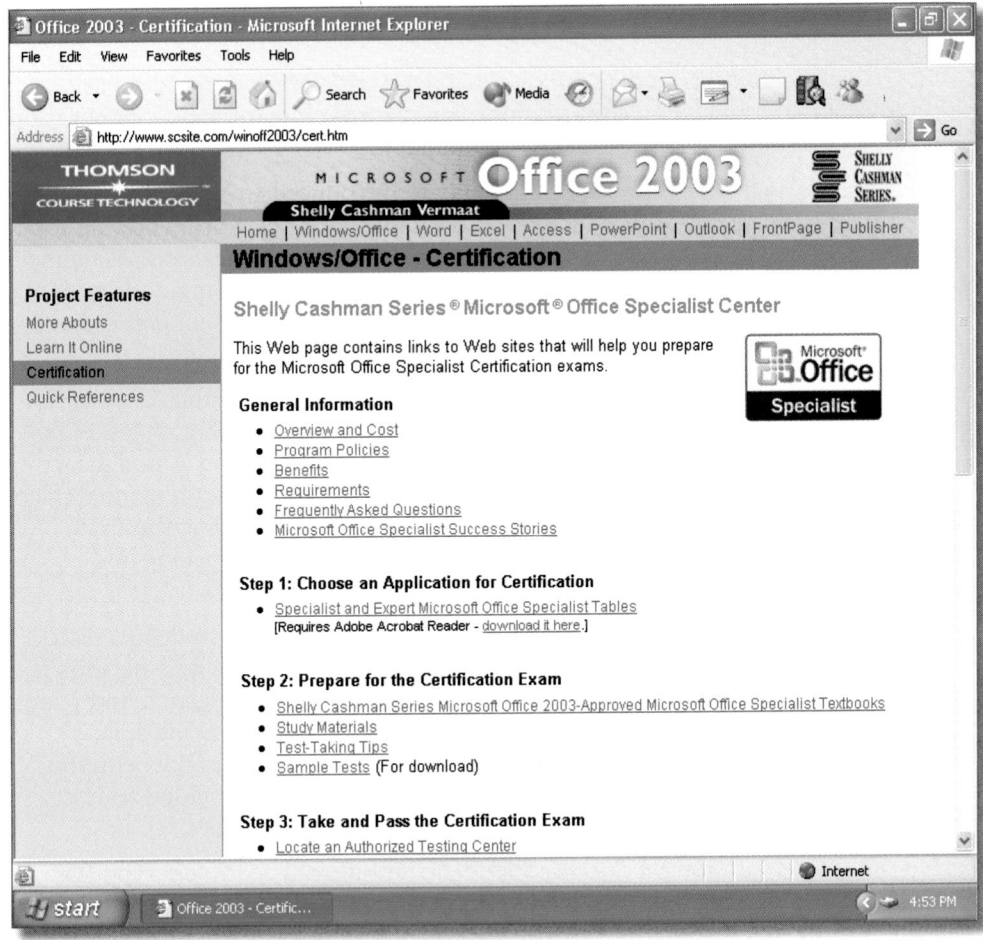

FIGURE 1

The Shelly Cashman Approach

Features of the Shelly Cashman Series *Microsoft Office Word 2003* books include:

- Project Orientation: Each project in the book presents a practical problem and complete solution using an easy-to-understand methodology.
- Step-by-Step, Screen-by-Screen Instructions: Each of the tasks required to complete a project is identified throughout the project. Full-color screens accompany the steps.
- Thoroughly Tested Projects: Unparalleled quality is ensured because every screen in the book is produced by the author only after performing a step, and then each project must pass Thomson Course Technology's award-winning Quality Assurance program.
- Other Ways Boxes and Quick Reference Summary: The Other Ways boxes displayed at the end of many of the step-by-step sequences specify the other ways to perform the task completed in the steps. Thus, the steps and the Other Ways box make a comprehensive reference unit.
- More About and Q&A Features: These marginal annotations provide background information, tips, and answers to common questions that complement the topics covered, adding depth and perspective to the learning process.
- Integration of the World Wide Web: The World Wide Web is integrated into the Word 2003 learning experience by (1) More About annotations that send students to Web sites for up-to-date information and alternative approaches to tasks; (2) a Microsoft Office Specialist Certification Web page so students can prepare for the certification examinations; (3) a Word 2003 Quick Reference Summary Web page that summarizes the ways to complete tasks (mouse, menu, shortcut menu, and keyboard); and (4) the Learn It Online page at the end of each project, which has project reinforcement exercises, learning games, and other types of student activities.

Organization of This Textbook

Microsoft Office Word 2003: Comprehensive Concepts and Techniques, CourseCard Edition provides basic instruction on how to use Word 2003. The material is divided into nine projects, a Web feature, a Collaboration feature, an Integration feature, five appendices, and a Quick Reference Summary.

Project 1 – Creating and Editing a Word Document   In Project 1, students are introduced to Word terminology and the Word window by preparing an announcement. Topics include starting and quitting Word; entering text; checking spelling while typing; saving a document; selecting characters, words, lines, and paragraphs; changing the font and font size of text; centering, right-aligning, bolding, and italicizing text; undoing commands and actions; inserting clip art in a document; resizing a graphic; printing a document; opening a document; correcting errors; and using the Word Help system.

Project 2 – Creating a Research Paper   In Project 2, students use the MLA style of documentation to create a research paper. Topics include changing margins; adjusting line spacing; using a header to number pages; entering text using Click and Type; first-line indenting paragraphs; using the AutoCorrect feature and AutoCorrect Options button; adding a footnote; modifying a style; inserting a symbol automatically; inserting a manual page break; creating a hanging indent; creating a text hyperlink; sorting paragraphs; moving text; using the Paste Options button; finding a synonym; counting and recounting words in a document; checking spelling and grammar at once; e-mailing a document; and using the Research task pane.

Project 3 – Creating a Resume Using a Wizard and a Cover Letter with a Table   In Project 3, students create a resume using Word's Resume Wizard and then create a cover letter with a letterhead. Topics include personalizing the resume; using print preview; adding color to characters; setting and using tab stops; collecting and pasting; adding a bottom border; clearing formatting; inserting the current date; inserting a nonbreaking space; creating and inserting an AutoText entry; creating a bulleted list while typing; inserting a Word table; entering data into a Word table; and formatting a Word table. Finally, students prepare and print an envelope address, use smart tags, and modify the document summary.

Web Feature – Creating Web Pages Using Word   In the Web feature, students are introduced to creating Web pages in Word. Topics include saving a Word document as a Web page; formatting an e-mail address as a hyperlink; applying a theme to a Web page; previewing a Web page; creating and modifying a frames page; and inserting and modifying hyperlinks.

Project 4 – Creating a Document with a Table, Chart, and Watermark   In Project 4, students work with a multi-page document that has a title page. Topics include learning how to border and shade paragraphs; changing paragraph indentation; formatting characters using the Font dialog box; modifying default font settings; clearing formatting; inserting clip art from the Web; centering the contents of a page vertically; inserting a section break; inserting an existing Word document in an open document; creating headers and footers different from previous headers and footers; changing the starting page number in a section; editing and formatting a Word table; summing columns in a table; selecting and formatting nonadjacent text; charting a Word table; modifying and formatting a chart; finding a format; adding picture bullets to a list; creating and applying a character style; creating a table using the Draw Table feature; changing the direction and alignment of text in table cells; inserting a text watermark; and revealing formatting.

Project 5 – Generating Form Letters, Mailing Labels, Envelopes, and Directories   In Project 5, students learn how to create and edit the main document for form letters, mailing labels, envelopes, and directories. Topics include using a letter template for the main document; inserting and formatting a drawing canvas; inserting and formatting an AutoShape; creating a folder while saving; creating and editing a data source; inserting a date field and editing its format; inserting and editing merge fields in a main document; using an IF field; creating an outline numbered list; applying a paragraph style; displaying and printing field codes; merging and printing the documents; selecting data records to merge and print; sorting data records and table contents; viewing merged data; modifying table properties; renaming a folder; formatting text as hidden; and printing a document in landscape orientation.

Project 6 – Creating a Professional Newsletter   In Project 6, students learn how to use Word's desktop publishing features to create a newsletter. Topics include creating and formatting a WordArt drawing object; adding ruling lines; inserting a symbol; changing a graphic's wrapping style; flipping and brightening a graphic; formatting a document in multiple columns; justifying a paragraph; formatting a character as a drop cap; inserting a column break; placing a vertical rule between columns; displaying a document in full screen view;

inserting, formatting, and positioning a text box; changing character spacing; shading a paragraph; using the Paste Special command; balancing columns; inserting and formatting a diagram; using the Format Painter button; adding a page border; highlighting text; animating text; changing background color and pattern; splitting a window; arranging open Word documents; and using reading layout view.

Collaboration Feature – Using Word's Collaboration Tools   In the Collaboration feature, students create an outline, use Word's collaboration tools to review the outline, and then send the final outline to PowerPoint for use in a slide show. Collaboration tools presented include e-mailing a document for review; inserting and editing comments; tracking changes; reviewing tracked changes; viewing comments; and comparing and merging documents.

Project 7 – Creating an Online Form   In Project 7, students learn how to create an online form and then use Word to fill in the form. Topics include creating a document template; adjusting a graphic's contrast; rotating a graphic; inserting a table into a form; inserting text form fields, drop-down form fields, and check box form fields; formatting form fields; using the Format Painter button; adding Help text to form fields; removing form field shading; drawing a rectangle; filling a drawing object with a texture; formatting drawing object; adding a shadow to a drawing object; protecting a form; saving form data in a text file; opening a text file in Word; and modifying the location of workgroup templates.

Project 8 – Working with Macros and Visual Basic for Applications (VBA)   In Project 8, students enhance an online form by modifying its appearance, adding macros, and inserting an ActiveX control. Topics include setting security levels in Word; cropping graphics; creating a new style assigned to a shortcut key; modifying a style; formatting a drawing object; recording and executing a macro; adding and deleting buttons to and from toolbars; adding and deleting commands to and from menus; copying, renaming, and deleting macros; viewing a macro's VBA code; adding comments and VBA code statements to a macro; attaching a macro to the exit property of a form field; inserting an ActiveX control; setting properties of an ActiveX control; writing VBA code statements for an ActiveX control; and attaching a digital signature.

Project 9 – Working with a Master Document, an Index, a Table of Contents, and XML   In Project 9, students learn how to organize and work with a long document. Topics include saving multiple versions of a document, adding a caption, converting a text box to a frame, creating a cross-reference, hyphenating a document, controlling widows and orphans, password-protecting a document, working with a master document and subdocuments, creating a subdocument, creating a table of figures, marking index entries, building an index, creating a table of contents, adding a bookmark, creating alternating headers and footers, setting a gutter margin, using the document map, working with AutoSummarize, analyzing readability statistics, customizing document properties, and structuring documents using XML.

Integration Feature – Linking an Excel Worksheet and Charting Its Data in Word   In this feature, students are introduced to linking Excel data to a Word document. Topics include linking an Excel worksheet to a Word document, creating a chart, linking Excel data to the chart, and editing a linked object.

Appendices   The book includes five appendices. Appendix A presents an introduction to the Microsoft Word Help system. Appendix B describes how to use the Word speech and handwriting recognition and speech playback capabilities. Appendix C explains how to publish Web pages to a Web server. Appendix D shows how to change the screen resolution and reset the menus and toolbars. Appendix E introduces students to Microsoft Office Specialist certification.

Quick Reference Summary   Summary In Word 2003, you can accomplish a task in a number of ways, such as using the mouse, menu, shortcut menu, and keyboard. The Quick Reference Summary at the back of the book provides a quick reference to each task presented.

Word 2003 CourseCard   New! Now includes a free, tear-off Word 2003 CourseCard that provides students with a great way to have Word skills at their fingertips.

End-of-Project Student Activities

A notable strength of the Shelly Cashman Series *Microsoft Office Word 2003* books is the extensive student activities at the end of each project. Well-structured student activities can make the difference between students merely participating in a class and students retaining the information they learn. The activities in the Shelly Cashman Series *Microsoft Office Word 2003* books include the following.

- **What You Should Know**   A listing of the tasks completed within a project together with the pages on which the step-by-step, screen-by-screen explanations appear.

- Learn It Online   Every project features a Learn It Online page that contains 12 exercises. These exercises include True/False, Multiple Choice, Short Answer, Flash Cards, Practice Test, Learning Games, Tips and Tricks, Newsgroup usage, Expanding Your Horizons, Search Sleuth, Office Online Training, and Office Marketplace.
- Apply Your Knowledge   This exercise usually requires students to open and manipulate a file on the Data Disk that parallels the activities learned in the project. To obtain a copy of the Data Disk, follow the instructions on the inside back cover of this textbook.
- In the Lab   Three in-depth assignments per project require students to utilize the project concepts and techniques to solve problems on a computer.
- Cases and Places   Five unique real-world case-study situations, including one small-group activity.

Instructor Resources CD-ROM

The Shelly Cashman Series is dedicated to providing you with all of the tools you need to make your class a success. Information on all supplementary materials is available through your Thomson Course Technology representative or by calling one of the following telephone numbers: Colleges and Universities, 1-800-648-7450; High Schools, 1-800-824-5179; Private Career Colleges, 1-800-347-7707; Canada, 1-800-268-2222; Corporations with IT Training Centers, 1-800-648-7450; and Government Agencies, Health-Care Organizations, and Correctional Facilities, 1-800-477-3692.

The Instructor Resources for this textbook include both teaching and testing aids. The contents of each item on the Instructor Resources CD-ROM (ISBN 0-619-20048-0) are described below.

INSTRUCTOR'S MANUAL   The Instructor's Manual is made up of Microsoft Word files, which include detailed lesson plans with page number references, lecture notes, teaching tips, classroom activities, discussion topics, projects to assign, and transparency references. The transparencies are available through the Figure Files described below.

LECTURE SUCCESS SYSTEM   The Lecture Success System consists of intermediate files that correspond to certain figures in the book, allowing you to step through the creation of an application in a project during a lecture without entering large amounts of data.

SYLLABUS   Sample syllabi, which can be customized easily to a course, are included. The syllabi cover policies, class and lab assignments and exams, and procedural information.

FIGURE FILES   Illustrations for every figure in the textbook are available in electronic form. Use this ancillary to present a slide show in lecture or to print transparencies for use in lecture with an overhead projector. If you have a personal computer and LCD device, this ancillary can be an effective tool for presenting lectures.

POWERPOINT PRESENTATIONS   PowerPoint Presentations is a multimedia lecture presentation system that provides slides for each project. Presentations are based on project objectives. Use this presentation system to present well-organized lectures that are both interesting and knowledge based. PowerPoint Presentations provides consistent coverage at schools that use multiple lecturers.

SOLUTIONS TO EXERCISES   Solutions are included for the end-of-project exercises, as well as the Project Reinforcement exercises.

RUBRICS AND ANNOTATED SOLUTION FILES   The grading rubrics provide a customizable framework for assigning point values to the laboratory exercises. Annotated solution files that correspond to the grading rubrics make it easy for you to compare students' results with the corect solutions whether you receive their homework as hard copy or via e-mail.

TEST BANK & TEST ENGINE   The ExamView test bank includes 110 questions for every project (25 multiple choice, 50 true/false, and 35 short answer) with page number references and, when appropriate, figure references. A version of the test bank you can print also is included. The test bank comes with a copy of the test engine, ExamView, the ultimate tool for your objective-based testing needs. ExamView is a state-of-the-art test builder that is easy to use. ExamView enables you to create paper-, LAN-, or Web-based tests from test banks designed specifically for your Thomson Course Technology textbook. Utilize the ultra-efficient QuickTest Wizard to create tests in less than five minutes by taking advantage of Thomson Course Technology's question banks, or customize your own exams from scratch.

LAB TESTS/TEST OUT   The Lab Tests/Test Out exercises parallel the In the Lab assignments and are supplied for the purpose of testing students in the laboratory on the material covered in the project or testing students out of the course.

DATA FILES FOR STUDENTS   All the files that are required by students to complete the exercises are included. You can distribute the files on the Instructor Resources CD-ROM to your students over a network, or you can have them follow the instructions on the inside back cover of this book to obtain a copy of the Data Disk.

ADDITIONAL ACTIVITIES FOR STUDENTS   These additional activities consist of Project Reinforcement Exercises, which are true/false, multiple choice, and short answer questions that help students gain confidence in the material learned.

SAM 2003

SAM 2003 helps you energize your class exams and training assignments by allowing students to learn and test important computer skills in an active, hands-on environment.

SAM 2003 ASSESSMENT   With SAM 2003 Assessment, you create powerful interactive exams on critical applications such as Word, Excel, Access, PowerPoint, Windows, Outlook, and the Internet.

SAM 2003 TRAINING   Invigorate your lesson plan with SAM 2003 Training. Using highly interactive text, graphics, and sound, SAM 2003 Training gives your students the flexibility to learn computer applications by choosing the training method that fits them best. Create customized training units that employ various approaches to teaching computer skills.

SAM 2003 ASSESSMENT AND TRAINING   Designed to be used with the Shelly Cashman Series, SAM 2003 Assessment and Training includes built-in page references so students can create study guides that match the Shelly Cashman Series textbooks you use in class.

Online Content

Thomson Course Technology offers textbook-based content for Blackboard, WebCT, and MyCourse 2.1.

BLACKBOARD AND WEBCT   As the leading provider of IT content for the Blackboard and WebCT platforms, Thomson Course Technology delivers rich content that enhances your textbook to give your students a unique learning experience.

MYCOURSE 2.1   MyCourse 2.1 is Thomson Course Technology's powerful online course management and content delivery system. MyCourse 2.1 allows nontechnical users to create, customize, and deliver Web-based courses; post content and assignments; manage student enrollment; administer exams; track results in the online grade book; and more.

To the Student... Getting the Most Out of Your Book

Welcome to *Microsoft Office Word 2003: Comprehensive Concepts and Techniques, CourseCard Edition*. You can save yourself a lot of time and gain a better understanding of Microsoft Office Word 2003 if you spend a few minutes reviewing the figures and callouts in this section.

1 Project Orientation

Each project presents a practical problem and shows the solution in the first figure of the project. The project orientation lets you see firsthand how problems are solved from start to finish using application software and computers.

2 Consistent Step-by-Step, Screen-by-Screen Presentation

Project solutions are built using a step-by-step, screen-by-screen approach. This pedagogy allows you to build the solution on a computer as you read through the project. Generally, each step is followed by an italic explanation that indicates the result of the step.

3 More Than Just Step-by-Step

More About and Q&A annotations in the margins of the book and substantive text in the paragraphs provide background information, tips, and answers to common questions that complement the topics covered, adding depth and perspective. When you finish with this book, you will be ready to use Word to solve problems on your own.

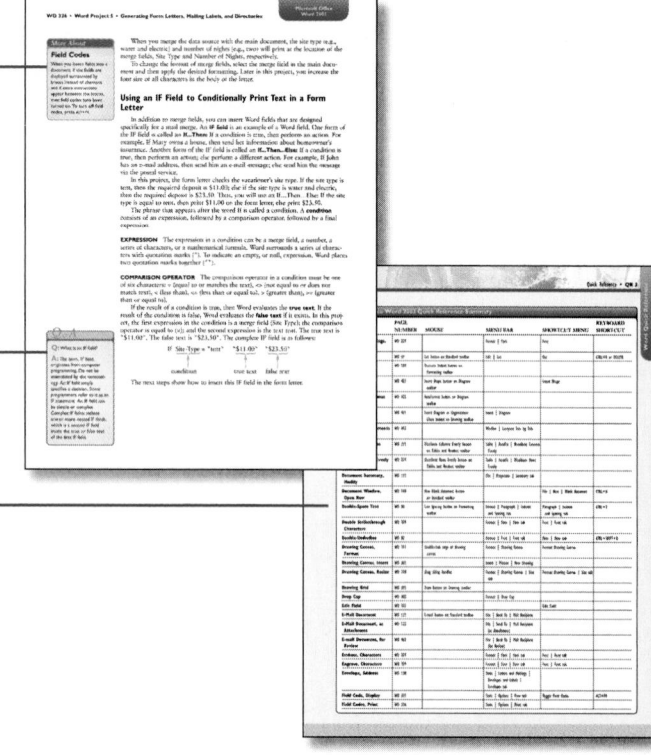

4 Other Ways Boxes and Quick Reference Summary

Other Ways boxes that follow many of the step sequences and a Quick Reference Summary at the back of the book explain the other ways to complete the task presented, such as using the mouse, menu, shortcut menu, and keyboard.

5 Emphasis on Getting Help When You Need It

The first project of each application and Appendix A show you how to use all the elements of the Word Help system. Being able to answer your own questions will increase your productivity and reduce your frustrations by minimizing the time it takes to learn how to complete a task.

6 Review

After you successfully step through a project, a section titled What You Should Know summarizes the project tasks with which you should be familiar. Terms you should know for test purposes are bold in the text.

7 Reinforcement and Extension

The Learn It Online page at the end of each project offers reinforcement in the form of review questions, learning games, and practice tests. Also included are Web-based exercises that require you to extend your learning beyond the book.

8 Laboratory Exercises

If you really want to learn how to use the applications, then you must design and implement solutions to problems on your own. Every project concludes with several carefully developed laboratory assignments that increase in complexity.

Shelly Cashman Series – Traditionally Bound Textbooks

The Shelly Cashman Series presents the following computer subjects in a variety of traditionally bound textbooks. For more information, see your Course Technology representative or call 1-800-648-7450. For Shelly Cashman Series information, visit Shelly Cashman Online at **scseries.com**

COMPUTERS	
Computers	Discovering Computers 2006: A Gateway to Information, Complete
	Discovering Computers 2006: A Gateway to Information, Introductory
	Discovering Computers 2006: A Gateway to Information, Brief
	Discovering Computers: Fundamentals, Second Edition
	Teachers Discovering Computers: Integrating Technology in the Classroom, Third Edition
	Essential Introduction to Computers, Sixth Edition (40-page)

WINDOWS APPLICATIONS	
Microsoft Office	Microsoft Office 2003: Essential Concepts and Techniques (5 projects)
	Microsoft Office 2003: Brief Concepts and Techniques (9 projects)
	Microsoft Office 2003: Introductory Concepts and Techniques, Second Edition (15 projects)
	Microsoft Office 2003: Advanced Concepts and Techniques (12 projects)
	Microsoft Office 2003: Post Advanced Concepts and Techniques (11 projects)
	Microsoft Office XP: Essential Concepts and Techniques (5 projects)
	Microsoft Office XP: Brief Concepts and Techniques (9 projects)
	Microsoft Office XP: Introductory Concepts and Techniques, Windows XP Edition (15 projects)
	Microsoft Office XP: Introductory Concepts and Techniques, Enhanced Edition (15 projects)
	Microsoft Office XP: Advanced Concepts and Techniques (11 projects)
	Microsoft Office XP: Post Advanced Concepts and Techniques (11 projects)
Integration	Teachers Discovering and Integrating Microsoft Office: Essential Concepts and Techniques, Second Edition
	Integrating Microsoft Office XP Applications and the World Wide Web: Essential Concepts and Techniques
PIM	Microsoft Outlook 2002: Essential Concepts and Techniques • Microsoft Office Outlook 2003: Introductory Concepts and Techniques
Microsoft Works	Microsoft Works 6: Complete Concepts and Techniques[1] • Microsoft Works 2000: Complete Concepts and Techniques[1]
Microsoft Windows	Microsoft Windows XP: Comprehensive Concepts and Techniques[2]
	Microsoft Windows XP: Brief Concepts and Techniques
	Microsoft Windows 2000: Comprehensive Concepts and Techniques[2]
	Microsoft Windows 2000: Brief Concepts and Techniques
	Microsoft Windows 98: Comprehensive Concepts and Techniques[2]
	Microsoft Windows 98: Essential Concepts and Techniques
	Introduction to Microsoft Windows NT Workstation 4
Notebook Organizer	Microsoft Office OneNote 2003: Introductory Concepts and Techniques
Word Processing	Microsoft Office Word 2003: Comprehensive Concepts and Techniques[2] • Microsoft Word 2002: Comprehensive Concepts and Techniques[2]
Spreadsheets	Microsoft Office Excel 2003: Comprehensive Concepts and Techniques[2] • Microsoft Excel 2002: Comprehensive Concepts and Techniques[2]
Database	Microsoft Office Access 2003: Comprehensive Concepts and Techniques[2] • Microsoft Access 2002: Comprehensive Concepts and Techniques[2]
Presentation Graphics	Microsoft Office PowerPoint 2003: Comprehensive Concepts and Techniques[2] • Microsoft PowerPoint 2002: Comprehensive Concepts and Techniques[2]
Desktop Publishing	Microsoft Office Publisher 2003: Comprehensive Concepts and Techniques[2] • Microsoft Publisher 2002: Comprehensive Concepts and Techniques[1]

PROGRAMMING	
Programming	Microsoft Visual Basic .NET: Comprehensive Concepts and Techniques[2] • Microsoft Visual Basic 6: Complete Concepts and Techniques[1] • Java Programming: Comprehensive Concepts and Techniques, Second Edition[2] • Structured COBOL Programming, Second Edition • Understanding and Troubleshooting Your PC • Programming Fundamentals Using Microsoft Visual Basic .NET

INTERNET	
Concepts	Discovering the Internet: Brief Concepts and Techniques • Discovering the Internet: Complete Concepts and Techniques
Browser	Microsoft Internet Explorer 6: Introductory Concepts and Techniques, Windows XP Edition • Microsoft Internet Explorer 5: An Introduction • Netscape Navigator 6: An Introduction
Web Page Creation	Web Design: Introductory Concepts and Techniques • HTML: Comprehensive Concepts and Techniques, Third Edition[2] • Microsoft Office FrontPage 2003: Comprehensive Concepts and Techniques[2] • Microsoft FrontPage 2002: Comprehensive Concepts and Techniques[2] • Microsoft FrontPage 2002: Essential Concepts and Techniques • JavaScript: Complete Concepts and Techniques, Second Edition[1] • Macromedia Dreamweaver MX: Comprehensive Concepts and Techniques[2]

SYSTEMS ANALYSIS	
Systems Analysis	Systems Analysis and Design, Sixth Edition

DATA COMMUNICATIONS	
Data Communications	Business Data Communications: Introductory Concepts and Techniques, Fourth Edition

[1] Also available as an Introductory Edition, which is a shortened version of the complete book, [2] Also available as an Introductory Edition and as a Complete Edition, which are shortened versions of the comprehensive book.

MICROSOFT OFFICE

WORD

MICROSOFT

Office Word 2003

Creating and Editing a Word Document

PROJECT

1

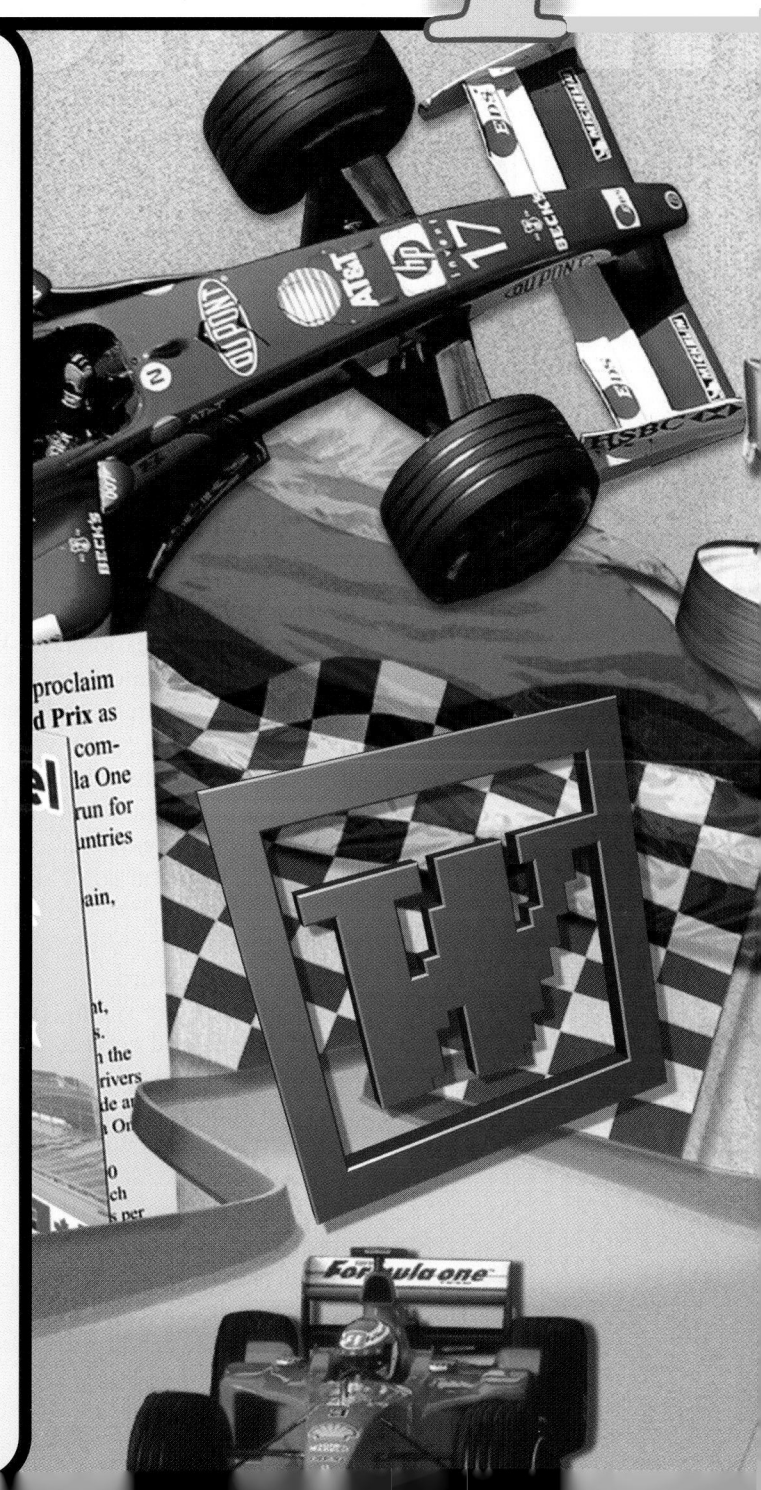

CASE PERSPECTIVE

Racing fans everywhere proclaim the Formula One Grand Prix as the most exhilarating racing competition in the world. Formula One Grand Prix events typically run for three days in a variety of countries including Brazil, Canada, England, Germany, Italy, Spain, and the United States. On the first day of each event, drivers practice on the tracks. Qualifying sessions begin on the second day. The fastest 26 drivers participate in a drivers' parade and then compete in the Formula One Grand Prix race on Sunday. During the race of nearly 200 miles, Formula One cars reach speeds that exceed 220 miles per hour.

When the Formula One Grand Prix season approaches, travel agents begin taking reservations for race packages. Jill Hall is a senior travel agent at Beacon Travel, where you are employed as a summer intern. Jill knows you have learned the guidelines for designing announcements in your marketing classes and has asked you to prepare a one-page flier announcing Beacon's Grand Prix race packages. You decide to use thick, bold characters to emphasize the headline and title. To attract attention to the announcement, you plan to include a large graphic of a Formula One race car. When you show the finished document to Jill, she is quite impressed. After Jill approves the completed flier, she wants you to distribute it to businesses for display on bulletin boards and in window fronts.

As you read through this project, you will learn how to use Word to create, save, and print a document that includes a graphical image.

Microsoft Office Word 2003

Creating and Editing a Word Document

PROJECT

Objectives

You will have mastered the material in this project when you can:

- Start and quit Word
- Describe the Word window
- Enter text in a document
- Check spelling as you type
- Save a document
- Format text and paragraphs

- Undo and redo commands or actions
- Insert clip art in a document
- Print a document
- Open a document
- Correct errors in a document
- Use Word's Help to answer questions

What Is Microsoft Office Word 2003?

Microsoft Office Word 2003 is a full-featured word processing program that allows you to create professional looking documents and revise them easily. With Word, you can develop announcements, letters, memos, resumes, reports, fax cover sheets, mailing labels, newsletters, and many other types of documents. Word also provides tools that enable you to create Web pages with ease. From within Word, you can place these Web pages directly on a Web server.

Word has many features designed to simplify the production of documents and make documents look visually appealing. Using Word, you easily can change the shape, size, and color of text. You also can include borders, shading, tables, images, pictures, and Web addresses in documents. With proper hardware, you can dictate or handwrite text instead of typing it in Word. You also can speak instructions to Word.

While you are typing, Word performs many tasks automatically. For example, Word detects and corrects spelling and grammar errors in several languages. Word's thesaurus allows you to add variety and precision to your writing. Word also can format text such as headings, lists, fractions, borders, and Web addresses as you type them. Within Word, you can e-mail a copy of a Word document to an e-mail address.

This latest version of Word has many new features to make you more productive. It supports XML documents, improves readability of documents, supports ink input from devices such as the Tablet PC, provides more control for protecting documents, allows two documents to be compared side by side, and includes the capability to search a variety of reference information.

WD 4

Project One — Grand Prix Announcement

To illustrate the features of Word, this book presents a series of projects that use Word to create documents similar to those you will encounter in academic and business environments. Project 1 uses Word to produce the announcement shown in Figure 1-1.

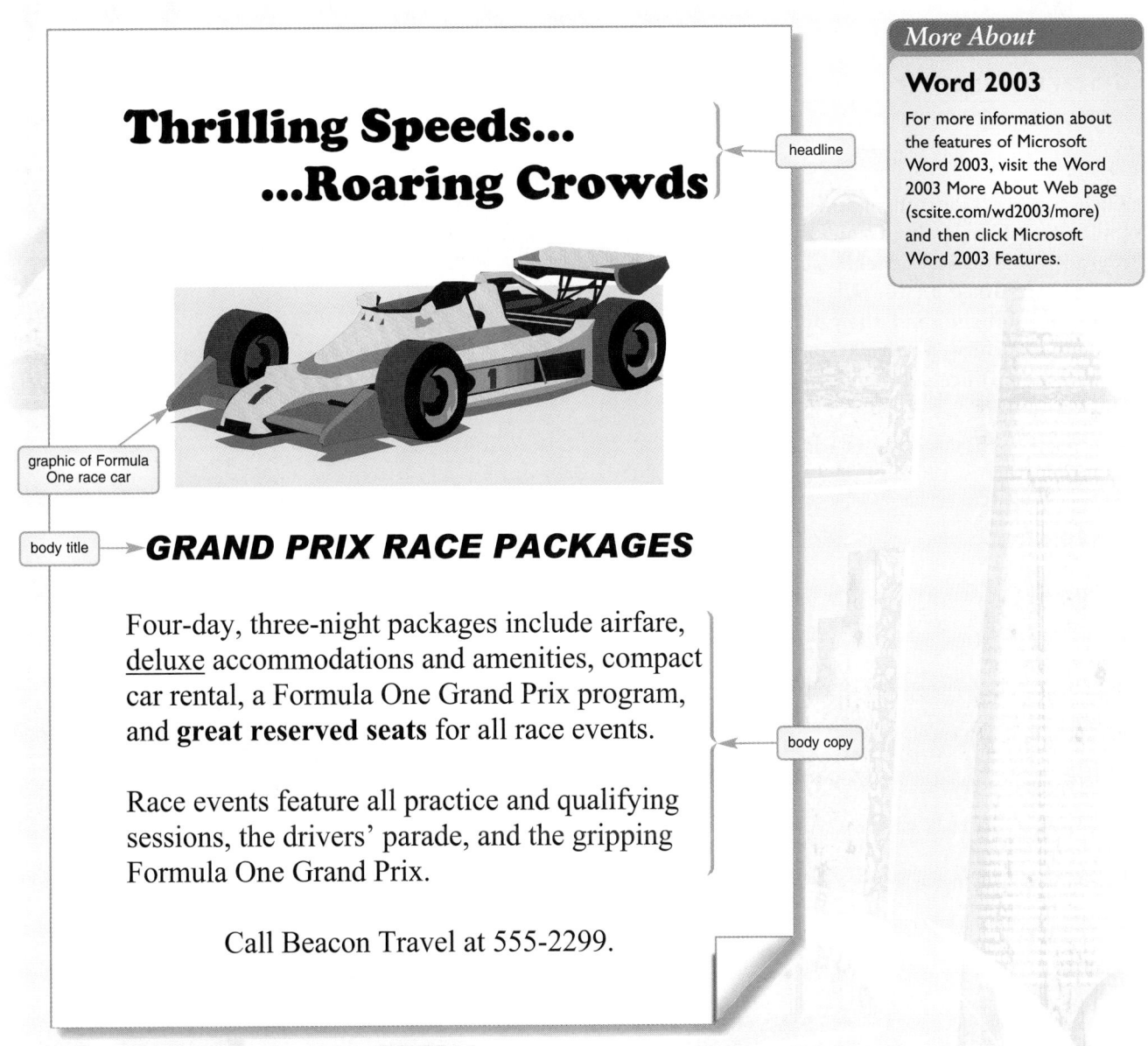

More About

Word 2003

For more information about the features of Microsoft Word 2003, visit the Word 2003 More About Web page (scsite.com/wd2003/more) and then click Microsoft Word 2003 Features.

FIGURE 1-1

The announcement informs potential customers about Grand Prix race packages available through Beacon Travel. The announcement begins with a headline in large, thick characters. Below the headline is a graphic of a Formula One race car, followed by the body title, GRAND PRIX RACE PACKAGES. The paragraphs of body copy below the body title briefly discuss the items included in the race packages. Finally, the last line of the announcement lists the telephone number of Beacon Travel.

Starting and Customizing Word

If you are stepping through this project on a computer and you want your screen to match the figures in this book, then you should change your computer's resolution to 800 × 600. For more information about how to change the resolution on your computer, read Appendix D.

To start Word, Windows must be running. The following steps show how to start Word. You may need to ask your instructor how to start Word for your system.

To Start Word

1

• **Click the Start button on the Windows taskbar, point to All Programs on the Start menu, point to Microsoft Office on the All Programs submenu, and then point to Microsoft Office Word 2003 on the Microsoft Office submenu.**

Windows displays the commands on the Start menu above the Start button and then displays the All Programs and Microsoft Office submenus (Figure 1-2).

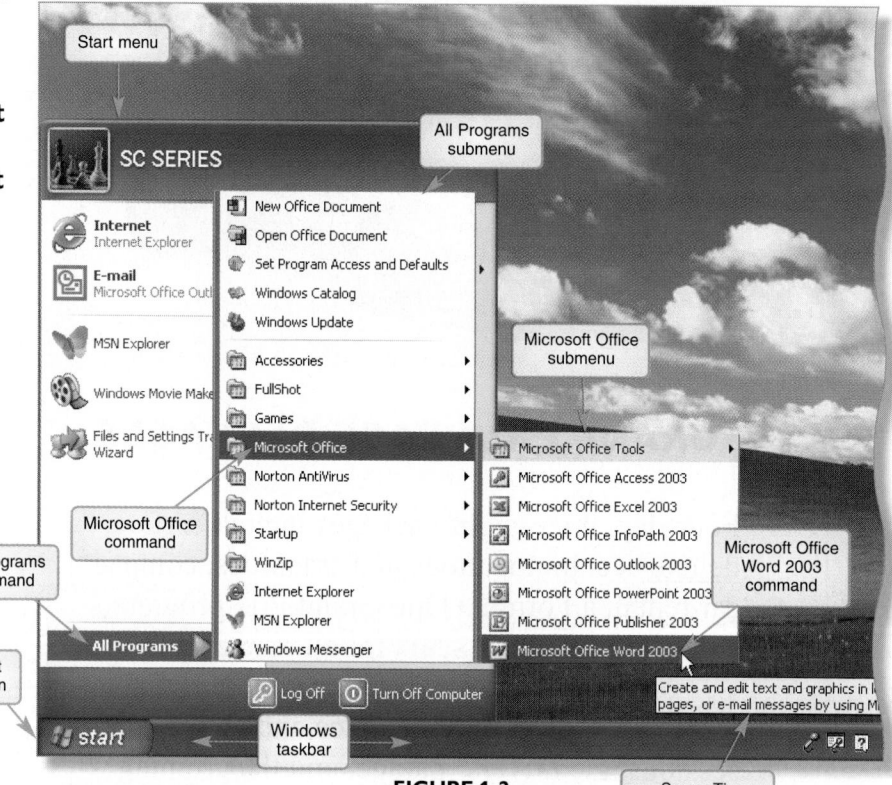

FIGURE 1-2

2

• **Click Microsoft Office Word 2003.**

Word starts. After a few moments, Word displays a new blank document titled Document1 in the Word window (Figure 1-3). The Windows taskbar displays the Word program button, indicating Word is running.

3

• **If the Word window is not maximized, double-click its title bar to maximize it.**

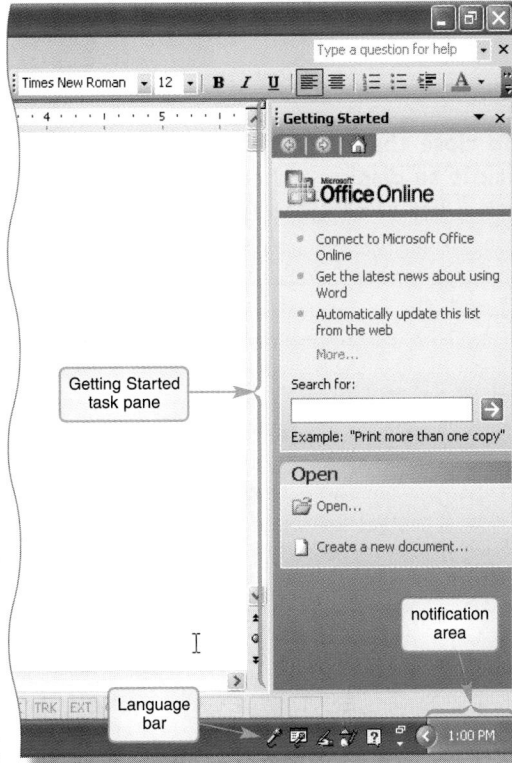

FIGURE 1-3

The screen in Figure 1-3 shows how the Word window looks the first time you start Word after installation on most computers. If the Office Speech Recognition software is installed and active on your computer, then when you start Word the Language bar is displayed on the screen. The **Language bar** contains buttons that allow you to speak commands and dictate text. It usually is located on the right side of the Windows taskbar next to the notification area, and it changes to include the speech recognition functions available in Word. In this book, the Language bar is closed because it takes up computer resources and with the Language bar active, the microphone can be turned on accidentally by clicking the Microphone button, causing your computer to act in an unstable manner. For additional information about the Language bar, see page WD 16 and Appendix B.

As shown in Figure 1-3, Word may display a task pane on the right side of the screen. A **task pane** is a separate window that enables users to carry out some Word tasks more efficiently. When you start Word, it automatically may display the Getting Started task pane, which is a task pane that allows you to search for Office-related topics on the Microsoft Web site, open files, or create new documents. In this book, the Getting Started task pane is closed to allow the maximum typing area in Word.

After installation, Word displays the toolbar buttons on a single row. A **toolbar** contains buttons and boxes that allow you to perform frequent tasks quickly. For more efficient use of the buttons, the toolbars should be displayed on two separate rows instead of sharing a single row.

The steps on the next page show how to customize the Word window by closing the Language bar, closing the Getting Started task pane, and displaying the toolbar buttons on two separate rows.

To Customize the Word Window

1

• **To close the Language bar, right-click it to display a shortcut menu with a list of commands.**

The Language bar shortcut menu appears (Figure 1-4).

FIGURE 1-4

2

• **Click Close the Language bar on the shortcut menu.**

• **If the Getting Started task pane is displayed, click the Close button in the upper-right corner of the task pane.**

The Language bar disappears. Word removes the Getting Started task pane from the screen (Figure 1-5).

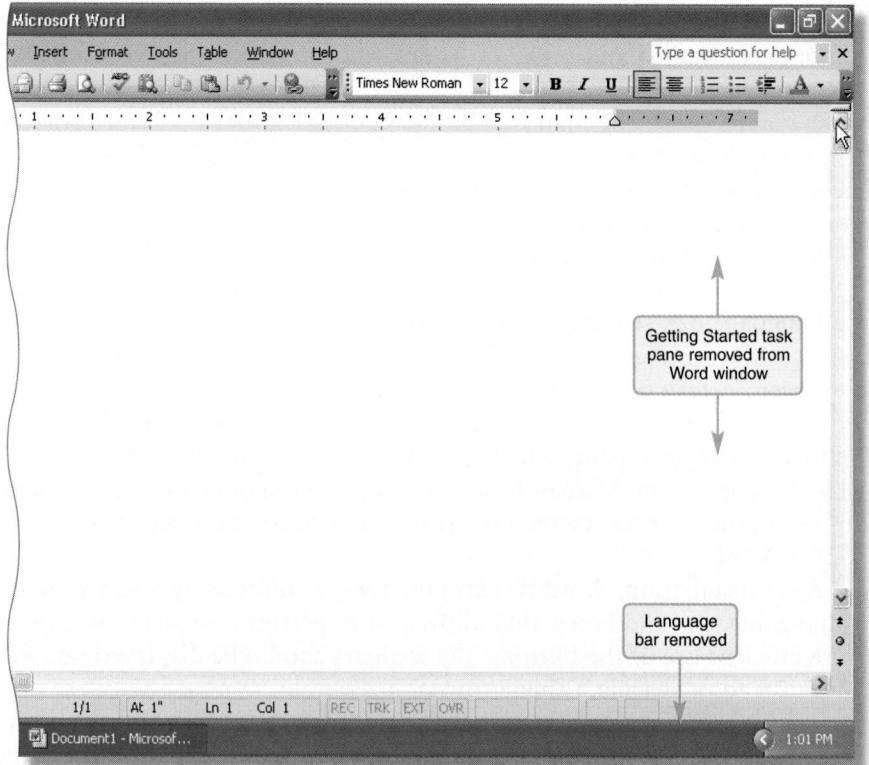

FIGURE 1-5

3

- **If the toolbar buttons are displayed on one row, click the Toolbar Options button.**

Word displays the Toolbar Options list, which shows the buttons that do not fit on the toolbars when they are displayed on one row (Figure 1-6).

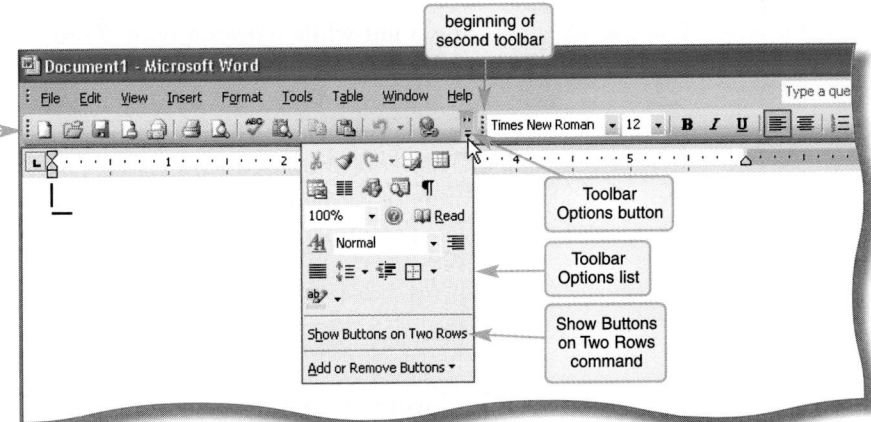

FIGURE 1-6

4

- **Click Show Buttons on Two Rows in the Toolbar Options list.**
- **If your screen differs from Figure 1-7, click the Normal View button on the horizontal scroll bar.**

Word displays the toolbars on two separate rows (Figure 1-7). The Toolbar Options list now is empty because all of the buttons fit on the toolbars when they display on two rows.

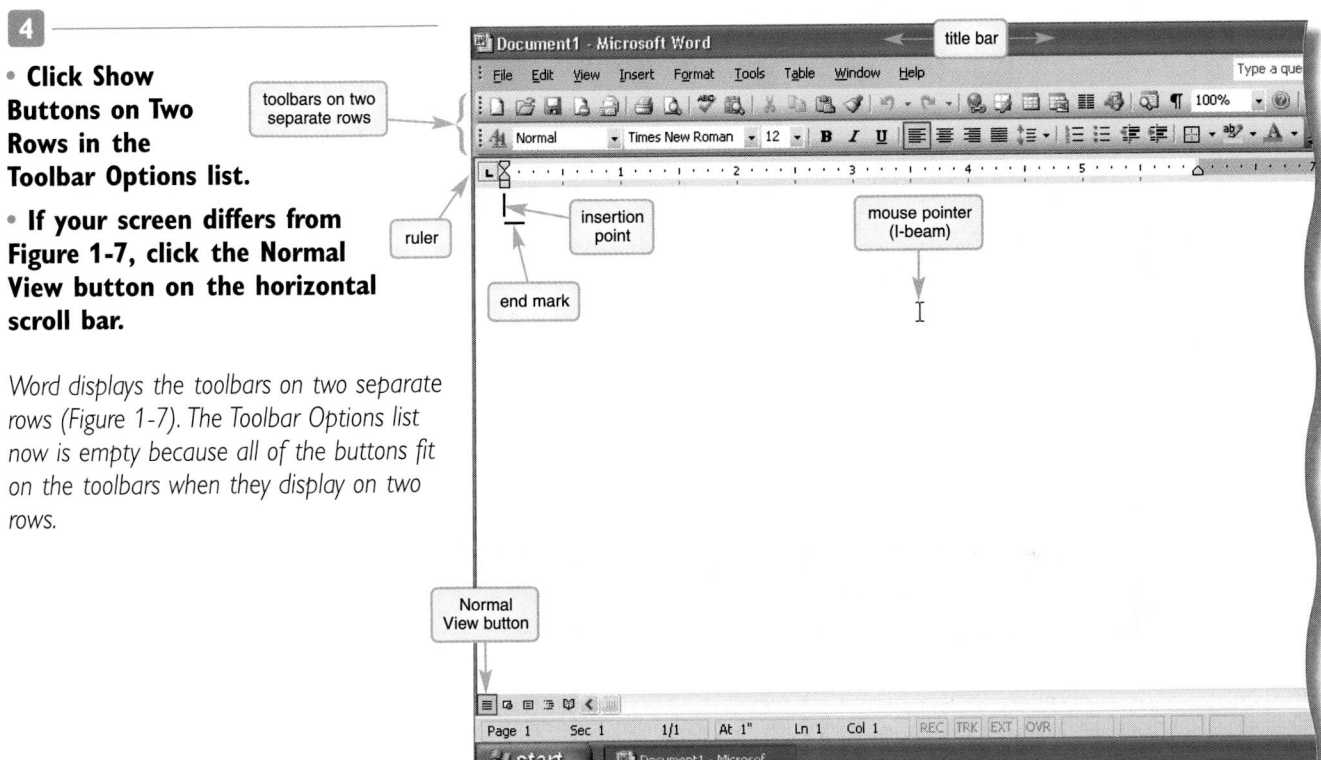

FIGURE 1-7

As an alternative to Steps 3 and 4 above, you can point to the beginning of the second toolbar (Figure 1-6), and when the mouse pointer changes to a four-headed arrow, drag the toolbar down to create two rows of toolbars.

Each time you start Word, the Word window appears the same way it did the last time you used Word. If the toolbar buttons are displayed on one row, then they will be displayed on one row the next time you start Word.

As you work through creating a document, you will find that certain Word operations automatically display a task pane. In addition to the Getting Started task pane shown in Figure 1-4, Word provides 13 other task panes. Some of the more important ones are the Help, Clip Art, Clipboard, and Research task panes. These task panes are discussed as they are used throughout the book.

At any point while working with Word, you can open or close a task pane by clicking View on the menu bar and then clicking Task Pane. To display a different task pane, click the Other Task Panes button to the left of the Close button on the task pane title bar (Figure 1-4 on page WD 8) and then click the desired task pane in the list. The Back and Forward buttons below the task pane title bar allow you to switch among task panes you have opened during a Word session. The Home button causes Word to display the Getting Started task pane.

The Word Window

The Word window consists of a variety of components to make your work more efficient and documents more professional. The following sections discuss these components, which are identified in either Figure 1-7 on the previous page or Figure 1-8.

Document Window

The **document window** displays text, tables, graphics, and other items as you type or insert them in a document. Only a portion of a document, however, appears on the screen at one time. You view the portion of the document displayed on the screen through a document window (Figure 1-8).

FIGURE 1-8

A document window contains several elements commonly found in other application software, as well as some elements unique to Word. The main elements of the Word document window are the insertion point, end mark, mouse pointer, rulers, scroll bars, and status bar.

INSERTION POINT The **insertion point** (Figure 1-7 on page WD 9) is a blinking vertical bar that indicates where text will be inserted as you type. As you type, the insertion point moves to the right and, when you reach the end of a line, it moves downward to the beginning of the next line. You also insert graphics, tables, and other items at the location of the insertion point.

END MARK The **end mark** (Figure 1-7) is a short horizontal line that indicates the end of the document. Each time you begin a new line, the end mark moves downward.

MOUSE POINTER The **mouse pointer** becomes different shapes depending on the task you are performing in Word and the pointer's location on the screen (Figure 1-7). The mouse pointer in Figure 1-7 has the shape of an I-beam. Other mouse pointer shapes are described as they appear on the screen during this and subsequent projects.

RULERS At the top edge of the document window is the horizontal ruler (Figure 1-8). You use the **horizontal ruler**, usually simply called the **ruler**, to set tab stops, indent paragraphs, adjust column widths, and change page margins.

An additional ruler, called the **vertical ruler**, sometimes is displayed at the left edge of the Word window when you perform certain tasks. The purpose of the vertical ruler is discussed in a later project. If your screen displays a vertical ruler, click View on the menu bar and then click Normal.

SCROLL BARS By using the **scroll bars**, you display different portions of your document in the document window (Figure 1-8). At the right edge of the document window is a vertical scroll bar. At the bottom of the document window is a horizontal scroll bar. On both the vertical and horizontal scroll bars, the position of the **scroll box** reflects the location of the portion of the document that is displayed in the document window.

On the left edge of the horizontal scroll bar are five buttons that change the view of a document. On the bottom of the vertical scroll bar are three buttons you can use to scroll through a document. These buttons are discussed as they are used in later projects.

STATUS BAR The **status bar** displays at the bottom of the document window, above the Windows taskbar (Figure 1-8). The status bar presents information about the location of the insertion point and the progress of current tasks, as well as the status of certain commands, keys, and buttons.

From left to right, Word displays the following information on the status bar in Figure 1-8: the page number, the section number, the page containing the insertion point followed by the total number of pages in the document, the position of the insertion point in inches from the top of the page, the line number and column number of the insertion point, and then several status indicators.

More About

The Horizontal Ruler

If the horizontal ruler is not displayed on your screen, click View on the menu bar and then click Ruler. To hide the ruler, also click View on the menu bar and then click Ruler.

More About

Scroll Bars

You can use the vertical scroll bar to scroll through multi-page documents. As you drag the scroll box up or down the scroll bar, Word displays a page indicator to the left of the scroll box. When you release the mouse button, the document window displays the page shown in the page indicator.

You use the **status indicators** to turn certain keys or modes on or off. Word displays the first four status indicators (REC, TRK, EXT, and OVR) darkened when they are on and dimmed when they are off. For example, the dimmed OVR indicates overtype mode is off. To turn these four status indicators on or off, double-click the status indicator on the status bar. Each of these status indicators is discussed as it is used in the projects.

The remaining status indicators display icons as you perform certain tasks. For example, when you begin typing in the document window, Word displays a Spelling and Grammar Status icon. When Word is saving your document, it displays a Background Save icon. When you print a document, Word displays a Background Print icon. If you perform a task that requires several seconds (such as saving a document), the status bar usually displays a message informing you of the progress of the task.

Menu Bar and Toolbars

The menu bar and toolbars display at the top of the screen just below the title bar (Figure 1-9).

FIGURE 1-9

MENU BAR The **menu bar** is a special toolbar that displays the Word menu names. Each menu name represents a menu. A **menu** contains a list of commands you use to perform tasks such as retrieving, storing, printing, and formatting data in a document.

When you point to a menu name on the menu bar, the area of the menu bar containing the name is displayed as a selected button. Word shades selected buttons in light orange and surrounds them with a blue outline.

To display a menu, click the menu name on the menu bar. For example, to display the Edit menu, click the Edit menu name on the menu bar. When you click a menu name on the menu bar, Word initially displays a **short menu** listing your most recently used commands (Figure 1-10a). If you wait a few seconds or click the arrows at the bottom of the short menu, it expands into a full menu. A **full menu** lists all the commands associated with a menu (Figure 1-10b). You also can display a full menu immediately by double-clicking the menu name on the menu bar.

(a) Short Menu

FIGURE 1-10

(b) Full Menu

In this book, when you display a menu, use one of the following techniques to ensure that Word always displays a full menu:

1. Click the menu name on the menu bar and then wait a few seconds.
2. Click the menu name on the menu bar and then click the arrows at the bottom of the short menu.
3. Click the menu name on the menu bar and then point to the arrows at the bottom of the short menu.
4. Double-click the menu name on the menu bar.

Both short and full menus may display some dimmed commands. A **dimmed command** appears gray, or dimmed, instead of black, which indicates it is not available for the current selection. A command with medium blue shading in the rectangle to its left on a full menu is called a **hidden command** because it does not appear on a short menu. As you use Word, it automatically personalizes the short menus for you based on how often you use commands. That is, as you use hidden commands on the full menu, Word *unhides* them and places them on the short menu.

Some commands have an arrow at the right edge of the menu. If you point to this arrow, Word displays a **submenu**, which is a list of additional commands associated with the selected command.

TOOLBARS Word has many predefined, or built-in, toolbars. A toolbar contains buttons, boxes, and menus that allow you to perform tasks more quickly than using the menu bar. For example, to print a document, you can click the Print button on a toolbar instead of navigating through the File menu to reach the Print command.

Each button on a toolbar displays an image to help you remember its function. Also, when you position the mouse pointer on, or point to, a button or box, Word displays the name of the button or box in a ScreenTip. A **ScreenTip** is a short on-screen note associated with the object to which you are pointing.

Two built-in toolbars are the Standard toolbar and the Formatting toolbar. Figure 1-11a shows the **Standard toolbar** and identifies its buttons and boxes. Figure 1-11b shows the **Formatting toolbar**. Each of these buttons and boxes will be explained in detail when it is used in this book.

(a) Standard Toolbar

(b) Formatting Toolbar

FIGURE 1-11

When you first install Word, the buttons on both the Standard and Formatting toolbars are preset to display on the same row immediately below the menu bar (Figure 1-12a). Unless the resolution of your display device is greater than 800 × 600, many of the buttons that belong to these toolbars are hidden when the two toolbars share one row. The buttons that display on the toolbar are the more frequently used buttons. Hidden buttons display in the Toolbar Options list (Figure 1-12b). You can display all the buttons on either toolbar by double-clicking the **move handle**, which is the vertical dotted line on the left edge of the toolbar.

As an alternative, you can instruct Word to display the buttons on the Standard and Formatting toolbars on separate rows, one below the other, by clicking the Show Buttons on Two Rows command in the Toolbar Options list (Figure 1-12b). In this book, the Standard and Formatting toolbars are shown on separate rows so that all buttons are displayed on a screen with the resolution set to 800 × 600 (Figure 1-12c).

In the previous figures, the Standard and Formatting toolbars are docked. A **docked toolbar** is a toolbar that is attached to an edge of the Word window. Depending on the task you are performing, Word may display additional toolbars on the screen. These additional toolbars either are docked or floating in the Word window. A **floating toolbar** is not attached to an edge of the Word window; that is, it appears in the middle of the Word window. You can rearrange the order of docked toolbars and can move floating toolbars anywhere in the Word window. Later in this book, steps are presented that show you how to float a docked toolbar or dock a floating toolbar.

More About

The Word Help System

Need Help? It is no further away than the Type a question for help box on the menu bar in the upper-right corner of the window. Click the box that contains the text, Type a question for help (Figure 1-12c), type help, and then press the ENTER key. Word responds with a list of topics you can click to learn about obtaining help on any Word-related topic. To find out what is new in Word 2003, type what is new in Word in the Type a question for help box.

(a) Standard and Formatting Toolbars on One Row

(b) Toolbar Options List

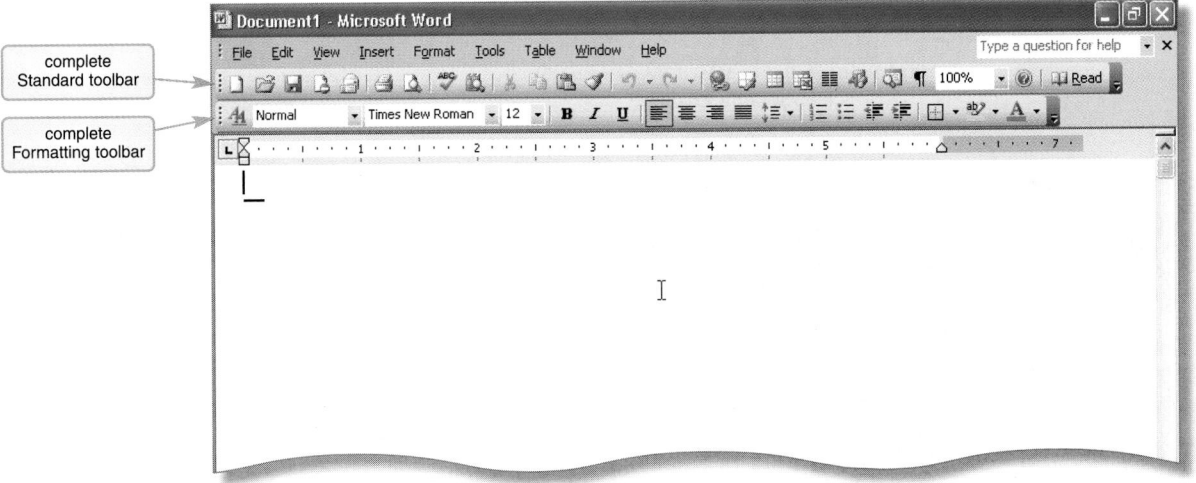

(c) Standard and Formatting Toolbars on Two Rows

FIGURE 1-12

Resetting Menus and Toolbars

Each project in this book begins with the menus and toolbars appearing as they did at the initial installation of the software. If you are stepping through this project on a computer and you want your menus and toolbars to match the figures in this book, then you should reset your menus and toolbars. For more information about how to reset menus and toolbars, read Appendix D.

More About

Toolbar Buttons

If you have difficulty seeing the small buttons on the toolbars, you can increase their size. Click View on the menu bar, point to Toolbars, click Customize on the Toolbars submenu, click the Options tab, place a check mark in the Large icons check box, and then click the Close button.

More About

Speech Recognition

If Office Speech Recognition software is installed on your computer, you can speak instructions to Word including toolbar button names, menu names and commands, and items in dialog boxes and task panes. You also can dictate so Word writes exactly what you say. The microphone picks up others' voices and background sounds, so speech recognition is most effective when used in a quiet environment.

Speech Recognition

With the **Office Speech Recognition software** installed and a microphone, you can speak the names of toolbar buttons, menus, menu commands, list items, alerts, and dialog box controls, such as OK and Cancel. You also can dictate text, such as words and sentences. To indicate whether you want to speak commands or dictate text, you use the Language bar. The Language bar can be in one of four states: (1) **restored**, which means it is displayed somewhere in the Word window (Figure 1-13a); (2) **minimized**, which means it is displayed on the Windows taskbar (Figure 1-13b); (3) **hidden**, which means you do not see it on the screen but it will be displayed the next time you start your computer; or (4) **closed**, which means it is hidden permanently until you enable it. If the Language bar is hidden and you want it to be displayed, then do the following:

1. Right-click an open area on the Windows taskbar at the bottom of the screen.
2. Point to Toolbars and then click Language bar on the Toolbars submenu.

(a) **Language Bar in Word Window with Microphone Enabled**   (b) **Language Bar Minimized on Windows Taskbar**

FIGURE 1-13

If the Language bar command is dimmed on the Toolbars submenu or if the Speech command is dimmed on the Tools menu, the Office Speech Recognition software is not installed.

In this book, the Language bar does not appear in the figures. If you want to close the Language bar so that your screen is identical to what you see in the book, right-click the Language bar and then click Close the Language bar on the shortcut menu. Additional information about the speech recognition capabilities of Word is available in Appendix B.

Q&A

Q: What font size should I use in an announcement?

A: An announcement usually is posted on a bulletin board. Thus, its font size should be as large as possible so that all potential readers easily can see the announcement.

Entering Text

Characters that display on the screen are a specific shape, size, and style. The **font**, or typeface, defines the appearance and shape of the letters, numbers, and special characters. The preset, or **default**, font is Times New Roman (Figure 1-14). **Font size** specifies the size of the characters and is determined by a measurement system called points. A single **point** is about 1/72 of one inch in height. Thus, a character with a font size of 12 is about 12/72 or 1/6 of one inch in height. On most computers, the default font size in Word is 12.

If more of the characters in your document require a larger font size than the default, you easily can change the font size before you type. In Project 1, many of the characters in the body copy of the announcement are a font size of 22. The following steps show how to increase the font size before you begin typing text.

To Increase the Font Size before Typing

1

• **Click the Font Size box arrow on the Formatting toolbar.**

Word displays a list of available font sizes in the Font Size list (Figure 1-14). The available font sizes depend on the current font, which is Times New Roman.

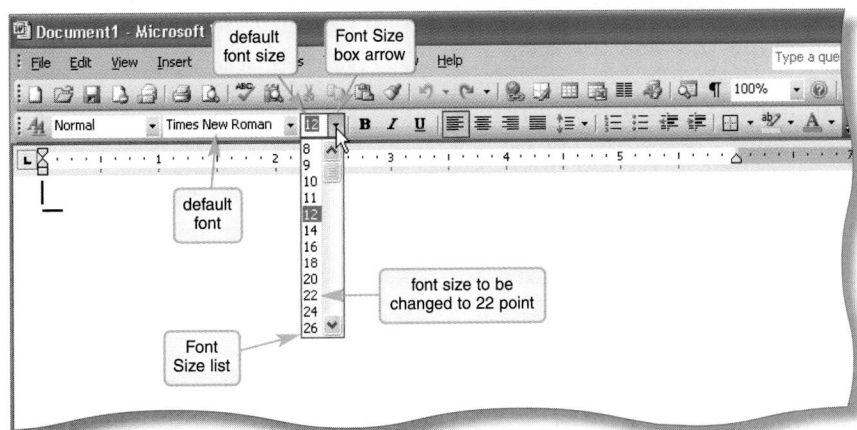

FIGURE 1-14

2

• **Click 22 in the Font Size list.**

The font size for characters to be entered in this document changes to 22 (Figure 1-15). The size of the insertion point increases to reflect the new font size.

FIGURE 1-15

The new font size takes effect immediately in the document. Word uses this font size for characters you enter in this announcement.

Typing Text

To enter text in a document, you type on the keyboard or speak into the microphone. The example on the next page illustrates the steps required to type both lines of the headline in the announcement. By default, Word positions these lines at the left margin. In a later section, this project will show how to make all of the characters in the headline larger and thicker, and how to position the second line of the headline at the right margin.

The steps on the next page show how to begin typing text in the announcement.

Other Ways

1. On Format menu click Font, click Font tab, select desired font size in Size list, click OK button
2. Right-click paragraph mark above end mark, click Font on shortcut menu, click Font tab, select desired font size in Size list, click OK button
3. Press CTRL+SHIFT+P, type desired font size, press ENTER
4. Press CTRL+SHIFT+> repeatedly
5. In Voice Command mode, say "Font Size, [select font size]"

To Type Text

1

• **Type** Thrilling Speeds **and then press the** PERIOD (.) **key three times. If you make an error while typing, press the** BACKSPACE **key until you have deleted the text in error and then retype the text correctly.**

As you type, the insertion point moves to the right (Figure 1-16).

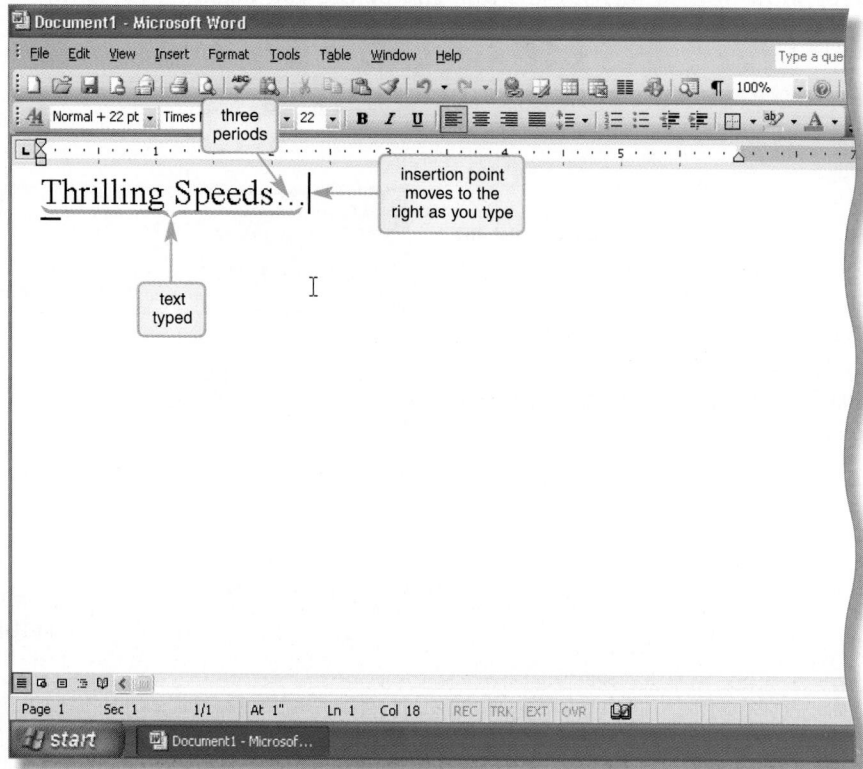

FIGURE 1-16

2

• **Press the** ENTER **key.**

Word moves the insertion point to the beginning of the next line (Figure 1-17). Notice the status bar indicates the current position of the insertion point. That is, the insertion point currently is on line 2 column 1.

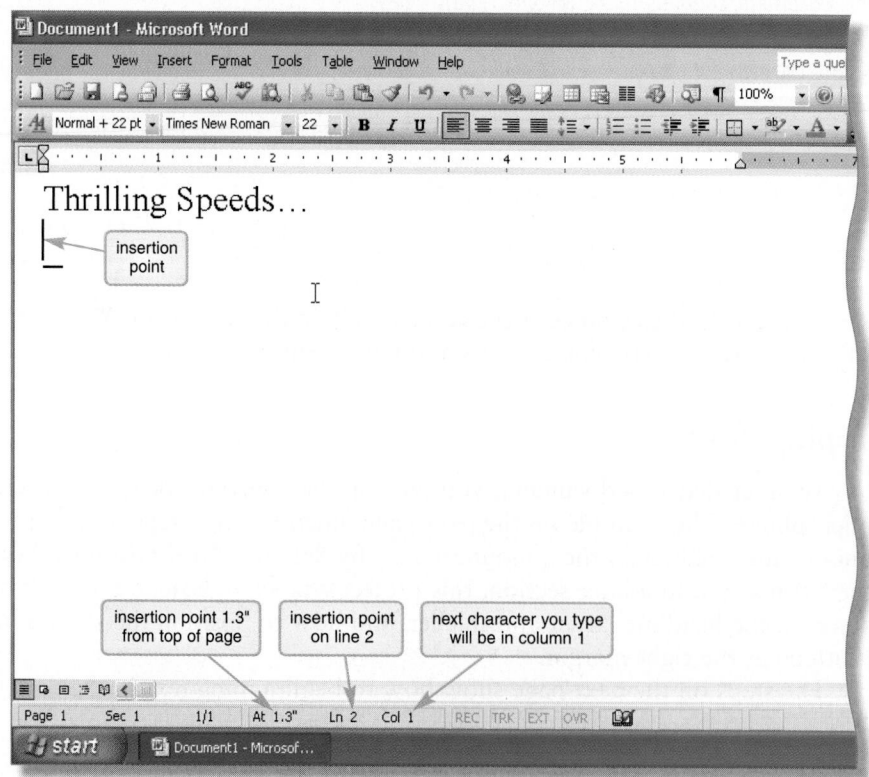

FIGURE 1-17

3

- **Press the PERIOD key three times.**
- **Type** Roaring Crowds **and then press the ENTER key.**

The headline is complete (Figure 1-18). The insertion point is on line 3.

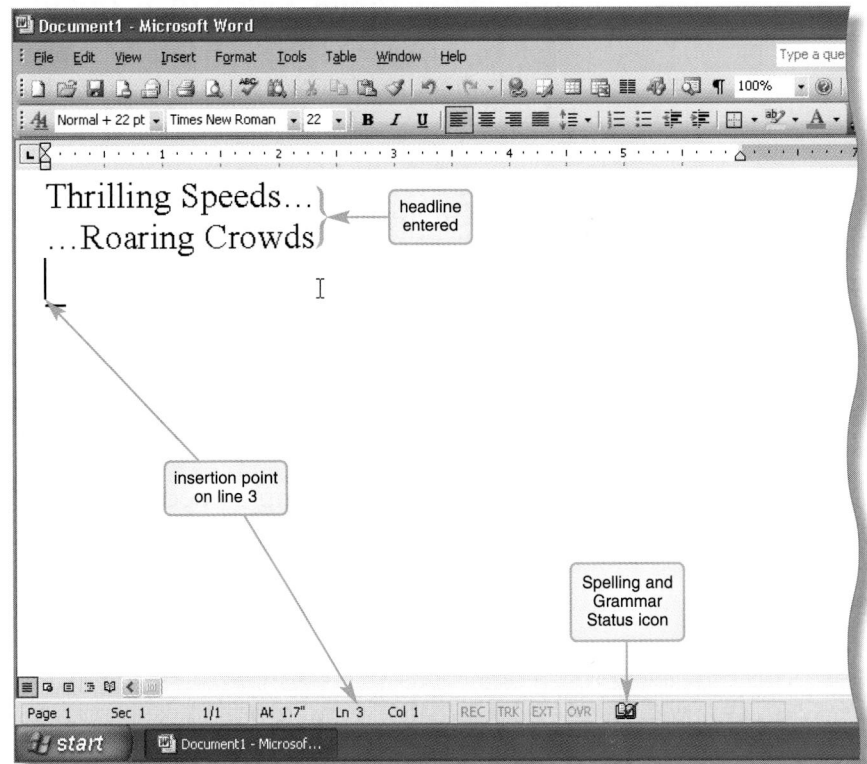

FIGURE 1-18

When you begin entering text in a document, the **Spelling and Grammar Status icon** appears at the right of the status bar (Figure 1-18). As you type, the Spelling and Grammar Status icon shows an animated pencil writing on paper, which indicates Word is checking for possible errors. When you stop typing, the pencil changes to either a red check mark or a red X. In Figure 1-18, the Spelling and Grammar Status icon contains a red check mark.

In general, if all of the words you have typed are in Word's dictionary and your grammar is correct, the Spelling and Grammar Status icon contains a red check mark. If you type a word not in the dictionary (because it is a proper name or misspelled), a red wavy underline appears below the word. If you type text that may be incorrect grammatically, a green wavy underline appears below the text. When Word flags a possible spelling or grammar error, it also changes the red check mark on the Spelling and Grammar Status icon to a red X. As you enter text in a document, your Spelling and Grammar Status icon may show a red X instead of a red check mark. Later, this project will show how to check the spelling of these flagged words. At that time, the red X returns to a red check mark.

Entering Blank Lines in a Document

To enter a blank line in a document, press the ENTER key without typing any text on the line. The following example shows how to enter three blank lines below the headline.

To Enter Blank Lines in a Document

* **Press the ENTER key three times.**

Word inserts three blank lines in the document below the headline (Figure 1-19).

FIGURE 1-19

Displaying Formatting Marks

To indicate where in a document you press the ENTER key or SPACEBAR, you may find it helpful to display formatting marks. A **formatting mark**, sometimes called a **nonprinting character**, is a character that Word displays on the screen but is not visible on a printed document. For example, the paragraph mark (¶) is a formatting mark that indicates where you pressed the ENTER key. A raised dot (•) shows where you pressed the SPACEBAR. Other formatting marks are discussed as they appear on the screen.

Depending on settings made during previous Word sessions, the Word screen already may display formatting marks (Figure 1-20). The following step shows how to display formatting marks, if they are not displayed already on the screen.

To Display Formatting Marks

1

• **If it is not selected already, click the Show/Hide ¶ button on the Standard toolbar.**

Word displays formatting marks on the screen (Figure 1-20). The Show/Hide ¶ button is selected. That is, the button is light orange and surrounded with a blue outline.

FIGURE 1-20

Notice several changes to the Word document window (Figure 1-20). A paragraph mark appears at the end of each line to indicate you pressed the ENTER key. Each time you press the ENTER key, Word creates a new paragraph. The size of paragraph marks is 22 point because the font size was changed earlier in the project. Between each word, a raised dot appears, indicating you pressed the SPACEBAR. Finally, the Show/Hide ¶ button changes from blue to light orange and has a blue outline, which indicates it is selected.

If you feel the formatting marks clutter the screen, you can hide them by clicking the Show/Hide ¶ button again. It is recommended that you display formatting marks; therefore, the document windows presented in this book show the formatting marks.

More About

Zooming

If text is too small to read on the screen, you can zoom the document by clicking View on the menu bar, clicking Zoom, selecting the desired percentage, and then clicking the OK button. Changing the zoom percent has no effect on the printed document.

More About

Caps Lock

If you leave the CAPS LOCK key on and begin typing a new sentence, Word automatically corrects the problem for you. That is, it disengages the CAPS LOCK key and capitalizes only the first letter of the first word in the next sentence.

Entering More Text

Every character in the body title (GRAND PRIX RACE PACKAGES) of the announcement is in capital letters. The next step is to enter this body title in all capital letters in the document window, as explained below.

To Type More Text

1 **Press the CAPS LOCK key on the keyboard to turn on capital letters. Verify the caps lock indicator is lit on the keyboard.**

2 **Type** GRAND PRIX RACE PACKAGES **and then press the CAPS LOCK key to turn off capital letters.**

3 **Press the ENTER key twice.**

Word displays the body title on line 6 (Figure 1-21). Depending on your Word settings, your screen may not display the smart tag indicator below the word, RACE.

More About

Smart Tags

A smart tag is a button that automatically appears on the screen when Word performs a certain action. You then can use the smart tag to perform tasks more efficiently. Word notifies you of a smart tag by displaying a smart tag indicator, such as the purple dotted underline shown in Figure 1-21.

FIGURE 1-21

Using Wordwrap

Wordwrap allows you to type words in a paragraph continually without pressing the ENTER key at the end of each line. When the insertion point reaches the right margin, Word automatically positions the insertion point at the beginning of the next line. As you type, if a word extends beyond the right margin, Word also automatically positions that word on the next line with the insertion point.

As you type text in the document window, do not press the ENTER key when the insertion point reaches the right margin. Word creates a new paragraph each time you press the ENTER key. Thus, press the ENTER key only in these circumstances:

1. To insert blank lines in a document
2. To begin a new paragraph
3. To terminate a short line of text and advance to the next line
4. In response to certain Word commands

The following step illustrates wordwrap.

To Wordwrap Text as You Type

1

• **Type** Four-day, three-night packages include airfare, deluxe **and then press the SPACEBAR.**

The word, deluxe, wraps to the beginning of line 9 because it is too long to fit on line 8 (Figure 1-22). Your document may wordwrap differently depending on the type of printer you are using.

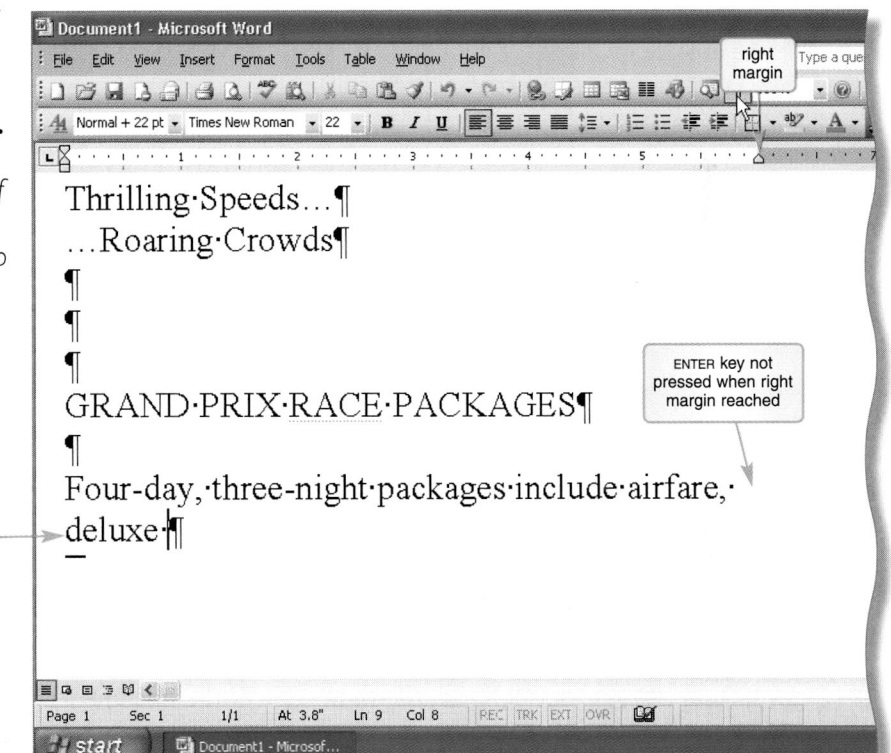

the word, deluxe, could not fit on line 8, so it wrapped to beginning of line 9

ENTER key not pressed when right margin reached

FIGURE 1-22

Entering Text that Scrolls the Document Window

As you type more lines of text than Word can display in the document window, Word **scrolls** the top portion of the document upward off the screen. Although you cannot see the text once it scrolls off the screen, it remains in the document. As previously discussed, the document window allows you to view only a portion of your document at one time (Figure 1-8 on page WD 10).

Microsoft Office
Word 2003

The following step shows how Word scrolls text through the document window.

To Enter Text that Scrolls the Document Window

1

• **Type** accommodations and amenities, compact car rental, a Formula One Grand Prix program, and great reserved seats for all race events.

• **Press the ENTER key twice.**

Word scrolls the headline off the top of the screen (Figure 1-23). Your screen may scroll differently depending on the type of monitor you are using.

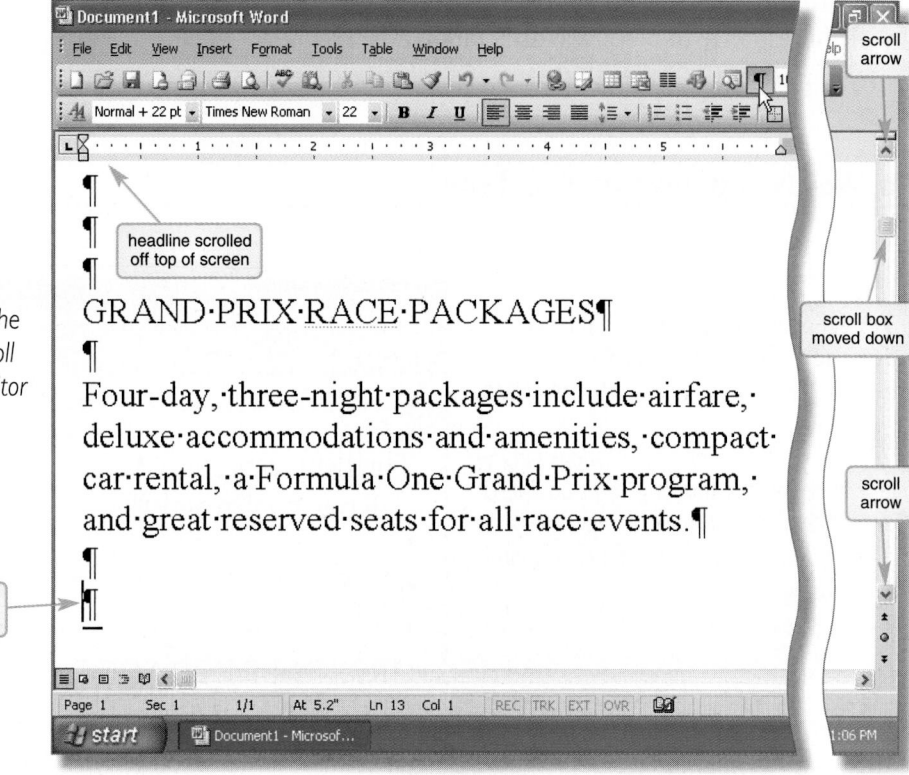

FIGURE 1-23

When Word scrolls text off the top of the screen, the scroll box on the vertical scroll bar at the right edge of the document window moves downward (Figure 1-23). The scroll box indicates the current relative location of the portion of the document that is displayed in the document window. You may use either the mouse or the keyboard to scroll to a different location in a document.

With the mouse, you can use the scroll arrows or the scroll box on the scroll bar to display a different portion of the document in the document window, and then click the mouse to move the insertion point to that location. Table 1-1 explains various techniques for using the scroll bar to scroll vertically with the mouse.

Table 1-1 Using the Scroll Bar to Scroll with the Mouse	
SCROLL DIRECTION	**MOUSE ACTION**
Up	Drag the scroll box upward.
Down	Drag the scroll box downward.
Up one screen	Click anywhere above the scroll box on the vertical scroll bar.
Down one screen	Click anywhere below the scroll box on the vertical scroll bar.
Up one line	Click the scroll arrow at the top of the vertical scroll bar.
Down one line	Click the scroll arrow at the bottom of the vertical scroll bar.

When you use the keyboard to scroll, the insertion point automatically moves when you press the appropriate keys. Table 1-2 outlines various techniques to scroll through a document using the keyboard.

Table 1-2 Scrolling with the Keyboard	
SCROLL DIRECTION	**KEY(S) TO PRESS**
Left one character	LEFT ARROW
Right one character	RIGHT ARROW
Left one word	CTRL+LEFT ARROW
Right one word	CTRL+RIGHT ARROW
Up one line	UP ARROW
Down one line	DOWN ARROW
To end of a line	END
To beginning of a line	HOME
Up one paragraph	CTRL+UP ARROW
Down one paragraph	CTRL+DOWN ARROW
Up one screen	PAGE UP
Down one screen	PAGE DOWN
To top of document window	ALT+CTRL+PAGE UP
To bottom of document window	ALT+CTRL+PAGE DOWN
To beginning of a document	CTRL+HOME
To end of a document	CTRL+END

Q & A

Q: How can I help prevent wrist injury while working on a computer?

A: Typical computer users frequently switch between the keyboard and the mouse during a word processing session, an action that strains the wrist. To help prevent wrist injury, minimize switching. If your fingers already are on the keyboard, use keyboard keys to scroll. If your hand already is on the mouse, use the mouse to scroll.

Checking Spelling and Grammar as You Type

As you type text in the document window, Word checks your typing for possible spelling and grammar errors. If a word you type is not in the dictionary, a red wavy underline appears below the word. Similarly, if text you type contains a possible grammar error, a green wavy underline appears below the text. In both cases, the Spelling and Grammar Status icon on the status bar shows a red X, instead of a check mark. Although you can check the entire document for spelling and grammar errors at once, you also can check these flagged errors immediately.

To verify that the check spelling as you type feature is enabled, right-click the Spelling and Grammar Status icon on the status bar and then click Options on the shortcut menu. When Word displays the Spelling & Grammar dialog box, be sure Check spelling as you type has a check mark and Hide spelling errors in this document does not have a check mark.

When a word is flagged with a red wavy underline, it is not in Word's dictionary. To display a list of suggested corrections for a flagged word, you right-click the word. A flagged word, however, is not necessarily misspelled. For example, many names, abbreviations, and specialized terms are not in Word's main dictionary. In these cases, you tell Word to ignore the flagged word. As you type, Word also detects duplicate words. For example, if your document contains the phrase, to the the store, Word places a red wavy underline below the second occurrence of the word, the.

In the example on the next page, the word, feature, has been misspelled intentionally as feture to illustrate Word's check spelling as you type. If you are doing this project on a personal computer, your announcement may contain different misspelled words, depending on the accuracy of your typing.

To Check Spelling and Grammar as You Type

 1

• **Type** Race events feture **and then press the** SPACEBAR.

• **Position the mouse pointer in the flagged word (feture, in this case).**

Word flags the misspelled word, feture, by placing a red wavy underline below it (Figure 1-24). The Spelling and Grammar Status icon on the status bar now contains a red X, indicating Word has detected a possible spelling or grammar error.

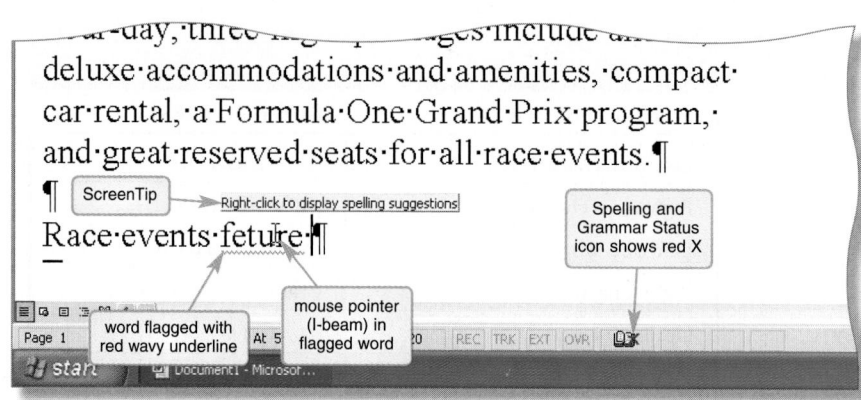

FIGURE 1-24

2

• **Right-click the flagged word, feture.**

Word displays a shortcut menu that lists suggested spelling corrections for the flagged word (Figure 1-25).

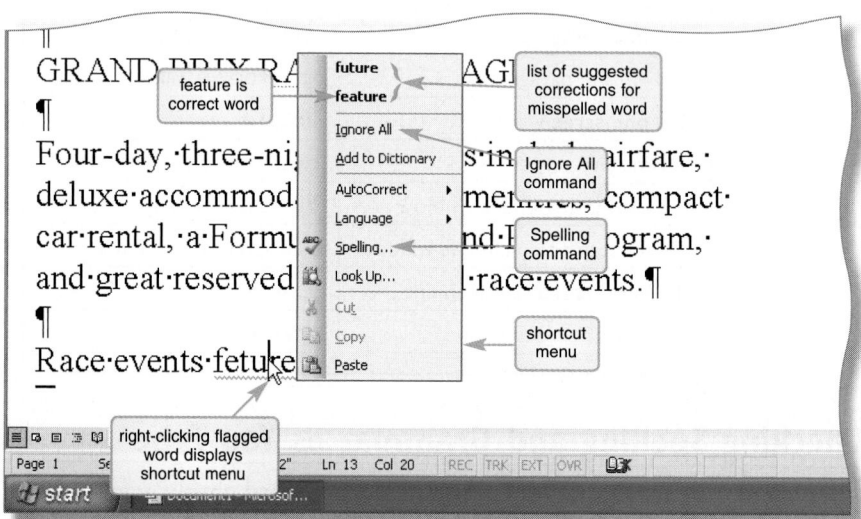

FIGURE 1-25

3

• **Click feature on the shortcut menu.**

Word replaces the misspelled word with the word selected on the shortcut menu (Figure 1-26). The Spelling and Grammar Status icon once again contains a red check mark.

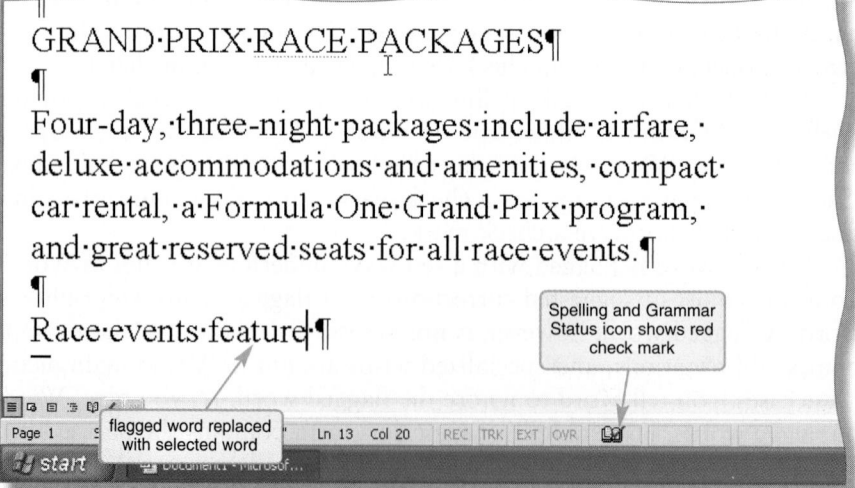

Other Ways

1. Double-click Spelling and Grammar Status icon on status bar, click correct word on shortcut menu
2. In Voice Command mode, say "Spelling and Grammar"

FIGURE 1-26

If a flagged word actually is spelled correctly and, for example, is a proper name, you can right-click it and then click Ignore All on the shortcut menu (Figure 1-25). If, when you right-click the misspelled word, your desired correction is not in the list on the shortcut menu, you can click outside the shortcut menu to close the menu and then retype the correct word, or you can click Spelling on the shortcut menu to display the Spelling dialog box. Project 2 discusses the Spelling dialog box.

If you feel the wavy underlines clutter the document window, you can hide them temporarily until you are ready to check for spelling and grammar errors. To hide spelling errors, right-click the Spelling and Grammar Status icon on the status bar and then click Hide Spelling Errors on the shortcut menu. To hide grammar errors, right-click the Spelling and Grammar Status icon on the status bar and then click Hide Grammatical Errors on the shortcut menu.

The next step is to type the remainder of text in the announcement, as described in the following steps.

To Enter More Text

1 Press the END key to move the insertion point to the end of the line.

2 Type all practice and qualifying sessions, the drivers' parade, and the gripping Formula One Grand Prix.

3 Press the ENTER key twice.

4 Type Call Beacon Travel at 555-2299.

The text of the announcement is complete (Figure 1-27).

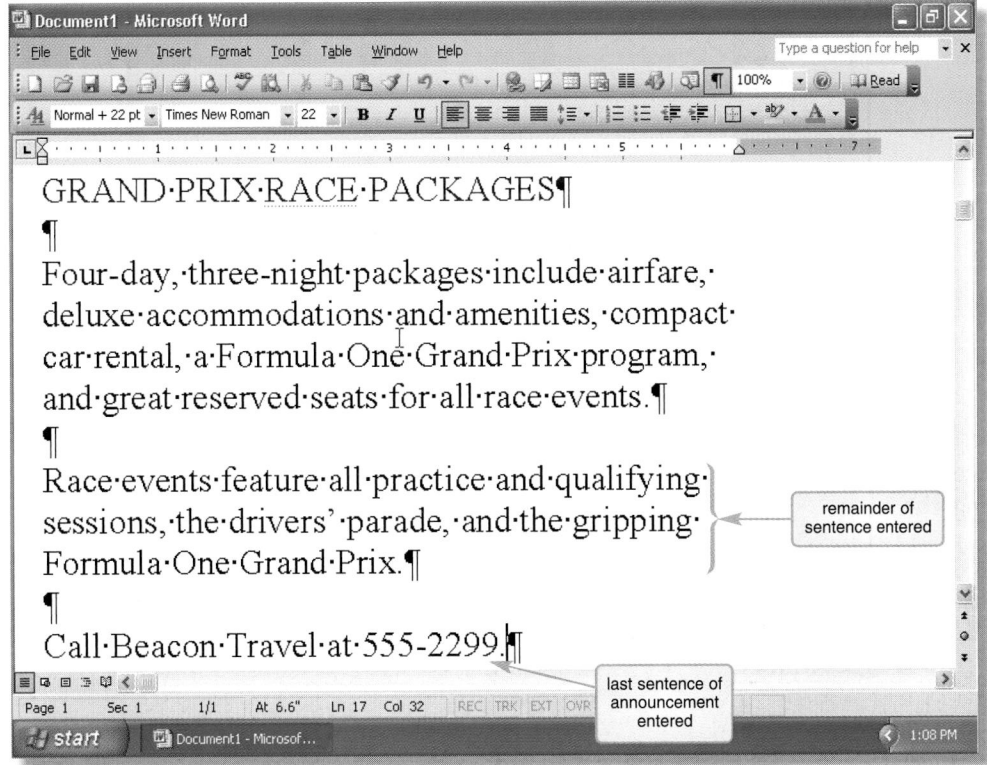

FIGURE 1-27

Saving a Document

As you create a document in Word, the computer stores it in memory. If the computer is turned off or if you lose electrical power, the document in memory is lost. Hence, if you plan to use the document later, you must save it on disk.

A saved document is called a **file**. A **file name** is the name assigned to a file when it is saved. This project saves the announcement with the file name, Grand Prix Announcement. Depending on your Windows settings, the file type .doc may display immediately after the file name. The file type **.doc** indicates the file is a Word document.

The following steps illustrate how to save a document on a floppy disk in drive A using the Save button on the Standard toolbar.

To Save a New Document

1

• **With a formatted floppy disk in drive A, click the Save button on the Standard toolbar.**

Word displays the Save As dialog box (Figure 1-28). The first line from the document (Thrilling Speeds) is selected in the File name text box as the default file name. You can change this selected file name by immediately typing the new name.

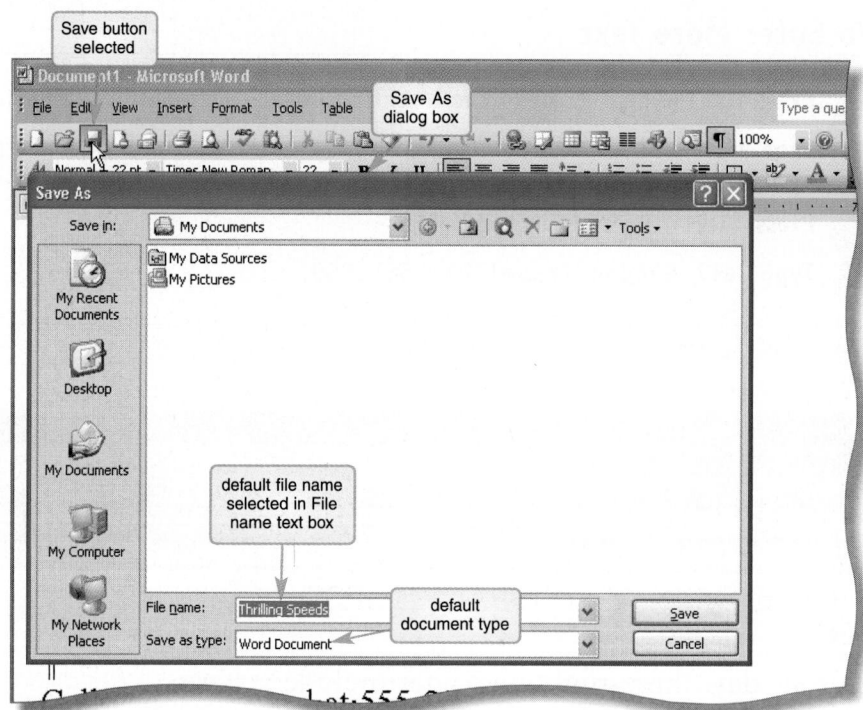

FIGURE 1-28

2

• **Type** Grand Prix Announcement **in the File name text box. Do not press the ENTER key after typing the file name.**

The file name, Grand Prix Announcement, replaces the text, Thrilling Speeds, in the File name text box (Figure 1-29).

FIGURE 1-29

3

• **Click the Save in box arrow.**

*Word displays a list of the available drives and folders in which you can save the document (Figure 1-30). A **folder** is a specific location on a disk. Your list may differ depending on your computer's configuration.*

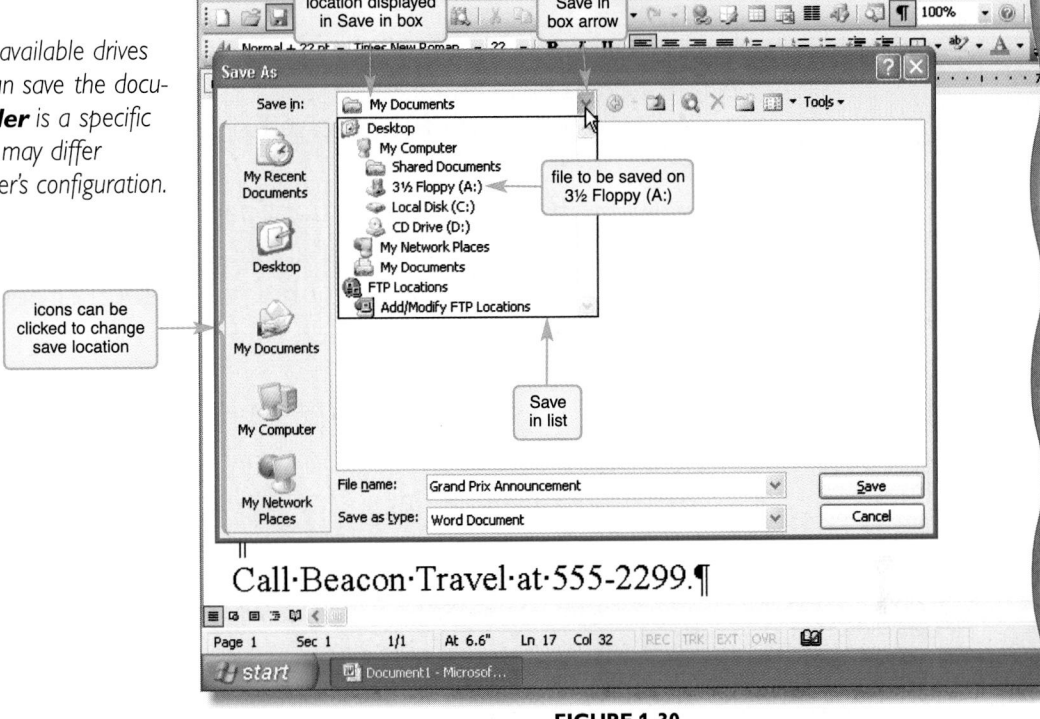

FIGURE 1-30

4

• **Click 3½ Floppy (A:) in the Save in list.**

Drive A becomes the new save location (Figure 1-31). The Save As dialog box now shows names of existing files stored on the floppy disk in drive A. In Figure 1-31, the list is empty because no Word files currently are stored on the floppy disk in drive A.

FIGURE 1-31

5

• **Click the Save button in the Save As dialog box.**

Word saves the document on the floppy disk in drive A with the file name, Grand Prix Announcement (Figure 1-32). Although the announcement is saved on a floppy disk, it also remains in main memory and on the screen.

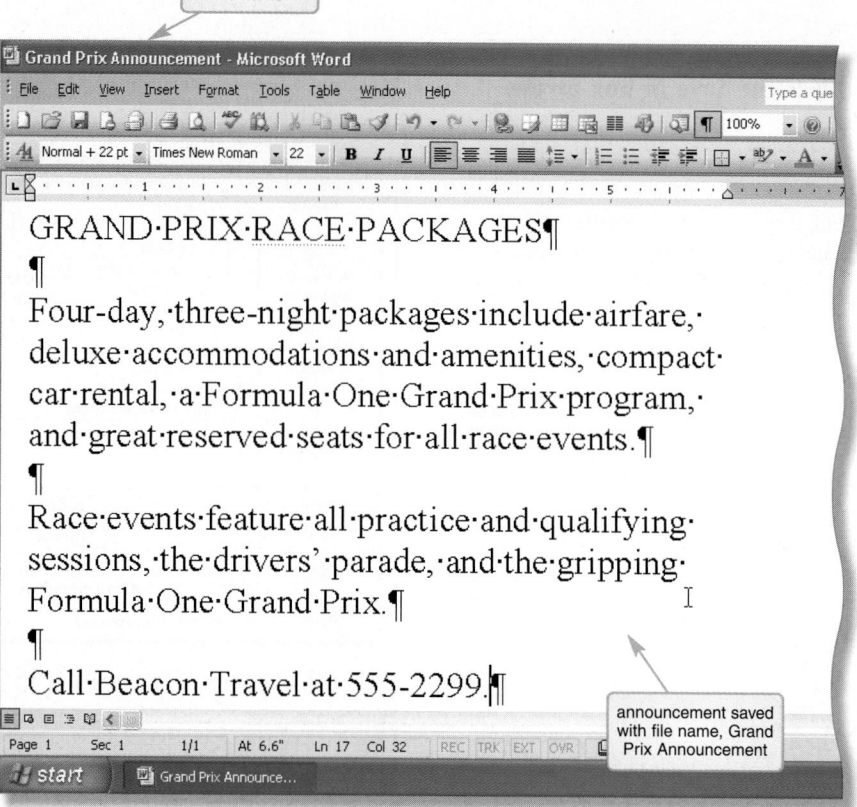

title bar displays
file name

announcement saved
with file name, Grand
Prix Announcement

FIGURE 1-32

While Word is saving the document, it displays a message on the status bar indicating the progress of the save. After the save operation is complete, Word changes the name of the document on the title bar from Document1 to Grand Prix Announcement (Figure 1-32).

You can use the seven buttons at the top of the Save As dialog box (Figure 1-30 on the previous page) and the five icons along the left edge to change the save location and other tasks. Table 1-3 lists the function of the buttons and icons in the Save As dialog box.

When you click the Tools button in the Save As dialog box, Word displays the Tools menu. The Save Options command on the Tools menu allows you to save a backup copy of the document, create a password to limit access to the document, and carry out other functions that are discussed later.

BUTTON OR ICON	BUTTON OR ICON NAME	FUNCTION
Table 1-3 Save As Dialog Box Buttons and Icons		
	Default File Location	Displays contents of default file location
	Up One Level	Displays contents of folder one level up from current folder
	Search the Web	Starts Web browser and displays search engine
	Delete	Deletes selected file or folder
	Create New Folder	Creates new folder
	Views	Changes view of files and folders
Tools	Tools	Lists commands to print or modify file names and folders
My Recent Documents	My Recent Documents	Displays contents of My Recent Documents in Save in list (you cannot save to this location)

BUTTON OR ICON	BUTTON OR ICON NAME	FUNCTION
Table 1-3 Save As Dialog Box Buttons and Icons		
Desktop	Desktop	Displays contents of Windows desktop folder in Save in list to save quickly to the Windows desktop
My Documents	My Documents	Displays contents of My Documents in Save in list to save quickly to the My Documents folder
My Computer	My Computer	Displays contents of My Computer in Save in list to save quickly to another drive on the computer
My Network Places	My Network Places	Displays contents of My Network Places in Save in list to save quickly to My Network Places

Formatting Paragraphs and Characters in a Document

The text for Project 1 now is complete. The next step is to format the paragraphs and characters in the announcement.

Paragraphs encompass the text up to and including a paragraph mark (¶). **Paragraph formatting** is the process of changing the appearance of a paragraph. For example, you can center or indent a paragraph.

Characters include letters, numbers, punctuation marks, and symbols. **Character formatting** is the process of changing the way characters appear on the screen and in print. You use character formatting to emphasize certain words and improve readability of a document. For example, you can italicize or underline characters.

In many cases, you apply both paragraph and character formatting to the same text. For example, you may center a paragraph (paragraph formatting) and bold the characters in a paragraph (character formatting).

With Word, you can format paragraphs and characters before you type, or you can apply new formats after you type. Earlier, this project showed how to change the font size (character formatting) before you typed any text. This section shows how to format existing text.

Q&A

Q: What is the difference between character formatting and paragraph formatting?

A: Character formatting includes changing the font, font style, font size; adding an underline, color, strikethrough, shadow, or outline; embossing; engraving; making a superscript or subscript; and changing the case of the letters. Paragraph formatting includes alignment; indentation; and spacing above, below, and in between lines.

Microsoft Office
Word 2003

Figure 1-33a shows the announcement before formatting its paragraphs and characters. Figure 1-33b shows the announcement after formatting. As you can see from the two figures, a document that is formatted is easier to read and looks more professional.

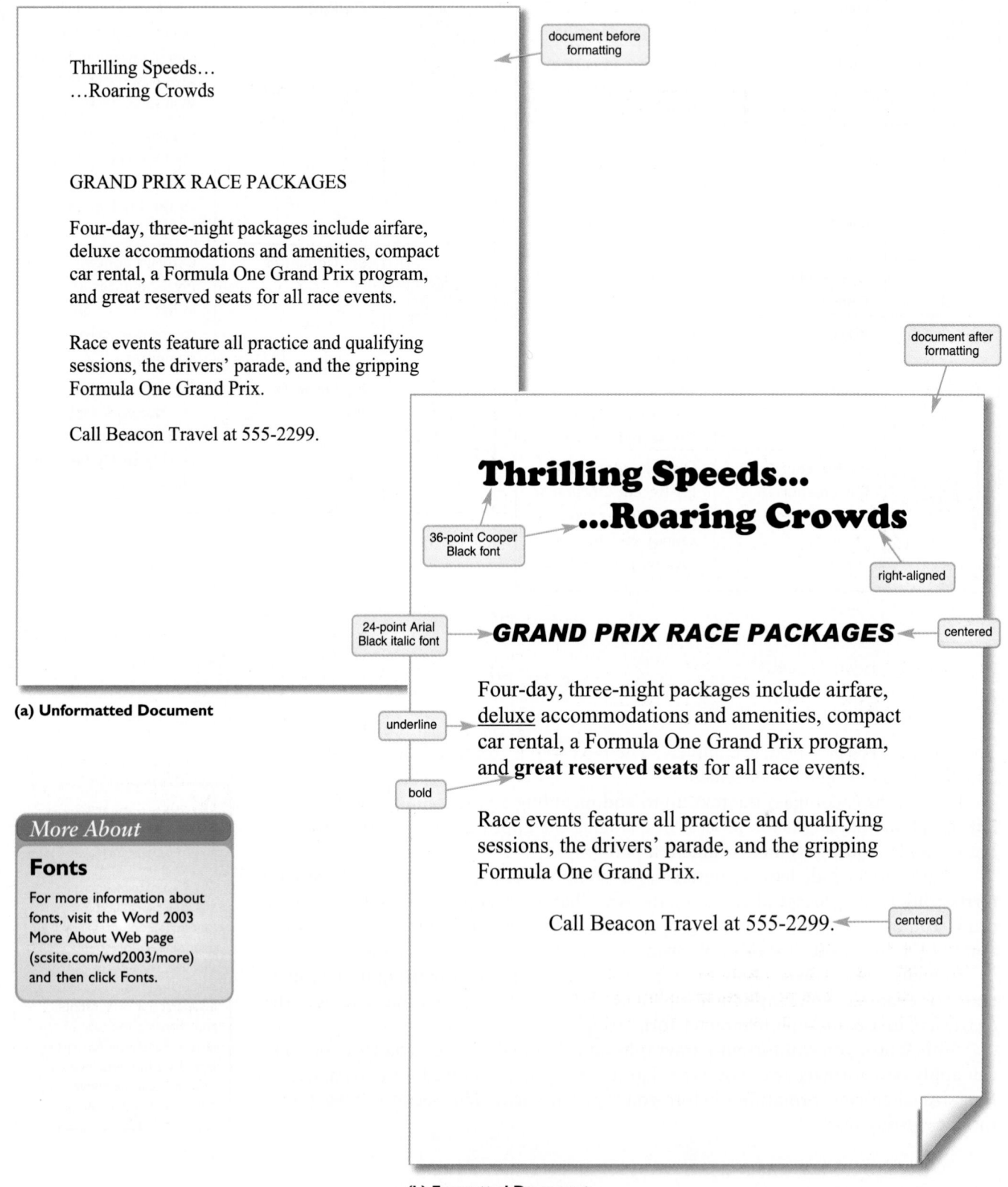

(a) Unformatted Document

(b) Formatted Document

FIGURE 1-33

More About

Fonts

For more information about fonts, visit the Word 2003 More About Web page (scsite.com/wd2003/more) and then click Fonts.

Selecting and Formatting Paragraphs and Characters

To format a single paragraph, move the insertion point in the paragraph and then format the paragraph. That is, you do not need to select a single paragraph to format it. To format *multiple* paragraphs, however, you first must select the paragraphs you want to format and then format them. In the same manner, to format a single word, position the insertion point in the word and then format the word. To format multiple characters or words, however, you first must select the characters or words to be formatted and then format the selection.

Selected text is highlighted text. If your screen normally displays dark letters on a light background, then selected text displays light letters on a dark background.

Selecting Multiple Paragraphs

The first formatting step in this project is to change the font size of the characters in the headline. The headline consists of two separate lines, each ending with a paragraph mark. As previously discussed, Word creates a new paragraph each time you press the ENTER key. Thus, the headline actually is two separate paragraphs.

To change the font size of the characters in the headline, you first must **select** (highlight) both paragraphs in the headline, as shown in the following steps.

To Select Multiple Paragraphs

1

- **Press CTRL+HOME; that is, press and hold down the CTRL key, press the HOME key, and then release both keys.**

- **Move the mouse pointer to the left of the first paragraph to be selected until the mouse pointer changes to a right-pointing block arrow.**

CTRL+HOME is a keyboard shortcut that positions the insertion point at the top of the document. The mouse pointer changes to a right-pointing block arrow when positioned to the left of a paragraph (Figure 1-34).

FIGURE 1-34

2

• **Drag downward until both paragraphs are selected.**

Word selects (highlights) both of the paragraphs (Figure 1-35). Dragging is the process of holding down the mouse button while moving the mouse and then releasing the mouse button.

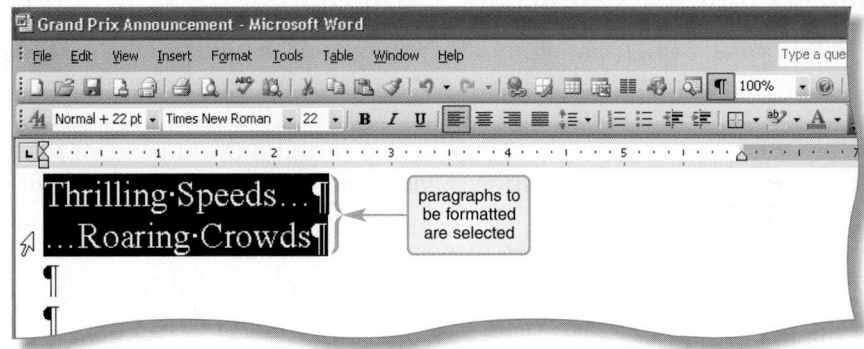

FIGURE 1-35

Other Ways

1. With insertion point at beginning of first paragraph, press CTRL+SHIFT+DOWN ARROW
2. In Voice Command mode, say "Select Paragraph"

Changing the Font Size of Text

The next step is to increase the font size of the characters in the selected headline. Recall that the font size specifies the size of the characters. Earlier, this project showed how to change the font size to 22 for characters typed in the entire announcement. To give the headline more impact, it has a font size larger than the body copy. The following steps show how to increase the font size of the headline from 22 to 36 point.

To Change the Font Size of Text

1

• **With the text selected, click the Font Size box arrow on the Formatting toolbar.**

Word displays a list of available font sizes (Figure 1-36). Available font sizes vary depending on the current font and the printer driver.

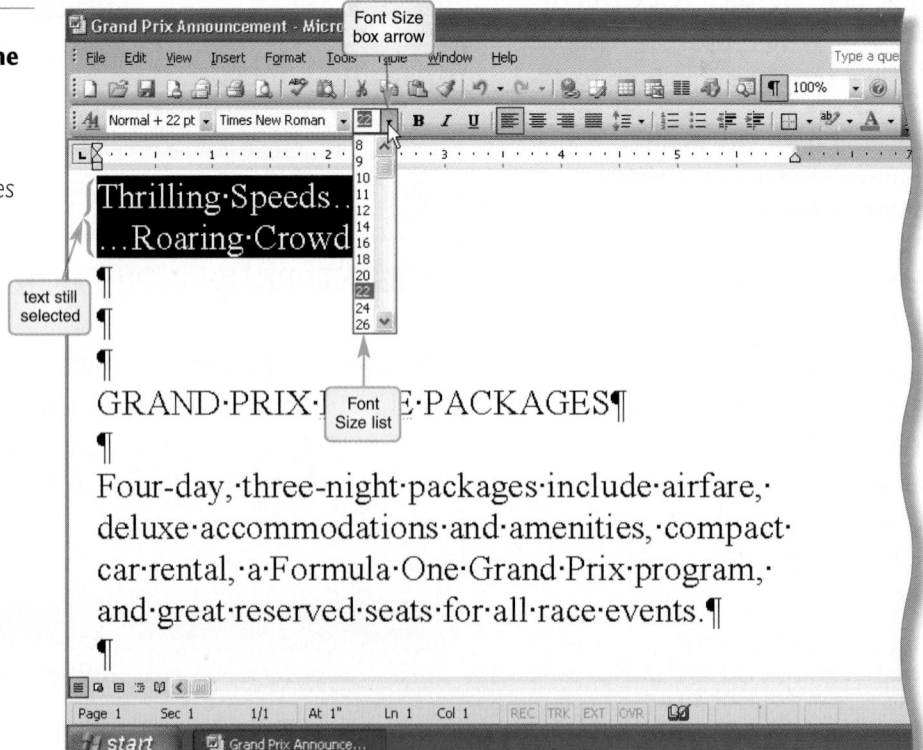

FIGURE 1-36

2

• **Click the down scroll arrow on the Font Size scroll bar until 36 appears in the list (Figure 1-37).**

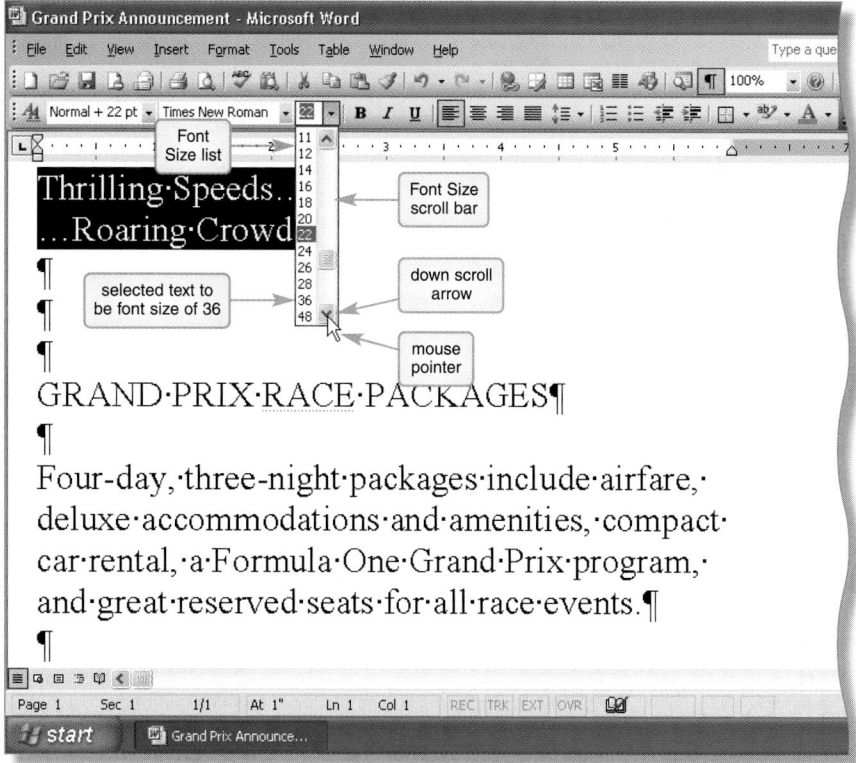

FIGURE 1-37

3

• **Click 36 in the Font Size list.**

Word increases the font size of the headline to 36 (Figure 1-38). The Font Size box on the Formatting toolbar displays 36, indicating the selected text has a font size of 36. Notice that when the mouse pointer is positioned in selected text, its shape is a left-pointing block arrow.

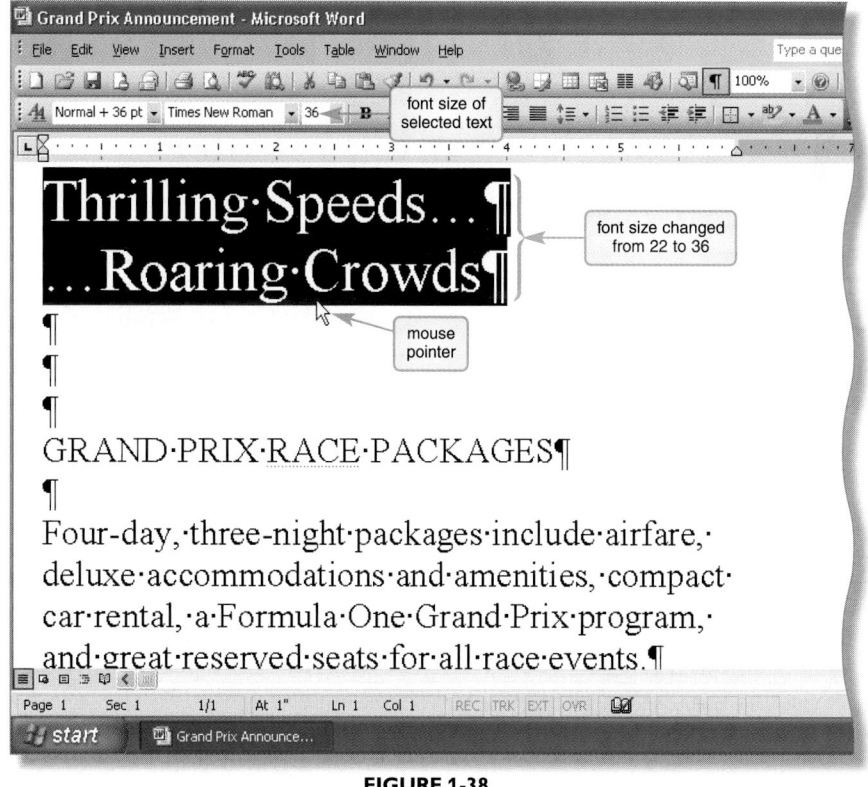

FIGURE 1-38

Other Ways

1. On Format menu click Font, click Font tab, select desired font size in Size list, click OK button
2. Right-click selected text, click Font on shortcut menu, click Font tab, select desired font size in Size list, click OK button
3. Press CTRL+SHIFT+P, type desired font size, press ENTER
4. In Voice Command mode, say "Font Size, [select font size]"

Changing the Font of Text

As mentioned earlier in this project, the default font in Word is Times New Roman. Word, however, provides many other fonts to add variety to your documents. The following steps show how to change the font of the headline in the announcement from Times New Roman to Cooper Black.

To Change the Font of Text

1

• **With the text selected, click the Font box arrow on the Formatting toolbar and then scroll through the Font list until Cooper Black (or a similar font) is displayed.**

Word displays a list of available fonts (Figure 1-39). Your list of available fonts may differ, depending on the type of printer you are using.

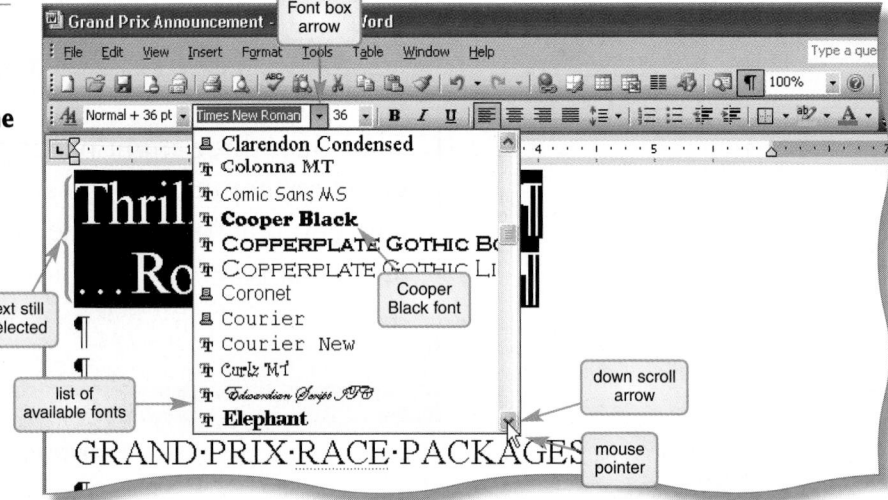

FIGURE 1-39

2

• **Click Cooper Black (or a similar font).**

Word changes the font of the selected text to Cooper Black (Figure 1-40).

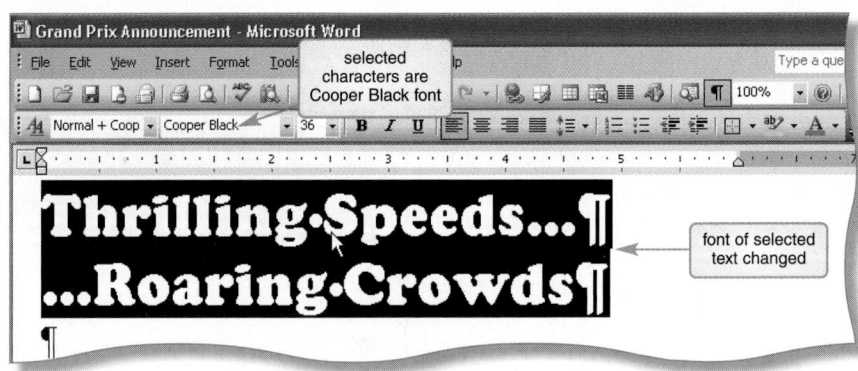

FIGURE 1-40

Right-Align a Paragraph

The default alignment for paragraphs is **left-aligned**, that is, flush at the left margin of the document with uneven right edges. In Figure 1-41, the Align Left button is selected to indicate the paragraph containing the insertion point is left-aligned.

The second line of the headline, however, is to be **right-aligned**, that is, flush at the right margin of the document with uneven left edges. Recall that the second line of the headline is a paragraph, and paragraph formatting does not require you to select the paragraph prior to formatting. Just position the insertion point in the paragraph to be formatted and then format it accordingly.

The following steps show how to right-align the second line of the headline.

To Right-Align a Paragraph

1

• **Click somewhere in the paragraph to be right-aligned.**

Word positions the insertion point at the location you clicked (Figure 1-41).

FIGURE 1-41

2

• **Click the Align Right button on the Formatting toolbar.**

The second line of the headline now is right-aligned (Figure 1-42). Notice that you did not have to select the paragraph before right-aligning it. Formatting a single paragraph requires only that the insertion point be positioned somewhere in the paragraph.

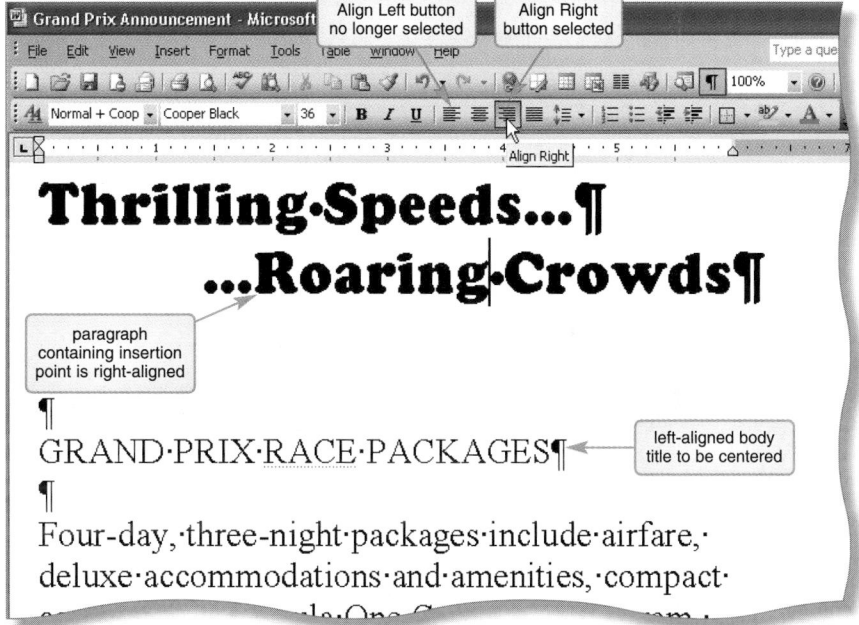

FIGURE 1-42

When a paragraph is right-aligned, the Align Right button on the Formatting toolbar is selected. If, for some reason, you wanted to return the paragraph to left-aligned, you would click the Align Left button on the Formatting toolbar.

Other Ways

1. On Format menu click Paragraph, click Indents and Spacing tab, click Alignment box arrow, click Right, click OK button
2. Right-click paragraph, click Paragraph on short-cut menu, click Indents and Spacing tab, click Alignment box arrow, click Right, click OK button
3. Press CTRL+R
4. In Voice Command mode, say "Align Right"

Center a Paragraph

The body title currently is left-aligned (Figure 1-42 on the previous page). The following step shows how to **center** the paragraph, that is, position its text horizontally between the left and right margins on the page.

To Center a Paragraph

1

• **Click somewhere in the paragraph to be centered.**

• **Click the Center button on the Formatting toolbar.**

Word centers the body title between the left and right margins (Figure 1-43). The Center button on the Formatting toolbar is selected, which indicates the paragraph containing the insertion point is centered.

FIGURE 1-43

When a paragraph is centered, the Center button on the Formatting toolbar is selected. If, for some reason, you wanted to return the paragraph to left-aligned, you would click the Align Left button on the Formatting toolbar.

More About

Centering

The Center button on the Formatting toolbar centers text horizontally between the left and right margins. You also can center text vertically between the top and bottom margins. To do this, click File on the menu bar, click Page Setup, click the Layout tab, click the Vertical alignment box arrow, click Center in the list, and then click the OK button.

Undoing, Redoing, and Repeating Commands or Actions

Word provides an Undo button on the Standard toolbar that you can use to cancel your recent command(s) or action(s). For example, if you format text incorrectly, you can undo the format and try it again. If, after you undo an action, you decide you did not want to perform the undo, you can use the Redo button to redo the undo. Word prevents you from undoing or redoing some actions, such as saving or printing a document.

The following steps show how to undo the center format to the body title using the Undo button and then re-center it using the Redo button.

To Undo and Redo an Action

* **Click the Undo button on the Standard toolbar.**

Word returns the body title to its formatting before you issued the center command (Figure 1-44). That is, Word left-aligns the body title.

* **Click the Redo button on the Standard toolbar.**

Word reapplies the center format to the body title (shown in Figure 1-43).

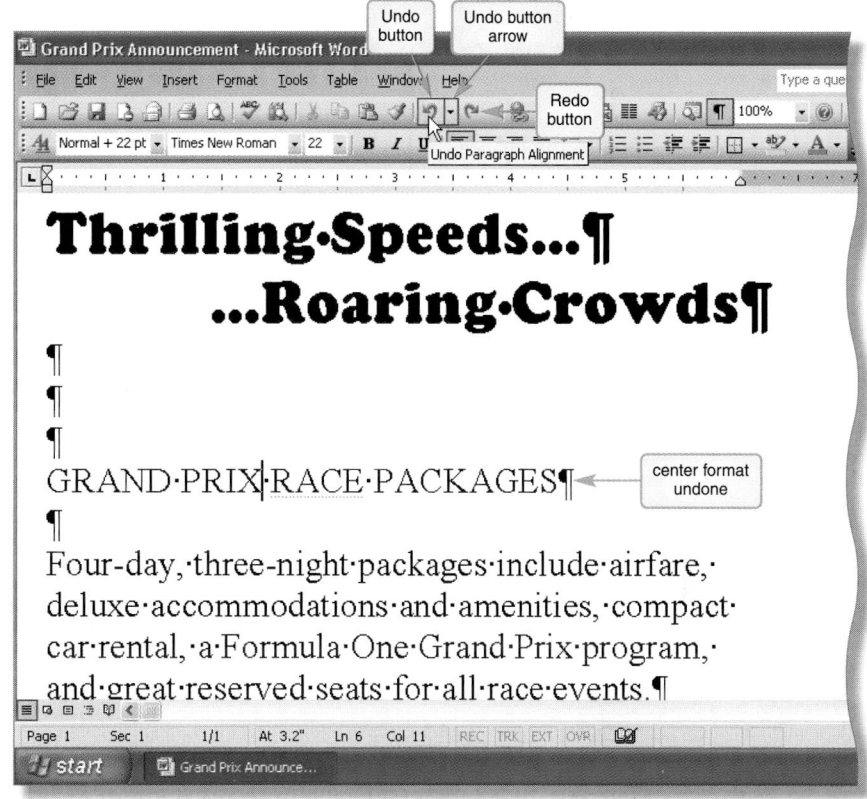

FIGURE 1-44

You also can cancel a series of prior actions by clicking the Undo button arrow on the Standard toolbar (Figure 1-44) to display the list of undo actions and then dragging through the actions you wish to undo.

Whereas the Undo command cancels an action you did not want to perform, Word also provides a **Repeat command** on the Edit menu, which duplicates your last command so you can perform it again. For example, if you centered a paragraph and wish to format another paragraph the exact same way, you could click in the second paragraph to format, click Edit on the menu bar, and then click Repeat Paragraph Alignment. The text listed after Repeat varies, depending on your most recent action. If the action cannot be repeated, Word displays the text, Can't Repeat, on the Edit menu.

Microsoft Office
Word 2003

Selecting a Line and Formatting It

The characters in the body title, GRAND PRIX RACE PACKAGES, are to be a different font, larger font size, and italicized. To make these changes, you must select the line of text containing the body title, as shown in the following step.

To Select a Line

1

• **Move the mouse pointer to the left of the line to be selected (in this case, GRAND PRIX RACE PACKAGES) until it changes to a right-pointing block arrow and then click.**

Word selects the entire line to the right of the mouse pointer (Figure 1-45).

FIGURE 1-45

Other Ways

1. Drag through the line
2. With insertion point at beginning of desired line, press SHIFT+DOWN ARROW
3. In Voice Command mode, say "Select Line"

The next step is to change the font of the selected characters from Times New Roman to Arial Black and increase the font size of the selected characters from 22 to 24, as explained below.

To Format a Line of Text

1 **With the text selected, click the Font box arrow on the Formatting toolbar and then scroll to Arial Black (or a similar font) in the list. Click Arial Black (or a similar font).**

2 **With the text selected, click the Font Size box arrow on the Formatting toolbar and then click 24 in the list.**

Word changes the characters in the body title to 24-point Arial Black (Figure 1-46).

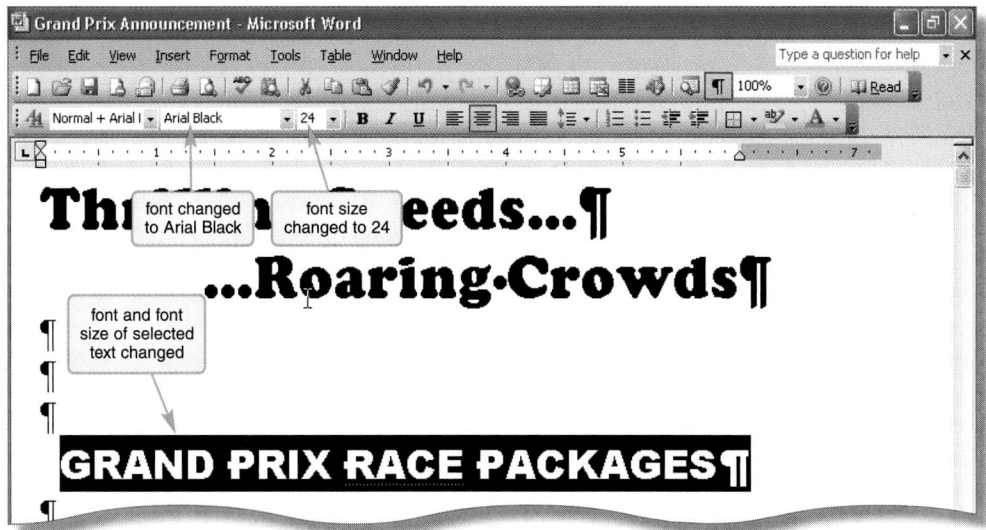

FIGURE 1-46

Italicizing Text

Italicized text has a slanted appearance. The following step shows how to italicize the selected characters in the body title.

To Italicize Text

1

• **With the text still selected, click the Italic button on the Formatting toolbar.**

Word italicizes the text (Figure 1-47). The Italic button on the Formatting toolbar is selected.

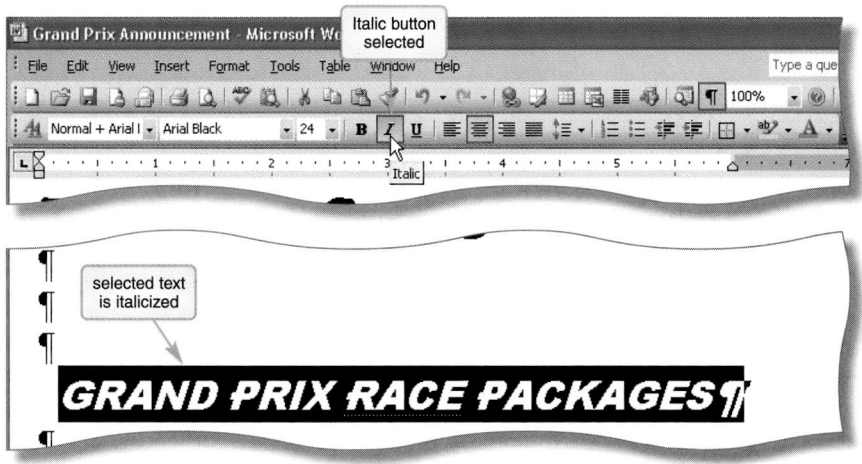

FIGURE 1-47

When the selected text is italicized, the Italic button on the Formatting toolbar is selected. If, for some reason, you wanted to remove the italic format from the selected text, you would click the Italic button a second time, or you immediately could click the Undo button on the Standard toolbar.

Underlining Text

The next step is to underline a word in the first paragraph below the body title. **Underlined** text prints with an underscore (_) below each character. Underlining is used to emphasize or draw attention to specific text.

As with a single paragraph, if you want to format a single word, you do not need to select the word. Simply position the insertion point somewhere in the word and apply the desired format. The following step shows how to underline a word.

To Underline a Word

1

• **Click somewhere in the word to be underlined (deluxe, in this case).**

• **Click the Underline button on the Formatting toolbar.**

Word underlines the word containing the insertion point (Figure 1-48). The Underline button on the Formatting toolbar is selected.

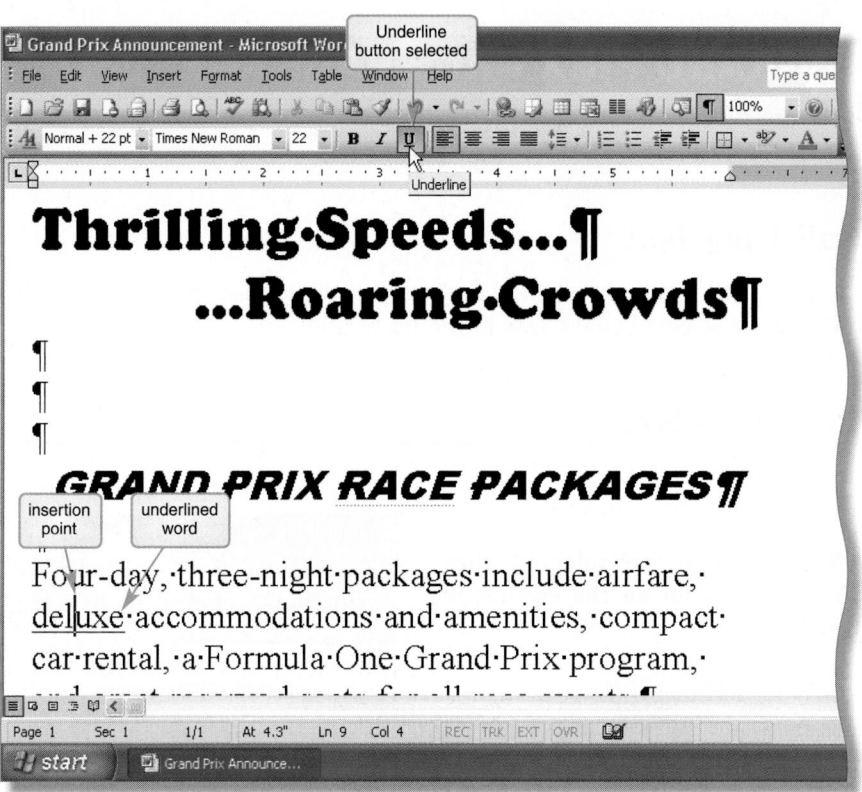

FIGURE 1-48

When the text containing the insertion point is underlined, the Underline button on the Formatting toolbar is selected. If, for some reason, you wanted to remove the underline from the text, you would click the Underline button a second time, or you immediately could click the Undo button on the Standard toolbar.

In addition to the basic underline shown in Figure 1-48, Word has many decorative underlines that are available through the Font dialog box. For example, you can use double underlines, dotted underlines, and wavy underlines. In the Font dialog box, you also can change the color of an underline and instruct Word to underline only the words and not the spaces between the words. To display the Font dialog box, click Format on the menu bar and then click Font.

Scrolling

The next text to format is in the lower portion of the announcement, which currently is not showing in the document window. To continue formatting the document, scroll down so the lower portion of the announcement is displayed in the document window, as shown in the following step.

To Scroll through a Document

• **Click the down scroll arrow on the vertical scroll bar nine times.**

Word scrolls through the document (Figure 1-49). Depending on your monitor type, your screen may scroll differently.

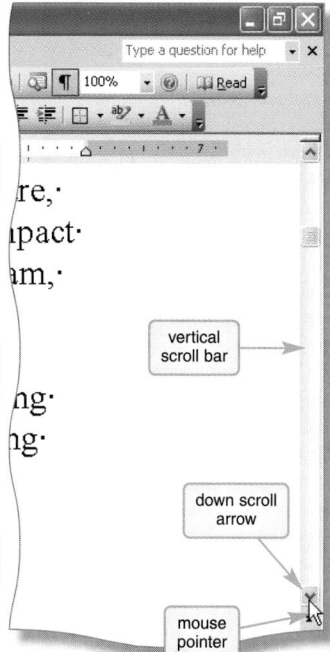

FIGURE 1-49

Other Ways

1. See Tables 1-1 and 1-2 on pages WD 24 and WD 25
2. In Dictation mode, say key name(s) in Table 1-2

Selecting a Group of Words

The next step is to bold the words, great reserved seats, in the announcement. To do this, you first must select this group of words. The following steps show how to select a group of words.

To Select a Group of Words

• **Position the mouse pointer immediately to the left of the first character of the text to be selected (in this case, the g in great).**

The mouse pointer's shape is an I-beam when positioned in unselected text in the document window (Figure 1-50).

FIGURE 1-50

2

• **Drag the mouse pointer through the last character of the text to be selected (in this case, the second s in seats).**

Word selects the phrase, great reserved seats (Figure 1-51).

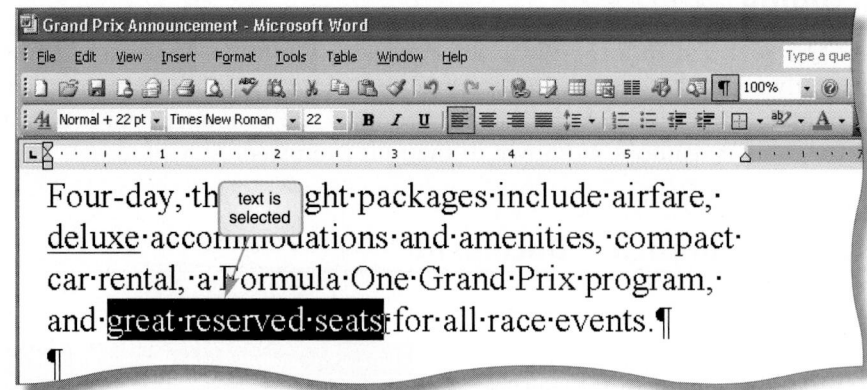

FiGURE 1-51

Bolding Text

Bold characters display somewhat thicker and darker than those that are not bold. The following step shows how to bold the selected phrase, great reserved seats.

To Bold Text

1

• **With the text selected, click the Bold button on the Formatting toolbar.**

• **Click inside the selected text to remove the selection (highlight).**

Word formats the selected text in bold and positions the insertion point inside the bold text (Figure 1-52). The Bold button on the Formatting toolbar is selected.

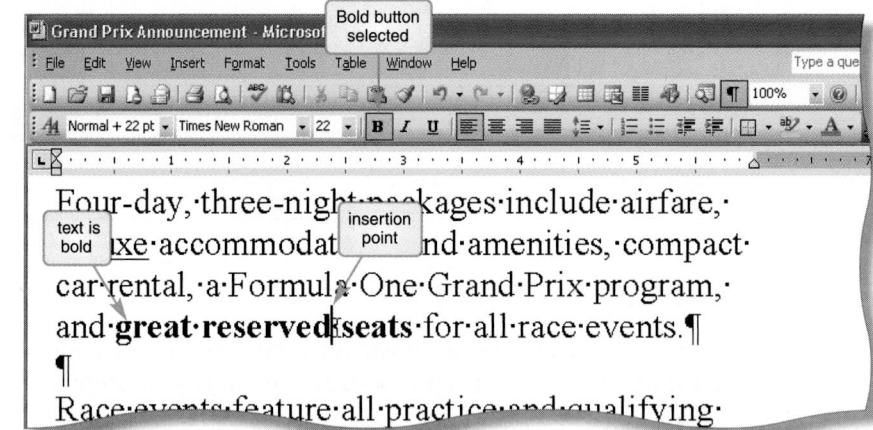

FIGURE 1-52

When you click in the document, Word positions the insertion point at the location you clicked and removes the selection (highlight) from the screen. If you click inside the selection, the Formatting toolbar displays the formatting characteristics of the characters and paragraphs containing the insertion point. For example, at the location of the insertion point, the characters are a 22-point Times New Roman bold font, and the paragraph is left-aligned.

When the selected text is bold, the Bold button on the Formatting toolbar is selected. If, for some reason, you wanted to remove the bold format from the selected text, you would click the Bold button a second time, or you immediately could click the Undo button on the Standard toolbar.

The next step is to center the last line of the announcement, as described in the following steps.

To Center a Paragraph

1 **Click somewhere in the paragraph to be centered (in this case, the last line of the announcement).**

2 **Click the Center button on the Formatting toolbar.**

Word centers the last line of the announcement (Figure 1-53).

FIGURE 1-53

The formatting for the announcement now is complete.

Inserting Clip Art in a Word Document

Files containing graphical images, also called **graphics**, are available from a variety of sources. Word includes many predefined graphics, called **clip art**, that you can insert in a document. Clip art is located in the **Clip Organizer**, which contains a collection of clips, including clip art, as well as photographs, sounds, and video clips.

More About

Toolbar Buttons

Many of the buttons on the Formatting toolbar are toggles; that is, click them once to format the selected text, and click them again to remove the format from the selected text. For example, clicking the Bold button bolds selected text; clicking the Bold button again removes the bold format.

More About

Graphics

If you have a scanner or digital camera attached to your computer, Word can insert a graphic directly from these devices. You also can scan a graphic into a file and then insert the scanned file into the Word document.

Inserting Clip Art

The next step in the project is to insert clip art of a race car in the announcement between the headline and the body title. Recall that Word has 14 task panes, some of which automatically appear as you perform certain operations. When you use the Clip Art command, Word automatically displays the Clip Art task pane. The following steps show how to use the Clip Art task pane to insert clip art in a document.

To Insert Clip Art in a Document

1

• **To position the insertion point where you want the clip art to be located, press CTRL+HOME and then press the DOWN ARROW key three times.**

• **Click Insert on the menu bar.**

Word positions the insertion point on the second paragraph mark below the headline, and displays the Insert menu (Figure 1-54). Remember that a short menu initially displays, which expands into a full menu after a few seconds.

FIGURE 1-54

2

• **Point to Picture on the Insert menu.**

Word displays the Picture submenu (Figure 1-55). As discussed earlier, when you point to a command that has a small arrow to its right, Word displays a submenu associated with that command.

FIGURE 1-55

3

• **Click Clip Art on the Picture submenu.**

• **If the Search for text box contains text, drag through the text to select it.**

• **Type** race car **in the Search for text box.**

Word displays the Clip Art task pane at the right edge of the Word window (Figure 1-56). Recall that a task pane is a separate window that enables you to carry out some Word tasks more efficiently. When you click the Go button, Word searches the Clip Organizer for clips that match the description you type in the Search for text box.

FIGURE 1-56

4

• **Click the Go button.**

Word displays a list of clips that match the description, race car (Figure 1-57). If you are connected to the Web, the Clip Art task pane displays clips from the Web, as well as those installed on your hard disk.

FIGURE 1-57

5

• **Click the image to be inserted in the document (in this case, the Formula One race car).**

Word inserts the clip art in the document at the location of the insertion point (Figure 1-58). In the Clip Art task pane, the selected clip art has a box arrow at its right edge.

6

• **Click the Close button on the Clip Art task pane title bar.**

Word removes the Clip Art task pane from the screen.

FIGURE 1-58

The clip art in the announcement is part of a paragraph. Because that paragraph is left-aligned, the clip art also is left-aligned. Notice the Align Left button on the Formatting toolbar is selected (Figure 1-58). You can use any of the paragraph alignment buttons on the Formatting toolbar to reposition the clip art. The following step shows how to center a graphic that is part of a paragraph.

To Center a Paragraph Containing a Graphic

1 **With the insertion point on the paragraph mark containing the clip art, click the Center button on the Formatting toolbar.**

Word centers the paragraph, which also centers the graphic in the paragraph (Figure 1-59).

More About

Clip Art

If you are not connected to the Web, Word displays clip art from your hard disk. If you are connected to the Web, Word displays clip art from your hard disk and also from Microsoft's Web site. Your results may differ from those shown in the preceding steps if you are not connected to the Web. When clip art images display in the Clip Art task pane, Web clips are identified by a small globe displayed in their lower-left corner (Figure 1-58).

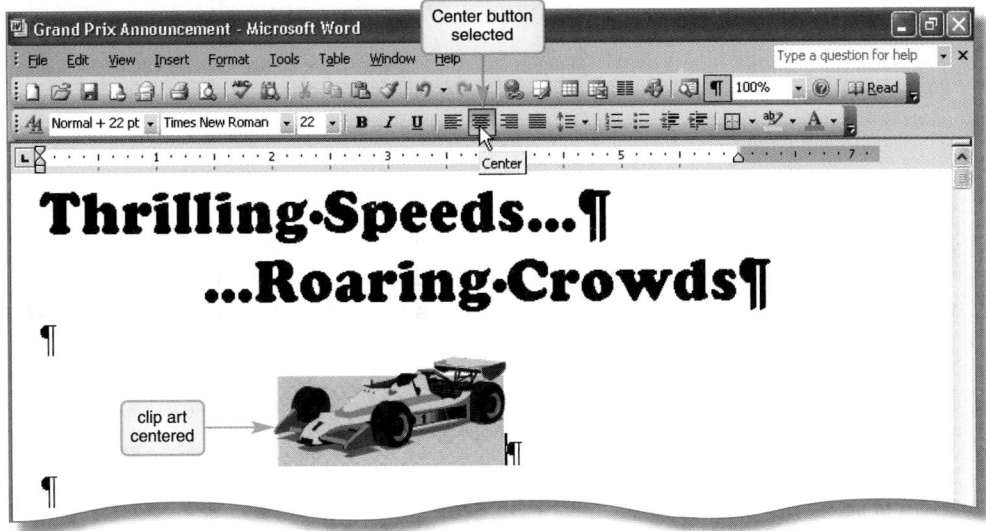

FIGURE 1-59

Resizing a Graphic

The clip art in this announcement is to be a larger size. Once you have inserted a graphic in a document, you easily can change its size. **Resizing** includes both enlarging and reducing the size of a graphic. To resize a graphic, you first must select it. Thus, the following step shows how to select a graphic.

To Select a Graphic

1

• **Click anywhere in the graphic.**

• **If your screen does not display the Picture toolbar, click View on the menu bar, point to Toolbars, and then click Picture.**

*Word selects the graphic (Figure 1-60). A selected graphic is displayed surrounded by a **selection rectangle**, which has small squares, called **sizing handles**, at each corner and middle location. You use the sizing handles to change the size of the graphic. When a graphic is selected, the Picture toolbar automatically should appear on the screen.*

FIGURE 1-60

The following steps show how to resize the graphic just inserted and selected.

To Resize a Graphic

1

• **With the graphic still selected, point to the upper-right corner sizing handle.**

The mouse pointer shape changes to a two-headed arrow when it is on a sizing handle (Figure 1-61). To resize a graphic, you drag the sizing handle(s) until the graphic is the desired size.

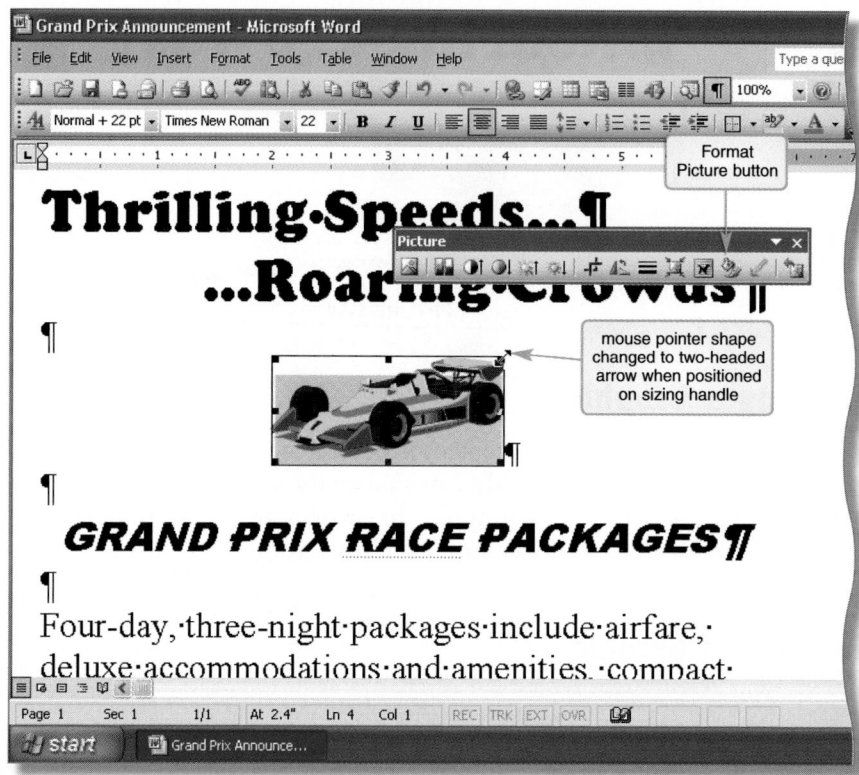

FIGURE 1-61

2

• **Drag the sizing handle diagonally outward until the dotted selection rectangle is positioned approximately as shown in Figure 1-62.**

When you drag a corner sizing handle, the proportions of the graphic remain intact.

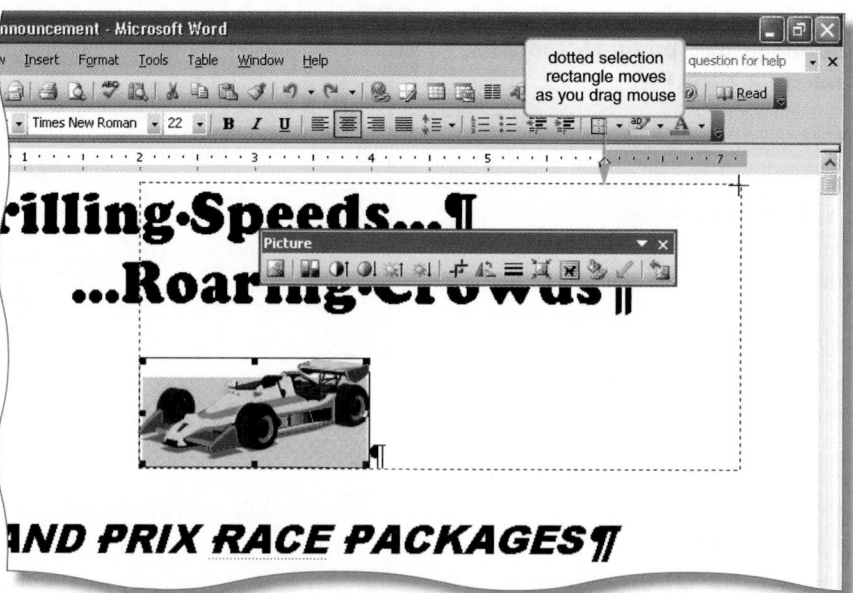

FIGURE 1-62

3

• **Release the mouse button. Press CTRL+HOME.**

Word resizes the graphic (Figure 1-63). When you click outside of a graphic or press a key to scroll through a document, Word deselects the graphic. The Picture toolbar disappears from the screen when you deselect a graphic.

FIGURE 1-63

Instead of resizing a selected graphic by dragging a sizing handle with the mouse, you also can use the Format Picture dialog box to resize a graphic by clicking the Format Picture button on the Picture toolbar (Figure 1-61) and then clicking the Size tab. In the Size sheet, you can enter exact height and width measurements. If you have a precise measurement for a graphic, use the Format Picture dialog box; otherwise, drag the sizing handles to resize a graphic.

Sometimes, you might resize a graphic and realize it is the wrong size. In this case, you may want to return the graphic to its original size and start again. To restore a resized graphic to its exact original size, click the graphic to select it and then click the Format Picture button on the Picture toolbar to display the Format Picture dialog box. Click the Size tab, click the Reset button, and then click the OK button.

Saving an Existing Document with the Same File Name

The announcement for Project 1 now is complete. To transfer the modified document with the formatting changes and graphic to the floppy disk in drive A, you must save the document again. When you saved the document the first time, you assigned a file name to it (Grand Prix Announcement). When you use the procedure on the next page, Word automatically assigns the same file name to the document each time you subsequently save it.

Other Ways

1. Click Format Picture button on Picture toolbar, click Size tab, enter desired height and width, click OK button
2. On Format menu click Picture, click Size tab, enter desired height and width, click OK button
3. In Voice Command mode, say "Format, Picture"

More About

The Picture Toolbar

The Picture toolbar is a floating toolbar. Thus, you can drag its title bar to move the toolbar to a different location on the screen.

To Save an Existing Document with the Same File Name

1

• **Click the Save button on the Standard toolbar.**

Word saves the document on a floppy disk inserted in drive A using the currently assigned file name, Grand Prix Announcement (Figure 1-64).

FIGURE 1-64

<img id="save button callout">Save button</img>

Word saved document with same file name, Grand Prix Announcement

Other Ways

1. On File menu click Save
2. Press CTRL+S
3. In Voice Command mode, say "Save"

While Word is saving the document, the Background Save icon appears near the right edge of the status bar. When the save is complete, the document remains in memory and on the screen.

If, for some reason, you want to save an existing document with a different file name, click Save As on the File menu to display the Save As dialog box. Then, fill in the Save As dialog box as discussed in Steps 2 through 5 on pages WD 28 through WD 30.

More About

Print Preview

To view a document before you print it, click the Print Preview button on the Standard toolbar. To return to the document window, click the Close Preview button on the Print Preview toolbar.

Printing a Document

The next step is to print the document you created. A printed version of the document is called a **hard copy** or **printout**. The following steps show how to print the announcement created in this project.

To Print a Document

1

• **Ready the printer according to the printer instructions.**

• **Click the Print button on the Standard toolbar.**

The mouse pointer briefly changes to an hourglass shape as Word prepares to print the document. While the document is print-ing, a printer icon appears in the notification area on the Windows taskbar (Figure 1-65).

2

• **When the printer stops printing the document, retrieve the printout, which should look like Figure 1-1 on page WD 5.**

FIGURE 1-65

When you use the Print button to print a document, Word prints the entire document automatically. You then may distribute the printout or keep it as a permanent record of the document.

If you wanted to print multiple copies of the document, display the Print dialog box by clicking File on the menu bar and then clicking Print. In addition to the number of copies, the Print dialog box has several printing options.

If you wanted to cancel your job that is printing or one you have waiting to be printed, double-click the printer icon on the taskbar (Figure 1-65). In the printer window, click the job to be canceled and then click Cancel on the Document menu.

Quitting Word

After you create, save, and print the announcement, Project 1 is complete.
The following steps show how to quit Word and return control to Windows.

To Quit Word

1

• **Position the mouse pointer on the Close button on the right side of the title bar (Figure 1-66).**

2

• **Click the Close button.**

The Word window closes.

FIGURE 1-66

When you quit Word, a dialog box may display asking if you want to save the changes. This occurs if you made changes to the document since the last save. Clicking the Yes button in the dialog box saves the changes; clicking the No button ignores the changes; and clicking the Cancel button returns to the document. If you did not make any changes since you saved the document, this dialog box usually is not displayed.

Starting Word and Opening a Document

Once you have created and saved a document, you often will have reason to retrieve it from disk. For example, you might want to revise the document or print it again. Earlier, you saved the Word document created in Project 1 on a floppy disk using the file name, Grand Prix Announcement.

The following steps, which assume Word is not running, show how to open the Grand Prix Announcement file from a floppy disk in drive A.

To Open a Document

1

• **With your floppy disk in drive A, click the Start button on the Windows taskbar, point to All Programs on the Start menu, point to Microsoft Office on the All Programs submenu, and then click Microsoft Office Word 2003 on the Microsoft Office submenu.**

Word starts. The Open area of the Getting Started task pane lists up to four of the most recently used files (Figure 1-67).

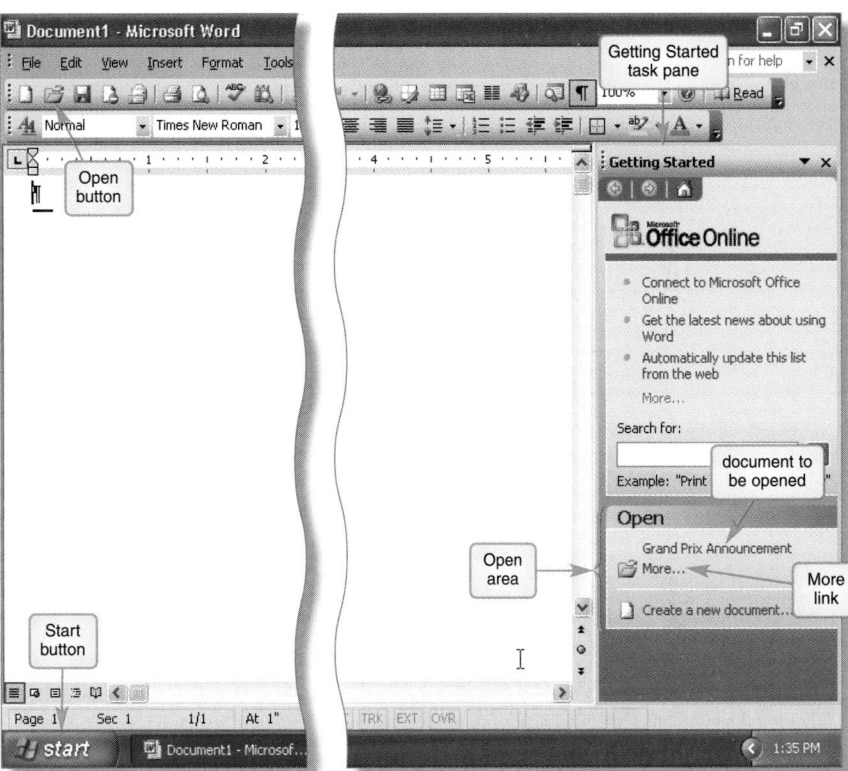

FIGURE 1-67

2

• **Click Grand Prix Announcement in the Getting Started task pane.**

Word opens the document, Grand Prix Announcement, from the floppy disk in drive A and displays it in the Word window (Figure 1-68). The Getting Started task pane closes.

file name on title bar

Grand Prix Announcement document is displayed in document window

FIGURE 1-68

Other Ways

1. Click Start Button, point to All Programs on Start menu, click Open Office Document, select desired drive, double-click file name
2. Right-click Start button, click Explore, display contents of desired drive and folder, double-click file name
3. In Word, click Open button on Standard toolbar, select file name, click Open button in dialog box
4. In Word, on File menu click Open, select file name, click Open button in dialog box
5. In Word, press CTRL+O, select file name, press ENTER
6. In Word, in Voice Command mode, say "Open, [select file name], Open"

If you want to open a document other than one of the four most recently opened ones, click the Open button on the Standard toolbar or the More link in the Getting Started task pane. Clicking the Open button or the More link displays the Open dialog box, which allows you to navigate to a document stored on disk.

Correcting Errors

After creating a document, you often will find you must make changes to it. For example, the document may contain an error or new circumstances may require you add text to the document.

Types of Changes Made to Documents

The types of changes made to documents normally fall into one of the three following categories: additions, deletions, or modifications.

ADDITIONS Additional words, sentences, or paragraphs may be required in a document. Additions occur when you omit text from a document and want to insert it later. For example, the travel agency may decide to add breakfast as part of its Grand Prix race packages.

DELETIONS Sometimes, text in a document is incorrect or is no longer needed. For example, the travel agency may stop including car rental in their Grand Prix race packages. In this case, you would delete the words, compact car rental, from the announcement.

MODIFICATIONS If an error is made in a document or changes take place that affect the document, you might have to revise a word(s) in the text. For example, the travel agency might change the Grand Prix race packages from four-day, three-night to five-day, four-night.

Inserting Text in an Existing Document

Word inserts text to the left of the insertion point. The text to the right of the insertion point moves to the right and downward to fit the new text. The following steps show how to insert the word, fun, to the left of the word, drivers', in the announcement.

To Insert Text in an Existing Document

1

- **Scroll through the document and then click to the left of the location of text to be inserted (in this case, the d in drivers').**

Word positions the insertion point at the clicked location (Figure 1-69).

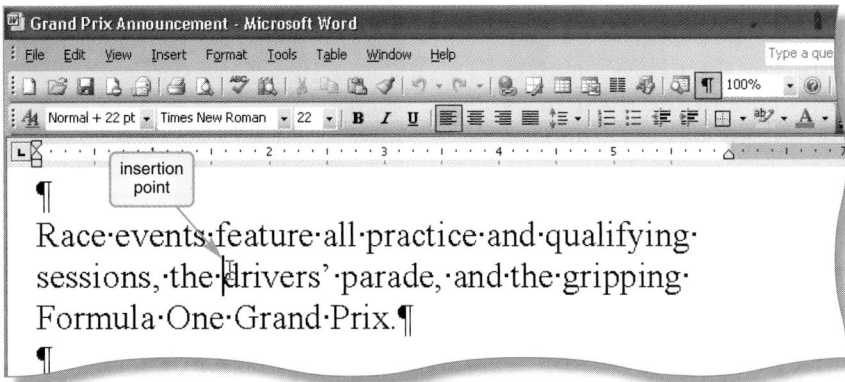

FIGURE 1-69

2

- **Type** fun **and then press the SPACEBAR.**

Word inserts the word, fun, to the left of the insertion point (Figure 1-70).

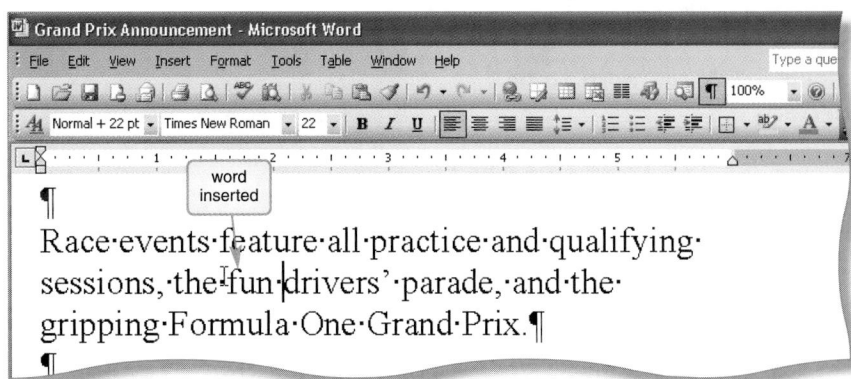

FIGURE 1-70

In Word, the default typing mode is insert mode. In **insert mode**, as you type a character, Word inserts the character and moves all the characters to the right of the typed character one position to the right. You can change to overtype mode by double-clicking the OVR status indicator on the status bar (Figure 1-8 on page WD 10). In **overtype mode**, Word replaces characters to the right of the insertion point. Double-clicking the OVR status indicator again returns Word to insert mode.

More About

Overtype

As you type, if existing text is overwritten with new text, you probably are in overtype mode. Double-click the OVR status indicator to turn overtype mode off. You also can press the INSERT key on the keyboard to turn off overtype mode.

More About

The Clipboard Task Pane

If you click the Cut button (or Copy button) twice in a row, Word displays the Clipboard task pane. You use the Clipboard task pane to copy and paste items within a document or from one Office document to another. To close the Clipboard task pane, click the Close button on the task pane title bar.

Deleting Text from an Existing Document

It is not unusual to type incorrect characters or words in a document. As discussed earlier in this project, you can click the Undo button on the Standard toolbar to immediately undo a command or action — this includes typing. Word also provides other methods of correcting typing errors.

To delete an incorrect character in a document, simply click next to the incorrect character and then press the BACKSPACE key to erase to the left of the insertion point, or press the DELETE key to erase to the right of the insertion point.

To delete a word or phrase you first must select the word or phrase. The following steps show how to select the word, fun, that was just added in the previous steps and then delete the selection.

To Select a Word

1

• **Position the mouse pointer somewhere in the word to be selected (in this case, fun), as shown in Figure 1-71.**

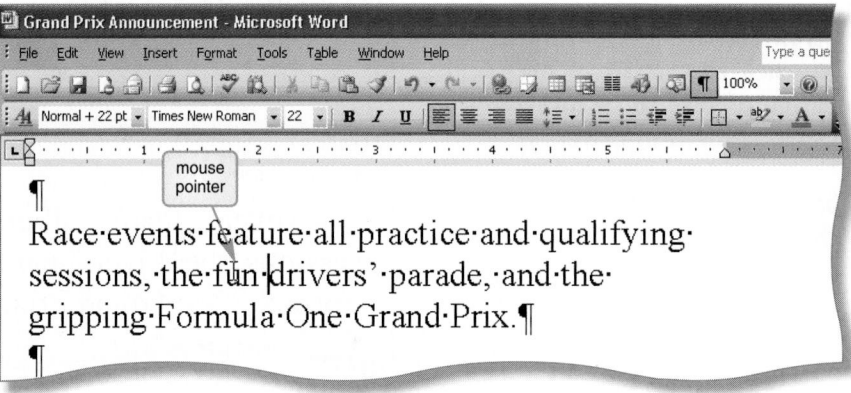

FIGURE 1-71

2

• **Double-click the word to be selected.**

The word, fun, is selected (Figure 1-72).

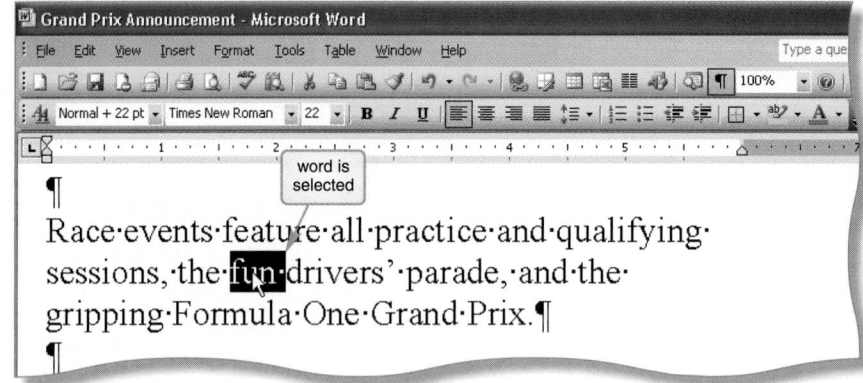

FIGURE 1-72

Other Ways

1. Drag through the word
2. With insertion point at beginning of desired word, press CTRL+SHIFT+RIGHT ARROW
3. With insertion point at beginning of desired word, in Voice Command mode, say "Select Word"

The next step is to delete the selected text.

To Delete Text

1

• **With the text selected, press the** DELETE **key.**

Word deletes the selected word from the document (Figure 1-73).

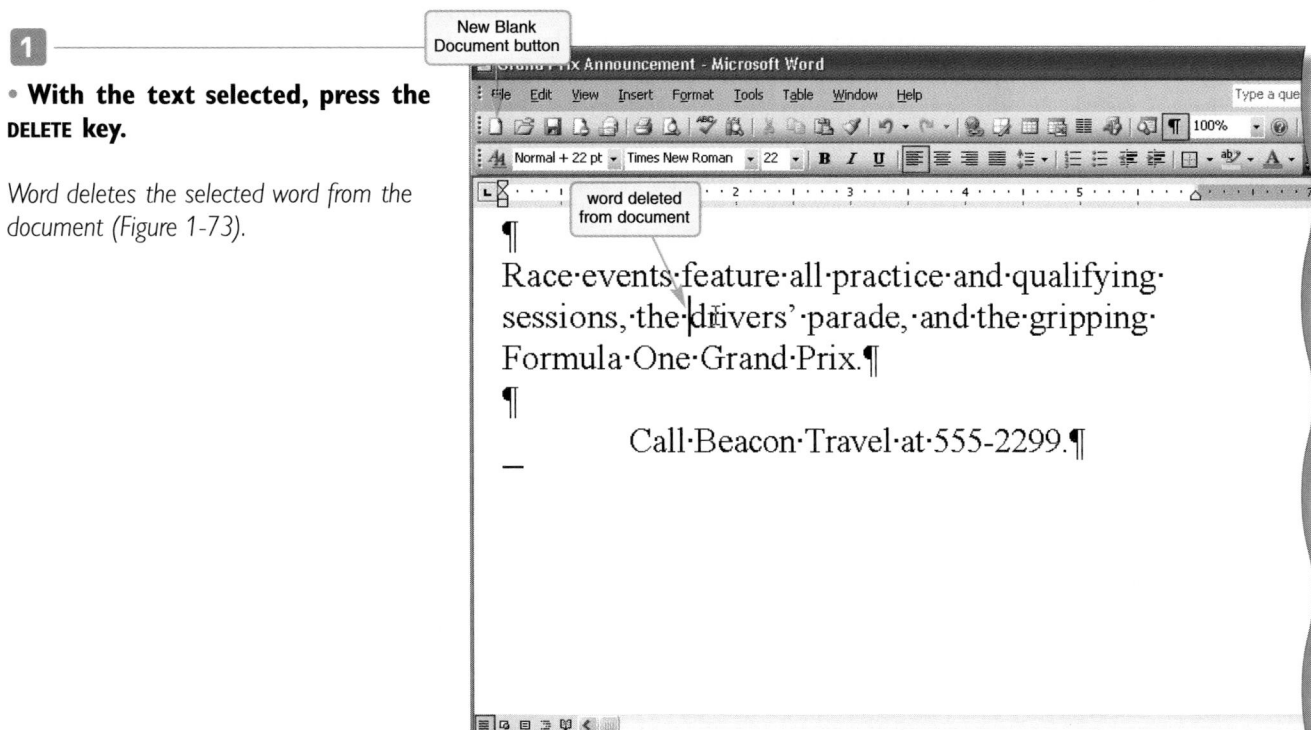

FIGURE 1-73

Closing the Entire Document

Sometimes, everything goes wrong. If this happens, you may want to close the document entirely and start over. You also may want to close a document when you are finished with it so you can begin your next document.

To Close the Entire Document and Start Over

1. Click File on the menu bar and then click Close.
2. If Word displays a dialog box, click the No button to ignore the changes since the last time you saved the document.
3. Click the New Blank Document button (Figure 1-73) on the Standard toolbar.

You also can close the document by clicking the Close button at the right edge of the menu bar.

More About

The Word Help System

The best way to become familiar with the Word Help system is to use it. Appendix A includes detailed information on the Word Help system and exercises that will help you gain confidence in using it.

Word Help System

At anytime while you are using Word, you can get answers to questions through the **Word Help system**. You activate the Word Help system by using the Type a question for help box on the menu bar, the Microsoft Office Word Help button on the Standard toolbar, or the Help menu (Figure 1-74). Used properly, this form of online assistance can increase your productivity and reduce your frustrations by minimizing the time you spend learning how to use Word.

The following section shows how to obtain answers to your questions using the Type a question for help box. Additional information about using the Word Help system is available in Appendix A.

Using the Type a Question for Help Box

Through the Type a question for help box on the right side of the menu bar (Figure 1-66 on page WD 54), you type free-form questions, such as *how do I save* or *how do I create a Web page*, or you type terms, such as *copy*, *save*, or *format*. Word responds by displaying a list of topics related to the word or phrase you typed. The following steps show how to use the Type a question for help box to obtain information about shortcut keys.

To Use the Type a Question for Help Box

1

• **Click the Type a question for help box on the right side of the menu bar and then type** shortcut keys **(Figure 1-74).**

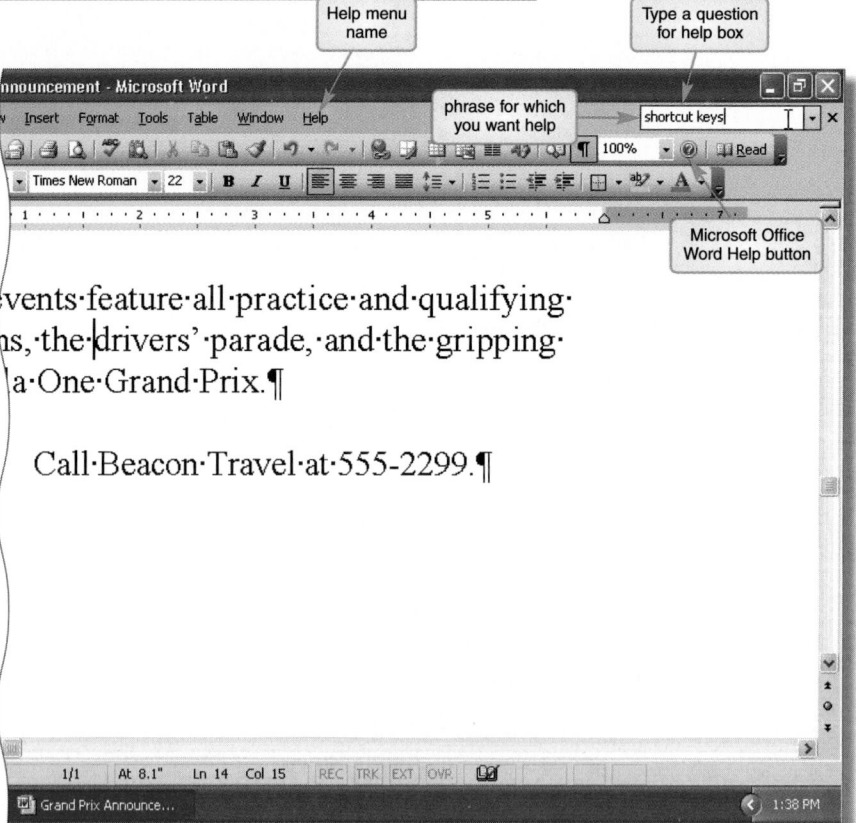

FIGURE 1-74

2

- **Press the ENTER key.**
- **When Word displays the Search Results task pane, if necessary, scroll to display the topic, About shortcut keys.**
- **Click About shortcut keys.**
- **If the Microsoft Office Help window has an Auto Tile button, click it so the Word window and Help window display side-by-side.**

Word displays the Search Results task pane with a list of topics relating to the phrase, shortcut keys. When the About shortcut keys link is clicked, Word opens the Microsoft Office Word Help window on the right side of the screen (Figure 1-75).

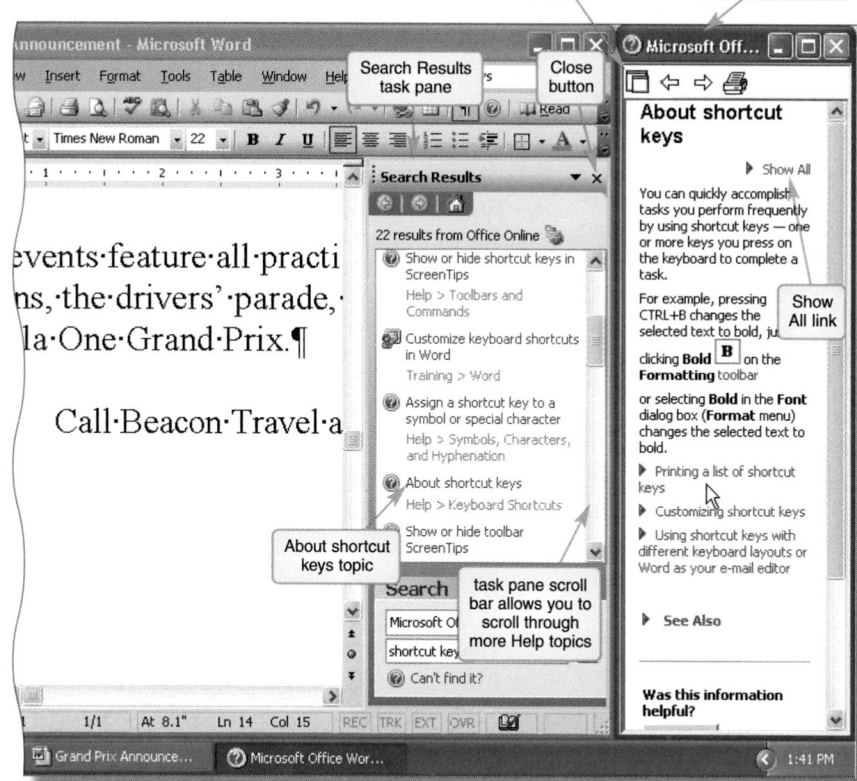

FIGURE 1-75

3

- **Click the Show All link on the right side of the Microsoft Office Word Help window to expand the links in the window.**
- **Double-click the Microsoft Office Word Help window title bar to maximize the window.**

The links in the Microsoft Office Word Help window are expanded and the window is maximized (Figure 1-76).

4

- **Click the Close button on the Microsoft Office Word Help window title bar.**
- **Click the Close button on the Search Results task pane.**

Word closes the Microsoft Office Word Help window. The Word document window again is active.

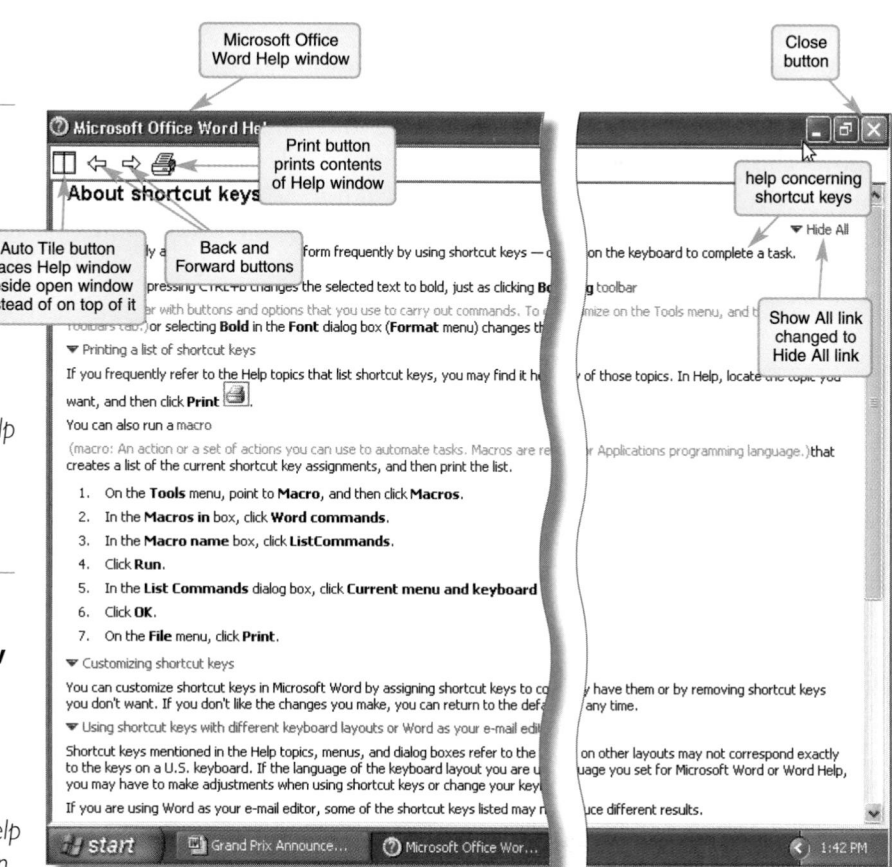

FIGURE 1-76

Use the buttons in the upper-left corner of the Microsoft Office Word Help window (Figure 1-76 on the previous page) to navigate through the Help system, change the display, or print the contents of the window.

You can use the Type a question for help box to search for Help about any topic concerning Word. As you enter questions and terms in the Type a question for help box, Word adds them to the Type a question for help list. Thus, if you click the Type a question for help box arrow, Word displays a list of previously typed questions and terms.

More About

Certification

The Microsoft Office Specialist Certification program provides an opportunity for you to obtain a valuable industry credential - proof that you have the Word 2003 skills required by employers. For more information, see Appendix E or visit the Word 2003 Certification Web page (scsite.com/wd2003/cert).

Quitting Word

The final step in this project is to quit Word.

To Quit Word

1 Click the Close button on the right side of the Word title bar (Figure 1-66 on page WD 54).

2 If Word displays a dialog box, click the No button to ignore the changes since the last time you saved the document.

The Word window closes.

Project Summary

In creating the Grand Prix Announcement document in this project, you gained a broad knowledge of Word. First, you were introduced to starting Word. You learned about the Word window. Before entering any text in the document, you learned how to change the font size. You then learned how to type in the Word document window. The project showed how to use Word's check spelling as you type feature.

Once you saved the document, you learned how to format its paragraphs and characters. Then, the project showed how to insert and resize a clip art image. You also learned how to save the document again, print it, and then quit Word. You learned how to open a document, and insert, delete, and modify text. Finally, you learned how to use the Word Help system to answer questions.

 If you have a SAM user profile, you may have access to hands-on instruction, practice, and assessment of the skills covered in this project. Log in to your SAM account and go to your assignments page to see what your instructor has assigned.

What You Should Know

Having completed this project, you should be able to perform the tasks below. The tasks are listed in the same order they were presented in this project. For a list of the buttons, menus, toolbars, and commands introduced in this project, see the Quick Reference Summary at the back of this book and refer to the Page Number column.

1. Start Word   (WD 6)
2. Customize the Word Window   (WD 8)
3. Increase the Font Size before Typing   (WD 17)
4. Type Text   (WD 18)
5. Enter Blank Lines in a Document   (WD 20)
6. Display Formatting Marks   (WD 21)
7. Type More Text   (WD 22)
8. Wordwrap Text as You Type   (WD 23)
9. Enter Text that Scrolls the Document Window (WD 24)
10. Check Spelling and Grammar as You Type (WD 26)
11. Enter More Text   (WD 27)
12. Save a New Document   (WD 28)
13. Select Multiple Paragraphs   (WD 33)
14. Change the Font Size of Text   (WD 34)
15. Change the Font of Text   (WD 36)
16. Right-Align a Paragraph   (WD 37)
17. Center a Paragraph   (WD 38)
18. Undo and Redo an Action   (WD 39)
19. Select a Line   (WD 40)
20. Format a Line of Text   (WD 40)
21. Italicize Text   (WD 41)
22. Underline a Word   (WD 42)
23. Scroll through a Document   (WD 43)
24. Select a Group of Words   (WD 43)
25. Bold Text   (WD 44)
26. Center a Paragraph   (WD 45)
27. Insert Clip Art in a Document   (WD 46)
28. Center a Paragraph Containing a Graphic (WD 48)
29. Select a Graphic   (WD 49)
30. Resize a Graphic   (WD 50)
31. Save an Existing Document with the Same File Name   (WD 52)
32. Print a Document   (WD 53)
33. Quit Word   (WD 54, WD 62)
34. Open a Document   (WD 55)
35. Insert Text in an Existing Document   (WD 57)
36. Select a Word   (WD 58)
37. Delete Text   (WD 59)
38. Close the Entire Document and Start Over (WD 59)
39. Use the Type a Question for Help Box   (WD 60)

More About

Quick Reference

For a table that lists how to complete the tasks covered in this book using the mouse, menu, shortcut menu, and keyboard, see the Quick Reference Summary at the back of this book, or visit the Word 2003 Quick Reference Web page (scsite.com/ wd2003/qr).

Learn It Online

Instructions: To complete the Learn It Online exercises, start your browser, click the Address bar, and then enter the Web address scsite.com/wd2003/learn. When the Word 2003 Learn It Online page is displayed, follow the instructions in the exercises below. Each exercise has instructions for printing your results, either for your own records or for submission to your instructor.

1 Project Reinforcement TF, MC, and SA

Below Word Project 1, click the Project Reinforcement link. Print the quiz by clicking Print on the File menu for each page. Answer each question.

2 Flash Cards

Below Word Project 1, click the Flash Cards link and read the instructions. Type 20 (or a number specified by your instructor) in the Number of playing cards text box, type your name in the Enter your Name text box, and then click the Flip Card button. When the flash card is displayed, read the question and then click the ANSWER box arrow to select an answer. Flip through Flash Cards. If your score is 15 (75%) correct or greater, click Print on the File menu to print your results. If your score is less than 15 (75%) correct, then redo this exercise by clicking the Replay button.

3 Practice Test

Below Word Project 1, click the Practice Test link. Answer each question, enter your first and last name at the bottom of the page, and then click the Grade Test button. When the graded practice test is displayed on your screen, click Print on the File menu to print a hard copy. Continue to take practice tests until you score 80% or better.

4 Who Wants To Be a Computer Genius?

Below Word Project 1, click the Computer Genius link. Read the instructions, enter your first and last name at the bottom of the page, and then click the PLAY button. When your score is displayed, click the PRINT RESULTS link to print a hard copy.

5 Wheel of Terms

Below Word Project 1, click the Wheel of Terms link. Read the instructions, and then enter your first and last name and your school name. Click the PLAY button. When your score is displayed, right-click the score and then click Print on the shortcut menu to print a hard copy.

6 Crossword Puzzle Challenge

Below Word Project 1, click the Crossword Puzzle Challenge link. Read the instructions, and then enter your first and last name. Click the SUBMIT button. Work the crossword puzzle. When you are finished, click the Submit button. When the crossword puzzle is redisplayed, click the Print Puzzle button to print a hard copy.

7 Tips and Tricks

Below Word Project 1, click the Tips and Tricks link. Click a topic that pertains to Project 1. Right-click the information and then click Print on the shortcut menu. Construct a brief example of what the information relates to in Word to confirm you understand how to use the tip or trick.

8 Newsgroups

Below Word Project 1, click the Newsgroups link. Click a topic that pertains to Project 1. Print three comments.

9 Expanding Your Horizons

Below Word Project 1, click the Expanding Your Horizons link. Click a topic that pertains to Project 1. Print the information. Construct a brief example of what the information relates to in Word to confirm you understand the contents of the article.

10 Search Sleuth

Below Word Project 1, click the Search Sleuth link. To search for a term that pertains to this project, select a term below the Project 1 title and then use the Google search engine at google.com (or any major search engine) to display and print two Web pages that present information on the term.

11 Word Online Training

Below Word Project 1, click the Word Online Training link. When your browser displays the Microsoft Office Online Web page, click the Word link. Click one of the Word courses that covers one or more of the objectives listed at the beginning of the project on page WD 4. Print the first page of the course before stepping through it.

12 Office Marketplace

Below Word Project 1, click the Office Marketplace link. When your browser displays the Microsoft Office Online Web page, click the Office Marketplace link. Click a topic that relates to Word. Print the first page.

Apply Your Knowledge

1 Checking Spelling and Grammar, Modifying Text, and Formatting a Document

Instructions: Start Word. Open the document, Apply 1-1 Paris Announcement Unformatted, on the Data Disk. See the inside back cover of this book for instructions for downloading the Data Disk or see your instructor for information about accessing files required in this book.

The document on the Data Disk is an unformatted announcement that contains some spelling errors. You are to fix the spelling mistakes, modify text, format paragraphs and characters, and insert clip art in the announcement, so it looks like Figure 1-77 on the next page.

1. Correct each spelling and grammar error by right-clicking the flagged word and then clicking the appropriate correction on the shortcut menu, so the announcement text matches Figure 1-77 on the next page. The unformatted announcement on the Data Disk contains several spelling errors (red wavy underline) and grammar errors (green wavy underline). Word may flag some proper names that are spelled correctly. In these cases, click Ignore Once or Ignore All on the shortcut menu. If your screen does not display the wavy underlines, right-click the Spelling and Grammar Status icon on the status bar and be sure Hide Spelling Errors and Hide Grammatical Errors do not have check marks beside them. If they do, remove the check mark(s) by the appropriate command. If your screen still does not display the wavy underlines, right-click the Spelling and Grammar Status icon on the status bar, click Options on the shortcut menu, click the Recheck Document button, and then click the OK button.
2. At the end of the first sentence of body copy, change the period to an exclamation point. The sentence should read: See Paris this spring – on a shoestring!
3. Delete the word, morning, in the first sentence of the second paragraph of body copy.
4. Insert the word, event, between the text, Discount tickets, in the second sentence of the second paragraph of body copy. The text should read: Discount event tickets...
5. Change the font and font size of the first line of the headline to 72-point Lucida Calligraphy, or a similar font.
6. Change the font and font size of the second line of the headline to 48-point Lucida Calligraphy, or a similar font.
7. Right-align the second line of the headline.
8. Change the font size of the two paragraphs of body copy to 20 point.
9. Change the font and font size of the last line of the announcement to 24-point Arial.
10. Italicize the word, shoestring, in the first paragraph of body copy.
11. Bold the phrase, unbelievably low price, in the same paragraph.
12. Underline the telephone number in the last line of the announcement.
13. Italicize the text in the last line of the announcement.
14. Center the last line of the announcement.
15. Insert the clip art between the first and second lines of the headline. Use the search text, Paris, to locate this, or a similar, clip art image. Center the clip art.
16. Click File on the menu bar and then click Save As. Save the document using Apply 1-1 Paris Announcement Formatted as the file name.
17. Print the revised document, shown in Figure 1-77.

(continued)

Apply Your Knowledge

Checking Spelling and Grammar, Modifying Text, and Formatting a Document *(continued)*

FIGURE 1-77

1 Creating an Announcement with Clip Art

Problem: You work part-time for the events coordinator at Memorial Hall. She has asked you to prepare an announcement for the upcoming annual charity costume ball. First, you prepare the unformatted announcement shown in Figure 1-78a, and then you format it so it looks like Figure 1-78b on the next page. *Hint:* Remember, if you make a mistake while formatting the announcement, you can click the Undo button on the Standard tool-bar to undo your last action.

1. Before entering any text, change the font size from 12 to 20.
2. Display formatting marks on the screen.
3. Type the unformatted announcement shown in Figure 1-78a. If Word flags any misspelled words as you type, check the spelling of these words and correct them.
4. Save the document on a floppy disk with Lab 1-1 Costume Ball Announcement as the file name.

> Come One...
> ...Come All
>
>
> Charity Costume Ball
>
> Mark your calendar for a fun-filled gala on Saturday, August 6, at 8:00 p.m. at Memorial Hall. Tickets are $50.00 per couple, with dinner prepared by Chef Jeffery Vincent of Le Chic and live entertainment by The Class Act. All proceeds go to charity.
>
> As in past years, this event includes prizes for the best costumes, door prizes, a silent auction, and the traditional unmasking at midnight. Have an enjoyable evening while promoting a good cause.
>
> Call 555-6344 for reservations.

(a) Unformatted Document

FIGURE 1-78

5. Change the font of both lines of the headline to Cooper Black, or a similar font. Change the font size from 20 to 48.
6. Right-align the second line of the headline.
7. Center the body title line.

(continued)

In the Lab

Creating an Announcement with Clip Art *(continued)*

8. Change the font of the body title line to Harrington, or a similar font. Change the font size to 36. Bold the body title line.

9. In the first paragraph of the body copy, bold the text, fun-filled.

10. In the same paragraph, italicize the word, live.

11. In the same paragraph, underline the word, All.

12. Center the last line of the announcement.

13. Insert the clip art of a mask between the headline and the body title line. Search for the text, mask, in the Clip Art task pane to locate this, or a similar, graphic.

14. Center the clip art.

15. Save the announcement again with the same file name.

16. Print the formatted announcement, as shown in Figure 1-78b.

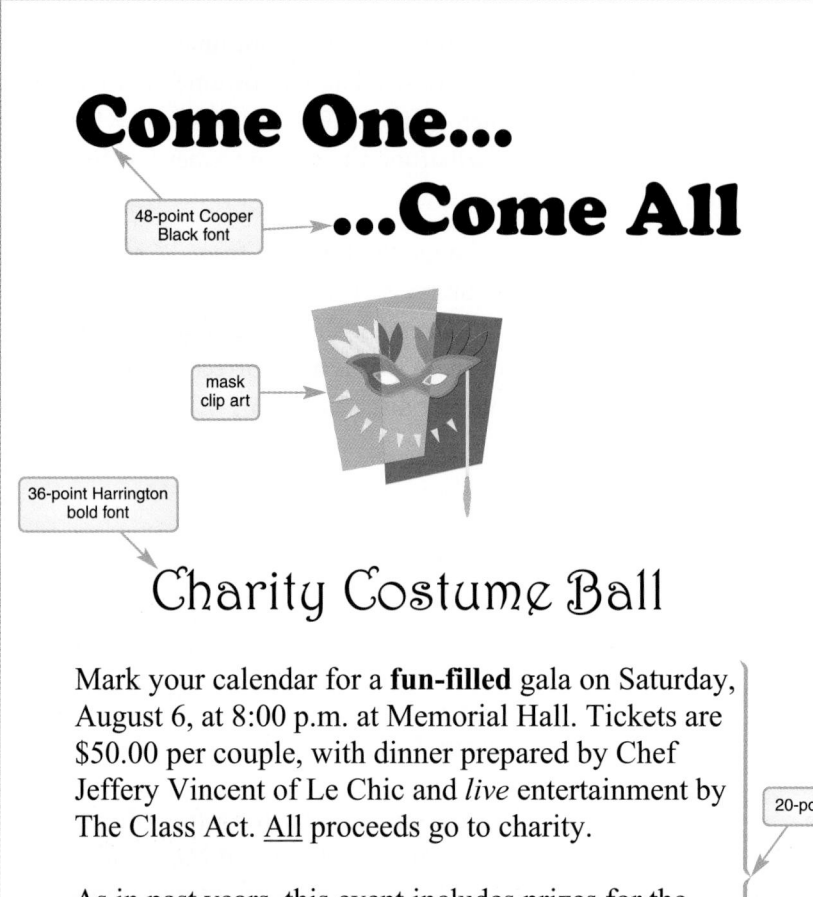

Come One...
...Come All

48-point Cooper Black font

mask clip art

36-point Harrington bold font

Charity Costume Ball

Mark your calendar for a **fun-filled** gala on Saturday, August 6, at 8:00 p.m. at Memorial Hall. Tickets are $50.00 per couple, with dinner prepared by Chef Jeffery Vincent of Le Chic and *live* entertainment by The Class Act. <u>All</u> proceeds go to charity.

20-point

As in past years, this event includes prizes for the best costumes, door prizes, a silent auction, and the traditional unmasking at midnight. Have an enjoyable evening while promoting a good cause.

Call 555-6344 for reservations.

(b) Formatted Document

FIGURE 1-78

2 Creating an Announcement with Resized Clip Art

Problem: Your boss at Southside Physicians Group has requested that you prepare an announcement for the upcoming Public Health Clinic. You prepare the announcement shown in Figure 1-79. *Hint:* Remember, if you make a mistake while formatting the announcement, you can click the Undo button on the Standard toolbar to undo your last action.

1. Before entering any text, change the font size from 12 to 20.

2. Display formatting marks on the screen.

In the Lab

3. Create the announcement shown in Figure 1-79. Enter the text of the document first without the clip art and unformatted; that is, without any bold, underlined, italicized, right-aligned, or centered text. If Word flags any misspelled words as you type, check the spelling of these words and correct them.

4. Save the document on a floppy disk with Lab 1-2 Health Clinic Announcement as the file name.

5. Change the font of both lines of the headline to Brush Script MT, or a similar font. Change the font size from 20 to 48.

6. Right-align the second line of the headline.

7. Center the body title line.

8. Change the font and font size of the body title line to 28-point Bookman Old Style. Bold the body title line.

9. Underline the word, free, in the first paragraph of the body copy.

10. In the next paragraph, italicize these words: Qualified, licensed physicians and nurse practitioners.

11. Center the last line of the announcement.

12. Insert the clip art between the headline and the body title line. Search for the text, medicine, in the Clip Art task pane to locate this, or a similar, graphic. Center the graphic.

13. Enlarge the graphic. If you make the graphic too large, the announcement may flow onto two pages. If this occurs, reduce the size of the graphic so the announcement fits on a single page. *Hint:* Use Help to learn about print preview, which is a way to see the page before you print it. To exit print preview and return to the document window, click the Close button on the Print Preview toolbar.

14. Save the announcement again with the same file name.

15. Print the announcement.

Free...

...Public Health Clinic

48-point Brush Script MT font

medicine clip art

28-point Bookman Old Style bold font

Southside Physicians Group

Our annual, <u>free</u> Public Health Clinic will be held at the concourse of Woodstar Mall from 9:30 a.m. until 6:30 p.m. on Thursday, November 3. No appointment is necessary.

Flu shots, cholesterol tests, hearing and eye exams, and blood pressure screening will be offered to the public. *Qualified, licensed physicians and nurse practitioners* conduct the exams and dispense advice.

Call 555-7225 for more information.

20-point

FIGURE 1-79

In the Lab

3 Creating an Announcement with Resized Clip Art, a Bulleted List, and Color

Problem: The owner of Zachary Sports Complex has requested that each student in your class prepare an announcement advertising the sports complex. The student that creates the winning announcement will receive a complimentary membership. You prepare the announcement shown in Figure 1-80. *Hint:* Remember, if you make a mistake while formatting the announcement, you can click the Undo button on the Standard toolbar to undo your last action.

1. Type the announcement shown in Figure 1-80, using the fonts and font sizes indicated in the figure. Check spelling as you type.
2. Save the document on a floppy disk with Lab 1-3 Training Camp Announcement as the file name.
3. Change the font color of the headline to red, the body title to blue, and the last line of the announcement to green. *Hint:* Use Help to learn how to change the font color of text.
4. Add a brown double underline below the text, Space is limited. *Hint:* Use Help to learn how to add a decorative underline to text.
5. Add bullets to the three paragraphs of body copy. *Hint:* Use Help to learn how to add bullets to a list of paragraphs.
6. Insert clip art of a baseball player between the headline and the body title line. If you have access to the Web, select the clip art from the Web. Otherwise, select the clip art from the hard disk. In the Clip Art task pane, images from the Web display an icon of a small globe in their lower-left corner.
7. Enlarge the graphic of the baseball player. If you make the graphic too large, the announcement may flow onto two pages. If this occurs, reduce the size of the graphic so the announcement fits on a single page. *Hint:* Use Help to learn about print preview, which is a way to see the page before you print it. To exit print preview and return to the document window, click the Close button on the Print Preview toolbar.
8. Save the announcement again with the same file name.
9. Print the announcement.

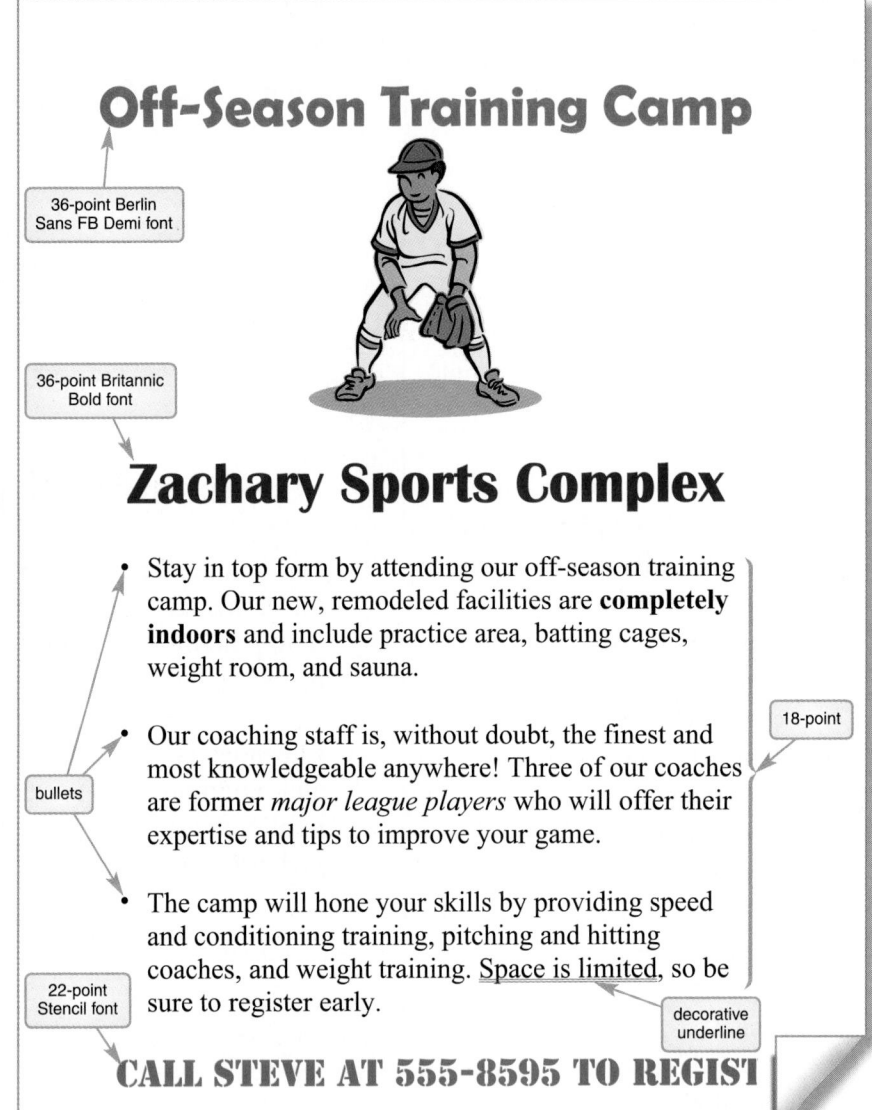

FIGURE 1-80

Cases and Places

The difficulty of these case studies varies:
■ are the least difficult and ■■ are more difficult. The last exercise is a group exercise.

1 ■ You have been assigned the task of preparing an announcement for The Gridiron Club. The announcement is to contain clip art related to football. Use the following text: first line of headline – Gridiron Club…; second line of headline – …Tailgate Party; body title – GO TROJANS!; first paragraph of body copy – Join us on Friday, October 28, for a pre-game tailgate party. Help us celebrate our beloved Trojans' undefeated season! The Gridiron Club will provide grills, brats, hamburgers, hot dogs, and buns. Please bring a side dish to share and your own nonalcoholic beverages.; second paragraph of body copy – The party starts at 5:30 p.m. in the parking lot by the Administration Center. Kick-off for the first playoff game is at 7:00 p.m.; last line – Call 555-1995 for more information. Use the concepts and techniques presented in this project to create and format this announcement. Be sure to check spelling and grammar in the announcement.

2 ■ You have been assigned the task of preparing an announcement for an upcoming camp at the Sherman Planetarium. The announcement is to contain clip art of a telescope. Use the following text: first line of headline – Reach for…; second line of headline – …the Stars; body title – Space, Stars, and Skies Camp; first paragraph of body copy – Have you always been fascinated by the planets, stars, and space travel? Enroll in our Space, Stars, and Skies Camp to learn more about the cosmos. The camp will meet June 6 through June 9 from 8:30 a.m. until 12:30 p.m. at the Sherman Planetarium.; second paragraph of body copy – Our facilities include simulators, lecture halls, virtual rooms, and a planetarium. Learn about space travel from our staff, two of whom are former astronauts.; third paragraph of body copy – Register early to reserve your seat. Space is limited to 25 participants.; last line – Call 555-9141 to register. Use the concepts and techniques presented in this project to create and format this announcement. Be sure to check spelling and grammar in the announcement.

3 ■■ Your boss at Cornucopia Health Foods has asked you to prepare an announcement for a grand opening. You are to include appropriate clip art. He gives you the following information for the announcement. The doors of its newest store will open in Centerbrook Mall at 9:00 a.m. on Monday, September 26. You will find great deals throughout the store. Discount coupons and free samples will be distributed all day. The first 50 customers at the register will receive a free bottle of vitamin C tablets. Cornucopia Health Foods offers a huge selection of health food and organics. Tofu, carob, soy products, herbal teas, vitamin supplements, and organically grown produce are just a few items in our extensive product line. The store's slogan is as follows: Cornucopia ~ good food for good health! Use the concepts and techniques presented in this project to create the announcement. Change the color of text in the headline, body title, and last line of the announcement. Use a decorative underline in the announcement. Add bullets to the paragraphs of the body copy. Be sure to check spelling and grammar in the announcement.

Cases and Places

4 ■ ■ You have been assigned the task of preparing an announcement for Stone Bay Apartments advertising an apartment for rent. You are to include appropriate clip art. These details have been provided. Stone Bay Apartments has a two-bedroom apartment available for rent now. This upper-level unit has an eat-in kitchen, central air, and a large living room with southern exposure. Rent is $925.00 a month. Utilities are included in rent. Pets are welcome. Interested parties should call 555-8265 to arrange a showing. Stone Bay Apartments provide amenities galore, including laundry facilities, garage parking, clubhouse, pool, and tennis courts. We are located close to Lake Park Mall, grocery stores, restaurants, and Victor Community College. Use the concepts and techniques presented in this project to create the announcement. Change the color of text in the headline, body title, and last line of the announcement. Use a decorative underline in the announcement. Add bullets to some of the paragraphs of the body copy. Be sure to check spelling and grammar in the announcement.

5 ■ ■ **Working Together** Schools, churches, libraries, grocery stores, and other public places have bulletin boards for announcements and other postings. Often, these bulletin boards have so many announcements that some go unnoticed. Look at a bulletin board at one of the locations mentioned above and find a posted announcement that you think might be overlooked. Copy the text from the announcement and distribute it to each team member. Each member then independently should use this text, together with the techniques presented in this project, to create an announcement that would be more likely to catch a reader's eye. Be sure to check spelling and grammar. As a group, critique each announcement and have each member redesign their announcement based on the group's recommendations. Hand in printouts of each team member's original and final announcements.

Creating a Research Paper

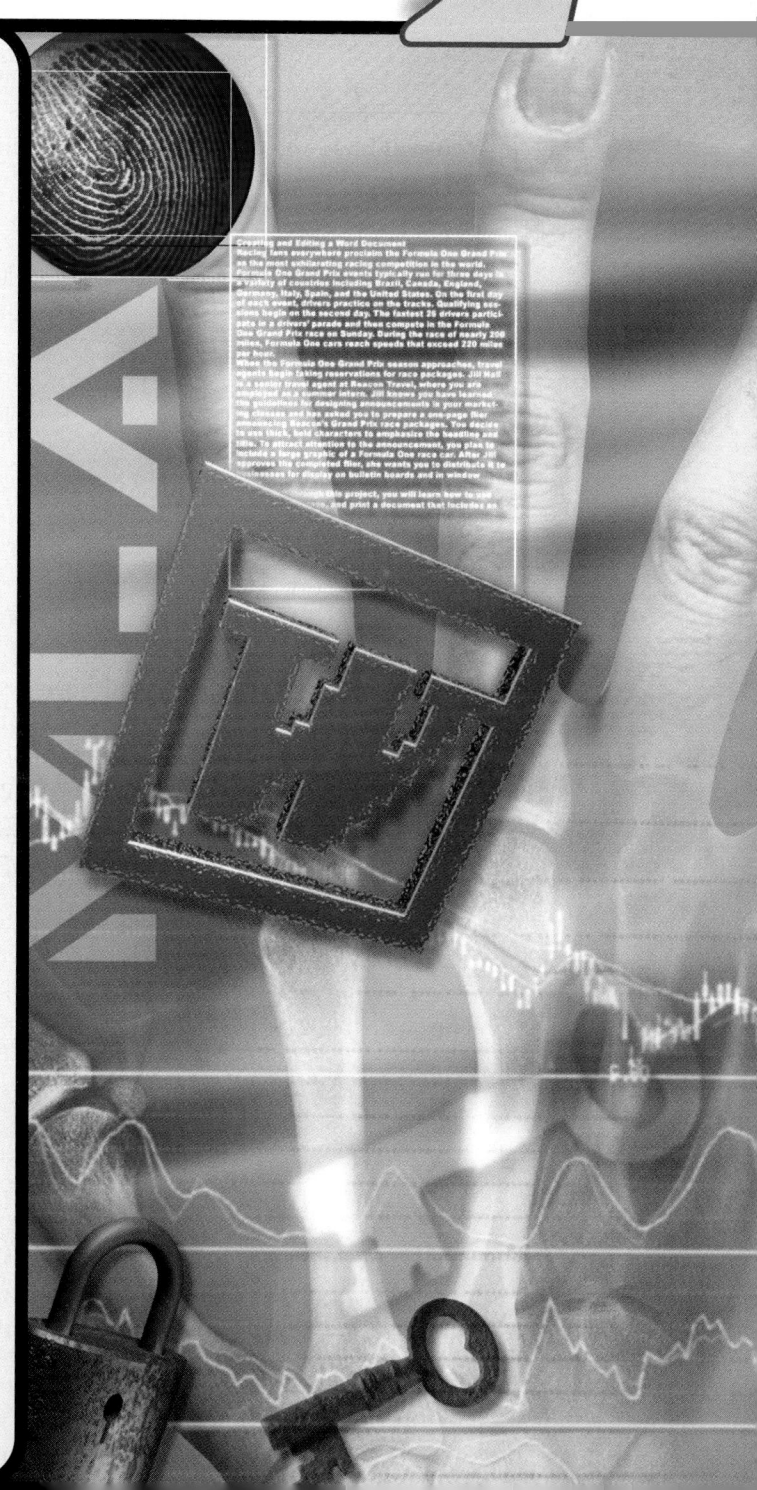

CASE PERSPECTIVE

Suzy Zhao is a full-time college student, majoring in Finance. Mr. Ortiz, the instructor in her introductory computer class, has assigned a short research paper that should contain a minimum of 325 words. The paper must discuss some aspect of computer security. It also must be written according to the MLA documentation style, which specifies guidelines for report preparation. The paper is to contain one footnote and three references — one of which must be obtained from the World Wide Web. Finally, all students are to submit their papers electronically via e-mail to Mr. Ortiz.

When Suzy graduates from college, she plans to work in the banking sector. She is interested in ways to ensure that users are legitimate before allowing them access to a computer. Suzy recently read a short article about computer security that mentioned computers can use biometrics to authenticate a person's identity by verifying a personal characteristic. Examples include fingerprints, hand geometry, facial features, voice, signatures, and eye patterns. Suzy decides to write her research paper about biometrics. She intends to review computer magazines at the school's library, surf the Internet, and e-mail a few biometrics vendors for information about their products. She also plans to use the Internet to obtain the guidelines for the MLA style of documentation. Suzy knows that you are a computer major and quite skilled at searching the Internet. She asks you to assist her with the Web searches. You immediately agree to help your friend.

As you read through this project, you will learn how to use Word to create a research paper and e-mail a copy of the finished paper.

Creating a Research Paper

Objectives

You will have mastered the material in this project when you can:

- Describe the MLA documentation style for research papers
- Change the margin settings and line spacing in a document
- Use a header to number pages of a document
- Apply formatting using shortcut keys
- Modify paragraph indentation
- Add a footnote to a document
- Count the words in a document
- Insert a manual page break
- Create a hyperlink
- Sort selected paragraphs
- Proof and revise a document
- Display the Web page associated with a hyperlink
- E-mail a copy of a document
- Use the Research task pane to locate information

Introduction

In both academic and business environments, you will be asked to write reports. Business reports range from proposals to cost justifications to five-year plans to research findings. Academic reports focus mostly on research findings. Whether you are writing a business report or an academic report, you should follow a standard style when preparing it.

Many different styles of documentation exist for report preparation, depending on the nature of the report. Each style requires the same basic information; the differences among styles relates to how the information is presented. For example, one documentation style may use the term bibliography, whereas another uses references, and yet a third prefers works cited. Two popular documentation styles for research papers are the **Modern Language Association of America** (**MLA**) and **American Psychological Association** (**APA**) styles. This project uses the MLA documentation style.

Project 2 — Biometrics Research Paper

Project 2 illustrates the creation of a short research paper about biometrics. As shown in Figure 2-1, the paper follows the MLA documentation style. The first two pages present the research paper, and the third page alphabetically lists the works cited.

Zhao 3

Works Cited

paragraphs in alphabetical order

Carter, Donnell W., and Louis C. Juarez. *Securing Confidential Data Entered into a Computer*.

Boston: Thomas Publishing, 2005.

Computers and Biometrics. Shelly Cashman Series®. Course Technology. 3 Oct. 2005.

http://www.scsite.com/wd2003/pr2/wc.htm.

Schmidt, Karl J. "Biometrics and Authenticating Computer Users." *Computers and the Internet*

Aug. 2005: 54-62.

Zhao 2

Law enforcement, surveillance systems, airports, day-care centers, financial institutions,

the military, and other organizations that deal with highly sensitive data use other types of

biometrics. A face recognition system captures a live face image and compares it with a stored

image. A hand geometry system measures the shape and size of a person's hand (*Computers and*

Biometrics). A voice verification system compares a person's live speech with his or her stored

voice pattern. A signature verification system recognizes the shape of a handwritten signature, as

well as measures the pressure exerted and the motion used to write the signature. Finally, an iris

recognition system reads patterns in the iris of the eye.

parenthetical citation

header contains last name followed by page number → Zhao 1

Suzy Zhao

Mr. Ortiz

Information Systems 101

October 13, 2005

Biometrics **parenthetical citation**

Biometrics is the technology of authenticating a person's identity by verifying a personal

characteristic. Biometric devices grant users access to programs, systems, or rooms by analyzing

some biometric identifier (Schmidt 54-62). A biometric identifier is a physical or behavioral

characteristic. Examples include fingerprints, facial features, hand geometry, voice patterns,

signatures, and eye patterns.

A biometric device translates a personal characteristic into a digital code that is compared

with a digital code stored in the computer. If the digital code in the computer does not match the

personal characteristic's code, the computer denies access to the individual.

The most widely used biometric device today is a fingerprint scanner. A fingerprint

scanner captures curves and indentations of a fingerprint. With the cost of fingerprint scanners

less than $100, experts believe this technology will become the home user's authentication

device for e-commerce transactions. To conduct a credit-card transaction, the Web site would

require users to hold a finger on the scanner. External fingerprint scanners usually plug into a

parallel or USB port.[1] Businesses use fingerprint scanners to authenticate users before they can

access a personal computer. Grade schools use fingerprint scanners as an alternative to lunch

money. Students' account balances adjust for each lunch purchased.

superscripted note reference mark

_____

[1] According to Carter and Juarez, newer keyboards and notebook computers have a

fingerprint scanner built into them (42-53).

explanatory note positioned as footnote

More About

MLA and APA

The MLA documentation style is the standard in the humanities, and the APA style is preferred in the social sciences. For more information about the MLA and APA guidelines, visit the Word 2003 More About Web page (scsite.com/wd2003/more) and then click MLA or APA, respectively.

FIGURE 2-1

MLA Documentation Style

When writing papers, you should adhere to some style of documentation. The research paper in this project follows the guidelines presented by the MLA. To follow the MLA style, double-space text on all pages of the paper using one-inch top, bottom, left, and right margins. Indent the first word of each paragraph one-half inch from the left margin. At the right margin of each page, place a page number one-half inch from the top margin. On each page, precede the page number by your last name.

The MLA style does not require a title page. Instead, place your name and course information in a block at the left margin beginning one inch from the top of the page. Center the title one double-space below your name and course information.

In the body of the paper, place author references in parentheses with the page number(s) of the referenced information. The MLA style uses in-text **parenthetical citations** instead of noting each source at the bottom of the page or at the end of the paper. In the MLA style, notes are used only for optional explanatory notes.

If used, explanatory notes elaborate on points discussed in the body of the paper. Use a superscript (raised number) to signal that an explanatory note exists, and also sequence the notes. Position explanatory notes either at the bottom of the page as footnotes or at the end of the paper as endnotes. Indent the first line of each explanatory note one-half inch from the left margin. Place one space following the superscripted number before beginning the note text. Double-space the note text. At the end of the note text, you may list bibliographic information for further reference.

The MLA style uses the term **works cited** for the bibliographical references. The works cited page alphabetically lists works that are referenced directly in the paper. List works by each author's last name, or, if the author's name is not available, by the title of the work. Italicize or underline the title of the work. Place the works cited on a separate numbered page. Center the title, Works Cited, one inch from the top margin. Double-space all lines. Begin the first line of each entry at the left margin, indenting subsequent lines of the same entry one-half inch from the left margin.

Starting and Customizing Word

To start and customize Word, Windows must be running. If you are stepping through this project on a computer and you want your screen to match the figures in this book, then you should change your computer's resolution to 800 × 600 and reset the toolbars and menus. For information about changing the resolution and resetting toolbars and menus, read Appendix D.

The next steps show how to start Word and customize the Word window. You may need to ask your instructor how to start Word for your system.

To Start and Customize Word

1 Click the Start button on the Windows taskbar, point to All Programs on the Start menu, point to Microsoft Office on the All Programs submenu, and then click Microsoft Office Word 2003 on the Microsoft Office submenu.

2 If the Word window is not maximized, double-click its title bar to maximize it.

3 If the Language bar appears, right-click it and then click Close the Language bar on the shortcut menu.

4 If the Getting Started task pane is displayed in the Word window, click its Close button.

5 If the Standard and Formatting toolbar buttons are displayed on one row, click the Toolbar Options button and then click Show Buttons on Two Rows in the Toolbar Options list.

6 If your screen differs from Figure 2-2 on the next page, click View on the menu bar and then click Normal.

7 If your zoom percent is not 100 (shown in Figure 2-2), click View on the menu bar, click Zoom on the View menu, click 100%, and then click the OK button.

Word starts and, after a few moments, displays an empty document titled Document1 in the Word window (shown in Figure 2-2).

Displaying Formatting Marks

As discussed in Project 1, it is helpful to display formatting marks that indicate where in the document you pressed the ENTER key, SPACEBAR, and other keys. The following step discusses how to display formatting marks.

To Display Formatting Marks

1 If the Show/Hide ¶ button on the Standard toolbar is not selected already, click it.

Word displays formatting marks in the document window, and the Show/Hide ¶ button on the Standard toolbar is selected (shown in Figure 2-2).

Changing the Margins

Word is preset to use standard 8.5-by-11-inch paper, with 1.25-inch left and right margins and 1-inch top and bottom margins. These margin settings affect every page in the document.

Periodically, you may want to change the default margin settings. The MLA documentation style, for example, requires one-inch top, bottom, left, and right margins throughout the paper. Thus, the steps on the next page show how to change the margin settings for a document when the window is in normal view. To verify the document window is in normal view, click View on the menu bar and then click Normal.

More About

Writing Papers

The Web contains numerous sites with information, tips, and suggestions about writing research papers. College professors and fellow students develop many of these Web sites. For links to Web sites about writing research papers, visit the Word 2003 More About Web page (scsite.com/wd2003/more) and then click one of the Writing Research Papers links.

More About

Changing Margins

In print layout view, you can change margin settings using the horizontal and vertical rulers. Current margin settings are shaded in gray. The margin boundary is located where the gray meets the white. To change a margin setting, drag the margin boundary on the ruler. To see the numeric margin settings, hold down the ALT key while dragging the margin boundary on the ruler.

To Change the Margin Settings

1

• **Click File on the menu bar (Figure 2-2).**

FIGURE 2-2

2

• **Click Page Setup on the File menu.**

• **When Word displays the Page Setup dialog box, if necessary, click the Margins tab.**

Word displays the current margin settings in the text boxes of the Page Setup dialog box (Figure 2-3).

FIGURE 2-3

3

- **With 1" selected in the Top text box, press the TAB key twice to select 1.25" in the Left text box.**
- **Type 1 and then press the TAB key.**
- **Type 1 in the Right text box.**

The new left and right margin settings are 1 inch (Figure 2-4). Instead of typing margin values, you can click the text box arrows to increase or decrease the number in the text box.

4

- **Click the OK button in the Page Setup dialog box.**

Word changes the left and right margins.

FIGURE 2-4

The new margin settings take effect immediately in the document. Word uses these margins for the entire document.

When you change the margin settings in the text boxes in the Page Setup dialog box, the Preview area (Figure 2-4) does not adjust to reflect a changed margin setting until the insertion point leaves the respective text box. That is, you must press the TAB or ENTER key or click another text box if you want to view a changed margin setting in the Preview area.

Adjusting Line Spacing

Line spacing is the amount of vertical space between lines of text in a document. By default, Word single-spaces between lines of text and automatically adjusts line height to accommodate various font sizes and graphics.

The MLA documentation style requires that you **double-space** the entire paper; that is, one blank line should be between each line of text. The steps on the next page show how to adjust the line spacing from single to double.

Other Ways

1. In print layout view, drag margin boundary(s) on ruler
2. In Voice Command mode, say "File, Page Setup, Margins, Left, [type left margin setting], Tab, [type right margin setting], OK"

More About

The Page Setup Dialog Box

A document printed in portrait orientation is taller than it is wide. A document printed in landscape orientation is wider than it is tall. If you want to change the orientation of a printout from portrait to landscape, click Landscape in the Orientation area in the Page Setup dialog box (Figure 2-4).

To Double-Space Text

1

• **Click the Line Spacing button arrow on the Formatting toolbar.**

Word displays a list of line spacing options (Figure 2-5).

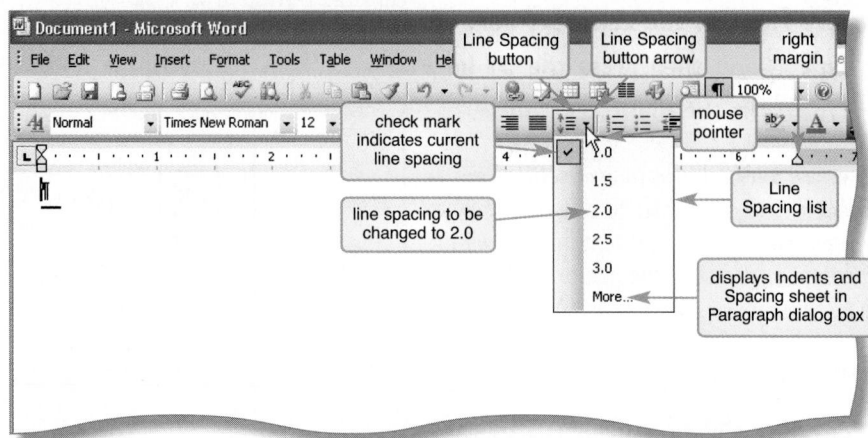

FIGURE 2-5

2

• **Click 2.0 in the Line Spacing list.**

Word changes the line spacing to double at the location of the insertion point (Figure 2-6).

FIGURE 2-6

Other Ways

1. On Format menu click Paragraph, click Indents and Spacing tab, click Line spacing box arrow, click Double, click OK button
2. Right-click paragraph, click Paragraph on shortcut menu, click Indents and Spacing tab, click Line spacing box arrow, click Double, click OK button
3. Press CTRL+2
4. In Voice Command mode, say "Line Spacing, [select 2]"

More About

Line Spacing

If the top of characters or a graphic is chopped off, then line spacing may be set to Exactly in the Paragraph dialog box. To remedy the problem, change the line spacing to Single (1.0), 1.5, Double (2.0), 2.5, 3.0, or At least, all of which accommodate the largest font or graphic.

Notice when line spacing is double (Figure 2-6), the end mark displays one blank line below the insertion point.

The Line Spacing list (Figure 2-5) contains a variety of settings for the line spacing. The default, 1 (for single), and the options 1.5, 2 (for double), 2.5, and 3 (for triple) instruct Word to adjust line spacing automatically to accommodate the largest font or graphic on a line. For additional line spacing options, click More in the Line Spacing list and then click the Line spacing box arrow in the Indents and Spacing sheet in the Paragraph dialog box.

If you wanted to apply the most recently set line spacing to the current or selected paragraphs, you would click the Line Spacing button instead of the Line Spacing button arrow.

To change the line spacing of existing text, select the text first and then change the line spacing. For example, to change an existing paragraph to double-spacing, triple-click the paragraph to select it, click the Line Spacing button arrow on the Formatting toolbar, and then click 2.0 in the list.

Using a Header to Number Pages

In Word, you easily can number pages by clicking Insert on the menu bar and then clicking Page Numbers. Using the Page Numbers command, you can specify the location (top or bottom of the page) and alignment (right, left, or centered) of the page numbers.

The MLA style requires that your last name display to the left of the page number on each page. The Page Numbers command, however, does not allow you to enter text along with the page number. Thus, to place your name to the left of the page number, you must create a header that contains the page number.

Headers and Footers

A **header** is text you want printed at the top of each page in a document. A **footer** is text you want printed at the bottom of every page. In Word, headers print in the top margin one-half inch from the top of every page, and footers print in the bottom margin one-half inch from the bottom of each page, which meets the MLA style. Headers and footers can include text and graphics, as well as the page number, total number of pages, current date, and current time.

In this project, you are to precede the page number with your last name placed one-half inch from the top of each page. Your last name and the page number should print right-aligned; that is, at the right margin.

To create the header, first you display the header area in the document window. Then, you can enter the header text into the header area. The procedures on the following pages show how to create the header with page numbers, according to the MLA documentation style.

To Display the Header Area

1

• **Click View on the menu bar (Figure 2-7).**

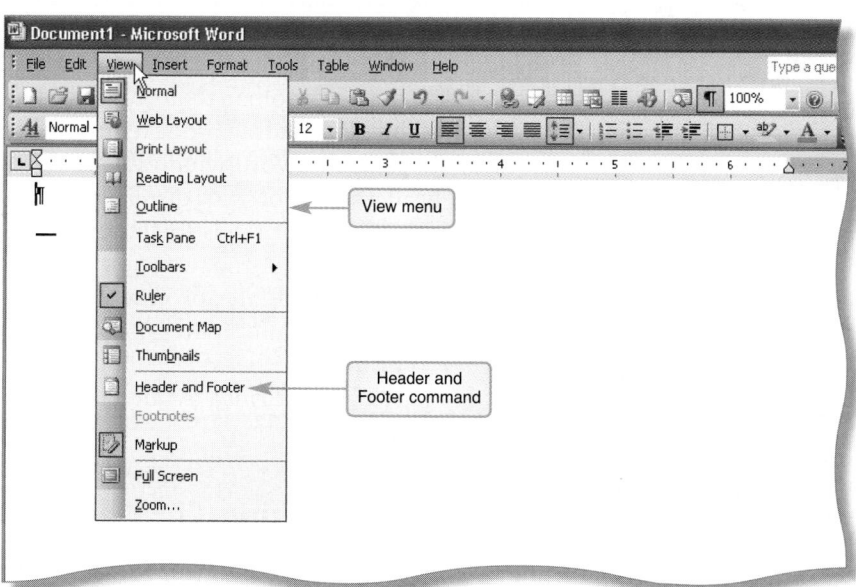

FIGURE 2-7

2

• **Click Header and Footer on the View menu.**

• **If your zoom percent is not 100, click View on the menu bar, click Zoom on the View menu, click 100%, and then click the OK button.**

Word switches from normal view to print layout view and displays the Header and Footer toolbar (Figure 2-8). You type header text in the header area.

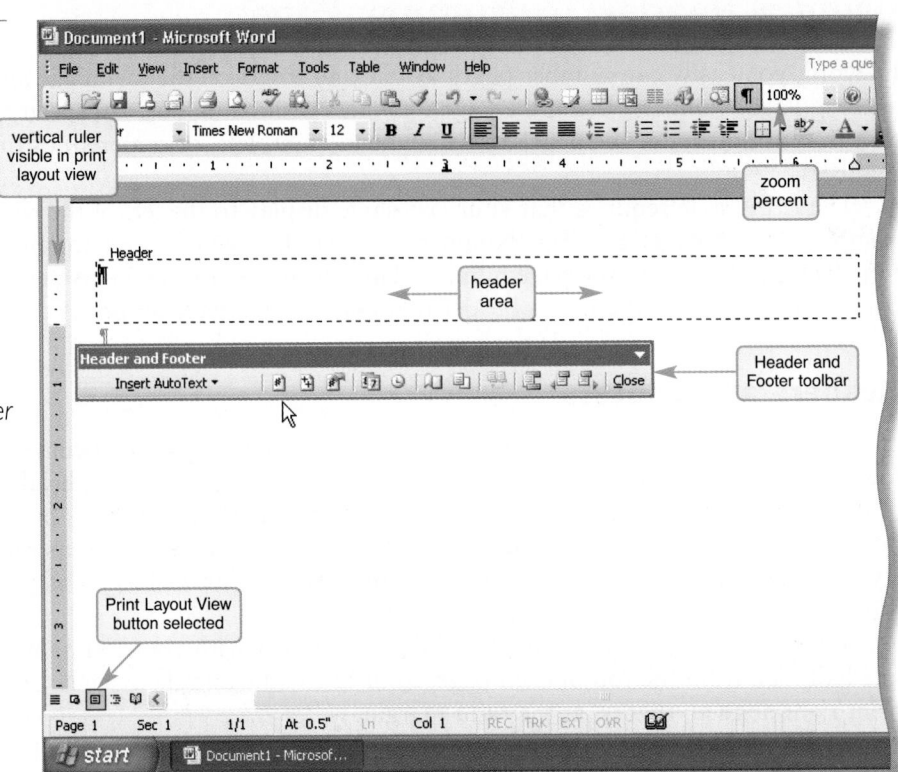

FIGURE 2-8

The Header and Footer toolbar initially floats in the document window. To move a floating toolbar, drag its title bar. You can **dock,** or attach, a floating toolbar above or below the Standard and Formatting toolbars by double-clicking the floating tool-bar's title bar. To move a docked toolbar, drag its move handle. Recall that the move handle is the vertical dotted bar to the left of the first button on a docked toolbar. If you drag a floating toolbar to an edge of the window, the toolbar snaps to the edge of the window. If you drag a docked toolbar to the middle of the window, the toolbar floats in the Word window.

The header area does not display on the screen when the document window is in normal view because it tends to clutter the screen. To see the header in the document window with the rest of the text, you can display the document in print preview, which is discussed in a later project, or you can switch to print layout view. When you click the Header and Footer command on the View menu, Word automatically switches to **print layout view,** which displays the document exactly as it will print. In print layout view, the Print Layout View button on the horizontal scroll bar is selected (Figure 2-8).

Entering Text Using Click and Type

When in print layout view, you can use **Click and Type** to format and enter text, graphics, and other items. To use Click and Type, you double-click a blank area of the document window. Word automatically formats the item you enter according to the location where you double-click. The next steps show how to use Click and Type to right-align and then type the last name into the header area.

To Click and Type

1

• **Position the mouse pointer at the right edge of the header area to display a right-align icon next to the I-beam.**

As you move the Click and Type pointer around the window, the icon changes to represent formatting that will be applied if you double-click at that location (Figure 2-9).

FIGURE 2-9

2

• **Double-click.**

• **Type** Zhao **and then press the SPACEBAR.**

Word displays the last name, Zhao, right-aligned in the header area (Figure 2-10).

FIGURE 2-10

Entering a Page Number into the Header

The next task is to enter the page number into the header area, as shown in the following steps.

To Enter a Page Number

• **Click the Insert Page Number button on the Header and Footer toolbar.**

Word displays the page number 1 in the header area (Figure 2-11).

FIGURE 2-11

2

• **Click the Close Header and Footer button on the Header and Footer toolbar.**

Word closes the Header and Footer toolbar and returns the screen to normal view (Figure 2-12).

FIGURE 2-12

Word does not display the header on the screen in normal view. Although it disappears from the screen when you switch from print layout view to normal view, the header still is part of the document. To view the header, you can click View on the menu bar and then click Header and Footer; you can switch to print layout view; or you can display the document in print preview. Project 3 discusses print layout view and print preview.

Figure 2-13 identifies the buttons on the Header and Footer toolbar. Just as the Insert Page Number button on the Header and Footer toolbar inserts the page number into the document, three other buttons on the Header and Footer toolbar insert items into the document. The Insert Number of Pages button inserts the total number of pages in the document; the Insert Date button inserts the current date; and the Insert Time button inserts the current time.

To edit an existing header, you can follow the same procedure that you use to create a new header. That is, click View on the menu bar and then click Header and Footer to display the header area. If you have multiple headers, click the Show Next button on the Header and Footer toolbar until the appropriate header displays in the header area. Edit the header as you would any Word text and then click the Close Header and Footer button on the Header and Footer toolbar.

To create a footer, click View on the menu bar, click Header and Footer, click the Switch Between Header and Footer button on the Header and Footer toolbar, and then follow the same procedure as you would to create a header.

Later projects explain other buttons on the Header and Footer toolbar.

FIGURE 2-13

Typing the Body of a Research Paper

The body of the research paper in this project encompasses the first two pages of the research paper. You will type the body of the research paper and then modify it later in the project, so it matches Figure 2-1 on page WD 75.

As discussed earlier in this project, the MLA style does not require a separate title page for research papers. Instead, place your name and course information in a block at the top of the page at the left margin. The next steps describe how to begin typing the body of the research paper.

To Enter Name and Course Information

1 **Type** `Suzy Zhao` **and then press the** ENTER **key.**

2 **Type** `Mr. Ortiz` **and then press the** ENTER **key.**

3 **Type** `Information Systems 101` **and then press the** ENTER **key.**

4 **Type** `October 13, 2005` **and then press the** ENTER **key.**

Word displays the student name on line 1, the instructor name on line 2, the course name on line 3, and the paper due date on line 4 (Figure 2-14). Depending on your Word settings, the smart tag indicator may not appear below the date on the screen.

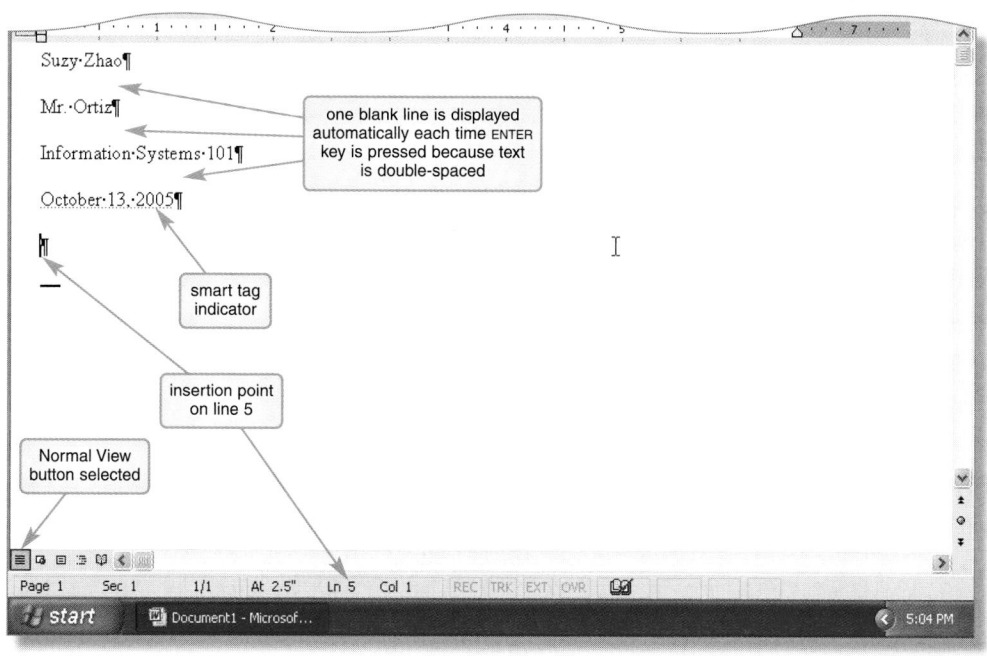

FIGURE 2-14

Notice in Figure 2-14 that the insertion point currently is on line 5. Each time you press the ENTER key, Word advances two lines on the screen. The line counter on the status bar is incremented by only one, however, because earlier you set line spacing to double.

If you watch the screen as you type, you may have noticed that as you typed the first few characters in the month, Octo, Word displayed the **AutoComplete tip**, October, above the characters. To save typing, you could press the ENTER key while the AutoComplete tip appears, which instructs Word to place the text of the AutoComplete tip at the location of your typing.

Applying Formatting Using Shortcut Keys

The next step is to enter the title of the research paper centered between the page margins. As you type text, you may want to format paragraphs and characters as you type them, instead of typing the text and then formatting it later. In Project 1, you typed the entire document, selected the text to be formatted, and then applied the desired formatting using toolbar buttons. When your fingers are already on the keyboard, it often is more efficient to use **shortcut keys**, or keyboard key combinations, to format text as you type it.

The following steps show how to center a paragraph using the shortcut keys CTRL+E and then left-align a paragraph using the shortcut keys CTRL+L. (Recall from Project 1 that a notation such as CTRL+E means to press the letter e on the keyboard while holding down the CTRL key.)

To Format Text Using Shortcut Keys

1

• **Press CTRL+E.**

• **Type** Biometrics **and then press the ENTER key.**

Word centers the title between the left and right margins (Figure 2-15). The paragraph mark and insertion point are centered because the formatting specified in the previous paragraph is carried forward to the next paragraph.

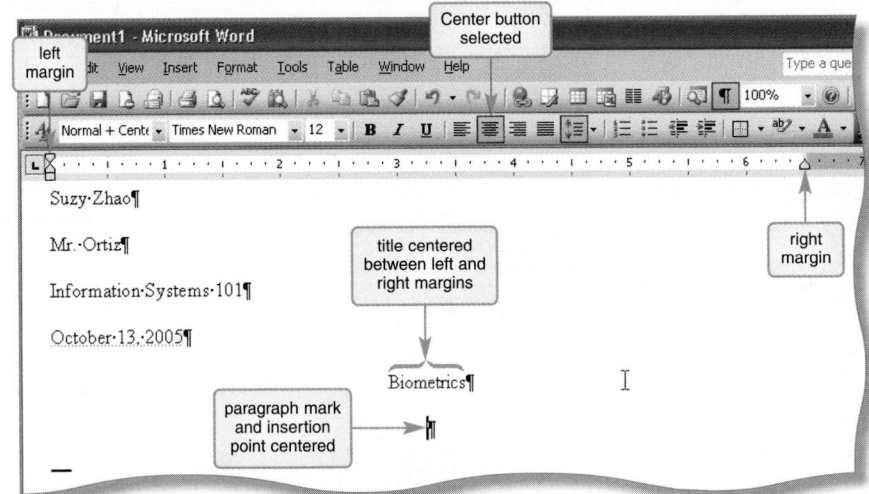

FIGURE 2-15

2

• **Press CTRL+L.**

Word positions the paragraph mark and the insertion point at the left margin (Figure 2-16). The next text you type will be left-aligned.

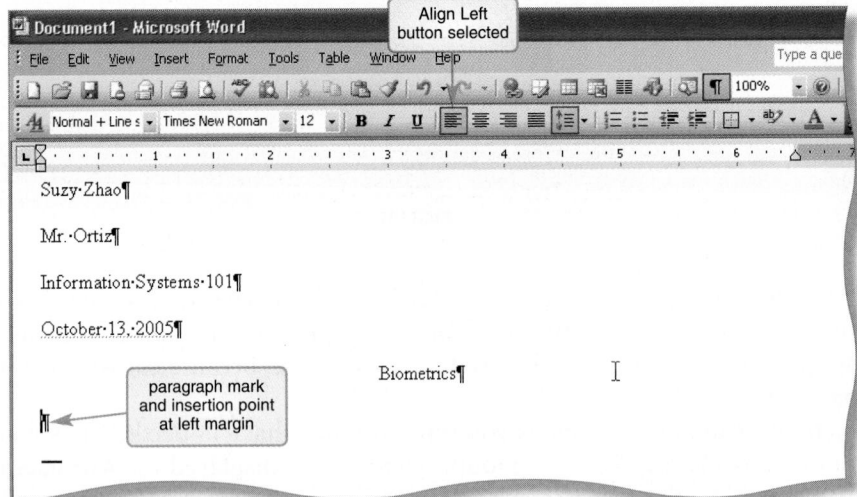

FIGURE 2-16

Word has many shortcut keys for your convenience while typing. Table 2-1 lists the common shortcut keys for formatting characters. Table 2-2 lists common shortcut keys for formatting paragraphs.

Table 2-1 Shortcut Keys for Formatting Characters	
CHARACTER FORMATTING TASK	SHORTCUT KEYS
All capital letters	CTRL+SHIFT+A
Bold	CTRL+B
Case of letters	SHIFT+F3
Decrease font size	CTRL+SHIFT+<
Decrease font size 1 point	CTRL+[
Double-underline	CTRL+SHIFT+D
Increase font size	CTRL+SHIFT+>
Increase font size 1 point	CTRL+]
Italic	CTRL+I
Remove character formatting (plain text)	CTRL+SPACEBAR
Small uppercase letters	CTRL+SHIFT+K
Subscript	CTRL+=
Superscript	CTRL+SHIFT+PLUS SIGN
Underline	CTRL+U
Underline words, not spaces	CTRL+SHIFT+W

Table 2-2 Shortcut Keys for Formatting Paragraphs	
PARAGRAPH FORMATTING TASK	SHORTCUT KEYS
1.5 line spacing	CTRL+5
Add/remove one line above	CTRL+0 (zero)
Center paragraph	CTRL+E
Decrease paragraph indent	CTRL+SHIFT+M
Double-space lines	CTRL+2
Hanging indent	CTRL+T
Increase paragraph indent	CTRL+M
Justify paragraph	CTRL+J
Left-align paragraph	CTRL+L
Remove hanging indent	CTRL+SHIFT+T
Remove paragraph formatting	CTRL+Q
Right-align paragraph	CTRL+R
Single-space lines	CTRL+1

Saving the Research Paper

You now should save the research paper. For a detailed example of the procedure summarized below, refer to pages WD 28 through WD 30 in Project 1.

To Save a Document

1 **Insert a floppy disk into drive A.**

2 **Click the Save button on the Standard toolbar.**

3 **Type** Biometrics Paper **in the File name text box.**

4 **Click the Save in box arrow and then click 3½ Floppy (A:).**

5 **Click the Save button in the Save As dialog box.**

Word saves the document with the file name, Biometrics Paper (shown in Figure 2-17 on the next page).

Indenting Paragraphs

According to the MLA style, the first line of each paragraph in the research paper is to be indented one-half inch from the left margin. You can instruct Word to indent just the first line of a paragraph, called **first-line indent**, using the horizontal ruler. The left edge of the horizontal ruler contains two triangles above a square. The **First Line Indent marker** is the top triangle at the 0" mark on the ruler (Figure 2-17). The bottom triangle is discussed later in this project. The small square at the 0" mark is the Left Indent marker. The **Left Indent marker** allows you to change the entire left margin, whereas the First Line Indent marker indents only the first line of the paragraph.

More About

Shortcut Keys

To print a complete list of shortcut keys in Word, type keyboard shortcuts in the Type a question for help box on the right side of the menu bar. In the Search Results task pane, click the Keyboard shortcuts link. In the upper-right corner of the Office Word Help window, click the Show All link. Click the Print button in the Help window and then click the Print button in the Print dialog box.

More About

First-Line Indent

Some users may find it confusing to use the ruler to indent paragraphs. In this case, you can use the Paragraph dialog box to first-line indent a paragraph. To do this, click Format on the menu bar, click Paragraph, click the Indents and Spacing tab, click the Special box arrow, click First line, and then click the OK button.

The following steps show how to first-line indent paragraphs in the research paper.

To First-Line Indent Paragraphs

1

• **If the horizontal ruler is not displayed on your screen, click View on the menu bar and then click Ruler.**

• **With the insertion point on the paragraph mark in line 6, point to the First Line Indent marker on the ruler (Figure 2-17).**

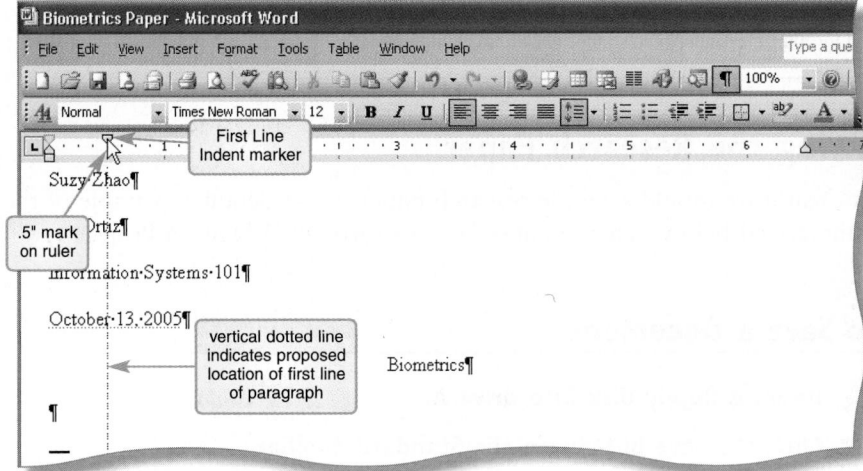

FIGURE 2-17

2

• **Drag the First Line Indent marker to the .5" mark on the ruler.**

As you drag the mouse, Word displays a vertical dotted line in the document window, indicating the proposed location of the first line of the paragraph (Figure 2-18).

FIGURE 2-18

3

• **Release the mouse button.**

Word displays the First Line Indent marker at the .5" mark on the ruler, or one-half inch from the left margin (Figure 2-19). The paragraph mark containing the insertion point in the document window also moves one-half inch to the right.

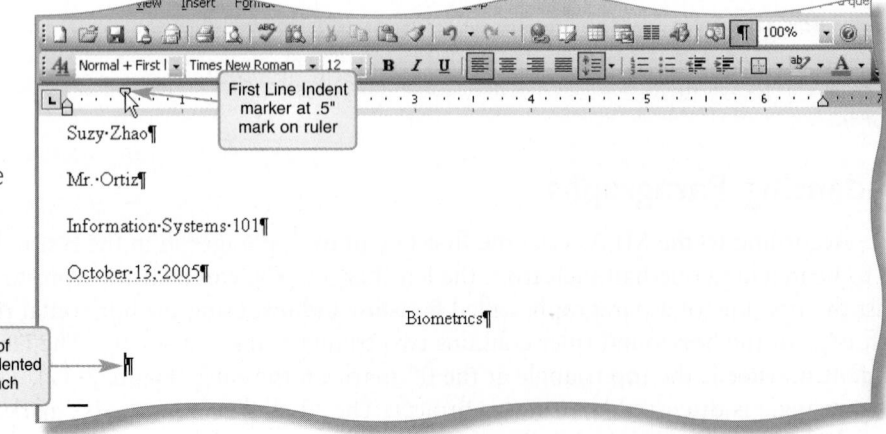

FIGURE 2-19

4

- **Type the first paragraph of the research paper body, as shown in Figure 2-20.**
- **Press the ENTER key.**
- **Type** A biometric device translates a personal characteristic into a digital code that is compared with a digital code stored in the computer.

Word automatically indents the first line of the second paragraph by one-half inch (Figure 2-20).

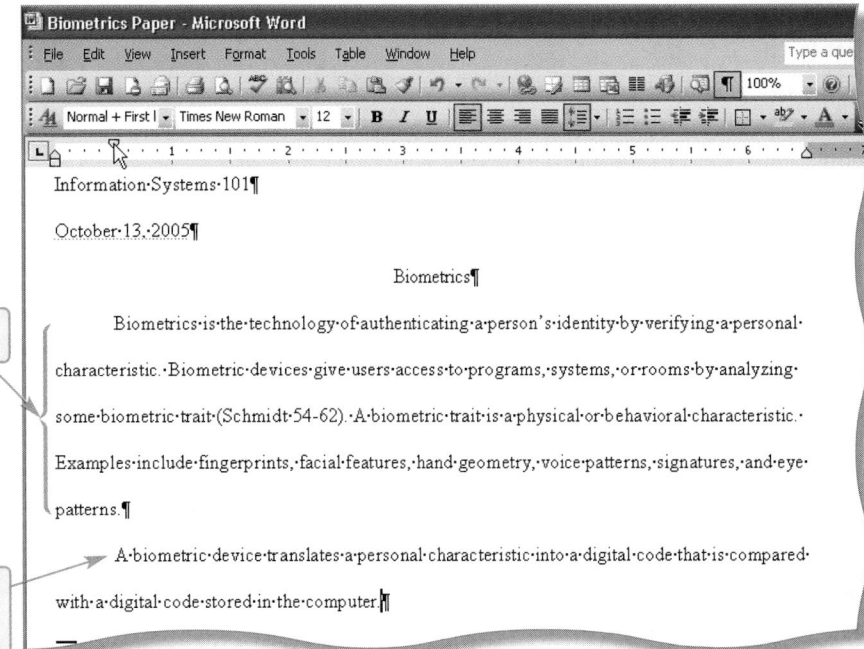

first paragraph

first line of subsequent paragraph indented automatically when ENTER key is pressed

Information·Systems·101¶

October·13,·2005¶

Biometrics¶

Biometrics·is·the·technology·of·authenticating·a·person's·identity·by·verifying·a·personal· characteristic.·Biometric·devices·give·users·access·to·programs,·systems,·or·rooms·by·analyzing· some·biometric·trait·(Schmidt·54-62).·A·biometric·trait·is·a·physical·or·behavioral·characteristic.· Examples·include·fingerprints,·facial·features,·hand·geometry,·voice·patterns,·signatures,·and·eye· patterns.¶

A·biometric·device·translates·a·personal·characteristic·into·a·digital·code·that·is·compared· with·a·digital·code·stored·in·the·computer.¶

FIGURE 2-20

Recall that each time you press the ENTER key, the paragraph formatting in the previous paragraph is carried forward to the next paragraph. Thus, once you set the first-line indent, its format carries forward automatically to each subsequent paragraph you type.

Using Word's AutoCorrect Feature

As you type, you may make typing, spelling, capitalization, or grammar errors. For this reason, Word provides an **AutoCorrect** feature that automatically corrects these kinds of errors as you type them in the document. For example, if you type the text, ahve, Word automatically changes it to the correct spelling, have, when you press the SPACEBAR or a punctuation mark key such as a period or comma.

Word has predefined many commonly misspelled words, which it automatically corrects for you. In the following steps the word, the, is misspelled intentionally as teh to illustrate the AutoCorrect as you type feature.

To AutoCorrect as You Type

1

- **Press the SPACEBAR.**
- **Type the beginning of the next sentence, misspelling the word, the, as follows:** If the digital code in the computer does not match teh **(Figure 2-21).**

Other Ways

1. On Format menu click Paragraph, click Indents and Spacing tab, click Special box arrow, click First line, click OK button
2. Right-click paragraph, click Paragraph on shortcut menu, click Indents and Spacing tab, click Special box arrow, click First line, click OK button
3. Press TAB key at beginning of paragraph
4. In Voice Command mode, say "Format, Paragraph, Indents and Spacing, Special, First line, OK"

insertion point immediately follows last character in misspelled word

A·biometric·device·translates·a·personal·characteristic·into·a·digital·code·that·is·compared· with·a·digital·code·stored·in·the·computer.·If·the·digital·code·in·the·computer·does·not·match·teh¶

misspelled word

FIGURE 2-21

2

• **Press the SPACEBAR.**

• **Type the rest of the sentence:** personal characteristic's code, the computer denies access to the individual.

As soon as the SPACEBAR is pressed, Word's AutoCorrect feature detects the misspelling and corrects the misspelled word (Figure 2-22).

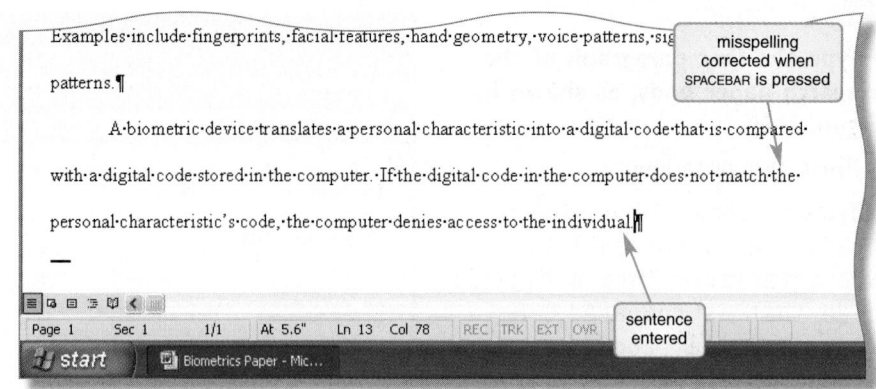

FIGURE 2-22

Word has a list of predefined typing, spelling, capitalization, and grammar errors that AutoCorrect detects and corrects. If you do not like a change that Word automatically makes in a document and you immediately notice the automatic correction, you can undo the change by clicking the Undo button on the Standard toolbar; clicking Edit on the menu bar and then clicking Undo; or pressing CTRL+Z.

If you do not immediately notice the change, you still can undo a correction automatically made by Word through the AutoCorrect Options button. When you position the mouse pointer on text that Word automatically corrected, a small blue box appears below the text. If you point to the small blue box, Word displays the AutoCorrect Options button. When you click the **AutoCorrect Options button**, Word displays a menu that allows you to undo a correction or change how Word handles future automatic corrections of this type. The following steps show how to use the AutoCorrect Options button and menu.

To Use the AutoCorrect Options Button

1

• **Position the mouse pointer at the beginning of the text automatically corrected by Word (in this case, the t in the).**

Word displays a small blue box below the automatically corrected word (Figure 2-23).

FIGURE 2-23

2

- **Point to the small blue box to display the AutoCorrect Options button.**
- **Click the AutoCorrect Options button.**

Word displays the AutoCorrect Options menu (Figure 2-24).

3

- **Press the ESCAPE key to remove the AutoCorrect Options menu from the screen.**

When you move the mouse pointer, the AutoCorrect Options button disappears from the screen, or you can press the ESCAPE key a second time to remove the AutoCorrect Options button from the screen.

FIGURE 2-24

In addition to the predefined list of AutoCorrect spelling, capitalization, and grammar errors, you can create your own AutoCorrect entries to add to the list. For example, if you tend to type the word, computer, as comptuer, you should create an AutoCorrect entry for it, as shown in these steps.

To Create an AutoCorrect Entry

1

- **Click Tools on the menu bar (Figure 2-25).**

FIGURE 2-25

2

- **Click AutoCorrect Options on the Tools menu.**
- **When Word displays the AutoCorrect dialog box, type** comptuer **in the Replace text box.**
- **Press the TAB key and then type** computer **in the With text box.**

In the AutoCorrect dialog box, the Replace text box contains the misspelled word, and the With text box contains its correct spelling (Figure 2-26).

3

- **Click the Add button in the AutoCorrect dialog box. (If your dialog box displays a Replace button instead, click it and then click the Yes button in the Microsoft Office Word dialog box.)**
- **Click the OK button.**

Word adds the entry alphabetically to the list of words to correct automatically as you type.

FIGURE 2-26

In addition to creating AutoCorrect entries for words you commonly misspell or mistype, you can create entries for abbreviations, codes, and so on. For example, you could create an AutoCorrect entry for asap, indicating that Word should replace this text with the phrase, as soon as possible.

If, for some reason, you do not want Word to correct automatically as you type, you can turn off the Replace text as you type feature by clicking Tools on the menu bar, clicking AutoCorrect Options, clicking the AutoCorrect tab (Figure 2-26), clicking the Replace text as you type check box to remove the check mark, and then clicking the OK button.

The AutoCorrect sheet (Figure 2-26) contains other check boxes that correct capitalization errors if the check boxes are selected. If you type two capital letters in a row, such as TH, Word makes the second letter lowercase, Th. If you begin a sentence with a lowercase letter, Word capitalizes the first letter of the sentence. If you type the name of a day in lowercase, such as tuesday, Word capitalizes the first letter of the day, Tuesday. If you leave the CAPS LOCK key on and begin a new sentence such as aFTER, Word corrects the typing, After, and turns off the CAPS LOCK key.

Sometimes you do not want Word to AutoCorrect a particular word or phrase. For example, you may use the code WD. in your documents. Because Word automatically capitalizes the first letter of a sentence, the character you enter following the period will be capitalized (in the previous sentence, it would capitalize the letter i in the word, in). To allow the code WD. to be entered into a document and still leave the AutoCorrect feature turned on, you should set an exception. To set an exception to an AutoCorrect rule, click Tools on the menu bar, click AutoCorrect Options, click the AutoCorrect tab, click the Exceptions button in the AutoCorrect sheet (Figure 2-26), click the appropriate tab in the AutoCorrect Exceptions dialog box, type the exception entry in the text box, click the Add button, click the Close button in the AutoCorrect Exceptions dialog box, and then click the OK button in the AutoCorrect dialog box.

The next step is to continue typing text in the body of the research paper, up to the location of the footnote, as described below.

To Enter More Text

1 Press the ENTER key.

2 Type the first five sentences in the third paragraph of the paper as shown in Figure 2-27.

Word displays the first five sentences in the third paragraph in the document window (Figure 2-27).

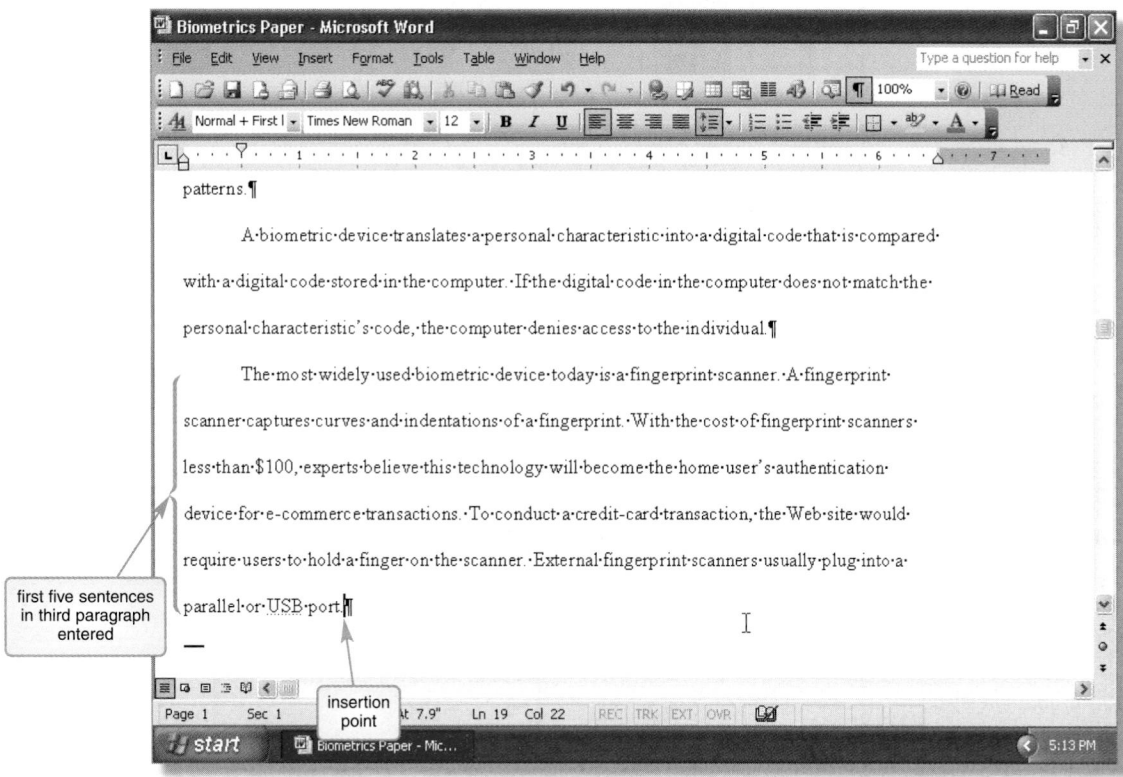

FIGURE 2-27

Adding Footnotes

As discussed earlier in this project, explanatory notes are optional in the MLA documentation style. They are used primarily to elaborate on points discussed in the body of a research paper. The MLA style specifies that a superscript (raised number) be used for a **note reference mark** to signal that an explanatory note exists either at the bottom of the page as a **footnote** or at the end of the document as an **endnote**.

Word, by default, places notes at the bottom of each page as footnotes. In Word, **note text** can be any length and format. Word automatically numbers notes sequentially by placing a note reference mark in the body of the document and also to the left of the note text. If you insert, rearrange, or remove notes, Word renumbers any subsequent note reference marks according to their new sequence in the document.

Q&A

Q: Should I footnote sources in a research paper?

A: Both the MLA and APA guidelines suggest the use of in-text parenthetical citations, instead of footnoting each source of material in a paper. These parenthetical acknowledgments guide the reader to the end of the paper for complete information on the source.

The following steps show how to add a footnote to the research paper.

To Add a Footnote

1

• **With the insertion point positioned as shown in Figure 2-28, click Insert on the menu bar and then point to Reference (Figure 2-28).**

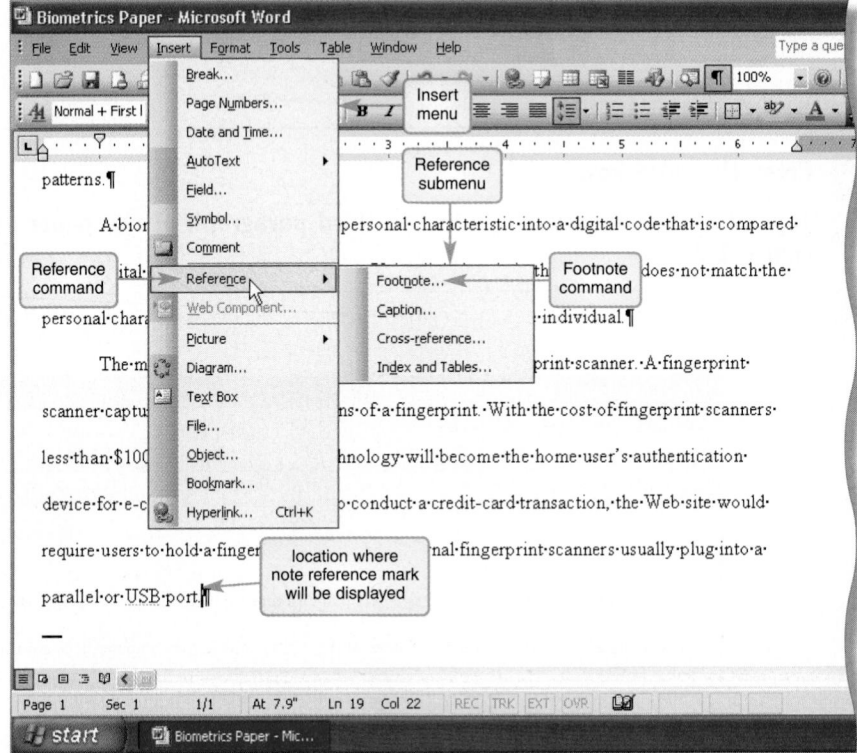

FIGURE 2-28

2

• **Click Footnote on the Reference submenu.**

Word displays the Footnote and Endnote dialog box (Figure 2-29). If you wanted to create endnotes instead of footnotes, you would click Endnotes in the Footnote and Endnote dialog box.

FIGURE 2-29

3

• **Click the Insert button in the Footnote and Endnote dialog box.**

Word opens a note pane in the lower portion of the Word window with the note reference mark (a superscripted 1) positioned at the left margin of the note pane (Figure 2-30). Word also displays the note reference mark in the document window at the location of the insertion point. Note reference marks are, by default, superscripted; that is, raised above other letters.

FIGURE 2-30

4

• **Type** According to Carter and Juarez, newer keyboards and notebook computers have a fingerprint scanner built into them (42-53).

Word displays the note text in the note pane (Figure 2-31).

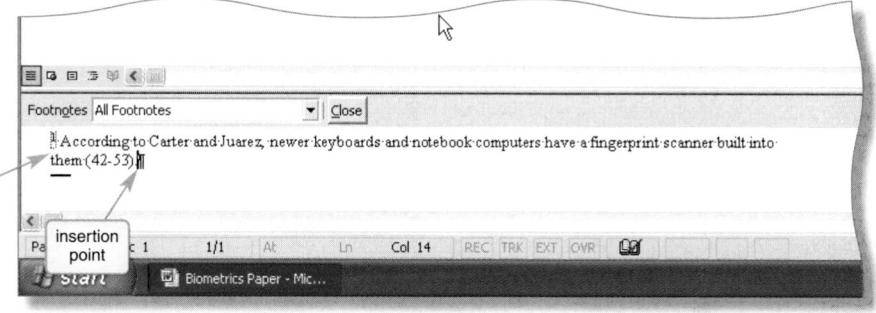

FIGURE 2-31

The footnote is not formatted according to the MLA requirements. Thus, the next step is to modify the style of the footnote.

Modifying a Style

A **style** is a named group of formatting characteristics that you can apply to text. Word has many built-in, or predefined, styles that you may use to format text. The formats defined by these styles include character formatting, such as the font and font size; paragraph formatting, such as line spacing and text alignment; table formatting; and list formatting.

Whenever you create a document, Word formats the text using a particular style. The underlying style, called the **base style**, for a new Word document is the Normal style. For a new installation of Word 2003, the **Normal style** most likely uses 12-point Times New Roman font for characters and single-spaced, left-aligned paragraphs. As you type, you can apply different predefined styles to the text or you can create your own styles. A later project discusses applying and creating styles.

Other Ways

1. In Voice Command mode, say "Insert, Reference, Footnote, Insert, Dictation, [note text]"

More About

Styles

To view the list of styles associated with the current document, click the Style box arrow on the Formatting toolbar or display the Styles and Formatting task pane by clicking the Styles and Formatting button on the Formatting toolbar. To apply a style, click the desired style name in the Style list or in the Styles and Formatting task pane.

When the insertion point is in the note text area, the entered note text is formatted using the Footnote Text style. The Footnote Text style defines characters as 10-point Times New Roman and paragraphs as single-spaced and left-aligned.

You could change the paragraph formatting of the footnote text to first-line indent and double-spacing as you did for the text in the body of the research paper. Then, you would change the font size from 10 to 12 point. If you use this technique, however, you will need to change the format of the footnote text for each footnote you enter into the document.

A more efficient technique is to modify the format of the Footnote Text style to first-line indent and double-spaced paragraphs and a 12-point font size. By changing the formatting of the Footnote Text style, every footnote you enter into the document will use the formats defined in this style. The following steps show how to modify the Footnote Text style.

To Modify a Style

1

• **Right-click the note text in the note pane.**

Word displays a shortcut menu related to footnotes (Figure 2-32).

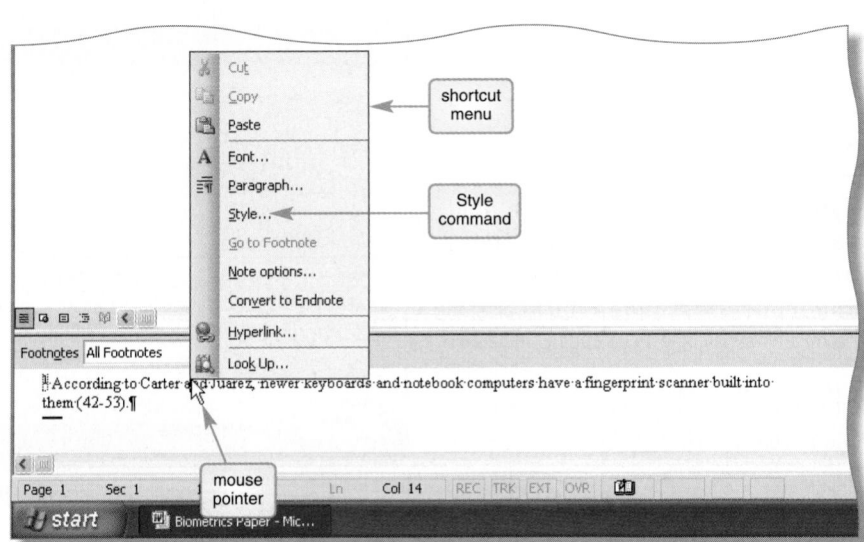

FIGURE 2-32

2

• **Click Style on the shortcut menu.**

• **When Word displays the Style dialog box, if necessary, click Footnote Text in the Styles list.**

The Preview area of the Style dialog box shows the formatting associated with the selected style (Figure 2-33). The selected style is Footnote Text.

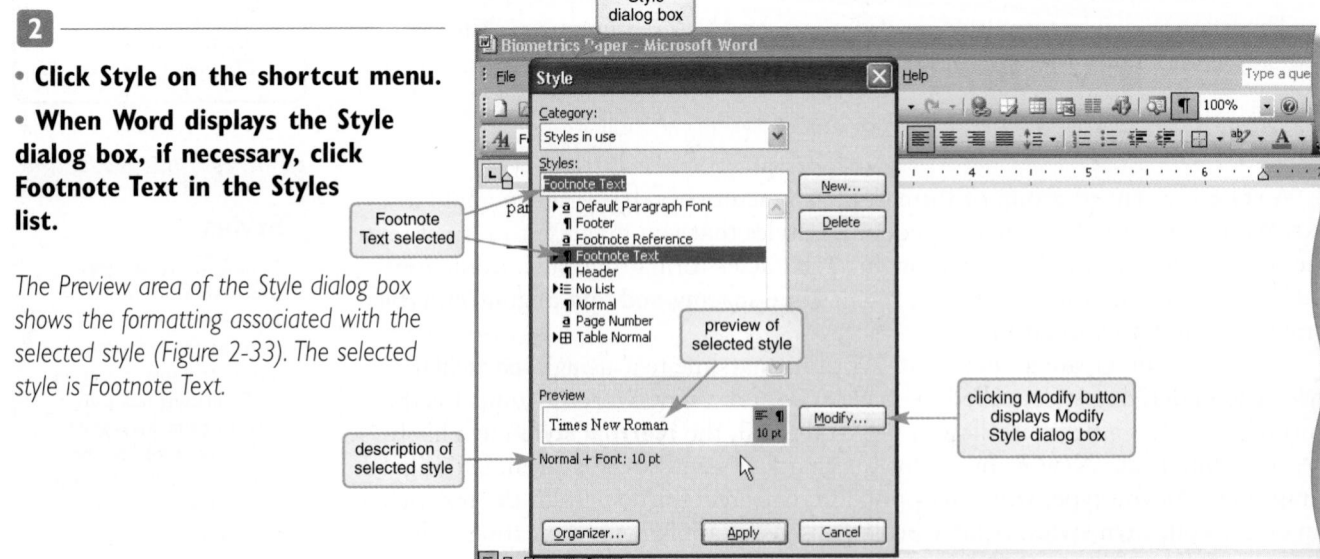

FIGURE 2-33

3

• **Click the Modify button in the Style dialog box.**

• **When Word displays the Modify Style dialog box, click the Font Size box arrow in the Formatting area and then click 12 in the Font Size list.**

• **Click the Double Space button in the Modify Style dialog box.**

In the Modify Style dialog box, the font size for the Footnote Text style is changed to 12, and paragraph spacing is changed to double (Figure 2-34). The first-line indent still must be set.

FIGURE 2-34

4

• **Click the Format button in the Modify Style dialog box.**

Word displays the Format button menu above the Format button (Figure 2-35).

FIGURE 2-35

5

• **Click Paragraph on the Format button menu.**

• **When Word displays the Paragraph dialog box, click the Special box arrow and then click First line.**

In the Paragraph dialog box, Word displays First line in the Special box (Figure 2-36). Notice the default first-line indent is 0.5".

FIGURE 2-36

6

• **Click the OK button in the Paragraph dialog box.**

Word modifies the Footnote Text style to first-line indented paragraphs and closes the Paragraph dialog box (Figure 2-37). The Modify Style dialog box is visible again.

7

• **Click the OK button in the Modify Style dialog box.**

• **When Word closes the Modify Style dialog box, click the Apply button in the Style dialog box.**

Word displays the note text using the modified Footnote Text style, that is, the font size of the note text is changed to 12, the line spacing for the note is set to double, and the first line of the note is indented by one-half inch (Figure 2-38).

FIGURE 2-37

1. Click Styles and Formatting button on Formatting toolbar, right-click style name in Pick formatting to apply list, click Modify
2. In Voice Command mode, say "Context menu, Style, Modify, Font Size, [select font size], Double Space, Format, Paragraph, Special, First line, OK, OK, Apply"

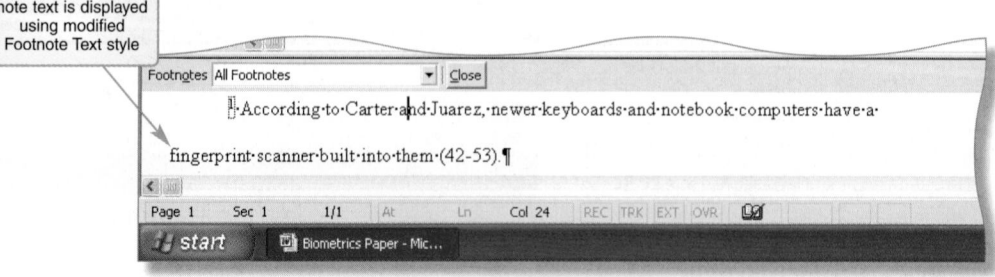

FIGURE 2-38

Any future footnotes entered into the document will use a 12-point font with the paragraphs first-line indented and double-spaced. The footnote now is complete. The next step is to close the note pane.

To Close the Note Pane

1

• **Position the mouse pointer on the Close button in the note pane (Figure 2-39).**

2

• **Click the Close button to remove the note pane from the document window.**

FIGURE 2-39

When Word closes the note pane and returns to the document window, the note text disappears from the screen. Although the note text still exists, it usually is not visible as a footnote in normal view. If, however, you position the mouse pointer on the note reference mark, the note text displays above the note reference mark as a ScreenTip. To remove the ScreenTip, move the mouse pointer.

If you want to verify that the note text is positioned correctly on the page, you must switch to print layout view or display the document in print preview. Project 3 discusses print preview and print layout view.

To delete a note, select the note reference mark in the document window (not in the note pane) by dragging through the note reference mark and then click the Cut button on the Standard toolbar. Another way to delete a note is to click immediately to the right of the note reference mark in the document window and then press the BACKSPACE key twice, or click immediately to the left of the note reference mark in the document window and then press the DELETE key twice.

To move a note to a different location in a document, select the note reference mark in the document window (not in the note pane), click the Cut button on the Standard toolbar, click the location where you want to move the note, and then click the Paste button on the Standard toolbar. When you move or delete notes, Word automatically renumbers any remaining notes in the correct sequence.

You edit note text using the note pane that is displayed at the bottom of the Word window. To display the note text in the note pane, double-click the note reference mark in the document window, or click View on the menu bar and then click Footnotes. In the note pane, you can edit the note as you would any Word text. When finished editing the note text, click the Close button in the note pane.

If you want to change the format of note reference marks in footnotes or endnotes (i.e., from 1, 2, 3, to A, B, C), click Insert on the menu bar, point to Reference, and then click Footnote. When Word displays the Footnote and Endnote dialog box, click the Number format box arrow, click the desired number format in the list, and then click the OK button.

Using Word Count

Often when you write papers, you are required to compose the papers with a minimum number of words. The minimum requirement for the research paper in this project is 325 words. Word provides a command that displays the number of words, as well as the number of pages, characters, paragraphs, and lines in the current document. The following steps show how to use word count and display the Word Count toolbar, which allows you easily to recount words as you type more text.

To Count Words

• **Click Tools on the menu bar (Figure 2-40).**

FIGURE 2-40

2

• **Click Word Count on the Tools menu.**

• **When Word displays the Word Count dialog box, if necessary, click Include footnotes and endnotes to place a check mark in the check box.**

• **Click the Show Toolbar button in the Word Count dialog box.**

In the Word Count dialog box, the number of pages, words, characters, paragraphs, and lines is displayed (Figure 2-41). The Word Count toolbar is displayed floating in the Word window.

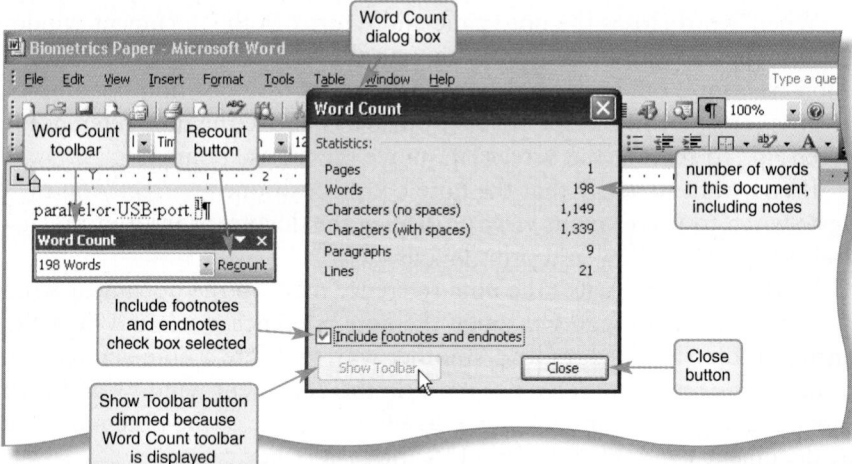

FIGURE 2-41

3

• **Click the Close button in the Word Count dialog box.**

Word removes the Word Count dialog box from the screen, but the Word Count toolbar remains on the screen (Figure 2-42). Your Word Count toolbar may be displayed at a different location on the screen.

Other Ways

1. Click Recount button on Word Count toolbar
2. On File menu click Properties, click Statistics tab, click OK button
3. In Voice Command mode, say "Tools, Word Count, Include footnotes and endnotes, Show Toolbar, Close"

FIGURE 2-42

The Word Count toolbar floats on the screen. As discussed earlier in this project, you can move a floating toolbar by dragging its title bar.

The Word Count dialog box (Figure 2-41) presents a variety of statistics about the current document, including number of pages, words, characters, paragraphs, and lines. You can choose to have note text included or not included in these statistics. If you want statistics on only a section of the document, select the section and then issue the Word Count command.

At anytime, you can recount the number of words in a document by clicking the Recount button on the Word Count toolbar.

Automatic Page Breaks

As you type documents that exceed one page, Word automatically inserts page breaks, called **automatic page breaks** or **soft page breaks**, when it determines the text has filled one page according to paper size, margin settings, line spacing, and other settings. If you add text, delete text, or modify text on a page, Word recomputes the location of automatic page breaks and adjusts them accordingly.

Word performs page recomputation between the keystrokes, that is, in between the pauses in your typing. Thus, Word refers to the automatic page break task as **background repagination**. In normal view, automatic page breaks display on the Word screen as a single dotted horizontal line. The following step illustrates Word's automatic page break feature.

To Page Break Automatically

1

• **With the insertion point positioned as shown in Figure 2-42, press the SPACEBAR and then type the last three sentences of the third paragraph of the paper, as shown in Figure 2-43.**

• **Press the ENTER key and then type the fourth paragraph. Italicize the text in the parenthetical citation.**

• **Drag the title bar of the Word Count toolbar to the location shown in Figure 2-43.**

As you type, Word places an automatic page break between the third and fourth paragraphs in the paper (Figure 2-43). The status bar now displays Page 2 as the current page.

More About

Word Count

You also can display statistics about a document by clicking File on the menu bar, clicking Properties, and then clicking the Statistics tab. This information, however, does not include words and characters in the footnotes or endnotes.

end of third paragraph entered

Word Count toolbar moved

parallel or USB port. Businesses use fingerprint scanners to authenticate users before they can access a personal computer. Grade schools use fingerprint scanners as an alternative to lunch money. Students' account balances adjust for each lunch purchased.

Word Count <Click Recount to view> Recou

mouse pointer

single dotted line indicates automatic page break

Law enforcement, surveillance systems, airports, day-care centers, financial institutions, the military, and other organizations that deal with highly sensitive data use other types of biometrics. A hand geometry system measures the shape and size of a person's hand (*Computers and Biometrics*). A face recognition system captures a live face image and compares it with a stored image. A voice verification system compares a person's live speech with his or her stored voice pattern. A signature verification system recognizes the shape of a handwritten signature, as well as measures the pressure exerted and the motion used to write the signature. Finally, an iris recognition system reads patterns in the iris of the eye.

fourth paragraph entered

status bar shows page 2

text in parenthetical citation italicized because it is a title

Page 2   Sec 1   2/2   At 3.6"   Ln 8   Col 58

insertion point now on page 2

start   Biometrics Paper - Mic...

FIGURE 2-43

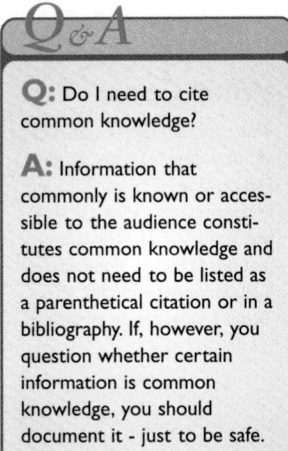

Your page break may occur at a different location, depending on the type of printer connected to the computer.

The header, although not shown in normal view, contains the name Zhao followed by the page number 2. If you wanted to view the header, click View on the menu bar and then click Header and Footer. Then, click the Close Header and Footer button on the Header and Footer toolbar to return to normal view.

Recounting Words in a Document

Now that the last paragraph of the body of the paper is typed, you want to recount the number of words to see if you have met the minimum requirement of 325 words. The following steps show how to use the Word Count toolbar to recount words in a document.

To Recount Words

• **Click the Recount button on the Word Count toolbar.**

The Word Count toolbar displays the number of words in the document (Figure 2-44). You now close the Word Count toolbar because the research paper contains the required minimum of 325 words.

• **Click the Close button on the Word Count toolbar.**

Word removes the Word Count toolbar from the screen.

FIGURE 2-44

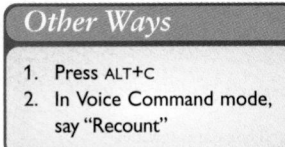

Creating an Alphabetical Works Cited Page

According to the MLA style, the **works cited page** is a bibliographical list of works that are referenced directly in a research paper. You place the list on a separate numbered page with the title, Works Cited, centered one inch from the top margin. The works are to be alphabetized by the author's last name or, if the work has no author, by the work's title. The first line of each entry begins at the left margin. Indent subsequent lines of the same entry one-half inch from the left margin.

The first step in creating the works cited page is to force a page break so the works cited display on a separate page.

Manual Page Breaks

The works cited are to display on a separate numbered page. Thus, you must insert a manual page break following the body of the research paper. A **manual page break**, or **hard page break**, is one that you force into the document at a specific location. Word displays a manual page break on the screen as a horizontal dotted line, separated by the words, Page Break. Word never moves or adjusts manual page breaks; however, Word adjusts any automatic page breaks that follow a manual page break. Word inserts manual page breaks just before the location of the insertion point.

The following step shows how to insert a manual page break after the body of the research paper.

To Page Break Manually

1

• **With the insertion point at the end of the body of the research paper, press the ENTER key.**

• **Then, press CTRL+ENTER.**

*The shortcut keys, **CTRL+ENTER**, instruct Word to insert a manual page break immediately above the insertion point and position the insertion point immediately below the manual page break (Figure 2-45). The status bar indicates the insertion point now is on page 3.*

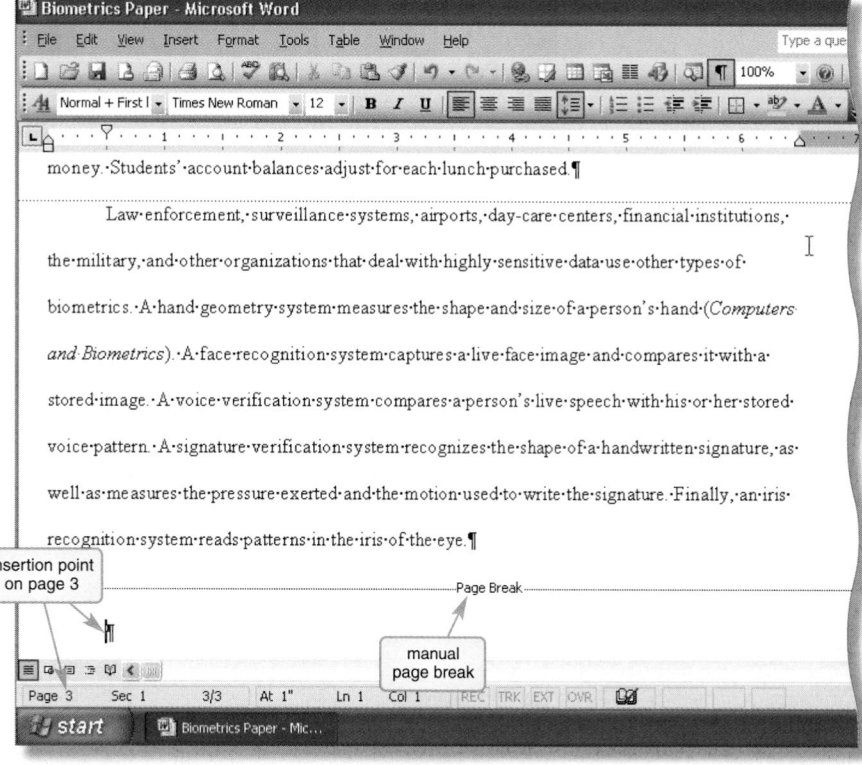

FIGURE 2-45

Word displays the manual page break as a horizontal dotted line with the words, Page Break, in the middle of the line. The header, although not shown in normal view, contains the name Zhao followed by the page number 3. If you wanted to view the header, click View on the menu bar and then click Header and Footer. Then, click the Close Header and Footer button on the Header and Footer toolbar to return to normal view.

If, for some reason, you wanted to remove a manual page break from a document, you must first select the page break by double-clicking it. Then, press the DELETE key; or click the Cut button on the Standard toolbar; or right-click the selection and then click Cut on the shortcut menu.

Centering the Title of the Works Cited Page

The works cited title is to be centered between the margins of the paper. If you simply click the Center button on the Formatting toolbar, the title will not be centered properly. Instead, it will be one-half inch to the right of the center point because earlier you set first-line indent at one-half inch. That is, Word indents the first line of every paragraph one-half inch.

To properly center the title of the works cited page, you must move the First Line Indent marker back to the left margin before clicking the Center button, as described in the following steps.

To Center the Title of the Works Cited Page

1 **Drag the First Line Indent marker to the 0" mark on the ruler, which is at the left margin.**

2 **Click the Center button on the Formatting toolbar.**

3 **Type** Works Cited **as the title.**

4 **Press the ENTER key.**

5 **Because your fingers already are on the keyboard, press CTRL+L to left-align the paragraph mark.**

Word centers the title properly, and the insertion point is left-aligned (Figure 2-46).

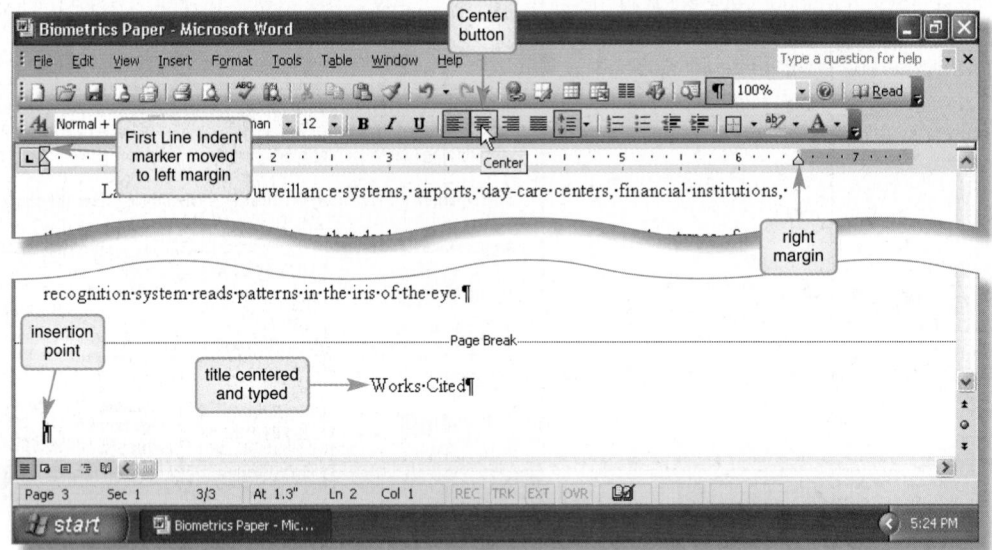

FIGURE 2-46

Creating a Hanging Indent

On the works cited page, the first line of each entry begins at the left margin. Subsequent lines in the same paragraph are to be indented one-half inch from the left margin. In essence, the first line hangs to the left of the rest of the paragraph; thus, this type of paragraph formatting is called a **hanging indent**.

One method of creating a hanging indent is to use the horizontal ruler. The **Hanging Indent marker** is the bottom triangle at the 0" mark on the ruler (Figure 2-47). The next steps show how to create a hanging indent using the horizontal ruler.

To Create a Hanging Indent

1

• **With the insertion point in the paragraph to format, point to the Hanging Indent marker on the ruler (Figure 2-47).**

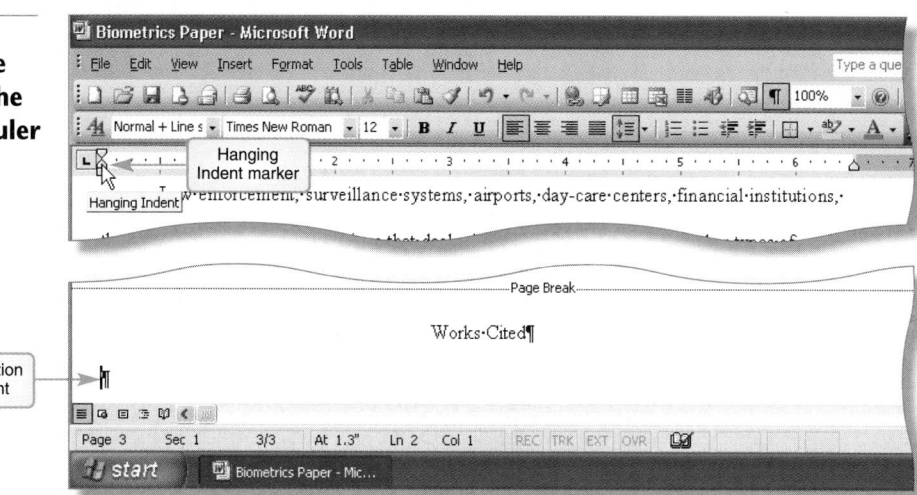

FIGURE 2-47

2

• **Drag the Hanging Indent marker to the .5" mark on the ruler.**

The Hanging Indent marker and Left Indent marker display one-half inch from the left margin (Figure 2-48). When you drag the Hanging Indent marker, the Left Indent marker moves with it. The insertion point in the document window remains at the left margin because only subsequent lines in the paragraph are to be indented.

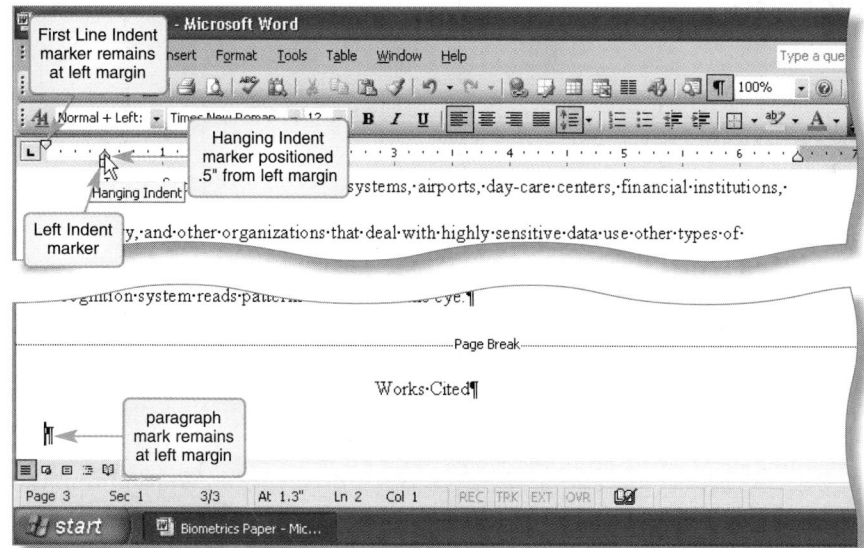

FIGURE 2-48

The next step is to enter the works in the works cited. As you type the works, Word will format them with a hanging indent. The following steps describe how to type the first two works in the works cited.

To Enter Works Cited Paragraphs

1 **Type** Schmidt, Karl J. "Biometrics and Authenticating Computer Users."

2 **Press the SPACEBAR. Press CTRL+I to turn on the italic format. Type** Computers and the Internet **and then press CTRL+I to turn off the italic format.**

3 **Press the SPACEBAR. Type** Aug. 2005: 54-62.

4 **Press the ENTER key.**

5 **Type** Carter, Donnell W., and Louis C. Juarez.

6 **Press the SPACEBAR. Press CTRL+I to turn on the italic format. Type** Securing Confidential Data Entered into a Computer. **Press CTRL+I to turn off the italic format.**

7 **Press the SPACEBAR. Type** Boston: Thomas Publishing, 2005.

8 **Press the ENTER key.**

Word displays two of the works cited paragraphs in the document window (Figure 2-49).

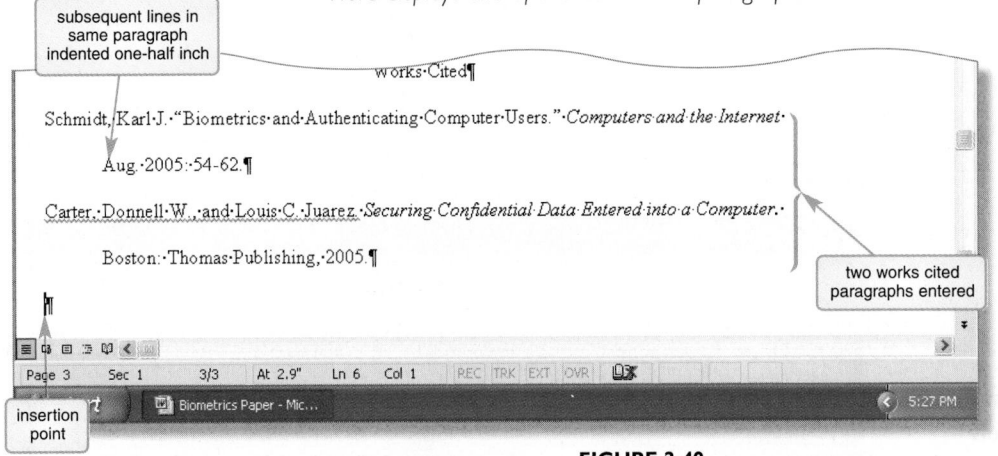

FIGURE 2-49

When Word wraps the text in each works cited paragraph, it automatically indents the second line of the paragraph by one-half inch. When you press the ENTER key at the end of the first paragraph of text, the insertion point returns automatically to the left margin for the next paragraph. Recall that each time you press the ENTER key, Word carries forward the paragraph formatting from the previous paragraph to the next paragraph.

Inserting Arrows, Faces, and Other Symbols Automatically

As discussed earlier in this project, Word has predefined many commonly misspelled words, which it automatically corrects for you as you type. In addition to words, this built-in list of **AutoCorrect entries** also contains some commonly used symbols. For example, to insert a smiling face in a document, you type :) and Word automatically changes it to ☺. Table 2-3 lists the characters you type to insert arrows, faces, and other symbols in a Word document.

You also can enter the first four symbols in Table 2-3 and other symbols by clicking Insert on the menu bar, clicking Symbol, clicking the Special Characters tab, clicking the desired symbol in the Character list, clicking the Insert button, and then clicking the Close button in the Symbol dialog box.

As discussed earlier in this project, if you do not like a change that Word automatically makes in a document and you immediately notice the automatic correction, you can undo the change by clicking the Undo button on the Standard toolbar; clicking Edit on the menu bar and then clicking Undo; or pressing CTRL+Z.

If you do not immediately notice the change, you can undo a correction automatically made by Word using the AutoCorrect Options button. Figures 2-23 and 2-24 on pages WD 90 and WD 91 illustrated how to display and use the AutoCorrect Options button.

Table 2-3	Word's Automatic Symbols	
TO DISPLAY	DESCRIPTION	TYPE
©	copyright symbol	(c)
®	registered trademark symbol	(r)
™	trademark symbol	(tm)
…	ellipsis	...
☺	smiling face	:) or :-)
😐	indifferent face	:| or :-|
☹	frowning face	:(or :-(
→	thin right arrow	-->
←	thin left arrow	<
→	thick right arrow	==>
←	thick left arrow	<==
⇔	double arrow	<=>

The next step in the research paper is to enter text that uses the registered trademark symbol. The following steps show how to insert automatically the registered trademark symbol in the research paper.

To Insert a Symbol Automatically

1

• **With the insertion point positioned as shown in Figure 2-49, press CTRL+I to turn on the italic format.**

• **Type** Computers and Biometrics.

• **Press CTRL+I to turn off the italic format.**

• **Press the SPACEBAR.**

• **Type** Shelly Cashman Series(r **as shown in Figure 2-50.**

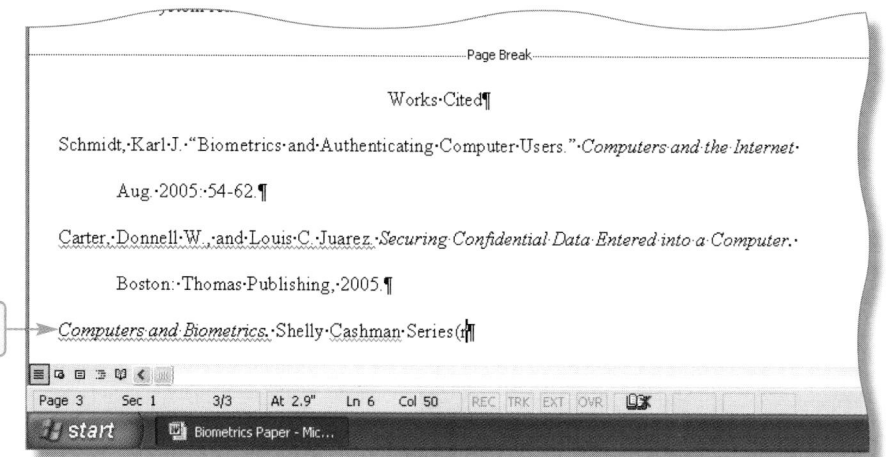

FIGURE 2-50

2

• **Press the RIGHT PARENTHESIS key.**

Word automatically converts the typed (r) to ®, the registered trademark symbol (Figure 2-51).

3

• **Press the PERIOD key.**

• **Press the SPACEBAR.**

• **Type** Course Technology. 3 Oct. 2005.

• **Press the SPACEBAR.**

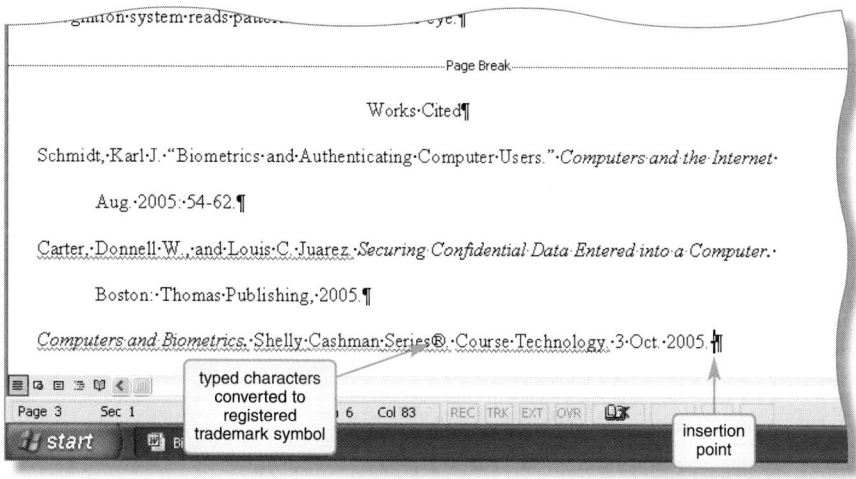

FIGURE 2-51

Creating a Hyperlink

A **hyperlink** is a shortcut that allows a user to jump easily and quickly to another location in the same document or to other documents or Web pages. **Jumping** is the process of following a hyperlink to its destination. For example, by clicking a hyperlink in the document window while pressing the CTRL key (called **CTRL+clicking**), you jump to another document on your computer, on your network, or on the World Wide Web. When you close the hyperlink destination page or document, you return to the original location in your Word document. In Word, you can create a hyperlink simply by typing the address of the file or Web page to which you want to link and then pressing the SPACEBAR or the ENTER key.

Other Ways

1. On Insert menu click Symbol, click Special Characters tab, click Registered in Character list, click Insert button, click Close button
2. In Dictation mode, say "Right Parenthesis, R, Left Parenthesis"

In this project, one of the works cited is from a Web page on the Internet. When someone displays your research paper on the screen, you want him or her to be able to CTRL+click the Web address in the work to jump to the associated Web page for more information.

To create a hyperlink to a Web page in a Word document, you do not have to be connected to the Internet. The following steps show how to create a hyperlink as you type.

To Create a Hyperlink

1

• **With the insertion point positioned as shown in Figure 2-51 on the previous page, type** http://www.scsite.com/ wd2003/pr2/wc.htm.

Word does not format the entry as a hyperlink until you press the ENTER key or SPACEBAR (Figure 2-52).

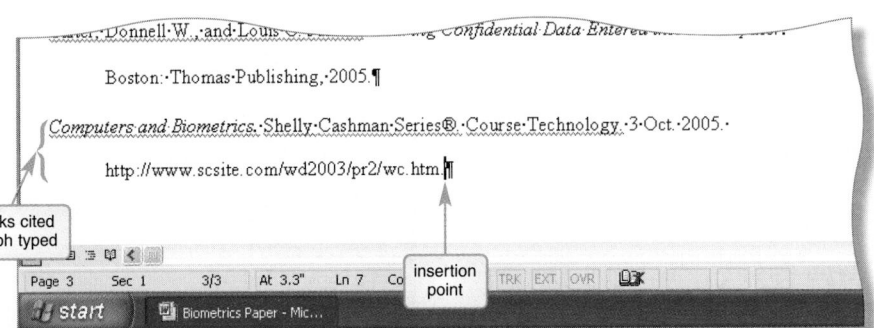

FIGURE 2-52

2

• **Press the ENTER key.**

As soon as you press the ENTER key after typing the Web address, Word formats it as a hyperlink (Figure 2-53). That is, the Web address is underlined and colored blue.

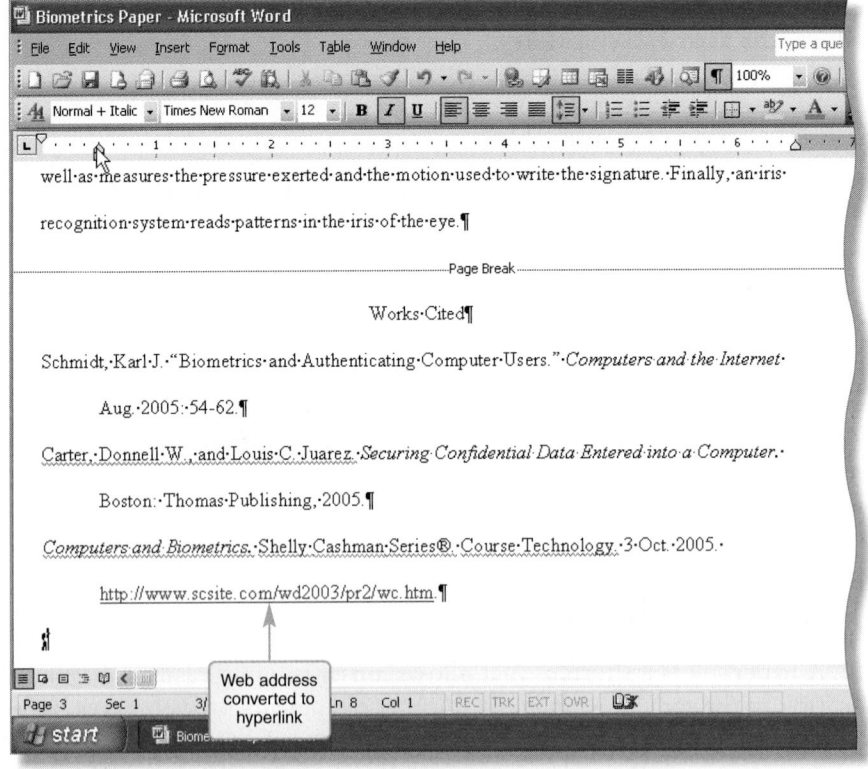

FIGURE 2-53

Other Ways

1. Select text, click Insert Hyperlink button on Standard toolbar, click Existing File or Web Page in the Link to bar, type Web address in Address text box, click OK button
2. Right-click selected text, click Hyperlink on short-cut menu, click Existing File or Web Page in the Link to bar, type Web address in Address text box, click OK button

Later, this project will show how to jump to the hyperlink just created.

Sorting Paragraphs

The MLA style requires that the works cited be listed in alphabetical order by the first character in each work. In Word, you can arrange paragraphs in alphabetic, numeric, or date order based on the first character in each paragraph. Ordering characters in this manner is called **sorting**.

The following steps show how to sort the works cited paragraphs alphabetically.

More About

Hyperlinks

If Word does not convert Web addresses to hyperlinks automatically, click Tools on the menu bar, click AutoCorrect Options, click the AutoFormat As You Type tab, select the Internet and network paths with hyperlinks check box, and then click the OK button.

To Sort Paragraphs

1

• **Select all the works cited paragraphs by pointing to the left of the first paragraph and then dragging down.**

• **Click Table on the menu bar.**

Word displays the Table menu (Figure 2-54). All of the paragraphs to be sorted are selected.

FIGURE 2-54

2

• **Click Sort on the Table menu.**

Word displays the Sort Text dialog box (Figure 2-55). In the Sort by area, Ascending, the default, is selected. The term, ascending, means to sort in alphabetic, numeric, or earliest to latest date order.

FIGURE 2-55

3

- **Click the OK button in the Sort Text dialog box.**
- **Click inside the selected text to remove the selection.**

Word sorts the works cited paragraphs alphabetically (Figure 2-56).

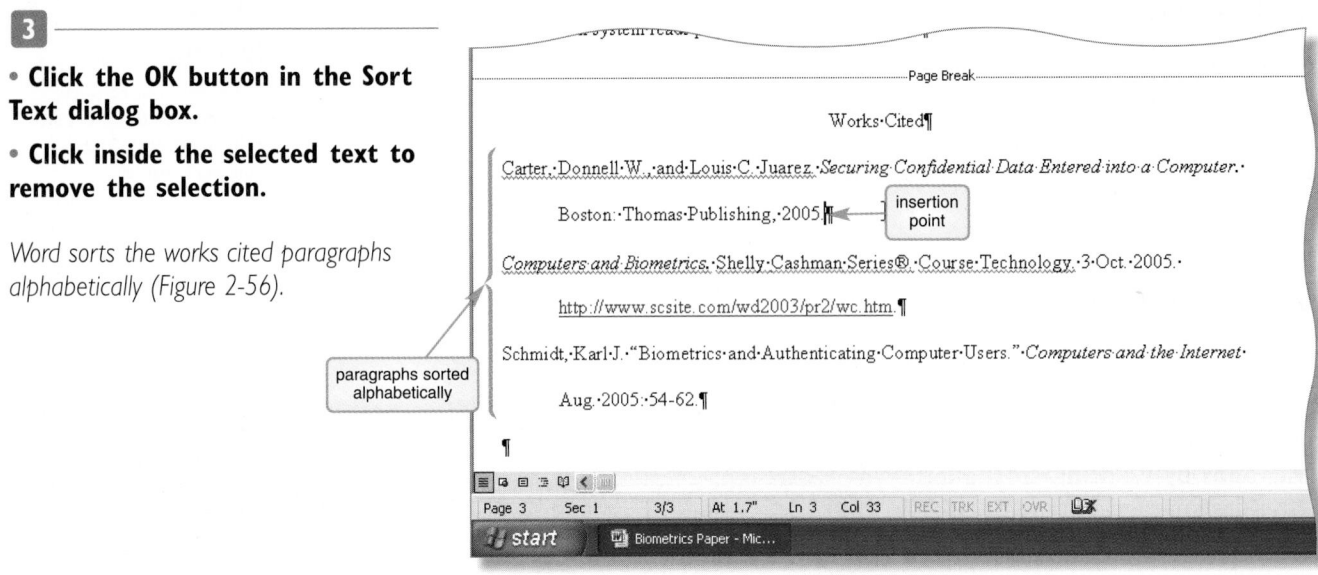

FIGURE 2-56

If you accidentally sort the wrong paragraphs, you can undo a sort by clicking the Undo button on the Standard toolbar.

In the Sort Text dialog box (Figure 2-55 on the previous page), the default sort order is Ascending. By default, Word orders in **ascending sort order**, which means from the beginning of the alphabet to the end of the alphabet, smallest number to the largest number, or earliest date to the most recent date. For example, if the first character of each paragraph to be sorted is a letter, Word sorts the selected paragraphs alphabetically.

You also can sort in descending order by clicking Descending in the Sort Text dialog box. **Descending sort order** means sorting from the end of the alphabet to the beginning of the alphabet, the largest number to the smallest number, or the most recent date to the earliest date.

Q: How should I go about proofreading a research paper?

A: Ask yourself these questions: Is the purpose clear? Does the title suggest the topic? Does the paper have an introduction, body, and conclusion? Is the thesis clear? Does each paragraph in the body relate to the thesis? Is the conclusion effective? Are all sources acknowledged?

Proofing and Revising the Research Paper

As discussed in Project 1, once you complete a document, you might find it necessary to make changes to it. Before submitting a paper to be graded, you should proofread it. While **proofreading**, you look for grammatical errors and spelling errors. You want to be sure the transitions between sentences flow smoothly and the sentences themselves make sense. To assist you with the proofreading effort, Word provides several tools. The following pages discuss these tools.

Going to a Specific Location in a Document

Often, you would like to bring a certain page, footnote, or other object into view in the document window. To accomplish this, you could scroll through the document to find a desired page, footnote, or item. Instead of scrolling through the document, however, Word provides an easier method of going to a specific location via the Select Browse Object menu.

The next steps show how to go to the top of page two in the research paper using the Select Browse Object menu.

To Browse by Page

1

• **Click the Select Browse Object button on the vertical scroll bar.**

• **When Word displays the Select Browse Object menu, position the mouse pointer on the Browse by Page icon.**

When you point to an icon on the Select Browse Object menu, Word displays the associated command name at the bottom of the menu (Figure 2-57).

FIGURE 2-57

2

• **Click the Browse by Page icon.**

• **Position the mouse pointer on the Previous Page button on the vertical scroll bar.**

Word closes the Select Browse Object menu and displays the top of page 3 at the top of the document window (Figure 2-58).

FIGURE 2-58

3

• **Click the Previous Page button.**

Word places the top of page 2 (the previous page) at the top of the document window (Figure 2-59).

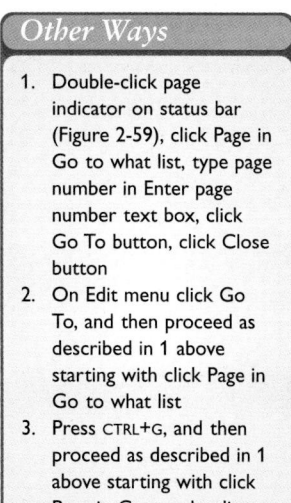

Other Ways

1. Double-click page indicator on status bar (Figure 2-59), click Page in Go to what list, type page number in Enter page number text box, click Go To button, click Close button
2. On Edit menu click Go To, and then proceed as described in 1 above starting with click Page in Go to what list
3. Press CTRL+G, and then proceed as described in 1 above starting with click Page in Go to what list

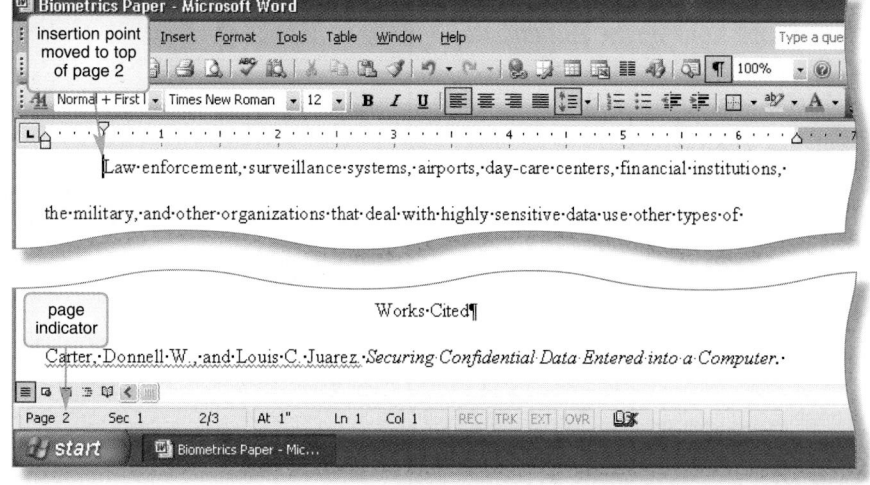

FIGURE 2-59

Depending on the icon you click on the Select Browse Object menu, the function of the buttons above and below the Select Browse Object button on the vertical scroll bar changes. When you select Browse by Page, the buttons become Previous Page and Next Page buttons. If you select Browse by Footnote, however, the buttons become Previous Footnote and Next Footnote buttons, and so on.

Moving Text

While proofreading the research paper, you realize that text in the fourth paragraph would flow better if the third sentence was moved so it followed the first sentence. That is, you want to move the third sentence so it is the second sentence in the fourth paragraph.

To move text, such as words, characters, sentences, or paragraphs, you first select the text to be moved and then use drag-and-drop editing or the cut-and-paste technique to move the selected text. With **drag-and-drop editing**, you drag the selected item to the new location and then insert, or *drop*, it there. **Cutting** involves removing the selected item from the document and then placing it on the Clipboard. The **Clipboard** is a temporary Windows storage area. **Pasting** is the process of copying an item from the Clipboard into the document at the location of the insertion point. The next steps demonstrate drag-and-drop editing.

To drag-and-drop a sentence in the research paper, first select a sentence as shown in the next step.

To Select a Sentence

1

• **Position the mouse pointer (an I-beam) in the sentence to be moved (shown in Figure 2-60).**

• **Press and hold down the CTRL key. While holding down the CTRL key, click the sentence.**

• **Release the CTRL key.**

Word selects the entire sentence (Figure 2-60). Notice that Word includes the space following the period in the selection.

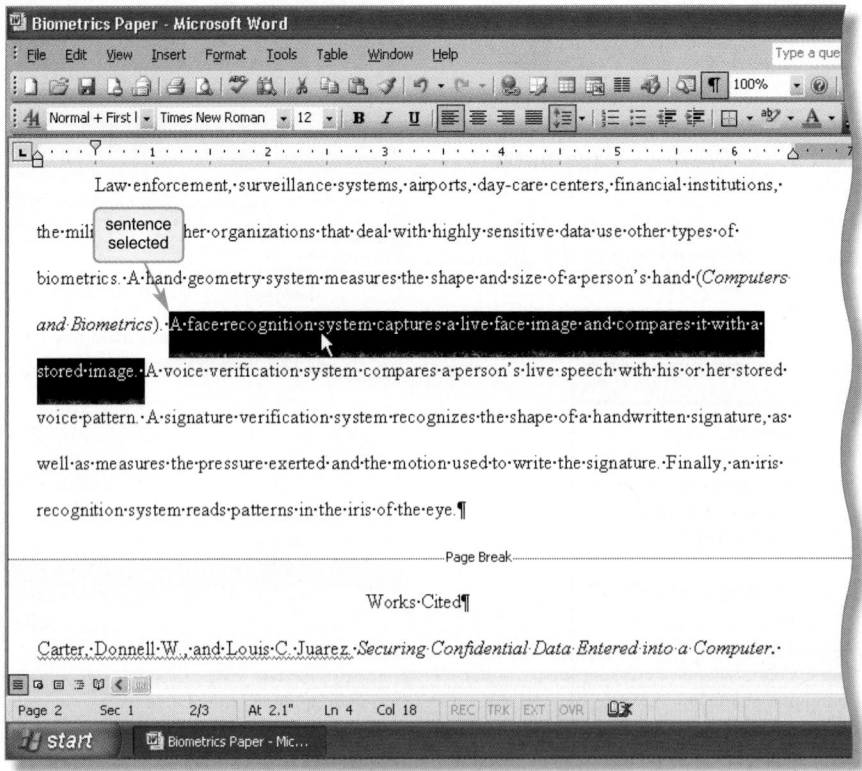

FIGURE 2-60

In the previous steps and throughout Projects 1 and 2, you have selected text. Table 2-4 summarizes the techniques used to select various items with the mouse.

Table 2-4 Techniques for Selecting Items with the Mouse	
ITEM TO SELECT	**MOUSE ACTION**
Block of text	Click at beginning of selection, scroll to end of selection, position mouse pointer at end of selection, hold down SHIFT key and then click; or drag through the text
Character(s)	Drag through character(s)
Document	Move mouse to left of text until mouse pointer changes to a right-pointing block arrow and then triple-click
Graphic	Click the graphic
Line	Move mouse to left of line until mouse pointer changes to a right-pointing block arrow and then click
Lines	Move mouse to left of first line until mouse pointer changes to a right-pointing block arrow and then drag up or down
Paragraph	Triple-click paragraph; or move mouse to left of paragraph until mouse pointer changes to a right-pointing block arrow and then double-click
Paragraphs	Move mouse to left of paragraph until mouse pointer changes to a right-pointing block arrow, double-click and then drag up or down
Sentence	Press and hold down CTRL key and then click sentence
Word	Double-click the word
Words	Drag through words

More About

Selecting Text

In Word, you can select nonadjacent text. This is helpful when you are formatting multiple items the same way. To select items that are not next to each other (nonadjacent), do the following. Select the first item, such as a word or paragraph, as usual. Press and hold down the CTRL key. While holding down the CTRL key, select any additional items. All selected items are displayed highlighted on the screen.

With the sentence to be moved selected, you can use drag-and-drop editing to move it. You should be sure that drag-and-drop editing is enabled by clicking Tools on the menu bar, clicking Options, clicking the Edit tab, verifying the Drag-and-drop text editing check box is selected, and then clicking the OK button.

The following steps show how to move the selected sentence so it becomes the second sentence in the paragraph.

To Move Selected Text

1

• **With the mouse pointer in the selected text, press and hold down the mouse button.**

When you begin to drag the selected text, the insertion point changes to a dotted insertion point (Figure 2-61).

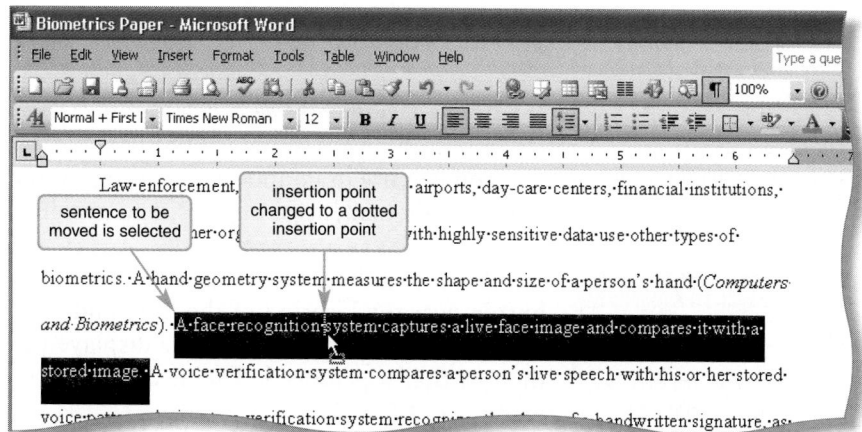

FIGURE 2-61

2

• **Drag the dotted insertion point to the location where the selected text is to be moved, as shown in Figure 2-62.**

The dotted insertion point follows the space after the first sentence in the paragraph (Figure 2-62).

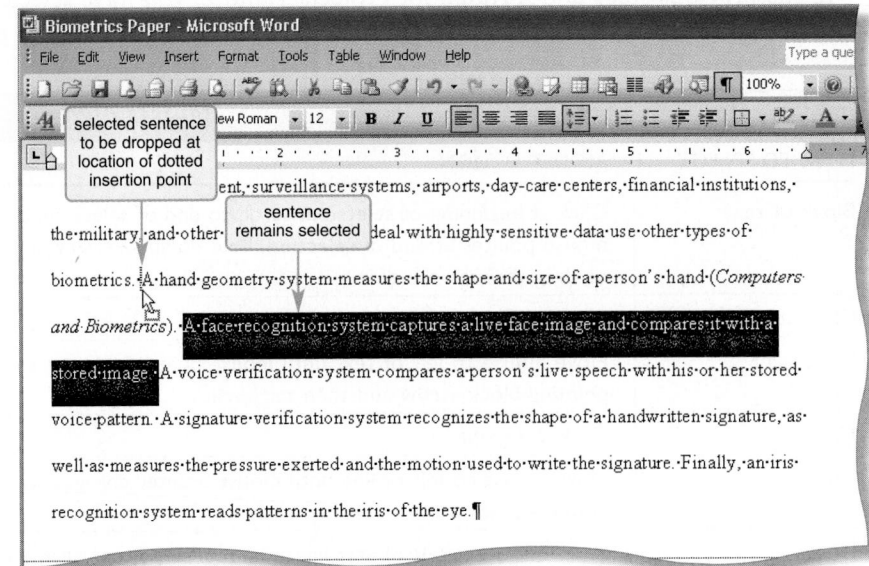

FIGURE 2-62

3

• **Release the mouse button. Click outside the selected text to remove the selection.**

Word moves the selected text to the location of the dotted insertion point (Figure 2-63).

FIGURE 2-63

If you accidentally drag selected text to the wrong location, you can click the Undo button on the Standard toolbar.

You can use drag-and-drop editing to move any selected item. That is, you can select words, sentences, phrases, and graphics and then use drag-and-drop editing to move them.

When you drag-and-drop text, Word automatically displays a Paste Options button near the location of the drag-and-dropped text (Figure 2-63). If you click the **Paste Options button**, a menu is displayed that allows you to change the format of the text that was moved. The next steps show how to display the Paste Options menu.

To Display the Paste Options Menu

1 ————————————————————

• **Click the Paste Options button.**

Word displays the Paste Options menu (Figure 2-64).

2 ————————————————————

• **Press the ESCAPE key to remove the Paste Options menu from the window.**

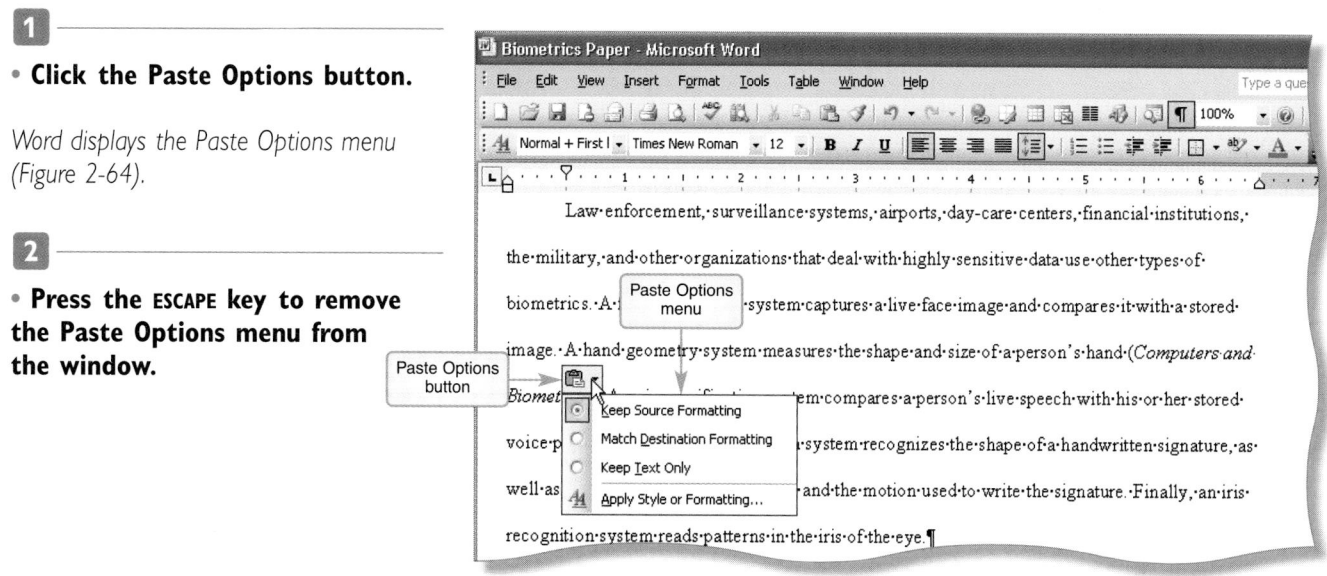

FIGURE 2-64

Smart Tags

A **smart tag** is a button that automatically appears on the screen when Word performs a certain action. In this project, you used two smart tags: AutoCorrect Options (Figures 2-23 and 2-24 on pages WD 90 and WD 91) and Paste Options (Figure 2-64). In addition to AutoCorrect Options and Paste Options, Word provides other smart tags. Table 2-5 summarizes the smart tags available in Word.

Table 2-5	Smart Tags in Word	
BUTTON	**NAME**	**MENU FUNCTION**
⚡	AutoCorrect Options	Undoes an automatic correction, stops future automatic corrections of this type, or displays the AutoCorrect Options dialog box
📋	Paste Options	Specifies how moved or pasted items should display, e.g., with original formatting, without formatting, or with different formatting
ⓘ	Smart Tag Actions	
	• Person name	Adds this name to Outlook Contacts folder, sends an e-mail, or schedules a meeting in Outlook Calendar with this person
	• Date or time	Schedules a meeting in Outlook Calendar at this date or time or displays your calendar
	• Address	Adds this address to Outlook Contacts folder or displays a map or driving directions
	• Place	Adds this place to Outlook Contacts folder or schedules a meeting in Outlook Calendar at this location

More About

Smart Tags

If your screen does not display smart tag indicators, click Tools on the menu bar, click AutoCorrect Options, click the Smart Tags tab, select the Label text with smart tags check box, and then click the OK button. If AutoCorrect Options buttons do not appear on your screen, click Tools on the menu bar, click AutoCorrect Options, click the AutoCorrect tab, select the Show AutoCorrect Options buttons check box, and then click the OK button.

More About

**Smart Tag
Actions**

The commands in the Smart
Tag Actions menu vary
depending on the smart tag.
For example, the Smart Tag
Actions menu for a date
includes commands that allow
you to schedule a meeting in
Outlook Calendar or display
your Outlook Calendar. The
Smart Tag Actions menu for
an address includes com-
mands for displaying a map of
the address or driving directions to or from the address.

With the AutoCorrect Options and Smart Tag Actions, Word notifies you that the smart tag is available by displaying a **smart tag indicator** on the screen. The smart tag indicator for the AutoCorrect Options smart tag is a small blue box. The smart tag indicator for Smart Tag Actions is a purple dotted underline, as shown in Figure 2-14 on page WD 85. To display a smart tag button, you point to the smart tag indicator.

Clicking a smart tag button displays a menu that contains commands relative to the action performed at the location of the smart tag. For example, if you want to add a name in your Word document to the Outlook Contacts folder, point to the purple dotted line below the name to display the Smart Tag Actions button, click the Smart Tag Actions button to display the Smart Tag Actions menu, and then click Add to Contacts on the Smart Tag Actions menu to display the Contact window in Outlook.

Finding and Replacing Text

While proofreading the paper, you notice that it contains the word, trait, in the first paragraph (Figure 2-65). You prefer to use the word, identifier. Therefore, you wish to change all occurrences of trait to identifier. To do this, you can use Word's find and replace feature, which automatically locates each occurrence of a word or phrase and then replaces it with specified text, as shown in these steps.

To Find and Replace Text

1

• **Press CTRL+HOME to position the insertion point at the top of the document.**

• **Double-click the status bar anywhere to the left of the status indicators.**

• **When Word displays the Find and Replace dialog box, click the Replace tab.**

• **Type** trait **in the Find what text box.**

• **Press the TAB key. Type** identifier **in the Replace with text box.**

Word displays entered text in the Find and Replace dialog box (Figure 2-65).

FIGURE 2-65

2

• **Click the Replace All button in the Find and Replace dialog box.**

A Microsoft Office Word dialog box displays indicating the total number of replacements made (Figure 2-66). The word, identifier, displays in the document instead of the word, trait.

3

• **Click the OK button in the Microsoft Office Word dialog box.**

• **Click the Close button in the Find and Replace dialog box.**

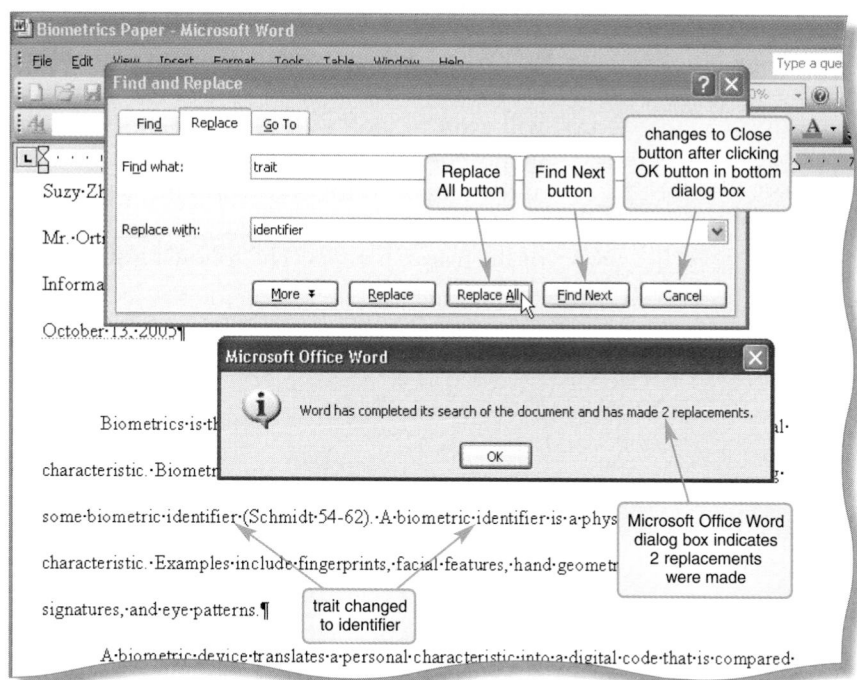

FIGURE 2-66

The Replace All button replaces all occurrences of the Find what text with the Replace with text. In some cases, you may want to replace only certain occurrences of a word or phrase, not all of them. To instruct Word to confirm each change, click the Find Next button in the Find and Replace dialog box (Figure 2-65), instead of the Replace All button. When Word locates an occurrence of the text, it pauses and waits for you to click either the Replace button or the Find Next button. Clicking the Replace button changes the text; clicking the Find Next button instructs Word to disregard the replacement and look for the next occurrence of the Find what text.

If you accidentally replace the wrong text, you can undo a replacement by clicking the Undo button on the Standard toolbar. If you used the Replace All button, Word undoes all replacements. If you used the Replace button, Word undoes only the most recent replacement.

Finding Text

Sometimes, you may want only to find text, instead of finding *and* replacing text. To search for just a single occurrence of text, you would follow these steps.

To Find Text

1. Click the Select Browse Object button on the vertical scroll bar and then click the Find icon on the Select Browse Object menu; or click Edit on the menu bar and then click Find; or press CTRL+F.
2. Type the text to locate in the Find what text box and then click the Find Next button. To edit the text, click the Cancel button in the Find and Replace dialog box; to find the next occurrence of the text, click the Find Next button.

More About

Synonyms

For access to an online thesaurus, visit the Word 2003 More About Web page (scsite.com/wd2003/more) and then click Online Thesaurus.

Finding and Inserting a Synonym

When writing, you may discover that you used the same word in multiple locations or that a word you used was not quite appropriate. In these instances, you will want to look up a **synonym**, or word similar in meaning, to the duplicate or inappropriate word. A **thesaurus** is a book of synonyms. Word provides synonyms and a thesaurus for your convenience.

In this project, you would like a synonym for the word, give, in the first paragraph of the research paper. The following steps show how to find an appropriate synonym.

To Find and Insert a Synonym

1

• **Right-click the word for which you want to find a synonym (give, in this case).**

• **Point to Synonyms on the shortcut menu.**

Word displays a list of synonyms for the word that you right-clicked (Figure 2-67).

2

• **Click the synonym you want (grant) on the Synonyms submenu.**

Word replaces the word, give, in the document with the word, grant (Figure 2-68).

FIGURE 2-67

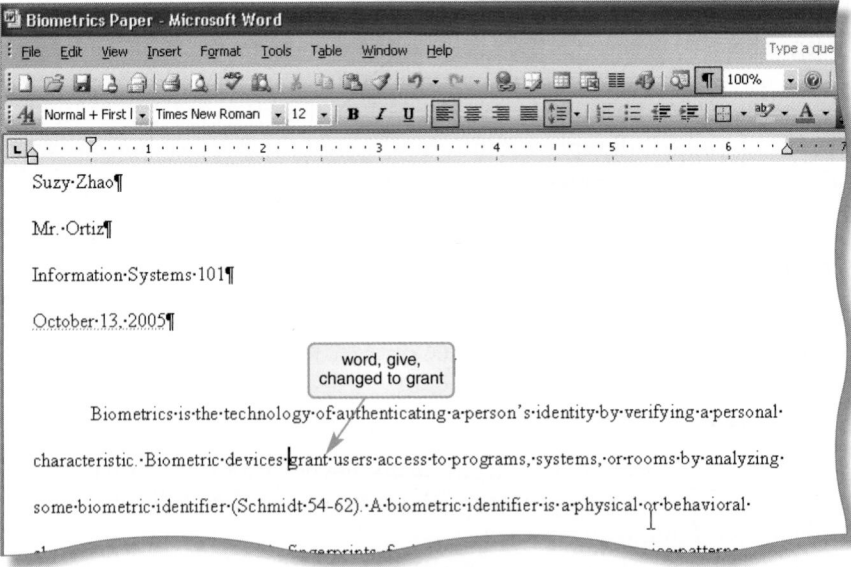

FIGURE 2-68

Other Ways

1. Select word, on Tools menu point to Language, on Language submenu click Thesaurus, scroll to appropriate meaning in Research task pane, point to desired synonym in Research task pane, click the box arrow to the right of the synonym, click Insert on submenu, close Research task pane
2. Select word, press SHIFT+F7, scroll to appropriate meaning in Research task pane, point to desired synonym in Research task pane, click the box arrow to the right of the synonym, click Insert on submenu, close Research task pane
3. In Voice Command mode, with insertion point in word, say "Right Click, Synonyms, [select synonym]"

If the synonyms list on the shortcut menu does not display an appropriate word, you can display the thesaurus in the Research task pane by clicking Thesaurus on the Synonyms submenu (Figure 2-67). The Research task pane displays a complete thesaurus, in which you can look up synonyms for various meanings of a word. You also can look up an **antonym**, or word with an opposite meaning. The Research task pane is discussed later in this project.

Checking Spelling and Grammar at Once

As discussed in Project 1, Word checks spelling and grammar as you type and places a wavy underline below possible spelling or grammar errors. Project 1 illustrated how to check these flagged words immediately. As an alternative, you can wait and check the entire document for spelling and grammar errors at once.

The following steps illustrate how to check spelling and grammar in the Biometrics Paper at once. In the following example the word, hand, has been misspelled intentionally as han to illustrate the use of Word's check spelling and grammar at once feature. If you are completing this project on a personal computer, your research paper may contain different misspelled words, depending on the accuracy of your typing.

To Check Spelling and Grammar at Once

1

• **Press CTRL+HOME to move the insertion point to the beginning of the document.**

• **Click the Spelling and Grammar button on the Standard toolbar.**

Word displays the Spelling and Grammar dialog box (Figure 2-69). The spelling and grammar check begins at the location of the insertion point, which, in this case, is at the beginning of the document. Word did not find the misspelled word, han, in its dictionary. The Suggestions list displays suggested corrections for the flagged word.

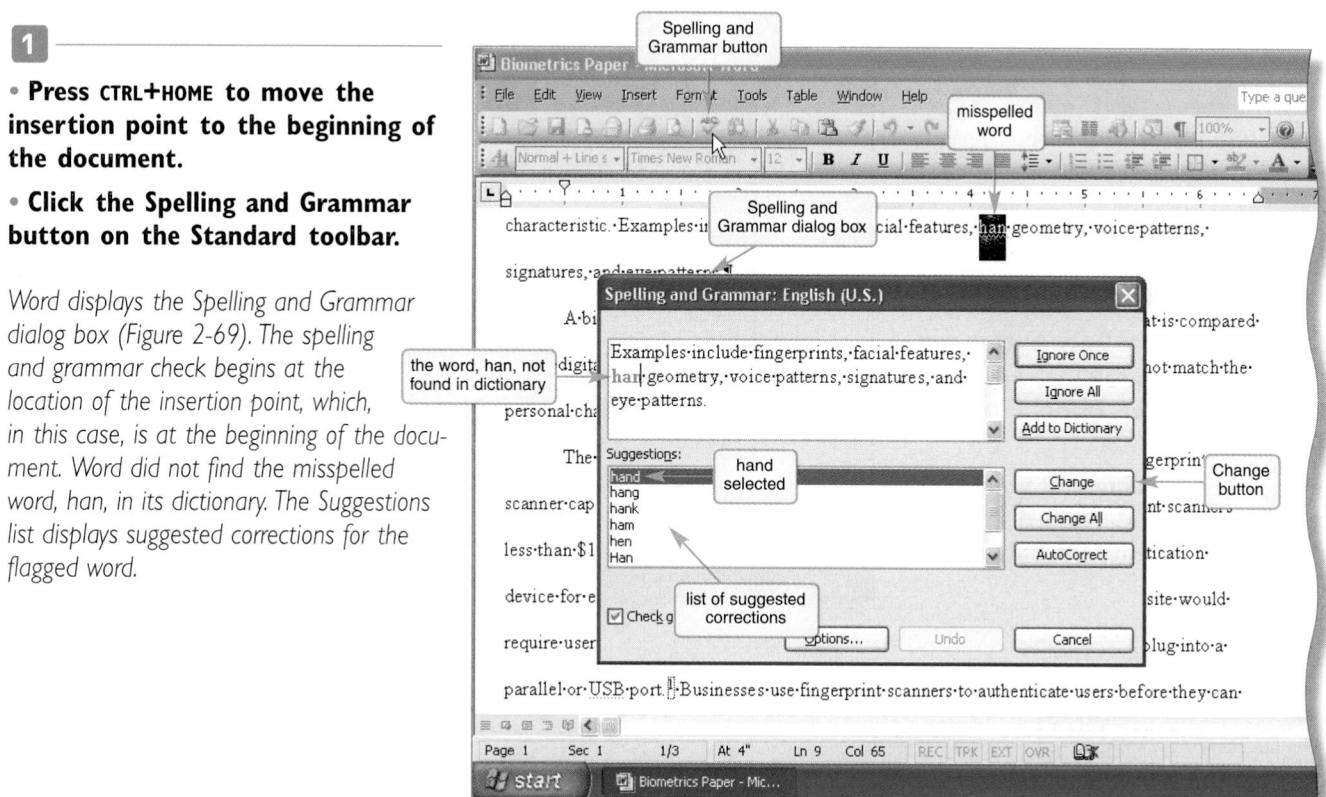

FIGURE 2-69

2

• **Click the Change button in the Spelling and Grammar dialog box.**

Word corrects the misspelled word and then continues the spelling and grammar check until it finds the next error or reaches the end of the document. In this case, it flags an error on the Works Cited page (Figure 2-70). The entry is correct, so you instruct Word to ignore it.

FIGURE 2-70

3

• **Click the Ignore Once button.**

• **Click the Ignore Once button for the next grammar error that Word flags on the Works Cited page.**

Word continues the spelling and grammar check and does not find Cashman in its dictionary (Figure 2-71). Cashman is a proper name and is spelled correctly.

4

• **Click the Ignore All button.**

• **Click the Ignore Once button for each remaining grammar error that Word flags on the Works Cited page.**

• **When the spelling and grammar check is done and Word displays a dialog box, click its OK button.**

FIGURE 2-71

Your document no longer displays red and green wavy underlines below words and phrases. In addition, the red X on the Spelling and Grammar Status icon has returned to a red check mark.

Saving Again and Printing the Document

The document now is complete. You should save the research paper again and print it, as described in the following steps.

To Save a Document Again and Print It

1 **Click the Save button on the Standard toolbar.**

2 **Click the Print button on the Standard toolbar.**

Word saves the research paper with the same file name, Biometrics Paper. The completed research paper prints as shown in Figure 2-1 on page WD 75.

Working with Main and Custom Dictionaries

As shown in the previous steps, Word often flags proper names as errors because these names are not in its main dictionary. To prevent Word from flagging proper names as errors, you can add the names to the custom dictionary. To add a correctly spelled word to the custom dictionary, click the Add to Dictionary button in the Spelling and Grammar dialog box (Figure 2-71) or right-click the flagged word and then click Add to Dictionary on the shortcut menu. Once you have added a word to the custom dictionary, Word no longer will flag it as an error. To view or modify the list of words in a custom dictionary, you would follow these steps.

To View or Modify Entries in a Custom Dictionary

1. Click Tools on the menu bar and then click Options.
2. Click the Spelling & Grammar tab in the Options dialog box.
3. Click the Custom Dictionaries button.
4. When Word displays the Custom Dictionaries dialog box, place a check mark next to the dictionary name to view or modify. Click the Modify button. (In this dialog box, you can add or delete entries to and from the selected custom dictionary.)
5. When finished viewing and/or modifying the list, click the OK button in the dialog box.
6. Click the OK button in the Custom Dictionaries dialog box.
7. If the Suggest from main dictionary only check box is selected in the Spelling & Grammar sheet in the Options dialog box, remove the check mark. Click the OK button in the Options dialog box.

If you have multiple custom dictionaries, you can specify which one Word should use when checking spelling. The following steps describe how to set the default custom dictionary.

To Set the Default Custom Dictionary

1. Click Tools on the menu bar and then click Options.
2. Click the Spelling & Grammar tab in the Options dialog box.
3. Click the Custom Dictionaries button.
4. When the Custom Dictionaries dialog box displays, place a check mark next to the desired dictionary name. Click the Change Default button.
5. Click the OK button in the Custom Dictionaries dialog box.
6. If the Suggest from main dictionary only check box is selected in the Spelling & Grammar dialog box, remove the check mark. Click the OK button in the Spelling & Grammar dialog box.

More About

Certification

The Microsoft Office Specialist Certification program provides an opportunity for you to obtain a valuable industry credential - proof that you have the Word 2003 skills required by employers. For more information, see Appendix E or visit the Word 2003 Certification Web page (scsite.com/wd2003/cert).

Navigating to a Hyperlink

Recall that a requirement of this research paper is that one of the works be a Web page and be formatted as a hyperlink. The following steps show how to check the hyperlink in the document.

To Navigate to a Hyperlink

1

• **Display the third page of the research paper in the document window and then position the mouse pointer in the hyperlink.**

When you position the mouse pointer in a hyperlink in a Word document, a ScreenTip is displayed above the hyperlink (Figure 2-72).

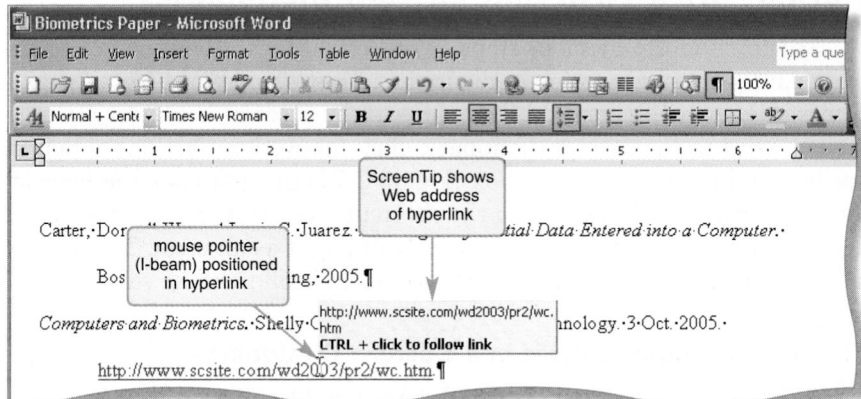

FIGURE 2-72

Close button

2

• **While holding down the CTRL key, click the hyperlink. Release the CTRL key.**

If you currently are not connected to the Web, Word connects you using your default browser. The www.scsite.com/wd2003/pr2/wc.htm Web page is displayed in a browser window (Figure 2-73).

3

• **Close the browser window.**

• **If necessary, click the Microsoft Word program button on the taskbar to redisplay the Word window.**

• **Press CTRL+HOME.**

Word displays the first page of the research paper on the screen.

Web page associated with hyperlink in research paper

Microsoft Word program button

FIGURE 2-73

The hyperlink in the document changes color, which indicates you CTRL+clicked the hyperlink to display its associated Web page.

E-Mailing a Copy of the Research Paper

Your instructor, Mr. Ortiz, has requested you e-mail him a copy of your research paper so he can verify your hyperlink. The following steps show how to e-mail the document from within Word if you use Outlook as your e-mail program.

To E-Mail a Document

1

- **Click the E-mail button on the Standard toolbar.**
- **Fill in the To text box with Mr. Ortiz's e-mail address and the Introduction text box as shown in Figure 2-74.**

Word displays certain buttons and boxes from the e-mail editor inside the Word window. The file name is displayed automatically in the Subject text box.

2

- **Click the Send a Copy button.**

The document is e-mailed to the recipient named in the To text box.

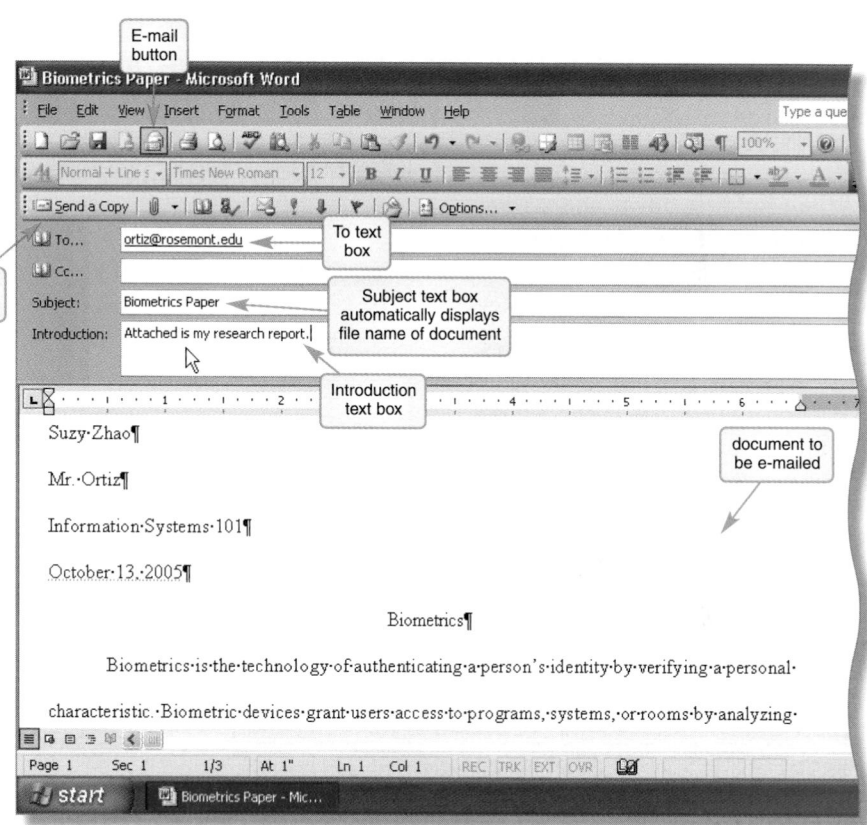

FIGURE 2-74

If you want to cancel the e-mail operation, click the E-mail button again.

In the steps above, the Word document becomes part of the e-mail message. If you wanted to send the Word document as an attachment to the e-mail message instead, do the following.

To E-Mail a Document as an Attatchment

1. Click File on the menu bar, point to Send To, and then click Mail Recipient (as Attachment).
2. Fill in the text boxes.
3. Click the Send button.

Other Ways

1. On File menu point to Send To, on Send To submenu click Mail Recipient
2. In Voice Command mode, say "E-mail"

More About

**The Research
Task Pane**

Other Office applications,
such as Excel and PowerPoint,
also use the Research task
pane. Internet Explorer uses
it, too. Thus, once you learn
how to use the Research task
pane in Word, you will be
able to use it in many other
programs.

Using the Research Task Pane

From within Word, you can search through various forms of online reference information. Earlier, this project discussed the Research task pane with respect to looking up a synonym in a thesaurus. Other services available in the Research task pane include the Microsoft Encarta English dictionary, bilingual dictionaries, the Microsoft Encarta Encyclopedia (with a Web connection), and Web sites that provide information such as stock quotes, news articles, and company profiles.

After reading a document you create, you might want to know the meaning of a certain word. For example, in the research paper, you might want to look up the definition of the word, e-commerce. The following step shows how to use the Research task pane to look up the definition of a word.

To Use the Research Task Pane to Locate Information

1

• **While holding down the ALT key, click the word for which you want a definition (in this case, e-commerce). Release the ALT key.**

• **If the Research task pane does not display the definition of the ALT+CLICKED word, click the Search for box arrow and then click All Reference Books.**

Word displays the Research task pane with the ALT+CLICKED word in the Search for text box (Figure 2-75). The Research button on the Standard toolbar is selected and the insertion point is in the ALT+CLICKED word. The contents of your reference book entry in the Research task pane may be different.

FIGURE 2-75

Other Ways

1. On Tools menu click Research
2. Right-click selected word, click Look Up on shortcut menu
3. In Voice Command mode, say "Tools, Research"

After you have looked up information in the Research task pane, you either can close the task pane or you can insert certain pieces of the information into the document. The next steps illustrate the procedure of copying information displayed in the Research task pane and inserting the copied text in a Word document.

To Insert Text from the Research Task Pane in a Word Document

1

- **In the Research task pane, double-click the word, Internet.**
- **Right-click the selected word.**

The word, Internet, is selected in the Research task pane and a shortcut menu is displayed (Figure 2-76).

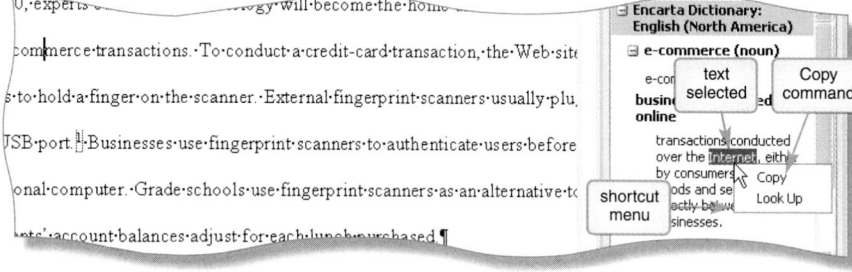

FIGURE 2-76

2

- **Click Copy on the shortcut menu to copy the selected text to the Clipboard.**
- **Drag through the word, e-commerce, in the research paper.**
- **Right-click the selected text in the document (Figure 2-77).**

The word, e-commerce, is selected in the document and a shortcut menu is displayed.

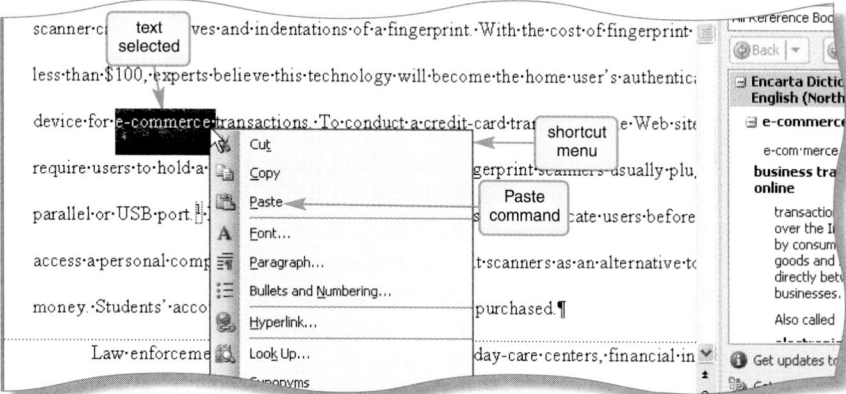

FIGURE 2-77

3

- **Click Paste on the shortcut menu.**
- **If necessary, press the SPACEBAR to insert a space after the inserted word.**
- **Click the Close button in the Research task pane.**

Word removes the selected word, e-commerce, and inserts the word, Internet, in its place (Figure 2-78).

FIGURE 2-78

Microsoft Office
Word 2003

More About

Quick Reference

For a table that lists how to complete the tasks covered in this book using the mouse, menu, shortcut menu, and keyboard, see the Quick Reference Summary at the back of this book, or visit the Word 2003 Quick Reference Web page (scsite.com/ wd2003/qr).

When using Word to insert material from the Research task pane or any other online reference, be very careful not to plagiarize, or copy other's work and use it as your own. Not only is plagiarism unethical, but it is considered an academic crime that can have severe punishments such as failing a course or being expelled from school.

The final step in this project is to quit Word, as described below.

To Quit Word

1 **Click the Close button in the Word window.**

2 **If Word displays a dialog box, click the No button.**

The Word window closes.

Project Summary

In creating the Biometrics Paper in this project, you learned how to use Word to enter and format a research paper using the MLA documentation style. You learned how to change margin settings, adjust line spacing, create headers with page numbers, enter text using Click and Type, and first-line indent paragraphs. You learned how to use Word's AutoCorrect feature. Then, you added a footnote in the research paper and modified the Footnote Text style. You also learned how to count words in a document. In creating the Works Cited page, you learned how to insert a manual page break, create a hanging indent, create a hyperlink, and sort paragraphs.

Once you finished typing text into the entire paper, you learned how to browse through a Word document, move text, and find and replace text. You looked up a synonym for a word and checked spelling and grammar in the entire document. Finally, you navigated to a hyperlink, e-mailed a copy of a document, and looked up information using the Research task pane.

If you have a SAM user profile, you may have access to hands-on instruction, practice, and assessment of the skills covered in this project. Log in to your SAM account and go to your assignments page to see what your instructor has assigned.

What You Should Know

Having completed this project, you should be able to perform the tasks below. The tasks are listed in the same order they were presented in this project. For a list of the buttons, menus, toolbars, and commands introduced in this project, see the Quick Reference Summary at the back of this book and refer to the Page Number column.

1. Start and Customize Word   (WD 77)
2. Display Formatting Marks   (WD 77)
3. Change the Margin Settings   (WD 78)
4. Double-Space Text   (WD 80)
5. Display the Header Area   (WD 81)
6. Click and Type   (WD 83)
7. Enter a Page Number   (WD 83)
8. Enter Name and Course Information   (WD 85)
9. Format Text Using Shortcut Keys   (WD 86)
10. Save a Document   (WD 87)
11. First-Line Indent Paragraphs   (WD 88)
12. AutoCorrect as You Type   (WD 89)
13. Use the AutoCorrect Options Button   (WD 90)
14. Create an AutoCorrect Entry   (WD 91)
15. Enter More Text   (WD 93)
16. Add a Footnote   (WD 94)
17. Modify a Style   (WD 96)
18. Close the Note Pane   (WD 99)
19. Count Words   (WD 100)
20. Page Break Automatically   (WD 101)
21. Recount Words   (WD 102)
22. Page Break Manually   (WD 103)
23. Center the Title of the Works Cited Page   (WD 104)
24. Create a Hanging Indent   (WD 105)
25. Enter Works Cited Paragraphs   (WD 105)
26. Insert a Symbol Automatically   (WD 107)
27. Create a Hyperlink   (WD 108)
28. Sort Paragraphs   (WD 109)
29. Browse by Page   (WD 111)
30. Select a Sentence   (WD 112)
31. Move Selected Text   (WD 113)
32. Display the Paste Options Menu   (WD 115)
33. Find and Replace Text   (WD 116)
34. Find Text   (WD 117)
35. Find and Insert a Synonym   (WD 118)
36. Check Spelling and Grammar at Once   (WD 119)
37. Save a Document Again and Print It   (WD 121)
38. View or Modify Entries in a Custom Dictionary   (WD 121)
39. Set the Default Custom Dictionary   (WD 121)
40. Navigate to a Hyperlink   (WD 122)
41. E-Mail a Document   (WD 123)
42. E-Mail a Document as an Attachment   (WD 123)
43. Use the Research Task Pane to Locate Information   (WD 124)
44. Insert Text from the Research Task Pane in a Word Document   (WD 125)
45. Quit Word   (WD 126)

Learn It Online

Instructions: To complete the Learn It Online exercises, start your browser, click the Address bar, and then enter the Web address scsite.com/wd2003/learn. When the Word 2003 Learn It Online page is displayed, follow the instructions in the exercises below. Each exercise has instructions for printing your results, either for your own records or for submission to your instructor.

1 Project Reinforcement TF, MC, and SA

Below Word Project 2, click the Project Reinforcement link. Print the quiz by clicking Print on the File menu for each page. Answer each question.

2 Flash Cards

Below Word Project 2, click the Flash Cards link and read the instructions. Type 20 (or a number specified by your instructor) in the Number of playing cards text box, type your name in the Enter your Name text box, and then click the Flip Card button. When the flash card is displayed, read the question and then click the ANSWER box arrow to select an answer. Flip through Flash Cards. If your score is 15 (75%) correct or greater, click Print on the File menu to print your results. If your score is less than 15 (75%) correct, then redo this exercise by clicking the Replay button.

3 Practice Test

Below Word Project 2, click the Practice Test link. Answer each question, enter your first and last name at the bottom of the page, and then click the Grade Test button. When the graded practice test is displayed on your screen, click Print on the File menu to print a hard copy. Continue to take practice tests until you score 80% or better.

4 Who Wants To Be a Computer Genius?

Below Word Project 2, click the Computer Genius link. Read the instructions, enter your first and last name at the bottom of the page, and then click the PLAY button. When your score is displayed, click the PRINT RESULTS link to print a hard copy.

5 Wheel of Terms

Below Word Project 2, click the Wheel of Terms link. Read the instructions, and then enter your first and last name and your school name. Click the PLAY button. When your score is displayed, right-click the score and then click Print on the shortcut menu to print a hard copy.

6 Crossword Puzzle Challenge

Below Word Project 2, click the Crossword Puzzle Challenge link. Read the instructions, and then enter your first and last name. Click the SUBMIT button. Work the crossword puzzle. When you are finished, click the Submit button. When the crossword puzzle is redisplayed, click the Print Puzzle button to print a hard copy.

7 Tips and Tricks

Below Word Project 2, click the Tips and Tricks link. Click a topic that pertains to Project 2. Right-click the information and then click Print on the shortcut menu. Construct a brief example of what the information relates to in Word to confirm you understand how to use the tip or trick.

8 Newsgroups

Below Word Project 2, click the Newsgroups link. Click a topic that pertains to Project 2. Print three comments.

9 Expanding Your Horizons

Below Word Project 2, click the Expanding Your Horizons link. Click a topic that pertains to Project 2. Print the information. Construct a brief example of what the information relates to in Word to confirm you understand the contents of the article.

10 Search Sleuth

Below Word Project 2, click the Search Sleuth link. To search for a term that pertains to this project, select a term below the Project 2 title and then use the Google search engine at google.com (or any major search engine) to display and print two Web pages that present information on the term.

11 Word Online Training

Below Word Project 2, click the Word Online Training link. When your browser displays the Microsoft Office Online Web page, click the Word link. Click one of the Word courses that covers one or more of the objectives listed at the beginning of the project on page WD 74. Print the first page of the course before stepping through it.

12 Office Marketplace

Below Word Project 2, click the Office Marketplace link. When your browser displays the Microsoft Office Online Web page, click the Office Marketplace link. Click a topic that relates to Word. Print the first page.

Apply Your Knowledge

1 Revising a Document

Instructions: Start Word. Open the document, Apply 2-1 Authentication Paragraph, on the Data Disk. See the inside back cover of this book for instructions for downloading the Data Disk or see your instructor for information about accessing the files in this book.

The document on the Data Disk is a paragraph of text. You are to revise the paragraph as follows: move a sentence; change the format of the moved sentence; change paragraph indentation, change line spacing, change margin settings, replace all occurrences of the word, memorized, with the word, remembered; add a sentence; remove an automatic hyperlink format, and modify the header. The revised paragraph is shown in Figure 2-79.

Perform the following tasks:

1. Select the first sentence of the paragraph. Use drag-and-drop editing to move this sentence to the end of the paragraph, so it is the last sentence in the paragraph.

2. Click the Paste Options button that displays to the right of the moved sentence. Remove the italic format from the moved sentence by clicking Keep Text Only on the shortcut menu.

3. Use first-line indent to indent the first line of the paragraph.

> Revised Authentication Paragraph
> 10/17/2005 12:35:34 PM
>
> Three common types of authentication are remembered information, biometric devices, and possessed objects. With remembered information, the user enters a word or series of characters that match an entry in the computer's security file. Examples of remembered information are passwords, user IDs, and logon codes. A password is confidential, usually known only by the user and possibly the system administrator. A user ID typically identifies the user, and a logon code identifies an application program. A possessed object is any item the user must carry to access the computer facility. Some examples are keys, badges, and cards. Possessed objects often are used together with a personal identification number (PIN), which is a numeric password. For more information about passwords, visit www.scsite.com/dc2003/apply.htm and click Apply It #1 below Chapter 11.

FIGURE 2-79

4. Change the line spacing of the paragraph from single to double.

5. Change the left and right margins of the document to .75".

6. Use the Find and Replace dialog box to replace all occurrences of the word, memorized, with the word, remembered.

7. Use Word's thesaurus to change the word, usually, to the word, typically, in the sentence that starts, A user ID usually...

8. At the end of the paragraph, press the SPACEBAR and then type this sentence: For more information about passwords, visit www.scsite.com/dc2003/apply.htm and click Apply It #1 below Chapter 11.

9. Remove the hyperlink automatic format from the Web address by positioning the mouse pointer at the beginning of the Web address (that is, the w in www), pointing to the small blue box below the w, clicking the AutoCorrect Options button, and then clicking Undo Hyperlink on the shortcut menu.

10. Display the header on the screen. Change the alignment of the text in the header from left to centered. Insert the word, Revised, in the text so it reads: Revised Authentication Paragraph. On the second line of the header, insert and center the current date and the current time using buttons on the Header and Footer toolbar. Place one space between the current date and current time.

11. Click File on the menu bar and then click Save As. Save the document using the file name, Apply 2-1 Revised Authentication Paragraph.

12. Print the revised paragraph, shown in Figure 2-79.

13. Use the Research task pane to look up the definition of the word, passwords, in the third sentence of the paragraph. Handwrite the definition on your printout.

1 Preparing a Short Research Paper

Problem: You are a college student currently enrolled in an introductory computer class. Your assignment is to prepare a short research paper (350-400 words) about a computer component. The requirements are that the paper be presented according to the MLA documentation style and have three references. One of the three references must be from the Web and formatted as a hyperlink on the Works Cited page. You prepare the paper shown in Figure 2-80, which discusses the system unit.

Marks 1

Nicholas Marks

Ms. White

Computer Literacy 100

August 6, 2005

The System Unit

The system unit is a case that houses the electronic components of the computer used to process data. Although many system units resemble a box, they are available in many shapes and sizes. The case of the system unit, sometimes called a chassis, is made of metal or plastic and protects the internal electronic components from damage. All computers have a system unit (Alvarez 102).

Components of the system unit include the processor, memory modules, adapter cards, drive bays, power supply, ports, and connectors. The processor interprets and carries out the basic instructions that operate a computer. A memory module houses memory chips. An adapter card is a circuit board that provides connections and functions not built into the motherboard.[1] A drive bay holds a disk drive. The power supply allows electricity to travel into a computer.

On a personal computer, the electronic components and most storage devices reside inside the system unit. Other devices, such as a keyboard, mouse, microphone, monitor, printer, speakers, scanner, and digital camera, normally occupy space outside the system unit (*How to Use a Computer*). On a desktop personal computer, the system unit usually is a device separate from the monitor and keyboard. Some system units sit on top of a desk. Other models, called tower models, can stand vertically on the floor.

---

[1] According to Wilson, four adapter cards most commonly found in desktop personal computers today are sound cards, modem cards, video cards, and network cards (18-32).

FIGURE 2-80a

In the Lab

Marks 2

To conserve space, an all-in-one computer houses the system unit in the same physical case as the monitor. On notebook computers, the keyboard and pointing device often occupy the area on the top of the system unit. The display attaches to the system unit by hinges. The system unit on a PDA (personal digital assistant) or handheld computer usually consumes the entire device. On these small mobile devices, the display is part of the system unit, too.

FIGURE 2-80b

Marks 3

Works Cited

Alvarez, Juan. *Understanding Computer Basics: Stepping Toward Literacy*. Chicago: Martin Publishing, 2005.

How to Use a Computer. Shelly Cashman Series®. Course Technology. 3 Aug. 2005. www.scsite.com/wd2003/pr2/wc1.htm.

Wilson, Tracey M. "Personal Computers and their Applications." *Computing and Information Systems Weekly* May 2005: 18-32.

FIGURE 2-80c

Instructions:

1. If necessary, display formatting marks on the screen.
2. Change all margins to one inch.
3. Adjust line spacing to double.
4. Create a header to number pages.
5. Type the name and course information at the left margin. Center and type the title.
6. Set first-line indent for paragraphs in the body of the research paper.
7. Type the body of the paper as shown in Figure 2-80a and Figure 2-80b. Add the footnote as shown in Figure 2-80a. At the end of the body of the research paper, press the ENTER key and then insert a manual page break.
8. Create the works cited page (Figure 2-80c).
9. Check the spelling of the paper at once.
10. Save the document on a floppy disk using Lab 2-1 System Unit Paper as the file name.
11. Use the Select Browse Object button to go to page 3. If you have access to the Web, CTRL+click the hyperlink to test it.
12. Print the research paper. Handwrite the number of words, paragraphs, and characters in the research paper above the title of your printed research paper.

2 Preparing a Research Report with a Footnote(s)

Problem: You are a college student currently enrolled in an introductory computer class. Your assignment is to prepare a short research paper in any area of interest to you. The requirements are that the paper be presented according to the MLA documentation style, contain at least one explanatory note positioned as a footnote, and have three references. One of the three references must be from the Internet and formatted as a hyperlink on the works cited page. You decide to prepare a paper about employee monitoring (Figure 2-81).

Mills 1

Francis Mills

Mr. Rugenstein

Information Systems 101

August 27, 2005

Employee Monitoring

Employee monitoring involves the use of computers to observe, record, and review an employee's use of a computer, including communications such as e-mail, keyboard activity (used to measure productivity), and Web sites visited. Many computer programs exist that easily allow employers to monitor employees.[1] Further, it is legal for employers to use these programs.

A frequently debated issue is whether an employer has the right to read employee e-mail messages. Actual policies vary widely. Some companies declare that they will review e-mail messages regularly; others state that e-mail messages are private. If a company does not have a formal e-mail policy, it can read e-mail messages without employee notification. One recent survey discovered that more than 73 percent of companies search and/or read employee files, voice mail, e-mail messages, Web connections, and other networking communications. Another claimed that 25 percent of companies have fired employees for misusing communications technology.

Currently, no privacy laws exist relating to employee e-mail (*Privacy Laws and Personal Data*). The 1986 Electronic Communications Privacy Act provides the same right of privacy protection that covers the postal delivery service and telephone companies to various forms of

---

[1] According to Lang, software currently is being developed that can track and record what employees are doing while they work, using a digital video camera with real-time image recognition (33-45).

FIGURE 2-81a

Mills 2

electronic communications, such as e-mail, voice mail, and cellular telephones. The Electronic Communications Privacy Act, however, does not cover communications within a company. This is because any piece of mail sent from an employer's computer is considered company property. Several lawsuits have been filed against employers because many people believe that such internal employee communications should be private (Slobovnik and Stuart 144-160).

FIGURE 2-81b

In the Lab

Instructions Part 1: Perform the following tasks to create the research paper:

1. If necessary, display formatting marks on the screen. Change all margin settings to one inch. Adjust line spacing to double. Create a header to number pages. Type the name and course information at the left margin. Center and type the title. Set first-line indent for paragraphs in the body of the research paper.

2. Type the body of the paper as shown in Figure 2-81a and Figure 2-81b. Add the footnote as shown in Figure 2-81a. Change the Footnote Text style to the format specified in the MLA style. At the end of the body of the research paper, press the ENTER key once and insert a manual page break.

3. Create the works cited page. Enter the works cited shown below as separate paragraphs. Format the works according to the MLA documentation style and then sort the works cited paragraphs.
   (a) Slobovnik, Victor W., and Janel K. Stuart. Workplace Challenges. Dallas: Techno-Cyber Publishing, 2005.
   (b) Privacy Laws and Personal Data. Shelly Cashman Series®. Course Technology. 3 Aug. 2005. www.scsite.com/wd2003/pr2/wc2.htm.
   (c) Lang, Stefanie. "The New Invasion: Employee Monitoring and Privacy Issues." Technology Issues Aug. 2005: 33-45.

4. Check the spelling of the paper.

5. Save the document on a floppy disk using Lab 2-2 Employee Monitoring Paper as the file name.

6. If you have access to the Web, CTRL+click the hyperlink to test it.

7. Print the research paper. Handwrite the number of words, including the footnotes, in the research paper above the title of your printed research paper.

Instructions Part 2: Perform the following tasks to modify the research paper:

1. Use Word to find a synonym of your choice for the word, issue, in the first sentence of the second paragraph.

2. Change all occurrences of the word, employers, to the word, companies.

3. Insert a second footnote at the end of the fourth sentence in the last paragraph of the research paper. Use the following footnote text: Some companies even use automated software that searches e-mail messages for derogatory language. One unidentified woman, for example, was fired for using her office e-mail to complain about her boss.

4. In the first footnote, find the word, developed, and change it to the word, written.

5. Save the document on a floppy disk using Lab 2-2 Employee Monitoring Paper - Part 2 as the file name.

6. Print this revised research paper that has notes positioned as footnotes. Handwrite the number of words, including the footnotes, in the research paper above the title of the printed research paper.

Instructions Part 3: Perform the following tasks to modify the research paper created in Part 2:

1. Convert the footnotes to endnotes. Recall that endnotes display at the end of a document. Switch to print layout view to see the endnotes. *Hint:* Use Help to learn about print layout view and converting footnotes to endnotes.

2. Modify the Endnote text style to 12-point font, double-spaced text with a first-line indent. Insert a page break so the endnotes are placed on a separate, numbered page. Center the title, Endnotes, double-spaced above the notes.

3. Change the format of the note reference marks to capital letters (A, B, etc.). *Hint:* Use Help to learn about changing the number format of note reference marks.

4. Save the document on a floppy disk using Lab 2-2 Employee Monitoring Paper - Part 3 as the file name.

5. Print the revised research paper with notes positioned as endnotes. Handwrite the number of words, including the endnotes, in the research paper above the title of the printed research paper.

In the Lab

3 Composing a Research Paper from Notes

Problem: You have drafted the notes shown in Figure 2-82. Your assignment is to prepare a short research paper from these notes.

Instructions: Perform the following tasks:

1. Review the notes in Figure 2-82 and then rearrange and reword them. Embellish the paper as you deem necessary. Present the paper according to the MLA documentation style. Create an AutoCorrect entry that automatically corrects the spelling of the misspelled word, softare, to the correct spelling, software. Add a footnote that refers the reader to the Web for more information. Create the works cited page from the listed sources. Be sure to sort the works.

2. Check the spelling and grammar of the paper. Save the document on a floppy disk using Lab 2-3 Computer Software Paper as the file name.

3. Use the Research task pane to look up a definition. Copy and insert the definition into the document as a footnote. Be sure to quote the definition and cite the source.

4. Print the research paper. Handwrite the number of words, including the footnotes, in the research paper above the title of the printed research paper. Circle the definition inserted into the document from the Research task pane.

5. Use Word to e-mail the research paper to your instructor, if your instructor gives you permission to do so.

Software, also called a program, is a series of instructions that tells the computer hardware what to do and how to do it. Two categories of software are system software and application software.

System software (source: "The Future of Application Software," an article on page 39-55 in the May 2005 issue of Computers and Peripherals, authors James A. Naylor and Joseph I. Vincent.)
- System software is an interface between the application software, the user, and the computer's hardware.
- An operating system is a popular type of system software. Microsoft Windows is an operating system that has a graphical user interface. Users interact with software through its user interface.
- System software consists of the programs that control or maintain the operations of the computer and its devices.

Application software (source: a Web site titled Guide to Application Software, sponsored by the Shelly Cashman Series® at Course Technology, site visited on October 3, 2005, Web address is www.scsite.com/wd2003/pr2/wc3.htm)
- Application software consists of programs that perform specific tasks for users. Examples are word processing software, spreadsheet software, database software, presentation graphics software, and Web browsers.
- Database software - store data in an organized fashion, and retrieve, manipulate, and display that data in a variety of formats.
- Word processing software - create documents such as letters, reports, and brochures.
- Spreadsheet software - calculate numbers arranged in rows and columns.
- Web browser - connect to the Internet to access and view Web pages.
- Presentation graphics software - create documents called slides that add visual appeal to presentations.
- Other types of application software are available that enable users to perform a variety of tasks, including personal information management, project management, accounting, desktop publishing, photo and video editing, personal finance, tax preparation, reference, education, entertainment, and communications.

Software suites (source: Hardware and Software Made Simple, a book published by Cyber Press Publishing in New York, 2005, written by Nanette Allen and Clint Muhr.)
- When installing the software suite, you install the entire collection of programs at once instead of installing each one individually. Business software suites typically include word processing, spreadsheet, e-mail, and presentation graphics programs.
- Software vendors often bundle and sell individual programs together as a single package called a software suite. This costs much less than buying the applications individually.
- Two widely used business software suites are Microsoft Office and Sun StarOffice.

FIGURE 2-82

Cases and Places

The difficulty of these case studies varies:
■ are the least difficult and ■■ are more difficult. The last exercise is a group exercise.

1 ■ This project discussed the requirements of the MLA documentation style on page WD 76 and in several More About boxes dispersed throughout the project. Using the material presented in this project, write a short research paper (400-450 words) that describes the requirements of the MLA documentation style. Include at least two references and one explanatory note positioned as a footnote. Add an AutoCorrect entry to correct a word you commonly mistype. Use the concepts and techniques presented in this project to format the paper. Type the paper with the Word screen in normal view. Switch to print layout view to proof the paper.

2 ■■ The ever-increasing presence of computers in everyone's lives has generated an awareness of the need to address computing requirements for those who have or may develop physical limitations. The Americans with Disabilities Act (ADA) requires any company with 15 or more employees to make reasonable attempts to accommodate the needs of physically challenged workers. Whether at work or at home, you may find it necessary to acquire devices that address physical limitations. Using Word's Research task pane, the school library, other textbooks, magazines, the Internet, friends and family, or other resources, research the types of input and/or output devices designed for physically challenged computer users. Then, prepare a brief research paper (400-450 words) that discusses your findings. Include at least one explanatory note and two references, one of which must be a Web site on the Internet. Use the concepts and techniques presented in this project to format the paper.

3 ■■ Computers process input (data) into output (information). A computer often holds data, information, and instructions in storage for future use. Most computers today also can communicate with other computers. Computers perform input, output, storage, and communications operations with amazing speed, reliability, consistency, and accuracy. Using Word's Research task pane, the school library, other textbooks, the Internet, magazines, or other resources, research one of the following computer operations: input, output, storage, or communications. Then, prepare a brief research paper (400-450 words) that discusses how the computer operation works and/or the types of devices used for that activity. Include at least one explanatory note and two references, one of which must be a Web site on the Internet. Use the concepts and techniques presented in this project to format the paper.

4 ■■ A programming language is a set of words, symbols, and codes that enables a programmer to communicate instructions to a computer. Just as humans speak a variety of languages (English, Spanish, French, and so on), programmers use a variety of programming languages and program development tools to write computer programs. Using Word's Research task pane, the school library, other textbooks, the Internet, magazines, interviews with programmers, or other resources, research the types of programming languages or program development tools on the market today. Then, prepare a brief research paper (400-450 words) that discusses one or more programming languages or program development tools. Include at least one explanatory note and two references, one of which must be a Web site on the Internet. Use the concepts and techniques presented in this project to format the paper.

Cases and Places

5 ■■ **Working Together** PDAs are one of the more popular lightweight mobile devices in use today. A PDA (personal digital assistant) can provide a variety of personal information management functions including calendar, appointment book, address book, calculator, and notepad, as well as access to the Internet and telephone capabilities. Many different PDAs are on the market. Each team member is to research the features, price, and accessories of one type of PDA by looking through newspapers, magazines, searching the Web, and/or visiting an electronics or computer store. Each team member is to write a minimum of 200 words summarizing his or her findings. Each team member also is to write at least one explanatory note and supply his or her reference for the works cited page. Then, the team should meet as a group to compose a research paper that includes all team members' write-ups. Start by copying and pasting the text into a single document and then write an introduction and conclusion as a group. Use the concepts and techniques presented in this project to format the paper according to the MLA documentation style. Set the default dictionary. If Word flags any of your last names as an error, add the name(s) to the custom dictionary. Hand in printouts of each team member's original write-up, as well as the final research paper.

Creating a Resume Using a Wizard and a Cover Letter with a Table

P R O J E C T

3

CASE PERSPECTIVE

Hartford College offers many educational courses of study, such as certificate (vocational training), associate, and bachelor degree programs. Benjamin Kane Okamoto recently graduated from Hartford with a bachelor's degree in information and computer technology. You had classes with Benjamin and counseled him while you worked as an intern in Hartford College's Office of Career Development.

Benjamin is ready to embark on a full-time career in computer sales. He buys several local newspapers to begin his job hunt. While reading through the classified section of the *New England Tribune*, Benjamin notices a computer sales position available at National Computer Sales that seems perfect. The ad requests that all applicants send a resume and a cover letter to the personnel director, Ms. Helen Weiss. Benjamin contacts you and asks you to help him create a professional resume and cover letter. You immediately agree to help your schoolmate.

With Benjamin's educational background, work experience, and communications skills, and your resume-writing abilities, Benjamin will be prepared for success in acquiring the computer sales position. You suggest he use Word's Resume Wizard to create the resume because the wizard saves time by formatting much of the document. You also advise Benjamin to include all essential business letter components in the cover letter. Then, you mention he can use Word to prepare and print an envelope, so the entire presentation looks professional.

As you read through this project, you will learn how to use Word to create a resume, a cover letter, and an addressed envelope.

Creating a Resume Using a Wizard and a Cover Letter with a Table

PROJECT

Objectives

You will have mastered the material in this project when you can:

- Create a resume using Word's Resume Wizard
- Fill in a document template
- Use print preview to view and print a document
- Set and use tab stops
- Collect and paste using the Clipboard task pane
- Format paragraphs and characters
- Remove formatting from text
- Identify the components of a business letter

- Insert the current date
- Create and insert an AutoText entry
- Insert a Word table, enter data into the table, and format the table
- Address and print an envelope
- Work with smart tags
- Modify file properties

Introduction

At some time in your professional life, you will prepare a resume along with a personalized cover letter to send to a prospective employer(s). In addition to some personal information, a **resume** usually contains the applicant's educational background and job experience. Employers review many resumes for each vacant position. Thus, you should design your resume carefully so it presents you as the best candidate for the job. You also should attach a personalized cover letter to each resume you send. A **cover letter** enables you to elaborate on positive points in your resume; it also provides you with an opportunity to show a potential employer your written communications skills. Accordingly, it is important that your cover letter is written well and follows proper business letter rules.

Composing documents from scratch can be a difficult process for many people. To assist with this task, Word provides wizards and templates. A **wizard** asks you several basic questions and then, based on your responses, uses a template to prepare and format a document for you. A **template** is similar to a form with prewritten text; that is, Word prepares the requested document with text and/or formatting common to all documents of this nature. After Word creates a document from a template, you fill in the blanks or replace prewritten words in the document. In addition to templates used by wizards, Word provides other templates you can use to create documents.

Project Three — Resume and Cover Letter

Benjamin Kane Okamoto, a recent college graduate, is seeking a full-time position in computer sales. Project 3 uses Word to produce his resume, shown in Figure 3-1, and a personalized cover letter and an envelope, shown in Figure 3-2 on the next page.

78 Larkspur Road
Plantsville, CT 06479

Phone (860) 555-4499
Fax (860) 555-4490
E-mail okamoto@earth.net

resume

Benjamin Kane Okamoto

Objective	To obtain a full-time sales position with a major computer or electronics company in the New England area.
Education	2001-2005 Hartford College Hartford, CT
	Information and Computer Technology
	▪ B.S., December 2005
	▪ A.S., December 2003
Areas of concentration	Computer Hardware Computer Software and Programming Professional Communications Business
Awards received	Dean's List, every semester Gamma Phi Sigma Honors Society, 2002-2005 Hartford College Outstanding Senior, 1st Place, 2005
Interests and activities	Association of Sales Representatives, junior member Big Brothers Big Sisters of Hartford, volunteer Computer Club, treasurer New England Ski Club, publicity coordinator
Languages	English (fluent) Japanese (fluent) Knowledge of sign language
Work experience	2002-2005 Computer Discount Sales Plantsville, CT
	Intern
	▪ Sold hardware and software components to home and small business customers
	▪ Arranged and configured in-store computer hardware, software, and network displays
	▪ Logged and replied to computer-related customer e-mail, fax, and telephone inquiries
Volunteer experience	As a Big Brother, I spend at least eight hours every week with my Little Brother – hoping to make a difference in this youth's life.

FIGURE 3-1

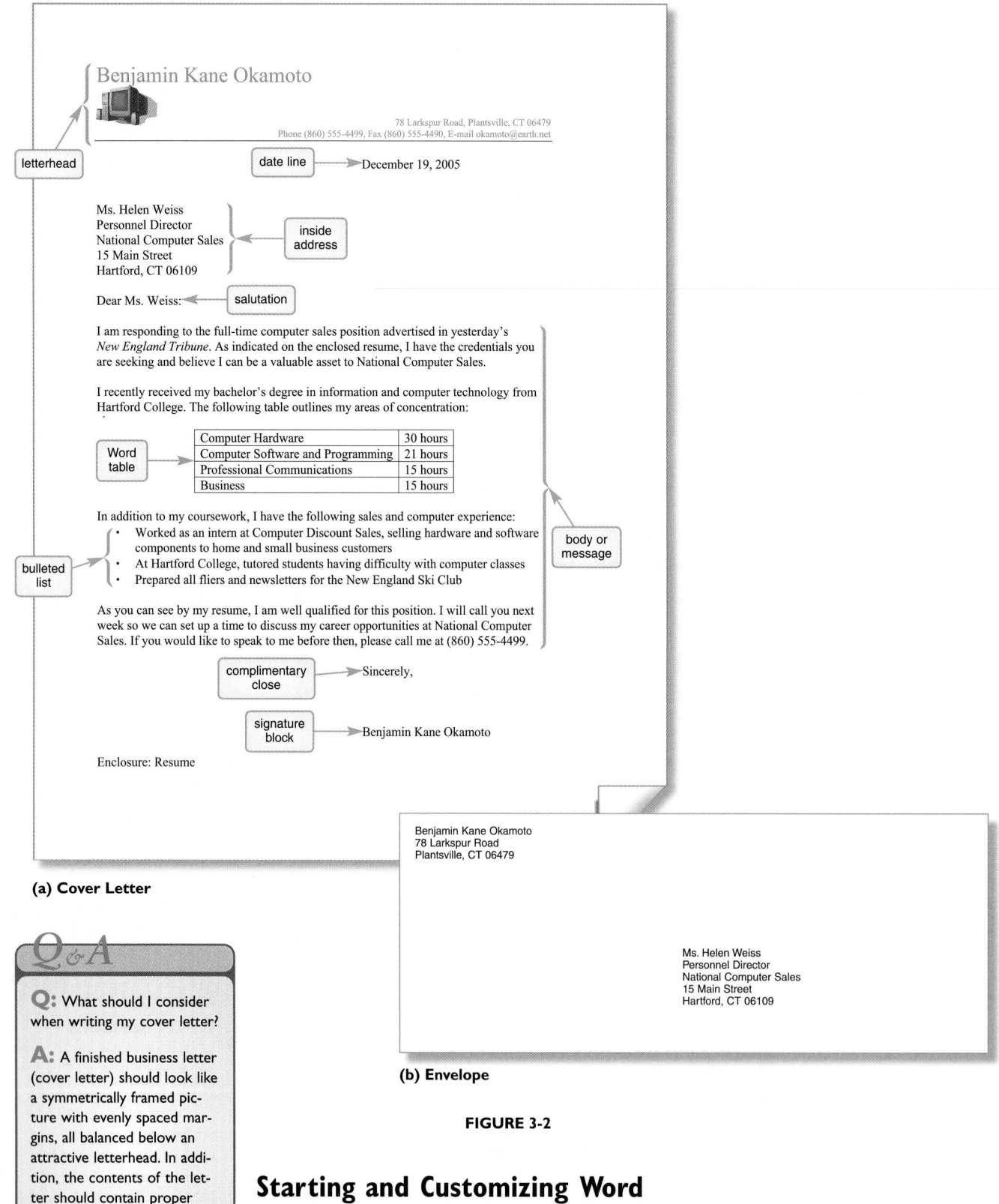

Benjamin Kane Okamoto

78 Larkspur Road, Plantsville, CT 06479
Phone (860) 555-4499, Fax (860) 555-4490, E-mail okamoto@earth.net

letterhead

date line → December 19, 2005

Ms. Helen Weiss
Personnel Director
National Computer Sales ← inside address
15 Main Street
Hartford, CT 06109

Dear Ms. Weiss: ← salutation

I am responding to the full-time computer sales position advertised in yesterday's *New England Tribune*. As indicated on the enclosed resume, I have the credentials you are seeking and believe I can be a valuable asset to National Computer Sales.

I recently received my bachelor's degree in information and computer technology from Hartford College. The following table outlines my areas of concentration:

Word table

Computer Hardware	30 hours
Computer Software and Programming	21 hours
Professional Communications	15 hours
Business	15 hours

In addition to my coursework, I have the following sales and computer experience:

bulleted list

- Worked as an intern at Computer Discount Sales, selling hardware and software components to home and small business customers
- At Hartford College, tutored students having difficulty with computer classes
- Prepared all fliers and newsletters for the New England Ski Club

body or message

As you can see by my resume, I am well qualified for this position. I will call you next week so we can set up a time to discuss my career opportunities at National Computer Sales. If you would like to speak to me before then, please call me at (860) 555-4499.

complimentary close → Sincerely,

signature block → Benjamin Kane Okamoto

Enclosure: Resume

(a) Cover Letter

Benjamin Kane Okamoto
78 Larkspur Road
Plantsville, CT 06479

Ms. Helen Weiss
Personnel Director
National Computer Sales
15 Main Street
Hartford, CT 06109

(b) Envelope

FIGURE 3-2

Q&A

Q: What should I consider when writing my cover letter?

A: A finished business letter (cover letter) should look like a symmetrically framed picture with evenly spaced margins, all balanced below an attractive letterhead. In addition, the contents of the letter should contain proper grammar, correct spelling, logically constructed sentences, flowing paragraphs, and sound ideas.

Starting and Customizing Word

To start and customize Word, Windows must be running. If you are stepping through this project on a computer and you want your screen to match the figures in this book, then you should change your computer's resolution to 800 × 600 and reset the toolbars and menus. For information about changing the resolution and resetting toolbars and menus, read Appendix D.

The following steps describe how to start Word and customize the Word window. You may need to ask your instructor how to start Word for your system.

To Start and Customize Word

1 Click the Start button on the Windows taskbar, point to All Programs on the Start menu, point to Microsoft Office on the All Programs submenu, and then click Microsoft Office Word 2003 on the Microsoft Office submenu.

2 If the Word window is not maximized, double-click its title bar to maximize it.

3 If the Language bar appears, right-click it and then click Close the Language bar on the shortcut menu.

4 If the Getting Started task pane is displayed in the Word window, click its Close button.

5 If the Standard and Formatting toolbar buttons are displayed on one row, click the Toolbar Options button and then click Show Buttons on Two Rows in the Toolbar Options list.

6 If your screen differs from Figure 3-3 on the next page, click View on the menu bar and then click Normal.

Word starts and, after a few moments, displays an empty document in the Word window (shown in Figure 3-3).

Displaying Formatting Marks

As discussed in Project 1, it is helpful to display formatting marks that indicate where in the document you pressed the ENTER key, SPACEBAR, and other keys. The following step describes how to display formatting marks.

To Display Formatting Marks

1 If the Show/Hide ¶ button on the Standard toolbar is not selected already, click it.

Word displays formatting marks in the document window, and the Show/Hide ¶ button on the Standard toolbar is selected (shown in Figure 3-3).

Using Word's Resume Wizard to Create a Resume

You can type a resume from scratch into a blank document window, or you can use the **Resume Wizard** and let Word format the resume with appropriate headings and spacing. After answering several questions, you customize the resume created by the Resume Wizard by filling in blanks or selecting and replacing text.

When you use a wizard, Word displays a dialog box with the wizard's name on its title bar. A wizard's dialog box displays a list of **panel names** along its left side with the currently selected panel displaying on the right side of the dialog box (shown in Figure 3-6 on page WD 143). Each panel presents a different set of options, in which you select preferences or enter text. To move from one panel to the next within the wizard's dialog box, click the Next button or click the panel name on the left side of the dialog box.

> **More About**
>
> ### The Getting Started Task Pane
>
> If you do not want the Getting Started task pane to be displayed each time you start Word, click Tools on the menu bar, click Options, remove the check mark from the Startup Task Pane check box, and then click the OK button.

> **More About**
>
> ### Wizards and Templates
>
> After you create a document using a wizard or template, Word displays the wizard or template name in the Recently used templates area in the New Document task pane. In addition to those installed on your hard disk, Microsoft has more wizards and templates available on the Web that you can download. To access these templates, click the Templates on Office Online link in the Template area in the New Document task pane.

The following steps show how to create a resume using the Resume Wizard. A wizard retains the settings selected by the last person who used the wizard. Thus, the wizard initially may display some text and selections different from the figures shown here. If you are stepping through this project on a computer, be sure to verify that your settings match the screens shown in the following steps before clicking the Next button in each dialog box.

To Create a Resume Using Word's Resume Wizard

1

• **Click File on the menu bar (Figure 3-3).**

FIGURE 3-3

2

• **Click New on the File menu.**

Word displays the New Document task pane (Figure 3-4). You access wizards through the Templates area in the task pane.

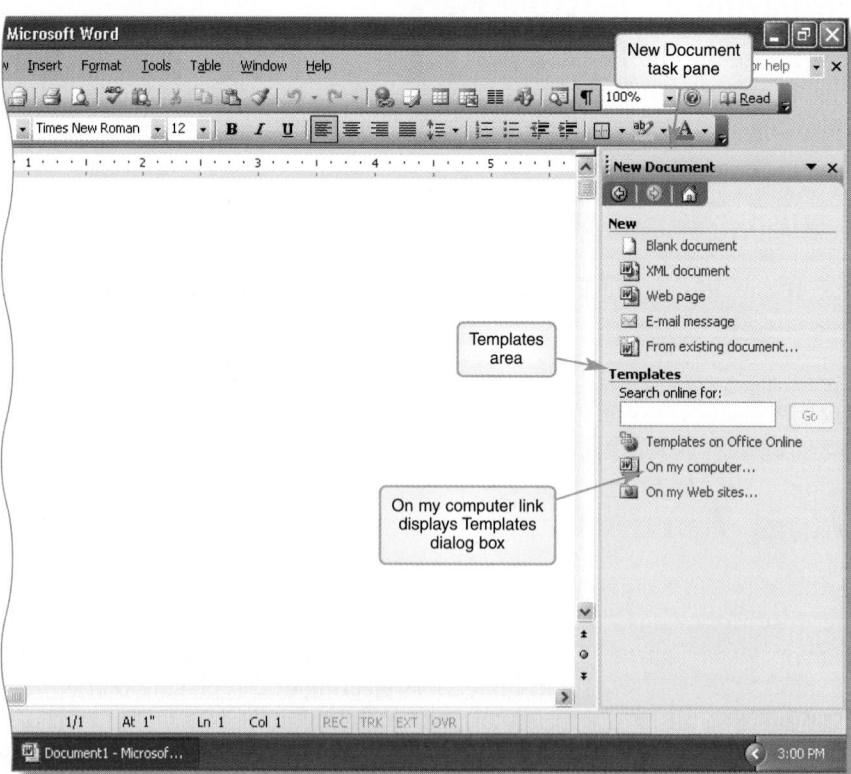

FIGURE 3-4

3

• **Click the On my computer link in the Templates area in the New Document task pane.**

• **When Word displays the Templates dialog box, click the Other Documents tab.**

• **Click the Resume Wizard icon.**

Word displays several wizard and template icons in the Other Documents sheet in the Templates dialog box (Figure 3-5). Icons without the word, wizard, are templates. If you click an icon, the Preview area shows a sample of the resulting document.

FIGURE 3-5

4

• **Click the OK button.**

After a few seconds, Word displays the Start panel in the Resume Wizard dialog box, informing you the Resume Wizard has started (Figure 3-6). This dialog box has a Microsoft Word Help button you can click to obtain help while using the wizard. When you create a document based on a wizard, Word creates a new document window, which is called Document2 in this figure.

FIGURE 3-6

5

• **Click the Next button in the Resume Wizard dialog box.**

• **When the wizard displays the Style panel, if necessary, click Professional.**

The Style panel in the Resume Wizard dialog box requests the style of your resume (Figure 3-7). Three styles of wizards and templates are available in Word: Professional, Contemporary, and Elegant. A sample of each resume style is displayed in this panel.

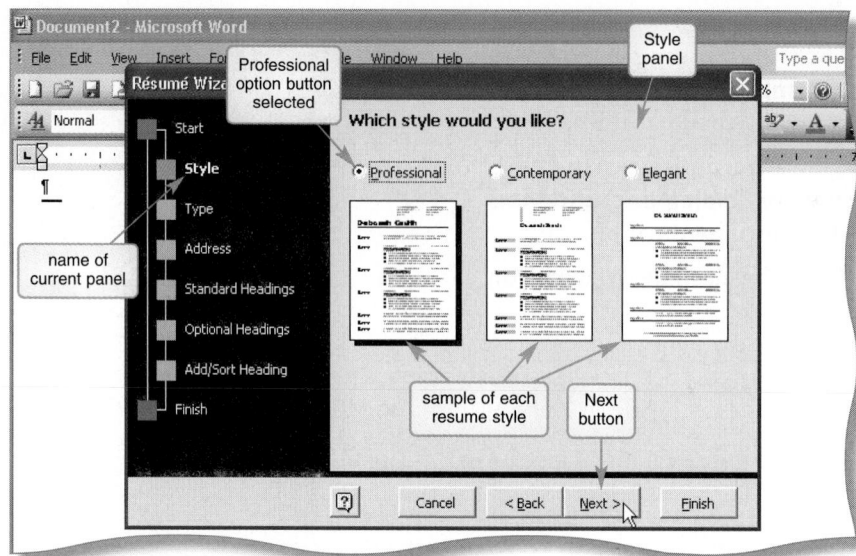

FIGURE 3-7

6

• **Click the Next button.**

• **When the wizard displays the Type panel, if necessary, click Entry-level resume.**

The Type panel in the Resume Wizard dialog box asks for the type of resume that you want to create (Figure 3-8).

FIGURE 3-8

7

• **Click the Next button.**

The Address panel in the Resume Wizard dialog box requests name and mailing address information (Figure 3-9). The name displayed and selected in your Name text box will be different, depending on the name of the last person who used the Resume Wizard.

FIGURE 3-9

8

• **With the name in the Name text box selected, type** Benjamin Kane Okamoto **and then press the TAB key.**

• **Type** 78 Larkspur Road **and then press the ENTER key.**

• **Type** Plantsville, CT 06479 **and then press the TAB key.**

• **Type** (860) 555-4499 **and then press the TAB key.**

• **Type** (860) 555-4490 **and then press the TAB key.**

• **Type** okamoto@earth.net **as the e-mail address.**

As you type the new text, it automatically replaces any selected text (Figure 3-10).

FIGURE 3-10

9

• **Click the Next button.**

• **When the wizard displays the Standard Headings panel, if necessary, click Hobbies and References to remove the check marks. All other check boxes should have check marks. If any do not, place a check mark in the check box by clicking it.**

The Standard Headings panel in the Resume Wizard dialog box requests the headings you want on your resume (Figure 3-11). You want all headings, except for these two: Hobbies and References.

FIGURE 3-11

10

• **Click the Next button.**

• **When the wizard displays the Optional Headings panel, if necessary, remove any check marks from the check boxes.**

The Optional Headings panel in the Resume Wizard dialog box allows you to choose additional headings for your resume (Figure 3-12). All of these check boxes should be empty because none of these headings are on the resume in this project.

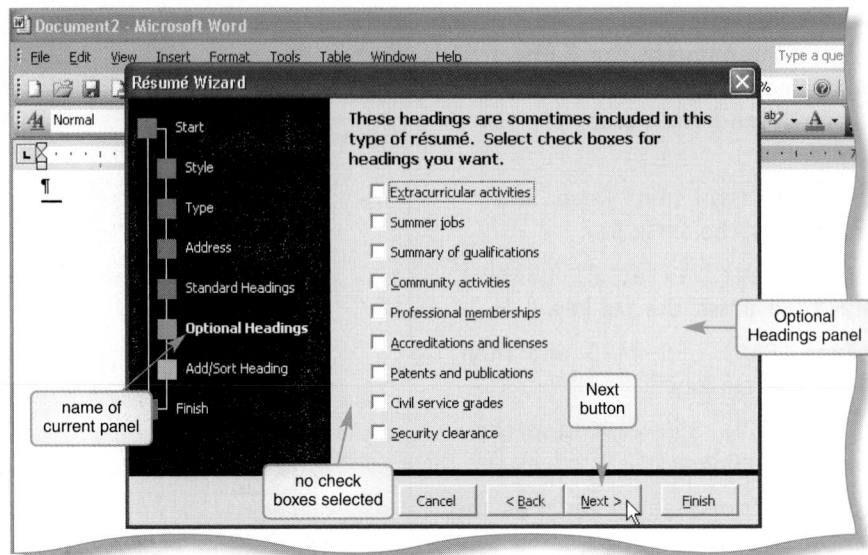

FIGURE 3-12

11

• **Click the Next button.**

• **When the wizard displays the Add/Sort Heading panel, type** Areas of concentration **in the additional headings text box.**

The Add/Sort Heading panel in the Resume Wizard dialog box allows you to enter any additional headings you want on the resume (Figure 3-13).

FIGURE 3-13

12

• **Click the Add button.**

• **Scroll to the bottom of the list of resume headings and then click Areas of concentration.**

The Areas of concentration heading is selected (Figure 3-14). You can rearrange the order of the headings on your resume by selecting a heading and then clicking the appropriate button (Move Up button or Move Down button).

FIGURE 3-14

13

• **Click the Move Up button five times.**

The wizard moves the heading, Areas of concentration, above the Awards received heading (Figure 3-15).

14

• **If the last person using the Resume Wizard included additional headings, you may have some unwanted headings. Your heading list should be as follows: Objective, Education, Areas of concentration, Awards received, Interests and activities, Languages, Work experience, and Volunteer experience. If you have an additional heading(s), click the unwanted heading and then click the Remove button.**

FIGURE 3-15

15

• **Click the Next button.**

The Finish panel in the Resume Wizard dialog box indicates the wizard is ready to create your document (Figure 3-16).

FIGURE 3-16

16

• **Click the Finish button in the Resume Wizard dialog box.**

• **If the Office Assistant appears on the screen, click its Cancel button.**

Word uses a template of an entry-level professional style resume to format a resume on the screen (Figure 3-17). You are to personalize the resume as indicated.

FIGURE 3-17

Other Ways

1. On View menu click Task Pane, click Other Task Panes button on task pane title bar and then click New Document, click On my computer, click Other Documents tab, double-click Resume Wizard icon
2. Click Start button on Windows taskbar, point to All Programs, click New Office Document, click Other Documents tab, double-click Resume Wizard icon
3. With task pane displaying, in Voice Command mode, say "On my computer, Other Documents, [select Resume Wizard], OK"

When you create a resume using the Resume Wizard (Figure 3-16 on the previous page), you can click the panel name or the Back button in any panel of the Resume Wizard dialog box to change the previously selected options. To exit from the Resume Wizard and return to the document window without creating the resume, click the Cancel button in any panel of the Resume Wizard dialog box.

In addition to the Resume Wizard, Word provides many other wizards to assist you in creating documents: agenda for a meeting, calendar, envelope, fax cover sheet, legal pleading, letter, mailing label, and memorandum.

Word displays the resume in the document window in print layout view. You can tell that the document window is in print layout view by looking at the screen (Figure 3-17). In print layout view, the Print Layout View button on the horizontal scroll bar is selected. Also, a vertical ruler is displayed at the left edge of the document window, in addition to the horizontal ruler at the top of the window.

The Word screen was in normal view while creating documents in Project 1 and for most of Project 2. In Project 2, the Word window switched to print layout view when the header was created. In both normal view and print layout view, you can type and edit text. The difference is that **print layout view** shows you an exact view of the printed page. That is, in print layout view, Word places a piece of paper in the document window, showing precisely the positioning of the text, margins, headers, footers, and footnotes.

To display more of the document on the screen in print layout view, you can hide the white space at the top and bottom of the pages and the gray space between pages. The next steps show how to hide the white space, if your screen displays it.

To Hide White Space

1

• **Point to the top of the page in the document window until the Hide White Space button appears.**

The mouse pointer changes to the Hide White Space button when positioned at the top of the page (Figure 3-18).

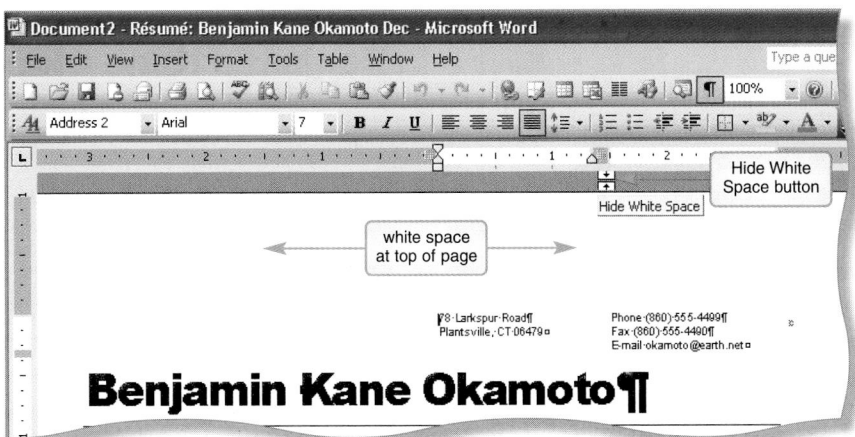

FIGURE 3-18

2

• **Click the Hide White Space button.**

Word removes white space, which causes the page to move up in the document window (Figure 3-19).

FIGURE 3-19

If you wanted to show the white space again, you would point between two pages and click when the mouse pointer changes to a Show White Space button.

To see the entire resume created by the Resume Wizard, print the document shown in the Word window, as described in the following steps.

To Print the Resume Created by the Resume Wizard

1 Ready the printer and then click the Print button on the Standard toolbar.

2 When the printer stops, retrieve the hard copy resume from the printer.

The printed resume is shown in Figure 3-20 on the next page.

resume
generated by
Resume Wizard

78 Larkspur Road
Plantsville, CT 06479

Phone (860) 555-4499
Fax (860) 555-4490
E-mail okamoto@earth.net

Benjamin Kane Okamoto

Objective	[Type Objective Here]
Education	[Dates Attended] [Company/Institution Name] [City, State] **[Degree/Major]** [Details of position, award, or achievement.]
Areas of concentration	[Click here and enter information.]
Awards received	[Click here and enter information.]
Interests and activities	[Click here and enter information.]
Languages	[Click here and enter information.]
Work experience	[Dates Attended] [Company/Institution Name] [City, State] **[Job Title]** [Details of position, award, or achievement.]
Volunteer experience	[Click here and enter information.]

first column
of table

second column
of table

FIGURE 3-20

Personalizing the Resume

The next step is to personalize the resume. Where Word has indicated, you type the objective, education, areas of concentration, awards received, interests and activities, languages, work experience, and volunteer experience next to the respective headings. The following pages show how to personalize the resume generated by the Resume Wizard.

Tables

When the Resume Wizard prepares a resume, it arranges the body of the resume as a table. A Word **table** is a collection of rows and columns. As shown in Figure 3-21, the first column of the table in the resume contains the section headings (Objective, Education, Areas of concentration, Awards received, Interests and activities, Languages, Work experience, and Volunteer experience). The second column of the table contains the details for each of these sections. Thus, this table contains two columns. It also contains eight rows — one row for each section of the resume.

FIGURE 3-21

More About

The Ruler

When the insertion point is in a table, the ruler shows the boundaries of each column in the table. For example, in Figure 3-21, the address information at the top of the resume is a separate table of one row and two columns. The ruler shows the width of each column.

The intersection of a row and a column is called a **cell**, and cells are filled with text. Each cell has an **end-of-cell mark**, which is a formatting mark that assists you with selecting and formatting cells. Recall that formatting marks do not print on a hard copy.

To see the rows, columns, and cells clearly in a Word table, some users prefer to show gridlines. As illustrated in Figure 3-21, **gridlines** help identify the rows and columns in a table. If you want to display gridlines in a table, position the insertion point somewhere in the table, click Table on the menu bar, and then click Show Gridlines. If you want to hide the gridlines, click somewhere in the table, click Table on the menu bar, and then click Hide Gridlines.

You can resize a table, add or delete rows or columns in a table, and format a table. When you point to the upper-left corner of the table, the table move handle appears. Using the table move handle, you can select or move a table. To select a table, click the table move handle; to move the table to a new location, drag the table move handle. These and other features of tables are discussed in more depth later in this project.

Styles

When you use a wizard to create a document, Word formats the document using styles. As discussed in Project 2, a **style** is a named group of formatting characteristics that you can apply to text. The Style box on the Formatting toolbar displays the name of the style associated with the location of the insertion point or selection. You can identify many of the characteristics assigned to a style by looking at the Formatting toolbar. For example, in Figure 3-22 on the next page, the characters in the selected paragraph are formatted with the Objective style, which uses 10-point Arial font.

If you click the Style box arrow on the Formatting toolbar, Word displays the list of styles associated with the current document. You also can select the appropriate style from the Style list before typing text so that the text you type will be formatted according to the selected style.

Another way to work with styles is by clicking the Styles and Formatting button on the Formatting toolbar, which displays the Styles and Formatting task pane. Through the **Styles and Formatting task pane**, you can view, create, and apply styles. The Styles and Formatting task pane is shown later when it is used.

In Word, four basic styles exist: paragraph styles, character styles, list styles, and table styles. **Paragraph styles** affect formatting of an entire paragraph, whereas **character styles** affect formats of only selected characters. **List styles** affect alignment and fonts in a numbered or bulleted list, and **table styles** affect the borders, shading, alignment, and fonts in a Word table. In the Style list and Styles and Formatting task pane, paragraph style names usually are followed by a proofreader's paragraph mark (¶); character style names usually are followed by an underlined letter a (a); list styles usually are followed by a bulleted list icon (≣); and table styles usually are followed by a table icon (⊞).

Selecting and Replacing Text

The next step in personalizing the resume is to select text that the Resume Wizard inserted into the resume and replace it with personal information. The first heading on the resume is the objective. You enter the objective where the Resume Wizard inserted the words, Type Objective Here, which is called **placeholder text**.

To replace text in Word, select the text to be removed and then type the desired text. To select the placeholder text, Type Objective Here, you click it. Then, type the objective. As soon as you begin typing, Word deletes the selected placeholder text. Thus, you do not need to delete the selection before you begin typing.

The following steps show how to enter the objective into the resume.

To Select and Replace Placeholder Text

1

• **Click the placeholder text, Type Objective Here.**

Word selects the placeholder text in the resume (Figure 3-22). Notice the style is Objective in the Style box on the Formatting toolbar.

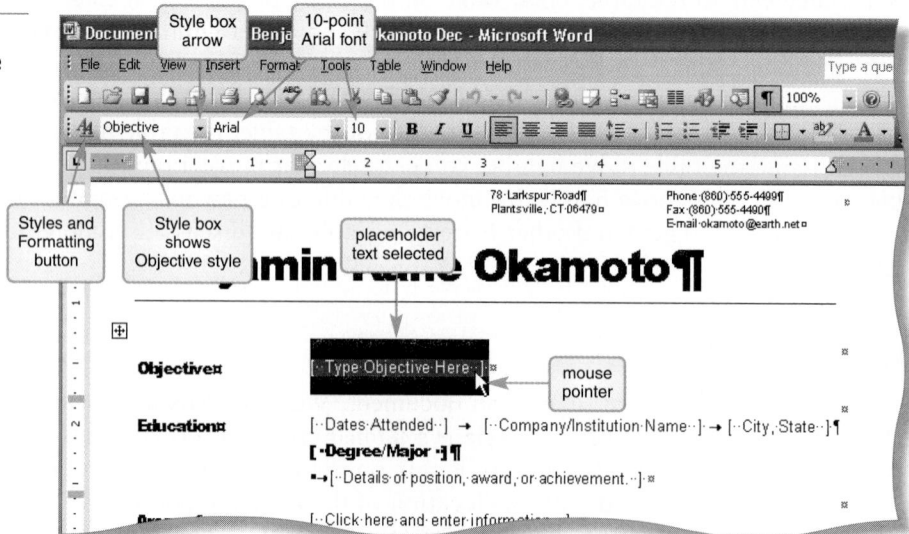

FIGURE 3-22

2

• **Type** To obtain a full-time sales position with a major computer or electronics company in the New England area.

Word replaces the selected placeholder text, Type Objective Here, with the typed objective (Figure 3-23). Your document may wordwrap differently depending on the type of printer you are using.

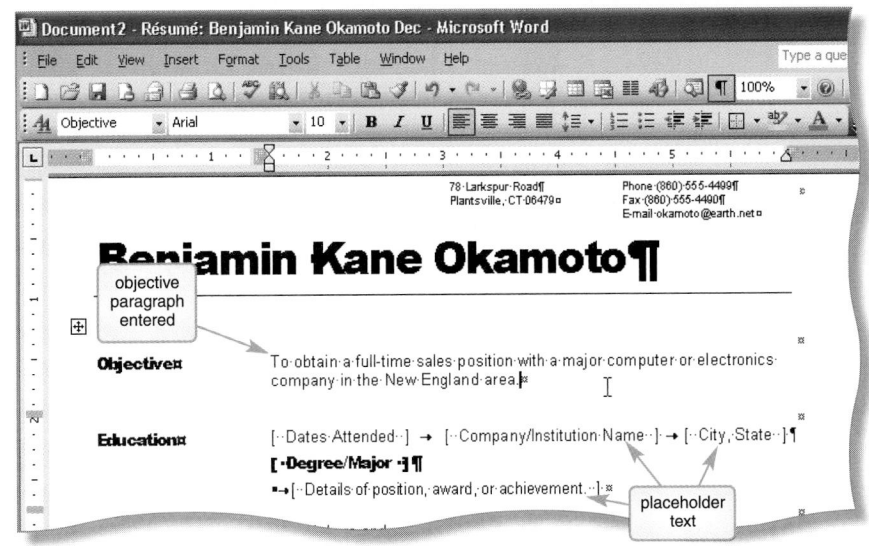

FIGURE 3-23

The next step in personalizing the resume is to replace the placeholder text in the education section of the resume with your own words and phrases, as described in the following steps.

To Select and Replace More Placeholder Text

1 If necessary, scroll down to display the entire education section of the resume. Click, or if necessary drag through, the placeholder text, Dates Attended. **Type** 2001-2005 **and then click the placeholder text, Company/ Institution Name.**

2 **Type** Hartford College **and then click the placeholder text, City, State. Type** Hartford, CT **and then click the placeholder text, Degree/Major. Type** Information and Computer Technology **and then click the placeholder text, Details of position, award, or achievement.**

3 **Type** B.S., December 2005 **and then press the ENTER key. Type** A.S., December 2003 **as the last item in the list.**

The education section is entered (Figure 3-24).

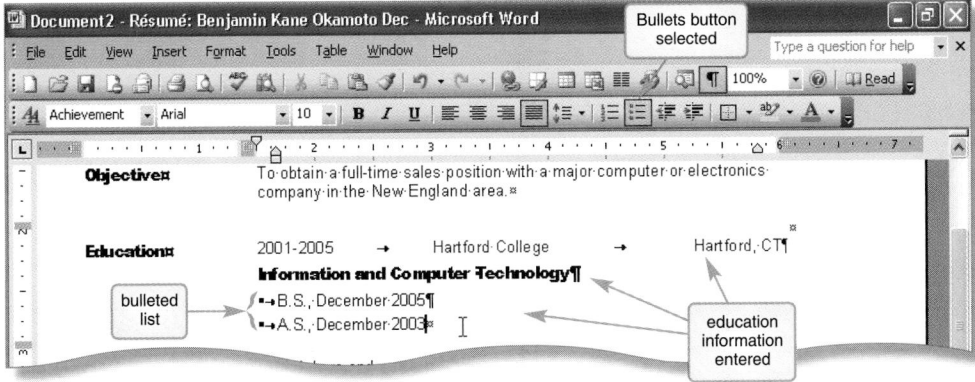

FIGURE 3-24

A **bullet** is a dot or other symbol positioned at the beginning of a paragraph. A **bulleted list** is a list of paragraphs that each begin with a bullet character. For example, the list of degrees in the education section of the resume is a bulleted list (Figure 3-24 on the previous page). When the insertion point is in a paragraph containing a bullet, the Bullets button on the Formatting toolbar is selected. In a bulleted list, each time you press the ENTER key, a bullet displays at the beginning of the new paragraph. This is because Word carries forward paragraph formatting when you press the ENTER key.

Entering a Line Break

The next step in personalizing the resume is to enter four lines of text in the areas of concentration section. The style used for the characters in the areas of concentration section of the resume is the Objective style. A paragraph formatting characteristic of the Objective style is that when you press the ENTER key, the insertion point advances downward at least 11 points, which leaves nearly an entire blank line between each paragraph.

You want the lines within the areas of concentration section to be close to each other, as shown in Figure 3-1 on page WD 139. Thus, you will not press the ENTER key between each area of concentration. Instead, you press SHIFT+ENTER to create a **line break**, which advances the insertion point to the beginning of the next physical line.

The following steps show how to enter text in the areas of concentration section using a line break, instead of a paragraph break, between each line.

To Enter a Line Break

1

• **If necessary, scroll down to display the areas of concentration section of the resume.**

• **In the areas of concentration section, click the placeholder text, Click here and enter information.**

• **Type** Computer Hardware **and then press SHIFT+ENTER.**

*Word inserts a **line break character**, which is a formatting mark for a line break at the end of a line, and moves the insertion point to the beginning of the next physical line (Figure 3-25).*

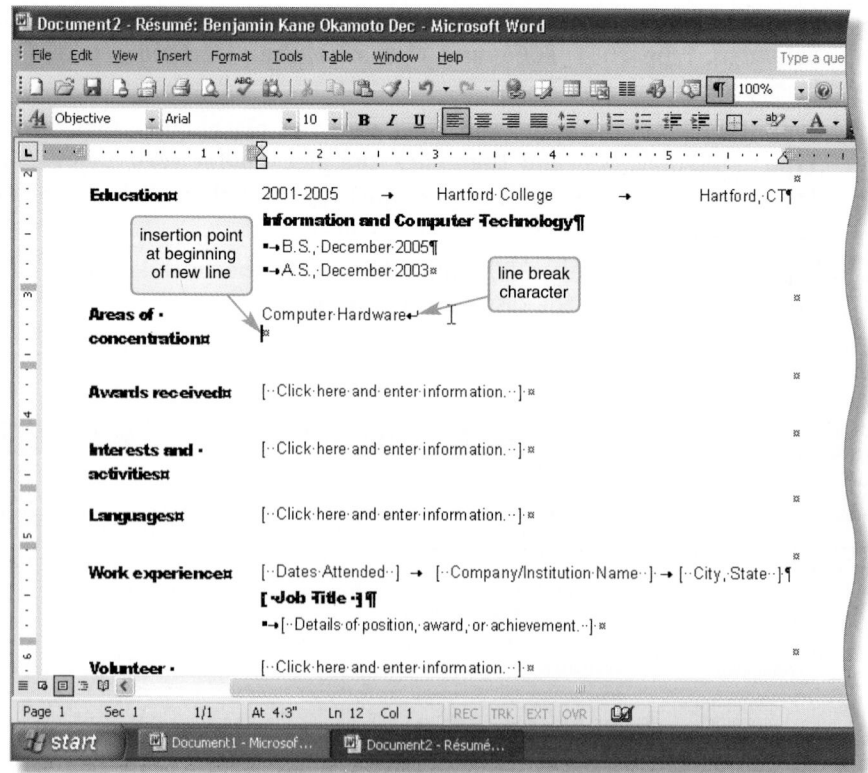

FIGURE 3-25

2

• **Type** Computer Software and Programming **and then press** SHIFT+ENTER.

• **Type** Professional Communications **and then press** SHIFT+ENTER.

• **Type** Business **as the last entry. Do not press** SHIFT+ENTER **at the end of this line.**

The areas of concentration section is entered (Figure 3-26).

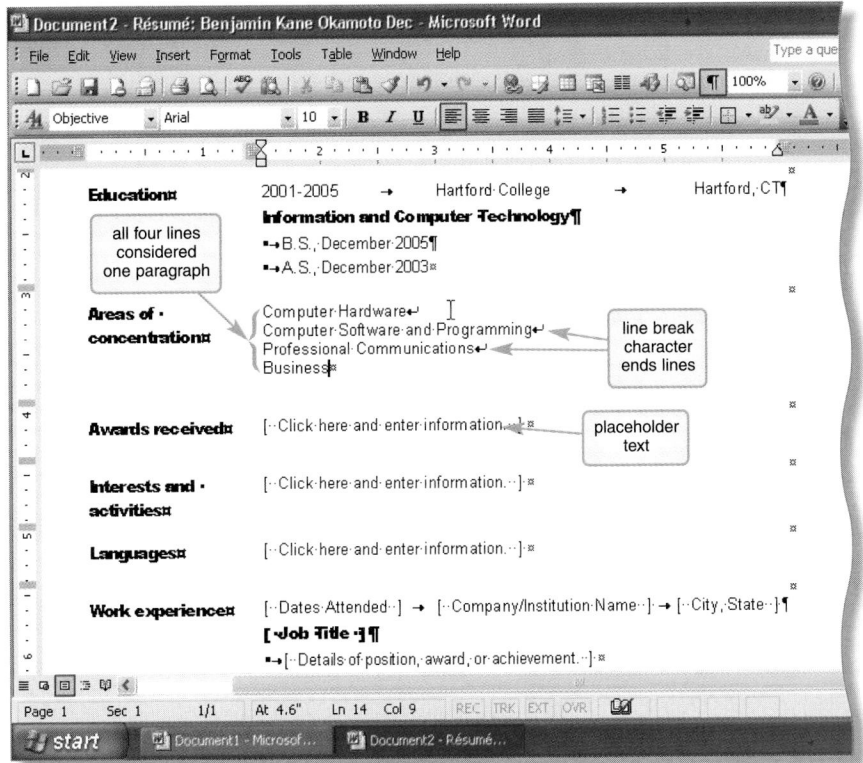

FIGURE 3-26

The next step is to enter the first two awards in the awards received section of the resume.

To Enter More Text with Line Breaks

1 If necessary, scroll down to display the awards received section of the resume. In the awards received section, click the placeholder text, Click here and enter information. **Type** Dean's List, every semester **and then press** SHIFT+ENTER.

2 **Type** Gamma Phi Sigma Honors Society, 2002-2005 **and then press** SHIFT+ENTER.

The first two awards are entered in the awards received section (shown in Figure 3-27 on the next page).

AutoFormat As You Type

As you type text in a document, Word automatically formats it for you. Table 3-1 on the next page outlines commonly used AutoFormat As You Type options and their results.

More About

AutoFormat

For an AutoFormat option to work as expected, it must be turned on. To check if an AutoFormat option is enabled, click Tools on the menu bar, click AutoCorrect Options, click the AutoFormat As You Type tab, select the appropriate check boxes, and then click the OK button.

Table 3-1   Commonly Used AutoFormat As You Type Options

TYPED TEXT	AUTOFORMAT FEATURE	EXAMPLE
Quotation marks or apostrophes	Changes straight quotation marks or apostrophes to curly ones	"the" becomes "the"
Text, a space, one hyphen, one or no spaces, text, space	Changes the hyphen to an en dash	ages 20 - 45 becomes ages 20 – 45
Text, two hyphens, text, space	Changes the two hyphens to an em dash	Two types--yellow and red becomes Two types—yellow and red
Web or e-mail address followed by space or ENTER key	Formats Web or e-mail address as a hyperlink	www.scsite.com becomes www.scsite.com
Three hyphens, underscores, equal signs, asterisks, tildes, or number signs and then ENTER key	Places a border above a paragraph	--- This line becomes _____ This line
Number followed by a period, hyphen, right parenthesis, or greater than sign and then a space or tab followed by text	Creates a numbered list when you press the ENTER key	1. Word 2. Excel becomes 1. Word 2. Excel
Asterisk, hyphen, or greater than sign and then a space or tab followed by text	Creates a bulleted list when you press the ENTER key	* Standard toolbar * Formatting toolbar becomes • Standard toolbar • Formatting toolbar
Fraction and then a space or hyphen	Converts the entry to a fraction-like notation	1/2 becomes ½
Ordinal and then a space or hyphen	Makes the ordinal a superscript	3rd becomes 3rd

The next step in this project is to enter an ordinal (1st) and see how Word automatically makes the ordinal a superscript.

To AutoFormat As You Type

• **Type** Hartford College Outstanding Senior, 1st **(Figure 3-27).**

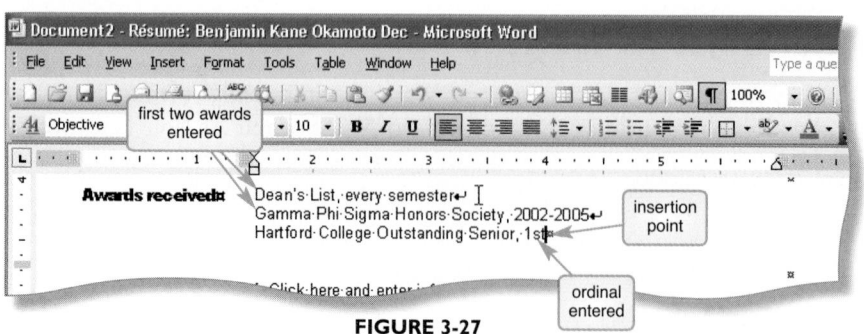

FIGURE 3-27

2

- **Press the SPACEBAR.**

- **Type** Place, 2005 **as the end of the award.**

Word automatically converts the st in 1st to a superscript (Figure 3-28).

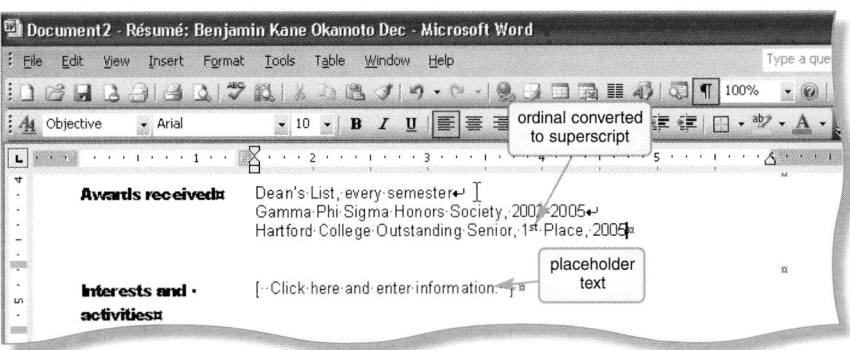

FIGURE 3-28

The next step is to enter the remaining text for the resume, as described below.

To Enter the Remaining Sections of the Resume

1 **If necessary, scroll down to display the interests and activities section of the resume. Click the placeholder text, Click here and enter information. Type** Association of Sales Representatives, junior member **and then press SHIFT+ENTER.**

2 **Type** Big Brothers Big Sisters of Hartford, volunteer **and then press SHIFT+ENTER.**

3 **Type** Computer Club, treasurer **and then press SHIFT+ENTER.**

4 **Type** New England Ski Club, publicity coordinator **as the last activity. Do not press SHIFT+ENTER at the end of this line.**

5 **If necessary, scroll down to display the languages section of the resume. Click the placeholder text, Click here and enter information. Type** English (fluent) **and then press SHIFT+ENTER.**

6 **Type** Japanese (fluent) **and then press SHIFT+ENTER.**

7 **Type** Knowledge of sign language **as the last language. Do not press SHIFT+ENTER at the end of this line.**

8 **If necessary, scroll down to display the work experience section of the resume. Click, or if necessary drag through, the placeholder text, Dates Attended. Type** 2002-2005 **as the years.**

9 **Click the placeholder text, Company/Institution Name. Type** Computer Discount Sales **and then click the placeholder text, City, State. Type** Plantsville, CT **and then click the placeholder text, Job Title. Type** Intern **as the title.**

10 **Click the placeholder text, Details of position, award, or achievement. Type** Sold hardware and software components to home and small business customers **and then press the ENTER key.**

11 **Type** Arranged and configured in-store computer hardware, software, and network displays **and then press the ENTER key.**

12 **Type** Logged and replied to computer-related customer e-mail, fax, and telephone inquiries **as the last item in the list.**

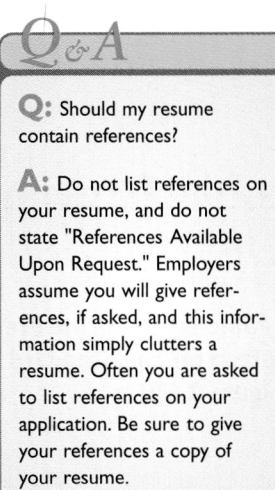

Q: Should my resume contain references?

A: Do not list references on your resume, and do not state "References Available Upon Request." Employers assume you will give references, if asked, and this information simply clutters a resume. Often you are asked to list references on your application. Be sure to give your references a copy of your resume.

13 If necessary, scroll down to display the volunteer experience section of the resume. Click the placeholder text, Click here and enter information. Type `As a Big Brother, I spend at least eight hours every week with my Little Brother - hoping to make a difference in this youth's life.` **Do not press the ENTER key at the end of this line.**

The interests and activities, languages, work experience, and volunteer experience sections of the resume are complete (Figure 3-29).

FIGURE 3-29

Notice when you typed the hyphen in the volunteer experience section of the resume (Step 13) that Word automatically formatted it as an en dash as you typed.

Viewing and Printing the Resume in Print Preview

To see exactly how a document will look when you print it, you could display it in print preview. **Print preview** displays the entire document in reduced size on the Word screen. In print preview, you can edit and format text, adjust margins, view multiple pages, reduce the document to fit on a single page, and print the document.

The following steps show how to view and print the resume in print preview.

To Print Preview a Document

1

• **Point to the Print Preview button on the Standard toolbar (Figure 3-30).**

FIGURE 3-30

2

• **Click the Print Preview button.**

Word displays the document in print preview (Figure 3-31). The Print Preview toolbar is displayed below the menu bar; the Standard and Formatting toolbars disappear from the screen.

3

• **Click the Print button on the Print Preview toolbar.**

• **Click the Close Preview button on the Print Preview toolbar.**

Word prints the resume, as shown in Figure 3-1 on page WD 139. When you close print preview, Word redisplays the resume in the document window.

FIGURE 3-31

Saving the Resume

The resume now is complete. Thus, you should save it. For a detailed example of the procedure summarized below, refer to pages WD 28 through WD 30 in Project 1.

To Save a Document

1 **Insert your floppy disk into drive A.**

2 **Click the Save button on the Standard toolbar.**

3 **Type** Okamoto Resume **in the File name text box. Do not press the ENTER key.**

4 **Click the Save in box arrow and then click 3½ Floppy (A:).**

5 **Click the Save button in the Save As dialog box.**

Word saves the document on a floppy disk in drive A with the file name, Okamoto Resume.

Do not close the Okamoto Resume. You will use it again later in this project to copy the address, telephone, fax, and e-mail information.

Creating a Letterhead

You have created a resume to send to prospective employers. Along with the resume, you will enclose a personalized cover letter. Thus, the next step in Project 3 is to create a cover letter to send with the resume to a potential employer. You would like the cover letter to have a professional looking letterhead (Figure 3-2a on page WD 140).

In many businesses, letterhead is preprinted on stationery that everyone in a company uses for correspondence. For personal letters, the cost of preprinted letterhead can be high. An alternative is to create your own letterhead and save it in a file. At a later time, when you want to create a letter using the letterhead, simply open the letterhead file and then save the file with a new name – to preserve the original letterhead file.

The steps on the following pages illustrate how to use Word to create a personal letterhead file.

Opening a New Document Window

The resume currently is displayed in the document window. The resume document should remain open because you intend to use it again during this Word session. That is, you will be working with two documents at the same time: the resume and the letterhead. Word will display each of these documents in a separate document window.

The following step opens a new document window for the letterhead file.

To Open a New Document Window

1

• **Click the New Blank Document button on the Standard toolbar.**

Word opens a new document window (Figure 3-32).

FIGURE 3-32

The Okamoto Resume document still is open. The program buttons on the taskbar display the names of the open Word document windows. The Document3 button on the taskbar is selected, indicating that it is the active document currently displayed in the Word document window.

The next step is to change the font size to 20 because you want the name in the letterhead to be a larger font size than the body of the letter. The next steps describe how to change the font size.

To Change the Font Size

1 **Click the Font Size box arrow on the Formatting toolbar.**

2 **Click 20 in the Font Size list.**

Word changes the font size to 20 (shown in Figure 3-33 below).

Changing Color of Text

The text in the letterhead is to be brown. The following steps show how to change the color of the text before you type.

To Color Text

1

• **Click the Font Color button arrow on the Formatting toolbar.**

Word displays a list of available colors on the color palette (Figure 3-33). The color that displays below the letter A on the Font Color button is the most recently used text color. Your button may show a different color.

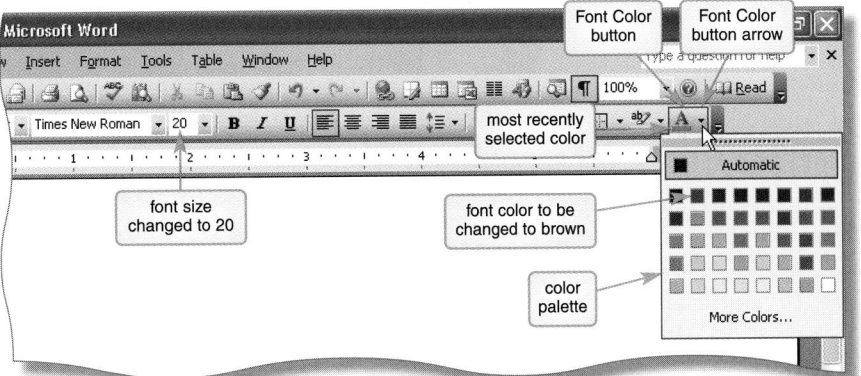

FIGURE 3-33

2

• **Click Brown, which is the second color on the first row of the color palette.**

• **Type** Benjamin Kane Okamoto **and then press the ENTER key.**

Word displays the first line of the letterhead in brown (Figure 3-34).

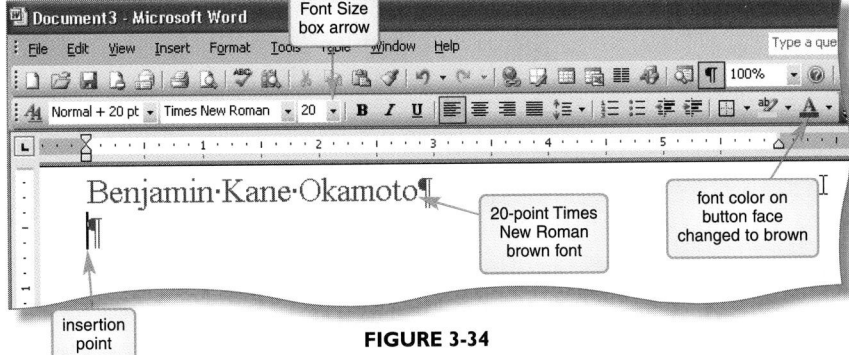

FIGURE 3-34

Notice the paragraph mark on line 2 is brown. Recall that each time you press the ENTER key, Word carries forward formatting to the next paragraph. If, for some reason, you wanted to change the text back to black at this point, you would click the Font Color button arrow on the Formatting toolbar and then click Automatic on the color palette. Automatic is the default color, which usually is black.

The next step is to reduce the font size of text entered into the second line in the letterhead. The address, telephone, fax, and e-mail information is to be a font size of 9. The steps on the next page describe how to change the font size.

To Change the Font Size

1 **With the insertion point on line 2 as shown in Figure 3-34 on the previous page, click the Font Size box arrow on the Formatting toolbar.**

2 **Click 9 in the Font Size list.**

At the location of the insertion point, Word changes the font size to 9 (shown in Figure 3-37).

Inserting and Resizing a Graphic

The letterhead has a graphic of a computer on line 2 below the job seeker's name. The following steps describe how to insert this graphic.

To Insert a Graphic

1 **With the insertion point below the name on line 2, click Insert on the menu bar, point to Picture, and then click Clip Art on the Picture submenu.**

2 **When Word displays the Clip Art task pane, if necessary, drag through any text in the Search for text box to select the text. Type** computer **and then click the Go button.**

3 **Scroll through the list of results until you locate the graphic of a computer that matches, or is similar to, the one shown in Figure 3-35. Click the graphic of the computer to insert it in the document.**

4 **Click the Close button on the Clip Art task pane title bar.**

Word inserts the graphic of the computer at the location of the insertion point (shown in Figure 3-35).

The next step is to reduce the size of the graphic to 40 percent of its current size. Instead of dragging the sizing handle, you can use the Format Picture dialog box to set exact size measurements. The following steps show how to resize a graphic using the Format Picture dialog box.

To Resize a Graphic

1

• **Position the mouse pointer in the graphic (in this case, the computer) and then double-click.**

• **When Word displays the Format Picture dialog box, click the Size tab.**

The Size sheet allows you to specify exact measurements of the selected graphic (Figure 3-35).

FIGURE 3-35

2

- **In the Scale area, double-click the Height box to select it.**
- **Type** 40 **and then press the TAB key.**

Word displays 40 % in the Height and Width boxes (Figure 3-36). When you press the TAB key from the Height box, the insertion point moves to the Width box and automatically changes the width to 40 % - to match the height proportionately.

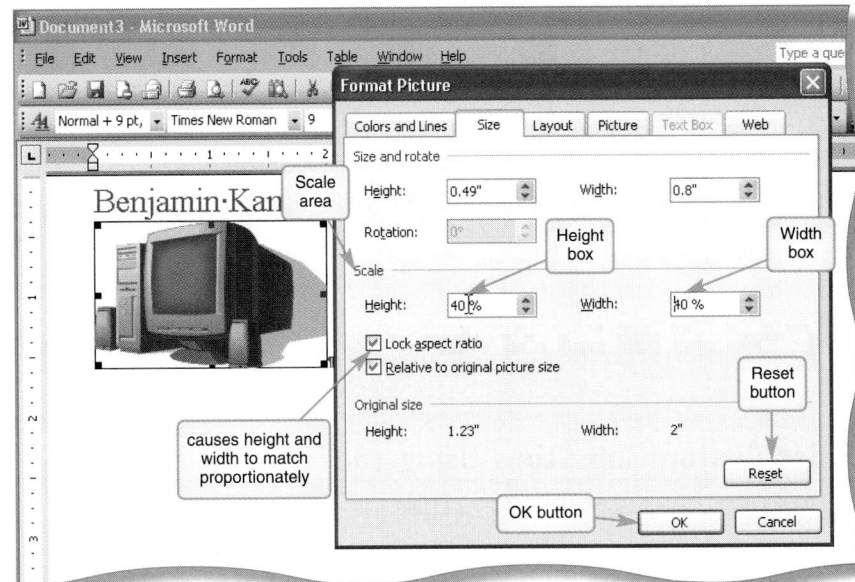

FIGURE 3-36

3

- **Click the OK button in the Format Picture dialog box.**
- **Press the END key to move the insertion point to the paragraph mark to the right of the graphic.**

Word resizes the graphic to 40 percent of its original size (Figure 3-37).

FIGURE 3-37

Sometimes, you might resize a graphic and realize it is the wrong size. In this case, you may want to return the graphic to its original size and start again. To restore a resized graphic to its exact original size, click the Reset button in the Format Picture dialog box (Figure 3-36).

Setting Tab Stops Using the Tabs Dialog Box

The graphic of the computer is left-aligned (Figure 3-37). The address information in the letterhead is to be positioned at the right margin of the same line. If you click the Align Right button, the graphic will be right-aligned. In Word, a paragraph cannot be both left-aligned and right-aligned. To place text at the right margin of a left-aligned paragraph, you set a tab stop at the right margin.

A **tab stop** is a location on the horizontal ruler that tells Word where to position the insertion point when you press the TAB key on the keyboard. A tab stop is useful for indenting and aligning text.

Other Ways

1. Select the graphic, drag the graphic's sizing handle
2. Click Format Picture button on Picture toolbar, click Size tab, enter desired height and width, click OK button
3. In Voice Command mode, say "Format, Picture"

Word, by default, places a tab stop at every .5" mark on the ruler (shown in Figure 3-39). These default tab stops are indicated at the bottom of the horizontal ruler by small vertical tick marks. You also can set your own custom tab stops. When you set a **custom tab stop**, Word clears all default tab stops to the left of the custom tab stop. You specify how the text will align at a tab stop: left, centered, right, or decimal. Tab settings are a paragraph format. Thus, each time you press the ENTER key, any custom tab stops are carried forward to the next paragraph.

In the letterhead for this project, you want the tab stop to be right-aligned with the right margin, that is, at the 6" mark on the ruler. One method of setting custom tab stops is to click the ruler at the desired location of the tab stop. You cannot click, however, at the right margin location. Thus, use the Tabs dialog box to set a custom tab stop at the 6" mark, as shown in the following steps.

To Set Custom Tab Stops Using the Tabs Dialog Box

1

• **With the insertion point positioned between the paragraph mark and the graphic, click Format on the menu bar (Figure 3-38).**

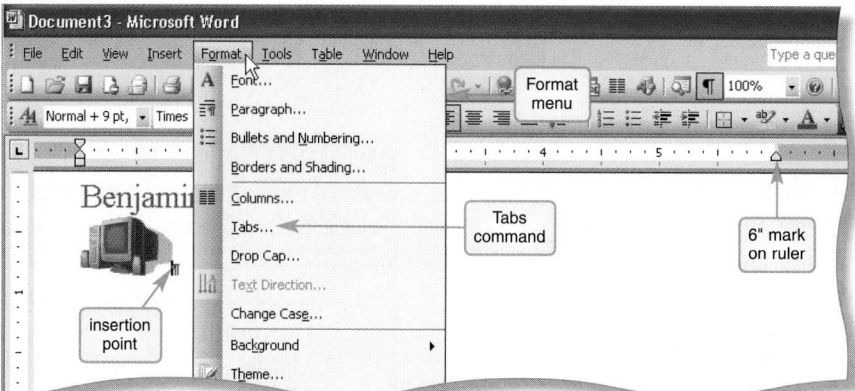

FIGURE 3-38

2

• **Click Tabs on the Format menu.**

• **When Word displays the Tabs dialog box, type 6 in the Tab stop position text box.**

• **Click Right in the Alignment area.**

The Tabs dialog box allows you to set and clear custom tabs (Figure 3-39).

FIGURE 3-39

3

• **Click the Set button in the Tabs dialog box.**
• **Click the OK button.**

*Word places a right tab marker at the 6"
mark on the ruler and removes all default
tab stops to the left of the tab marker on
the ruler (Figure 3-40).*

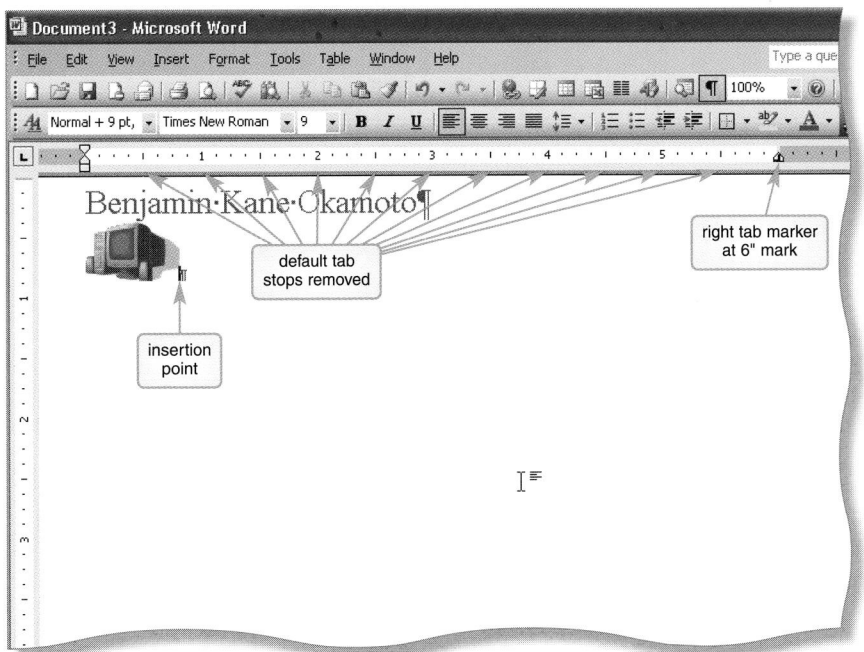

FIGURE 3-40

When you set a custom tab stop, the tab marker on the ruler reflects the alignment of the characters at the location of the tab stop. A capital letter L (⌐) indicates a left-aligned tab stop. A mirror image of a capital letter L (⌐) indicates a right-aligned tab stop. An upside down T (⊥) indicates a centered tab stop. An upside down T with a dot next to it (⊥) indicates a decimal-aligned tab stop. Specific tab markers are discussed as they are presented in these projects. The tab marker on the ruler in Figure 3-40 indicates text entered at that tab stop will be right-aligned.

To move the insertion point from one tab stop to another, press the TAB key on the keyboard. When you press the TAB key, a **tab character** formatting mark appears in the empty space between the tab stops.

Collecting and Pasting

The next step in creating the letterhead is to copy the address, telephone, fax, and e-mail information from the resume to the letterhead. To copy multiple items from one Office document to another, you use the Office Clipboard. The **Office Clipboard** is a temporary storage area that holds up to 24 items (text or graphics) copied from any Office application. You copy, or **collect**, items and then paste them in a new location. **Pasting** is the process of copying an item from the Office Clipboard into the document at the location of the insertion point. When you paste an item into a document, the contents of the Office Clipboard are not erased.

To copy the address, telephone, fax, and e-mail information from the resume to the letterhead, you first switch to the resume document, copy the items from the resume to the Office Clipboard, switch back to the letterhead document, and then paste the information from the Office Clipboard into the letterhead. The following pages illustrate this process.

The step below switches from the letterhead document to the resume document.

To Switch from One Open Document to Another

1

• **Click the Okamoto Resume - Microsoft Word program button on the Windows taskbar.**

Word switches from the letterhead document to the resume document (Figure 3-41). The letterhead document (Document3) still is open.

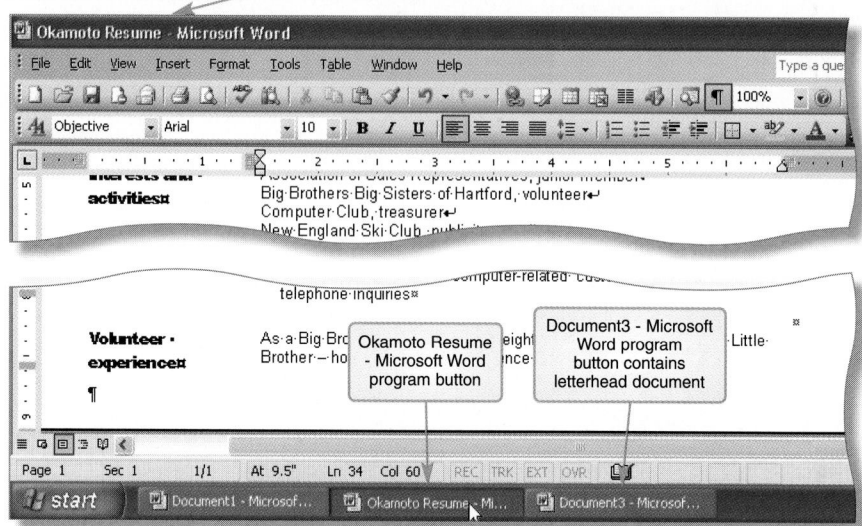

FIGURE 3-41

Other Ways

1. On Window menu click document name
2. Press ALT+TAB
3. In Voice Command mode, say "Window [document number]"

You can copy multiple items to the Office Clipboard and then can paste them later. Each copied item appears as an entry in the Office Clipboard gallery in the Clipboard task pane. The entry displays an icon that indicates the Office program from which the item was copied. The entry also displays a portion of text that was copied or a thumbnail of a graphic that was copied. The most recently copied item is displayed at the top of the gallery.

The following steps show how to copy five items to the Office Clipboard.

To Copy Items to the Office Clipboard

1

• **Press CTRL+HOME to display the top of the resume in the document window.**

• **Click Edit on the menu bar (Figure 3-42).**

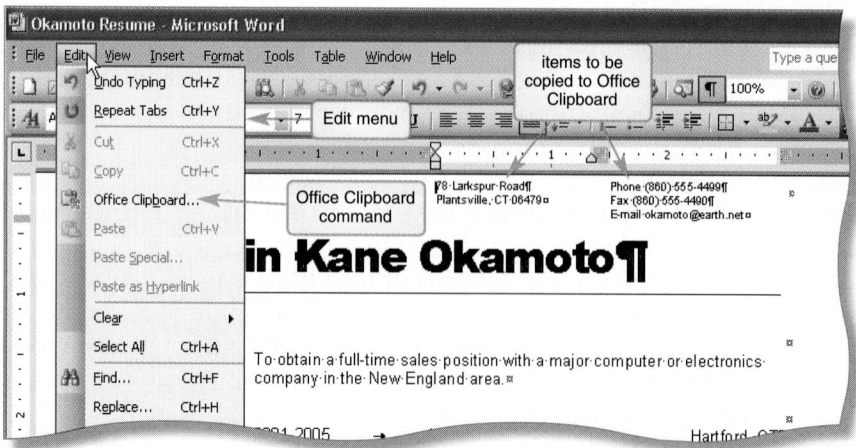

FIGURE 3-42

2

• **Click Office Clipboard on the Edit menu.**

• **If the Office Clipboard gallery in the Clipboard task pane is not empty, click the Clear All button in the Clipboard task pane.**

• **Scroll to the right to display all of the telephone, fax, and e-mail information in the resume.**

• **In the resume, drag through the street address, 78 Larkspur Road.**

Word displays the Clipboard task pane on the screen (Figure 3-43). The Office Clipboard icon appears in the notification area on the Windows taskbar, indicating the Office Clipboard is displayed in at least one open Office program.

FIGURE 3-43

3

• **Click the Copy button on the Standard toolbar.**

Word copies the selection to the Office Clipboard and places an entry in the Office Clipboard gallery in the Clipboard task pane (Figure 3-44).

FIGURE 3-44

4

- Drag through the city, state, and postal code information and then click the Copy button on the Standard toolbar.

- Drag through the telephone information and then click the Copy button on the Standard toolbar.

- Drag through the fax information and then click the Copy button on the Standard toolbar.

- Drag through the e-mail information and then click the Copy button on the Standard toolbar (Figure 3-45).

FIGURE 3-45

Each time you copy an item to the Office Clipboard, a ScreenTip appears above the Office Clipboard icon in the notification area on the Windows taskbar, indicating the number of entries currently in the Office Clipboard. The Office Clipboard stores up to 24 items at one time. When you copy a 25th item, Word deletes the first item to make room for the new item. When you point to a text entry in the Office Clipboard gallery in the Clipboard task pane, the first several characters of text in the item display as a ScreenTip.

The next step is to paste the copied items into the letterhead. When you switch to another document, the Clipboard task pane might not be displayed on the screen. You could display it by clicking Edit on the menu bar and then clicking Office Clipboard. If the Office Clipboard icon is displayed in the notification area on the Windows taskbar, however, you can double-click the icon to display the Clipboard task pane, as described in the next step.

To Display the Clipboard Task Pane

1

- **Click the Document3 - Microsoft Word button on the Windows taskbar to display the letterhead.**
- **Double-click the Office Clipboard icon in the notification area on the Windows taskbar.**

Word displays the Clipboard task pane on the screen (Figure 3-46). The Office Clipboard gallery shows the items contained on the Clipboard.

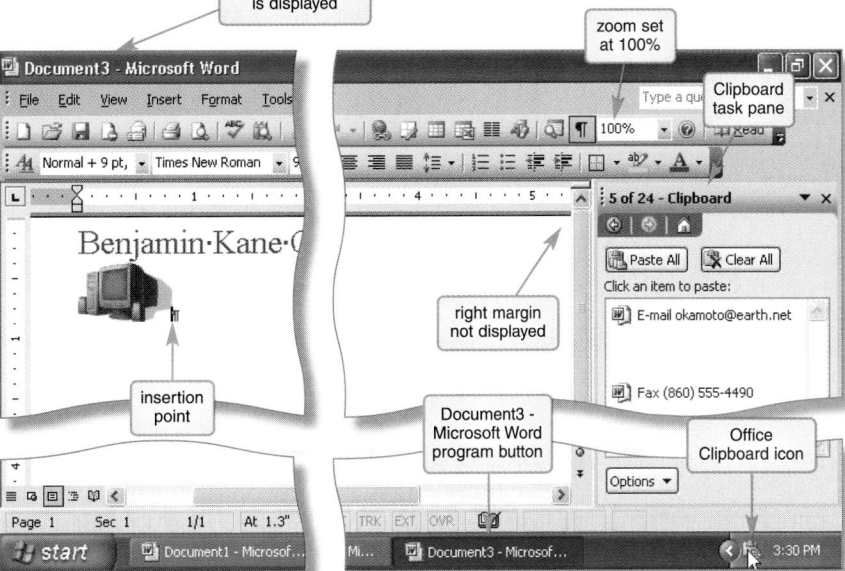

FIGURE 3-46

The next step is to press the TAB key to position the insertion point at the location where the text will be copied. Recall that the address information is to be located at the right margin of the document window. Notice in Figure 3-46 that the right margin is not displayed on the screen when the task pane also is on the screen.

Depending on your Windows and Word settings, the horizontal ruler at the top of the document window may show more inches or fewer inches than the ruler shown in Figure 3-46. Two factors that affect how much of the ruler displays in the document window are the Windows screen resolution and the Word zoom percentage. The more inches of ruler that display, the smaller the text will be on the screen. The fewer inches of ruler that display, the larger the text will be on the screen.

To view both the right and left margins on the screen beside the Clipboard task pane, you need to change the zoom percent, which in this project is set at 100 percent. The following steps show how to let Word determine the best percentage to zoom when showing both the left and right margins at the same time.

More About

The Office Clipboard Icon

If the Office Clipboard icon does not appear on the Windows taskbar, click the Options button at the bottom of the Clipboard task pane and then click Show Office Clipboard icon on Taskbar.

To Zoom Text Width

1

- **Click the Zoom box arrow on the Standard toolbar (Figure 3-47).**

FIGURE 3-47

2

• **Click Text Width in the Zoom list.**

Word places the margins of the document in the window (Figure 3-48).

FIGURE 3-48

If Text Width is not available in your Zoom list, then your document window is in normal view. Text Width is available only in print layout view. To switch to print layout view, click View on the menu bar and then click Print Layout.

The Zoom box in Figure 3-48 displays 89%, which Word computes based on a variety of settings. Your percentage may be different depending on your computer configuration.

When you paste items into a document, Word displays the Paste Options button on the screen. The Paste Options button allows you to change the format of pasted items. For example, you can instruct Word to format the pasted text the same as the text from where it was copied or format it the same as the text to where it was pasted. You also can have Word remove all extra non-text characters that were pasted. For example, if you included a paragraph mark when copying at the end of a line in the address of the resume, the Paste Options button allows you to remove the paragraph marks from the pasted text.

The following steps show how to paste the address information from the Office Clipboard into the letterhead – removing any extraneous paragraph marks after pasting.

To Paste from the Office Clipboard

1

• **With the insertion point between the paragraph mark and the computer graphic (shown in Figure 3-48), press the TAB key.**

• **Click the bottom (first) entry in the Office Clipboard gallery.**

• **Click the Paste Options button.**

Word pastes the contents of the clicked item at the location of the insertion point, which is at the 6" mark on the ruler, and then displays the Paste Options menu (Figure 3-49). Depending on the format of the copied text, the pasted text may not be aligned or formatted as shown in this figure. The next step fixes any formatting problems in the pasted text.

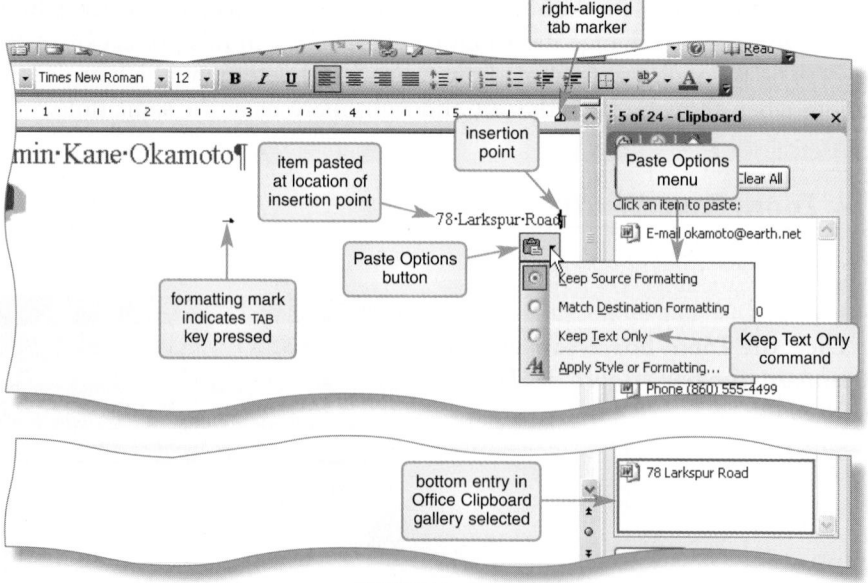

FIGURE 3-49

2

• **Click Keep Text Only on the Paste Options menu.**

• **Press the COMMA key. Press the SPACEBAR.**

• **Click the second entry (city, state, postal code) in the Office Clipboard gallery.**

• **Click the Paste Options button and then click Keep Text Only.**

The city, state, and postal code from the Office Clipboard are pasted into the letterhead (Figure 3-50). The Keep Text Only command removes any extraneous paragraph marks from the pasted text.

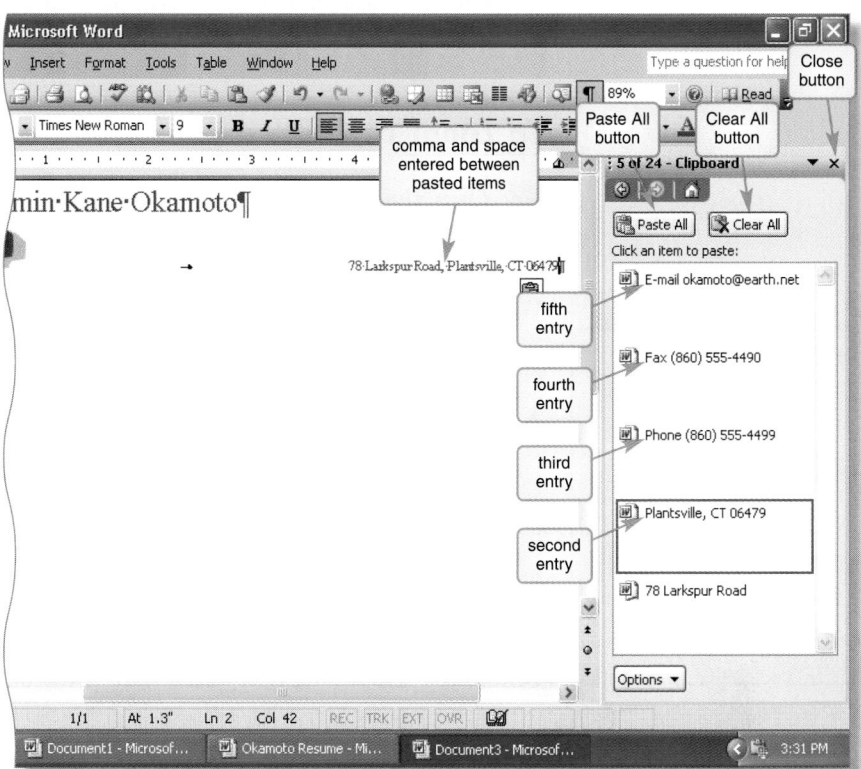

FIGURE 3-50

If you wanted to paste all items in a row without any characters in between them, you would click the Paste All button in the Clipboard task pane. If you wanted to erase all items on the Office Clipboard, you would click the Clear All button in the Clipboard task pane.

The following steps discuss how to paste the telephone, fax, and e-mail information into the letterhead from the resume.

To Paste More Information from the Office Clipboard

1 Press the ENTER key. Press the TAB key. Click the third entry (telephone) in the Office Clipboard gallery. Click the Paste Options button and then click Keep Text Only.

2 Press the COMMA key. Press the SPACEBAR. Click the fourth entry (fax) in the Office Clipboard gallery. Click the Paste Options button and then click Keep Text Only.

3 Press the COMMA key. Press the SPACEBAR. Click the fifth entry (e-mail) in the Office Clipboard gallery. Click the Paste Options button and then click Keep Text Only.

4 Click the Close button in the upper-right corner of the Clipboard task pane title bar to close the task pane.

All items are pasted from the Office Clipboard into the letterhead (shown in Figure 3-51 on the next page). The Clipboard task pane is closed.

Other Ways

1. With Clipboard task pane displayed, on Edit menu click Paste
2. With Clipboard task pane displayed, right-click selected item, click Paste on shortcut menu
3. With Clipboard task pane displayed, press CTRL+V
4. With Clipboard task pane displayed, in Voice Command mode, say "Paste"

More About

The Office Clipboard Gallery

To delete an item from the Office Clipboard gallery, point to the item in the gallery, click the box arrow to the right of the item, and then click Delete.

With the task pane closed, you now can return the zoom percentage of the document window to 100 percent, as described in the following steps.

To Zoom to 100%

1 **Click the Zoom box arrow on the Standard toolbar.**

2 **Click 100% in the Zoom list.**

Word changes the zoom to 100% (shown in Figure 3-51).

Adding a Bottom Border to a Paragraph

To add professionalism to the letterhead, you can draw a horizontal line from the left margin to the right margin immediately below the telephone, fax, and e-mail information. In Word, you draw a solid line, called a **border**, at any edge of a paragraph. That is, borders may be added above or below a paragraph, to the left or right of a paragraph, or any combination of these sides.

The following steps show how to add a bottom border to the paragraph containing telephone, fax, and e-mail information.

To Bottom Border a Paragraph

1

• **With the insertion point in the paragraph to border, click the Border button arrow on the Formatting toolbar.**

Word displays the border palette either horizontally or vertically below the Border button (Figure 3-51). Using the border palette, you can add a border to any edge of a paragraph.

FIGURE 3-51

2

• **Click Bottom Border on the border palette.**

Word places a border below the paragraph containing the insertion point (Figure 3-52). The Border button on the Formatting toolbar now displays the icon for a bottom border.

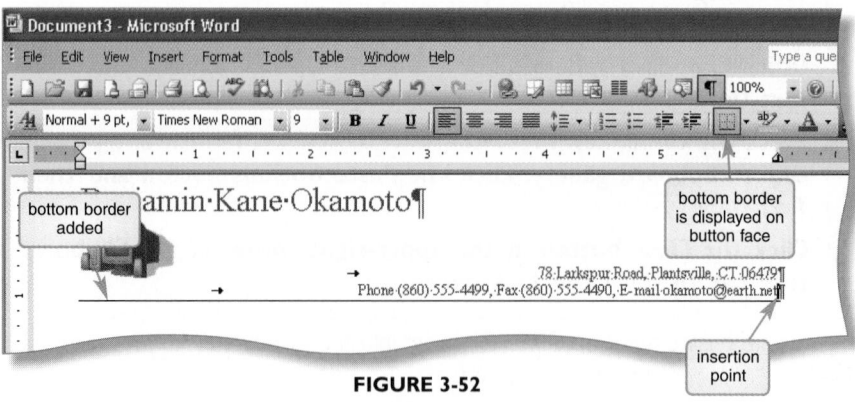

FIGURE 3-52

If, for some reason, you wanted to remove a border from a paragraph, you would position the insertion point in the paragraph, click the Border button arrow on the Formatting toolbar, and then click the No Border button (Figure 3-51) on the border palette.

Clearing Formatting

The next step is to position the insertion point below the letterhead, so that you can type the content of the letter. When you press the ENTER key at the end of a paragraph containing a border, Word moves the border forward to the next paragraph. It also retains all current settings. That is, the paragraph text will be brown and will have a bottom border. Instead, you want the paragraph and characters on the new line to use the Normal style: black font with no border. In Word the term, **clear formatting**, refers to returning the formatting to the Normal style.

The following steps show how to clear formatting at the location of the insertion point.

Other Ways

1. Click Style box arrow on Formatting toolbar, click Clear Formatting
2. On Format menu click Styles and Formatting, click Show box arrow, click Available formatting, click Clear Formatting
3. Press CTRL+SPACEBAR, press CTRL+Q
4. In Voice Command mode, say "Styles and Formatting, Clear Formatting, Styles and Formatting"

To Clear Formatting

- **With the insertion point at the end of line 3 (Figure 3-52), press the ENTER key.**
- **Click the Styles and Formatting button on the Formatting toolbar.**

Word displays the Styles and Formatting task pane (Figure 3-53). The insertion point is on line 4. Formatting at the insertion point consists of a bottom border and a brown font. You want to clear this formatting.

FIGURE 3-53

- **Click Clear Formatting in the Pick formatting to apply area in the Styles and Formatting task pane.**

Word applies the Normal style to the location of the insertion point (Figure 3-54).

3

- **Click the Close button in the upper-right corner of the Styles and Formatting task pane title bar.**

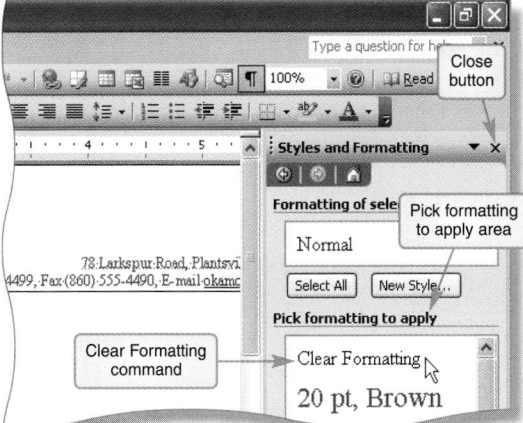

FIGURE 3-54

The next step is to remove the hyperlink autoformat from the e-mail address in the letterhead. As discussed earlier in this project, Word automatically formats text as you type. When you press the ENTER key or SPACEBAR after entering an e-mail address or Web address, Word automatically formats the address as a hyperlink, that is, colored blue and underlined. In Step 1 on the previous page, Word formatted the e-mail address as a hyperlink because you pressed the ENTER key at the end of the line. You want to remove the hyperlink format from the e-mail address.

The following steps show how to convert the e-mail address from a hyperlink to regular text.

To Convert a Hyperlink to Regular Text

1

• **Right-click the hyperlink, in this case, the e-mail address (Figure 3-55).**

FIGURE 3-55

2

• **Click Remove Hyperlink on the shortcut menu.**

• **Position the insertion point on the paragraph mark below the border.**

Word removes the hyperlink format from the e-mail address (Figure 3-56).

FIGURE 3-56

Other Ways

1. With insertion point in hyperlink, click Insert Hyperlink button on Standard toolbar, click Remove Link button
2. With insertion point in hyperlink, on Insert menu click Hyperlink, click Remove Link button
3. With insertion point in hyperlink, press CTRL+K, press ALT+R
4. With insertion point in hyperlink, in Voice Command mode, say "Right Click, Remove Hyperlink"

The letterhead now is complete. Thus, you should save it in a file, as described in the following steps.

To Save the Letterhead

1 **Insert your floppy disk into drive A.**

2 **Click the Save button on the Standard toolbar.**

3 **Type the file name** `Okamoto Letterhead` **in the File name text box.**

4 **If necessary, click the Save in box arrow and then click 3½ Floppy (A:).**

5 **Click the Save button in the Save As dialog box.**

Word saves the document on a floppy disk in drive A with the file name, Okamoto Letterhead.

Each time you wish to create a letter, you would open the letterhead file (Okamoto Letterhead) and then immediately save it with a new file name. By doing this, the letterhead file will remain unchanged for future use.

Creating a Cover Letter

You have created a letterhead for the cover letter. The next step is to compose the cover letter. The following pages outline how to use Word to compose a cover letter that contains a table and a bulleted list.

Components of a Business Letter

During your professional career, you most likely will create many business letters. A cover letter is one type of business letter. All business letters contain the same basic components.

When preparing business letters, you should include all essential elements. Essential business letter elements include the date line, inside address, message, and signature block (Figure 3-2a on page WD 140). The **date line**, which consists of the month, day, and year, is positioned two to six lines below the letterhead. The **inside address**, placed three to eight lines below the date line, usually contains the addressee's courtesy title plus full name, business affiliation, and full geographical address. The **salutation**, if present, begins two lines below the last line of the inside address. The body of the letter, the message, begins two lines below the salutation. Within the **message**, paragraphs are single-spaced with double-spacing between paragraphs. Two lines below the last line of the message, the **complimentary close** is displayed. Capitalize only the first word in a complimentary close. Type the **signature block** at least four lines below the complimentary close, allowing room for the author to sign his or her name.

You can follow many different styles when you create business letters. The cover letter in this project follows the modified block style. Table 3-2 outlines the differences among three common styles of business letters.

Table 3-2 Common Business Letter Styles	
LETTER STYLES	**FEATURES**
Block	All components of the letter begin flush with the left margin.
Modified Block	The date, complimentary close, and signature block are positioned approximately ½" to the right of center, or at the right margin. All other components of the letter begin flush with the left margin.
Modified Semi-Block	The date, complimentary close, and signature block are centered, positioned approximately ½" to the right of center, or at the right margin. The first line of each paragraph in the body of the letter is indented ½" to 1" from the left margin. All other components of the letter begin flush with the left margin.

Saving the Cover Letter with a New File Name

The document in the document window currently has the name Okamoto Letterhead, the name of the personal letterhead. You want the letterhead to remain intact. Thus, you should save the document with a new file name, as described in steps on the next page.

To Save the Document with a New File Name

1 **If necessary, insert your floppy disk into drive A.**

2 **Click File on the menu bar and then click Save As.**

3 **Type the file name** Okamoto Cover Letter **in the File name text box.**

4 **If necessary, click the Save in box arrow and then click 3½ Floppy (A:).**

5 **Click the Save button in the Save As dialog box.**

Word saves the document on a floppy disk in drive A with the file name, Okamoto Cover Letter (shown in Figure 3-57).

Setting Tab Stops Using the Ruler

The first required element of the cover letter is the date line, which in this letter is to be positioned two lines below the letterhead. The date line contains the month, day, and year, and begins 3.5 inches from the left margin, or one-half inch to the right of center. Thus, you should set a custom tab stop at the 3.5" mark on the ruler.

Earlier you used the Tabs dialog box to set a tab stop because you could not use the ruler to set a tab stop at the right margin. The following steps show how to set a left-aligned tab stop using the ruler.

To Set Custom Tab Stops Using the Ruler

1

• **With the insertion point on the paragraph mark below the border, press the ENTER key.**

• **If necessary, click the button at the left edge of the horizontal ruler until it displays the Left Tab icon.**

• **Position the mouse pointer on the 3.5" mark on the ruler.**

Each time you click the button at the left of the horizontal ruler, its icon changes (Figure 3-57). The left tab icon looks like a capital letter L (⌊).

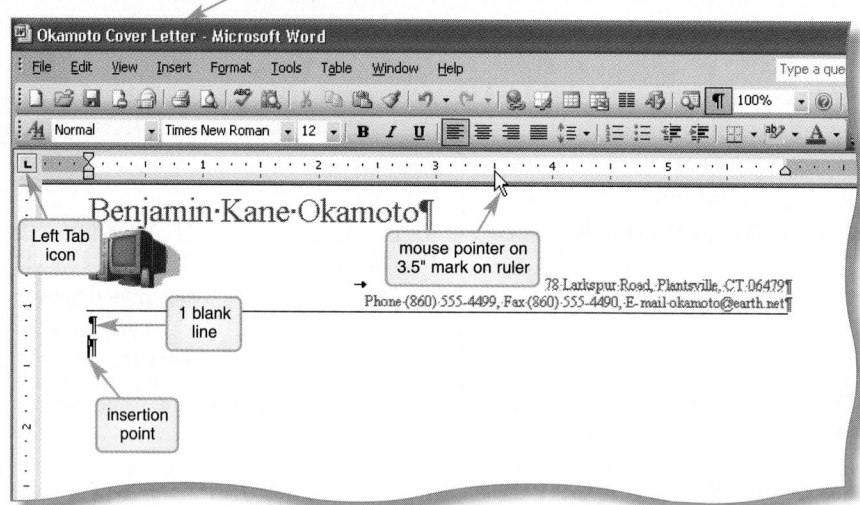

FIGURE 3-57

2

• **Click the 3.5" mark on the ruler.**

Word places a left tab marker at the 3.5" mark on the ruler (Figure 3-58). The text you type at this tab stop will be left-aligned.

FIGURE 3-58

If, for some reason, you wanted to move a custom tab stop, you would drag the tab marker to the desired location on the ruler.

If you wanted to change the alignment of a custom tab stop, you could remove the existing tab stop and then insert a new one as described in the previous steps. To remove a custom tab stop, point to the tab marker on the ruler and then drag the tab marker down and out of the ruler. You also could use the Tabs dialog box to change an existing tab stop's alignment or position. As discussed earlier in this project, you click Format on the menu bar and then click Tabs to display the Tabs dialog box. To remove all tab stops, click the Clear All button in the Tabs dialog box.

Inserting the Current Date in a Document

The next step is to enter the current date at the 3.5" tab stop in the document. Word provides a method of inserting a computer's system date in a document. The following steps show how to insert the current date in the cover letter.

To Insert the Current Date in a Document

1

- **Press the TAB key.**
- **Click Insert on the menu bar (Figure 3-59).**

2

- **Click Date and Time on the Insert menu.**
- **When Word displays the Date and Time dialog box, click the desired format (in this case, December 19, 2005).**
- **If the Update automatically check box is selected, click the check box to remove the check mark.**

The Date and Time dialog box lists a variety of date and time formats (Figure 3-60). Your dialog box will differ, showing the current system date stored in your computer.

3

- **Click the OK button.**

Word inserts the current date at the location of the insertion point (shown in Figure 3-61 on the next page).

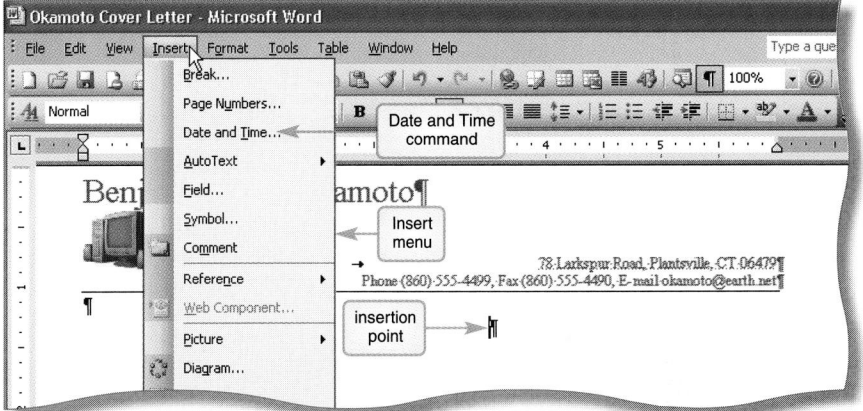

FIGURE 3-59

FIGURE 3-60

Microsoft Office
Word 2003

Dates

A field is a set of codes that instructs Word to perform a certain action. If you want Word to display the current date or time when you print a document, make it a field. That is, place a check mark in the Update automatically check box in the Date and Time dialog box (Figure 3-60 on the previous page) when you insert the current date or time.

The next step is to type the inside address and salutation in the cover letter, as described in the following steps.

To Enter the Inside Address and Salutation

1 **With the insertion point at the end of the date, press the ENTER key three times.**

2 **Type** Ms. Helen Weiss **and then press the ENTER key.**

3 **Type** Personnel Director **and then press the ENTER key.**

4 **Type** National Computer Sales **and then press the ENTER key.**

5 **Type** 15 Main Street **and then press the ENTER key.**

6 **Type** Hartford, CT 06109 **and then press the ENTER key twice.**

7 **Type** Dear Ms. Weiss **and then press the COLON key (:).**

The inside address and salutation are entered (Figure 3-61).

Inside Addresses

Pay close attention to the spelling, punctuation, and official abbreviations of company names. For example, does the company name spell out the word, and, or does it use the ampersand character (&)? Is the word, Company, spelled out or abbreviated?

FIGURE 3-61

Creating an AutoText Entry

If you use the same text frequently, you can store the text in an **AutoText entry** and then use the stored entry throughout the open document, as well as future documents. That is, you type the entry only once, and for all future occurrences of the text, you access the stored entry as you need it. In this way, you avoid entering the text inconsistently or incorrectly in different locations throughout the same document.

The next steps show how to create an AutoText entry for the prospective employer's name.

To Create an AutoText Entry

1

- **Drag through the text to be stored, in this case, National Computer Sales. Do not select the paragraph mark at the end of the text.**

- **Click Insert on the menu bar and then point to AutoText.**

The employer name, National Computer Sales, in the inside address is selected (Figure 3-62). Notice the paragraph mark is not part of the selection.

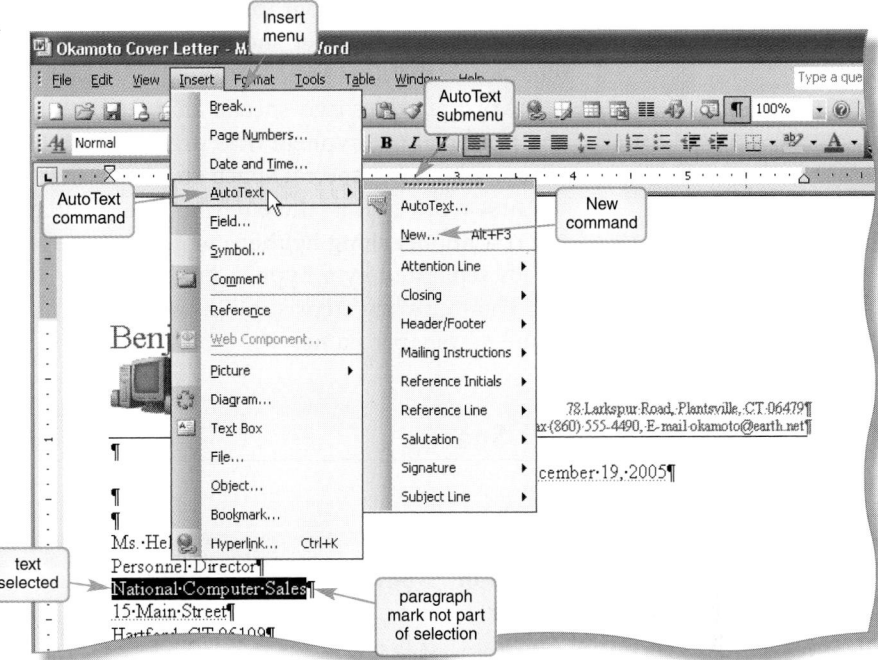

FIGURE 3-62

2

- **Click New on the AutoText submenu.**

- **When Word displays the Create AutoText dialog box, type** ncs **as the AutoText entry name.**

When the Create AutoText dialog box first appears, Word proposes a name for the AutoText entry. You change Word's suggestion to ncs (Figure 3-63).

3

- **Click the OK button.**

- **If Word displays another dialog box, click the Yes button.**

Word stores the AutoText entry and closes the AutoText dialog box.

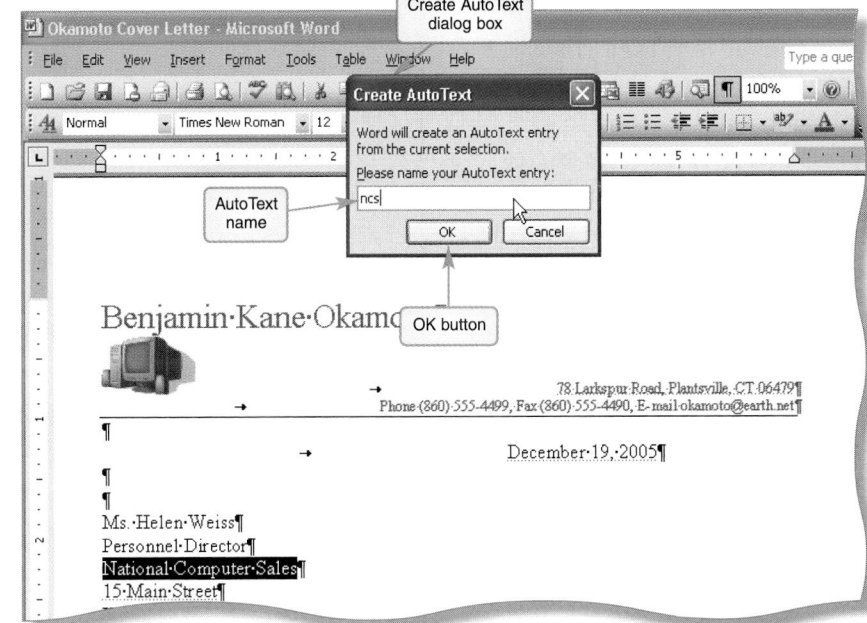

FIGURE 3-63

The name, ncs, has been stored as an AutoText entry. Later in the project, you will use the AutoText entry, ncs, instead of typing the employer name, National Computer Sales.

Other Ways

1. Select text, press ALT+F3, type AutoText name, click OK button
2. In Voice Command mode, say "Insert, AutoText, New, [AutoText name], OK"

Q&A

Q: What is an appropriate salutation if I do not know the recipient's name?

A: Avoid using the salutation "To whom it may concern" - it is extremely impersonal. If you cannot obtain the name and gender of the company officer to whom you are addressing the letter, then use the recipient's title in the salutation, e.g., Dear Personnel Supervisor.

Entering a Nonbreaking Space

Some compound words, such as proper names, dates, units of time and measure, abbreviations, and geographic destinations, should not be divided at the end of a line. These words either should fit as a unit at the end of a line or be wrapped together to the next line.

Word provides two special characters to assist with this task: nonbreaking space and nonbreaking hyphen. You press CTRL+SHIFT+SPACEBAR to insert a **nonbreaking space**, which is a special space character that prevents two words from splitting if the first word falls at the end of a line. Similarly, you press CTRL+SHIFT+HYPHEN to insert a **nonbreaking hyphen**, which is a special type of hyphen that prevents two words separated by a hyphen from splitting at the end of a line.

The following steps show how to enter a nonbreaking space between the words in the newspaper name.

To Insert a Nonbreaking Space

• **Scroll the salutation to the top of the document window. Click after the colon in the salutation and then press the ENTER key twice.**

• **Type** I am responding to the full-time computer sales position advertised in yesterday's **and then press the SPACEBAR.**

• **Press CTRL+I to turn on italics. Type** New **and then press CTRL+SHIFT+SPACEBAR.**

Word inserts a nonbreaking space after the word, New (Figure 3-64).

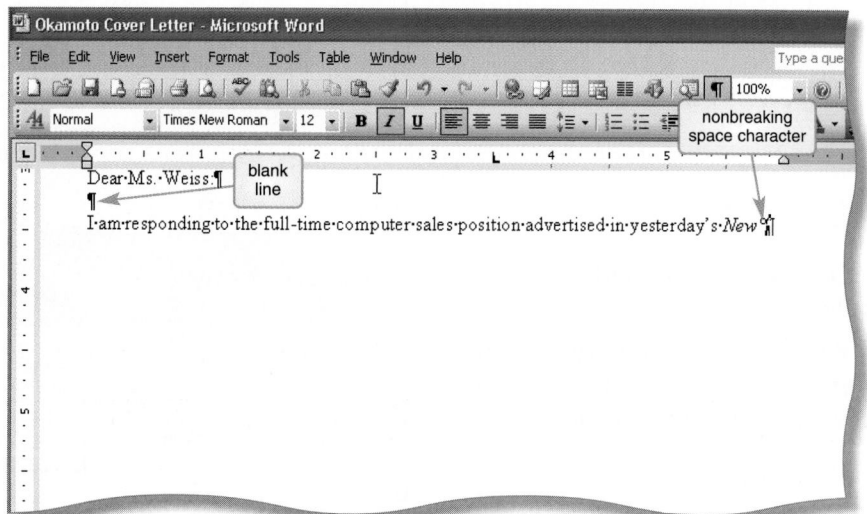

FIGURE 3-64

2

• **Type** England **and then press CTRL+SHIFT+SPACEBAR.**

• **Type** Tribune **and then press CTRL+I to turn off italics. Press the PERIOD key.**

Word wraps the words in the newspaper title, New England Tribune, to the next line (Figure 3-65).

1. On Insert menu click Symbol, click Special Characters tab, click Nonbreaking Space in Character list, click Insert button, click Close button

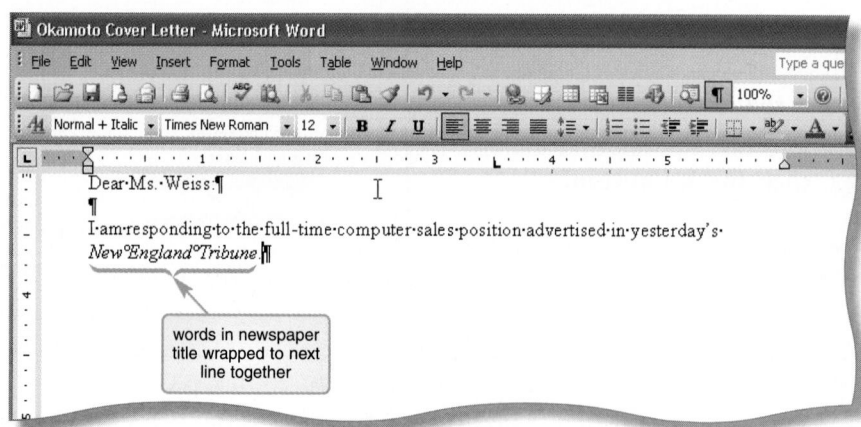

FIGURE 3-65

Inserting an AutoText Entry

At the end of the next sentence in the body of the cover letter, you want the prospective employer name, National Computer Sales, to be displayed. Recall that earlier in this project, you created an AutoText entry name of ncs for National Computer Sales. Thus, you will type the AutoText entry's name and then instruct Word to replace the AutoText entry's name with the stored entry of National Computer Sales.

The following steps show how to insert an AutoText entry.

To Insert an AutoText Entry

1

• **Press the SPACEBAR. Type** As indicated on the enclosed resume, I have the credentials you are seeking and believe I can be a valuable asset to ncs **as shown in Figure 3-66.**

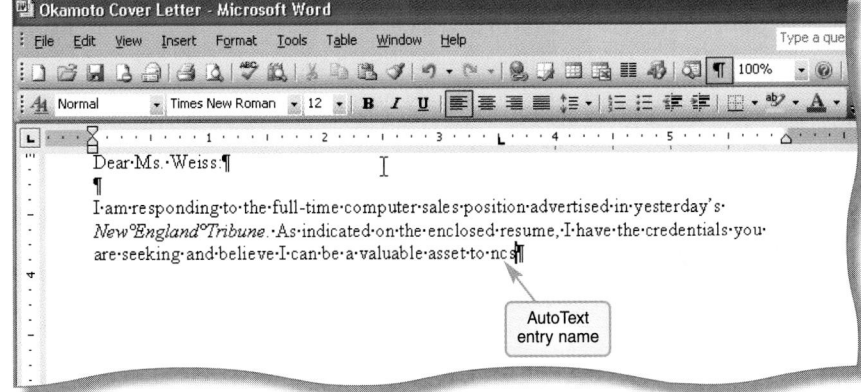

FIGURE 3-66

2

• **Press the F3 key.**
• **Press the PERIOD key.**

Word replaces the characters, ncs, with the stored AutoText entry, National Computer Sales, when you press the F3 key (Figure 3-67).

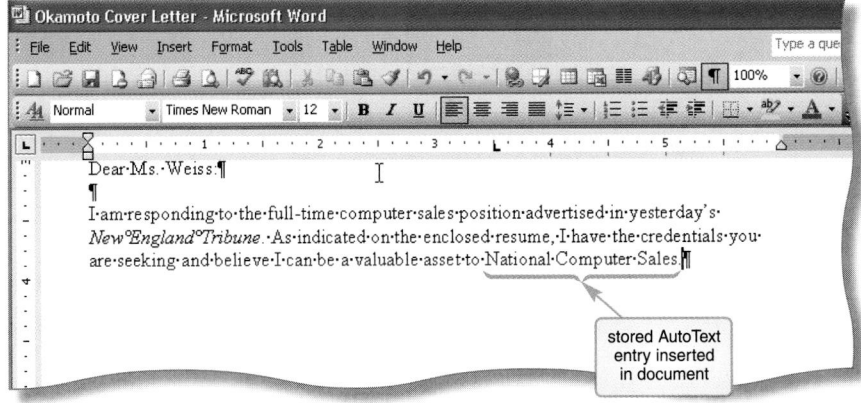

FIGURE 3-67

Pressing the F3 key instructs Word to replace the AutoText entry name with the stored AutoText entry. In Project 2, you learned how to use the AutoCorrect feature, which enables you to insert and also create AutoCorrect entries (just as you did for this AutoText entry). The difference between an AutoCorrect entry and an AutoText entry is that the AutoCorrect feature makes corrections for you automatically as soon as you press the SPACEBAR or type a punctuation mark, whereas you must press the F3 key or click the AutoText command to instruct Word to make an AutoText correction.

Other Ways

1. Type first few characters to display AutoComplete tip, press ENTER
2. On Insert menu point to AutoText, point to appropriate AutoText entry, click desired AutoText entry on submenu
3. On Insert menu point to AutoText, click AutoText, select desired AutoText entry name, click OK button

More About

AutoText

Word provides many AutoText categories of entries for business letters. Categories include attention line, closing, mailing instructions, salutation, and subject line. To insert an AutoText entry, click Insert on the menu bar, point to AutoText, point to the desired category, and then click the desired entry. Or, click the All Entries button on the AutoText toolbar, point to the desired category, and then click the desired entry.

If you watch the screen as you type, you may discover that AutoComplete tips appear on the screen. As you type, Word searches the list of AutoText entry names, and if one matches your typing, Word displays its complete name above your typing as an **AutoComplete tip**. If you press the ENTER key while an AutoComplete tip is displayed on the screen, Word places the text in the AutoComplete tip at the location of your typing. To ignore an AutoComplete tip proposed by Word, simply continue typing to remove the AutoComplete tip from the screen.

In addition to AutoText entries, Word proposes AutoComplete tips for the current date, days of the week, months, and so on. If your screen does not display AutoComplete tips, click Tools on the menu bar, click AutoCorrect Options, click the AutoText tab, click Show AutoComplete suggestions, and then click the OK button. To view the complete list of entries, click Tools on the menu bar, click AutoCorrect Options, click the AutoText tab, and then scroll through the list of entries.

The next step is to enter a paragraph of text into the cover letter, as described below.

To Enter a Paragraph

1 **Press the ENTER key twice.**

2 **Type** I recently received my bachelor's degree in information and computer technology from Hartford College. The following table outlines my areas of concentration **and then press the COLON key.**

3 **Press the ENTER key twice.**

The paragraph is entered (shown in Figure 3-68).

More About

Word Tables

Although you can use the TAB key to align data in a table, many Word users prefer to use a table. With a Word table, you can arrange numbers and text in columns. For emphasis, tables can be shaded and have borders. The contents of Word tables can be sorted, and you can have Word sum the contents of an entire row or column.

Creating a Table with the Insert Table Button

The next step in composing the cover letter is to place a table listing your areas of concentration (Figure 3-2a on page WD 140). You create this table using Word's table feature. As discussed earlier in this project, a Word table is a collection of rows and columns, and the intersection of a row and a column is called a cell.

Within a Word table, you easily can rearrange rows and columns, change column widths, sort rows and columns, and sum the contents of rows and columns. You also can format and chart table data.

The first step in creating a table is to insert an empty table into the document. When inserting a table, you must specify the total number of rows and columns required, which is called the **dimension** of the table. The table in this project has two columns. You often do not know the total number of rows in a table. Thus, many Word users create one row initially and then add more rows as needed. The first number in a dimension is the number of rows, and the second is the number of columns.

The following steps show how to insert a 1 × 2 (pronounced one by two) table; that is, a table with one row and two columns.

To Insert an Empty Table

1

• **Click the Insert Table button on the Standard toolbar.**

• **Position the mouse pointer on the cell in the first row and second column of the grid.**

Word displays a grid so you can select the desired table dimension (Figure 3-68). Word will insert the table immediately above the insertion point.

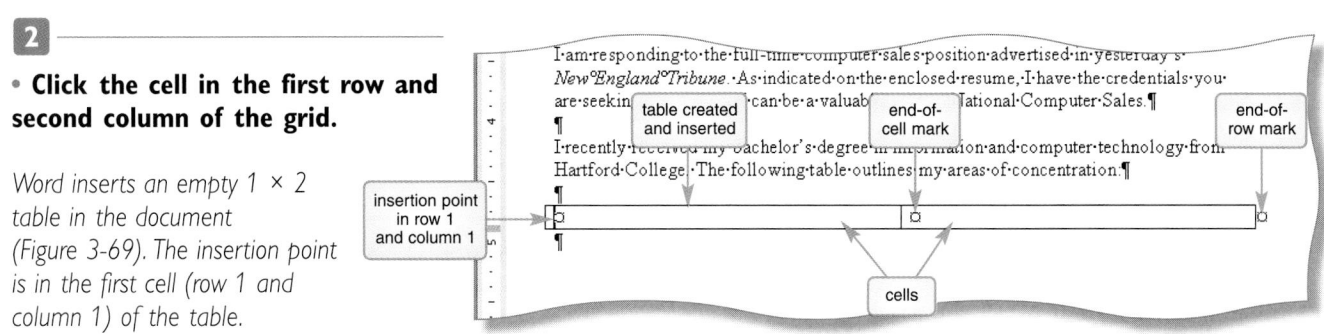

FIGURE 3-68

2

• **Click the cell in the first row and second column of the grid.**

Word inserts an empty 1 × 2 table in the document (Figure 3-69). The insertion point is in the first cell (row 1 and column 1) of the table.

FIGURE 3-69

As discussed earlier in this project, each row of a table has an end-of-row mark, which you can use to add columns to the right of a table. Each cell has an end-of-cell mark, which you can use to select a cell. The end-of-cell mark currently is left-aligned; thus, it is positioned at the left edge of each cell. You can use any of the paragraph formatting buttons on the Formatting toolbar to change the alignment of the text within the cells. For example, if you click the Align Right button on the Formatting toolbar, the end-of-cell mark and any entered text will be displayed at the right edge of the cell.

For simple tables, such as the one just created, Word users click the Insert Table button to create a table. For more complex tables, such as one with a varying number of columns per row, Word has a Draw Table feature that allows you to use a pencil pointer to draw a table on the screen.

Entering Data in a Word Table

The next step is to enter data into the cells of the empty table. The data you enter within a cell wordwraps just as text does between the margins of a document. To place data in a cell, you click the cell and then type. To advance rightward from one cell to the next, press the TAB key. When you are at the rightmost cell in a row, also press the TAB key to move to the first cell in the next row; do not press the ENTER key. The ENTER key is used to begin a new paragraph within a cell.

Other Ways

1. On Table menu point to Insert, click Table on Insert submenu, enter number of columns, enter number of rows, click OK button
2. In Voice Command mode, say "Insert Table, [select table dimension]"

More About

Draw Table

To use Draw Table, click the Tables and Borders button on the Standard toolbar to change the mouse pointer to a pencil. Use the pencil to draw from one corner to the opposite diagonal corner to define the perimeter of the table. Then, draw the column and row lines inside the perimeter. To remove a line, use the Eraser button on the Tables and Borders toolbar.

To add new rows to a table, press the TAB key with the insertion point positioned in the bottom-right corner cell of the table.

The following steps show how to enter data in the table.

To Enter Data in a Table

1

• **If necessary, scroll the table up in the document window.**

• **With the insertion point in the left cell of the table, type** Computer Hardware **and then press the TAB key.**

• **Type** 30 hours **and then press the TAB key.**

Word enters the table data in the first row of the table and adds a second row to the table (Figure 3-70). The insertion point is positioned in the first cell of the second row.

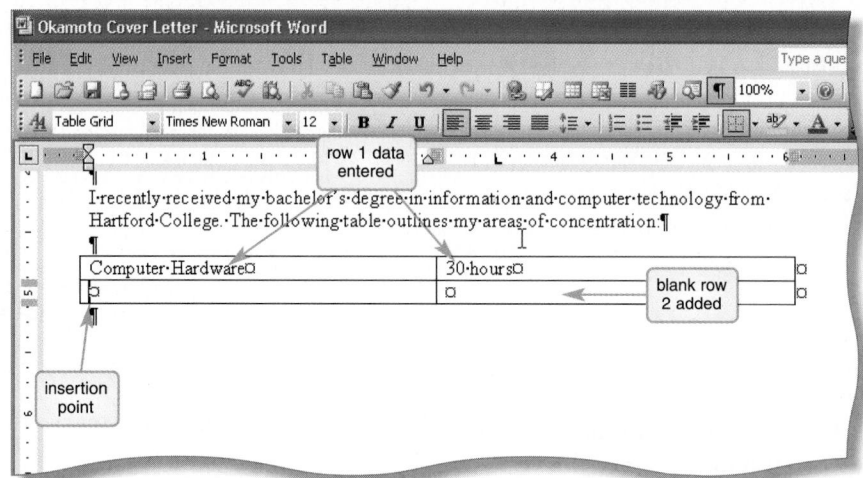

FIGURE 3-70

2

• **Type** Computer Software and Programming **and then press the TAB key. Type** 21 hours **and then press the TAB key.**

• **Type** Professional Communications **and then press the TAB key. Type** 15 hours **and then press the TAB key.**

• **Type** Business **and then press the TAB key. Type** 15 hours **as shown in Figure 3-71.**

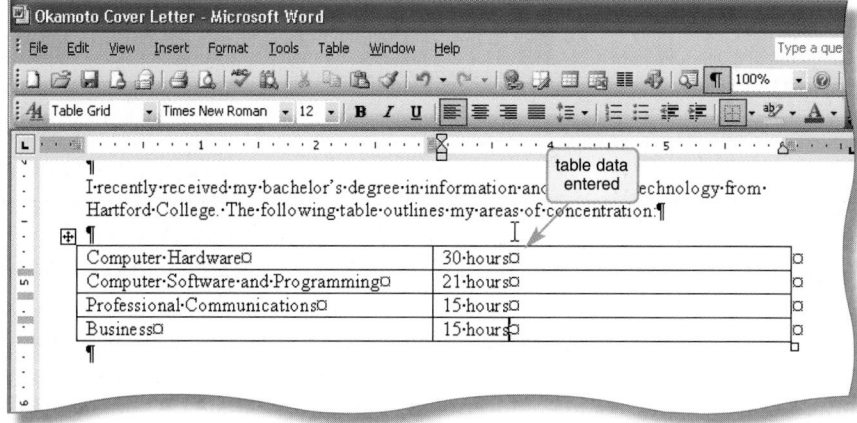

FIGURE 3-71

Other Ways

1. In Dictation mode, say "Computer Hardware, Tab, 30 hours, Tab," etc.

More About

Tabs

The TAB key advances the insertion point from one cell to the next in a table. Thus, press CTRL+TAB to insert a tab character into a cell.

You modify the contents of cells just as you modify text in a document. To delete the contents of a cell, select the cell contents by pointing to the left edge of a cell and clicking when the mouse pointer changes direction, and then press the DELETE key. To modify text in a cell, click in the cell and then correct the entry. You can double-click the OVR indicator on the status bar to toggle between insert and overtype modes. You also can drag and drop or cut and paste the contents of cells.

As discussed in the previous steps, you add a row to the end of a table by positioning the insertion point in the bottom-right corner cell and then pressing the TAB key. To add a row in the middle of a table, select the row below where the new row is to be inserted, then click the Insert Rows button on the Standard toolbar (the same button you clicked to insert a table); or click Insert Rows on the shortcut menu; or click Table on the menu bar, point to Insert, and then click Rows Above.

To add a column in the middle of a table, select the column to the right of where the new column is to be inserted and then click the Insert Columns button on the Standard toolbar (the same button you clicked to insert a table); or click Insert Columns on the shortcut menu; or click Table on the menu bar, point to Insert, and then click Columns to the Left. To add a column to the right of a table, select the end-of-row marks at the right edge of the table, then click the Insert Columns button; or click Insert Columns on the shortcut menu; or click Table on the menu bar, point to Insert, and then click Columns to the Right.

If you want to delete row(s) or delete column(s) from a table, select the row(s) or column(s) to delete and then click Delete Rows or Delete Columns on the shortcut menu, or click Table on the menu bar, click Delete, and then click the appropriate item to delete.

More About

Table Commands

If a Table command is dimmed on the Table menu, the insertion point might not be positioned in the table.

Resizing Table Columns

The table in this project currently extends from the left margin to the right margin of the document. You want each column only to be as wide as the longest entry in the table. That is, the first column must be wide enough to accommodate the words, Computer Software and Programming; and the second column must be wide enough for the phrase, 30 hours.

The following steps show how to instruct Word to fit the width of the columns to the contents of the table automatically.

Other Ways

1. Double-click column boundary
2. On Table menu point to AutoFit, click AutoFit to Contents
3. In Voice Command mode, say "Table, AutoFit, AutoFit to Contents"

To Fit Columns to Table Contents

1

• **Right-click the table and then point to AutoFit on the shortcut menu (Figure 3-72).**

FIGURE 3-72

2

• **Click AutoFit to Contents on the AutoFit submenu.**

Word automatically adjusts the widths of the columns based on the text in the table (Figure 3-73). In this case, Word reduces the widths of the columns.

FIGURE 3-73

More About

Table Formats

You can change the width of a column to an exact measurement. Hold down the ALT key while dragging markers on the ruler. Or, click Table on the menu bar, click Table Properties, click the Column tab, enter desired measurements, and then click the OK button. Similarly, to change the row height to an exact measurement, click the Row tab in the Table Properties dialog box, enter desired measurements, and then click the OK button.

If you do not want to resize the columns to the table widths, Word provides other options. You can drag a **column boundary**, the border to the right of a column (Figure 3-73 on the previous page), until the column is the desired width. Similarly, you can resize a row by dragging the **row boundary**, the border at the bottom of a row, until the row is the desired height. You also can resize the entire table by dragging the **table resize handle**, which is a small square that appears when you point to the bottom-right corner of the table (shown in Figure 3-74).

Changing the Table Alignment

When you first create a table, it is left-aligned; that is, flush with the left margin. In this cover letter, the table should be centered. To center a table, select the entire table and then center it using the Center button on the Formatting toolbar, as shown in the following series of steps.

To Select a Table

1

• **Position the mouse pointer in the table so the table move handle appears.**

• **Click the table move handle.**

Word selects the entire table (Figure 3-74).

Other Ways

1. On Table menu point to Select, click Table
2. With insertion point in table, press ALT+5 (using the 5 on the numeric keypad with NUM LOCK off)
3. In Voice Command mode, say "Table, Select, Table"

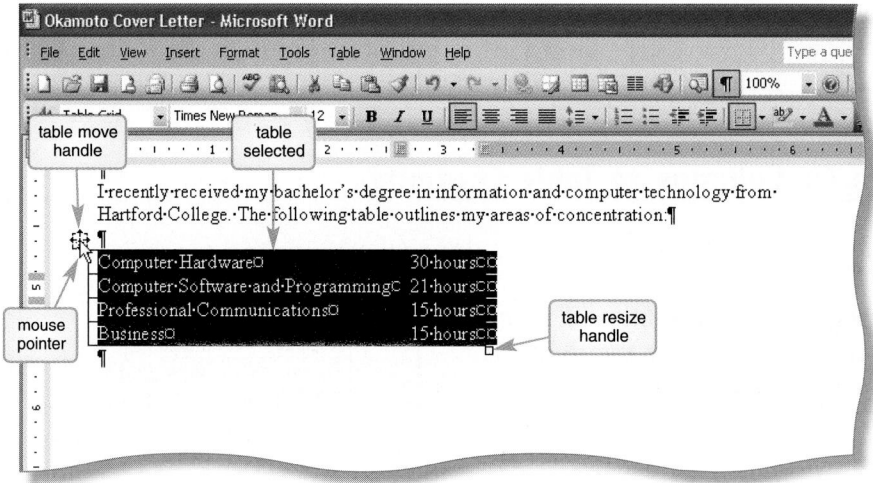

FIGURE 3-74

When working with tables, you may need to select the contents of cells, rows, columns, or the entire table. Table 3-3 identifies ways to select various items in a table.

Table 3-3 Selecting Items in a Table	
ITEM TO SELECT	ACTION
Cell	Click left edge of cell
Column	Click border at top of column
Multiple cells, rows, or columns adjacent to one another	Drag through cells, rows, or columns
Multiple cells, rows, or columns not adjacent to one another	Select first cell, row, or column and then hold down CTRL key while selecting next cell, row, or column
Next cell	Press TAB key
Previous cell	Press SHIFT+TAB
Row	Click to left of row
Table	Click table move handle

The following step centers the selected table between the margins.

To Center a Selected Table

1 **Click the Center button on the Formatting toolbar.**

Word centers the selected table between the left and right margins (shown in Figure 3-75).

When an entire table is selected and you click the Center button on the Formatting toolbar, Word centers the entire table. If you wanted to center the contents of the cells, you would select the cells by dragging through them and then click the Center button.

The next step is to add more text below the table, as described here.

To Add More Text

1 **If necessary, scroll up. Click the paragraph mark below the table.**

2 **Press the ENTER key.**

3 **Type** In addition to my coursework, I have the following sales and computer experience **and then press the COLON key. Press the ENTER key.**

The text is entered (shown in Figure 3-75).

Bulleting a List

You can type a list and then add bullets to the paragraphs at a later time, or you can use Word's AutoFormat As You Type feature to bullet the paragraphs as you type them (Table 3-1 on page WD 156).

The following steps show how to add bullets automatically to a list as you type.

To Bullet a List as You Type

1

• **Press the ASTERISK key (*).**

• **Press the SPACEBAR.**

• **Type** Worked as an intern at Computer Discount Sales, selling hardware and software components to home and small business customers **(Figure 3-75).**

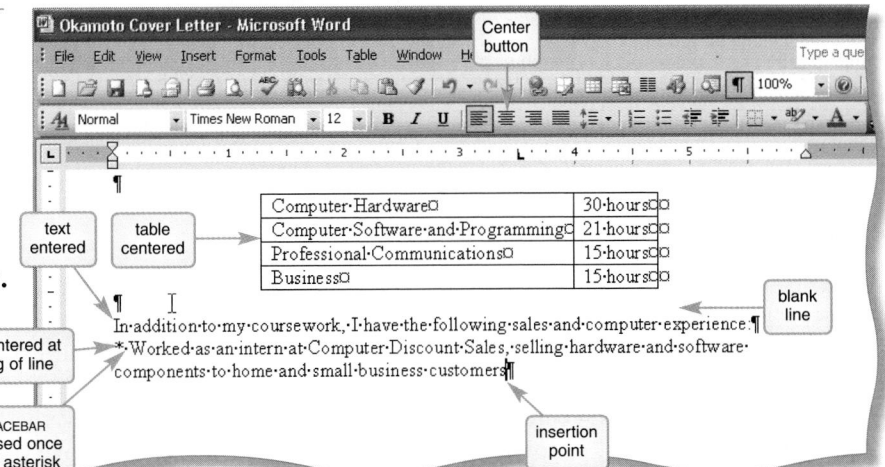

FIGURE 3-75

2

• **Press the ENTER key.**

Word converts the asterisk to a bullet character, places another bullet on the second list item, and indents the two bulleted paragraphs.

3

• **Type** At Hartford College, tutored students having difficulty with computer classes **and then press the ENTER key.**

• **Type** Prepared all fliers and newsletters for the New England Ski Club **and then press the ENTER key.**

Word places a bullet on the next line (Figure 3-76).

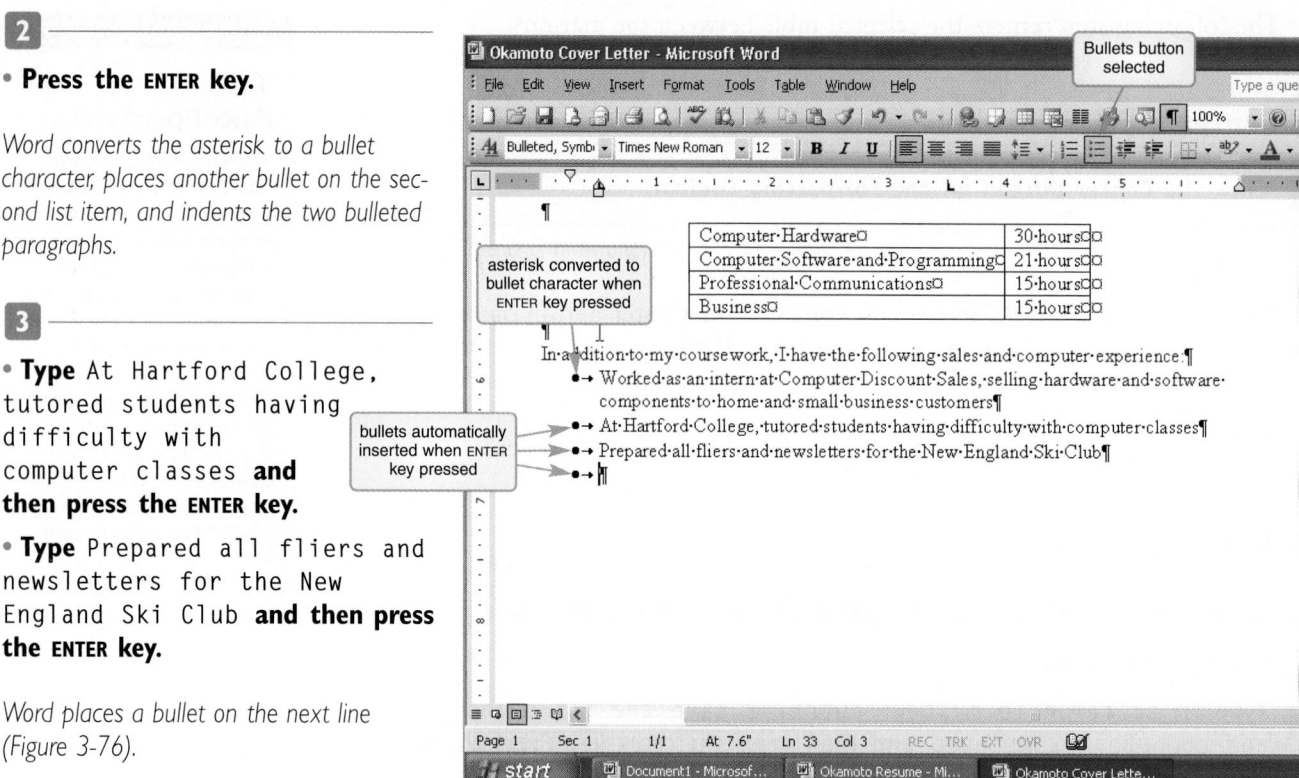

FIGURE 3-76

4

• **Press the ENTER key.**

Word removes the lone bullet because you pressed the ENTER key twice (Figure 3-77). The Bullets button no longer is selected.

FIGURE 3-77

When the insertion point is in a bulleted list, the Bullets button on the Formatting toolbar is selected (Figure 3-76). To instruct Word to stop bulleting paragraphs, press the ENTER key twice, click the Bullets button on the Formatting toolbar, or press the BACKSPACE key to remove the bullet.

You may have noticed that Word displayed the AutoCorrect Options button when it formatted the list automatically as a bulleted list. If you did not want the list to be a bulleted list, you could click the AutoCorrect Options button and then click Undo Automatic Bullets on the shortcut menu.

You can add numbers as you type, just as you can add bullets as you type. To number a list, type the number one followed by a period and then a space (1.) at the beginning of the first item and then type your text. When you press the ENTER key, Word places the number two (2.) at the beginning of the next line automatically. As with bullets, press the ENTER key twice at the end of the list or click the Numbering button (Figure 3-77) on the Formatting toolbar to stop numbering.

The next step is to enter the remainder of the cover letter, as described below.

To Enter the Remainder of the Cover Letter

1 Type the paragraph shown in Figure 3-78, making certain you use the AutoText entry, ncs, to insert the employer name.

2 Press the ENTER key twice. Press the TAB key. Type `Sincerely` and then press the COMMA key.

3 Press the ENTER key four times. Press the TAB key. Type `Benjamin Kane Okamoto` and then press the ENTER key twice.

4 Type `Enclosure: Resume` as the final text.

The cover letter text is complete (Figure 3-78).

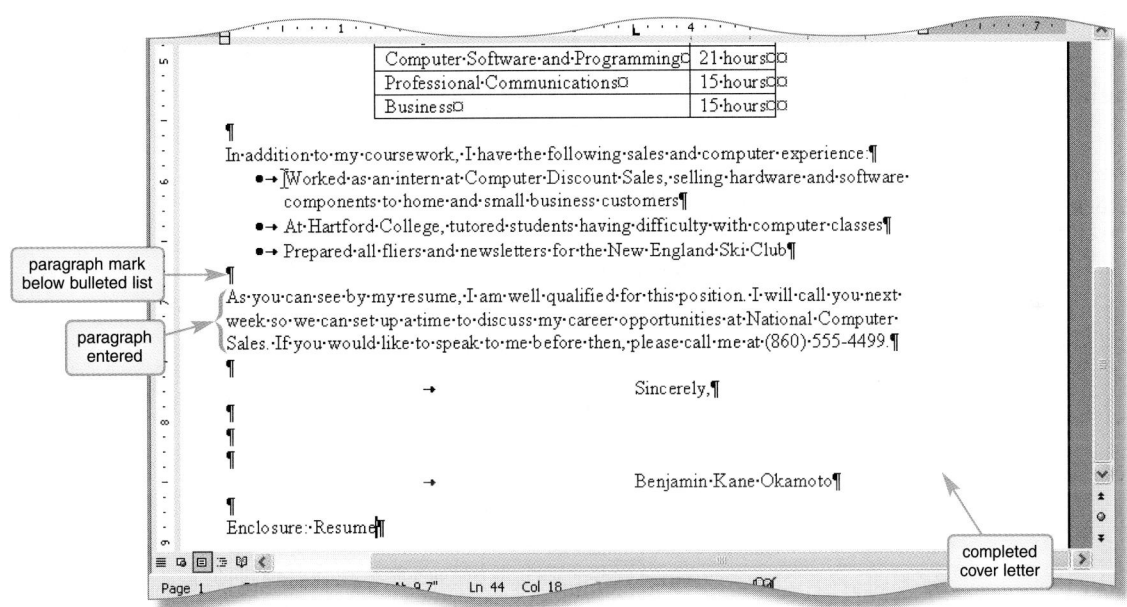

FIGURE 3-78

Saving Again and Printing the Cover Letter

The cover letter for the resume now is complete. You should save the cover letter again and then print it, as described in the following steps.

To Save a Document Again

1 Click the Save button on the Standard toolbar.

Word saves the cover letter with the same file name, Okamoto Cover Letter.

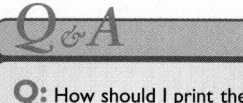
To Print a Document

1 **Click the Print button on the Standard toolbar.**

The completed cover letter prints as shown in Figure 3-2a on page WD 140.

Addressing and Printing Envelopes and Mailing Labels

With Word, you can print address information on an envelope or on a mailing label. Computer-printed addresses look more professional than handwritten ones. Thus, the following steps show how to address and print an envelope.

To Address and Print an Envelope

1

• **Scroll through the cover letter to display the inside address in the document window.**

• **Drag through the inside address to select it.**

• **Click Tools on the menu bar and then point to Letters and Mailings (Figure 3-79).**

FIGURE 3-79

2

- **Click Envelopes and Labels on the Letters and Mailings submenu.**

- **When Word displays the Envelopes and Labels dialog box, if necessary, click the Envelopes tab.**

- **Click the Return address text box.**

- **Type** Benjamin Kane Okamoto **and then press the ENTER key.**

- **Type** 78 Larkspur Road **and then press the ENTER key.**

- **Type** Plantsville, CT 06479 **(Figure 3-80).**

3

- **Insert an envelope into your printer, as shown in the Feed area of the dialog box (your Feed area may be different depending on your printer).**

- **Click the Print button in the Envelopes and Labels dialog box.**

- **If a dialog box is displayed, click the No button.**

Word prints the envelope (shown in Figure 3-2b on page WD 140).

FIGURE 3-80

Instead of printing the envelope immediately, you can add it to the document by clicking the Add to Document button in the Envelopes and Labels dialog box. To specify a different envelope or label type (identified by a number on the box of envelopes or labels), click the Options button in the Envelopes and Labels dialog box.

Instead of printing an envelope, you can print a mailing label. To do this, click the Labels tab in the Envelopes and Labels dialog box (Figure 3-80). Type the delivery address in the Address box. To print the same address on all labels on the page, click Full page of the same label. Click the Print button in the dialog box.

More About

Office Supplies

For more information about where to obtain supplies for printing documents, visit the Word 2003 More About Web page (scsite.com/wd2003/more) and then click Online Office Supplies.

Smart Tags

A **smart tag** is a button that automatically appears on the screen when Word performs a certain action. In this and previous projects, you worked with the AutoCorrect Options and Paste Options smart tags. This section discusses the third type of smart tag, called Smart Tag Actions, which performs various functions depending on the object identified by the smart tag indicator.

The smart tag indicator for Smart Tag Actions is a purple dotted underline. As shown throughout this project, a smart tag indicator appears below addresses and dates. A smart tag indicator also may appear below names, places, times, and financial symbols. To view or change the list of objects recognized as smart tags, click Tools on the menu bar, click AutoCorrect Options, and then click the Smart Tags tab.

When you point to a smart tag indicator, the Smart Tag Actions button appears on the screen. Clicking the Smart Tag Actions button displays a Smart Tag Actions menu. The commands in the Smart Tag Actions menu vary depending on the smart tag. For example, the Smart Tag Actions menu for a date includes commands that allow you to schedule a meeting in Outlook Calendar or display your Outlook Calendar. The Smart Tag Actions menu for an address includes commands for adding the address to your Outlook contacts list.

The following steps illustrate using a smart tag to display your Outlook Calendar. If you are stepping through this project on a computer and you want your screen to match the figures in the following steps, then your computer must have Outlook installed.

To Use the Smart Tag Actions Button

• **Click anywhere to remove the highlight from the inside address.**

• **Position the mouse pointer on the smart tag indicator below the date line, December 19, 2005, in the cover letter. (If the smart tag indicator is not displayed, click Tools on the menu bar, click AutoCorrect Options, click the Smart Tags tab, click Date, and then click the OK button.)**

Word displays the Smart Tag Actions button (Figure 3-81).

FIGURE 3-81

• **Click the Smart Tag Actions button.**

Word displays the Smart Tag Actions menu (Figure 3-82).

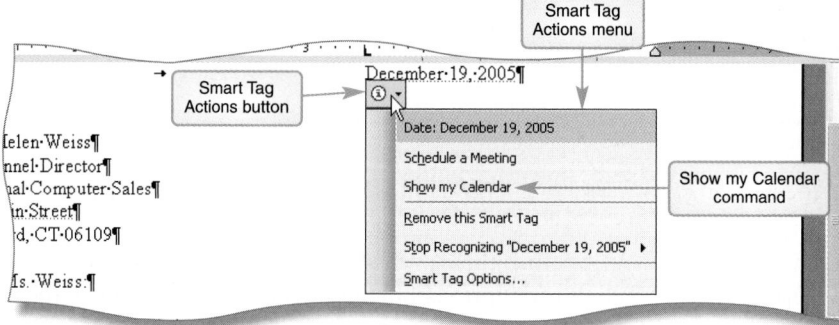

FIGURE 3-82

3

• **Click Show my Calendar on the Smart Tag Actions menu.**

Outlook starts and displays your calendar for today's date (Figure 3-83). Your date will differ, depending on the computer's system date.

4

• **Click the Close button on the Outlook title bar to close Outlook.**

FIGURE 3-83

Document Summary

When you create and save many documents on a computer, you may not remember the name of each individual document. To help locate documents at a later time, you can store additional information about the document, called **file properties** or the **document summary**, when you save it. For example, you can specify items such as a title, subject, category, keyword(s), and comment(s).

The following steps show how to modify and view the document summary for the cover letter.

Other Ways

1. In Voice Command mode, say "File, Properties, Summary"

To Modify the Document Summary

1

- **Click File on the menu bar (Figure 3-84).**

2

- **Click Properties on the File menu.**
- **When Word displays the Okamoto Cover Letter Properties dialog box, if necessary, click the Summary tab.**
- **Type** National Computer Sales **in the Title text box.**
- **Type** Cover Letter **in the Subject text box.**
- **Type** Cover Letter **in the Category text box.**
- **Type** cover letter, National Computer Sales **in the Keywords text box.**
- **Type** Cover letter to Ms. Helen Weiss at National Computer Sales **in the Comments text box (Figure 3-85).**

3

- **Click the OK button to close the dialog box.**
- **Click the Save button on the Standard toolbar.**
- **Click File on the menu bar and then click Close to close the cover letter document window.**

FIGURE 3-84

FIGURE 3-85

The updated file properties become part of the document when you save the document.

Word automatically pulls the author information from the user information stored on the computer. To change the user information, click Tools on the menu bar, click Options, click the User Information tab, enter the new information in the text boxes, and then click the OK button.

When opening a document at a later time, you can display the document properties to help you locate a particular file, as shown in the following steps.

To Display File Properties in the Open Dialog Box

1

• **Click the Open button on the Standard toolbar.**

• **When Word displays the Open dialog box, if necessary, click the Look in box arrow, click 3½ Floppy (A:), and then click Okamoto Cover Letter.**

• **Click the Views button arrow in the Open dialog box.**

Word displays the Views menu in the Open dialog box (Figure 3-86).

FIGURE 3-86

2

• **Click Properties on the Views menu.**

Word displays the file properties to the right of the selected file (Figure 3-87).

3

• **Click the Cancel button in the dialog box.**

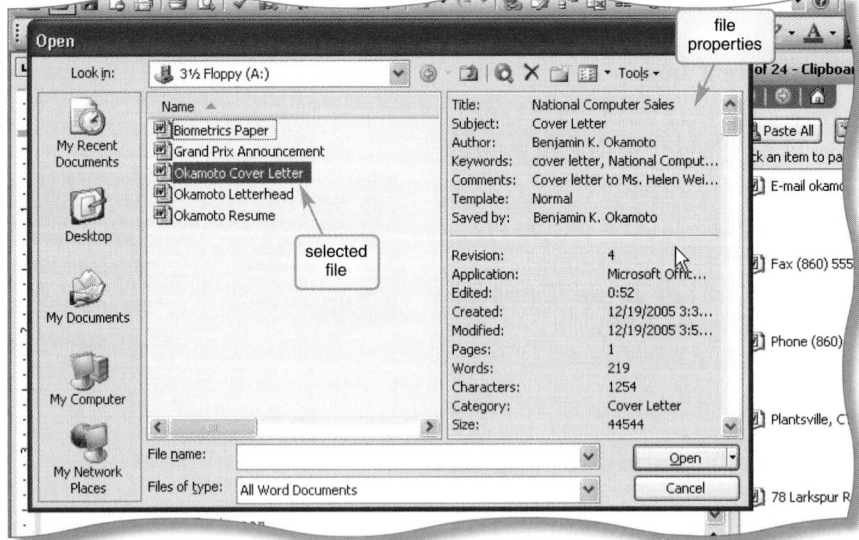

FIGURE 3-87

The final step in this project is to quit Word, as described in the next step.

To Quit Word

1 **Click File on the menu bar and then click Exit. (If Word displays a dialog box about saving changes, click the No button.)**

Word closes any open documents (in this case, the resume) and then the Word window closes.

Project Summary

In creating the Okamoto Resume and Okamoto Cover Letter in this project, you learned how to use Word to enter and format a resume and cover letter. You learned how to use the Resume Wizard to create a resume. Then, you selected and replaced placeholder text in the document created by the resume. In personalizing the resume, you learned how to hide white space, enter a line break, and use Word's AutoFormat As You Type feature. This project also discussed how to view and print the resume in print preview.

Next, this project showed how to create a letterhead and then the cover letter. While creating the letterhead, you learned how to add color to characters, set custom tab stops, collect and paste between documents, add a border to a paragraph, and clear formatting. In the cover letter, this project showed how to insert a date, create and insert an AutoText entry, create and format a table, and enter a bulleted list. Finally, the project showed how to address and print an envelope, use smart tags, and modify the document summary.

 If you have a SAM user profile, you may have access to hands-on instruction, practice, and assessment of the skills covered in this project. Log in to your SAM account and go to your assignments page to see what your instructor has assigned.

What You Should Know

Having completed this project, you should be able to perform the tasks below. The tasks are listed in the same order they were presented in this project. For a list of the buttons, menus, toolbars, and commands introduced in this project, see the Quick Reference Summary at the back of this book and refer to the Page Number column.

1. Start and Customize Word   (WD 141)
2. Display Formatting Marks   (WD 141)
3. Create a Resume Using Word's Resume Wizard (WD 142)
4. Hide White Space   (WD 149)
5. Print the Resume Created by the Resume Wizard (WD 149)
6. Select and Replace Placeholder Text   (WD 152)
7. Select and Replace More Placeholder Text (WD 153)
8. Enter a Line Break   (WD 154)
9. Enter More Text with Line Breaks   (WD 155)
10. AutoFormat As You Type   (WD 156)
11. Enter the Remaining Sections of the Resume (WD 157)
12. Print Preview a Document   (WD 158)
13. Save a Document   (WD 159)
14. Open a New Document Window   (WD 160)
15. Change the Font Size   (WD 161, WD 162)
16. Color Text   (WD 161)
17. Insert a Graphic   (WD 162)
18. Resize a Graphic   (WD 162)
19. Set Custom Tab Stops Using the Tabs Dialog Box (WD 164)
20. Switch from One Open Document to Another (WD 166)
21. Copy Items to the Office Clipboard   (WD 166)
22. Display the Clipboard Task Pane   (WD 169)
23. Zoom Text Width   (WD 169)
24. Paste from the Office Clipboard   (WD 170)
25. Paste More Information from the Office Clipboard   (WD 171)

26. Zoom to 100%   (WD 172)

27. Bottom Border a Paragraph   (WD 172)

28. Clear Formatting   (WD 173)

29. Convert a Hyperlink to Regular Text   (WD 174)

30. Save the Letterhead   (WD 174)

31. Save the Document with a New File Name (WD 176)

32. Set Custom Tab Stops Using the Ruler (WD 176)

33. Insert the Current Date in a Document (WD 177)

34. Enter the Inside Address and Salutation (WD 178)

35. Create an AutoText Entry   (WD 179)

36. Insert a Nonbreaking Space   (WD 180)

37. Insert an AutoText Entry   (WD 181)

38. Enter a Paragraph   (WD 182)

39. Insert an Empty Table   (WD 183)

40. Enter Data in a Table   (WD 184)

41. Fit Columns to Table Contents   (WD 185)

42. Select a Table   (WD 186)

43. Center a Selected Table   (WD 187)

44. Add More Text   (WD 187)

45. Bullet a List as You Type   (WD 187)

46. Enter the Remainder of the Cover Letter (WD 189)

47. Save a Document Again   (WD 189)

48. Print a Document   (WD 190)

49. Address and Print an Envelope   (WD 190)

50. Use the Smart Tag Actions Button   (WD 192)

51. Modify the Document Summary   (WD 193)

52. Display File Properties in the Open Dialog Box (WD 194)

53. Quit Word   (WD 195)

More About

Certification

The Microsoft Office Specialist Certification program provides an opportunity for you to obtain a valuable industry credential - proof that you have the Word 2003 skills required by employers. For more information, see Appendix E or visit the Word 2003 Certification Web page (scsite.com/wd2003/cert).

More About

Quick Reference

For a table that lists how to complete the tasks covered in this book using the mouse, menu, shortcut menu, and keyboard, see the Quick Reference Summary at the back of this book, or visit the Word 2003 Quick Reference Web page (scsite.com/wd2003/qr).

Learn It Online

Instructions: To complete the Learn It Online exercises, start your browser, click the Address bar, and then enter the Web address scsite.com/wd2003/learn. When the Word 2003 Learn It Online page is displayed, follow the instructions in the exercises below. Each exercise has instructions for printing your results, either for your own records or for submission to your instructor.

1 Project Reinforcement TF, MC, and SA

Below Word Project 3, click the Project Reinforcement link. Print the quiz by clicking Print on the File menu for each page. Answer each question.

2 Flash Cards

Below Word Project 3, click the Flash Cards link and read the instructions. Type 20 (or a number specified by your instructor) in the Number of playing cards text box, type your name in the Enter your Name text box, and then click the Flip Card button. When the flash card is displayed, read the question and then click the ANSWER box arrow to select an answer. Flip through Flash Cards. If your score is 15 (75%) correct or greater, click Print on the File menu to print your results. If your score is less than 15 (75%) correct, then redo this exercise by clicking the Replay button.

3 Practice Test

Below Word Project 3, click the Practice Test link. Answer each question, enter your first and last name at the bottom of the page, and then click the Grade Test button. When the graded practice test is displayed on your screen, click Print on the File menu to print a hard copy. Continue to take practice tests until you score 80% or better.

4 Who Wants To Be a Computer Genius?

Below Word Project 3, click the Computer Genius link. Read the instructions, enter your first and last name at the bottom of the page, and then click the PLAY button. When your score is displayed, click the PRINT RESULTS link to print a hard copy.

5 Wheel of Terms

Below Word Project 3, click the Wheel of Terms link. Read the instructions, and then enter your first and last name and your school name. Click the PLAY button. When your score is displayed, right-click the score and then click Print on the shortcut menu to print a hard copy.

6 Crossword Puzzle Challenge

Below Word Project 3, click the Crossword Puzzle Challenge link. Read the instructions, and then enter your first and last name. Click the SUBMIT button. Work the crossword puzzle. When you are finished, click the Submit button. When the crossword puzzle is redisplayed, click the Print Puzzle button to print a hard copy.

7 Tips and Tricks

Below Word Project 3, click the Tips and Tricks link. Click a topic that pertains to Project 3. Right-click the information and then click Print on the shortcut menu. Construct a brief example of what the information relates to in Word to confirm you understand how to use the tip or trick.

8 Newsgroups

Below Word Project 3, click the Newsgroups link. Click a topic that pertains to Project 3. Print three comments.

9 Expanding Your Horizons

Below Word Project 3, click the Expanding Your Horizons link. Click a topic that pertains to Project 3. Print the information. Construct a brief example of what the information relates to in Word to confirm you understand the contents of the article.

10 Search Sleuth

Below Word Project 3, click the Search Sleuth link. To search for a term that pertains to this project, select a term below the Project 3 title and then use the Google search engine at google.com (or any major search engine) to display and print two Web pages that present information on the term.

11 Word Online Training

Below Word Project 3, click the Word Online Training link. When your browser displays the Microsoft Office Online Web page, click the Word link. Click one of the Word courses that covers one or more of the objectives listed at the beginning of the project on page WD 138. Print the first page of the course before stepping through it.

12 Office Marketplace

Below Word Project 3, click the Office Marketplace link. When your browser displays the Microsoft Office Online Web page, click the Office Marketplace link. Click a topic that relates to Word. Print the first page.

Apply Your Knowledge

1 Working with Tabs and a Table

Instructions: Start Word. Open the document, Apply 3-1 Expenses Table, on the Data Disk. See the inside back cover of this book for instructions for downloading the Data Disk or see your instructor for information about accessing the files in this book.

The document is a Word table that you are to edit and format. The revised table is shown in Figure 3-88.

Perform the following tasks:

1. In the line containing the table title, Personal Expenses Table, remove the tab stop at the 1" mark on the ruler.

2. Set a centered tab at the 3" mark on the ruler.

3. Bold the characters in the title. Change their color to dark red.

4. Add a new row to the bottom of the table. In the first cell of the new row, type Total as the entry.

Personal Expenses Table

	January	February	March	April
Rent	425.00	425.00	425.00	425.00
Utilities	130.92	126.33	99.12	96.54
Entertainment	88.95	75.50	91.17	101.49
Telephone	33.24	36.22	35.67	34.80
Cable/Internet	62.19	62.19	62.19	62.19
Car Payment	205.14	205.14	205.14	205.14
Total	**945.44**	**930.38**	**918.29**	**925.16**

FIGURE 3-88

5. Delete the row containing the Miscellaneous expenses.

6. Insert a column between the February and April columns. Fill in the column as follows: Column Title – March; Rent – 425.00; Utilities – 99.12; Entertainment – 91.17; Telephone – 35.67; Cable/Internet – 62.19; Car Payment – 205.14.

7. Click the Tables and Borders button on the Standard toolbar to display the Tables and Borders toolbar. If necessary, click the Draw Table button on the Tables and Borders toolbar to deselect the button. Position the insertion point in the January Total cell (second column, last row). Click the AutoSum button on the Tables and Borders toolbar to sum the contents of the column. Repeat for February, March, and April totals. Click the Tables and Borders button on the Standard toolbar to remove the Tables and Borders toolbar from the screen. Leave the screen in print layout view.

8. Right-align all cells containing numbers.

9. Apply the Table Contemporary style to the table. *Hint:* You may need to click the Show box arrow in the Styles and Formatting task pane and then click All styles to display all available styles.

10. Make all columns as wide as their contents (AutoFit to Contents).

11. Center the table between the left and right margins of the page.

12. Change the color of the table contents to dark blue.

13. Bold the last row of the table, which contains the totals.

14. Click File on the menu bar and then click Save As. Save the document using the file name, Apply 3-1 Modified Expenses Table.

15. Print the revised table.

In the Lab

1 Using Word's Resume Wizard to Create a Resume

Problem: You are a student at Midway University expecting to receive your Bachelor of Arts degree in Technical Writing this May. As graduation is approaching quickly, you prepare the resume shown in Figure 3-89 using Word's Resume Wizard.

Instructions:

1. Use the Resume Wizard to create a Professional style resume. Use your own name and address information when the Resume Wizard requests it.

2. Hide white space on the screen. Personalize the resume as shown in Figure 3-89. When entering multiple lines in the areas of concentration, awards received, interests and activities, and languages sections, be sure to enter a line break at the end of each line, instead of a paragraph break.

3. Check the spelling of the resume.

4. Save the resume with Lab 3-1 Malone Resume as the file name.

5. View and print the resume from within print preview.

2 Creating a Cover Letter with a Table

Problem: You prepared the resume shown in Figure 3-89 and now are ready to create a cover letter to send to a prospective employer (Figure 3-90 on the next page).

Instructions:

1. Create the letterhead shown at the top of Figure 3-90. If you completed In the Lab 1, use the Office Clipboard to copy and paste the address information from the resume to the letterhead. Save the letterhead with the file name, Lab 3-2 Malone Letterhead.

1225 Schilton Court   Phone (312) 555-6380
Chicago, IL 60602   Fax (312) 555-6391
                         E-mail malone@earthnet.com

Leah A. Malone

Objective	To obtain a full-time editorial position with a publishing company in the Chicago area.
Education	2001-2005 Midway University Chicago, IL **Technical Writing** • B.A., May 2005 • A.A., May 2003
Areas of concentration	Technical Publications Journalism Research Writing and Techniques Information Technology
Awards received	Dean's List, 2002-2005 Excellence in Student Publications Award, 1st Place, 2004-2005 Alpha Omega Honors Society, 2003-2005
Interests and activities	Reading Buddy program, participant Technical Buzz, contributor Regional Writers Association, member Literacy Council, member
Languages	English (fluent) Spanish (fluent)
Work experience	2001-2005 Midway Community Center Chicago, IL **Assistant Program Coordinator** • Assisted with developing programs aimed at increasing literacy and reading skills • Conducted reading programs aimed at children, adults, and seniors, as well as new readers • Composed, proofread, and edited the center's monthly newsletter advertising new offerings and services
Volunteer experience	Participant in Midway Library's Reading Buddy program, in which adults read to school-aged children on a weekly basis.

FIGURE 3-89

(continued)

In the Lab

Creating a Cover Letter with a Table *(continued)*

2. Create the letter shown in Figure 3-90. Set a tab stop at the 3.5" mark on the ruler for the date line, complimentary close, and signature block. Insert the current date. After entering the inside address, create an AutoText entry for Greyton Publications, and insert the AutoText entry whenever you have to enter the company name. Remove the hyperlink format from the e-mail address. Insert and center the table.

3. Modify the document summary as follows: Title – Greyton Publications; Subject – Cover Letter; Category – Cover Letter; Keywords – cover letter, Greyton Publications; Comments – Cover letter to Mr. Roger Grandy at Greyton Publications.

4. Check the spelling. Save the letter with Lab 3-2 Malone Cover Letter as the file name.

5. View and print the cover letter from within print preview.

6. View the document summary. On the printout, write down the edited time.

7. Address and print an envelope and a mailing label using the inside and return addresses in the cover letter.

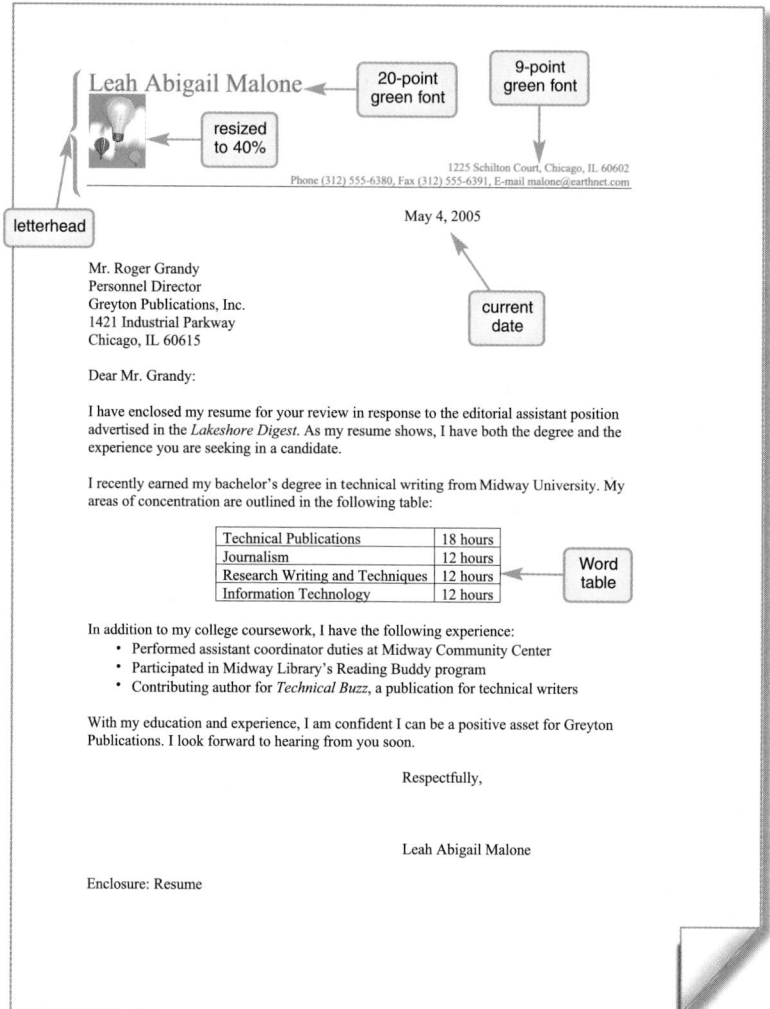

FIGURE 3-90

3 Creating a Resume and Cover Letter

Problem: You are to create a personal resume and cover letter. Assume you are graduating this semester.

Instructions:

1. Use the Resume Wizard to create a personal resume using whichever style you desire. Try to be as accurate as possible when personalizing the resume. Check spelling and grammar in the resume.

2. Obtain a copy of last Sunday's newspaper. Look through the classified section and cut out a want ad in an area of your major. Create a cover letter for your resume, gearing the letter to the job advertised in the newspaper. Use the job advertisement information for the inside address and your personal information for the return address. After setting tabs at the 3.5" mark, change them to the 3" mark. Include a table and a numbered list in the cover letter. *Hint:* Use Help to learn how to create a numbered list.

3. Address and print an envelope. Then, print an entire page of mailing labels using your home address. Submit the want ad with your cover letter, resume, envelope, and mailing labels.

Cases and Places

The difficulty of these case studies varies:
■ are the least difficult and ■■ are more difficult. The last exercise is a group exercise.

1 ■ Your boss has asked you to create a calendar for June so he can post it on the office bulletin board. Use the Calendar Wizard in the Other Documents sheet in the Templates dialog box. Use the following settings in the wizard: Boxes & borders style, portrait print direction, leave room for a picture, June 2005 for both the start and end date. With the calendar on the screen, click the current graphic and delete it. Insert a clip art image of a sailboat graphic (he loves to sail) and then resize the image so it fits in the entire space for the graphic.

2 ■ You have been asked to prepare the agenda for an insurance benefits meeting. Use the Agenda Wizard in the Other Documents sheet in the Templates dialog box. Use the following settings in the wizard: style – standard; meeting date – September 15, 2005; meeting time – 8:00 a.m. to 10:15 a.m.; title – Insurance Benefits Meeting; meeting location – Conference Room G; include Type of meeting and Special notes headings; include these names on agenda – Meeting called by and Attendees; Topics, People, and Minutes – Introduction, Keith Brazil, 10; New information system, Kelly Walters, 60; Benefits update, Sharon Gonzalez, 20; Break, 15; Updated claim forms, Bryant Jenkins, 30; do not add a form for recording the minutes. On the agenda created by the wizard, add the following names in the appropriate spaces: Marsha Goldfarb, Employee Insurance and Benefits director called the meeting; all people listed in this assignment will be attending – along with T. Ryan, D. Bleuer, M. Kiddle, and you. The meeting is an informational meeting. As a special note, remind attendees to bring paper and pen to the meeting.

3 ■ A customer has asked you to fax information about a rental home in Panama City, Florida so he can review it for an upcoming vacation. Use the Fax Wizard and the following settings: create the fax cover sheet with a note and print the fax so you can send it on a separate fax machine. It must be faxed to Terrell Bryce. His fax number is (317) 555-2202 and his telephone number is (317) 555-2214. You will fax him a total of four pages of information using the subject of Vacation home rental inquiry. In the fax notes, write a message informing Terrell that the following pages contain the information he requested on the rental home in Panama City, Florida, and that he should let you know if you can help with any other part of his vacation planning. Use your own name, address, and telephone information in the fax and use whichever fax style you like best.

4 ■■ As director of employee insurance and benefits, you are responsible for keeping all Employee Insurance and Benefits staff members informed of changes in procedures or policies. You will be scheduling a meeting on Thursday, September 15, at 8:30 a.m. in Conference Room G to discuss the new information system, along with new claim forms and benefits. It is important all staff members attend. If they will be on vacation or are unavailable, they need to contact you to arrange to receive the informational packet that will be distributed at the meeting. You prepare a memorandum about the meeting. A copy of the memo should be sent to Marsha Goldfarb. Use the Memo Wizard or a memo template, together with the concepts and techniques presented in this project, to create and format the interoffice memorandum.

Cases and Places

5 ■■ **Working Together** The office of career development at your school is looking for a team of students to create a sample resume to be used as a reference for other students in your major. The department also would like you to submit a list of resume-writing tips they could share with other students. Each member of your team is to identify a minimum of five resume-writing tips by searching the Web, visiting a library, and/or talking to an expert in the area of human resources. Then, the team should meet as a group to create a numbered list of resume-writing tips. Next, all team members are to look through the headings available in the Resume Wizard and select the ones best suited to students in your major, adding any not included in the wizard. Then, the members should divide up the headings among the team. After each team member writes his or her section(s) of the resume, the group should meet to copy and paste the individual sections into a single resume. Finally, write a memo indicating the work the team has completed. Use the concepts and techniques presented in this project to format the memo, resume-writing tips, and resume.

MICROSOFT
Office Word 2003

Creating Web Pages Using Word

CASE PERSPECTIVE

In Project 3, Benjamin Kane Okamoto created his resume with your assistance (Figure 3-1 on page WD 139). Recently, Benjamin has been surfing the Internet and has discovered that many people have their own personal Web pages. Their Web pages contain links to other Web sites and also to personal Web pages such as resumes and schedules. These personal Web pages are very impressive.

To make himself more marketable to a potential employer, Benjamin has asked you to help him create a personal Web page. He wants his Web page to contain a hyperlink to his resume – with the hyperlink on the left side of the page and his resume on the right side of the page. On the left side of the Web page, Benjamin would like another hyperlink called My Favorite Site. When a Web site visitor clicks this link, Benjamin's favorite Web site (www.scsite.com) will be displayed on the right side of his personal Web page. Finally, Benjamin wants the e-mail address on his resume Web page to be a hyperlink to an e-mail program. This way, potential employers easily can send him an e-mail message to schedule an interview or request additional information. You show Benjamin how to save his resume as a Web page and incorporate frames and hyperlinks into a Web page.

As you read through this Web Feature, you will learn how to use Word to create a Web page. If you are stepping through this feature on a computer, you will need the resume document created in Project 3. (If you did not create the resume, see your instructor for a copy of it.)

Objectives

You will have mastered the material in this feature when you can:

- Save a Word document as a Web page
- Format and preview a Web page
- Create and modify a frames page
- Insert and modify hyperlinks

Introduction

Word provides two techniques for creating Web pages. If you have an existing Word document, you can save it as a Web page. If you do not have an existing Word document, you can use Word to create a Web page from scratch. Word has many Web page authoring tools that allow you to incorporate objects such as frames, hyperlinks, sounds, videos, pictures, scrolling text, bullets, horizontal lines, check boxes, option buttons, list boxes, text boxes, and scripts on Web pages.

This Web Feature illustrates how to save the resume created in Project 3 as a Web page. Then, it uses Word to create another Web page that contains two frames (Figure 1a on the next page). A **frame** is a rectangular section of a Web page that can display another separate Web page. Thus, a Web page with multiple frames can display multiple Web pages simultaneously. Word stores all frames associated with a Web page in a single file called the **frames page**. When you open the frames page in Word or a Web browser, all frames associated with the Web page are displayed on the screen.

In this Web Feature, the file name of the frames page is Okamoto Personal Web Page. When you initially open this frames page, the left frame contains the title, Benjamin Okamoto, and two hyperlinks — My Resume and My Favorite Site; the right frame displays Benjamin's resume (Figure 1a). As discussed in Project 3, a hyperlink is a shortcut that allows a user to jump easily and quickly to another location in the same document or to other documents or Web pages. In the left frame, the My Resume hyperlink is a link to the resume Web page, and the My Favorite Site hyperlink is a link to www.scsite.com.

(a) **Web Page Displaying Resume**

(c) **E-Mail Program**

(b) **Web Page Displaying Web Site**

FIGURE 1

When you click the My Favorite Site hyperlink in the left frame, the www.scsite.com Web site is displayed in the right frame (Figure 1b). When you click the My Resume hyperlink in the left frame, the resume Web page is displayed in the right frame. The resume itself contains a hyperlink to an e-mail address. When you click the e-mail address, Word starts your e-mail program automatically with the recipient's address (okamoto@earth.net) already filled in (Figure 1c). You simply type a subject and message and then click the Send button, which places the message in the Outbox or sends it if you are connected to an e-mail server.

Once you have created Web pages, you can publish them. **Publishing** is the process of making Web pages available to others, for example on the World Wide Web or on a company's intranet. In Word, you can publish Web pages by saving them to a Web folder or to an FTP location. The procedures for publishing Web pages in Microsoft Office are discussed in Appendix C.

This Web Feature is for instructional purposes. Thus, you create and save your frames page and associated Web pages to a floppy disk rather than to the Web.

Saving a Word Document as a Web Page

Once you have created a Word document, you can save it as a Web page so that it can be published and then viewed by a Web browser, such as Internet Explorer. The following steps show how to save the resume created in Project 3 as a Web page.

To Save a Word Document as a Web Page

1

• **Start Word and then open the file named Okamoto Resume created in Project 3. Click File on the menu bar (Figure 2).**

FIGURE 2

2

• **Click Save as Web Page on the File menu.**

• **When Word displays the Save As dialog box, type** Okamoto Resume Web Page **in the File name text box and then, if necessary, change the Save in location to 3½ Floppy (A:).**

• **Click the Change Title button.**

• **When Word displays the Set Page Title dialog box, type** Okamoto Resume Web Page **in the Page title text box (Figure 3).**

When the Web page is displayed in a browser, it will show the text, Okamoto Resume Web Page, on the title bar.

FIGURE 3

3

• **Click the OK button in the Set Page Title dialog box.**

• **Click the Save button in the Save As dialog box.**

Word saves the resume as a Web page and displays it in the Word window (Figure 4).

FIGURE 4

Other Ways

1. On File menu click Save As, click Save as type box arrow, click Single File Web Page, click Save button

Word switches to Web layout view and also changes some of the toolbar buttons and menu commands to provide Web page authoring features. For example, the Standard toolbar now displays a New Web Page button (Figure 4 on the previous page). The Web Layout View button on the horizontal scroll bar is selected.

The resume is displayed in the Word window much like it will be displayed in a Web browser. Some of Word's formatting features are not supported by Web pages. Thus, your Web page may look slightly different from the original Word document.

When you save a file as a Web page, Word converts the contents of the document into **HTML** (hypertext markup language), which is a language that browsers can interpret. The Save as Web Page command, by default, saves the document in a format called single file Web page (shown in Figure 3 on the previous page). The **single file Web page format** saves all of the components of the Web page in a single file that has an .mht extension. This format is particularly useful for e-mailing documents in HTML format. Another format, called **Web Page format**, saves the Web page in a file and some of its components in a folder. This format is useful if you need access to the individual components, such as images, that make up the Web page. The **filtered Web Page format** saves the file in Web page format and then reduces the size of the file by removing specific Microsoft Office formats.

If you wanted to save a file using the Web Page format or the filtered Web page format, or any other type of format, you would follow these steps.

To Save a File in a Different Format

1. Click File on the menu bar and then click Save As.
2. When Word displays the Save As dialog box, type the desired file name in the File name box.
3. Click the Save as type box arrow.
4. Select the desired file format in the Save as type list.
5. Click the Save button in the Save As dialog box.

If you have access to a Web server and it allows you to save files to a Web folder, then you can save the Web page directly to the Web server by clicking My Network Places in the lower-left corner of the Save As dialog box (Figure 3). If you have access to a Web server that allows you to save to an FTP site, then you can select the FTP site under FTP locations in the Save in box just as you select any folder to which you save a file. To learn more about publishing Web pages to a Web folder or FTP location using Microsoft Office applications, refer to Appendix C.

Formatting and Previewing a Web Page

In this feature, the e-mail address on the Okamoto Resume Web page is to be formatted as a hyperlink. Also, the colors and formats of elements on the Web page should follow a standard theme. The following sections describe how to modify the Web page to include these enhancements. After modifying the Web page, you will see how to preview the Web page in Word.

Formatting the E-Mail Address as a Hyperlink

The e-mail address in the resume is to be formatted as a hyperlink so that when someone clicks the e-mail address on the Web page, his or her e-mail program starts automatically and displays an e-mail window with the e-mail address already filled in.

The next steps show how to format the e-mail address as a hyperlink.

More About

HTML

If you wish to view the HTML source code associated with a Web page, click View on the menu bar and then click HTML Source, which starts the Script Editor. To close the Script Editor, click File on the menu bar and then click Exit.

More About

Web Page Design

For information on guidelines for designing Web pages, visit the Word 2003 More About Web page (scsite.com/wd2003/more) and then click Web Page Design.

To Format Text as a Hyperlink

 1

- **Select the e-mail address (okamoto@earth.net) and then right-click the selected text (Figure 5).**

FIGURE 5

2

- **Click Hyperlink on the shortcut menu.**

- **When Word displays the Insert Hyperlink dialog box, click E-mail Address in the Link to bar.**

- **In the Text to display text box, type** okamoto@earth.net **and then click the E-mail address text box.**

- **Type** okamoto@earth.net **in the E-mail address text box.**

As soon as you begin typing the e-mail address, Word inserts mailto: in front of the address, which connects the hyperlink to your e-mail program (Figure 6). The text in the Text to display text box will be displayed as the hyperlink text on the screen.

3

- **Click the OK button.**

Word formats the e-mail address as a hyperlink; that is, it is colored blue and underlined (shown in Figure 7 on the next page).

FIGURE 6

If you want to test the e-mail address hyperlink, CTRL+click the mouse while pointing to the hyperlink. This should open an e-mail window.

To edit a hyperlink, right-click the hyperlink and then click Edit Hyperlink on the shortcut menu.

Other Ways

1. Click Insert Hyperlink button on Standard toolbar
2. On Insert menu click Hyperlink
3. Press CTRL+K
4. In Voice Command mode, say "Insert, Hyperlink"

Applying a Theme to the Web Page

The next step is to apply a theme to the Web page. A **theme** is a predefined set of colors, fonts, and other design elements for backgrounds, graphics, headings, lists, lines, hyperlinks, and tables. By using themes, you easily can make Web pages and other online documents consistent with one another.

The steps on the next page show how to apply a theme to the Okamoto Resume Web Page document.

To Apply a Theme

1

• **Click Format on the menu bar (Figure 7).**

FIGURE 7

2

• **Click Theme on the Format menu.**
• **When Word displays the Theme dialog box, scroll to Rice Paper in the Choose a Theme list and then click Rice Paper.**

Word presents a variety of themes in the Theme dialog box (Figure 8).

3

• **Click the OK button.**

Word applies the Rice Paper theme to the open document (shown in Figure 9).

FIGURE 8

If you like all elements except for the background in a theme, remove the check mark from the Background Image check box in the Theme dialog box (Figure 8) before clicking the OK button.

Viewing the Web Page in Your Default Browser

In Word, you can see how a Web page looks in your default browser – before publishing it and without actually connecting to the Internet. To do this, use the Web Page Preview command, which displays on the File menu when Word is in Web layout view. The next steps show how to preview a Web page in Word.

To Preview a Web Page

1

• **Click File on the menu bar (Figure 9).**

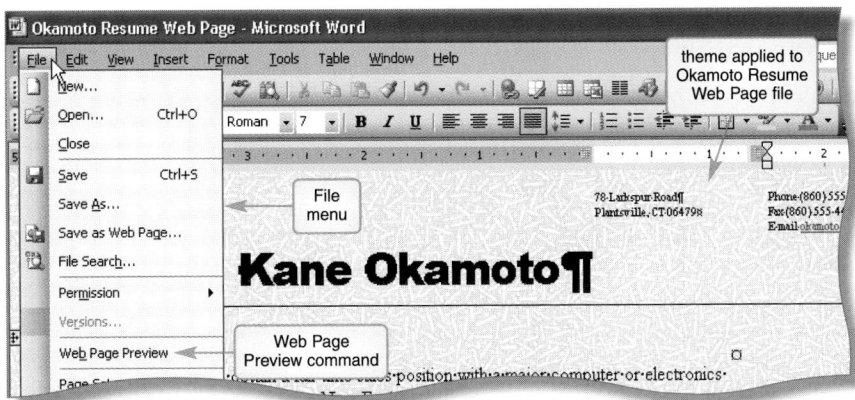

FIGURE 9

2

• **Click Web Page Preview on the File menu.**

• **If necessary, maximize the browser window.**

Word opens the Web browser in a separate window and displays the open Web page file in the browser window (Figure 10).

3

• **Click the Close button on the browser title bar to close the browser window.**

FIGURE 10

Other Ways

1. In Windows Explorer, double-click Web page file name
2. In Voice Command mode, say "File, Web Page Preview"

You now are finished modifying the Okamoto Resume Web Page file. The following step describes saving the file again.

To Save a Web Page

1 **Click the Save button on the Standard toolbar.**

Word saves the file.

Creating and Modifying a Frames Page

In the previous section, you saved an existing Word document as a Web page. Next, you want to create the frames page that will be divided into two separate frames. The left frame is to contain two links: one to the Okamoto Resume Web Page file just created and one to www.scsite.com.

The following steps show how to create a frames page and then add a frame so the frames page contains two frames side-by-side.

To Create a Frames Page

 1

• **Click Format on the menu bar and then point to Frames (Figure 11).**

FIGURE 11

2

• **Click New Frames Page on the Frames submenu.**

Word opens a new document window that contains the Okamoto Resume Web Page in the current frame (called Frame1) and displays the Frames toolbar on the screen (Figure 12).

FIGURE 12

3

• **Click the New Frame Left button on the Frames toolbar.**

Word opens a new frame to the left of the current frame (Figure 13). The new frame is called Frame2.

FIGURE 13

More About

Web Pages

You can use horizontal lines to separate sections of a Web page. To add a horizontal line at the location of the insertion point, click Format on the menu bar, click Borders and Shading, click the Horizontal Line button, click the desired line type in the Horizontal Line dialog box, and then click the OK button.

The frames page is divided into two frames, one on the left and one on the right. A **frame border** separates the frames. The next step is to add text to the left frame, as described below.

To Add Text to a Frame

1 **With the insertion point in the left frame (Frame2), click the Font Size box arrow. Click 16 in the Font Size list. Type** Benjamin Okamoto **and then click the Font Size box arrow. Click 12 in the Font Size list. Press the ENTER key twice.**

2 **Type** My Resume **and then press the ENTER key twice.**

3 **Type** My Favorite Site **as the last entry in the left frame.**

Word displays the text in the left frame (shown in Figure 14).

The next step is to make the left frame narrower. To do this, you drag the frame border. When you point to and drag the frame border, the mouse pointer shape changes to a double-headed arrow. The following step shows how to resize a Web page frame.

To Resize a Web Page Frame

1

• **Drag the frame border to the left until it is positioned between the letters a and m in Okamoto in the left frame (Figure 14).**

Word narrows the left frame and widens the right frame (shown in Figure 15).

FIGURE 14

In this feature the left frame uses the Rice Paper theme, except it does not contain a background image. The following steps describe how to apply a theme, without a background image.

To Apply a Theme

1 **With the insertion point in the left frame, click Format on the menu bar and then click Theme.**

2 **When the Theme dialog box is displayed, scroll to and then click Rice Paper in the Choose a Theme list.**

3 **Place a check mark in the Vivid Colors check box.**

4 **Remove the check mark from the Background Image check box (Figure 15).**

5 **Click the OK button.**

FIGURE 15

Word applies the Rice Paper theme, without a background image (shown in Figure 16 on the next page).

In the left frame, you want the text, My Resume, to be a hyperlink to the Okamoto Resume Web Page document. This means when you click the My Resume link in the left frame, the Okamoto Resume Web Page file will be displayed in the right frame. Similarly, you want the My Favorite site text to be a hyperlink. That is, when you click the hyperlink in the left frame, the www.scsite.com Web site should be displayed in the right frame.

The following steps describe how to link the My Resume text in the left frame to an existing Web Page file that will be displayed in the right frame (Frame1) when the user clicks the My Resume link in the left frame (Frame2).

To Insert and Modify a Hyperlink

1

• **Drag through the text, My Resume, in the left frame to select it.**

• **Click the Insert Hyperlink button on the Standard toolbar.**

• **When Word displays the Insert Hyperlink dialog box, if necessary, click Existing File or Web Page in the Link to bar.**

• **If necessary, click the Look in box arrow and then click 3½ Floppy (A:).**

• **Click Okamoto Resume Web Page.**

Word displays the Okamoto Resume Web Page file name in the Address box (Figure 16).

FIGURE 16

2

• **Click the Target Frame button.**

• **When Word displays the Set Target Frame dialog box, click the right frame in the Current frames page diagram.**

The Set Target Frame dialog box displays a diagram of the left and right frames in the frames page (Figure 17).

3

• **Click the OK button in the Set Target Frame dialog box.**

• **Click the OK button in the Insert Hyperlink dialog box.**

FIGURE 17

Word formats the selected text as a hyperlink (shown in Figure 18). When you click the My Resume link in the left frame, the Okamoto Resume Web Page file will be displayed in the right frame.

The following steps describe how to link the My Favorite Site text in the left frame to a Web site that will be displayed in the right frame.

To Insert and Modify a Hyperlink

1 Drag through the text, My Favorite Site, in the left frame.

2 Click the Insert Hyperlink button on the Standard toolbar.

3 When Word displays the Insert Hyperlink dialog box, if necessary, click Existing File or Web Page in the Link to bar. Type www.scsite.com in the Address text box.

4 Click the Target Frame button. When Word displays the Set Target Frame dialog box, click the right frame in the diagram (Figure 18).

5 Click the OK button in each dialog box.

Word formats the text, My Favorite Site, as a hyperlink that, when clicked, displays the associated Web site in the right frame (shown in Figure 1b on page WD 204).

FIGURE 18

If you wanted to edit an existing hyperlink, you right-click the hyperlink text and then click Edit Hyperlink on the shortcut menu. Word will display the Edit Hyperlink dialog box instead of the Insert Hyperlink dialog box. Other than the title bar, these two dialog boxes are the same.

The next task is to modify the frame properties of the left frame so it does not display a scroll bar between the left and right frames, as shown on the next page.

More About

Quick Reference

For a table that lists how to complete the tasks covered in this book using the mouse, menu, shortcut menu, and keyboard, see the Quick Reference Summary at the back of this book, or visit the Word 2003 Quick Reference Web page (scsite.com/wd2003/qr).

More About

Highlighting

To add color to an online document or e-mail message, highlight the text. Highlighting alerts the reader to the text's importance, much like a highlight marker does in a textbook. To highlight text, select it, click the Highlight button arrow on the Formatting toolbar, and then click the desired highlight color.

To Modify Frame Properties

1

• **With the insertion point in the left frame, click the Frame Properties button on the Frames toolbar.**

• **When Word displays the Frame Properties dialog box, if necessary, click the Borders tab.**

• **Click the Show scrollbars in browser box arrow and then click Never.**

The Borders sheet in the Frame Properties dialog box allows you to set options related to the frame borders (Figure 19).

2

• **Click the OK button.**

Word formats the border to no scroll bar.

FIGURE 19

The next step is to save the frames page with a file name and specify the title to be displayed on the Web page title bar, as described below.

To Save the Frames Page

1 **Insert your floppy disk into drive A. Click File on the menu bar and then click Save as Web Page.**

2 **When Word displays the Save As dialog box, type** Okamoto Personal Web Page **in the File name box. Do not press the ENTER key.**

3 **If necessary, click the Save in box arrow and then click 3½ Floppy (A:).**

4 **Click the Change Title button. When Word displays the Set Page Title dialog box, type** Okamoto Personal Web Page **in the Page title text box.**

5 **Click the OK button in the Set Page Title dialog box. Click the Save button in the Save As dialog box.**

Word saves the frames page on a floppy disk in drive A with the file name, Okamoto Personal Web Page. When a user displays the Web page in a browser, the title bar also will show this same name.

The final step is to quit Word, as described next.

To Quit Word

1 **Click the Close button on the Word title bar.**

The Word window closes.

You can start Windows Explorer and double-click the file name, Okamoto Personal Web Page to display the Web page in your browser. From the browser window (Figure 1a on page WD 204), you can test your hyperlinks to be sure they work — before publishing them to the Web. For example, in the left frame, click the My Favorite Site link to display the Web site www.scsite.com in the right frame. (If you are not connected to the Internet, your browser will connect you and then display the Web site.) Click the My Resume link to display the Okamoto Resume Web Page in the right frame. Click the e-mail address to start your e-mail program with the address, okamoto@earth.net, entered in the recipient's address box.

The final step is to make your Web pages and associated files available to others on a network, on an intranet, or on the World Wide Web. Read Appendix C for instructions about publishing Web pages and then talk to your instructor about how you should do this for your system.

More About

Editing Web Pages

You can edit a Web page directly from Internet Explorer. With the Internet Explorer window open and the Web page to edit displaying in the browser window, click the Edit with Microsoft Word button on the toolbar. Internet Explorer starts Word and displays the Web page in the Word window - ready for editing. Or, you can start Word and open the Web page directly in Word by clicking the Open button on the Standard toolbar, clicking the Files of type box arrow, clicking All Web Pages, selecting the Web page document, and then clicking the Open button in the dialog box.

Web Feature Summary

This Web Feature introduced you to creating a Web page by illustrating how to save an existing Word document as a Web page file. The feature then showed how to modify and format the Web page file. Next, you learned how to create a new Web page with frames and then modify the frames page. Finally, the project showed how to create one hyperlink to an e-mail address, one to a Web page file, and another to a Web site.

 If you have a SAM user profile, you may have access to hands-on instruction, practice, and assessment of the skills covered in this project. Log in to your SAM account and go to your assignments page to see what your instructor has assigned.

What You Should Know

Having completed this feature, you should be able to perform the tasks below. The tasks are listed in the same order they were presented in this project. For a list of the buttons, menus, toolbars, and commands introduced in this feature, see the Quick Reference Summary at the back of this book and refer to the Page Number column.

1. Save a Word Document as a Web Page (WD 205)
2. Save a File in a Different Format   (WD 206)
3. Format Text as a Hyperlink   (WD 207)
4. Apply a Theme   (WD 208, WD 211)
5. Preview a Web Page   (WD 209)
6. Save a Web Page   (WD 209)
7. Create a Frames Page   (WD 210)
8. Add Text to a Frame   (WD 210)
9. Resize a Web Page Frame   (WD 211)
10. Insert and Modify a Hyperlink   (WD 212, WD 213)
11. Modify Frame Properties   (WD 214)
12. Save the Frames Page   (WD 214)
13. Quit Word   (WD 215)

In the Lab

1 Saving a Word Document as a Web Page and in Other Formats

Problem: You created the research paper shown in Figure 2-80 on pages WD 130 and WD 131 in Project 2. You decide to save this research paper in a variety of formats.

Instructions:

1. Open the Lab 2-1 Brain Implant Paper shown in Figure 2-80. (If you did not create the research paper, see your instructor for a copy.)
2. Save the paper as a single file Web page using the file name, Lab WF-1 Brain Implant Paper Web Page A. Print the Web page.
3. Use the Web Page Preview command to view the Web page.
4. If you have access to a Web server or FTP site, save the Web page to the server or site (see Appendix C for instructions).
5. Using Windows Explorer, look at the contents of the disk containing the Web page. Write down the names of the files. Open the original Lab 2-1 Brain Implant Paper. Save it as a Web page (not single file) using the file name, Lab WF-1 Brain Implant Paper Web Page B. That is, change the file type in the Save as type box to Web Page. Again, look at the contents of the disk using Windows Explorer. Write down any additional file names. How many more files and folders are created by the Web Page format?
6. Open the original Lab 2-1 Brain Implant Paper. Save it as plain text using the file name, Lab WF-1 Brain Implant Paper Plain Text. That is, change the file type in the Save as type box to Plain Text. Click the OK button when Word displays the File Conversion dialog box. Open the plain text file. *Hint:* In the Open dialog box, click the Files of type box arrow and then click All Files. Write down the difference between the plain text file and the original file.

2 Creating a Web Page with Frames and Hyperlinks

Problem: You created the resume shown in Figure 3-89 on page WD 199 in Project 3. You decide to create a personal Web page with a link to this resume. Thus, you also must save the resume as a Web page.

Instructions:

1. Open the Lab 3-1 Faddis Resume shown in Figure 3-89. (If you did not create the resume, see your instructor for a copy.)
2. Save the resume as a single file Web page using the file name, Lab WF-2 Faddis Resume Web Page. Convert the e-mail address to a hyperlink. Apply the Blends theme to the Web page. Preview the Web page using the Web Page Preview command. Save the Web page again.
3. Create a frames page. Insert a left frame. Add the following text to the left frame on three separate lines: Heather Faddis, My Resume, My Favorite Site. Apply the Blends theme to the left frame. Resize the left frame to the width of its text.
4. In the left frame of the frames page, format the text, My Resume and My Favorite Site, as hyperlinks. When clicked, the My Resume hyperlink should display the Lab WF-2 Faddis Resume Web Page in the right frame. The My Favorite Site hyperlink, when clicked, should display your favorite Web site in the right frame.
5. Modify the properties of the left frame to never display a scroll bar. Save the frames page using the file name, Lab WF-2 Faddis Personal Web Page and change the title of the Web page. Use the Web Page Preview command to view the Web page in your browser.
6. In Windows Explorer, double-click the name of the frames page. Test your Web page links. Print the Web page.
7. If you have access to a Web server or FTP site, save the Web page to the server or site (see Appendix C).

Creating a Document with a Table, Chart, and Watermark

PROJECT

4

CASE PERSPECTIVE

The Minooka Park District provides facilities and services for the citizens of Minooka, Nebraska. For the past 55 years, residents have been enjoying these amenities at no cost. This will change if the bond referendum does not pass next month. The Minooka Park District needs community support to renovate parks, purchase land, and upgrade facilities. It plans to use the bond funds to update playground equipment, replace picnic tables and benches, refurbish concession stands, maintain kitchen and restroom facilities, pave parking lots, and develop an outdoor community skating/ice hockey rink and two playing fields.

Last year, the park district attempted to acquire similar bonds for park renovations and facility upgrades. Although the referendum did not pass, it was a close vote. Board members feel the referendum failed because they did not properly inform the community about the proposed use of funds from the bonds and the estimated tax impact to homeowners. This year, the board has a plan. To better educate community members about the referendum and persuade them to cast a yes vote, the board approved expenses for preparing and mailing a proposal to every Minooka homeowner. The park district director has asked you to design the proposal because she knows you are a marketing major with a minor in computer technology. You are thrilled to participate in this assignment. You will complete the proposal for her review within a week.

As you read through this project, you will learn how to use Word to create a proposal with a table, chart, and watermark.

MICROSOFT
Office Word 2003

Creating a Document with a Table, Chart, and Watermark

PROJECT

Objectives

You will have mastered the material in this project when you can:

- Add a border and shading to a paragraph
- Center page contents vertically on a page
- Insert a section break
- Insert a Word document into an open document
- Create and format a header and footer different from the previous header and footer
- Modify and format a Word table
- Sum columns in a table using the AutoSum button
- Select and format nonadjacent text
- Create a chart from a Word table and modify the chart in Microsoft Graph
- Add picture bullets to a list
- Create and apply a character style
- Use the Draw Table feature to create a table
- Insert a text watermark
- Reveal formatting

Introduction

Sometime during your professional life, you most likely will find yourself placed in a sales role. You might be selling a tangible product, such as vehicles or books, or a service, such as Web page design or interior decorating. Within an organization, you might be selling an idea, such as a benefits package to company employees or a budget plan to upper management. Instead of selling a product, you might be trying to persuade people to take an action, such as signing a petition, joining a club, or donating to a cause. To sell an item or persuade the public, you may find yourself writing a proposal. Proposals vary in length, style, and formality, but all are designed to elicit acceptance from the reader.

A proposal generally is one of three types: planning, research, or sales. A **planning proposal** offers solutions to a problem or improvement to a situation. A **research proposal** usually requests funding for a research project. A **sales proposal** sells an idea, a product, or a service.

Project Four — Sales Proposal

Project 4 uses Word to produce the sales proposal shown in Figure 4-1. The sales proposal is designed to persuade readers to cast a yes vote for the upcoming Minooka Park District bond referendum. The proposal has a colorful title page to attract the readers' attention. To add impact, the sales proposal has a watermark containing the words, YES, behind the text and uses tables and a chart to summarize data.

(a) Title Page

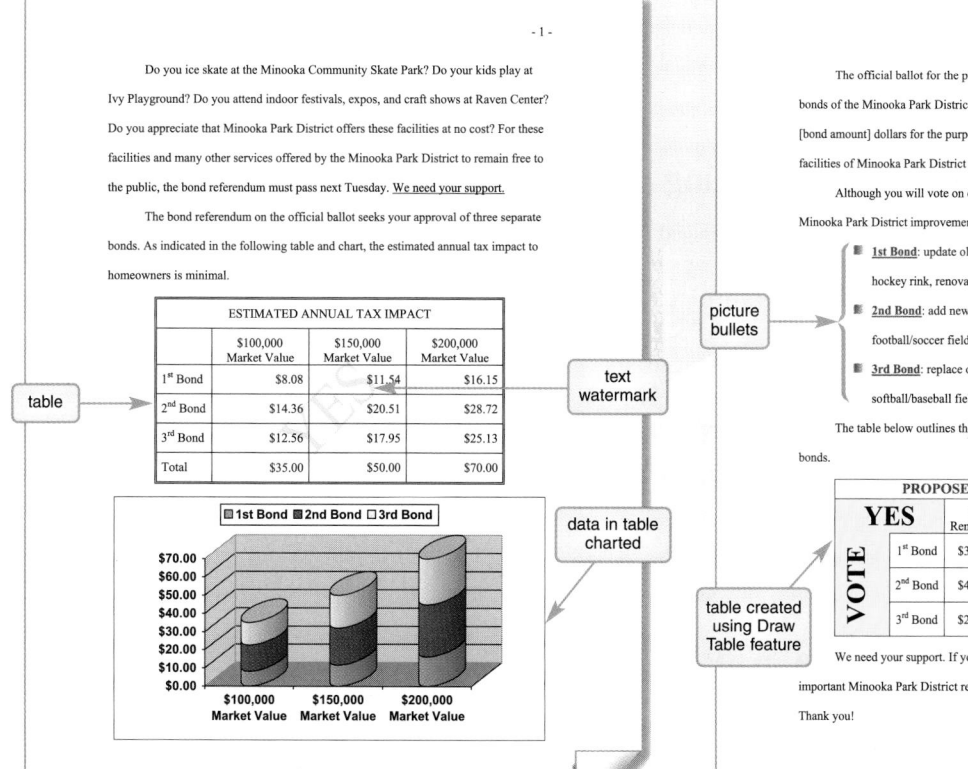

(b) First Page of Body of Sales Proposal

(c) Second Page of Body of Sales Proposal

FIGURE 4-1

More About

Writing Proposals

For more information about writing proposals, visit the Word 2003 More About Web page (scsite.com/wd2003/more) and then click Writing Proposals.

Starting and Customizing Word

To start and customize Word, Windows must be running. If you are stepping through this project on a computer and you want your screen to match the figures in this book, then you should change your computer's resolution to 800 × 600 and reset the toolbars and menus. For information about changing the resolution and resetting toolbars and menus, read Appendix D.

The following steps describe how to start Word and customize the Word window. You may need to ask your instructor how to start Word for your system.

To Start and Customize Word

1 Click the Start button on the Windows taskbar, point to All Programs on the Start menu, point to Microsoft Office on the All Programs submenu, and then click Microsoft Office Word 2003 on the Microsoft Office submenu.

2 If the Word window is not maximized, double-click its title bar to maximize it.

3 If the Language bar appears, right-click it and then click Close the Language bar on the shortcut menu.

4 If the Getting Started task pane is displayed in the Word window, click its Close button.

5 If the Standard and Formatting toolbar buttons are displayed on one row, click the Toolbar Options button and then click Show Buttons on Two Rows in the Toolbar Options list.

6 Click View on the menu bar and then click Print Layout.

Word starts and, after a few moments, displays an empty document in the Word window. You will use print layout view in this project because the proposal contains tables. Thus, the Print Layout View button on the horizontal scroll bar is selected (shown in Figure 4-2 on page WD 222).

Displaying Formatting Marks

As discussed in Project 1, it is helpful to display formatting marks that indicate where in the document you pressed the ENTER key, SPACEBAR, and other keys. The following step displays formatting marks.

To Display Formatting Marks

1 If the Show/Hide ¶ button on the Standard toolbar is not selected already, click it.

Word displays formatting marks in the document window, and the Show/Hide ¶ button on the Standard toolbar is selected (shown in Figure 4-2).

Zooming Page Width

In print layout view, many users **zoom page width** so they can see all edges of the page in the document window at once. The next steps zoom page width.

Q: Do all sales proposals have the same content?

A: A sales proposal may be solicited or unsolicited. If someone else requests that you develop the proposal, it is solicited. If you write the proposal because you recognize a need, the proposal is unsolicited. A sales proposal is successful if it addresses how its product or service meets the reader's needs better than the competition does.

To Zoom Page Width

1 Click the Zoom box arrow on the Standard toolbar.

2 Click Page Width in the Zoom list.

Word computes the zoom percentage and displays it in the Zoom box (shown in Figure 4-2 on the next page). Your percentage may be different depending on your computer.

Creating a Title Page

A **title page** should attract a readers' attention. The title page of the sales proposal in Project 4 (Figure 4-1a on page WD 219) contains color, shading, an outside border, shadowed text, clip art, and a variety of fonts, font sizes, and font styles. The steps on the following pages discuss how to create this title page. The text watermark, which displays on all pages of the sales proposal, is created at the end of this project.

Formatting and Entering Characters

The first step in creating the title page is to enter the phrase, Vote Yes!, centered and using 72-point Cooper Black bold dark red font, as described below.

To Format Characters

1 Click the Center button on the Formatting toolbar.

2 Click the Font box arrow on the Formatting toolbar. Scroll to and then click Cooper Black (or a similar font) in the list of available fonts.

3 Click the Font Size box arrow on the Formatting toolbar. Scroll to and then click 72.

4 Click the Bold button on the Formatting toolbar.

5 Click the Font Color button arrow on the Formatting toolbar and then click Dark Red on the color palette.

6 Type Vote Yes!

Word enters the phrase, Vote Yes!, centered and using 72-point Cooper Black bold dark red font (shown in Figure 4-2).

Adding a Border and Shading to a Paragraph

The next step is to surround the phrase, Vote Yes!, with a 4½-point dark teal outside border and then shade inside the border in tan.

In Project 2, you added a bottom border to a paragraph using the Border button on the Formatting toolbar. When you click this button, Word applies the most recently defined border or the default border to the current paragraph. One method of specifying a different point size, color, shading, and placement of a border is to use the **Tables and Borders toolbar**.

To display the Tables and Borders toolbar, click the **Tables and Borders button** on the Standard toolbar. When you click the Tables and Borders button, Word displays the Tables and Borders toolbar in the Word window. Also, if your Word

Q: What are the guidelines for a title page on a proposal?

A: Formal proposals often require a specific format for the title page. Beginning about 3 to 4 inches from the top margin, the following components are each centered and on a separate line: title; the word, For; reader's name, position, organization, and address; the word, by; your name, position, and organization; and the date the proposal was written.

More About

Borders

You can add a border to any edge of a paragraph. That is, borders may be added above or below a paragraph, to the left or right of a paragraph, or any combination of these sides. To add the most recently defined border, click the Border button on the Formatting toolbar. To change border specifications, use the Tables and Borders toolbar.

window is not already in print layout view, Word automatically switches to print layout view. The Tables and Borders button on the Standard toolbar remains selected until you close the Tables and Borders toolbar.

The following steps show how to add a 4½-point dark teal outside border around a paragraph using the Tables and Borders toolbar.

To Border a Paragraph

1

• **If the Tables and Borders toolbar is not displayed in the Word window, click the Tables and Borders button on the Standard toolbar.**

• **If the Tables and Borders toolbar is floating in the Word window, double-click the title bar of the Tables and Borders toolbar.**

• **With the insertion point on line 1, click the Line Weight box arrow on the Tables and Borders toolbar.**

Word displays a list of available line weights (Figure 4-2).

2

• **Click 4 ½ pt in the Line Weight list.**

Word changes the line weight to 4½ point.

FIGURE 4-2

3

• **Click the Border Color button arrow on the Tables and Borders toolbar.**

Word displays a color palette for border colors (Figure 4-3).

4

• **Click Dark Teal, which is the fifth color on the first row of the color palette.**

Word changes the color of the border to dark teal, as shown in the Line Style box and on the Border Color button.

FIGURE 4-3

5

• **Click the Outside Border button on the Tables and Borders toolbar. (If your Border button does not show an outside border, click the Border button arrow on the Tables and Borders toolbar and then click Outside Border.)**

Word places a 4½-point dark teal outside border around the phrase, Vote Yes! (Figure 4-4).

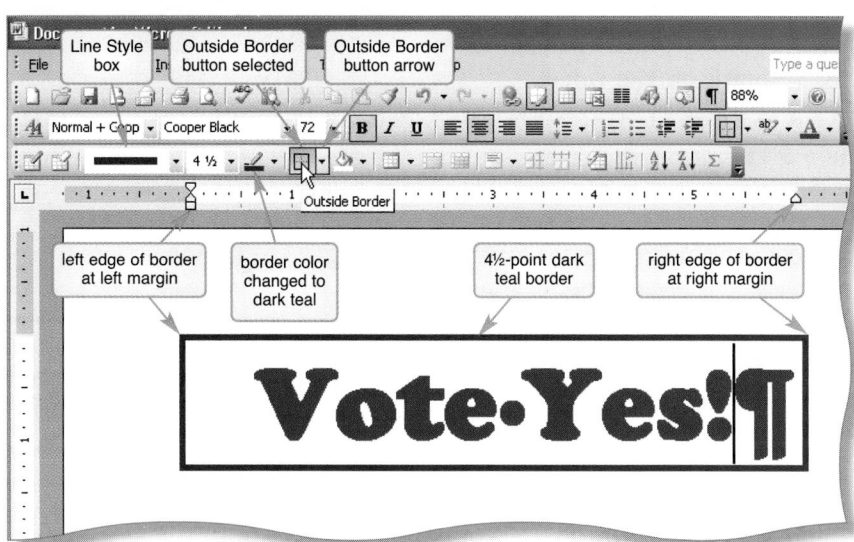

FIGURE 4-4

Depending on the last position of the Tables and Borders toolbar, it may be floating or it may be docked. To dock a floating toolbar, double-click its title bar. Word docks the Tables and Borders toolbar above or below the Formatting toolbar. You can move the toolbar by dragging its move handle, which is the dotted vertical line at the left edge of the toolbar.

When the Draw Table button on the Tables and Borders toolbar is selected, the mouse pointer shape is a pencil — ready to draw a table. If you want to edit a document when the Tables and Borders toolbar is displayed, click the Draw Table button to deselect it.

As previously discussed, Word provides two Border buttons: one on the Formatting toolbar and one on the Tables and Borders toolbar. To place a border using the same settings as the most recently defined border, simply click the Border button on the Formatting toolbar. To change the size, color, or other settings of a border, use the Tables and Borders toolbar or the Borders and Shading dialog box.

Notice in Figure 4-4 that the border extends from the left margin to the right margin. If you want the border to start and end at a different location, you change the left and right paragraph indent. One way to change a paragraph indent is to drag the markers on the ruler, as shown in the following steps.

To Change Left and Right Paragraph Indent

1

• **Position the mouse pointer on the Left Indent marker on the ruler.**

The Left Indent marker is the small square at the 0" mark on the ruler (Figure 4-5).

FIGURE 4-5

2

• **Drag the Left Indent marker to the .5" mark on the ruler.**

• **Drag the Right Indent marker to the 5.5" mark on the ruler.**

Word indents the left and right edges of the paragraph one-half inch from the margin, which causes the paragraph borders to move in one-half inch (Figure 4-6).

> ### Other Ways
>
> 1. On Format menu click Paragraph, click Indents and Spacing tab, enter indentation values in Left and Right boxes, click OK button
> 2. Right-click paragraph, click Paragraph on shortcut menu, click Indents and Spacing tab, enter indentation values in Left and Right boxes, click OK button
> 3. In Voice Command mode, say "Format, Paragraph, Indents and Spacing, [enter indentation values in Left and Right boxes], OK"

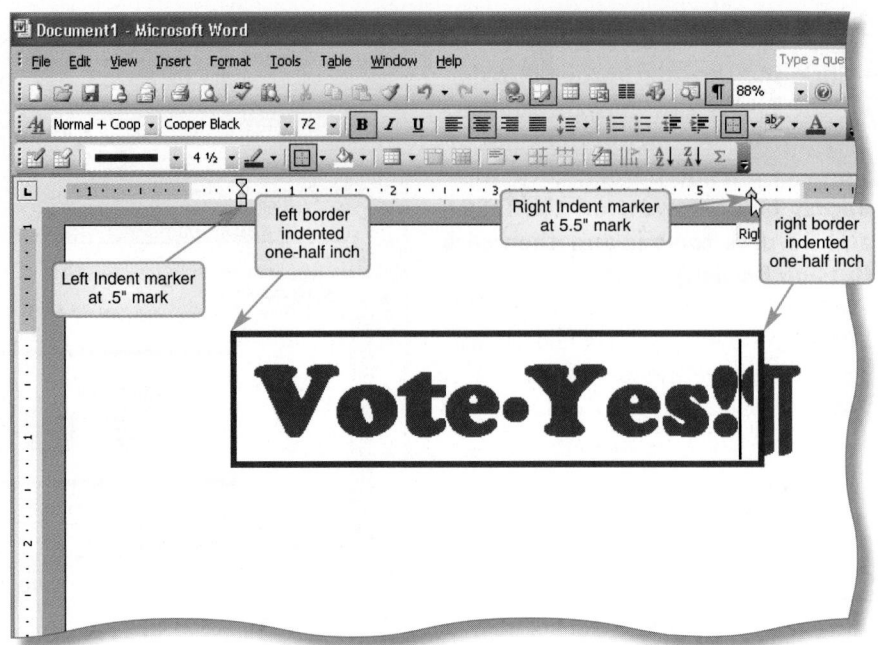

FIGURE 4-6

The next step is to shade the paragraph containing the words, Vote Yes!, in the color tan. When you shade a paragraph, Word shades the rectangular area containing the paragraph from the left edge of the paragraph to the right edge. If the paragraph is surrounded by a border, Word shades inside the border.

The following steps show how to shade a paragraph.

To Shade a Paragraph

1

• **With the insertion point on line 1, click the Shading Color button arrow on the Tables and Borders toolbar.**

Word displays a color palette for shading (Figure 4-7).

FIGURE 4-7

2

• **Click Tan, which is the second color on the bottom row of the color palette.**

• **Click the Tables and Borders button on the Standard toolbar to remove the Tables and Borders toolbar from the Word screen.**

Word shades the current paragraph tan (Figure 4-8). The Tables and Borders toolbar no longer is displayed on the screen.

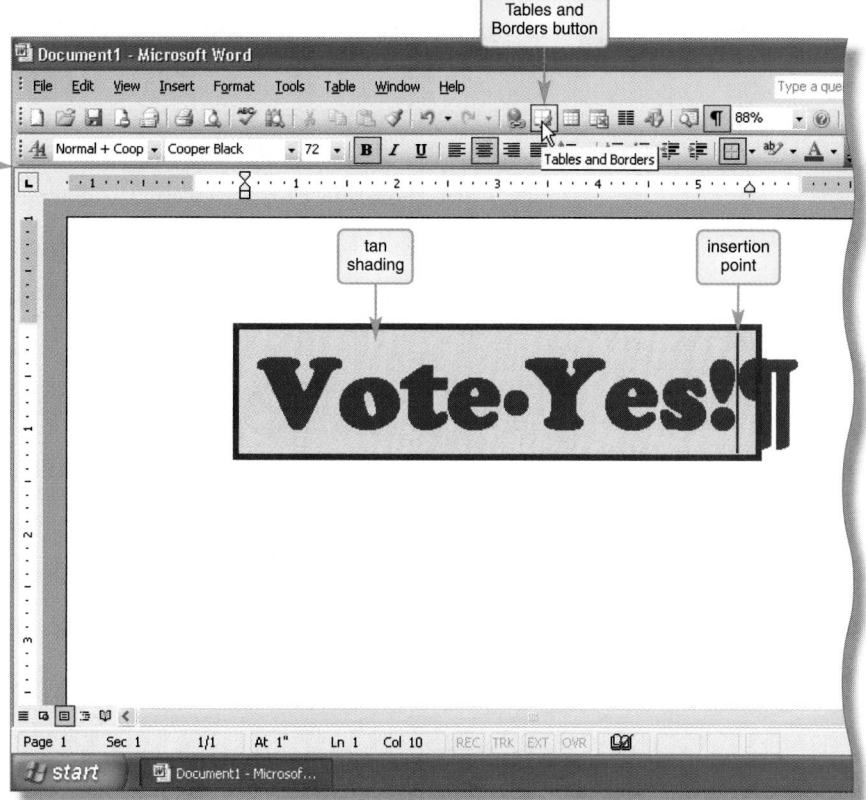

FIGURE 4-8

The first line of the title page is entered and formatted. When you press the ENTER key to advance the insertion point to the next line on the title page, the border and shading also will be displayed on line 2 and the characters will be 72-point Cooper Black bold dark red font, because Word carries forward formatting each time you press the ENTER key. The paragraphs and characters on line 2 should not have the same formatting as line 1. Instead, they should be formatted using the Normal style.

Recall from Project 2 that the base style for a new Word document is the Normal style, which for a new installation of Word 2003 typically uses 12-point Times New Roman font for characters and single-spaced, left-aligned paragraphs (shown in Figure 4-10 on page WD 227). A previous project used the Styles and Formatting task pane to clear formatting, which returns the current paragraph to the Normal style. The steps on the next page clear formatting using the Style box on the Formatting toolbar.

More About

Removing Borders

If you wanted to remove a border from a paragraph, position the insertion point somewhere in the paragraph containing the border, click the Border button arrow on either the Formatting toolbar or on the Tables and Borders toolbar, and then click No Border on the border palette.

To Clear Formatting

1 **With the insertion point positioned at the end of line 1 (shown in Figure 4-8 on the previous page), press the ENTER key.**

2 **Click the Style box arrow on the Formatting toolbar (Figure 4-9).**

3 **Click Clear Formatting in the Style list.**

Word applies the Normal style to the location of the insertion point (shown in Figure 4-10).

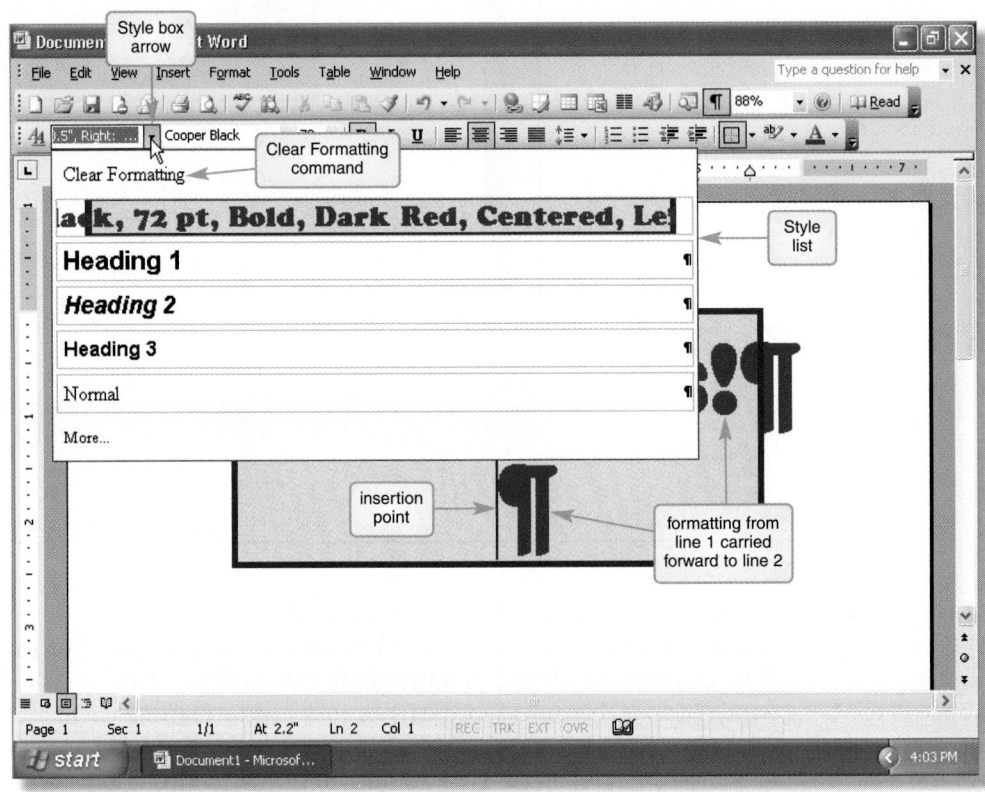

FIGURE 4-9

Depending on your installation of Word, the Normal style might be a different font or font size.

Formatting Characters Using the Font Dialog Box

The next step is to enter the text, MINOOKA PARK DISTRICT REFERENDUM, on the title page. This text is to be 48-point Britannic Bold italic dark teal font. Each letter in this text is to display a shadow. A **shadow** is a light gray duplicate image that appears on the lower-right edge of a character or object. Also, you want extra space between each character so the text spans across the width of the page.

You could use buttons on the Formatting toolbar to format much of the text. The shadow effect and expanded spacing, however, are applied using the Font dialog box. Thus, the next steps show how to apply all formats using the Font dialog box.

To Format Characters and Modify Character Spacing

1

• **With the insertion point positioned on line 2, press the ENTER key two times.**

• **Press CTRL+E to center the paragraph on line 4.**

• **Press the CAPS LOCK key. Type** MINOOKA **and then press the ENTER key.**

• **Type** PARK DISTRICT **and then press the ENTER key.**

• **Type** REFERENDUM **and then press the CAPS LOCK key.**

• **Drag through the three lines of text on lines 4 through 6 to select them. Right-click the selected text.**

Word displays a shortcut menu (Figure 4-10). The text in lines 4 through 6 of the document is selected.

FIGURE 4-10

2

• **Click Font on the shortcut menu. When Word displays the Font dialog box, if necessary, click the Font tab.**

• **Scroll through the Font list and then click Britannic Bold (or a similar font).**

• **Click Italic in the Font style list.**

• **Scroll through the Size list and then click 48.**

• **Click the Font color box arrow and then click Dark Teal on the color palette.**

• **Click Shadow in the Effects area.**

Word displays the Font dialog box (Figure 4-11). The Preview area reflects the current selections.

FIGURE 4-11

3

- **Click the Character Spacing tab.**
- **Click the Spacing box arrow and then click Expanded.**
- **Press the TAB key. Type** 5 **in the Spacing By box and then press the TAB key.**

Word displays the Character Spacing sheet in the Font dialog box (Figure 4-12). The Preview area displays the text with five points between each character.

FIGURE 4-12

4

- **Click the OK button.**
- **Click at the end of line 6 to position the insertion point after the word, REFERENDUM.**

Word displays the characters in the text, MINOOKA PARK DISTRICT REFERENDUM, formatted to 48-point Britannic Bold italic dark teal font with a shadow and expanded by 5 points (Figure 4-13).

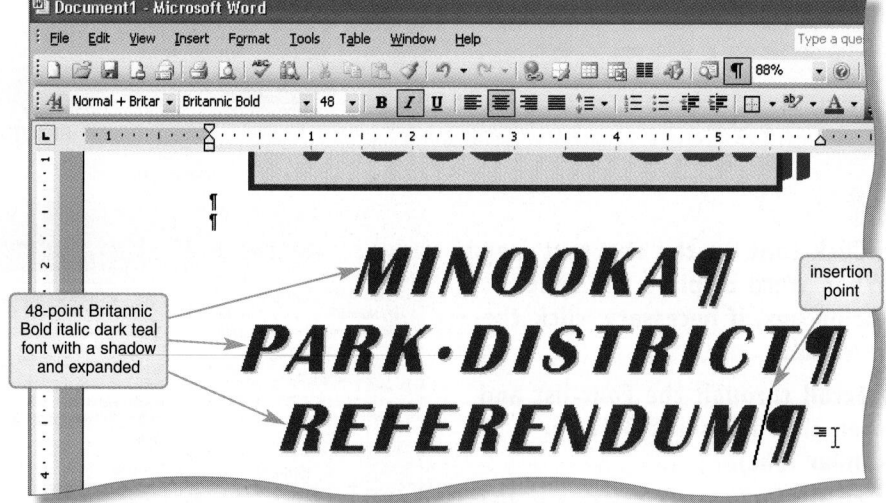

FIGURE 4-13

Other Ways

1. On Format menu click Font, [select formats], click OK button
2. In Voice Command mode, say "Format, Font, [select formats], OK"

In addition to a shadow, the Font sheet in the Font dialog box (Figure 4-11 on the previous page) contains many other character effects you can add to text in a document. Table 4-1 illustrates the result of each of these effects.

Hidden text does not print but is part of the document. When the Show/Hide ¶ button on the Standard toolbar is not selected, hidden text does not appear on the screen. When the Show/Hide ¶ button is selected, Word displays hidden text on the screen.

If you wanted to change the default font from 12-point Times New Roman to another font, font style, font size, font color, and/or font effects, you would use the Default button in the Font dialog box (Figure 4-11), as described in the next steps.

To Modify the Default Font Settings

1. Click Format on the menu bar and then click Font.
2. Make desired changes to the font in the Font dialog box.
3. Click the Default button.
4. When the Microsoft Word dialog box is displayed, click the Yes button.

Table 4-1 Character Effects Available in the Font Dialog Box		
TYPE OF EFFECT	PLAIN TEXT	FORMATTED TEXT
Strikethrough	MINOOKA	~~MINOOKA~~
Double strikethrough	PARK DISTRICT	~~PARK DISTRICT~~
Superscript	1st	1st
Subscript	H2O	H$_2$O
Shadow	Referendum	Referendum
Outline	Referendum	Referendum
Emboss	Referendum	Referendum
Engrave	Referendum	Referendum
Small caps	Referendum	REFERENDUM
All caps	Referendum	REFERENDUM
Hidden	Referendum	

When you change the default font as described above, the current document and all future documents will use the new font settings. That is, if you quit Word, restart the computer, and restart Word, documents you create will use the new default font.

The insertion point currently is at the end of line 6 in the document window (Figure 4-13). When you press the ENTER key, the paragraph and character formatting will carry forward to line 7. You want to return formatting on line 7 to the Normal style. The following steps clear formatting below line 6.

To Clear Formatting

1 With the insertion point positioned at the end of line 6 (shown in Figure 4-13), press the ENTER key.

2 Click the Style box arrow on the Formatting toolbar and then click Clear Formatting (shown in Figure 4-9 on page WD 226).

Word applies the Normal style to the location of the insertion point, which is on line 7.

Inserting Clip Art from the Web in a Word Document

As discussed in Project 1, Word 2003 includes a series of predefined graphics called **clip art** that you can insert in a Word document. This clip art is located in the **Clip Organizer**, which contains a collection of clip art, as well as photographs, sounds, and video clips.

To insert clip art, you use the Clip Art task pane. Word displays miniature clip art images, called **thumbnails**, in the Clip Art task pane. When the thumbnails appear in the Clip Art task pane, some display a small icon in their lower-left corner. Thumbnails with these icons link to clip art images that are not installed on your computer. For example, if you are connected to the Web while searching for clip art images, thumbnails from the Web appear in the Clip Art task pane with a small globe icon in their lower-left corner. Table 4-2 identifies various icons that may appear on a thumbnail in the Clip Art task pane.

If a thumbnail displays a small icon of a star (☒) in its lower-right corner, the clip art contains animation. These clip art images have the appearance of motion when displayed in some Web browsers.

More About

Clip Art

For more information about clip art, visit the Word 2003 More About Web page (scsite.com/wd2003/more) and then click Clip Art.

Table 4-2 Icons on Thumbnails in Clip Art Task Pane	
ICON	LOCATION OF CLIP
	CD-ROM or DVD-ROM
	Microsoft's Web site
	Web site partnering with Microsoft (free clip)
	Web site partnering with Microsoft (clip available for a fee)
	Unavailable clip

The following steps illustrate how to insert a clip art image from the Web in a Word document.

> **Note:** The following steps assume your computer is connected to the Internet. If it is not, go directly to the shaded steps at the top of the next page.

To Insert Clip Art from the Web

1

• **With the insertion point on line 7, press the ENTER key twice.**

• **Press CTRL+E to center the insertion point.**

• **Click Insert on the menu bar, point to Picture, and then click Clip Art.**

• **If necessary, click the Results should be box arrow and then select All media file types.**

• **In the Clip Art task pane, drag through any text in the Search for text box. Type** ballot box **and then click the Go button.**

• **If necessary, scroll through the clips until the one shown in Figure 4-14 appears (or a similar clip).**

FIGURE 4-14

2

• **Click the clip to be inserted.**

• **Click the Close button on the Clip Art task pane title bar. If necessary, scroll to display the image in the document window.**

Word inserts the clip in the document at the location of the insertion point (Figure 4-15).

FIGURE 4-15

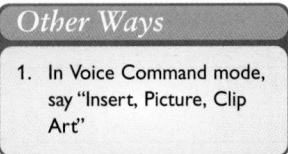

Other Ways

1. In Voice Command mode, say "Insert, Picture, Clip Art"

If you do not have access to the Web, you can insert the clip art file in the Word document from the Data Disk, as described in the following steps. If you did not download the Data Disk, see the inside back cover for instructions for downloading the Data Disk or see your instructor.

To Insert a Graphic File from the Data Disk

1 With the insertion point on line 7, press the ENTER key twice. Press CTRL+E to center the insertion point.

2 Click Insert on the menu bar, point to Picture, and then click From File.

3 Insert the Data Disk into drive A. When Word displays the Insert Picture dialog box, click the Look in box arrow and then click 3½ Floppy (A:). Click the file name g1utss1r[1] and then click the Insert button.

Word inserts the clip in your document at the location of the insertion point (shown in Figure 4-15).

The graphic of the ballot box is too small for the title page. The next step is to increase its size to about 250 percent, as described below.

To Resize a Graphic Using the Format Picture Dialog Box

1 Double-click the graphic. When Word displays the Format Picture dialog box, if necessary, click the Size tab.

2 In the Scale area, double-click the number in the Height box to select it. Type 250 and then press the TAB key (Figure 4-16).

3 Click the OK button.

Word resizes the graphic to 250 percent of its original size (shown in Figure 4-17 on the next page).

More About

Inserting Graphics

If you have a file containing a graphic image, you can insert the file by following the shaded steps to the left. Graphic files Word can use include those with extensions or file types of .gif, .jpg, .png, .bmp, .wmf, .tif, and .eps. When you scan a photograph or other image and save it as a graphic file, you can select the file type for the saved graphic through the photo editing or illustration software. Word also can insert graphic files directly from a scanner or camera (through the Picture submenu).

FIGURE 4-16

If you want a graphic to be an exact height and width, you can type the measurements in the Height and Width boxes in the Size and rotate area in the Size sheet in the Format Picture dialog box. If you want to return a graphic to its original size and start resizing it again, click the Reset button (Figure 4-16 on the previous page) in the Size sheet in the Format Picture dialog box.

To see the layout of the title page, the following steps display an entire page in the document window.

To Zoom Whole Page

1 **Click the Zoom box arrow on the Standard toolbar.**

2 **Click Whole Page in the Zoom list.**

Word displays the title page in reduced form so that the entire page is displayed in the document window (Figure 4-17).

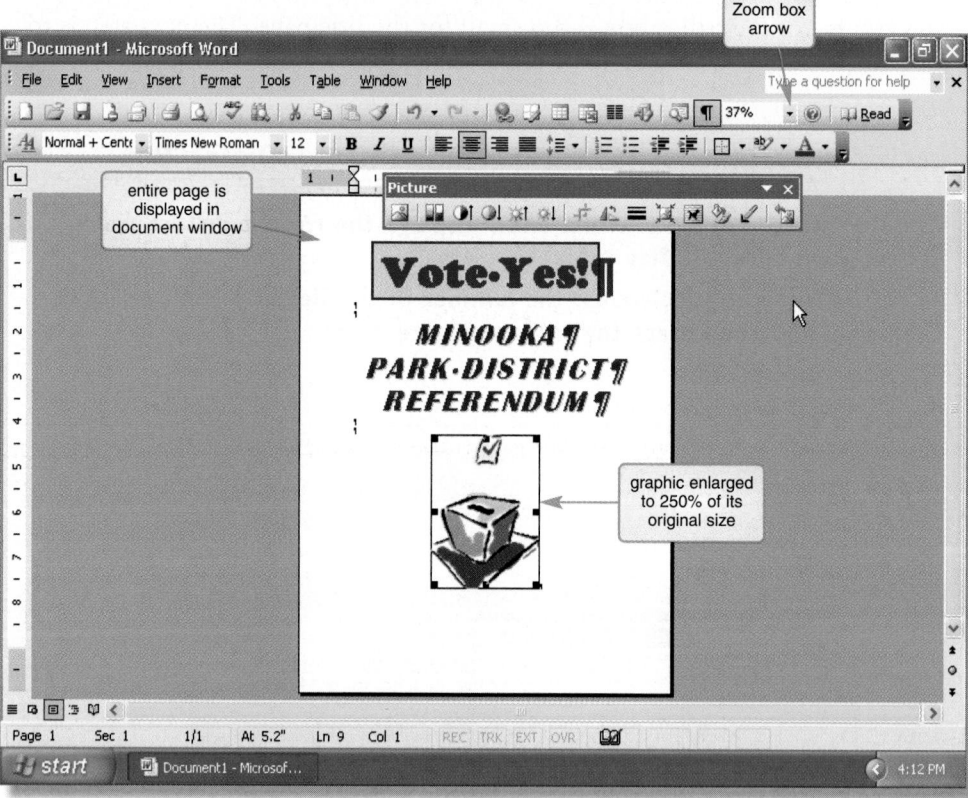

FIGURE 4-17

Centering the Title Page Contents Vertically on the Page

For visual appeal, you would like to center the contents of the title page vertically, that is, between the top and bottom margins. As discussed in previous projects, the default top margin in Word is one inch, which includes a one-half inch header. Notice in Figure 4-18 that the insertion point, which is at the top of the title page text, is 1" from the top of the page.

The next steps show how to center the contents of a page vertically.

To Center Page Contents Vertically

1

• **Press CTRL+HOME to position the insertion point at the top of the document.**

• **Click File on the menu bar (Figure 4-18).**

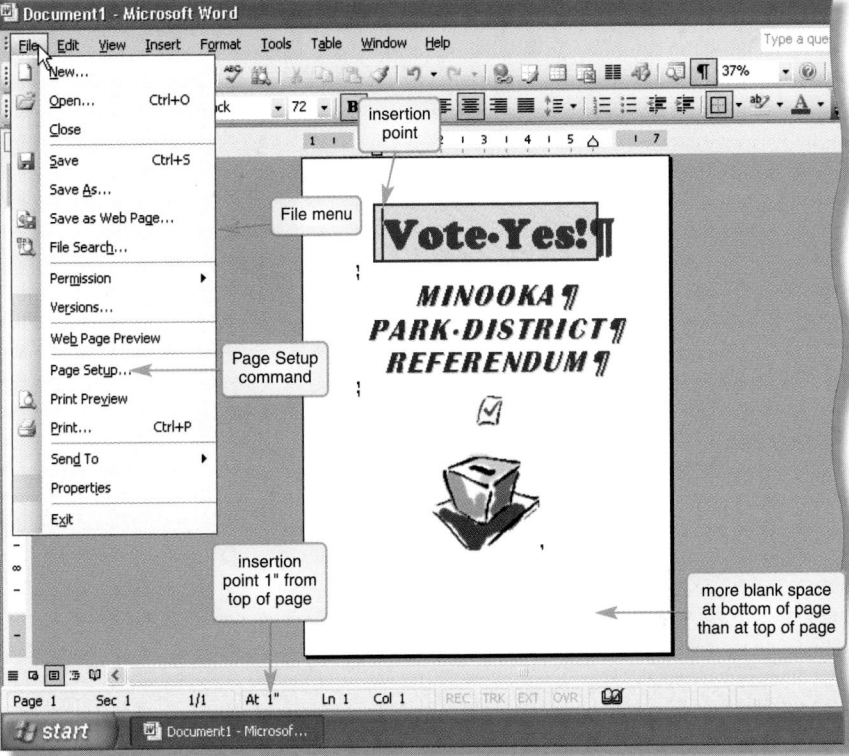

FIGURE 4-18

2

• **Click Page Setup on the File menu.**

• **When Word displays the Page Setup dialog box, if necessary, click the Layout tab.**

• **Click the Vertical alignment box arrow and then click Center.**

Word changes the vertical alignment to Center in the Page Setup dialog box (Figure 4-19).

FIGURE 4-19

3

• **Click the OK button.**

Word centers the contents of the title page vertically (Figure 4-20). The status bar shows the insertion point now is 1.6" from the top of the document, which means the empty space above and below the page content totals approximately 3.2".

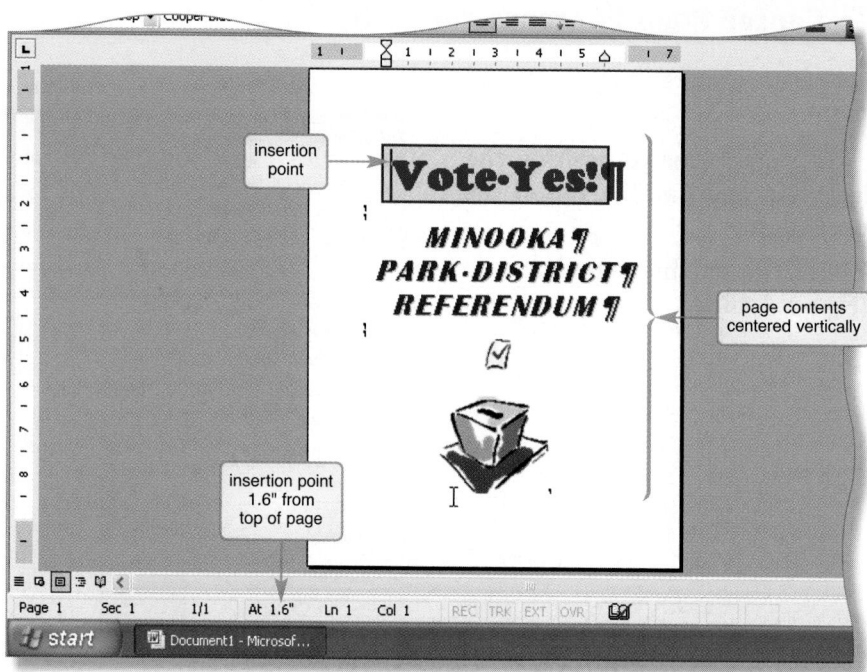

insertion point

Vote·Yes!¶

MINOOKA¶
PARK·DISTRICT¶
REFERENDUM¶

page contents centered vertically

insertion point 1.6" from top of page

FIGURE 4-20

The following step changes the zoom back to page width.

To Zoom Page Width

1 Click the Zoom box arrow on the Standard toolbar and then click Page Width.

Word computes the zoom percentage and displays it in the Zoom box (shown in Figure 4-21 on page WD 236). Your percentage may be different depending on your computer.

Saving the Title Page

The title page for the sales proposal is complete. Thus, the next step is to save it, as described below.

To Save a Document

1 Insert a floppy disk into drive A. Click the Save button on the Standard toolbar.

2 Type Park District Title Page in the File name box.

3 Click the Save in box arrow and then click 3½ Floppy (A:).

4 Click the Save button in the Save As dialog box.

Word saves the document on a floppy disk in drive A with the file name, Park District Title Page (shown in Figure 4-21).

Inserting an Existing Document into an Open Document

Assume you already have prepared a draft of the body of the proposal and saved it with the file name, Park District Draft. You would like the draft to display on a separate page following the title page. Once the two documents are displayed on the screen together as one document, you save this active document with a new name so each of the original documents remains intact.

The inserted pages of the sales proposal are to use the Times New Roman font and be left-aligned. When you press the ENTER key at the bottom of the title page, the paragraph and character formatting will carry forward to the next line. Thus, you return formatting on the new line to the Normal style. The following steps describe how to clear formatting so the inserted pages use the Normal style.

To Clear Formatting

1 Press CTRL+END to move the insertion point to the end of the title page. If necessary, scroll down to display the insertion point in the document window. Press the ENTER key.

2 Click the Style box arrow on the Formatting toolbar and then click Clear Formatting (shown in Figure 4-9 on page WD 226).

Word applies the Normal style to the location of the insertion point, which now is on line 10 (shown in Figure 4-21 on the next page).

Inserting a Section Break

The body of the sales proposal requires page formatting different from that of the title page. Earlier in this project, you vertically centered the contents of the title page. The body of the proposal should have top alignment; that is, it should begin one inch from the top of the page.

Whenever you want to change page formatting for a portion of a document, you must create a new **section** in the document. Each section then may be formatted differently from the others. Thus, the title page formatted with centered vertical alignment must be in one section, and the body of the proposal formatted with top alignment must be in another section.

A Word document can be divided into any number of sections. All Word documents have at least one section. During the course of creating a document, if you need to change the top margin, bottom margin, page alignment, paper size, page orientation, page number position, or contents or position of headers, footers, or footnotes, you must create a new section.

When you create a new section, a **section break** is displayed on the screen as a double dotted line separated by the words, Section Break. Section breaks do not print. When you create a section break, you specify whether or not the new section should begin on a new page.

The body of the sales proposal is to be on a separate page following the title page. The steps on the next page show how to insert a section break that instructs Word to begin the new section on a new page in the document.

To Insert a Next Page Section Break

1

• **Be sure the insertion point is positioned on the paragraph mark on line 10.**

• **Click Insert on the menu bar (Figure 4-21).**

FIGURE 4-21

2

• **Click Break on the Insert menu.**

• **When Word displays the Break dialog box, click Next page in the Section break types area.**

The Next page option in the Break dialog box instructs Word to place the new section on the next page (Figure 4-22).

3

• **Click the OK button.**

Word inserts a next page section break in the document (shown in Figure 4-24).

FIGURE 4-22

Other Ways

1. In Voice Command mode, say "Insert, Break, Next page, OK"

Word places the insertion point and paragraph mark in the new section, which is on a new page. Notice in Figure 4-23 that the status bar indicates the insertion point is on page 2 in section 2. Also, the insertion point is positioned 5.4" from the top of the page because earlier you changed the page formatting to centered vertical alignment. The body of the proposal should have top alignment; that is, the insertion point should be one inch from the top of the page. The next steps show how to change the alignment of section two from center to top.

To Change Page Alignment of a Section

1

- **Be sure the insertion point is in section 2.**
- **Click File on the menu bar and then click Page Setup. When Word displays the Page Setup dialog box, if necessary, click the Layout tab.**
- **Click the Vertical alignment box arrow and then click Top.**

Word changes the vertical alignment to Top in the Page Setup dialog box (Figure 4-23).

FIGURE 4-23

2

- **Click the OK button.**
- **Scroll up so Word displays the bottom of page 1 and the top of page 2 in the document window.**

Word changes the vertical alignment of section 2 to top (Figure 4-24). Notice the status bar indicates the insertion point now is positioned 1" from the top of the page, which is the top margin setting for section 2.

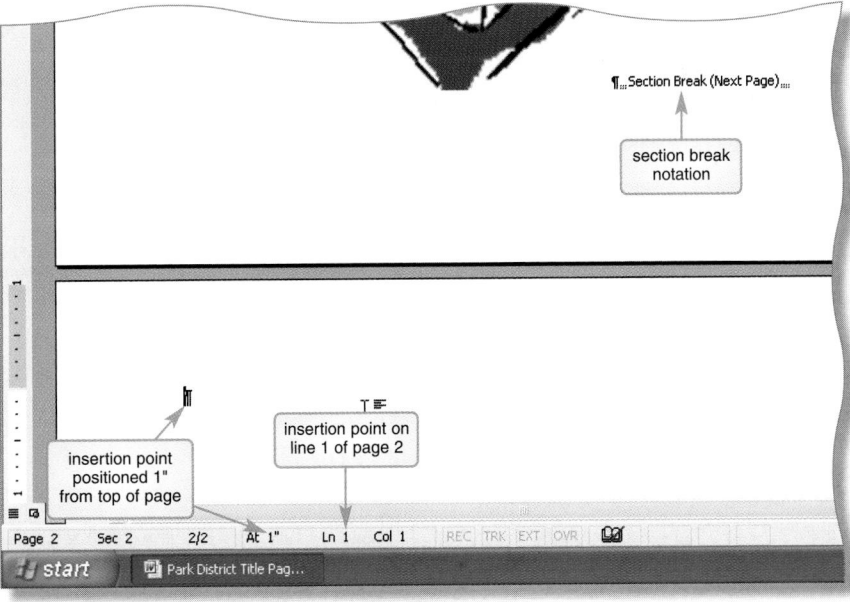

FIGURE 4-24

Word stores all section formatting in the section break. You can delete a section break and all associated section formatting using a variety of techniques: (1) select the section break notation, right-click the selection, and then click Cut on the shortcut menu; (2) select the section break notation and then press the DELETE key; or (3) position the insertion point immediately to the right of the section break notation and then press the BACKSPACE key. To select a section break, point to its left until the mouse pointer changes direction and then click. If you accidentally delete a section break, you can restore it by clicking the Undo button on the Standard toolbar.

Inserting a Word Document into an Open Document

The next step is to insert the draft of the sales proposal at the top of the second page of the document. The draft is located on the Data Disk. If you did not download the Data Disk, see the inside back cover for instructions for downloading the Data Disk or see your instructor.

If you created a Word file at an earlier time, you may have forgotten its name. For this reason, Word provides a means to display the contents of, or **preview**, any file before you insert it. The following steps show how to preview and then insert the draft of the proposal into the open document.

To Insert a Word Document into an Open Document

1

• **Be sure the insertion point is positioned on the paragraph mark at the top of section 2.**

• **If necessary, insert the Data Disk into drive A.**

• **Click Insert on the menu bar (Figure 4-25).**

FIGURE 4-25

2

• **Click File on the Insert menu.**

• **When Word displays the Insert File dialog box, click the Look in box arrow and then click 3½ Floppy (A:).**

• **Click the Views button arrow and then click Preview.**

• **Click Park District Draft in the Name list.**

In the Insert File dialog box, the contents of the selected file (Park District Draft) are displayed on the right side of the dialog box (Figure 4-26).

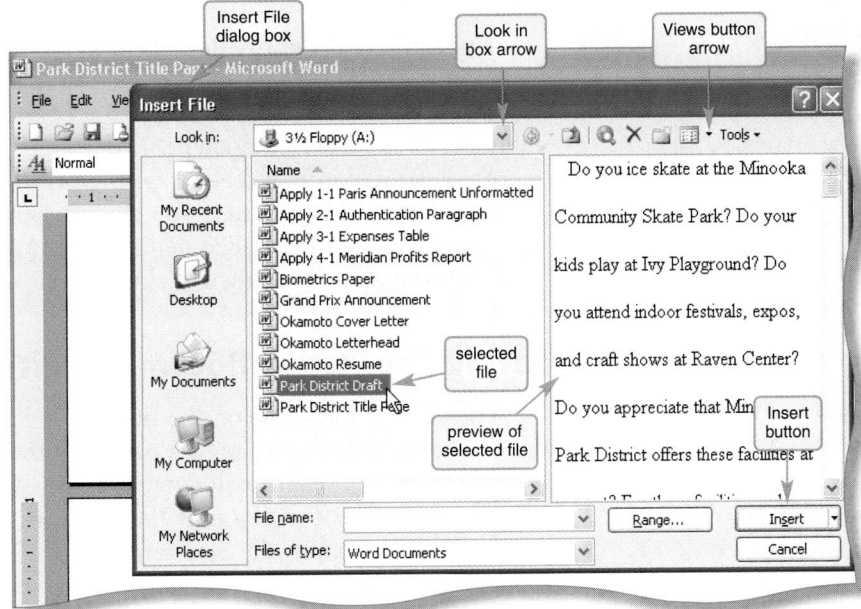

FIGURE 4-26

3

• **Click the Insert button in the dialog box.**

Word inserts the file, Park District Draft, into the open document at the location of the insertion point. The insertion point is at the end of the inserted document.

4

• **Press SHIFT+F5.**

*Word positions the insertion point on line 1 of page 2, which was its location prior to inserting the new Word document (Figure 4-27). Pressing **SHIFT+F5** instructs Word to place the insertion point at your last editing location.*

FIGURE 4-27

Other Ways

1. In Voice Command mode, say "Insert, File, [select file], Insert"

More About

Files

In the Insert File and Open dialog boxes, click the Views button arrow to change how the files are displayed in the dialog box. Click the Tools button arrow and then click Delete to delete the selected file. Click the Tools button arrow and then click Properties to display information about the selected file.

Word inserts the entire document at the location of the insertion point. If the insertion point, therefore, is positioned in the middle of the open document when you insert another Word document, the open document continues after the last character of the inserted document.

As illustrated in Figure 4-26 on the previous page, previewing files before opening them can be useful if you have forgotten the name of a file. For this reason, both the Open and Insert File dialog boxes allow you to preview files by clicking the Views button arrow and then clicking Preview.

Saving the Active Document with a New File Name

The current file name on the title bar is Park District Title Page, yet the active document contains both the title page and the draft of the sales proposal. To keep the title page as a separate document called Park District Title Page, you should save the active document with a new file name. If you save the active document by clicking the Save button on the Standard toolbar, Word will assign it the current file name. You want the active document to have a new file name.

The following steps describe how to save the active document with a new file name.

More About

File Types

Through the Save As dialog box, you also can change the file type. The default file type is Word document, which is a Word 2003 format. You also can save documents in other file types, including XML Document, Web Page, Document Template, Rich Text Format, Plain Text, several versions of Works, and earlier versions of Word. Use the File menu or press F12 to display the Save As dialog box.

To Save an Active Document with a New File Name

1 If necessary, insert the floppy disk containing your title page into drive A.

2 Click File on the menu bar and then click Save As.

3 Type Park District Proposal in the File name box. Do not press the ENTER key.

4 If necessary, click the Save in box arrow and then click 3½ Floppy (A:).

5 Click the Save button in the Save As dialog box.

Word saves the document on a floppy disk in drive A with the file name, Park District Proposal (shown in Figure 4-28).

Printing Specific Pages in a Document

The title page is the first page of the proposal. The body of the proposal spans the second and third pages. The next steps show how to print a hard copy of only the body of the proposal.

More About

Printing Pages

If you want to print from a certain page to the end of the document, enter the page number followed by a dash in the Pages text box. For example, 5- will print from page 5 to the end of the document. To print up to a certain page, put the dash first (e.g., -5 will print pages 1 through 5).

To Print Specific Pages in a Document

1

• **Ready the printer. Click File on the menu bar and then click Print.**

• **When Word displays the Print dialog box, click Pages in the Page range area.**

• **Type** 2-3 **in the Pages text box.**

The Print dialog box displays 2-3 in the Pages text box (Figure 4-28).

2

• **Click the OK button.**

Word prints the inserted draft of the sales proposal (shown in Figure 4-29a on the next page).

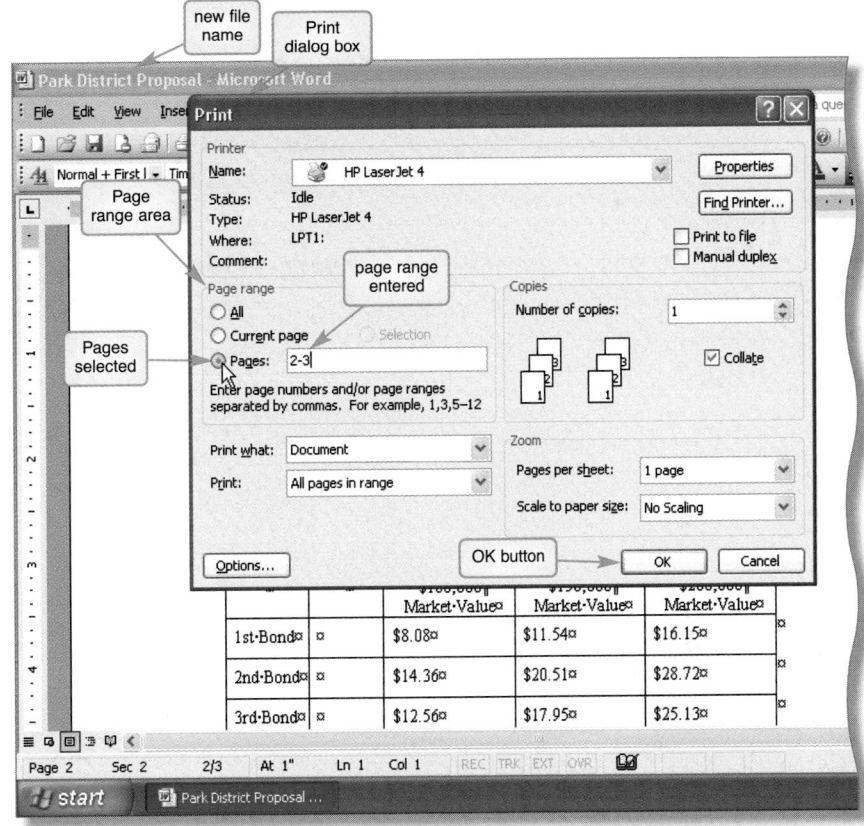

FIGURE 4-28

When you remove the document from the printer, review it carefully. Depending on your printer, wordwrap may occur in different locations from those shown in Figure 4-29a.

By adding a header and a footer, formatting and charting the table, changing the bullets to picture bullets, inserting another table into the document, and adding a watermark, you can make the body of the proposal more attention-grabbing. These enhancements to the body of the sales proposal are shown in Figure 4-29b on page WD 243.

The following pages illustrate how to change the document in Figure 4-29a so it looks like Figure 4-29b.

Other Ways

1. Press CTRL+P
2. In Voice Command mode, say "File, Print"

Q: How can I save ink, print faster, or decrease printer overrun errors?

A: Print a draft. Click File on the menu bar, click Print, click the Options button, place a check mark in the Draft output check box, and then click the OK button in each dialog box.

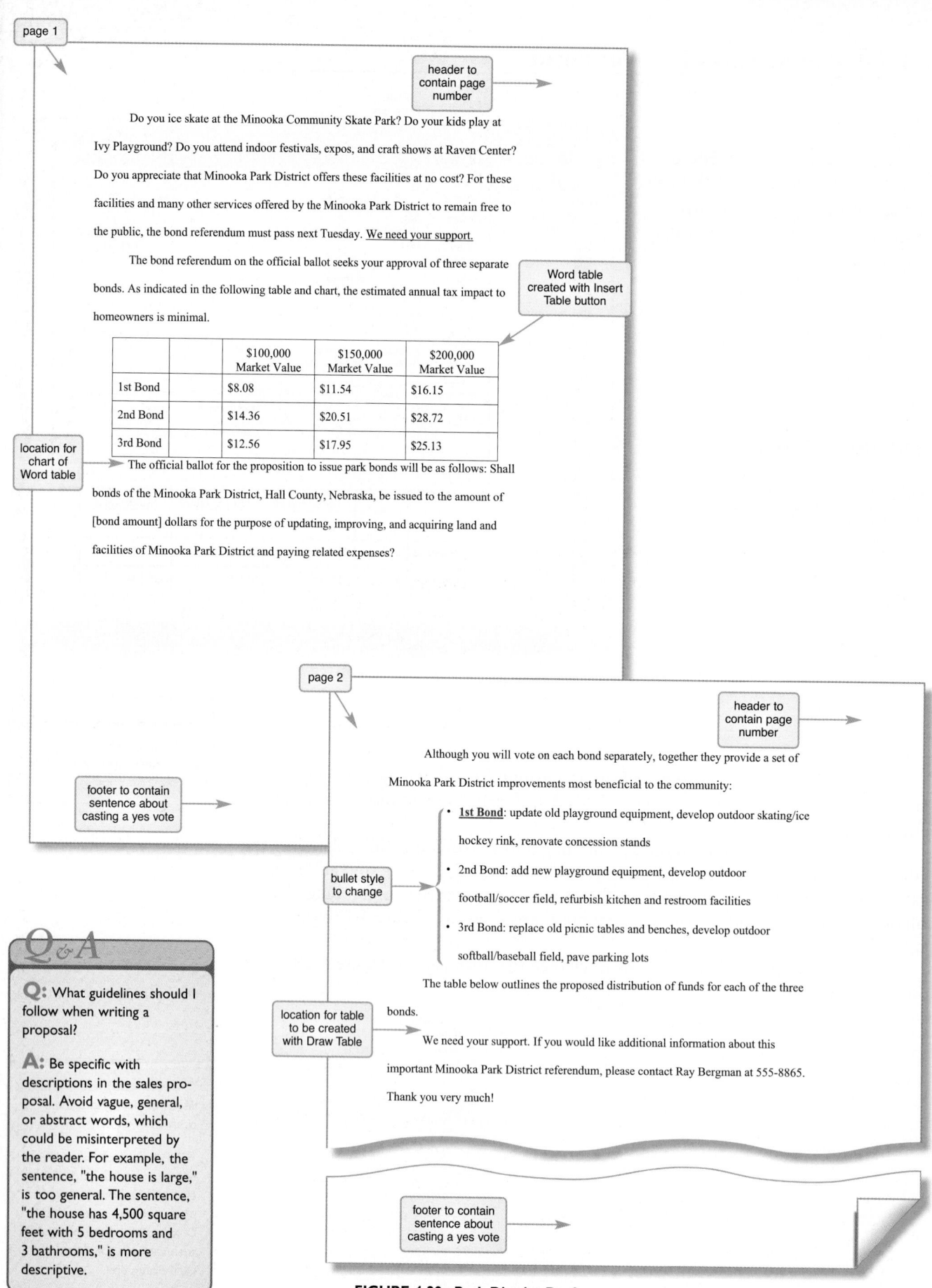

FIGURE 4-29a Park District Draft

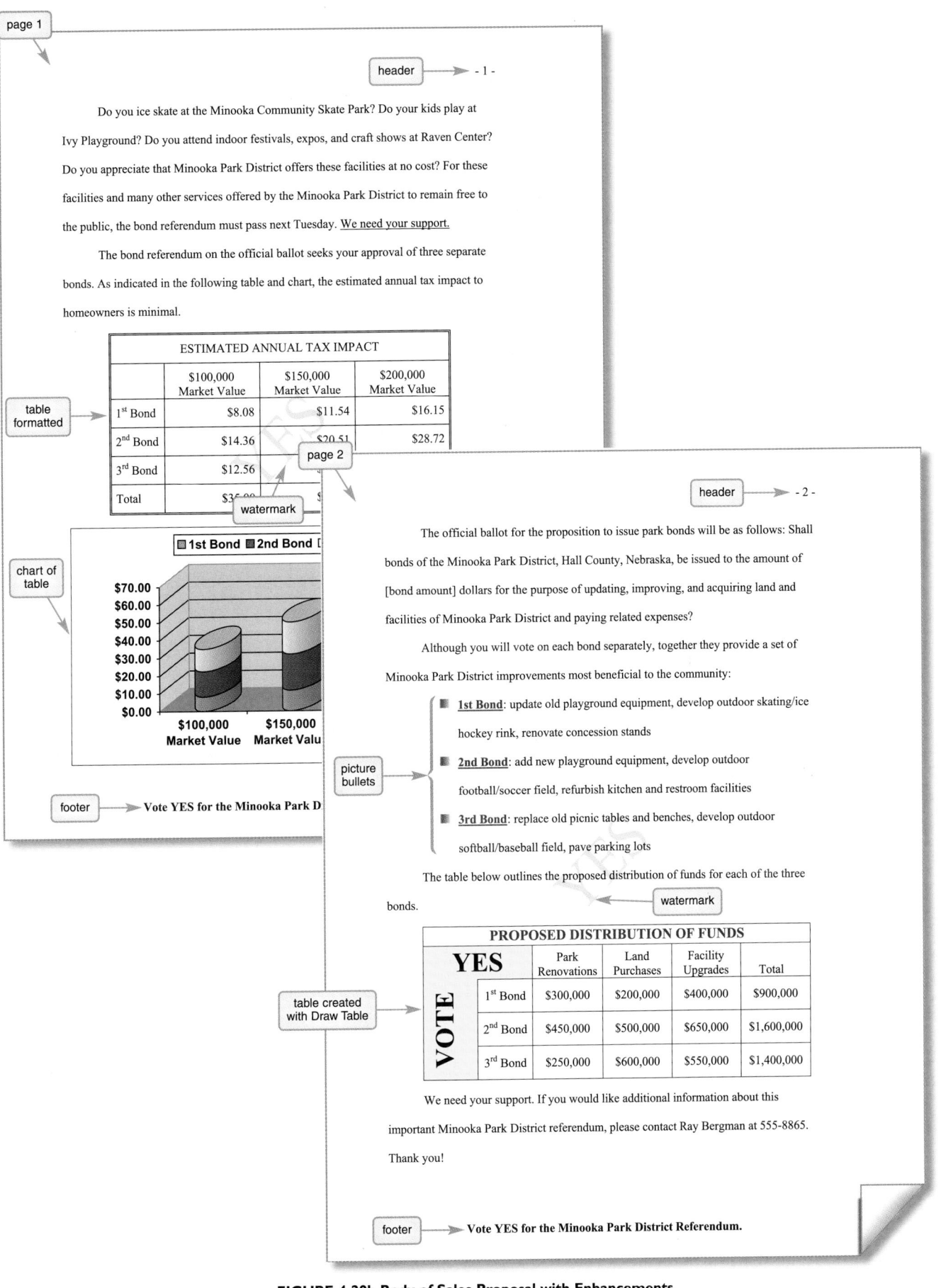

FIGURE 4-29b Body of Sales Proposal with Enhancements

Deleting a Page Break

After reviewing the draft, you notice the document contains a page break below the third paragraph. The following steps show how to delete the page break.

To Delete a Page Break

1

• **Scroll to the bottom of page 2 to display the page break notation in the document window.**

• **Position the mouse pointer to the left of the page break and click when it changes to a right-pointing arrow.**

Word selects the page break notation (Figure 4-30).

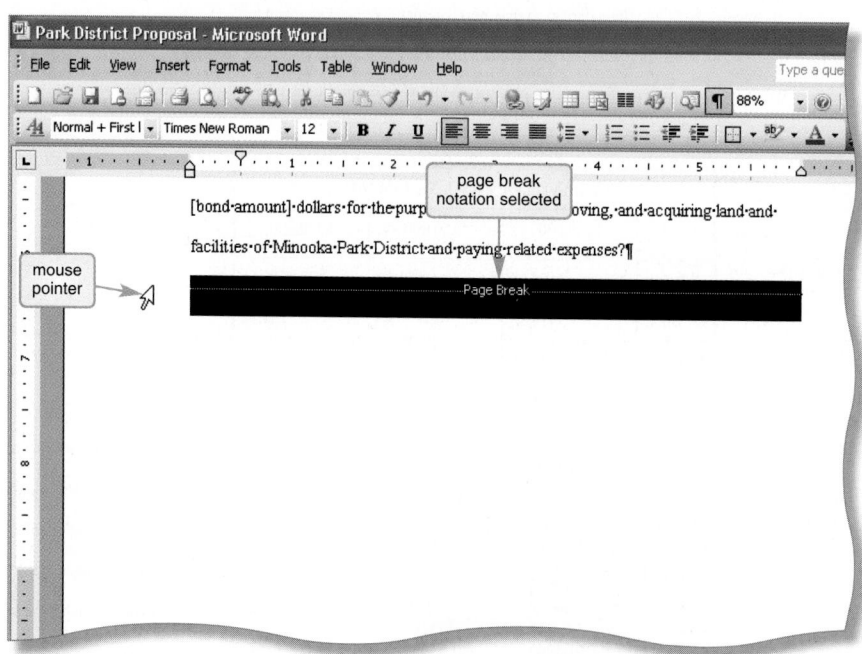

FIGURE 4-30

2

• **Press the DELETE key.**

Word removes the page break from the document (Figure 4-31).

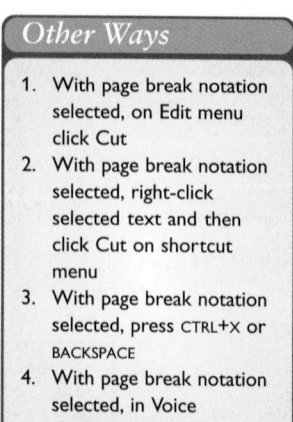

Other Ways

1. With page break notation selected, on Edit menu click Cut
2. With page break notation selected, right-click selected text and then click Cut on shortcut menu
3. With page break notation selected, press CTRL+X or BACKSPACE
4. With page break notation selected, in Voice Command mode, say "Delete"

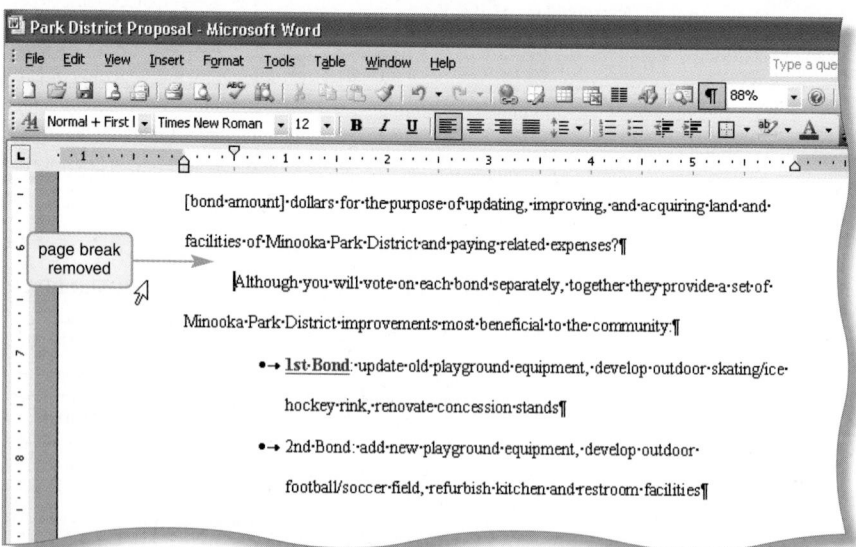

FIGURE 4-31

Cutting Text

The last line of the document contains the phrase, Thank you very much! You decide to shorten it simply to say, Thank you! The following steps show how to cut the text from the document.

To Cut Text

1

• **Scroll to the bottom of the document.**

• **Drag through the words, very much.**

Word selects the text (Figure 4-32).

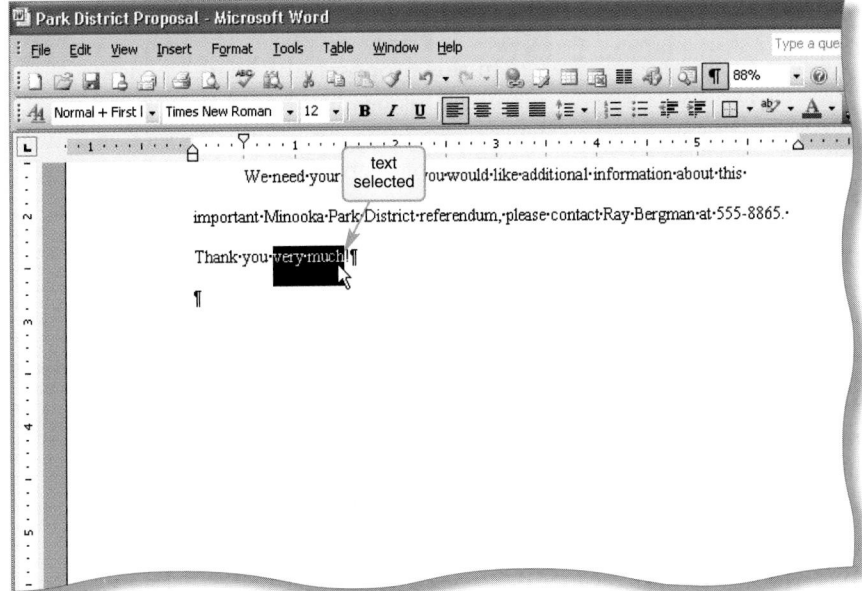

FIGURE 4-32

2

• **Click the Cut button on the Standard toolbar.**

Word removes the selected text from the document (Figure 4-33).

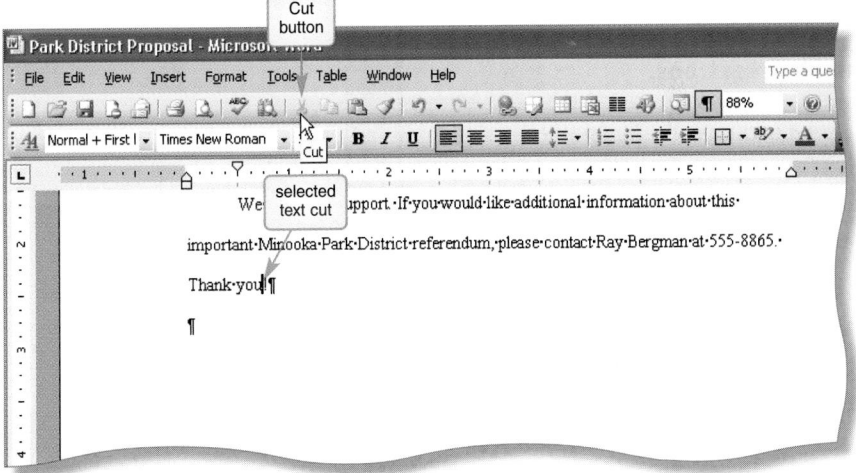

FIGURE 4-33

When you cut text or objects from a document, Word places the cut item(s) on the Clipboard. Recall from Project 3 that you can paste items on the Clipboard by clicking the Paste button on the Standard toolbar or by using the Clipboard task pane.

Other Ways

1. Right-click selected text and then click Cut on shortcut menu
2. Press CTRL+X
3. In Voice Command mode, say "Cut"

More About

Headers and Footers

If a portion of a header or footer does not print, it may be in a nonprintable area. Check the printer manual to see how close it can print to the edge of the paper. Then, click File on the menu bar, click Page Setup, click the Layout tab, adjust the From edge box to a value that is larger than the printer's minimum margin setting, and then click the OK button.

Creating Headers and Footers

As discussed in Project 2, a **header** is text that prints at the top of each page in the document. A **footer** is text that prints at the bottom of each page. In this proposal, you want the header and footer to display on each page in the body of the sales proposal. You do not want the header and footer on the title page. Recall that the title page and the body of the sales proposal are in two separate sections. Thus, the header and footer should not be in section 1, but they should be in section 2.

Creating a Header Different from a Previous Section Header

In this proposal, the header consists of the page number aligned at the right margin. This header should be only on the pages in section 2 of the document. Thus, be sure the insertion point is in section 2 when you create the header.

The next steps go to the beginning of section 2 in the document.

To Go To a Section

1

• **Double-click the status bar anywhere to the left of the status indicators.**

• **When Word displays the Find and Replace dialog box, if necessary, click the Go To tab.**

• **Click Section in the Go to what area.**

• **Type** 2 **in the Enter section number text box.**

Word displays the Go To sheet in the Find and Replace dialog box (Figure 4-34).

2

• **Click the Go To button in the dialog box.**

• **Click the Close button in the dialog box.**

Word displays the top of section 2 in the document window (shown in Figure 4-35).

Other Ways

1. Click Select Browse Object button on vertical scroll bar, click Browse by Section
2. On Edit menu click Go To
3. Press CTRL+G
4. In Voice Command mode, say "Edit, Go To"

FIGURE 4-34

In addition to sections, you can go to pages, lines, bookmarks, comments, footnotes, and endnotes through the Go To sheet (Figure 4-34) in the Find dialog box.

The next steps show how to add a header only to the second section of the document so it does not appear on the title page but does appear on all pages in the body of the proposal.

To Create a Header Different from the Previous Section Header

1

• **Verify the insertion point is in section 2 by looking at the status bar.**

• **Click View on the menu bar and then click Header and Footer.**

• **Click the Align Right button on the Formatting toolbar.**

Word right-aligns the insertion point in the header area (Figure 4-35). The header area title displays, Header -Section 2-. Notice the label, Same as Previous, at the top of the header area, which indicates any text you type in this header will be copied to section 1. You do not want text you type to be in section 1.

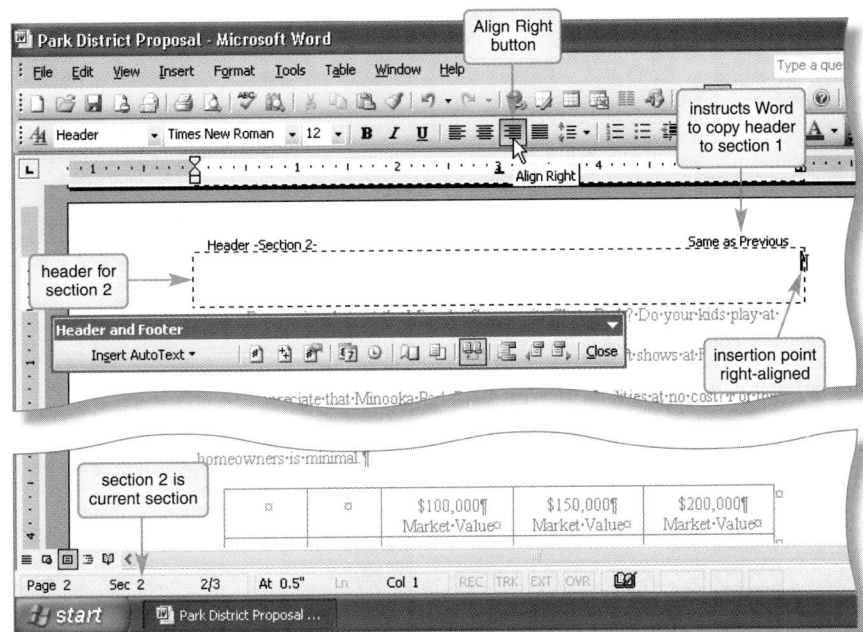

FIGURE 4-35

2

• **If the header area displays the label, Same as Previous, click the Link to Previous button on the Header and Footer toolbar to deselect the button.**

• **Click the Insert Page Number button on the Header and Footer toolbar.**

Word removes the Same as Previous label from the header area and inserts the page number at the location of the insertion point (Figure 4-36).

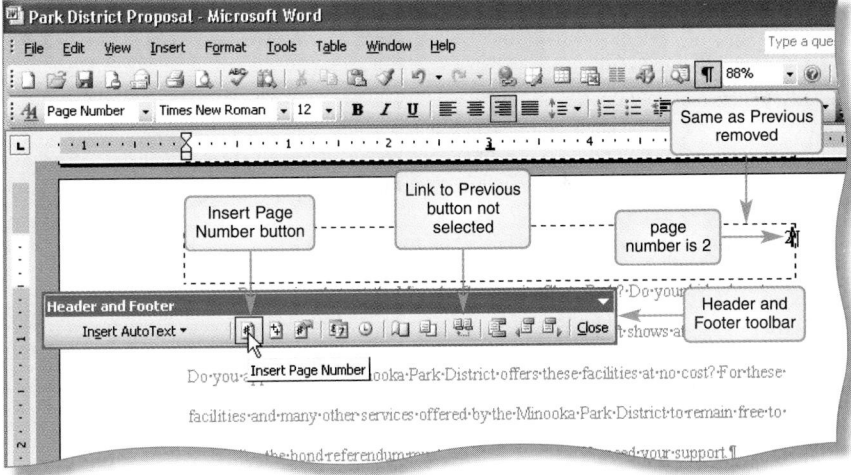

FIGURE 4-36

> *Other Ways*
>
> 1. In Voice Command mode, say "View, Header and Footer, Link to Previous"

When the Link to Previous button is not selected on the Header and Footer toolbar, Word does not copy the typed header into the previous section. If you wanted the header typed in section 2 also to be in section 1, you would leave the Link to Previous button selected on the Header and Footer toolbar.

In Figure 4-36, the page number is 2 because Word begins numbering pages from the beginning of the document. You want to begin numbering the body of the sales proposal with a number 1. Thus, you need to instruct Word to begin numbering the pages in section 2 with the number 1.

The following steps show how to change the format of page numbers and how to page number differently in a section.

To Change Page Number Format and Page Number Differently in a Section

1

• **Click the Format Page Number button on the Header and Footer toolbar.**

• **When Word displays the Page Number Format dialog box, click the Number format box arrow and then click the second format in the list.**

• **Click Start at in the Page numbering area.**

By default, Word displays the number 1 in the Start at box in the Page Number Format dialog box (Figure 4-37).

2

• **Click the OK button.**

Word changes the starting page number for section 2 to the number 1 (Figure 4-38).

More About

Page Numbers

If Word displays {PAGE} instead of the actual page number, press ALT+F9 to turn off field codes. If Word prints {PAGE} instead of the page number, click File on the menu bar, click Print, click the Options button, remove the check mark from the Field codes check box, and then click the OK button in each dialog box.

FIGURE 4-37

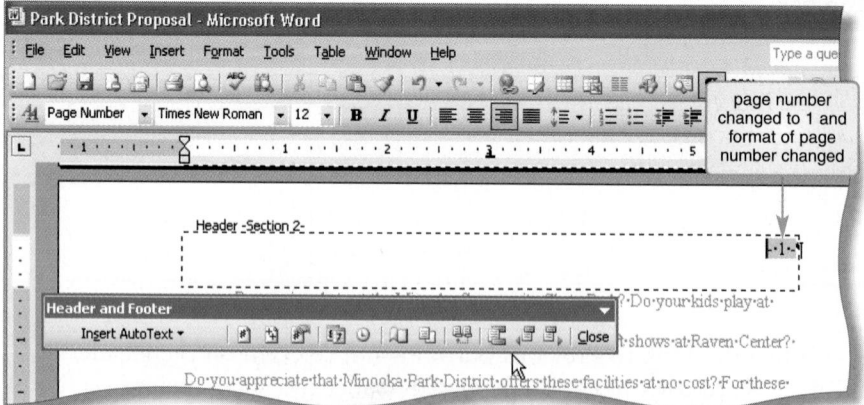

FIGURE 4-38

Creating a Footer Different from a Previous Section Footer

In this proposal, the footer consists of the following sentence: Vote YES for the Minooka Park District Referendum. This footer should be only on the pages in section 2 of the document. Thus, be sure the insertion point is in section 2 when you create the footer.

The following steps show how to add a footer only to the second section of the document.

To Create a Footer Different from the Previous Section Footer

1

• **Click the Switch Between Header and Footer button on the Header and Footer toolbar.**

• **If the footer area displays the label, Same as Previous, click the Link to Previous button on the Header and Footer toolbar to deselect the button.**

• **Click the Bold button on the Formatting toolbar.**

• **Click the Center button on the Formatting toolbar.**

• **Type** Vote YES for the Minooka Park District Referendum.

Word displays the text in the footer area (Figure 4-39). The footer area displays the title, Footer -Section 2-, at its left edge.

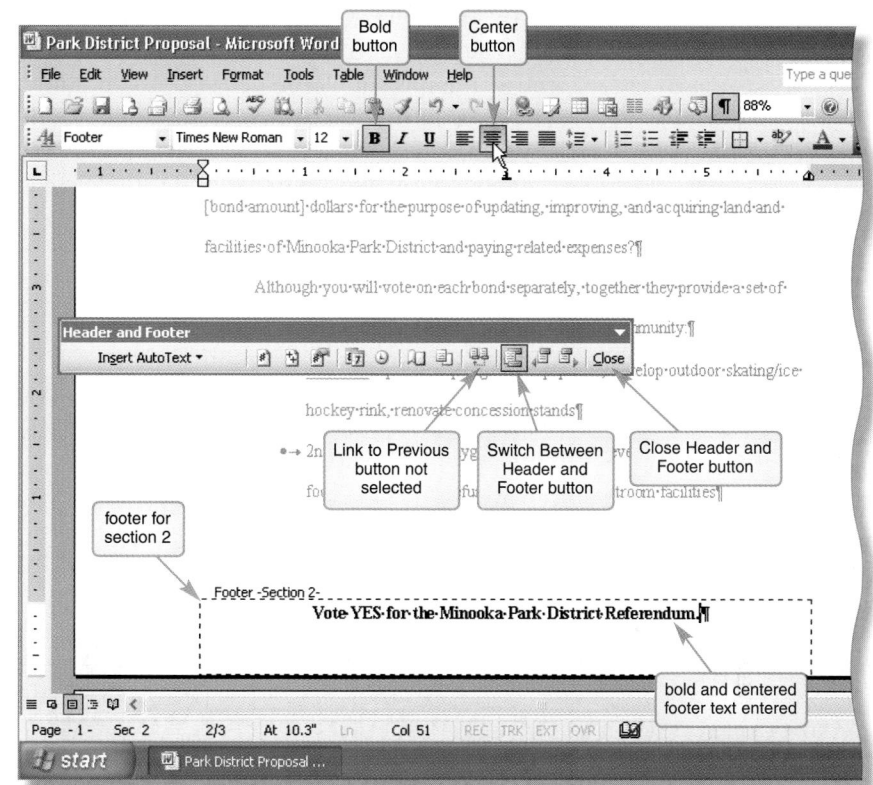

FIGURE 4-39

2

• **Click the Close Header and Footer button to remove the Header and Footer toolbar from the screen.**

Notice you used the same technique as for the header. That is, the Link to Previous button on the Header and Footer toolbar is not selected. When this button is not selected, Word does not copy the typed footer into the previous section. If you wanted the footer typed in section 2 also to be in section 1, you would leave the Link to Previous button selected on the Header and Footer toolbar.

Other Ways

1. With Header and Footer toolbar displaying, in Voice Command mode, say "Switch Between Header and Footer"

Formatting and Charting a Table

The sales proposal draft contains a Word table (shown in Figure 4-29a on page WD 242) that was created using the Insert Table button on the Standard toolbar. This table contains four rows and five columns. The first row identifies the market value of homes; the remaining rows show the estimated annual tax for each bond. The first column identifies the bond, and the remaining columns show the taxes for each home market value. The following pages explain how to modify the table, sum the contents of the table, format the table, chart the table's contents, modify the chart, and then format the chart.

Adding and Deleting Table Rows and Columns

The table needs several modifications. The blank column between the first and third columns should be deleted. A title should be added in a row at the top of the table, and a row that shows total dollar amounts needs to be added to the bottom of the table.

The following steps show how to delete a column from the middle of the table.

To Delete a Column

1

• **If necessary, scroll to display the table in the document window.**

• **Position the mouse pointer at the top of the column to be deleted and click when it changes to a downward pointing arrow.**

Word selects the entire column below the mouse pointer (Figure 4-40).

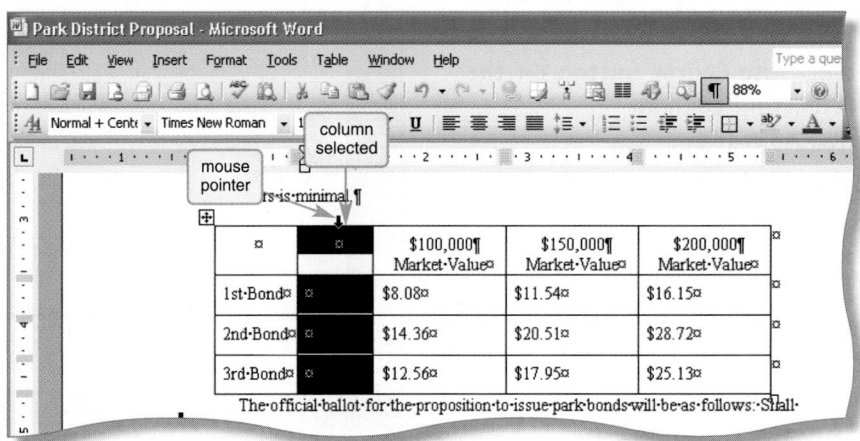

FIGURE 4-40

2

• **Right-click the selected column.**

Word displays a shortcut menu related to tables with a selected column(s) (Figure 4-41).

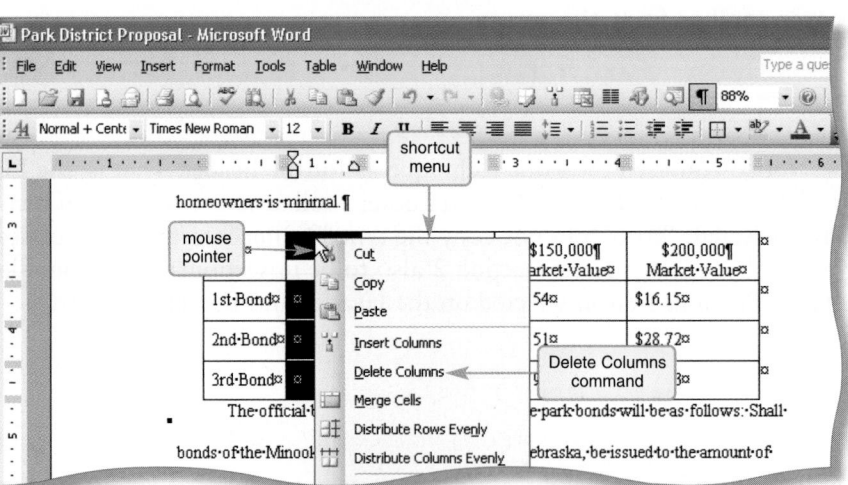

FIGURE 4-41

3

- **Click Delete Columns on the shortcut menu.**

Word deletes the selected column (Figure 4-42).

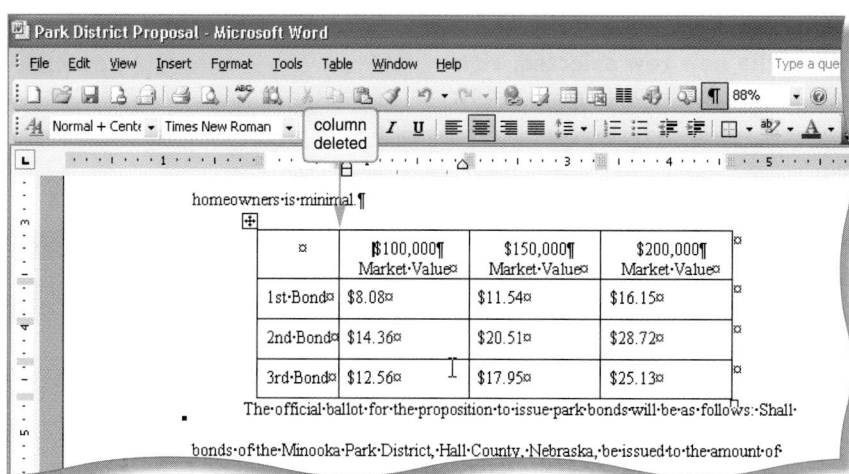

FIGURE 4-42

Other Ways

1. With the column selected, on Table menu point to Delete, click Columns
2. With the column selected, in Voice Command mode, say "Table, Delete, Columns"

If you want to **delete a row**, instead of a column, from a table, you would select the row(s) to delete and then click Delete Rows on the shortcut menu, or click Table on the menu bar, click Delete, and then click Rows.

The top row of the table is to contain the table title, which should be centered above the columns of the table. When you add a row, it will have one cell for each column, in this case, four cells. The title of the table, however, should be in a single cell that spans across all rows. Thus, the first step is to add a row to the top of the table and then merge its cells, as shown in the following steps.

To Add a Row and Merge Cells

1

- **Position the mouse pointer to the left of the first row of the table (the column headings) until it changes to a right-pointing arrow and then click to select the entire row.**
- **Right-click inside the selected row.**

Word displays a shortcut menu related to a table with a selected row(s) (Figure 4-43).

2

- **Click Insert Rows on the shortcut menu.**

Word adds a row above the selected row and selects the newly added row (shown in Figure 4-44 on the next page).

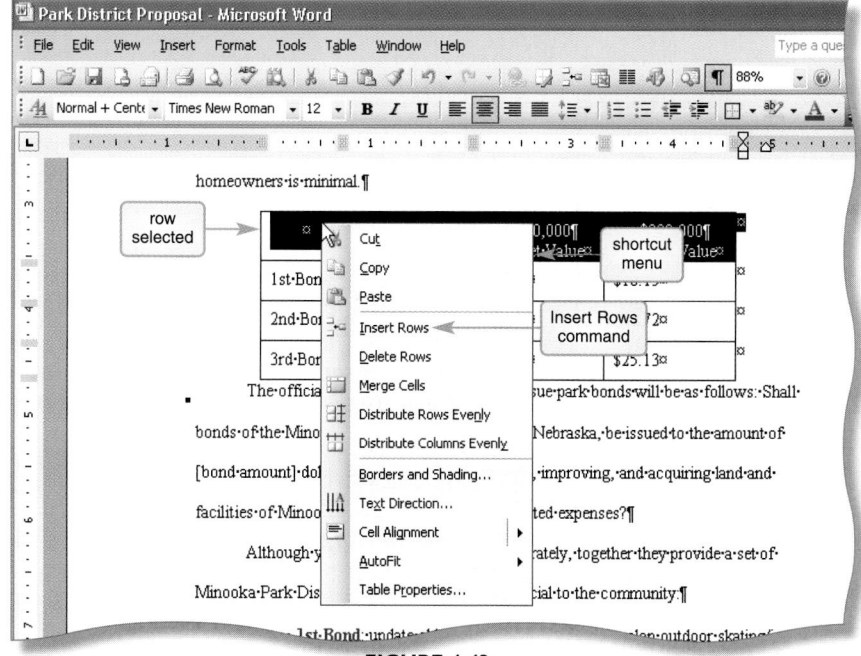

FIGURE 4-43

Microsoft Office
Word 2003

3

• **With the new row selected, right-click the added row (Figure 4-44).**

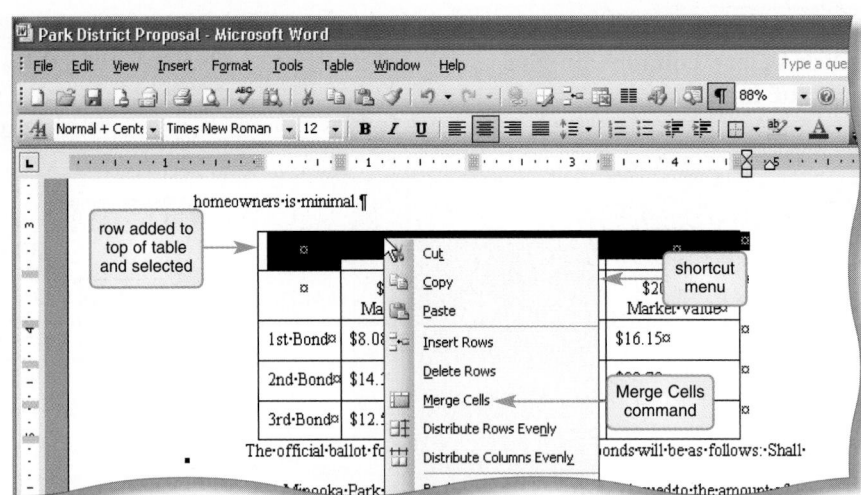

FIGURE 4-44

4

• **Click Merge Cells on the shortcut menu.**

• **Click inside the top row to remove the highlight.**

Word merges the four selected cells into a single cell (Figure 4-45). Text entered into this cell automatically will be centered.

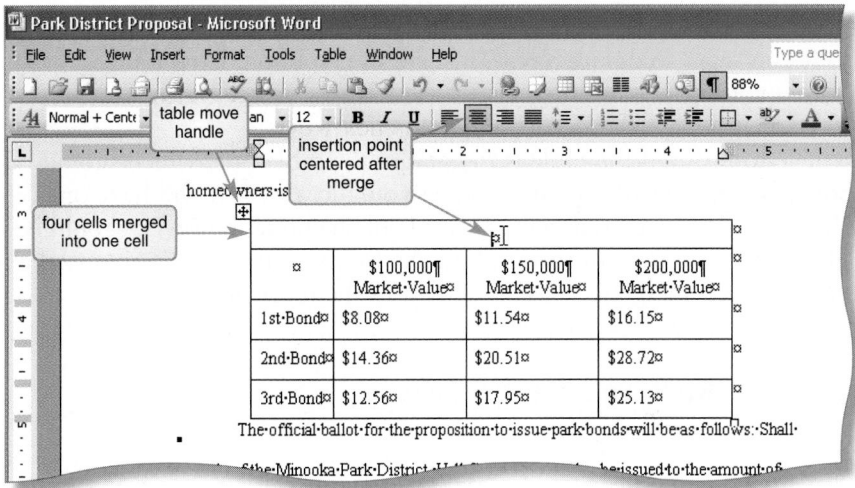

FIGURE 4-45

The next task is to add text into the merged cell, as described in the following steps.

To Enter and Format Text in a Table Cell

1 **With the insertion point in the cell at the top of the table, press the CAPS LOCK key. Type** ESTIMATED ANNUAL TAX IMPACT **and then press the CAPS LOCK key.**

2 **Press CTRL+5.**

*Pressing **CTRL+5** instructs Word to change the line spacing of the cell to 1.5 lines (shown in Figure 4-46).*

Instead of merging multiple cells into a single cell, sometimes you want to split a cell into more cells. To split cells, you would perform the following steps.

To Split Cells

1. Select the cell to split.
2. Right-click the selected cell and then click Split Cells on the shortcut menu; or click the Split Cells button on the Tables and Borders toolbar; or click Table on the menu bar and then click Split Cells.
3. When Word displays the Split Cells dialog box, enter the number of rows and columns into which you want the cell split.
4. Click the OK button.

The next step is to add a row to the bottom of the table that shows totals of the dollar amounts in the second, third, and fourth columns. As discussed in Project 3, to add a row to the end of a table, position the insertion point in the bottom-right corner cell and then press the TAB key, as described below.

To Add a Row to the End of a Table

1 **Position the insertion point at the end of the lower-right corner cell of the table (after the $25.13).**

2 **Press the TAB key to create a new row at the bottom of the table.**

3 **Type** Total **and then press the TAB key.**

Word adds a row to the bottom of the table (Figure 4-46). The first cell in the new row contains the word, Total. The remaining cells in the new row are empty.

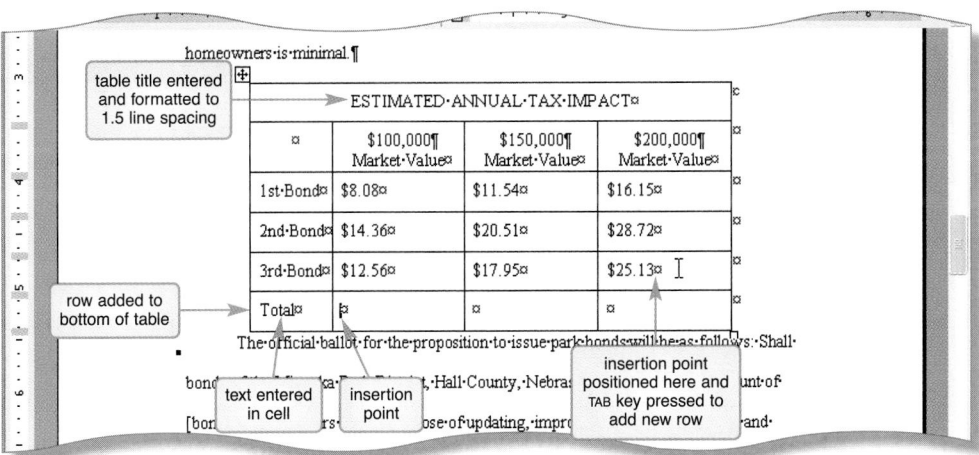

FIGURE 4-46

If you wanted to **add a column** in the middle of a table, you would select the column to the right of where the new column is to be inserted and then click the Insert Columns button on the Standard toolbar (the same button you click to insert a table); or click Insert Columns on the shortcut menu; or click Table on the menu bar, point to Insert, and then click Columns to the Left. To add a column to the right of a table, select the end-of-row marks at the right edge of the table, then click the Insert Columns button; or click Insert Columns on the shortcut menu; or click Table on the menu bar, point to Insert, and then click Columns to the Right.

Summing Table Contents

To quickly total a column or a row, Word provides an **AutoSum button** on the Tables and Borders toolbar. The following steps show how to sum columns in the table.

To Sum Columns in a Table

1

• **If the Tables and Borders toolbar is not displayed in the Word window, click the Tables and Borders button on the Standard toolbar.**

• **If the Draw Table button on the Tables and Borders toolbar is selected, click it to deselect it.**

• **With the insertion point in the cell to contain the sum (shown in Figure 4-46 on the previous page), click the AutoSum button on the Tables and Borders toolbar.**

Word places the sum of the numbers in the column in the current cell.

2

• **Press the TAB key. Click the AutoSum button on the Tables and Borders toolbar.**

• **Press the TAB key. Click the AutoSum button on the Tables and Borders toolbar.**

Word places a sum in each of the remaining columns (Figure 4-47).

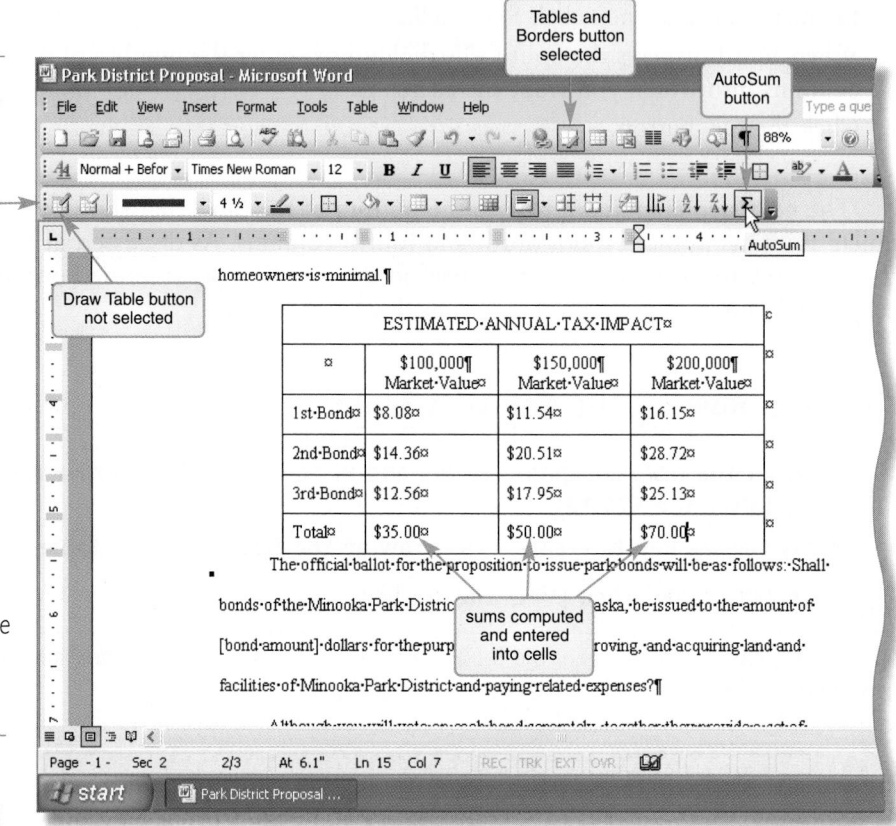

FIGURE 4-47

Other Ways

1. On Table menu click Formula, if necessary type =SUM(ABOVE) in Formula text box, click OK button
2. With Tables and Borders toolbar displayed, in Voice Command mode, say "AutoSum"

If you wanted to sum the contents of a row instead of a column, you would place the insertion point in the empty cell at the right of the row and then click the AutoSum button. Depending on the location of the insertion point, Word determines if it should sum a row or a column. If Word uses the wrong formula, you can change it. The formula for summing a column is =SUM(ABOVE), and the formula for summing a row is =SUM(LEFT). To change an existing formula, click Table on the menu bar and then click Formula. Make the change in the Formula dialog box and then click the OK button. You also use the Formula dialog box if you want to enter a formula into a cell other than summing a row or column.

Formatting a Table

The table in the document looks dull. Although you can format each row, column, and cell of a table individually, Word provides a Table AutoFormat feature that contains predefined styles for tables. The following steps show how to format the entire table using Table AutoFormat.

More About

Table Borders

Instead of using AutoFormat, you can use buttons and boxes on the Tables and Borders toolbar to apply your own borders to a table.

To AutoFormat a Table

1

• **With the insertion point in the table, click the Table AutoFormat button on the Tables and Borders toolbar.**

• **When Word displays the Table AutoFormat dialog box, if necessary, scroll through the Table styles list and then click Table Elegant. Be sure all check boxes in the Apply special formats to area at the bottom of the dialog box contain check marks.**

Word displays a preview of the table style in the Table AutoFormat dialog box (Figure 4-48).

FIGURE 4-48

2

• **Click the Apply button in the dialog box.**

• **Click the Tables and Borders button on the Standard toolbar to remove the Tables and Borders toolbar from the screen.**

Word formats the table according to the Table Elegant style (Figure 4-49).

FIGURE 4-49

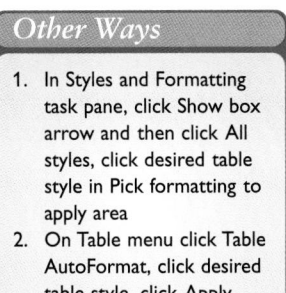

Other Ways

1. In Styles and Formatting task pane, click Show box arrow and then click All styles, click desired table style in Pick formatting to apply area
2. On Table menu click Table AutoFormat, click desired table style, click Apply button

The next step is to center the table horizontally between the page margins, as described below.

To Center a Table

1 **Position the mouse pointer in the table to display the table move handle in the upper-left corner of the table. Position the mouse pointer on the table move handle and then click to select the table.**

2 **With the entire table selected, click the Center button on the Formatting toolbar.**

3 **Click anywhere to remove the selection in the table.**

Word centers the selected table (shown in Figure 4-50).

As with paragraphs, you can left-align, center, or right-align data in table cells. By default, the data you enter into the cells is left-aligned. You can change the alignment just as you would for a paragraph. If you want to change the alignment of multiple cells, first select the cells. The following step right-aligns the contents of all the cells that contain dollar amounts.

To Right-Align Cell Contents

1

• **Drag through the cells to right-align.**

• **Click the Align Right button on the Formatting toolbar.**

Word right-aligns the data in the selected cells (Figure 4-50).

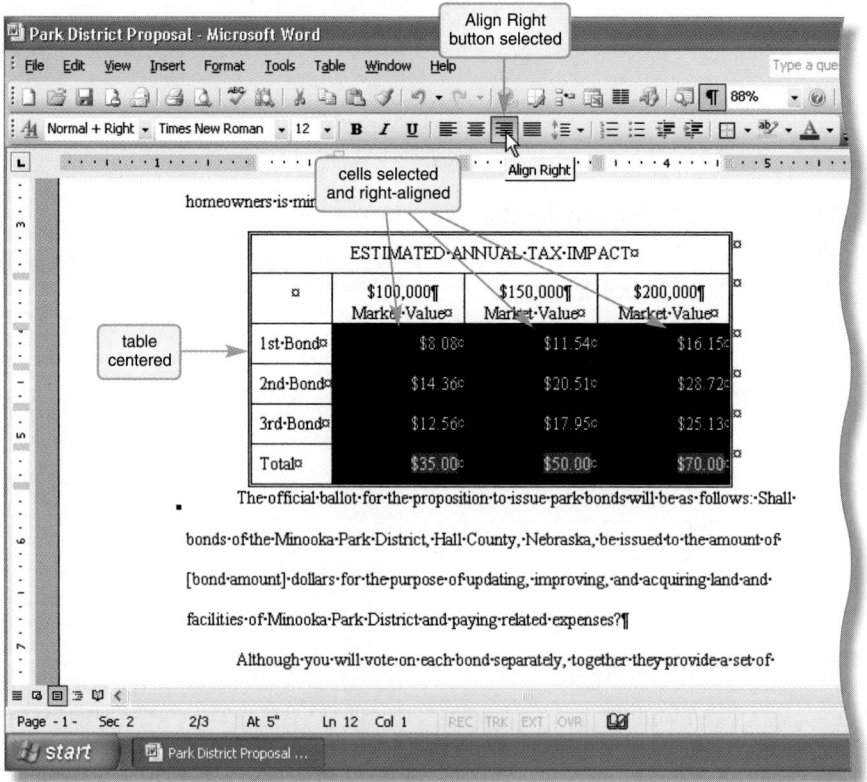

FIGURE 4-50

Formatting Nonadjacent Characters

The next step is to change the ordinals in the first column of the table to be superscripts. That is, the 1st should display as 1st, the 2nd as 2nd, and so on. To do this, select the characters to be superscripted and then use the Font dialog box to apply this character effect to the selected text.

You want to select the st in 1st, the nd in 2nd, and the rd in 3rd. In Word, you can select several segments of text that are not next to each other, called **nonadjacent text** or **noncontiguous text**, by selecting the first segment of text and then pressing and holding down the CTRL key while selecting each additional segment of text.

The following steps show how to select nonadjacent text.

To Select Nonadjacent Text

1

• **Drag through the st in 1st.**

Word selects the st (Figure 4-51).

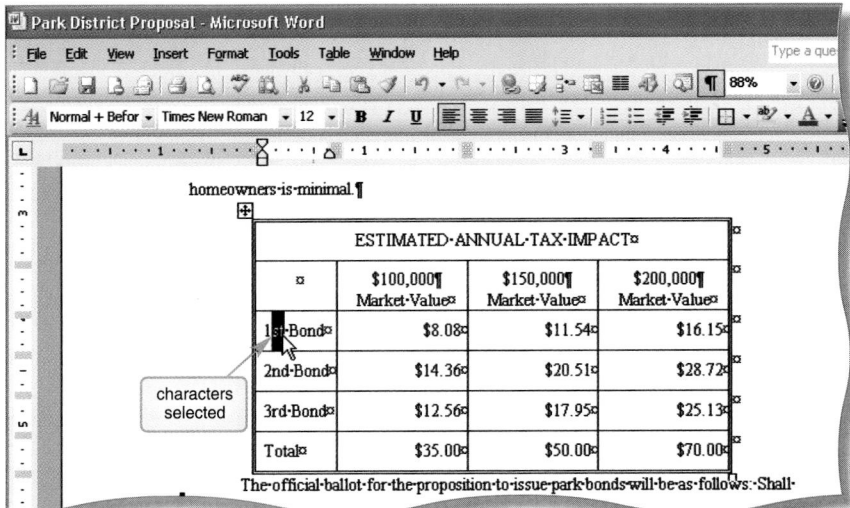

FIGURE 4-51

2

• **While holding down the CTRL key, drag through the nd in 2nd.**

• **While holding down the CTRL key, drag through the rd in 3rd. Release the CTRL key.**

Word selects the nonadjacent text (Figure 4-52).

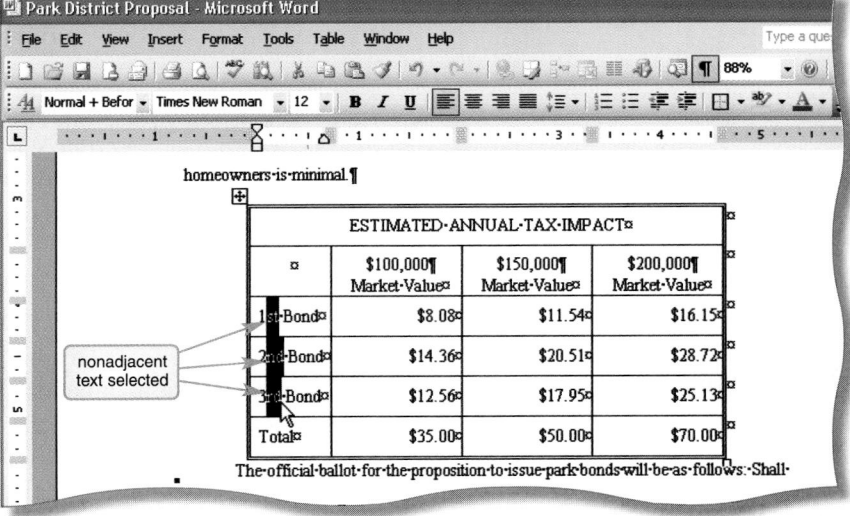

FIGURE 4-52

The next step is to apply the superscript character effect to the selected text, as described below.

To Superscript Selected Characters

1 With the text selected, click Format on the menu bar and then click Font. When Word displays the Font dialog box, if necessary, click the Font tab.

2 Click Superscript in the Effects area to place a check mark in the check box (Figure 4-53).

3 Click the OK button. Click anywhere to remove the selections.

Word superscripts the selected text (shown in Figure 4-54).

FIGURE 4-53

As discussed earlier in this project and shown in Figure 4-53, the Font sheet in the Font dialog box contains many other character effects you can add to text in a document. Table 4-1 on page WD 229 identified all of the available character effects.

Charting a Word Table

When you create a Word table, you easily can chart its data using an embedded charting application called **Microsoft Graph**. Graph has its own menus and commands because it is an application embedded in the Word program. Using Graph commands, you can modify the appearance of the chart once you create it.

To create a chart from a Word table, the first row and left column of the selected cells in the table must contain text labels, and the other cells in the selected cells must contain numbers. The table in the Park District Proposal meets these criteria.

More About

Word 2003 Features

For more information about the features and capabilities of Word 2003, visit the Word 2003 More About Web page (scsite.com/wd2003/more) and then click Features and Capabilities of Word 2003.

To chart a Word table, first select the rows and columns in the table to be charted. In this project, you do not want to chart the first row in the table that contains the title or the last row in the table that contains the totals. Thus, you will select the middle four rows in the table and then instruct Word to chart the selected cells, as shown in the following steps.

To Chart a Table

1

• **Point to the left of (outside) the second row in the table (the column headings) until the mouse pointer changes to a right-pointing arrow and then drag downward until the middle four rows in the table are selected.**

The rows to be charted are selected (Figure 4-54). Notice the first and last rows of the table are not selected.

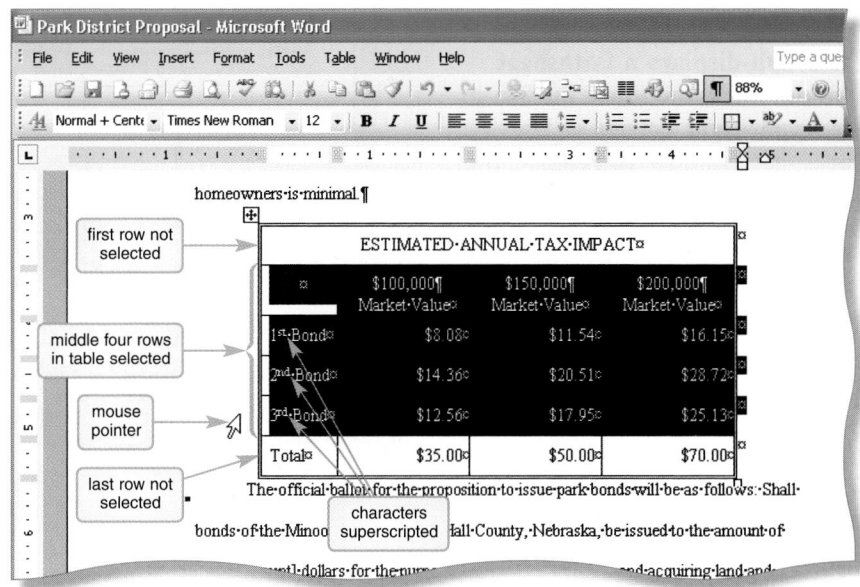

FIGURE 4-54

2

• **Click Insert on the menu bar and then point to Picture (Figure 4-55).**

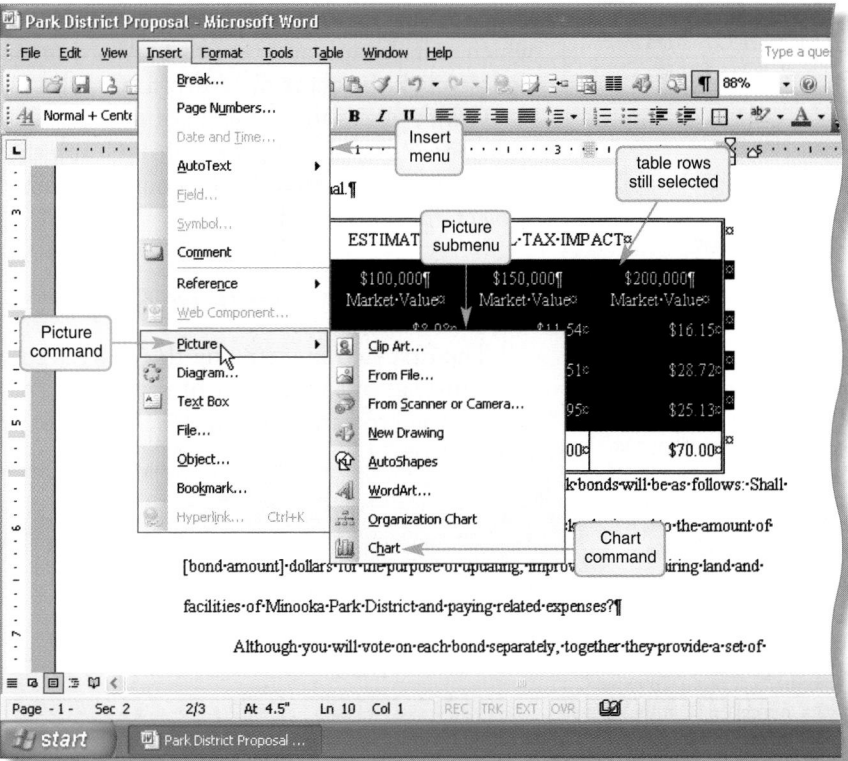

FIGURE 4-55

3

• **Click Chart on the Picture submenu.**

Graph menu bar and toolbars are displayed

Word starts the Microsoft Graph program (Figure 4-56). Graph creates a chart of the selected rows in the table.

4

• **If Graph displays a Datasheet window, click the Close button in the upper-right corner of the Datasheet window to remove the Datasheet window from the screen.**

FIGURE 4-56

The menus on the menu bar and buttons on the toolbars change to Graph menus and toolbars because the Graph program is running inside the Word program. While you are working in Graph, you may inadvertently click somewhere outside the chart, which exits Graph and returns to Word menus and toolbars. If this occurs, simply double-click the chart to return to Graph.

Graph places the contents of the table into a **Datasheet window**, also called a **datasheet** (shown in Figure 4-56). Graph then charts the contents of the datasheet. Although you can modify the contents of the datasheet, it is not necessary in this project and, thus, is closed.

Changing the Chart in Graph

The first step in changing the chart is to move the legend so it displays above the chart instead of to the right of the chart. The **legend** is a box that identifies the colors assigned to categories in the chart. The next steps show how to move the legend in the chart.

To Move Legend Placement in a Chart

1
• **If necessary, scroll to display the chart in the document window.**

• **Right-click the legend in the chart.**

Word displays a shortcut menu related to legends (Figure 4-57).

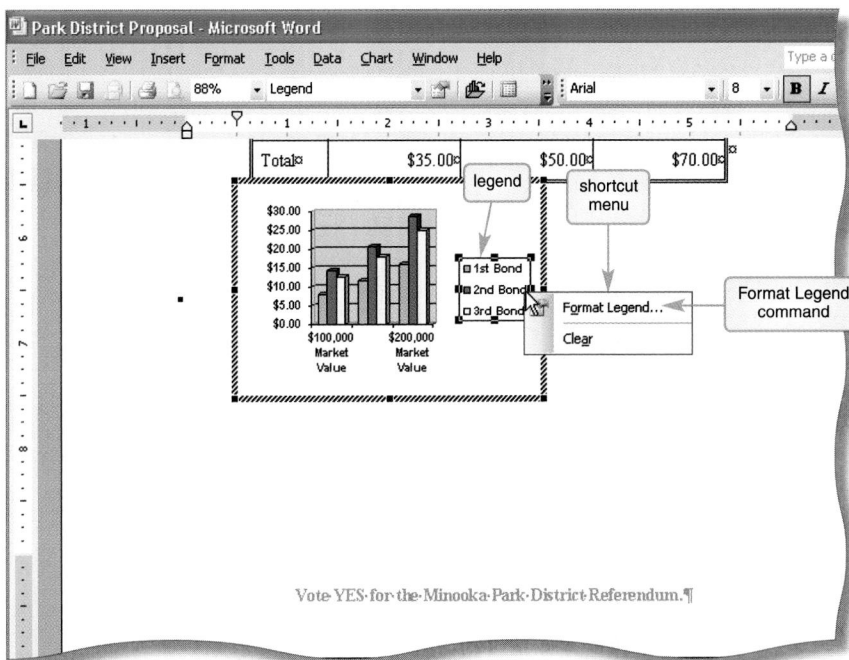
FIGURE 4-57

2
• **Click Format Legend on the shortcut menu.**

• **When Word displays the Format Legend dialog box, if necessary, click the Placement tab.**

• **Click Top in the Placement area.**

Graph displays the Format Legend dialog box (Figure 4-58).

3
• **Click the OK button.**

Graph places the legend above the chart (shown in Figure 4-59 on the next page).

FIGURE 4-58

The next step is to resize the chart so it is bigger. You resize a chart the same way you resize any other graphical object. That is, you drag the chart's sizing handles, as shown in the following steps.

To Resize a Chart

1

• **Point to the bottom-right sizing handle on the chart and drag downward and to the right as shown in Figure 4-59.**

2

• **Release the mouse button.**

Graph resizes the chart (shown in Figure 4-60).

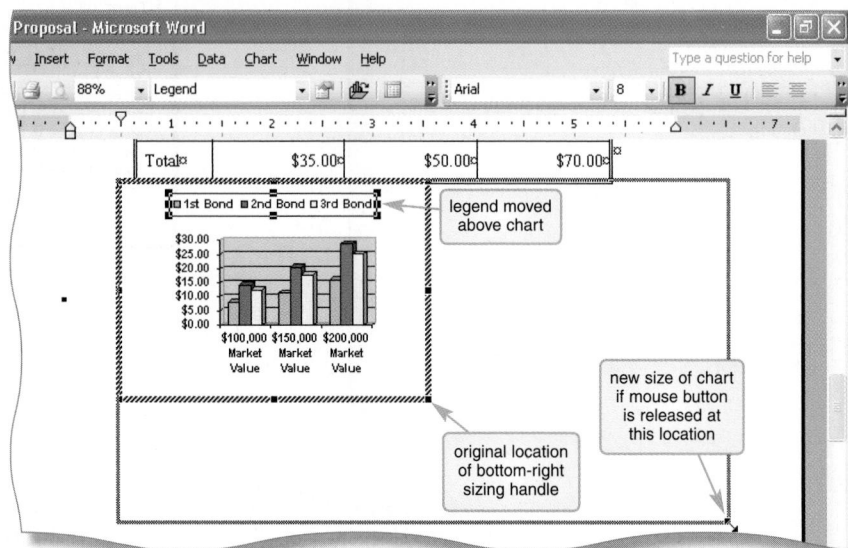

FIGURE 4-59

The next task is to change the chart type so the columns have a cylindrical shape instead of a rectangular shape, as shown in the following steps.

To Change the Chart Type

1

• **Point to the right of the columns in the chart and then right-click when the words, Plot Area, appear as the ScreenTip (Figure 4-60).**

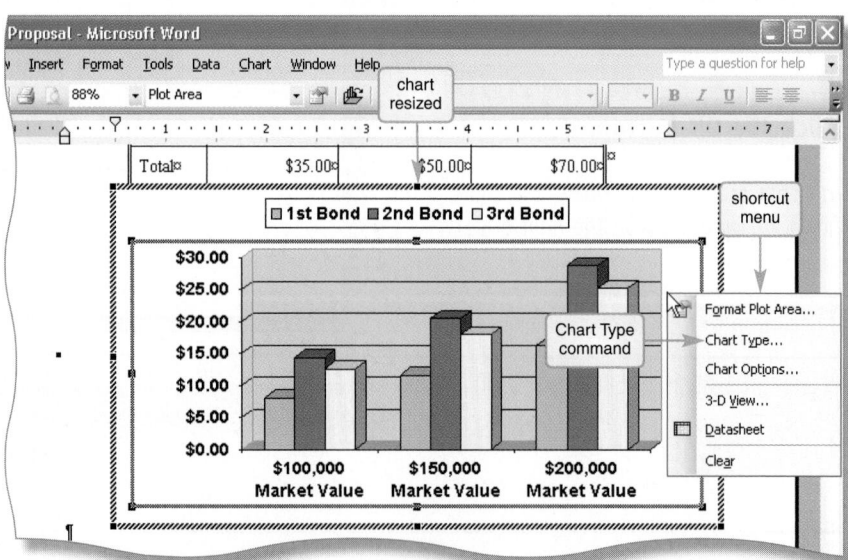

FIGURE 4-60

2

• **Click Chart Type on the shortcut menu.**

• **When Graph displays the Chart Type dialog box, if necessary, click the Standard Types tab.**

• **In the Chart type list, scroll to and then click Cylinder.**

• **In the Chart sub-type area, click the second graphic in the first row (Figure 4-61).**

3

• **Click the OK button.**

Graph changes the shape of the columns to a stacked column with a cylindrical shape (shown in Figure 4-62).

FIGURE 4-61

The modified chart is finished. The next step is to exit Graph and return to Word.

To Exit Graph and Return to Word

1

• **Click somewhere outside the chart. If necessary, scroll to display the chart in the document window.**

Word closes the Graph application (Figure 4-62). Word's menu bar and toolbars are redisplayed below the title bar.

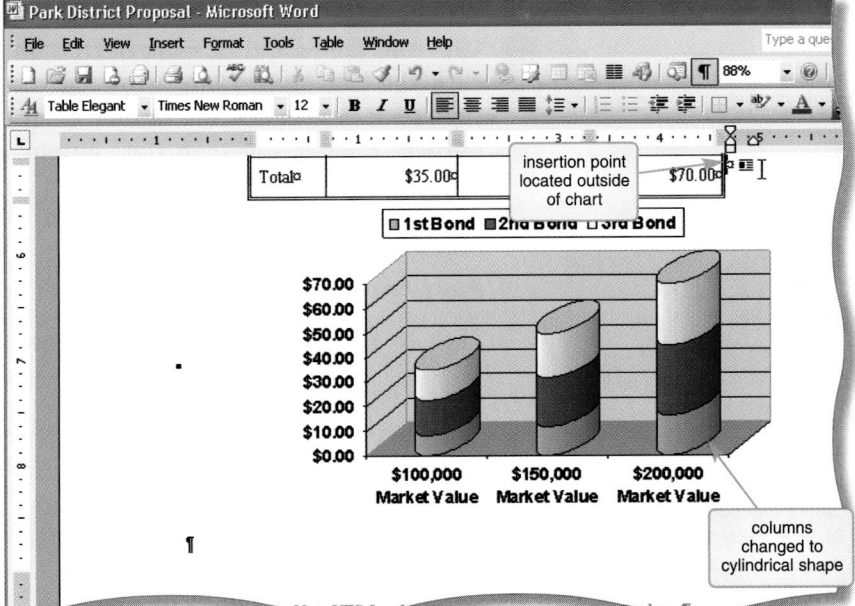

FIGURE 4-62

If you wanted to modify an existing chart in a document, you would double-click the chart to reopen the Microsoft Graph program. Then, you can make changes to the chart. When you are finished making changes to the chart, click anywhere outside the chart to return to Word.

Formatting the Chart Object in Word

The chart now is part of the paragraph below the table. Thus, you can apply any paragraph alignment settings to the chart. The chart should be centered. If you select the chart and then click the Center button on the Formatting toolbar, the chart will not be centered properly. Instead, it will be one-half inch to the right of the center point because first-line indent is set at one-half inch. Thus, you need to remove the first-line indent setting in order to center the paragraph (chart) properly.

You also want to add an outside border to the chart and insert a blank line between the chart and the table. Earlier in this project, you added an outside border to a paragraph on the title page. Its line weight was 4½ point, and its color was dark teal. You do not want this same border definition for the chart. Instead, you want a ½-point border in black.

The chart is part of the paragraph. To insert a blank line above a paragraph, position the insertion point in the paragraph and then press CTRL+0 (the numeral zero).

The following steps describe how to center, outline, and insert a blank line above the chart.

To Format a Chart Object

1 **Click anywhere in the chart to select it, so it displays sizing handles at its corner and middle locations.**

2 **Drag the First Line Indent marker to the 0" mark on the ruler. Click the Center button on the Formatting toolbar.**

3 **Click the Tables and Borders button on the Standard toolbar. If necessary, click the Line Weight box arrow on the Tables and Borders toolbar and then click ½ pt. Click the Border Color button arrow on the Tables and Borders toolbar and then click Automatic on the color palette. Click the Outside Border button on the Tables and Borders toolbar. Click the Tables and Borders button on the Standard toolbar to close the Tables and Borders toolbar.**

4 **Press CTRL+0 (the numeral zero) to insert a blank line above the chart.**

5 **Click to the right of the chart to deselect it.**

Word centers the chart between the left and right margins, places an outside border around the chart, and inserts a blank line above the chart (Figure 4-63).

More About

Charts

If you have an Excel chart or worksheet that you want to be displayed in a Word document, open the Excel workbook and display the chart or worksheet you want to copy. Select the chart or worksheet in Excel. Click the Copy button on Excel's Standard toolbar. Switch to the Word document. Click Edit on the menu bar, click Paste Special, click Paste, click Microsoft Office Excel Worksheet Object in the As list, and then click the OK button.

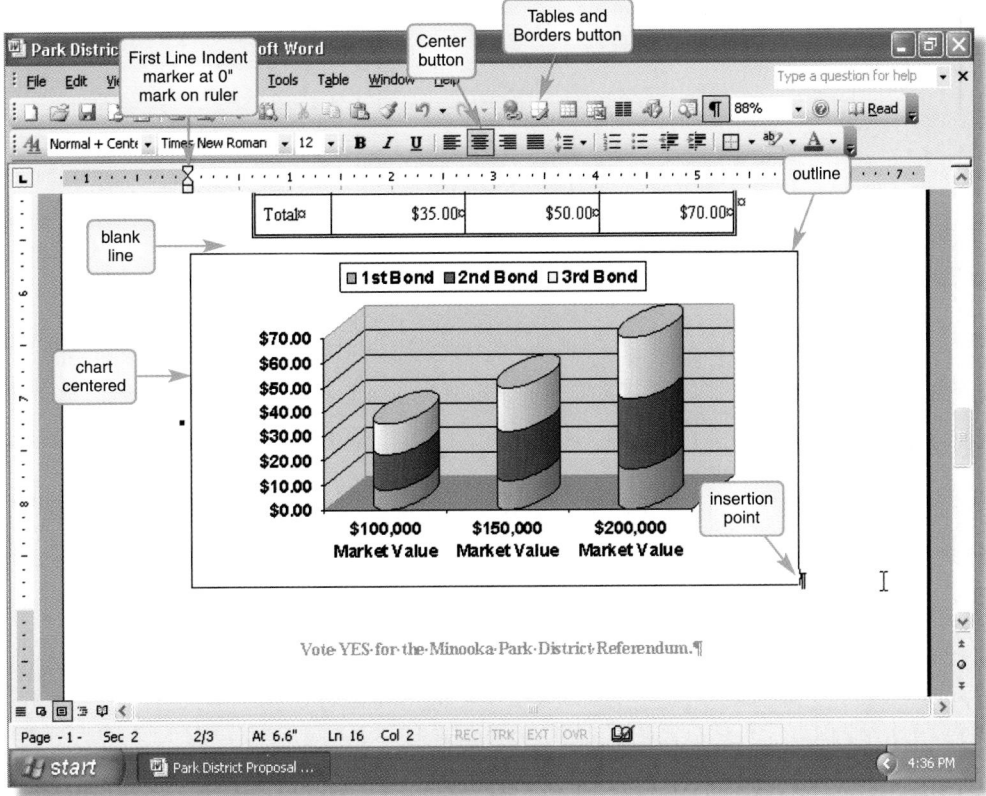

FIGURE 4-63

Working with Formats, Styles, and Bulleted Lists

In this document, the bond names at the beginning of each bulleted item and the bullet character in the bulleted list should be emphasized. The following pages illustrate each of these formatting changes.

Finding a Format

The second page of the body of the proposal has a bulleted list. The text at the beginning of each bulleted paragraph identifies a specific bond. The first bullet, identified with the text, 1st Bond, has been formatted as bold, underlined, and dark red. To find this text in the document, you could scroll through the document until it is displayed on the screen. A more efficient way is to find the bold, underlined, dark red format using the Find and Replace dialog box, as shown in the steps on the next page.

More About

Finding Special Characters

In addition to finding formats, you can use the Find and Replace dialog box to find special characters such as paragraph marks, page breaks, and line breaks. Click the Special button arrow in the Find and Replace dialog box and then click the special character in the list.

To Find a Format

1

• **Press CTRL+F to display the Find and Replace dialog box.**

• **If Word displays a More button in the Find and Replace dialog box, click it so it changes to a Less button.**

• **Click the Format button in the Find and Replace dialog box.**

Word displays the Format button menu above the Format button in the dialog box (Figure 4-64).

FIGURE 4-64

2

• **Click Font on the Format button menu in the Find and Replace dialog box.**

• **When Word displays the Find Font dialog box, click Bold in the Font style list.**

• **In the Find Font dialog box, click the Font color box arrow and then click Dark Red on the color palette.**

• **In the Find Font dialog box, click the Underline style box arrow and then click the first underline style in the list.**

The Preview area displays a sample of the selected font to find (Figure 4-65).

FIGURE 4-65

3

• Click the OK button in the Find Font dialog box.

• When the Find and Replace dialog box is active again, click its Find Next button.

Word locates and highlights the first occurrence of the specified format in the document (Figure 4-66).

4

• Click the Cancel button in the Find and Replace dialog box.

FIGURE 4-66

Other Ways

1. Click Select Browse Object button on vertical scroll bar, click Find on Select Browse Object menu
2. On Edit menu click Find
3. Press CTRL+F
4. In Voice Command mode, say "Edit, Find"

In addition to finding occurrences of text and formatting, you also can use the Find and Replace dialog box to find special characters such as paragraph marks, page breaks, and section breaks. For a complete list of special characters, click the Special button in the Find and Replace dialog box. To remove formatting specified in the Find and Replace dialog box, click the No Formatting button.

Creating and Applying a Character Style

In this project, the bond names at the beginning of the second and third bulleted paragraphs are to have the same character format as the bond name at the beginning of the first bulleted paragraph (bold, underlined, and dark red). As discussed in Project 1, **character formats** affect the way characters appear on the screen and in print. Character formats emphasize certain characters, words, and phrases to improve readability of a document.

You could select each of the bond names and then format them. A more efficient technique is to create a character style. If you decide to modify the formats of the bond names at a later time, you simply change the formats assigned to the style. All characters in the document based on that style will change automatically. Without a style, you would have to select all the bond names again and then change their format. Thus, creating a style saves time in the long run.

Recall that a **style** is a named group of formatting characteristics that you can apply to text. Whenever you create a document, Word formats the text using a particular style. The base style for a new Word document is the Normal style, which for a new installation of Word 2003 mostly likely uses 12-point Times New Roman font for characters. For the bulleted list, you also want the bond names to be bold, underlined, and dark red.

More About

Styles

If you want to create a new style that is based on text that you already have formatted, select the text and then display the Styles and Formatting task pane. When you click the New Style button, the formats of the selected text will display in the New Style dialog box.

The following steps show how to create a character style called Bonds.

To Create a Character Style

1

• **If necessary, click the bond name, 1st Bond, to position the insertion point in the first bulleted paragraph.**

• **Click the Styles and Formatting button on the Formatting toolbar.**

• **Click the New Style button in the Styles and Formatting task pane.**

• **When Word displays the New Style dialog box, type** Bonds **in the Name text box.**

• **Click the Style type box arrow and then click Character.**

The New Style dialog box displays formats assigned to the location of the insertion point (Figure 4-67).

FIGURE 4-67

2

• **Click the OK button.**

Word inserts the new style, Bonds, alphabetically in the Pick formatting to apply area in the Styles and Formatting task pane (Figure 4-68).

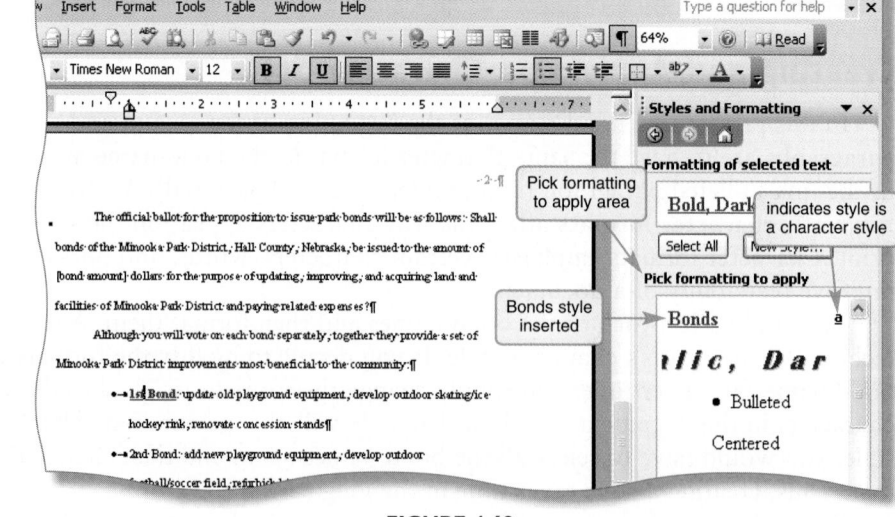

FIGURE 4-68

Other Ways

1. On Format menu click Styles and Formatting, click New Style button, define style, click OK button
2. In Voice Command mode, say "Styles and Formatting, New Style, [define style], OK"

The next step is to apply the style to the bond names in the bulleted list, as shown below.

To Apply a Character Style

1

• **Drag through the text, 2nd Bond, to select it.**

• **Press and hold down the CTRL key and then drag through the text, 3rd Bond, to select it also. Release the CTRL key.**

Word selects the nonadjacent text that is to be based on the Bonds style (Figure 4-69).

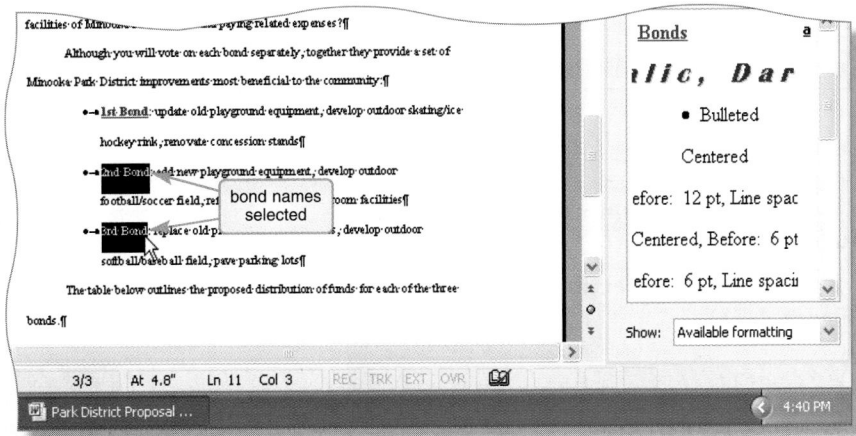

FIGURE 4-69

2

• **With the Styles and Formatting task pane displaying in the Word window, click Bonds in the Pick formatting to apply area.**

• **Click in the bulleted list to remove the selection.**

Word applies the character format, Bonds, to the selected bond names in the bulleted list (Figure 4-70).

3

• **Close the Styles and Formatting task pane by clicking its Close button.**

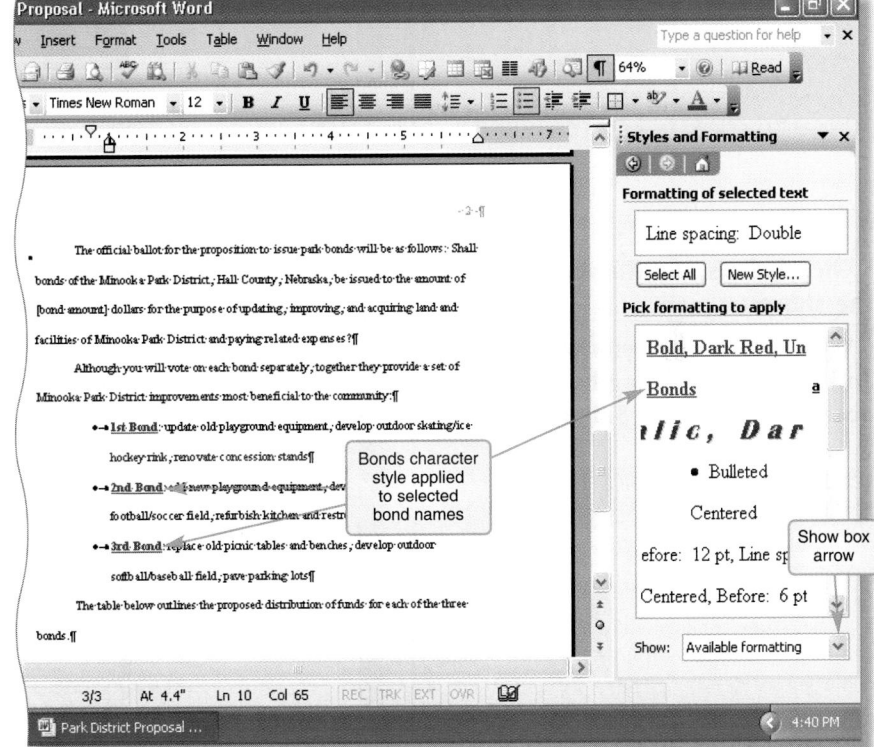

FIGURE 4-70

If a style you wish to use is not displayed in the Pick formatting to apply area of the Styles and Formatting task pane and you know the style exists, click the Show box arrow in the Styles and Formatting task pane and then click All styles.

Other Ways

1. Click Style box arrow on Formatting toolbar and then click style name
2. In Voice Command mode, say "Style, [select style name]"

Customizing Bullets in a List

The bulleted list uses default bullet characters (shown in Figure 4-71). To change the bullet symbol from a small, solid circle to the picture bullets shown in Figure 4-29b on page WD 243, use the Bullets and Numbering dialog box. The following steps show how to change the bullets in the list to picture bullets.

To Add Picture Bullets to a List

1

• **Select the paragraphs in the bulleted list.**

• **Right-click the selection (Figure 4-71).**

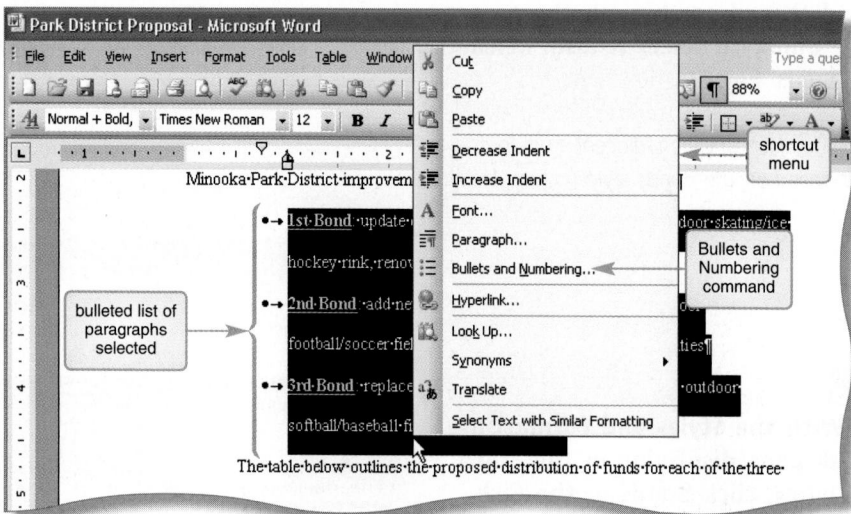

FIGURE 4-71

2

• **Click Bullets and Numbering on the shortcut menu.**

• **When Word displays the Bullets and Numbering dialog box, if necessary, click the Bulleted tab.**

Word displays several bullet styles in the Bullets and Numbering dialog box (Figure 4-72).

FIGURE 4-72

3

- **Click the Customize button in the Bullets and Numbering dialog box.**
- **When Word displays the Customize Bulleted List dialog box, click the Picture button.**
- **When Word displays the Picture Bullet dialog box, click the desired picture bullet (third row, second column).**

In the Picture Bullet dialog box, the selected picture bullet has a box around it, indicating it is selected (Figure 4-73).

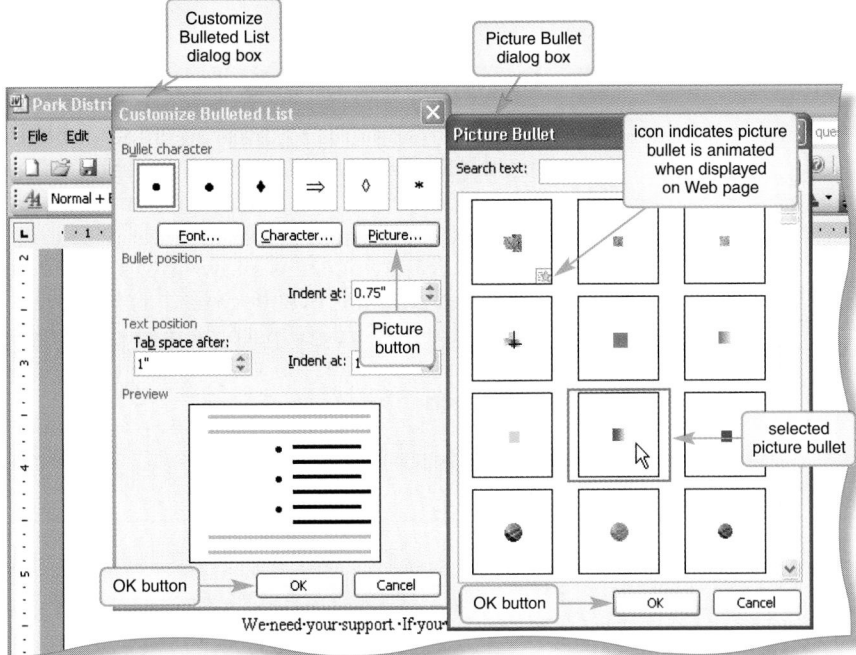

FIGURE 4-73

4

- **Click the OK button in the Picture Bullet dialog box.**
- **Click the OK button in the Customize Bulleted List dialog box.**
- **When the Word window is visible again, click in the selected list to remove the selection.**

Word changes the default bullets to picture bullets (Figure 4-74).

FIGURE 4-74

In addition to picture bullets, the Bullets and Numbering dialog box (Figure 4-72) provides a number of other bullet styles. To use one of these styles, simply click the desired style in the dialog box and then click the OK button.

Drawing a Table

The next step is to insert a table above the last paragraph of the proposal (Figure 4-29b on page WD 243). As previously discussed, a Word table is a collection of rows and columns; the intersection of a row and a column is called a cell. Cells are filled with data.

When you want to create a simple table, one with the same number of rows and columns, use the Insert Table button on the Standard toolbar to create the table. To create a more complex table, use Word's **Draw Table feature**. The table to be created at this point in the project is a complex table because it does not contain the same number of rows and columns. The following pages discuss how to use Word's Draw Table feature.

Other Ways

1. Select list, on Format menu click Bullets and Numbering, click Bulleted tab, click Customize button, click Picture button, click desired bullet style, click OK button, click OK button
2. Select list, in Voice Command mode, say "Format, Bullets and Numbering, Bullets, Customize, Picture, [select desired bullet style], OK, OK"

More About

Drawing Tables

To draw a table, the Draw
Table button on the Tables
and Borders toolbar must be
selected (Figure 4-75). If it is
not selected, click it.

Drawing an Empty Table

The first step is to draw an empty table in the document. To draw a table, you use the **Draw Table button** on the Tables and Borders toolbar. When the Draw Table button is selected, the mouse pointer shape changes to a pencil. To draw the boundary, rows, and columns of the table, you drag the pencil pointer on the screen.

The following steps show how to draw an empty table. Do not try to make the rows and columns evenly spaced as you draw them. After you draw the table, you will instruct Word to space them evenly. If you make a mistake while drawing the table, you can click the Undo button on the Standard toolbar to undo your most recent action(s).

To Draw an Empty Table

1

• **Position the insertion point at the beginning of the last paragraph.**

• **If the Tables and Borders toolbar is not displayed, click the Tables and Borders button on the Standard toolbar.**

• **If it is not selected, click the Draw Table button on the Tables and Borders toolbar.**

• **Position the mouse pointer, which has a pencil shape, immediately above the insertion point (Figure 4-75).**

• **Verify the insertion point is positioned exactly as shown in Figure 4-75.**

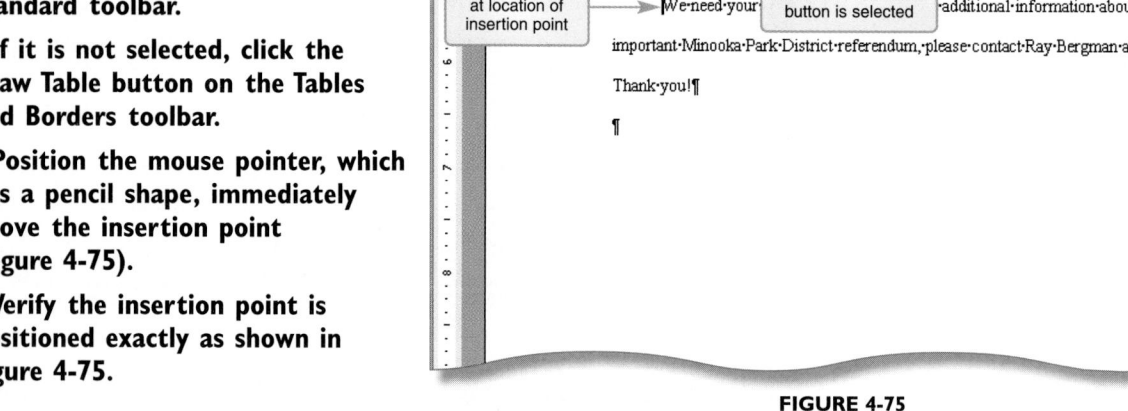

FIGURE 4-75

2

• **Drag the pencil pointer downward and to the right until the dotted rectangle is positioned similarly to the one shown in Figure 4-76.**

Word displays a dotted rectangle to indicate the proposed table's size (Figure 4-76).

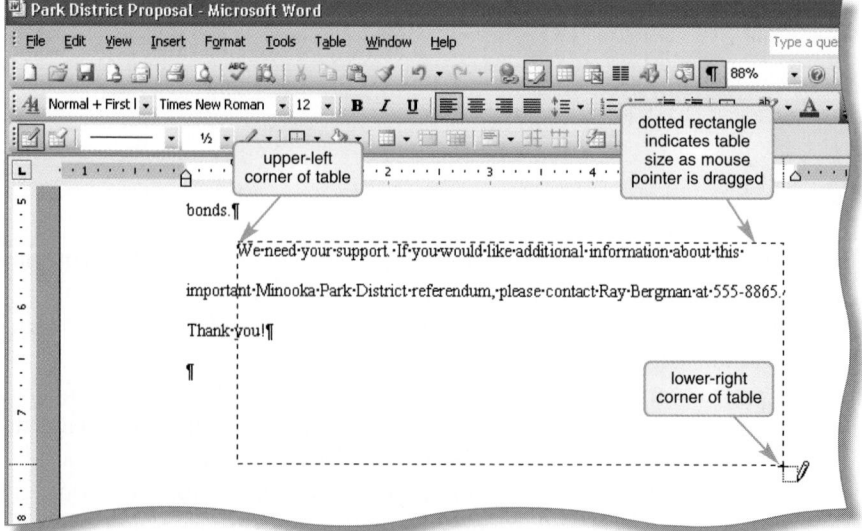

FIGURE 4-76

3

- Release the mouse button.

- If Word wraps the text around the table, right-click the table, click Table Properties on the shortcut menu, click the Table tab, click None in the Text wrapping area, and then click the OK button.

- If the table is not positioned as shown here, click the Undo button on the Standard toolbar and then repeat Step 2.

- Position the pencil pointer in the table as shown in Figure 4-77.

Word draws the table border (Figure 4-77).

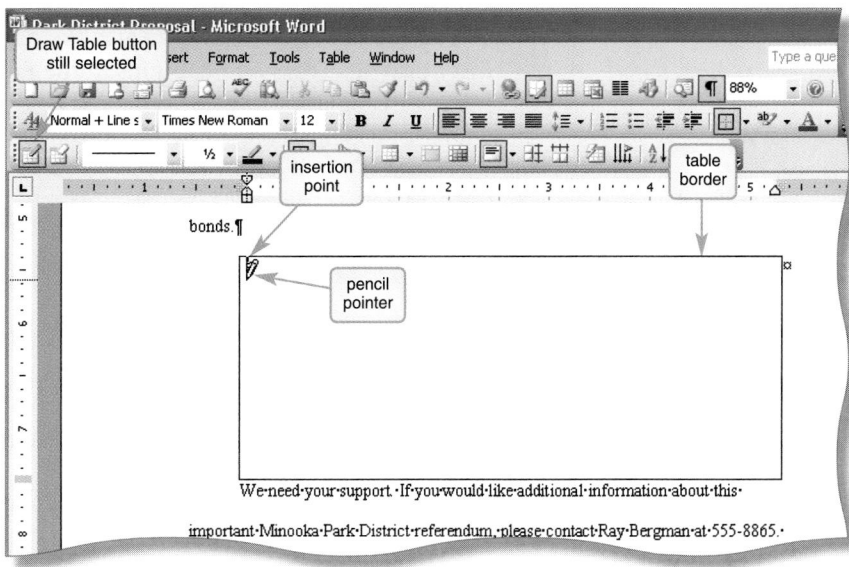

FIGURE 4-77

4

- Drag the pencil pointer to the right to draw a horizontal line.

- Drag the pencil pointer from left to right three more times to draw three more horizontal lines, as shown in Figure 4-78.

- Position the pencil pointer in the table as shown in Figure 4-78.

Word draws four horizontal lines, which form the rows in the table (Figure 4-78).

FIGURE 4-78

5

- Draw five vertical lines to form the column borders, similarly to those shown in Figure 4-79.

The empty table displays as shown in Figure 4-79.

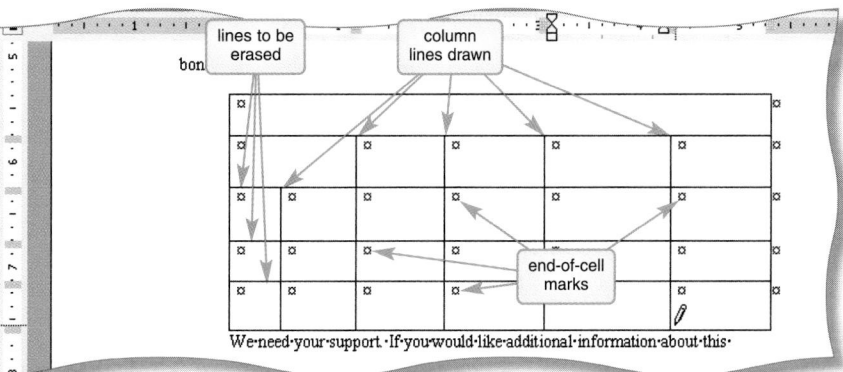

FIGURE 4-79

Other Ways

1. On Table menu click Draw Table, use pencil pointer to draw table
2. In Voice Command mode, say "Tables and Borders, [use pencil pointer to draw table]"

All Word tables that you draw have a one-half-point border, by default. To change this border, you can use the Tables and Borders toolbar, as described earlier in this project.

Notice the end-of-cell marks currently are left-aligned in each cell (Figure 4-79 on the previous page), which indicates the data will be left-aligned in the cells.

After drawing rows and columns in the table, you may want to remove a line. In this table, three lines need to be removed (shown in Figure 4-79). The following steps show how to use the **Eraser button** on the Tables and Borders toolbar to remove lines.

To Erase Lines in a Table

1

• **Click the Eraser button on the Tables and Borders toolbar.**

The mouse pointer shape changes to an eraser.

2

• **Drag the mouse pointer (eraser shape) through each line you wish to erase (Figure 4-80).**

3

• **Click the Eraser button on the Tables and Borders toolbar to turn off the eraser.**

FIGURE 4-80

Because you drew the table borders with the mouse, some of the rows may be varying heights. The following step shows how to make the row spacing in the table even.

To Distribute Rows Evenly

1

• **With the insertion point somewhere in the table, click the Distribute Rows Evenly button on the Tables and Borders toolbar.**

Word makes the height of the rows uniform (Figure 4-81).

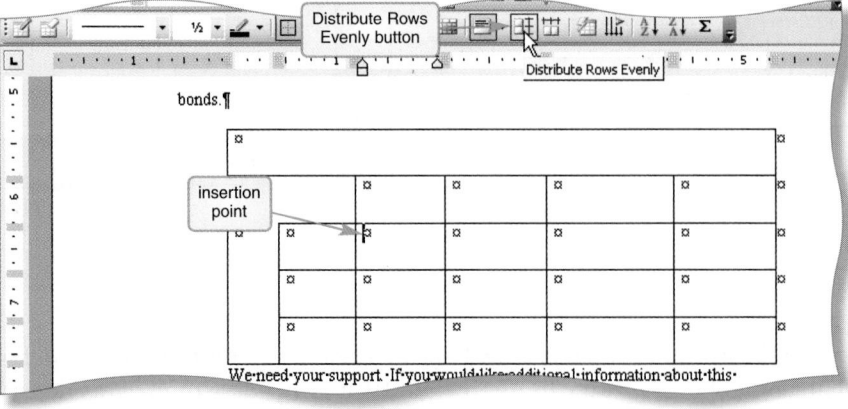

FIGURE 4-81

You want the last four columns in the table to be the same width. Because you drew the borders of these columns, they may be varying widths. The following steps show how to evenly size these columns.

To Distribute Columns Evenly

1

- **Drag through the 16 cells shown in Figure 4-82 to select them.**
- **Click the Distribute Columns Evenly button on the Tables and Borders toolbar.**

Word applies uniform widths to the selected columns (Figure 4-82).

2

- **Click inside the table to remove the selection.**

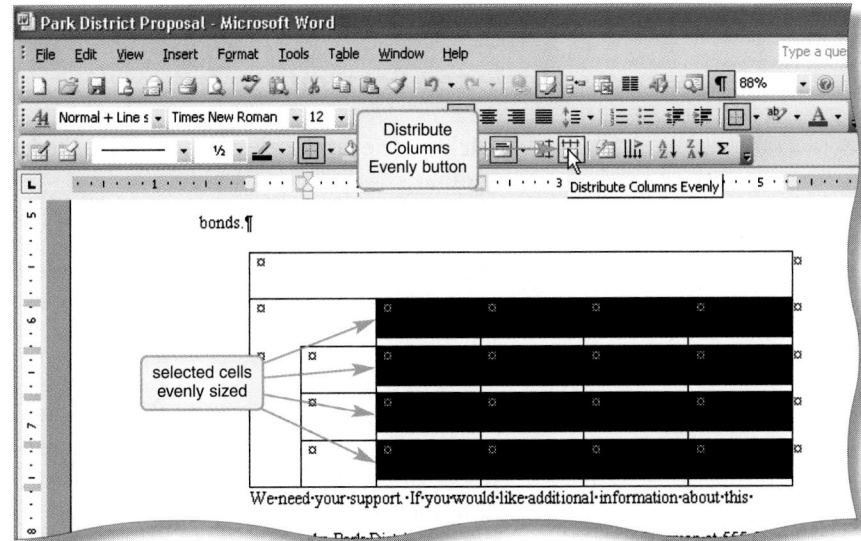

FIGURE 4-82

Single-Space the Table Contents

You want the data you type within the cells to be single-spaced, instead of double-spaced. Thus, the following steps describe how to single-space the table cells.

To Single-Space Table Contents

1 Position the mouse pointer in the table to display the table move handle in the upper-left corner of the table. Position the mouse pointer on the table move handle and then click to select the table.

2 With the entire table selected, press CTRL+1.

3 Click anywhere to remove the selection in the table.

Word single-spaces the cells in the table. The size of the table does not change.

When you enter data that wraps within a cell, it will be single-spaced instead of double-spaced.

Entering Data into the Table

The next step is to enter the data into the table. To advance from one column to the next, press the TAB key. To advance from one row to the next, also press the TAB key; do not press the ENTER key. Use the ENTER key only to begin a new paragraph within a cell.

More About

Nested Tables

You can create a table within a table, or a nested table, using the Drawing toolbar. To do this, click the Draw Table button on the Tables and Borders toolbar to display the pencil pointer. Draw the new table inside the current table. When you are finished, click the Draw Table button to turn off the pencil pointer.

Earlier in this project, the AutoSum button was used to enter row and column totals. The AutoSum button automatically inserts totals as dollars and cents, even when the numbers being summed are whole numbers. If you want the totals to display as whole numbers, you must edit the totals as you edit the contents of any other cell. In this case, because the numbers are easy to add up, you simply type the totals into the cells.

The following steps describe how to enter the data into this table (shown in Figure 4-83).

To Enter Data into a Table

1 **Click in the first cell of the table. Click the Center button on the Formatting toolbar.**

2 **Type** PROPOSED DISTRIBUTION OF FUNDS **and then press the TAB key.**

3 **Type** YES **and then press the TAB key. Type** Park Renovations **and then press the TAB key. Type** Land Purchases **and then press the TAB key. Type** Facility Upgrades **and then press the TAB key. Type** Total **and then press the TAB key.**

4 **Type** VOTE **and then press the TAB key. Type** 1st Bond **and then press the TAB key. Type** $300,000 **and then press the TAB key. Type** $200,000 **and then press the TAB key. Type** $400,000 **and then press the TAB key. Type** $900,000 **and then press the TAB key twice.**

5 **Type** 2nd Bond **and then press the TAB key. Type** $450,000 **and then press the TAB key. Type** $500,000 **and then press the TAB key. Type** $650,000 **and then press the TAB key. Type** $1,600,000 **and then press the TAB key twice.**

6 **Type** 3rd Bond **and then press the TAB key. Type** $250,000 **and then press the TAB key. Type** $600,000 **and then press the TAB key. Type** $550,000 **and then press the TAB key. Type** $1,400,000 **as the last entry in the table.**

The table data is entered (shown in Figure 4-83). As you type an ordinal, such as 2nd, Word automatically formats it as a superscript (e.g., 2nd).

Formatting the Table

The data you enter in cells displays horizontally. You can rotate the text so it displays vertically. Changing the direction of text adds variety to your tables.

The following steps show how to display text in a table cell vertically.

To Vertically Display Text in a Cell

1

• **Select the cell containing the word, VOTE.**

The cell to be formatted is selected (Figure 4-83).

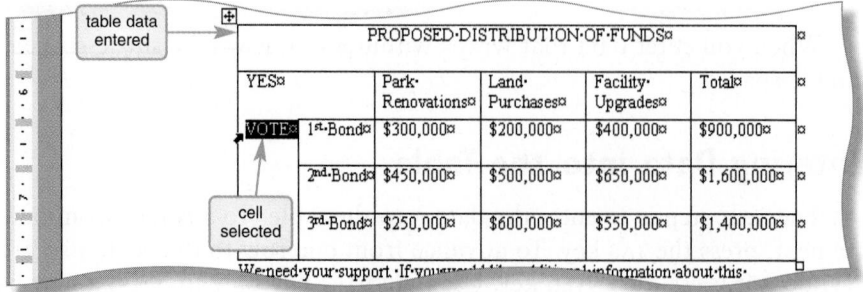

PROPOSED·DISTRIBUTION·OF·FUNDS¤					¤
YES¤		Park·Renovations¤	Land·Purchases¤	Facility·Upgrades¤	Total¤	¤
VOTE¤	1ˢᵗ·Bond¤	$300,000¤	$200,000¤	$400,000¤	$900,000¤	¤
	2ⁿᵈ·Bond¤	$450,000¤	$500,000¤	$650,000¤	$1,600,000¤	¤
	3ʳᵈ·Bond¤	$250,000¤	$600,000¤	$550,000¤	$1,400,000¤	¤

table data entered

cell selected

We·need·your·support.·If·you···········information·about·this·

FIGURE 4-83

2
• **Click the Change Text Direction button on the Tables and Borders toolbar twice.**

Word displays the text vertically so that it reads from bottom to top (Figure 4-84).

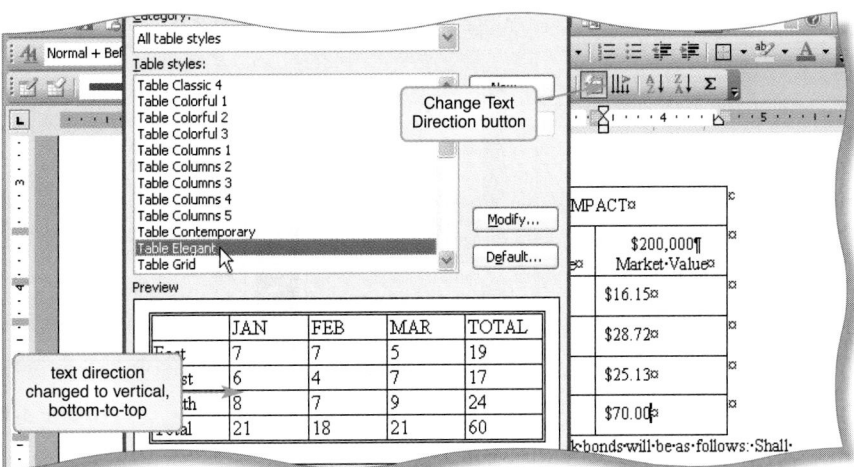

FIGURE 4-84

The first time you click the Change Text Direction button, Word displays the text vertically so it reads from top to bottom. The second time you click the Change Text Direction button, Word displays the text vertically so it reads from bottom to top (Figure 4-84). If you click the button a third time, the text would display horizontally again.

The words, VOTE YES, in the table are to be 26-point bold font and centered. The following steps describe how to format this text in the table.

To Format Table Text

1 **With the word VOTE selected, hold down the CTRL key and select the cell containing the word YES in the table. Release the CTRL key.**

2 **With both words, VOTE and YES, selected, click the Font Size box arrow on the Formatting toolbar and then click 26. Click the Bold button on the Formatting toolbar. Click the Center button on the Formatting toolbar.**

Word formats the table text (shown in Figure 4-85 on the next page).

The next step is to shade cells containing the words, VOTE and YES, in light yellow. The following steps describe how to shade selected cells.

To Shade Table Cells

1 **With the cells containing the words, VOTE and YES, selected, click the Shading Color button arrow on the Tables and Borders toolbar (Figure 4-85).**

2 **Click Light Yellow (third color in bottom row of color palette).**

Word shades the cells in light yellow (shown in Figure 4-86 on the next page).

More About

Table Wrapping

If you want text to wrap around a table, instead of displaying above and below the table, do the following. Right-click the table, click Table Properties on the shortcut menu, click the Table sheet, click Around in the Text wrapping area, and then click the OK button.

More About

Shading

To remove shading from a cell(s), select the cell(s), click the Shading Color button arrow on the Tables and Borders toolbar, and then click No Fill on the palette.

FIGURE 4-85

The title of the table should be 14-point Times New Roman bold dark red font. The following steps describe how to format the table title.

To Format the Table Title

1 Drag through the table title, **PROPOSED DISTRIBUTION OF FUNDS.**

2 Click the Font Size button arrow on the Formatting toolbar and then click 14. Click the Bold button on the Formatting toolbar. Click the Font Color button arrow on the Formatting toolbar and then click Dark Red.

3 Click in the first row to remove the selection.

Word formats the table title (shown in Figure 4-86).

The next step is to narrow the height of the row containing the table title. The steps below show how to change a row's height.

To Change Row Height

1

• **Point to the bottom border of the first row. When the mouse pointer changes to a double-headed arrow, drag up until the proposed row border looks like Figure 4-86.**

When you release the mouse button, Word will resize the row according to the location to which you dragged the row border.

2

• **Release the mouse button.**

Word resizes the row (shown in Figure 4-87).

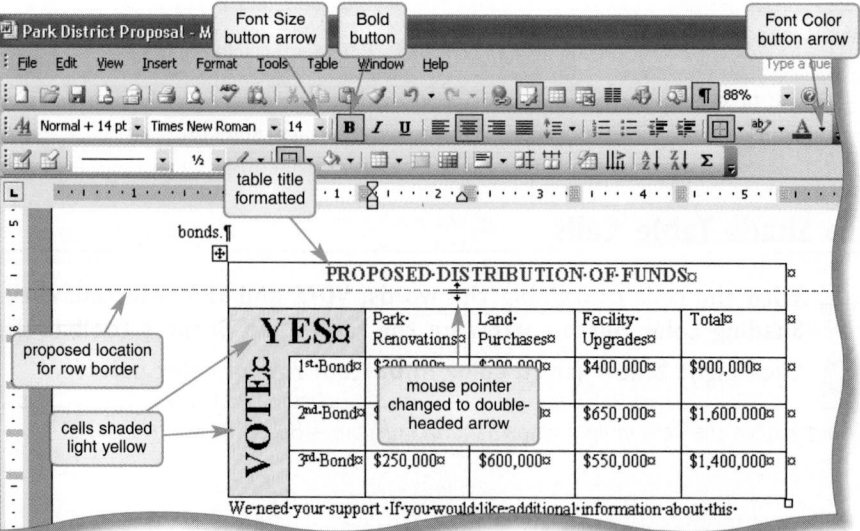

FIGURE 4-86

If you wanted to change the width of a column, you would drag the column border similarly to the way you dragged the row border in the previous steps.

The next step is to change the alignment of the data in the last three rows. In addition to aligning text horizontally in a cell (left, centered, or right) by clicking the appropriate button on the Formatting toolbar, you can center it vertically within a cell using the Align button arrow on the Tables and Borders toolbar. The following steps show how to align data in cells.

To Align Data in Cells

- **Select the cells in the bottom three rows of the table by dragging through them.**
- **Click the Align button arrow on the Tables and Borders toolbar.**

Word displays a list of cell alignment options (Figure 4-87).

- **Click Align Center in the list.**

Word changes the alignment of the selected cells to center (Figure 4-88).

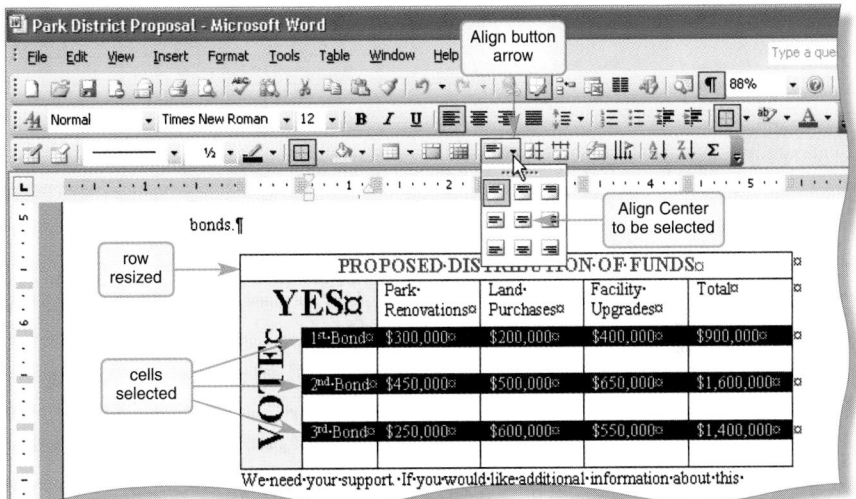

FIGURE 4-87

3

- **Select the four column headings by dragging through them.**
- **Click the Align button arrow on the Tables and Borders toolbar (Figure 4-88).**

4

- **Click Align Bottom Center in the list.**
- **Click the Tables and Borders button on the Standard toolbar to remove the toolbar from the screen.**

Word changes the alignment of selected cells to bottom center (shown in Figure 4-89 on the next page).

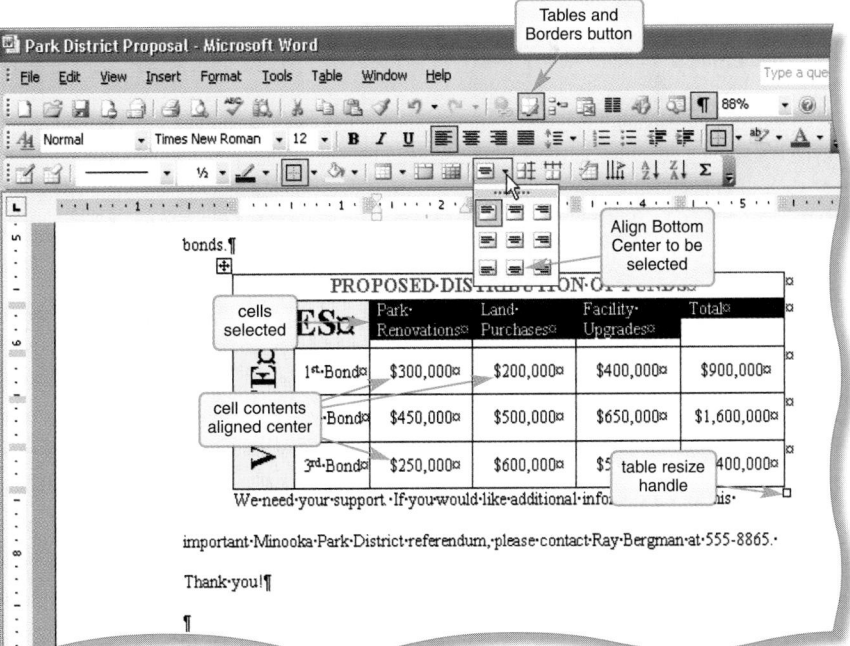

FIGURE 4-88

Notice in Figure 4-88 on the previous page that when you click the Align button arrow on the Tables and Borders toolbar, Word provides several cell alignment options. Table 4-3 illustrates the various alignment options.

Table 4-3 Cell Alignment Options		
Align Top Left	$300,000	
Align Top Center		$300,000	
Align Top Right		$300,000
Align Center Left	$300,000	
Align Center		$300,000	
Align Center Right		$300,000
Align Bottom Left	$300,000	
Align Bottom Center		$300,000	
Align Bottom Right		$300,000

The final step in formatting the table is to add a blank line between the table and the paragraph below it, as described in the following step.

To Add a Blank Line Above a Paragraph

1 **Position the insertion point in the last paragraph of the proposal and then press CTRL+0 (the numeral zero).**

*The shortcut key, **CTRL+0**, instructs Word to add a blank line above the paragraph (Figure 4-89).*

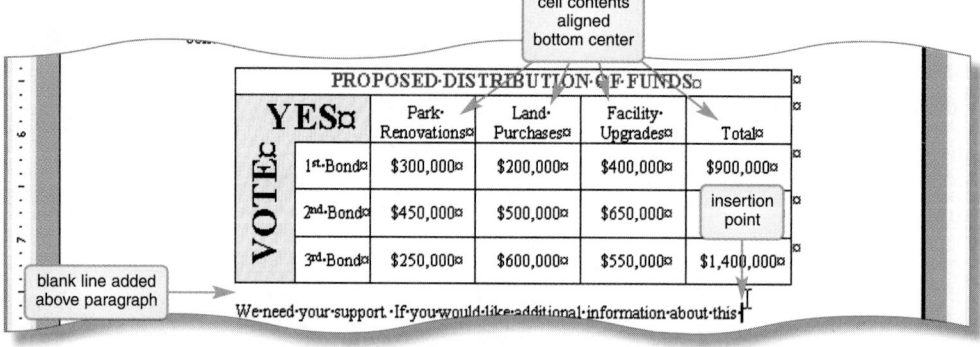

FIGURE 4-89

If the last paragraph spills onto the next page, you can make the table smaller so the paragraph fits at the bottom of the page. To do this, drag the table resize handle (shown in Figure 4-88) that appears in the lower-right corner of the table inward.

Creating a Watermark

A **watermark** is text or a graphic that is displayed on top of or behind the text in a document. For example, a catalog may print the words, Sold Out, on top of sold-out items. A product manager may want the word, Draft, to print behind his or her first draft of a five-year plan. Some companies use their logos or other graphics as watermarks on documents to add visual appeal to the document.

In this project, you would like the word, YES, to display on all pages of the proposal. The following steps show how to create this watermark.

To Create a Text Watermark

1

• **Click Format on the menu bar and then point to Background (Figure 4-90).**

2

• **Click Printed Watermark on the Background submenu.**

• **When Word displays the Printed Watermark dialog box, click Text watermark.**

• **Drag through the text in the Text box to select it. Type YES in the Text box.**

• **Click the Size box arrow and then click 54.**

• **Click the Color box arrow and then click Tan on the color palette.**

In the Printed Watermark dialog box, the Semitransparent setting adjusts the brightness and contrast so the text is faded (Figure 4-91).

3

• **Click the Apply button.**

The Cancel button in the dialog box changes to a Close button.

4

• **Click the Close button in the dialog box.**

Word displays the watermark faded behind the text of the proposal (shown in Figure 4-92 on the next page).

FIGURE 4-90

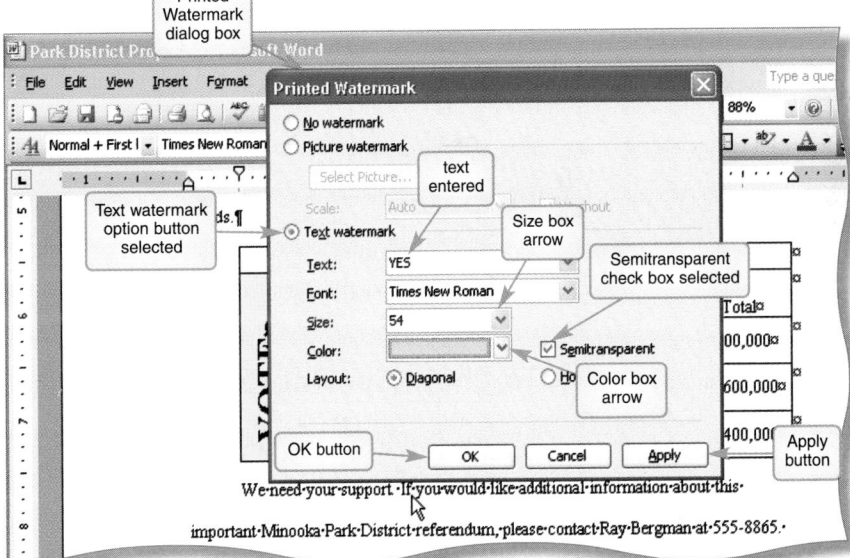

FIGURE 4-91

If you want to remove a watermark, click No watermark in the Printed Watermark dialog box (Figure 4-91). To see how the watermark looks in the entire document, print the document or view the document in print preview, as described in the steps on the next page.

Other Ways

1. In Voice Command mode, say "Format, Background, Printed Watermark, [enter settings], OK"

To Print Preview a Document

1 Click the Print Preview button on the Standard toolbar. If necessary, click the Multiple Pages button on the Print Preview toolbar and then click the third icon in the first row of the grid (1 × 3 Pages) to display all three pages of the proposal as shown in Figure 4-92.

2 When finished viewing the document, click the Close Preview button on the Print Preview toolbar.

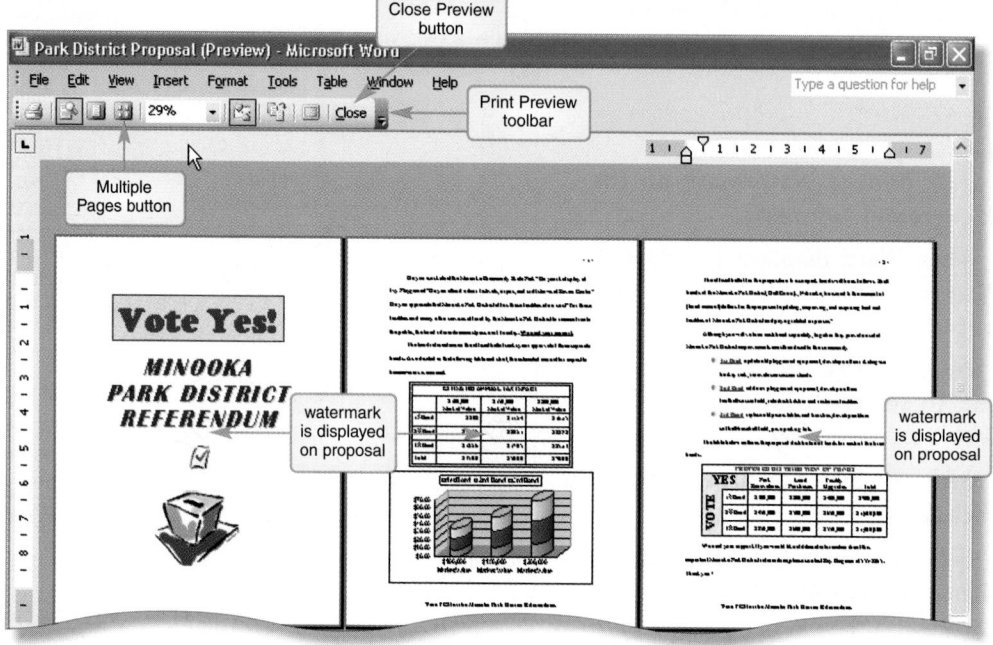

FIGURE 4-92

Checking Spelling, Saving Again, and Printing the Sales Proposal

The following steps describe how to check the spelling of the document, save the document, and then print the document.

To Check Spelling, Save, and Print the Document

1 Click the Spelling and Grammar button on the Standard toolbar. Correct any misspelled words.

2 Click the Save button on the Standard toolbar.

3 Click the Print button on the Standard toolbar.

The document prints as shown in Figure 4-1 on page WD 219.

Revealing Formatting

Sometimes, when you review a document, you want to know what formats were applied to certain text items. For example, you may wonder what font, font size, font color, border size, border color, or shading color you used on the first line of the title page. To display formatting applied to text, use the **Reveal Formatting task pane**. The next steps illustrate how to reveal formatting.

To Reveal Formatting

1

• **Press CTRL+HOME and then verify that the insertion point in the first line of the document, Vote Yes!**

• **Click Format on the menu bar (Figure 4-93).**

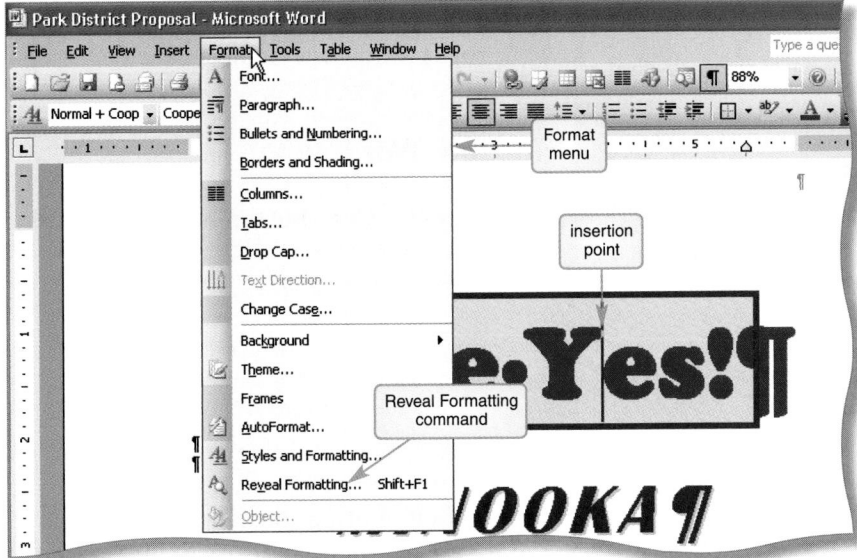

FIGURE 4-93

2

• **Click Reveal Formatting on the Format menu.**

Word displays the Reveal Formatting task pane (Figure 4-94). The Reveal Formatting task pane shows formatting applied to the location of the insertion point.

3

• **Click the Close button on the Reveal Formatting task pane to close the task pane.**

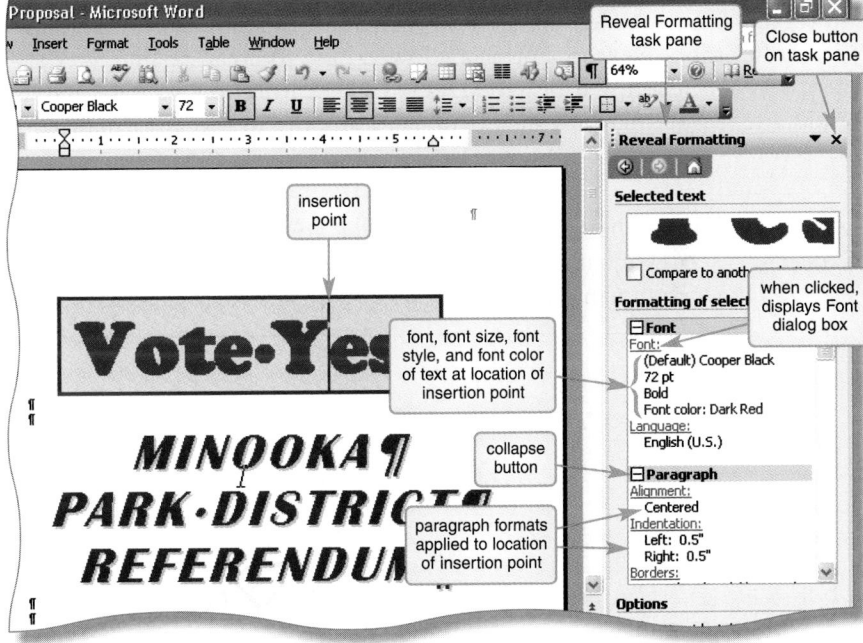

FIGURE 4-94

Other Ways

1. Press SHIFT+F1
2. In Voice Command mode, say "Format, Reveal Formatting"

When the Reveal Formatting task pane is displayed, you can click any text in the document window and the contents of the Reveal Formatting task pane changes to show formatting applied to the location of the insertion point. To display or hide items in the Formatting of selected text area of the Reveal Formatting task pane, click the expand (+) or collapse (-) buttons. For example, clicking the collapse button to the left of Paragraph hides the paragraph formats applied to the text.

More About

Certification

The Microsoft Office Specialist Certification program provides an opportunity for you to obtain a valuable industry credential - proof that you have the Word 2003 skills required by employers. For more information, see Appendix E or visit the Word 2003 Certification Web page (scsite.com/wd2003/cert).

If you want to change the format of text through the Reveal Formatting task pane, select the text and then click the blue underlined word in the Formatting of selected text area to display the linked dialog box. For example, clicking Font in the Reveal Formatting task pane displays the Font dialog box. As soon as you click the OK button in the dialog box, Word changes the format of the selected text.

Project 4 now is complete. The next step is to quit Word.

To Quit Word

1 **Click the Close button in the Word window.**

The Word window closes.

Project Summary

In creating the Minooka Park District Proposal in this project, you learned how to create a document with a title page, table, chart, and a watermark. On the title page, you learned how to add a border and shading to a paragraph and how to change the paragraph indentation. Then, the project showed how to add a shadow effect to characters and expand them by several points. You learned how to insert a graphic from the Web and center the contents of the title page vertically.

Next, you learned how to insert an existing Word document into the active document. The project showed how to insert a header and also a footer in the body of the proposal that was different from the title page header and footer. Then, you learned how to format an existing Word table and chart it using the embedded program, Microsoft Graph. Next, the project showed how to create a character style and add picture bullets to a list. Then, you learned how to use the Draw Table feature to create a complex table. Finally, the project showed how to add a text watermark to the document and how to reveal formatting of a document.

 If you have a SAM user profile, you may have access to hands-on instruction, practice, and assessment of the skills covered in this project. Log in to your SAM account and go to your assignments page to see what your instructor has assigned.

More About

Quick Reference

For a table that lists how to complete the tasks covered in this book using the mouse, menu, shortcut menu, and keyboard, see the Quick Reference Summary at the back of this book, or visit the Word 2003 Quick Reference Web page (scsite.com/wd2003/qr).

What You Should Know

Having completed this project, you should be able to perform the tasks below. The tasks are listed in the same order they were presented in this project. For a list of the buttons, menus, toolbars, and commands introduced in this project, see the Quick Reference Summary at the back of this book and refer to the Page Number column.

1. Start and Customize Word   (WD 220)
2. Display Formatting Marks   (WD 220)
3. Zoom Page Width   (WD 221, WD 234)
4. Format Characters   (WD 221)
5. Border a Paragraph   (WD 222)
6. Change Left and Right Paragraph Indent (WD 223)
7. Shade a Paragraph   (WD 224)
8. Clear Formatting   (WD 226, WD 229, WD 235)
9. Format Characters and Modify Character Spacing   (WD 227)
10. Modify the Default Font Settings   (WD 229)
11. Insert Clip Art from the Web   (WD 230)
12. Insert a Graphic File from the Data Disk (WD 231)
13. Resize a Graphic Using the Format Picture Dialog Box   (WD 231)
14. Zoom Whole Page   (WD 232)
15. Center Page Contents Vertically   (WD 232)
16. Save a Document   (WD 234)
17. Insert a Next Page Section Break   (WD 236)
18. Change Page Alignment of a Section   (WD 237)
19. Insert a Word Document into an Open Document (WD 238)
20. Save an Active Document with a New File Name (WD 240)
21. Print Specific Pages in a Document   (WD 241)
22. Delete a Page Break   (WD 244)
23. Cut Text   (WD 245)
24. Go To a Section   (WD 246)
25. Create a Header Different from the Previous Section Header   (WD 247)
26. Change Page Number Format and Page Number Differently in a Section   (WD 248)
27. Create a Footer Different from the Previous Section Footer   (WD 249)
28. Delete a Column   (WD 250)
29. Add a Row and Merge Cells   (WD 251)
30. Enter and Format Text in a Table Cell   (WD 252)
31. Split Cells   (WD 253)
32. Add a Row to the End of a Table   (WD 253)
33. Sum Columns in a Table   (WD 254)
34. AutoFormat a Table   (WD 255)
35. Center a Table   (WD 256)
36. Right-Align Cell Contents   (WD 256)
37. Select Nonadjacent Text   (WD 257)
38. Superscript Selected Characters   (WD 258)
39. Chart a Table   (WD 259)
40. Move Legend Placement in a Chart   (WD 261)
41. Resize a Chart   (WD 262)
42. Change the Chart Type   (WD 262)
43. Exit Graph and Return to Word   (WD 263)
44. Format a Chart Object   (WD 264)
45. Find a Format   (WD 266)
46. Create a Character Style   (WD 268)
47. Apply a Character Style   (WD 269)
48. Add Picture Bullets to a List   (WD 270)
49. Draw an Empty Table   (WD 272)
50. Erase Lines in a Table   (WD 274)
51. Distribute Rows Evenly   (WD 274)
52. Distribute Columns Evenly   (WD 275)
53. Single-Space Table Contents   (WD 275)
54. Enter Data into a Table   (WD 276)
55. Vertically Display Text in a Cell   (WD 276)
56. Format Table Text   (WD 277)
57. Shade Table Cells   (WD 277)
58. Format the Table Title   (WD 278)
59. Change Row Height   (WD 278)
60. Align Data in Cells   (WD 279)
61. Add a Blank Line Above a Paragraph   (WD 280)
62. Create a Text Watermark   (WD 281)
63. Print Preview a Document   (WD 282)
64. Check Spelling, Save, and Print the Document (WD 282)
65. Reveal Formatting   (WD 283)
66. Quit Word   (WD 284)

Learn It Online

Instructions: To complete the Learn It Online exercises, start your browser, click the Address bar, and then enter the Web address scsite.com/wd2003/learn. When the Word 2003 Learn It Online page is displayed, follow the instructions in the exercises below. Each exercise has instructions for printing your results, either for your own records or for submission to your instructor.

1 Project Reinforcement TF, MC, and SA

Below Word Project 4, click the Project Reinforcement link. Print the quiz by clicking Print on the File menu for each page. Answer each question.

Flash Cards

Below Word Project 4, click the Flash Cards link and read the instructions. Type 20 (or a number specified by your instructor) in the Number of playing cards text box, type your name in the Enter your Name text box, and then click the Flip Card button. When the flash card is displayed, read the question and then click the ANSWER box arrow to select an answer. Flip through Flash Cards. If your score is 15 (75%) correct or greater, click Print on the File menu to print your results. If your score is less than 15 (75%) correct, then redo this exercise by clicking the Replay button.

3 Practice Test

Below Word Project 4, click the Practice Test link. Answer each question, enter your first and last name at the bottom of the page, and then click the Grade Test button. When the graded practice test is displayed on your screen, click Print on the File menu to print a hard copy. Continue to take practice tests until you score 80% or better.

4 Who Wants To Be a Computer Genius?

Below Word Project 4, click the Computer Genius link. Read the instructions, enter your first and last name at the bottom of the page, and then click the PLAY button. When your score is displayed, click the PRINT RESULTS link to print a hard copy.

5 Wheel of Terms

Below Word Project 4, click the Wheel of Terms link. Read the instructions, and then enter your first and last name and your school name. Click the PLAY button. When your score is displayed, right-click the score and then click Print on the shortcut menu to print a hard copy.

6 Crossword Puzzle Challenge

Below Word Project 4, click the Crossword Puzzle Challenge link. Read the instructions, and then enter your first and last name. Click the SUBMIT button. Work the crossword puzzle. When you are finished, click the Submit button. When the crossword puzzle is redisplayed, click the Print Puzzle button to print a hard copy.

7 Tips and Tricks

Below Word Project 4, click the Tips and Tricks link. Click a topic that pertains to Project 4. Right-click the information and then click Print on the shortcut menu. Construct a brief example of what the information relates to in Word to confirm you understand how to use the tip or trick.

8 Newsgroups

Below Word Project 4, click the Newsgroups link. Click a topic that pertains to Project 4. Print three comments.

9 Expanding Your Horizons

Below Word Project 4, click the Expanding Your Horizons link. Click a topic that pertains to Project 4. Print the information. Construct a brief example of what the information relates to in Word to confirm you understand the contents of the article.

10 Search Sleuth

Below Word Project 4, click the Search Sleuth link. To search for a term that pertains to this project, select a term below the Project 4 title and then use the Google search engine at google.com (or any major search engine) to display and print two Web pages that present information on the term.

11 Word Online Training

Below Word Project 4, click the Word Online Training link. When your browser displays the Microsoft Office Online Web page, click the Word link. Click one of the Word courses that covers one or more of the objectives listed at the beginning of the project on page WD 218. Print the first page of the course before stepping through it.

12 Office Marketplace

Below Word Project 4, click the Office Marketplace link. When your browser displays the Microsoft Office Online Web page, click the Office Marketplace link. Click a topic that relates to Word. Print the first page.

Apply Your Knowledge

1 Working with Complex Tables

Instructions: Start Word. Open the document, Apply 4-1 Meridian Profits Report, on the Data Disk. If you did not download the Data Disk, see the inside back cover for instructions for downloading the Data Disk or see your instructor.

The document contains a table created with the Draw Table feature. You are to modify the table so it looks like Figure 4-95.

Meridian Sports Leagues					
		Yearly Profits by Season			
		Concessions	Fund-raisers	Raffle	Total
Spring	Baseball	$2,504.35	$1,255.55	$1,480.00	**$5,239.90**
	Soccer	$1,753.87	$982.40	$1,199.00	**$3,935.27**
Fall	Football	$3,004.25	$2,125.83	$2,860.00	**$7,990.08**
	Soccer	$1,512.65	$876.07	$995.00	**$3,383.72**
Total Yearly Sales		**$8,775.12**	**$5,239.85**	**$6,534.00**	**$20,548.97**

FIGURE 4-95

Perform the following tasks.

1. Use the Split Cells command or the Split Cells button on the Tables and Borders toolbar to split the first row into two rows (one column). In the new cell below the company title, type Yearly Profits by Season as the subtitle.

2. Select the cell containing the title, Meridian Sports Leagues. Center it, bold it, change its font size to 28, and change its font color to brown. Shade the cell in the color light orange.

3. Select the row containing the subtitle, Yearly Profits by Season. Center and bold the subtitle. Change the font color to brown.

4. Select the cell containing the label, Total Yearly Sales, and the cell immediately to its right. Use the Merge Cells command or the Merge Cells button on the Tables and Borders toolbar to merge the two cells into a single cell. Bold the text in the cell. Center align the text in the cell.

(continued)

Working with Complex Tables *(continued)*

5. Select the cells containing the row headings, Spring and Fall. Use the Change Text Direction button on the Tables and Borders toolbar to position the text vertically from bottom to top. Change the alignment of these two cells to Align Center.

6. Click in the table to remove the selection. Drag the left edge of the table rightward to make the cells containing Spring and Fall narrower. The cell containing the words, Total Yearly Sales, should fit on one line (that is, it should not wrap).

7. Select the last four columns containing Concessions, Fund-raisers, Raffle, and Total. Use the Distribute Columns Evenly button on the Tables and Borders toolbar to make the columns the same widths.

8. Center the entire table across the width of the page.

9. Use the AutoSum button on the Tables and Borders toolbar to place totals in the bottom row for the concessions, fund-raisers, and raffle columns.

10. Use the AutoSum button on the Tables and Borders toolbar to place totals in the right column. Start in the bottom-right cell and work your way up the table. If your totals are incorrect, click Table on the menu bar, click Formula, be sure the formula is =SUM(LEFT) and then click the OK button.

11. Align center the cells containing the column headings, Concessions, Fund-raisers, Raffle, and Total.

12. Align center right the cells containing numbers.

13. Align center left the cells containing these labels: Baseball, Soccer, Football, Soccer, and Total Yearly Sales.

14. Select the rows below the subtitle, Yearly Profits by Season, and distribute the rows evenly.

15. Bold the numbers in the last row and also in the rightmost column.

16. Click File on the menu bar and then click Save As. Use the file name, Apply 4-1 Revised Meridian Profits Report.

17. Print the revised document.

18. Position the insertion point in the first row of the table. Display the Reveal Formatting task pane. On your printout, write down all the formatting assigned to this row.

19. Select the table and then clear formatting. Write down the purpose of the Clear Formatting command. Undo the clear formatting and then save the file again.

In the Lab

1 Creating a Proposal that Uses the Draw Table Feature

Problem: The owner of the Costume Barn has hired you to prepare a sales proposal describing the facility (Figures 4-96a and 4-96b on the next page), which will be mailed to all community residents.

Instructions:

1. Create the title page as shown in Figure 4-96a. Be sure to resize the clip art; change the fonts, font sizes, font colors, and font effects; and include the border, paragraph shading and indentation, and expanded character spacing, as indicated in the figure.
2. Center the contents of the title page vertically. Insert a next page section break. Clear formatting. Change the vertical alignment for the second section to top. Adjust line spacing to double.

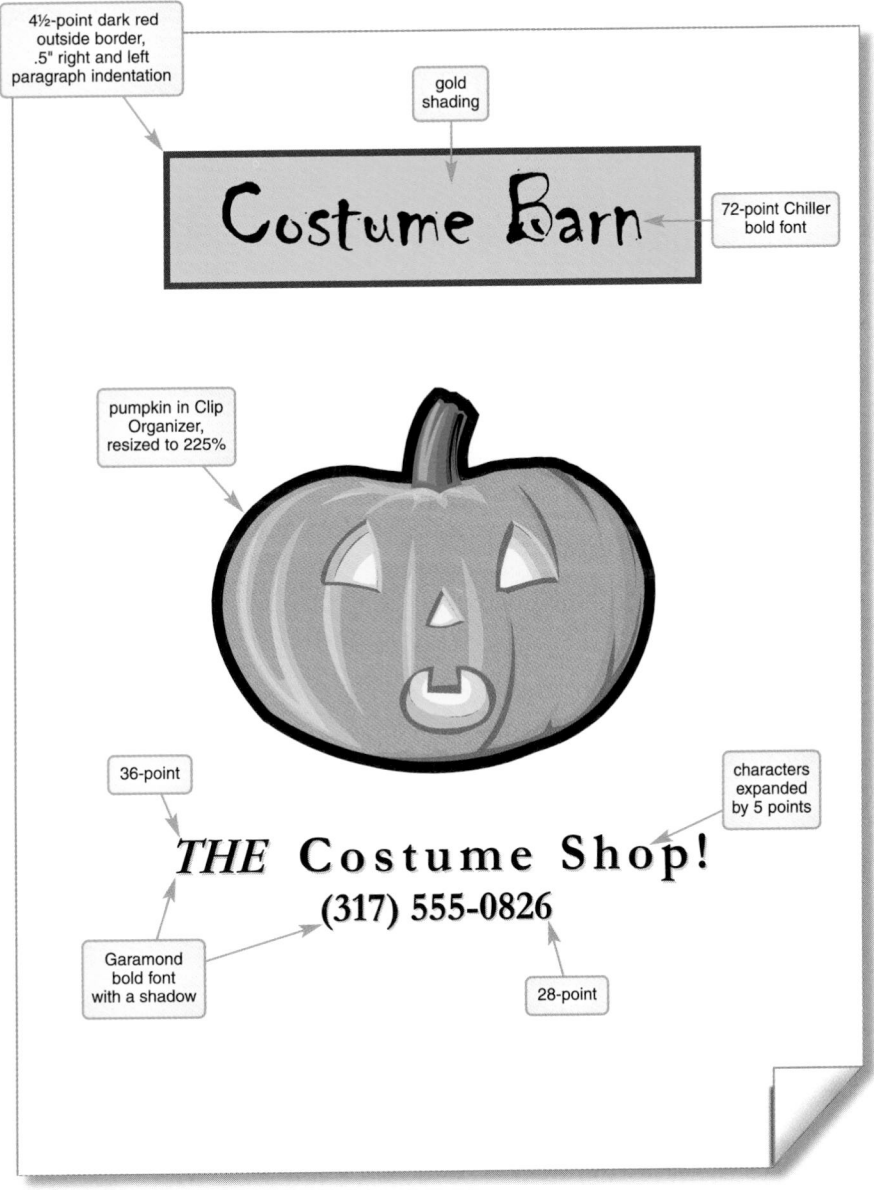

4½-point dark red outside border, .5" right and left paragraph indentation

gold shading

72-point Chiller bold font

pumpkin in Clip Organizer, resized to 225%

36-point

characters expanded by 5 points

Garamond bold font with a shadow

28-point

Costume Barn

THE Costume Shop!
(317) 555-0826

FIGURE 4-96a

(continued)

In the Lab

Creating a Proposal that Uses the Draw Table Feature *(continued)*

3. Type the body of the proposal as shown in Figure 4-96b.
   (a) Create the table with the Draw Table feature. Distribute rows evenly in the table. Center the table. Single-space the contents of the table. Bold and change the font color of text in the table as specified in the figure. Change the direction of the row titles, Vampire and Jester, and then align center the titles. Change the alignment of the title and column headings to align center; the second column to align center left; and the cells with numbers to align center right. Shade the table cells as specified in the figure.
   (b) The body of the proposal has a list with yellow picture bullets.
   (c) Create a character style of 12-point Arial brown bold characters. Apply the character style to the text in the bulleted list.
4. Check the spelling. Save the document with Lab 4-1 Costume Barn Proposal as the file name. View and print the document in print preview.

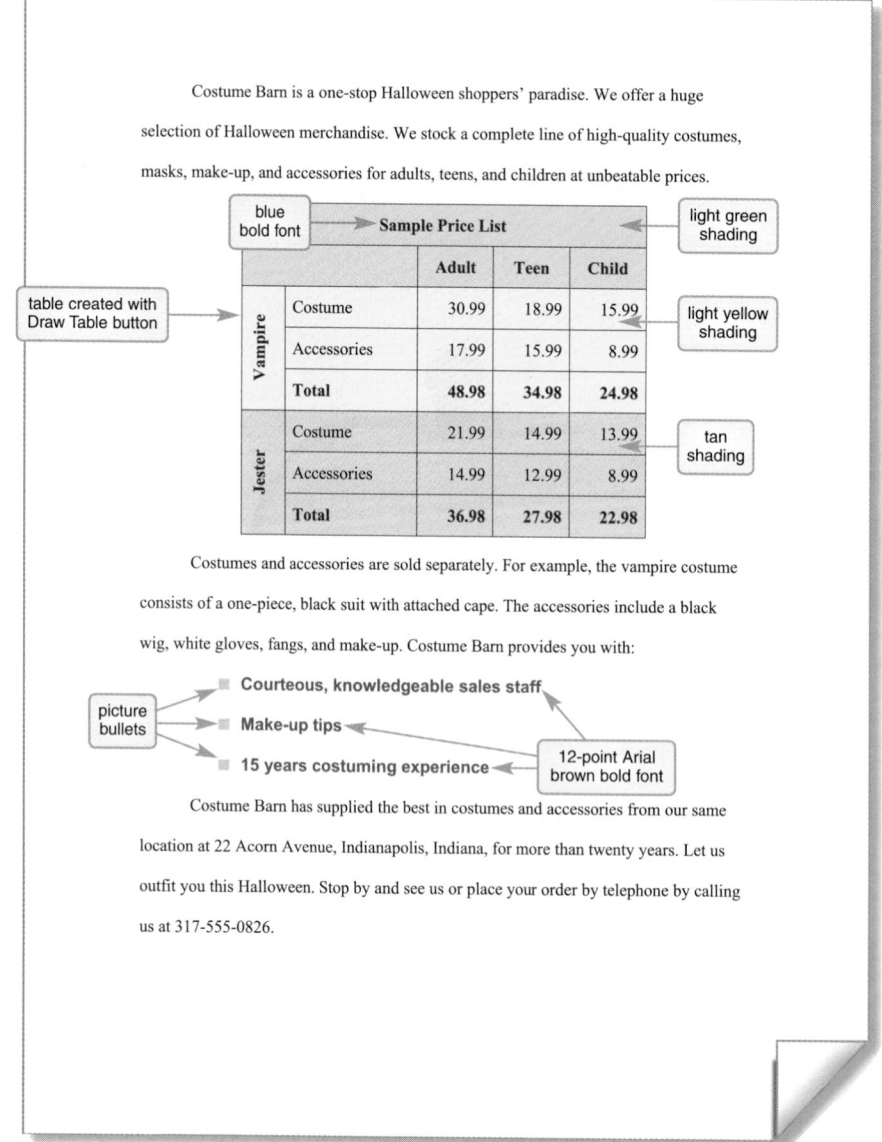

FIGURE 4-96b

In the Lab

2 Creating a Proposal that Contains Clip Art from the Web and a Chart

Problem: Your neighbor owns Peerless Office Rentals and has hired you to create a sales proposal for her business. You develop the proposal shown in Figures 4-97a and 4-97b on the next page.

Instructions:

1. Create the title page as shown in Figure 4-97a. Be sure to resize the clip art; change the fonts, font sizes, font colors, and font effects; and include the borders, paragraph shading and indentation, and expanded character spacing, as indicated in the figure. Use the keyword, office buildings, to locate the clip art image, which is located on the Web. If you do not have access to the Web, you can insert the file (file name j0234930.wmf) from the Data Disk. If you did not download the Data Disk, see the inside back cover for instructions for downloading the Data Disk or see your instructor.

2. Center the contents of the title page vertically. Insert a next page section break. Clear formatting. Change the vertical alignment for the second section to top. Adjust line spacing to double.

3. Create the body of the proposal as shown in Figure 4-97b.

   (a) Use the Insert Table button to create the table. Use the Table AutoFormat dialog box to format the table as specified in the figure. Center the title, column headings, and numbers. Center the table between the page margins. Distribute the rows evenly.

   (b) Chart the table. Resize the chart so it is wider. Change the chart type to cylinder. Move the legend. Add a ½-point indigo outline around the chart. Insert a blank line above the chart.

   (c) Add picture bullets to the list at the end of the page. Create a character style of 12-point Trebuchet MS bold indigo characters. Apply the character style to the text in the bulleted list.

FIGURE 4-97a

(continued)

Creating a Proposal that Contains Clip Art from the Web and a Chart *(continued)*

4. Check the spelling. Save the document with Lab 4-2 Office Rentals Proposal as the file name. View and print the document in print preview.

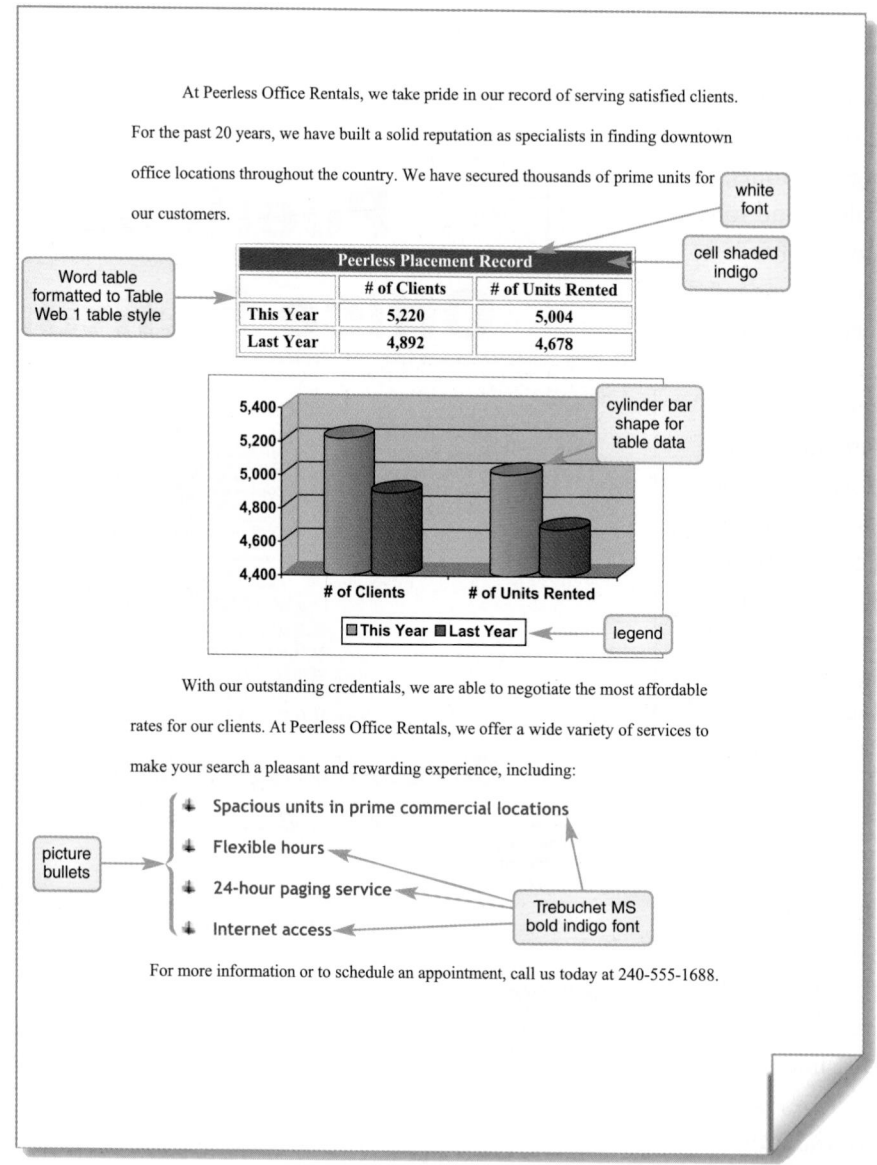

FIGURE 4-97b

3 Enhancing a Draft of a Proposal

Problem: You work for the transportation director at Centerton School Corporation. You create a title page (Figure 4-98a) for an informal sales proposal that your boss has drafted (Figure 4-98b on page WD 294) to be sent to the school board. You decide to add picture bullets, another table, a chart, and a watermark to the proposal.

   This lab uses the Data Disk. If you did not download the Data Disk, see the inside back cover for instructions for downloading the Data Disk or see your instructor.

In the Lab

Instructions:

1. Create the title page as shown in Figure 4-98a. *Hint:* Use the Font dialog box to apply the decorative underline in color and the emboss and small caps effects.

2. Center the contents of the title page vertically. Insert a next page section break. Clear formatting. Insert the draft of the body of the proposal below the title page using the File command on the Insert menu. The draft is called Lab 4-3 Bus Route Draft on the Data Disk (shown in Figure 4-98b on the next page). Be sure to change the vertical alignment to top for section 2.

3. On the first page of the body of the draft, do the following:
   (a) Cut the first line of text in the draft.
   (b) Delete the page break at the bottom of the first page.
   (c) Below the second paragraph, use the Draw Table button to create a table that is similar to the one below at right. Format the table titles in bold, shade important cells, add a colorful border around the table, align data in the cells as shown, and expand the word, Total, by 10 points.
   (d) Change the style of bullet characters in the list to picture bullets.
   (e) Use the Find and Replace dialog box to find the format 14-point Britannic Bold dark red characters. Create a character style for this format. Apply the character style to the rest of the text in the bulleted list.

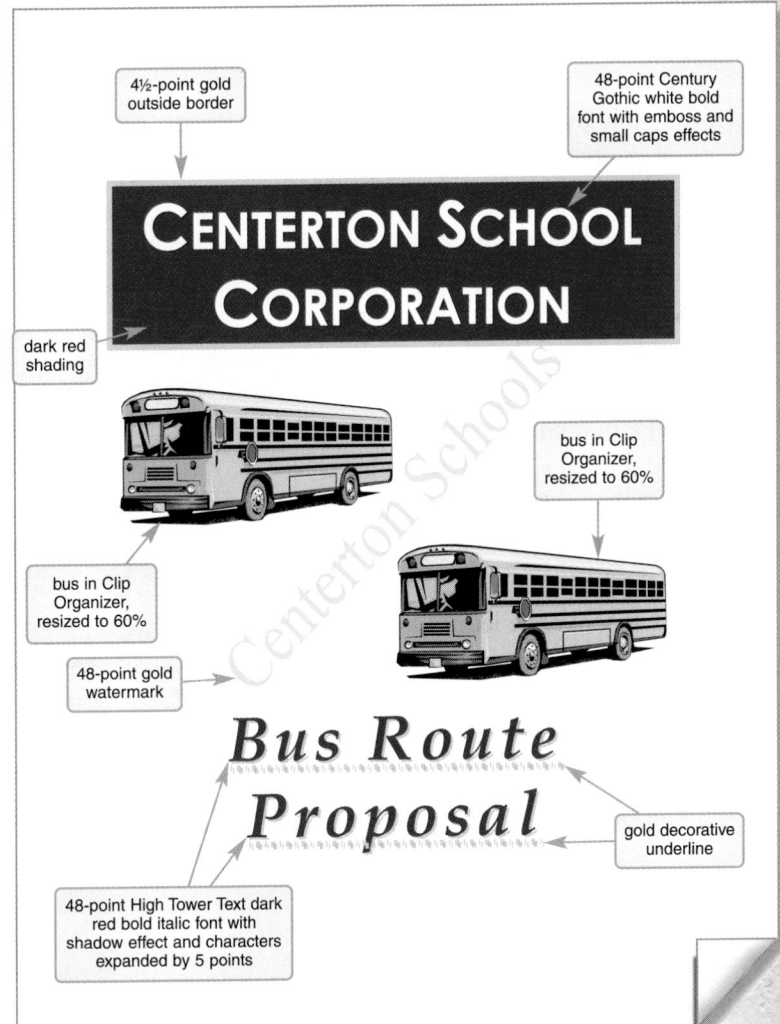

FIGURE 4-98a

CENTERTON SCHOOLS ENROLLMENT			
	School	Current Enrollment	Projected Enrollment
Bus 4 & 14	Pleasant Elementary	101	125
	North Elementary	85	100
Bus 8, 11, 17	Center Elementary	94	105
	West Elementary	80	120
	Total	360	450

4. Change the formatting of the paragraph that follows the bulleted list in Step 3(d) to Keep lines together and Page break before. *Hint:* Use Help to search for the text, control pagination, to determine how to keep lines together and page break before a paragraph.

5. Set all paragraph formatting in the entire document so that no widows or orphans occur. *Hint:* Use Help to search for the text, control pagination, to determine how to control widows and orphans.

(continued)

In the Lab

Enhancing a Draft of a Proposal

(continued)

6. On the table on the second page of the body of the proposal,
   (a) delete the duplicate row for Bus 8
   (b) delete the blank column
   (c) add a row to the table that totals the values in the two right columns
   (d) align center all data in second and third columns; align center left the first column of data
   (e) apply a table style to the table
   (f) center the table

7. Chart the first six rows of the table (all but the total row). Enlarge the chart so it is wider. Move the legend below the chart. Change the chart type to clustered bar with 3-D visual effect. Add the title, Breakdown by Bus, to the chart. *Hint:* Use the Chart Options command.

8. Add a header containing the page number to section 2 of the proposal. Change the starting page number to 1. Format the page number so it has dashes on each side (e.g., -1-).

9. Add a footer containing the words, Centerton Schools – Excellence, to section 2 of the proposal.

10. Create a text watermark on the proposal that contains the words, Centerton Schools, using 48-point gold font.

11. Modify the footer so it includes the words, A Tradition of, to the left of the word, Excellence.

12. Make any other formatting changes you feel would improve the document.

13. Save the active document with the file name, Lab 4-3 Bus Route Proposal.

14. View and print the document in print preview.

15. Position the insertion point in the first line of the title page. Display the Reveal Formatting task pane. On your print-out, write down all formatting assigned to this paragraph.

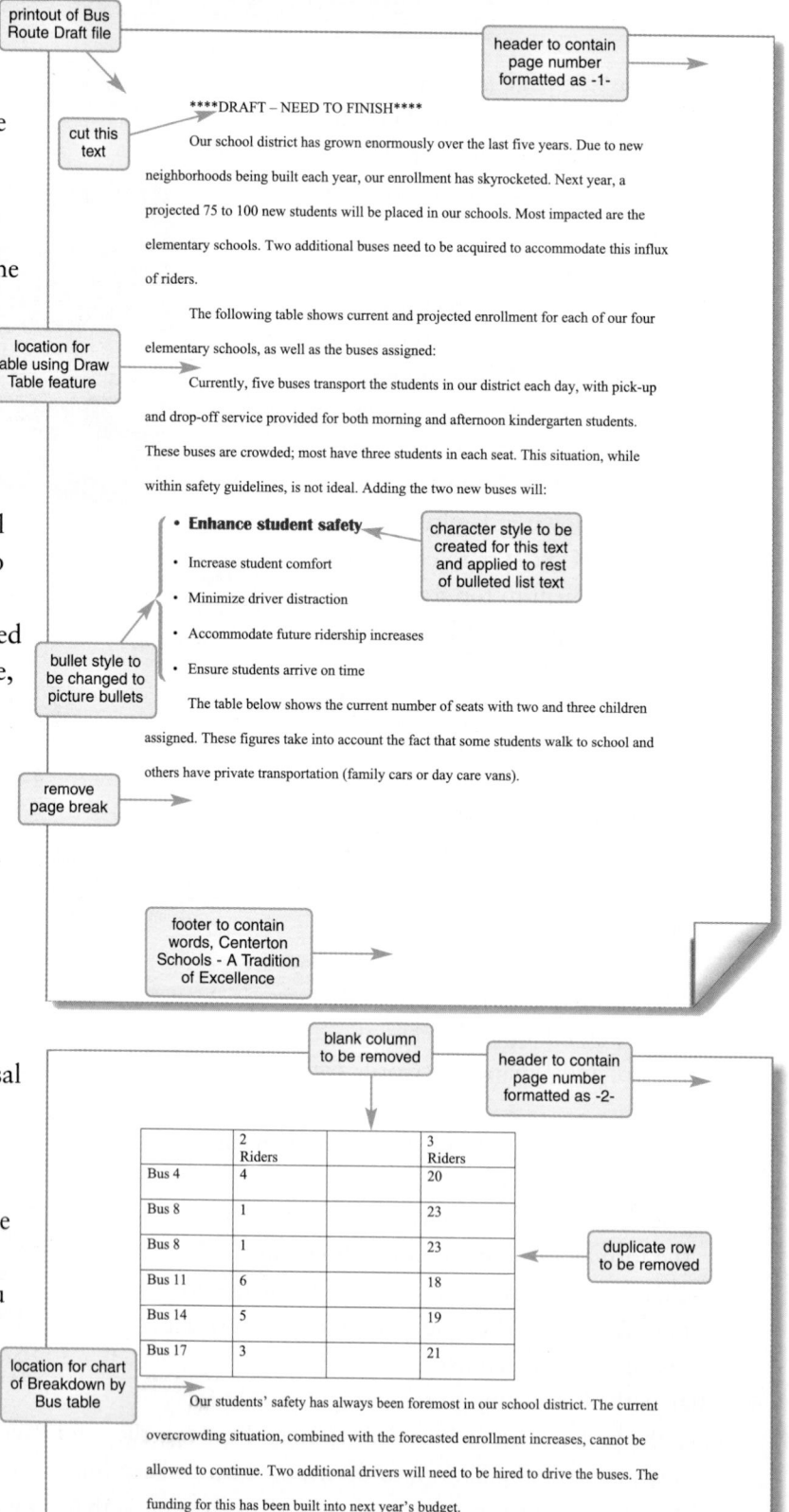

FIGURE 4-98b

Cases and Places

The difficulty of these case studies varies:
■ are the least difficult and ■■ are more difficult. The last exercise is a group exercise.

1 ■ As assistant to the owner of Happy Homes, you have been assigned the task of preparing a sales proposal that sells the business to prospective customers. The title page is to contain the name, Happy Homes, followed by an appropriate graphic, and then the slogan, A Clean House Is a Happy Home! The body of the proposal should contain the following: first paragraph — We know how busy you are. Between your job, family, and appointments, you barely have time for yourself, let alone the drudgery of cleaning your house. Let Happy Homes take care of your cleaning needs. We offer:, list with picture bullets — Bonded, licensed housekeepers; Light or heavy cleaning; Daily, weekly, or monthly service; Reasonable rates; next paragraph — We can clean your home and restore its sparkle, letting you devote your time to better projects. A sample price list follows:; the data for the table is shown in the table at right; paragraph below table — Standard service includes vacuuming; dusting; bathroom and kitchen cleaning; and floor mopping. Deluxe service provides additional services, including linen changes, window cleaning, and wall washing. We also perform one-time cleaning jobs, such as spring cleaning, pre-event cleaning, etc.; last paragraph – Whether you need us once a week or just once before your big party, call us to arrange an appointment time. Make your life easier and call Happy Homes today!

All prices weekly		
SQUARE FEET	STANDARD SERVICE	DELUXE SERVICE
1000	$25.00	$40.00
1500	35.00	50.00
2000	50.00	75.00
3000	90.00	125.00

2 ■■ Your boss at Greenfield Lawns has asked you to design a sales proposal that sells his business. He plans to post the proposal around the community and mail to local residents and businesses. Create a proposal that discusses various types of lawn treatments (grub and pest control, weed control, seeding and sodding, aeration, and fertilizer and nutrients). The proposal also should discuss the preferred customer discount program that is tailored to the customer – as long as the customer commits to one year of lawn care by Greenfield Lawns. For example, the regular price of weed control is $55.00 and the preferred customer price is $42.25; regular price of grub and pest control is $48.00 and the preferred customer price is $31.95; regular price of fertilizer and nutrients is $43.00 and the preferred customer price is $30.00. Greenfield Lawns also has a 100 percent satisfaction guarantee. The company slogan is "A Greener Lawn – Guaranteed!" Place the company name, an appropriate graphic, and the company slogan on the title page. Be sure the body of the proposal includes the following items: a list with picture bullets, a table with totals, a chart, a watermark, a header with a formatted page number, and a footer.

Cases and Places

3 ■■ Your boss at RSM Industries has asked you to design a planning proposal that outlines a utility upgrade. Create a proposal using the following pertinent information. The plant is powered by an on-site power house, which provides and generates all utilities (steam, electricity, gas, water treating, and sewer). Excess needs of utilities are purchased from CTM Utilities. Lately, RSM is purchasing as much as it is generating. It needs to upgrade the following equipment to more effectively manage its energy needs: chillers, boilers, co-gen, turbines, automated controls, and water treating facility. The upgrade will allow RSM to combat rising utility costs. For example, current gas prices are $25,000, proposed prices with upgrade is $12,900; current electric prices are $19,998, proposed prices are $10,500; current water prices are $7,500, proposed prices are $4,500. Without the upgrade, RSM either will reduce its profit margin or pass the cost onto its customers. Place the company name, an appropriate graphic, and the name of the proposal on the title page. Be sure the body of the proposal includes the following items: a list with picture bullets, a table with totals, a chart, a watermark, a header with a formatted page number, and a footer.

4 ■■ As an assistant at Market Solutions, Inc., you have been asked to design a research proposal that outlines a computer system upgrade. Create a proposal that discusses that the current problems with employees and customers related to the existing computer system: complaints about late mailings, slow order processing, and poor inventory control. Upgrading will enable Market Solutions to network workstations, access the Internet, process orders faster, respond to customers quicker, maintain accurate inventory data, provide a Web site for customer inquiries, reduce redundant data, and increase customer satisfaction. Currently, 60 hours a week are spent on hardware maintenance, 25 hours on software queries, and 105 hours on customer queries. With the new system, these numbers reduce to 10, 5, and 10, respectively. The cost of this project will be negligible compared with the expected gain in benefits. Place the company name, an appropriate graphic, and the name of the proposal on the title page. Be sure the body of the proposal includes the following items: a list with picture bullets, a table with totals, a chart, a watermark, a header with a formatted page number, and a footer.

5 ■■ **Working Together**   Your school provides several facilities and services such as registration, advising, cafeteria, day care, computer lab, career development, fitness center, library, bookstore, parking, and a tutoring center. Your team is to select an item from this list, or another facility or service that the group feels needs improvement at your school. The team is to develop a planning proposal that could be submitted to the Dean of Students. Visit the library or surf the Internet for guidelines about preparing a planning proposal. Team members can divide work as follows: create an appropriate title page, give details about the current situation, identify the problems, explain how the problems can be solved, identify any costs associated with the proposed solutions, and recommend a course(s) of action the school could take to improve the situation. Modify the default font settings to a font, font size, font style(s), font color, and effects to which the entire team agrees upon. Be sure the body of the proposal includes the following items: a list with picture bullets, a table, a chart, a header with a formatted page number, a footer, and a watermark.

Generating Form Letters, Mailing Labels, and Directories

PROJECT

5

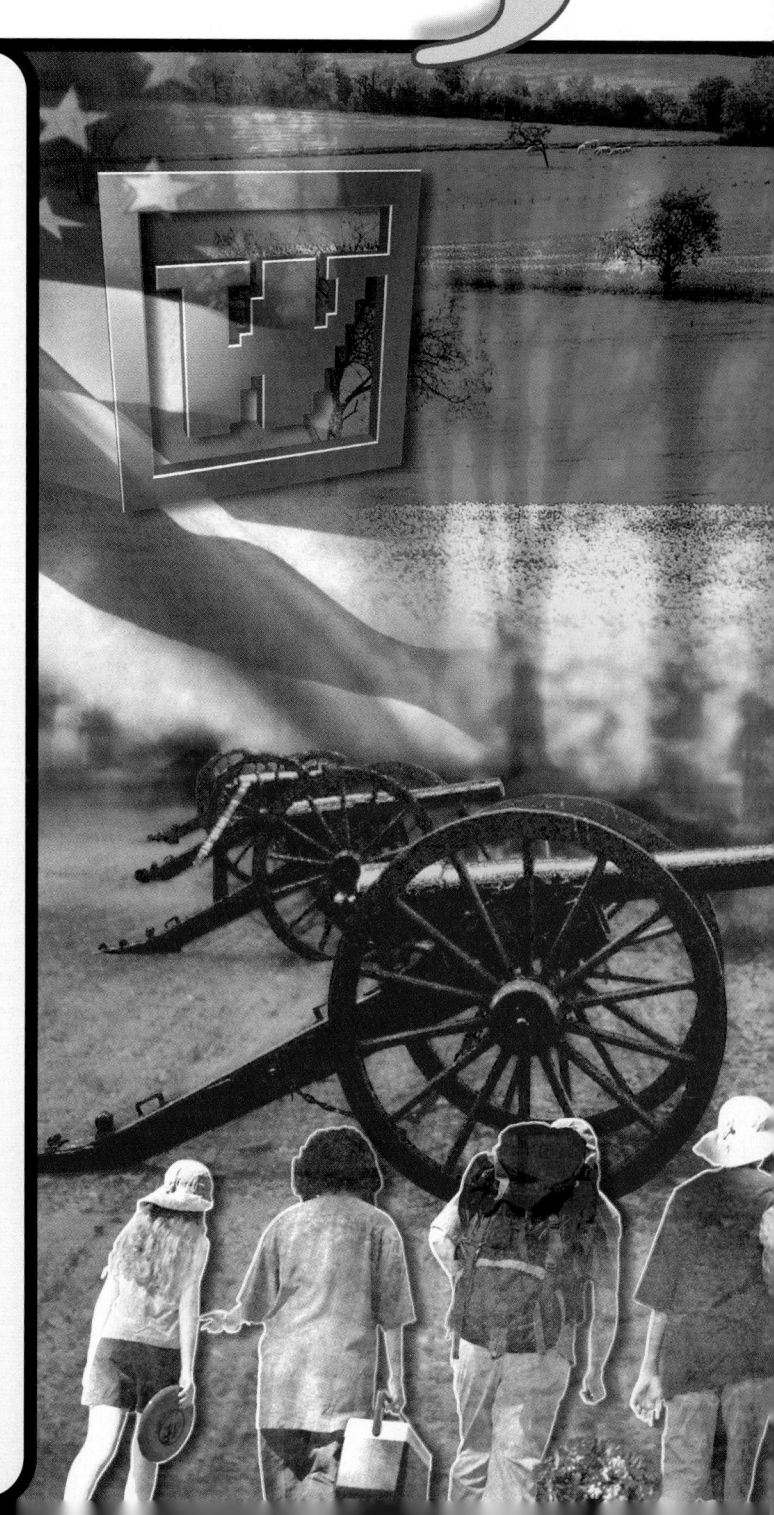

CASE PERSPECTIVE

Located in the popular destination of Gettysburg, Pennsylvania, River Run Campground is a favorite vacation spot for travelers from around the country. In addition to its scenic beauty, the main attraction is the historic battlefield of Gettysburg situated 15 minutes from the campground.

On Monday, you started working part-time for Tom and Deanna Rosatti, the campground's owners. The job allows you to meet many new people and obtain real-world computer experience. Your responsibilities include responding to e-mail questions, maintaining the campground Web site, and handling all correspondence.

The first day, you realize that you can simplify the correspondence procedures. Currently, each time a vacationer reserves a campsite, the owners type a confirmation letter. Instead of typing a separate letter for each reservation, you want to use Word to create a form letter because so much of the information is identical. To personalize each letter, you will need to create a separate file, called a data source, that contains the names and addresses of the guests as they make their reservations. Then, you will merge the guest data in the data source with the form letter so an individual letter prints for each guest. Each form letter should include the type of site, the deposit amount, and the arrival date. The deposit for a water and electric site is $23.50; tent sites require a deposit of $11.00.

As you read through this project, you will learn how to use Word to create and generate form letters, mailing labels, and a directory.

Office Word 2003

Generating Form Letters, Mailing Labels, and Directories

Objectives

You will have mastered the material in this project when you can:

- Explain the merge process
- Use the Mail Merge task pane and the Mail Merge toolbar
- Use a letter template
- Insert and format an AutoShape on a drawing canvas
- Create and edit a data source
- Insert and edit merge fields in a main document
- Use an IF field in a main document
- Create an outline numbered list
- Merge and print form letters
- Sort data records
- Address and print mailing labels and envelopes
- Merge all data records to a directory
- Change page orientation
- Modify table properties

Introduction

Individuals and business people are more likely to open and read a personalized letter than a letter addressed as Dear Sir, Dear Madam, or To Whom It May Concern. Typing individual personalized letters, though, can be a time-consuming task. Thus, Word provides the capability of creating a form letter, which is an easy way to generate mass mailings of personalized letters. The basic content of a group of form letters is similar. Items such as name, address, city, state, and ZIP code, however, vary from one letter to the next. With Word, you easily can address and print mailing labels or envelopes for the form letters.

Both business and personal correspondence regularly uses form letters to communicate via the postal service or e-mail with groups of people. **Business form letters** include announcements of sales to customers, confirmation letters (Figure 5-1), or notices of benefits to employees. **Personal form letters** include letters of application for a job or invitations to participate in a sweepstakes giveaway.

(a) Main Document for the Form Letter

(b) Data Source

Title	First Name	Last Name	Address Line 1	Address Line 2	City	State	ZIP Code	Site Type	Reservation Date	Number of Nights
Mr.	Jonah	Weinberg	22 Fifth Avenue		Auburn	AL	36830	water and electric	September 16	two
Ms.	Shannon	Murray	33099 Clark Street	Apt. D	Maple Park	IL	60151	tent	September 10	three
Mr.	Tyrone	Davis	P.O. Box 45	4430 Fifth Avenue	Dover	FL	33527	water and electric	September 10	four
Mrs.	Allison	Popovich	33 Parker Road		Memphis	TN	38101	tent	September 9	two
Dr.	Mae	Ling	13239 Oak Street		Hammond	IN	46323	water and electric	September 16	two

placeholder for address fields

**River
Camp...**

16 August 2005

«AddressBlock»   **placeholder for salutation fields**   **merge fields**   **IF field**

«GreetingLine»

We would like to thank you for reserving a «Site_Type» site for «Number_of_Nights» nights at our campground. To guarantee your reservation, we must receive a deposit of « IF Site_Type = "tent" "$11.00" "$23.50" » one week before your arrival date of «Reservation_Date» at the address shown at the bottom of this letter.

Our goal is to make your stay comfortable and enjoyable. The facilities and recreational activities at our campground continue to receive the highest ratings from *Camping Today* magazine.

1) Facilities
  a) Spotless restrooms and showers
  b) Two laundry rooms
  c) Groceries and snack bar
  d) Modem, telephone, and CATV hookup at each site

2) Recreational Activities
  a) Heated swimming pool
  b) Recreation hall and game room
  c) Freshwater fishing and boat rental
  d) Horseback riding

outline numbered list

We look forward to making your stay with us a memorable cam...

Sincerely,

Tom and Dea...
Owners

campground name in banner shape

form letter 1

**River Run
Campground**

16 August 2005

vacationer name and address in first data record

Mr. Jonah Weinberg
22 Fifth Avenue
Auburn, AL 36830

title and last name in first data record

Dear Mr. Weinberg:

We would like to thank you for reserving a water and electric site for two nights at our campground. To guarantee your reservation, we must receive a deposit of $23.50 one week before your arrival date of September 16 at the address shown at the bottom of this letter.

Our goal is to make your stay comfortable and enjoyable. The facilities and recreational activities at our campground continue to receive the highest ratings from *Camping Today* magazine.

1) Facilities
  a) Spotless restrooms and showers
  b) Two laundry rooms
  c) Groceries and snack bar
  d) Modem, telephone, and CATV hookup at each site

deposit is $23.50 because site type is water and electric

2) Recreational Activities
  a) Heated swimming pool
  b) Recreation hall and game room
  c) Freshwater fishing and boat rental
  d) Horseback riding

We look forward to making your stay with us a memorable camping adventure.

Sincerely,

Tom and Deanna Rosatti
Owners

vacationer name and address in second data record

**River Run
Campgroun...**

16 August 2005

Ms. Shannon Murray
33099 Clark Street
Apt. D
Maple Park, IL 60151

title and last name in second data record

Dear Ms. Murray:

We would like to thank you for reserving a tent site for three guarantee your reservation, we must receive a deposit of $11.00 one w... September 10 at the address shown at the bottom of this letter.

Our goal is to make your stay comfortable and enjoyable. The fac... at our campground continue to receive the highest ratings from *Campi...*

deposit is $11.00 because site type is tent

1) Facilities
  a) Spotless restrooms and showers
  b) Two laundry rooms
  c) Groceries and snack bar
  d) Modem, telephone, and CATV hookup at each site

2) Recreational Activities
  a) Heated swimming pool
  b) Recreation hall and game room
  c) Freshwater fishing and boat rental
  d) Horseback riding

We look forward to making your stay with us a memorable camping adventure.

Sincerely,

13 KNOB ROAD • GETTYSBURG, PA • 17325
PHONE: 717-555-6543 • FAX: 717-555-6544

form letter 2

form letter 3

(c) Form Letters

form letter 4

FIGURE 5-1

form letter 5

More About

Writing Letters

For more information about writing letters, visit the Word 2003 More About Web page (scsite.com/wd2003/more) and then click Writing Letters.

Project Five — Form Letters, Mailing Labels, and Directories

Project 5 illustrates how to create a business form letter and address and print corresponding mailing labels. The form letter is sent to future campground guests, confirming their reservation. Each form letter also identifies the type of site the vacationer reserved and specifies the deposit amount due. The type of site determines the deposit required.

The process of generating form letters involves creating a main document for the form letter and a data source, and then merging, or *blending*, the two together into a series of individual letters as shown in Figure 5-1 on the previous page.

Merging is the process of combining the contents of a data source with a main document. A **main document** contains the constant, or unchanging, text, punctuation, spaces, and graphics. In Figure 5-1a, the main document represents the portion of the form letter that repeats from one merged letter to the next. Conversely, the **data source** contains the variable, or changing, values for each letter. In Figure 5-1b, the data source contains five different vacationers. Thus, one form letter is generated for each vacationer listed in the data source.

Starting and Customizing Word

To start and customize Word, Windows must be running. If you are stepping through this project on a computer and you want your screen to match the figures in this book, then you should change your computer's resolution to 800 × 600 and reset the toolbars and menus. For information about changing the resolution and resetting toolbars and menus, read Appendix D.

The following steps describe how to start Word and customize the Word window. You may need to ask your instructor how to start Word for your system.

To Start and Customize Word

1. **Click the Start button on the Windows taskbar, point to All Programs on the Start menu, point to Microsoft Office on the All Programs submenu, and then click Microsoft Office Word 2003 on the Microsoft Office submenu.**

2. **If the Word window is not maximized, double-click its title bar to maximize it.**

3. **If the Language bar appears, right-click it and then click Close the Language bar on the shortcut menu.**

4. **If the Getting Started task pane is displayed in the Word window, click its Close button.**

5. **If the Standard and Formatting toolbar buttons are displayed on one row, click the Toolbar Options button and then click Show Buttons on Two Rows in the Toolbar Options list.**

6. **Click View on the menu bar and then click Print Layout.**

Word starts and, after a few moments, displays an empty document in the Word window. You use print layout view in this project because the letterhead contains a shape, and shapes are displayed properly only in print layout view. The Print Layout View button on the horizontal scroll bar is selected (shown in Figure 5-2 on page WD 302).

Displaying Formatting Marks

It is helpful to display formatting marks that indicate where in the document you pressed the ENTER key, SPACEBAR, and other keys. The following step describes how to display formatting marks.

To Display Formatting Marks

1 If the Show/Hide ¶ button on the Standard toolbar is not selected already, click it.

Word displays formatting marks in the document window, and the Show/Hide ¶ button on the Standard toolbar is selected (shown in Figure 5-2 on the next page).

Zooming Page Width

In print layout view, many users **zoom page width** so they can see all edges of the page in the document window at once. The following steps zoom page width.

To Zoom Page Width

1 Click the Zoom box arrow on the Standard toolbar (shown in Figure 5-2).

2 Click Page Width in the Zoom list.

Word computes the zoom percentage and displays it in the Zoom box. Your percentage may be different depending on your computer.

Identifying the Main Document for Form Letters

Creating form letters requires merging a main document with a data source. To create form letters using Word's mail merge, you perform these tasks: (1) identify the main document, (2) create or specify the data source, (3) enter text, graphics, and fields into the main document for the form letter, and (4) merge the data source with the main document to generate and print the form letters. The following pages illustrate these tasks.

Word provides two methods of merging documents: the Mail Merge task pane and the Mail Merge toolbar. The **Mail Merge task pane** guides you through the process of merging. The **Mail Merge toolbar** provides buttons and boxes you use to merge documents. This project first illustrates the Mail Merge task pane and then later uses the Mail Merge toolbar.

Identifying the Main Document

The first step in the mail merge process is to identify the type of document you are creating for the main document. Basic installations of Word support five types of main documents: letters, e-mail messages, envelopes, labels, and a directory. In this section, you are creating letters as the main document. Later in this project, you will specify labels and a directory as the main document.

When creating letters, such as the form letter in this project, you have three basic options: type the letter from scratch into a blank document window, as you did with the cover letter in Project 3; use the letter wizard and let Word format the letter based on your responses to the wizard; or use a letter template. As discussed in Project 3, a **template** is similar to a form with prewritten text; that is, Word prepares the requested document with text and/or formatting common to all documents of this nature. In the case of the letter template, Word prepares a letter with text and/or formatting common to all letters. Then, you customize the resulting letter by selecting and replacing prewritten text.

Word provides three styles of wizards and templates: Professional, Contemporary, and Elegant. The form letter in this project uses the Elegant Merge Letter template. The following steps show how to use a template as the main document for a form letter.

To Use a Template

1

• **Click File on the menu bar and then click New.**

Word displays the New Document task pane (Figure 5-2). You access templates through the Templates area in the task pane.

FIGURE 5-2

2

• **Click the On my computer link in the Templates area in the New Document task pane.**

• **When Word displays the Templates dialog box, click the Mail Merge tab.**

• **Click the Elegant Merge Letter icon.**

Word displays several template icons in the Mail Merge sheet in the Templates dialog box (Figure 5-3). If you click an icon, the Preview area shows a sample of the resulting document.

FIGURE 5-3

3

- **Click the OK button in the Templates dialog box.**

In the document window, Word displays a document that is based on the Elegant Merge Letter template (Figure 5-4). Word also opens the Mail Merge task pane at the right edge of the screen. Because you are not ready to continue with the merge process, you close the task pane.

4

- **Click the Close button in the upper-right corner of the Mail Merge task pane title bar.**
- **Click the Zoom box arrow and then click Page Width.**

FIGURE 5-4

The letter template instructs Word to display the current date in the letter (Figure 5-4). More than likely, your date line will display a different date.

Recall from Project 3 that a template displays prewritten text, called **placeholder text**, that you select and replace to personalize the document. Figure 5-4 identifies some of the placeholder text created by the Elegant Merge Letter template.

Also recall that all business letters have common elements such as a date line, inside address, message, and signature block. The Elegant Merge Letter template uses formatting for a **modified block style** letter; that is, the date line, complimentary close, and signature block are slightly to the right of the center point, and all other letter components begin flush with the left margin.

In creating a letter from a template, Word uses styles to represent various elements of the letter. As discussed in previous projects, a style is a named group of formatting characteristics that you can apply to text. Figure 5-5 on the next page identifies the styles used by the Elegant Merge Letter template.

The Style box on the Formatting toolbar displays the name of the style associated with the location of the insertion point or the current selection (shown in Figure 5-4). When you modify the form letter, the style associated with the location of the insertion point will be applied to the text you type.

At this point, you closed the Mail Merge task pane because you want to create the letterhead for the letter. With the Mail Merge task pane closed, Word displays the document window larger on the screen. Later, this project shows how to redisplay the Mail Merge task pane to continue the Mail Merge process.

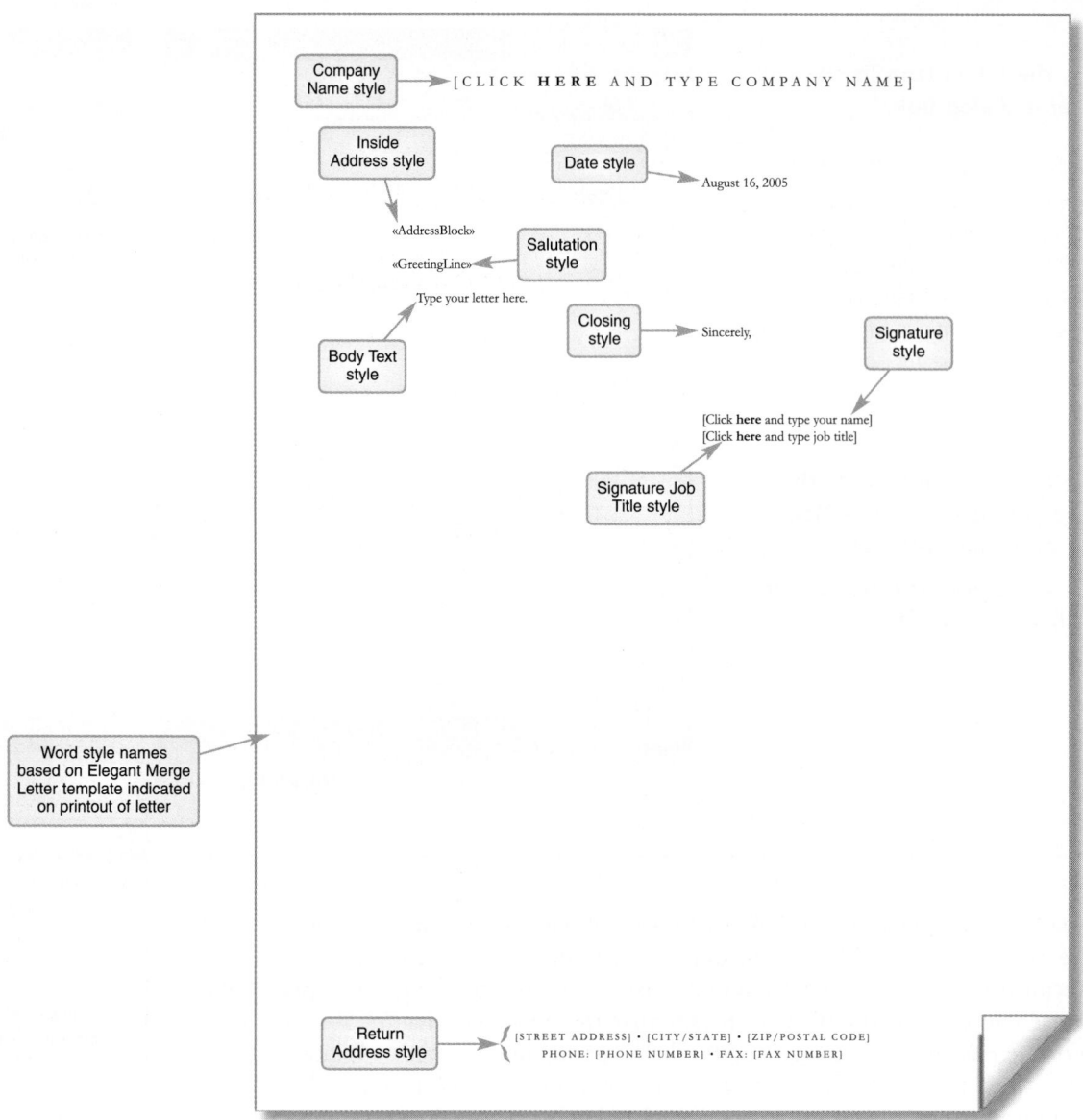

FIGURE 5-5

Working with AutoShapes and the Drawing Canvas

You can insert two types of graphics into a Word document: a picture and a drawing object. A **picture** is a graphic that was created in another program. Examples of pictures include scanned images, photographs, and clip art. A **drawing object** is a graphic that you create using Word.

Adding an AutoShape in a Drawing Canvas

In this project, the campground name is in a banner at the top of the form letter. A banner is a type of drawing object. This drawing object is in a drawing canvas. A **drawing canvas** is a container that helps you to resize and arrange shapes on the page. In this project, the banner is one color and the drawing canvas is another color. Also, the drawing canvas is surrounded with a border.

The following steps show how to insert a drawing canvas in a document and then format the drawing canvas.

To Insert a Drawing Canvas

1

• **Click the placeholder text, CLICK HERE AND TYPE COMPANY NAME, to select it.**

• **Click Insert on the menu bar and then point to Picture.**

Word selects the placeholder text (Figure 5-6). As soon as you instruct word to create a new drawing, it removes the selected placeholder text and inserts a drawing canvas in its place.

FIGURE 5-6

2

• **Click New Drawing on the Picture submenu.**

Word removes the selected placeholder text and inserts a drawing canvas at the location of the selection (Figure 5-7). When the drawing canvas is selected, Word automatically displays the Drawing Canvas toolbar.

FIGURE 5-7

Other Ways

1. In Voice Command mode, say "Insert, Picture, New Drawing"

Notice in Figure 5-7 that the drawing canvas is surrounded by a patterned rectangle. This rectangle does not print; you use it to resize or move the drawing canvas and its contents.

The next step is to draw a banner AutoShape on the drawing canvas. An **AutoShape** is a shape that Word has predefined. Examples of AutoShapes include rectangles, circles, triangles, arrows, flowcharting symbols, stars, banners, and callouts. The steps on the next page show how to insert a banner AutoShape into a document.

To Insert an AutoShape

1

• If the Drawing toolbar is not displayed on your screen, click the Drawing button on the Standard toolbar to display the Drawing toolbar.

• Click the AutoShapes button on the Drawing toolbar and then point to Stars and Banners on the AutoShapes menu (Figure 5-8).

FIGURE 5-8

2

• Click the Double Wave shape on the Stars and Banners submenu (bottom-right shape).

• Position the mouse pointer (a crosshair) in the upper-left corner of the drawing canvas, as shown in Figure 5-9.

FIGURE 5-9

3

• Drag the mouse to the right and downward to form a banner, as shown in Figure 5-10.

FIGURE 5-10

4

• **Release the mouse button. Once the shape is drawn, if you need to resize it, simply drag the sizing handles.**

Word places sizing handles at the middle and corner locations of the shape, allowing you to resize it if necessary (Figure 5-11).

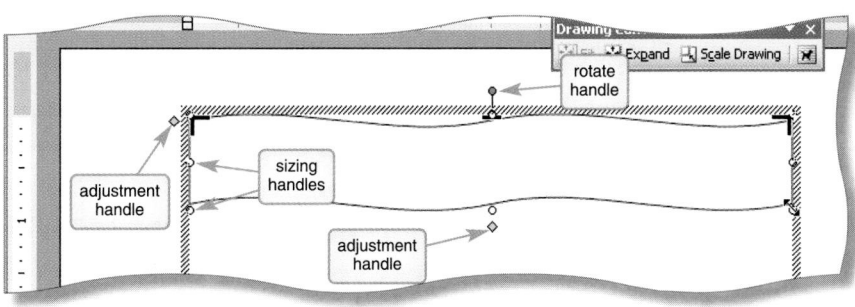

FIGURE 5-11

Many objects, such as the banner AutoShape shown in Figure 5-11, have an adjustment handle(s) and a rotate handle. When you drag an object's **adjustment handle**, which is a yellow diamond, Word changes the object's shape. When you drag an object's **rotate handle**, which is a green circle, Word rotates the object in the direction you drag the mouse.

If, for some reason, you wanted to delete an AutoShape, you would click it to select it and then press the DELETE key or click the Cut button on the Standard toolbar.

Formatting an AutoShape

The next step is to color the inside of the banner light green and remove the line that surrounds the banner. You could use the Fill Color and Line Color buttons on the Drawing toolbar to change the fill color to light green and to remove the line, respectively. You also want to check the size of the banner. To fit the campground name properly in the banner, its width should be approximately six inches and its height approximately one inch. To check an object's size, you use the Format AutoShape dialog box. Thus, you will use the Format AutoShape dialog box for all formatting changes to the banner.

The following steps show how to format an AutoShape.

To Format an AutoShape

1

• **Position the mouse pointer inside the banner and then double-click when the mouse pointer has a four-headed arrow attached to it.**

• **When Word displays the Format AutoShape dialog box, if necessary, click the Colors and Lines tab.**

• **In the Fill area, click the Color box arrow and then click Light Green.**

• **In the Line area, click the Color box arrow and then click No Line.**

Word displays the Colors and Lines sheet in the Format AutoShape dialog box (Figure 5-12).

FIGURE 5-12

2

• **Click the Size tab.**

• **In the Size and rotate area, verify that the height and width values are approximately 1" and 6", respectively. If they are not, change the values so they are close to those in Figure 5-13.**

3

• **Click the OK button.**

Word fills the banner with light green and removes its line (shown in Figure 5-14).

Other Ways

1. On Format menu click AutoShape
2. Right-click AutoShape, click Format AutoShape on shortcut menu
3. In Voice Command mode, say "Format, AutoShape"

FIGURE 5-13

The next step is to add the campground name inside the AutoShape. Thus, the following steps show how to add text to an AutoShape.

To Add Formatted Text to an AutoShape

1

• **Right-click the AutoShape.**

Word displays a shortcut menu (Figure 5-14).

2

• **Click Add Text on the shortcut menu.**

Word places an insertion point in the AutoShape.

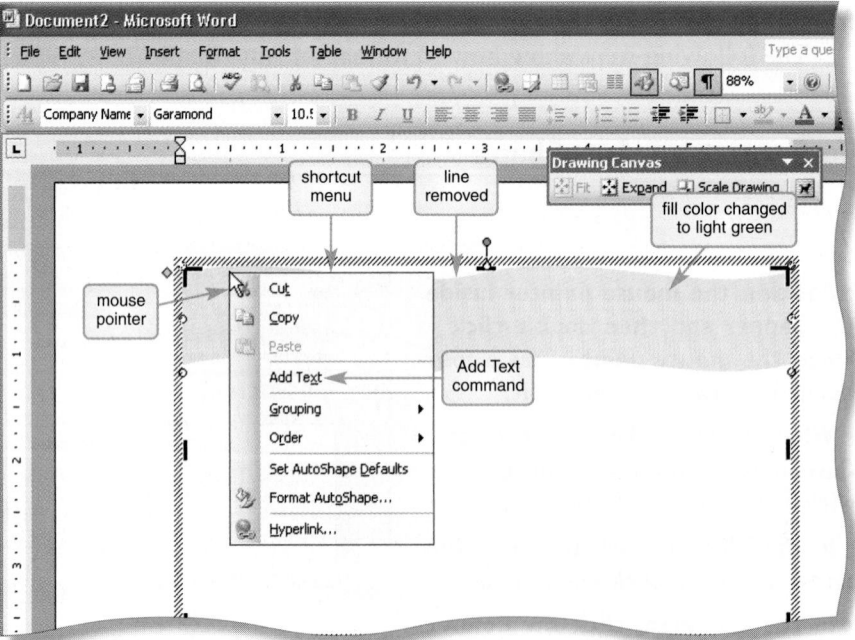

FIGURE 5-14

3

- Click the **Font box arrow** on the Formatting toolbar, scroll to and then click **Wide Latin** (or a similar font).

- Click the **Font Size box arrow** on the Formatting toolbar and then click **20**.

- Click the **Bold button** and then click the **Center button** on the Formatting toolbar.

- Click the **Font Color button arrow** on the Formatting toolbar and then click **Green** on the color palette.

- **Type** River Run **and then press the** ENTER **key. Type** Campground **in the banner.**

Word formats and displays the campground name in the banner AutoShape (Figure 5-15). The Text Box toolbar also may appear on the screen.

FIGURE 5-15

Other Ways

1. In Voice Command mode, say "Right Click, Add Text, [enter text]"

Resizing and Formatting the Drawing Canvas

Recall that the banner AutoShape was drawn on a drawing canvas. The height of the drawing canvas is about 3.5 inches, which is too big for this letter. You want the drawing canvas to touch the widest part of the wave in the AutoShape. Thus, you must resize the drawing canvas by dragging its bottom border up.

The steps on the next page show how to resize a drawing canvas.

More About

AutoShape Text and Drawing Canvas

To resize a text box to be as wide as its text, double-click an edge of the AutoShape, click the Text Box tab in the Format AutoShape dialog box, place a check mark in the Resize AutoShape to fit text check box, and then click the OK button. To make the drawing canvas larger and leave the AutoShape object the same size, click the Expand button on the Drawing Canvas toolbar. To make the drawing canvas fit tightly around the AutoShape, click the Fit button on the Drawing Canvas toolbar. To resize the drawing canvas and AutoShape object proportionately, click the Scale button on the Drawing Canvas toolbar and then drag the drawing canvas boundary.

To Resize a Drawing Canvas

1

• **Click in the drawing canvas in an area outside the AutoShape to select the drawing canvas.**

A selected drawing canvas has sizing handles at its corner and middle locations.

2

• **Scroll down until the bottom of the drawing canvas is displayed in the document window.**

• **Position the mouse pointer on the bottom-middle sizing handle until the mouse pointer shape changes to a T.**

• **Drag the bottom-middle sizing handle upward until the dotted line is positioned as shown in Figure 5-16.**

When you release the mouse, the bottom of the drawing canvas will be resized to the location of the dotted line.

FIGURE 5-16

3

• **Release the mouse button.**

• **If the banner AutoShape is not centered properly inside the drawing canvas, click it and drag it to the desired location.**

Word resizes the drawing canvas (Figure 5-17).

FIGURE 5-17

Other Ways

1. On Format menu click Drawing Canvas, click Size tab, enter height and width values in the Size and rotate area, click OK button

The next step is to fill the drawing canvas with a transparent (see-through) shade of pale blue. If you simply wanted to fill the drawing canvas, you would select it and then click the Fill Color button arrow on the Drawing toolbar. To make the fill color transparent, however, you must use the Format Drawing Canvas dialog box. You also want to change the line color and style, which requires you use the Format Drawing Canvas dialog box. The next steps show how to format the drawing canvas.

To Format a Drawing Canvas

1

• **Point to an edge of the drawing canvas and double-click when the mouse pointer has a four-headed arrow attached to it.**

• **When Word displays the Format Drawing Canvas dialog box, if necessary, click the Colors and Lines tab.**

• **In the Fill area, click the Color box arrow and then click Pale Blue. Drag the Transparency slider until the Transparency box displays 50%.**

• **In the Line area, click the Color box arrow and then click Green on the color palette.**

• **Click the Dashed box arrow and then click the fifth line in the list.**

• **Click the Style box arrow and then click the next to last style in the list (Figure 5-18).**

FIGURE 5-18

2

• **Click the OK button.**

• **Click outside the drawing canvas to deselect it.**

• **Click the Drawing button on the Standard toolbar to remove the Drawing toolbar from the screen.**

Word fills the drawing canvas with a transparent shade of pale blue and adds a dashed box around it (Figure 5-19).

FIGURE 5-19

Notice in Figure 5-19 that the bottom of the drawing canvas is too close to the top of the date. To be more readable, additional white space should be placed between the drawing canvas and the date. In a previous project, you pressed CTRL+0 (the numeral zero) to add one blank line, which is equal to 12 points, above a paragraph. In this project, you want 6 points above the date.

The steps on the next page show how to use the Reveal Formatting task pane to change paragraph formatting.

Other Ways

1. On Format menu click Drawing Canvas
2. Right-click edge of drawing canvas in area outside AutoShape, click Format Drawing Canvas on shortcut menu
3. In Voice Command mode, say "Format, Drawing Canvas"

To Change Paragraph Formatting Using the Reveal Formatting Task Pane

1

• **Position the insertion point in the date line in the letter.**

• **Click Format on the menu bar and then click Reveal Formatting.**

• **In the Reveal Formatting task pane, scroll to display the Spacing link.**

Word displays the Reveal Formatting task pane (Figure 5-20).

FIGURE 5-20

2

• **Click the Spacing link.**

• **In the Spacing area in the Paragraph dialog box, click the Before box up arrow.**

Word displays 6 pt in the Before box in the Paragraph dialog box (Figure 5-21).

FIGURE 5-21

3

• **Click the OK button.**

• **Click the Close button on the Reveal Formatting task pane title bar to close the task pane.**

Word adds 6 points above the paragraph containing the date (Figure 5-22).

Other Ways

1. On Format menu click Paragraph
2. Right-click date line, click Paragraph on shortcut menu
3. In Voice Command mode, say "Format, Paragraph"

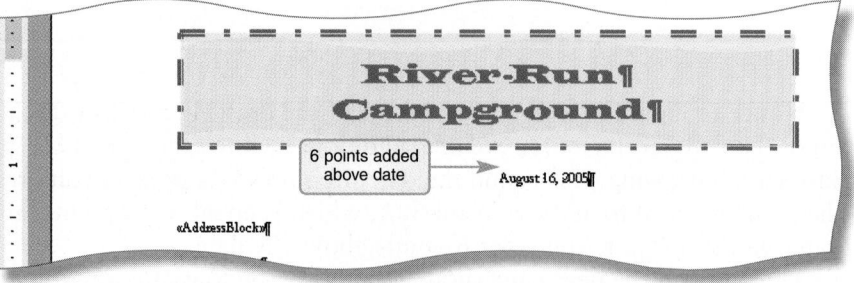

FIGURE 5-22

Through the Paragraph dialog box, you also can adjust the amount of space that is displayed after a paragraph by changing the value in the After box in the Spacing area (Figure 5-21).

Creating a Folder

You have performed several tasks to the form letter and should save it. You want to save this and all other documents created in this project in a folder called River Run. This folder does not exist, so you must create it. Rather than creating the folder in Windows, you can create folders in Word, which saves time.

The following steps show how to create a folder during the process of saving a document.

To Create a Folder while Saving

1

• **With a floppy disk in drive A, click the Save button on the Standard toolbar.**

• **When Word displays the Save As dialog box, type** Campground Form Letter **in the File name box. Do not press the ENTER key after typing the file name.**

• **If necessary, click the Save in box arrow and then click 3½ Floppy (A:).**

• **Click the Create New Folder button in the Save As dialog box.**

• **When Word displays the New Folder dialog box, type** River Run **(Figure 5-23).**

2

• **Click the OK button.**

• **Click the Save button in the Save As dialog box.**

Word saves the Campground Form Letter in the River Run folder on a disk in drive A.

FIGURE 5-23

Other dialog boxes, such as the Open and Insert File dialog boxes, also have a Create New Folder button, saving the time of using Windows to create a new folder for document storage.

Creating a Data Source

A data source is a file that contains the data that changes from one merged document to the next. As shown in Figure 5-24, a data source often is shown as a table that consists of a series of rows and columns. Each row is called a **record**. The first row of a data source is called the **header record** because it identifies the name of each column. Each row below the header row is called a **data record**. Data records contain the text that varies in each copy of the merged document. The data source for this project contains five data records. In this project, each data record identifies a different vacationer. Thus, five form letters will be generated from this data source.

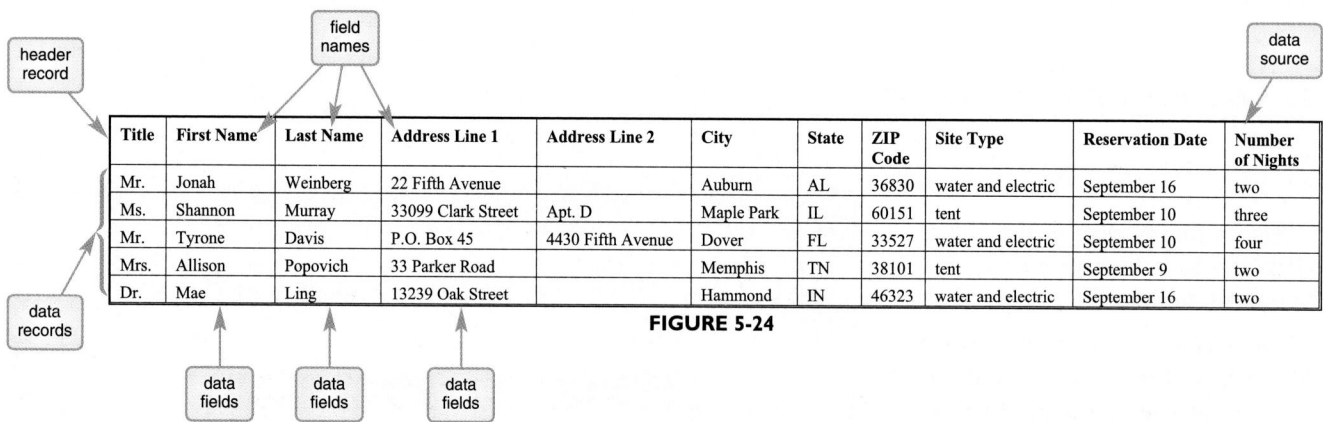

Title	First Name	Last Name	Address Line 1	Address Line 2	City	State	ZIP Code	Site Type	Reservation Date	Number of Nights
Mr.	Jonah	Weinberg	22 Fifth Avenue		Auburn	AL	36830	water and electric	September 16	two
Ms.	Shannon	Murray	33099 Clark Street	Apt. D	Maple Park	IL	60151	tent	September 10	three
Mr.	Tyrone	Davis	P.O. Box 45	4430 Fifth Avenue	Dover	FL	33527	water and electric	September 10	four
Mrs.	Allison	Popovich	33 Parker Road		Memphis	TN	38101	tent	September 9	two
Dr.	Mae	Ling	13239 Oak Street		Hammond	IN	46323	water and electric	September 16	two

FIGURE 5-24

Each column in the data source is called a **data field**. A data field represents a group of similar data. Each data field must be identified uniquely with a name, called a **field name**. For example, First Name is the name of the field (column) that contains the first names of vacationers. In this project, the data source contains 11 data fields with the following field names: Title, First Name, Last Name, Address Line 1, Address Line 2, City, State, ZIP Code, Site Type, Reservation Date, and Number of Nights.

The first step in creating a data source is to decide which fields it will contain. That is, you must identify the data that will vary from one merged document to the next. For each field, you must decide on a field name. Field names must be unique; that is, no two field names may be the same.

Data sources often contain the same fields. For this reason, Word provides you with a list of 13 commonly used field names. This project uses eight of the 13 field names supplied by Word: Title, First Name, Last Name, Address Line 1, Address Line 2, City, State, and ZIP Code. The other five field names are deleted from the list supplied by Word. That is, this project deletes Company Name, Country, Home Phone, Work Phone, and E-mail Address. Then, three new field names (Site Type, Reservation Date, and Number of Nights) are added to the data source.

Fields may be listed in any order in the data source. That is, the order of fields has no effect on the order in which they will print in the main document.

The next steps show how to type a new data source for a mail merge.

To Type a New Data Source

1

• **Click Tools on the menu bar and then point to Letters and Mailings (Figure 5-25).**

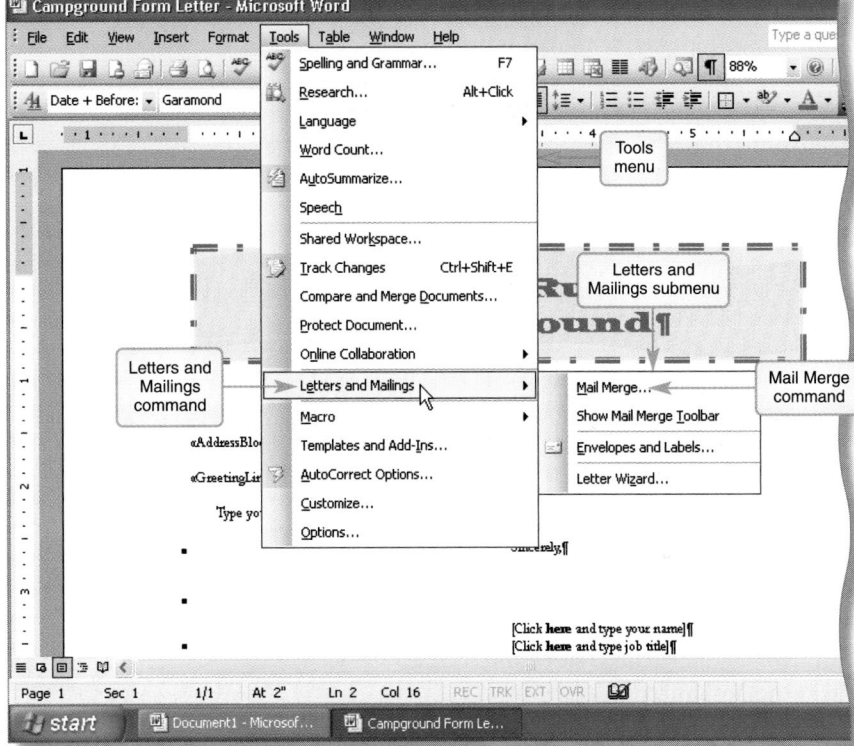

FIGURE 5-25

2

• **Click Mail Merge on the Letters and Mailings submenu.**

• **When Word displays the Mail Merge task pane, click Type a new list in the Select recipients area.**

When Word displays the Mail Merge task pane, it remembers where you left off in the merge process. You have three choices for the data source: use an existing list, select from Outlook contacts, or type a new list.

3

• **Click the Create link in the Mail Merge task pane.**

Word displays the New Address List dialog box with a list of commonly used field names (Figure 5-26). You can modify this list by clicking the Customize button.

FIGURE 5-26

4

• **Click the Customize button in the New Address List dialog box.**

• **When Word displays the Customize Address List dialog box, click Company Name in the Field Names list and then click the Delete button.**

Word displays a dialog box asking if you are sure you want to delete the selected field (Figure 5-27). The field name, Company Name, is selected for removal.

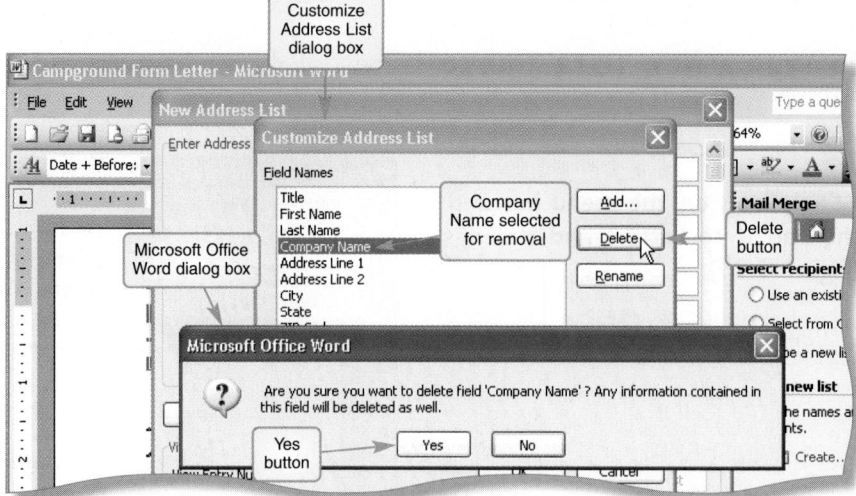

FIGURE 5-27

5

• **Click the Yes button.**

• **Click Country in the Field Names list. Click the Delete button. Click the Yes button.**

• **Click Home Phone in the Field Names list. Click the Delete button. Click the Yes button.**

• **Click Work Phone in the Field Names list. Click the Delete button. Click the Yes button.**

• **Click E-mail Address in the Field Names list. Click the Delete button. Click the Yes button.**

Word removes five field names from the list (Figure 5-28). The next step is to add the Site Type, Reservation Date, and Number of Nights field names to the list.

FIGURE 5-28

6

• **Click the Add button.**

• **When Word displays the Add Field dialog box, type** Site Type **in the text box (Figure 5-29).**

7

• **Click the OK button.**

Word adds the Site Type field name to the bottom of the Field Names list (shown in Figure 5-30).

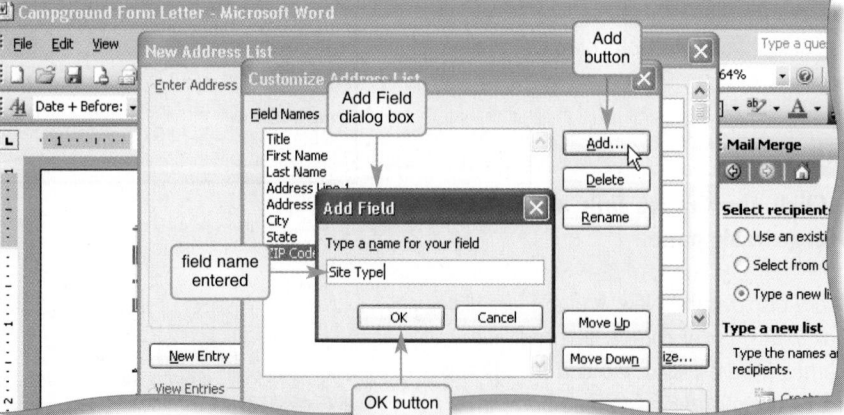

FIGURE 5-29

8

- **Click the Add button.**
- **When Word displays the Add Field dialog box, type** Reservation Date **in the text box and then click the OK button.**
- **Click the Add button.**
- **When Word displays the Add Field dialog box, type** Number of Nights **in the text box and then click the OK button.**

Word adds the Reservation Date and Number of Nights field names to the bottom of the Field Names list (Figure 5-30).

FIGURE 5-30

9

- **Click the OK button to close the Customize Address List dialog box.**
- **When the New Address List dialog box is active again, click the Title text box.**

Word displays the new list of field names in the Enter Address information area in the New Address List dialog box (Figure 5-31). The insertion point is displayed in the Title text box, ready for the first data record entry. Text entered in this dialog box becomes records in the data source.

FIGURE 5-31

10

• **Type** Mr. **and then press the ENTER key.**

• **Type** Jonah **and then press the ENTER key.**

• **Type** Weinberg **and then press the ENTER key.**

• **Type** 22 Fifth Avenue **and then press the ENTER key twice.**

• **Type** Auburn **and then press the ENTER key.**

• **Type** AL **as the state (Figure 5-32).**

If you notice an error in a text box, click the text box and then correct the error as you would in the document window.

FIGURE 5-32

11

• **Press the ENTER key.**

• **Type** 36830 **and then press the ENTER key.**

• **Type** water and electric **and then press the ENTER key.**

• **Type** September 16 **and then press the ENTER key.**

• **Type** two **as the last field value in this record.**

The first few fields scroll off the top of the dialog box to make room for the last three fields (Figure 5-33).

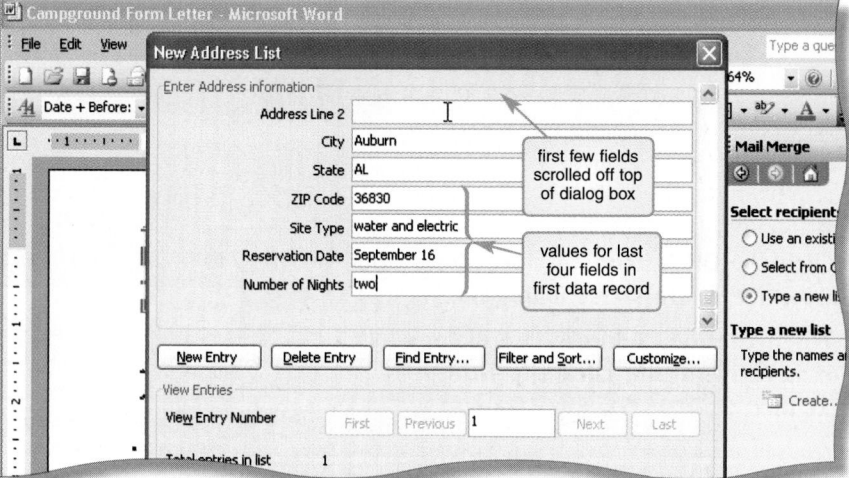

FIGURE 5-33

12

• **Click the New Entry button.**

Word adds the entered data to the data source and clears the text boxes in the Enter Address information area in preparation for the next data record to be entered (Figure 5-34).

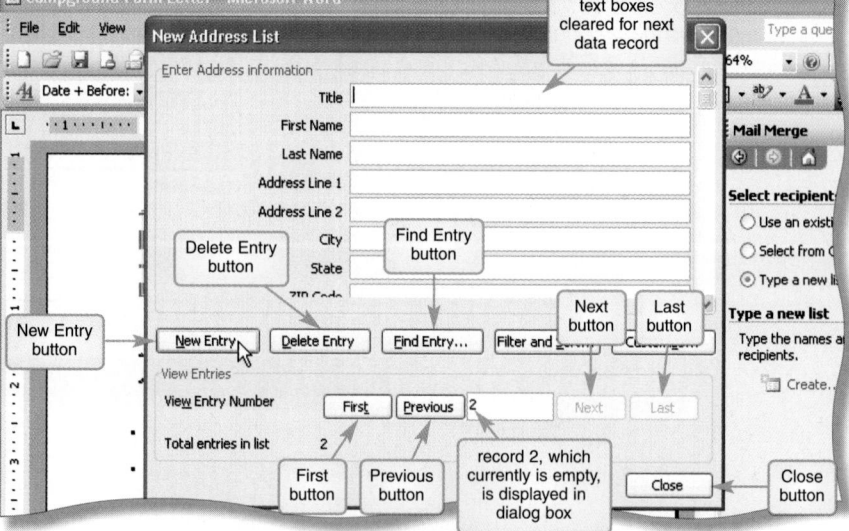

FIGURE 5-34

The next step is to enter the remaining four records into the New Address List dialog box, as described in the steps below.

To Enter More Records

1 **Type** Ms. **and then press the ENTER key. Type** Shannon **and then press the ENTER key. Type** Murray **and then press the ENTER key. Type** 33099 Clark Street **and then press the ENTER key. Type** Apt. D **and then press the ENTER key. Type** Maple Park **and then press the ENTER key. Type** IL **and then press the ENTER key. Type** 60151 **and then press the ENTER key. Type** tent **and then press the ENTER key. Type** September 10 **and then press the ENTER key. Type** three **and then click the New Entry button.**

2 **Type** Mr. **and then press the ENTER key. Type** Tyrone **and then press the ENTER key. Type** Davis **and then press the ENTER key. Type** P.O. Box 45 **and then press the ENTER key. Type** 4430 Fifth Avenue **and then press the ENTER key. Type** Dover **and then press the ENTER key. Type** FL **and then press the ENTER key. Type** 33527 **and then press the ENTER key. Type** water and electric **and then press the ENTER key. Type** September 10 **and then press the ENTER key. Type** four **and then click the New Entry button.**

3 **Type** Mrs. **and then press the ENTER key. Type** Allison **and then press the ENTER key. Type** Popovich **and then press the ENTER key. Type** 33 Parker Road **and then press the ENTER key twice. Type** Memphis **and then press the ENTER key. Type** TN **and then press the ENTER key. Type** 38101 **and then press the ENTER key. Type** tent **and then press the ENTER key. Type** September 9 **and then press the ENTER key. Type** two **and then click the New Entry button.**

4 **Type** Dr. **and then press the ENTER key. Type** Mae **and then press the ENTER key. Type** Ling **and then press the ENTER key. Type** 13239 Oak Street **and then press the ENTER key twice. Type** Hammond **and then press the ENTER key. Type** IN **and then press the ENTER key. Type** 46323 **and then press the ENTER key. Type** water and electric **and then press the ENTER key. Type** September 16 **and then press the ENTER key. Type** two **and then click the Close button (shown in Figure 5-34).**

The data records are entered in the data source.

When you click the Close button in the New Address List dialog box, Word displays a Save Address List dialog box so you can save the data source. The steps on the next page show how to save the data source in the River Run folder created earlier in this project.

Q&A

Q: How should I organize data in a data source?

A: Organize the items in a data source so it is reusable. For example, you may want to print a person's title, first name, middle initial, and last name (e.g., Mr. Roger A. Bannerman) in the inside address but only the title and last name in the salutation (Dear Mr. Bannerman). Thus, you should break the name into separate fields: title, first name, middle initial, and last name.

To Save the Data Source when Prompted by Word

1

• **When Word displays the Save Address List dialog box, type** `Camper List` **in the File name box.**

• **If necessary, change the drive to 3½ Floppy (A:) and then double-click the River Run folder.**

*The data source for this project will be saved with the file name, Camper List (Figure 5-35). Word saves the data source as a **Microsoft Office Address List**, which is a Microsoft Access database file.*

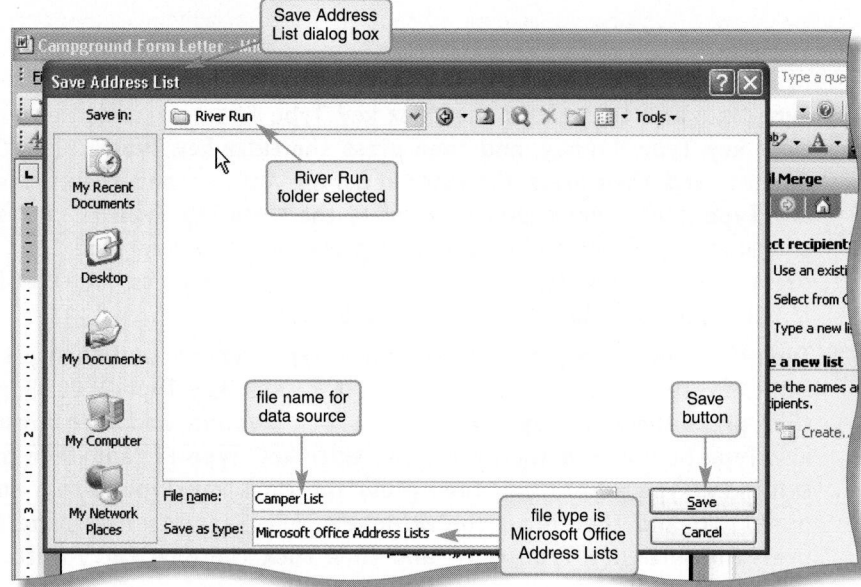

FIGURE 5-35

2

• **Click the Save button in the Save Address List dialog box.**

Word saves the data source in the River Run folder on the disk in drive A using the file name, Camper List, and then displays the Mail Merge Recipients dialog box (Figure 5-36).

FIGURE 5-36

3

• **Click the OK button.**

• **Click the Close button on the Mail Merge task pane title bar.**

• **If the Mail Merge toolbar is not displayed on the screen, click Tools on the menu bar, point to Letters and Mailings, and then click Show Mail Merge Toolbar.**

FIGURE 5-37

Word displays the Mail Merge toolbar docked above or below the Formatting toolbar (Figure 5-37).

The Mail Merge task pane is closed because the next step is to enter the contents of the form letter, and the document window is larger if the task pane is closed.

If you are familiar with Microsoft Access, you can open the Camper List file in Access. You do not have to be familiar with Access, however, to continue with this mail merge process. Word simply stores a data source as an Access table because it is an efficient method of storing a data source.

Editing Records in the Data Source

The Mail Merge toolbar is displayed on the screen because you have identified a main document and a data source. Figure 5-38 identifies the buttons and boxes on the Mail Merge toolbar. These buttons and boxes are explained as they are used.

FIGURE 5-38

All of the data records have been entered into the data source and saved with the file name, Camper List. To add more data records to the data source, click the Mail Merge Recipients button on the Mail Merge toolbar to display the Mail Merge Recipients dialog box (shown in Figure 5-36). Click the Edit button in the Mail Merge Recipients dialog box to display the data records in a dialog box similar to the one shown in Figure 5-34 on page WD 318. Then add records as described in the previous steps.

To change an existing data record in the data source, display the data record by clicking the Mail Merge Recipients button on the Mail Merge toolbar to display the Mail Merge Recipients dialog box. Click the data record to change in the Mail Merge Recipients dialog box. If the list of data records is long, you can click the Find button to locate an item, such as the first name, quickly in the list. With the record to change selected, click the Edit button in the Mail Merge Recipients dialog box to display the selected data record in a dialog box similar to the one shown in Figure 5-34.

To delete a record, display it using the same procedure described in the previous paragraph. Then, click the Delete Entry button in the dialog box (Figure 5-34).

Composing the Main Document for the Form Letters

The next step is to enter and format the text and fields in the main document, which in this case is the form letter (shown in Figure 5-1a on page WD 299). The banner containing the campground name is complete. The steps on the following pages illustrate how to compose the rest of the main document for the form letter.

More About

Saving Data Sources

Word, by default, saves a data source in the My Data Sources folder on your hard disk. Likewise, when you open a data source, Word initially looks in the My Data Sources folder for the file. The default file type for a new data source created in Word is called a Microsoft Office Address List. If you are familiar with Microsoft Access, you can open and view these file types in Access using the Microsoft Office Access file type.

More About

Docked Toolbars

Word docks the Mail Merge toolbar at the top of the Word window. If you want to move the docked toolbar above or below the Standard and Formatting toolbars, drag the move handle on the Mail Merge toolbar to position the toolbar in a new location.

More About

Date Formats

Most business letters use the following date format: month day, year (August 16, 2005). Thus, Word uses this format as its default date format. Some people, however, prefer other date formats. This project demonstrates how to change the date format from this standard to another format.

Modifying a Field

In the elegant letter template, Word automatically displays the current computer date in the date line because the date actually is a field. Earlier in this project, you worked with data fields – the fields in the data source. A field, however, does not have to be associated with a data source. A **field** can be any placeholder for a value that changes. For example, when you print a document that contains a date field, Word always prints the current date on the document. If you want to update a field on the screen, for example if the date displayed is not the current computer date, click the field and then press the **F9** key.

The date line at the top of the form letter displays the date August 16, 2005 in the form: month day, year. In this project, the date should be displayed as 16 August 2005, that is, in the form: day month year. To make this change, you edit the date field. The following steps show how to edit a field.

To Edit a Field

1

• **Right-click the field, in this case, the date field (Figure 5-39).**

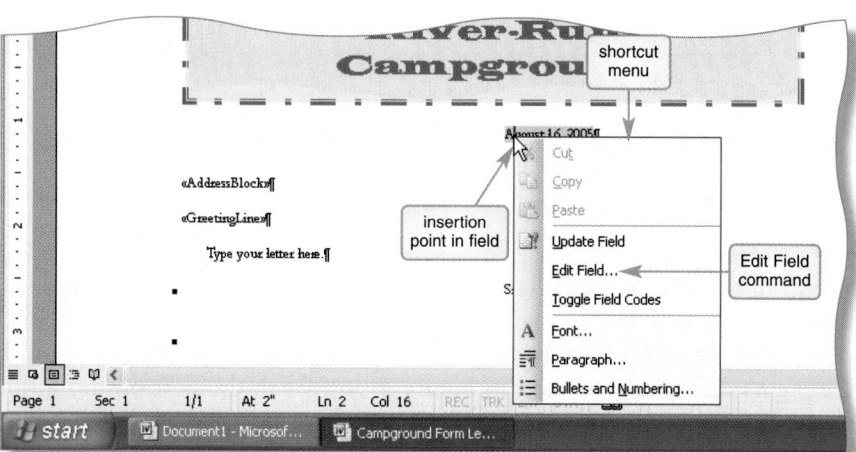

FIGURE 5-39

2

• **Click Edit Field on the shortcut menu.**

• **When Word displays the Field dialog box, click the desired format in the Date formats list (in this case, 16 August 2005).**

The Field dialog box shows a list of available formats for dates and times with the format d MMMM yyyy shown in the Date formats text box (Figure 5-40). Your screen probably will not show 16 August 2005; instead, it will display the current system date stored in your computer.

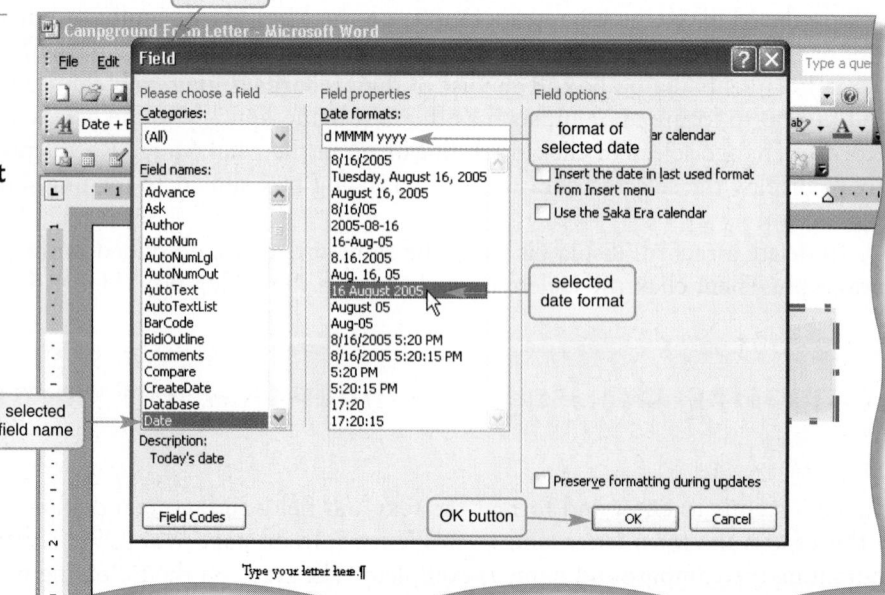

FIGURE 5-40

3

• **Click the OK button.**

Word displays the current date in the d MMMM yyyy format in the form letter (Figure 5-41).

FIGURE 5-41

Inserting Merge Fields in the Main Document

In a letter, the inside address is below the date line, and the salutation is below the inside address. The contents of the inside address are located in the data source. That is, data in the data source is to be displayed in the main document.

Earlier, this project showed how to create the data source for this form letter. Recall that each field in the data source was assigned a field name. To link the data source to the main document, you insert these field names into the main document.

In the main document, these field names are called **merge fields** because they merge, or combine, the main document with the contents of the data source. When a merge field is inserted into the main document, Word surrounds the field name with merge field characters (shown in Figure 5-42). The **merge field characters**, which are chevrons, mark the beginning and ending of a merge field. Merge field characters are not on the keyboard; therefore, you cannot type them directly into the document. Word automatically displays them when a merge field is inserted into the main document.

Most letters contain an address and salutation. For this reason, Word provides an AddressBlock merge field and a GreetingLine merge field. The **AddressBlock merge field** contains several fields related to an address: title, first name, middle name, last name, suffix, company, street address 1, street address 2, city, state, and ZIP code. When Word is instructed to use the AddressBlock merge field, it automatically looks for any fields in the associated data source that are related to an address and then formats the address block properly when you merge the data source with the main document. For example, if your inside address does not use a middle name, suffix, or company, Word omits these items from the inside address and adjusts the spacing so the address prints correctly.

The **GreetingLine merge field** contains text and fields related to a salutation. The default greeting for the salutation is in the format, Dear Mr. Randall, followed by a comma. In this letter, you want a more formal ending to the salutation – a colon. The following steps show how to edit the GreetingLine merge field.

To Edit the GreetingLine Merge Field

1

• **If necessary, scroll down to display the GreetingLine merge field in the document window.**

• **Right-click the GreetingLine merge field (Figure 5-42).**

FIGURE 5-42

• **Click Edit Greeting Line on the shortcut menu.**

• **When Word displays the Greeting Line dialog box, click the right box arrow in the Greeting line format area and then click the colon (:).**

In the Greeting Line dialog box, the first box arrow displays a list of initial phrases in the greeting line; the second box arrow displays a list of formats for the name; the third box arrow displays a list of punctuation formats to end the salutation (Figure 5-43).

3

• **Click the OK button.**

Word modifies the format of the greeting line.

FIGURE 5-43

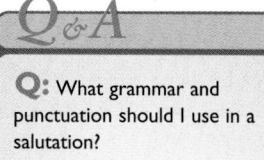
You will not notice a change in the GreetingLine merge field at this time. The new format will be displayed when you merge the form letter to the data source later in this project.

The next step is to begin typing the body of the letter, which is to be located where Word has the placeholder text, Type your letter here (shown in Figure 5-43).

The following steps describe how to begin typing the body of the form letter.

To Begin Typing the Body of the Form Letter

1 Triple-click the placeholder text containing the sentence, Type your letter here., to select it.

2 With the sentence selected, type We would like to thank you for reserving a and then press the SPACEBAR.

The beginning of the first sentence below the GreetingLine merge field is entered (shown in Figure 5-44).

The first sentence in the first paragraph of the letter identifies the type of campsite the vacationer reserved, for example, water and electric, and the number of nights in the reservation. Both the site type and number of nights are data fields in the data source. To instruct Word to use data fields from the data source, you insert merge fields in the main document for the form letter, as shown in the next steps.

To Insert Merge Fields in the Main Document

1

• **With the insertion point positioned as shown in Figure 5-44, click the Insert Merge Fields button on the Mail Merge toolbar.**

• **When Word displays the Insert Merge Field dialog box, click Site Type in the Fields list.**

Word displays a list of field names in the data source file associated with this main document (Figure 5-44). The field you select will be inserted in the main document at the location of the insertion point.

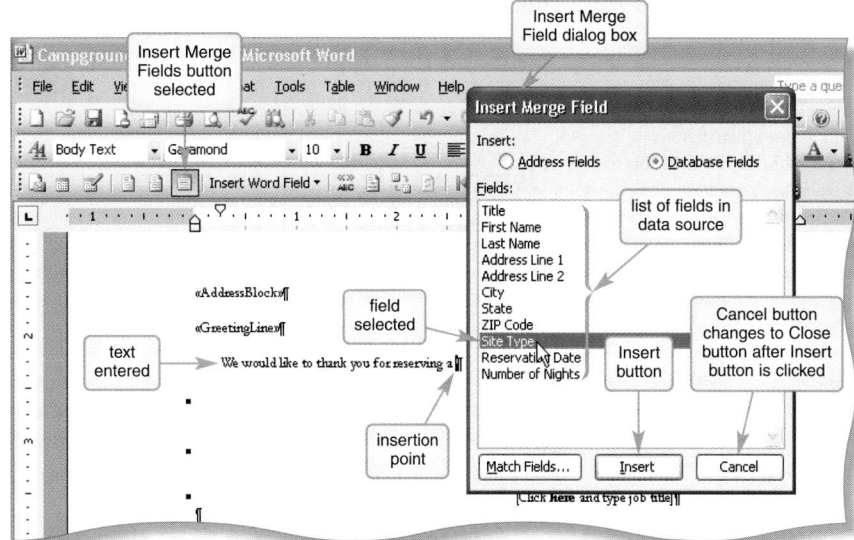

FIGURE 5-44

2

• **Click the Insert button in the dialog box.**

• **Click the Close button in the dialog box.**

• **Press the SPACEBAR. Type** site for **and then press the SPACEBAR.**

• **Click the Insert Merge Fields button on the Mail Merge toolbar, click Number of Nights in the Fields list, click the Insert button, and then click the Close button in the dialog box.**

• **Press the SPACEBAR and then type** nights at our campground.

Word displays the merge fields, Site Type and Number of Nights, surrounded by merge field characters in the main document (Figure 5-45).

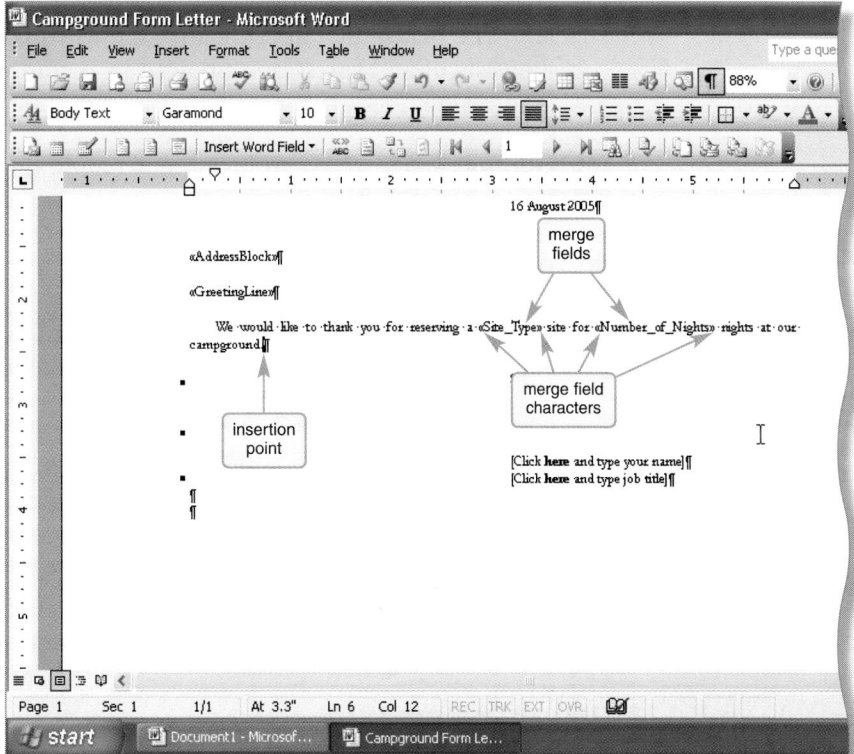

FIGURE 5-45

Other Ways

1. With Mail Merge toolbar displaying, in Voice Command mode, say "Insert Merge Fields, [select field], Insert, Close"

More About

Field Codes

When you insert fields into a document, if the fields are displayed surrounded by braces instead of chevrons and if extra instructions appear between the braces, then field codes have been turned on. To turn off field codes, press ALT+F9.

When you merge the data source with the main document, the site type (e.g., water and electric) and number of nights (e.g., two) will print at the location of the merge fields, Site Type and Number of Nights, respectively.

To change the format of merge fields, select the merge field in the main document and then apply the desired formatting. Later in this project, you increase the font size of all characters in the body of the letter.

Using an IF Field to Conditionally Print Text in a Form Letter

In addition to merge fields, you can insert Word fields that are designed specifically for a mail merge. An **IF field** is an example of a Word field. One form of the IF field is called an **If...Then:** If a condition is true, then perform an action. For example, If Mary owns a house, then send her information about homeowner's insurance. Another form of the IF field is called an **If...Then...Else:** If a condition is true, then perform an action; else perform a different action. For example, If John has an e-mail address, then send him an e-mail message; else send him the message via the postal service.

In this project, the form letter checks the vacationer's site type. If the site type is tent, then the required deposit is $11.00; else if the site type is water and electric, then the required deposit is $23.50. Thus, you will use an If...Then...Else: If the site type is equal to tent, then print $11.00 on the form letter, else print $23.50.

The phrase that appears after the word If is called a condition. A **condition** consists of an expression, followed by a comparison operator, followed by a final expression.

EXPRESSION The expression in a condition can be a merge field, a number, a series of characters, or a mathematical formula. Word surrounds a series of characters with quotation marks ("). To indicate an empty, or null, expression, Word places two quotation marks together (" ").

COMPARISON OPERATOR The comparison operator in a condition must be one of six characters: = (equal to or matches the text), <> (not equal to or does not match text), < (less than), <= (less than or equal to), > (greater than), >= (greater than or equal to).

If the result of a condition is true, then Word evaluates the **true text**. If the result of the condition is false, Word evaluates the **false text** if it exists. In this project, the first expression in the condition is a merge field (Site Type); the comparison operator is equal to (=); and the second expression is the text tent. The true text is "$11.00". The false text is "$23.50". The complete IF field is as follows:

Q&A

Q: What is an IF field?

A: The term, IF field, originates from computer programming. Do not be intimidated by the terminology. An IF field simply specifies a decision. Some programmers refer to it as an IF statement. An IF field can be simple or complex. Complex IF fields include one or more nested IF fields, which is a second IF field inside the true or false text of the first IF field.

If Site-Type = "tent"   "$11.00"   "$23.50"

       condition   true text   false text

The next steps show how to insert this IF field in the form letter.

To Insert an IF Field in the Main Document

1

• **With the insertion point positioned as shown in Figure 5-45 on page WD 325, press the SPACEBAR. Type** To guarantee your reservation, we must receive a deposit of **and then press the SPACEBAR.**

• **Click the Insert Word Field button on the Mail Merge toolbar.**

A list of Word fields that may be inserted in the main document is displayed (Figure 5-46).

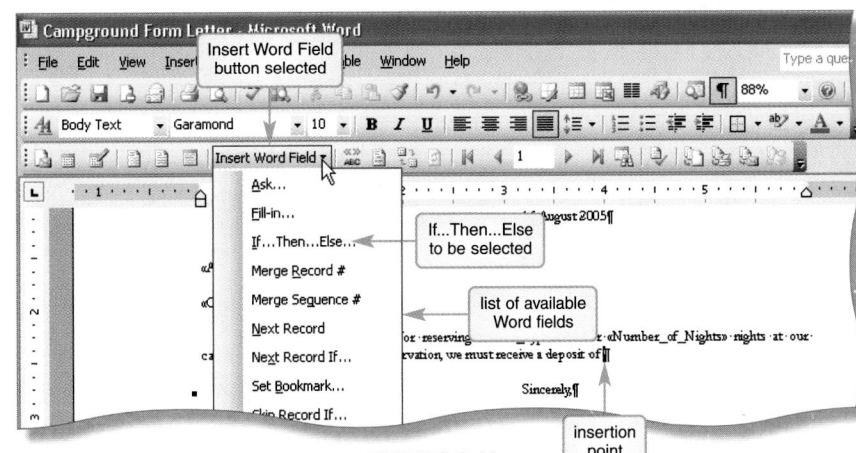

FIGURE 5-46

2

• **Click If...Then...Else in the list.**

Word displays the Insert Word Field: IF dialog box (Figure 5-47). You can specify the IF condition in the IF area of this dialog box.

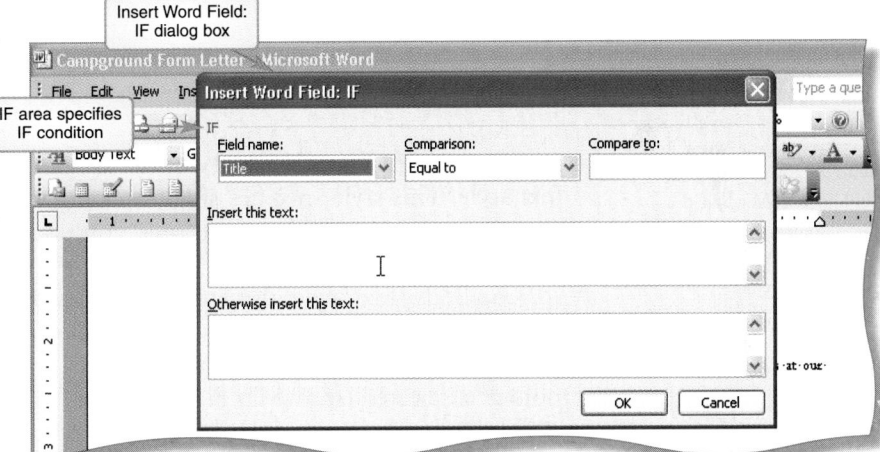

FIGURE 5-47

3

• **Click the Field name box arrow. Scroll through the list of fields and then click Site_Type.**

• **Click the Compare to text box. Type** tent **and then press the TAB key.**

• **Type** $11.00 **and then press the TAB key.**

• **Type** $23.50 **as the false text.**

The entries in the Insert Word Field: IF dialog box are complete (Figure 5-48).

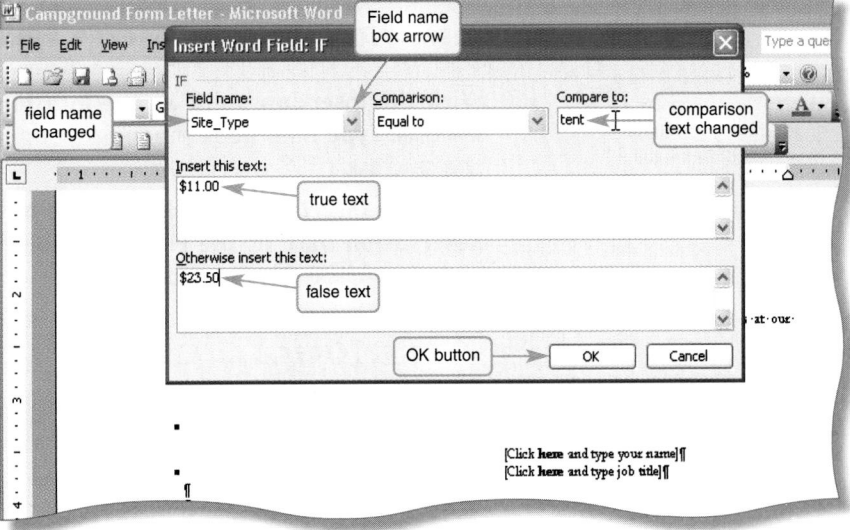

FIGURE 5-48

4

• **Click the OK button.**

Word displays $23.50 at the location of the insertion point in the main document because the first record in the data source has a site type of water and electric (Figure 5-49).

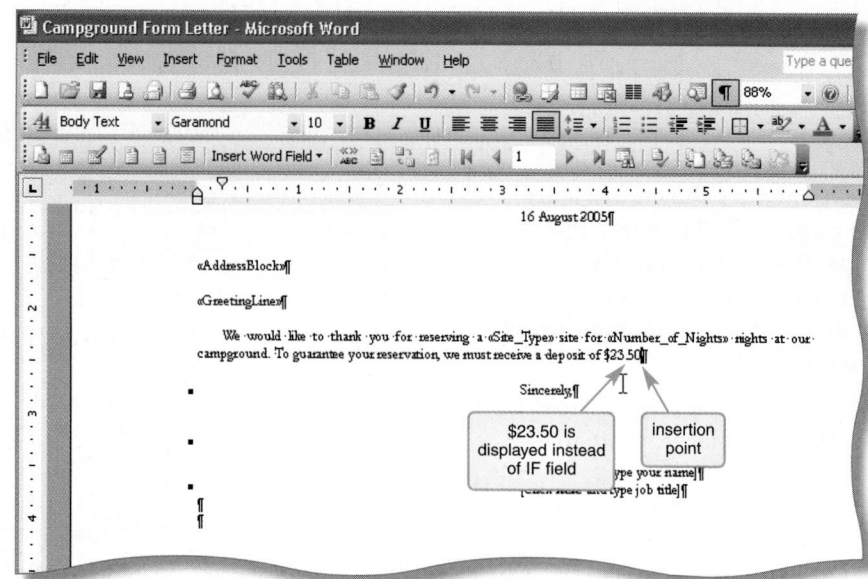

FIGURE 5-49

Other Ways

1. With Mail Merge toolbar displaying, in Voice Command mode, say "Insert Word Field, If...Then...Else, [enter condition], OK"

More About

Word Fields

In addition to the IF field, Word provides other fields that may be used in form letters. For example, the ASK and FILLIN fields prompt the user to enter data for each record in the data source. The SKIP RECORD IF field instructs the mail merge to not generate a form letter for a data record if a specific condition is met.

The paragraphs of the body of the Elegant Merge Letter template use the Body Text style. This style specifies single-spacing within paragraphs and double-spacing between paragraphs. Thus, each time you press the ENTER key, Word places a blank line between paragraphs.

The Body Text style also specifies to **justify** paragraphs, which means the left and right edges of the paragraphs are aligned with the left and right margins, respectively, like the edges of newspaper columns. Thus, the Justify button on the Formatting toolbar is selected (shown in Figure 5-50).

The following steps describe how to enter the remaining text in the current paragraph, which contains another merge field, and to enter another paragraph of text into the form letter.

To Enter More Text and Merge Fields

1 **With the insertion point at the location shown in Figure 5-49, press the SPACEBAR. Type** one week before your arrival date of **and then press the SPACEBAR.**

2 **Click the Insert Merge Fields button on the Mail Merge toolbar. Click Reservation Date in the Fields list. Click the Insert button in the dialog box and then click the Close button.**

3 **Press the SPACEBAR and then type** at the address shown at the bottom of this letter.

4 **Press the ENTER key.**

5 **Type** Our goal is to make your stay comfortable and enjoyable. The facilities and recreational activities at our campground continue to receive the highest ratings from *Camping Today* magazine. **Press the ENTER key.**

Word enters the text and merge field in the form letter (Figure 5-50).

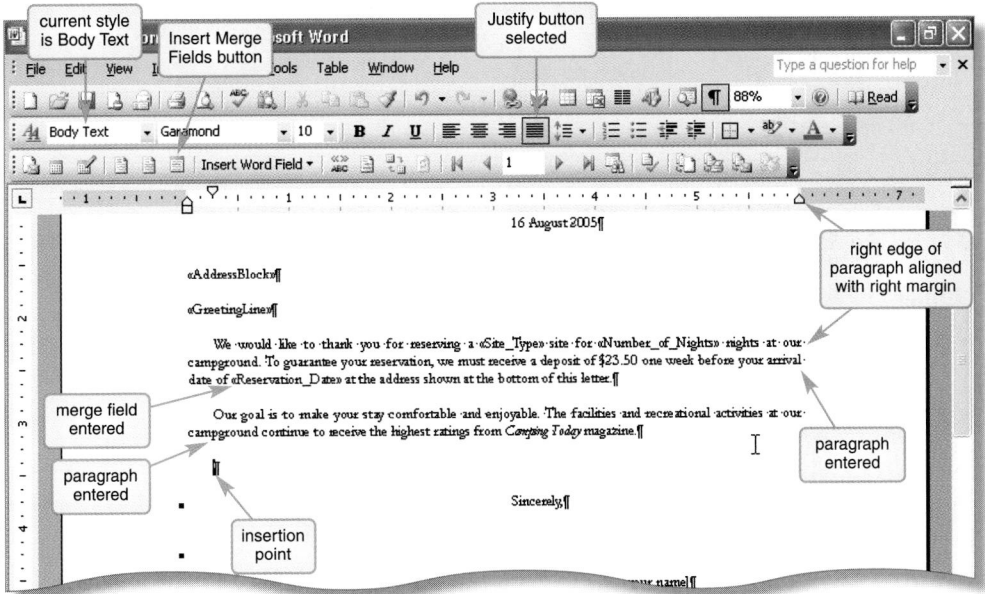

FIGURE 5-50

Creating an Outline Numbered List

The next step is to enter an outline numbered list in the form letter (shown in Figure 5-1a on page WD 299). An **outline numbered list** is a list that contains several levels of items, with each level displaying a different numeric, alphabetic, or bullet symbol.

To ensure that no existing formatting will affect the outline numbered list, the first step in creating the list is to clear formatting, which changes the paragraph from the Body Text style to the Normal style. The following steps show how to create an outline numbered list.

To Create an Outline Numbered List

1

• **If necessary, scroll down to display the insertion point in the document window.**

• **With the insertion point positioned as shown in Figure 5-50, click the Style box arrow on the Formatting toolbar and then click Clear Formatting.**

• **Click Format on the menu bar.**

Word clears formatting of the paragraph at the location of the insertion point (Figure 5-51). The Style box now displays Normal, instead of Body Text.

FIGURE 5-51

2

- Click **Bullets and Numbering** on the Format menu.

- When Word displays the Bullets and Numbering dialog box, if necessary, click the Outline Numbered tab.

- Click the desired number or bullet style in the list (Figure 5-52).

FIGURE 5-52

3

- Click the **OK button**.

- Type `Facilities` **and then press the ENTER key.**

*Word places the number one, 1), on the first item in the list (Figure 5-53). The number two, 2), is displayed on the next line. This list item needs to be **demoted** to a second-level list item, indented below the first list item.*

FIGURE 5-53

4

- **Press the TAB key to demote the current list item.**

- **Type** `Spotless restrooms and showers` **and then press the ENTER key.**

- **Type** `Two laundry rooms` **and then press the ENTER key.**

- **Type** `Groceries and snack bar` **and then press the ENTER key.**

- **Type** `Modem, telephone, and CATV hookup at each site` **and then press the ENTER key.**

The second level list items are entered (Figure 5-54). The letter e displays on the next line. This list item needs to be promoted to a first-level list item, aligned below the number one.

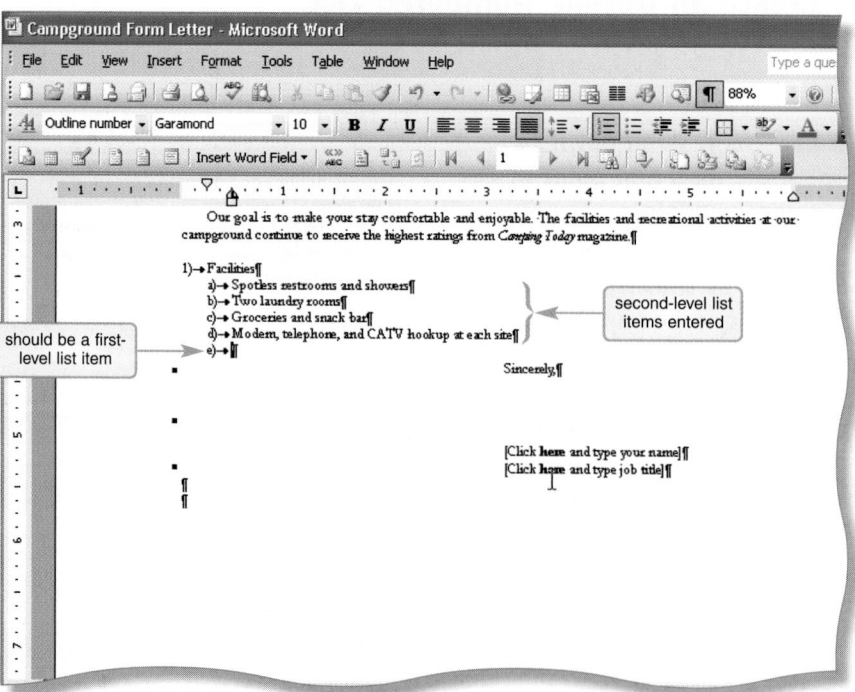

FIGURE 5-54

5

• **Press SHIFT+TAB to promote the current list item.**

• **Press CTRL+0 (the numeral zero) to add a blank line above the paragraph containing the number two list item.**

• **Type** Recreational Activities **and then press the ENTER key.**

• **Press the TAB key to demote the current list item.**

• **Press CTRL+0 (the numeral zero) to remove the blank line above the paragraph containing the letter a) list item.**

Recall that pressing CTRL+0 is a toggle that adds or removes a blank line above a paragraph (Figure 5-55).

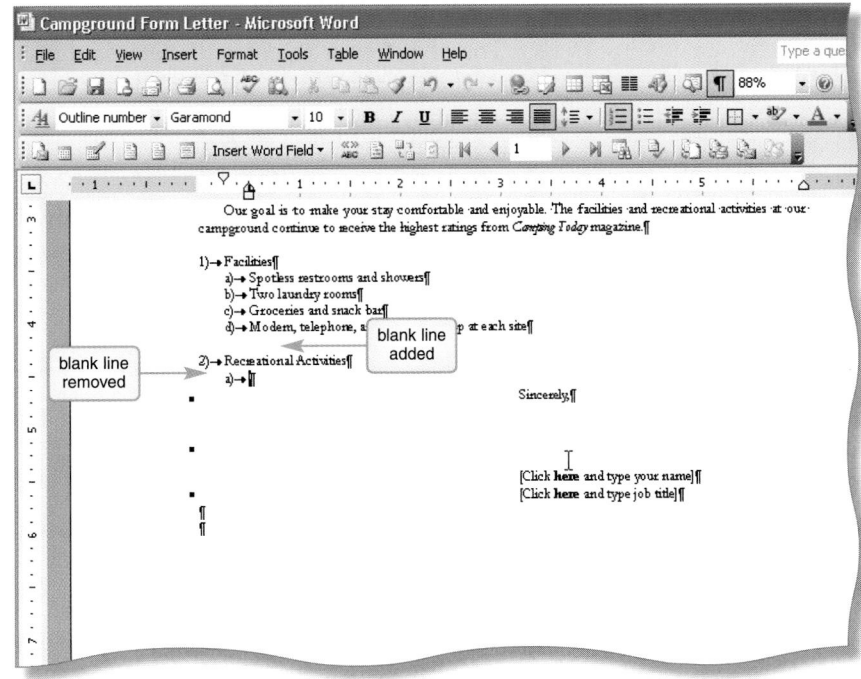

FIGURE 5-55

6

• **Type** Heated swimming pool **and then press the ENTER key.**

• **Type** Recreation hall and game room **and then press the ENTER key.**

• **Type** Freshwater fishing and boat rental **and then press the ENTER key.**

• **Type** Horseback riding **and then press the ENTER key twice.**

The outline numbered list is complete (Figure 5-56). Word removes the numbered list symbol from the current paragraph when you press the ENTER key twice at the end of a numbered or bulleted list.

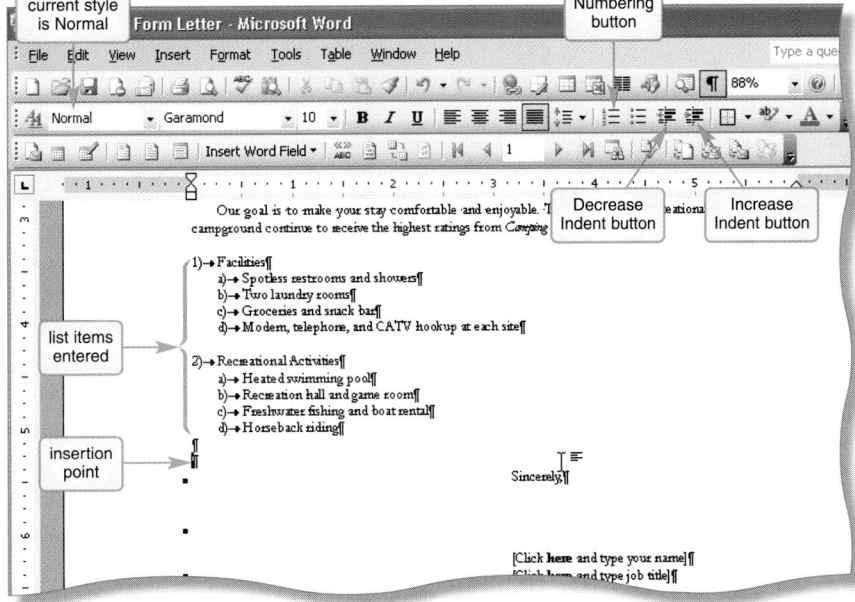

FIGURE 5-56

Instead of pressing the TAB key to demote a list item, you can click the Increase Indent button (Figure 5-56) on the Formatting toolbar. Likewise, you can click the Decrease Indent button on the Formatting toolbar to promote a list item – instead of pressing SHIFT+TAB.

As an alternative to pressing the ENTER key twice at the bottom of a list to stop Word from automatically numbering, you can click the Numbering button on the Formatting toolbar (Figure 5-56) to remove a number from a list item.

Other Ways

1. Right-click paragraph, click Bullets and Numbering on shortcut menu, click Outline Numbered tab, click numbering style, click OK button
2. In Voice Command mode, say "Format, Bullets and Numbering, Outline Numbered, [select numbering style], OK"

Applying a Paragraph Style

The next step is to enter the last paragraph of text into the body of the cover letter. The paragraphs in the cover letter use the Body Text style, which specifies spacing above and below the paragraph, first-line indents the paragraph, and justifies the text in the paragraph. The current paragraph is set to the Normal style because you cleared formatting before creating the outline numbered list.

The following steps show how to apply the Body Text paragraph style to the current paragraph.

To Apply a Paragraph Style

1

- **With the insertion point positioned two lines below the outline numbered list as shown in Figure 5-56 on the previous page, click the Style box arrow on the Formatting toolbar. If necessary, scroll until Body Text appears in the list.**

Word displays a list of styles associated with the current document (Figure 5-57).

2

- **Click Body Text.**

The entered paragraph will be formatted according to the Body Text paragraph style (shown in Figure 5-58).

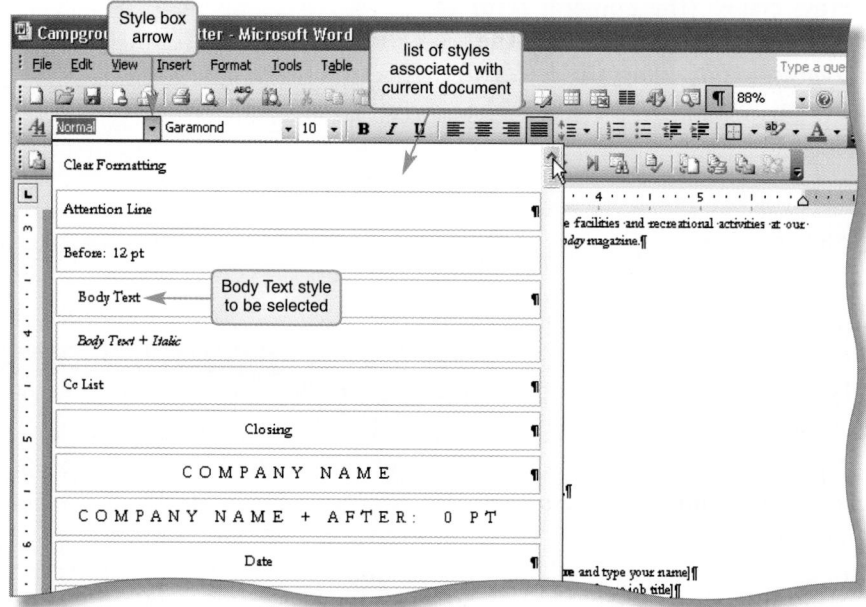

FIGURE 5-57

Other Ways

1. On Format menu click Styles and Formatting, click style name in Pick formatting to apply area
2. Click Styles and Formatting button on Formatting toolbar, click style name in Pick formatting to apply area
3. In Voice Command mode, say "Style, [select style]"

Many different styles are associated with a document. To view the complete list, click the Style box arrow on the Formatting toolbar or click the Styles and Formatting button on the Formatting toolbar (Figure 5-58) to display the Styles and Formatting task pane.

The following steps describe how to enter the text in the remainder of the letter.

To Enter More Text

1 **Type** We look forward to making your stay with us a memorable camping adventure.

2 **If necessary, scroll down to display the signature block. Click the placeholder text in the signature block, Click here and type your name, and then type** Tom and Deanna Rosatti **as the name.**

3 **Click the placeholder text in the signature block, Click here and type your job title, and then type** Owners **as the title.**

The body and signature block portions of the letter are complete (Figure 5-58).

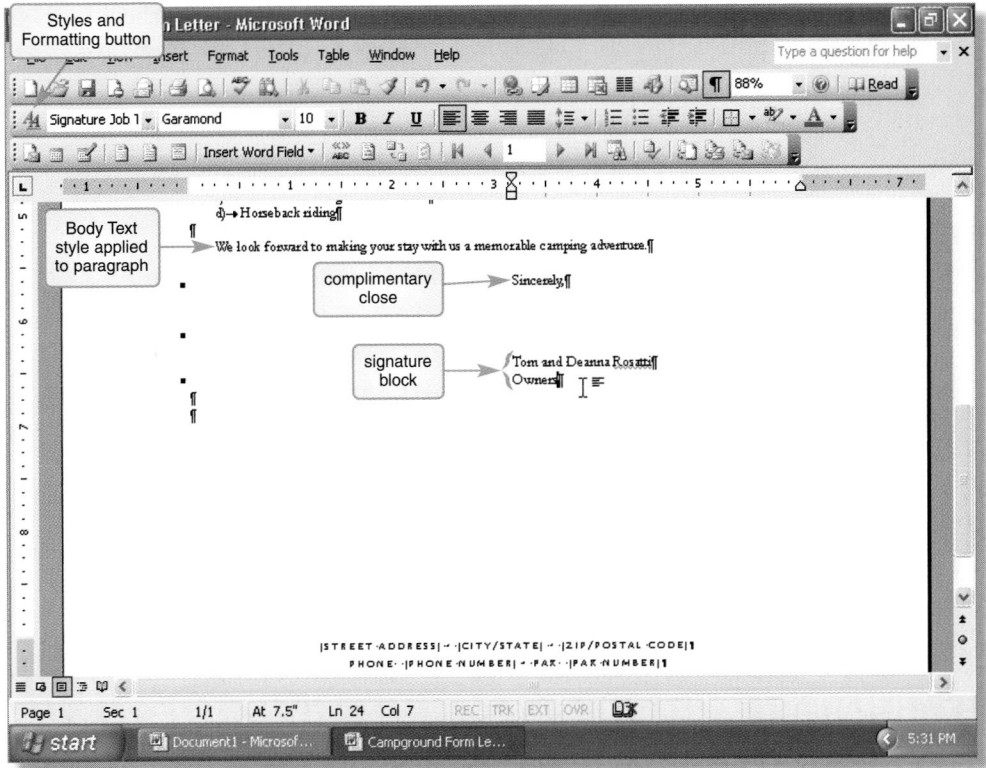

FIGURE 5-58

The return address at the bottom of the letter is formatted using the All Caps character effect (shown in Figure 5-5 on page WD 304). Thus, as you type characters, Word automatically converts them to capital letters. The following steps describe how to enter the return address at the bottom of the letter.

To Select and Replace More Placeholder Text

1 Scroll to the bottom of the letter to display the return address in the document window. Click the placeholder text, STREET ADDRESS. Type 13 KNOB ROAD and then click the placeholder text, CITY/STATE.

2 Type GETTYSBURG, PA and then click the placeholder text, ZIP/POSTAL CODE.

3 Type 17325 and then click the placeholder text, PHONE NUMBER.

4 Type 717-555-6543 and then click the placeholder text, FAX NUMBER.

5 Type 717-555-6544 as the fax number.

Word displays the return address at the bottom of the letter (Figure 5-59).

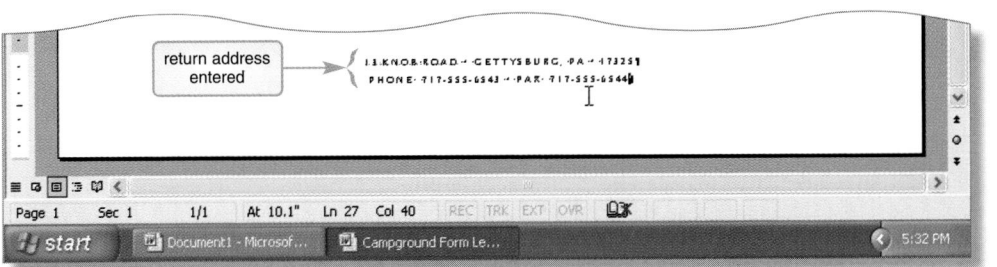

FIGURE 5-59

> **More About**
>
> ### Character Effects
>
> To apply other character effects, click Format on the menu bar, click Font, click the Font tab, click the desired effect in the Effects area, and then click the OK button.

More About

Locking Fields

If you wanted to lock a field so that its field results cannot be changed, click the field and then press CTRL+F11. To subsequently unlock a field so that it may be updated, click the field and then press CTRL+SHIFT+F11.

The next step is to change the font size of characters below the letterhead, including the return address, to 11 point. The following steps describe how to change the font size of characters in the form letter.

To Change the Font Size of Text

1 Click the Zoom box arrow on the Standard toolbar and then click Whole Page to display the entire form letter in the document window.

2 Drag from the date line down through the bottom of the letter to select all the text below the campground name.

3 Click the Font Size box arrow on the Formatting toolbar and then click 11 (Figure 5-60).

4 Click anywhere in the document to remove the selection.

5 Click the Zoom box arrow on the Standard toolbar and then click Page Width.

Word changes the font size to 11.

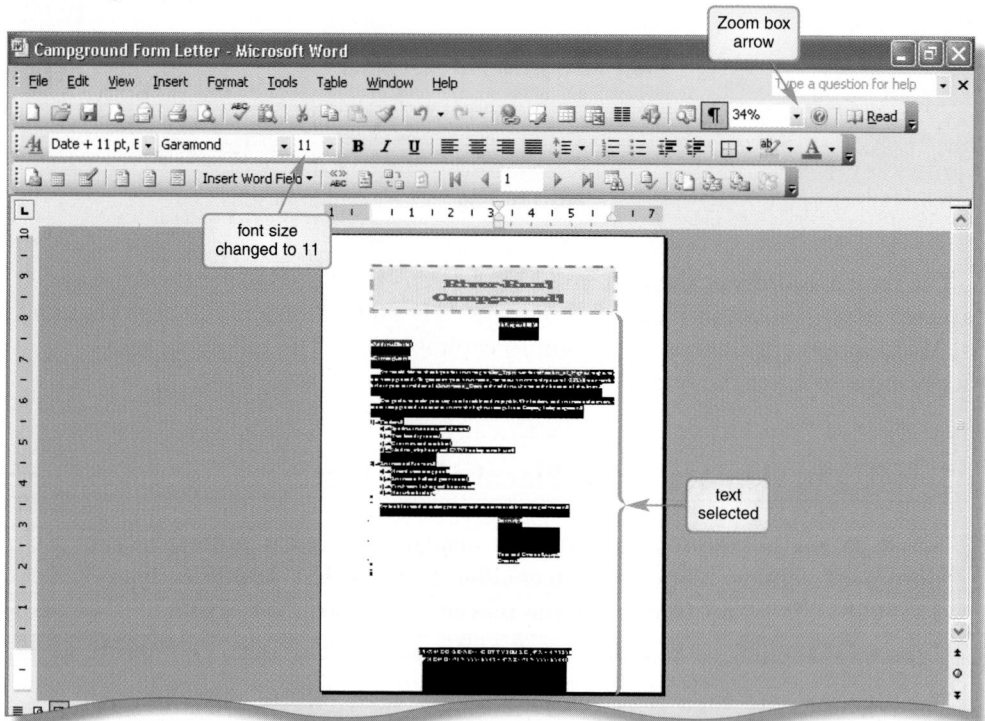

FIGURE 5-60

More About

Electronic Signatures

For more information about electronic signatures, visit the Word 2003 More About Web page (scsite.com/wd2003/more) and then click Electronic Signatures.

Saving the Document Again

The main document for the form letter now is complete. Thus, you should save it again, as described in the following step.

To Save a Document Again

1 Click the Save button on the Standard toolbar.

Word saves the main document for the form letter with the same name, Campground Form Letter, in the River Run folder.

Displaying Field Codes

The instructions in the IF field are not displayed in the document; instead, the field results are displayed. **Field results** represent the value to display after Word evaluates the instructions of the IF field. For example, Word displays the dollar amount, $23.50, in the document window (Figure 5-61) because the site type in the first data record is water and electric.

The instructions of an IF field are referred to as **field codes**, and the default for Word is field codes off. Thus, field codes do not print or show on the screen unless you turn them on. You use one procedure to show field codes on the screen and a different procedure to print them on a hard copy.

The following steps illustrate how to turn on a field code so you can see it on the screen. Most Word users turn on a field code only to verify its accuracy or to modify it. Field codes tend to clutter the screen. Thus, you should turn them off after viewing them.

More About

Main Documents

When you open a main document, Word attempts to open the associated data source file, too. If the data source is not in exactly the same location (i.e., drive and folder) as when it originally was saved, Word displays a dialog box indicating that it could not find the data source. When this occurs, click the Find Data Source button to display the Open Data Source dialog box, where you can locate the data source file.

To Display a Field Code

1

- **Scroll to and then right-click the dollar amount, $23.50.**

Word displays a shortcut menu (Figure 5-61).

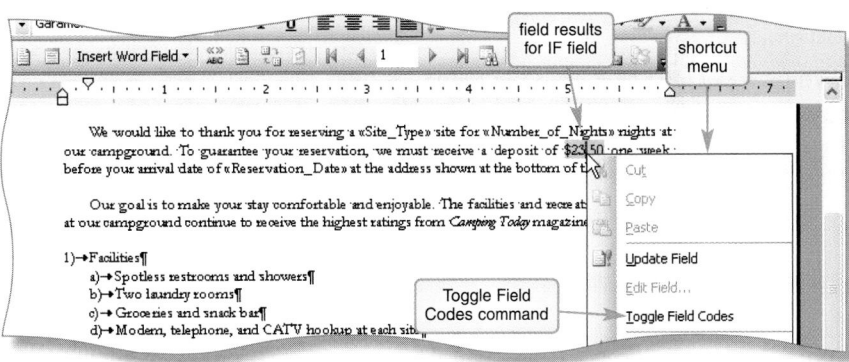

FIGURE 5-61

2

- **Click Toggle Field Codes on the shortcut menu.**

Word displays the field code instead of the field results, which means the instructions in the IF field are displayed (Figure 5-62). With field codes on, braces surround a field instead of chevrons.

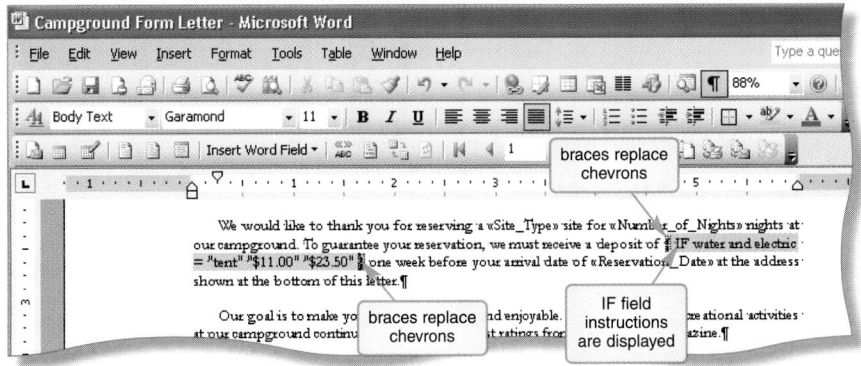

FIGURE 5-62

Other Ways

1. With insertion point in field, press SHIFT+F9
2. With insertion point in field, in Voice Command mode, say "Right-Click, Toggle Field Codes"

If you wanted all field codes in a document to be displayed on the screen, you would press **ALT+F9**. Then, to hide all the field codes, press ALT+F9 again.

Whether field codes are on or off on your screen has no effect on the merge process.

Printing Field Codes

When you merge or print a document, Word automatically converts field codes that show on the screen to field results. You may want to print the field codes version of the form letter, however, so you have a hard copy of the field codes for future reference. When you print field codes, you must remember to turn off the field codes option so that future documents print field results instead of field codes. For example, with field codes on, merged form letters will display field codes instead of data.

The following steps show how to print the field codes in the main document and then turn off the field codes print option for future printing.

To Print Field Codes in the Main Document

1

• **Click File on the menu bar and then click Print.**

• **When Word displays the Print dialog box, click the Options button.**

• **When Word displays another Print dialog box, place a check mark in the Field codes check box.**

Word displays a Print dialog box within another Print dialog box (Figure 5-63). The Field codes check box is selected.

FIGURE 5-63

2

• **Click the OK button.**

• **Click the OK button in the remaining Print dialog box.**

Word prints the main document with all field codes showing (Figure 5-64). Notice the contents of the letter are cluttered with many fields. Your printout also may show the banner at the top.

3

• **Click Tools on the menu bar and then click Options.**

• **When Word displays the Options dialog box, if necessary, click the Print tab.**

• **Click Field codes in the Include with document area to remove the check mark.**

• **Click the OK button.**

Word turns off field codes for printed documents.

field codes show on hard copy

{ SHAPE * MERGEFORMAT }

instructions in AddressBlock field

instructions in Date field → { DATE \@ "d MMMM yyyy" }

{ ADDRESSBLOCK \f "<<_TITLE0_ >><<_FIRST0_>><< _MIDDLE0_>><< _LAST0_>><< _SUFFIX0_>>
<<_COMPANY_ >><<_STREET1_ >><<_STREET2_ >><<_CITY_>><<, _STATE_>><< _POSTAL_>>" \l 1033 \c 0 \e "" }

MERGEFIELD precedes a merge field name

{ GREETINGLINE \f "<<_BEFORE_ Dear >><<_TITLE0_>><< _LAST0_>><<_AFTER_ :>>" \l 1033 \e "Dear Sir or Madam:" }

instructions in GreetingLine field

We would like to thank you for reserving a { MERGEFIELD "Site_Type" } site for { MERGEFIELD "Number_of_Nights" } nights at our campground. To guarantee your reservation, we must receive a deposit of { IF { MERGEFIELD Site_Type } = "tent" "$11.00" "$23.50" } one week before your arrival date of { MERGEFIELD "Reservation_Date" } at the address shown at the bottom of this letter.

Our goal is to make your stay comfortable and enjoyable. The facilities and recreational activities at our campground cont[ ]e highest ratings from *Camping Today* magazine.

instructions in IF field

1) Facilities
    a) Spotless restrooms and showers
    b) Two laundry rooms
    c) Groceries and snack bar
    d) Modem, telephone, and CATV hookup at each site

2) Recreational Activities
    a) Heated swimming pool
    b) Recreation hall and game room
    c) Freshwater fishing and boat rental
    d) Horseback riding

We look forward to making your stay with us a memorable camping adventure.

{ AUTOTEXTLIST }

Tom and Deanna Rosatti
Owners

13 KNOB ROAD • GETTYSBURG, PA • 17325
PHONE: 717-555-6543 • FAX: 717-555-6544

FIGURE 5-64

Other Ways

1. On Tools menu click Options, click Print tab, click Field codes, click OK button, click Print button on Standard toolbar
2. In Voice Command mode, say "File, Print, Options, Field codes, OK, OK"

Merging the Documents and Printing the Letters

The data source and main document for the form letter are complete. The next step is to merge them to generate the individual form letters. The following steps show how to merge form letters, sending the merged letters to the printer.

To Merge the Form Letters to the Printer

1

• **Click the Merge to Printer button on the Mail Merge toolbar.**

• **When Word displays the Merge to Printer dialog box, if necessary, click All to select it.**

In the Merge to Printer dialog box, you indicate which data records should be merged (Figure 5-65).

2

• **Click the OK button.**

• **When Word displays the Print dialog box, click the OK button.**

• **If Word displays a message about locked fields, click the OK button whenever the dialog box appears.**

Word prints five separate letters, one for each vacationer in the data source (shown in Figure 5-1c on page WD 299).

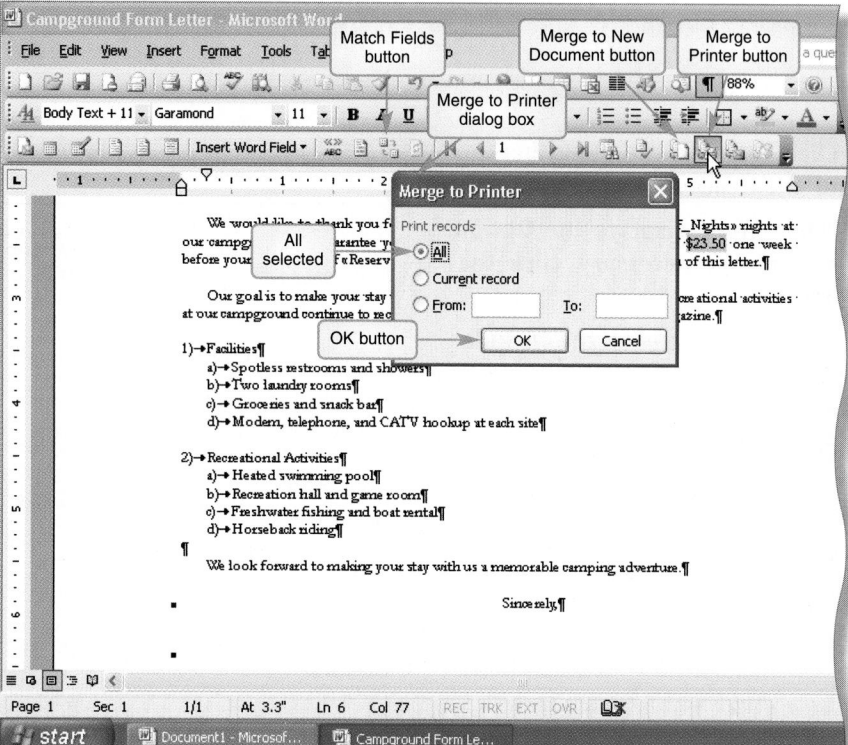

FIGURE 5-65

The contents of the data source merge with the merge fields in the main document to generate the form letters. Word prints five form letters because the data source contains five records. The address lines suppress blanks. That is, vacationers without a second address line begin the city on the line immediately below the first address line. In addition, the deposit amount in each letter varies – depending on the type of campsite reserved.

If you notice errors in the printed form letters, edit the main document the same way you edit any other document. Then, save the changes and merge again. If the wrong field results print, Word may be mapping the fields incorrectly. To view fields, click the Match Fields button on the Mail Merge toolbar (Figure 5-65). Then, review the list of fields in the list. For example, the Last Name should map to the Last Name field in the data source. If it does not, click the box arrow to change the name of the data source field.

Instead of immediately printing the merged form letters, you could send them into a new document window by clicking the Merge to New Document button on the Mail Merge toolbar (shown in Figure 5-65). With this button, you view the merged form letters in a new document window on the screen to verify their accuracy before printing the letters. When you are finished viewing the merged form letters, you can print them by clicking the Print button on the Standard toolbar. In addition, you can save these merged form letters in a file. If you do not want to save the merged form letters, close the document window by clicking the Close button at the right edge of the menu bar. When the Microsoft Word dialog box is displayed asking if you want to save the document, click the No button.

Selecting Data Records to Merge and Print

Instead of merging and printing all of the records in the data source, you can choose which records will merge, based on a condition you specify. The dialog box in Figure 5-65 allows you to specify by record number which records to merge. Often you merge based on the contents of a specific field. For example, you may want to merge and print only those vacationers in the mailing list who are arriving on September 10.

The following steps show how to select records for a merge.

To Select Records to Merge

1

• **Click the Mail Merge Recipients button on the Mail Merge toolbar.**

Word displays the Mail Merge Recipients dialog box (Figure 5-66). You must scroll to the right to display the Reservation Date field in this dialog box.

FIGURE 5-66

• **Drag the scroll box to the right edge of the scroll bar in the Mail Merge Recipients dialog box.**

• **Click the arrow to the left of the field name, Reservation Date.**

Word displays a list of selection criteria for the Reservation Date field (Figure 5-67).

• **Click September 10.**

Word reduces the number of data records that is displayed in the Mail Merge Recipients dialog box to two, because two vacationers have a reservation date of September 10.

FIGURE 5-67

The next step is to merge the selected records. To do this, you follow the same steps described earlier. The difference is that Word will merge only those records that meet the criteria just specified, that is, those with a reservation date of September 10.

To Merge the Form Letters to the Printer

1 **Click the Merge to Printer button on the Mail Merge toolbar.**

2 **When Word displays the Merge to Printer dialog box, if necessary, click All.**

3 **Click the OK button.**

4 **When Word displays the Print dialog box, click the OK button.**

5 **If Word displays a message about locked fields, click the OK button whenever the dialog box appears.**

Word prints the form letters that match the specified condition: Reservation Date equal to September 10 (Figure 5-68). Two form letters print because two vacationers have a reservation date of September 10.

River Run Campground

16 August 2005

Ms. Shannon Murray
33099 Clark Street
Apt. D
Maple Park, IL 60151

Dear Ms. Murray:

We would like to thank you for reserving a tent site for three nights at our campground. To guarantee your reservation, we must receive a deposit of $11.00 one week before your arrival date of September 10 at the address shown at the bottom of this letter.

Our goal is to make your stay comfortable and enjoyable. The facilities and recreational activities at our campground continue to receive the highest ratings from *Camping Today* magazine.

[vacationer with reservation date of September 10]

ities
potless restrooms and showers
Two laundry rooms
Groceries and snack bar
d) Modem, telephone, and CATV hookup at each

2) Recreational Activities
a) Heated swimming pool
b) Recreation hall and game room
c) Freshwater fishing and boat rental
d) Horseback riding

We look forward to making your stay with us a mem

Sir

To
O

13 KNOB ROAD • GETTY
PHONE: 717-555-6543 •

River Run Campground

16 August 2005

Mr. Tyrone Davis
P.O. Box 45
4430 Fifth Avenue
Dover, FL 33527

Dear Mr. Davis:

We would like to thank you for reserving a water and electric site for four nights at our campground. To guarantee your reservation, we must receive a deposit of $23.50 one week before your arrival date of September 10 at the address shown at the bottom of this letter.

Our goal is to make your stay comfortable and enjoyable. The facilities and recreational activities at our campground continue to receive the highest ratings from *Camping Today* magazine.

1) [vacationer with reservation date of September 10]

and showers

c) Groceries and snack bar
d) Modem, telephone, and CATV hookup at each site

2) Recreational Activities
a) Heated swimming pool
b) Recreation hall and game room
and boat rental

FIGURE 5-68

More About

Date Fields

The template used in this project contained a date field. To insert a date and/or time field into a Word document, click Insert on the menu bar, click Date and Time, select the desired date and/or time format, place a check mark in the Update automatically check box, and then click the OK button.

You should remove the merge condition so that future merges will not be restricted to vacationers with a September 10 reservation date.

To Remove a Merge Condition

1 Click the Mail Merge Recipients button on the Mail Merge toolbar.

2 Scroll to the right of the dialog box and then click the arrow to the left of the field name, Reservation Date. Click (All) in the list.

3 Click the OK button.

Word removes the specified condition.

In addition to selecting records based on values in a field, Word provides other choices by which you can select the data records (Figure 5-67 on page WD 340). The (Blanks) option selects records that contain blanks in that field, and the (Nonblanks) option selects records that do not contain blanks in that field. The (Advanced) option displays the Filter and Sort dialog box, which allows you to perform more advanced record selection operations.

Sorting Data Records to Merge and Print

If you mail the form letters using the U.S. Postal Service's bulk rate mailing service, the post office requires you to sort and group the form letters by ZIP code. Thus, the following steps show how to sort the data records by ZIP code.

To Sort the Data Records in a Data Source

1

• **Click the Mail Merge Recipients button on the Mail Merge toolbar.**

• **When Word displays the Mail Merge Recipients dialog box, scroll to the right until the ZIP Code field shows in the dialog box (Figure 5-69).**

• **Position the mouse pointer on the ZIP Code field name.**

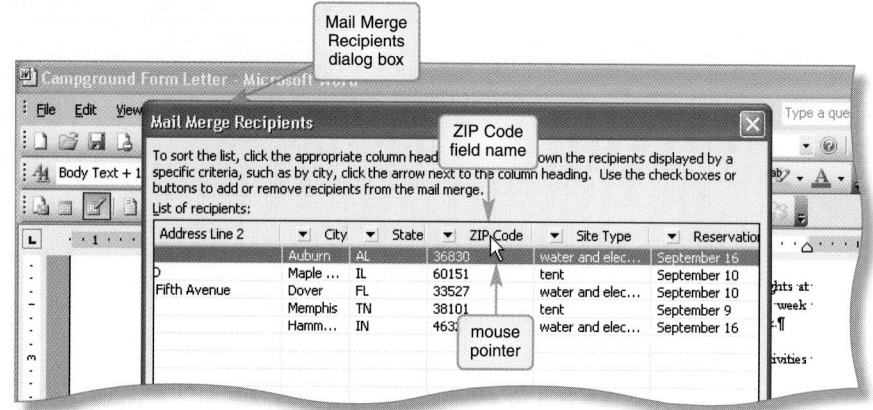

FIGURE 5-69

2

• **Click the ZIP Code field name.**

• **If necessary, scroll to the right to display the ZIP Code field again.**

The data records are sorted in ZIP code order (Figure 5-70). Future merged documents will print in ZIP code order.

3

• **Click the OK button in the Mail Merge Recipients dialog box.**

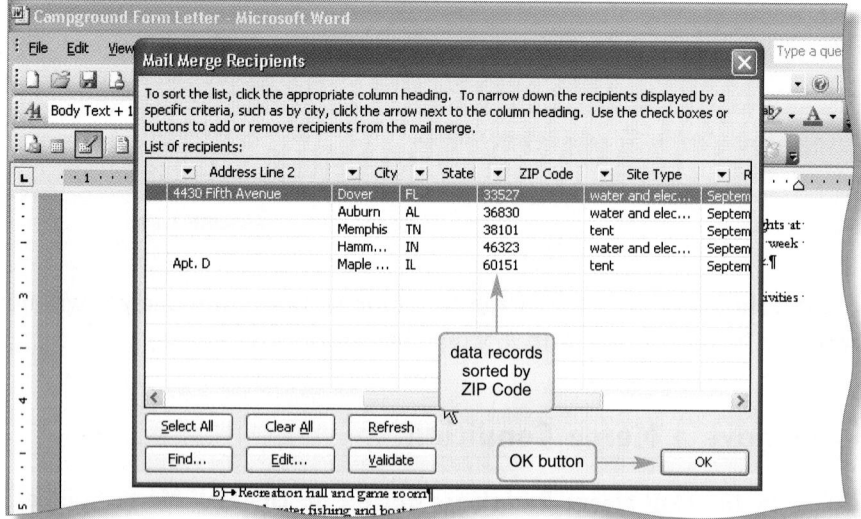

FIGURE 5-70

If you chose to merge the form letters again at this point, Word would print them in ZIP code order; that is, Tyrone Davis's letter would print first and Shannon Murray's letter would print last.

Viewing Merged Data

You can verify the order of the data records without printing them by using the **View Merged Data button** on the Mail Merge toolbar, as shown in the following steps.

To View Merged Data in the Main Document

1

• **If necessary, scroll up to display the AddressBlock merge field in the document window.**

• **Click the View Merged Data button on the Mail Merge toolbar.**

Word displays the contents of the first data record in the main document, instead of the merge fields (Figure 5-71). The View Merged Data button is selected.

2

• **Click the View Merged Data button on the Mail Merge toolbar again.**

Word displays the merge fields in the main document, instead of the field values.

FIGURE 5-71

When you are viewing merged data in the main document (the View Merged Data button is selected), you can click the **Last Record button** (Figure 5-71) on the Mail Merge toolbar to display the values from the last record in the data source, the **First Record button** to display the values in record one, the **Next Record button** to display the values in the next consecutive record number, or the **Previous Record button** to display the values from the previous record number. You also can display a specific record by clicking the **Go to Record text box**, typing the record number you would like to be displayed in the main document, and then pressing the ENTER key.

The campground form letter is complete. Thus, the next step is to close the document as described below.

To Close a Document

1 Click File on the menu bar and then click Close.

2 When the Microsoft Office Word dialog box is displayed, click the Yes button to save the changes.

Word saves the Campground Form Letter in the River Run folder on a disk in drive A.

Renaming a Folder

After reviewing folder names on a disk, you may decide to change a folder name. For example, you may want to change the folder name from River Run to Campground. Rather than renaming the folder in Windows, you can rename a folder through the Open, Save As, and Insert File dialog boxes in Word.

To rename a folder, you must be sure the folder is not in use. That is, all documents must be closed that are in the folder. The following steps show how to use the Open dialog box to rename the River Run folder.

To Rename a Folder in Word

• **With the floppy disk containing the River Run folder in drive A, click the Open button on the Standard toolbar.**

• **When Word displays the Open dialog box, if necessary, click the Look in box arrow and then click 3½ Floppy (A:).**

• **If necessary, click the Up One Level button to display the River Run folder in the Name list.**

• **Right-click the River Run folder.**

Word displays a shortcut menu (Figure 5-72).

FIGURE 5-72

• **Click Rename on the shortcut menu.**

• **Type** Campground **as the new folder name (Figure 5-73).**

3

• **Press the ENTER key.**

• **Click the Cancel button in the dialog box.**

Word changes the name of the folder on the disk in drive A from River Run to Campground.

Other Ways

1. Select folder and then press F2
2. In Voice Command mode, say "Right-Click, Rename"

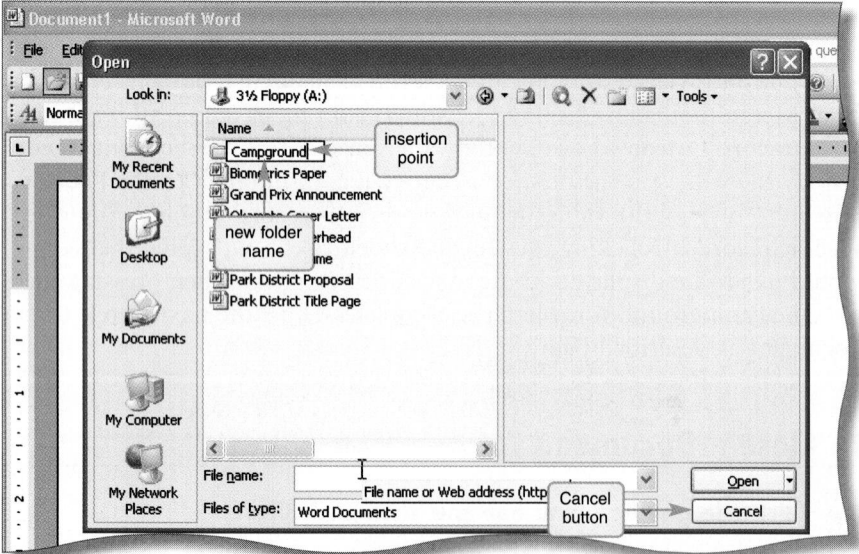

FIGURE 5-73

If a file in the folder is in use when you attempt to rename the folder, Word will display a dialog box indicating you cannot rename the folder at this time. If this occurs, simply close the open document and try to rename the folder again.

Addressing and Printing Mailing Labels

Now that you have merged and printed the form letters, the next step is to print addresses on mailing labels to be affixed to envelopes for the form letters. The mailing labels will use the same data source as the form letter, Camper List. The format and content of the mailing labels will be exactly the same as the inside address in the main document for the form letter. That is, the first line will contain the vacationer's title and first name followed by the last name. The second line will contain his or her street address, and so on. Thus, you will use the AddressBlock merge field in the mailing labels.

You follow the same basic steps to create the main document for the mailing labels as you did to create the main document for the form letters. The major difference is that the data source already exists because you created it earlier in this project.

To address mailing labels, you specify the type of labels you intend to use. Word will request the manufacturer's name, as well as a product number and name. You can obtain this information from the box of labels. For illustration purposes in addressing these labels, the manufacturer is Avery, and the product name is address labels, which has a product number of 5160.

The following steps illustrate how to address and print these mailing labels using an existing data source.

More About

Mailing Labels

Instead of addressing mailing labels from a data source, you can print a label(s) for a single address. Click Tools on the menu bar, point to Letters and Mailings, click Envelopes and Labels, click the Labels tab, type the name and address in the Address text box, click the Options button and select the label type, click the OK button, and then click the Print button in the Envelopes and Labels dialog box.

To Address and Print Mailing Labels Using an Existing Data Source

1

• **If necessary, open a new blank document.**

• **Click Tools on the menu bar, point to Letters and Mailings, and then click Mail Merge.**

• **When Word displays the Mail Merge task pane, click Labels in the Select document type area.**

Word displays Step 1 of the mail merge process in the Mail Merge task pane (Figure 5-74). In Step 1, you select a main document type.

FIGURE 5-74

2

• **Click the Next: Starting document link.**

• **In the Mail Merge task pane, click the Label options link.**

• **When Word displays the Label Options dialog box, click the desired Avery product number in the Product number list (in this case, 5160 - Address).**

Step 2 of the mail merge process allows you to specify the label product information (Figure 5-75). If you have a dot matrix printer, your printer information will differ from this figure. The Product number list displays the product numbers for Avery mailing labels compatible with your printer.

FIGURE 5-75

3

• **Click the OK button in the Label Options dialog box.**

Word displays the selected label layout in the main document (Figure 5-76). The next step is to select the data source. You will open and use the same data source you created for the form letters.

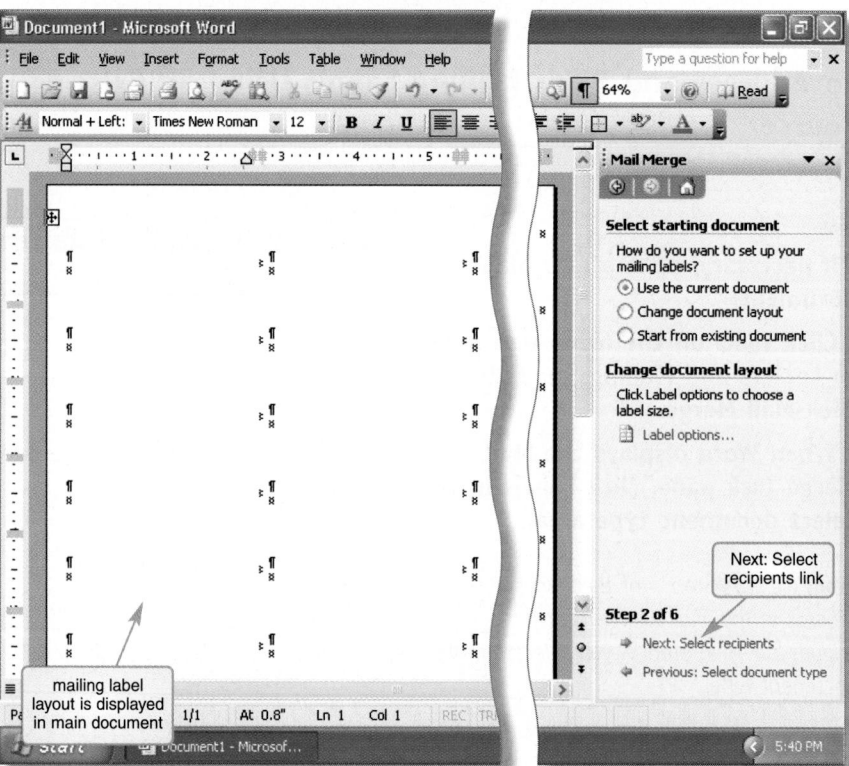

FIGURE 5-76

4

• **In the Mail Merge task pane, click the Next: Select recipients link (Figure 5-76) to display the next step of the mail merge process.**

• **In the Select recipients area, if necessary, click Use an existing list.**

• **In the Use an existing list area, click the Browse link.**

• **When Word displays the Select Data Source dialog box, if necessary, click the Look in box arrow, click 3½ Floppy (A:), and then double-click the Campground folder.**

• **Click the file name, Camper List.**

In the Select Data Source dialog box, you select the existing data source, Camper List, to address the mailing labels (Figure 5-77).

FIGURE 5-77

5

• **Click the Open button in the Select Data Source dialog box.**

Word displays the Mail Merge Recipients dialog box (Figure 5-78).

FIGURE 5-78

• **Click the OK button in the Mail Merge Recipients dialog box.**

• **At the bottom of the Mail Merge task pane, click the Next: Arrange your labels link (Figure 5-78 on the previous page).**

• **In the Mail Merge task pane, in the Arrange your labels area, click the Address block link.**

Word displays the Insert Address Block dialog box (Figure 5-79). Word automatically matches fields and suppresses blank lines. Thus, the address information will print according to the data in the data source.

7

• **Click the OK button.**

The next step is to copy the layout of the first label to the rest of the labels in the main document.

FIGURE 5-79

8

• **Point to the down arrow at the bottom of the Mail Merge task pane (Figure 5-79) to scroll to the bottom of the task pane.**

• **Click the Update all labels button.**

Word copies the layout of the first label to the remaining label layouts in the main document (Figure 5-80).

FIGURE 5-80

9

• **Click the Next: Preview your labels link at the bottom of the Mail Merge task pane.**

Word displays a preview of the mailing labels in the document window (Figure 5-81).

FIGURE 5-81

10

• **Click the Next: Complete the merge link at the bottom of the Mail Merge task pane.**

• **In the Mail Merge task pane, in the Merge area, click the Print link.**

• **If necessary, insert a sheet of blank mailing labels into the printer.**

• **When Word displays the Merge to Printer dialog box, if necessary, click All (Figure 5-82).**

• **Click the OK button.**

• **When the Print dialog box is displayed, click the OK button.**

The mailing labels print.

FIGURE 5-82

11

• **Retrieve the mailing labels from the printer (Figure 5-83).**

• **Click the Close button at the right edge of the Mail Merge task pane.**

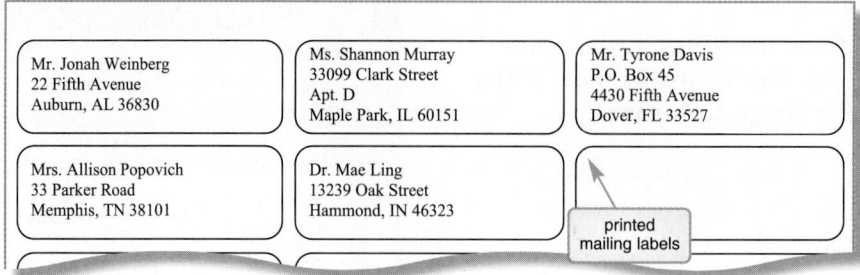

Mr. Jonah Weinberg
22 Fifth Avenue
Auburn, AL 36830

Ms. Shannon Murray
33099 Clark Street
Apt. D
Maple Park, IL 60151

Mr. Tyrone Davis
P.O. Box 45
4430 Fifth Avenue
Dover, FL 33527

Mrs. Allison Popovich
33 Parker Road
Memphis, TN 38101

Dr. Mae Ling
13239 Oak Street
Hammond, IN 46323

printed
mailing labels

FIGURE 5-83

Mailing Label Bar Codes

If your printer can print graphics, you can add a POSTNET (POSTal Numeric Encoding Technique) delivery-point bar code, usually referred to simply as a bar code, below the address on each mailing label or envelope. Using a bar code speeds up delivery by the U.S. Postal Service. The POSTNET bar code represents the addressee's ZIP code and first street address. To insert a bar code, click the Postal bar code link in the Mail Merge task pane (shown in Figure 5-79 on page WD 348).

As an alternative to using the Mail Merge task pane, you can use the buttons on the Mail Merge toolbar for the entire mailing label mail merge. Click the Main document setup button (Figure 5-38 on page WD 321) and then click Labels in the dialog box. Click the Open Data Source button to display the Select Data Source dialog box. Click the Insert Address Block button to display the Insert Address Block dialog box. Click the Propagate Labels button to copy the layout of the first label to the remaining labels in the main document. Click the Merge to Printer button to merge and print the mailing labels.

Saving the Mailing Labels

The following steps describe how to save the mailing labels.

To Save the Mailing Labels

1 **If necessary, insert your floppy disk into drive A.**

2 **Click the Save button on the Standard toolbar.**

3 **Type the file name** Campground Labels **in the File name box. Do not press the ENTER key after typing the file name.**

4 **If necessary, click the Save in box arrow, click 3½ Floppy (A:), and then double-click the Campground folder.**

5 **Click the Save button in the Save As dialog box.**

Word saves the document with the file name, Campground Labels, in the Campground folder on the floppy disk in drive A.

Addressing and Printing Envelopes

Instead of addressing mailing labels to affix to envelopes, your printer may have the capability of printing directly onto envelopes. To print the label information directly on envelopes, follow the same basic steps as you did to address the mailing labels. The next steps describe how to address envelopes using an existing data source.

Note: If your printer does not have the capability of printing envelopes, skip these steps and proceed to the next section titled, Merging All Data Records to a Directory. If you are in a laboratory environment, ask your instructor if you should perform these steps or skip them.

To Address and Print Envelopes Using an Existing Data Source

1 Click the New Blank Document button on the Standard toolbar. Click Tools on the menu bar, point to Letters and Mailings, and then click Mail Merge.

2 In the Mail Merge task pane, in the Select document type area, click Envelopes. Click the Next: Starting document link.

3 In the Mail Merge task pane, click the Envelope options link. When Word displays the Envelope Options dialog box, select the envelope size and then click the OK button to create the envelope layout as the main document.

4 If your envelope does not have a pre-printed return address, position the insertion point in the upper-left corner of the envelope layout and then type a return address.

5 Click the paragraph mark in the middle of the envelope layout (Figure 5-84). Click the Next: Select recipients link at the bottom of the Mail Merge task pane.

6 In the Mail Merge task pane, in the Select recipients area, if necessary, click Use an existing list. In the Use an existing list area, click the Browse link. When Word displays the Select Data Source dialog box, if necessary, click the Look in box arrow, click 3½ Floppy (A:), and then double-click the Campground folder. Click the file name, Camper List. Click the Open button in the Select Data Source dialog box. Click the OK button in the Mail Merge Recipients dialog box. At the bottom of the Mail Merge task pane, click the Next: Arrange your envelope link.

7 In the Mail Merge task pane, in the Arrange your envelope area, click the Address block link. When Word displays the Insert Address Block dialog box, click the OK button.

8 Click the Next: Preview your envelopes link at the bottom of the Mail Merge task pane. Click the Next: Complete the merge link at the bottom of the Mail Merge task pane. In the Mail Merge task pane, in the Merge area, click the Print link. If necessary, insert blank envelopes into the printer. When Word displays the Merge to Printer dialog box, if necessary, click All. Click the OK button. When the Print dialog box displays, click the OK button to print the envelopes. Click the Close button in the Mail Merge task pane.

More About

Data Sources

Word initially looks in the My Data Sources folder for a data source when it displays the Select Data Source dialog box. To find a data source in a different location, click the Look in box arrow, locate the file, and then click the Open button in the dialog box.

FIGURE 5-84

As an alternative to using the Mail Merge task pane, you can use the buttons on the Mail Merge toolbar for the entire envelope mail merge. Click the Main document setup button (Figure 5-38 on page WD 321) and then click Envelopes in the dialog box. Click the Open Data Source button to display the Select Data Source dialog box. Click the Insert Address Block button to display the Insert Address Block dialog box. Click the Merge to Printer button to merge and print the mailing labels.

The following steps describe how to save the envelopes.

To Save the Envelope

1 **If necessary, insert your floppy disk into drive A.**

2 **Click the Save button on the Standard toolbar.**

3 **Type the file name** Campground Envelopes **in the File name box. Do not press the ENTER key after typing the file name.**

4 **If necessary, click the Save in box arrow, click 3½ Floppy (A:), and then double-click the Campground folder.**

5 **Click the Save button in the Save As dialog box.**

Word saves the document with the file name, Campground Envelopes, in the Campground folder on the floppy disk in drive A.

Merging All Data Records to a Directory

You may want to print the data records in the data source. Recall that the data source is saved as a Microsoft Access database table. Thus, you cannot open the data source in Word. To view the data source, you click the Mail Merge Recipients button on the Mail Merge toolbar. The Mail Merge Recipients dialog box, however, does not have a Print button.

One way to print the contents of the data source is to merge all data records in the data source into a single document, called a **directory**, instead of merging to a separate document for each data record. The next steps show how to merge the data records in the data source into a directory. These steps illustrate the use of the buttons on the Mail Merge toolbar, instead of using the Mail Merge task pane, for the merge.

Q: How do I convert a mail merge main document into a regular Word document?

A: Open the main document. Click the Main document setup button on the Mail Merge toolbar, click Normal Word document in the Document type list, and then click the OK button.

To Merge to a Directory

1

• **Click the New Blank Document button on the Standard toolbar.**

• **If the Mail Merge toolbar is not displayed, click Tools on the menu bar, point to Letters and Mailings, and then click Show Mail Merge Toolbar.**

• **Click the Main document setup button on the Mail Merge toolbar.**

• **When Word displays the Main Document Type dialog box, click Directory.**

In the Main Document Type dialog box, you select the document type (Figure 5-85).

FIGURE 5-85

2

• **Click the OK button.**

• **Click the Open Data Source button on the Mail Merge toolbar.**

• **When Word displays the Select Data Source dialog box, if necessary, click the Look in box arrow, click 3½ Floppy (A:), and then double-click the Campground folder.**

• **Click the file name, Camper List.**

Word selects the data source, Camper List, in the Select Data Source dialog box (Figure 5-86).

3

• **Click the Open button in the Select Data Source dialog box.**

FIGURE 5-86

4

• **Click the Insert Merge Fields button on the Mail Merge toolbar.**

• **When Word displays the Insert Merge Field dialog box, click Title in the Fields list and then click the Insert button.**

Word inserts the field name in the document window (Figure 5-87).

5

• **Click the Close button in the dialog box.**

• **Press the ENTER key.**

FIGURE 5-87

6

• **Repeat Steps 4 and 5 for each remaining field in the Fields list.**

Word displays the fields in the data source, each on a separate line in the document window (Figure 5-88).

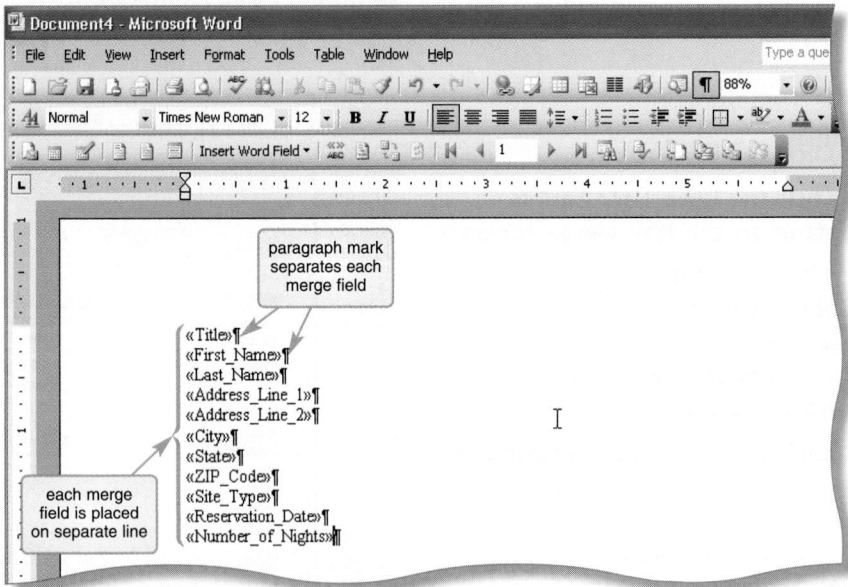

FIGURE 5-88

If you merge the records now, they will print in one long list, one record below the next. Instead of a long list, you want each data record to be in a single row and each merge field to be in a column. That is, you want the directory to be in a table form. The next steps show how to convert the text containing the merge fields to a table.

To Convert Text to a Table

1

- **Click Edit on the menu bar and then click Select All to select the entire document.**
- **Click Table on the menu bar and then point to Convert.**

Word selects all merge fields in the document (Figure 5-89).

FIGURE 5-89

2

- **Click Text to Table on the Convert submenu.**
- **When Word displays the Convert Text to Table dialog box, type 11 in the Number of columns box.**

The resulting table should have 11 columns and 1 row (Figure 5-90). The one row will contain the merge field names.

FIGURE 5-90

3

- **Click the OK button.**
- **If necessary, you can change column widths to match this figure.**

Word converts the text of the merge fields to a table (Figure 5-91). Each merge field is in its own column.

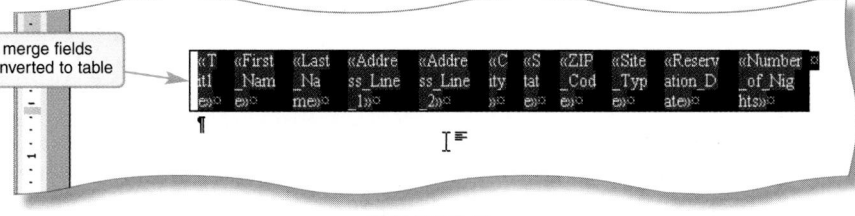

FIGURE 5-91

Notice in Figure 5-91 that the merge fields wrap in the first row and consume three lines in the document. This is because the table is too wide to fit on a piece of paper in **portrait orientation**; that is, with the short edge of the paper at the top. You can instruct Word to print a document in **landscape orientation** so the long edge of the paper is at the top. The steps on the next page show how to change the orientation of the document from portrait to landscape.

To Change Page Orientation

1

- **Click File on the menu bar and then click Page Setup.**
- **When Word displays the Page Setup dialog box, if necessary, click the Margins tab.**
- **Click Landscape in the Orientation area.**

In the Margins sheet, you can choose between Portrait and Landscape orientation (Figure 5-92).

2

- **Click the OK button.**
- **Click the Zoom box arrow on the Standard toolbar and then click Page Width.**

Word changes the print orientation to landscape (shown in Figure 5-93). With the zoom set to page width, the entire page in landscape orientation is displayed in the document window.

FIGURE 5-92

The next step is to merge the data records in the data source into the directory in a new document window, as described in the following steps.

To Merge to a New Document Window

1

- **Click the Merge to New Document button on the Mail Merge toolbar.**
- **When Word displays the Merge to New Document dialog box, if necessary, click All (Figure 5-93).**

FIGURE 5-93

2

• **Click the OK button.**

Word merges the data records into a directory in a new document window (Figure 5-94).

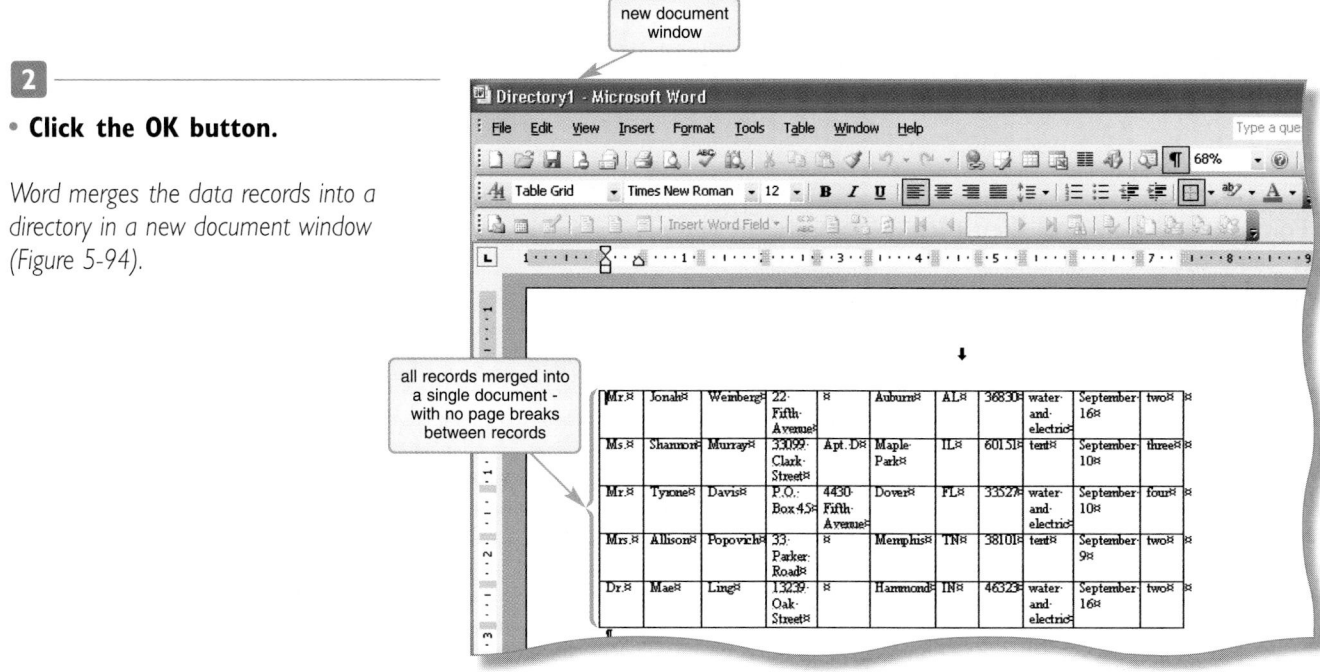

new document window

all records merged into a single document - with no page breaks between records

FIGURE 5-94

The table would be more descriptive if the field names were displayed in a row above the actual data. Thus, the following steps describe how to add a row to the top of a table and format it.

To Modify and Format a Table

1 Click in the upper-left cell of the table. Click Table on the menu bar, point to Insert, and then click Rows Above.

2 Click in the left cell of the new row. Type Title and then press the TAB key. Type First Name and then press the TAB key. Type Last Name and then press the TAB key. Type Address Line 1 and then press the TAB key. Type Address Line 2 and then press the TAB key. Type City and then press the TAB key. Type State and then press the TAB key. Type ZIP Code and then press the TAB key. Type Site Type and then press the TAB key. Type Reservation Date and then press the TAB key. Type Number of Nights as the last entry in the row.

3 Select this first row by pointing to the left of the new row and then clicking when the mouse pointer changes to a right-pointing arrow. Click the Bold button on the Formatting toolbar. Click anywhere in the document to remove the selection.

4 Double-click the border between the last two rows so the Reservation Dates are displayed on a single line. (You may have to double-click the border twice.)

Word adds and formats a row at the top of the table (shown in Figure 5-95 on the next page).

The next step is to add a .05 inch margin at the top of each cell and place a .05 inch space between each cell in the table using the Table Properties dialog box. You also can center the table between the left and right margins in this dialog box, as shown in the steps on the next page.

To Modify Table Properties

1

• **Point in the table and then click the table move handle in the upper-left corner of the table to select the table.**

• **Right-click somewhere in the table.**

Word displays a shortcut menu (Figure 5-95).

FIGURE 5-95

2

• **Click Table Properties on the shortcut menu.**

• **When Word displays the Table Properties dialog box, if necessary, click the Table tab.**

• **Click Center in the Alignment area.**

• **Click the Options button.**

• **When Word displays the Table Options dialog box, click the Top box up arrow until 0.05" is displayed in the Top box.**

• **Place a check mark in the Allow spacing between cells check box and then click the up arrow until 0.05" is displayed in this box also (Figure 5-96).**

3

• **Click the OK button in both dialog boxes.**

Word modifies the table (shown in Figure 5-97).

FIGURE 5-96

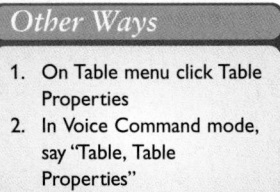

Other Ways

1. On Table menu click Table Properties
2. In Voice Command mode, say "Table, Table Properties"

The next step is to sort the table. You want its records to be displayed in order of reservation date. Within each reservation date, the records should be sorted by vacationer last name. The following steps show how to sort a table.

To Sort a Table

1

• **Position the insertion point in the table. Click Table on the menu bar and then click Sort.**

• **When Word displays the Sort dialog box, click the Sort by box arrow, scroll to and then click Reservation Date.**

• **Click the first Then by box arrow and then click Last Name.**

With the Header row option button selected in the Sort dialog box, Word will leave row one alone when it sorts the records (Figure 5-97).

2

• **Click the OK button.**

• **Click anywhere in the document to remove the highlight.**

Word sorts the records in the table in ascending Last Name order within ascending Reservation Date order (shown in Figure 5-99 on the next page).

FIGURE 5-97

With the Last Name, ascending means alphabetical. With the Reservation Date, ascending means the earliest date is at the top of the list. If you were sorting a list of numbers in ascending order, it would put the smallest numbers first.

You may want to add a note to the top of this table, but do not want the note to print. To do this, you format the text as hidden. The steps on the next page show how to format text as hidden.

Other Ways

1. In Voice Command mode, say "Table, Sort"

To Format Text as Hidden

1

• **Click in the top-left corner of the table and then press the ENTER key twice.**

Word places two paragraph marks above the table.

2

• **Click the first paragraph mark above the table and then type** Table last updated on August 16.

• **Drag through the added text to select it.**

• **Click Format on the menu bar and then click Font.**

• **When Word displays the Font dialog box, if necessary, click the Font tab.**

• **In the Effects area, click Hidden (Figure 5-98).**

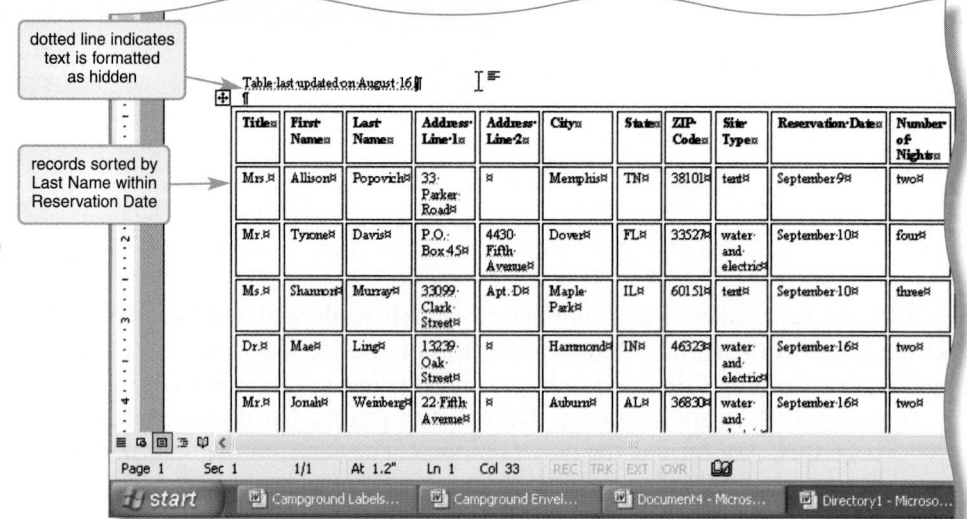

FIGURE 5-98

3

• **Click the OK button.**

• **Click anywhere in the document to remove the highlight.**

Word places a dotted line below the text, which indicates it is hidden (Figure 5-99).

FIGURE 5-99

Hidden text appears on the screen only when the Show/Hide ¶ button on the Standard toolbar is selected, as shown in the step on the next page.

To Hide Hidden Text

1

- **If the Show/Hide ¶ button on the Standard toolbar is selected, click it to deselect it.**

Word hides the hidden text (Figure 5-100).

FIGURE 5-100

To reveal the hidden text, simply click the Show/Hide ¶ button on the Standard toolbar to toggle it on.

The following step prints the directory.

To Print a Document

1 **Click the Print button on the Standard toolbar.**

Word prints the directory in landscape orientation (Figure 5-101). Notice that hidden text does not print on the hard copy.

Title	First Name	Last Name	Address Line 1	Address Line 2	City	State	Zip	Site Type	Reservation Date	Number of Nights
Mrs.	Allison	Popovich	33 Parker Road		Memphis	TN	38101	tent	September 9	two
Mr.	Tyrone	Davis	P.O. Box 45	4430 Fifth Avenue	Dover	FL	33527	water and electric	September 10	four
Ms.	Shannon	Murray	33099 Clark Street	Apt. D	Maple Park	IL	60151	tent	September 10	three
Dr.	Mae	Ling	13239 Oak Street		Hammond	IN	46323	water and electric	September 16	two
Mr.	Jonah	Weinberg	22 Fifth Avenue		Auburn	AL	36830	water and electric	September 16	two

FIGURE 5-101

As an alternative to merging to a directory and printing the results, if you are familiar with Microsoft Access, you can open and print the data source in Access.

Saving the Directory

The following steps save the directory.

To Save the Directory

1 If necessary, insert your floppy disk into drive A.

2 Click the Save button on the Standard toolbar.

3 Type the file name `Camper Directory` in the File name text box. Do not press the ENTER key after typing the file name.

4 If necessary, click the Save in box arrow, click 3½ Floppy (A:), and then double-click the Campground folder.

5 Click the Save button in the Save As dialog box.

Word saves the document with the file name, Camper Directory, in the Campground folder on the floppy disk on drive A.

Closing All Open Word Documents

More than one Word document currently is open: Campground Labels, Campground Envelopes, Document4, and Campground Directory. Instead of closing each file individually, you can close all open files at once, as shown in the following steps.

To Close All Open Word Documents

1

• **Press and hold the SHIFT key.**

• **While holding down the SHIFT key, click File on the menu bar. Release the SHIFT key.**

Word displays a Close All command, instead of a Close command, on the File menu because you pressed the SHIFT key when you clicked the menu name (Figure 5-102).

2

• **Click Close All.**

• **If a Microsoft Word dialog box is displayed, click the Yes button to save any changes made to the Campground Labels, Campground Envelopes, and Camper Directory files. For the Document4 file, click the No button.**

Word closes all open documents.

FIGURE 5-102

Notice the Save command also changes to a Save All command (Figure 5-102) when you SHIFT+click File on the menu bar. The **Save All command** saves all open documents at once.

Project 5 now is complete. The following step quits Word.

To Quit Word

1 **Click the Close button in the Word window.**

The Word window closes.

More About

Certification

The Microsoft Office Specialist Certification program provides an opportunity for you to obtain a valuable industry credential - proof that you have the Word 2003 skills required by employers. For more information, see Appendix E or visit the Word 2003 Certification Web page (scsite.com/wd2003/cert).

Project Summary

In Project 5, you learned how to create and print form letters and address corresponding mailing labels and envelopes. First, the project showed how to use a letter template to begin creating the main document for the form letter. Next, you learned how to insert and format an AutoShape on a drawing canvas. Then, the project showed how to create a data source. You learned how to enter text, merge fields, and an IF field into the main document for the form letter. The form letter also included an outline numbered list. You learned how to merge and print all the records in the data source, as well as only records that meet a certain criterion. You also learned how to sort the data source records.

The project illustrated how to address mailing labels and envelopes to accompany the form letters. Finally, you learned how merge all data records into a directory and print the resulting directory.

If you have a SAM user profile, you may have access to hands-on instruction, practice, and assessment of the skills covered in this project. Log in to your SAM account and go to your assignments page to see what your instructor has assigned.

What You Should Know

Having completed this project, you should be able to perform the tasks below. The tasks are listed in the same order they were presented in this project. For a list of the buttons, menus, toolbars, and commands introduced in this project, see the Quick Reference Summary at the back of this book and refer to the Page Number column.

1. Start and Customize Word   (WD 300)
2. Display Formatting Marks   (WD 301)
3. Zoom Page Width   (WD 301)
4. Use a Template   (WD 302)
5. Insert a Drawing Canvas   (WD 305)
6. Insert an AutoShape   (WD 306)
7. Format an AutoShape   (WD 307)
8. Add Formatted Text to an AutoShape (WD 308)
9. Resize a Drawing Canvas   (WD 310)
10. Format a Drawing Canvas   (WD 311)
11. Change Paragraph Formatting Using the Reveal Formatting Task Pane   (WD 312)
12. Create a Folder while Saving   (WD 313)
13. Type a New Data Source   (WD 315)
14. Enter More Records   (WD 319)
15. Save the Data Source when Prompted by Word (WD 320)
16. Edit a Field   (WD 322)
17. Edit the GreetingLine Merge Field   (WD 323)
18. Begin Typing the Body of the Form Letter (WD 324)
19. Insert Merge Fields in the Main Document (WD 325)
20. Insert an IF Field in the Main Document (WD 327)
21. Enter More Text and Merge Fields   (WD 328)

(continued)

What You Should Know *(continued)*

22. Create an Outline Numbered List   (WD 329)

23. Apply a Paragraph Style   (WD 332)

24. Enter More Text   (WD 332)

25. Select and Replace More Placeholder Text (WD 333)

26. Change the Font Size of Text   (WD 334)

27. Save a Document Again   (WD 334)

28. Display a Field Code   (WD 335)

29. Print Field Codes in the Main Document (WD 336)

30. Merge the Form Letters to the Printer (WD 338, WD 340)

31. Select Records to Merge   (WD 339)

32. Remove a Merge Condition   (WD 341)

33. Sort the Data Records in a Data Source (WD 342)

34. View Merged Data in the Main Document (WD 343)

35. Close a Document   (WD 343)

36. Rename a Folder in Word   (WD 344)

37. Address and Print Mailing Labels Using an Existing Data Source   (WD 345)

38. Save the Mailing Labels   (WD 350)

39. Address and Print Envelopes Using an Existing Data Source   (WD 351)

40. Save the Envelope   (WD 352)

41. Merge to a Directory   (WD 353)

42. Convert Text to a Table   (WD 355)

43. Change Page Orientation   (WD 356)

44. Merge to a New Document Window   (WD 356)

45. Modify and Format a Table   (WD 357)

46. Modify Table Properties   (WD 358)

47. Sort a Table   (WD 359)

48. Format Text as Hidden   (WD 360)

49. Hide Hidden Text   (WD 361)

50. Print a Document   (WD 361)

51. Save the Directory   (WD 362)

52. Close All Open Word Documents   (WD 362)

53. Quit Word   (WD 363)

More About

Quick Reference

For a table that lists how to complete the tasks covered in this book using the mouse, menu, shortcut menu, and keyboard, see the Quick Reference Summary at the back of this book, or visit the Word 2003 Quick Reference Web page (scsite.com/wd2003/qr).

Learn It Online

Instructions: To complete the Learn It Online exercises, start your browser, click the Address bar, and then enter the Web address scsite.com/wd2003/learn. When the Word 2003 Learn It Online page is displayed, follow the instructions in the exercises below. Each exercise has instructions for printing your results, either for your own records or for submission to your instructor.

1 Project Reinforcement TF, MC, and SA

Below Word Project 5, click the Project Reinforcement link. Print the quiz by clicking Print on the File menu for each page. Answer each question.

2 Flash Cards

Below Word Project 5, click the Flash Cards link and read the instructions. Type 20 (or a number specified by your instructor) in the Number of playing cards text box, type your name in the Enter your Name text box, and then click the Flip Card button. When the flash card is displayed, read the question and then click the ANSWER box arrow to select an answer. Flip through Flash Cards. If your score is 15 (75%) correct or greater, click Print on the File menu to print your results. If your score is less than 15 (75%) correct, then redo this exercise by clicking the Replay button.

3 Practice Test

Below Word Project 5, click the Practice Test link. Answer each question, enter your first and last name at the bottom of the page, and then click the Grade Test button. When the graded practice test is displayed on your screen, click Print on the File menu to print a hard copy. Continue to take practice tests until you score 80% or better.

4 Who Wants To Be a Computer Genius?

Below Word Project 5, click the Computer Genius link. Read the instructions, enter your first and last name at the bottom of the page, and then click the PLAY button. When your score is displayed, click the PRINT RESULTS link to print a hard copy.

5 Wheel of Terms

Below Word Project 5, click the Wheel of Terms link. Read the instructions, and then enter your first and last name and your school name. Click the PLAY button. When your score is displayed, right-click the score and then click Print on the shortcut menu to print a hard copy.

6 Crossword Puzzle Challenge

Below Word Project 5, click the Crossword Puzzle Challenge link. Read the instructions, and then enter your first and last name. Click the SUBMIT button. Work the crossword puzzle. When you are finished, click the Submit button. When the crossword puzzle is redisplayed, click the Print Puzzle button to print a hard copy.

7 Tips and Tricks

Below Word Project 5, click the Tips and Tricks link. Click a topic that pertains to Project 5. Right-click the information and then click Print on the shortcut menu. Construct a brief example of what the information relates to in Word to confirm you understand how to use the tip or trick.

8 Newsgroups

Below Word Project 5, click the Newsgroups link. Click a topic that pertains to Project 5. Print three comments.

9 Expanding Your Horizons

Below Word Project 5, click the Expanding Your Horizons link. Click a topic that pertains to Project 5. Print the information. Construct a brief example of what the information relates to in Word to confirm you understand the contents of the article.

10 Search Sleuth

Below Word Project 5, click the Search Sleuth link. To search for a term that pertains to this project, select a term below the Project 5 title and then use the Google search engine at google.com (or any major search engine) to display and print two Web pages that present information on the term.

11 Word Online Training

Below Word Project 5, click the Word Online Training link. When your browser displays the Microsoft Office Online Web page, click the Word link. Click one of the Word courses that covers one or more of the objectives listed at the beginning of the project on page WD 298. Print the first page of the course before stepping through it.

12 Office Marketplace

Below Word Project 5, click the Office Marketplace link. When your browser displays the Microsoft Office Online Web page, click the Office Marketplace link. Click a topic that relates to Word. Print the first page.

Apply Your Knowledge

1 Working with a Form Letter

Instructions: Start Word. Open the document, Apply 5-1 Wellness Form Letter, on the Data Disk. If you did not download the Data Disk, see the inside back cover for instructions for downloading the Data Disk or see your instructor. When you open the main document, if Word displays a dialog box about an SQL command, click the Yes button. If Word prompts for the name of the data source, select Apply 5-1 Donor List on the Data Disk.

The document is a main document for the Child Wellness Council (Figure 5-103). You are to edit the date and greeting line fields, print the form letter with field codes displaying and then without field codes, add a record to the data source, and then merge the form letters to a file.

Perform the following tasks:

1. Edit the date field so it is displayed in the format d MMMM yyyy.
2. Edit the GreetingLine merge field so the salutation ends with a colon (:).
3. Save the revised form letter with the name Apply 5-1 Wellness Form Letter Revised in a folder called Apply 5-1 Wellness Council. *Hint:* Create a folder while saving the document.
4. Print the form letter with field codes; that is, with the Field codes check box selected. Be sure to deselect the Field codes check box after printing the field codes version of the letter.
5. Add a record to the data source that contains your personal information. Type North in the Region field and $75.00 in the Donation field. *Hint:* Click the Edit button in the Mail Merge Recipients dialog box.

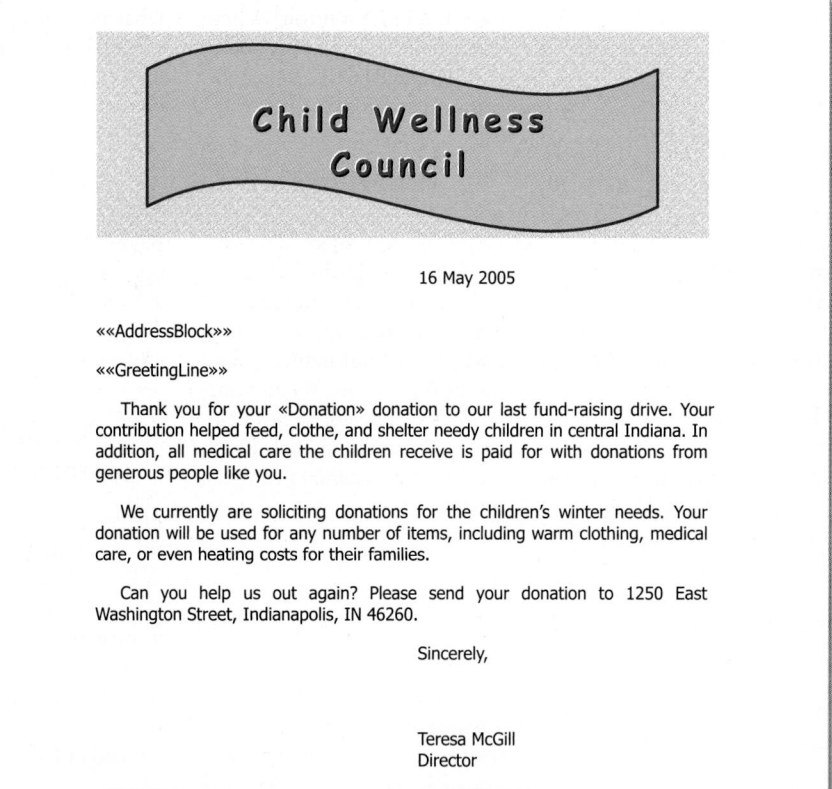

16 May 2005

««AddressBlock»»

««GreetingLine»»

Thank you for your «Donation» donation to our last fund-raising drive. Your contribution helped feed, clothe, and shelter needy children in central Indiana. In addition, all medical care the children receive is paid for with donations from generous people like you.

We currently are soliciting donations for the children's winter needs. Your donation will be used for any number of items, including warm clothing, medical care, or even heating costs for their families.

Can you help us out again? Please send your donation to 1250 East Washington Street, Indianapolis, IN 46260.

Sincerely,

Teresa McGill
Director

FIGURE 5-103

6. Sort the data source by the Last Name field.
7. Save the form letter again.
8. Merge the form letters to a new document. Save the new document with the name Apply 5-1 Merged Form Letters. Print the document containing the merged form letters.
9. Save all open documents using the Save All command.
10. Close all open documents using the Close All command.
11. Rename the Apply 5-1 Wellness Council folder to the name Apply 5-1 Child Wellness.

In the Lab

1 Creating a Form Letter, Data Source, Mailing Labels, and Directory

Problem: Ray Fleischner, the service manager at TLC Auto Care, has asked you to send a letter to customers that are due for a service call. You decide to use a form letter (Figure 5-104a).

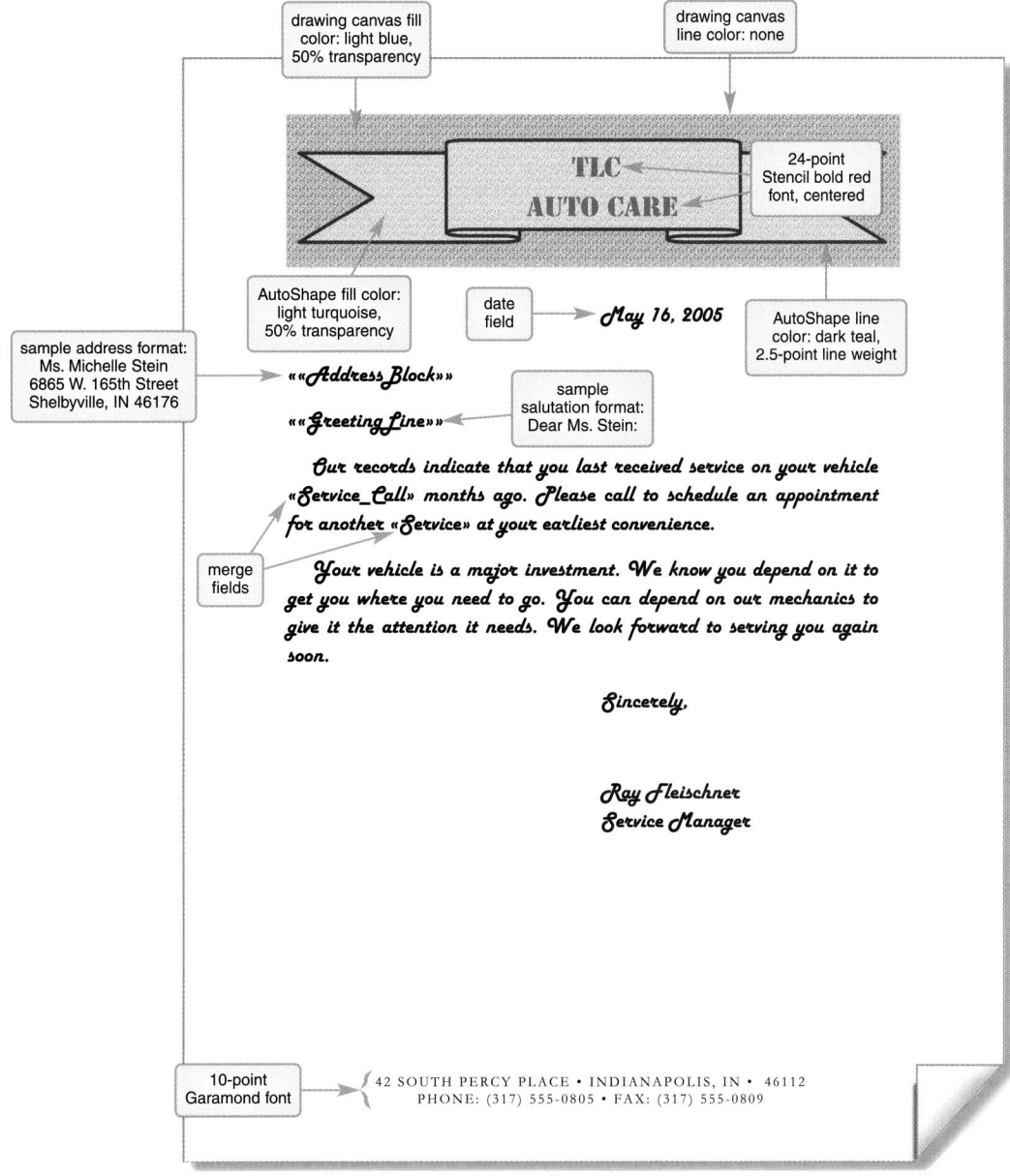

FIGURE 5-104a

Instructions:

1. Use the Elegant Merge Letter template to create a form letter.
2. Insert the up ribbon AutoShape in place of the placeholder text at the top of the letterhead. Add text to and format the AutoShape as shown in Figure 5-104a.

(continued)

Creating a Form Letter, Data Source, Mailing Labels, and Directory *(continued)*

3. Use the Reveal Formatting task pane to insert 24 points above the date line.
4. Type a new data source using the data shown in Figure 5-104b. Delete field names not used, and add two field names: Service Call and Service. Save the data source with the file name, Lab 5-1 TLC Auto Care List, in a folder called Lab 5-1 TLC Auto. *Hint*: You will need to create the folder while saving.

Title	First Name	Last Name	Address Line 1	Address Line 2	City	State	ZIP Code	Service Call	Service
Ms.	Michelle	Stein	6865 W. 165th Street		Shelbyville	IN	46176	six	tune-up
Mr.	Walter	Benjamin	9025 Wilson Court	Apt. 1E	Indianapolis	IN	46259	six	oil change
Mr.	Timothy	Jackson	2 East Penn Drive		Pittsboro	IN	46167	12	emission test
Ms.	Louella	Drake	33 Timmons Place	P.O. Box 12	Plainfield	IN	46168	12	emission test
Mr.	Adelbert	Ruiz	1722 East Lincoln Park Place		Carmel	IN	46033	six	tune-up

FIGURE 5-104b

5. Save the main document for the form letter with the file name, Lab 5-1 TLC Auto Care Form Letter, in the folder called Lab 5-1 TLC Auto. Compose the form letter for the main document as shown in Figure 5-104a on the previous page. Edit the GreetingLine field so it ends with a colon, instead of a comma. Insert the merge fields as shown in Figure 5-104a. Change the font of the body of the letter to 16-point Harrow Solid Italic, or a similar font.
6. Save the main document for the form letter again. Print the main document twice: once with field codes displaying and once without field codes.
7. Merge the form letters to the printer.
8. In a new document window, address mailing labels using the same data source you used for the form letters. Save the mailing labels with the name, Lab 5-1 TLC Auto Care Labels, in the Lab 5-1 TLC Auto folder. Print the mailing labels.
9. In a new document window, specify the main document type as a directory. Insert all merge fields into the document. Convert the list of fields to a Word table (the table will have 10 columns). Change the page layout to landscape orientation. Merge the directory layout to a new document window. Add a row to the top of the table and insert field names into the empty cells. Bold the first row. Resize the columns so the table looks like Figure 5-104b. Add 0.05" above each table cell using the Table Properties dialog box.
10. Insert your name as text above the table. Format your name as hidden text. Hide the text on the screen. Then, reveal the text on the screen.
11. Save the directory with the name, Lab 5-1 TLC Auto Care Directory, in the folder named Lab 5-1 TLC Auto. Print the directory (your name should not print because it is hidden).
12. Sort the table in the directory by the Last Name field. Print the sorted directory.
13. Save the directory again.
14. Close all open documents. Rename the folder from Lab 5-1 TLC Auto to Lab 5-1 TLC Auto Care.

2 Creating a Form Letter with an IF Field and an Outline Numbered List

Problem: As the computer specialist at Global Choice Coffee Club, the owner has asked you to send a letter to new members, outlining the details of their membership. You have decided to use a form letter (Figure 5-105a). The contact telephone number will vary, depending if the new member resides in the west or the east sales zone.

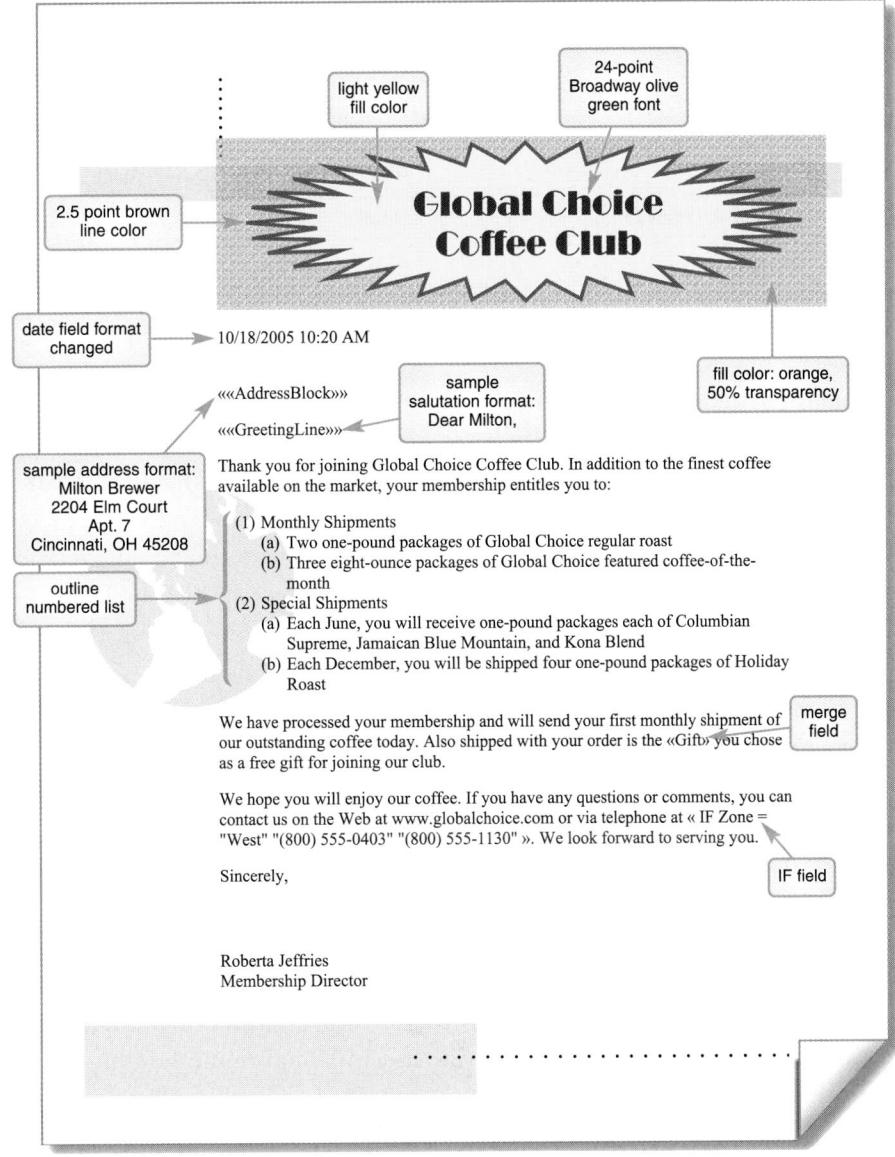

FIGURE 5-105a

Instructions:

1. Use the Contemporary Merge Letter template to create a form letter.
2. Insert a 32-point star AutoShape in place of the placeholder text at the top of the letterhead. Add text to and format the AutoShape as shown in Figure 5-105a.
3. Use the Reveal Formatting task pane to insert 6 points above the date line. Edit the date line field so it displays the date and time as shown in Figure 5-105a.

(continued)

In the Lab

Creating a Form Letter with an IF Field and an Outline Numbered List *(continued)*

4. Type a new data source using the data shown in Figure 5-105b. Delete field names not used, and add two field names: Zone and Gift. Save the data source with the file name, Lab 5-2 Global Coffee Customer List, in a folder called Lab 5-2 Global. *Hint:* You will need to create the folder while saving.

First Name	Last Name	Address Line 1	Address Line 2	City	State	ZIP Code	Zone	Gift
Milton	Brewer	2204 Elm Court	Apt. 7	Cincinnati	OH	45208	East	carafe
Benjamin	Tu	54 Lacy Court		Ipswich	MA	01938	East	mug set
Elena	Gupta	99 E. 101st Place	Suite 9	Brea	CA	92821	West	carafe
Ronald	Hidalgo	7676 Independence Parkway		Orange	CA	92866	West	frothing pitcher
Adam	Rosen	8802 E. Schilling Avenue		Boston	MA	02219	East	mug set

FIGURE 5-105b

5. Save the main document for the form letter with the file name, Lab 5-2 Global Coffee Form Letter, in the folder named Lab 5-2 Global. Compose the form letter for the main document as shown in Figure 5-105a on the previous page. Edit the GreetingLine field so it just shows the first name (e.g., Dear Mike,). Insert the merge fields as shown in Figure 5-105a. Change the font of the body of the letter to 12-point Footlight MT Light, or a similar font. Be sure to clear formatting before starting the outline numbered list. Apply the Body Text paragraph style to the paragraphs below the outline numbered list. The IF field tests if Zone is equal to West; if it is, then print the text, (800) 555-0403; otherwise print the text, (800) 555-1130.

6. Save the main document for the form letter again. Print the main document twice: once with field codes displaying and once without field codes.

7. Merge the form letters to the printer.

8. In a new document window, address mailing labels using the same data source you used for the form letters. Save the mailing labels with the name, Lab 5-2 Global Coffee Labels, in the Lab 5-2 Global folder. Print the mailing labels (Figure 5-105c).

9. If your printer allows or your instructor requests it, in a new document window, address envelopes using the same data source you used for the form letters. Save the envelopes with the file name, Lab 5-2 Global Coffee Envelopes, in the folder named Lab 5-2 Global. Print the envelopes.

10. In a new document window, specify the main document type as a directory. Insert all merge fields into the document. Convert the list of fields to a Word table (the table will have nine columns). Change the page layout to landscape orientation. Merge the directory layout to a new document window. Add a row to the top of the table and insert field names into the empty cells. Bold the first row. Change the top, bottom, left, and right page margins to one-half inch (*Hint:* Use the Page Setup dialog box). Resize the columns so the table looks like Figure 5-105b. Add 0.05" above and below each table cell using the Table Properties dialog box.

Milton Brewer 2204 Elm Court Apt. 7 Cincinnati, OH 45208	Benjamin Tu 54 Lacy Court Ipswich, MA 01938	Elena Gupta 99 E. 101st Place Suite 9 Brea, CA 92821
Ronald Hidalgo 7676 Independence Parkway Orange, CA 92866	Adam Rosen 8802 E. Schilling Avenue Boston, MA 02219	

FIGURE 5-105c

11. Insert your name as text above the table. Format your name as hidden text.
12. Save the directory with the name, Lab 5-2 Global Coffee Member Directory, in the folder named Lab 5-2 Global. Print the directory (your name should not print because it is hidden).
13. Sort the table in the directory by the Last Name field within the State field. Print the sorted directory.
14. Save the directory again.
15. Close all open documents. Rename the folder from Lab 5-2 Global to Lab 5-2 Global Coffee.

In the Lab

3 Designing a Data Source, Form Letter, and Mailing Labels from Sample Memos

Problem: The benefits director at CADdesign, Inc., would like to schedule an insurance benefits meeting. Two separate session times will be scheduled: salaried employees will meet on Thursday, October 6, and hourly employees will meet on Friday, October 7. Sample drafted memos for each type of employee are shown in Figure 5-106.

Instructions:

1. Decide which fields should be in the data source. Write the field names down on a piece of paper.
2. Use the Professional Memo template to create a form letter for the memorandums.

FIGURE 5-106a

In the Lab

3. Create a data source containing two records that will generate the memos shown in Figure 5-106. Save the data source with the file name, Lab 5-3 CADdesign Data Source, in a folder named Lab 5-3 CADdesign.

4. Save the main document for the form letter with the file name, Lab 5-3 CADdesign Form Letter. Enter the text of the main document for the form letter shown in Figure 5-106. The IF field tests if Employee Type is equal to Salary; if it is, then print the text, Thursday, October 6; otherwise print the text, Friday, October 7. Resize the contents of the memorandum to 10-point Arial.

5. Print the main document twice, once with field codes displaying and once without field codes.

6. Merge and print the form letters.

7. Merge the data source to a directory. Convert it to a Word table. Add an attractive border to the table and apply any other formatting you feel necessary. Print the table. Save the file using the name Lab 5-3 CADdesign Directory.

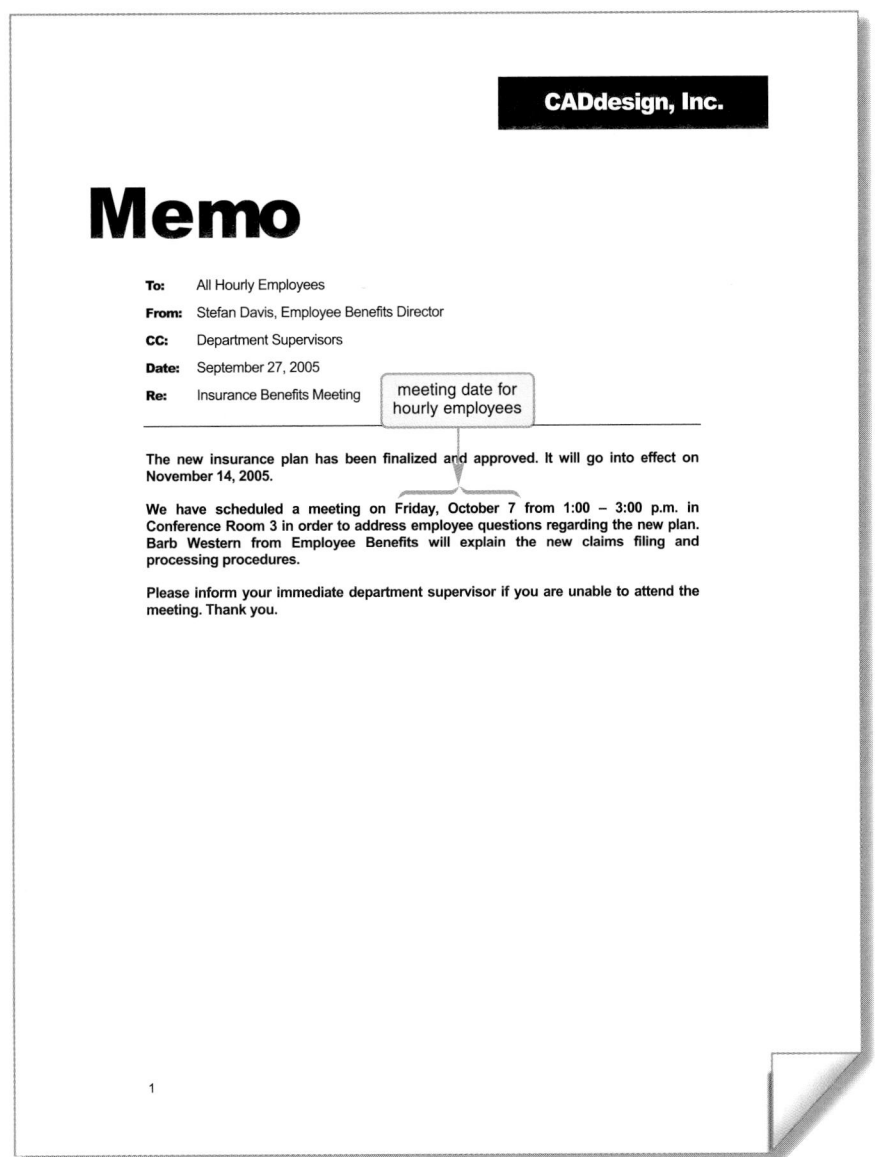

FIGURE 5-106b

Cases and Places

The difficulty of these case studies varies:
■ are the least difficult and ■■ are more difficult. The last exercise is a group exercise.

1 ■ You work for Darren Wilkins, membership director, at Royal Oaks Health club. You are responsible for sending letters to current members, inviting them to upgrade their membership. Create a form letter using the following information: In an AutoShape at the top of the letter, insert the text Royal Oaks Health Club. Place the AutoShape in a drawing canvas. Format both the AutoShape and drawing canvas. The address of the health club is 575 Commerce Drive, Denver, CO 80033; Telephone: 555-0914; Fax: 555-0920. Create the data source shown in Figure 5-107. Edit the date field so it shows the day of the week in addition to the month day and year. A sample salutation is as follows: Dear Juanita,. First paragraph: Thank you, «First_Name», for your recent membership contract with Royal Oaks Health Club. Our facility boasts the latest in state-of-the-art fitness equipment in addition to a truly top-notch staff. We do, however, offer enhancements to your standard membership. Create an outline numbered list for the following list items: 1) Silver membership upgrade ($20.00 per month) – eligibility for premium court times, admission to lap pool for one hour before and one hour after regular open pool hours, and one hour per week with a personal trainer; and 2) Gold membership upgrade ($30.00 per month) – all privileges of silver membership upgrade, one free hour court time per week, discount membership at Royal Oaks Tennis Club, and 30-minute massage weekly. Last paragraph: If you are interested in upgrading your current membership, call 555-9910. Enjoy your new membership! Use your name in the signature block. Sort the data source by the ZIP code field. Then, address and print accompanying labels or envelopes for the form letters. Save all documents in a folder called Case 5-1 Royal Oaks.

Title	First Name	Last Name	Address Line 1	Address Line 2	City	State	ZIP Code
Ms.	Juanita	Mendez	85 Cottage Grove Lane	Unit 2	Denver	CO	80002
Mr.	Steven	Gold	3404 Scherton Drive		Denver	CO	80012
Mr.	Chad	Nicholas	P.O. Box 72	802 Drury Place	Denver	CO	80033
Ms.	Tiffany	Goldstein	7074 Keyway Drive		Denver	CO	80010
Ms.	Bethany	Ames	11234 W. 72nd Street	Apt. 3C	Denver	CO	80201

FIGURE 5-107

Cases and Places

2 ▪▪ You currently are seeking an employment position in your field of study. You already have prepared a resume and would like to send it to a group of potential employers. You decide to design a cover letter to send along with the resume. Obtain a recent newspaper and cut out three classified advertisements pertaining to your field of study. Locate two job advertisements on the Internet. Create the cover letter for your resume as a form letter. Be sure the cover letter contains your name, address, and telephone number. The data source should contain the five potential employers' names, addresses, and position being sought. Use the information in the classified ads from newspapers and the Internet for the data source. Address accompanying labels or envelopes for the cover letters. Then, create a directory of the data source records. Save all documents in a folder called Case 5-2 Cover Letter. Use the concepts and techniques presented in this project to format the form letter and directory. Turn in the want ads with your printouts.

3 ▪▪ Your neighbor, Lynette Galens, owns a lawn care service, called Lynette's Lawn Care. She has asked you to assist her in preparing a form letter that thanks customers for their recent contracts with her business. Contracts include weekly care of mowing, watering, and weeding; and monthly care of fertilizing, edging, and pest/grub control. It also includes troubleshooting additional problems. Depending on the contract type, the customer contact person varies: Tammy at 555-1717 handles summer contracts; Sam at 555-1720 handles annual contracts. Create a form letter thanking customers, outlining contract services, outlining additional problems (you will need to research these), and informing them of their contact person (use an IF for this). Use an outline numbered list in the form letter. Place the business name at the top of the letter in an AutoShape in a drawing canvas. Obtain the names and addresses of five of your friends or family members and use them as records in the data source. Create a directory of the data source records. Address accompanying labels or envelopes for the form letters. Save all documents in a folder called Case 5-3 Lawn Care. Use the concepts and techniques presented in this project to format the form letter and directory.

4 ▪▪ You work part-time for Latisha Adams, credit manager, at American Fashions. One of your responsibilities is to inform applicants when their credit card is approved – and let them know the credit card will be mailed separately within a week. American Fashions assigns credit ratings of good or excellent. With a good rating, the letter includes a 15 percent off coupon to be used on their first credit purchase; with an excellent rating, they get a 25 percent off coupon. Be sure the top of the form letter has an AutoShape in a drawing canvas with appropriate text. Obtain the names and addresses of five of your classmates and use them as records in the data source. Create a directory of the data source records. Address accompanying labels or envelopes for the form letters. Save all documents in a folder called Case 5-4 American Fashions. Use the concepts and techniques presented in this project to format the form letter and directory.

Cases and Places

5 ■■ **Working Together** This team project investigates other types of data sources in form letters and other ways to merge. Select the Project 5 form letter, the Apply Your Knowledge form letter, or one of the assignments in this project as a starting point for the content of your form letter and data source. Team members are to create and merge form letters as follows:

1) One or more team members are to use Microsoft Office Excel to create a table and then use that table as the data source in the mail merge document. It may be necessary to use Help in Word and also Help in Excel to assist in the procedure for creating and saving a worksheet in the proper format for a mail merge;

2) One or more team members are to use Microsoft Office Outlook recipients as a data source in a mail merge document. It may be necessary to use Help in Word and also Help in Outlook;

3) One or more team members are to use Microsoft Office Access to view, format, and print the contents of a data source created in Word. It may be necessary to use Help in Access; and

4) One or more team members are to merge the contents of the data source to e-mail addresses. It may be necessary to use Help in Word.

Then, your team is to develop a PowerPoint slide show that outlines the steps required to complete these four tasks and present the results to your classmates.

MICROSOFT
Office Word 2003

Creating a Professional Newsletter

P R O J E C T

6

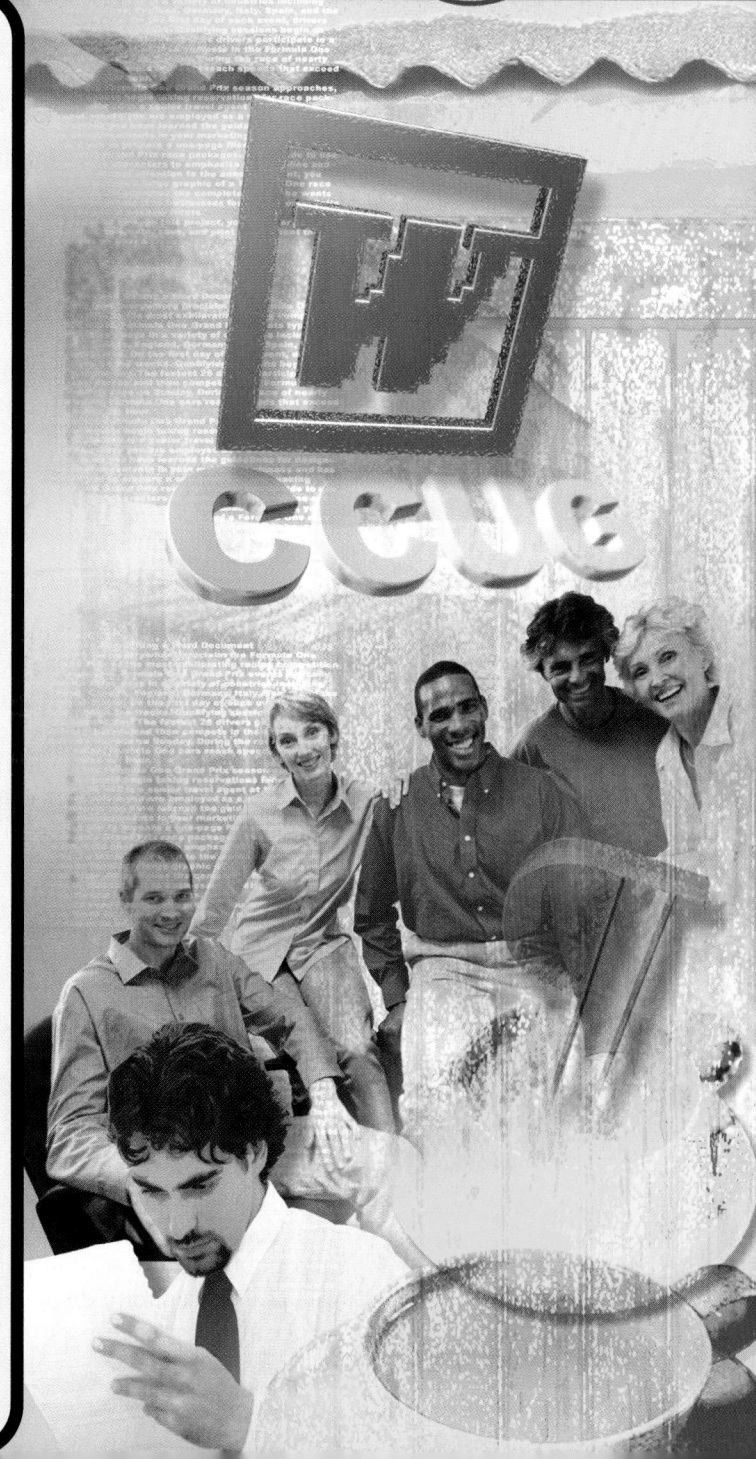

CASE PERSPECTIVE

With a membership ranging from students to professionals, Clever Clicks User Group (CCUG) provides a means for novice to expert computer users to meet and converse. At the bimonthly meetings, CCUG members listen to a presentation by one or more industry experts and then network with each other in a casual setting. In addition to meetings, members communicate on CCUG's newsgroup, via instant messaging, and by e-mail. CCUG also distributes a monthly newsletter called *Clever Clicks* designed to provide computing tips and important user group information to all members.

As a member of CCUG, you are required to serve on one committee. This year, you chose the Publicity Committee. Your responsibility is to prepare the monthly newsletter. Each issue of *Clever Clicks* contains a feature article and announcements. This month's feature article will discuss how to safeguard computers from virus infections. You plan to create the article as a Word document. The article will discuss how computer viruses infect a computer and then present a variety of precautions users can take to protect their computers from viruses. The article also will have a diagram showing the symptoms of a computer virus infection. The announcements section will remind members about the upcoming user group meeting, inform them of a new CCUG member discount, and advise them of the topic of the next month's feature article.

Your task now is to design the newsletter so the feature article spans the first two columns of page 1 and then continues on page 2. The announcements should be located in the third column of page 1 of the newsletter. As you read through this project, you will learn how to use Word to create a newsletter.

Creating a Professional Newsletter

Objectives

You will have mastered the material in this project when you can:

- Create and format a WordArt drawing object
- Insert a symbol into a document
- Insert and format a floating graphic
- Format a document into multiple columns
- Format a character as a drop cap
- Insert a column break
- Place a vertical rule between columns
- Insert and format a text box
- Use the Paste Special command to link items in a document
- Balance columns
- Insert and format a diagram
- Use the Format Painter button
- Add a page border
- Enhance a document for online viewing

Introduction

Professional looking documents, such as newsletters and brochures, often are created using desktop publishing software. With desktop publishing software, you can divide a document into multiple columns, wrap text around diagrams and other objects, change fonts and font sizes, add color and lines, and so on, to create an attention-grabbing document. A traditionally held opinion of desktop publishing software, such as Adobe PageMaker or QuarkXpress, is that it enables you to open an existing word processing document and enhance it through formatting not provided in your word processing software. Word, however, provides many of the formatting features that you would find in a desktop publishing package. Thus, you can use Word to create eye-catching newsletters and brochures.

Project Six — Clever Clicks Newsletter

Project 6 uses Word to produce the newsletter shown in Figure 6-1. The newsletter is a monthly publication for members of Clever Clicks User Group (CCUG). Notice that it incorporates the desktop publishing features of Word. The body of each page of the newsletter is divided into three columns. A variety of fonts, font sizes, and colors add visual appeal to the document. The first page has text wrapped around a pull-quote, and the second page has text wrapped around a diagram. Horizontal and vertical lines separate distinct areas of the newsletter, including a page border around the perimeter of each page.

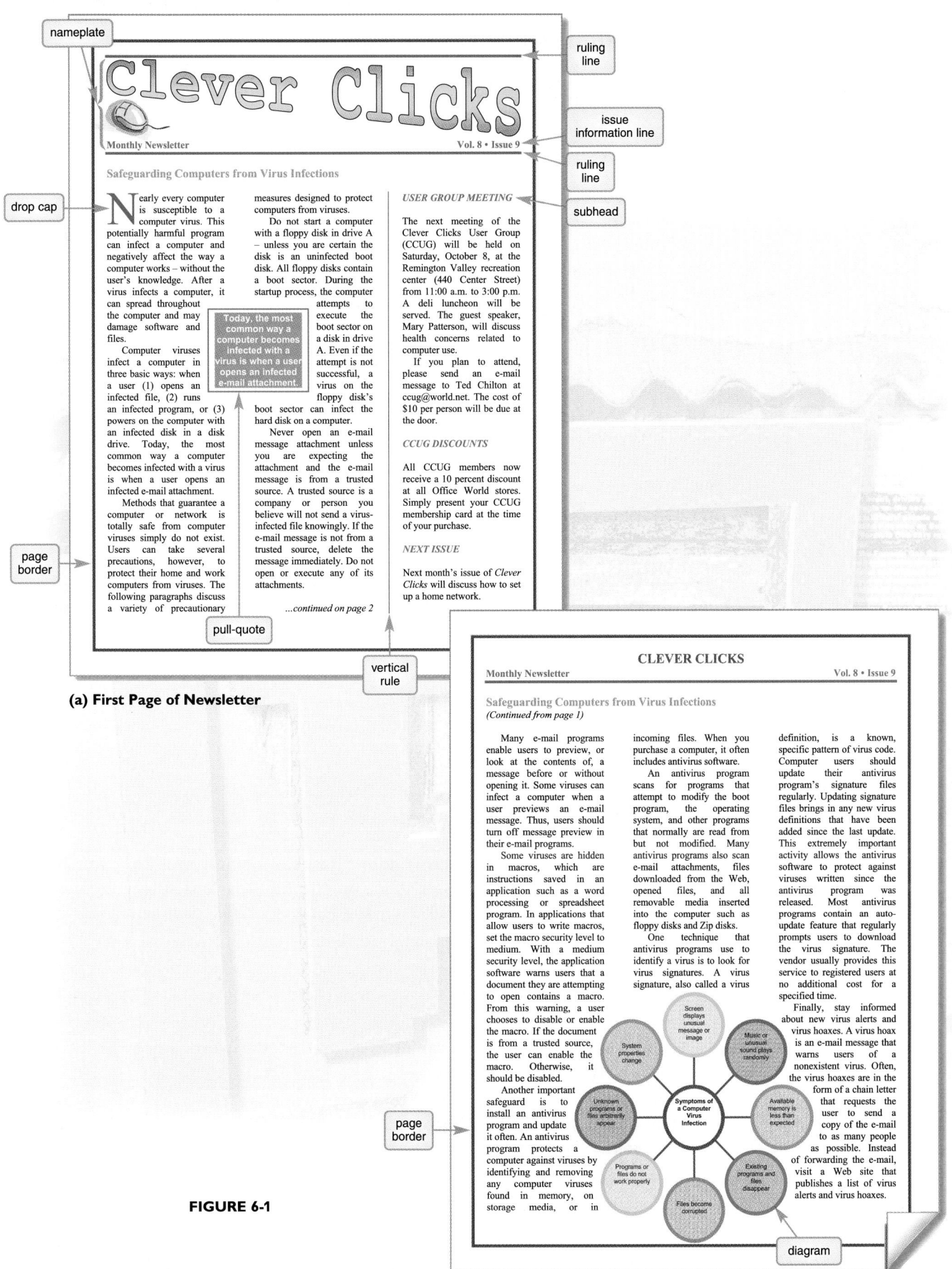

(a) First Page of Newsletter

FIGURE 6-1

(b) Second Page of Newsletter

More About

Desktop Publishing

For more information about desktop publishing, visit the Word 2003 More About Web page (scsite.com/wd2003/more) and then click Desktop Publishing.

Desktop Publishing Terminology

As you create professional looking newsletters and brochures, you should understand several desktop publishing terms. In Project 6 (Figure 6-1 on the previous page), the **nameplate**, or **banner**, is the top portion of the newsletter above the three columns. The nameplate on the first page contains more graphical enhancements than the one on the second page. A nameplate usually contains the name of the newsletter and the **issue information line**. The horizontal lines in the nameplate are called **rules**, or **ruling lines**.

Within the body of the newsletter, a heading, such as USER GROUP MEETING, is called a **subhead**. The vertical line dividing the second and third columns on the first page of the newsletter is a **vertical rule**.

The first page of the newsletter contains a pull-quote (Figure 6-1a). A **pull-quote** is text that is *pulled*, or copied, from the text of the document and given graphical emphasis so it stands apart and commands the reader's attention.

The text that wraps around an object, such as the pull-quote or the diagram, is referred to as **wrap-around text**. The space between the object and the text is called the **run-around**.

This project involves several steps requiring you to drag the mouse. Thus, you may want to cancel an action if you drag to the wrong location. Remember that you always can click the Undo button on the Standard toolbar to cancel your most recent action.

Starting and Customizing Word

To start and customize Word, Windows must be running. If you are stepping through this project on a computer and you want your screen to match the figures in this book, then you should change your computer's resolution to 800 × 600 and reset the toolbars and menus. For information about changing the resolution and resetting toolbars and menus, read Appendix D.

The following steps describe how to start Word and customize the Word window. You may need to ask your instructor how to start Word for your system.

To Start and Customize Word

1 Click the Start button on the Windows taskbar, point to All Programs on the Start menu, point to Microsoft Office on the All Programs submenu, and then click Microsoft Office Word 2003 on the Microsoft Office submenu.

2 If the Word window is not maximized, double-click its title bar to maximize it.

3 If the Language bar appears, right-click it and then click Close the Language bar on the shortcut menu.

4 If the Getting Started task pane is displayed in the Word window, click its Close button.

5 If the Standard and Formatting toolbar buttons are displayed on one row, click the Toolbar Options button and then click Show Buttons on Two Rows in the Toolbar Options list.

6 If necessary, click View on the menu bar and then click Print Layout.

Word starts and, after a few moments, displays an empty document in the Word window. You use print layout view in this project because the newsletter contains columns and a diagram, and these display properly only in print layout view. The Print Layout View button on the horizontal scroll bar is selected (shown in Figure 6-2 on page WD 382).

Displaying Formatting Marks

It is helpful to display formatting marks that indicate where in the document you pressed the ENTER key, SPACEBAR, and other keys. The following step describes how to display formatting marks.

To Display Formatting Marks

1 **If the Show/Hide ¶ button on the Standard toolbar is not selected already, click it.**

Word displays formatting marks in the document window, and the Show/Hide ¶ button on the Standard toolbar is selected (shown in Figure 6-2 on the next page).

Zooming Page Width

In print layout view, many users zoom page width so they can see all edges of the page in the document window at once. The following steps zoom page width.

To Zoom Page Width

1 **Click the Zoom box arrow on the Standard toolbar.**

2 **Click Page Width in the Zoom list.**

Word computes the zoom percentage and displays it in the Zoom box (shown in Figure 6-2). Your percentage may be different depending on your computer.

Changing All Margin Settings

Word is preset to use standard 8.5-by-11-inch paper, with 1.25-inch left and right margins and 1-inch top and bottom margins. For the newsletter in this project, you want all margins (left, right, top, and bottom) to be .75 inches.

The following steps describe how to change margin settings.

To Change All Margin Settings

1 **Click File on the menu bar and then click Page Setup.**

2 **When Word displays the Page Setup dialog box, if necessary, click the Margins tab. Type** .75 **in the Top box and then press the TAB key.**

3 **Type** .75 **in the Bottom box and then press the TAB key.**

4 **Type** .75 **in the Left box and then press the TAB key.**

5 **Type** .75 **in the Right box (Figure 6-2).**

6 **Click the OK button to change the margin settings for this document.**

Depending on the printer you are using, you may need to set the margins differently for this project. In this case, Word displays a message when you attempt to print the newsletter.

FIGURE 6-2

Creating the Nameplate

The nameplate on the first page of this newsletter consists of the information above the multiple columns (Figure 6-1a on page WD 379). In this project, the nameplate includes the newsletter title, Clever Clicks, the issue information line, and the title of the feature article. The steps on the following pages illustrate how to create the nameplate for the first page of the newsletter in this project.

Inserting a WordArt Drawing Object

In Project 5, you added an AutoShape drawing object to a document. Recall that a **drawing object** is a graphic you create using Word. You can create another type of drawing object, called **WordArt**, which enables you to create special effects such as shadowed, rotated, stretched, skewed, and wavy text.

On the first page of the newsletter in this project, the newsletter name, Clever Clicks, is a WordArt drawing object. The next steps show how to insert a WordArt drawing object.

Q: What elements should a nameplate contain?

A: A nameplate should contain, at a minimum, the title and date of the newsletter. The title should be shown in as large a font size as possible. You also may include a logo in the nameplate. Many nameplates include a headline outlining the function of the newsletter. Some nameplates also include a short table of contents.

To Insert a WordArt Drawing Object

1

• **If the Drawing toolbar is not displayed in the Word window, click the Drawing button on the Standard toolbar.**

• **Click the Insert WordArt button on the Drawing toolbar.**

• **When Word displays the WordArt Gallery dialog box, if necessary, click the style in the upper-left corner.**

Word displays the WordArt Gallery dialog box (Figure 6-3). You will add your own special text effects. Thus, you will use the default style in the WordArt Gallery.

FIGURE 6-3

2

• **Click the OK button.**

• **When Word displays the Edit WordArt Text dialog box, type** Clever Clicks **in the Text text box.**

• **Click the Font box arrow in the dialog box. Scroll to and then click Courier New, or a similar font.**

• **Click the Size box arrow in the dialog box, scroll to and then click 72.**

• **Click the Bold button in the dialog box.**

In the Edit WordArt Text dialog box, you enter the WordArt text and change its font, font size, and font style (Figure 6-4).

FIGURE 6-4

3

• **Click the OK button.**

A WordArt drawing object is displayed in the document window (Figure 6-5).

WordArt drawing object inserted in newsletter

FIGURE 6-5

To change the WordArt text, its font, its font size, or its font style, display the Edit WordArt Text dialog box (Figure 6-4 on the previous page) by clicking the Edit Text button on the WordArt toolbar (shown in Figure 6-6). To display the WordArt toolbar, click the WordArt drawing object. If the WordArt toolbar does not appear on your screen when you select the WordArt drawing object, right-click the WordArt drawing object and then click Show WordArt Toolbar on the shortcut menu.

If, for some reason, you wanted to delete the WordArt drawing object, you could right-click it and then click Cut on the shortcut menu, or click it and then press the DELETE key.

Formatting a WordArt Drawing Object

The next step is to change the size and color of the WordArt drawing object. It is to be slightly taller and display an orange to yellow to orange gradient color effect. **Gradient** colors blend into one another. Thus, an orange color at the top of the characters should blend into a yellow color in the middle of the characters, which will blend into the orange color again at the bottom of the characters. To make these formatting changes, use the Format WordArt dialog box.

The following steps show how to resize and change the color of the WordArt drawing object.

To Format a WordArt Drawing Object

1

• **Click the WordArt drawing object to select it.**

• **If the WordArt toolbar does not appear on the screen, right-click the WordArt drawing object and then click Show WordArt Toolbar on the shortcut menu.**

When a WordArt drawing object is selected, the WordArt toolbar is displayed in the Word window (Figure 6-6).

Edit Text button

WordArt toolbar

sizing handles are displayed around selected WordArt drawing object

FIGURE 6-6

2

• **Click the Format WordArt button on the WordArt toolbar.**

• **When Word displays the Format WordArt dialog box, if necessary, click the Size tab.**

• **In the Size and rotate area, select the text in the Height box and then type** 1.3 **as the new height.**

Word displays the Size sheet in the Format WordArt dialog box (Figure 6-7).

FIGURE 6-7

3

• **Click the Colors and Lines tab.**

• **In the Fill area, click the Color box arrow.**

Word displays the Colors and Lines sheet in the Format WordArt dialog box (Figure 6-8). You can add a gradient color effect through the Fill Effects button.

FIGURE 6-8

4

• **Click the Fill Effects button.**

• **When Word displays the Fill Effects dialog box, if necessary, click the Gradient tab.**

• **In the Colors area, click Two colors.**

When you select two colors for a drawing object, Word uses a gradient effect to blend them into one another (Figure 6-9).

FIGURE 6-9

5

• **Click the Color 1 box arrow and then click Orange on the color palette.**

• **Click the Color 2 box arrow and then click Yellow on the color palette.**

• **Click the bottom-left variant in the Variants area.**

The selected colors and variant for the WordArt object are displayed in the Sample box (Figure 6-10). The default gradient shading style is horizontal, and the selected variant blends color 2 from the middle outward into color 1.

FIGURE 6-10

6

• **Click the OK button.**

• **Click the OK button in the Format WordArt dialog box.**

Word changes the colors of the WordArt object (Figure 6-11).

FIGURE 6-11

Instead of using the Size sheet in the Format WordArt dialog box to change the size (width and height) of a WordArt drawing object, you can drag its sizing handles, just as with any other graphic.

Changing the WordArt Shape

Word provides a variety of shapes to make your WordArt drawing object more interesting. The next steps show how to change the WordArt drawing object to a cascade down shape.

To Change the Shape of a WordArt Drawing Object

1

• **Click the WordArt Shape button on the WordArt toolbar.**

Word displays a graphical list of available shapes (Figure 6-12). When you click a shape, the WordArt drawing object forms itself into the selected shape.

FIGURE 6-12

2

• **Click Cascade Down (the bottom-right shape) in the list of shapes.**

• **Click the paragraph mark to the right of the WordArt text.**

The newsletter title is displayed in a cascade down shape (Figure 6-13). The WordArt drawing object no longer is selected. Thus, the WordArt toolbar no longer appears in the Word window.

FIGURE 6-13

The Drawing toolbar still is displayed in the Word window because it will be used again later in this project.

The next step is to center the WordArt drawing object, as described below.

To Center the Newsletter Title

1 **Click the Center button on the Formatting toolbar.**

Word centers the WordArt drawing object between the left and right margins (shown in Figure 6-14 on the next page). Because the WordArt object extends from the left to the right margins, you may not notice a difference in its position after you click the Center button.

Adding Ruling Lines

In Word, you use borders to create ruling lines. As discussed in previous projects, Word can place borders on any edge of a paragraph(s), that is, the top, bottom, left, or right edges.

The following steps describe how to place ruling lines above the newsletter title.

To Use Borders to Add Ruling Lines

1 If the Tables and Borders toolbar is not displayed on the screen, click the Tables and Borders button on the Standard toolbar. Click the Line Style box arrow on the Tables and Borders toolbar, scroll to and then click the diagonally stroked line (just below the double wavy lines) in the list.

2 Click the Border Color button arrow on the Tables and Borders toolbar and then click Teal on the color palette.

3 Click the Border button arrow on the Tables and Borders toolbar and then click Top Border.

The newsletter title and Tables and Borders toolbar display as shown in Figure 6-14.

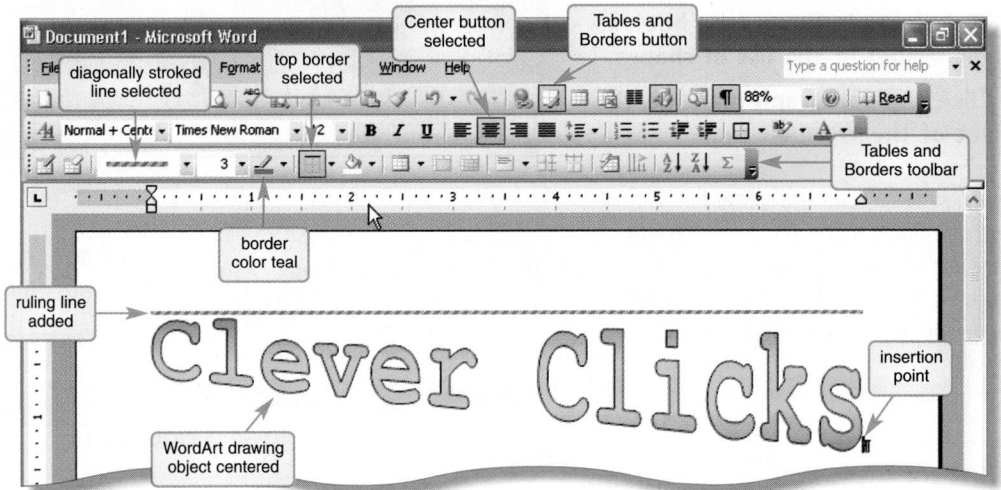

FIGURE 6-14

When you press the ENTER key at the end of the newsletter title to advance the insertion point to the next line, Word carries forward formatting. You do not want the paragraphs and characters on line 2 to have the same formatting as line 1. Instead, you clear formatting so the characters on line 2 use the Normal style.

The following steps describe how to clear formatting.

To Clear Formatting

1 With the insertion point positioned at the end of line 1 (shown in Figure 6-14), press the ENTER key.

2 Click the Style box arrow on the Formatting toolbar (Figure 6-15).

3 Click Clear Formatting in the Style list.

Word applies the Normal style to the location of the insertion point.

FIGURE 6-15

Depending on your installation of Word, the Normal style might be a different font or font size.

Inserting Symbols

The issue information line in this newsletter contains the text, Monthly Newsletter, at the left margin and the volume and issue number at the right margin (shown in Figure 6-1a on page WD 379). As discussed previously, a paragraph cannot be formatted as both left-aligned and right-aligned. To place text at the right margin of a left-aligned paragraph, you must set a tab stop at the right margin.

In this newsletter, between the volume number and issue number is a large round dot. This special symbol is not on the keyboard. You insert dots and other symbols, such as letters in the Greek alphabet and mathematical characters, using the Symbol dialog box.

The following steps explain how to enter the text in the issue information line. First, text is entered at the left margin and a right-aligned tab stop is set at the right margin. Then, text is entered at the right margin, with a dot symbol between the volume and issue numbers.

To Set a Right-Aligned Tab Stop

1 **Click the Bold button on the Formatting toolbar. Click the Font Color button arrow on the Formatting toolbar and then click Teal on the color palette. Type** Monthly Newsletter **on line 2 of the newsletter.**

2 **Click Format on the menu bar and then click Tabs. When Word displays the Tabs dialog box, type** 7 **in the Tab stop position text box and then click Right in the Alignment area. Click the Set button (Figure 6-16 on the next page).**

3 **Click the OK button.**

After clicking the OK button, Word places a right-aligned tab stop at the right margin (shown in Figure 6-17 on the next page).

FIGURE 6-16

The next step is to insert a symbol in the middle of text, as shown below.

To Insert a Symbol

1

• **Press the TAB key. Type** Vol. 8
and then press the SPACEBAR.

• **Click Insert on the menu bar.**

*The volume number displays at the right
margin (Figure 6-17). Notice the right tab
marker is positioned directly on top of the
right margin on the ruler.*

FIGURE 6-17

2

- Click **Symbol** on the Insert menu.

- When Word displays the Symbol dialog box, if necessary, click the Symbols tab.

- In the Symbol dialog box, if necessary, click the Font box arrow, scroll to and then click Symbol.

- In the list of symbols, if necessary, scroll to and then click the dot symbol.

- Click the Insert button.

As soon as you click the Insert button, the dot symbol is placed in the document to the left of the insertion point (Figure 6-18). At this point, you can insert additional symbols or close the Symbol dialog box.

3

- Click the **Close** button in the Symbol dialog box.

FIGURE 6-18

When you insert a symbol, Word places it in the Recently used symbols list in the Symbol dialog box (Figure 6-18).

You also can insert ANSI (American National Standards Institute) characters in a document by entering the ANSI code directly into the document. The **ANSI characters** are a predefined set of characters, including both characters on the keyboard and special characters, such as the dot symbol. To enter the ANSI code, make sure the NUM LOCK key on the numeric keypad is on. Press and hold the ALT key and then type the numeral zero followed by the ANSI code for the symbol. You must use the numeric keypad when entering the ANSI code. For a complete list of ANSI codes, see your Microsoft Windows documentation.

The next step is to finish entering text in the issue information line and then place a border immediately below the line, as described below.

To Enter Text and Add a Border

1 Press the SPACEBAR. Type `Issue 9` at the end of the issue information line.

2 Click the Border button arrow on the Tables and Borders toolbar and then click Bottom Border (Figure 6-19 on the next page).

3 Click the Tables and Borders button on the Standard toolbar to remove the Tables and Borders toolbar from the screen.

The issue information line is complete. Word uses the previously defined line style (diagonal stroked line) and color (teal) for the bottom border.

Other Ways

1. Press ALT+0 (zero) and then with the NUM LOCK key on, use numeric keypad to type ANSI character code for symbol
2. In Voice Command mode, say "Insert, Symbol, [select symbol], Insert, Close"

More About

Inserting Special Characters

Through the Symbol dialog box, in addition to symbols you can insert special characters including a variety of dashes, hyphens, spaces, apostrophes, and quotation marks. Click Insert on the menu bar, click Symbol, click the Special Characters tab, click the desired character in the Character list, click the Insert button, and then click the Close button.

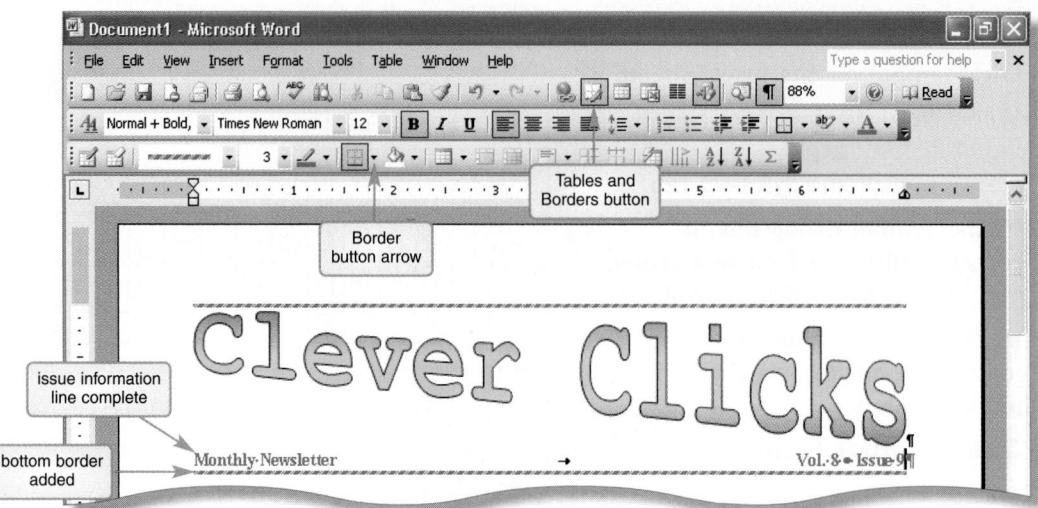

FIGURE 6-19

Inserting and Formatting a Floating Graphic

The next step is to insert a computer mouse clip art image from the Web into the nameplate. When you insert a clip art image in a paragraph in a document, Word inserts the image as an inline object. An **inline object** is an object that is part of a paragraph. With inline objects, you change the location of the object by setting paragraph options, such as centered, right-aligned, and so on.

In many cases, you want more flexibility in positioning graphics. That is, you want to position a graphic at a specific location in a document. To do this, the object must be floating. A **floating object** is an object that can be positioned at a specific location in a document or in a layer over or behind text in a document. You can position a floating object anywhere on the page.

In this project, for example, the computer mouse image is to be positioned at the left edge of the nameplate below the title of the newsletter. The following steps describe how to insert a clip art image and then change it from an inline object to a floating object.

> **Note:** The following steps assume your computer is connected to the Internet. If it is not, go directly to the shaded steps on the opposite page that are titled To Insert a Graphic File from the Data Disk.

To Insert Clip Art from the Web

1 Click Insert on the menu bar, point to Picture, and then click Clip Art on the Picture submenu.

2 In the Clip Art task pane, drag through any text in the Search for text box to select the text. Type `computer hardware mouse` and then press the ENTER key.

3 Scroll to and then click the clip that matches the one shown in Figure 6-20. (If the clip does not display in the task pane, click the Close button on the Clip Art task pane to close the task pane and then proceed to the shaded steps on the opposite page.)

4 Click the Close button on the Clip Art task pane title bar.

Word inserts the computer mouse graphic at the location of the insertion point (Figure 6-20). The graphic is an inline object, that is, part of the current paragraph.

computer mouse
graphic inserted
as inline object

Monthly·Newsletter   →   Vol.·8·•·Issue·9

FIGURE 6-20

If you do not have access to the Web, you can insert the clip art file in the Word document from the Data Disk, as described in the following steps. If you did not download the Data Disk, see the inside back cover for instructions for downloading the Data Disk or see your instructor.

To Insert a Graphic File from the Data Disk

1 Click Insert on the menu bar, point to Picture, and then click From File.

2 Insert the Data Disk into drive A. When the Insert Picture dialog box is displayed, click the Look in box arrow and then click 3½ Floppy (A:). Click the file name laq4py2r[1] and then click the Insert button.

Word inserts the computer mouse graphic at the location of the insertion point (shown in Figure 6-20). The graphic is an inline object, that is, part of the current paragraph.

More About

Inserting Graphics

If you have a scanned image or photograph on disk that you would like to insert in a document, you would follow the steps to the left to insert the graphic file in the document.

Depending on the location of the insertion point, the computer mouse graphic may be in a different position.

The following steps show how to change the computer mouse graphic from inline to floating, which will enable you to move the graphic to any location on the page.

To Format a Graphic as Floating

1

• **In the document window, click the graphic to select it.**

• **If the Picture toolbar does not appear, right-click the graphic and then click Show Picture Toolbar on the shortcut menu.**

• **Click the Text Wrapping button on the Picture toolbar.**

Notice that a selected inline object has small squares as sizing handles (Figure 6-21).

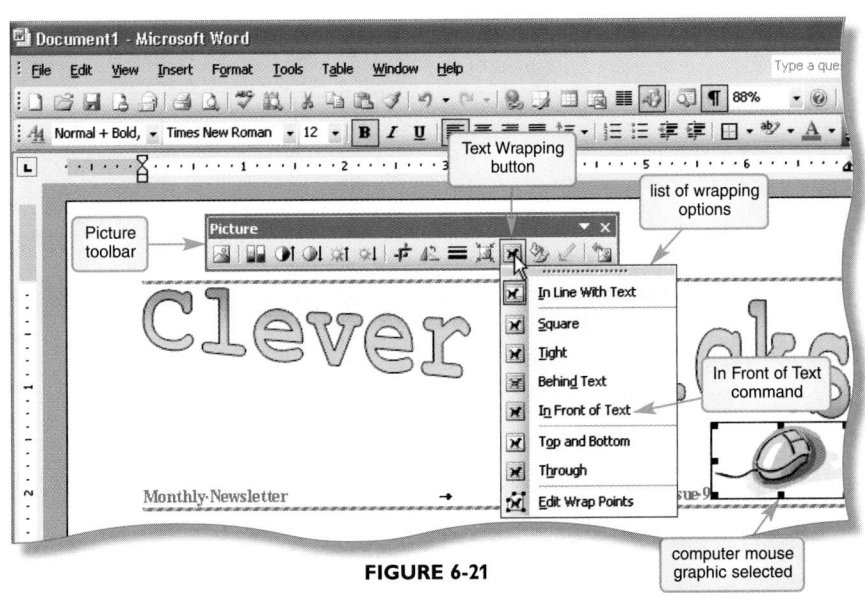

FIGURE 6-21

2

• **In the list of wrapping options, click In Front of Text.**

Word changes the format of the graphic from inline to floating (Figure 6-22). You can position a floating object anywhere in the document. The sizing handles on a floating object display as small circles.

Other Ways

1. Click Format Picture button on Picture toolbar, click Layout tab, click In front of text, click OK button
2. On Format menu click Picture, click Layout tab, click In front of text, click OK button
3. In Voice Command mode, say "Format, Picture, Layout, In front of text, OK"

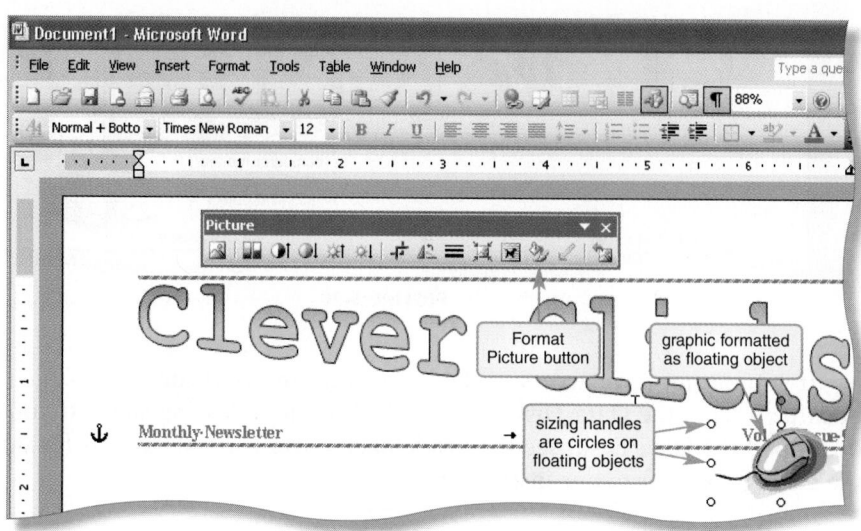

FIGURE 6-22

The next step is to flip the computer mouse graphic so the tail (cord) points toward the right instead of the left. The following steps show how to flip a graphic horizontally.

To Flip a Graphic

1

• **With the graphic still selected, click the Draw button on the Drawing toolbar.**

• **Point to Rotate or Flip on the Draw menu.**

Word displays the Draw menu above the Draw button (Figure 6-23). The Rotate or Flip submenu is displayed to the right of the Draw menu.

FIGURE 6-23

2

• **Click Flip Horizontal on the Rotate or Flip submenu.**

Word flips the graphic to display its mirror image (Figure 6-24).

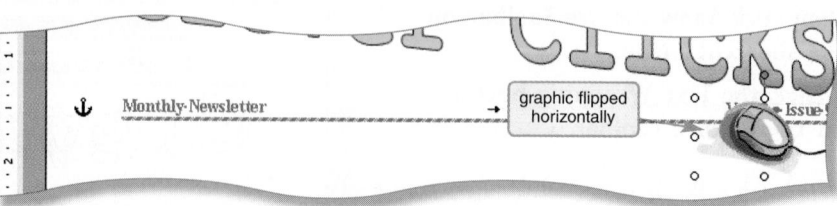

FIGURE 6-24

The next step is to move the computer mouse graphic to the left edge of the nameplate below the C in Clever. When you move an object, such as this graphic, Word automatically attaches it to an invisible set of horizontal and vertical lines, called the **drawing grid**. If you want to position an object at a precise spot, you must instruct Word to not use the drawing grid, as shown in the following steps.

To Not Use the Drawing Grid

1

• **Click the Draw button on the Drawing toolbar.**

Word displays the Draw menu above the Draw button (Figure 6-25).

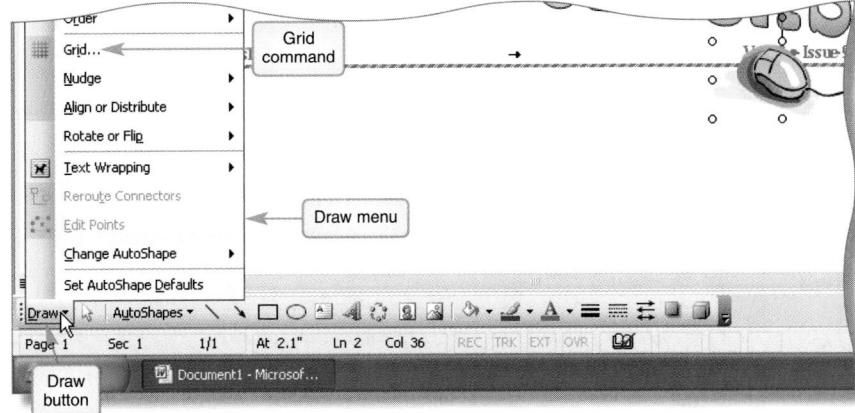

FIGURE 6-25

2

• **Click Grid on the Draw menu.**

• **When Word displays the Drawing Grid dialog box, if necessary, remove the check mark from the Snap objects to grid check box.**

The Drawing Grid dialog box allows you to specify many settings related to the drawing grid (Figure 6-26).

3

• **Click the OK button.**

When you drag objects in the document, Word will not attach them to the drawing grid.

FIGURE 6-26

If you wanted to restore the drawing grid to its default settings, you would click the Default button in the Drawing Grid dialog box and then click the Yes button in the Microsoft Word dialog box.

The next step is to move the computer mouse graphic to the left edge of the nameplate so its left edge is immediately below the letter C in Clever, as described on the next page.

Other Ways

1. With Drawing toolbar displaying, in Voice Command mode, say "Draw, Grid, Snap objects to grid, OK"

To Move a Graphic

1 **Point to the middle of the graphic, and when the mouse pointer has a four-headed arrow attached to it, drag the graphic to the location shown in Figure 6-27.**

Word places the graphic at the exact location you desire.

The color on the computer mouse graphic is a bit dark. With Word, you can brighten or darken a graphic. The following step shows how to brighten the graphic in this project.

To Brighten a Graphic

1

• **With the computer mouse graphic selected, click the More Brightness button on the Picture toolbar four times.**

Word brightens the selected graphic (Figure 6-27). A brightened graphic has lighter colors.

FIGURE 6-27

Instead of making a graphic's colors lighter, you can darken its colors. To darken a graphic, you would perform this step.

TO DARKEN A GRAPHIC

1. Click the Less Brightness button on the Picture toolbar.

If you wanted to return the brightness to its original settings, you would click the Format Picture button on the Picture toolbar, click the Picture tab, click the Reset button, and then click the OK button.

The next step is to enter the name of the feature article below the ruling line. To do this, you position the insertion point at the end of the issue information line (after the 9 in Issue 9) and then press the ENTER key. Recall that the issue information line has a bottom border. As mentioned earlier, when you press the ENTER key in a bordered paragraph, Word carries forward the border to the next paragraph. Thus, after you press the ENTER key, you should clear formatting to format the new paragraph to the Normal style.

The following steps describe how to clear formatting.

To Clear Formatting

1 Click at the end of line 2 (the issue information line) so the insertion point is immediately after the 9 in Issue 9. Press the ENTER key.

2 With the insertion point on line 3, click the Style box arrow on the Formatting toolbar and then click Clear Formatting.

Word applies the Normal style to the location of the insertion point.

One blank line below the bottom border is the name of the feature article, Safeguarding Computers from Virus Infections, in 14-point Times New Roman bold orange font. The following steps describe how to enter this text and then clear formatting on the line below the text.

To Format and Enter Text

1 With the insertion point on line 3, press the ENTER key.

2 Click the Font Size box arrow on the Formatting toolbar and then click 14. Click the Bold button on the Formatting toolbar. Click the Font Color button arrow on the Formatting toolbar and then click Orange on the color palette.

3 Type Safeguarding Computers from Virus Infections **and then press the ENTER key.**

4 Click the Style box arrow on the Formatting toolbar and then click Clear Formatting.

The article title is entered (Figure 6-28). The paragraph at the location of the insertion point is returned to the Normal style.

More About

Graphics

If you have multiple graphics in a single area on a page, you can group them together so they become one single object. To do this, select the first object by clicking it and then select each additional object by holding down the CTRL key while clicking it. With all objects selected, click the Draw button on the Drawing toolbar and then click Group on the Draw menu.

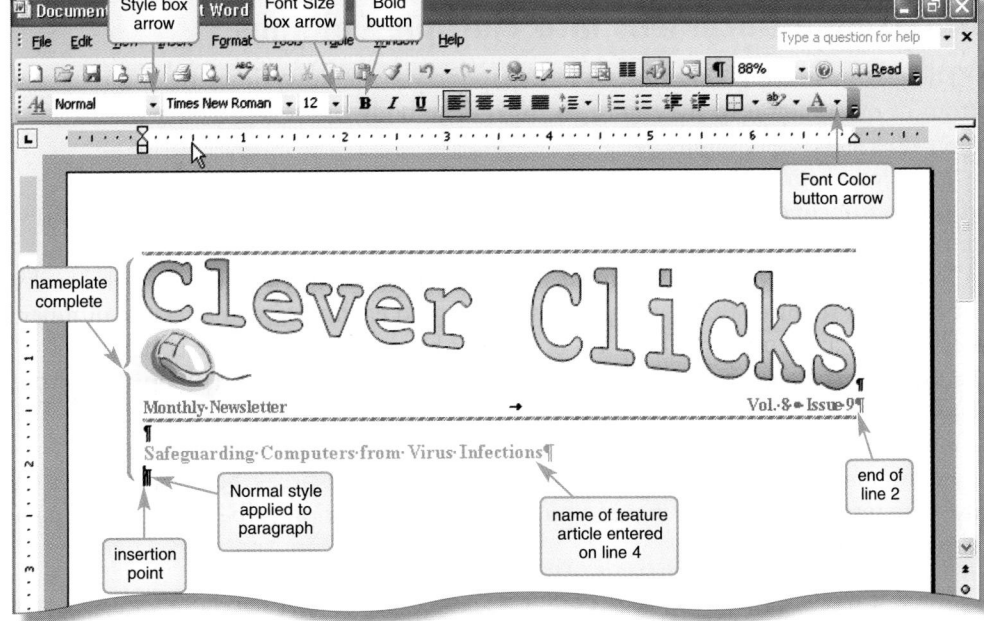

FIGURE 6-28

Saving the Newsletter

You have made several changes to this newsletter. Thus, you should save it, as described in the following steps.

To Save a Document

1 **Insert a floppy disk into drive A.**

2 **Click the Save button on the Standard toolbar.**

3 **Type** Clever Clicks Newsletter **in the File name box. Do not press the ENTER key.**

4 **Click the Save in box arrow and then click 3½ Floppy (A:).**

5 **Click the Save button in the Save As dialog box.**

Word saves the document on a floppy disk in drive A with the file name, Clever Clicks Newsletter (shown in Figure 6-29).

The nameplate for the newsletter is complete.

Formatting the First Page of the Body of the Newsletter

The next step is to format the first page of the body of the newsletter. The body of the newsletter in this project is divided into three columns (Figure 6-1a on page WD 379). The characters in the paragraphs are aligned on both the right and left edges — similar to newspaper columns. The first letter in the first paragraph is much larger than the rest of the characters in the paragraph. A vertical rule separates the second and third columns. The steps on the following pages illustrate how to format the first page of the body of the newsletter using these desktop publishing features.

Formatting a Document into Multiple Columns

The text in **snaking columns,** or newspaper-style columns, flows from the bottom of one column to the top of the next. The body of the newsletter in this project uses snaking columns.

When you begin a document in Word, it has one column. You can divide a portion of a document or the entire document into multiple columns. Within each column, you can type, modify, or format text.

To divide a portion of a document into multiple columns, you use section breaks. That is, Word requires that a new section be created each time you alter the number of columns in a document. Thus, if a document has a nameplate (one column) followed by an article of three columns followed by an article of two columns, then the document would be divided into a total of three sections.

In this project, the nameplate is one column and the body of the newsletter is three columns. Thus, you must insert a continuous section break below the nameplate. The term, continuous, means you want the new section to be on the same page as the previous section.

Q&A

Q: How many newspaper-style columns should be across a page?

A: Narrow columns generally are easier to read than wide ones. Columns, however, can be too narrow. Try to have between five and fifteen words per line. To do this, you may need to adjust the column width, the font size, or the leading. Leading is the line spacing, which can be adjusted through the Paragraph dialog box in Word.

The following steps show how to divide the body of the newsletter into three columns.

To Insert a Continuous Section Break

1

• **With the insertion point on line 5 (shown in Figure 6-28 on page WD 397), press the ENTER key. Scroll the document down a few lines.**

• **Click Insert on the menu bar and then click Break.**

• **When Word displays the Break dialog box, click Continuous in the Section break types area.**

In the Break dialog box, continuous means you want the new section on the same page as the previous section (Figure 6-29).

FIGURE 6-29

2

• **Click the OK button.**

Word inserts a continuous section break above the insertion point (Figure 6-30). The insertion point now is located in section 2.

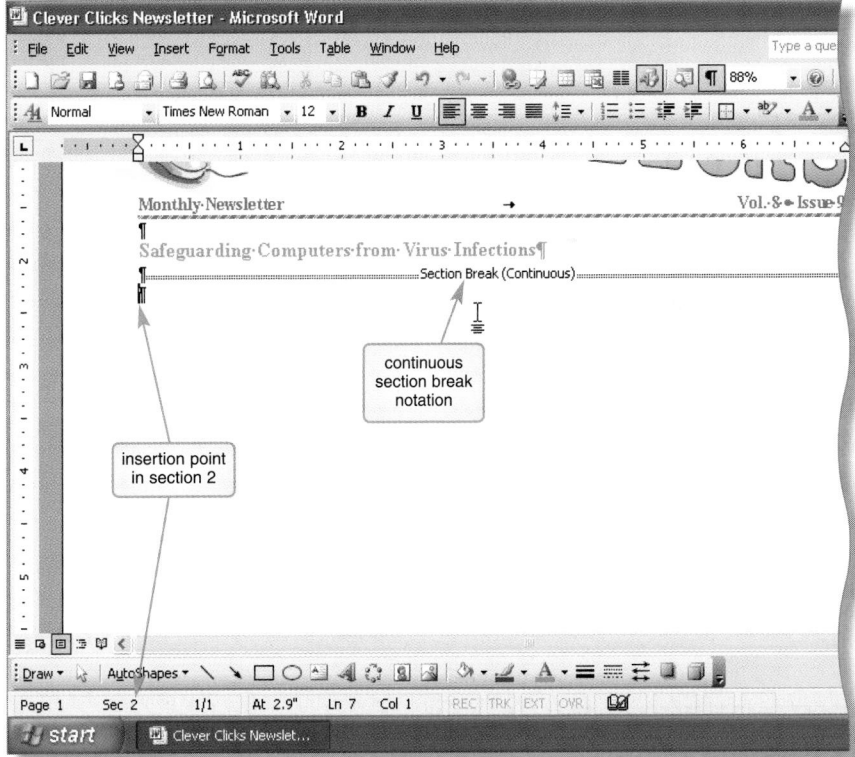

FIGURE 6-30

Other Ways

1. In Voice Command mode, say "Insert, Break, Continuous, OK"

The document now has two sections. The nameplate is in the first section, and the insertion point is in the second section. The second section is to be formatted to three columns. Thus, the steps on the next page show how to format the second section in the document to three columns.

To Change the Number of Columns

1

• **Be sure the insertion point is in section 2. Click the Columns button on the Standard toolbar.**

Word displays a columns list graphic below the Columns button (Figure 6-31).

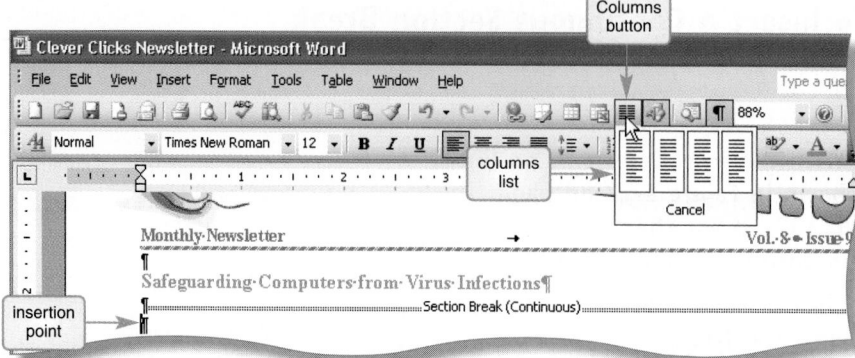

FIGURE 6-31

2

• **Position the mouse pointer on the third column in the columns list (Figure 6-32).**

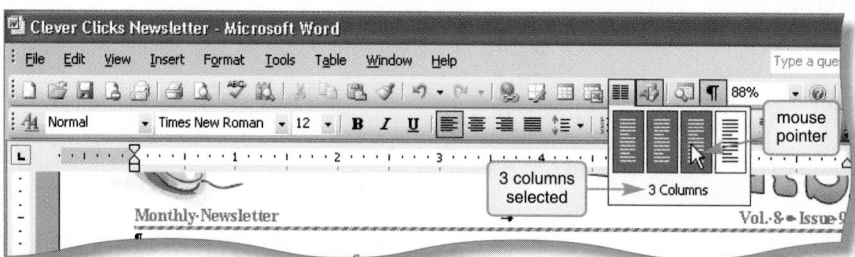

FIGURE 6-32

3

• **Click the third column in the list.**

Word divides the section containing the insertion point into three evenly sized and spaced columns (Figure 6-33). Notice that the ruler indicates the width of each column.

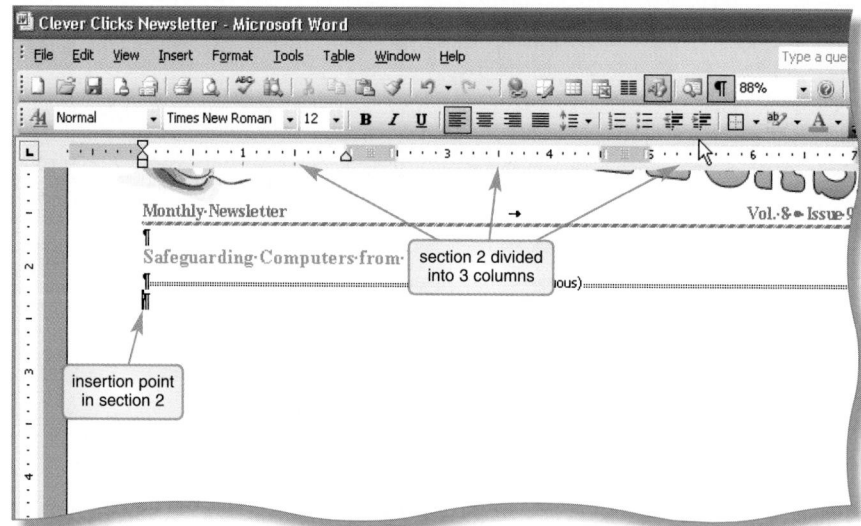

FIGURE 6-33

When you use the Columns button to change the number of columns, Word creates columns of equal width. You can create columns of unequal width by clicking the Columns command on the Format menu.

Justifying a Paragraph

The text in the paragraphs of the body of the newsletter is **justified**, which means that the left and right margins are aligned, like the edges of newspaper columns. The following step shows how to enter the first paragraph of the feature article using justified alignment.

To Justify a Paragraph

1

• **Click the Justify button on the Formatting toolbar.**

• **Type the first paragraph of the feature article, as shown in Figure 6-34.**

• **Press the ENTER key.**

Word aligns both the left and right edges of the paragraph (Figure 6-34). Notice that Word places extra space between some words when text is justified.

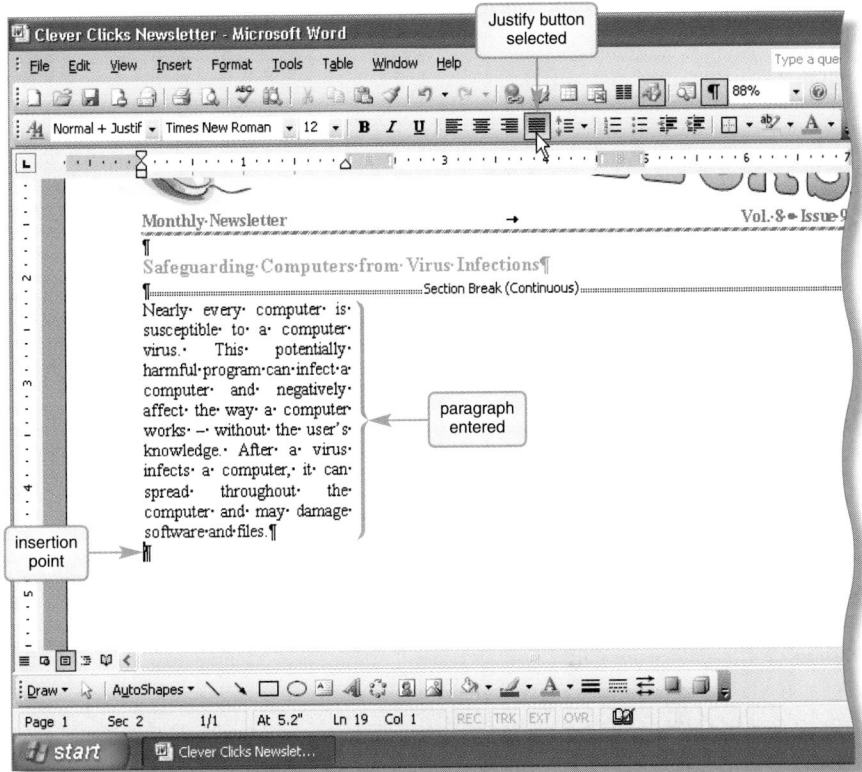

FIGURE 6-34

Other Ways

1. On Format menu click Paragraph, click Indents and Spacing tab, click Alignment box arrow, click Justified, click OK button
2. Press CTRL+J
3. In Voice Command mode, say "Justify"

Inserting the Remainder of the Feature Article

Instead of typing the rest of the feature article into the newsletter for this project, the next step is to insert a file named Computer Virus Article in the newsletter. This file, which contains the remainder of the feature article, is located on the Data Disk. If you did not download the Data Disk, see the inside back cover for instructions for downloading the Data Disk or see your instructor.

The steps on the next page show how to insert the Computer Virus Article file in the newsletter.

To Insert a File in the Newsletter

1

• **If necessary, insert the Data Disk into drive A. Click Insert on the menu bar and then click File.**

• **When Word displays the Insert File dialog box, if necessary, click the Look in box arrow and then click 3½ Floppy (A:).**

• **Click Computer Virus Article.**

The selected file in the Insert File dialog box will be inserted at the location of the insertion point in the document (Figure 6-35).

FIGURE 6-35

2

• **Click the Insert button.**

Word inserts the file, Computer Virus Article, in the file Clever Clicks Newsletter at the location of the insertion point (Figure 6-36). The text automatically is formatted into columns.

FIGURE 6-36

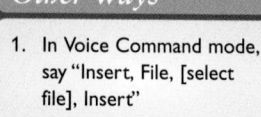

Other Ways

1. In Voice Command mode, say "Insert, File, [select file], Insert"

Formatting a Letter as a Drop Cap

You can format the first character in a paragraph to be a **drop cap**, which is a large, dropped capital letter. That is, a drop cap is larger than the rest of the characters in the paragraph. The text in the paragraph then wraps around the drop cap.

The following steps show how to create a drop cap in the first paragraph of the feature article in the newsletter.

To Format a Letter as a Drop Cap

1

• **Press CTRL+HOME to scroll to the top of the document. Scroll down and then click anywhere in the first paragraph of the feature article.**

• **Click Format on the menu bar.**

The insertion point is in the first paragraph of the feature article (Figure 6-37).

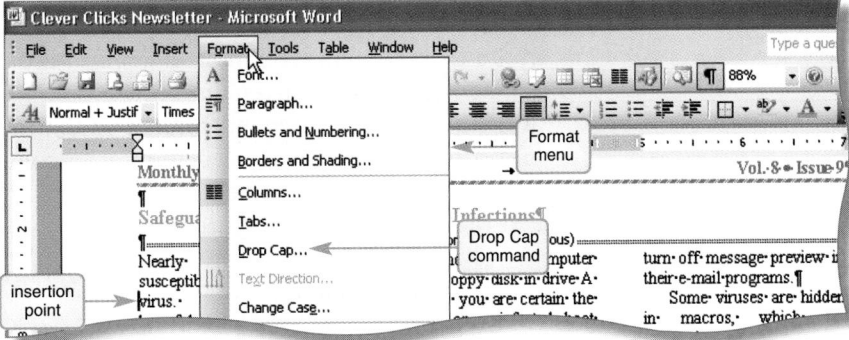

FIGURE 6-37

2

• **Click Drop Cap on the Format menu.**

• **When Word displays the Drop Cap dialog box, click Dropped in the Position area.**

Word displays the Drop Cap dialog box (Figure 6-38).

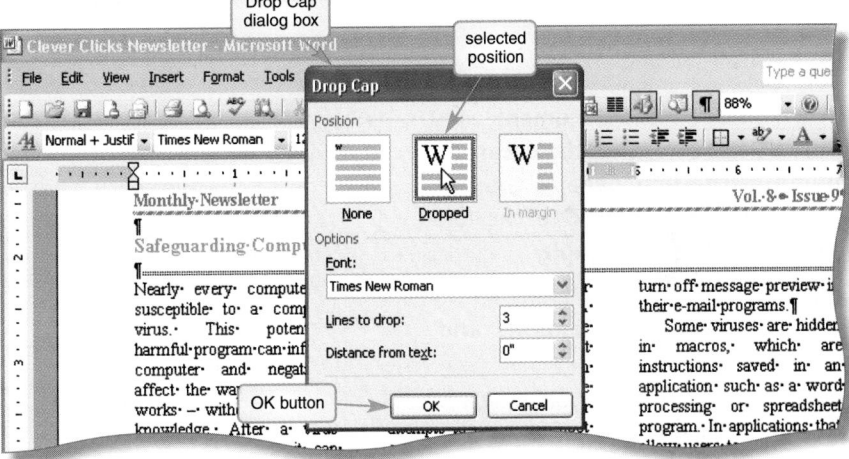

FIGURE 6-38

3

• **Click the OK button.**

Word drops the letter N in the word, Nearly, and wraps subsequent text around the drop cap (Figure 6-39).

FIGURE 6-39

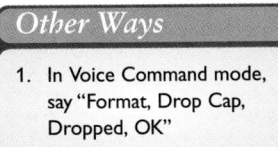

Other Ways

1. In Voice Command mode, say "Format, Drop Cap, Dropped, OK"

More About

Drop Caps

A drop cap often is used to mark the beginning of an article. To format the entire first word as a drop cap, select the word. An alternative to a drop cap is a stick-up cap, which extends into the left margin, instead of sinking into the first few lines of the text. To insert a stick-up cap, click In margin in the Drop Cap dialog box (Figure 6-38 on the previous page).

When you drop cap a letter, Word places a frame around it. A **frame** is a container for text that allows you to position the text anywhere on the page. As illustrated in the previous steps, Word can format a frame so that text wraps around it.

To remove the frame from displaying in the document window, simply click outside the frame to display the insertion point elsewhere in the document.

Inserting a Column Break

The next step is to insert a column break at the bottom of the second column. Notice in Figure 6-1a on page WD 379 that the third column on the first page of the newsletter is not a continuation of the feature article. The third column, instead, contains several member announcements. The feature article continues on the second page of the newsletter (Figure 6-1b). For the member announcements to be displayed in the third column, you insert a **column break** at the bottom of the second column.

Before inserting the column break, you first must insert a next page section break at the bottom of the second column so that the remainder of the feature article moves to the second page. Then, insert a column break at the bottom of the second column so the announcements always display in the third column, even if you add text or graphics to the feature article.

The following steps show how to insert a next page section break at the bottom of the second column.

To Insert a Next Page Section Break

1

• **Scroll through the document to display the bottom of the second column of the first page in the document window. Click to the left of the M in the paragraph beginning with the word, Many.**

• **Click Insert on the menu bar and then click Break.**

• **When Word displays the Break dialog box, click Next page in the Section break types area.**

The insertion point is to the left of the M in the word, Many (Figure 6-40).

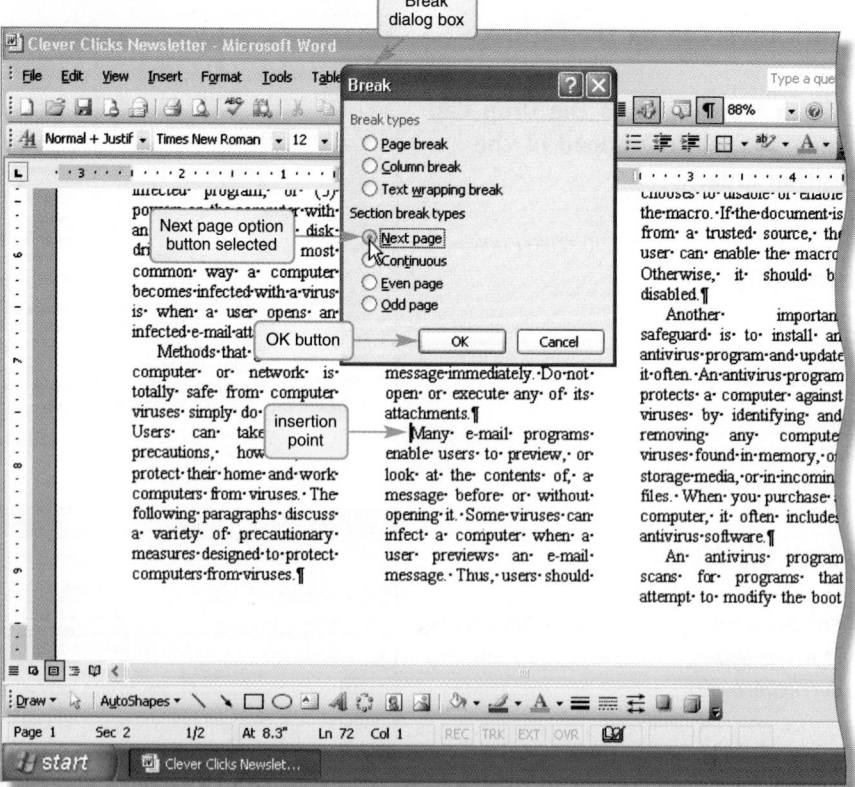

FIGURE 6-40

2

• **Click the OK button.**

Word inserts a section break at the location of the insertion point (Figure 6-41). The remainder of the article moves to page 2 of the document because a next page section break includes a page break. On page 1, the bottom of the second column and the entire third column are empty.

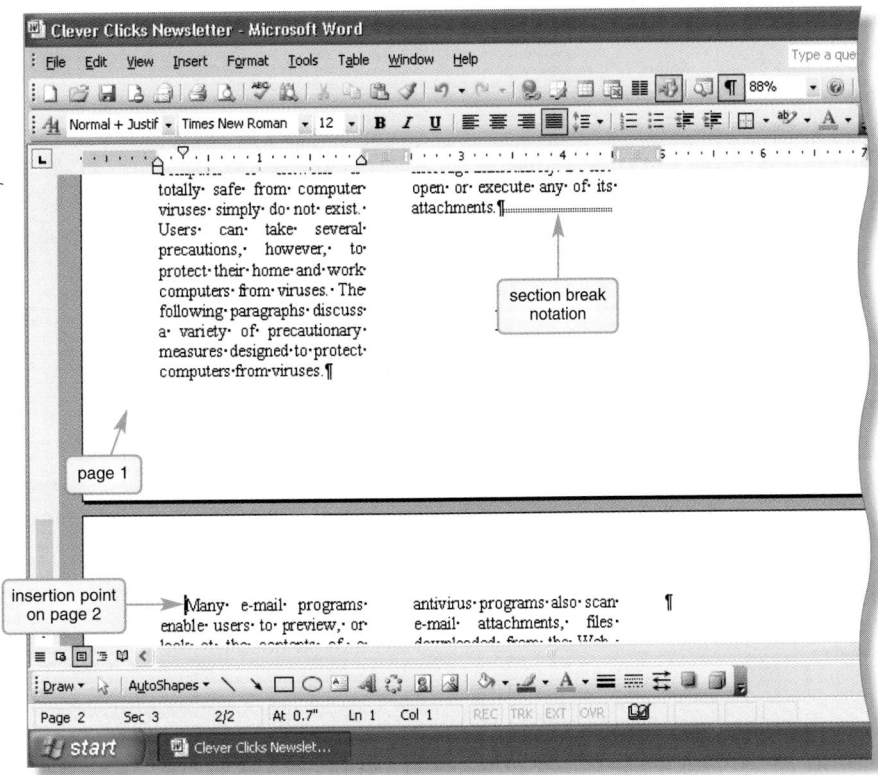

FIGURE 6-41

Other Ways

1. In Voice Command mode, say "Insert, Break, Next page, OK"

You want the member announcements to begin at the top of the third column, even though a small amount of room is available at the bottom of the second column. To move the insertion point to the top of the third column, you will insert a column break at the end of the text in the second column.

First, you add a note to the reader that the feature article continues on page 2, and then you insert a column break.

To Enter Text

1 Scroll up to display the bottom of the second column of the first page of the newsletter and then position the insertion point between the paragraph mark and the section break notation.

2 Press the ENTER key three times. Press the UP ARROW key.

3 Press CTRL+R to right align the paragraph mark. Press CTRL+I to turn on italics. Type ...continued on page 2 and then press CTRL+I again to turn off italics.

The continued message is entered at the bottom of the second column (shown in Figure 6-42 on the next page).

The steps on the next page show how to insert a column break below the continued message.

Q: Should multi-page articles contain jump lines?

A: An article that spans multiple pages should contain a jump or jump line, which informs the reader where to look for the rest of the article or story. The message on the first page is called a jump-to line, and a jump-from line marks the beginning of the continuation.

To Insert a Column Break

1

• **Press the ENTER key. Press CTRL+L to left-align the insertion point.**

• **Click Insert on the menu bar and then click Break.**

• **When Word displays the Break dialog box, click Column break in the Break types area (Figure 6-42).**

FIGURE 6-42

2

• **Click the OK button.**

Word inserts a column break at the bottom of the second column on page 1 and places the insertion point at the top of the third column (Figure 6-43).

FIGURE 6-43

...continued on page 2¶

More About

Column Breaks

A column break is displayed on the screen with the words Column Break separated by a thinly dotted horizontal line. Figure 6-44 shows the column break notation at the bottom of the second column. To remove a column break, select it and then click the Cut button on the Standard toolbar or press the DELETE key.

The following step saves the newsletter again.

To Save a Document

1 **With the disk containing the newsletter file in drive A, click the Save button on the Standard toolbar.**

Word saves the document again with the file name, Clever Clicks Newsletter.

Inserting Text from a File, Viewing the Document, and Modifying the Inserted Text

To eliminate having to enter the entire third column of announcements into the newsletter, the next step in the project is to insert the file named Volume 8 Issue 9 Announcements in the third column of the newsletter. This file contains the three announcements: the first about a user group meeting, the second about member discounts, and the third about the topic of the next newsletter issue.

The Volume 8 Issue 9 Announcements file is located on the Data Disk. If you did not download the Data Disk, see the inside back cover for instructions for downloading the Data Disk or see your instructor.

The following steps describe how to insert a file in the newsletter.

To Insert a File in a Column of the Newsletter

1 If necessary, insert the Data Disk into drive A. With the insertion point at the top of the third column, click Insert on the menu bar and then click File.

2 When Word displays the Insert File dialog box, if necessary, click the Look in box arrow and then click 3½ Floppy (A:). Click the file name, Volume 8 Issue 9 Announcements.

3 Click the Insert button.

Word inserts the file, Volume 8 Issue 9 Announcements, in the third column of the newsletter (shown in Figure 6-45 on the next page).

Word provides a **full screen view** that places the current document in a window that fills the entire screen; that is, it removes the title bar, menu bar, toolbars, rulers, scroll bars, and taskbar. In full screen view, reading through a document is easier because more of the document is displayed. You scroll through a document in full screen view the same as when it is in the document window.

To see the announcements just inserted into the third column more easily, the next task is to switch to full screen view. The following steps show how to display a document in full screen view and then exit full screen view.

To Display a Document in Full Screen View

1

• Click View on the menu bar.

Word displays the View menu (Figure 6-44).

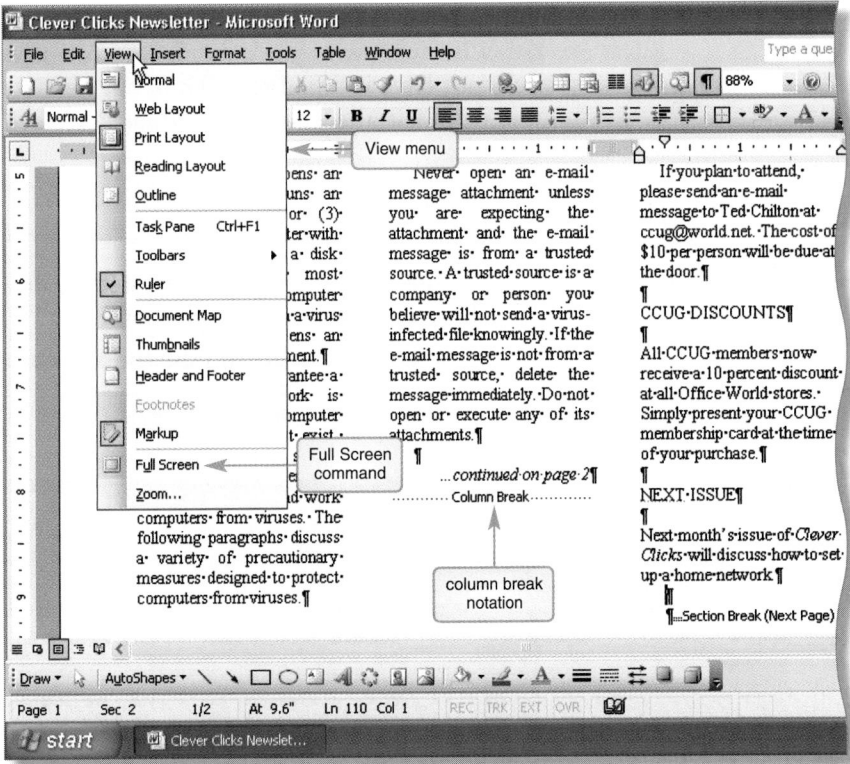

FIGURE 6-44

2

- Click **Full Screen** on the **View** menu.
- **Scroll through the document to display the announcements on the screen.**

Word displays the newsletter in full screen view (Figure 6-45). The newsletter fills the entire screen. The only toolbar on the screen is the Full Screen toolbar, which contains just the Close Full Screen button. You can scroll through the document in full screen view using the mouse or keyboard.

3

- Click the **Close Full Screen button** on the **Full Screen toolbar** to return to print layout view.

full screen view

Volume 8 Issue 9 Announcements file inserted in column 3

Nearly every computer is susceptible to a computer virus. This potentially harmful program can infect a computer and negatively affect the way a computer works—without the user's knowledge. After a virus infects a computer, it can spread throughout the computer and may damage software and files.¶

Computer viruses infect a computer in three basic ways: when a user (1) opens an infected file, (2) runs an infected program, or (3) powers on the computer with an infected disk in a disk drive. Today, the most common way a computer becomes infected with a virus is when a user opens an infected e-mail attachment.¶

Methods that guarantee a computer or network is totally safe from computer viruses simply do not exist. Users can take several precautions, however, to protect their home and work computers from viruses following paragraphs a variety of precautionary measures designed

Do not start a computer with a floppy disk in drive A —unless you are certain the disk is an uninfected boot disk. All floppy disks contain a boot sector. During the startup process, the computer attempts to execute the boot sector on a disk in drive A. Even if the attempt is not successful, a virus on the floppy disk's boot sector can infect the hard disk on a computer.¶

Never open an e-mail message attachment unless you are expecting the attachment and the e-mail message is from a trusted source. A trusted source is a company or person you believe will not send a virus-infected file knowingly. If the e-mail message is not from a trusted source, delete the message immediately. Do not open or execute any of its attachments.¶

¶
...continued on page 2¶

Column Break

Full Screen toolbar

Close Full Screen button

Full Screen
Close Full Screen

USER GROUP MEETING¶
¶
The next meeting of the Clever Clicks User Group (CCUG) will be held on Saturday, October 8, at the Remington Valley recreation center (440 Center Street) from 11:00 a.m. to 3:00 p.m. A deli luncheon will be served. The guest speaker, Mary Patterson, will discuss health concerns related to computer use.¶
If you plan to attend, please send an e-mail message to Ted Chilton at ccug@world.net. The cost of $10 per person will be due at the door.¶
¶
CCUG DISCOUNTS¶
¶
All CCUG members now receive a 10 percent discount at all Office World stores. Simply present your CCUG membership card at the time of your purchase.¶
NEXT ISSUE¶
¶
Next month's issue of *Clever Clicks* will discuss how to set up a home network.¶

FIGURE 6-45

text is left-aligned instead of justified

Instead of clicking the Full Screen button on the Full Screen toolbar, you can press the ESCAPE key to exit full screen view.

While reviewing the document in full screen view, you notice that the last column does not have justified text. Thus, the next step is to change the formatting of the text from left-aligned to justified, as described below.

To Justify Paragraphs

1 On the first page of the newsletter, drag the mouse from the top of the third column down to the bottom of the third column.

2 Click the **Justify button** on the **Formatting toolbar**.

Word changes the alignment of the selected paragraphs from left-aligned to justified (Figure 6-46).

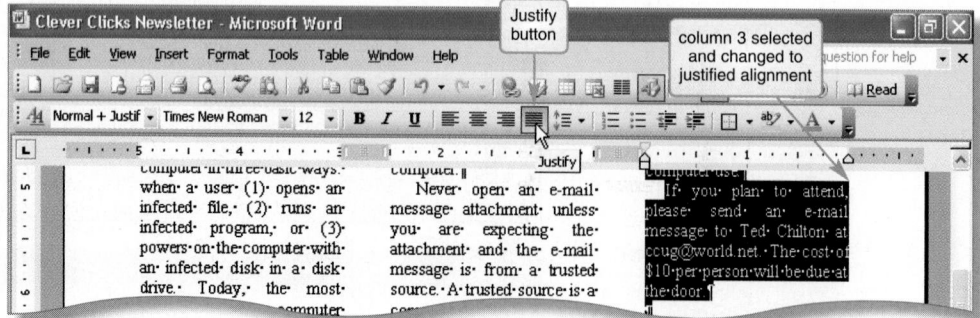

Justify button

column 3 selected and changed to justified alignment

FIGURE 6-46

Adding a Vertical Rule between Columns

In newsletters, you often see a vertical rule separating columns. With Word, you can place a vertical rule between all columns by clicking the Columns command on the Format menu and then clicking the Line between check box.

In this project, you want a vertical rule between only the second and third columns. To do this, place a left border spaced several points from the text. A point is approximately 1/72 of an inch.

The following steps place a vertical rule between the second and third columns of the newsletter.

To Place a Vertical Rule between Columns

1

• **With the third column of page 1 in the newsletter still selected, click Format on the menu bar.**

The entire third column of page 1 in the newsletter is selected (Figure 6-47).

FIGURE 6-47

2

• **Click Borders and Shading on the Format menu.**

• **When Word displays the Borders and Shading dialog box, if necessary, click the Borders tab.**

• **Click the Left Border button in the Preview area.**

In the Borders and Shading dialog box, the border diagram graphically shows the selected borders (Figure 6-48).

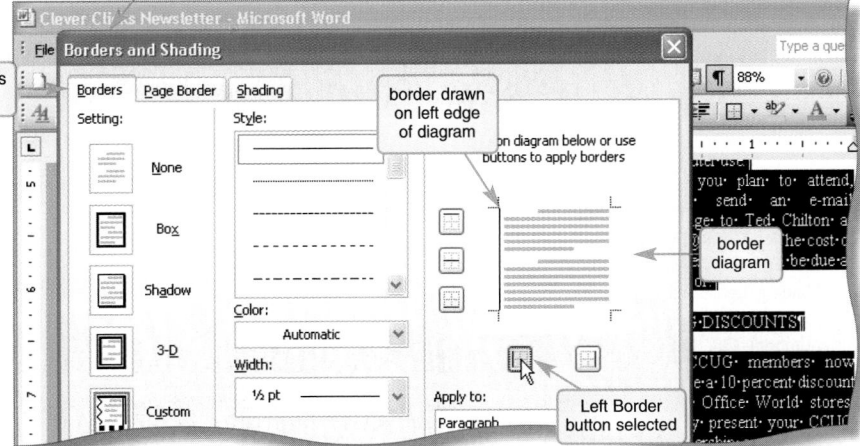

FIGURE 6-48

Q&A

Q: When should a vertical rule be used in a newsletter?

A: A vertical rule is used to guide the reader through the newsletter. If a multi-column newsletter contains a single article, place a vertical rule between every column. If different columns present different articles, place a vertical rule between each article.

3

• **Click the Options button.**

• **When Word displays the Border and Shading Options dialog box, change the Left box to 15 pt.**

The Preview area shows the border positioned 15 points from the left edge of the paragraph (Figure 6-49).

FIGURE 6-49

4

• **Click the OK button.**

• **When the Borders and Shading dialog box is visible again, click its OK button.**

• **Click in the document to remove the selection from the third column.**

Word draws a border positioned 15 points from the left edge of the text in the third column (Figure 6-50). The border is displayed as a vertical rule between the second and third columns of the newsletter.

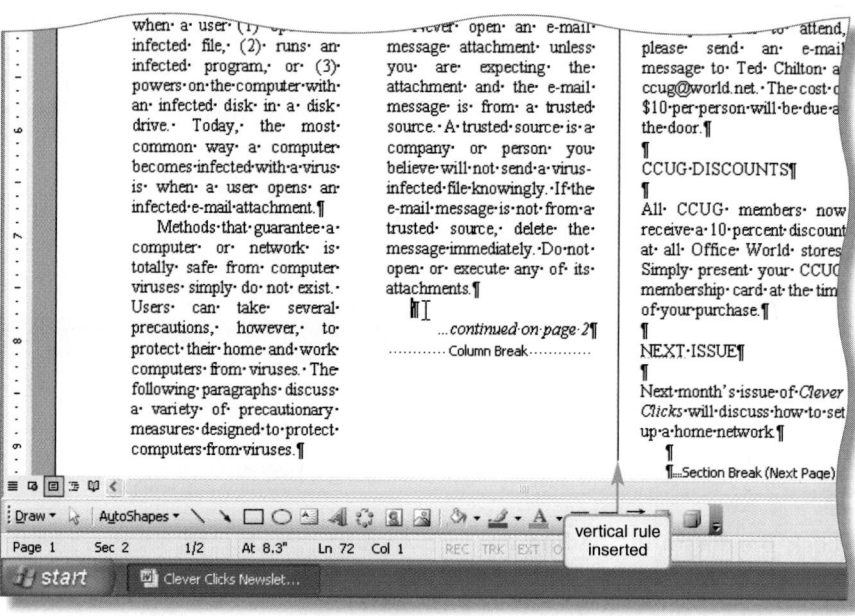

FIGURE 6-50

...continued·on·page·2¶

Other Ways

1. In Voice Command mode, say "Format, Borders and Shading, Left Border, Options, Left, [enter number], OK, OK"

Creating a Pull-Quote

A pull-quote is text pulled, or copied, from the text of the document and given graphical emphasis so it stands apart and commands the reader's attention. The newsletter in this project has a pull-quote on the first page between the first and second columns (Figure 6-1a on page WD 379).

To create a pull-quote, copy the text in the existing document to the Clipboard and then paste it into a column of the newsletter. To position the text between columns, place a text box around it. A **text box**, like a frame, is a container for text that allows you to position the text anywhere on the page. The difference between a text box and a frame is that a text box has more graphical formatting options than does a frame.

The steps on the following pages discuss how to create the pull-quote shown in Figure 6-1a on page WD 379.

Inserting a Text Box

The first step in creating the pull-quote is to copy the text to be used in the pull-quote and then insert a text box around it, as shown in the following steps.

Q: What guidelines should I follow when using pull-quotes?

A: Because of their bold emphasis, pull-quotes should be used sparingly in a newsletter. Pull-quotes are useful for breaking the monotony of long columns of text. Typically, quotation marks are used only if you are quoting someone directly. If you use quotation marks, use curly (or smart) quotation marks instead of straight quotation marks.

To Insert a Text Box

1

• **Scroll to display the second paragraph in the newsletter and then select its last sentence: Today, the most common way a computer becomes infected with a virus is when a user opens an infected e-mail attachment.**

• **With the text selected, click the Copy button on the Standard toolbar.**

The text for the pull-quote is selected (Figure 6-51).

FIGURE 6-51

2

• **Click at the end of the paragraph that contains the selected sentence and then click the Paste button on the Standard toolbar to create a duplicate of the sentence at the end of the paragraph.**

• **Select the entire sentence to be in the pull-quote.**

The sentence to be in the text box is selected (Figure 6-52).

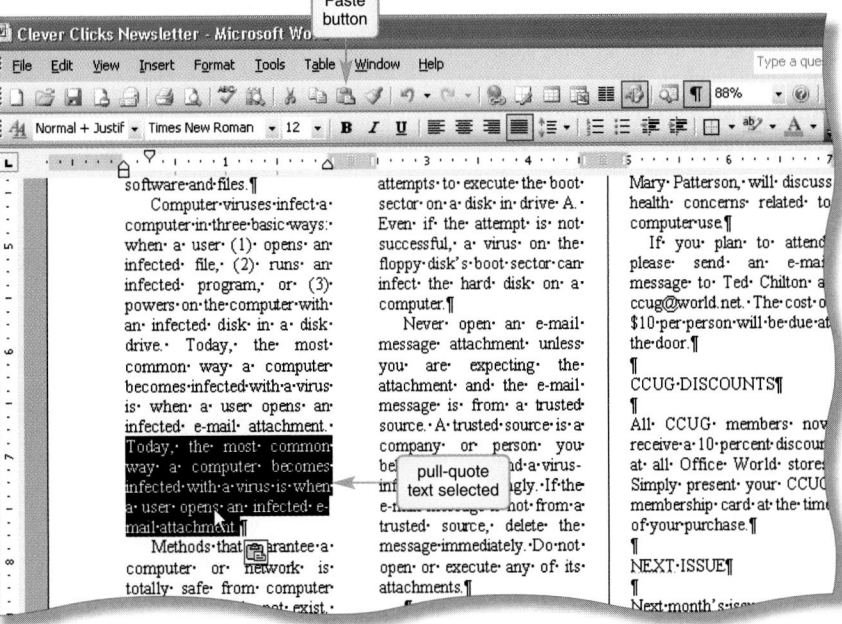

FIGURE 6-52

Microsoft Office
Word 2003

3

• **Click the Text Box button on the Drawing toolbar.**

Word places a text box around the pull-quote (Figure 6-53). The pull-quote now may be positioned anywhere on the page. The Text Box toolbar may appear on the screen when the text box is selected.

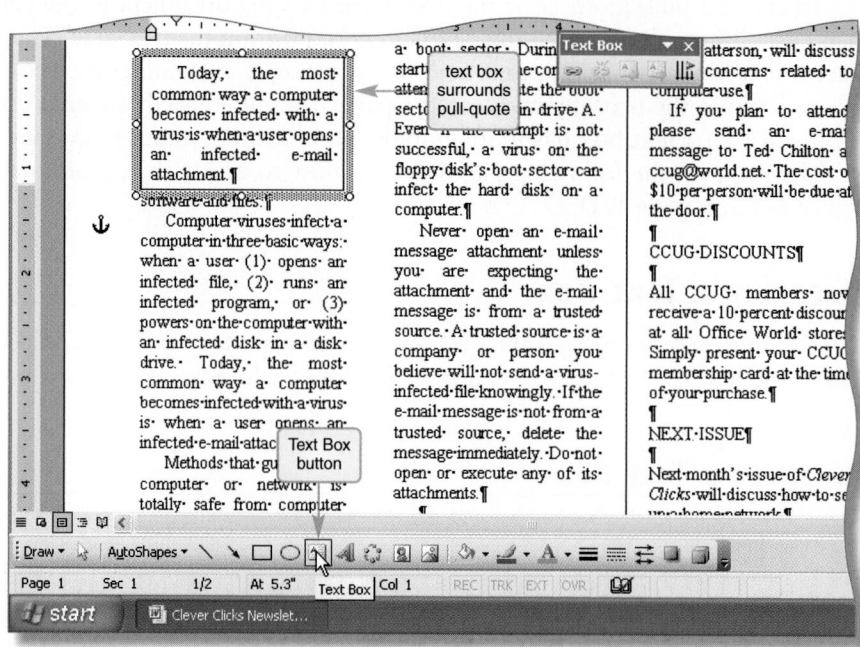

FIGURE 6-53

Other Ways

1. On Insert menu click Text Box
2. In Voice Command mode, say "Insert, Text Box"

Depending on your printer, the text in the text box may wrap differently than shown in Figure 6-53.

The next step in formatting the pull-quote is to change the color and increase the weight of the text box, as described in the following steps.

To Format a Text Box

1

• **Point to an edge of the text box and double-click when the mouse pointer has a four-headed arrow attached to it.**

• **When Word displays the Format Text Box dialog box, if necessary, click the Colors and Lines tab.**

• **In the Line area, click the Color box arrow and then click Teal on the color palette.**

• **Change the line weight to 1.5 pt.**

In the Colors and Lines sheet in the Format Text Box dialog box, you can modify characteristics of the fill color, lines, and arrows (Figure 6-54).

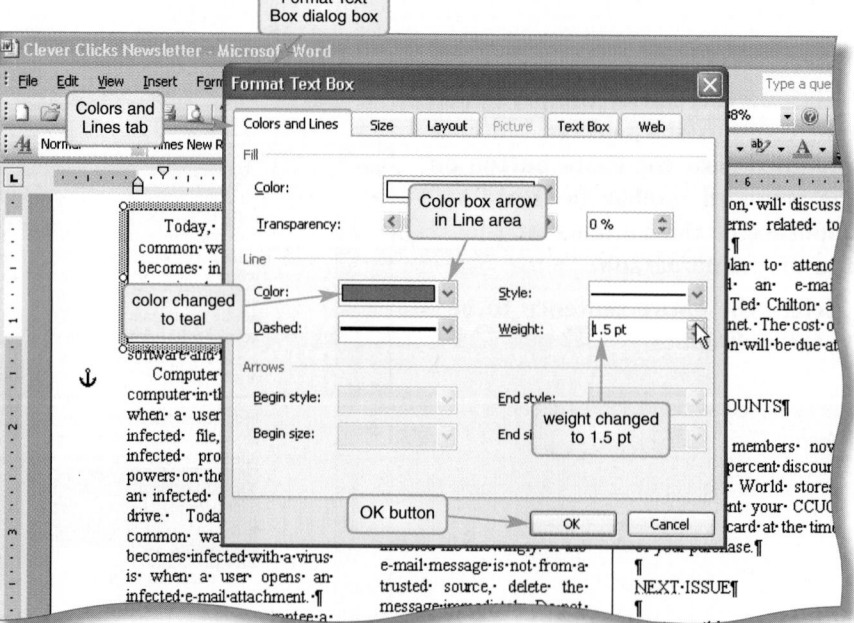

FIGURE 6-54

2

• **Click the OK button.**

Word formats the text box to a 1.5-point teal line (Figure 6-55).

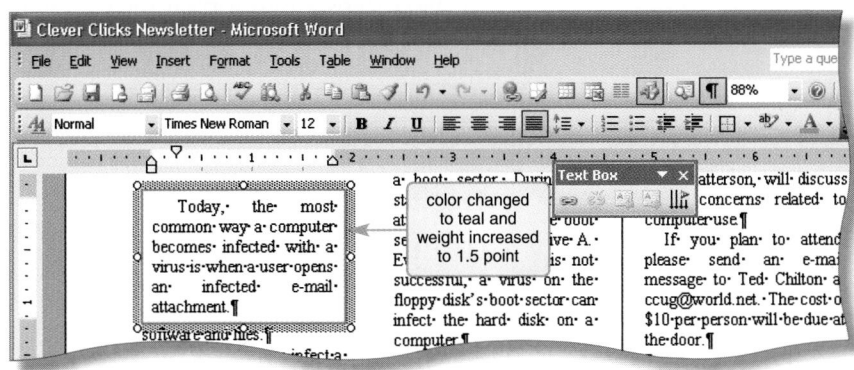

FIGURE 6-55

Other Ways

1. On Format menu click Text Box
2. Right-click edge of text box, click Format Text Box on shortcut menu
3. In Voice Command mode, say "Format, Text Box"

The next step in formatting the pull-quote is to shade the pull-quote paragraph orange, as shown in the following steps.

To Shade a Paragraph

1

• **Click in the pull-quote paragraph to position the insertion point in the pull-quote.**

• **Click Format on the menu bar and then click Borders and Shading.**

• **When Word displays the Borders and Shading dialog box, if necessary, click the Shading tab.**

• **In the Fill area, click Orange.**

Word displays the Shading sheet in the Borders and Shading dialog box (Figure 6-56).

2

• **Click the OK button.**

Word shades the paragraph orange (Figure 6-57).

FIGURE 6-56

Other Ways

1. Click Shading Color button arrow on Tables and Borders toolbar, click color on color palette
2. In Voice Command mode, say "Format, Borders and Shading, Shading, [select color on color palette], OK"

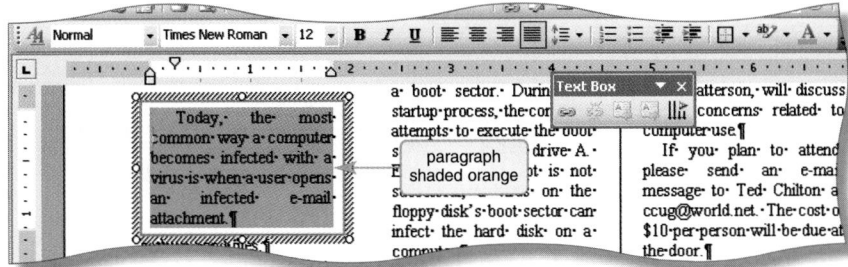

FIGURE 6-57

The next steps are to format the characters and center the text in the pull-quote, as described below.

To Format Text

1 **Drag through the pull-quote text to select it.**

2 **Click the Font box arrow on the Formatting toolbar and then click Arial.**

3 **Click the Font Size box arrow on the Formatting toolbar and then click 11.**

4 **Click the Bold button on the Formatting toolbar.**

5 **Click the Center button on the Formatting toolbar.**

6 **Click the Font Color button arrow on the Formatting toolbar and then click White on the color palette.**

7 **Drag the First Line Indent marker to the 0" mark on the ruler.**

8 **Click inside the pull-quote text to remove the selection.**

Word formats the text in the pull-quote (shown in Figure 6-58).

The next step in formatting the pull-quote is to resize the text box. You resize a text box in the same way as any other object. That is, you drag its sizing handles, as described below.

To Resize a Text Box

1 **Click the edge of the text box to select it.**

2 **Drag the right-middle sizing handle inward about one-half inch to make the pull-quote a bit narrower so that the pull-quote text looks more balanced.**

The text box is resized (Figure 6-58).

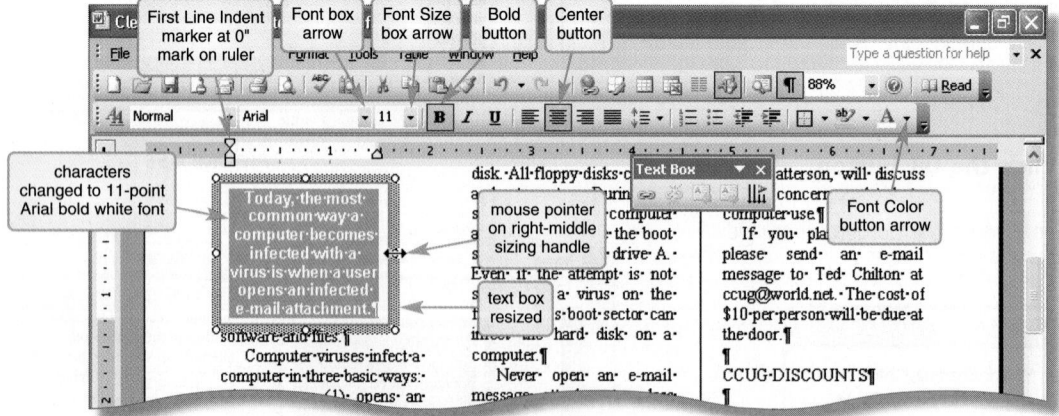

FIGURE 6-58

The final step is to position the pull-quote text box between the first and second columns of the newsletter, as shown next.

To Position a Text Box

1

• **With the text box still selected, drag the text box to its new location (Figure 6-59). You may need to drag the text box a couple of times to position it similarly to this figure.**

• **Click outside the text box to remove the selection.**

The pull-quote is complete (Figure 6-59). Depending on your printer, your wordwrap around the text box may occur in different locations.

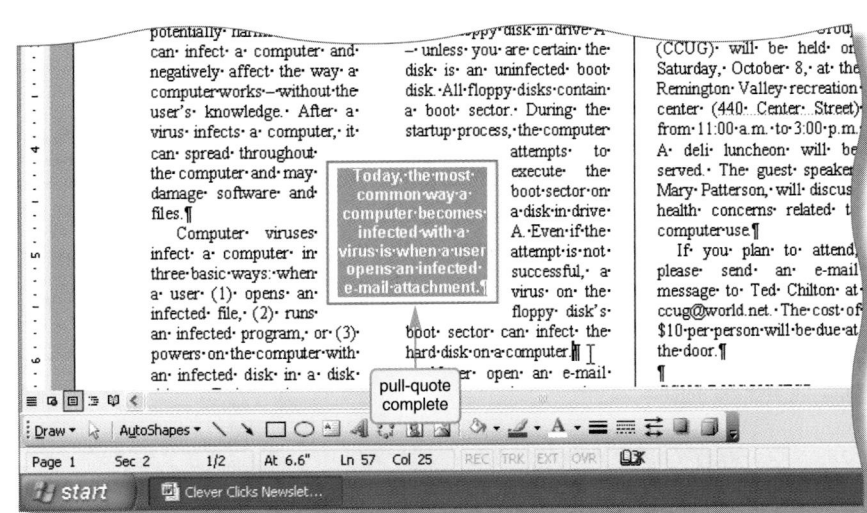

FIGURE 6-59

The following step saves the document again.

To Save a Document

1 **With the disk containing the newsletter file in drive A, click the Save button on the Standard toolbar.**

Word saves the document again with the file name, Clever Clicks Newsletter.

The first page of the newsletter is finished, with the exception of the page border and subhead colors, which will be added later in this project.

More About

Moving Text Boxes

To move a text box using the keyboard, select the text box and then press the arrow keys on the keyboard. For example, each time you press the DOWN ARROW key, the selected text box moves down one line.

Formatting the Second Page of the Newsletter

The second page of the newsletter (Figure 6-1b on page WD 379) continues the feature article that began in the first two columns on the first page. The nameplate on the second page is simpler than the one on the first page of the newsletter. In addition to the text in the feature article, page two contains a diagram. The following pages illustrate how to format the second page of the newsletter in this project.

Changing Column Formatting

The document currently is formatted into three columns. The nameplate at the top of the second page, however, should be in a single column. The next step, then, is to change the number of columns at the top of the second page from three to one.

As discussed earlier in this project, Word requires a new section each time you change the number of columns in a document. Thus, you first must insert a continuous section break and then format the section to one column so the title can be entered on the second page of the newsletter, as shown in the steps on the next page.

Microsoft Office
Word 2003

To Change Column Formatting

1

• **Scroll through the document and then position the mouse pointer at the upper-left corner of the second page of the newsletter (to the left of M in Many).**

• **Click Insert on the menu bar and then click Break.**

• **When Word displays the Break dialog box, click Continuous in the Section break types area.**

A continuous section break will place the nameplate on the same physical page as the three columns of the continued feature article (Figure 6-60).

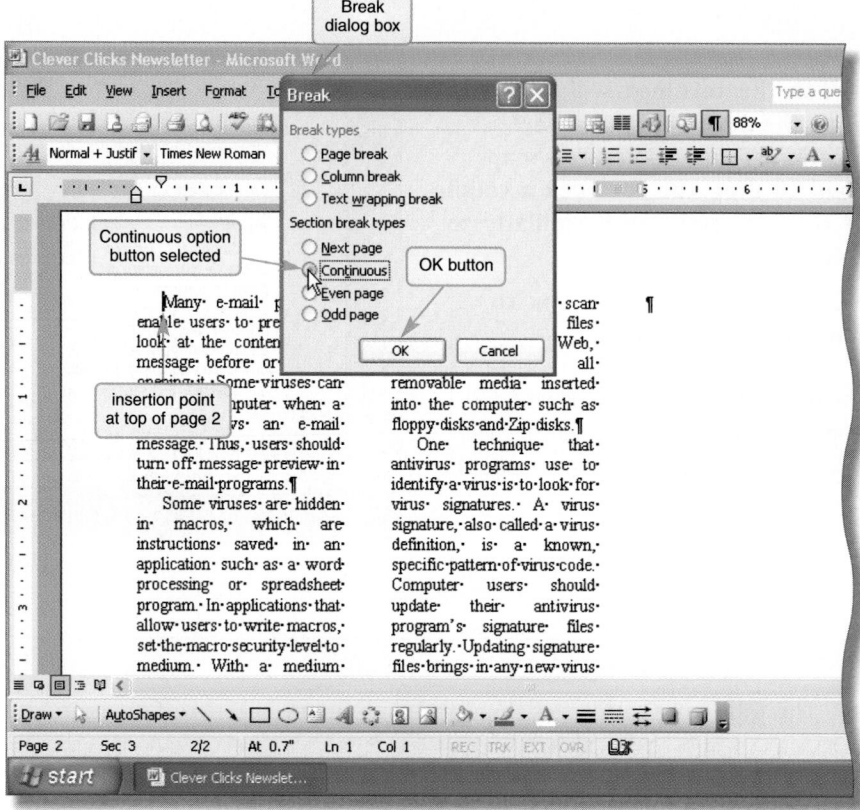

FIGURE 6-60

2

• **Click the OK button.**

Word inserts a continuous section break above the insertion point.

3

• **Press the UP ARROW key to position the insertion point in section 3 to the left of the section break notation.**

• **Click the Style box arrow and then click Clear Formatting to remove the paragraph formatting from the section break.**

• **Click the Columns button on the Standard toolbar.**

• **Position the mouse pointer on the first column in the columns list.**

Word displays the columns list (Figure 6-61).

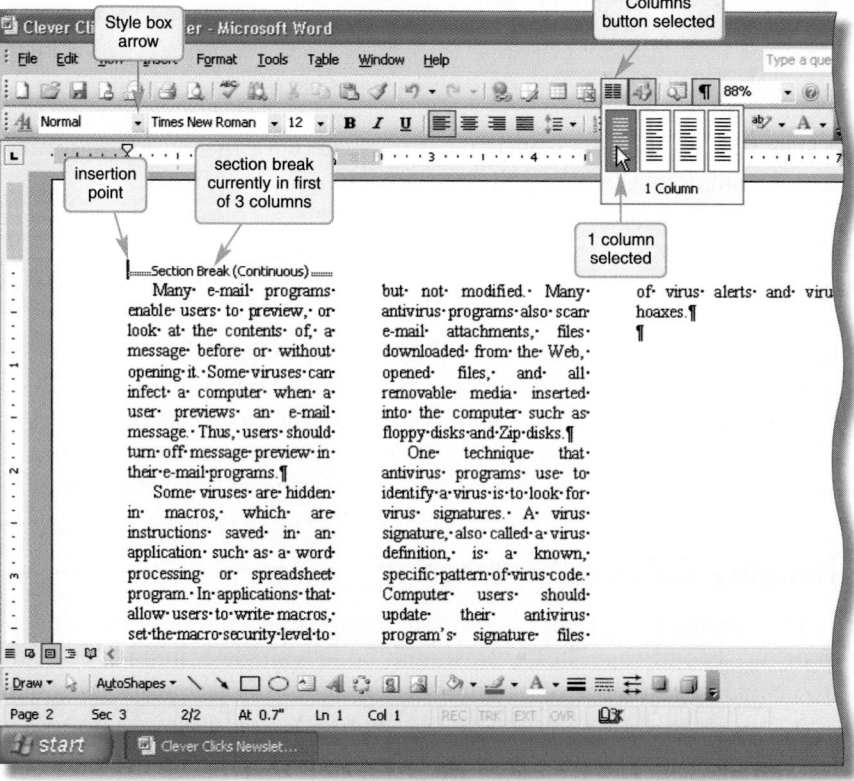

FIGURE 6-61

4

• **Click the first column in the columns list.**

Word formats the current section to one column (Figure 6-62). The section break now extends from the left margin to the right margin.

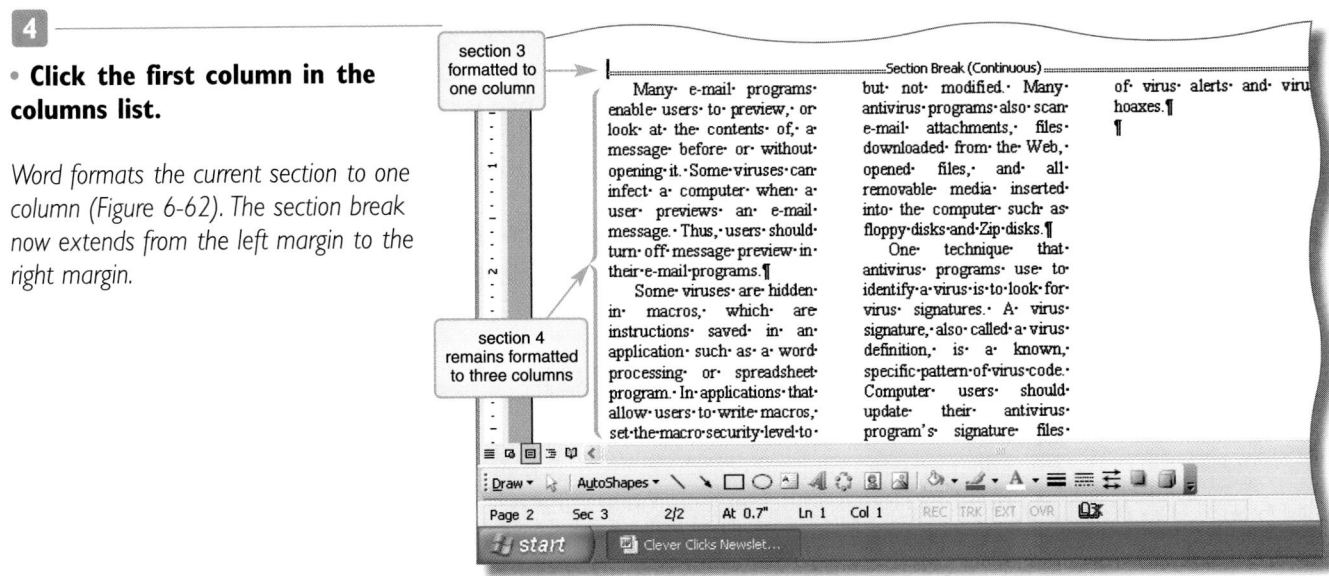

FIGURE 6-62

The following steps describe how to enter the newsletter title at the top of the second page in section 3.

To Format and Enter Text

1 **With the insertion point in section 3 to the left of the section break notation, press the ENTER key twice. Press the UP ARROW key.**

2 **Click the Font Size box arrow on the Formatting toolbar and then click 16. Click the Bold button on the Formatting toolbar. Click the Center button on the Formatting toolbar. Click the Font Color button arrow and then click Brown on the color palette.**

3 **Type** CLEVER CLICKS **and then press the ENTER key.**

4 **Click the Style box arrow on the Formatting toolbar and then click Clear Formatting.**

The title is formatted and entered at the top of the second page of the newsletter (Figure 6-63).

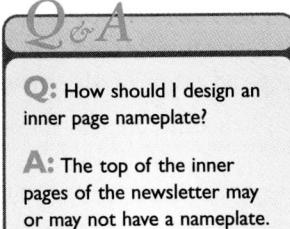

Q&A

Q: How should I design an inner page nameplate?

A: The top of the inner pages of the newsletter may or may not have a nameplate. If you choose to create one for your inner pages, it should not be the same as, or compete with, the one on the first page. Inner page nameplates usually contain only a portion of the nameplate from the first page of a newsletter.

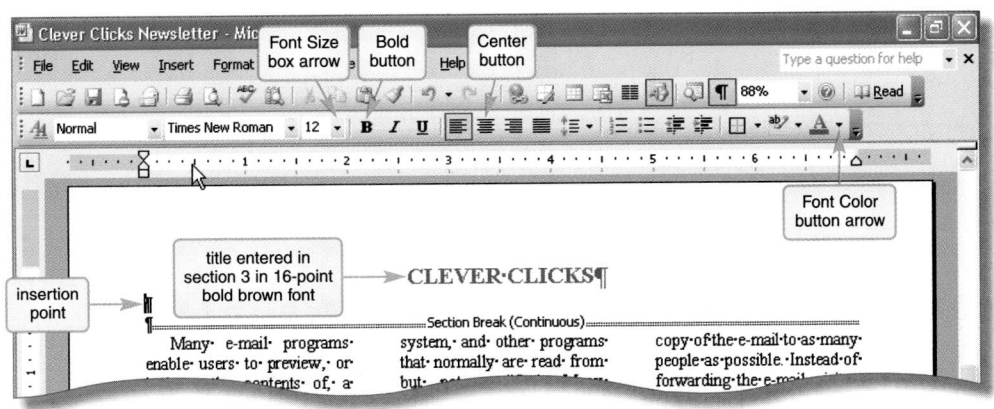

FIGURE 6-63

Using the Paste Special Command to Link Text

The rest of the nameplate on the second page is identical to the nameplate on the first page. That is, the issue information line is below the newsletter title. A ruling line is below the issue information line. Then, the title of the feature article is one blank line below the bottom border. Thus, the next step is to copy these lines of text from the nameplate on the first page and then paste them on the second page.

The item being copied is called the **source object**. The item being pasted is called the **destination object**. Thus, the source object is the bottom part of the nameplate on the first page, and the destination object will be the bottom part of the nameplate on the second page of the newsletter.

Instead of using the Paste button to paste the source object to the destination object, this project uses the Paste Special command. The **Paste Special command** allows you to link the pasted (destination) object to the copied (source) object. The advantage of linking these objects is that if the source object ever changes, the destination object also will change automatically. That is, if you change the bottom part of the nameplate on page 1, the bottom part of the nameplate on page 2 also will change.

The following steps show how to link a copied item.

More About

Links

If you wanted to modify the location of the source file in a link or remove a link while leaving the source text in the destination document, click the link, click Edit on the menu bar and then click Links to display the Links dialog box. Follow instructions in the dialog box to remove or modify the link.

To Link a Copied Item

1

• **Scroll up to display the top of page 1 in the document window.**

• **Drag through lines 2, 3, and 4 in the nameplate.**

• **Click the Copy button on the Standard toolbar.**

Word copies the second, third, and fourth lines on the first page of the newsletter to the Clipboard (Figure 6-64).

FIGURE 6-64

2

• **Press SHIFT+F5 to reposition the insertion point on line 2 of the second page of the newsletter.**

• **Click Edit on the menu bar.**

Recall that pressing SHIFT+F5 repositions the insertion point at your last editing location (Figure 6-65).

FIGURE 6-65

- **Click Paste Special on the Edit menu.**
- **When Word displays the Paste Special dialog box, click Paste link.**
- **Click Formatted Text (RTF) in the As list.**

In the Paste Special dialog box, the Formatted Text (RTF) option pastes the destination object using the same formatting as the source object (Figure 6-66).

FIGURE 6-66

- **Click the OK button.**

Word pastes the copied object at the location of the insertion point (Figure 6-67).

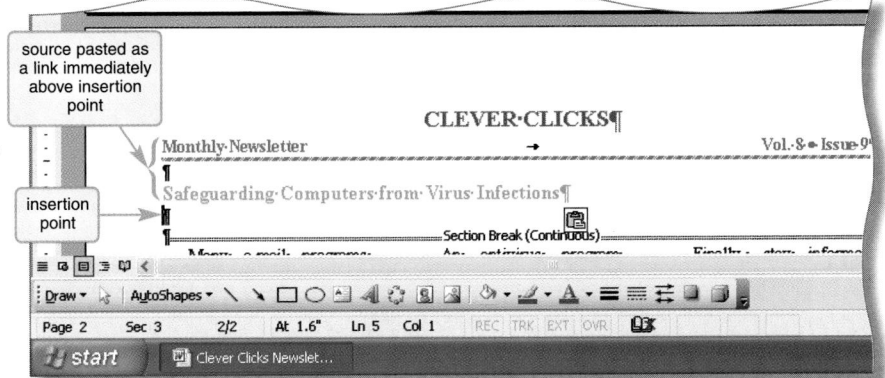

FIGURE 6-67

Other Ways

1. In Voice Command mode, say "Edit, Paste Special, Paste link, [select Formatted Text (RTF)], OK"

If a link, for some reason, is not updated automatically, click the link and then press the F9 key to update it manually. When you click in the link, it displays shaded in gray. This shading does not print; it helps you identify this item as a link.

The next step is to add a continued message immediately below the pasted link, as described below.

To Enter Text

1. **With the insertion point on the line immediately below the pasted link, press CTRL+I to turn on italics. Type** (Continued from page 1) **and then press CTRL+I to turn off italics.**

The continued message is entered below the pasted link (shown in Figure 6-68 on the next page).

Balancing Columns

Currently, the text on the second page of the newsletter completely fills up the first and second columns and spills into a portion of the third column. The text in the three columns is to consume the same amount of vertical space. That is, the three columns should be balanced.

To balance columns, you insert a continuous section break at the end of the text, as shown in the following steps.

To Balance Columns

1

• **Scroll to the bottom of the text in the third column on the second page of the newsletter and then click the paragraph mark below the text.**

• **Click Insert on the menu bar and then click Break.**

• **When Word displays the Break dialog box, click Continuous in the Section break types area.**

Word displays the Break dialog box (Figure 6-68).

FIGURE 6-68

2

• **Click the OK button.**

Word inserts a continuous section break, which balances the columns on the second page of the newsletter (Figure 6-69).

FIGURE 6-69

Other Ways

1. In Voice Command mode, say "Insert, Break, Continuous, OK"

The following step saves the document again.

To Save a Document

1 **With the disk containing the newsletter file in drive A, click the Save button on the Standard toolbar.**

Word saves the document again with the file name, Clever Clicks Newsletter.

Creating a Diagram

The next step is to insert a diagram between the second and third columns on the second page of the newsletter. In Word, you can insert an organization chart and five other types of diagrams in your documents: cycle, pyramid, radial, target, and Venn. Table 6-1 briefly describes the purpose of each of these diagrams.

When working with these diagrams, it is best to insert the diagram in a single column layout so that you easily can see all its components. At this point in the newsletter, the number of columns is three. Thus, the next step is to open a new document window, which has one column, insert and format the diagram, and then copy it to the newsletter.

The newsletter in this project has a radial diagram on the second page that identifies various symptoms of a computer virus infection. The following steps show how to insert a radial diagram in a new document window.

Table 6-1	Word Diagrams
DIAGRAM TYPE	**PURPOSE**
Cycle	Shows a process with continuous steps that form a loop
Organization	Shows hierarchical relationships
Pyramid	Shows items that relate to one another
Radial	Shows elements that relate to a central item
Target	Shows steps toward a goal
Venn	Shows overlapping items

To Insert a Diagram

1

• **Click the New Blank Document button on the Standard toolbar.**

• **When Word displays a blank document window, click the Insert Diagram or Organization Chart button on the Drawing toolbar.**

• **When Word displays the Diagram Gallery dialog box, click the radial diagram.**

Word displays the Diagram Gallery dialog box in a new document window (Figure 6-70).

2

• **Click the OK button.**

Word inserts a radial diagram in the document window (shown in Figure 6-71 on the next page). The Diagram toolbar appears on the screen.

FIGURE 6-70

The entire radial diagram does not fit in the document window. Thus, the following steps change the zoom percentage so more of the radial diagram is displayed.

To Zoom to a Percentage

1 Click the Zoom box arrow on the Standard toolbar.

2 Click 75% in the Zoom list.

3 If necessary, scroll up or down so the entire radial diagram is displayed in the document window.

By changing the zoom percentage to 75%, more of the radial diagram shows in the document window (Figure 6-71).

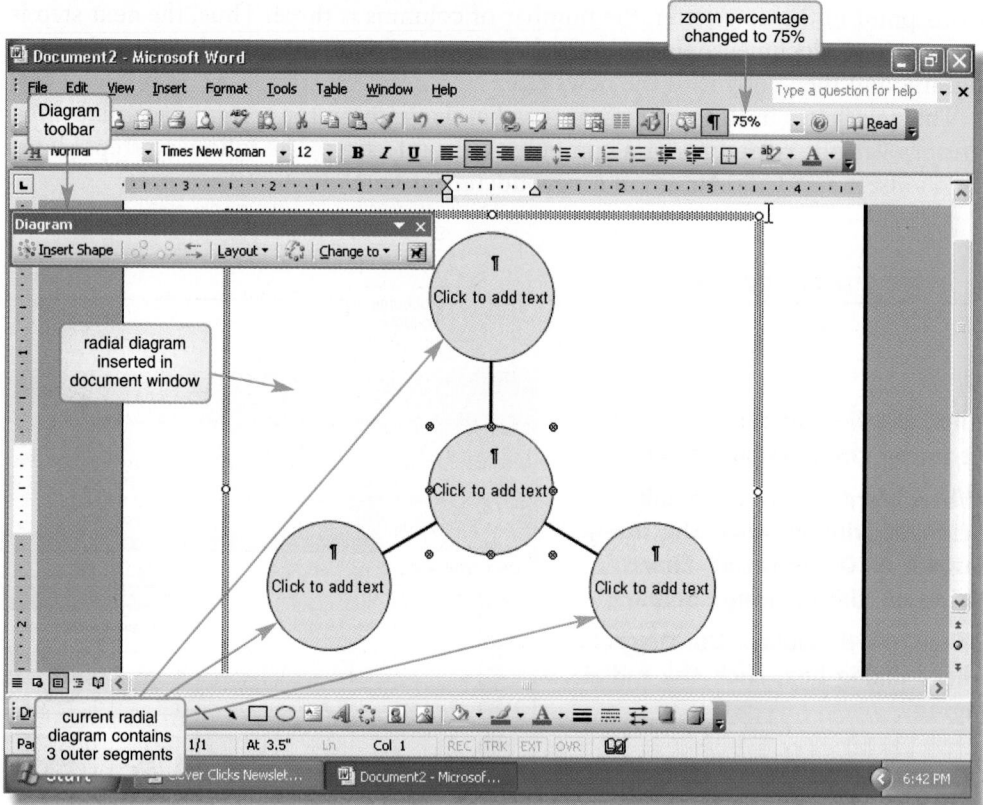

FIGURE 6-71

More About

Diagram Segment Color

To change the fill color in a diagram segment, click the segment, click the Fill Color button arrow on the Drawing toolbar, and then click the desired color. To remove a fill color, click the Fill Color button arrow on the Drawing toolbar and then click No Fill on the color palette.

The radial diagram in this newsletter is to contain a total of eight segments (Figure 6-1b on page WD 379). The current radial diagram contains only three segments. Thus, the next task is to add five more segments to the diagram.

The next step shows how to add segments to a diagram.

To Add Segments to a Diagram

1

• **With the diagram selected, click the Insert Shape button on the Diagram toolbar five times.**

Word adds five segments to the diagram (Figure 6-72).

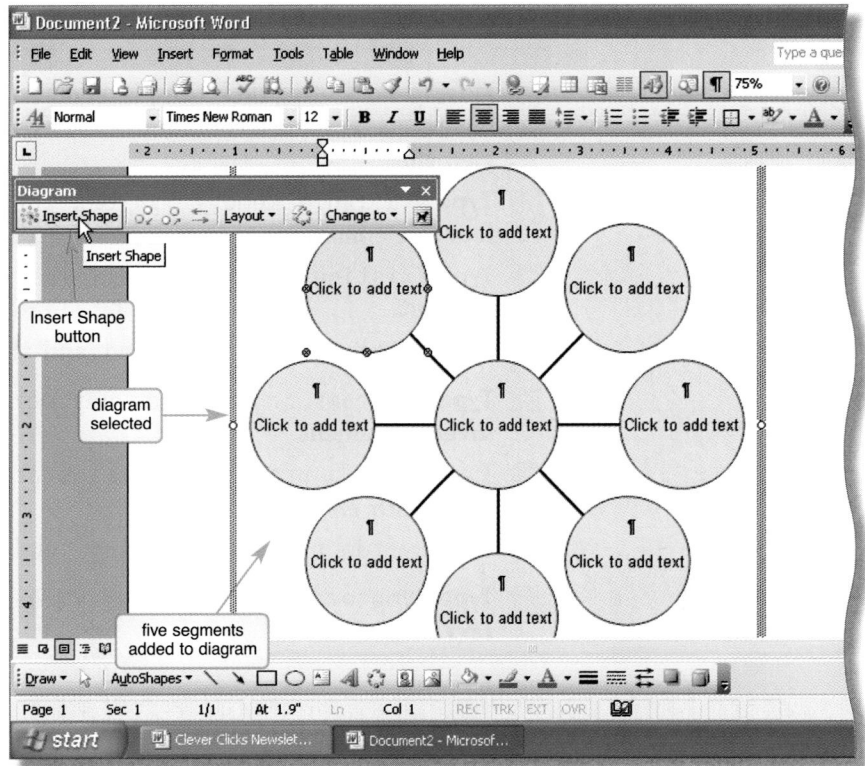

FIGURE 6-72

Other Ways

1. Right-click edge of outer element, click Insert Shape on shortcut menu
2. With Diagram toolbar displaying, in Voice Command mode, say "Insert Shape"

If you add too many elements (segments) to a diagram, you can remove an element(s). Simply click the edges of an element to select it and then click the Cut button on the Standard toolbar or press the DELETE key.

The next task is to add text to the elements of the diagram, as shown in the following step.

To Add Text to a Diagram

1

• **In the top element in the radial diagram, click the placeholder text, Click to add text.**

• **Type** Screen displays unusual message or image **as the element text.**

Word selects and adds text to the top element of the radial diagram (Figure 6-73).

FIGURE 6-73

The following steps enter the text in the remaining elements of the radial diagram.

To Enter More Diagram Text

1 **Moving clockwise, click the placeholder text in the second element. Type** Music or unusual sound plays randomly **and then click the third element.**

2 **Type** Available memory is less than expected **and then click the fourth element.**

3 **Type** Existing programs and files disappear **and then click the fifth element.**

4 **Type** Files become corrupted **and then click the sixth element.**

5 **Type** Programs or files do not work properly **and then click the seventh element.**

6 **Type** Unknown programs or files arbitrarily appear **and then click the eighth element.**

7 **Type** System properties change **and then click the middle (core) element.**

8 **Type** Symptoms of a Computer Virus Infection **as the core element text.**

The text is added to the diagram (Figure 6-74).

FIGURE 6-74

More About

Moving Diagram Segments

To move a segment of a diagram, select the segment and then click either the Move Shape Forward button or the Move Shape Backward button on the Diagram toolbar. For example, each time you click the Move Shape Forward button, the selected segment moves down one position in the diagram.

The next task is to format the diagram using one of the built-in AutoFormat styles, as shown in the following steps.

To AutoFormat a Diagram

1

• **Click the AutoFormat button on the Diagram toolbar.**

• **When Word displays the Diagram Style Gallery dialog box, click Thick Outline in the Select a Diagram Style list.**

The selected style in the Diagram Style Gallery dialog box will be applied to the diagram in the document window (Figure 6-75).

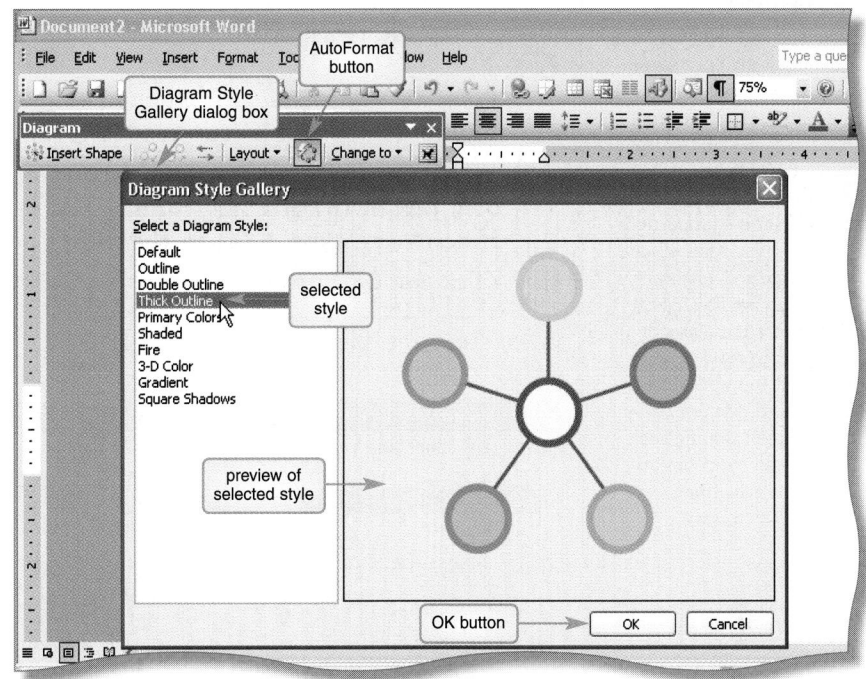

FIGURE 6-75

2

• **Click the OK button.**

Word applies the thick outline style to the diagram (Figure 6-76).

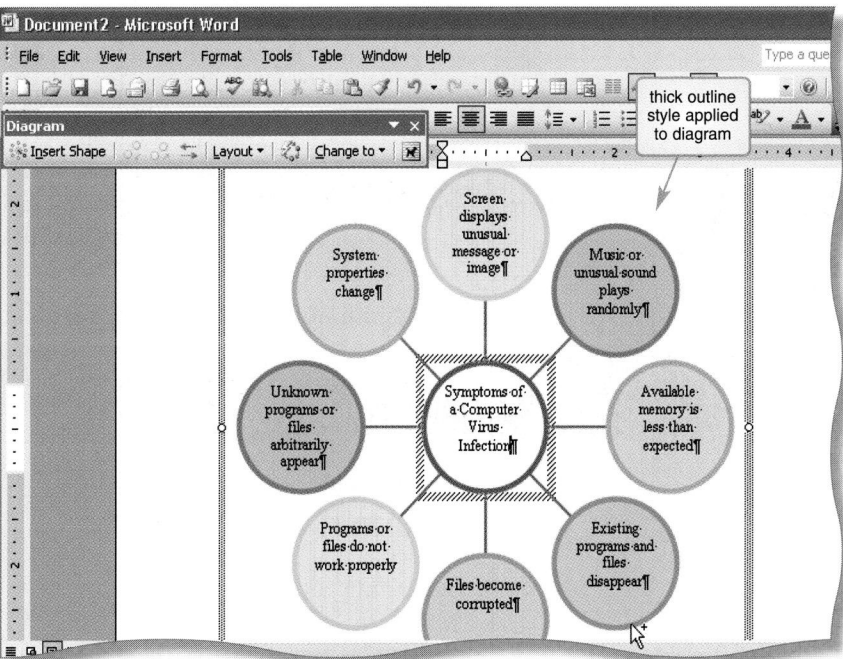

FIGURE 6-76

The next task is to reduce the size of the diagram so it will fit at the bottom of the second page of the newsletter. You resize a diagram the same as any other graphic object. That is, you can drag its sizing handles or enter exact measurements into the Format Diagram dialog box.

More About

Formatting Graphics

In the Format Diagram dialog box, when the Lock aspect ratio check box in the Scale area in the Size sheet contains a check mark, Word keeps the height and width percentage values the same to maintain the proportions of the graphic. Thus, if you type height and width values in the Size and rotate area that distort these proportions, Word readjusts your entries. If you want the percentages to differ, remove the check mark from the Lock aspect ratio check box so Word will allow the proportions to vary.

This diagram should be 4.25 inches tall and 4.25 inches wide. The following steps describe how to enter these measurements into the Format Diagram dialog box.

To Resize a Diagram

1 Point to the frame surrounding the diagram and double-click when the mouse pointer has a four-headed arrow attached to it.

2 When Word displays the Format Diagram dialog box, if necessary, click the Size tab. In the Size and rotate area, type 4.25 in the Height box and then, if necessary, type 4.25 in the Width box.

3 Click the OK button.

Word resizes the diagram (Figure 6-77).

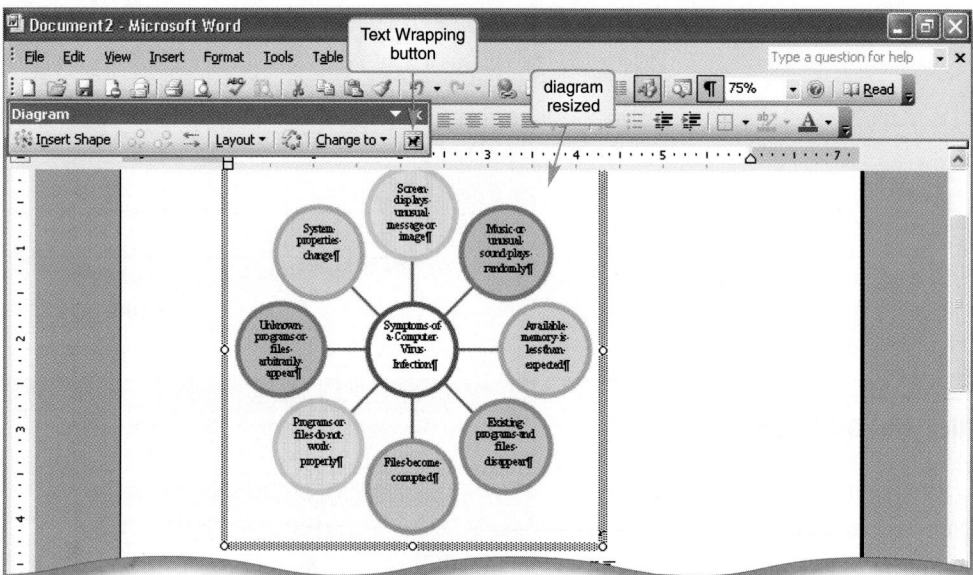

FIGURE 6-77

The diagram now is too small to read. The following steps zoom to 100%.

To Zoom to 100%

1 Click the Zoom box arrow on the Standard toolbar.

2 Click 100% in the Zoom list.

When you zoom to 100%, the text in the diagram is more readable (shown in Figure 6-78).

You want text in the newsletter to wrap around the diagram – fitting the form of the diagram. Thus, the next step is to change the graphic from inline to floating with a wrapping style of tight, as described in the next steps.

To Format a Graphic as Floating

1 **Click the frame around the diagram to select the diagram.**

2 **Click the Text Wrapping button on the Diagram toolbar and then click Tight.**

The diagram is formatted to a tight wrapping style, which means text will wrap tightly around the graphic. This format will become apparent when you copy the diagram into the newsletter.

Using the Format Painter Button

The next step is to reduce the font size of the text in each element of the AutoShape to 7.5 point, so the text fits completely in the elements. Instead of selecting each element one at a time and then changing its font size, you can format the text in the first element and then copy its formatting to the other elements. To copy formatting, use the Format Painter button on the Standard toolbar, as shown in the following steps.

To Use the Format Painter Button

1

• **Triple-click the text in the top element of the radial diagram to select the text.**

• **If necessary, drag the Diagram toolbar off of the Formatting toolbar.**

• **Click the Font button arrow on the Formatting toolbar and then click Arial.**

• **Click the Font Size box arrow on the Formatting toolbar. Type** 7.5 **in the Font Size box and then press the ENTER key.**

• **Double-click the Format Painter button on the Standard toolbar.**

• **Moving clockwise, position the mouse pointer to the left of the text in the second element.**

The format painter copies the format of the selected text (Figure 6-78). When you double-click the Format Painter button, it remains selected until you click it again. This enables you to copy the format to multiple locations. Word attaches a paintbrush to the mouse pointer when the Format Painter button is selected.

FIGURE 6-78

2

• **Select the text in the second element by triple-clicking the text.**

• **Triple-click the text in each of the remaining elements, including the core (center) element.**

• **Click the Format Painter button on the Standard toolbar to turn off the format painter.**

Word copies the 7.5-point Arial font to the text in the remaining elements (Figure 6-79).

FIGURE 6-79

If you want to copy formatting to just one location in a document, you would click the Format Painter button, instead of double-clicking it. When you click the Format Painter button, it copies formatting to the next item you select and then immediately turns off the format painter.

The next step is to bold the text in the core (center) element and then add some space above the text in two elements in the diagram, as described below.

To Format Text

1 **With the text in the core (center) element still selected, click the Bold button on the Formatting toolbar.**

2 **Click the text in the bottom (fifth) element and then press CTRL+0 (the numeral zero) to add a blank line above the text.**

3 **Moving clockwise, click the text in the eighth element and then press CTRL+0.**

Word bolds the text in the core element and adds space above text in two other elements in the diagram (Figure 6-80). The bold format is difficult to see because the text is small. It will become apparent when you print the document.

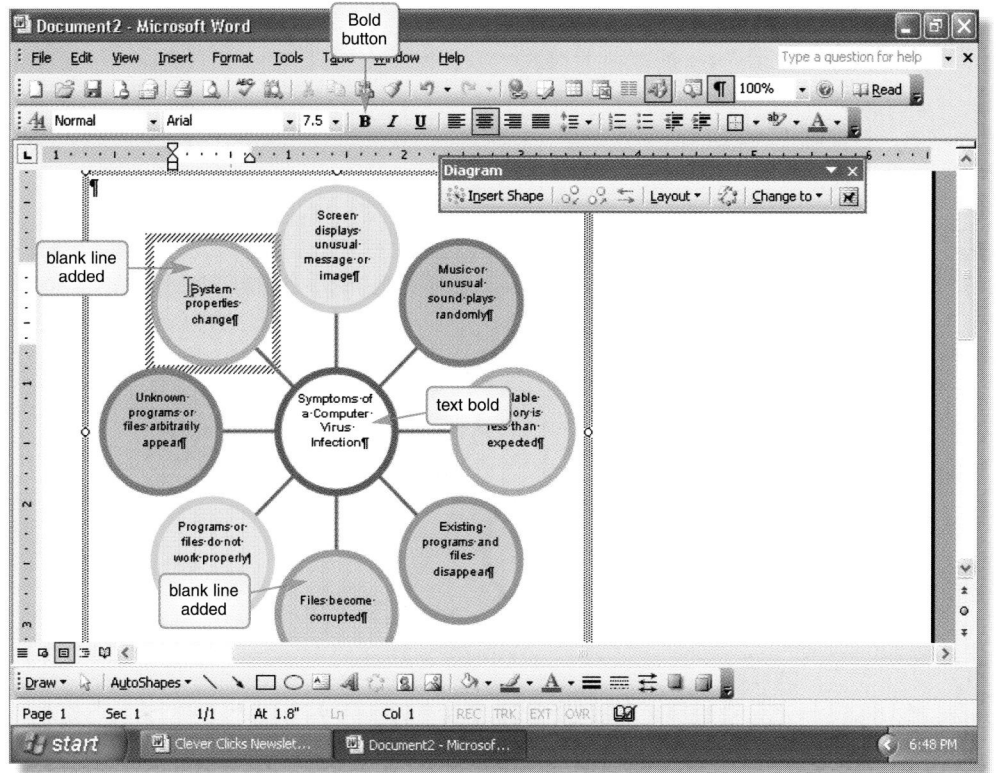

FIGURE 6-80

The next step is to save the diagram, as described below.

To Save a Document

1. **With the disk containing the newsletter in drive A, click the Save button on the Standard toolbar.**

2. **Type** Computer Virus Symptoms Diagram **in the File name box. Do not press the ENTER key.**

3. **If necessary, click the Save in box arrow and then click 3½ Floppy (A:).**

4. **Click the Save button in the Save As dialog box.**

Word saves the document on a floppy disk in drive A with the file name, Computer Virus Symptoms Diagram (shown in Figure 6-81 on the next page).

Copying, Pasting, and Positioning a Diagram

The diagram is finished. The next step is to copy it from this document window and then paste it in the newsletter. The steps on the next page show how to copy and paste the diagram in the second page of the newsletter.

More About

Go To

Recall that you can go to a certain page, section, line, or other object in a document through the Go To sheet in the Find and Replace dialog box. To display the Go To sheet, click Edit on the menu bar and then click Go To or press CTRL+G. In the Go to what list, click the item you want to go to, enter the item number (e.g., 2 for page 2), and then click the Go To button.

To Copy and Paste a Diagram

1

• **Click the frame around the diagram to select the diagram.**
• **Click the Copy button on the Standard toolbar (Figure 6-81).**

Word copies the diagram to the Clipboard.

2

• **Click File on the menu bar and then click Close.**

Word closes the file containing the diagram.

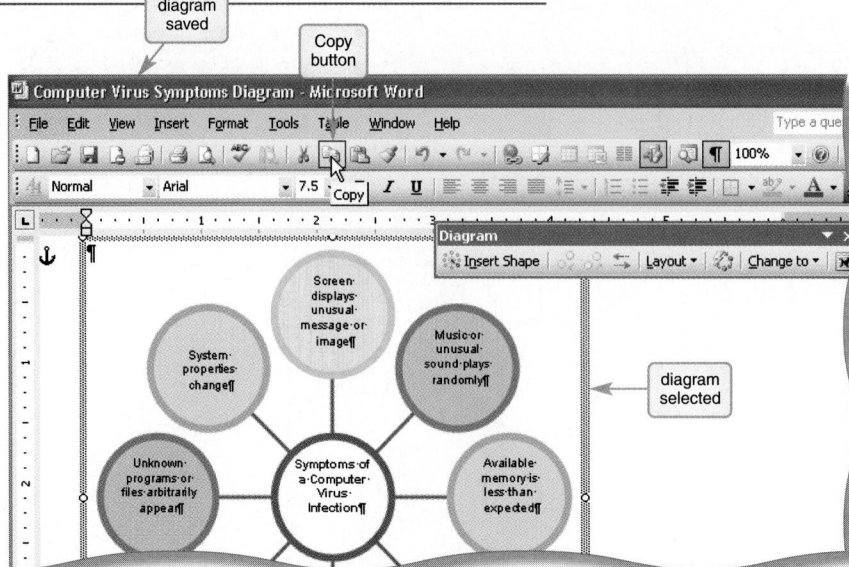

FIGURE 6-81

3

• **When Word redisplays the newsletter document window, right-click somewhere on page 2 in the feature article.**

Word displays a shortcut menu (Figure 6-82).

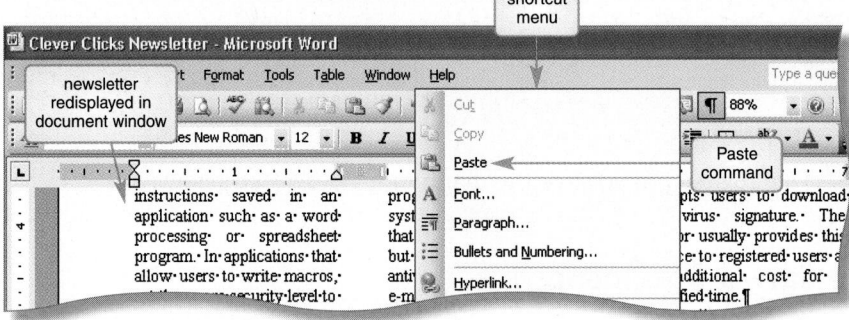

FIGURE 6-82

4

• **Click Paste on the shortcut menu.**

Word pastes the diagram from the Clipboard into the document (Figure 6-83). Your diagram may be pasted at a different location in the newsletter. The next step is to reposition the pasted diagram.

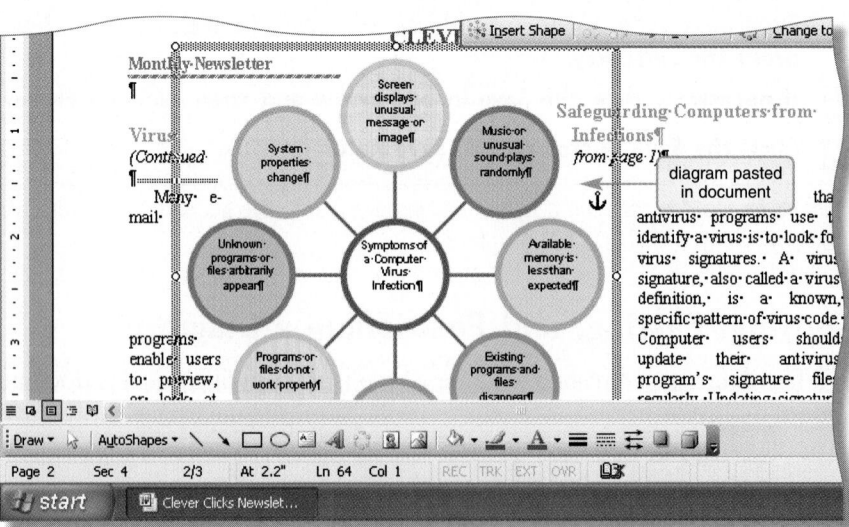

FIGURE 6-83

5

• **Point to the frame on the diagram and when the mouse has a four-headed arrow attached to it, drag the diagram to the desired location. You may have to drag the graphic a couple of times to position it similarly to Figure 6-84.**

Depending on the printer you are using, the wordwrap around the diagram may occur in different locations (Figure 6-84).

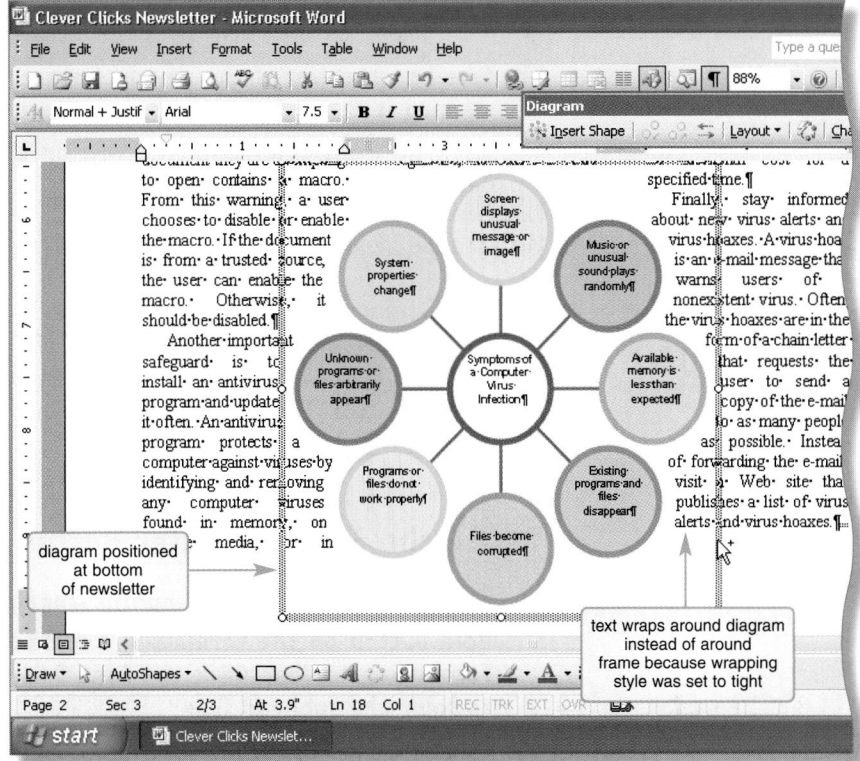

FIGURE 6-84

Notice in Figure 6-84 that the wrap-around text in the first and third columns wraps around the diagram, instead of the frame. This is because earlier you set the wrapping style to Tight. If you wanted the text to wrap around the frame in a square, you would set the wrapping style to Square.

The following step saves the document again.

To Save a Document

1 **With the disk containing the newsletter file in drive A, click the Save button on the Standard toolbar.**

Word saves the document again with the file name, Clever Clicks Newsletter.

Enhancing the Newsletter with Color and a Page Border

Many of the characters and lines in the newsletter in this project are in color. The drop cap and the subheads in the announcements columns also should be in color. Lastly, a border should surround each page of the newsletter. The following pages illustrate these tasks.

The first step is to color the drop cap, as described on the next page.

Q&A

Q: How much space should be in the run-around?

A: The run-around, which is the space between the diagram and the text, should be at least 1/8" and should be the same for all graphics in the newsletter. Adjust the run-around of a selected graphic by clicking the Format Picture button on the Picture toolbar, clicking the Layout tab, clicking the Advanced button, adjusting the Distance from text text boxes, and then clicking the OK button.

To Color a Drop Cap

1 **Scroll to the top of the newsletter and then select the drop cap by double-clicking it.**

2 **Click the Font Color button arrow on the Formatting toolbar and then click Teal on the color palette.**

Word changes the color of the drop cap to teal (shown in Figure 6-1b on page WD 379).

The rightmost column on the first page of the newsletter contains three subheads: USER GROUP MEETING, CCUG DISCOUNTS, and NEXT ISSUE. Currently, all characters in the subheads are capitalized. They also should be bold, italicized, and teal. The next step is to format the first subhead and then use the format painter to copy its formatting to the other two subheads, as described below.

To Use the Format Painter Button

1 **Select the subhead, USER GROUP MEETING, by clicking to its left. Click the Bold button on the Formatting toolbar. Click the Italic button on the Formatting toolbar. Click the Font Color button on the Formatting toolbar to color the subhead Teal.**

2 **Double-click the Format Painter button on the Standard toolbar. Scroll through the newsletter to the next subhead, CCUG DISCOUNTS. Select the subhead by clicking to its left.**

3 **Scroll through the newsletter to the next subhead, NEXT ISSUE. Select the subhead by clicking to its left.**

4 **Click the Format Painter button on the Standard toolbar to turn off the format painter. Click outside the selection to remove the highlight.**

Word copies the bold, italic, teal font from the first subhead to the other two subheads (Figure 6-85).

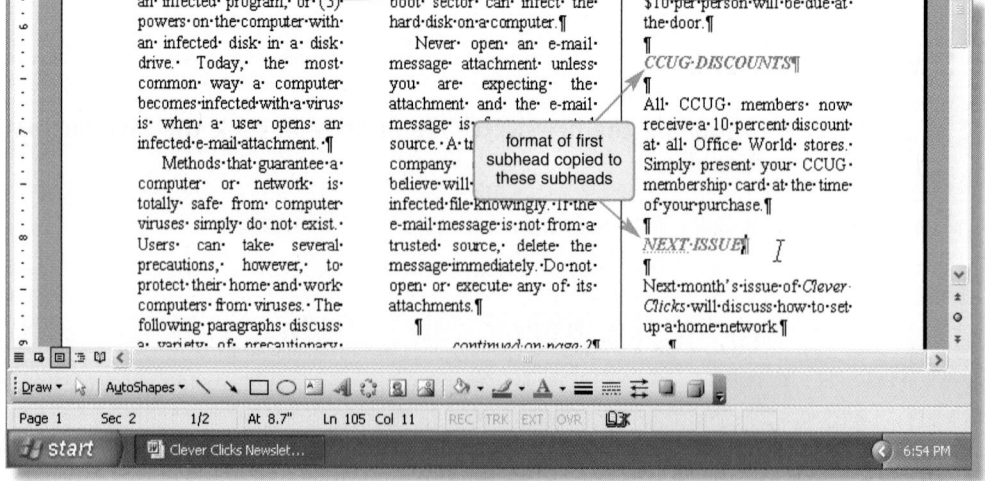

FIGURE 6-85

Adding a Page Border

In this and previous projects, you have added borders to the edges of a paragraph(s). In Word, you also can add a border around the perimeter of an entire page. Page borders add professionalism to documents.

In Word, page borders are positioned 24 points from the edge of the page. Many printers cannot print text and graphics that close to the edge of the page. To alleviate this problem, this project changes the border to be positioned from the edge of the text, instead of the edge of the page.

The following steps show how to add a light orange page border around the pages of the newsletter.

To Add a Page Border

1

- **Click Format on the menu bar and then click Borders and Shading.**
- **When Word displays the Borders and Shading dialog box, if necessary, click the Page Border tab.**
- **Click Box in the Setting area.**
- **Scroll through the Style list and click the style shown in Figure 6-86.**
- **Click the Color box arrow and then click Light Orange on the color palette.**
- **Click the Width box arrow and then click 2 ¼ pt.**

The page border is set to a 2¼-point light orange box in the Borders and Shading dialog box (Figure 6-86).

FIGURE 6-86

• **Click the Options button.**

• **When Word displays the Border and Shading Options dialog box, click the Measure from box arrow and then click Text.**

• **Change the Top box, Bottom box, Left box, and Right box to 15 pt.**

In the Borders and Shading Options dialog box, you specify the distance of the border from the edge of the page or from the text (Figure 6-87).

3

• **Click the OK button in each dialog box.**

Word places a page border on each page of the newsletter (shown in Figure 6-88).

FIGURE 6-87

To see the borders on the newsletter, display both pages in the document window, as described in the following step.

To Zoom Two Pages

1 **Click the Zoom box arrow on the Standard toolbar and then click Two Pages.**

Word displays the pages of the newsletter in reduced form so that two pages display in the document window (Figure 6-88).

FIGURE 6-88

The following step returns the display to zoom page width.

To Zoom Page Width

1 **Click the Zoom box arrow on the Standard toolbar and then click Page Width.**

Word displays the page as wide as possible in the document window.

The newsletter now is complete. You should save the document again and print it, as described in the following series of steps.

To Save a Document

1 **With the disk containing the newsletter file in drive A, click the Save button on the Standard toolbar.**

Word saves the document again with the file name, Clever Clicks Newsletter.

To Print a Document

1 **Click the Print button on the Standard toolbar.**

The printed newsletter is shown in Figure 6-1 on page WD 379.

More About

Printing

If you want to save ink, print faster, or decrease printer overrun errors, print a draft. Click File on the menu bar, click Print, click the Options button, place a check mark in the Draft output check box, and then click the OK button in each dialog box.

Enhancing a Document for Online Viewing

Often, you will send documents to others online. For example, you may e-mail the Clever Clicks Newsletter instead of sending it via the postal service or you may publish it on the Web. Word provides some additional features for online documents. These include highlighted text, animated text, and backgrounds. The following pages illustrate each of these features.

Highlighting Text

Highlighting alerts a reader to online text's importance, much like a highlight marker does in a textbook. The following steps show how to highlight text yellow.

To Highlight Text

1

• **Scroll to display the feature article title, Safeguarding Computers from Virus Infections, on page 1.**

• **If the Highlight button on the Formatting toolbar displays yellow on its face, click the Highlight button; otherwise, click the Highlight button arrow and then click Yellow.**

• **Position the mouse pointer in the document window.**

The Highlight button is selected and displays yellow on its face (Figure 6-89). The mouse pointer is displayed as an I-beam with a highlighter attached to it when the Highlight button is selected.

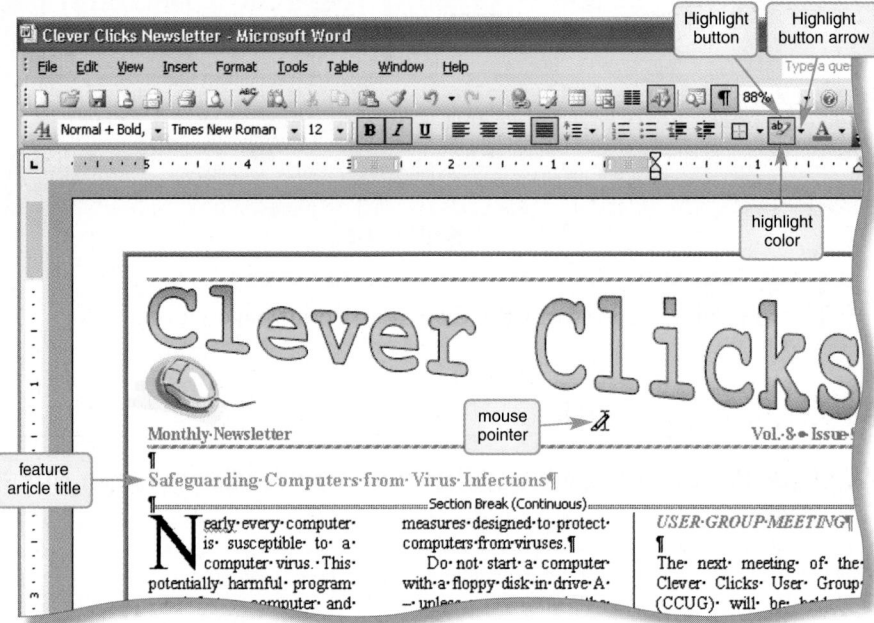

FIGURE 6-89

2

• **Drag through the feature article title, Safeguarding Computers from Virus Infections, to select it.**

Word highlights the selection yellow (Figure 6-90).

3

• **Click the Highlight button on the Formatting toolbar to turn off highlighting (shown in Figure 6-91).**

FIGURE 6-90

Word provides a variety of colors for highlighting text. If the Highlight button already displays your desired highlight color on its face, simply click the Highlight button to begin highlighting text. If you want to use a different highlight color, click the Highlight button arrow, select the desired highlight color, and then begin highlighting text.

If you wanted to remove a highlight, you would select the highlighted text, click the Highlight button arrow, and then click None.

If you scroll down to the second page of the newsletter, you will notice that the feature article title on the second page also is highlighted (shown in Figure 6-97 on page WD 440). Word automatically highlighted this text because earlier this project linked the nameplate on the second page to the nameplate on the first page. (In some instances, the highlight may not appear immediately.)

Animating Text

When you **animate text**, it has the appearance of motion. To animate text in Word, you select it and then apply one of the predefined text effects in the Text Effects sheet in the Font dialog box.

In this newsletter, you want to apply the Marching Black Ants text effect to the subhead USER GROUP MEETING. Once applied, the text has a moving black dashed rectangle around it.

The following steps show how to animate the words, USER GROUP MEETING, at the top of the announcements in the third column of the newsletter.

To Animate Text

1

• **Drag through the text to animate (in this case, USER GROUP MEETING).**

• **Right-click the selected text and then click Font on the shortcut menu.**

• **When Word displays the Font dialog box, if necessary, click the Text Effects tab.**

• **Click Marching Black Ants in the Animations list.**

The Preview area in the Font dialog box shows a sample of the selected animation (Figure 6-91).

FIGURE 6-91

2

• **Click the OK button.**

• **Click outside the selected text.**

Word applies the selected animation to the text (Figure 6-92).

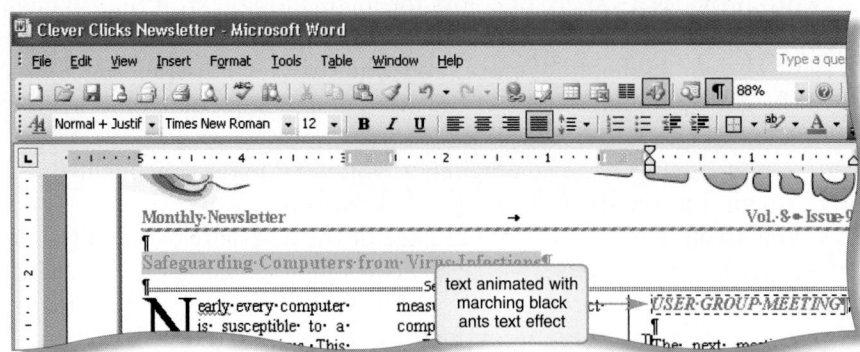

FIGURE 6-92

If you wanted to remove animation from text, you would select the text, right-click the selection, click Font on the shortcut menu, click the Text Effects tab, click (none) in the Animations list, and then click the OK button.

If you print a document that contains animated text, the animations do not show on the hard copy; instead the text prints as regular text. Thus, animations are designed specifically for documents that will be viewed online.

Changing a Document's Background

In Word, the default background color is No Fill, which means the background displays in the color white. For documents viewed online, you may wish to change the background color so the document is more visually appealing. The following steps show how to change the background color of the newsletter to light turquoise.

To Change Background Color

1

• **Click Format on the menu bar and then point to Background.**

Word displays the Background submenu, which contains a color palette (Figure 6-93).

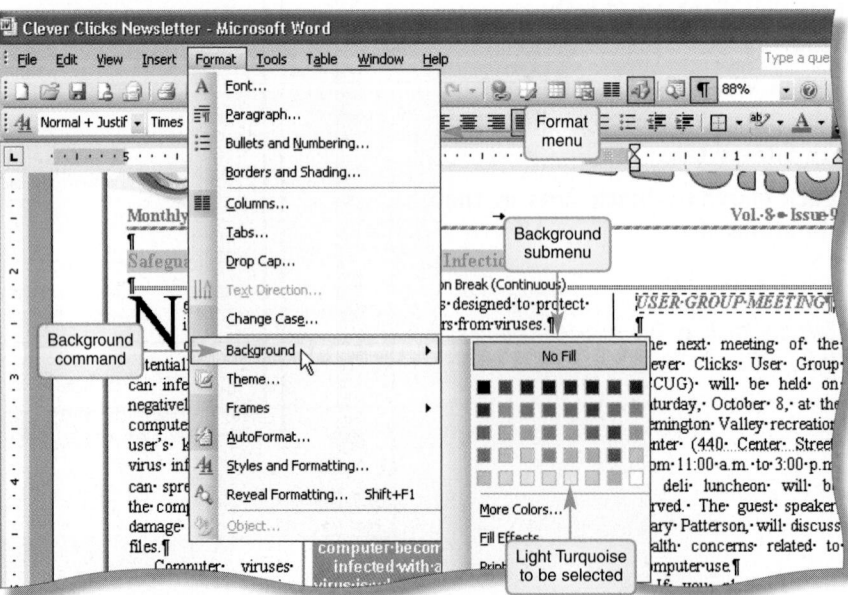

FIGURE 6-93

2

- **Click Light Turquoise on the color palette.**

Word changes the background color of the document to light turquoise (Figure 6-94).

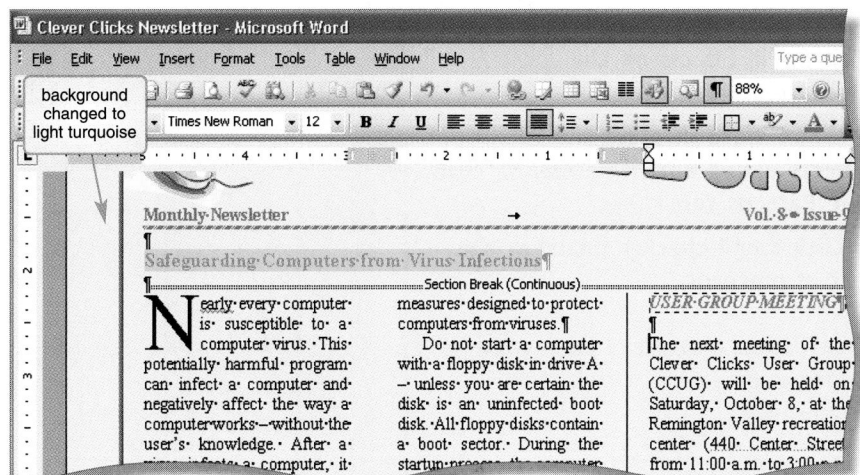

FIGURE 6-94

When you change the background color of a document, Word places the solid color behind all text and graphics on the page. To soften the background, you can add patterns to the color. The following steps show how to add a pattern to the light turquoise background color.

To Add a Pattern Fill Effect to a Background

1

- **Click Format on the menu bar and then point to Background (Figure 6-95).**

FIGURE 6-95

2

• **Click Fill Effects on the Background submenu.**

• **When Word displays the Fill Effects dialog box, if necessary, click the Pattern tab.**

• **Click Small checker board in the list of patterns.**

Word displays a sample of the selected pattern in the Fill Effects dialog box (Figure 6-96).

3

• **Click the OK button.**

Word applies the selected pattern to the document (shown in Figure 6-97).

FIGURE 6-96

Other Ways

1. In Voice Command mode, say "Format, Background, Fill Effects, Pattern, [select pattern], OK"

To see the enhancements to the entire newsletter, display both pages in the document window, as described in the following step.

To Zoom Two Pages

1 **Click the Zoom box arrow on the Standard toolbar and then click Two Pages.**

Word displays the pages of the newsletter in reduced form so that two pages display in the document window (Figure 6-97).

FIGURE 6-97

The following step returns the display to zoom page width.

To Zoom Page Width

1 **Click the Zoom box arrow on the Standard toolbar and then click Page Width.**

Word displays the page as wide as possible in the document window.

To keep the original newsletter intact, you should save the newsletter that was enhanced for online viewing with a new file name, as described in the following steps.

To Save a File with a New File Name

1 **Insert a floppy disk in drive A. Click File on the menu bar and then click Save As.**

2 **Type** Clever Clicks Online Newsletter **in the File name box. Do not press the ENTER key.**

3 **If necessary, click the Save in box arrow and then click 3½ Floppy (A:).**

4 **Click the Save button in the Save As dialog box.**

Word saves the document on a floppy disk in drive A with the file name, Clever Clicks Online Newsletter.

Splitting the Window and Arranging Open Windows

On some occasions, you may want to view two different portions of a document on the screen at the same time. For example, you may want to see the nameplate on the first page and the nameplate on the second page on the screen simultaneously.

Word allows you to split the window into two separate panes, each containing the current document and having its own scroll bar. This enables you to scroll to and view two different portions of the same document at the same time. The following steps show how to split the Word window.

To Split the Window

1

• **Position the mouse pointer on the split box at the top of the vertical scroll bar.**

*The mouse pointer changes to a **resize pointer**, which has two small horizontal lines each with a vertical arrow (Figure 6-98).*

FIGURE 6-98

2

• **Drag the resize pointer about half-way down the screen.**

Word displays a split bar at the location of the resize pointer (Figure 6-99). The split bar will be positioned at the location you release the mouse.

3

• **Release the mouse button.**

Word places the current document in both the top and bottom panes.

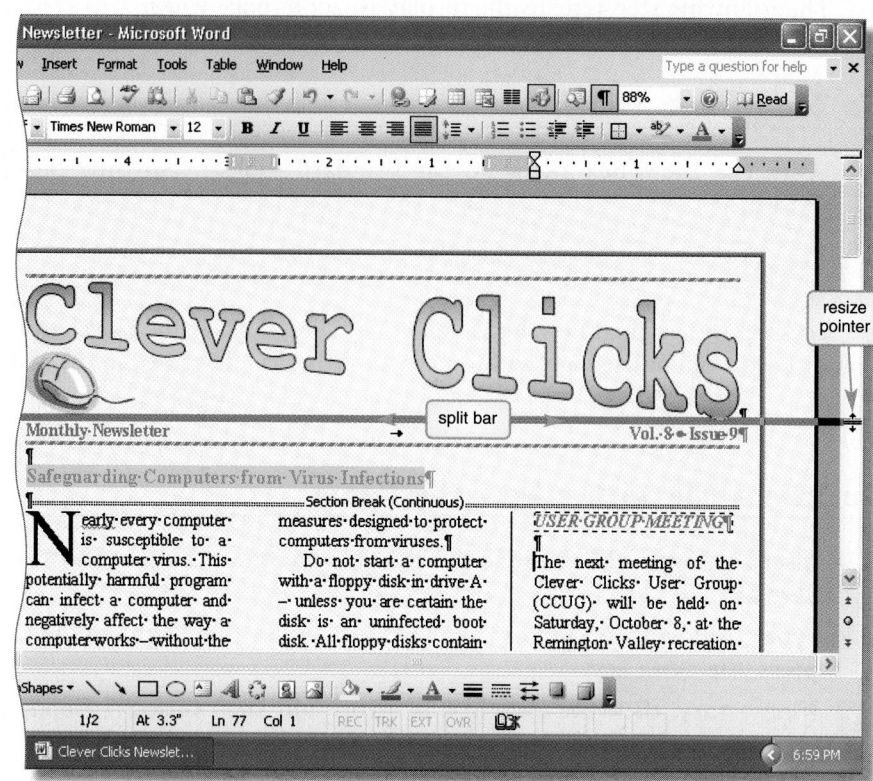

FIGURE 6-99

4

• **In the top pane, scroll to display the nameplate on page 1.**

• **In the bottom pane, scroll to display the nameplate on page 2.**

Word displays two separate parts of the same document on the screen simultaneously (Figure 6-100). The bottom pane does not show the background.

5

• **Double-click the split bar to return to a single Word window on the screen.**

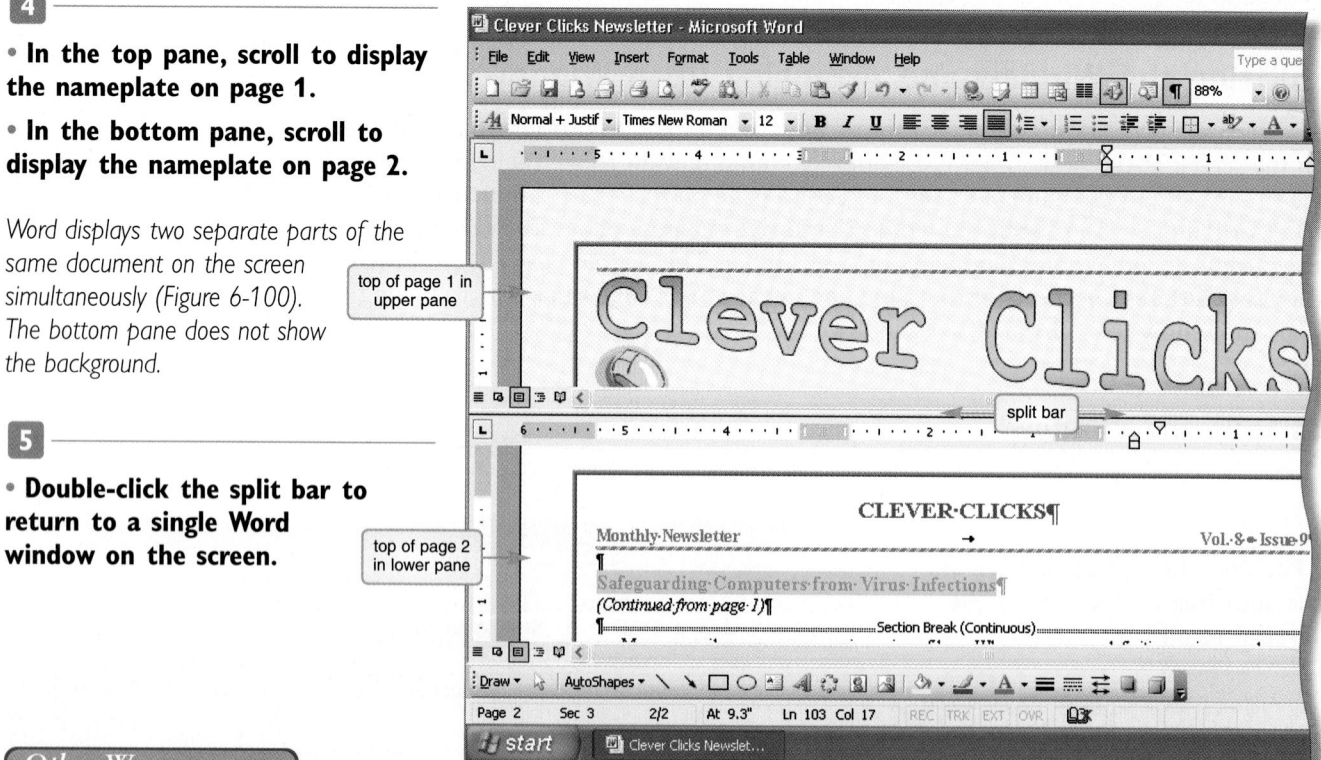

FIGURE 6-100

Instead of double-clicking the split bar to return to a single Word window, you can click Window on the menu bar and then click Remove Split.

If you have multiple Word documents open and want to view all of them at the same time on the screen, you can instruct Word to arrange all the open documents on the screen from top to bottom.

TO ARRANGE ALL OPEN WORD DOCUMENTS ON THE SCREEN

1. Click Window on the menu bar and then click Arrange All.
Word displays each open Word document on the screen.

To make one of the arranged documents fill the entire screen again, maximize the window by clicking its Maximize button or double-clicking its title bar.

If you have two documents that have similar content and you want to view and scroll through them at the same time, you can instruct Word to display them side by side.

TO DISPLAY TWO DOCUMENTS SIDE BY SIDE

1. Open the documents that you want to be displayed beside each other.
2. Click Window on the menu bar and then click Compare Side by Side with [file name].
*Word displays the **Compare Side by Side toolbar** on the screen. The two documents are beside each other, each in a separate window.*

You can scroll through each document as you do any other document. If you want to scroll through the two documents at the same time, click the Synchronous Scrolling button on the Compare Side by Side toolbar. To stop viewing the documents beside each other, click the Close Side by Side button on the Compare Side by Side toolbar.

Viewing a Document in Reading Layout

When you are finished with a document, you may want to proofread it. You could proofread a printout of the document or you could read it on the screen. If you prefer reading on the screen, Word provides a **reading layout view** that increases the readability and legibility of an onscreen document. Reading layout view is not WYSIWYG (what you see is what you get), which means the document in reading layout view does not represent how the document will look when it is printed.

The following steps show how to switch to reading layout view.

To Use Reading Layout View

1

• **Position the mouse pointer on the Read button on the Standard toolbar (Figure 6-101).**

FIGURE 6-101

2

• **Click the Read button on the Standard toolbar.**

*Word switches to reading layout view (Figure 6-102). In reading layout view, Word hides all toolbars, except for the **Reading Layout toolbar** and the Reviewing toolbar.*

3

• **To close reading layout, click the Close button on the Reading Layout toolbar or press the ESCAPE key.**

FIGURE 6-102

Notice in reading layout view that the text is larger and easier to read. If you want to make the text on the screen even larger, click the Increase Text Size button on the Reading Layout toolbar. To make the text on the screen smaller, click the Decrease Text Size button on the Reading Layout toolbar. Adjusting text size in reading layout view does not change the font size of characters in the document.

In reading layout view, graphics and other elements do not display in their correct position because the view is designed for onscreen readability. To see the actual page layout, print the document by clicking the Print button on the Reading Layout toolbar or click the Actual Page button on the Reading Layout toolbar. To return to reading layout view, click the Actual Page button again.

You can edit the document in reading layout view the same way you edit a document in any other view. In reading layout view, Word displays the Reviewing toolbar so you can track changes as you edit the document. The Collaboration Feature that follows this project shows how to track changes using the Reviewing toolbar.

This project now is finished. The following step quits Word.

To Quit Word

1 **Click File on the menu bar and then click Exit.**

The Word window closes.

Project Summary

In creating the *Clever Clicks Newsletter* in this project, you learned how to create a professional looking newsletter using Word's desktop publishing features. First, the project discussed how to create a nameplate using a WordArt drawing object, borders for ruling lines, and a floating graphic. Next, you learned how to format the body of the newsletter into three columns and add a vertical rule between the second and third columns. You learned how to link one section of the document to another. The project showed how to create and format a pull-quote and also a diagram, and then how to move these graphical objects between columns. You learned how to use the Format Painter button and add a page border to the newsletter.

For documents that will be viewed online, the project showed how to highlight text, animate text, and add background colors and patterns. Finally, you learned how to split a document into two windows.

 If you have a SAM user profile, you may have access to hands-on instruction, practice, and assessment of the skills covered in this project. Log in to your SAM account and go to your assignments page to see what your instructor has assigned.

What You Should Know

Having completed this project, you should be able to perform the tasks below. The tasks are listed in the same order they were presented in this project. For a list of the buttons, menus, toolbars, and commands introduced in this project, see the Quick Reference Summary at the back of this book and refer to the Page Number column.

1. Start and Customize Word   (WD 380)
2. Display Formatting Marks   (WD 381)
3. Zoom Page Width   (WD 381, WD 435, WD 441)
4. Change All Margin Settings   (WD 381)
5. Insert a WordArt Drawing Object   (WD 383)
6. Format a WordArt Drawing Object   (WD 384)
7. Change the Shape of a WordArt Drawing Object (WD 387)
8. Center the Newsletter Title   (WD 387)
9. Use Borders to Add Ruling Lines   (WD 388)
10. Clear Formatting   (WD 388, WD 397)
11. Set a Right-Aligned Tab Stop   (WD 389)
12. Insert a Symbol   (WD 390)
13. Enter Text and Add a Border   (WD 391)
14. Insert Clip Art from the Web   (WD 392)
15. Insert a Graphic File from the Data Disk (WD 393)
16. Format a Graphic as Floating   (WD 393)
17. Flip a Graphic   (WD 394)
18. Not Use the Drawing Grid   (WD 395)
19. Move a Graphic   (WD 396)
20. Brighten a Graphic   (WD 396)
21. Darken a Graphic   (WD 396)
22. Format and Enter Text   (WD 397, WD 417)
23. Save a Document   (WD 398, WD 406, WD 415, WD 420, WD 429, WD 431, WD 435)
24. Insert a Continuous Section Break   (WD 399)
25. Change the Number of Columns   (WD 400)
26. Justify a Paragraph   (WD 401)
27. Insert a File in the Newsletter   (WD 402)
28. Format a Letter as a Drop Cap   (WD 403)
29. Insert a Next Page Section Break   (WD 404)
30. Enter Text   (WD 405, WD 419)
31. Insert a Column Break   (WD 406)
32. Insert a File in a Column of the Newsletter (WD 407)
33. Display a Document in Full Screen View (WD 407)
34. Justify Paragraphs   (WD 408)
35. Place a Vertical Rule between Columns (WD 409)
36. Insert a Text Box   (WD 411)
37. Format a Text Box   (WD 412)
38. Shade a Paragraph   (WD 413)
39. Format Text   (WD 414, WD 428)

(continued)

What You Should Know *(continued)*

40. Resize a Text Box   (WD 414)

41. Position a Text Box   (WD 415)

42. Change Column Formatting   (WD 416)

43. Link a Copied Item   (WD 418)

44. Balance Columns   (WD 420)

45. Insert a Diagram   (WD 421)

46. Zoom to a Percentage   (WD 422)

47. Add Segments to a Diagram   (WD 423)

48. Add Text to a Diagram   (WD 423)

49. Enter More Diagram Text   (WD 424)

50. AutoFormat a Diagram   (WD 425)

51. Resize a Diagram   (WD 426)

52. Zoom to 100%   (WD 426)

53. Format a Graphic as Floating   (WD 427)

54. Use the Format Painter Button   (WD 427, WD 432)

55. Copy and Paste a Diagram   (WD 430)

56. Color a Drop Cap   (WD 432)

57. Add a Page Border   (WD 433)

58. Zoom Two Pages   (WD 434, WD 440)

59. Print a Document   (WD 435)

60. Highlight Text   (WD 436)

61. Animate Text   (WD 437)

62. Change Background Color   (WD 438)

63. Add a Pattern Fill Effect to a Background (WD 439)

64. Save a File with a New File Name   (WD 441)

65. Split the Window   (WD 441)

66. Arrange All Open Word Documents on the Screen   (WD 443)

67. Display Two Documents Side by Side   (WD 443)

68. Use Reading Layout View   (WD 443)

69. Quit Word   (WD 444)

More About

Certification

The Microsoft Office Specialist Certification program provides an opportunity for you to obtain a valuable industry credential - proof that you have the Word 2003 skills required by employers. For more information, see Appendix E or visit the Word 2003 Certification Web page (scsite.com/wd2003/cert).

Learn It Online

Instructions: To complete the Learn It Online exercises, start your browser, click the Address bar, and then enter the Web address scsite.com/wd2003/learn. When the Word 2003 Learn It Online page is displayed, follow the instructions in the exercises below. Each exercise has instructions for printing your results, either for your own records or for submission to your instructor.

1 Project Reinforcement TF, MC, and SA

Below Word Project 6, click the Project Reinforcement link. Print the quiz by clicking Print on the File menu for each page. Answer each question.

2 Flash Cards

Below Word Project 6, click the Flash Cards link and read the instructions. Type 20 (or a number specified by your instructor) in the Number of playing cards text box, type your name in the Enter your Name text box, and then click the Flip Card button. When the flash card is displayed, read the question and then click the ANSWER box arrow to select an answer. Flip through Flash Cards. If your score is 15 (75%) correct or greater, click Print on the File menu to print your results. If your score is less than 15 (75%) correct, then redo this exercise by clicking the Replay button.

3 Practice Test

Below Word Project 6, click the Practice Test link. Answer each question, enter your first and last name at the bottom of the page, and then click the Grade Test button. When the graded practice test is displayed on your screen, click Print on the File menu to print a hard copy. Continue to take practice tests until you score 80% or better.

4 Who Wants To Be a Computer Genius?

Below Word Project 6, click the Computer Genius link. Read the instructions, enter your first and last name at the bottom of the page, and then click the PLAY button. When your score is displayed, click the PRINT RESULTS link to print a hard copy.

5 Wheel of Terms

Below Word Project 6, click the Wheel of Terms link. Read the instructions, and then enter your first and last name and your school name. Click the PLAY button. When your score is displayed, right-click the score and then click Print on the shortcut menu to print a hard copy.

6 Crossword Puzzle Challenge

Below Word Project 6, click the Crossword Puzzle Challenge link. Read the instructions, and then enter your first and last name. Click the SUBMIT button. Work the crossword puzzle. When you are finished, click the Submit button. When the crossword puzzle is redisplayed, click the Print Puzzle button to print a hard copy.

7 Tips and Tricks

Below Word Project 6, click the Tips and Tricks link. Click a topic that pertains to Project 6. Right-click the information and then click Print on the shortcut menu. Construct a brief example of what the information relates to in Word to confirm you understand how to use the tip or trick.

8 Newsgroups

Below Word Project 6, click the Newsgroups link. Click a topic that pertains to Project 6. Print three comments.

9 Expanding Your Horizons

Below Word Project 6, click the Expanding Your Horizons link. Click a topic that pertains to Project 6. Print the information. Construct a brief example of what the information relates to in Word to confirm you understand the contents of the article.

10 Search Sleuth

Below Word Project 6, click the Search Sleuth link. To search for a term that pertains to this project, select a term below the Project 6 title and then use the Google search engine at google.com (or any major search engine) to display and print two Web pages that present information on the term.

11 Word Online Training

Below Word Project 6, click the Word Online Training link. When your browser displays the Microsoft Office Online Web page, click the Word link. Click one of the Word courses that covers one or more of the objectives listed at the beginning of the project on page WD 378. Print the first page of the course before stepping through it.

12 Office Marketplace

Below Word Project 6, click the Office Marketplace link. When your browser displays the Microsoft Office Online Web page, click the Office Marketplace link. Click a topic that relates to Word. Print the first page.

Apply Your Knowledge

1 Enhancing a Document for Online Viewing

Instructions: Start Word. Open the document, Apply 6-1 Certification Information, on the Data Disk. If you did not download the Data Disk, see the inside back cover for instructions for downloading the Data Disk or see your instructor.

You are to modify the document for online viewing (Figure 6-103).

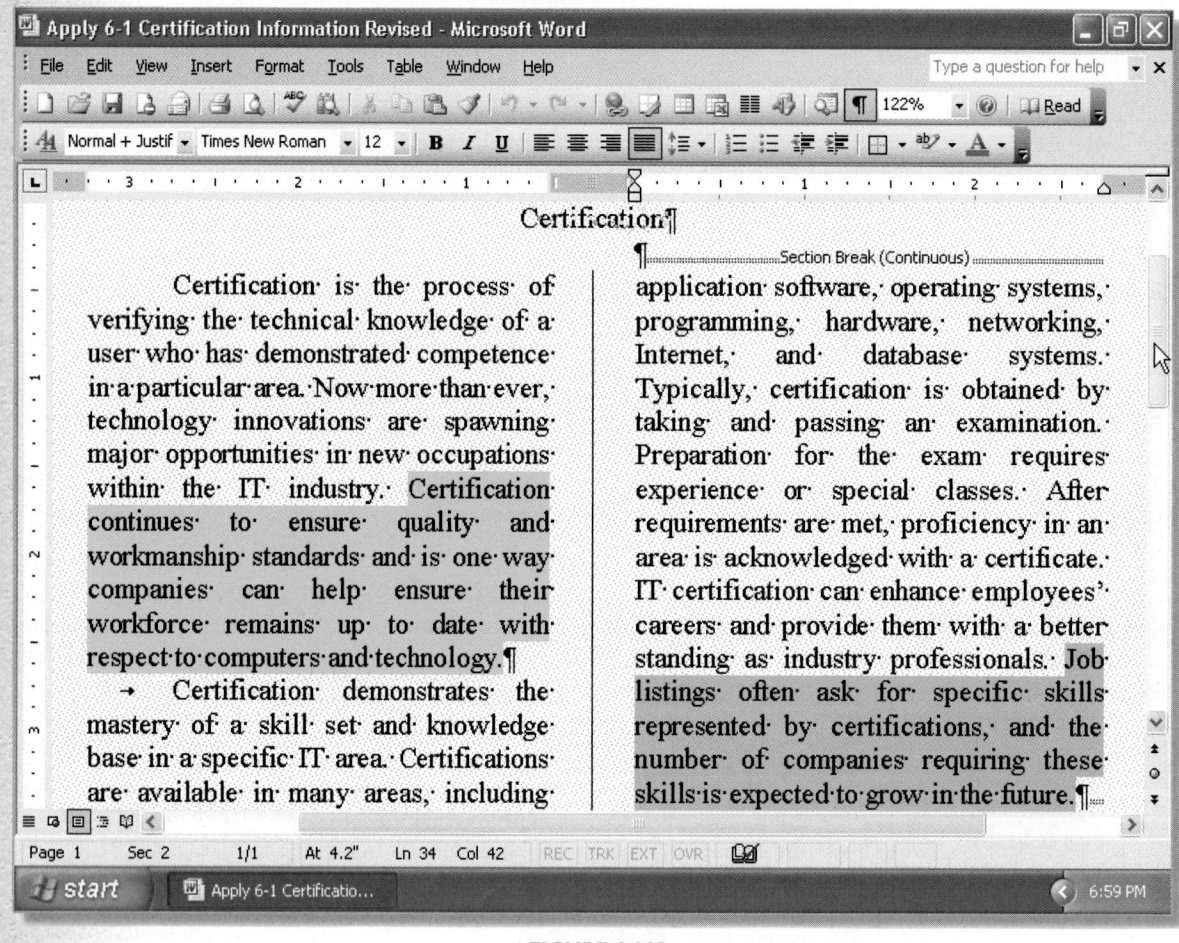

FIGURE 6-103

Apply Your Knowledge

Perform the following tasks:

1. For the two paragraphs below the title, change their alignment from left-aligned to justified.
2. Insert a continuous section break to the left of the first paragraph of text. In section 2, change the number of columns from one to two.
3. Balance the two columns by inserting a continuous section break at the end of the text.
4. Use the Columns dialog box (Format menu, Columns command) to draw a line between the two columns in section 2 of the document. *Hint*: Be sure the insertion point is in section 2 before displaying the Columns dialog box.
5. Highlight the last sentence in the first paragraph in turquoise. Highlight the last sentence in the second paragraph in yellow.
6. Apply the Sparkle Text animation text effect to the title above the columns.
7. Change the background color of the document to rose.
8. Change the pattern fill effect of the background color to Small confetti.
9. Save the revised document with the name Apply 6-1 Certification Information Revised.
10. Print the document.
11. View the document in full screen view. In reading layout view, increase the text size and then decrease the text size. On the printout, write down how a document looks in full screen view. Close full screen view.
12. View the document in reading layout view. On the printout, write down how a document looks in reading layout view. Close reading layout view.
13. Split the window. Scroll through the document in the top window. Scroll through the document in the bottom window. Remove the split window. On the printout, write down the purpose of splitting a window.

In the Lab

1 Creating a Newsletter with a Pull-Quote and an Article on File

Problem: You are an editor of the newsletter, Old Town Historical. The next edition is due out in one week. This issue's article will discuss the funding of a historic home renovation (Figure 6-104). The text for the feature article is on the Data Disk. If you did not download the Data Disk, see the inside back cover for instructions for downloading the Data Disk or see your instructor. You need to create the nameplate and the pull-quote.

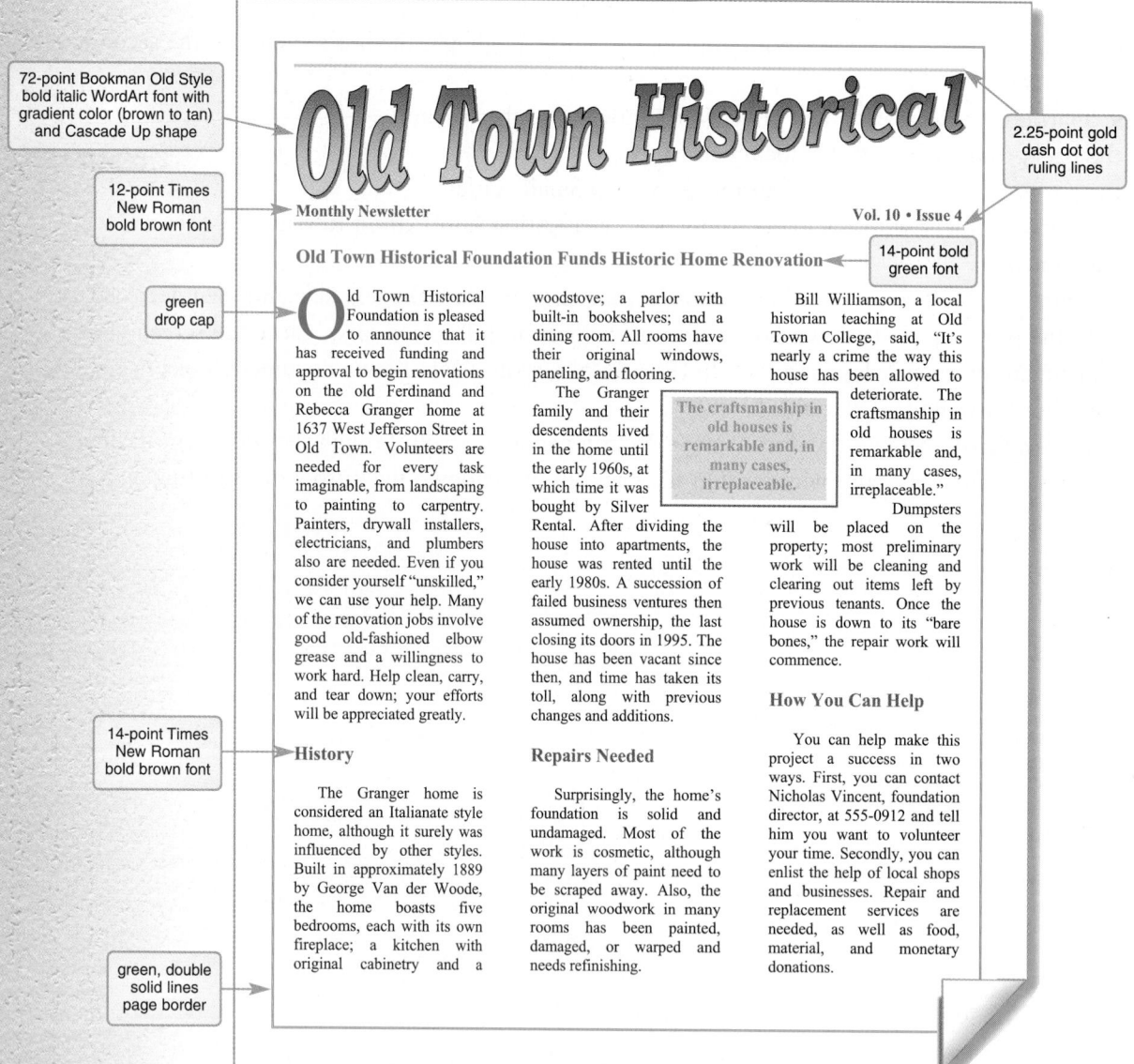

72-point Bookman Old Style bold italic WordArt font with gradient color (brown to tan) and Cascade Up shape

12-point Times New Roman bold brown font

green drop cap

14-point Times New Roman bold brown font

green, double solid lines page border

2.25-point gold dash dot dot ruling lines

14-point bold green font

FIGURE 6-104

Instructions:

1. Change all margins to .75 inches. Depending on your printer, you may need different margin settings.
2. Create the nameplate using the formats identified in Figure 6-104. Insert the dot symbol between the volume and issue.
3. Create a continuous section break below the nameplate.
4. Format section 2 to three columns.
5. Insert the Lab 6-1 Home Renovation Article on the Data Disk into section 2 below the nameplate.
6. Format the newsletter according to Figure 6-104. Use the Format Painter button to copy formatting from the first subhead to remaining subheads.
7. Insert a continuous section break at the end of the document to balance the columns.
8. The text for the pull-quote is in the Repairs Needed section of the article. Copy the text and then insert it into a text box. Change the line color of the text box to brown, and the line weight to 1½ point. Format the characters in the pull-quote to bold orange font. Shade the paragraph tan. Resize the text box so it matches Figure 6-104. Position the text box as shown in Figure 6-104.
9. Add the page border as shown in the figure.
10. View the document in print preview. If it does not fit on a single page, click the Shrink to Fit button on the Print Preview toolbar or reduce the size of the WordArt object.
11. Save the document with Lab 6-1 Old Town Newsletter as the file name.
12. Print the newsletter.

2 Creating a Newsletter with a Diagram and an Article on File

Problem: You are responsible for the monthly preparation of Northside Newcomers, a newsletter for community members. The next edition welcomes those new to the community (Figure 6-105 on the next page). This article already has been prepared and is on the Data Disk. If you did not download the Data Disk, see the inside back cover for instructions for downloading the Data Disk or see your instructor. You need to create the nameplate and the diagram.

Instructions:

1. Change all margins to .75 inches. Depending on your printer, you may need different margin settings.
2. Create the nameplate using the formats identified in Figure 6-105. If necessary, resize the WordArt object. Insert the dot symbol between the volume and issue. Use the Clip Art task pane to locate the image shown, or use a similar graphic. Change its wrapping style to In front of text. Darken the graphic. If necessary, resize the graphic.
3. Create a continuous section break below the nameplate.
4. Format section 2 to three columns.
5. Insert the Lab 6-2 Northside Newcomers Article on the Data Disk into section 2 below the nameplate.
6. Format the newsletter according to Figure 6-105. Use the Format Painter button to format the subheads.
7. Insert a continuous section break at the end of the document to balance the columns.
8. Place a border to the left of the Next Month section.
9. Add the page border as shown in the figure.

(continued)

In the Lab

Creating a Newsletter with a Diagram and an Article on File *(continued)*

10. Create the pyramid diagram shown in Figure 6-105 in a separate document window. Change its height to 3.78 inches and its width to 3.39 inches. Remember to deselect the Lock aspect ratio check box. AutoFormat it to the square shadows style. Change its wrapping style to tight. Save the diagram with the file name Lab 6-2 Clubs Diagram. Copy and paste the diagram into the newsletter.

11. Save the document using Lab 6-2 Northside Newcomers Newsletter as the file name.

12. Arrange both documents (the diagram and the newsletter) on the screen. Scroll through both open windows. Maximize the newsletter window.

13. Switch to full screen view and read through the newsletter. Close full screen view.

14. Print the newsletter.

60-point Verdana bold WordArt font with gradient color (dark blue to sky blue) and Deflate Bottom shape

12-point Times New Roman bold dark red font

16-point Times New Roman bold dark blue font

dark red drop cap

14-point Times New Roman bold dark blue font for subheads

3-point indigo single solid line page border

2.25-point dark red double ruling lines

Northside Newcomers

Monthly Newsletter   **Vol. 17 • Issue 8**

Welcome to the Northside Newcomers!

Welcome to the latest edition of the newsletter for those new to the Melville area, Northside Newcomers. We are in our fifteenth year and growing strong! At last count, our membership topped 150. This number, while impressive, makes it well-nigh impossible to meet at members' homes. For that happy reason, all future meetings will be held at the Community Center, 15175 Serene Way, Mellville.

Meet New Friends

As might be expected with such a large membership, a variety of offshoot groups have evolved from common hobbies and interests. Check out the seasonal club, the Armchair Quarterbacks, who attend all high school and professional league football games.

Or maybe your tastes are more intellectual. If so, perhaps you would be interested in joining the Bibliophiles, a group that meets monthly to discuss books. The Quilters Guild, another offshoot group, meets weekly, as does the Travel Club and the Northside Gastronomes, a group of self-styled gourmets. For the outdoorsy types among you, our Garden Club's own Larry and Susan McMillen had their home featured in last year's Annual Garden Walk.

The diagram shown at left lists all current clubs. No matter what your interests, you are sure to find like-minded souls.

Travel Club
Bibliophiles
Northside Gastronomes
Quilters' Guild
Armchair Quarterbacks

Surveys

Each member who attended the last meeting was given a survey to complete. The survey asked members to list their favorite restaurant,

music genre, sport activity, and pastime. Once we tally the survey results, we will use them to schedule future outings. For example, based on survey responses, we will schedule a dinner at the restaurant the most members cite as their favorite. We will try to secure tickets for musical venues, museum tours, sporting events, and the like based on survey results. Don't delay! Return your surveys as soon as possible to George Alizondo, Activities Chairman.

Next Month...

Be sure to attend next month's meeting, which is scheduled for 7:00 p.m. on Tuesday, September 13, at the Community Center. We hope to announce survey results at the meeting. We also plan to discuss our upcoming holiday outings.

The 50/50 drawing will be held the last week of August. Estimated winnings are at least $72.00 at this point. Mail in your 50/50 drawing envelopes if you are interested in participating.

FIGURE 6-105

In the Lab

3 Creating a Newsletter from Scratch

Problem: You work part-time for Valley Vista Apartments, which publishes a newsletter for all tenants. Figure 6-106 shows the contents of the next issue.

Instructions:

1. Change all margins to .75 inches. Depending on your printer, you may need different margin settings.
2. Create the nameplate using the formats identified in Figure 6-106. *Hint:* Use the Shadow Style button on the Drawing toolbar to apply the shadow effect to the WordArt object in the nameplate. *Hint:* Use a tab leader character to fill the space in the middle of the issue information line. Insert the diamond symbol between the volume and issue.

72-point Harlow Solid Italic bold WordArt font (or a similar font) with gold fill color, 1.5-point red line color, and Inflate shape

0.75-point gold double wavy ruling lines

shadow

14-point Times New Roman bold green font

14-point Times New Roman bold red font

12-point Times New Roman bold green font for subheads

1.5-point blue line around picture

10-point Times New Roman bold font

12-point Times New Roman bold red font

gold shading

green confetti art page border

Community Chatter

Monthly Newsletter---Vol. 7 ◊ Issue 5

Three New Tenants Arrive in May

We are happy to announce that we will be getting two new neighbors! Valley Vista Apartments sends a warm welcome to our new tenants. Because the entire complex has only five buildings, most tenants know one another fairly well. This "family" atmosphere is what makes our community so attractive.

Meet the New Folks

On Friday, June 10, at 7:30 p.m., join us in the Valley View Clubhouse for an informal party to welcome the new neighbors. Bring your own beverages. If you want to donate snacks or desserts, feel free to do so. No R.S.V.P. is necessary -- the more the merrier! In the meantime, here is who is moving into our complex.

Harry Martensen is moving into building D, apartment 10. Harry teaches math at the exclusive Shreve Preparatory School. He is new to the area, having relocated here from Chicago. Darren and Sylvia Barnett and their children, Derek and Phoebe, have moved into building A, apartment 4. Darren works for A-1 Engine Systems, and Sylvia is a full-time mom to Derek and Phoebe. Both children are preschoolers, and we look forward to hearing their laughter!

Clubhouse Renovation

Renovation on the Clubhouse finally is complete! New decks, landscaping, and pool renovation were included in the outdoor projects. Interior work included painting, replacing the carpeting, remodeling the kitchen and bathroom areas, and installing new draperies and furnishings. We all can look forward to enjoying the many amenities available at the Clubhouse, some of which are listed in the table at the bottom of this newsletter.

To reserve the Clubhouse for your event, call the Office at 555-8875.

Clubhouse pool after recent renovations.

Upcoming Clubhouse Events

Date	Event
June 10 at 7:30 p.m.	Welcome new neighbors
July 3 at dusk	Celebration, fireworks, and cookout
July 30 from 11:00 a.m. until ?	Pool party
August 4-6	Community garage sale
September 4 at 12:00 p.m.	Cookout

FIGURE 6-106

(continued)

Creating a Newsletter from Scratch *(continued)*

3. Create a continuous section break below the nameplate.

4. Format section 2 to three columns.

5. Enter the text into section 2 using justified paragraph formatting.

6. Insert the pool picture into the newsletter. The picture is called pool and is located on the Data Disk. If you did not download the Data Disk, see the inside back cover for instructions for downloading the Data Disk or see your instructor. *Hint:* Use Help to learn about inserting pictures. If necessary, resize the picture. Add a sky blue border around the picture. Add a text box below the picture as shown in Figure 6-106 on the previous page. Group the text box and the picture together. Be sure the newsletter text wraps around the picture and text box. *Hint:* Use Help to learn about grouping objects.

7. Compress the picture. *Hint:* Use Help to learn about compressing pictures.

8. Insert a continuous section break at the end of the third column in section 2. Format section 3 to one column. Create the table as shown at the bottom of the newsletter in section 3.

9. Format the newsletter according to Figure 6-106. Place a vertical rule between all columns in section 2. Use the Columns dialog box (Format menu) to do this. Use the Format Painter button to automate some of your formatting tasks. Add the art page border as shown in the figure.

10. Save the document with Lab 6-3 Community Chatter Newsletter as the file name.

11. Switch to reading layout view and read through the newsletter. Close reading layout view.

12. Print the newsletter.

Cases and Places

The difficulty of these case studies varies:
■ are the least difficult and ■■ are more difficult. The last exercise is a group exercise.

1 ■ As your final project in your computer concepts class, you have been assigned the task of creating page WD 447 in this textbook. The page contains many desktop publishing elements: nameplate in one column and text in four columns, balanced columns, and a variety of font sizes and font colors. Apply an animation text effect to the fill effect page title, Learn It Online. Highlight each exercise heading. Change the background color and pattern of the background color. Switch to full screen view and read through the document. Print the document. Change the exercise section from four to three columns. Switch to reading layout view and proofread the document. Print the revised document.

2 ■■ You work part-time at a local nature center. One of your responsibilities is to write articles for the Green Thumb Gazette, a one-page newsletter published by the nature center. Your assignment is to decide on a feature article for the next edition of the Green Thumb Gazette. The article can discuss any garden-related item such as planting or maintaining flowers or trees, controlling weeds or garden pests, cleaning out flower beds, using compost, protecting gardens in cold weather, gardening tips and tricks, etc. As a basis for the feature article, use personal experiences, the school library, the Internet, magazines, friends and family, or other resources. The newsletter should contain a clip art image or a picture with article text wrapping around the graphic. Adjust the lightness or darkness of the graphic as necessary. Enhance the newsletter with a drop cap, WordArt, color, ruling lines, and a page border.

3 ■■ Pennywise Press is a one-page newsletter that presents money-saving ideas and tips. As a part-time assistant at the village hall, one of your responsibilities is to write articles for Pennywise Press. One issue, for example, discussed the keys to smart shopping: buying in bulk, using coupons, stocking up on sale items, and resisting impulse buys. Your assignment is to decide on a feature article for the next edition of Pennywise Press. Select a money-saving topic with which you are familiar. As a basis for the feature article, use personal experiences, the school library, the Internet, magazines, friends and family, or other resources. The newsletter should contain a pull-quote taken from the article. Enhance the newsletter with a drop cap, WordArt, color, ruling lines, and a page border.

4 ■■ As an assistant in the admissions office at your school, you are responsible for writing the monthly newsletter, Frosh World. This newsletter is geared specifically for the school's college freshmen. Articles in the newsletter cover a wide range of topics such as campus life, school tours, clubs, study groups, tutoring, registering for classes, and upcoming events. Your assignment is to write the next edition of Frosh World. As a basis for the feature article, use personal experiences, friends and family, the school library, the Internet, magazines, or other resources. The newsletter should contain a diagram with the text wrapped around the diagram. Enhance the newsletter with a drop cap, WordArt, color, ruling lines, and a page border.

Cases and Places

5 ■■ **Working Together**   The local newspaper has a two-page newsletter in its Wednesday edition each week that reviews current movies, live performances, books, restaurants, and local events. Your team is to design and write the next newsletter. The newsletter should have a feature article that contains the reviews and some announcements for community members. As a group, decide on the name of the newsletter and design the nameplate. Each team member independently is to see or rent a current movie, watch a live performance, read a book, dine at a local restaurant, or attend a local event and then write at least a three paragraph review. Then, the team should meet as a group to combine all the reviews into a single article. Before inserting the documents into a single file, arrange the open Word documents so you can see all of them on the screen at the same time. Once verified, insert each document into the newsletter in the appropriate location. The feature article should span both pages of the newsletter. Announcements should be on the first page of the newsletter. Use the Paste Special command to copy and then paste link some lines of the nameplate from page 1 to page 2. Split the window so you can verify that both nameplates were updated properly. Be sure the newsletter contains a drop cap, WordArt, color, shading, ruling lines, and a page border. Use an appropriate graphic, a diagram, and a pull-quote in the newsletter. Use the Go To sheet in the Find and Replace dialog box to move to specific pages in the newsletter. Proofread the document in reading layout view. Save the newsletter. Enhance the newsletter for online viewing: highlight text, animate text, change the background color, and add a pattern fill effect to the background color.

MICROSOFT
Office Word 2003

Using Word's Collaboration Tools

CASE PERSPECTIVE

Nestled on 5,000 acres in the Colorado foothills, Tri-Circle Ranch has hosted Rocky Mountain excursions for the past decade. People from all walks of life thoroughly enjoy vacationing at this spectacular location where they see unspoiled wilderness, breathtaking snow-capped mountaintops, and a variety of wildlife including moose, antelope, coyote, fox, bighorn sheep, mule deer, elk, and water fowl. Expert guides lead the single-day, overnight, and week-long excursions. Daily activities consist of walking, hiking, backpacking, trout fishing, and rafting on the Colorado and Eagle Rivers.

As a part-time employee at Tri-Circle Ranch, you are responsible for all the company's computer work. Thus far, you have created a brochure, a fax cover sheet, several letters, mailing labels, a member newsletter, and a company Web page. Next week, your boss will be discussing Tri-Circle Ranch's Rocky Mountain excursions at a college fair. He has asked you to create an outline and corresponding slide show for his presentation. After creating the outline, you e-mail it to your boss for his review. He adds a couple of comments and incorporates some changes in the document and then e-mails it back to you. You review his comments and changes and then finalize the outline. Then, you send the final outline to Microsoft PowerPoint so your boss has an electronic slide show for his presentation. He is quite impressed!

As you read through this feature, you will learn how to create an outline, track changes in a document, and send an outline to PowerPoint.

Objectives

You will have mastered the material in this project when you can:

- Create an outline
- E-mail a document for review
- Insert comments
- Track changes
- Review tracked changes
- Send an outline to PowerPoint

Introduction

Word provides many tools that allow users to work with others, or **collaborate**, on a document. One set of collaboration tools allows you to track changes to a document and review the changes. That is, one computer user creates a document and another user(s) makes changes and inserts comments to the same document. Those changes then display on the screen with options that allow the originator (author) to accept or reject the changes and delete the comments. With another collaboration tool, you can compare and merge two documents to determine the differences between them.

As shown in Figure 1 on the next page, this feature illustrates how to track changes in Word and how to send a Word outline to PowerPoint for use in a slide show. Figure 1a shows the author's original outline. Figure 1b shows the reviewer's tracked changes and comments. Figure 1c shows the final outline, and Figure 1d shows the PowerPoint slide show created from the Word final outline.

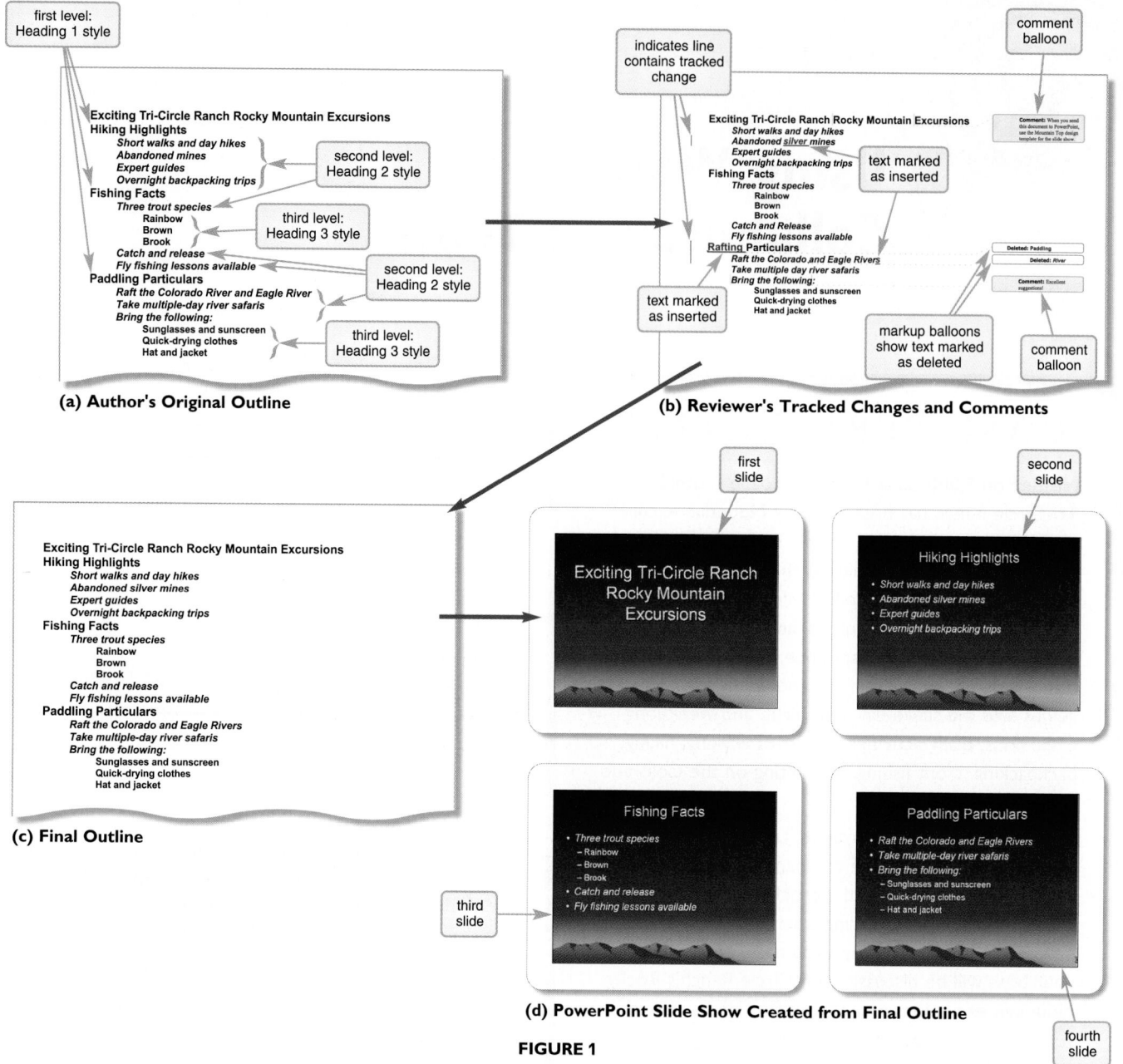

FIGURE 1

Creating an Outline

In an outline, the major (first level) headings are displayed at the left margin with each lower, or subordinate, level indented. The outline in this feature contains three major headings (shown in Figure 1a): Hiking Highlights, Fishing Facts, and Paddling Particulars.

To create an outline in Word, you use its built-in heading styles. When the document is displayed in **outline view**, Heading 1 style is displayed at the left margin, Heading 2 style is indented, Heading 3 style is indented further, and so on.

The following steps show how to create an outline. First, you switch to outline view. Then, you enter headings in the outline using heading styles.

To Enter Headings in an Outline

1

• **With Word started and a new document window open, click the Outline View button on the horizontal scroll bar.**

• **If your screen does not display the Outlining toolbar, click View on the menu bar, point to Toolbars, and then click Outlining.**

• **Type** Exciting Tri-Circle Ranch Rocky Mountain Excursions **and then press the ENTER key.**

• **Type** Hiking Highlights **and then press the ENTER key.**

Word switches to outline view, which shows an outline symbol to the left of each paragraph (Figure 2). The Outline Level box on the Outlining toolbar indicates the current heading is at the first level of the outline. The next heading entered is to be demoted to the second level.

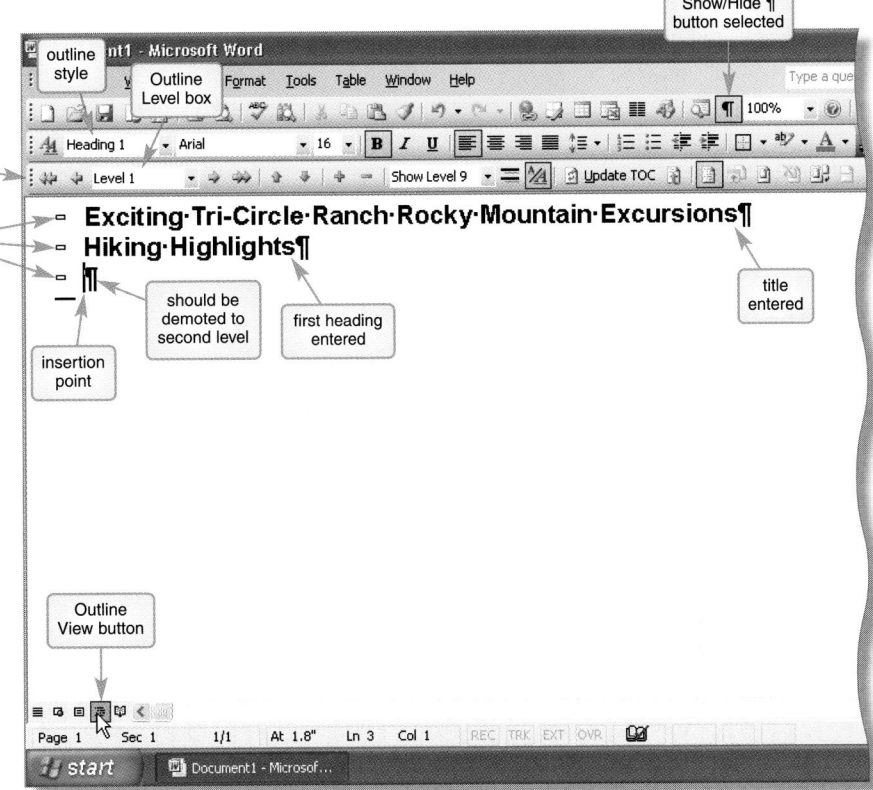

FIGURE 2

2

• **Press the TAB key.**

Word demotes the current paragraph to the second level, indented below the first heading.

3

• **Type** Short walks and day hikes **and then press the ENTER key.**

• **Type** Abandoned mines **and then press the ENTER key.**

• **Type** Expert guides **and then press the ENTER key.**

• **Type** Overnight backpacking trips **and then press the ENTER key.**

The Outline Level button on the Outlining toolbar shows Level 2 (Figure 3). The next item to be entered needs to be promoted to the first level.

FIGURE 3

4

• **Press SHIFT+TAB.**

Word promotes the paragraph containing the insertion point to the first level (Figure 4).

FIGURE 4

Other Ways

1. On View menu click Outline
2. In Voice Command mode, say "View, Outline"

The buttons and boxes on the left half of the Outlining toolbar allow you to promote and demote items in an outline and change an item's level. The buttons on the right half of the Outlining toolbar allow you to work with master and subdocuments.

Instead of pressing the TAB key to demote a paragraph, you can click the Demote button on the Outlining toolbar. Likewise, you can click the Promote button on the Outlining toolbar instead of pressing SHIFT+TAB to promote a paragraph. To promote a paragraph directly to the first level, you can click the Promote to Heading 1 button on the Outlining toolbar.

You use outline symbols to rearrange text or display and hide text. Notice in Figure 4 that the outline symbol is either a plus sign or a minus sign. A plus sign means the heading is **expanded**; that is, all lower-level headings are displayed on the screen. A minus sign means the heading has no lower levels or that the heading is **collapsed**; that is, lower-level headings are hidden from the screen. To expand a collapsed heading, double-click its outline symbol (the minus sign). To collapse an expanded heading, double-click its outline symbol (the plus sign).

If you wanted to rearrange headings in an outline, position the insertion point in the heading to be moved and then click the Move Up or Move Down button on the Outlining toolbar, or you can drag the outline symbol upward or downward.

The next step is to enter the remaining headings into the outline, as described below.

To Enter Headings in an Outline

1 **Type** Fishing Facts **and then press the ENTER key.**

2 **Press the TAB key. Type** Three trout species **and then press the ENTER key.**

3 **Press the TAB key. Type** Rainbow **and then press the ENTER key. Type** Brown **and then press the ENTER key. Type** Brook **and then press the ENTER key.**

4 **Press SHIFT+TAB. Type** Catch and release **and then press the ENTER key. Type** Fly fishing lessons available **and then press the ENTER key.**

5 **Press SHIFT+TAB. Type** Paddling Particulars **and then press the ENTER key.**

6 **Press the TAB key. Type** Raft the Colorado River and Eagle River **and then press the ENTER key. Type** Take multiple-day river safaris **and then press the ENTER key. Type** Bring the following: **and then press the ENTER key.**

7 **Press the TAB key. Type** Sunglasses and sunscreen **and then press the ENTER key. Type** Quick-drying clothes **and then press the ENTER key. Type** Hat and jacket **as the last heading in the outline.**

The outline headings are entered (Figure 5).

FIGURE 5

The following steps save the outline.

To Save a File

1 **With a floppy disk in drive A, click the Save button on the Standard toolbar.**

2 **Type** Rocky Mountain Outline **in the File name box. Do not press the ENTER key.**

3 **If necessary, click the Save in box arrow and then click 3½ Floppy (A:).**

4 **Click the Save button in the Save As dialog box.**

Word saves the document on a floppy disk in drive A with the file name, Rocky Mountain Outline.

Reviewing a Document

Reviewing a document is one of the collaboration tools provided in Word. After the originator (author) creates a document, reviewers make changes to the same document. For demonstration purposes, this project illustrates how both an originator and a reviewer work with a document.

E-Mailing a Document for Review

With the first draft of the outline complete, the next step in this feature is to e-mail the Rocky Mountain Outline document to another user for review. To e-mail a document for review, it should be displayed in the document window. A document sent for review becomes an attachment to the e-mail message. When the reviewer (recipient) opens the attached document in Word, the TRK indicator on the status bar is darkened, which means the document is ready to be reviewed.

The steps on the next page show how to e-mail a document for review.

To E-Mail a Document for Review

1

• **Click File on the menu bar and then point to Send To (Figure 6).**

2

• **Click Mail Recipient (for Review).**

• **When Word opens the Please review 'Rocky Mountain Outline' window, type the recipient's e-mail address in the To text box (in this case, type your own e-mail address or an address provided by your instructor).**

Word automatically displays a message in the Subject text box and includes the Rocky Mountain Outline file as an attachment in the Please review 'Rocky Mountain Outline' window (Figure 7). The **E-mail toolbar** *is displayed below the menu bar.*

3

• **Click the Send button on the E-mail toolbar, if directed to do so by your instructor.**

Word sends the Rocky Mountain Outline document to the recipient named in the To text box.

FIGURE 6

FIGURE 7

Other Ways
1. In Voice Command mode, say "File, Send To, Mail Recipient for Review, [enter e-mail address], Send"

When an e-mail recipient receives a document that has been sent to him or her for review, the subject line in the e-mail program shows the name of the attached file, and a paper clip denotes the attachment. The reviewer simply double-clicks the document attachment in the mail message to start the application and open the document. If Word opens the document in reading layout view, simply click View on the menu bar and then click Outline to switch to outline view.

Instead of sending a document for review, you can send an open document as an attachment (not for review) to an e-mail message from within Word.

TO E-MAIL AN OPEN DOCUMENT AS AN ATTACHMENT (NOT FOR REVIEW)

1. Click File on the menu bar, point to Send To, and then click Mail Recipient (as Attachment).
2. When Word displays the e-mail window with the document attached, type the recipient's e-mail address in the To text box.
3. Click the Send button on the E-mail toolbar.

If you wanted to cancel an e-mail operation, simply close the e-mail window.

Inserting, Viewing, and Editing Comments

After reading through the Rocky Mountain Outline document, your boss has a couple of comments. A **comment**, or annotation, is a note inserted in a document that does not affect the text of the document. Reviewers often use comments to communicate suggestions, tips, and other messages to the author of a document.

For example, your boss (Kyle Chambers) suggests using a mountain background in PowerPoint for the slide show of this outline. He also likes your list of items to bring on the rafting trips. Instead of writing his comments on a printout of the document, he plans to use Word to insert them. Then, you can delete the comments after viewing them.

The following steps show how a reviewer inserts a comment in a document.

> *Other Ways*
>
> 1. On Insert menu click Comment
> 2. In Voice Command mode, say "Insert, Comment"

To Insert a Comment in the Reviewing Pane

1

• **If the Reviewing toolbar is not displayed in the Word window, click View on the menu bar, point to Toolbars, and then click Reviewing.**

• **Select the text on which you wish to comment (in this case, Rocky Mountain, in the first line in the outline).**

• **Click the Insert Comment button on the Reviewing toolbar.**

When you insert a comment and the Word window is in outline view, the Reviewing Pane is displayed at the bottom of the window (Figure 8). The Reviewing Pane button is selected on the Reviewing toolbar. **Comment marks**, *which look like parentheses, surround the selected text in the document window. The reviewer's initials and comment number are displayed immediately after the last comment mark and also in the Reviewing Pane.*

FIGURE 8

2

• **Type** In PowerPoint, use a mountain background for the slide show.

Word displays the comment in the Reviewing Pane (Figure 9).

FIGURE 9

As with footnotes, if you point to the comment marks (parentheses) in the document window, Word displays the comment and the name of the comment's author above the comment mark as a ScreenTip.

Instead of selecting text on which you wish to comment (as shown in Step 1 on the previous page), you simply can click the location where you want to insert the comment. In this case, the comment marks (parentheses) display side by side at the location of the insertion point.

As an alternative to inserting comments in the Reviewing Pane, some users prefer to work with **comment balloons** that display to the right of the text in the document window. Comment balloons are not displayed in outline view or normal view; they are displayed only in print layout view, Web layout view, and reading layout view.

The following steps describe how to edit a comment when the Word window is in print layout view.

More About

Voice Comments

If your computer is equipped with a sound card and a microphone, you can record a voice comment in a document. Click the Insert Voice button on the Reviewing toolbar and then record the comment. If the Reviewing toolbar does not contain the Insert Voice button, click the Toolbar Options button at the right edge of the toolbar, point to Add or Remove Buttons, point to Reviewing, and then click Insert Voice on the submenu.

To Edit a Comment in a Comment Balloon

1 Click the Reviewing Pane button on the Reviewing toolbar to remove the Reviewing Pane from the screen.

2 Click the Print Layout View button on the horizontal scroll bar.

3 If necessary, click the Zoom box to select its percentage. Type 85 and then press the ENTER key.

4 If necessary, scroll to display the comment balloon in the document window.

5 In the comment balloon, delete the word, In, at the beginning of the sentence. Type When you send this document to **(Figure 10)**.

Word modifies the contents of the comment in the comment balloon. The insertion point is positioned in the comment balloon.

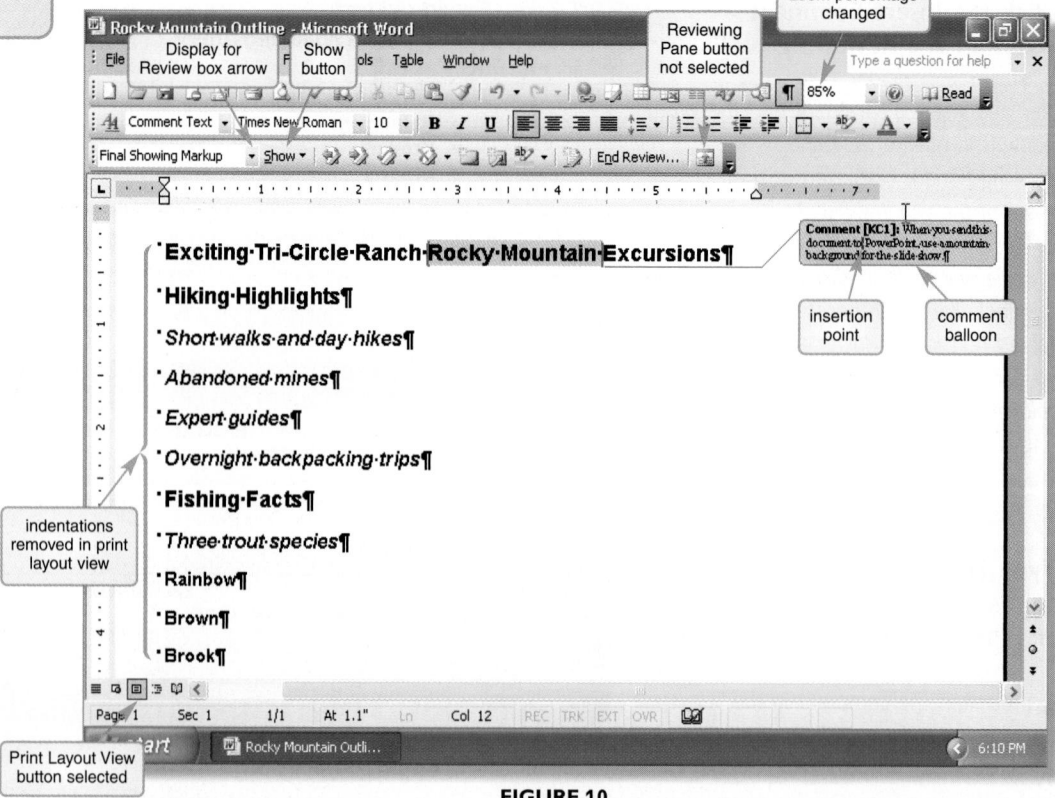

FIGURE 10

Notice in print layout view that Word removes the indentations for lower levels in the outline. That is, all text begins at the left margin. If you print the document while it is displayed in print layout view, it prints as shown on the screen – with all text at the left margin. To print the document so it looks like an outline, switch to outline view first and then print the document.

If comment marks do not appear on the screen, verify comments are showing by clicking the Show button on the Reviewing toolbar and then clicking Comments. Also, if necessary, click the Display for Review box arrow and then click Final Showing Markup. If comments still do not appear, click View on the menu bar and then click Markup.

Sometimes, Word cannot display the complete text of a comment in the comment balloon. If this occurs, simply display the Reviewing Pane to see the entire comment. The Reviewing Pane also is used to see comments in normal view and outline view, and to see items such as inserted or deleted graphics and text boxes. To display the Reviewing Pane, click the Reviewing Pane button on the Reviewing toolbar or right-click the TRK status indicator on the status bar and then click Reviewing Pane on the shortcut menu. To close the Reviewing Pane, click the Reviewing Pane button on the Reviewing toolbar again.

The next step is to insert another comment, as described below.

To Insert a Comment in a Comment Balloon

1 If necessary, scroll down to display the text, Bring the following:, in the document window.

2 Select the text, Bring the following.

3 Click the Insert Comment button on the Reviewing toolbar.

4 In the comment balloon, type Excellent suggestions!

Word inserts the comment in a comment balloon (Figure 11). Notice the number 2 follows the user initials in the comment balloon to indicate this is the second comment in the document.

FIGURE 11

More About

Ink Comments

If you are using Word on a Tablet PC, then you can insert ink comments into a document. Click Insert on the menu bar and then click Ink Comment. Use the Tablet PC's digital pen to write the comment in the comment balloon. Word saves the handwritten comment with the document.

You modify comments in a comment balloon by clicking inside the comment balloon and editing as you edit text in the document window.

If multiple users review the same document, each reviewer's comments are shaded in a different color to help you visually differentiate among multiple reviewers' comments.

Word uses predefined settings for the reviewer's name that are displayed in the ScreenTip and for the reviewer's initials that are displayed in the document window, the comment balloon, and the Reviewing Pane. If the reviewer's name or initials are not correct, you can modify them.

TO CHANGE REVIEWER INFORMATION

1. Click Tools on the menu bar and then click Options.
2. When Word displays the Options dialog box, click the User Information tab and enter the correct name or initials in the respective text boxes.

When you print a document with comments, Word chooses the zoom percentage and page orientation to best display the comments in the printed document. If you want to print the comments only (without printing the document), click File on the menu bar, click Print, click the Print what box arrow, click List of markup, and then click the OK button. If you want to print the document without comments, click File on the menu bar, click Print, click the Print what box arrow, click Document, and then click the OK button.

Tracking Changes

Kyle has three suggested changes for the Rocky Mountain Outline document: (1) insert the word, silver, between Abandoned mines, (2) change the word, Paddling, to the word, Rafting, and (3) delete the word, River, after Colorado and then add the letter s to the end of the word River after Eagle.

To track changes in a document, you must turn on the change-tracking feature. When you edit a document that has the change-tracking feature enabled, Word marks all text or graphics that you insert, delete, or modify and calls the revisions a **markup**. Thus, an author can identify the changes a reviewer has made by looking at the markup in the document. The author also has the ability to accept or reject any change that a reviewer has made to a document.

The following pages illustrate how a reviewer tracks changes to a document and then how the author (originator) reviews the tracked changes made to the document.

To Track Changes

1

- **Press CTRL+HOME to position the insertion point at the beginning of the document.**

- **Double-click the TRK status indicator on the status bar.**

- **Position the insertion point immediately to the left of the word, mines, in the fourth paragraph.**

- **Type** silver **and then press the SPACEBAR.**

*Word marks the inserted text, silver, as inserted (Figure 12). That is, it is displayed in color and underlined. When tracking changes is turned on, the characters in the TRK status indicator on the status bar appear darkened. Word places a **changed line** (a vertical bar) at the left edge of each line that contains a tracked change.*

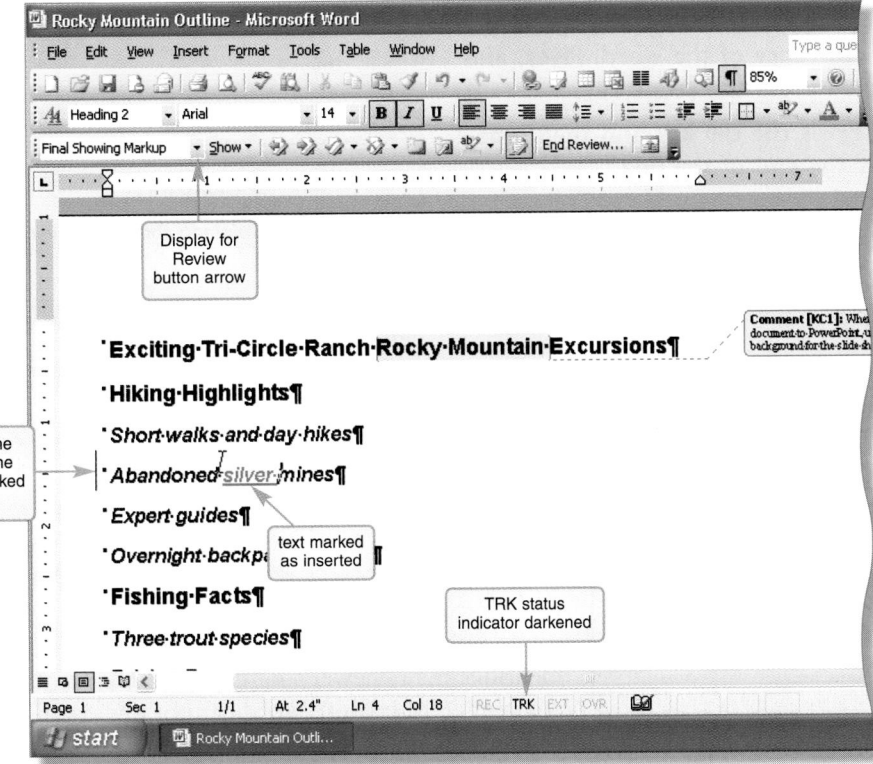

FIGURE 12

2

- **Scroll down and select the word, Paddling, in the third major heading of the outline by double-clicking it.**

- **Type** Rafting **as the replacement text.**

- **If necessary, click the right scroll arrow to display the markup balloon.**

*Word marks the selected word, Paddling, as deleted, and marks the word, Rafting, as inserted (Figure 13). In print layout view, deleted text displays in a **markup balloon**, and inserted text displays in the document in color and underlined.*

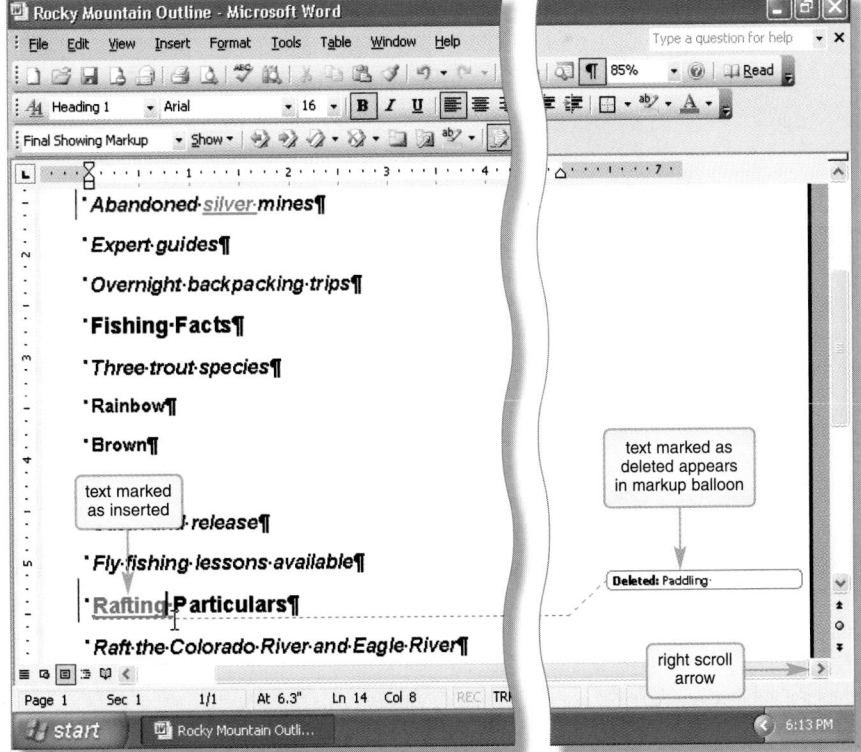

FIGURE 13

3

• **If necessary, scroll down to display the next line on the screen.**

• **In the next line, select the first occurrence of the word, River, and then press the DELETE key.**

• **Press the END key and then type s at the end of the line.**

The first occurrence of the word, River, is marked for deletion, and the second occurrence of the word River has been changed to Rivers (Figure 14).

FIGURE 14

Tracked changes, which are called **revision marks**, are displayed in markup balloons in print layout view, Web layout view, and reading layout view. In normal view and outline view, tracked changes display as strikethroughs for deleted text and underlined for inserted text.

In any view, if you point to a tracked change, Word displays a ScreenTip that identifies the reviewer's name and the type of change made by that reviewer. As with comments, Microsoft Word cannot always display the complete text of a tracked change in a markup balloon. Use the Reviewing Pane to view longer revisions.

The next step is to turn off the change-tracking feature, as described below.

To Stop Tracking Changes

1 **Double-click the TRK status indicator on the status bar.**

Word dims the characters in the TRK status indicator on the status bar (shown in Figure 15).

Reviewing Tracked Changes and Comments

Next, you would like to read the tracked changes and comments from Kyle. You could scroll through the document and point to each markup to read it, but you might overlook one or more changes using this technique. A more efficient method is to use the Reviewing toolbar to review the changes and comments one at a time, deciding whether to accept, modify, or delete them.

To do this, be sure the markups are displayed on the screen. Click the Show button on the Reviewing toolbar and verify that Comments, Insertions and Deletions, and Formatting each have a check mark beside them. Click the Display for Review box arrow and then click Final Showing Markup. If markups still are not displayed, click View on the menu bar and then click Markup.

The next steps show how to review the changes and comments from Kyle.

To Review Tracked Changes and View Comments

1

- **Press CTRL+HOME to position the insertion point at the beginning of the document.**
- **Click the Next button on the Reviewing toolbar.**
- **If necessary, click the right scroll arrow on the horizontal scroll bar so that the comment balloon is visible.**

The review of tracked changes and comments begins at the location of the insertion point, in this case, the top of the document (Figure 15). Word selects the comment and positions the insertion point in the comment balloon.

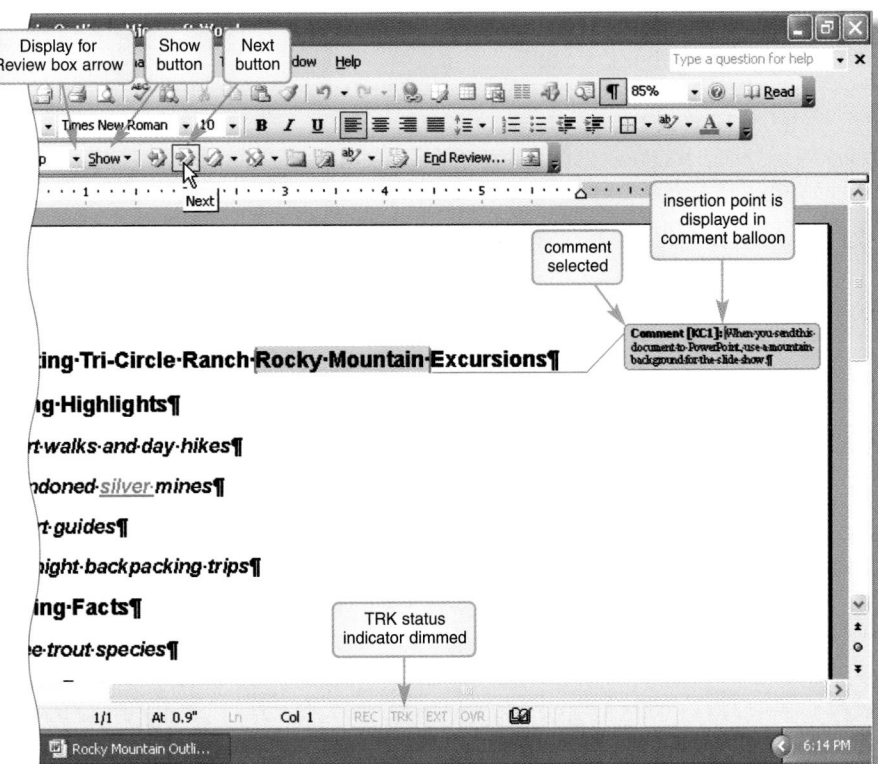

FIGURE 15

2

- **Read through the comment and then click the Reject Change/Delete Comment button on the Reviewing toolbar.**

Word deletes the comment balloon and the comment marks in the document (Figure 16).

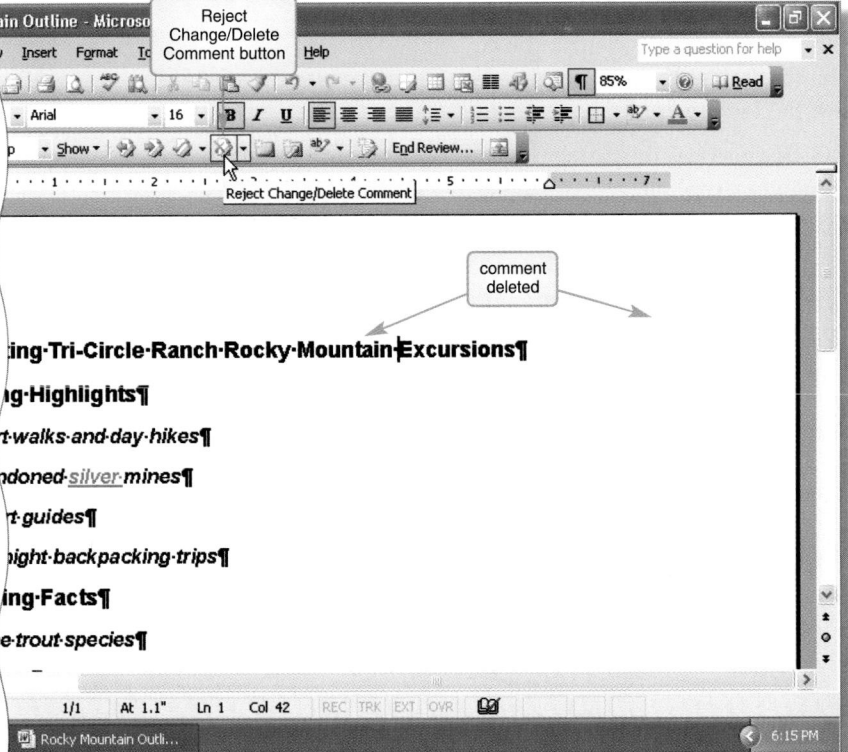

FIGURE 16

3

• **Click the Next button on the Reviewing toolbar again.**

• **Click the Accept Change button on the Reviewing toolbar to accept the insertion of the word, silver.**

Word selects the next tracked change or comment, in this case, the inserted word, silver (Figure 17). You agree with this change and, thus, instruct Word to accept it.

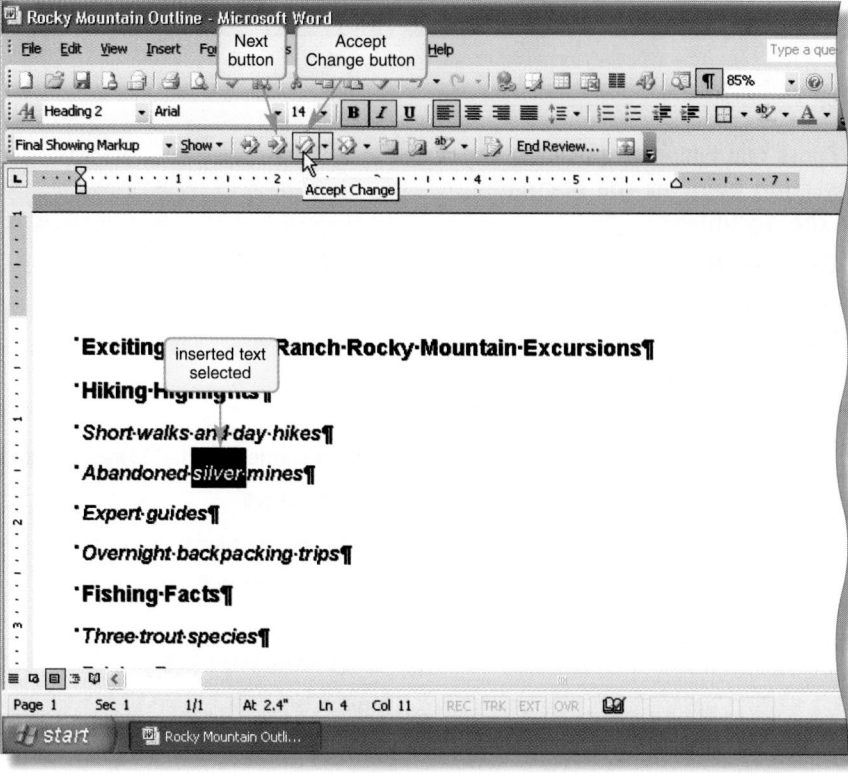

FIGURE 17

4

• **Click the Next button on the Reviewing toolbar.**

• **When Word selects the deletion of the word, Paddling, click the Reject Change/Delete Comment button on the Reviewing toolbar.**

• **Click the Next button on the Reviewing toolbar.**

• **When Word selects the insertion of the word, Rafting, click the Reject Change/Delete Comment button on the Reviewing toolbar.**

Because you do not agree with the change to replace the word, Paddling, with the word, Rafting, you instruct Word to reject it (Figure 18).

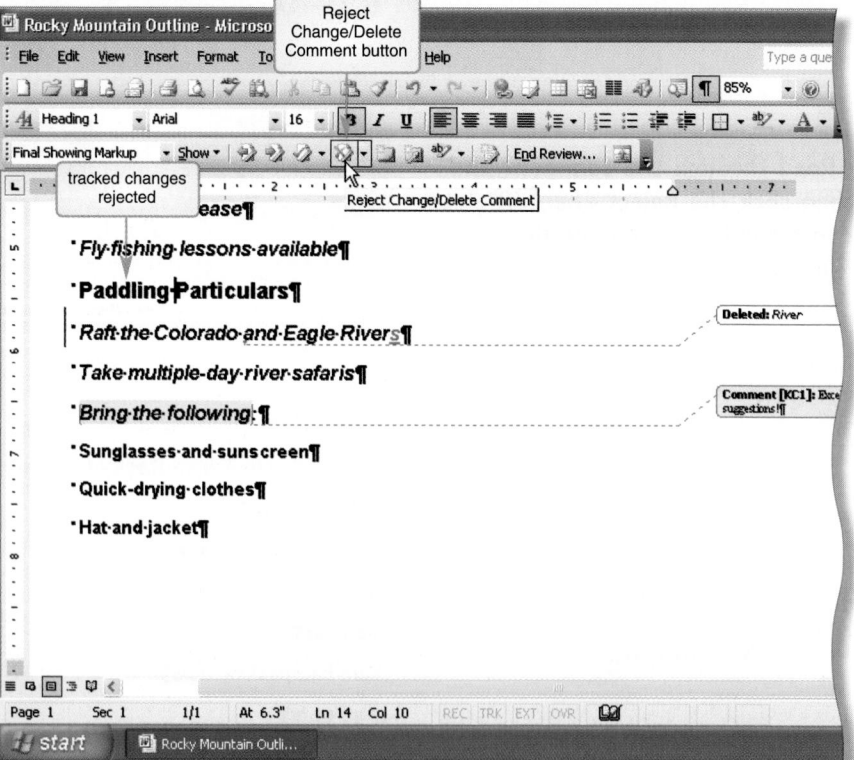

FIGURE 18

5

- **Click the Next button on the Reviewing toolbar.**

- **Click the Accept Change button to accept the deletion of the word, River.**

- **Click the Next button on the Reviewing toolbar.**

- **Click the Accept Change button to accept the insertion of the letter, s.**

- **Click the Next button on the Reviewing toolbar.**

- **Read through the selected comment and then click the Reject Change/Delete Comment button on the Reviewing toolbar to delete the comment.**

The review of tracked changes is complete (Figure 19).

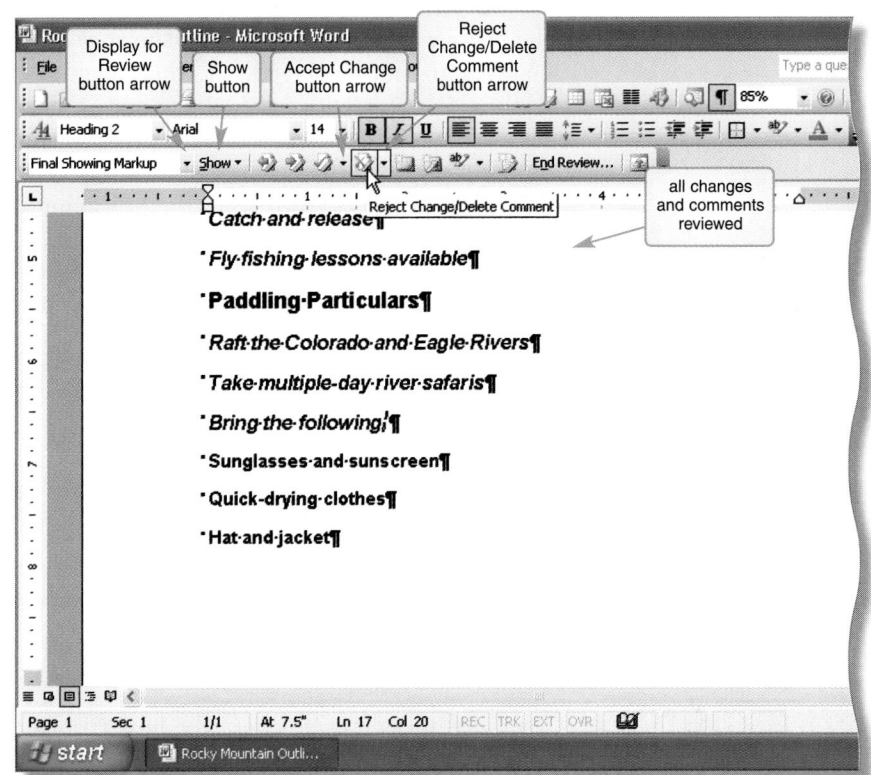

FIGURE 19

You also may accept or reject a change or comment by right-clicking it. On the shortcut menu, choices are displayed that allow you to accept or reject the changes and delete comments.

If you are certain you plan to accept all changes in a document containing tracked changes, you can accept all the changes at once by clicking the Accept Change button arrow on the Reviewing toolbar and then clicking Accept All Changes in Document. Likewise, you can click the Reject Change/Delete Comment button arrow on the Reviewing toolbar and then click Reject All Changes in Document or Delete All Comments in Document to reject all the changes or delete all the comments at once. If you click either of these commands by mistake, you can click the Undo button on the Standard toolbar to undo the action.

If you click the Next button and no tracked changes remain, Word displays a dialog box informing you the document contains no more changes. If this occurs, click the OK button.

To see how a document will look if you accept all the changes, without actually accepting them, click View on the menu bar and then click Markup, or click the Display for Review button arrow on the Reviewing toolbar and then click Final.

To show just a single reviewer's changes, click the Show button on the Reviewing toolbar, point to Reviewers, and then place a check mark beside the reviewer name whose changes you want the document to display. To hide a reviewer's changes, remove the check mark from beside the reviewer's name. Then, you can accept or reject changes and read and delete comments for one reviewer at a time.

More About

The Reviewing Toolbar

When you send a document for review, as shown on page WD 462, Word adds the End Review button to the Reviewing toolbar. After you have accepted/rejected all reviewer changes, you can click the End Review button to stop the reviewing process. Clicking the End Review button turns off tracking changes and removes the Reviewing toolbar from the Word window.

To print a hard copy that shows how the document will look if you accept all the changes, click View on the menu bar and then click Markup so the tracked changes are not displayed, and then print in the usual manner. To print a hard copy of the document with tracked changes, click the Print what box arrow in the Print dialog box and then click Document showing markup.

To keep the original outline intact, you should save the modified outline with a new file name, as described in the following steps.

To Save a File with a New File Name

1 With a floppy disk in drive A, click File on the menu bar and then click Save As.

2 Type Rocky Mountain Outline Final in the File name box. Do not press the ENTER key.

3 If necessary, click the Save in box arrow and then click 3½ Floppy (A:).

4 Click the Save button in the Save As dialog box.

Word saves the document on a floppy disk in drive A with the file name, Rocky Mountain Outline Final.

The following steps describe how to print the final outline.

Word prints the outline as shown in Figure 1c on page WD 458.

To Print the Outline

1 Click the Outline View button on the horizontal scroll bar to switch to outline view.

2 Click the Print button on the Standard toolbar.

Changing Review Settings

If you wanted to change the color and markings reviewers use for tracked changes or change how balloons are displayed, use the Track Options dialog box.

TO MODIFY REVIEWER INK COLORS AND BALLOON OPTIONS

1. Click Tools on the menu bar and then click Options.
2. When Word displays the Options dialog box, click the Track Changes tab.
3. To change how Word marks a change or the color a reviewer uses for changes, modify the settings in the Markup area in the dialog box. To change balloon options, modify settings in the Balloons area in the dialog box.
4. Click the OK button.

Other ways to display the Track Options dialog box include clicking the Show button on the Reviewing toolbar and then clicking Options, and right-clicking the TRK status indicator on the status bar and then clicking Options.

If you wanted to change the size or appearance of text in markup balloons, you would modify the Balloon Text style. The next steps describe how to modify the Balloon Text style.

More About

Printing Outlines

If you print the outline while in print layout view or normal view, Word does not indent levels of the outline. Instead, all levels print at the left margin. To print the outline with sublevels indented, switch to outline view first and then click the Print button.

More About

The Show Button

When you click the Show button on the Reviewing toolbar, Word displays a list of items. Those with a check mark beside them are displayed; those without a check mark are hidden. To hide a displayed item, such as comments or formatting marks, click its name in the list. For example, to hide comments, click the Show button and then click Comments to remove the check mark.

TO MODIFY THE BALLOON TEXT STYLE

1. Click the Styles and Formatting button on the Formatting toolbar.
2. In the Pick formatting to apply area in the Styles and Formatting task pane, scroll to Balloon Text. (If Balloon Text is not in the list, click the Show box arrow in the Styles and Formatting task pane, click Custom, place a check mark in the Balloon Text check box, and then click the OK button.)
3. Right-click Balloon Text and then click Modify on the shortcut menu.
4. Make desired changes to the Balloon Text style in the Modify Style dialog box and then click the OK button.

The size and appearance of text in comment balloons is controlled by the Comment Text style. To change the Comment Text style, follow the steps described above – replacing the occurrences of Balloon Text with Comment Text.

Comparing and Merging Documents

With Word, you can compare two documents to each other so you easily can identify any differences between the two files. Word displays the differences between the documents as tracked changes that you can review.

Assume you wanted to compare the original outline with the final outline so you easily can identify the changes made to the document. The following steps show how to compare and merge documents.

To Compare and Merge Documents

1

• **Be sure the Rocky Mountain Outline Final document is displayed on the screen and the disk that contains the original outline is in drive A.**

• **Click Tools on the menu bar (Figure 20).**

FIGURE 20

2

• **Click Compare and Merge Documents on the Tools menu.**

• **When Word displays the Compare and Merge Documents dialog box, if necessary, click the Look in box arrow and then click 3½ Floppy (A:). Click Rocky Mountain Outline in the list.**

• **Click the Merge button arrow.**

The Merge menu displays three commands: Merge, Merge into current document, and Merge into new document (Figure 21).

FIGURE 21

3

• **Click Merge into new document.**

• **If necessary, click the Outline View button on the horizontal scroll bar.**

Word displays the differences between the two documents as tracked changes (Figure 22).

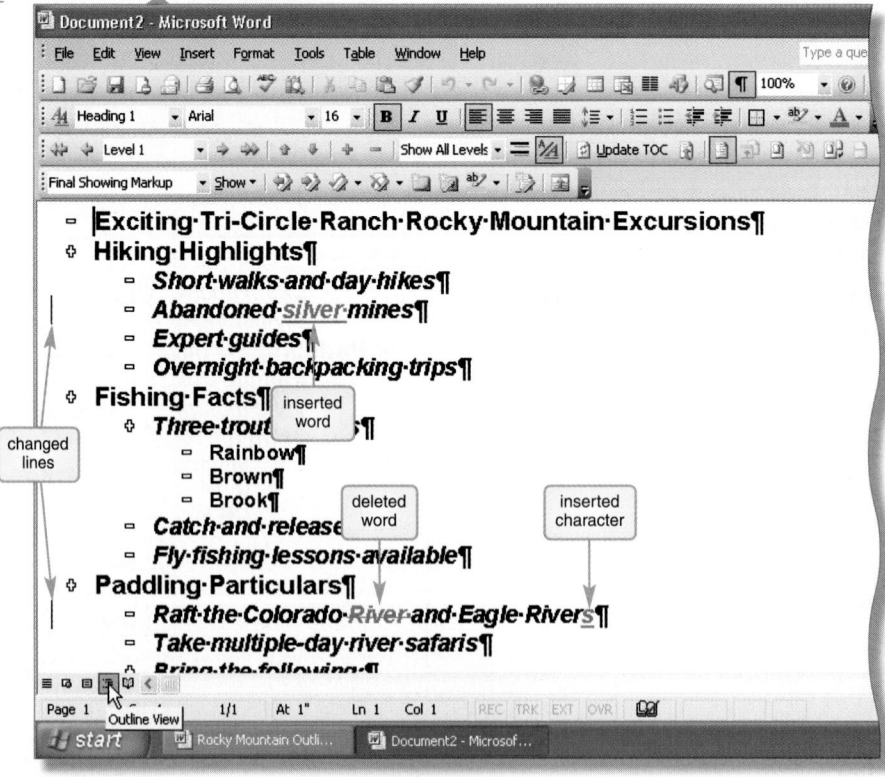

FIGURE 22

Other Ways

1. In Voice Command mode, say "Tools, Compare and Merge Documents"

Notice in Figure 22 that in outline view the deleted text is displayed as strikethrough text instead of in markup balloons. This is because markup balloons do not show on the screen in outline view or in normal view.

Word's Compare and Merge feature is useful if a reviewer does not remember to use the change-tracking feature while editing a document. That is, you can compare and merge the reviewer's document to your original document. Word tracks changes to display all differences between the two documents, which you later can accept or reject using the steps shown previously.

The following steps describe how to close the compared and merged document.

To Close a Document

1 **Click File on the menu bar and then click Close.**

2 **When Word displays a dialog box asking if you want to save changes, click the No button.**

Word closes the current document and redisplays the Rocky Mountain Outline Final document on the screen.

You now are finished tracking changes and reviewing tracked changes. Thus, you can hide the Reviewing toolbar, as described in the following steps.

To Hide the Reviewing Toolbar

1 **Right-click the Reviewing toolbar.**

2 **Click Reviewing on the shortcut menu.**

Word hides the Reviewing toolbar, which means it no longer is displayed in the Word window.

Sending an Outline to PowerPoint

Word has the capability of sending an outline to PowerPoint, which automatically creates a slide show from the outline. PowerPoint uses the heading styles (e.g., Heading 1, Heading 2, etc.) to set up the slides. Each Heading 1 begins on a new slide.

The steps on the next page show how to send a Word outline to PowerPoint.

Q&A

Q: Other than for merging reviewer changes, why would I use the Compare and Merge command?

A: If you have two files in a folder that you believe to have the same content, you can be sure they are the same by using the Compare and Merge command to compare the two files. If no tracked changes are found, then the two documents are identical.

More About

Certification

The Microsoft Office Specialist Certification program provides an opportunity for you to obtain a valuable industry credential - proof that you have the Word 2003 skills required by employers. For more information, see Appendix E or visit the Word 2003 Certification Web page (scsite.com/wd2003/cert).

To Send an Outline to PowerPoint

1

• **Click File on the menu bar and then point to Send To (Figure 23).**

FIGURE 23

2

• **Click Microsoft Office PowerPoint on the Send To submenu.**

Word sends the outline to PowerPoint, which starts and then displays the slide show on the screen (Figure 24). The Word outline has four paragraphs formatted as Heading 1. Thus, the PowerPoint slide show contains four slides.

FIGURE 24

You can use PowerPoint to make a few adjustments to the slide show so it looks like Figure 1d on page WD 458. For example, the first slide should use the slide layout called Title Slide, and all slides should use the Mountain Top design template.

To Modify a PowerPoint Slide Show

1 **Right-click the first slide in the Slides tab and then click Slide Layout on the shortcut menu.**

2 **When PowerPoint displays the Slide Layout task pane, click the top-left text layout (called Title Slide) to apply the Title Slide layout to the first slide.**

3 **Click the Slide Design button on the Formatting toolbar.**

4 **When PowerPoint displays the Slide Design task pane, scroll through the list of designs until Mountain Top is displayed. Click Mountain Top.**

PowerPoint changes the layout of the first slide and applies the Mountain Top design to all slides (shown in Figure 1d).

To view the slide show in PowerPoint, click the Slide Show from current slide button in the lower-left corner of the PowerPoint window above the status bar. To move through the slide show one slide at a time, simply click anywhere on the displayed slide.

The following steps describe how to save the slide show in PowerPoint.

To Save the Slide Show

1 **With a floppy disk in drive A, click File on the menu bar and then click Save As.**

2 **Type** Rocky Mountain Slide Show **in the File name box. Do not press the ENTER key.**

3 **If necessary, click the Save in box arrow and then click 3½ Floppy (A:).**

4 **Click the Save button in the Save As dialog box.**

PowerPoint saves the slide show on a floppy disk in drive A with the file name, Rocky Mountain Slide Show.

> *More About*
>
> ### PowerPoint Slide Shows
>
> When you save a slide show, PowerPoint appends the extension .ppt to the end of the file name. If your computer displays extensions for known file types, then this file will be displayed as Rocky Mountain Slide Show.ppt.

The outline and slide show are complete. The final tasks are to quit PowerPoint and Word.

To Quit PowerPoint and Word

1 **In PowerPoint, click File on the menu bar and then click Exit.**

2 **In Word, click File on the menu bar and then click Exit. If Word displays a dialog box about saving changes, click the No button.**

The PowerPoint and Word windows close.

Collaboration Feature Summary

In creating the outline for this feature, you learned how to work with Word's collaboration features and also how to send a Word outline to PowerPoint. First, you learned how to switch to outline view and then enter headings into the outline. Then, the feature showed how to e-mail a document for review, insert and edit comments, track changes, review tracked changes and view comments, and compare and merge documents. Finally, you learned how to send an outline to PowerPoint for use in a slide show.

 If you have a SAM user profile, you may have access to hands-on instruction, practice, and assessment of the skills covered in this project. Log in to your SAM account and go to your assignments page to see what your instructor has assigned.

What You Should Know

Having completed this feature, you should be able to perform the tasks below. The tasks are listed in the same order they were presented in this feature. For a list of the buttons, menus, toolbars, and commands introduced in this feature, see the Quick Reference Summary at the back of this book and refer to the Page Number column.

1. Enter Headings in an Outline (WD 459, WD 460)
2. Save a File (WD 461)
3. E-Mail a Document for Review (WD 462)
4. E-mail an Open Document as an Attachment (Not for Review) (WD 462)
5. Insert a Comment in the Reviewing Pane (WD 463)
6. Edit a Comment in a Comment Balloon (WD 464)
7. Insert a Comment in a Comment Balloon (WD 465)
8. Change Reviewer Information (WD 466)
9. Track Changes (WD 467)
10. Stop Tracking Changes (WD 468)
11. Review Tracked Changes and View Comments (WD 469)
12. Save a File with a New File Name (WD 472)
13. Print the Outline (WD 472)
14. Modify Reviewer Ink Colors and Balloon Options (WD 472)
15. Modify the Balloon Text Style (WD 473)
16. Compare and Merge Documents (WD 473)
17. Close a Document (WD 475)
18. Hide the Reviewing Toolbar (WD 475)
19. Send an Outline to PowerPoint (WD 476)
20. Modify a PowerPoint Slide Show (WD 477)
21. Save the Slide Show (WD 477)
22. Quit PowerPoint and Word (WD 477)

More About

Quick Reference

For a table that lists how to complete the tasks covered in this book using the mouse, menu, shortcut menu, and keyboard, see the Quick Reference Summary at the back of this book, or visit the Word 2003 Quick Reference Web page (scsite.com/wd2003/qr).

1 Creating an Outline and Sending It to PowerPoint

Problem: Fitness center employees present many classes on a variety of physical and emotional wellness topics. Carol O'Malley, coordinator at Mid-City College Fitness Center, has contacted you to help her prepare an outline and a presentation that will be delivered at community fairs and at the local shopping mall.

Instructions:

1. In Word, create the outline shown in Figure 25. Save the outline with the file name, Lab CF-1 Wellness Outline. Print the outline in outline view.
2. Send the Word outline to PowerPoint. In PowerPoint, change the first slide to the Title Slide layout and then apply an appropriate design template to the entire slide show. Save the slide show with the file name, Lab CF-1 Wellness Slide Show. View and then print the slide show.
3. If your instructor permits, send the outline to him or her as an e-mail attachment.

Enhance Your Wellness at Mid-City College Fitness Center
Mind/Body Programs
   Meditation
      Various techniques
      Practice time included
   Stress Management Workshop
      Relaxation strategies
      Four-part series
Lifestyle Programs
   CPR and First Aid
      Certification and recertification
      American Red Cross instructors
   Smoking Cessation
      Eight-session group program
      Individual consultations
Nutrition Programs
   Nutrition Connection
      Semester-long program
      Change your lifestyle to enhance your health
      Achieve your weight-management goals
      Increase your self-esteem
   Dining Out: Eat and Be Healthy

FIGURE 25

2 Working with Tracked Changes and Comments

Problem: As editor for the school newspaper, you review all articles before they are published. One section of the newspaper spotlights a student athlete of the month. For the next issue, the author has prepared an article about an outstanding athlete and sent it to you for review. When you review the article, you find several areas where you wish to make changes and offer suggestions. The document, named Lab CF-2 Spotlight Athlete First Draft, is located on the Data Disk. If you did not download the Data Disk, see the inside back cover for instructions for downloading the Data Disk or see your instructor.

Instructions:

1. Open the Lab CF-2 Spotlight Athlete First Draft file on the Data Disk.
2. Read (view) the comment and follow its instruction. Edit the comment so it includes a message that you completed the requested task.
3. Use Word's change-tracking feature to insert, delete, and replace text in the article. Make at least 10 changes to the article and insert at least three comments. Save the document with the file name, Lab CF-2 Spotlight Athlete Revision 1. Print the article with tracked changes showing and again without tracked changes showing.
4. Assume you are the author of the article and have received it back from the editor. Review the tracked changes and read the comments. Accept at least one-half of the changes, reject at least one of the changes, and delete all comments. Save the document with the file name, Lab CF-2 Spotlight Athlete Revision 2.
5. Compare and merge the original document with the revised document into a new document. Print the new document. Save the document with the file name, Lab CF-2 Spotlight Athlete Revision 3.
6. Obtain the revised article from another student in your class. Compare and merge your classmate's document into your document. Review all changes. Accept and reject the changes as you feel necessary. Save the document with the file name, Lab CF-2 Spotlight Athlete Revision 4. Print the revised document. If your instructor permits, e-mail the merged document for his or her review.

3 Modifying Tracking Changes Options

Problem: As editor for the Old Town Historical newsletter (shown in Figure 6-104 on page WD 450), you review all articles before they are published. For the next issue, the author has prepared an article about funding for a historic home renovation. The article, named Lab 6-1 Home Renovation Article, is located on the Data Disk. If you did not download the Data Disk, see the inside back cover for instructions for downloading the Data Disk or see your instructor. You are to review this article.

Instructions: After you open the file on the Data Disk, save it with the new name, Lab CF-3 Home Renovation Article Revised. Change your reviewer's ink colors for all markup options: insertions, deletions, formatting, changed lines, and comments. Change the balloon text style to 10-point Arial font. Change the balloon width to two inches. Make at least 10 changes to the article and insert at least three comments. Obtain the tracked changes documents from three other students in your class. Compare and merge the documents from these students into your document. Print this document with tracked changes showing. Hide all reviewer's changes, except for one. Accept and reject that reviewer's changes, as you deem appropriate. Show all remaining reviewer's changes. Accept and reject changes, as you deem appropriate. Save the final document. Print the final document. Turn in both the document with all reviewer's tracked changes and the final document.

Creating an Online Form

CASE PERSPECTIVE

A+ Dentist Locator is a Web site that has been matching patients to qualified, prescreened dentists for the past five years. The Web site has an online database of comprehensive background data about dentists worldwide. The site provides visitors with access to dentists' contact information; the number of years they have been in practice; their education, current licenses, and specialties; the types of equipment and technology they use; standards to which they adhere; and payment plans they offer. When visiting the Web site, a potential patient enters his or her postal code, required dental service, and preferred method of payment. A+ Dentist Locator uses this information to search the dentist database for the best matches. Potential patients have free access to information about each dentist and can make appointments online.

The number of people using the A+ Dentist Locator Web site is growing rapidly. Your friend, Milan Sciranka, is the founder of A+ Dentist Locator. He wants to be sure that visitors are pleased with the services offered at the Web site. Milan knows that satisfied patients will tell their friends and family about A+ Dentist Locator.

Today, you receive a call from Milan. He knows you are majoring in Computer Technology at school and asks if you would be willing to help him create a survey to e-mail to all Web site visitors. The survey should request the person's name, an opinion of the Web site navigation, a rating of the dentist he or she visited, and the type of dental services performed. You welcome the opportunity to help your friend, and let him know that you think designing and distributing the survey will be fun.

As you read through this project, you will learn how to use Word to create an online form.

MICROSOFT
Office Word 2003

Creating an Online Form

PROJECT

7

Objectives

You will have mastered the material in this project when you can:

- Design an online form
- Create a document template
- Insert a table in a form
- Insert text, drop-down, and check box form fields in a form
- Format form fields
- Add Help text to form fields
- Insert and format a rectangle drawing object
- Protect a form
- Open a new document based on a template
- Fill in a form
- Save data on a form in a text file
- Modify the location of workgroup templates

Introduction

During your personal and professional life, you undoubtedly have filled in countless forms. Whether a federal tax form, a time card, an application, an order, a deposit slip, or a survey, a form is designed to collect information. In the past, forms were printed; that is, you received the form on a piece of paper, filled it in with a pen or pencil, and then returned it manually.

Today, people are concerned with using resources efficiently. To minimize paper waste, save the world's trees, enhance office efficiency, and improve access to data, many businesses attempt to become a paperless office. Thus, the online form has emerged. With an **online form**, you use a computer to access, fill in, and then return the form. You may access the form at a Web site, on your company's intranet, or from your inbox if you receive it via e-mail.

Not only does an online form reduce the need for paper, it saves the time spent making copies of the form and distributing it. With more and more people owning a home computer, online forms have become a popular means of collecting personal information, as well.

In Word, you easily can create an online form for distribution electronically, which then also can be filled in using Word.

Project Seven — Online Form

Project 7 uses Word to create the online form shown in Figure 7-1. The form is a survey e-mailed to all dental patients that used the A+ Dentist Locator Web site. Upon receipt of the form, the patient fills it in, saves it, and then e-mails it back to the A+ Dentist Locator service. Figure 7-1a shows how the form is displayed on a user's screen initially (as a blank form); Figure 7-1b shows the form partially filled in by one user; and Figure 7-1c shows how the user filled in the entire form.

(a) Blank Form

(b) Partially Filled-In Form

(c) Filled-In Form

FIGURE 7-1

The form is designed so it fits completely within the Word window — without a user having to scroll while filling in the form. The data entry area of the form is enclosed by a rectangle that is shaded light blue. The rectangle has a shadow on its top and left edges. The line above the data entry area is highlighted bright green to draw the user's attention to the message.

The data entry area of the form contains four text boxes (First Name, Last Name, rating scale, and Other), one drop-down list box (ease of use), and five check boxes (Checkup, Cleaning, Toothache, Whiter Smile, and Other). As a user presses the TAB key to move the selection from one data entry item to the next, the status bar displays a brief Help message that is related to the location of the selection. Note that in Word the drop-down list box does not display the box arrow until you tab to the drop-down list box. The date in the lower-right corner of the data entry area is the date from the computer on which the form is being displayed.

Starting and Customizing Word

To start and customize Word, Windows must be running. If you are stepping through this project on a computer and you want your screen to match the figures in this book, then you should change your computer's resolution to 800 × 600 and reset the toolbars and menus. For information about changing the resolution and resetting toolbars and menus, read Appendix D.

The following steps describe how to start Word and customize the Word window. You may need to ask your instructor how to start Word for your system.

To Start and Customize Word

1 **Click the Start button on the Windows taskbar, point to All Programs on the Start menu, point to Microsoft Office on the All Programs submenu, and then click Microsoft Office Word 2003 on the Microsoft Office submenu.**

2 **If the Word window is not maximized, double-click its title bar to maximize it.**

3 **If the Language bar appears, right-click it and then click Close the Language bar on the shortcut menu.**

4 **If the Getting Started task pane is displayed in the Word window, click its Close button.**

5 **If the Standard and Formatting toolbar buttons are displayed on one row, click the Toolbar Options button and then click Show Buttons on Two Rows in the Toolbar Options list.**

6 **Click View on the menu bar and then click Print Layout.**

Word starts and, after a few moments, displays an empty document in the Word window.

More About

Online Forms

For a sample online form on the Web, visit the Word 2003 More About Web page (scsite.com/wd2003/more) and then click Sample Online Form.

Displaying Formatting Marks

It is helpful to display formatting marks that indicate where in the document you pressed the ENTER key, SPACEBAR, and other keys. The following step describes how to display formatting marks.

To Display Formatting Marks

1 **If the Show/Hide ¶ button on the Standard toolbar is not selected already, click it.**

Word displays formatting marks in the document window, and the Show/Hide ¶ button on the Standard toolbar is selected (shown in Figure 7-3 on page WD 487).

Zooming Page Width

When you zoom page width, Word displays the page on the screen as large as possible in print layout view. The following steps zoom page width.

To Zoom Page Width

1 **Click the Zoom box arrow on the Standard toolbar.**

2 **Click Page Width in the Zoom list.**

Word computes the zoom percentage and displays it in the Zoom box (shown in Figure 7-3). Your percentage may be different depending on your computer.

Designing an Online Form

To minimize the time spent creating a form while at the computer, you should sketch the form on a piece of paper first. Figure 7-2 on the next page shows a handwritten design for the online form in this project.

During **form design**, you should create a well-thought-out draft of the form – being sure to include all essential form elements. These elements include the form's title, placement of text and graphics, instructions for users of the form, and field specifications. A **field** is a placeholder for data. A **field specification** defines characteristics of a field such as the field's type, length, format, and a list of possible values that may be entered into the field. Many designers place Xs in fields where a user will be allowed to enter any type of character, and 9s in fields where a user will be allowed to enter numbers only. For example, in Figure 7-2, a user can enter up to 15 of any type of character in the First Name text box and up to two numbers in the rating scale text box.

With a draft of the form in hand, the next step is to create the form in Word.

A+ DENTIST LOCATOR
Matching Patients to Qualified Dentists

Patient Survey

Clip art of tooth and toothbrush

Please fill in the form below and then e-mail the saved document to dentist@link.com.

Press the TAB key to move from one area to the next.
For additional help completing this form, read the messages on the status bar.

First Name: XXXXXXXXXXXXXX _____   Last Name: XXXXXXXXXXXXXXXXX

How easy was it to find a dentist using our Web site? XXXXXXXXXXXXXX _____

On a scale of 1 to 10, with 10 being the best, rate the dentist you visited: 99

Reason(s) you needed a dentist's services (check all that apply):

☐ Checkup   ☐ Cleaning   ☐ Tooth ache   ☐ Whiten Smile

☐ Other (please specify): _____

mm/dd/yyyy

Thank you for your time!

possible values for Web site ease of use →

Ease of use choices: Very Easy, Easy, Fair, Difficult, Very Difficult

FIGURE 7-2

Creating an Online Form

The process of creating an online form begins with creating a template. Then, you insert and format any text, graphics, and fields where data is to be entered on the form. Finally, before you save the form for electronic distribution, you protect it. With a **protected form**, users can enter data only where you have inserted form fields; that is, they will not be able to modify any other items on the form. Many menu commands and toolbar buttons are dimmed, and thus unavailable, in a protected form. The steps on the following pages illustrate how to create an online form.

Creating a Template

A **template** is a file that contains the definition of the appearance of a Word document, including items such as default font, font size, margin settings, and line spacing; available styles; and even placement of text. Every Word document you create is based on a template. When you select Blank document in the New Document task pane or when you click the New Blank Document button on the Standard toolbar, Word creates a document based on the Normal template. Word also provides other templates for more specific types of documents such as memos, letters, and fax cover sheets. Creating a document based on these templates can improve your productivity because Word has defined much of the document's appearance for you.

If you create and save an online form as a Word document that is based on the Normal template, users will be required to open that Word document to display the form on the screen. Next, they will fill in the form. Then, to preserve the content of the original form, they will have to save the form with a new file name. If they accidentally click the Save button on the Standard toolbar, Word will replace the original blank form with a filled-in form.

If you create and save the online form as a **document template** instead, users will open a new document window that is based on that template. This displays the form on the screen as a brand new Word document; that is, the document does not have a file name. Thus, the user fills in the form and then simply saves it. By using a template for the form, the original form remains intact when the user clicks the Save button.

The following steps show how to create a document template to be used for the online form and then save the template with the file name, A+ Dentist Locator.

To Create a Document Template

1

- Click File on the menu bar and then click New.

- When Word displays the New Document task pane, click the On my computer link.

- When the Templates dialog box is displayed, if necessary, click the General tab.

- Click the Blank Document icon and then, if necessary, click Template in the Create New area.

In the Templates dialog box, the Template option button instructs Word to create a new template, instead of a new Word document (Figure 7-3).

FIGURE 7-3

• **Click the OK button.**

Word displays a blank template titled Template1 in the Word window (Figure 7-4).

• **With a disk in drive A, click the Save button on the Standard toolbar.**

• **Type** A+ Dentist Locator **in the File name box.**

• **Click the Save in box arrow.**

Word displays the Save As dialog box with Document Template listed in the Save as type box (Figure 7-5). The default save location for templates is the Templates folder.

4

• **Click 3½ Floppy (A:) in the Save in list.**

• **Click the Save button in the Save As dialog box.**

Word saves the template on the floppy disk in drive A with the file name, A+ Dentist Locator (shown in Figure 7-6).

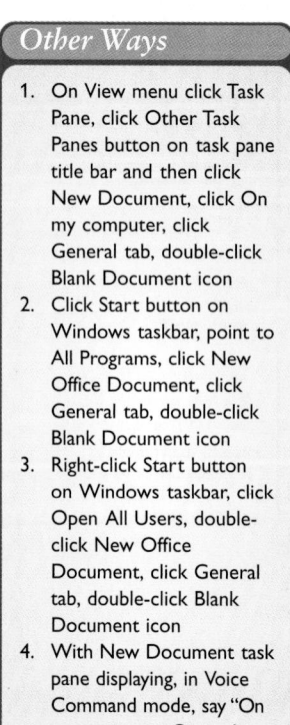

Other Ways

1. On View menu click Task Pane, click Other Task Panes button on task pane title bar and then click New Document, click On my computer, click General tab, double-click Blank Document icon

2. Click Start button on Windows taskbar, point to All Programs, click New Office Document, click General tab, double-click Blank Document icon

3. Right-click Start button on Windows taskbar, click Open All Users, double-click New Office Document, click General tab, double-click Blank Document icon

4. With New Document task pane displaying, in Voice Command mode, say "On my computer, General, Blank Document, OK"

FIGURE 7-4

FIGURE 7-5

The next step in creating the online form is to enter the text, graphics, and fields in the template. The steps below describe how to format and enter the company name, business tag line, and survey title in the template.

To Enter and Format Text

1 Click the Font box arrow on the Formatting toolbar, scroll to and then click Stencil (or a similar font). Click the Font Size box arrow on the Formatting toolbar and then click 36. Click the Bold button on the Formatting toolbar. Click the Font Color button arrow on the Formatting toolbar and then click Indigo on the color palette. Type A+ Dentist Locator and then press CTRL+B to turn off bold formatting. Press the ENTER key.

2 Click the Font box arrow on the Formatting toolbar and then click Times New Roman. Click the Font Size box arrow on the Formatting toolbar and then click 16. Click the Italic button on the Formatting toolbar. Click the Font Color button arrow on the Formatting toolbar and then click Sea Green on the color palette. Type Matching Patients to Qualified Dentists and then press CTRL+I to turn off italic formatting. Press the ENTER key twice.

3 Click the Font Size box arrow on the Formatting toolbar and then click 22. Click the Bold button and the Center button on the Formatting toolbar. Click the Font Color button arrow on the Formatting toolbar and then click Plum on the color palette. Type Patient Survey and then press CTRL+B to turn off bold formatting. Press the ENTER key.

Word displays the company name, business tag line, and survey title as shown in Figure 7-6.

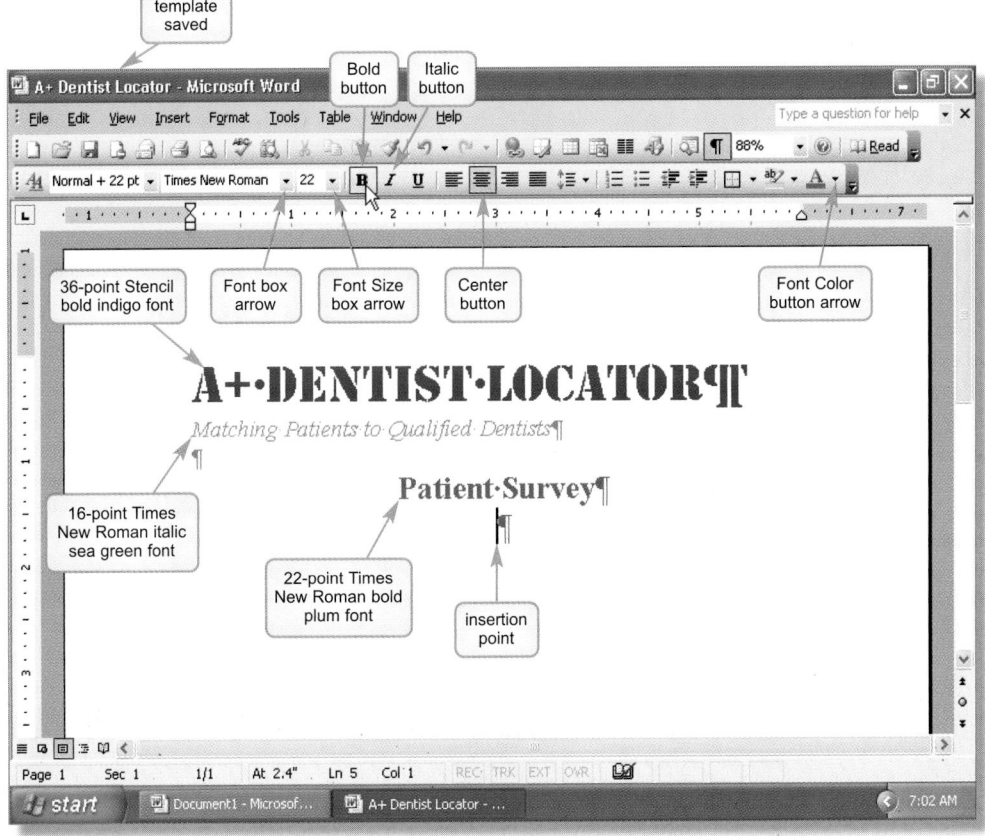

FIGURE 7-6

Formatting Graphics

The next step is to insert and format the clip art image of a tooth and toothbrush. First, you insert the clip art and reduce its size, as described below.

To Insert and Resize Clip Art

1 **With the insertion point on line 5, click Insert on the menu bar, point to Picture, and then click Clip Art. When Word displays the Clip Art task pane, drag through any text in the Search for text box. Type** `toothbrush` **and then press the ENTER key.**

2 **Click the clip that matches the one shown in Figure 7-7 (or a similar clip) and then click the Close button on the Clip Art task pane title bar.**

3 **Double-click the graphic to display the Format Picture dialog box and then, if necessary, click the Size tab. Change the Height and Width in the Scale area to 68%. Click the OK button.**

Word inserts and resizes the graphic (shown in Figure 7-7).

You would like the colors in the image of the tooth and toothbrush to stand out more, that is, have more contrast. The following step shows how to increase the contrast of the graphic in this project.

To Increase a Graphic's Contrast

1

• **With the graphic selected, click the More Contrast button on the Picture toolbar six times.**

Word adjusts the contrast of the selected graphic (Figure 7-7). A graphic with more contrast has a greater distinction between light and dark colors.

Other Ways

1. Click Format Picture button on Picture toolbar, click Picture tab, drag Contrast slider, click OK button
2. On Format menu click Picture, click Picture tab, drag Contrast slider, click OK button
3. Right-click graphic, click Format Picture on shortcut menu, click Picture tab, drag Contrast slider, click OK button
4. In Voice Command mode, say "Format, Picture, Picture, [adjust contrast], OK"

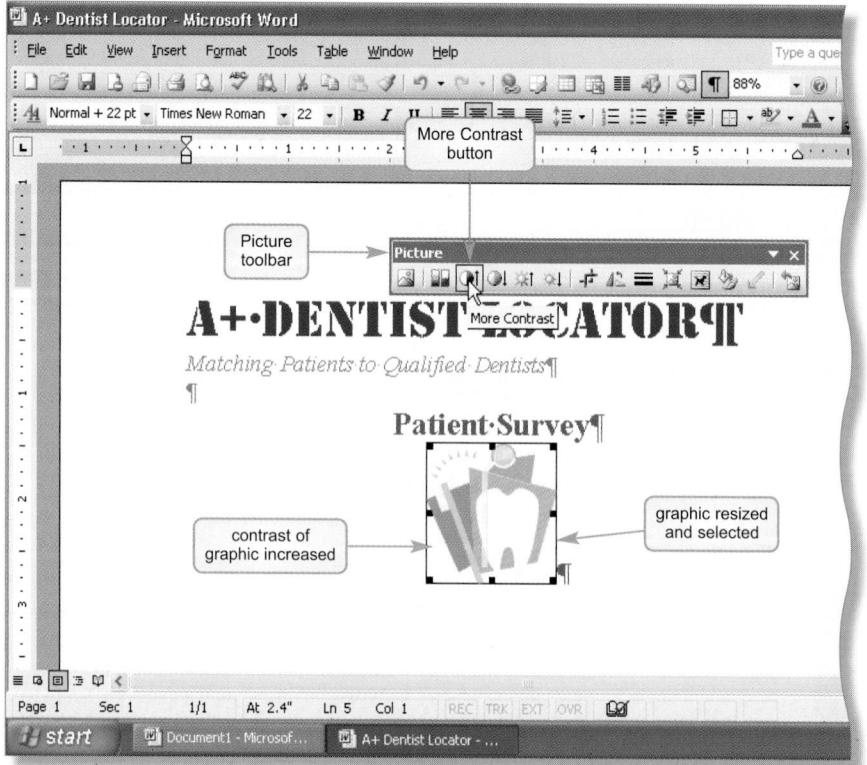

FIGURE 7-7

Instead of increasing a graphic's contrast, you can decrease the contrast. To decrease the contrast, you would perform this step.

TO DECREASE A GRAPHIC'S CONTRAST

1. Click the Less Contrast button on the Picture toolbar.

If you wanted to return the contrast to its original settings, you would click the Format Picture button on the Picture toolbar, click the Picture tab, click the Reset button, and then click the OK button. As an alternative, you could click the Undo button on the Standard toolbar. Each time you click the Undo button, Word undoes one level of contrast.

In this project, you also would like the colors to be a little darker, as described in the following step.

To Darken a Graphic

1 **Click the Less Brightness button on the Picture toolbar.**

Word slightly darkens the colors of the graphic (shown in Figure 7-8).

Word inserts clip art as an inline graphic, that is, as part of the current paragraph. You want to position the image to the right of the company name (shown in Figure 7-1 on page WD 483). Thus, the graphic needs to be a floating graphic instead of an inline graphic. To do this, you change the graphic's wrapping style. In previous projects, you have used the square and tight wrapping styles. In this project, you use the In Front of Text wrapping style, which allows the graphic to be placed over text. The following steps describe how to change a graphic's wrapping style.

To Change a Graphic's Wrapping Style

1 **Click the Text Wrapping button on the Picture toolbar (Figure 7-8).**

2 **Click In Front of Text on the Text Wrapping menu.**

Word converts the graphic from inline to floating and changes its wrapping style to In Front of Text (shown in Figure 7-9 on the next page).

More About

Contrast and Brightness

Instead of using the Picture toolbar to adjust contrast and brightness, you can use the Format Picture dialog box. To do this, double-click the graphic and then click the Picture tab in the Format Picture dialog box. To adjust the brightness, drag the Brightness slider or change the Brightness percent. To adjust the contrast, drag the Contrast slider or change the Contrast percent. When finished, click the OK button.

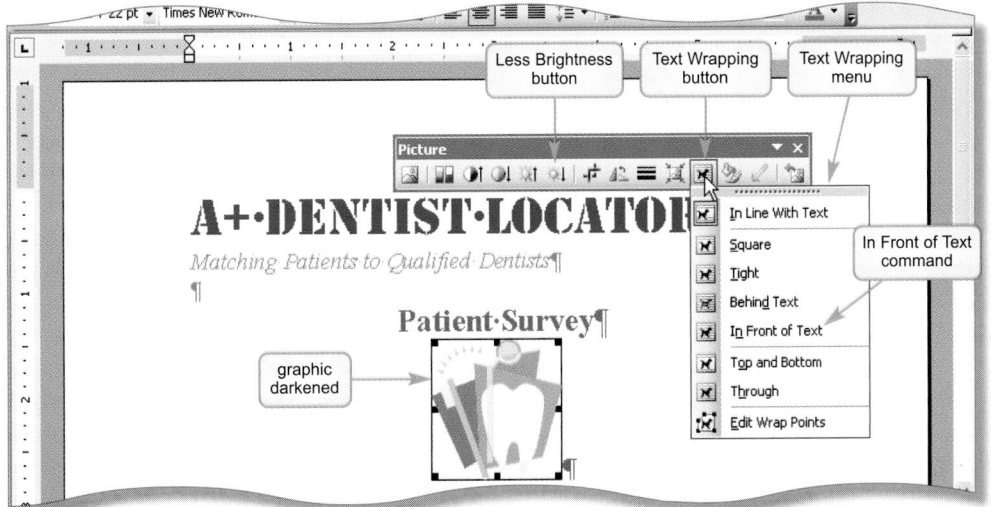

FIGURE 7-8

The next step is to move the graphic, as described below.

To Move a Graphic

1 **Position the mouse pointer in the graphic. When the mouse pointer has a four-headed arrow attached to it, drag the graphic to the right of the company name, as shown in Figure 7-9.**

Word moves the graphic to the new location.

In this project, the graphic is rotated so the toothbrush is more vertical. To rotate a graphic, you drag its rotate handle, as shown in the following steps.

To Rotate a Graphic

1

• **Position the mouse pointer on the graphic's rotate handle.**

Word changes the mouse pointer to a circular arrow wrapped around the rotate handle (Figure 7-9). You drag the rotate handle in the direction you want to rotate the graphic.

FIGURE 7-9

2

• **Drag the rotate handle about ¼" to the right, as shown in Figure 7-10.**

Word displays a dotted rectangle that rotates as you move the mouse.

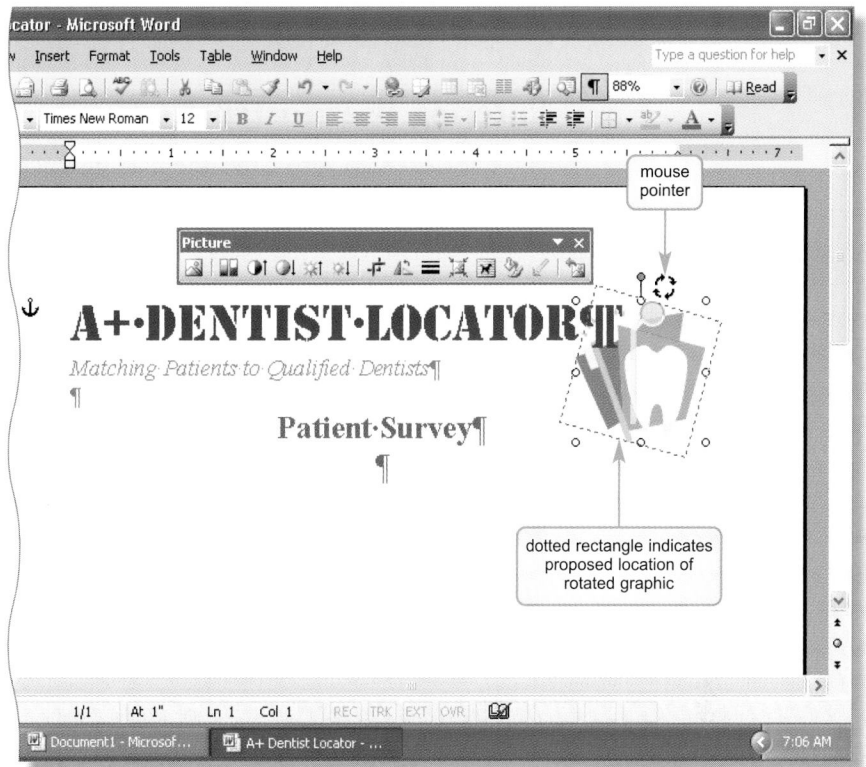

FIGURE 7-10

3

• **Release the mouse button. (You may need to rotate the graphic a few times to position it in the desired location.)**

Word rotates the graphic to the location where you release the mouse button (Figure 7-11).

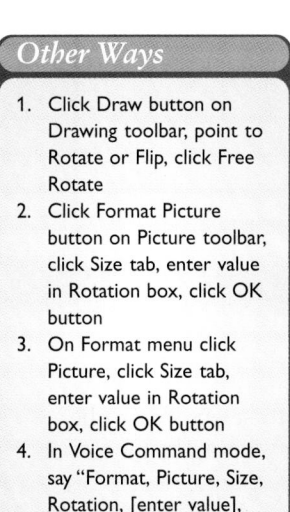

Other Ways

1. Click Draw button on Drawing toolbar, point to Rotate or Flip, click Free Rotate
2. Click Format Picture button on Picture toolbar, click Size tab, enter value in Rotation box, click OK button
3. On Format menu click Picture, click Size tab, enter value in Rotation box, click OK button
4. In Voice Command mode, say "Format, Picture, Size, Rotation, [enter value], OK"

FIGURE 7-11

The graphic is partly covered by the paragraph formatting mark. At the end of this project, you will hide formatting marks.

Entering User Instructions

The next step is to enter the user instructions and then highlight them bright green, as described in the following steps.

To Enter Text and Highlight It

1 **Position the insertion point on line 5. Click the Font Size box arrow on the Formatting toolbar and then click 12. Press the ENTER key.**

2 **Type** Please fill in the form below and then e-mail the saved document to dentist@link.com. **Press the ENTER key.**

3 **Click the Highlight button arrow on the Formatting toolbar and then click Bright Green. Click to the left of the sentence just entered, or drag through the sentence, to highlight it (Figure 7-12).**

4 **Click the Highlight button on the Formatting toolbar to turn off highlighting (shown in Figure 7-13).**

Word highlights the selected sentence bright green.

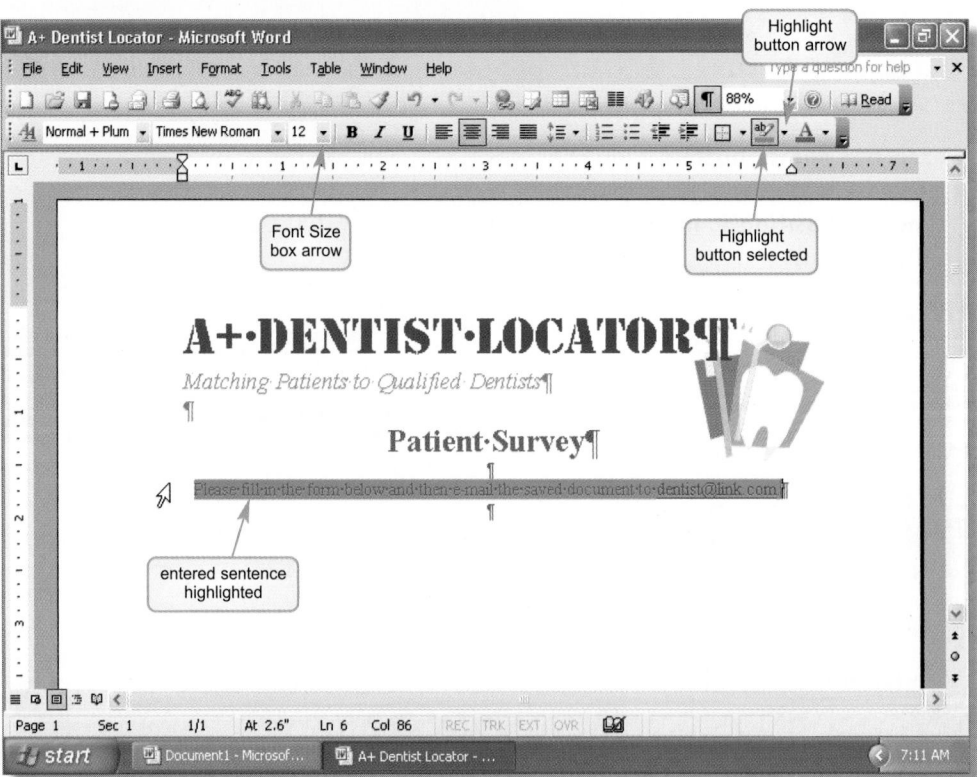

FIGURE 7-12

When the Highlight button is selected, you can continue to select text to be highlighted. The highlighter remains active until you click the Highlight button or press the ESC key to turn it off.

The next step is to enter the instructions for filling in the data entry area of the form.

To Enter Text

1 **Position the insertion point on the paragraph mark below the highlighted text and then press the ENTER key.**

2 **Click the Bold button on the Formatting toolbar. Type** `Press the TAB key to move from one area to the next.`

3 **Press the ENTER key. Type** `For additional help completing this form, read the messages on the status bar.`

4 **Press the ENTER key twice. Press CTRL+L to left-align the current paragraph.**

The data entry area instructions are entered (shown in Figure 7-1a on page WD 483).

Inserting a Table in a Form

The first line of data entry in the form consists of the First Name text box, which begins at the left margin, and the Last Name text box, which begins at the center point. Although you could set tab stops to align the data in a form, it is easier to insert a table. For example, the first line is a 1 × 2 table; that is, a table with one row and two columns. By inserting a 1 × 2 table, Word automatically positions the second column at the center point. Using tables in forms also keeps the data entered within the same region of the form, in case the user enters data that wraps to the next line on the screen.

When you insert a table, Word automatically surrounds it with a border. You do not want borders on tables in forms. The following steps show how to enter a 1 × 2 table in the form and then remove its border.

To Insert a Borderless Table in a Form

1

• **If the Forms toolbar is not displayed in the Word window, click View on the menu bar, point to Toolbars, and then click Forms.**

• **If necessary, scroll up so that the company name is positioned at the top of the document window.**

• **With the insertion point on line 11, click the Insert Table button on the Forms toolbar.**

• **Position the mouse pointer on the cell in the first row and second column of the grid.**

Word displays a grid to define the dimensions of the desired table (Figure 7-13). Word will insert the table immediately above the insertion point.

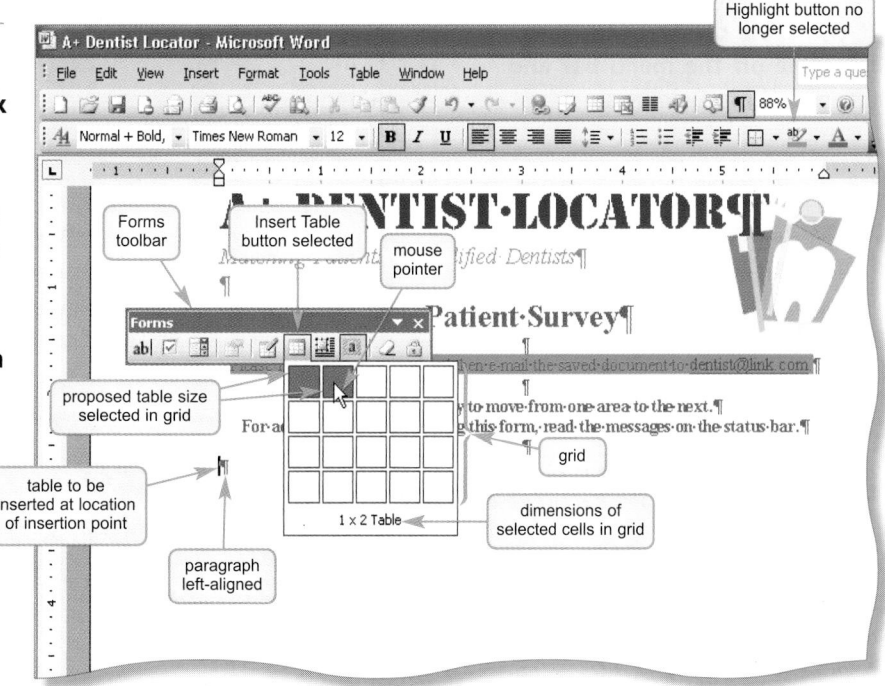

FIGURE 7-13

2

• **Click the cell in the first row and second column of the grid.**

Word inserts an empty 1 × 2 table in the form. The insertion point is in the first cell (row 1 and column 1) of the table.

3

• **Point to the first cell in the table to display the table move handle.**
• **Click the table move handle to select the table.**
• **Click the Border button arrow on the Formatting toolbar.**

Word displays a list of border types on the border palette (Figure 7-14). The table is selected in the document.

FIGURE 7-14

4

• **Click No Border on the border palette.**
• **Click the first cell of the table to remove the selection.**
• **If the table displays gridlines, click Table on the menu bar and then click Hide Gridlines.**

Word removes the border from the cells in the table (Figure 7-15). Only the end-of-row and end-of-cell marks are displayed in the document window to identify cells in the table.

Other Ways

1. Click Insert Table button on Standard toolbar, click grid
2. On Table menu point to Insert, click Table, enter number of columns, enter number of rows, click OK button
3. In Voice Command mode, say "Table, Insert, Table, [enter number of columns and rows], OK"

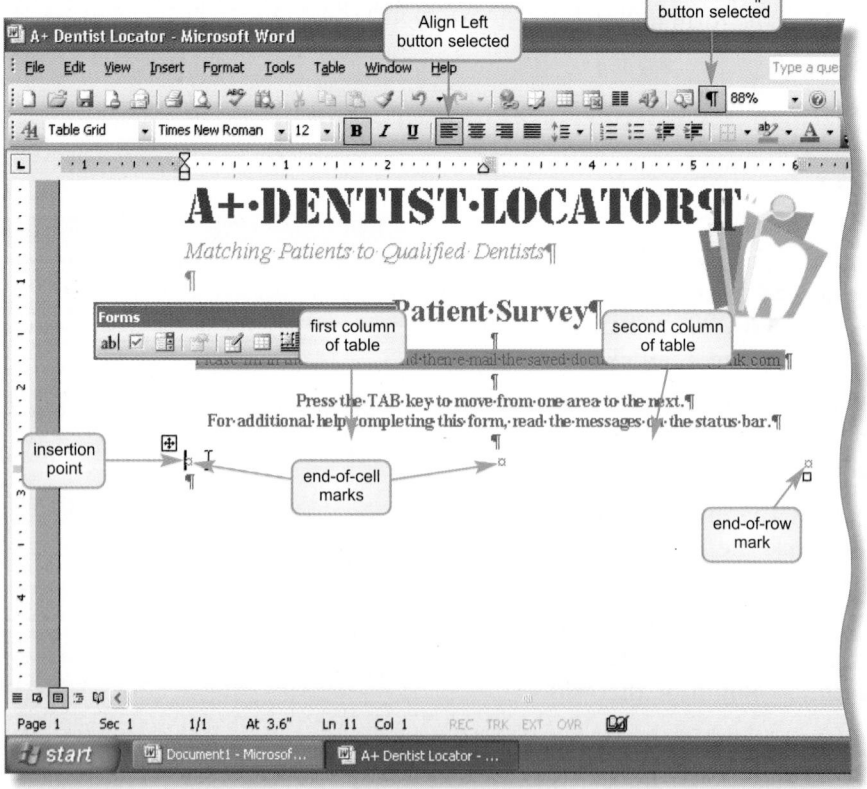

FIGURE 7-15

If your screen does not show end-of-cell marks, click the Show/Hide ¶ button on the Standard toolbar.

Each row of a table has an end-of-row mark, and each cell has an end-of-cell mark. The end-of-cell marks in Figure 7-15 are left-aligned because the cells are formatted as left-aligned. The data you enter within a cell wordwraps in that cell just as text does between the left and right margins of a document. To place data in a cell, click the cell and then type. To advance rightward from one cell to the next, press the TAB key.

Inserting a Text Form Field that Accepts Any Text

The first item that users enter on the Patient Survey is their first name. The field caption text, First Name, is to be displayed to the left of a text box. A field caption is the text on the screen that informs the user what to enter in the field. Often a colon or some other character follows a field caption to separate the field caption from a text box or other data entry field.

To place a text box in the document, you insert a text form field. A **text form field** allows users to enter letters, numbers, and other characters in the field. The following steps show how to insert the field caption and the text form field in the first cell of the table.

More About

Gridlines

If you want to see the table gridlines while developing a form, click Table on the menu bar and then click Show Gridlines. Gridlines are formatting marks that do not print. They are designed to help users easily identify table cells, rows, and columns.

To Insert a Text Form Field

1

• **With the insertion point in the first cell of the table as shown in Figure 7-15, type** First Name **and then press the COLON (:) key.**

• **Press the SPACEBAR.**

Word places the field caption in the first cell of the table.

2

• **Click the Text Form Field button on the Forms toolbar.**

• **If Word does not display the form field shaded in gray, click the Form Field Shading button on the Forms toolbar.**

Word inserts a text form field at the location of the insertion point (Figure 7-16). The form field is shaded in gray.

FIGURE 7-16

Other Ways

1. With Forms toolbar displaying, in Voice Command mode, say "Text Form Field" or say "Edit Box"

The text form field inserted by Word is five characters wide. You want to allow a user to enter up to 15 characters for the first name. You also want the first letter of each word that a user enters in the First Name text form field to be capitalized.

When Word displays the Patient Survey form on the screen initially (as a blank form), you want the text form fields to display an underline that signifies the data entry area. The text displayed initially in a field is called the **default text**. Thus, the default text for this text form field on the Patient Survey is to be an underline that spans 15 spaces.

The following steps show how to limit the user's entry to 15 characters, set the text form field for the first name so it displays 15 underscore characters as default text, and capitalize the first letter of each word the user enters.

To Specify Text Form Field Options

1

• **Double-click the text form field.**

• **When Word displays the Text Form Field Options dialog box, press the UNDERSCORE (_) key 15 times in the Default text text box.**

• **Double-click the Maximum length box and then type 15 as the length.**

• **Click the Text format box arrow and then click First capital in the Text format list.**

Word displays the new settings in the Text Form Field Options dialog box (Figure 7-17).

FIGURE 7-17

2

- **Click the OK button.**

- **Press the TAB key to move the insertion point to the beginning of the next cell in the table.**

The text form field options are set (Figure 7-18).

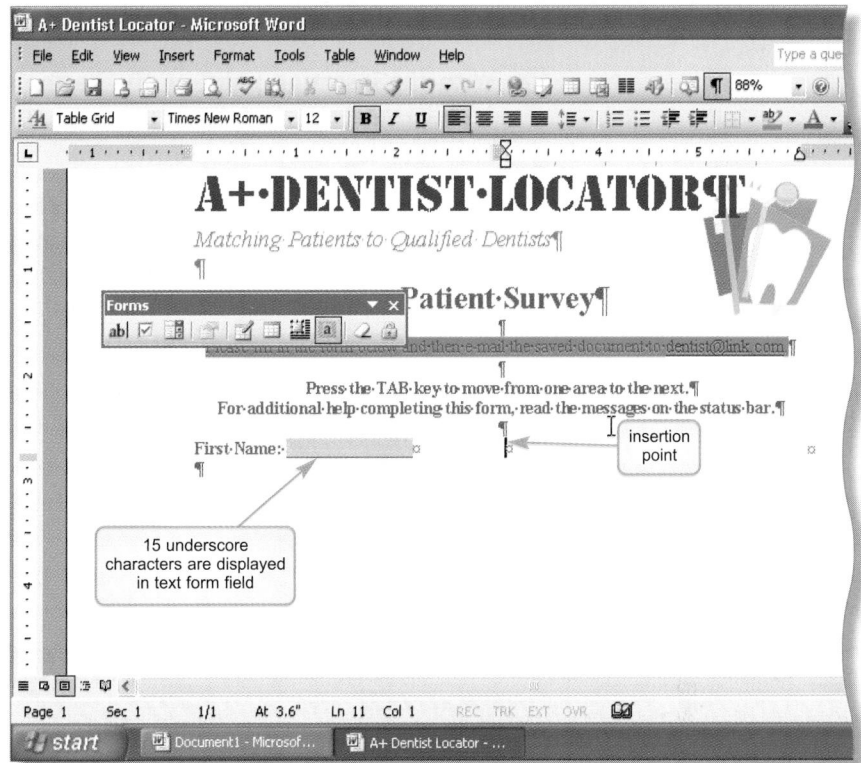

FIGURE 7-18

Other Ways

1. Click Form Field Options button on Forms toolbar
2. Right-click form field, click Properties on shortcut menu
3. With Forms toolbar displaying, in Voice Command mode, say "Form Field Options" or say "Properties"

When you click the Text format box arrow in the Text Form Field Options dialog box (Figure 7-17), four choices are displayed: Uppercase, Lowercase, First capital, and Title case. If you select one of these options, Word formats a user's entry according to your selection — after the user presses the TAB key to advance out of the form field. Table 7-1 shows how each option displays text that a user enters into the form field.

Table 7-1   Text Formats for Text Form Fields

TEXT FORMAT	EXAMPLE
Uppercase	ALL LETTERS IN ALL WORDS ARE CAPITALIZED.
Lowercase	all letters in all words are displayed as lowercase letters.
First capital	The first letter of the first word is capitalized.
Title case	The First Letter Of Every Word Is Capitalized.

The next form field to enter in the Patient Survey is the last name. The only difference between the options for the form fields for the last name and first name is that the last name allows up to 20 characters, instead of 15. The steps on the next page describe how to insert and specify options for another text form field.

To Insert and Specify Options for a Text Form Field

1 With the insertion point at the beginning of the second cell of the table, type Last Name **and then press the COLON (:) key. Press the SPACEBAR.**

2 Click the Text Form Field button on the Forms toolbar.

3 Double-click the text form field for the last name. When Word displays the Text Form Field Options dialog box, press the UNDERSCORE key 20 times in the Default text text box. Double-click the Maximum length box and then type 20 **as the length. Click the Text format box arrow and then click First capital in the Text format list (Figure 7-19).**

4 Click the OK button.

Word displays the form field for the last name according to the settings in the Text Form Field Options dialog box.

FIGURE 7-19

Inserting a Drop-Down Form Field

You use a **drop-down form field** when you want to present a set of choices to a user in the form of a drop-down list box. To view the set of choices, the user clicks an arrow at the right edge of the form field, which displays a list box (Figure 7-1b on page WD 483). In this online form, the drop-down form field to be inserted is to contain the user's opinion of how easy it is to use the Web site. The valid choices to be presented to the user are Very Easy, Easy, Fair, Difficult, and Very Difficult.

The following steps show how to insert a drop-down form field in the Patient Survey.

To Insert a Drop-Down Form Field

1

• **Click the paragraph mark below the 1 × 2 table to position the insertion point below the First Name caption and then press the ENTER key.**

• **Type** How easy was it to find a dentist using our Web site?

• **Press the SPACEBAR.**

Word enters the field caption.

2

• **Click the Drop-Down Form Field button on the Forms toolbar.**

Word inserts a drop-down form field at the location of the insertion point (Figure 7-20). The form field is shaded in gray.

FIGURE 7-20

Other Ways

1. With Forms toolbar displaying, in Voice Command mode, say "Combo Box" or say "Drop-Down Form Field"

Recall that when Word displays the form on the screen initially (as a blank form), underscore characters should be where the text form fields are located. Similarly, the drop-down form field should show underscore characters when the form initially is displayed on the screen. This will help the user identify all the data entry areas.

In the text form field, underscore characters were entered as the default text. With a drop-down form field, Word displays the first item in the list on a blank form. Thus, you should enter 15 underscore characters as the first list item.

The drop-down form field initially is five characters wide. As you enter items in the drop-down list, Word increases the width of the form field to accommodate the item with the largest number of characters.

The steps on the next page show how to specify options for the drop-down form field.

To Specify Drop-Down Form Field Options

1

• **Double-click the drop-down form field.**

• **When Word displays the Drop-Down Form Field Options dialog box, press the UNDERSCORE key 15 times in the Drop-down item text box.**

Word displays the Drop-Down Form Field Options dialog box (Figure 7-21).

FIGURE 7-21

2

• **Click the Add button.**

Word places 15 underscore characters as the first item in the Items in drop-down list list (Figure 7-22). The Drop-down item text box now is empty, awaiting the next entry.

FIGURE 7-22

3

• **With the insertion point positioned in the Drop-down item text box, type** Very Easy **and then click the Add button.**

• **Type** Easy **and then click the Add button.**

• **Type** Fair **and then click the Add button.**

• **Type** Difficult **and then click the Add button.**

• **Type** Very Difficult **and then click the Add button.**

The items in the drop-down list are entered (Figure 7-23).

FIGURE 7-23

4

• **Click the OK button.**

• **Press the END key to move the insertion point to the end of the line.**

• **Press the ENTER key twice.**

The list for the drop-down form field is defined (Figure 7-24). When you fill in the form, Word will display a box arrow at the right edge of the drop-down form field.

Other Ways

1. Click Form Field Options button on Forms toolbar
2. Right-click form field, click Properties on shortcut menu
3. With Forms toolbar displaying, in Voice Command mode, say "Form Field Options" or say "Properties"

FIGURE 7-24

Instead of clicking the Add button (Figure 7-21 on page WD 502) to move items from the Drop-down item text box to the Items in drop-down list, you can press the ENTER key. This alternative method is used later in this project.

Notice in Figure 7-24 on the previous page that the 15 underscore characters do not show on the screen yet. Word displays the first item in the drop-down list on the screen when you protect the form, which you will do later in this project.

After you enter items in a list box, if you want to modify their order, or add or delete one or more items, you would display the Drop-Down Form Field Options dialog box (Figure 7-23 on the previous page) by double-clicking the drop-down form field. To add more items, simply enter the text in the Drop-down item text box and then click the Add button. To remove an item, click it in the Items in drop-down list list and then click the Remove button. To reorder the list, click an item in the Items in drop-down list list and then click the Move Up button or Move Down button to move the item up or down one position each time you click the appropriate button.

Inserting a Text Form Field that Requires a Number

The next form field to be entered in the Patient Survey is for the dentist rating. The rating is a number between one and ten. Thus, a two-digit input area is sufficient. You, therefore, will instruct Word to display two underscore characters when the form initially is displayed on the screen (as a blank form).

If you ultimately will be analyzing the data entered in a form with another type of application software such as a database, you do not want non-numeric data in fields that require numeric entries. To address this problem, Word can convert a non-numeric entry such as AB to a zero.

The following steps describe how to insert and format this text form field.

To Insert and Specify Options for a Text Form Field

1 With the insertion point positioned two lines below the previous entry, as shown in Figure 7-24, type On a scale of 1 to 10, with 10 being the best, rate the dentist you visited: and then press the SPACEBAR.

2 Click the Text Form Field button on the Forms toolbar.

3 Double-click the newly inserted text form field for the dentist rating. When Word displays the Text Form Field Options dialog box, click the Type box arrow and then click Number in the Type list. Press the TAB key to position the insertion point in the Maximum length box and then type 2 as the length. Press the TAB key to position the insertion point in the Default number text box and then press the UNDERSCORE key two times (Figure 7-25).

4 Click the OK button.

Word displays the text form field for the dentist rating according to the settings in the Text Form Field Options dialog box (shown in Figure 7-26 on page WD 506).

More About

Text Form Field Types

When you click the Type box arrow in the Text Form Field Options dialog box (shown in Figure 7-25), you have six options: Regular text, Number, Date, Current date, Current time, and Calculation. Regular text accepts any keyboard character. Number requires a numeric entry. Date requires a valid date. The last three options display the date, time, or result of a calculation and do not allow a user to change the displayed value.

FIGURE 7-25

By changing the Type box to Number (Figure 7-25), Word will convert any non-numeric entry in this form field to a zero. Other valid text form field types are discussed later in this project.

Inserting a Check Box

The bottom of the data entry area of the Patient Survey contains five check boxes, one each for Checkup, Cleaning, Toothache, Whiter Smile, and Other. The Other check box also has a text form field to its right, which allows a user to explain further. Above the check boxes is a line of instructions pertaining to the check boxes. The following pages explain how to enter this section of the form.

The first step is to enter the line of text containing instructions for the check boxes, as described below.

To Enter Text

1 Press the END key to move the insertion point to the end of the line. Press the ENTER key twice. Type Reason(s) you needed a dentist's services (check all that apply) and then press the COLON (:) key.

2 Press the ENTER key.

Word displays the instructions for the check boxes (shown in Figure 7-26 on the next page).

You want four check boxes to be displayed horizontally below the check box instructions. To do this and align the check boxes evenly across the line, insert a 1 × 4 borderless table, that is, a table with one row and four columns. The following steps describe how to insert a 1 × 4 table in the form.

To Insert a Borderless Table in a Form

1 With the insertion point on the paragraph mark below the check box instructions, click the Insert Table button on the Forms toolbar and then point to the cell in the first row and fourth column of the grid (Figure 7-26).

2 Click the cell in the first row and fourth column of the grid.

3 When Word displays the table, point to the first cell and then, when the table move handle appears, click the table move handle to select the table. Click the Border button arrow on the Formatting toolbar and then click No Border on the border palette.

4 Click the first cell of the table.

Word inserts a 1 × 4 borderless table at the location of the insertion point (shown in Figure 7-27).

FIGURE 7-26

The next step is to insert the first check box in the first cell of the table, as shown next.

More About

Designing Questionnaires

For more information about how to design a good questionnaire, visit the Word 2003 More About Web page (scsite.com/wd2003/more) and then click Designing Questionnaires.

To Insert a Check Box Form Field

1

• **With the insertion point in the first cell of the table, click the Check Box Form Field button on the Forms toolbar.**

Word inserts a check box form field at the location of the insertion point (Figure 7-27).

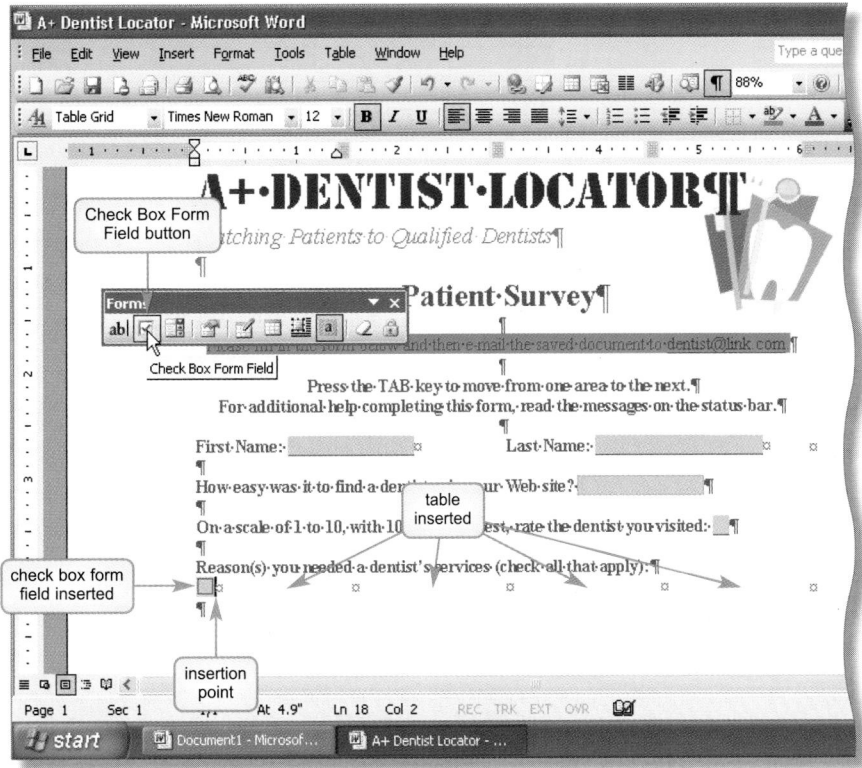

FIGURE 7-27

2

• **Press the SPACEBAR. Type** Checkup **and then press the TAB key.**

Word enters the caption in the first cell of the table after the check box form field (Figure 7-28).

Other Ways

1. With Forms toolbar displaying, in Voice Command mode, say "Check Box"

FIGURE 7-28

The next step is to enter the remaining check box fields in the form, as described below.

To Insert Additional Check Box Form Fields

1 With the insertion point in the second cell of the table, click the Check Box Form Field button on the Forms toolbar. Press the SPACEBAR. Type `Cleaning` and then press the TAB key.

2 With the insertion point in the third cell of the table, click the Check Box Form Field button on the Forms toolbar. Press the SPACEBAR. Type `Toothache` and then press the TAB key.

3 With the insertion point in the fourth cell of the table, click the Check Box Form Field button on the Forms toolbar. Press the SPACEBAR. Type `Whiter Smile` and then click the paragraph mark below the table.

4 With the insertion point below the table, click the Check Box Form Field button on the Forms toolbar. Press the SPACEBAR. Type `Other (please specify)` and then press the COLON (:) key. Press the SPACEBAR.

The check box form fields are inserted (Figure 7-29).

FIGURE 7-29

If users select the check box with the Other caption, you want them to explain the other type of dental service they required. To allow this entry, you insert a text form field as described next.

To Insert and Specify Options for a Text Form Field

1 Click the Text Form Field button on the Forms toolbar.

2 Double-click the text form field for Other (please specify). When Word displays the Text Form Field Options dialog box, press the UNDERSCORE key 30 times in the Default text text box (Figure 7-30).

3 Click the OK button.

Word displays the text form field for the other types of dental services according to the settings in the Text Form Field Options dialog box.

FIGURE 7-30

Inserting a Text Form Field that Displays the Current Date

The next form field to be entered in the Patient Survey is the current date. You do not want the user to enter the date; instead, you simply want the current date to be displayed on the form. When a user fills in and e-mails the completed form, Word automatically will display the date the user completed the form.

You could insert the current date as a field by clicking Insert on the menu bar and then clicking Date and Time. If, however, you plan to analyze the data later using a database or some other software and you want the current date to be part of the data saved with the form, then you must insert a text form field that displays the current date.

The steps on the next page show how to insert and specify options for this text form field as the current date.

To Insert and Specify Options for a Text Form Field as the Current Date

1

• **Click at the end of the last text form field entered and then press the ENTER key.**

• **Press CTRL+R to right-align the paragraph.**

• **Click the Text Form Field button on the Forms toolbar.**

• **Double-click the newly inserted text form field.**

• **When Word displays the Text Form Field Options dialog box, click the Type box arrow and then click Current date in the Type list.**

• **Click the Date format box arrow and then click M/d/yyyy (Figure 7-31).**

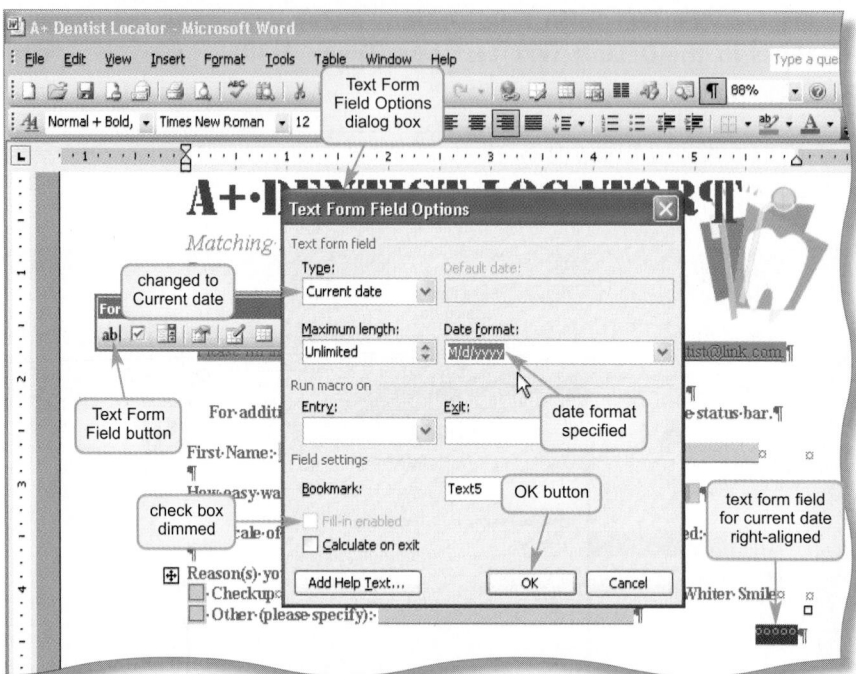

FIGURE 7-31

2

• **Click the OK button.**

• **Click outside the field to remove the selection.**

Word displays the current date in the form field (Figure 7-32). Your date displayed will be different.

FIGURE 7-32

Notice in the Text Form Field Options dialog box shown in Figure 7-31 that the Fill-in enabled check box in the Field settings area is dimmed. Word automatically dims this check box when you select Current date as the field type. When this check box is dimmed, a user is not allowed to modify the contents of the field when it is displayed on the screen. If you want a user to enter a date, you would select Date in the Type list instead of Current date.

Two other options in the Type list that also dim the Fill-in enabled check box are Current time and Calculation. That is, if you select Current time as the field type, Word displays the current time on the screen – so a user cannot change the time displayed. If you select Calculation as the field type, Word displays the result of a formula you enter.

More About

Date and Time

If a text form field type has been changed to Current date (shown in Figure 7-31) or Current time and you intend to print the form, you should ensure that the date and time are current on the hard copy. Click Tools on the menu bar, click Options, click the Print tab, place a check mark in the Update fields check box, and then click the OK button.

Formatting Form Fields

As users enter data in the text form fields and the drop-down form field on the form, you want the characters they type to be underlined in plum. Word prevents users from formatting data they enter in form fields. Thus, you should specify any desired field formatting to fields on the form template. To format a field, select the field and then format it as you do any other text. In this case, you use the Font dialog box to specify an underline color.

The following steps show how to underline the field for the first name in plum.

To Underline in Color

1

- **Click the text form field for the first name to select it.**
- **Right-click the selection.**

Word displays a shortcut menu (Figure 7-33).

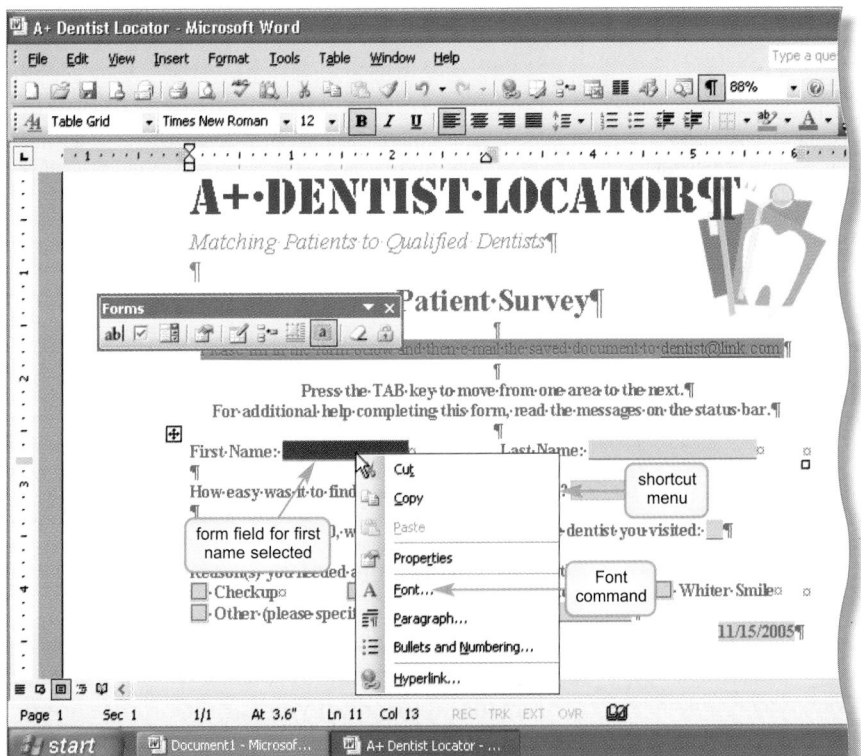

FIGURE 7-33

2

• **Click Font on the shortcut menu.**

• **When Word displays the Font dialog box, if necessary, click the Font tab.**

• **Click the Underline style box arrow and then click the first underline in the list.**

• **Click the Underline color box arrow and then click Plum on the color palette.**

Word displays the Font dialog box (Figure 7-34).

3

• **Click the OK button.**

Word formats the data entry for the first name field to 12-point Times New Roman bold underlined plum font (shown in Figure 7-35).

FIGURE 7-34

Other Ways

1. On Format menu click Font, click Font tab, select desired underline style, select desired underline color, click OK button
2. In Voice Command mode, say "Format, Font, Font, [select underline style and color], OK"

Earlier, this project showed how to set the text form fields so they show an underline when the form is displayed initially on the screen (as a blank form). Thus, you will not notice a change to the First Name text form field after formatting it. The formatting options will take effect when you enter data in the form.

Using the Format Painter Button

The next step is to copy this formatting from the First Name text form field to the other data entry fields on the screen. Instead of selecting each form field one at a time and then formatting it with the plum underline, you will copy the format assigned to the form field for the first name to the other text form fields and the drop-down form field.

To copy formats from one form field to another, select the form field from which you wish to copy formatting, click the Format Painter button on the Standard toolbar to copy the selected form field's formatting specifications, and then select the form field to which you wish to copy the formatting. To select a text form field, simply click it or drag through it. To select a drop-down form field, drag through it.

In this project, you are to copy formats from one form field to multiple form fields. Thus, you double-click the Format Painter button so that the format painter remains active until you turn it off, as shown in the next steps.

More About

Copying Formatting

If you want to copy paragraph formatting, too, such as alignment and line spacing, select the paragraph mark at the end of the paragraph prior to clicking the Format Painter button. If you want to copy only character formatting, such as fonts and font sizes, do not select the paragraph mark.

To Use the Format Painter Button

1

• **With the text form field for the first name selected as shown in Figure 7-33 on page WD 511, double-click the Format Painter button on the Standard toolbar.**

• **Click the text form field for the last name.**

Word copies the 12-point Times New Roman bold underlined plum font to the text form field for the last name (Figure 7-35). The last name field is selected, and the format painter remains active, allowing you to select more fields to which you wish to copy the format. Word attaches a paintbrush to the mouse pointer when the Format Painter button is selected.

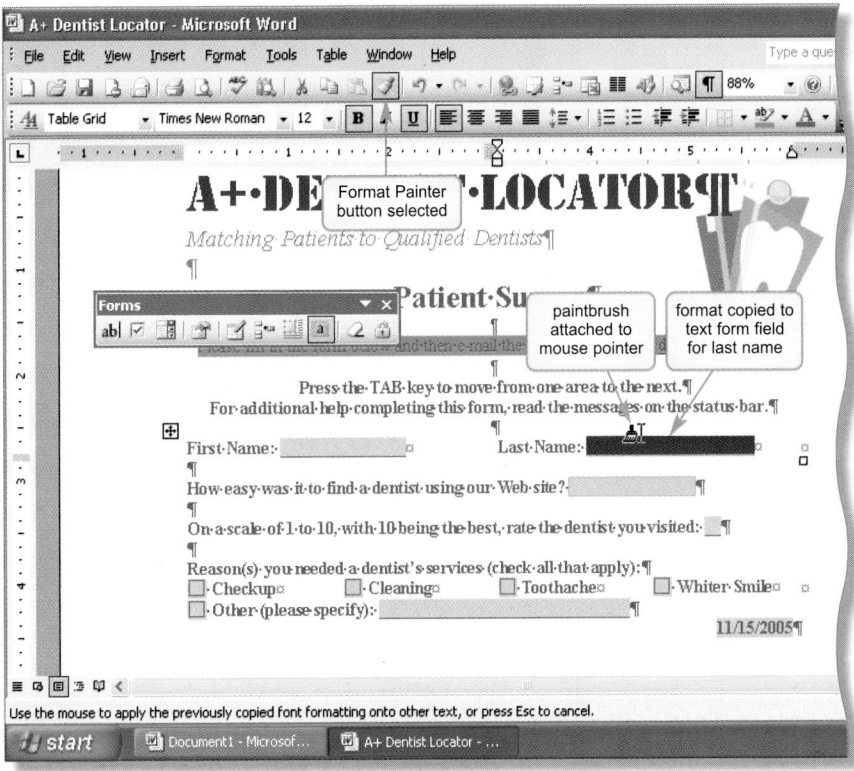

FIGURE 7-35

2

• **Drag through the ease of use drop-down form field.**

• **Click the text form field for the dentist rating.**

• **Click the text form field for Other (please specify).**

• **Click the Format Painter button on the Standard toolbar to turn off the format painter.**

The format in the text form field for the first name is copied to all other text form fields and to the drop-down form field (Figure 7-36). The Format Painter button no longer is selected.

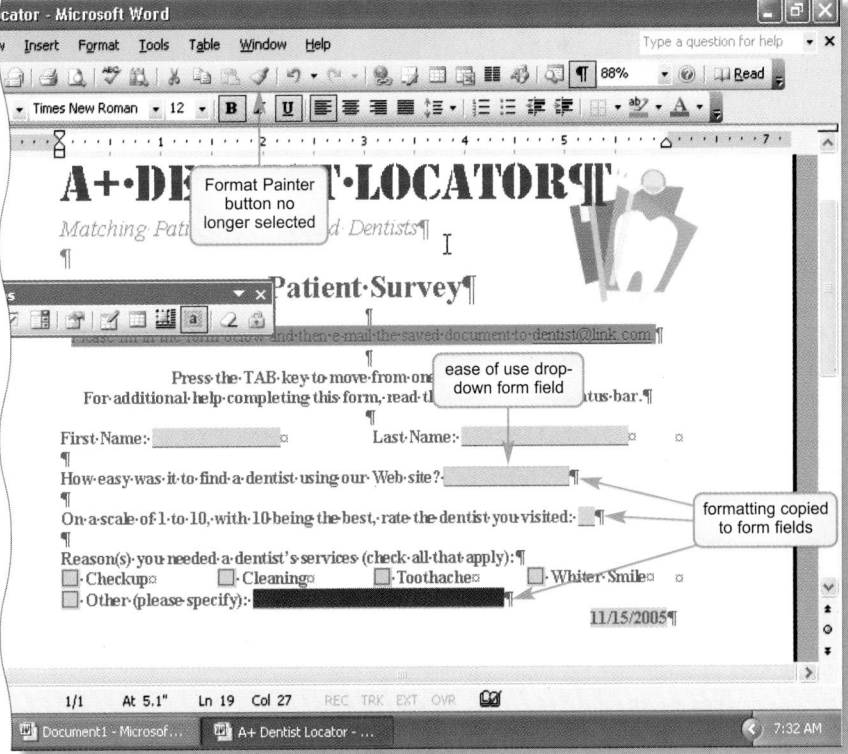

FIGURE 7-36

Adding Help Text to Form Fields

As users enter data in form fields, they may have a question about the purpose or function of a particular field. Thus, Word provides two Help mechanisms by which you can assist users during their data entry process. You can display a Help message on the status bar that relates to the current data entry field and/or you can display a Help dialog box when a user presses the F1 key. This project displays brief Help messages on the status bar as a user moves from form field to form field.

The following steps show how to display a Help message on the status bar when the user is entering the first name.

To Add Help Text to a Form Field

1

• **Double-click the text form field for the first name.**

Word displays the Text Form Field Options dialog box (Figure 7-37).

FIGURE 7-37

2

• **Click the Add Help Text button.**

• **When Word displays the Form Field Help Text dialog box, if necessary, click the Status Bar tab.**

• **Click Type your own.**

• **Type** Enter your first name.

Word displays the status bar Help text in the Form Field Help Text dialog box (Figure 7-38).

3

• **Click the OK button.**

• **Click the OK button in the Text Form Field Options dialog box.**

The Help text is entered for the first name text form field.

FIGURE 7-38

The Help text does not appear on the status bar until you protect the form, which you will do later in this project. At that time, you will enter data in the form and see the Help text on the status bar.

The next step is to enter the Help text for the remaining form fields on the form. You repeat the procedure in the previous steps for each data entry field on the form. The Help text for each field on the Patient Survey is shown in Table 7-2.

Table 7-2 Help Text for Fields on the Form		
FIELD	FIELD TYPE	HELP TEXT TO BE DISPLAYED ON STATUS BAR
First Name	Text Form Field	Enter your first name.
Last Name	Text Form Field	Enter your last name.
Ease of Use	Drop-Down Form Field	Click box arrow for list of choices.
Dentist Rating	Text Form Field	Enter rating in numbers.
Checkup	Check Box Form Field	Click check box to select or deselect.
Cleaning	Check Box Form Field	Click check box to select or deselect.
Toothache	Check Box Form Field	Click check box to select or deselect.
Whiter Smile	Check Box Form Field	Click check box to select or deselect.
Other (please specify)	Check Box Form Field	Click check box to select or deselect.
Other (please specify)	Text Form Field	Please list other dental services required.

The following steps describe how to add the Help text shown in Table 7-2 on the previous page.

To Add More Help Text

1 **Double-click the text form field for the last name.**

2 **Click the Add Help Text button in the Text Form Field Options dialog box. When Word displays the Form Field Help Text dialog box, if necessary, click the Status Bar tab. Click Type your own. Type** Enter your last name. **Click the OK button. Click the OK button in the Text Form Field Options dialog box.**

3 **Double-click the ease of use drop-down form field.**

4 **Click the Add Help Text button in the Drop-Down Form Field Options dialog box. When Word displays the Form Field Help Text dialog box, if necessary, click the Status Bar tab. Click Type your own. Type** Click box arrow for list of choices. **Click the OK button. Click the OK button in the Drop-Down Form Field Options dialog box.**

5 **Double-click the text form field for the dental rating.**

6 **Click the Add Help Text button in the Text Form Field Options dialog box. When Word displays the Form Field Help Text dialog box, if necessary, click the Status Bar tab. Click Type your own. Type** Enter rating in numbers. **Click the OK button. Click the OK button in the Text Form Field Options dialog box.**

7 **Double-click the check box form field for Checkup.**

8 **Click the Add Help Text button in the Check Box Form Field Options dialog box. When Word displays the Form Field Help Text dialog box, if necessary, click the Status Bar tab. Click Type your own. Type** Click check box to select or deselect. **Click the OK button. Click the OK button in the Check Box Form Field Options dialog box.**

9 **Double-click the check box form field for Cleaning. Repeat Step 8.**

10 **Double-click the check box form field for Toothache. Repeat Step 8.**

11 **Double-click the check box form field for Whiter Smile. Repeat Step 8.**

12 **Double-click the check box form field for Other (please specify). Repeat Step 8.**

13 **Double-click the text form field for Other (please specify).**

14 **Click the Add Help Text button in the Text Form Field Options dialog box. When Word displays the Form Field Help Text dialog box, if necessary, click the Status Bar tab. Click Type your own. Type** Please list other dental services required. **Click the OK button. Click the OK button in the Text Form Field Options dialog box.**

15 **Click outside the selected text to remove the selection.**

Help text is entered for all data entry fields according to Table 7-2.

More About

The F1 Key

If you want to enter Help text in a dialog box that is displayed when a user presses F1, click the Help Key (F1) tab in the Form Field Help Text dialog box (shown in Figure 7-38 on the previous page). You enter Help text in the Help Key (F1) sheet in the same manner as you do in the Status Bar sheet.

If you would like to change the Help text for any of the form fields, simply double-click the form field and then click the Add Help Text button in the dialog box. When Word displays the Form Field Help Text dialog box, if necessary, click the Status Bar tab. Make any necessary changes to the existing Help text and then click the OK button in the dialog boxes.

Removing Form Field Shading

The fields on the form currently are shaded (shown in Figure 7-36 on page WD 513). During the design of a form, it is helpful to display field shading so you easily can identify the fields. You do not want the fields to be shaded, however, when a user is entering data in a form. Thus, the following step shows how to remove form field shading.

To Remove Form Field Shading

More About

Form Field Shading

If you print a form that displays form field shading, the shading will not print. To add shading to a field on a printed form, you must select the form field, click the Shading Color button arrow on the Tables and Borders toolbar, and then click the desired shading color. Likewise, if you want a border surrounding a field, select the form field, click the Border button arrow on the Tables and Borders toolbar, and then click the Outside Border button.

1

• **Click the Form Field Shading button on the Forms toolbar.**

Word removes the shading from the form fields (Figure 7-39).

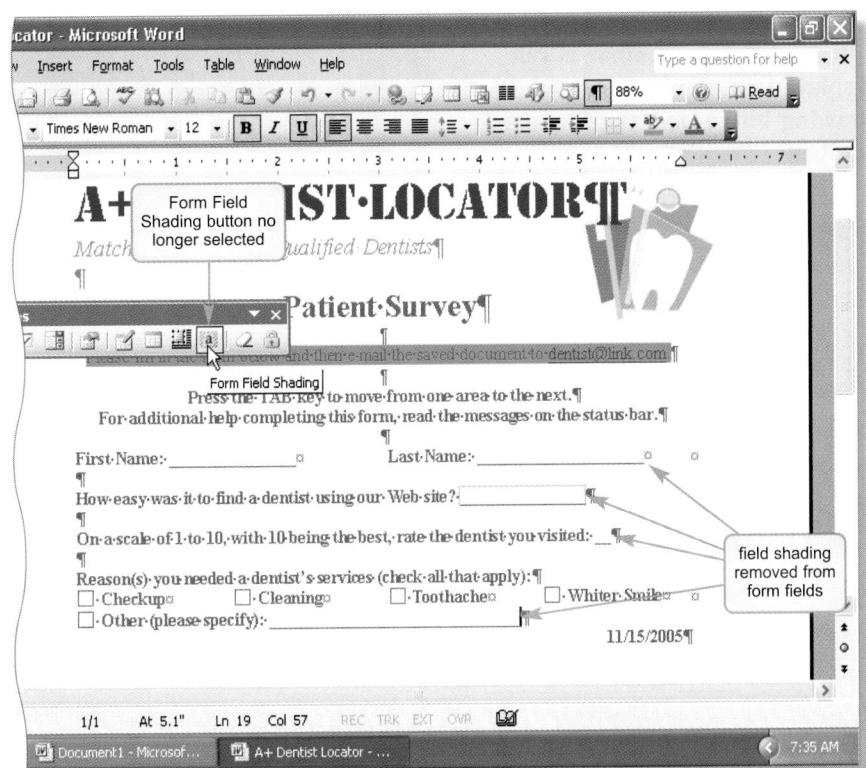

FIGURE 7-39

Other Ways

1. In Voice Command mode, say "Form Field Shading"

Inserting and Formatting a Rectangle Drawing Object

The next step is to emphasize the data entry area of the form. The data entry area of the form includes all the form fields in which a user enters data. You want to call attention to this area of the form. Thus, you decide to place a rectangle around the data entry area, fill the rectangle with a texture, change the line color of the rectangle, and add a shadow to the rectangle. In Word, a rectangle is an AutoShape, which is a type of drawing object.

The following pages explain how to insert and format a rectangle drawing object. The first step is to draw the rectangle, as shown next.

To Draw a Rectangle

1

• **Click at the end of the form, positioning the insertion point after the date field.**

• **If the Drawing toolbar is not displayed on the screen, click the Drawing button on the Standard toolbar.**

• **Click the Rectangle button on the Drawing toolbar.**

Word inserts a drawing canvas below the insertion point in the document and may display the Drawing Canvas toolbar (Figure 7-40). Recall that the drawing canvas is a container that helps you resize and arrange shapes on the page. You do not want the rectangle AutoShape on the drawing canvas in this project.

FIGURE 7-40

2

• **Press the ESC key to remove the drawing canvas.**

• **Scroll up and position the cross hair mouse pointer as shown in Figure 7-41.**

Word displays the mouse pointer as a cross hair, which you drag to form the size of the rectangle.

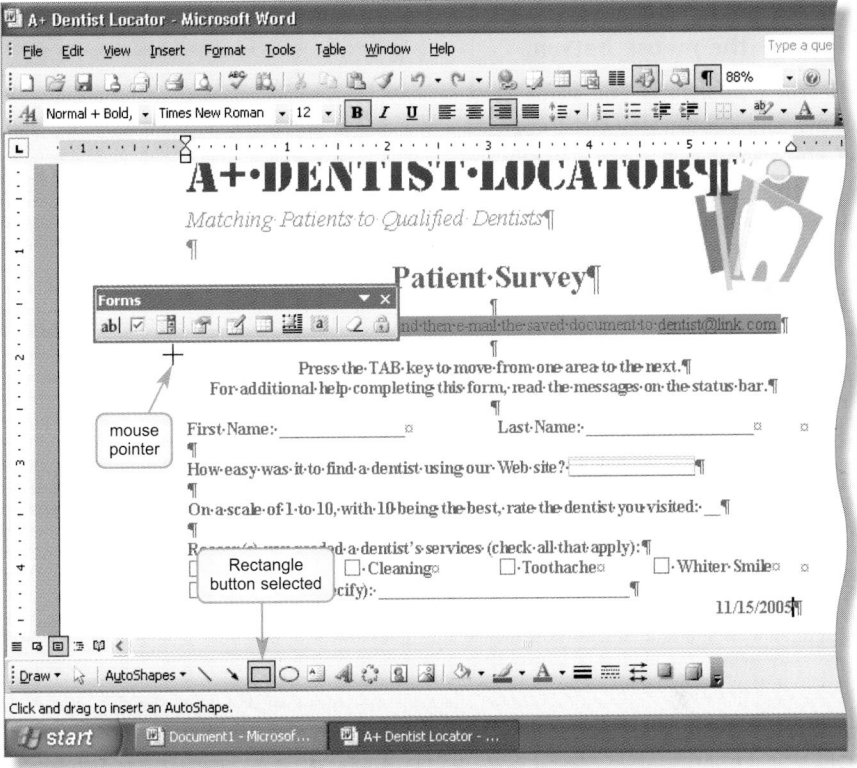

FIGURE 7-41

3

• **Drag the mouse pointer downward and rightward to form a rectangle around the data entry area, as shown in Figure 7-42.**

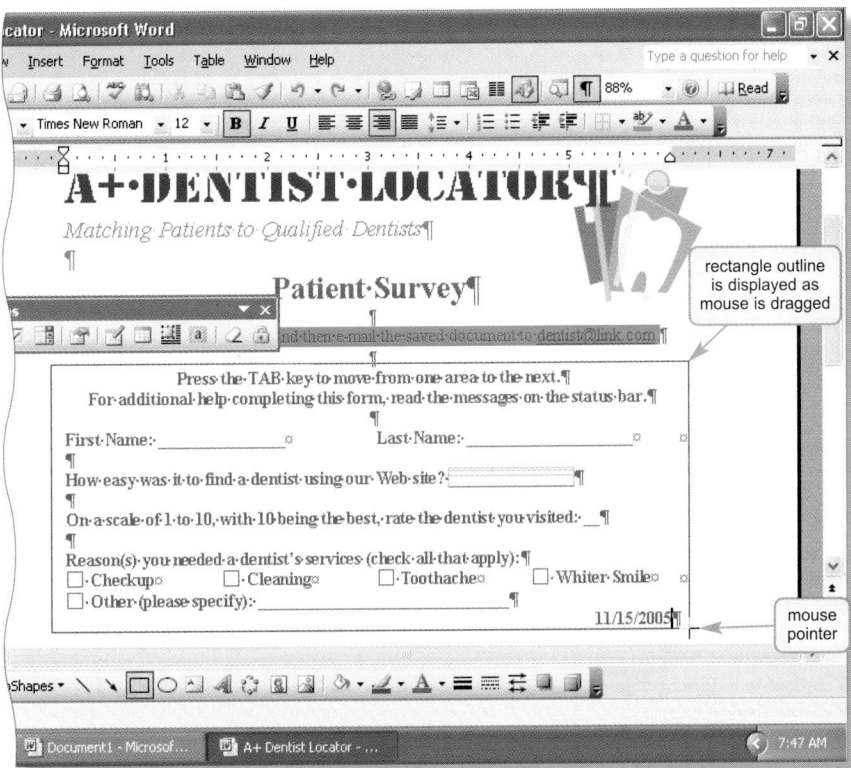

FIGURE 7-42

4

• **Release the mouse button.**

• **If Word positions the form text below the rectangle, click Format on the menu bar, click AutoShape, click the Layout tab, click In front of text, and then click the OK button.**

• **If you need to resize the rectangle after it is drawn, simply drag the sizing handles.**

When you release the mouse button, Word positions the rectangle on top of the text, thus hiding the data entry area from view (Figure 7-43).

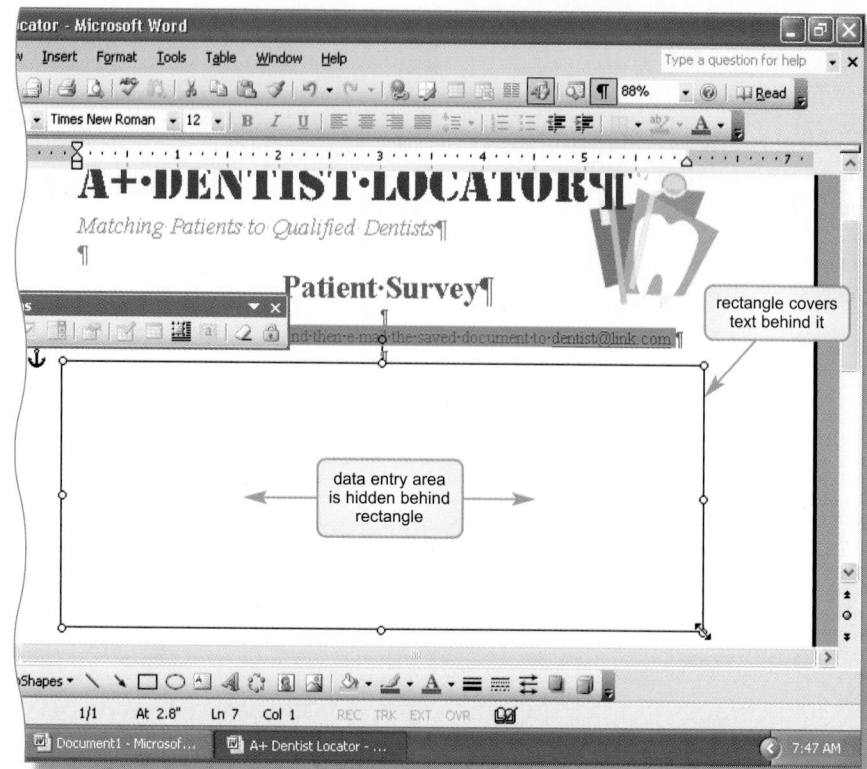

FIGURE 7-43

When you insert a drawing object in a document, Word initially places the drawing object in front of, or on top of, any text behind it. You can change the stacking order of the drawing object so that it is displayed behind the text. The next steps show how to send a drawing object behind text.

More About

Drawing Objects

To change the color of a drawing object, click the Line Color button arrow on the Drawing toolbar and then click the desired color. To add a shadow to a drawing object, click the Shadow button arrow on the Drawing tool-bar and then click the desired shadow. To add a 3-D effect to a drawing object, click the 3-D button arrow on the Drawing toolbar and then click the desired effect.

To Send a Drawing Object behind Text

1

• **Point to the edge of the drawing object (in this case, the rectangle) until the mouse pointer displays a four-headed arrow and then right-click.**

• **Point to Order on the shortcut menu (Figure 7-44).**

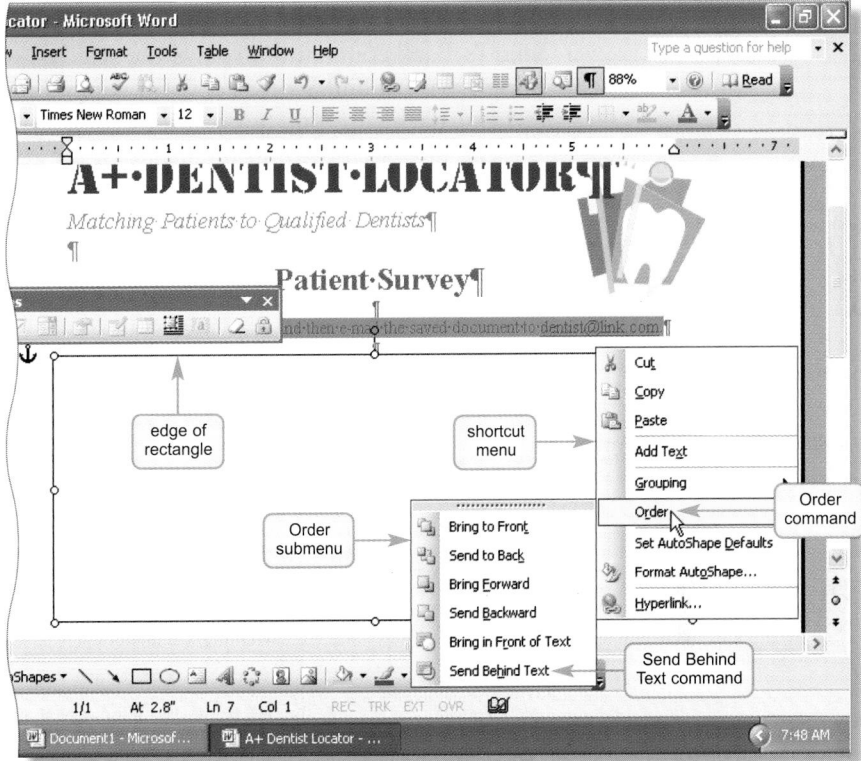

FIGURE 7-44

2

• **Click Send Behind Text on the Order submenu.**

Word positions the rectangle drawing object behind the text (Figure 7-45). The data entry area is visible again.

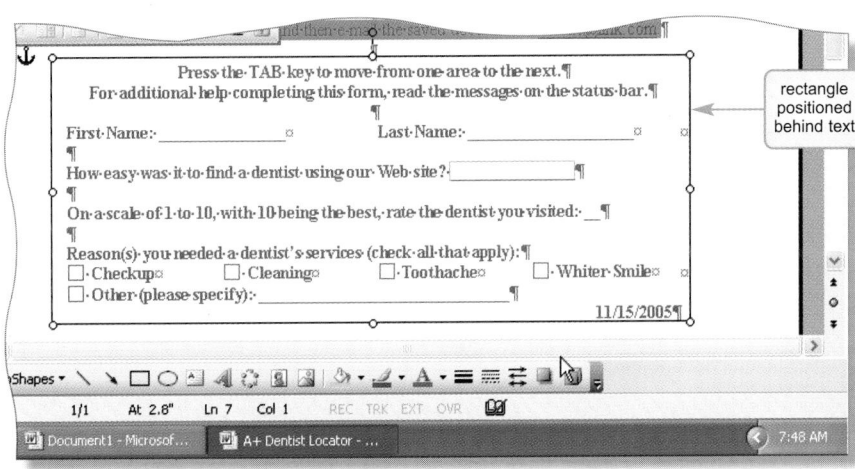

FIGURE 7-45

If you wanted to bring the drawing object on top of the text again, right-click one of its edges, point to Order on the shortcut menu, and then click Bring in Front of Text on the Order submenu (Figure 7-44).

Other Ways

1. Click drawing object, on Format menu click AutoShape, click Layout tab, click Behind text, click OK button
2. With drawing object selected, in Voice Command mode, say "Format, AutoShape, Layout, Behind text, OK"

If you have multiple graphics displaying on the screen and would like them to overlap, you can change their stacking order by right-clicking the graphic to reorder, pointing to Order on the shortcut menu, and then clicking one of the first four commands on the Order submenu (Figure 7-44 on the previous page). The Bring to Front command displays the selected object at the top of the stack, and the Send to Back command displays the selected object at the bottom of the stack. The Bring Forward and Send Backward commands each move the drawing object forward or backward one layer in the stack.

The next step is to fill the inside of the rectangle. In Word, you can **fill**, or paint, the inside of a drawing object with a color or with an effect. To fill a drawing object with a color, click the Fill Color button arrow on the Drawing toolbar and then click the desired color on the palette. **Fill effects** include gradient (two-toned) colors, textures, patterns, and pictures.

The following steps show how to format the drawing object, in this case the rectangle, using a texture fill effect.

To Fill a Drawing Object with a Texture

1

• **With the rectangle selected, click the Fill Color button arrow on the Drawing toolbar.**

Word displays the available predefined fill colors, as well as the More Fill Colors and Fill Effects buttons (Figure 7-46).

FIGURE 7-46

2

- **Click the Fill Effects button.**

- **When Word displays the Fill Effects dialog box, if necessary, click the Texture tab.**

- **Click the first texture in the third row (Blue tissue paper) in the list of textures.**

Word displays the Fill Effects dialog box (Figure 7-47). The selected texture name is displayed below the textures.

FIGURE 7-47

3

- **Click the OK button.**

Word fills the rectangle with the Blue tissue paper texture (Figure 7-48).

Other Ways

1. Select drawing object, click AutoShape on Format menu, click Colors and Lines tab, click Color box arrow in Fill area, click Fill Effects button, click Texture tab, click desired texture, click OK button in each dialog box
2. Right-click edge of drawing object, click Format AutoShape on shortcut menu, click Colors and Lines tab, click Color box arrow in Fill area, click Fill Effects button, click Texture tab, click desired texture, click OK button in each dialog box
3. With drawing object selected, in Voice Command mode, say "Format, AutoShape, Colors and Lines, Fill Color, Fill Effects, Texture, [select desired texture], OK, OK"

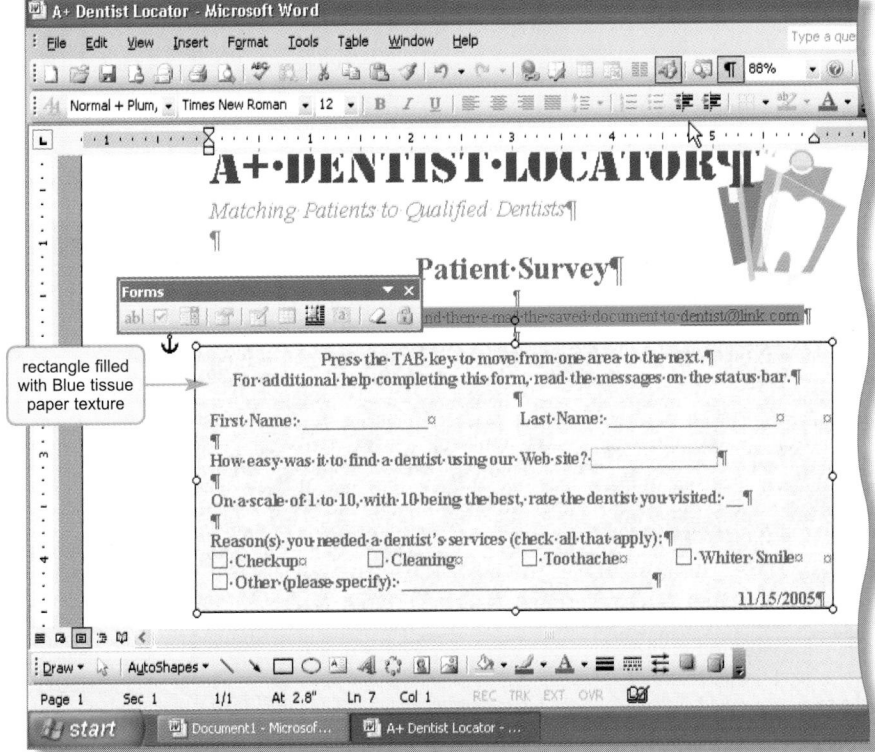

FIGURE 7-48

The next step is to change the line color of the rectangle from the default color (black) to plum so it matches the color of the text. The following steps show how to change the line color of the rectangle drawing object.

To Change the Line Color of a Drawing Object

1

• **With the rectangle selected, click the Line Color button arrow on the Drawing toolbar.**

Word displays the available predefined line colors, as well as the More Line Colors and Patterned Lines buttons (Figure 7-49).

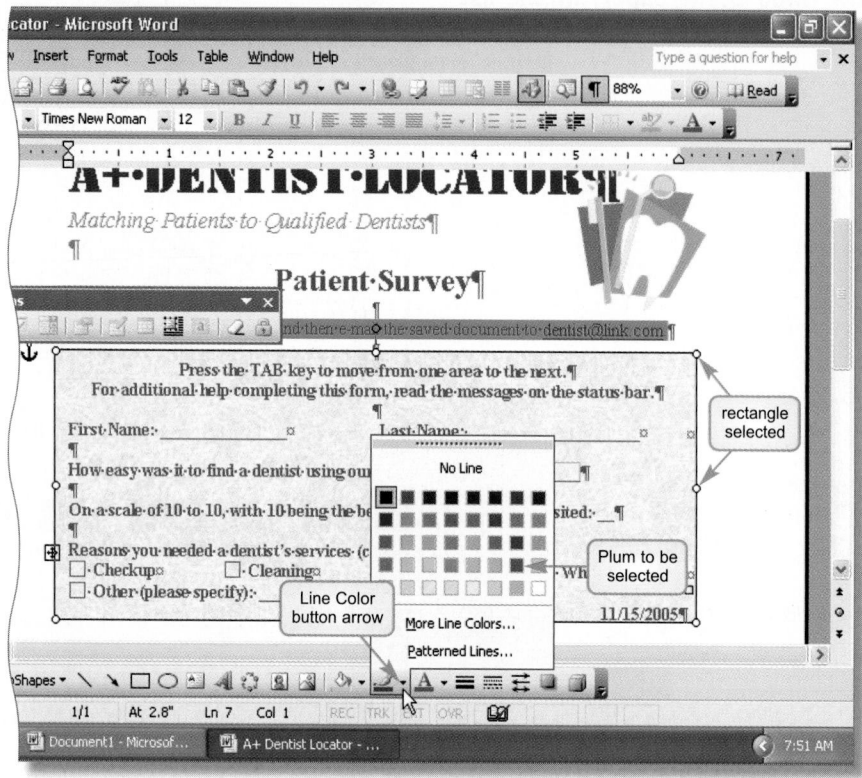

FIGURE 7-49

2

• **Click Plum.**

Word changes the rectangle's line color to plum (Figure 7-50).

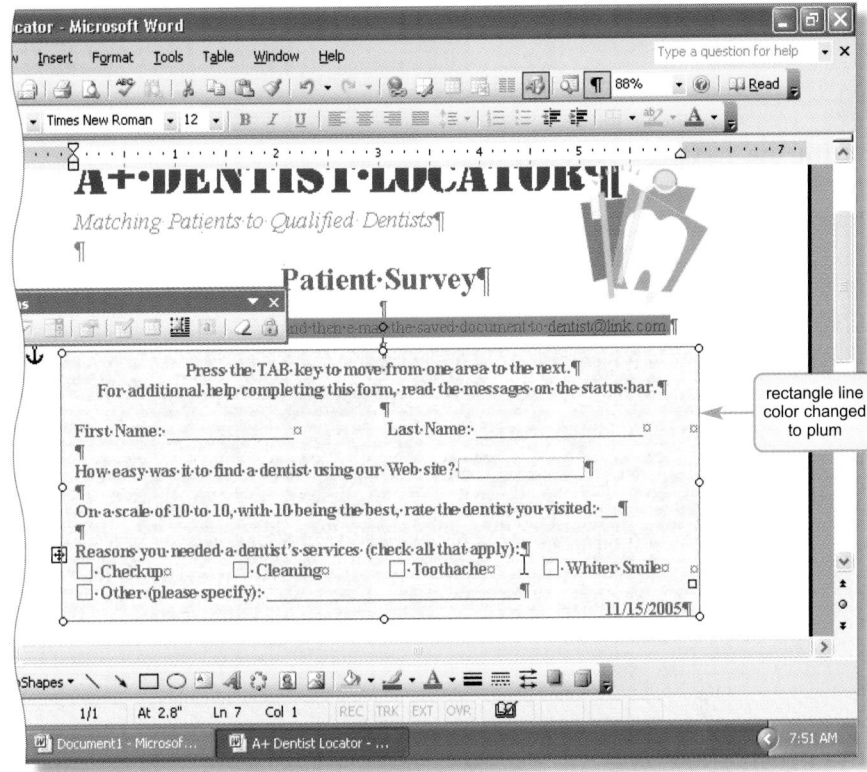

rectangle line color changed to plum

FIGURE 7-50

To offset the data entry area of the form, you can add a shadow to the rectangle. Thus, the next step is to add a shadow to the rectangle drawing object, as shown on the next page.

To Add a Shadow to a Drawing Object

1

• **With the rectangle selected, click the Shadow Style button on the Drawing toolbar.**

The available predefined shadow styles are displayed, as well as the Shadow Settings button (Figure 7-51).

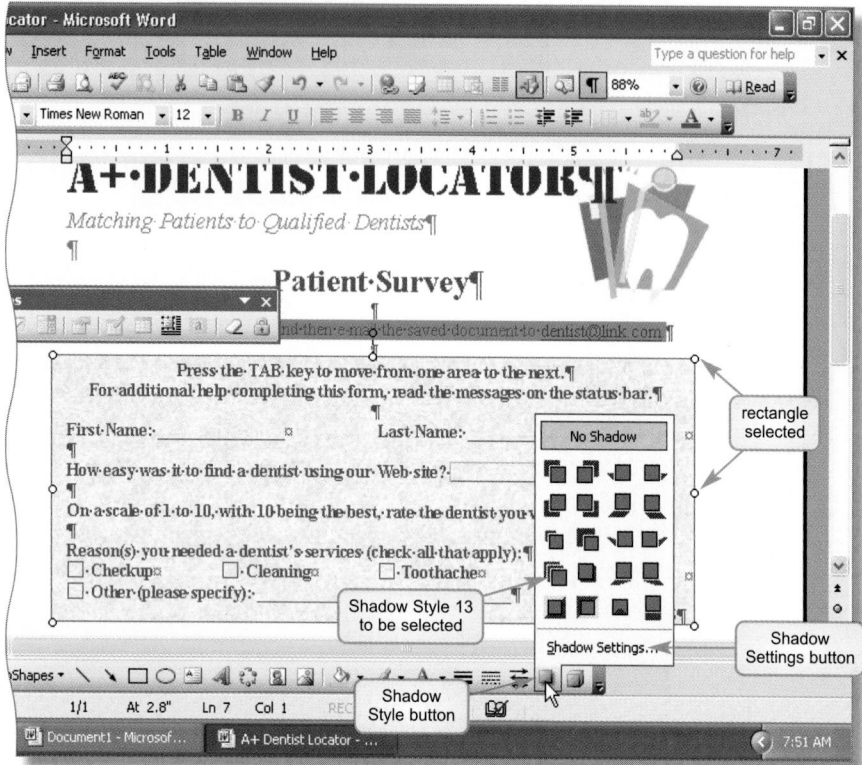

FIGURE 7-51

2

• **Click Shadow Style 13.**

• **Click inside the selected rectangle to remove the selection.**

Word adds a shadow to the top and left of the rectangle (Figure 7-52).

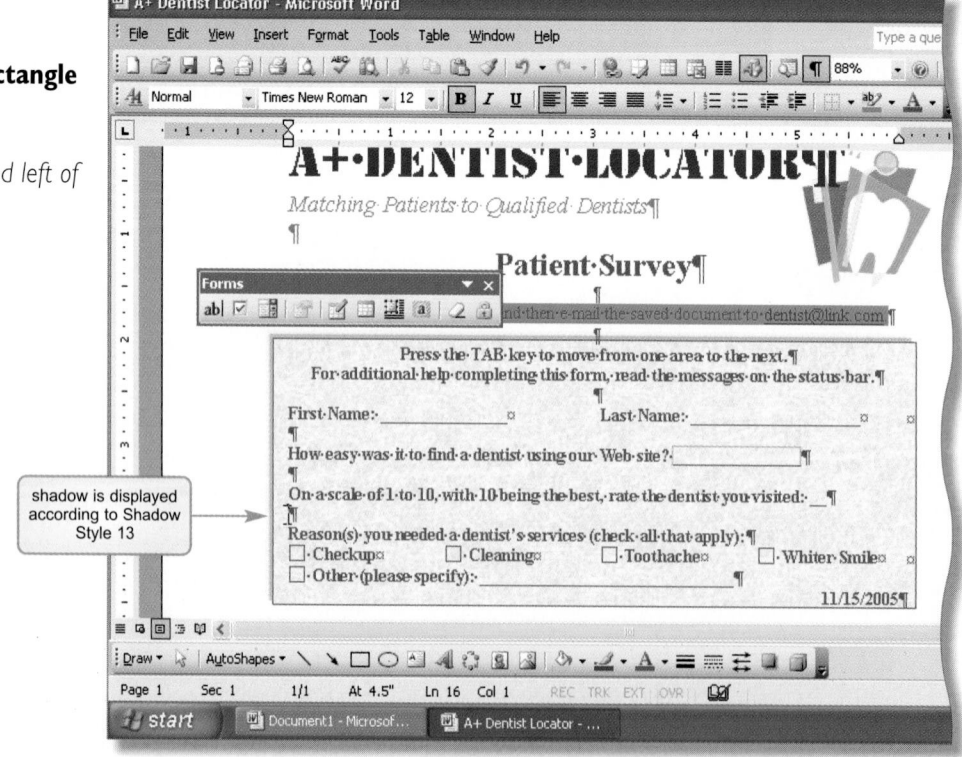

FIGURE 7-52

Other Ways

1. With Drawing toolbar displaying, in Voice Command mode, say "Shadow Style, [select shadow style]"

When you click the Shadow Settings button (Figure 7-51), Word displays the Shadow Settings toolbar. If you want Word to display a wider or narrower shadow, you can use this toolbar to move the shadow up, down, left, or right by clicking any of the four Nudge Shadow buttons to create the effect you want. Each time you click Nudge Shadow, the shadow moves one point in the specified direction. You also can change the shadow color using the Shadow Settings toolbar.

The next step is to enter and format the thank-you message below the data entry area, as described below.

To Enter Text

1 Click the Drawing button on the Standard toolbar to remove the Drawing toolbar from the screen.

2 Position the insertion point at the end of the current date in the data entry area and then press the ENTER key.

3 Click the Font box arrow on the Formatting toolbar and then click Monotype Corsiva in the Font list. Click the Font Size box arrow on the Formatting toolbar and then click 14 in the Font Size list. Click the Bold button on the Formatting toolbar to remove the bold format. Click the Center button on the Formatting toolbar. Click the Font Color button arrow on the Formatting toolbar and then click Sea Green on the color palette.

4 **Type** Thank you for your time!

The thank-you message is entered below the data entry area (Figure 7-53). Closing the Drawing toolbar allows you to see the entire form on the screen.

FIGURE 7-53

Protecting a Form

It is crucial that you protect a form before making it available to users. When you **protect a form**, you are allowing users to enter data only in designated areas — specifically, the form fields that are enabled.

The following steps show how to protect the Patient Survey.

To Protect a Form

1

• **Click the Protect Form button on the Forms toolbar.**

Word protects the form and then selects the first form field on the form (Figure 7-54).

2

• **Remove the Forms toolbar from the screen by clicking its Close button.**

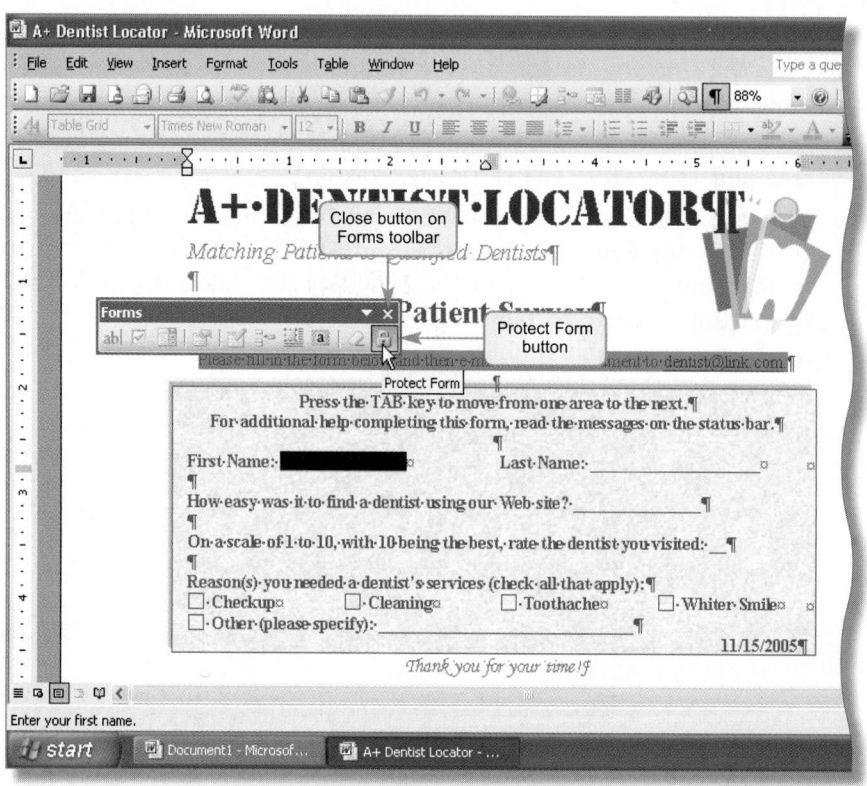

FIGURE 7-54

When a form is protected, Word selects the first form field. To advance to the next form field, press the TAB key. To move to a previous form field, press SHIFT+TAB. In a later section, this project shows how to enter data in this form.

The next step is to turn off the display of formatting marks. You do not want them on the form when a user opens it. The following step hides formatting marks.

To Hide Formatting Marks

1 **If the Show/Hide ¶ button on the Standard toolbar is selected, click it.**

Word hides the formatting marks (Figure 7-55).

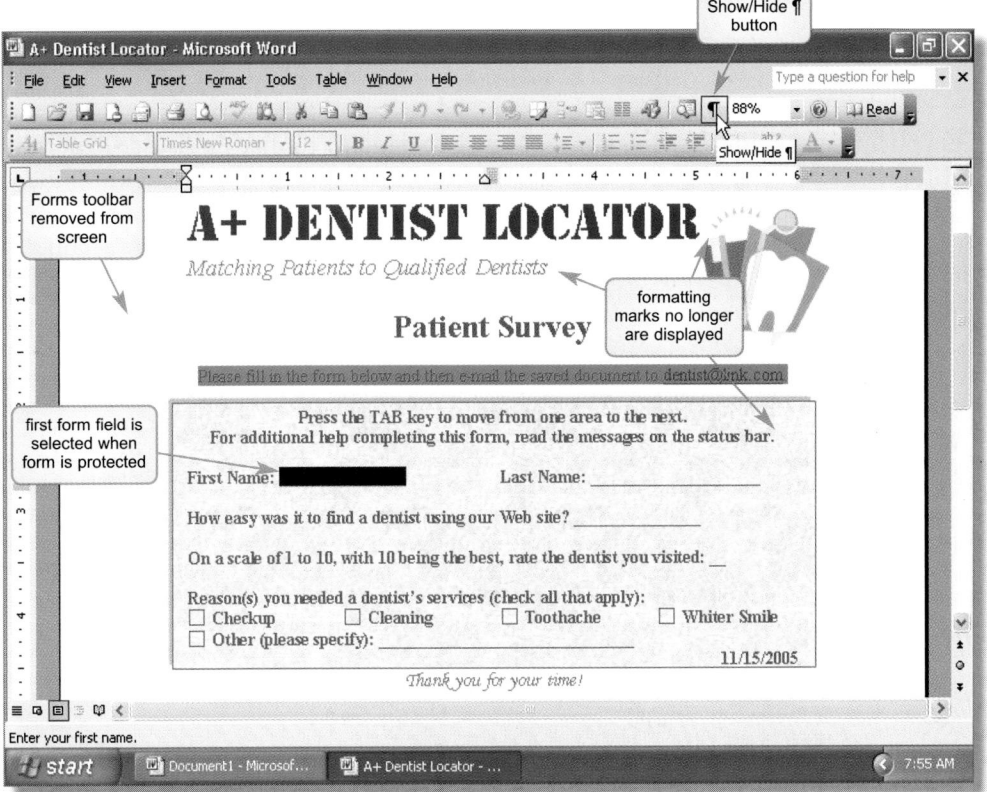

FIGURE 7-55

The online form template for this project now is complete. The following series of steps saves the template again and then closes the template window.

To Save the Template Again

1 **Click the Save button on the Standard toolbar.**

Word saves the template with the same file name, A+ Dentist Locator.

To Close the Template Window

1 **Click File on the menu bar and then click Close.**

The template window closes.

Working with an Online Form

Once you have created a template, you then can make it available to users. Users do not open templates with the Open button on the Standard toolbar in Word. A developer of a template uses the Open button to open the template so he or she can modify it. A user, by contrast, starts a new Word document that is based on the template. That is, when a user accesses a template, the title bar displays the default file name, Document1 (or a similar name). Instead of the Word window being blank, however, it contains text and formatting associated with the template that the user accesses. For example, Word provides a variety of templates such as those for memos, letters, fax cover sheets, and resumes. If a user accesses a memo template, Word displays the contents of a basic memo in a new document window.

When you save the template to a disk in drive A, as instructed earlier in this project, a user can access your template through the My Computer window or Windows Explorer. The following steps show how to display a new Word document window that is based on the Patient Survey template.

To Access a Template through Windows Explorer

1

• **Click the Start button on the Windows taskbar and then right-click My Computer on the Start menu (Figure 7-56).**

FIGURE 7-56

Q: Other than e-mail, how are online forms used?

A: Online forms frequently are used on Web pages to collect and provide data. For example, you might create a form on a Web page that allows users to search a database you have stored on a Web server or collect data from visitors. A Web form typically contains a Submit button that sends the data on the form back to a host computer. The Submit button and other Web form controls are available on the Web Tools toolbar.

2

- **Click Explore on the shortcut menu.**
- **When the Explorer window opens, if necessary, double-click its title bar to maximize the window.**
- **In the Folders bar, click 3½ Floppy (A:).**

The Explorer window opens (Figure 7-57). Your Explorer window may display differently. Notice the icon for the A+ Dentist Locator template has a small yellow bar at its top, which indicates the file has been saved as a template.

FIGURE 7-57

3

- **Double-click the A+ Dentist Locator icon in the Explorer window.**
- **Scroll down so the entire form is displayed in the Word window.**

Word displays a new document window that is based on the contents of the A+ Dentist Locator template (Figure 7-58). The first form field is selected, ready for a user's data entry. The corresponding Help message is displayed on the status bar.

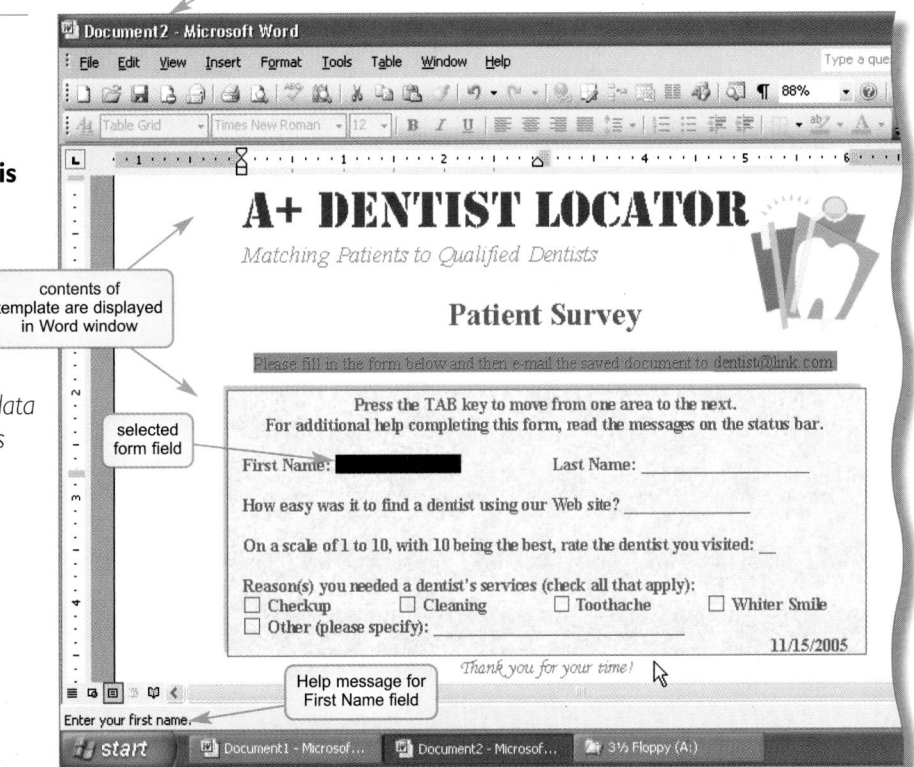

FIGURE 7-58

The next step is to enter data in the form. To advance to the next form field, a user presses the TAB key. To move to a previous form field, a user presses SHIFT+TAB. As a user tabs from one form field to the next, the status bar displays the Help messages related to the current field.

The following steps illustrate how to fill in the Patient Survey.

To Fill In a Form

1

• **With the First Name form field selected, type** Rick **and then press the TAB key.**

• **Type** Schultz **in the Last Name form field.**

• **Press the TAB key to select the ease of use form field and display its box arrow. Click the box arrow.**

The drop-down list is displayed (Figure 7-59).

FIGURE 7-59

2

• **Click Very Easy in the list and then press the TAB key.**

• **Type** 9 **in the dentist rating text box.**

• **Press the TAB key.**

• **Click the following check boxes: Checkup, Cleaning, and Other. Press the TAB key.**

• **Type** Sore Gums **in the Other text box.**

The form is filled in (Figure 7-60). Notice that the text box and drop-down list box entries are underlined in plum.

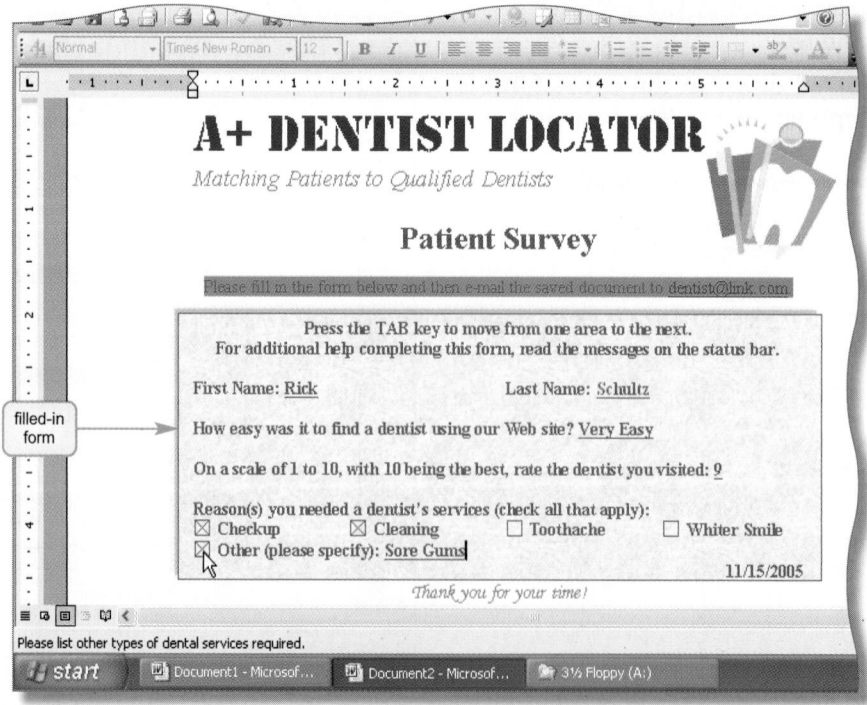

FIGURE 7-60

With the form filled in, a user can save it by clicking the Save button on the Standard toolbar. By basing the new document on a template, the blank A+ Dentist Locator template remains unchanged because users are saving a new document instead of saving a modification to the survey.

The following steps save the document that contains the user responses.

To Save a Document

1 **With a floppy disk in drive A, click the Save button on the Standard toolbar.**

2 **Type** `Schultz Form` **in the File name box.**

3 **If necessary, click the Save in box arrow and then click 3½ Floppy (A:).**

4 **Click the Save button in the Save As dialog box.**

Word saves the document with the file name, Schultz Form, on a disk in drive A (shown in Figure 7-61 on the next page).

You can print the document as you print any other document. Keep in mind, however, that the colors used were designed for viewing online. Thus, different color schemes would have been selected if the form had been designed for a printout.

Saving Data on the Form

You may wish to gather the responses from the completed surveys and analyze them. Depending on the number of forms completed, tabulating the data manually could be a time-consuming and monumental task. One alternative is to use database software, such as Access, to assist you in analyzing the responses. To do this, you must save the data on each survey in a manner that will be recognized by the database software.

Word provides a means through the Save As dialog box to save the data in a comma-delimited text file so that it can be recognized by database software. A **comma-delimited text** file is a file that separates each data item with a comma and places quotation marks around text data items. Figure 7-66 on page WD 537 shows an example of a comma-delimited text file.

The steps on the next page show how to save the data from the form in a text file.

More About

Microsoft Access 2003

For more information about features of Microsoft Access 2003, visit the Word 2003 More About Web page (scsite.com/wd2003/more) and then click Microsoft Access 2003.

More About

Printing Data Only

If you wanted to print only data instead of the entire form, click File on menu bar, click Print, click the Options button, place a check mark in Print data only for forms check box, click the OK button, and then click the OK button. Then, remove the check mark from the Print data only for forms check box so that future print jobs will print the entire form.

To Save Form Data in a Text File

1

• **Click File on the menu bar and then click Save As.**

• **When Word displays the Save As dialog box, click the Tools button (Figure 7-61).**

FIGURE 7-61

2

• **Click Save Options on the Tools button menu.**

• **When Word displays the Save dialog box, place a check mark in the Save data only for forms check box.**

Word displays the Save dialog box (Figure 7-62).

FIGURE 7-62

3

• **Click the OK button.**

Word changes the document type in the Save as type box to Plain Text (Figure 7-63).

FIGURE 7-63

4

• **Click the Save button in the Save As dialog box.**

Word displays the File Conversion dialog box, indicating that some formatting may be lost because the document is being saved as plain text (Figure 7-64).

5

• **Click the OK button.**

Word saves the data on the form in a text file called, Schultz Form, without formatting.

FIGURE 7-64

After you save the data to a text file, you should remove the check mark from the Save data only for forms check box so that Word will save the entire form the next time you save the document.

The following steps describe how to uncheck the Save data only for forms check box.

To Uncheck the Save Data Only for Forms Check Box

1 **Click Tools on the menu bar and then click Options. When Word displays the Options dialog box, click the Save tab.**

2 **Click the Save data only for forms check box to remove the check mark. Click the OK button.**

In the future, the entire form will be saved.

If you wanted to view the contents of the text file, you could open it in Word, as shown in the following steps.

To Open a Text File in Word

1

• **Click the Open button on the Standard toolbar.**

• **When Word displays the Open dialog box, if necessary, click the Files of type box arrow and then click All Files.**

• **Click the text file called Schultz Form in the list.**

Word displays the Open dialog box (Figure 7-65). The icon for a text file looks like a piece of paper with writing on it. Depending on previous settings, your screen may look different than this figure.

FIGURE 7-65

2

• **Click the Open button in the Open dialog box.**

The text file is displayed in the Word window (Figure 7-66).

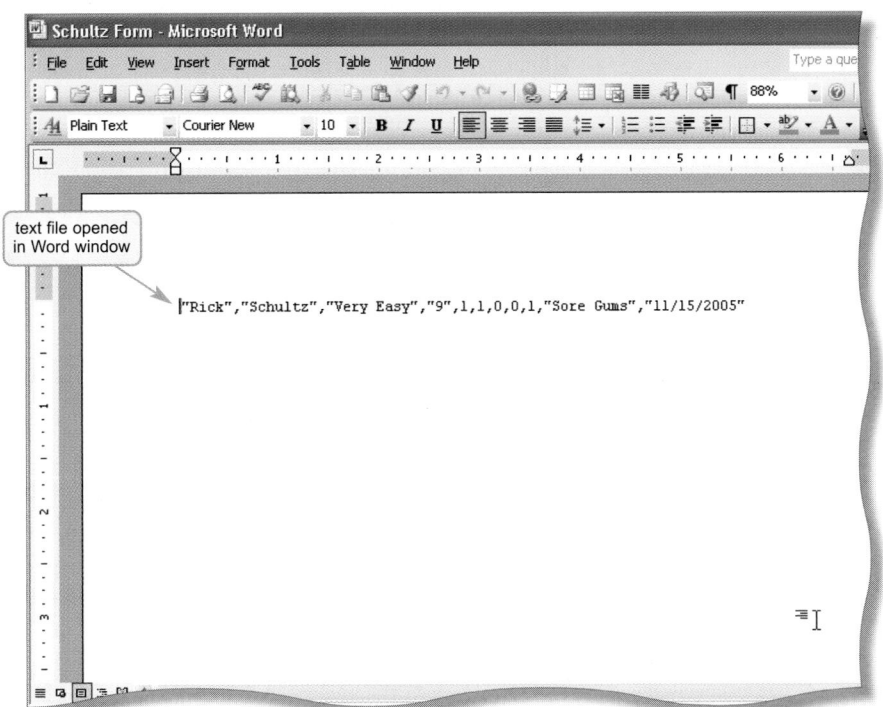

FIGURE 7-66

You also can display a text file in a text editor such as Notepad. To print the text file, click the Print button on the Standard toolbar.

Notice that the text file lists all data from the form fields, separating each form field with a comma. All text form fields and drop-down list form field entries are surrounded with quotation marks. Table 7-3 shows the form fields and their corresponding entries in the text file. Your date field will show the current date instead of 11/15/2005.

For the check boxes, a value of 1 (one) indicates that the user selected the check box, and a value of 0 (zero) indicates that a user did not select the check box. The text file is ready to be imported into a database table.

Other Ways

1. On File menu click Open, click Files of type box arrow, click All Files, double-click text file name
2. In Voice Command mode, say "File, Open, Files of type, All Files, [select file name], OK"

Table 7-3 Mapping of Form Fields to Contents of Text File

FORM FIELD	FORM FIELD TYPE	TEXT FILE ENTRY
First Name	Text	"Rick"
Last Name	Text	"Schultz"
Ease of Use	Drop-Down	"Very Easy"
Dentist Rating	Text	"9"
Checkup	Check Box	1
Cleaning	Check Box	1
Toothache	Check Box	0
Whiter Smile	Check Box	0
Other	Check Box	1
Other	Text	"Sore Gums"
Date	Text	"11/15/2005"

The following step closes the window displaying the text file.

To Close a Window

1 **Click File on the menu bar and then click Close.**

Word closes the window displaying the text file.

Working with Templates

If you want to modify the template, open it by clicking the Open button on the Standard toolbar, clicking the template name, and then clicking the Open button in the dialog box. Then, you must **unprotect the form** by clicking the Protect Form button on the Forms toolbar or by clicking Tools on the menu bar and then clicking Unprotect Document on the Tools menu. When you click the Unprotect Document command, Word displays the Protect Document task pane. Simply click the Close button on the task pane title bar to close the task pane. Project 8 discusses the Protect Document task pane in more depth.

When you created the template in this project, you saved it on a floppy disk in drive A. In environments other than an academic setting, you would not save the template on a floppy disk. Instead, you would save it in the Templates folder, which is the folder Word initially displays in the Save As dialog box for a document template file type (shown in Figure 7-5 on page WD 488). When you save a template in the Templates folder, Word places an icon for the template in the General sheet in the Templates dialog box. Thus, to open a new Word document that is based on a template that has been saved in the Templates folder, you click File on the menu bar, and then click New. When Word displays the New Document task pane, click On my computer, and then, in the General sheet, double-click the template icon. Figure 7-67 shows the template icon for the A+ Dentist Locator template in the General sheet in the Templates dialog box.

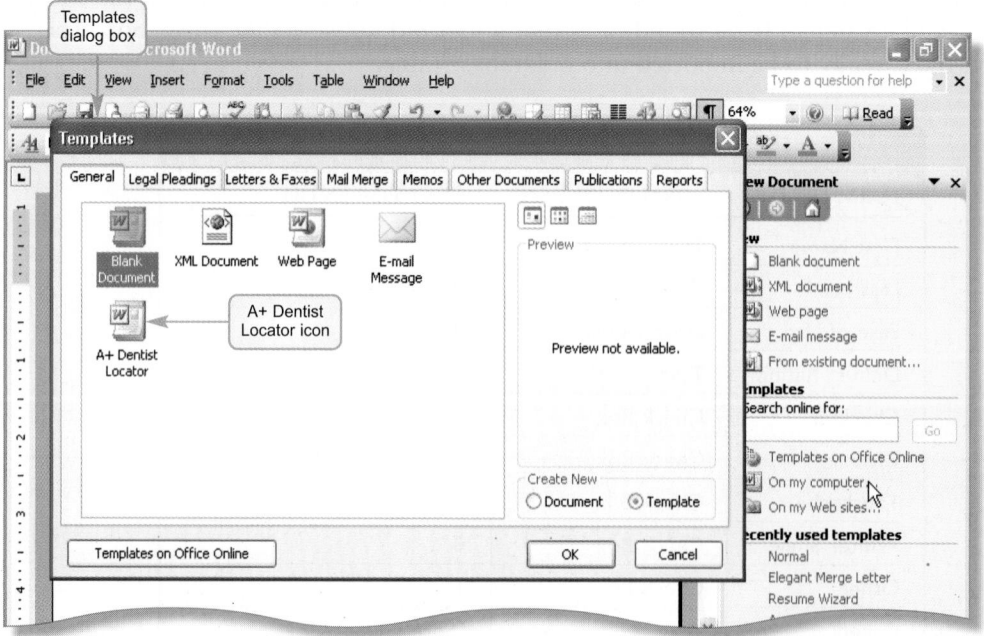

FIGURE 7-67

You also can make templates available on a network so others can share them. These templates, called **workgroup templates**, typically are stored on the network server by the network administrator as read-only files. This procedure prevents users from inadvertently modifying them. You can change the location of workgroup templates in the Options dialog box by using the following procedure.

TO MODIFY WORKGROUP TEMPLATE LOCATION

1. Click Tools on the menu bar and then click Options.
2. When Word displays the Options dialog box, click the File Locations tab. Click Workgroup templates in the File types list (Figure 7-68) and then click the Modify button.
3. Locate the folder assigned to workgroup templates (as specified by the network administrator) and then click the OK button in each dialog box.

With the workgroup template location specified, these templates also are displayed in the General sheet in the Templates dialog box.

FIGURE 7-68

Notice that the Options dialog box also lists locations of other files accessed by Word. Although you can change any of these locations through the Modify button, use caution when doing so because Word may not be able to access these types of files if you change their location.

Another way to share a form template is to e-mail it. You might want to e-mail the form template to co-workers for editing or collaboration, or you might e-mail a survey to respondents. Your computer must be connected to the Internet for the steps on the next page to work properly.

To E-Mail a Form

1. With the filled-in Patient Survey in the Word window, click File on the menu bar, point to Send To, and then click Mail Recipient (as Attachment).
2. Type your instructor's e-mail address in the To text box if your instructor gives you permission to do so. Type Patient Survey in the Subject text box.
3. If instructed to do so, click the Send button; otherwise, if you want to cancel the e-mail operation, close the e-mail window.

The filled-in form is e-mailed to the recipient named in the To text box.

The final steps are to quit Word and close Windows Explorer.

More About

Certification

The Microsoft Office Specialist Certification program provides an opportunity for you to obtain a valuable industry credential - proof that you have the Word 2003 skills required by employers. For more information, see Appendix E or visit the Word 2003 Certification Web page (scsite.com/wd2003/cert).

To Quit Word

1 **Click File on the menu bar and then click Exit.**

The Word window closes.

To Close Windows Explorer

1 **Click the Close button on the Explorer window's title bar.**

The Explorer window closes, and the desktop is displayed.

Project Summary

In creating the A+ Dentist Locator Patient Survey in this project, you learned how to create an online form. First, the project showed how to create a document template as the basis for the form. Next, you learned how to convert a graphic to floating, adjust the graphic's contrast, and rotate it. Then, the project illustrated how to add text form fields, a drop-down list form field, and check box form fields to the form. You also learned how to add Help text to each of these form fields. On the form, you learned how to add a rectangle drawing object around the data entry area and apply a fill effect and a shadow to the drawing object.

After the project showed how to protect the form, it discussed how to open a new document based on the template and then fill in the form. You also learned how to save the data on a form in a text file, how to unprotect a form so it can be edited, and how to modify the location of workgroup templates.

 If you have a SAM user profile, you may have access to hands-on instruction, practice, and assessment of the skills covered in this project. Log in to your SAM account and go to your assignments page to see what your instructor has assigned.

What You Should Know

Having completed this project, you should be able to perform the tasks below. The tasks are listed in the same order they were presented in the project. For a list of the buttons, menus, toolbars, and commands introduced in the project, see the Quick Reference Summary at the back of this book and refer to the Page Number column.

1. Start and Customize Word   (WD 484)
2. Display Formatting Marks   (WD 485)
3. Zoom Page Width   (WD 485)
4. Create a Document Template   (WD 487)
5. Enter and Format Text   (WD 489)
6. Insert and Resize Clip Art   (WD 490)
7. Increase a Graphic's Contrast   (WD 490)
8. Decrease a Graphic's Contrast   (WD 491)
9. Darken a Graphic   (WD 491)
10. Change a Graphic's Wrapping Style   (WD 491)
11. Move a Graphic   (WD 492)
12. Rotate a Graphic   (WD 492)
13. Enter Text and Highlight It   (WD 494)
14. Enter Text   (WD 495, WD 505, WD 527)
15. Insert a Borderless Table in a Form   (WD 495, WD 506)
16. Insert a Text Form Field   (WD 497)
17. Specify Text Form Field Options   (WD 498)
18. Insert and Specify Options for a Text Form Field   (WD 500, WD 504, WD 509)
19. Insert a Drop-Down Form Field   (WD 501)
20. Specify Drop-Down Form Field Options   (WD 502)
21. Insert a Check Box Form Field   (WD 507)
22. Insert Additional Check Box Form Fields   (WD 508)
23. Insert and Specify Options for a Text Form Field as the Current Date   (WD 510)
24. Underline in Color   (WD 511)
25. Use the Format Painter Button   (WD 513)
26. Add Help Text to a Form Field   (WD 514)
27. Add More Help Text   (WD 516)
28. Remove Form Field Shading   (WD 517)
29. Draw a Rectangle   (WD 518)
30. Send a Drawing Object behind Text   (WD 521)
31. Fill a Drawing Object with a Texture   (WD 522)
32. Change the Line Color of a Drawing Object   (WD 524)
33. Add a Shadow to a Drawing Object   (WD 526)
34. Protect a Form   (WD 528)
35. Hide Formatting Marks   (WD 528)
36. Save the Template Again   (WD 529)
37. Close the Template Window   (WD 529)
38. Access a Template through Windows Explorer   (WD 530)
39. Fill In a Form   (WD 532)
40. Save a Document   (WD 533)
41. Save Form Data in a Text File   (WD 534)
42. Uncheck the Save Data Only for Forms Check Box   (WD 536)
43. Open a Text File in Word   (WD 536)
44. Close a Window   (WD 538)
45. Modify Workgroup Template Location   (WD 539)
46. E-Mail a Form   (WD 540)
47. Quit Word   (WD 540)
48. Close Windows Explorer   (WD 540)

More About

Quick Reference

For a table that lists how to complete the tasks covered in this book using the mouse, menu, shortcut menu, and keyboard, see the Quick Reference Summary at the back of this book, or visit the Word 2003 Quick Reference Web page (scsite.com/wd2003/qr).

Learn It Online

Instructions: To complete the Learn It Online exercises, start your browser, click the Address bar, and then enter the Web address scsite.com/wd2003/learn. When the Word 2003 Learn It Online page is displayed, follow the instructions in the exercises below. Each exercise has instructions for printing your results, either for your own records or for submission to your instructor.

1 Project Reinforcement TF, MC, and SA

Below Word Project 7, click the Project Reinforcement link. Print the quiz by clicking Print on the File menu for each page. Answer each question.

2 Flash Cards

Below Word Project 7, click the Flash Cards link and read the instructions. Type 20 (or a number specified by your instructor) in the Number of playing cards text box, type your name in the Enter your Name text box, and then click the Flip Card button. When the flash card is displayed, read the question and then click the ANSWER box arrow to select an answer. Flip through Flash Cards. If your score is 15 (75%) correct or greater, click Print on the File menu to print your results. If your score is less than 15 (75%) correct, then redo this exercise by clicking the Replay button.

3 Practice Test

Below Word Project 7, click the Practice Test link. Answer each question, enter your first and last name at the bottom of the page, and then click the Grade Test button. When the graded practice test is displayed on your screen, click Print on the File menu to print a hard copy. Continue to take practice tests until you score 80% or better.

4 Who Wants To Be a Computer Genius?

Below Word Project 7, click the Computer Genius link. Read the instructions, enter your first and last name at the bottom of the page, and then click the PLAY button. When your score is displayed, click the PRINT RESULTS link to print a hard copy.

5 Wheel of Terms

Below Word Project 7, click the Wheel of Terms link. Read the instructions, and then enter your first and last name and your school name. Click the PLAY button. When your score is displayed, right-click the score and then click Print on the shortcut menu to print a hard copy.

6 Crossword Puzzle Challenge

Below Word Project 7, click the Crossword Puzzle Challenge link. Read the instructions, and then enter your first and last name. Click the SUBMIT button. Work the crossword puzzle. When you are finished, click the Submit button. When the crossword puzzle is redisplayed, click the Print Puzzle button to print a hard copy.

7 Tips and Tricks

Below Word Project 7, click the Tips and Tricks link. Click a topic that pertains to Project 7. Right-click the information and then click Print on the shortcut menu. Construct a brief example of what the information relates to in Word to confirm you understand how to use the tip or trick.

8 Newsgroups

Below Word Project 7, click the Newsgroups link. Click a topic that pertains to Project 7. Print three comments.

9 Expanding Your Horizons

Below Word Project 7, click the Expanding Your Horizons link. Click a topic that pertains to Project 7. Print the information. Construct a brief example of what the information relates to in Word to confirm you understand the contents of the article.

10 Search Sleuth

Below Word Project 7, click the Search Sleuth link. To search for a term that pertains to this project, select a term below the Project 7 title and then use the Google search engine at google.com (or any major search engine) to display and print two Web pages that present information on the term.

11 Word Online Training

Below Word Project 7, click the Word Online Training link. When your browser displays the Microsoft Office Online Web page, click the Word link. Click one of the Word courses that covers one or more of the objectives listed at the beginning of the project on page WD 482. Print the first page of the course before stepping through it.

12 Office Marketplace

Below Word Project 7, click the Office Marketplace link. When your browser displays the Microsoft Office Online Web page, click the Office Marketplace link. Click a topic that relates to Word. Print the first page.

Apply Your Knowledge

1 Filling In a Form

Instructions: In this assignment, you access a template through Windows Explorer. As shown in Figure 7-69, the template contains an online form. You are to fill in the form, save it, and print it. The template is located on the Data Disk. If you did not download the Data Disk, see the inside back cover for instructions for downloading the Data Disk or see your instructor.

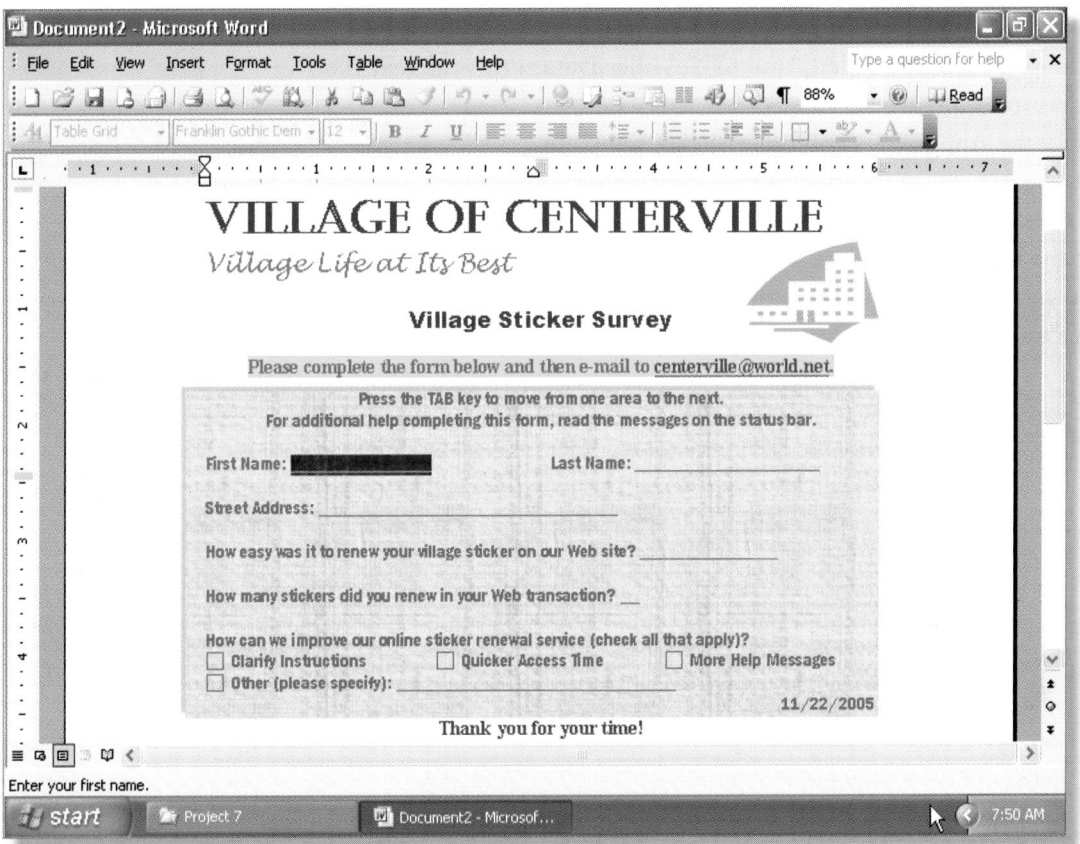

FIGURE 7-69

Perform the following tasks:

1. Start Windows Explorer. In the Explorer window, select drive A. Double-click the Apply 7-1 Centerville Sticker template icon in the Explorer window.
2. When Word displays a new document based on the Apply 7-1 Centerville Sticker template, scroll down so the entire form fits in the Word window. Only the Standard and Formatting toolbars should be displayed. Change the zoom percent to page width. Hide formatting marks. Your screen should look like Figure 7-69.
3. With the First Name text box selected, type Logan and then press the TAB key.
4. With the Last Name text box selected, type Miller and then press the TAB key.
5. With the Street Address text box selected, type 44 Western Boulevard and then press the TAB key.
6. With the drop-down list box selected, click the box arrow and then click Easy in the list. Press the TAB key.

(continued)

Apply Your Knowledge

Filling In a Form *(continued)*

7. Type 2 in response to How many stickers did you renew in your Web transaction? Press the TAB key.

8. Place an X in the Quicker Access Time and Other check boxes by clicking them. Press the TAB key. Type 24-hour access in the Other text box.

9. Save the file with the name Apply 7-1 Miller Form. Print the form.

10. Display the Save As dialog box. Save just the data on the form in a comma-delimited plain text file called Apply 7-1 Miller Data. When you are finished saving the data, be sure to remove the check mark from the Save data only for forms check box.

11. Open the plain text file called Apply 7-1 Miller Data. Print the text file.

12. Open the Apply 7-1 Centerville Sticker template.

13. Unprotect the Apply 7-1 Centerville Sticker template.

14. Change the date text form field to the format: M/d/yy.

15. Adjust the contrast of the graphic so it has less contrast (to about 35% or five clicks).

16. Protect the modified template.

17. Save the modified template with the file name, Apply 7-1 Center Sticker Modified.

18. Print the modified template.

1 Creating an Online Form with a Texture Fill Effect

Problem: You work part-time for Global Choice Coffee Club, a company that provides coffee memberships to customers. Your supervisor has asked you to prepare an online survey for Web customers. The survey should obtain the following information from the customer: first name, last name, the amount of time that elapses between ordering and delivery, their opinion of the coffee quality and flavor, and the types of items they order. You prepare the online form shown in Figure 7-70.

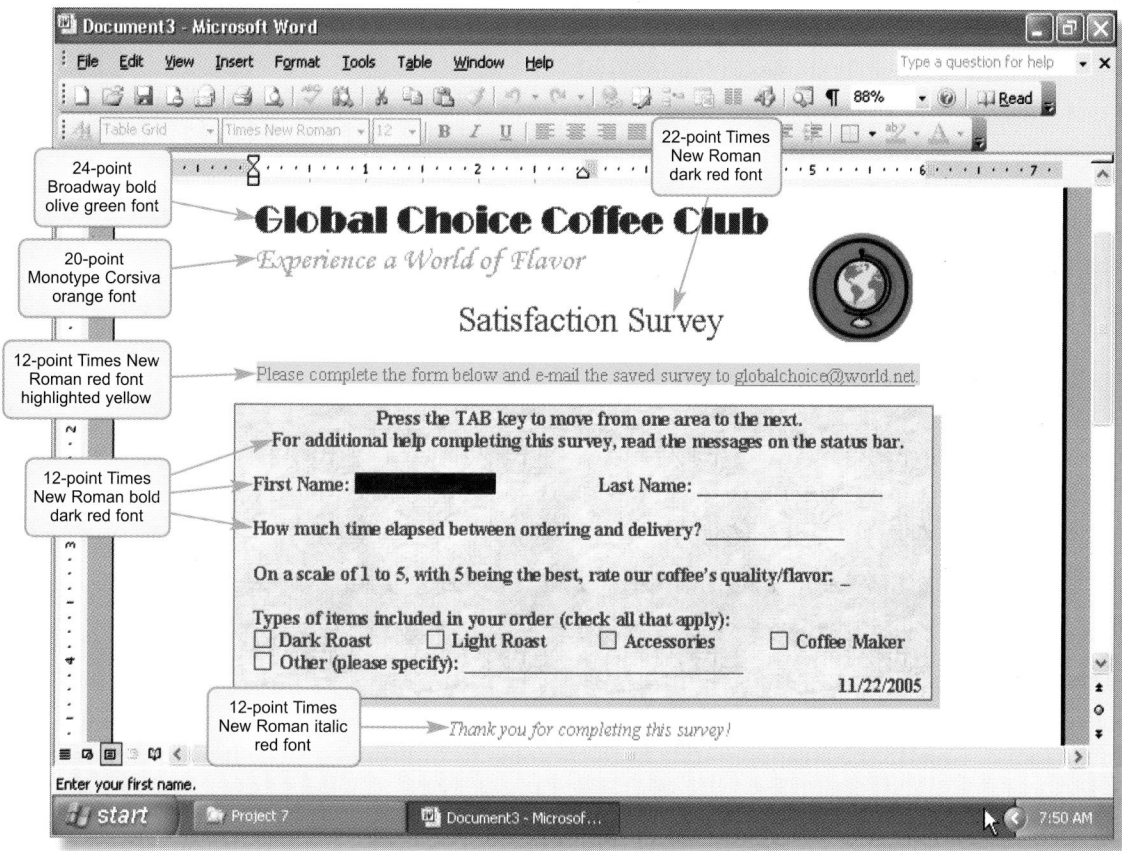

FIGURE 7-70

Instructions:

1. Create a template called Lab 7-1 Global Coffee for the online form.
2. Enter and format the company name, clip art, business tag line, and form title as shown in Figure 7-70 (or with similar fonts). Change the wrapping style of the graphic to In Front of Text. If necessary, resize the graphic.
3. Enter the user instructions and highlight them yellow.

(continued)

In the Lab

Creating an Online Form with a Texture Fill Effect *(continued)*

4. Enter the instructions in the data entry area, form field captions, and form fields as shown in Figure 7-70 on the previous page. First Name and Last Name are text form fields. How much time elapsed between ordering and delivery? is a drop-down form field with these choices: Less than 1 week, 1-2 weeks, and More than 2 weeks. On a scale of 1 to 5, with 5 being the best, rate our coffee's quality/flavor is a text form field requiring numeric input. The choices below Types of items included in your order are check box form fields. The Other check box also has a text form field to its right for further explanation. When the form initially is displayed on the screen as a blank form, the text form fields and drop-down form field should display underlines in dark red. The current date is a text form field.
5. Enter the thank-you message as shown in Figure 7-70.
6. Insert a rectangle drawing object around the data entry area. Fill the rectangle drawing object with the Stationery texture. Add Shadow Style 6 to the rectangle drawing object.
7. Add Help text to all the form fields.
8. Check the spelling of the form. Protect the form. Save the form again. Print the blank form.
9. Access the template through Windows Explorer. Fill in the form. Print the filled-in form.

2 Creating an Online Form with a Gradient Fill Effect and Modified Shadow

Problem: You work part-time for TechnoMart, Inc. Your supervisor has asked you to prepare an online shopping survey to be distributed to customers. The survey should obtain the following information from the customer: first name, last name, how they heard about the service, how long it took to place an order, and the types of supplies they ordered. You prepare the online form shown in Figure 7-71.

Instructions:

1. Create a template called Lab 7-2 TechnoMart for the online form.
2. Enter and format the company name, business tag line, clip art, and form title as shown in Figure 7-71 (or with similar fonts). Change the wrapping style of the graphic to In Front of Text. If necessary, resize the graphic.
3. Enter the user instructions and highlight them in bright green.
4. Enter the instructions in the data entry area, form field captions, and form fields as shown in Figure 7-71. First Name and Last Name are text form fields. How they heard about the service is a drop-down form field with these choices: Web ad, Printed ad, Business contact, and Friend. The number of minutes it took to place an order is a text form field that allows only a numeric entry. The types of supplies ordered are check box form fields. The Other field is both a check box form field and a text form field. When the form initially is displayed on the screen as a blank form, the text form fields and drop-down form field should display underlines in dark blue. The current date is a text form field.

WD 547

Word Project 7

In the Lab

5. Enter the thank-you message as shown in Figure 7-71.

6. Insert a rectangle drawing object around the data entry area. Change the rectangle line color to dark blue. Fill the rectangle with a two-color gradient of pale blue to white with a from center shading style.

7. Add Shadow Style 13 to the rectangle. With the rectangle selected, nudge the shadow to the left once and up once. Also, change the shadow color to plum. *Hint*: Use Help to learn about changing shadows.

8. Add Help text to all the form fields.

9. Check the spelling of the form. Protect the form. Save the form again. Print the blank form.

10. Access the template through Windows Explorer. Fill in the form. Print the filled-in form.

11. E-mail the template to your instructor, if your instructor gives you permission to do so.

FIGURE 7-71

3 Creating an Online Form with a Pattern Fill Effect

Problem: You have been hired to help with public relations at Click 'n' Save, an online grocer. Your supervisor has asked you to prepare an online survey to send to customers. The survey should obtain the following information from the customers: first name, last name, age group, employment status, number of people in household, whether or not they would use this service again, and the types of items they purchased. You prepare the online form shown in Figure 7-72.

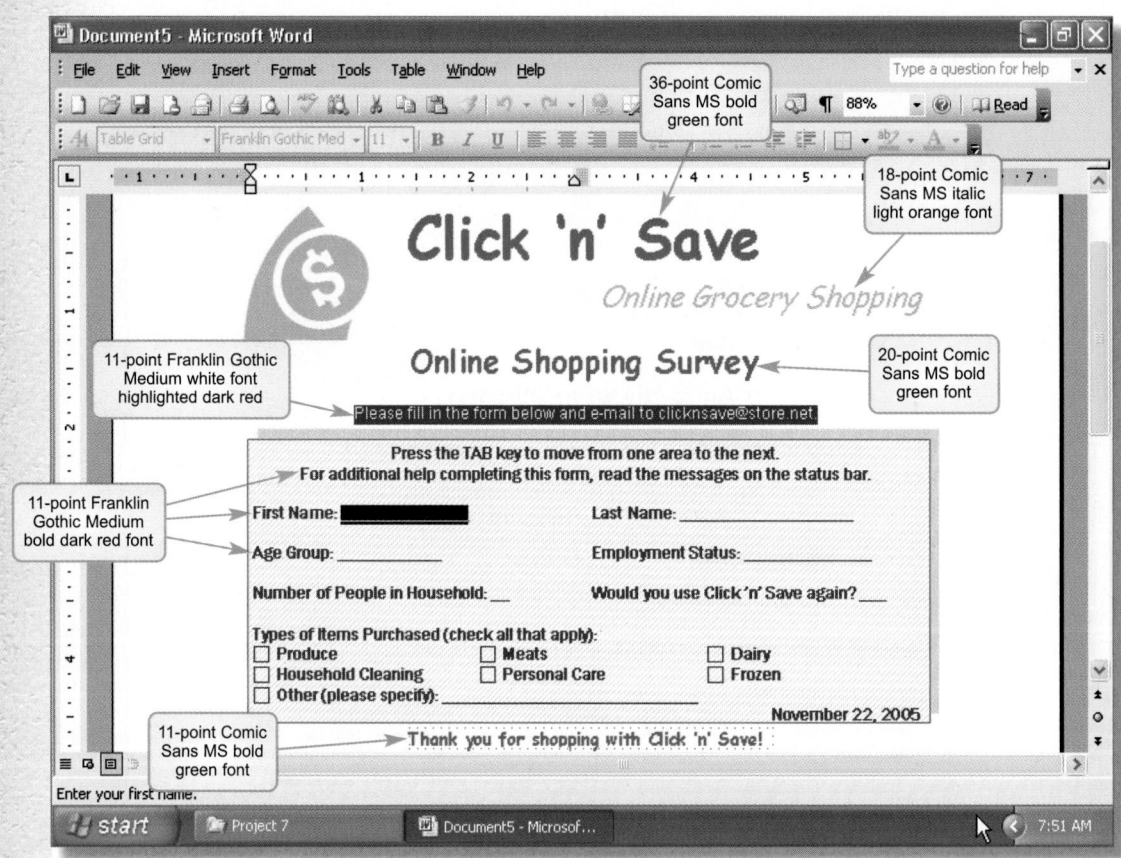

FIGURE 7-72

Instructions:

1. Create a template called Lab 7-3 Click N Save for the online form.
2. Enter and format the company name, clip art, and form title as shown in Figure 7-72 (or with similar fonts). Change the wrapping style of the graphic to In Front of Text. Rotate the graphic so the baseline is horizontal, as shown in Figure 7-72. If necessary, resize the graphic.
3. Enter the user instructions. Highlight them in dark red. Change the text font color to white.

In the Lab

4. Enter the instructions in the data entry area, form field captions, and form fields as shown in Figure 7-72. First Name and Last Name are text form fields. The age group should be a drop-down form field with these choices: < 21, 22-35, 36-50, > 50. Employment Status is a drop-down form field with these choices: Full-time, Part-time, Homemaker, Student, Retired, Other. The number of people in household is a text form field requiring a numeric entry. Would they use Click 'n' Save again is a text box. Types of items purchased are check box form fields and Other also has a text form field. The current date is a text form field. When the form initially is displayed on the screen as a blank form, the text form fields and drop-down form fields should display underlines in dark red.

5. Enter the thank-you message as shown in Figure 7-72. Animate the message using the Las Vegas Lights text effect.

6. Insert a rectangle drawing object around the data entry area. Change the rectangle line color to green. Fill the rectangle with a light upward diagonal pattern that has a foreground color of tan. Add a tan shadow to the rectangle as shown in the figure.

7. Add Help text to all the form fields. The Help text should display on the status bar, as well as when the user presses the F1 key.

8. Check the spelling of the form. Protect the form. Save the form again. Print the blank form.

9. Access the template through Windows Explorer. Fill in the form. Print the filled-in form.

10. If you have access to a Web server or FTP site, save the template to the server or site (see Appendix C for instructions). Access the template from the Web site or FTP site.

Cases and Places

The difficulty of these case studies varies:
▉ are the least difficult and ▉▉ are more difficult. The last exercise is a group exercise.

1 ▉ Your neighbor runs a business called Happy Handyman Service. He has asked you to help him develop a template for an online customer survey. The top of the form should contain the business name (Happy Handyman Service), the business tag line (Quality Household Repairs), appropriate clip art, the name of the form (Customer Survey), user instructions (Please fill in the form below and then e-mail to handyman@world.net.), and data entry area instructions (Press the TAB key to move from one area to the next. For additional help completing this form, check the status bar.). If necessary, adjust the contrast and brightness of the graphic and rotate it. The data entry area of the form should contain one text box form field with the label: On a scale of 1 to 10, with 10 being the best, rate our service. The drop-down form field should be labeled, How did you hear about our service?, and should contain these choices: Web ad, Newspaper ad, TV/Radio ad, and Referral. The check box form field heading is Types of repairs/work needed (check all that apply):, and the check box form fields required are plumbing, painting, remodeling, electrical, flooring, drywall, and other (please specify). Also, the current date should be a form field. Below the data entry area should be the message: Thank you for your time! Draw a rectangle around the data entry area of the form and add a fill effect and shadow to the rectangle. When the form is complete, protect it and then test it. If you have access to a Web server or FTP site, save the template to the server or site (see Appendix C for instructions). Access the template from the Web site or FTP site.

2 ▉▉ As a part-time worker at Fair Heart Fashions, you have been asked to create a template for a survey that will be sent to all online customers requesting feedback about their shopping experience. The company's tag line is Fashions You Will Love! Use the concepts and techniques presented in this project to create and format the online form. At a minimum, the form should contain text form fields for first name, last name, and the number of minutes it took to place an order; a drop-down form field asking the customer to rate the shopping experience; and check box form fields for the type of merchandise they ordered. The form should contain the current date as a form field. It also should have a thank-you message below the data entry area. Include an appropriate clip art image. If necessary, adjust the contrast and brightness of the graphic and rotate it. Draw a rectangle around the data entry area of the form and add a fill effect and shadow to the rectangle. When the form is complete, protect it and then test it. If you have access to a Web server or FTP site, save the template to the server or site (see Appendix C for instructions). Access the template from the Web site or FTP site.

Cases and Places

3 ■■ As a part-time assistant for Royal Oaks Health Club, you have been asked to create a template for a survey that will be sent to all customers requesting their opinion about the online racquetball court reservation process. The club's tag line is For All Your Fitness Needs. Use the concepts and techniques presented in this project to create and format the online form. At a minimum, the form should contain text form fields for first name, last name, and the number of minutes it took to reserve a court; a drop-down form field for how easy it was to use the Web site to make the reservation; a drop-down form field to request their membership type: standard, silver, or gold; and check box form fields to request other types of services they would like available through the Web, such as renewing memberships, signing up for tournaments, etc. The form should contain the current date as a form field. It also should have a thank-you message below the data entry area. Include an appropriate clip art image. If necessary, adjust the contrast and brightness of the graphic and rotate it. Draw a rectangle around the data entry area of the form and add a fill effect and shadow to the rectangle. When the form is complete, protect it and then test it. E-mail the form template to your instructor, if your instructor gives you permission to do so.

4 ■■ You are the computer specialist at Wheels on the Web, an online auto sales business. Your boss has asked you to create a template for a survey that will be sent to all recent customers. Use the concepts and techniques presented in this project to create and format the online form. At a minimum, the form should contain text form fields for first name, last name, the year and number of vehicles in which they are further interested; a drop-down form field for the type of vehicle being sought: sports car, sedan, SUV, truck, van, motorcycle, etc; check box form fields to request other types of services they would like to be able to view about a particular vehicle, such as previous accidents, number of owners, etc. The form should contain the current date as a form field. It also should have a thank-you message below the data entry area. Include an appropriate clip art image. If necessary, adjust the contrast and brightness of the graphic and rotate it. Draw a rectangle around the data entry area of the form and add a fill effect and shadow to the rectangle. When the form is complete, protect it and then test it. E-mail the form template to your instructor, if your instructor gives you permission to do so.

5 ■■ This team project investigates how to use Microsoft Office Access 2003 to create a database table and then use that table to analyze the data from Word forms. Your supervisor at A+ Dentist Locator would like to analyze the results of the surveys sent using Access. To generate data for the database table, each team member is to fill in the Project 7 Word form (Figure 7-1a on page WD 483) five times (acting as five separate users) and save the form data for each filled-in form in a separate text file. One or more team members should use Help in Access to learn how to create a blank database and import data from text files in a database table. When creating the database, use field names that match the field captions on the form. Each form field, including the current date, should have a field name. Other team members should use Help in Access to learn how to generate a report in Access that lists all the data collected from the forms. Next, your team is to create an outline in Word that describes the steps involved to import data from a Word text file into an Access database table. Finally, send the Word outline to a PowerPoint slide show and present the results to your classmates.

Working with Macros and Visual Basic for Applications (VBA)

PROJECT

8

CASE PERSPECTIVE

You recently designed an online survey for your friend, Milan Sciranka, the founder of A+ Dentist Locator. Before showing him the completed form, you decide to show it to your Web Page Design instructor for her opinion. She has the following suggestions for improving the form:

(1) Change the color scheme, fonts, and graphics on the form.

(2) Display the form without formatting marks showing, and position the Word window so the user does not have to scroll. She indicates you will need to create a macro for this task.

(3) Have the form display an error message if a user enters a letter or other nonnumeric value in the rating scale text box. This task also requires a macro, which uses Visual Basic for Applications (VBA).

(4) Place an X in the Other check box automatically (in case the user forgets to do this). For this task, she suggests creating a command button that users will click when they have finished completing the form. The command button would have VBA code associated with it that checks the Other check box, displays the Save As dialog box, and thanks the users for their time.

You incorporate her ideas in the form. When you present the completed form to Milan, he is thrilled with it. As a thank you for your time, he gives you three dental cleaning coupons.

As you read through this project, you will learn how to modify an online form to include macros and VBA. To complete this project, you will need the online form template created in Project 7. (If you did not create the template, see your instructor for a copy.)

Microsoft
Office Word 2003

Working with Macros and Visual Basic for Applications (VBA)

PROJECT

Objectives

You will have mastered the material in this project when you can:

- Unprotect a document
- Set a security level in Word
- Crop a graphic
- Create a new style that is associated with a shortcut key
- Modify a style
- Modify a drawing object
- Record and execute a macro

- Customize toolbars and menus
- View and edit a macro's VBA code
- Insert a VBA procedure
- Run a macro when a user exits a form field
- Insert an ActiveX control, set its properties, and write its VBA procedure
- Work with the Protect Document task pane
- Attach a digital signature to a document

Introduction

When you issue an instruction to Word by clicking a button or a command, Word must have a step-by-step description of the task you are attempting to perform. For example, when you click the Print button on the Standard toolbar, Word follows a precise set of steps to print the document. In Word, this precise step-by-step set of instructions is called a **procedure**. A procedure also is known as a **program** or **code**.

Computer programming is the process of writing a procedure. Every Word command on a menu and button on a toolbar has a corresponding procedure that executes when a user clicks the command or button. **Execute** means that the computer carries out step-by-step instructions. In a Windows environment, an event causes the instructions associated with a task to be executed. An **event** is an action such as clicking a button or a command, dragging a scroll box, or right-clicking selected text.

Although Word has many toolbar buttons and menu commands, it does not include a command or button for every possible task. Thus, Microsoft has included Visual Basic for Applications with Word. **Visual Basic for Applications** (**VBA**) is a powerful programming language that allows users to customize and extend the capabilities of Word.

Project Eight — Online Form Revised

In Project 8, you improve upon the online form created in Project 7 (shown in Figure 7-1 on page WD 483). Figure 8-1a shows the revised blank form, in which the

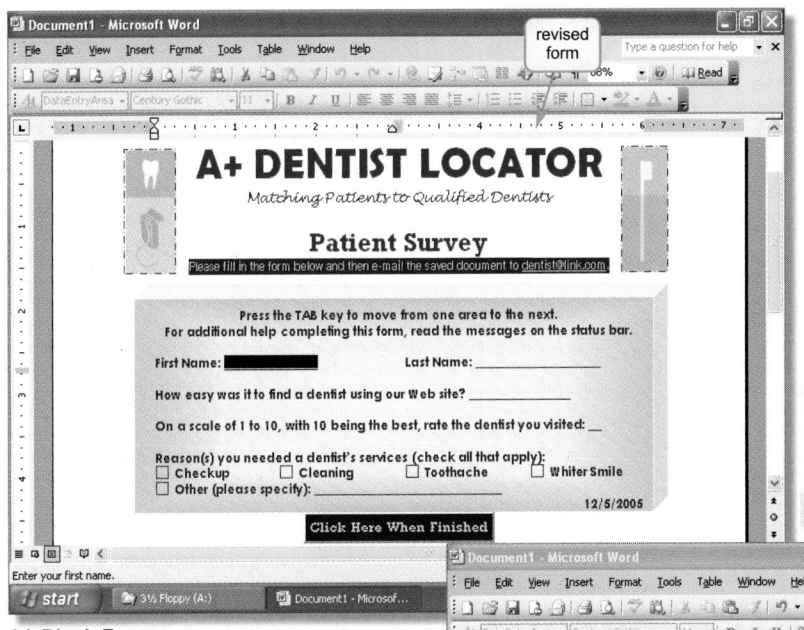

(b) Error Message Dialog Box

(a) Blank Form

fonts, font sizes, graphic, highlight color, and fill effect in the drawing object are changed. Figure 8-1b shows an error message box that appears if a user enters an incorrect value in the Rating Scale form field, and Figure 8-1c shows a thank-you message box that appears after the user clicks the button at the bottom of the form.

A **macro** is a set of commands and instructions grouped together to allow a user to accomplish a task automatically. In Word, macros consist of VBA code. This project shows how to create three macros and a VBA procedure:

1. The first macro prints the form data only, instead of printing the entire form.

2. The second macro controls how the form initially is displayed on the screen (as a blank form).

3. The third macro displays an error message if the user enters an invalid rating scale. Figure 8-1b shows the error message box.

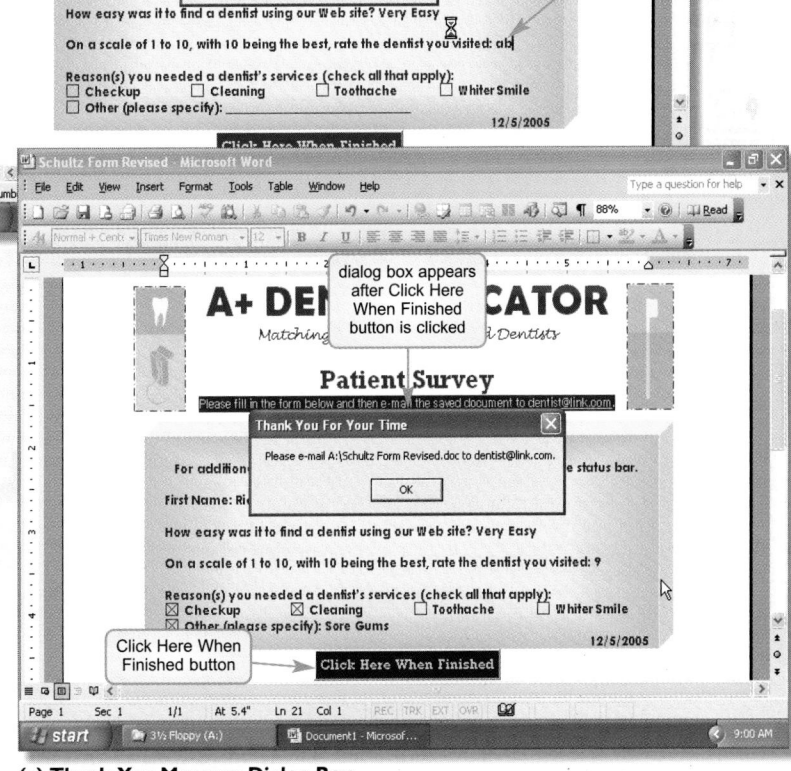

(c) Thank-You Message Dialog Box

FIGURE 8-1

```
NewMacros - 1

Sub PrintFormData()
'
' PrintFormData Macro
' Prints only the data on a form.
'
    With Options
        .UpdateFieldsAtPrint = False
        .UpdateLinksAtPrint = False
        .DefaultTray = "Use printer settings"
        .PrintBackground = True
        .PrintProperties = False
        .PrintFieldCodes = False
        .PrintComments = False
        .PrintHiddenText = False
        .PrintXMLTag = False
        .PrintDrawingObjects = True
        .PrintDraft = False
        .PrintReverse = False
        .MapPaperSize = True
        .PrintOddPagesInAscendingOrder = False
        .PrintEvenPagesInAscendingOrder = False
        .PrintBackgrounds = False
    End With
    With ActiveDocument
        .PrintPostScriptOverText = False
        .PrintFormsData = True
    End With
    Application.PrintOut FileName:="", Range:=wdPrintAllDocument, Item:= _
        wdPrintDocumentContent, Copies:=1, Pages:="", PageType:=wdPrintAllPages, _
        ManualDuplexPrint:=False, Collate:=True, Background:=True, PrintToFile:= _
        False, PrintZoomColumn:=0, PrintZoomRow:=0, PrintZoomPaperWidth:=0, _
        PrintZoomPaperHeight:=0
End Sub

Sub AutoNew()
'
' AutoNew Macro
' Controls how the form is displayed initially (as a blank form).
'
    ' Sets screen to page width zoom
    ActiveWindow.ActivePane.View.Zoom.PageFit = wdPageFitBestFit
    ' Scrolls down from to of page so entire form fits in window
    ActiveWindow.ActivePane.VerticalPercentScrolled = 0
    ActiveWindow.ActivePane.SmallScroll Down:=7
    ' Turns off table gridlines
    ActiveDocument.ActiveWindow.View.TableGridlines = False
    ' Turns off formatting marks
    ActiveDocument.ActiveWindow.View.ShowAll = False

End Sub

Public Sub RatingScaleValidation()
'
' RatingScaleValidation Macro
' Displays error message if entered number is not between 1 and 10.
'
    ' Assign value in Rating Scale form field to a variable
    RatingScaleEntered = ActiveDocument.FormFields("RatingScale").Result
    ' Test if entry in Rating Scale text form field is out of range
    If RatingScaleEntered < 1 Or RatingScaleEntered > 10 Then
        ' Display error message
        MsgBox "Rating scale must be between 1 and 10.", vbOKOnly + vbCritical
        ' Redisplay underscores in text form field
        ActiveDocument.FormFields("RatingScale").Result = "__"
        ' Reposition selection in text form field
        ActiveDocument.FormFields("EaseOfUse").Select
    End If

End Sub
```

> Print Form
> Data macro

> macro that executes
> when form initially is
> displayed on the screen
> (as a blank form)

> macro that executes
> when user TABS
> out of Rating Scale
> text box

4. The VBA procedure performs three actions when a user clicks the Click Here When Finished button (shown in Figure 8-1c on the previous page):

   a. If the user entered text in the Other text box, then Word places an X in the Other check box (just in case the user left it blank).

   b. The Save As dialog box appears so the user can assign a file name to the filled-in form.

   c. A thank-you message box appears on the screen (shown in Figure 8-1c) that informs the user what file should be e-mailed back to the dentist locator Web site.

   The macros and VBA procedure described above are saved with the template file so that they can be used anytime the template is open or when a document based on the template is displayed in the Word window. Figure 8-2 shows the VBA code for these macros.

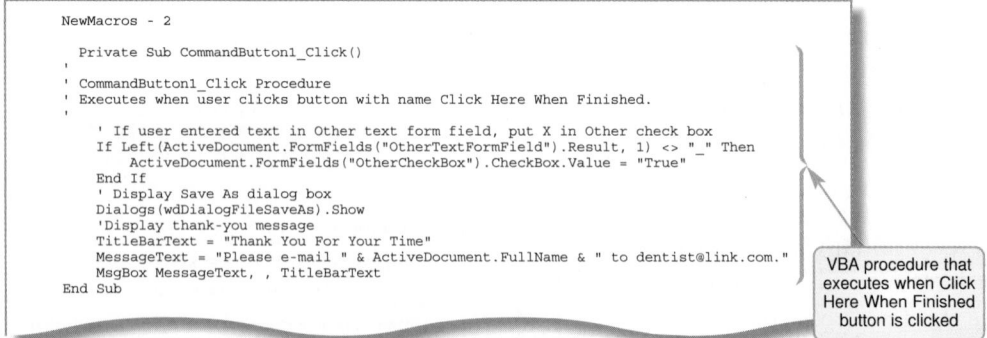

```
NewMacros - 2

 Private Sub CommandButton1_Click()
'
' CommandButton1_Click Procedure
' Executes when user clicks button with name Click Here When Finished.
'
    ' If user entered text in Other text form field, put X in Other check box
    If Left(ActiveDocument.FormFields("OtherTextFormField").Result, 1) <> "_" Then
        ActiveDocument.FormFields("OtherCheckBox").CheckBox.Value = "True"
    End If
    ' Display Save As dialog box
    Dialogs(wdDialogFileSaveAs).Show
    'Display thank-you message
    TitleBarText = "Thank You For Your Time"
    MessageText = "Please e-mail " & ActiveDocument.FullName & " to dentist@link.com."
    MsgBox MessageText, , TitleBarText
End Sub
```

> VBA procedure that
> executes when Click
> Here When Finished
> button is clicked

FIGURE 8-2

Starting and Customizing Word

To start and customize Word, Windows must be running. If you are stepping through this project on a computer and you want your screen to match the figures in this book, then you should change your computer's resolution to 800 × 600 and reset the toolbars and menus. For information about changing the resolution and resetting toolbars and menus, read Appendix D.

The following steps describe how to start Word and customize the Word window. You may need to ask your instructor how to start Word for your system.

To Start and Customize Word

1 Click the Start button on the Windows taskbar, point to All Programs on the Start menu, point to Microsoft Office on the All Programs submenu, and then click Microsoft Office Word 2003 on the Microsoft Office submenu.

2 If the Word window is not maximized, double-click its title bar to maximize it.

3 If the Language bar appears, right-click it and then click Close the Language bar on the shortcut menu.

4 If the Getting Started task pane is displayed in the Word window, click its Close button.

5 If the Standard and Formatting toolbar buttons are displayed on one row, click the Toolbar Options button and then click Show Buttons on Two Rows in the Toolbar Options list.

6 Click View on the menu bar and then click Print Layout.

Word starts and, after a few moments, displays an empty document in the Word window. This project uses floating graphics. Thus, the Word window is in print layout view. The Print Layout View button on the horizontal scroll bar is selected.

More About

Online Forms

For a sample online form on the Web, visit the Word 2003 More About Web page (scsite.com/wd2003/more) and then click Sample Online Form.

Opening a Word Template

The first step in this project is to open the template for the online form that was created in Project 7 so that you can modify it. (If you did not create the template, see your instructor for a copy.) The following steps describe how to open the A+ Dentist Locator template file.

To Open a Word Template

1 With the disk containing the A+ Dentist Locator template file in drive A, click the Open button on the Standard toolbar.

2 When Word displays the Open dialog box, if necessary, click the Look in box arrow and then click 3½ Floppy (A:). Click the Files of type box arrow and then click Document Templates.

3 Double-click the template, A+ Dentist Locator.

4 After Word opens the form, scroll down so the entire form is displayed in the Word window.

The online form titled, A+ Dentist Locator, is displayed in the Word window.

Saving the Document with a New File Name

To preserve the contents of the original A+ Dentist Locator template file created in Project 7, save a copy of it with a new file name as described below.

To Save a Document with a New File Name

1 With a floppy disk in drive A, click File on the menu bar and then click Save As.

2 When Word displays the Save As dialog box, type A+ Dentist Locator Revised in the File name box. Do not press the ENTER key.

3 If necessary, click the Save as type box arrow and then click Document Template.

4 If necessary, click the Save in box arrow and then click 3½ Floppy (A:).

5 Click the Save button in the Save As dialog box.

Word saves the document on a floppy disk in drive A with the new file name, A+ Dentist Locator Revised (shown in Figure 8-3).

Unprotecting a Document

The A+ Dentist Locator Revised template file is protected. Recall that Project 7 showed how to protect the form so users could enter data only in designated areas — specifically, the form fields that were enabled. Before this form can be modified, it must be unprotected, as shown in the following steps.

To Unprotect a Document

1

• Click Tools on the menu bar (Figure 8-3).

FIGURE 8-3

2

- **Click Unprotect Document on the Tools menu.**

Word unprotects the A+ Dentist Locator Revised file and displays the Protect Document task pane on the screen (Figure 8-4).

3

- **Click the Close button on the Protect Document task pane title bar.**

FIGURE 8-4

Other Ways

1. Click Protect Form button on Forms toolbar

With the template unprotected, you can change its contents. Later in this project, after you have completed the modifications, you will protect the document again — using the Protect Document task pane instead of the Forms toolbar.

Setting a Security Level in Word

A **computer virus** is a potentially damaging computer program designed to affect, or infect, your computer negatively by altering the way it works without your knowledge or permission. Currently, more than 80,000 known computer viruses exist and an estimated 6 new viruses are discovered each day. The increased use of networks, the Internet, and e-mail has accelerated the spread of computer viruses.

To combat this evil, most computer users run antivirus programs that search for viruses and destroy them before they ever have a chance to infect the computer. Macros are a known carrier of viruses, because of the ease with which a person can write code for a macro. For this reason, you can reduce the chance your computer will be infected with a macro virus by setting a **security level** in Word. These security levels allow users to enable or disable macros. An **enabled macro** is a macro that Word will execute, and a **disabled macro** is a macro that is unavailable to Word. Table 8-1 summarizes the four available security levels in Word.

More About

Viruses

For more information about viruses, visit the Word 2003 More About Web page (scsite.com/wd2003/more) and then click Viruses.

Table 8-1	Word Security Levels
SECURITY LEVEL	**CONDITION**
Very High	Word will execute only macros installed in trusted locations. All other macros, even those digitally signed, are disabled when the user opens the document.
High	Word will execute only macros that are digitally signed from trusted sources. All other macros are disabled when the user opens the document.
Medium	Upon opening a document that contains macros from an unknown source, Word displays a dialog box asking the user if he or she wishes to enable the macros.
Low	Word turns off macro virus protection. The document is opened with all macros enabled, including those from unknown sources.

If Word security is set to very high or high and you attach a macro to a document, Word will disable that macro when a user opens the document. This project shows how to create macros. Thus, the security level is set to medium. With a medium security level, each time a user opens this project or any document that contains a macro from an unknown source, Word displays a dialog box warning that a macro(s) is attached and allows the user to enable or disable the macros. If you are confident of the source (author) of the document and macros, click the Enable Macros button in the dialog box. If you are uncertain about the reliability of the source of the document and macros, click the Disable Macros button.

The following steps show how to set Word's security level to medium.

To Set a Security Level in Word

1

• **Click Tools on the menu bar and then point to Macro (Figure 8-5).**

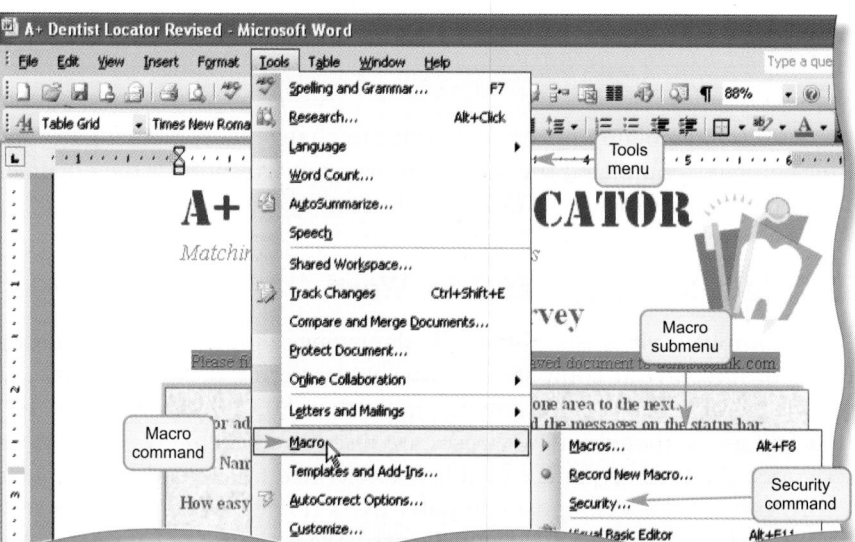

FIGURE 8-5

2

• **Click Security on the Macro submenu.**

• **When Word displays the Security dialog box, if necessary, click the Security Level tab.**

• **Click Medium.**

Word displays the Security dialog box (Figure 8-6). The Medium option button is selected.

3

• **Click the OK button.**

Word sets its security level to medium.

FIGURE 8-6

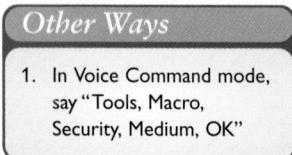

Other Ways

1. In Voice Command mode, say "Tools, Macro, Security, Medium, OK"

The next time you open a document that contains a macro from an unauthorized source, Word will ask if you wish to enable or disable the macro. In this project, you click the Enable Macros button.

Displaying Formatting Marks

It is helpful to display formatting marks that indicate where in the document you pressed the ENTER key, SPACEBAR, and other keys. The following step describes how to display formatting marks.

To Display Formatting Marks

1 If the Show/Hide ¶ button on the Standard toolbar is not selected already, click it.

Word displays formatting marks in the document window, and the Show/Hide ¶ button on the Standard toolbar is selected (shown in Figure 8-7 on the next page).

Zooming Page Width

When you zoom page width, Word displays the page on the screen as large as possible in print layout view. The following steps zoom page width.

To Zoom Page Width

1 Click the Zoom box arrow on the Standard toolbar.

2 Click Page Width in the Zoom list.

Word computes the zoom percentage and displays it in the Zoom box (shown in Figure 8-7). Your percentage may be different depending on your computer.

Modifying a Form

As suggested by your instructor, you will change the look of the Patient Survey. You will modify the fonts, font and highlight colors, font sizes, and alignment of the text on the form. Then, you will change the graphic and the fill color and shadow effects on the rectangle drawing object. The following pages discuss how to make these changes to the online form.

Formatting Text

The next step in modifying the Patient Survey is to delete the current clip art image and change the formats of the company name, business tag line, form name, and form instructions. The steps on the next page describe these changes.

More About

Macro Viruses

If Word's security level is set to low, Word does not warn you that a file contains a macro, thus leaving your computer open for infection from macro viruses. A macro virus is a type of computer virus that is stored in a macro within a file, template, or add-in. If Word's security level is set to medium, Word warns you before opening a document containing a macro. For the best protection against macro viruses, purchase and install specialized antivirus software.

For more information about using antivirus software, visit the Word 2003 More About Web page (scsite.com/wd2003/more) and then click Antivirus Software.

To Format Text

1 Click the clip art image of the tooth and then press the DELETE key to delete the graphic.

2 Select the first line of text, A+ Dentist Locator. Click the Font box arrow on the Formatting toolbar. Scroll to and then click Berlin Sans FB Demi (or a similar font). Click the Center button on the Formatting toolbar. Click the Font Color button arrow on the Formatting toolbar and then click Dark Red on the color palette. Press SHIFT+F3 to format the text as all capital letters.

3 Select the second line of text, which contains the business tag line: Matching Patients to Qualified Dentists. Click the Font box arrow on the Formatting toolbar. Scroll to and then click Lucida Handwriting (or a similar font). Click the Font Size box arrow on the Formatting toolbar and then click 12. Click the Center button on the Formatting toolbar. Click the Font Color button arrow on the Formatting toolbar and then click Dark Blue on the color palette.

4 Select the third line of text, which contains the form name, Patient Survey. Click the Font box arrow on the Formatting toolbar. Scroll to and then click Rockwell (or a similar font). Click the Font Color button arrow on the Formatting toolbar and then click Dark Red on the color palette.

5 Press the DOWN ARROW key to position the insertion point on the blank line between the form name and the user instructions. Press the DELETE key to delete the blank line.

6 Select the user instructions that currently are highlighted in bright green. Click the Font box arrow on the Formatting toolbar. Scroll to and then click Franklin Gothic Medium Cond (or a similar font). Click the Highlight button arrow on the Formatting toolbar and then click Dark Blue on the color palette. Click the Font Color button arrow on the Formatting toolbar and then click Tan on the color palette. Click anywhere in the document to remove the selection.

Word displays the company name, business tag line, form name, and form instructions as shown in Figure 8-7.

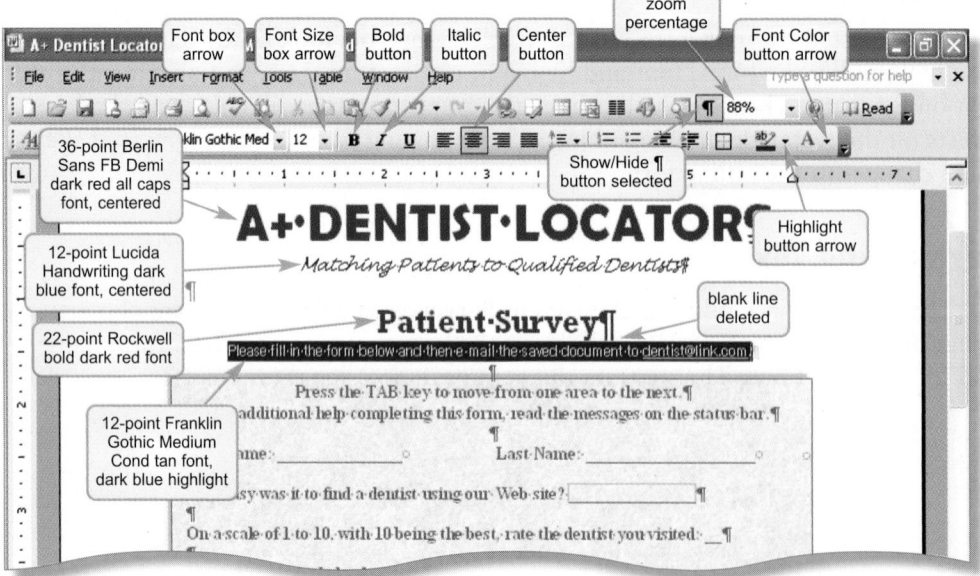

FIGURE 8-7

Cropping Graphics

The next step is to insert a graphic that shows a tooth, dental floss, and a toothbrush that is different from the tooth graphic used in Project 7. The new clip art image is on the Web. If you do not have access to the Web, you can insert the graphic from a file on the Data Disk that accompanies this book.

Note: The following steps assume your computer is connected to the Internet. If it is not, go directly to the shaded steps on this page.

To Insert Clip Art

1. Click Insert on the menu bar, point to Picture, and then click Clip Art. In the Clip Art task pane, if necessary, click the Results should be box arrow and then place a check mark in the All media types check box.

2. In the Clip Art task pane, drag through any text in the Search for text box to select the text. Type toothbrush and then press the ENTER key. If necessary, scroll through the clips until the one shown in Figure 8-8 on the next page appears.

3. Click the clip to be inserted. Click the Close button on the Clip Art task pane title bar.

Word inserts the clip art image in the document (shown in Figure 8-8). Word may insert your graphic in a different location.

If you do not have access to the Web, you can insert the clip art file in the Word document from the Data Disk, as described in the following steps. If you did not download the Data Disk, see the inside back cover for instructions for downloading the Data Disk or see your instructor.

To Insert a Graphic File from the Data Disk

1. Click Insert on the menu bar, point to Picture, and then click From File.

2. Insert the Data Disk into drive A. When Word displays the Insert Picture dialog box, click the Look in box arrow and then click 3½ Floppy (A:). Click the file name, j0213331[1], and then click the Insert button.

Word inserts the clip in your document (shown in Figure 8-8).

The next step is to change the clip art image from an inline graphic to a floating graphic. You want the graphic to have a square run-around, or space around it. Thus, you change the wrapping style to square, as described next.

To Format a Graphic with a Square Wrapping Style

1. Click the graphic to select it. If the Picture toolbar is not displayed on the screen, click View on the menu bar, point to Toolbars, and then click Picture.

2. Click the Text Wrapping button on the Picture toolbar (Figure 8-8).

3. Click Square in the list.

Word formats the graphic as a floating object with a square wrapping style.

More About

Clip Art on the Web

In the Clip Art task pane, the globe icon in the lower-left corner of a thumbnail indicates the clip art is located on the Web.

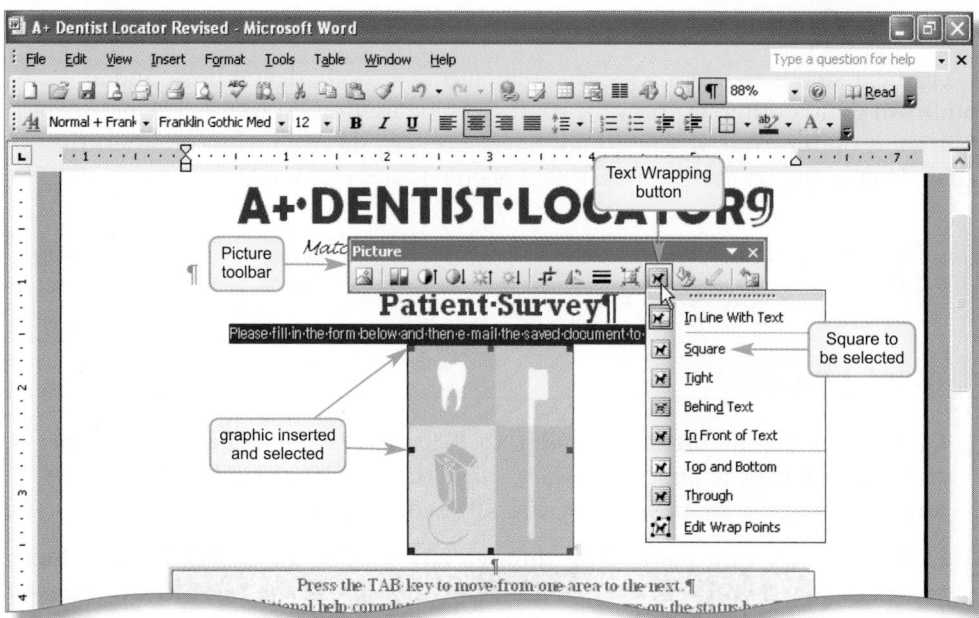

FIGURE 8-8

With the graphic formatted as floating, the text wraps around it. In its current location, the user instructions and the form instructions wrap around the graphic. When the graphic is moved to its new location, the user instructions and the form instructions will return to their correct position.

In this project, the left half of the graphic is to be displayed at the left edge of the Patient Survey, and the right half of the graphic is to be displayed at the right edge of the Patient Survey (shown in Figure 8-1a on page WD 555). In Word, you can cut out, or **crop**, a horizontal or vertical section of a graphic.

Usually, you want to crop to a precise location. Thus, you should instruct Word not to use the drawing grid, as described in the next set of steps.

To Not Use the Drawing Grid

1. **If the Drawing toolbar is not displayed in the Word window, click the Drawing button on the Standard toolbar.**

2. **Click the Draw button on the Drawing toolbar (shown in Figure 8-9) and then click Grid on the Draw menu.**

3. **When Word displays the Drawing Grid dialog box, if necessary, remove the check mark from the Snap objects to grid check box.**

4. **Click the OK button.**

Word will not use the drawing grid when you crop the graphic.

The next step is to crop the left half of the graphic, resize the cropped graphic, place a blue dashed border around it, and then position it on the left side of the form. You then will repeat this process with the right half of the graphic. That is, you will insert the graphic, crop the right half of it, resize it, border it, and then position this graphic on the right side of the form.

The following steps show how to crop a graphic.

To Crop a Graphic

1

• **Click the Crop button on the Picture toolbar.**

*Word attaches a cropping tool to the mouse pointer, and the graphic's sizing handles change to cropping handles (Figure 8-9). To crop the graphic, you drag a **cropping handle**. When you position the cropping tool on a cropping handle, the mouse pointer shape changes to a sideways capital letter T.*

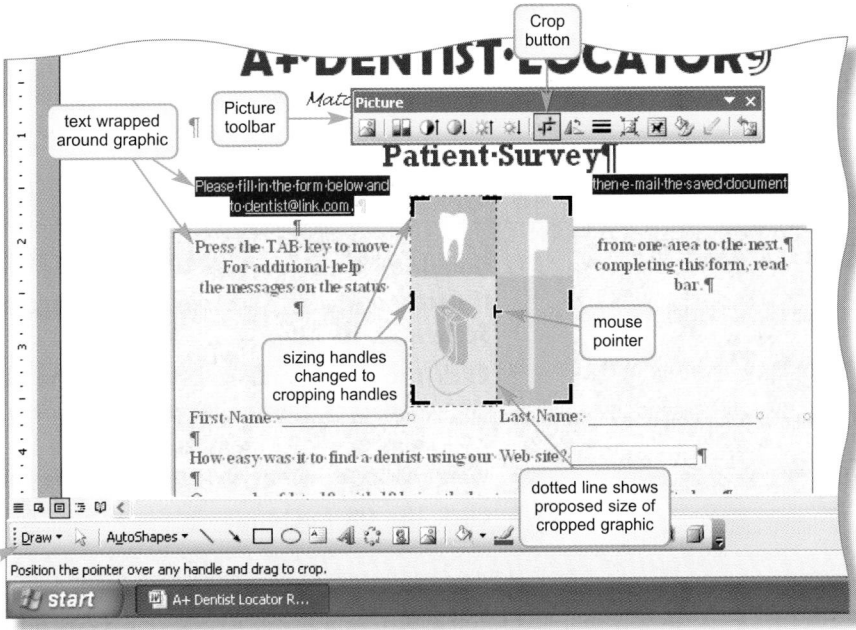

FIGURE 8-9

2

• **Drag the right-middle cropping handle leftward to the location of the mouse pointer shown in Figure 8-9.**

3

• **Release the mouse button.**

Word crops the graphic (Figure 8-10). The Crop button on the Picture toolbar remains selected.

4

• **Click the Crop button on the Picture toolbar again.**

Word deactivates the cropping tool. The cropping handles on the graphic change to sizing handles.

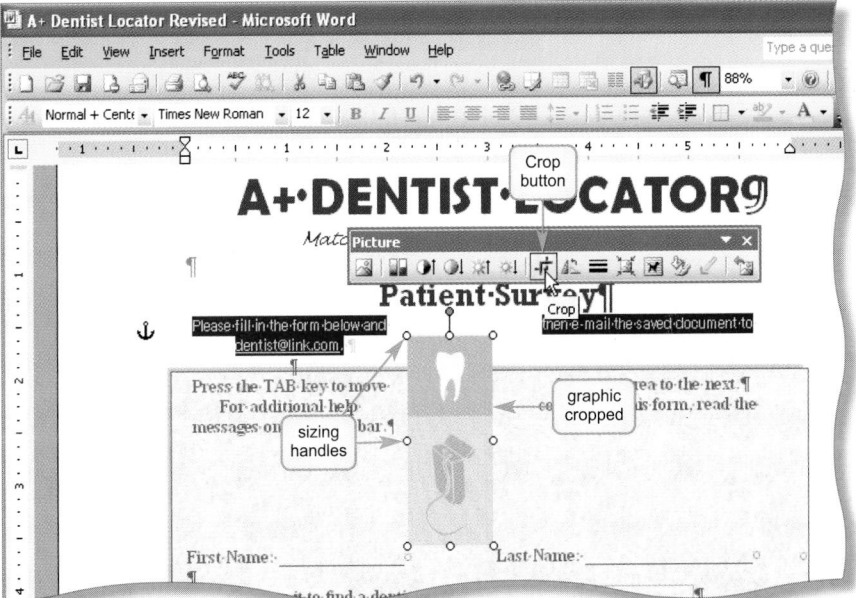

FIGURE 8-10

If you wanted to crop equally on two sides of a graphic at the same time, hold down the CTRL key while dragging a middle cropping handle inward. To crop equally on all four sides of a graphic, hold down the CTRL key while dragging a corner cropping handle inward.

The next step is to reduce the size of the graphic and add a border around it, as described in the following steps.

To Format a Graphic

1 **Double-click the graphic. When Word displays the Format Picture dialog box, if necessary, click the Size tab. Change the height and width values in the Scale area to 72%.**

2 **Click the Colors and Lines tab. In the Line area, click the Color box arrow and then click Dark Blue on the color palette. Click the Dashed box arrow and then click the next to last style in the list (long dash dot). Click the Weight box down arrow until the Weight box displays 0.25 pt (Figure 8-11).**

3 **Click the OK button.**

Word reduces the size of the graphic and places a dark blue .25-point dashed line around it (shown in Figure 8-12).

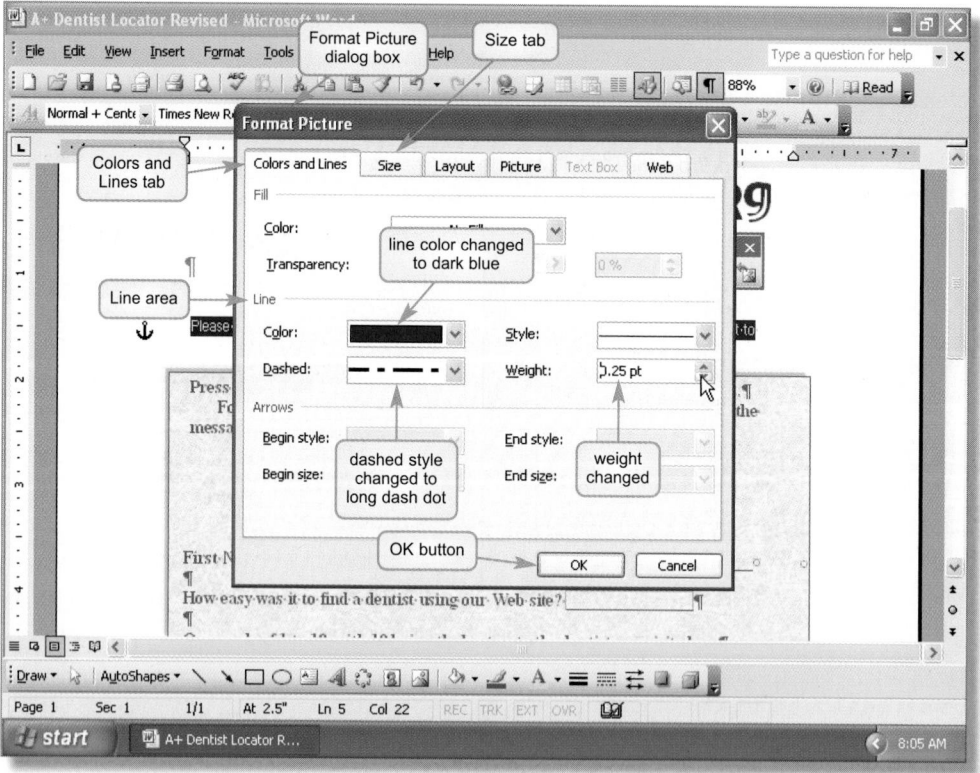

FIGURE 8-11

With the graphic formatted, the final step is to position the graphic in its proper location.

To Position a Graphic

1 **Drag the graphic so it is positioned as shown in Figure 8-12.**

The graphic is positioned as shown in Figure 8-12.

The next step is to insert the same clip art image, crop the right half (the toothbrush), format it the same as the first image, and position it on the right side of the form, as described below.

To Crop and Format a Graphic

1 **Click Insert on the menu bar, point to Picture, and then click Clip Art. In the Clip Art task pane, drag through any text in the Search for text box to select the text. Type** toothbrush **and then press the ENTER key. If necessary, scroll through the clips until the one shown in Figure 8-8 on page WD 564 appears. Click the clip to be inserted. Click the Close button on the Clip Art task pane title bar. (If you do not have access to the Web, you can insert the clip art file in the Word document from the Data Disk, as described in the steps on page WD 563).**

2 **Click the graphic to select it. If the Picture toolbar is not displayed on the screen, click View on the menu bar, point to Toolbars, and then click Picture. Click the Text Wrapping button on the Picture toolbar and then click Square in the list.**

3 **Click the Crop button on the Picture toolbar. Drag the left-middle cropping handle rightward until just the toothbrush is marked to be cropped. Release the mouse button. Click the Crop button on the picture toolbar again.**

4 **Double-click the graphic. When Word displays the Format Picture dialog box, if necessary, click the Size tab. Change the height and width values in the Scale area to 72%. Click the Colors and Lines tab. In the Line area, click the Color box arrow and then click Dark Blue on the color palette. Click the Dashed box arrow and then click the next to last style in the list (long dash dot). Click the Weight box down arrow until the Weight box displays 0.25 pt. Click the OK button.**

5 **Drag the graphic so it is positioned as shown in Figure 8-12.**

6 **Click outside the graphic to deselect it. If necessary, drag the scroll box on the vertical scroll bar to display the entire form in the document window.**

Both graphics have been cropped, resized, and positioned as shown in Figure 8-12.

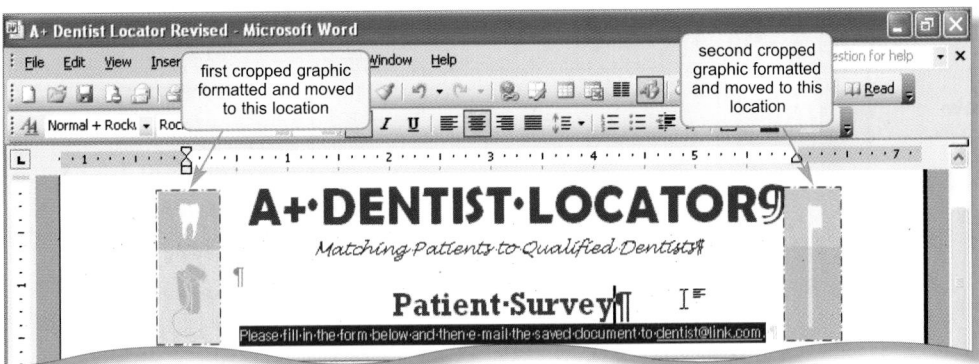

FIGURE 8-12

You may need to drag the graphics a couple of times to position them exactly as shown in Figure 8-12 on the previous page. If you feel the formatting marks clutter the screen while you try to position the graphics, you can hide them by clicking the Show/Hide ¶ button on the Standard toolbar. Then, redisplay the formatting marks by clicking the Show/Hide ¶ button again.

Creating a New Style with a Shortcut Key

You decide that all text in the data entry area should be formatted to 11-point Century Gothic bold dark red font. You could select each text item in the data entry area, one at a time, and change its font to Century Gothic, its font size to 11, its font style to bold, and its font color to dark red. A timesaving alternative, however, is to use a style. A **style** is a customized format that you apply to text. Although Word has many built-in styles, none of them is an 11-point Century Gothic bold dark red font. You can create your own new style, however, and then apply this style to the text in the data entry area of the form.

Word has two types of styles: character and paragraph. A **character style** defines attributes for text, such as font, font size, font style, and font color. A **paragraph style** defines formatting for a paragraph, such as line spacing, text alignment, bullet styles, and borders. Paragraph styles can include a character style definition. In the data entry area of this form, you want to change text to 11-point Century Gothic bold dark red font. Thus, you will create a character style.

A **shortcut key** is one or more keys you press on the keyboard to complete a task. Rather than selecting the newly created character style from a long list, you can use a shortcut key to apply the new style. In Word, you can assign the shortcut keys to commands that are not associated with a shortcut key already, remove shortcut keys that you do not use, or return to the default shortcut key settings at anytime.

The following steps illustrate how to create a new character style, called DataEntryArea, which formats selected text to 11-point Century Gothic bold dark red font. The steps also show how to assign the shortcut, ALT+D, to the new character style.

To Create a Style Associated with a Shortcut Key

1

- **Click the Styles and Formatting button on the Formatting toolbar.**
- **When Word displays the Styles and Formatting task pane, click the New Style button.**
- **When Word displays the New Style dialog box, type** DataEntryArea **in the Name text box.**
- **Click the Style type box arrow and then click Character.**

Word changes the style type to Character in the New Style dialog box (Figure 8-13). The list of formats in your Styles and Formatting task pane may be different.

FIGURE 8-13

2

- **In the Formatting area, click the Font box arrow and then click Century Gothic, click the Font Size box arrow and then click 11, click the Bold button (if necessary), click the Font Color button arrow and then click Dark Red on the color palette.**
- **Click the Format button.**

Word displays the font, font size, font styles, and font color settings and then displays a list of available formatting commands above or below the Format button (Figure 8-14). Some commands are dimmed because they relate to paragraph styles.

FIGURE 8-14

3

- **Click Shortcut key on the Format button menu.**
- **When Word displays the Customize Keyboard dialog box, press ALT+D.**
- **If necessary, click the Save changes in box arrow and then click A+ Dentist Locator Revised.**

Word displays the Customize Keyboard dialog box (Figure 8-15). The keys you pressed, ALT+D, appear in the Press new shortcut key text box. The Description area shows the characteristics of the style being assigned to the shortcut key.

4

- **Click the Assign button.**
- **Click the Close button to close the Customize Keyboard dialog box.**
- **Click the OK button in the New Style dialog box.**
- **Click the Close button on the Styles and Formatting task pane title bar.**

Word creates the DataEntryArea style and assigns it to the shortcut key, ALT+D.

FIGURE 8-15

To apply a character style, select the text to be formatted and then apply the style. To apply a paragraph style, you do not need to select text before applying the style — simply click in the paragraph to be formatted and then apply the style.

In the previous steps, you created a shortcut key of ALT+D for the DataEntryArea style. Instead of using the Style box on the Formatting toolbar to apply the style to text in the data entry area of the Patient Survey, you will use the shortcut key. The following step shows how to apply a style using a shortcut key.

To Apply a Style Using a Shortcut Key

1

• **If necessary, scroll to display the entire form in the document window.**

• **Drag through all of the text in the rectangle drawing object to select the text.**

• **Press ALT+D.**

The selected text in the rectangle now is formatted with the new style; that is, 11-point Century Gothic bold dark red font (Figure 8-16).

2

• **Click outside the selected text to remove the selection.**

FIGURE 8-16

After seeing the dark red font color of the text in the rectangle, you decide it would look better in dark blue. Instead of selecting the text and changing its font color, you simply can modify the DataEntryArea style to be a dark blue font. As soon as you modify the DataEntryArea style, all text in the document based on that style automatically will change to the new format.

The next steps show how to modify a style.

To Modify a Style

1

• **Click the Styles and Formatting button on the Formatting toolbar.**

• **When Word displays the Styles and Formatting task pane, if necessary scroll through the list of styles until DataEntryArea appears in the list.**

• **Right-click DataEntryArea in the list.**

Word displays the Styles and Formatting task pane (Figure 8-17). You modify or delete a style using commands in the list that appear when you right-click the style name.

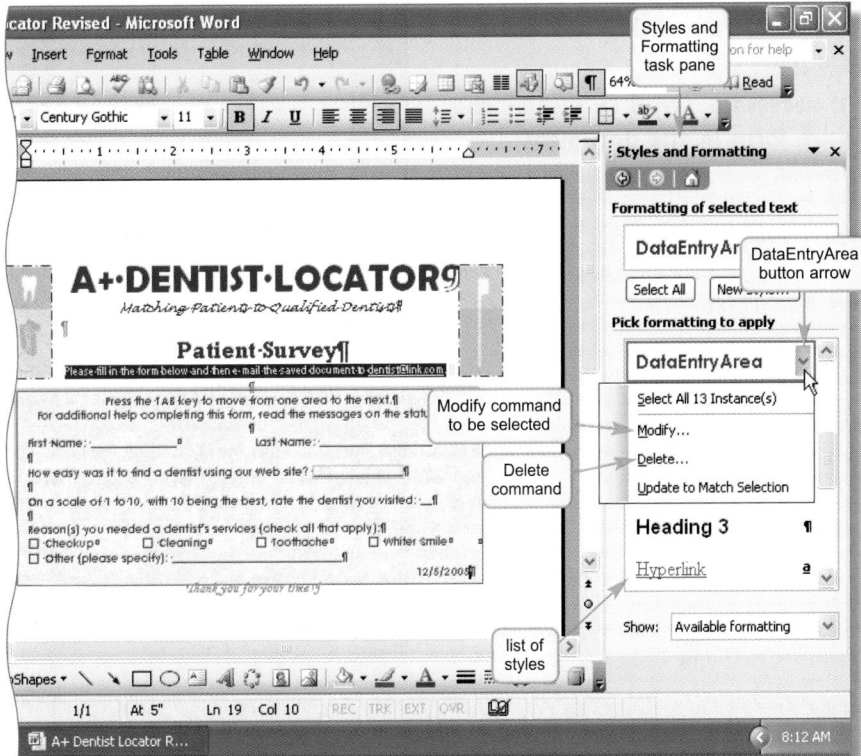

FIGURE 8-17

2

• **Click Modify in the list.**

• **When Word displays the Modify Style dialog box, click the Font Color button arrow and then click Dark Blue on the color palette.**

Word changes the style font color to dark blue (Figure 8-18).

FIGURE 8-18

3

- Click the **OK** button.
- Click the **Close** button on the Styles and Formatting task pane title bar.
- If necessary, scroll to display the entire form in the document window.

Word changes the font color of the text formatted with the DataEntryArea style to dark blue (Figure 8-19).

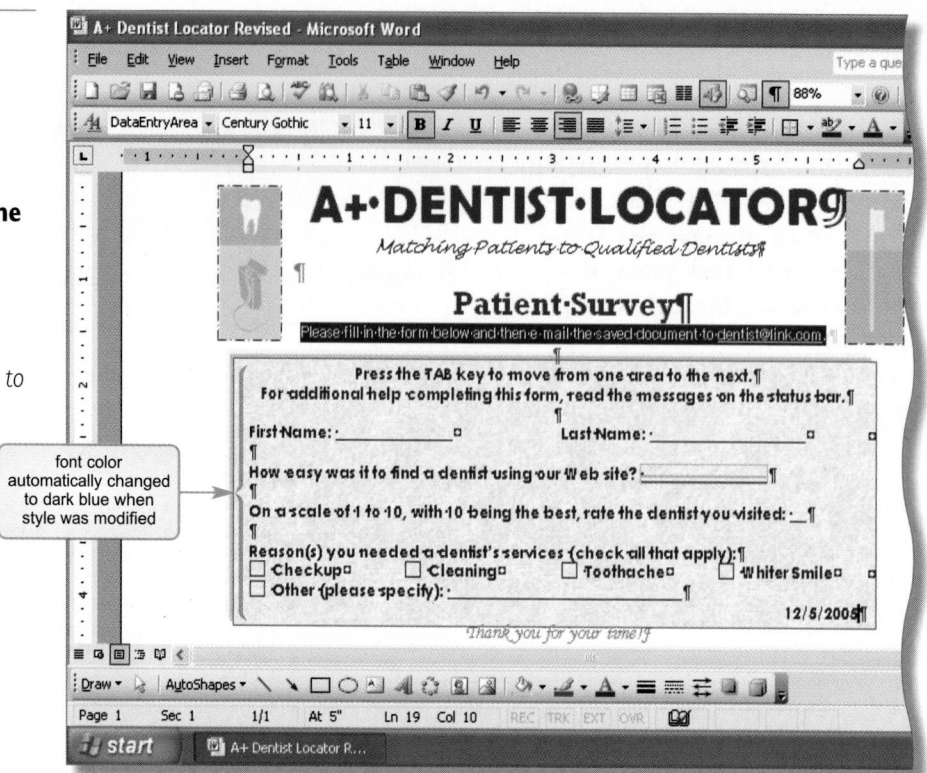

FIGURE 8-19

If you wanted to delete a style, you would right-click the style name in the Styles and Formatting task pane and then click Delete in the list (Figure 8-17 on the previous page). As an alternative to modifying a style using the Modify Style dialog box, you can modify one word of the style in the document, right-click the style name in the Styles and Formatting task pane, and then click Update to Match Selection in the list.

Filling a Drawing Object with a Preset Effect

A rectangle drawing object surrounds the data entry area in the form. Currently, the rectangle drawing object is filled with a texture. Other available fill effects include colors, patterns, and pictures. This project uses a preset color scheme fill effect in the rectangle drawing object.

The next steps show how to fill the rectangle drawing object with a preset color scheme fill effect.

To Fill a Drawing Object with a Preset Color Scheme Fill Effect

1

• **Select the rectangle by pointing to one of its edges and then clicking when the mouse pointer has a four-headed arrow attached to it.**

• **If the Drawing toolbar is not displayed on your screen, click the Drawing button on the Standard toolbar.**

• **Click the Fill Color button arrow on the Drawing toolbar and then click the Fill Effects button.**

• **When Word displays the Fill Effects dialog box, if necessary, click the Gradient tab.**

• **In the Colors area, click Preset.**

• **Click the Preset colors box arrow, scroll to and then click Parchment.**

The Sample area in the Fill Effects dialog box shows the Parchment preset color scheme (Figure 8-20).

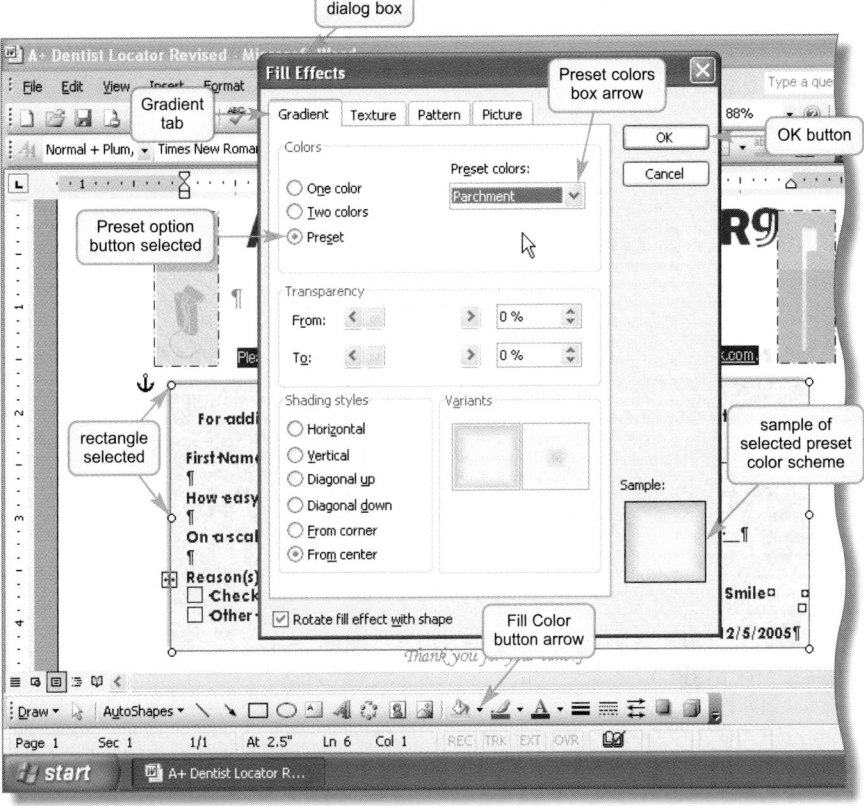

FIGURE 8-20

2

• **Click the OK button.**

Word fills the rectangle with the Parchment preset color scheme (Figure 8-21).

Other Ways

1. Right-click edge of drawing object, click Format AutoShape on shortcut menu, click Colors and Lines tab, click Color box arrow in Fill area, click Fill Effects button, click Gradient tab
2. Select drawing object, click AutoShape on Format menu, click Colors and Lines tab, click Color box arrow in Fill area, click Fill Effects button, click Gradient tab
3. In Voice command mode, say "Format, AutoShape"

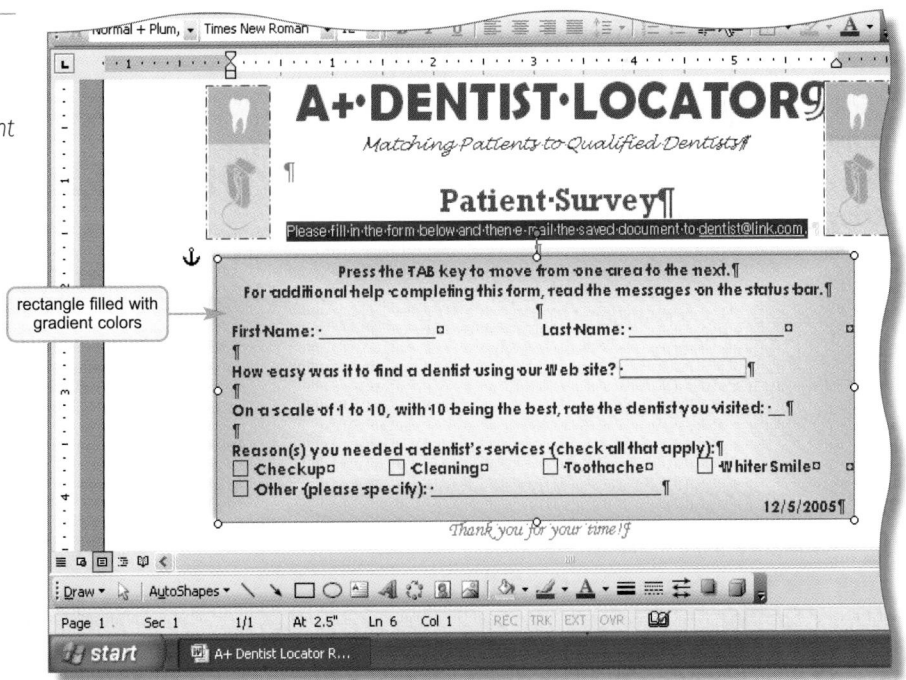

FIGURE 8-21

Adding a 3-D Effect to a Drawing Object

You can add a 3-D effect to a drawing object by using the 3-D Style button on the Drawing toolbar. Adding a 3-D effect changes the depth of the drawing object, its shadow color, the angle, the direction of lighting, and the surface reflection. When you add a 3-D effect, Word removes any previously applied shadow.

The following steps show how to add a 3-D effect to the rectangle drawing object that surrounds the data entry area of the Patient Survey.

To Add a 3-D Effect and Modify Its Settings

• **With the rectangle still selected, click the 3-D Style button on the Drawing toolbar.**

Word displays a list of 3-D styles (Figure 8-22).

2

• **Click 3-D Style 1.**

Word adds the 3-D Style 1 effect to the rectangle drawing object. The top shadow of the 3-D effect is too dark.

FIGURE 8-22

• **Click the 3-D Style button on the Drawing toolbar again.**

• **Click the 3-D Settings button in the list.**

• **When Word displays the 3-D Settings toolbar, click the Lighting button.**

Word displays the lighting options for the selected 3-D effect (Figure 8-23). To soften the shadow at the top of the 3-D effect, you will select the top-left lighting angle.

4

• **Click the top-left light in the list.**

• **Click the Close button on the 3-D Settings toolbar.**

Word adjusts the lighting of the 3-D effect (shown in Figure 8-24).

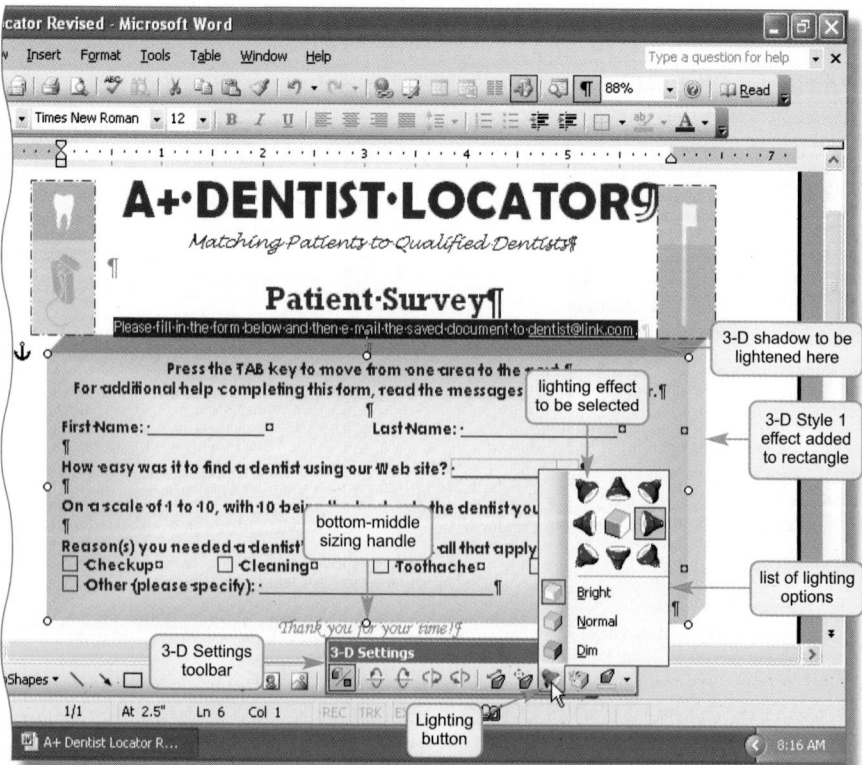

FIGURE 8-23

The final steps in modifying the form are to delete the thank-you message below the rectangle, resize the rectangle, and add a blank line above it, as described in the following steps.

To Finish Modifying the Form

1 Select the line below the data entry area that contains the thank-you message and then press the DELETE key.

2 Click the Drawing button on the Standard toolbar to remove the Drawing toolbar from the screen.

3 Point to an edge of the rectangle and click when the mouse pointer has a four-headed arrow attached to it. Drag the bottom-middle sizing handle on the rectangle (shown in Figure 8-23) up slightly so the bottom of the rectangle is immediately below the date.

4 Position the insertion point on the blank line between the user instructions and data entry area. Press the ENTER key to insert a blank line.

5 Scroll as necessary to display the entire form in the document window.

The online form appears as shown in Figure 8-24.

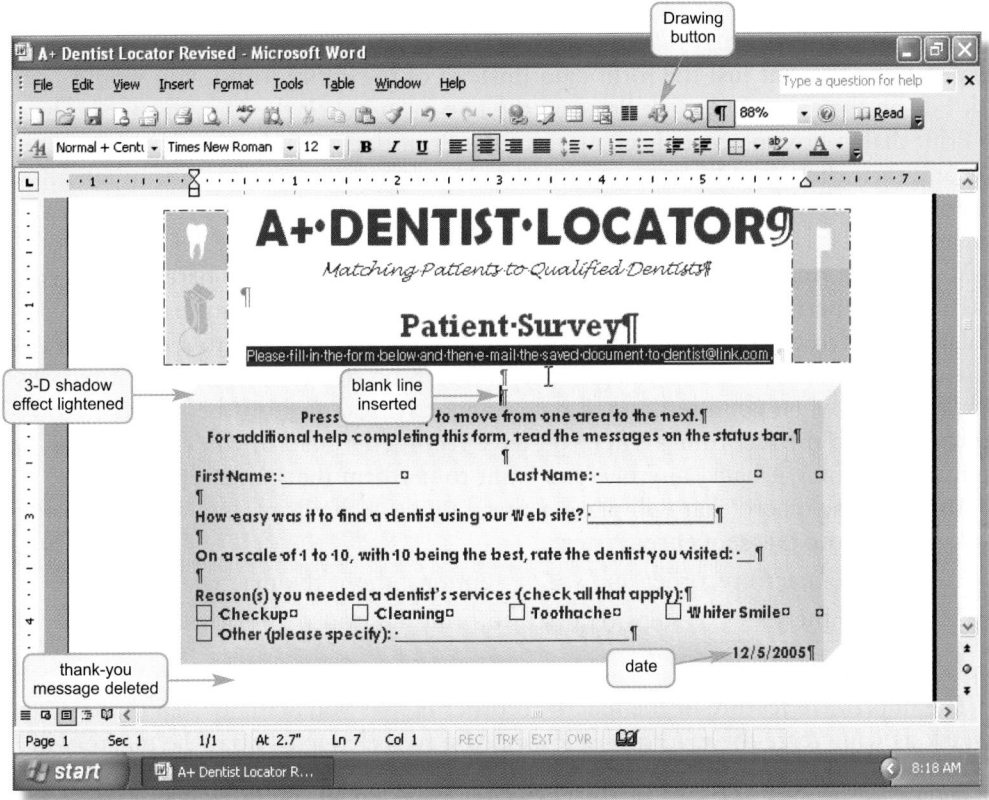

FIGURE 8-24

It is prudent to save the form again because many formatting tasks have been performed thus far.

To Save a Document

1 **Click the Save button on the Standard toolbar.**

Word saves the A+ Dentist Locator Revised template on a floppy disk in drive A.

Using a Macro to Automate a Task

As previously discussed, a macro consists of a series of Word commands or instructions that are grouped together as a single command. This single command is a convenient way to automate a difficult or lengthy task. Macros often are used for formatting or editing activities, to combine multiple commands into a single command, or to select an option in a dialog box with a single keystroke.

To create a macro, you can use the macro recorder or the Visual Basic Editor. The following pages illustrate how to use the macro recorder to create a macro. In a later section, this project discusses how to use the Visual Basic Editor to create a macro.

Recording and Executing a Macro

The purpose of the first macro you create in this project is to select an option in a dialog box. To print just the form data (instead of the entire form), you would click File on the menu bar, click Print on the File menu, click the Options button in the Print dialog box, place a check mark in the Print data only for forms check box, and then click the OK button in each dialog box. Instead of going through all these steps to print form data, this project shows how to create a macro to automate this task.

Word has a **macro recorder** that automatically creates a macro based on a series of actions you perform while the macro recorder is recording. The macro recorder is similar to a video camera in that it records all actions you perform to a document while the macro recorder is running. Once you turn on the macro recorder, it records your activities; when you are finished recording activities, turn off the macro recorder to stop the recording. After you have recorded a macro, you can **execute the macro**, or play it back, anytime you want to perform that same set of actions.

To create the macro that will place a check mark in the Print data only for forms check box, follow this sequence of steps:

1. Start the macro recorder and specify options about the macro.
2. Execute the series of steps required to print data only for forms.
3. Stop the macro recorder.

The impressive feature of the macro recorder is that you actually step through the task as you create the macro — allowing you to see exactly what the macro will do before you use it.

When you first create a macro, you have to name it. The name for this macro will be PrintFormData. **Macro names** can be up to 255 characters long; they can contain numbers, letters, and underscores; and they cannot contain spaces or other punctuation.

Earlier in this project, you assigned a shortcut key to a style. Likewise, you can assign a shortcut key to a macro. This allows you to run the macro by using its name or by pressing the shortcut key. The following steps show how to record the macro and assign ALT+P as its shortcut key.

To Record a Macro and Assign It a Shortcut Key

1

• **Double-click the REC status indicator on the status bar.**

• **When Word displays the Record Macro dialog box, type** `PrintFormData` **in the Macro name text box.**

• **If necessary, click the Store macro in box arrow and then click Documents Based On A+ Dentist Locator Revised.**

• **Select the text in the Description text box and then type** `Prints only the data on a form.`

The recorded macro will be saved with the document template, instead of the Normal template (Figure 8-25). Macros saved in the Normal template are available to all future documents; macros saved with the document template are available only with the document.

FIGURE 8-25

2

• **Click the Keyboard button.**

• **When Word displays the Customize Keyboard dialog box, press ALT+P.**

Word displays the Customize Keyboard dialog box (Figure 8-26). The characters you pressed, ALT+P, appear in the Press new shortcut key text box.

FIGURE 8-26

Microsoft Office
Word 2003

3

• **Click the Assign button.**

• **Click the Close button in the Customize Keyboard dialog box.**

Word assigns the shortcut key, ALT+P, to the PrintFormData macro, closes the Customize Keyboard and Record Macro dialog boxes, darkens the REC status indicator on the status bar, and then displays the Stop Recording toolbar in the document window (Figure 8-27). When you are finished recording the macro, you will click the Stop Recording button on the Stop Recording toolbar. The mouse pointer appears with a tape icon to remind you that you are recording. Any task you do will be part of the macro.

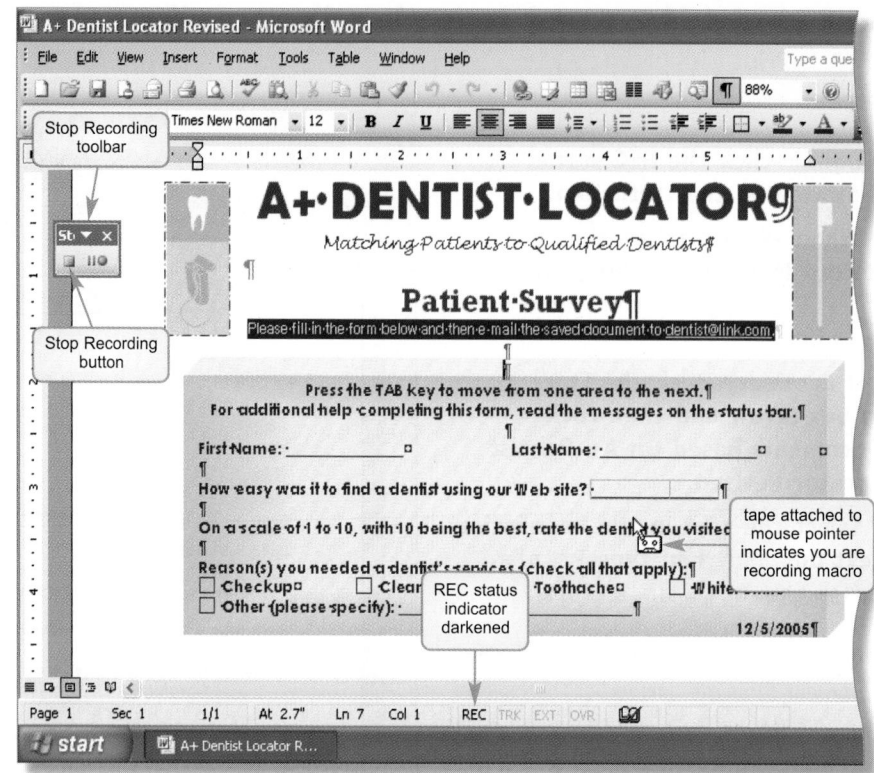

FIGURE 8-27

4

• **Click File on the menu bar.**

When you are recording a macro and the mouse pointer is in a menu or pointing to a toolbar button, the tape icon does not appear with the pointer (Figure 8-28).

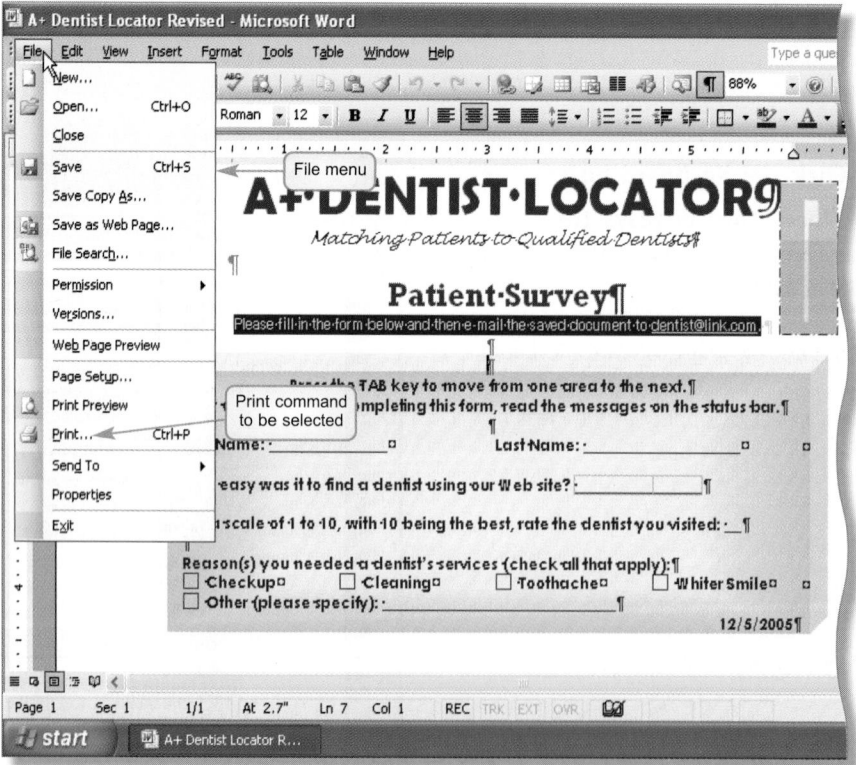

FIGURE 8-28

5

- **Click Print on the File menu.**

- **When Word displays the Print dialog box, click the Options button.**

- **When Word displays the second Print dialog box, place a check mark in the Print data only for forms check box.**

The Print dialog box displays as shown in Figure 8-29.

FIGURE 8-29

6

- **Click the OK button in each dialog box.**

Word closes the dialog boxes (Figure 8-30). The document prints.

7

- **Click the Stop Recording button on the Stop Recording toolbar.**

Word stops recording the keystrokes, closes the Stop Recording toolbar, and dims the REC status indicator on the status bar.

Other Ways

1. On Tools menu point to Macro, click Record New Macro, enter macro name, click Keyboard button, press shortcut keys, click Assign button, click Close button, record macro, click Stop Recording button on Stop Recording toolbar
2. In Voice command mode, say "Tools, Macro, Record New Macro"

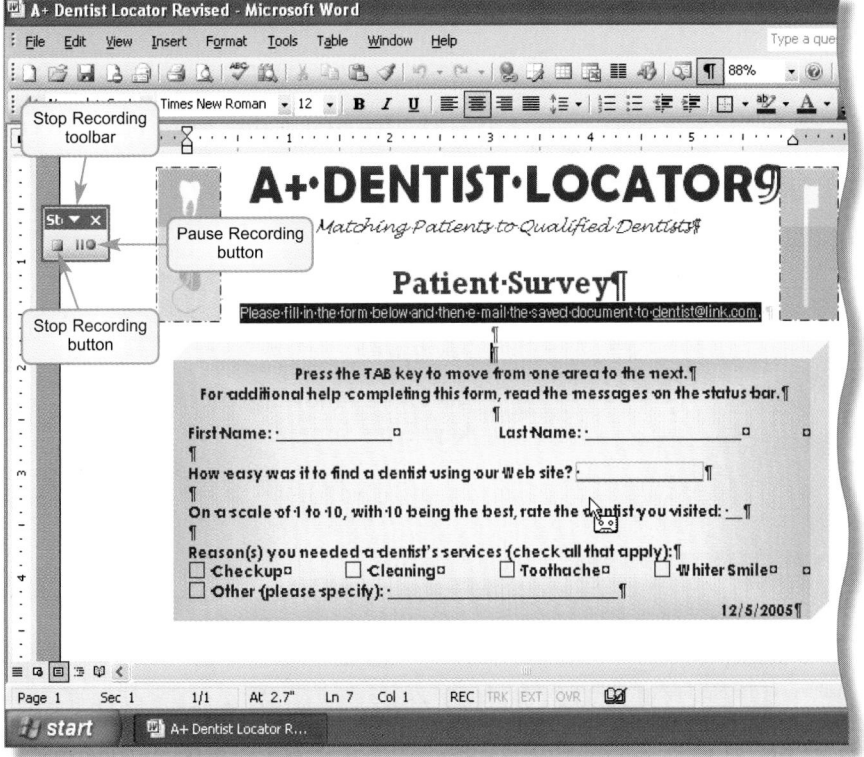

FIGURE 8-30

The macro has stored every command, button, and option clicked during the recording of the macro. If you record the wrong actions, delete the macro and record it again. You delete a macro by clicking Tools on the menu bar, pointing to Macro on the Tools menu, and then clicking Macros on the Macro submenu. When Word displays the Macro dialog box, click the name of the macro (PrintFormData), click the Delete button, and then click the Yes button. Finally, record the macro again.

If, while recording a macro, you want to perform some actions that should not be part of the macro, click the Pause Recording button on the Stop Recording toolbar (Figure 8-30 on the previous page) to suspend the macro recorder. The Pause Recording button changes to a Resume Recorder button that you click when you want to continue recording.

In the Record Macro dialog box (Figure 8-25 on WD 577), the location to store the macro was selected in the Store macro in box. If you wanted a macro to be available to all documents you create that are based on the Normal template, you would select All Documents (Normal.dot) in the Store macro in list. Most macros created with the macro recorder, however, are document specific, and thus are stored in the current template or document.

The next step is to execute, or run, the macro to ensure that it works. This macro prints form data. Thus, you need to protect the form and fill it in before running the macro, as described in the following steps.

To Protect and Fill In a Form

1. **If formatting marks are displayed on the screen, click the Show/Hide ¶ button on the Standard toolbar.**

2. **If the Forms toolbar is not displayed in the Word window, click View on the menu bar, point to Toolbars, and then click Forms.**

3. **Click the Protect Form button on the Forms toolbar.**

4. **With the First Name form field selected, type** Rick **and then press the TAB key.**

5. **Type** Schultz **in the Last Name form field.**

6. **Press the TAB key to select the ease of use form field. Click the box arrow and then click Very Easy in the list.**

7. **Press the TAB key and then type** 9 **in the rating scale form field. Press the TAB key.**

8. **Click the following check boxes: Checkup, Cleaning, and Other. Press the TAB key. Type** Sore Gums **in the Other text form field.**

The form is filled in (Figure 8-31).

More About

Storing Macros

Word, by default, stores macros in the Normal template. If you plan to use a macro in multiple documents, you should store it in the Normal template. If the macro is designed for a specific document, it is more efficient to store it with that document.

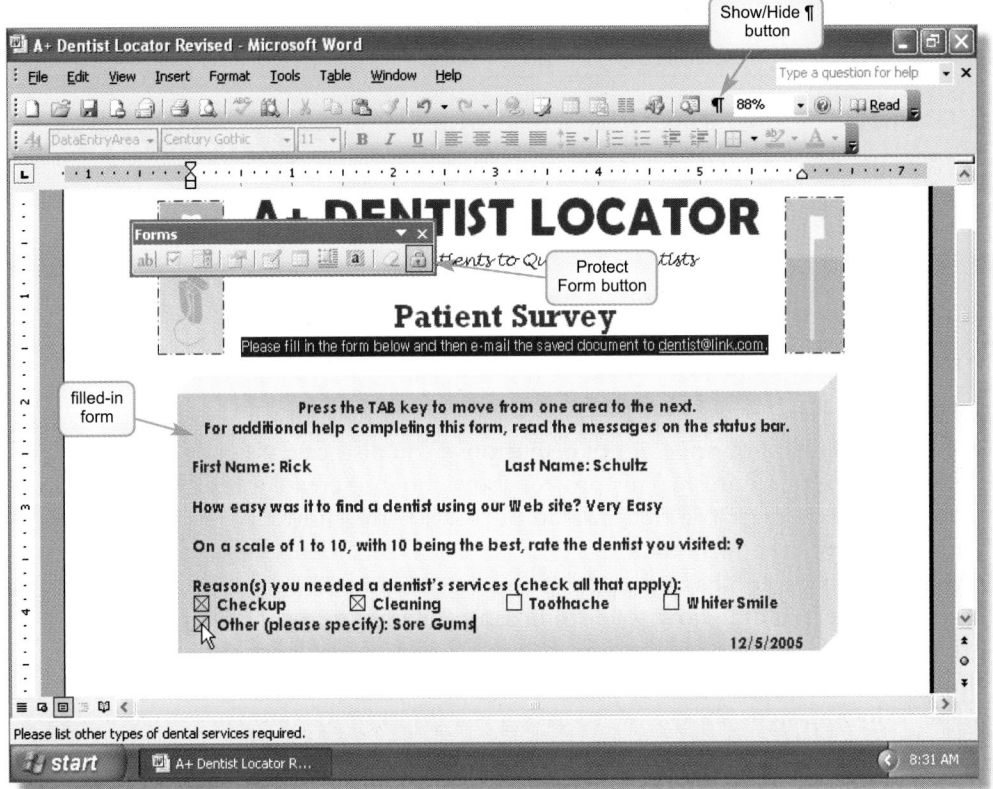

FIGURE 8-31

The following step describes how to run the PrintFormData macro using the shortcut key, ALT+P.

To Run a Macro

1

• **Press ALT+P.**

Word performs the instructions stored in the PrintFormData macro; that is, it prints a hard copy of the form data (Figure 8-32).

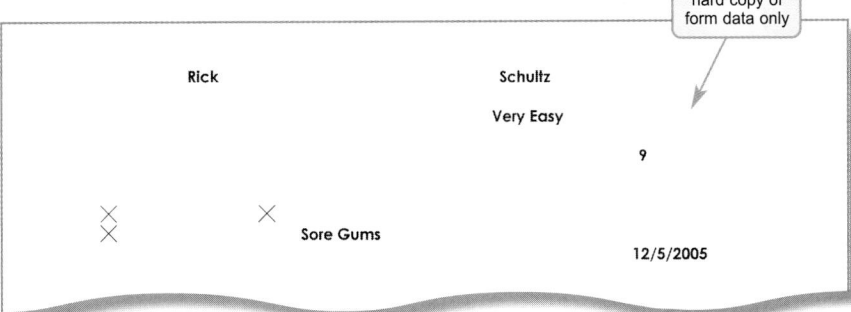

FIGURE 8-32

You are finished testing the macro and would like to continue working on the form for this project. Thus, you should unprotect the form, as described on the next page.

Other Ways

1. On Tools menu point to Macro, click Macros, click macro name in macro name list, click Run button
2. Press ALT+F8, click macro name in Macro name list, click Run button
3. Click Run Macro button on Standard toolbar in Visual Basic Editor
4. In Voice command mode, say, "Tools, Macro, Run"

To Unprotect a Document

1 **Click Tools on the menu bar and then click Unprotect Document.**

2 **Click the Close button on the Protect Document task pane title bar.**

3 **If necessary, scroll to display the entire form in the document window.**

Word unprotects the form.

Customizing Toolbars and Menus

Word allows you to customize toolbars by adding buttons, deleting buttons, and changing the function or appearance of buttons. You also can assign a command, such as a macro, to a button. This project shows how to create a toolbar button for the PrintFormData macro so that instead of pressing the shortcut keys, you can click the button to print the form data.

You customize a toolbar using the Customize command on the Tools menu. The key to understanding how to customize a toolbar is to recognize that when the Customize dialog box is displayed on the screen, Word's toolbars and menus are in Edit mode. **Edit mode** allows you to modify the toolbars and menus.

The following steps show how to assign the PrintFormData macro to a new button on the Standard toolbar and then change the button image.

To Add a Button to a Toolbar

1

• **Click Tools on the menu bar (Figure 8-33).**

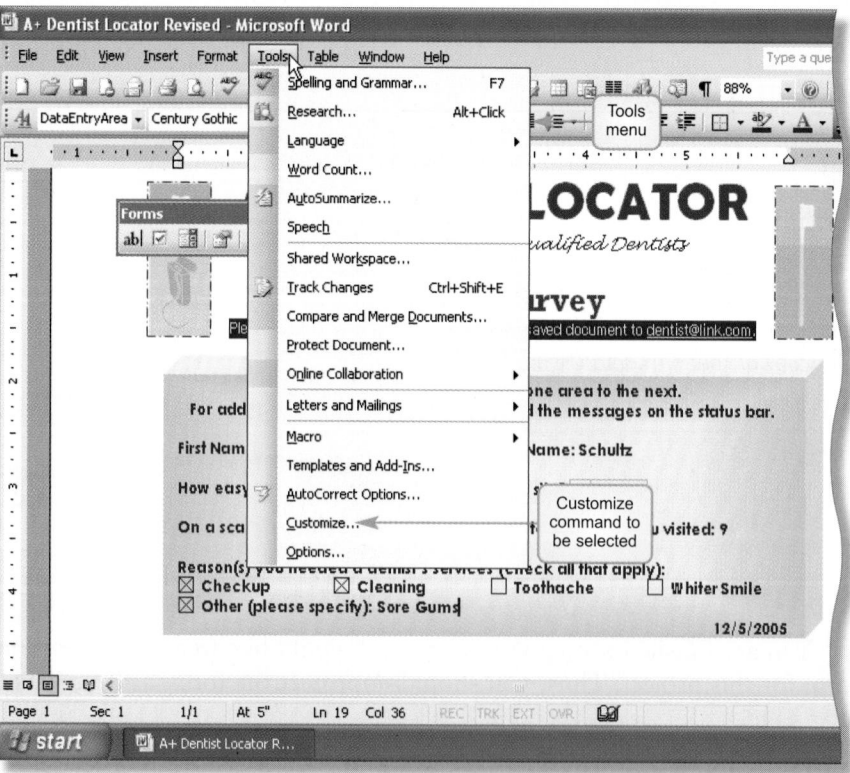

FIGURE 8-33

2

• **Click Customize on the Tools menu.**

• **When Word displays the Customize dialog box, if necessary, click the Commands tab.**

• **Scroll to and then click Macros in the Categories list.**

• **Click TemplateProject.NewMacros .PrintFormData in the Commands list.**

In the Commands sheet, you select the command to be added to a toolbar (Figure 8-34).

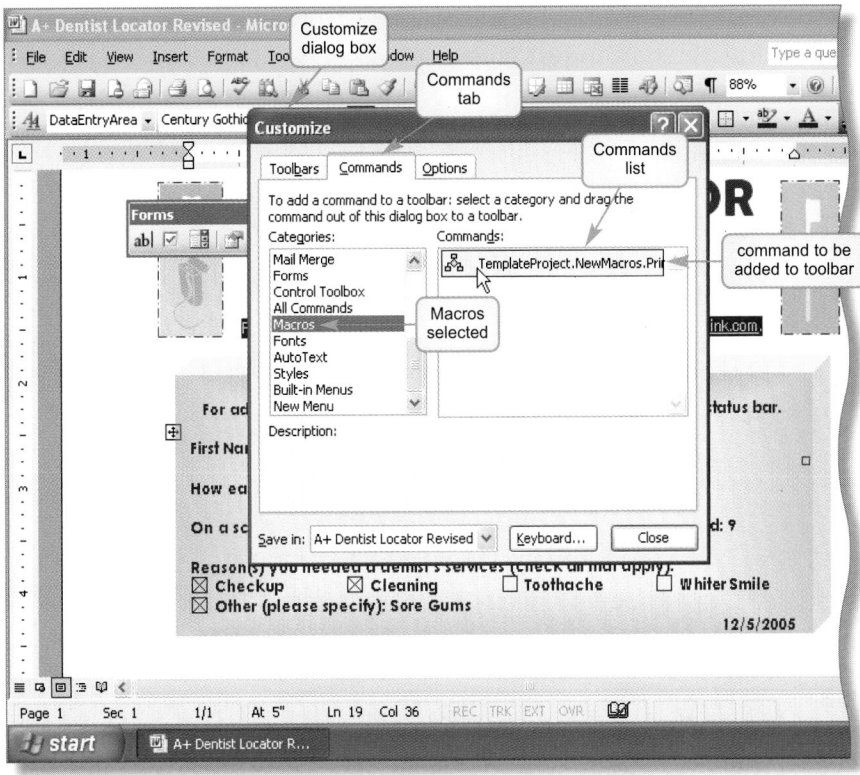

FIGURE 8-34

3

• **Drag the selected command in the Commands list to the Standard toolbar between the Print and Print Preview buttons.**

A button containing the text, TemplateProject.NewMacros.PrintFormData, appears to the right of the Print button on the Standard toolbar (Figure 8-35). A thick border surrounds the new button indicating Word is in Edit mode.

FIGURE 8-35

4

• **Right-click the button just added to the Standard toolbar and then point to Change Button Image on the shortcut menu.**

Word displays a palette of button images from which you can select (Figure 8-36).

FIGURE 8-36

5

• **In the palette of button images, click the button with the image of the text on pages.**

Word places the image to the left of the text on the button (Figure 8-37).

6

• **Right-click the button just added to the Standard toolbar.**

FIGURE 8-37

7

- **Click Text Only (in Menus).**

The text, TemplateProject.NewMacros .PrintFormData, no longer is displayed on the button (Figure 8-38).

8

- **Click the Close button in the Customize dialog box.**

Word quits Edit mode.

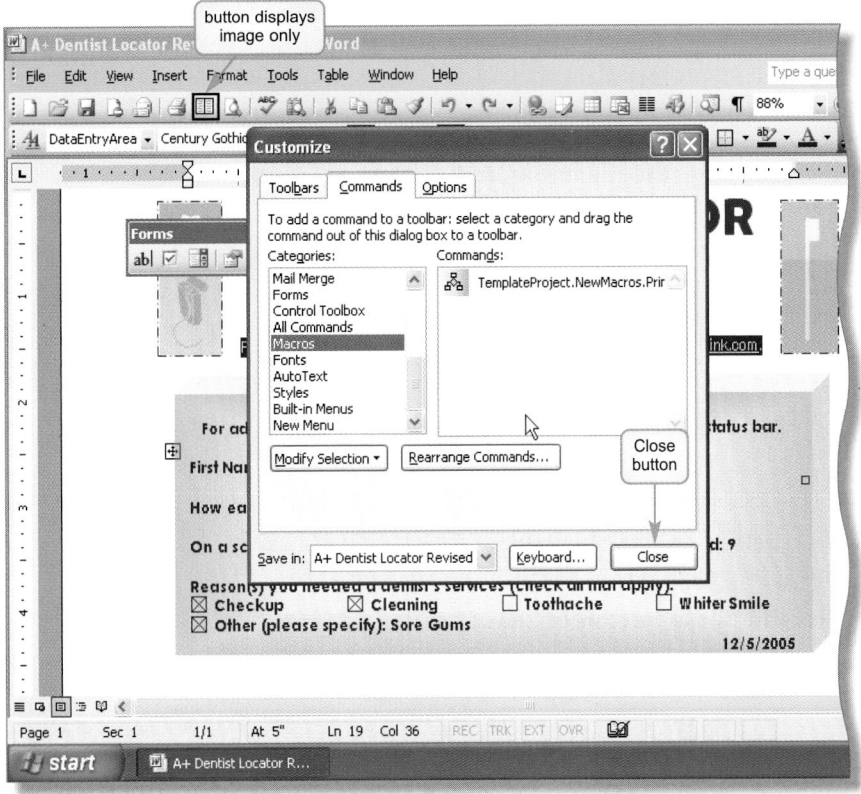

FIGURE 8-38

When you point to the button just added, Word displays the ScreenTip, Print Form Data. If you click the button, Word prints the form data only.

If you wanted to assign a Web address to a button so that when the user clicks the button, the associated Web page is displayed on the screen, you would right-click the button with the Customize dialog box displaying as shown in Figure 8-37, point to the Assign Hyperlink command on the shortcut menu, click Open, enter the Web address in the Assign Hyperlink dialog box, and then click the OK button.

You can add as many buttons as you want to a toolbar. As you add buttons, other buttons on the toolbar will be demoted to the More Buttons list.

Word allows you to change the image on any button or change an existing button's function. For example, when in Edit mode (the Customize dialog box is active), you can right-click the Save button on the Standard toolbar and assign it a command or a hyperlink. The next time you click the Save button, Word would execute the command or display the Web page associated with the hyperlink, instead of saving a document.

If you no longer use a button on a toolbar, you can delete it when in Edit mode, as shown in the steps on the next page.

Other Ways

1. On View menu point to Toolbars, click Customize, click Commands tab
2. Right-click toolbar, click Customize on shortcut menu, click Commands tab
3. In Voice command mode, say "View, Toolbars, Customize"

More About

Renaming Buttons and Menus

To rename a button or menu, click Tools on the menu bar, and then click Customize. In the Customize dialog box, click the Commands tab; click the button on the toolbar to be renamed or click the menu and then the command to be renamed; click the Modify Selection button; type a name in the Name text box, and then press the ENTER key; and then click the Close button in the dialog box. To rename a button, be sure the toolbar is displayed on the screen before beginning these steps.

To Delete a Button from a Toolbar

 1

• **Click Tools on the menu bar and then click Customize.**

• **Right-click the button to be deleted, in this case, the Print Form Data button.**

Word selects the button and displays an associated shortcut menu (Figure 8-39).

 2

• **Click Delete on the shortcut menu.**

• **Click the Close button in the Customize dialog box.**

Word deletes the Print Form Data button on the Standard toolbar (shown in Figure 8-40).

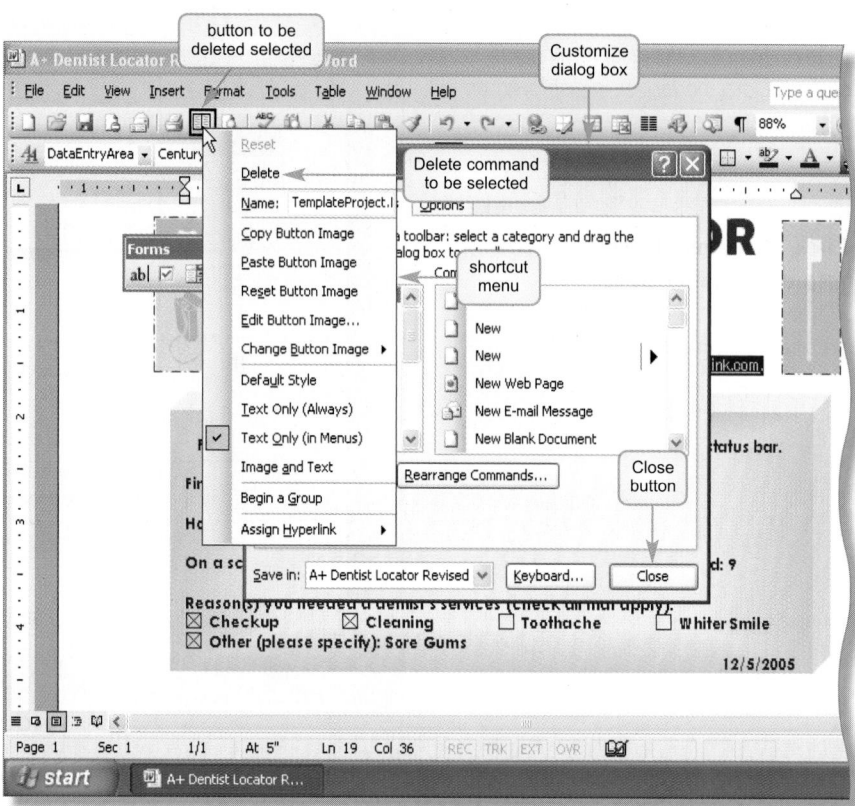

FIGURE 8-39

To reset the toolbars to their installation default, click the Toolbars tab in the Customize dialog box, select the toolbar name in the Toolbars list, and then click the Reset button. Each project in this book begins by resetting the toolbars because it is so easy to change the buttons on a toolbar.

In addition to customizing buttons and toolbars, Word allows you to customize menus. The procedure for customizing menus is very similar to customizing toolbars. The following steps describe how to add a command to a menu.

TO ADD A COMMAND TO A MENU

1. Click Tools on the menu bar and then click Customize.
2. Select the appropriate category in the Categories list.
3. Select the command name in the Commands list.
4. Drag the command to a menu name on the menu bar, and when the menu appears, drag the command to the desired location in the menu.

To change the name of a command, while in Edit mode, right-click the command, select the current name in the Name box on the shortcut menu, type a new name, and then press the ENTER key. To delete a command from a menu, while in Edit mode, right-click the command and then click Delete on the shortcut menu. For additional information about customizing menus and toolbars, see Appendix D.

To test the PrintFormData macro, you filled in the data entry form. To remove the sample data and return the fields to their default values, you use the Forms toolbar, as shown in the next step.

To Reset Form Fields

1

- **Click the Reset Form Fields button on the Forms toolbar.**

Word clears the values in the form fields and redisplays the fields with their defaults (Figure 8-40).

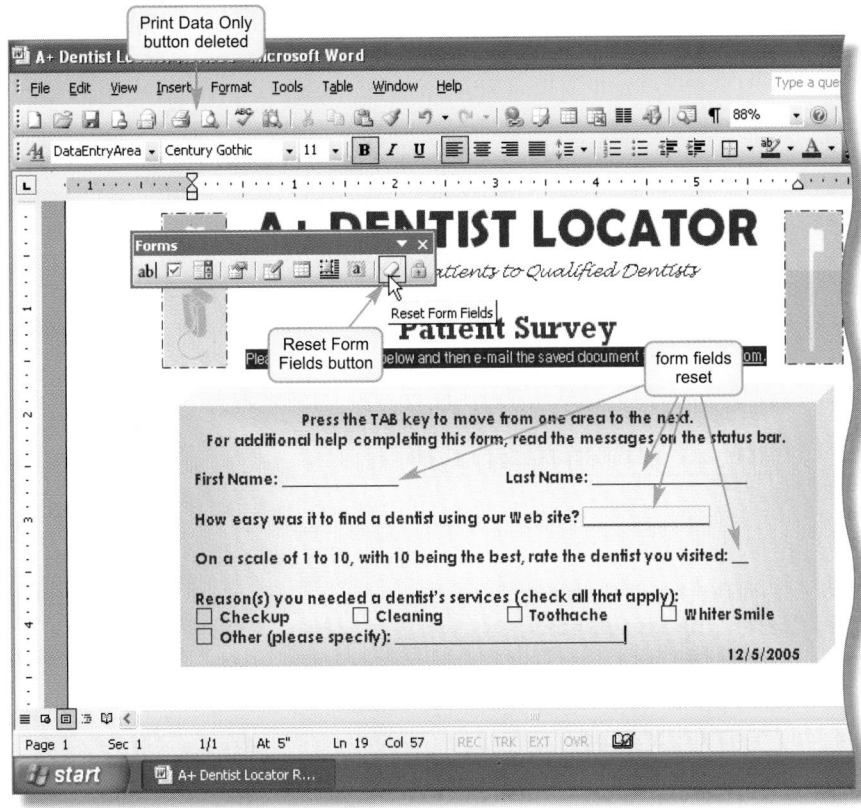

FIGURE 8-40

Recording an Automatic Macro

The previous section showed how to create a macro, assign it a unique name (PrintFormData), and then create a toolbar button that executed the macro. This section shows how to create an automatic macro. Word has five prenamed **automatic macros**, which execute automatically when a certain event occurs. Table 8-2 lists the name and function of these automatic macros.

Table 8-2 Automatic Macros	
MACRO NAME	**EVENT THAT CAUSES MACRO TO RUN**
AutoClose	Closing a document that contains the macro
AutoExec	Starting Word
AutoExit	Quitting Word
AutoNew	Creating a new document based on a template that contains the macro
AutoOpen	Opening a document that contains the macro

More About

Automatic Macros

A document can contain only one AutoClose, AutoNew, and AutoOpen macro. The AutoExec and AutoExit macro, however, are not stored with the document; instead, they must be stored in the Normal template. Thus, one AutoExec and only one AutoExit macro can exist for all Word documents.

The name you use for an automatic macro depends on when you want certain actions to occur. In this project, when a user creates a new Word document that is based on the A+ Dentist Locator Revised template, the online form should be displayed properly in the Word window. Thus, this project shows how to create an AutoNew macro.

The form is displayed properly when the zoom is set to page width. Thus, you will record the steps to zoom to page width. Also, the entire form should be displayed in the Word window so the user does not have to scroll to position the form. When you initially open the form in the Word window, the top of the form is displayed. To ensure the form is properly positioned, you drag the scroll box to the top of the vertical scroll bar and then click the scroll arrow at the bottom of the vertical scroll bar several times.

The following steps show how to create an AutoNew macro, using the macro recorder.

To Create an Automatic Macro

1

• **Double-click the REC status indicator on the status bar.**

• **When Word displays the Record Macro dialog box, type** AutoNew **in the Macro name text box.**

• **If necessary, click the Store macro in box arrow and then click Documents Based On A+ Dentist Locator Revised.**

• **Select the text in the Description text box and then type** Specifies how the form initially is displayed (as a blank form).

Word displays the Record Macro dialog box (Figure 8-41).

FIGURE 8-41

2

• **Click the OK button.**

Word closes the Record Macro dialog box and then displays the Stop Recording toolbar.

3

• **Click the Zoom box arrow on the Standard toolbar.**

Recall that when you are recording a macro and the mouse pointer is in a menu or pointing to a toolbar button, the tape icon does not display with the pointer (Figure 8-42).

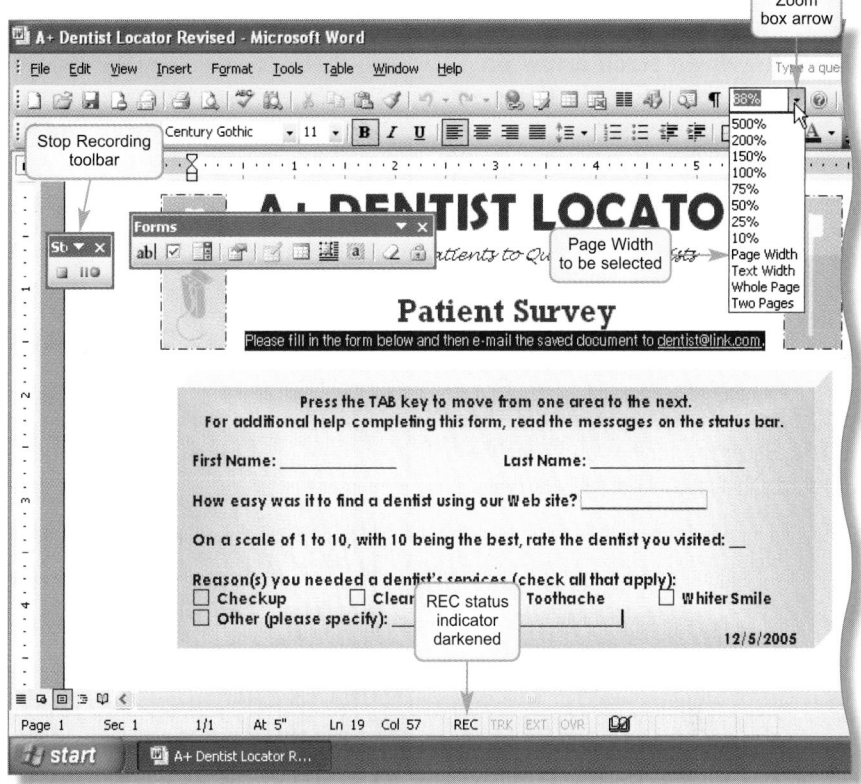

FIGURE 8-42

4

• **Click Page Width in the Zoom list.**

• **Drag the scroll box to the top of the vertical scroll bar.**

Word changes the zoom percentage and displays the top of the page in the document window (Figure 8-43).

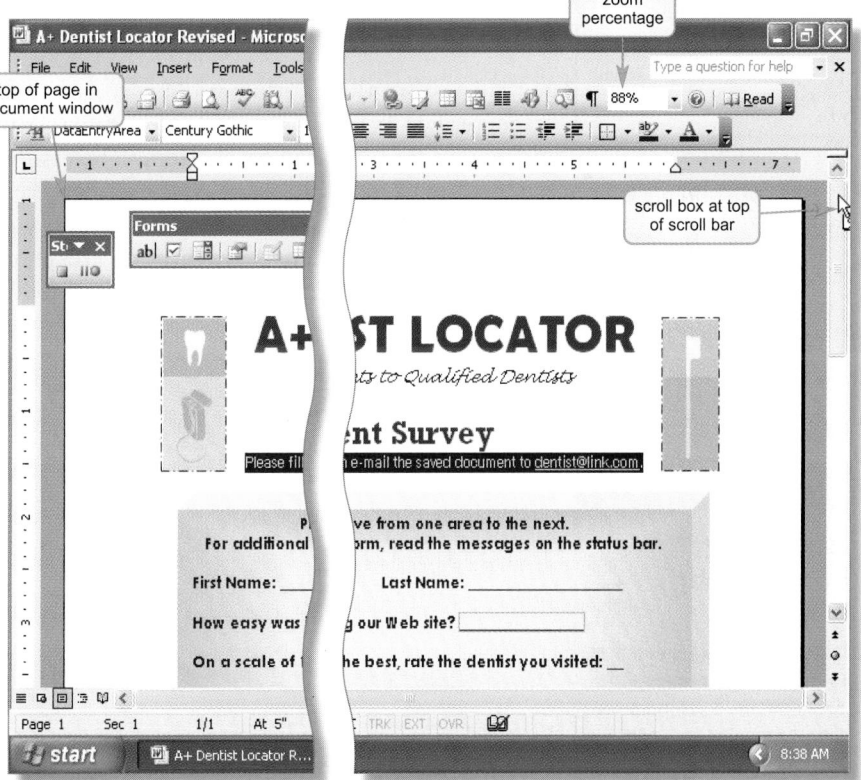

FIGURE 8-43

5

• **Click the down scroll arrow on the vertical scroll bar six times.**

The online form displays as shown in Figure 8-44.

6

• **Click the Stop Recording button on the Stop Recording toolbar.**

Word stops recording the keystrokes, closes the Stop Recording toolbar, and dims the REC status indicator on the status bar.

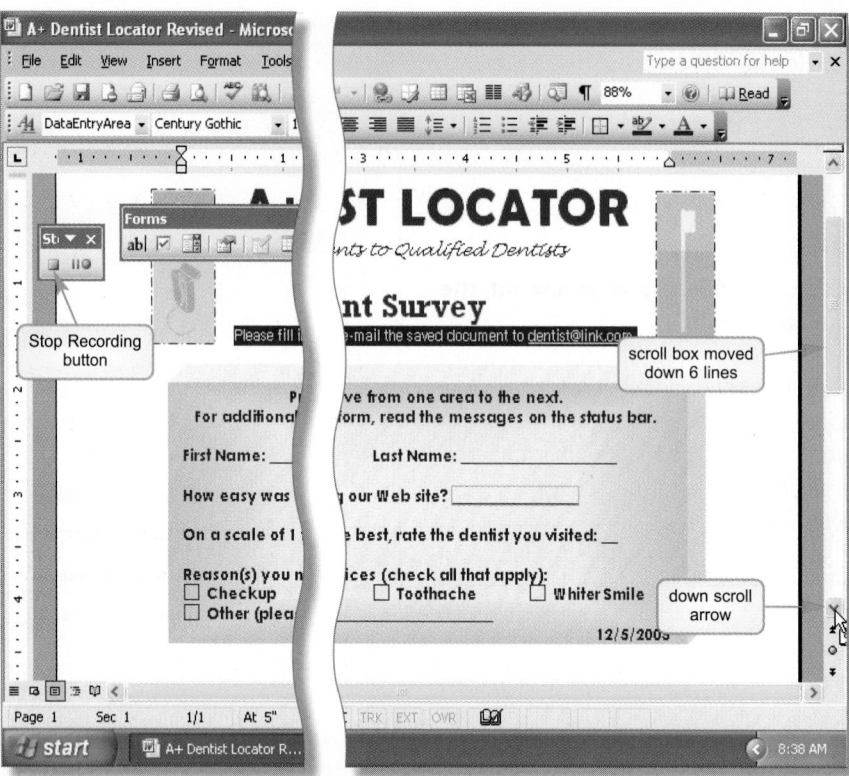

FIGURE 8-44

To test (run) the automatic macro, activate the event that causes the macro to execute. For example, the AutoNew macro runs whenever you create a new Word document that is based on the template. As discussed in Project 7, when you save a template to a disk in drive A, a user can create a Word document based on a template through the My Computer window or Windows Explorer.

The following steps show how to create a new Word document window that is based on the A+ Dentist Locator Revised template.

More About

Recording and Running Macros

If Word does not allow you to record or run a macro in a document, the document probably is marked as read-only. To record or run a macro in this document, save it with a new name using the Save As dialog box and then record or run the macro in the newly named document.

To Run the AutoNew Macro

1

- **Click the Save button on the Standard toolbar.**
- **Close the Forms toolbar.**
- **Click the Start button on the Windows taskbar, right-click My Computer on the Start menu, and then click Explore on the shortcut menu.**
- **When the Explorer window opens, if necessary, double-click its title bar to maximize the window.**
- **In the Folders list, click 3½ Floppy (A:).**

The Explorer window opens (Figure 8-45). Your list of files and folders will differ. Word still is running.

FIGURE 8-45

2

- **Double-click the A+ Dentist Locator Revised icon.**

Word opens a new document window that is based on the contents of the A+ Dentist Locator Revised template (Figure 8-46). The zoom is set to page width, and the screen scrolls down six lines as instructed by the AutoNew macro.

3

- **Click the Close button at the right edge of the Word title bar.**
- **If necessary, click the A+ Dentist Locator Revised - Microsoft Word program button on the taskbar.**

The new document window closes. The A+ Dentist Locator Revised template is displayed on the screen.

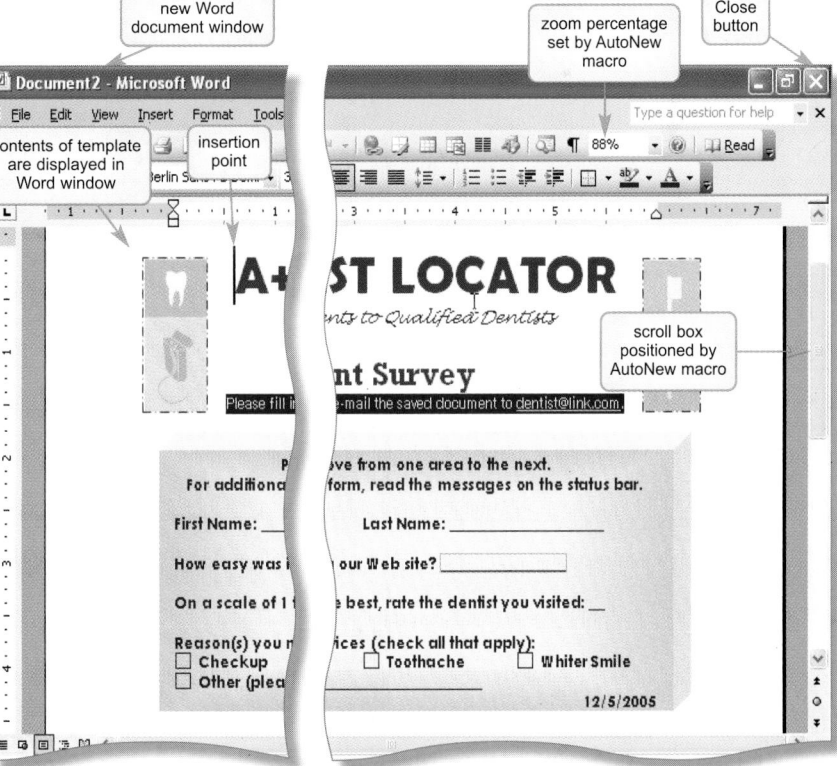

FIGURE 8-46

Notice in Figure 8-46 that the insertion point is at the top of the form. Recall that when you make a form available for users to access, you first protect the form. Protecting a form places the selection in the first form field and allows users to access only the form fields. You did not protect the form yet because you are not finished modifying it. You simply tested the AutoNew macro to be sure it worked properly.

Editing a Recorded Macro

The next step in this project is to edit the AutoNew macro. Word uses VBA to store a macro's instructions. To edit a recorded macro, you use the Visual Basic Editor. All Office applications use the Visual Basic Editor to enter, modify, and view VBA code associated with a document. The following pages explain how to use the Visual Basic Editor to view, enter, and modify VBA code.

Viewing a Macro's VBA Code

As described earlier, a macro consists of VBA code, which the macro recorder automatically creates as you record a macro. You view the VBA code assigned to a macro through the Visual Basic Editor. The following steps show how to view the VBA code associated with the AutoNew macro in the Patient Survey.

To View a Macro's VBA Code

1

• **Click Tools on the menu bar and then point to Macro (Figure 8-47).**

FIGURE 8-47

2

• **Click Macros on the Macro submenu.**

• **When Word displays the Macros dialog box, if necessary, click the Macros in box arrow and then click A+ Dentist Locator Revised (template).**

• **If necessary, click AutoNew in the Macro name list.**

Word displays the selected macro name in the Macro name text box (Figure 8-48).

FIGURE 8-48

3

• **Click the Edit button.**

• **If the Code window is not displayed in the Visual Basic Editor, click View on the menu bar and then click Code.**

• **If the Project Explorer window is displayed, click its Close button.**

• **If the Properties window is displayed, click its Close button.**

• **If the Code window is not maximized, double-click its title bar.**

The Visual Basic Editor starts and displays the VBA code for the AutoNew macro in the Code window (Figure 8-49). Your screen may appear differently depending on previous Visual Basic Editor settings.

FIGURE 8-49

The named set of instructions associated with a macro is called a procedure. It is this set of instructions — beginning with the words Sub AutoNew (shown in Figure 8-49) and continuing sequentially to the line with the words End Sub — that executes when you run the macro.

If you scroll up the Code window, you will see the code associated with the PrintFormData macro. By scrolling through the two procedures of VBA code, you can see that the macro recorder generates many instructions.

Other Ways

1. On Tools menu point to Macro, click Visual Basic Editor, scroll to desired procedure
2. Press ALT+F11, scroll to desired procedure
3. In Voice command mode, say "Tools, Macro, Visual Basic Editor"

The instructions within a procedure are called **code statements**. Each code statement can contain keywords, variables, constants, and operators. Table 8-3 explains the function of each of these elements of a code statement.

Table 8-3	Elements of a Code Statement	
CODE STATEMENT ELEMENT	**DEFINITION**	**EXAMPLES**
Keyword	Recognized by Visual Basic as part of its programming language. Keywords appear in blue in the Code window.	Sub End Sub
Variable	An item whose value can be modified during program execution.	ActiveWindow.ActivePane.SmallScroll TitleBarText
Constant	An item whose value remains unchanged during program execution.	6
Operator	A symbol that indicates a specific action.	= +

A procedure begins with a **Sub statement** and ends with an **End Sub statement**. As shown in Figure 8-49 on the previous page, the Sub statement is followed by the name of the procedure, which is the macro name (AutoNew). The parentheses following the macro name in the Sub statement are required. They indicate that arguments can be passed from one procedure to another. Passing arguments is beyond the scope of this project, but the parentheses still are required. The End Sub statement signifies the end of the procedure and returns control to Word. For clarity, code statement lines between the Sub statement and End Sub statement are indented four spaces.

Adding Comments to a Procedure

Adding comments before and within a procedure helps you remember the purpose of the macro and its code statements at a later date. **Comments** begin with the word, Rem, or with an apostrophe (') and appear in green in the Code window. In Figure 8-49, for example, the macro recorder placed four comment lines below the Sub statement. These comments display the name of the macro and its description, as entered in the Record Macro dialog box. Comments have no effect on the execution of a procedure; they simply provide information about the procedure, such as its name and description.

The macro recorder, however, does not add comments to the executable code statements in the procedures. Any code statement that is not a comment is considered an **executable code statement**. The AutoNew procedure in Figure 8-49 contains three executable code statements. The first statement,

```
ActiveWindow.ActivePane.View.Zoom.PageFit = wdPageFitBestFit
```

changes the zoom percentage to page width. The macro recorder generated this code statement when you clicked the Zoom box arrow on the Standard toolbar and then clicked Page Width.

More About

VBA Statements

Instead of a long VBA statement on a single line, you can continue a VBA statement on the next line by typing an underscore character (_) at the end of the line to be continued and then pressing the ENTER key. To place multiple VBA statements on the same line, type a colon (:) between each statement.

The next two code statements scroll the screen downward six lines from the top of the page. The macro recorder generated these code statements when you dragged the scroll box to the top of the vertical scroll bar and then clicked the down scroll arrow on the vertical scroll bar six times.

You would like to enter comments that explain the purpose of executable code statements in the AutoNew procedure. To make changes such as these, you use the Visual Basic Editor. The **Visual Basic Editor** is a full-screen editor, which allows you to enter a procedure by typing lines of VBA code as if you were using word processing software. At the end of a line, you press the ENTER key or use the DOWN ARROW key to move to the next line. If you make a mistake in a code statement, you can use the ARROW keys and the DELETE or BACKSPACE keys to correct it. You also can move the insertion point to lines requiring corrections.

The following steps show how to add comments above the executable code statements in the AutoNew procedure.

To Add Comments to a Procedure

1

• **Click to the left of the letter A in the first code statement beginning with the word ActiveWindow in the AutoNew procedure and then press the ENTER key to add a blank line above the code statement.**

• **Press the UP ARROW key.**

• **Type** ' Sets screen to page width zoom **and then press the DOWN ARROW key. Make sure you type the apostrophe at the beginning of the comment.**

The first comment is entered and appears in green (Figure 8-50).

comment added

FIGURE 8-50

2

• **Click to the left of the letter A in the second code statement beginning with the word ActiveWindow and then press the ENTER key.**

• **Press the UP ARROW key.**

• **Type** ' Scrolls down from top of page so entire form fits in window **and then press the DOWN ARROW key. Make sure you type the apostrophe at the beginning of the comment.**

The second comment is entered and appears in green (Figure 8-51).

comment added

number of lines to scroll currently set to 6

FIGURE 8-51

Modifying Existing Code in a Procedure

The next step is to modify existing code in the AutoNew macro. Suppose that when you tested the AutoNew macro, you noticed you should scroll down one more line so the company name is closer to the top of the screen (shown in Figure 8-46 on page WD 591). Thus, the next step is to change the 6 in the third executable code statement in the AutoNew procedure to a 7, as shown below.

To Modify Existing Code

1

• **Double-click the 6 at the end of the executable code statement above the End Sub statement.**

• **Type** 7 **as the new number of lines to scroll.**

The code statement is modified (Figure 8-52).

constant changed from 6 to 7

insertion point

FIGURE 8-52

Entering Code Statements

In addition to changing the zoom to page width and scrolling down seven lines, you would like to ensure that formatting marks and gridlines are hidden when a user initially opens this form (as a blank form). Thus, the next step is to add two executable code statements, each preceded by a comment. Table 8-4 shows the code statements to be entered.

Table 8-4 Code Statements to Be Added to AutoNew Procedure	
ORDER	CODE STATEMENT
First new code statement	`' Turns off table gridlines`
Second new code statement	`ActiveDocument.ActiveWindow.View.TableGridlines = False`
Third new code statement	`' Turns off formatting marks`
Fourth new code statement	`ActiveDocument.ActiveWindow.View.ShowAll = False`

The following step shows how to add these code statements to the procedure.

To Add Code Statements to a Procedure

1

• **With the insertion point following the 7 as shown in Figure 8-52, press the ENTER key.**

• **Type the first new code statement shown in Table 8-4 and then press the ENTER key.**

• **Enter the remaining three code statements shown in Table 8-4. Make sure you type an apostrophe at the beginning of both comment lines. Ignore any shortcut menus that appear as you type.**

The new code statements are entered in the AutoNew procedure (Figure 8-53).

FIGURE 8-53

You could add many more statements to this procedure to ensure the initial form screen is displayed properly. For example, you could close any open toolbars. For purposes of this project, you now are finished modifying the AutoNew macro. Thus, the step on the next page describes how to quit the Visual Basic Editor and return control to Word.

To Quit the Visual Basic Editor

1 **Click the Close button on the right edge of the Microsoft Visual Basic window title bar.**

The Visual Basic Editor window closes and control returns to Word.

Instead of clicking the Visual Basic window's Close button, you can click Close on the File menu or press ALT+Q to quit the Visual Basic Editor.

If you do not want to close the Visual Basic Editor, you can click the View Microsoft Word button on the Visual Basic Standard toolbar (Figure 8-49 on page WD 593) to minimize the Visual Basic Editor and return control to Word. If you plan to switch between Word and the Visual Basic Editor, use the View Microsoft Word button; otherwise use the Close button.

Creating a Macro from Scratch Using VBA

The next macro to be created in this project is the one that displays an error message if the user enters an out-of-range value in the rating scale form field (shown in Figure 8-1b on page WD 555). The macro is to execute when the user presses the TAB key to move the insertion point out of the rating scale form field. The following pages explain how to create this macro and attach it to the text form field for the rating scale.

Modifying Form Field Options

The rating scale is a text form field. To modify a text form field, double-click the text form field to display the Text Form Field Options dialog box. Two changes are to be made in the dialog box: change the type and enter a bookmark.

In Project 7, you wanted only numbers to be displayed in the rating scale text form field. Thus, you changed the text form field's type to Number. Doing so ensured that if a user entered a nonnumeric value in the text form field during data entry, the entry automatically was converted to a zero. In this project, you want to display an error message if the user enters an out-of-range value. Thus, you must change the text form field's type back to Regular text so that you can display an error message if a user makes an incorrect entry.

You also want to change the bookmark for this text form field because you will be writing VBA code that references this text form field. A **bookmark** is an item in a document that you name for future reference. Currently, the bookmark is Text3, which is not very descriptive. A more meaningful bookmark would be RatingScale. Notice this new bookmark does not have a space between the words, Rating and Scale. This is because a bookmark cannot contain any spaces. A bookmark also must begin with a letter.

The next steps describe how to change the text form field type and edit the bookmark.

To Change Options for a Text Form Field

1 Double-click the text form field for rating scale.

2 When Word displays the Text Form Field Options dialog box, click the Type box arrow and then click Regular text.

3 If necessary, enter two underscore characters in the Default text text box.

4 Select the text in the Bookmark text box and then type RatingScale as the new bookmark (Figure 8-54).

5 Click the OK button.

Word changes the form field options as specified in the Text Form Field Options dialog box.

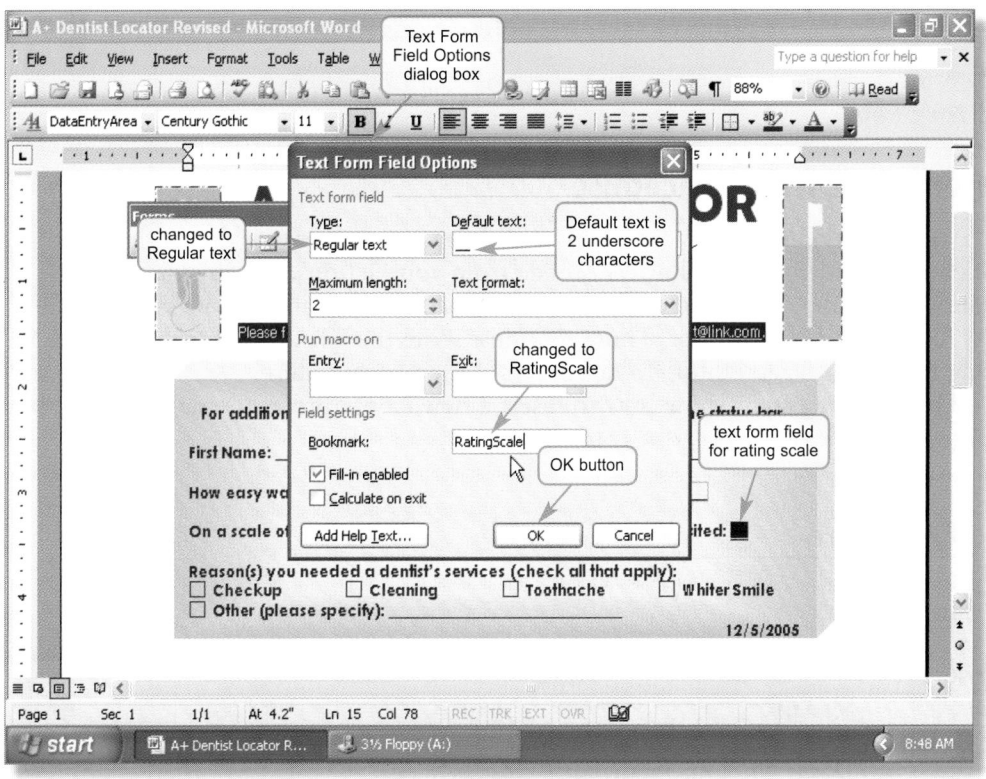

FIGURE 8-54

The ease of use form field also will be referenced in the VBA code. Thus, the next step is to change the bookmark for the ease of use form field from Dropdown3 to a more meaningful name, as described below.

To Change a Bookmark for a Drop-Down Form Field

1 Double-click the drop-down form field for ease of use.

2 When Word displays the Drop-Down Form Field Options dialog box, select the text in the Bookmark text box and then type EaseOfUse as the new bookmark (Figure 8-55 on the next page).

3 Click the OK button.

Word changes the form field options as specified in the Drop-Down Form Field Options dialog box.

FIGURE 8-55

Inserting a New Procedure

For the previous two macros, you used the macro recorder to create the macros, which generated corresponding VBA code from your actions. For this macro, you cannot record the displaying of the error message, because an error message for this text form field does not exist. Thus, you must write the VBA code for this macro using the Visual Basic Editor. To do this, you insert a procedure.

The following steps show how to insert a new empty procedure named RatingScaleValidation.

To Insert a Visual Basic Procedure

1

• **Press ALT+F11 to open the Visual Basic Editor in a new window.**

• **If the Project Explorer is displayed, click its Close button.**

• **If the Properties window is displayed, click its Close button.**

• **If the Code window is not displayed, click View on the menu bar and then click Code.**

• **If necessary, double-click the title bar of the Code window to maximize it.**

• **Click the Insert UserForm button arrow on the Standard toolbar.**

The Visual Basic Editor is displayed (Figure 8-56).

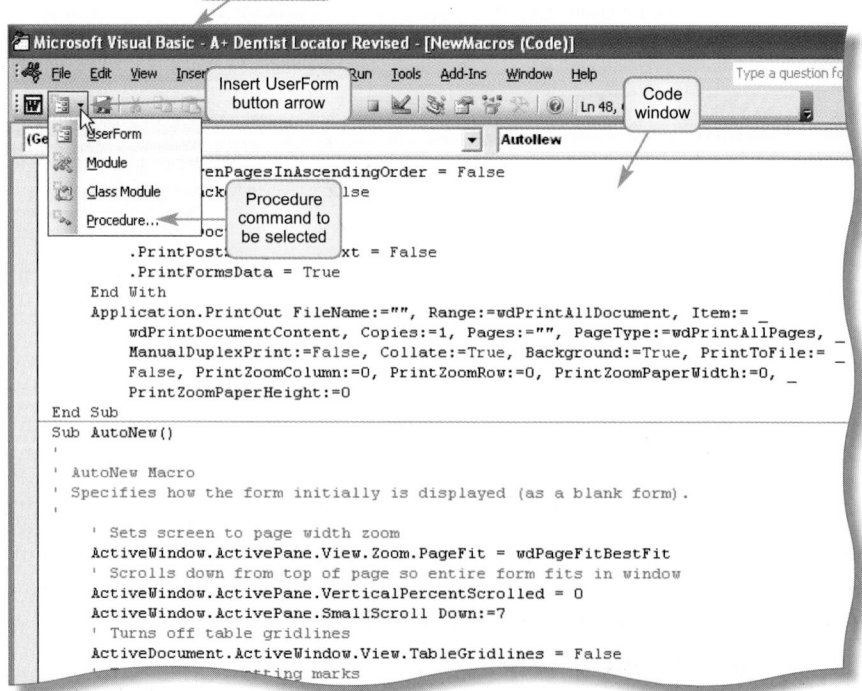

FIGURE 8-56

2

• **Click Procedure in the list.**

• **When Visual Basic displays the Add Procedure dialog box, type** RatingScaleValidation **in the Name text box.**

The Add Procedure dialog box is displayed (Figure 8-57).

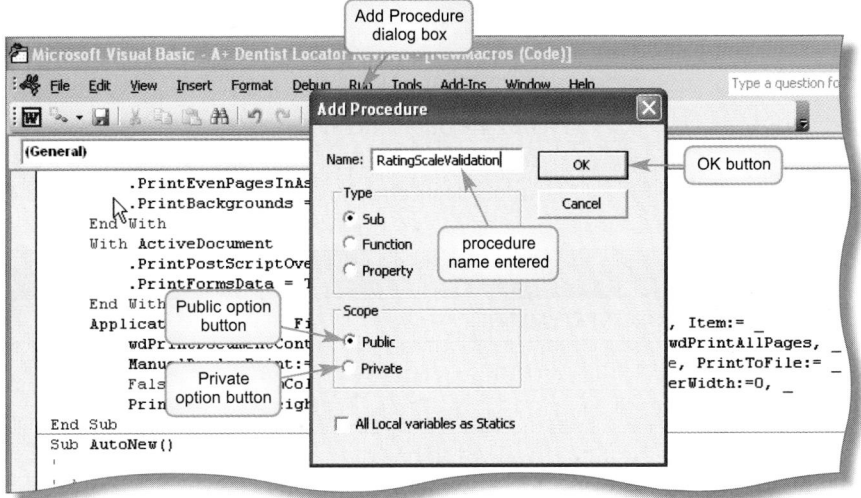

FIGURE 8-57

3

• **Click the OK button.**

Visual Basic displays a new procedure, called RatingScaleValidation, in the Code window (Figure 8-58).

FIGURE 8-58

Notice in Figure 8-58 that Visual Basic automatically inserts the Sub and End Sub statements in the procedure. The Sub statement, however, begins with the keyword Public, which means that this procedure can be executed from other documents or programs. Private, by contrast, means that the procedure can be executed only from this document. If you wanted a procedure to be private, you would click Private in the Scope area in the Add Procedure dialog box (Figure 8-57).

Planning and Writing a VBA Procedure

The next step is to write and then enter the code statements for the newly created RatingScaleValidation procedure. Before you write the statements, you should plan the procedure; that is, determine what tasks the procedure is to accomplish and the order in which the tasks should be executed. Planning the procedure is an extremely important activity because the order of statements determines the sequence of execution. If the order of statements is incorrect, the procedure will not execute properly.

Other Ways

1. On Insert menu click Procedure, enter procedure name, click OK button
2. In Voice command mode, say "Insert, Procedure"

Once you have planned the procedure thoroughly, the next step is to write the VBA code statements on paper similar to that shown in Table 8-5. Then, before entering the procedure, test it by putting yourself in the position of the computer and stepping through the instructions one at a time. As you step through the procedure, think about how it affects the Word document. Testing a procedure before entering it is called **desk checking** and is an extremely important part of the development process.

Table 8-5	Code Statements for RatingScaleValidation Procedure
LINE	**VBA CODE STATEMENT**
1	`Public Sub RatingScaleValidation()`
2	`'`
3	`' RatingScaleValidation Macro`
4	`' Displays error message if entered number is not between 1 and 10.`
5	`'`
6	`' Assign value in Rating Scale form field to a variable`
7	`RatingScaleEntered = ActiveDocument.FormFields("RatingScale").Result`
8	`' Test if entry in Rating Scale text form field is out of range`
9	`If RatingScaleEntered < 1 Or RatingScaleEntered > 10 Then`
10	`' Display error message`
11	`MsgBox "Rating scale must be between 1 and 10.", vbOKOnly + vbCritical`
12	`' Redisplay underscore characters in text form field`
13	`ActiveDocument.FormFields("RatingScale").Result = "__"`
14	`' Reposition selection in text form field`
15	`ActiveDocument.FormFields("EaseOfUse").Select`
16	`End If`
17	`End Sub`

In the code statements shown in Table 8-5, lines 2, 3, 4, 5, 6, 8, 10, 12, and 14 are comments. Lines 1 and 17 contain the Sub and End Sub statements that Visual Basic automatically inserted when you created the procedure. Line 7 is the first executable code statement.

Line 9 contains an If...Then statement because it executes the line(s) of code up to the End If statement if the result of a condition is true. The condition in line 9 is RatingScaleEntered < 1 Or RatingScaleEntered > 10. In nonprogramming terms, this condition is testing whether the user enters a number between 1 and 10 in the Rating Scale form field. If not, then the statements up to the End If statement will be executed. If the user did enter a number, then the statements up to the End If statement are not executed and control returns to Word.

Table 8-6	Types of Icons for a Message Box
ICON	**VISUAL BASIC CONSTANT**
Letter X	vbCritical
Question mark	vbQuestion
Exclamation point	vbExclamation
Information symbol	vbInformation

If the user enters an out-of-range value in the Rating Scale form field, the next executable code statement is in line 11, which uses the MsgBox keyword to display an error message box on the screen. The text inside the quotation marks is displayed inside the message box; vbOKOnly places an OK button in the message box, and vbCritical places an X icon in the dialog box. Table 8-6 lists the types of icons that can be displayed in a message box.

After a user reads the message in the error message box and clicks the OK button, the next executable code statement is in line 13, which replaces the user's invalid entry with underscore characters. Then, line 15 positions the selection in the EaseOfUse drop-down form field.

Having desk checked the code statements on paper, you now are ready to enter them in the Visual Basic Editor. The following steps describe how to add code statements to the RatingScaleValidation procedure.

To Add Code Statements to a Procedure

1 With the insertion point on the blank line between the Sub and End Sub statements in the Code window, type the code statements shown in lines 2 through 16 in Table 8-5. Make sure you enter an apostrophe at the beginning of each comment line. For clarity, indent code statements as shown in Table 8-5. To move the indent five spaces to the left, you will need to press SHIFT+TAB or the BACKSPACE key.

2 Verify your code statements by comparing them to Figure 8-59.

3 Click the Close button on the right edge of the Microsoft Visual Basic title bar to return to the template file.

The Microsoft Visual Basic window closes and control returns to Word.

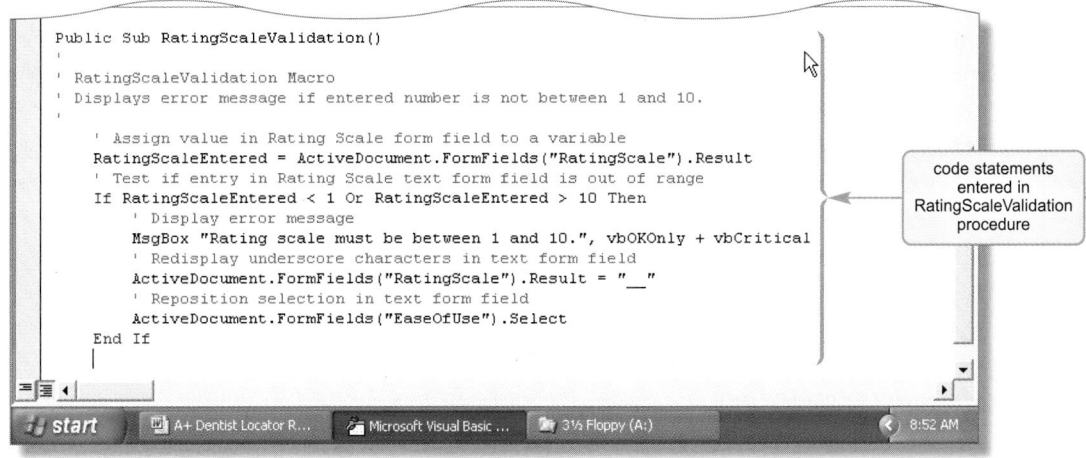

```
Public Sub RatingScaleValidation()
'
' RatingScaleValidation Macro
' Displays error message if entered number is not between 1 and 10.
'
    ' Assign value in Rating Scale form field to a variable
    RatingScaleEntered = ActiveDocument.FormFields("RatingScale").Result
    ' Test if entry in Rating Scale text form field is out of range
    If RatingScaleEntered < 1 Or RatingScaleEntered > 10 Then
        ' Display error message
        MsgBox "Rating scale must be between 1 and 10.", vbOKOnly + vbCritical
        ' Redisplay underscore characters in text form field
        ActiveDocument.FormFields("RatingScale").Result = "__"
        ' Reposition selection in text form field
        ActiveDocument.FormFields("EaseOfUse").Select
    End If
```

code statements entered in RatingScaleValidation procedure

🏁 start | A+ Dentist Locator R... | Microsoft Visual Basic ... | 3½ Floppy (A:) | 8:52 AM

FIGURE 8-59

Running a Macro when a User Exits a Form Field

The RatingScaleValidation macro just created in the Visual Basic Editor should execute whenever a user presses the TAB key to move the insertion point out of the rating scale text form field. That is, pressing the TAB key out of the rating scale text form field is the event that triggers execution of the procedure.

With respect to form fields, Word allows you to execute a macro under these two circumstances: (1) when the user enters a form field, and (2) when the user exits the form field. To specify when the macro should run, use the Text Form Field Options dialog box. The steps on the next page show how to instruct Word to execute the RatingScaleValidation macro when a user exits the rating scale text form field.

To Run a Macro when a User Exits a Form Field

 1

- **Double-click the text form field for the rating scale.**
- **When Word displays the Text Form Field Options dialog box, click the Exit box arrow and then click RatingScaleValidation.**

The selected macro name is displayed in the Exit box in the Text Form Field Options dialog box (Figure 8-60).

2

- **Click the OK button.**

Word sets the form field options as specified in the Text Form Field Options dialog box.

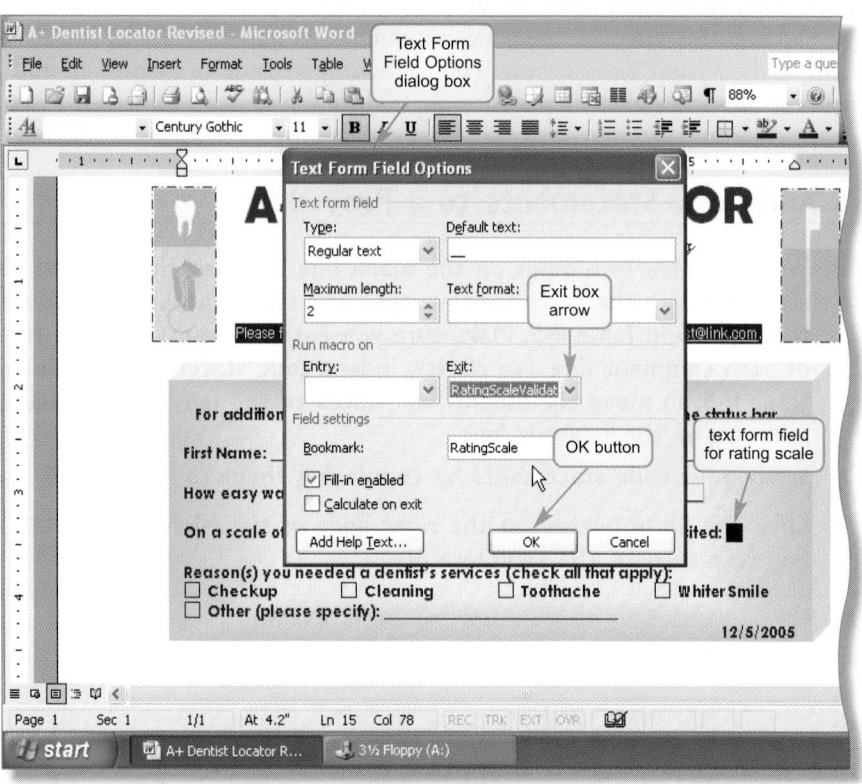

FIGURE 8-60

When you click the Entry or Exit box arrow in the Run macro on area in the Text Form Field Options dialog box, Word displays all available macros. You can select any one macro to run when the user enters or exits each form field in the form.

The RatingScaleValidation macro is complete. This macro will be tested at the end of this project.

Copying, Renaming, and Deleting Macros

You may find it necessary to copy a macro, rename a macro, or delete a macro. The following steps describe how to perform these tasks.

TO COPY A MACRO

1. Click Tools on the menu bar, point to Macro, and then click Macros on the Macro submenu. When Word displays the Macros dialog box, click the macro name to copy, and then click the Edit button to start the Visual Basic Editor and display the macro in the Code window.
2. Select all the text in the macro's VBA procedure; that is, drag from the Sub statement to the End Sub statement (including the Sub and End Sub statements).
3. Click Edit on the menu bar and then click Copy.
4. Position the insertion point in the destination area. Click Edit on the menu bar and then click Paste.

You can paste a macro into the same document or a different document.

TO RENAME A MACRO

1. Click Tools on the menu bar and then click Templates and Add-Ins.
2. When Word displays the Templates and Add-ins dialog box, click the Organizer button. When the Organizer dialog box is displayed, click the Macro Project Items tab.
3. In the document or template In list, click the macro name to be renamed and then click the Rename button. When Word displays the Rename dialog box, type the new name and then click the OK button.
4. Click the Close button.

TO DELETE A MACRO

1. Click Tools on the menu bar, point to Macro, and then click Macros on the Macro submenu.
2. When Word displays the Macros dialog box, click the macro name to be deleted, and then click the Delete button.
3. Click the Yes button in the Microsoft Word dialog box.

You also can delete macros in the Organizer dialog box.

Adding an ActiveX Control to a Form

In addition to the form fields available on the Forms toolbar, you can insert ActiveX controls in a Word form. An **ActiveX control** is an object, such as a button or check box, that can be included in a form to be published on the World Wide Web. The major difference between a form field and an ActiveX control is that form fields require the use of Word, whereas ActiveX controls do not. Thus, if you intend to create a Web page form, you should place ActiveX controls on the form instead of form fields.

ActiveX controls have the appearance and functionality of Windows controls. For example, the check box ActiveX control looks like a check box in a Windows dialog box. A check box form field, by contrast, has an appearance unique to Word. That is, it displays an X (instead of a check mark).

Users familiar with Windows applications will find it easier to work with ActiveX controls rather than working with form fields. With form fields, a user has to press the TAB key to move the insertion point from one form field to another. With an ActiveX control, the user can click in the form field or press the TAB key to move to it.

Adding an ActiveX control to a form involves three major activities: insert the ActiveX control, set properties of the ActiveX control, and write the procedure for the ActiveX control using VBA. Word refers to the time in which you perform these three activities as **design mode**. When you run the form (fill it in) as a user does, by contrast, you are in **run mode**.

The following pages explain how to add an ActiveX control to an online form.

More About

ActiveX

For more information about ActiveX, visit the Word 2003 More About Web page (scsite .com/wd2003/more) and then click ActiveX.

Inserting an ActiveX Control

For the form in this project, you would like to insert a command button that users click when they are finished filling in the form. When they click the button, three actions should occur:

1. If the user entered text in the Other text box, Word places an X in the Other check box (in case the user forgot to place an X in the check box).
2. Word displays the Save As dialog box so the user can assign a file name to the filled-in form.
3. Word displays a thank-you message box on the screen.

To insert an ActiveX control, such as a command button, use the Control Toolbox toolbar. The following steps show how to insert an ActiveX control command button in the online form.

To Insert an ActiveX Control

1

• **If the Control Toolbox toolbar is not displayed on the screen already, click View on the menu bar, point to Toolbars, and then click Control Toolbox.**

• **If formatting marks are not displayed on the screen already, click the Show/Hide ¶ button on the Standard toolbar.**

• **Click the paragraph mark at the end of the form and then press the ENTER key.**

• **Click the Center button on the Formatting toolbar.**

The Control Toolbox toolbar contains buttons to insert ActiveX controls (Figure 8-61).

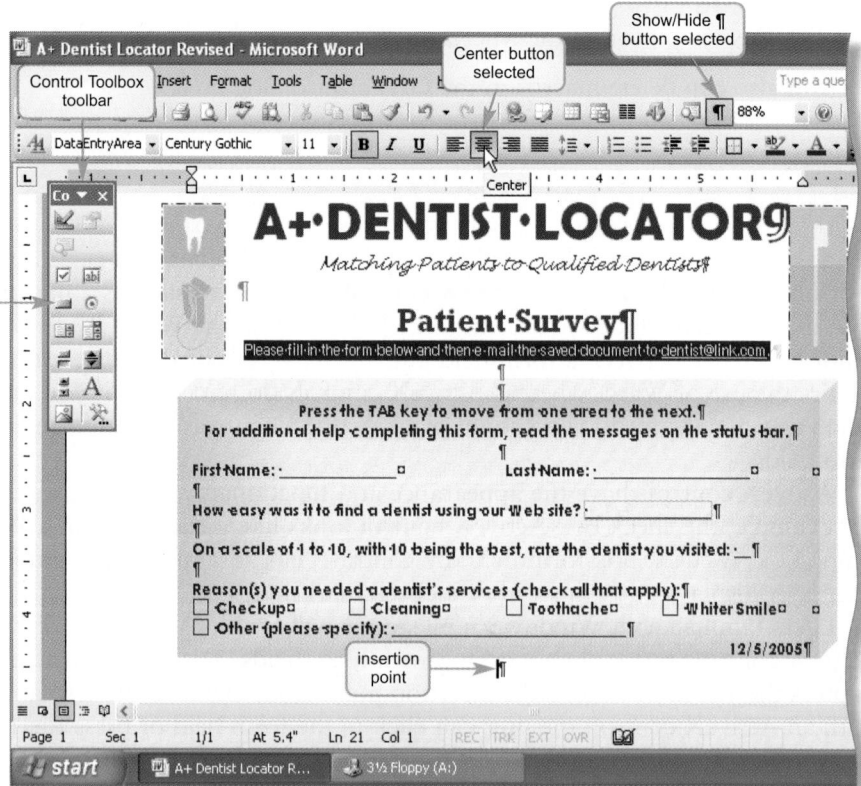

FIGURE 8-61

2

- **Click the Command Button button on the Control Toolbox toolbar.**

Word inserts a standard-sized command button at the location of the insertion point and switches to design mode (Figure 8-62). The text CommandButton1 partially appears on the face of the button. The button is selected and is surrounded by sizing handles.

FIGURE 8-62

When you click a button on the Control Toolbox toolbar, Word automatically switches to design mode, changes the Design Mode button on the Control Toolbox toolbar to an Exit Design Mode button, and selects the Exit Design Mode button. Word also may display an Exit Design Mode toolbar. The Control Toolbox toolbar buttons are summarized in Table 8-7.

Other Ways

1. Click Design Mode button on Visual Basic toolbar
2. In Voice command mode, say "Command Button"

Table 8-7   Summary of Buttons on the Control Toolbox Toolbar

BUTTON	NAME	FUNCTION	BUTTON	NAME	FUNCTION
	Design Mode	Changes to Exit Design Mode button when in design mode		Combo Box	Inserts a drop-down list box
	Properties	Opens Properties window		Toggle Button	Inserts a toggle button
	View Code	Opens Code window in Visual Basic Editor		Spin Button	Inserts a spin button
	Check Box	Inserts a check box		Scroll Bar	Inserts a scroll bar
	Text Box	Inserts a text box		Label	Inserts a label
	Command Button	Inserts a command button		Image	Inserts an image
	Option Button	Inserts an option button		More Controls	Displays a list of additional controls
	List Box	Inserts a list box			

Setting Properties of an ActiveX Control

In Word, an ActiveX control command button has many different properties (shown in Figure 8-63), such as the caption (the words on the face of the button), background color, foreground color, height, width, font, and so on. After you insert a command button in a form, you can change any of the properties to improve the button's appearance and modify its function.

This project requires the following settings of the command button be changed:

● Caption: should be the text, Click Here When Finished

● AutoSize: should be changed to True, which instructs Word to make the command button large enough to hold its entire caption

● BackColor: should be dark red

● ForeColor: should be tan

● Font: should be 12-point bold Rockwell

The following steps show how to change properties of an ActiveX control.

To Set Properties of an ActiveX Control

1

• **With the command button selected and Word in design mode, click the Properties button on the Control Toolbox toolbar (shown in Figure 8-62 on the previous page).**

• **When the Properties window opens, if necessary, click the Properties box arrow and then click CommandButton1 in the list.**

• **If necessary, click the Alphabetic tab.**

• **If necessary, drag the right edge of the Properties window to make it wider.**

• **In the list, click Caption in the left column and then drag through the value, CommandButton1, to its right.**

The Property names are displayed on the left of the Properties window, and the value of each property is displayed on the right (Figure 8-63). The caption appears on the face of the button.

FIGURE 8-63

2

• **Type** Click Here When Finished **as the new caption.**
• **Click the AutoSize property.**

Word changes the value of the caption property and displays the new caption on the button face (Figure 8-64). Notice the caption does not fit in the current button size. Thus, you will instruct Word to automatically size the button to the caption.

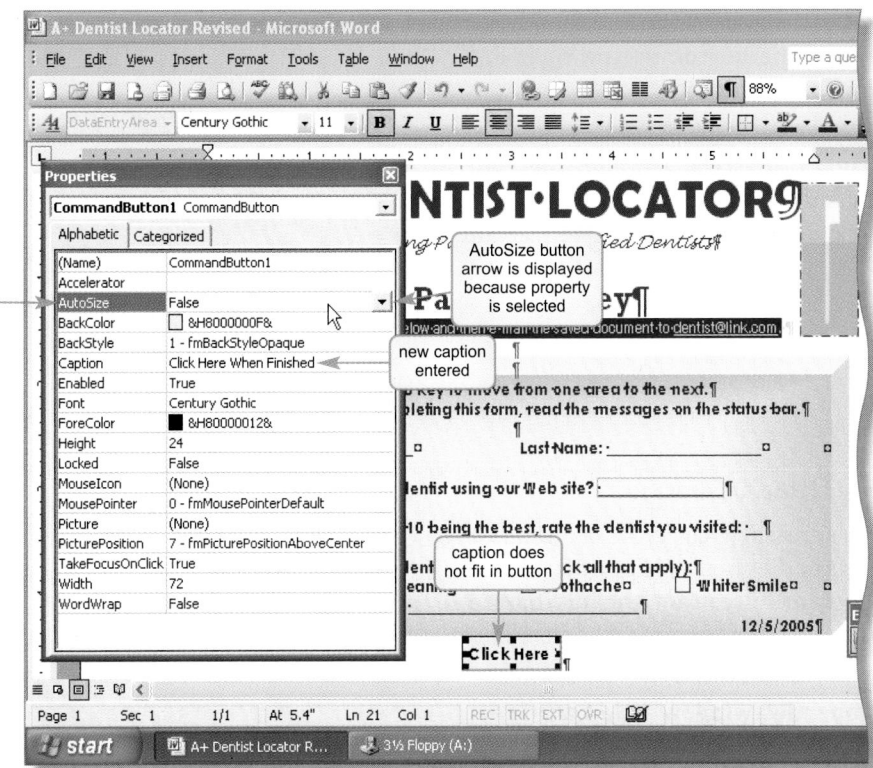

FIGURE 8-64

3

• **Click the AutoSize button arrow and then click True.**

Word changes the AutoSize value to True.

4

• **Click the BackColor property, click the BackColor button arrow, click the Palette tab, and then click Dark Red on the color palette.**
• **Click the ForeColor property, click the ForeColor button arrow, click the Palette tab, and then click Tan on the color palette.**
• **Click the Font property.**

Word changes the values of the BackColor and ForeColor properties (Figure 8-65).

FIGURE 8-65

5

• **Click the button at the right of the Font value box.**

• **When Word displays the Font dialog box, scroll through the Font list and click Rockwell; if necessary, click Bold in the Font style list; and then click 12 in the Size list.**

The font settings for the button are selected in the Font dialog box (Figure 8-66).

6

• **Click the OK button.**

• **If necessary, click the A+ Dentist Locator Revised – Microsoft Word program button on the taskbar to redisplay the form on the screen.**

• **Click the Close button on the Properties window title bar.**

Word closes the Font dialog box and the Properties window. The changed button is shown in Figure 8-67 on page WD 612.

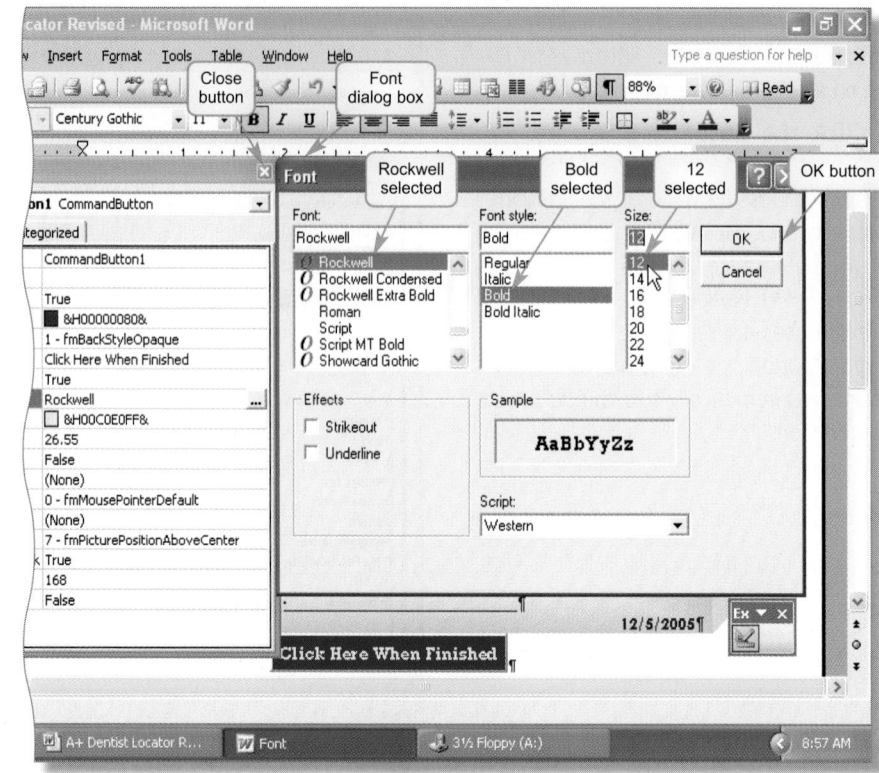

FIGURE 8-66

The Properties window (Figure 8-65 on the previous page) has two tabs, Alphabetic and Categorized. The Alphabetic sheet displays the properties in alphabetical order. The Categorized sheet displays the properties by subject, such as appearance, behavior, font, and miscellaneous.

Writing a Procedure for the ActiveX Control

The next step is to write and then enter the procedure that will execute when a user clicks the Click Here When Finished button. Clicking the button is the event that triggers execution of the procedure.

As mentioned earlier, you should plan a procedure by writing its VBA code on paper similar to that shown in Table 8-8. Then, before entering the procedure in the computer, desk check it.

Table 8-8   Click Here When Finished Button Procedure

LINE	VBA CODE STATEMENT
1	`Private Sub CommandButton1_Click()`
2	`'`
3	`' CommandButton1_Click Procedure`
4	`' Executes when user clicks button called Click Here When Finished.`
5	`'`
6	`    ' If user entered text in Other text form field, put X in Other check box`
7	`    If Left(ActiveDocument.FormFields("OtherTextFormField").Result, 1) <> "_" Then`
8	`        ActiveDocument.FormFields("OtherCheckBox").CheckBox.Value = True`
9	`    End If`
10	`    ' Display Save As dialog box`
11	`    Dialogs(wdDialogFileSaveAs).Show`
12	`    ' Display thank-you message`
13	`    TitleBarText = "Thank You For Your Time"`
14	`    MessageText = "Please e-mail " & ActiveDocument.FullName & " to dentist@link.com."`
15	`    MsgBox MessageText, , TitleBarText`
16	`End Sub`

Notice in line 1 that the name of the procedure in the Sub statement is CommandButton1_Click, which Word determines from the name of the button (shown in Figure 8-68 on page WD 613) and from the event that causes the procedure to execute (Click).

The first executable code statement is an If...Then statement in line 7. This statement tests if the user entered text in the Other text form field, which will have a bookmark of OtherTextFormField. If this text form field contains text, then line 8 instructs Word to place an X in the Other check box, which will have a bookmark of OtherCheckBox; otherwise, Word skips lines 8 and 9 and then proceeds to line 10.

The next executable code statement is in line 11, which displays the Save As dialog box on the screen — allowing the user to save the form. Finally, line 15 displays a message box that contains two variables. The first is for the message text, which is defined in line 14; and the second is for the title bar text, which is defined in line 13. Variables are used to define these elements of the message box, because the text for the title bar and message is so long.

As illustrated earlier in this project, you use the Visual Basic Editor to enter code statements in a procedure. With Word in design mode and the ActiveX control selected, you can click the View Code button on the Control Toolbox toolbar to display the control's procedure in the Code window of the Visual Basic Editor.

The code statements in lines 7 and 8 use bookmarks that need to be defined in the Form Field Options dialog box of these form fields. The steps on the next page describe how to change the default bookmarks for the Other check box form field and the Other text form field.

To Change Bookmarks for Form Fields

1 Double-click the check box form field for Other (shown in Figure 8-67).

2 When Word displays the Check Box Form Field Options dialog box, select the text in the Bookmark text box and then type OtherCheckBox as the new bookmark. Click the OK button.

3 Double-click the text form field for Other (shown in Figure 8-67).

4 When Word displays the Text Form Field Options dialog box, select the text in the Bookmark text box and then type OtherTextFormField as the new bookmark. Click the OK button.

Word changes form field options as specified in the Form Field Options dialog boxes.

The following steps show how to enter the code statements for the procedure that will execute when a user clicks the Click Here When Finished button.

To Enter the Click Here When Finished Button Procedure

1

• **With Word in design mode, click the Click Here When Finished button and then point to the View Code button on the Control Toolbox toolbar (Figure 8-67).**

FIGURE 8-67

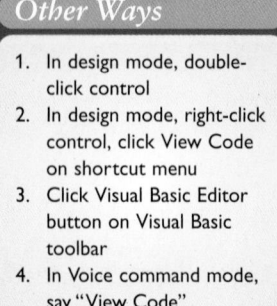

2

- Click the **View Code** button.

- If the Project Explorer window opens, click its Close button.

- If necessary, double-click the Code window title bar to maximize the window.

- With the insertion point on the blank line between the Sub and End Sub statements in the Code window, type the code statements shown in lines 2 through 15 in Table 8-8 on page WD 611. Make sure you type an apostrophe at the beginning of each comment line. For clarity, indent the code statements as shown in Table 8-8.

The command button procedure is entered (Figure 8-68).

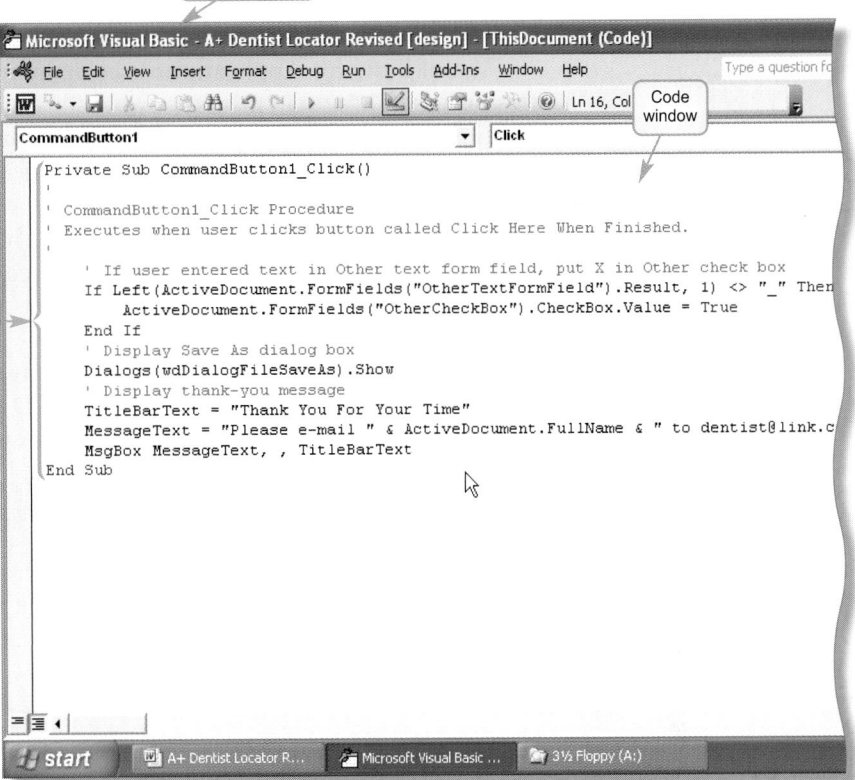

FIGURE 8-68

3

- Verify your code statements by comparing them to Figure 8-68.

4

- Click the **Close** button on the right edge of the Microsoft Visual Basic title bar to return to the online form (Figure 8-69).

5

- Click the **Exit Design Mode** button on the Control Toolbox toolbar.

- Click the Close button on the Control Toolbox toolbar title bar.

Word returns to run mode, which means if you click the Click Here When Finished button, Word will execute the associated procedure.

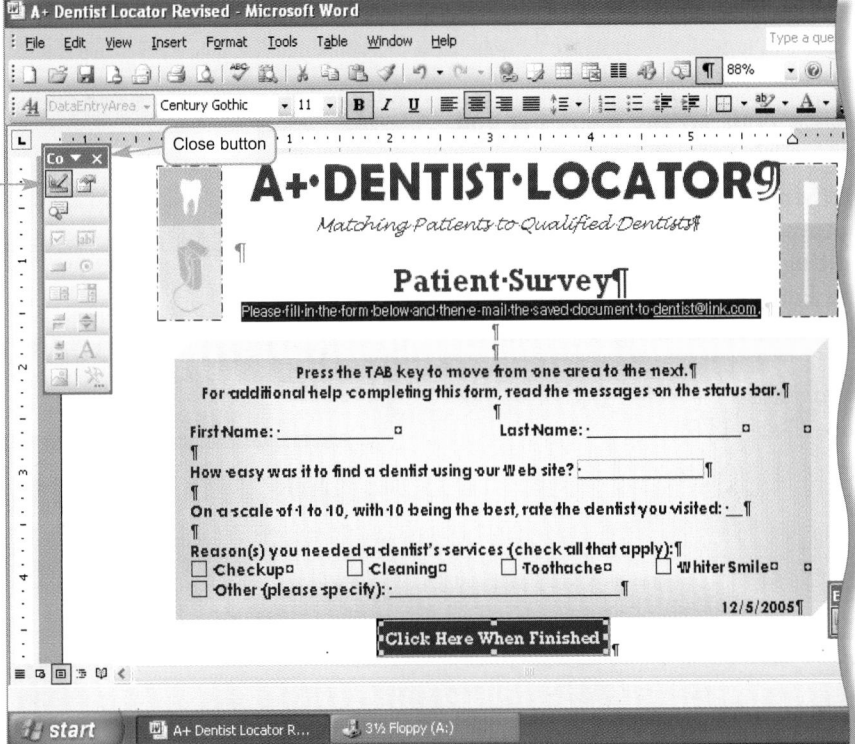

FIGURE 8-69

More About Visual Basic for Applications

Visual Basic for Applications uses many more statements than those presented in this project. These statements, however, should help you understand the basic composition of a Visual Basic statement. For example, the code statement in line 11 of Table 8-8 on page WD 611 that displays the Save As dialog box includes a period. The entry on the left side of the period tells Word which object you want to affect (in this case, the dialog box). An object can be a document, a form field, a bookmark, a dialog box, a button, or any other control on a form. The entry on the right side of the period tells Word what you want to do to the object (in this case, show it).

Earlier, this project showed how to change an object's properties using the Properties window (Figure 8-63 on page WD 608). Code statements also can change an object's property. For example, one code statement from the RatingScale macro is as follows:

```
ActiveDocument.ActiveWindow.View.TableGridlines = False
```

This statement changes the TableGridlines property of the View object in the ActiveWindow object in the ActiveDocument object to false; that is, it hides table gridlines. An equal sign in a code statement instructs Word to make an assignment to a property, variable, or other object.

Protecting a Form

The A+ Dentist Locator Revised form now is complete. Thus, you once again should protect the form and save it. The following steps show how to use the Protect Document task pane, instead of the Forms toolbar, to protect the form.

To Protect the Form Using the Protect Document Task Pane

1

• **Click Tools on the menu bar and then click Protect Document.**

• **When Word displays the Protect Document task pane, click the Editing restrictions check box, click the Editing restrictions box arrow, and then click Filling in forms.**

Word displays the Protect Document task pane (Figure 8-70).

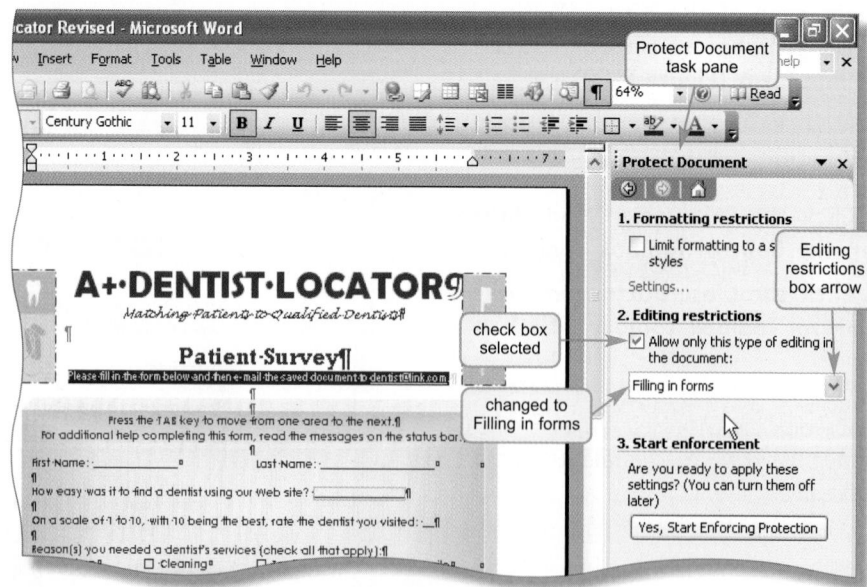

FIGURE 8-70

2

• **Click the Yes, Start Enforcing Protection button.**

Word displays the Start Enforcing Protection dialog box (Figure 8-71). If you enter a password, only a user who knows the password will be able to unprotect the document.

3

• **Click the OK button.**

• **Click the Close button on the Protect Document task pane title bar.**

• **If necessary, scroll to display the entire form in the document window.**

Word protects the form.

FIGURE 8-71

Other Ways

1. Click Protect Form button on Forms toolbar
2. In Voice Command mode, say "Tools, Protect Document, Yes Start Enforcing Protection, OK"

In addition to protecting a form so it only can be filled in, Word provides several other options in the Protect Document task pane. To limit the types of formatting that a user can make to a document, place a check mark in the Formatting restrictions check box, click the Settings link, check the types of formatting you want to allow, and then click the OK button. If you want to allow only tracked changes to be made to a document, click the Editing restrictions check box, click the box arrow, and then click Tracked changes. Similarly, to allow only comments to be entered in a document, click the box arrow and then click Comments. Another choice in this list is No changes, which makes the document read only.

When you select Tracked changes, Comments, and No changes as the editing restrictions, Word allows you to set exceptions. That is, you can select sections of the document and indicate certain groups of users to which the restriction does not apply.

The next step is to save the form.

To Save a Document

1 **Click the Save button on the Standard toolbar.**

Word saves the template with the same file name, A+ Dentist Locator Revised.

Testing the Online Form

The macros and procedures for the A+ Dentist Locator Revised file are complete. You now are ready to test the form. The steps on the next page test the form.

To Test the Form

1 Click the Windows Explorer [3½ Floppy (A:)] program button on the taskbar. Double-click the A+ Dentist Locator Revised icon.

2 If Word displays a Security Warning dialog box, click the Enable Macros button.

3 As instructed by the AutoNew macro, the Word document zooms page width, scrolls down seven lines, hides table gridlines, and hides formatting marks (shown in Figure 8-1a on page WD 555). With the First Name form field selected, type Rick and then press the TAB key. Type Schultz in the Last Name form field. Press the TAB key to select the ease of use form field. Click the box arrow and then click Very Easy in the list. Press the TAB key and then type ab in the rating scale text form field. Press the TAB key.

4 As instructed by the RatingScaleValidation procedure, an error message appears (shown in Figure 8-1b on page WD 555). Click the OK button in the message box. Type 9 in the rating scale form field. Press the TAB key. Click the following check boxes: Checkup and Cleaning. Press the TAB key four times. Type Sore Gums in the Other text form field.

5 Click the Click Here When Finished button.

6 As defined by the CommandButton1_Click procedure, Word displays the Save As dialog box. Change the Save in location to 3½ Floppy (A:). Type Schultz Form Revised in the File name box and then click the Save button in the Save As dialog box.

7 When the save process is complete, the CommandButton1_Click procedure then displays a thank-you message box that indicates the name and location of the file the user should e-mail back (shown in Figure 8-1c on page WD 555).

8 Click the OK button in the message box. Notice that Word placed an X in the Other check box.

If a Word or Visual Basic error message displayed while you tested the form, you will need to unprotect the form, make necessary corrections, protect the form again, save it, and then retest it. Repeat this procedure until the form runs as intended.

The next steps are to close the Schultz Form Revised form and then close Windows Explorer.

To Close a File

1 With the Schultz Form Revised form on the screen, click File on the menu bar and then click Close. If Word displays a dialog box asking to save the changes, click the No button.

2 With the A+ Dentist Locator Revised form on the screen, click File on the menu bar and then click Close. If Word displays a dialog box asking to save the changes, click the No button.

Word closes the open files.

To Close Windows Explorer

1 Click the Close button on the Explorer window's title bar.

Windows Explorer closes.

Digital Signatures

Some users attach a digital signature to a document to verify its authenticity. A **digital signature** is an electronic, encrypted, and secure stamp of authentication on a document. This signature confirms that the file originated from the signer (file developer) and that it has not been altered.

A digital signature references a digital certificate. A **digital certificate** is an attachment to a file, macro project, or e-mail message that vouches for its authenticity, provides secure encryption, or supplies a verifiable signature. Many users who receive online forms enable the macros based on whether they are digitally signed by a developer on the user's list of trusted sources.

You can obtain a digital certificate from a commercial **certification authority**, from your network administrator, or you can create a digital signature yourself. A digital certificate you create yourself is not issued by a formal certification authority. Thus, signed macros using such a certificate are referred to as **self-signed projects**. Certificates you create yourself are considered unauthenticated and still will generate a warning when opened if the security level is set to very high, high, or medium. Many users, however, consider self-signed projects safer to open than those with no certificates at all.

Attaching a Digital Signature to a File

A **file digital signature** is a digital signature that appears when you e-mail a document from Word. Word will display the digital signature whenever the document is opened. In the following steps, you will digitally sign a file from the Data Disk that accompanies this book. If you did not download the Data Disk, see the inside back cover for instructions for downloading the Data Disk or see your instructor.

The following steps describe how to open the file from the Data Disk and then save it with a new file name.

To Open a File from the Data Disk and Save It with a New File Name

1. With the Data Disk in drive A, click the Open button on the Standard toolbar.

2. When Word displays the Open dialog box, if necessary, click the Look in box arrow and then click 3½ Floppy (A:). Click the Files of type box arrow and then click Document Templates.

3. Double-click the template, Centerville Sticker.

4. When Word opens the file, click the Zoom box arrow and then click Page Width. Scroll down so the complete form is displayed on the screen.

5. Click Tools on the menu bar and then click Unprotect Document. Close the Protect Document task pane.

6. Click File on the menu bar and then click Save As.

7. When Word displays the Save As dialog box, if necessary, click Save in box arrow and then click 3½ Floppy (A:). Type Centerville Sticker Revised in the File name box and then click the Save button in the Save As dialog box.

The file is saved on the floppy disk with the name, Centerville Sticker Revised.

The steps on the next page show how to digitally sign the file.

More About

Certified Digital Signatures

Several companies provide authenticated, certified digital signatures via the Web. For more information about digital signatures, visit the Word 2003 More About Web page (scsite.com/wd2003/more) and then click Certified Digital Signatures.

More About

Digital Signatures

When you attach a digital signature to a macro project, Word will display the digital signature when the user of the file is asked to enable macros. When you modify code in a signed macro project, its digital signature usually is removed. For this reason, you should digitally sign macros only after your solution has been saved, tested, and is ready for distribution.

To Digitally Sign a File

1

• **Click Tools on the menu bar and then click Options.**

• **When Word displays the Options dialog box, if necessary, click the Security tab.**

The Security sheet displays options for password protecting a document and privacy, as well as for digital signatures (Figure 8-72).

FIGURE 8-72

2

• **Click the Digital Signatures button.**

Word displays the Digital Signature dialog box (Figure 8-73). Your Signer list may display previous certificates.

FIGURE 8-73

3

• **Click the Add button.**

• **If Word displays a dialog box, warning you about fonts, text, or pictures, click the Yes button.**

• **When Word displays the Select Certificate dialog box, click the certificate you wish to add. If your computer does not display any certificates, click the Cancel button in each dialog box and skip Step 4.**

Your certificate list will differ (Figure 8-74).

FIGURE 8-74

4

• **Click the OK button in each dialog box.**

Word displays a certificate icon on the status bar (Figure 8-75).

5

• **Click the Save button on the Standard toolbar.**

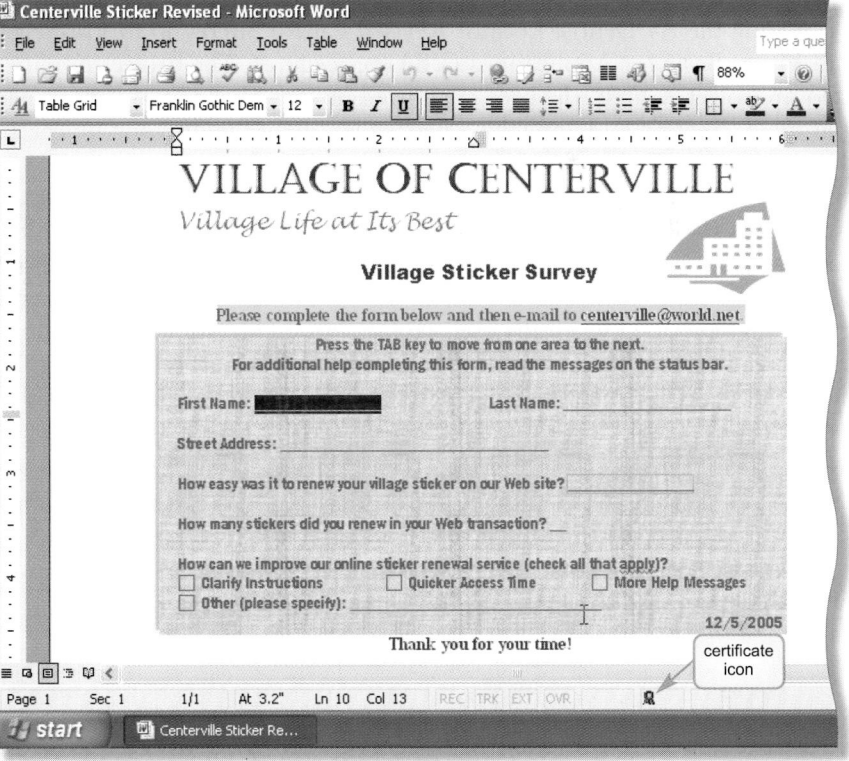

FIGURE 8-75

When you save or open a digitally signed document, Word displays a message announcing the signature on the status bar while the file opens. Once the file is opened, Word displays a certificate icon on the status bar. You can double-click the icon to see who digitally signed the document. The word, (Signed), also may be displayed on the title bar, indicating the document is digitally signed.

If you do not have any digital certificates on your computer, Office provides a method of creating your own. These self-signed projects that you create are not authenticated, which means Word still may display a warning about macros when the document is opened. Self-signed projects, however, are better than ones with no digital signature at all. To create your own digital signature, click the Start button on the taskbar, point to All Programs, point to Microsoft Office Tools, click Digital Certificate for VBA Projects, and then follow the instructions in the Create Digital Signature dialog box. Be aware that running this program multiple times can create duplicate digital signatures on the computer. You cannot remove duplicate digital signatures using Word.

You are finished with the form. The following step quits Word.

To Quit Word

1 **Click File on the menu bar and then click Exit.**

The Word window closes.

More About

Certification

The Microsoft Office Specialist Certification program provides an opportunity for you to obtain a valuable industry credential - proof that you have the Word 2003 skills required by employers. For more information, see Appendix E or visit the Word 2003 Certification Web page (scsite.com/wd2003/cert).

Project Summary

In creating the A+ Dentist Locator Revised Patient Survey in this project, you learned how to work with macros and Visual Basic for Applications (VBA) procedures. The project modified the template for the online form created in Project 7. First, the project showed how to change the appearance of the form by inserting and cropping a graphic, creating and applying a new style, filling the drawing object with a preset color scheme effect, and then adding a 3-D effect to the rectangle drawing object.

You learned how to create a macro using the macro recorder. Then, the project showed how to assign the macro to a toolbar button and a menu and then how to delete the toolbar button and menu command. Next, you learned how to record an automatic macro. The project showed how to view the macro's code using the Visual Basic Editor and add comments and code statements to the macro. You learned how to create another macro that executed when the user exits a form field. After showing how to insert an ActiveX control, the project showed how to set its properties and write a VBA procedure for it. Finally, you learned how to work with the Unprotect Document task pane and attach a digital signature to a document.

If you have a SAM user profile, you may have access to hands-on instruction, practice, and assessment of the skills covered in this project. Log in to your SAM account and go to your assignments page to see what your instructor has assigned.

What You Should Know

Having completed this project, you should be able to perform the tasks below. The tasks are listed in the same order they were presented in the project. For a list of the buttons, menus, toolbars, and commands introduced in the project, see the Quick Reference Summary at the back of this book and refer to the Page Number column.

1. Start and Customize Word (WD 557)
2. Open a Word Template (WD 557)
3. Save a Document with a New File Name (WD 558)
4. Unprotect a Document (WD 558, WD 582)
5. Set a Security Level in Word (WD 560)
6. Display Formatting Marks (WD 561)
7. Zoom Page Width (WD 561)
8. Format Text (WD 562)
9. Insert Clip Art (WD 563)
10. Insert a Graphic File from the Data Disk (WD 563)
11. Format a Graphic with a Square Wrapping Style (WD 563)
12. Not Use the Drawing Grid (WD 564)
13. Crop a Graphic (WD 565)
14. Format a Graphic (WD 566)
15. Position a Graphic (WD 567)
16. Crop and Format a Graphic (WD 567)
17. Create a Style Associated with a Shortcut Key (WD 568)
18. Apply a Style Using a Shortcut Key (WD 570)
19. Modify a Style (WD 571)
20. Fill a Drawing Object with a Preset Color Scheme Fill Effect (WD 573)
21. Add a 3-D Effect and Modify Its Settings (WD 574)
22. Finish Modifying the Form (WD 575)
23. Save a Document (WD 576, WD 615)
24. Record a Macro and Assign It a Shortcut Key (WD 577)
25. Protect and Fill In a Form (WD 580)
26. Run a Macro (WD 581)
27. Add a Button to a Toolbar (WD 582)
28. Delete a Button from a Toolbar (WD 586)
29. Add a Command to a Menu (WD 586)
30. Reset Form Fields (WD 587)
31. Create an Automatic Macro (WD 588)
32. Run the AutoNew Macro (WD 591)

33. View a Macro's VBA Code (WD 592)
34. Add Comments to a Procedure (WD 595)
35. Modify Existing Code (WD 596)
36. Add Code Statements to a Procedure (WD 597, WD 603)
37. Quit the Visual Basic Editor (WD 598)
38. Change Options for a Text Form Field (WD 599)
39. Change a Bookmark for a Drop-Down Form Field (WD 599)
40. Insert a Visual Basic Procedure (WD 600)
41. Run a Macro when a User Exits a Form Field (WD 604)
42. Copy a Macro (WD 604)
43. Rename a Macro (WD 605)
44. Delete a Macro (WD 605)
45. Insert an ActiveX Control (WD 606)
46. Set Properties of an ActiveX Control (WD 608)
47. Change Bookmarks for Form Fields (WD 612)
48. Enter the Click Here When Finished Button Procedure (WD 612)
49. Protect the Form Using the Protect Document Task Pane (WD 614)
50. Test the Form (WD 616)
51. Close a File (WD 616)
52. Close Windows Explorer (WD 616)
53. Open a File from the Data Disk and Save It with a New File Name (WD 617)
54. Digitally Sign a File (WD 618)
55. Quit Word (WD 620)

More About

Quick Reference

For a table that lists how to complete the tasks covered in this book using the mouse, menu, shortcut menu, and keyboard, see the Quick Reference Summary at the back of this book, or visit the Word 2003 Quick Reference Web page (scsite.com/wd2003/qr).

Learn It Online

Instructions: To complete the Learn It Online exercises, start your browser, click the Address bar, and then enter the Web address scsite.com/wd2003/learn. When the Word 2003 Learn It Online page is displayed, follow the instructions in the exercises below. Each exercise has instructions for printing your results, either for your own records or for submission to your instructor.

1 Project Reinforcement TF, MC, and SA

Below Word Project 8, click the Project Reinforcement link. Print the quiz by clicking Print on the File menu for each page. Answer each question.

2 Flash Cards

Below Word Project 8, click the Flash Cards link and read the instructions. Type 20 (or a number specified by your instructor) in the Number of playing cards text box, type your name in the Enter your Name text box, and then click the Flip Card button. When the flash card is displayed, read the question and then click the ANSWER box arrow to select an answer. Flip through Flash Cards. If your score is 15 (75%) correct or greater, click Print on the File menu to print your results. If your score is less than 15 (75%) correct, then redo this exercise by clicking the Replay button.

3 Practice Test

Below Word Project 8, click the Practice Test link. Answer each question, enter your first and last name at the bottom of the page, and then click the Grade Test button. When the graded practice test is displayed on your screen, click Print on the File menu to print a hard copy. Continue to take practice tests until you score 80% or better.

4 Who Wants To Be a Computer Genius?

Below Word Project 8, click the Computer Genius link. Read the instructions, enter your first and last name at the bottom of the page, and then click the PLAY button. When your score is displayed, click the PRINT RESULTS link to print a hard copy.

5 Wheel of Terms

Below Word Project 8, click the Wheel of Terms link. Read the instructions, and then enter your first and last name and your school name. Click the PLAY button. When your score is displayed, right-click the score and then click Print on the shortcut menu to print a hard copy.

6 Crossword Puzzle Challenge

Below Word Project 8, click the Crossword Puzzle Challenge link. Read the instructions, and then enter your first and last name. Click the SUBMIT button. Work the crossword puzzle. When you are finished, click the Submit button. When the crossword puzzle is redisplayed, click the Print Puzzle button to print a hard copy.

7 Tips and Tricks

Below Word Project 8, click the Tips and Tricks link. Click a topic that pertains to Project 8. Right-click the information and then click Print on the shortcut menu. Construct a brief example of what the information relates to in Word to confirm you understand how to use the tip or trick.

8 Newsgroups

Below Word Project 8, click the Newsgroups link. Click a topic that pertains to Project 8. Print three comments.

9 Expanding Your Horizons

Below Word Project 8, click the Expanding Your Horizons link. Click a topic that pertains to Project 8. Print the information. Construct a brief example of what the information relates to in Word to confirm you understand the contents of the article.

10 Search Sleuth

Below Word Project 8, click the Search Sleuth link. To search for a term that pertains to this project, select a term below the Project 8 title and then use the Google search engine at google.com (or any major search engine) to display and print two Web pages that present information on the term.

11 Word Online Training

Below Word Project 8, click the Word Online Training link. When your browser displays the Microsoft Office Online Web page, click the Word link. Click one of the Word courses that covers one or more of the objectives listed at the beginning of the project on page WD 554. Print the first page of the course before stepping through it.

12 Office Marketplace

Below Word Project 8, click the Office Marketplace link. When your browser displays the Microsoft Office Online Web page, click the Office Marketplace link. Click a topic that relates to Word. Print the first page.

Apply Your Knowledge

1 Debugging VBA Code

Instructions: In this assignment, you access a template through Windows Explorer. As shown in Figure 8-76, the template contains an online form. The form contains a macro that executes when you initially open the form on the screen and a procedure that executes when you click the command button at the bottom of the screen. Both the macro and the procedure each contain one coding error. You are to test the code by filling in the form. Then, correct the Visual Basic errors as they appear on the screen.

The template is located on the Data Disk. If you did not download the Data Disk, see the inside back cover for instructions for downloading the Data Disk or see your instructor.

FIGURE 8-76

(continued)

Debugging VBA Code *(continued)*

Perform the following tasks:

1. Start Windows Explorer.
2. Double-click the Apply 8-1 Centerville Sticker icon to display a new document based on the template.
3. If Word displays a dialog box about macros, click the Enable Macros button.
4. When Visual Basic displays an error message, click its OK button. If necessary, maximize the Microsoft Visual Basic window. Notice the text, .ZoomPageFit =, is highlighted because Visual Basic did not recognize it. The text should say, .Zoom.PageFit = (it is missing the period). Insert the missing period. Then, click the Continue button on the Visual Basic Standard toolbar. Close the Microsoft Visual Basic window by clicking its Close button.
5. With the selection in the First Name text form field, type your first name and then press the TAB key. Type your last name in the Last Name text form field and then press the TAB key. Enter your street address in the Street Address text form field and then press the TAB key. Click the ease of use box arrow and then click Easy in the list. Press the TAB key and then type 2 in the number of stickers text form field. Check the Clarify Instructions and More Help Messages check boxes.
6. Click the Click Here When Finished button. When Visual Basic displays an error message, click the OK button. If necessary, click the Microsoft Visual Basic - Apply 8-1 Centerville Sticker program button on the taskbar to display the Visual Basic Editor. Notice the code statement that displays the Save As dialog box is highlighted as an error. To the right of the text, Dialogs(wdDialogFileSaveAs)., the word, Show, is missing. Type the word Show after the period. Click the Continue button on the Visual Basic Standard toolbar.
7. When Word displays the Save As dialog box, type Apply 8-1 My Form in the File name box, change the Save in location to drive A, and then click the Save button in the Save As dialog box. When Word asks if you want to save changes to the template, click the No button. Click the OK button in the Thank You For Your Time message box.
8. Print the filled-in form.
9. Print the data only.
10. Press ALT+F11 or click the appropriate taskbar button to switch to the Visual Basic window. In the Microsoft Visual Basic window, click File on the menu bar and then click Print. When the Print dialog box appears, click Current Project and then click the OK button.
11. Close all open windows.

In the Lab

1 Creating an Automatic Macro for an Online Form

Problem: You created the online form shown in Figure 7-70 on page WD 545 for Global Choice Coffee Club. Your supervisor has asked you to change its appearance and create a macro for the form so it is displayed properly on the screen when a user first opens it (as a blank form). You modify the form so it looks like the one shown in Figure 8-77.

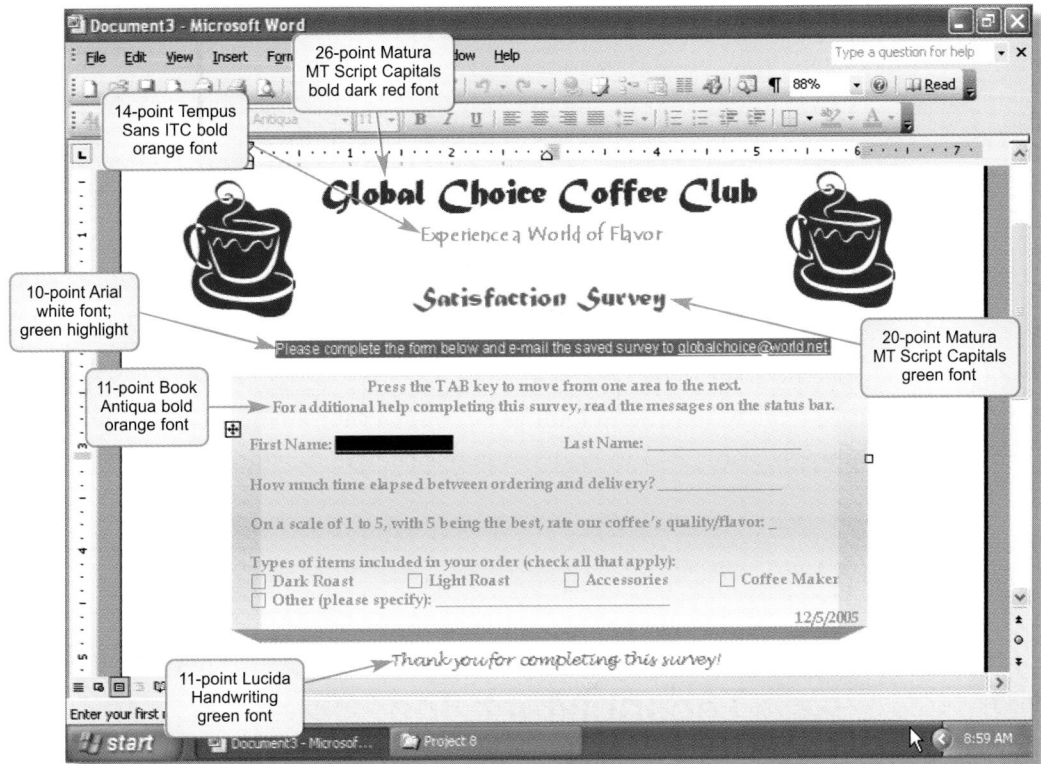

FIGURE 8-77

Instructions:

1. Open the template called Lab 7-1 Global Coffee that you created in Lab 1 of Project 7 on page WD 545. Save the template with a new file name of Lab 8-1 Global Coffee. If you did not complete this lab, see your instructor for a copy.
2. Modify the formats of the company name, business tag line, form title, user instructions, and thank-you message as shown in Figure 8-77 (or with similar fonts). Remove the current clip art and insert the ones shown in Figure 8-77 (or a similar image). Format the images as floating with a square wrapping style. Resize the clip art images to 66 percent of their original size.
3. Change the fill effect in the rectangle drawing object to the preset Wheat color scheme with 50 percent transparency. Add the 3-D effect called 3-D Style 7.
4. Create a new character style called DataEntryArea that is formatted with an 11-point Book Antiqua bold green font. Assign a shortcut key of ALT+D. Apply the style to all text in the data entry area.
5. Modify the character style to use an orange font, instead of green.

(continued)

In the Lab

Creating an Automatic Macro for an Online Form *(continued)*

6. Create an automatic macro called AutoNew using the macro recorder. The macro should change the zoom to page width and scroll down so the entire form fits in the document window. Run the macro to be sure it works.

7. Modify (edit) the macro in the Visual Basic Editor so that it also hides formatting marks and table gridlines. Also, modify the number of lines it scrolls down, if necessary. Run the macro again.

8. Print the Visual Basic code for the macro (in the Visual Basic Editor window, click File on the menu bar, click Print, click Current Project, click the OK button).

9. Protect the form. Save the form. Print the blank form.

10. Access the template through Windows Explorer. Fill in the form. Print the filled-in form.

2 Creating an Online Form with an Automatic Macro, an ActiveX Control, and a Digital Signature

Problem: You created the online form shown in Figure 7-71 on page WD 547 for TechnoMart, Inc. Your supervisor has asked you to change its appearance, create a macro for the form so it displays properly on the screen when a user first opens it (as a blank form), and add a button that automatically displays the Save As dialog box for the user. You modify the form so it looks like the one shown in Figure 8-78.

FIGURE 8-78

Instructions:

1. Open the template called Lab 7-2 TechnoMart that you created in Lab 2 of Project 7 on page WD 547. If you did not complete this lab, see your instructor for a copy. Save the template with a new file name of Lab 8-2 TechoMart.

2. Remove the current clip art and insert the one shown in Figure 8-78 (or a similar clip). Format the image as floating with a square wrapping style. Crop the edge of the clip art so just the computer shows. Resize the graphic to 57 percent of its original size. Add a 1-point red dashed border around the clip art. Copy and paste the clip to the right side of the form.

3. Modify the formats of the company name, tag line, form title, and user instructions as shown in Figure 8-78 (or with similar fonts).

4. Change the fill effect in the rectangle drawing object to the preset Gold color scheme. Add the 3-D effect called 3-D Style 1. Modify the lighting of the 3-D style so the light shines down from the top-right corner.

5. Create a new character style called DataEntryArea that is formatted with an 11-point Arial bold green font. Assign a shortcut key of ALT+D. Apply the style to all text in the data entry area.

6. Create an automatic macro called AutoNew using the macro recorder. The macro should change the zoom percentage to page width and scroll down so the entire form fits in the document window. Run the macro to be sure it works.

7. Modify (edit) the macro in the Visual Basic Editor so that it also hides formatting marks and table gridlines. Also, modify the number of lines it scrolls down, if necessary. Run the macro again.

8. Remove the thank-you message line. Insert a command button ActiveX control. Change its caption property to the text, Click Here When Finished. Change the AutoSize property so all text fits in the button. Add code to the button so that when the user clicks the button it displays the Save As dialog box and then displays a thank-you message.

9. Print the Visual Basic code for the macros (in the Visual Basic Editor window, click File on the menu bar, click Print, click Current Project, click the OK button).

10. Protect the form by setting appropriate editing restrictions in the Protect Document task pane. Save the form. Print the blank form.

11. Attach a digital signature to the form, if you have a digital signature on the computer. If you do not have a digital signature, create one – if your instructor gives you permission.

12. Access the template through Windows Explorer. Fill in the form. Print the filled-in form.

3 Creating an Automatic Macro, Data Entry Macros, and an ActiveX Control for an Online Form

Problem: You created the online form shown in Figure 7-72 on page WD 548 for Click 'n' Save. Your supervisor has asked you to change its appearance, create a macro for the form so it is displayed properly on the screen when a user first opens it (as a blank form), and create a macro that displays an error message when the user enters an out-of-range value in the number of people form field. Add a button that automatically displays the Save As dialog box for the user, and create a macro and corresponding button on the toolbar that prints form data only. You modify the form so it looks like the one shown in Figure 8-79.

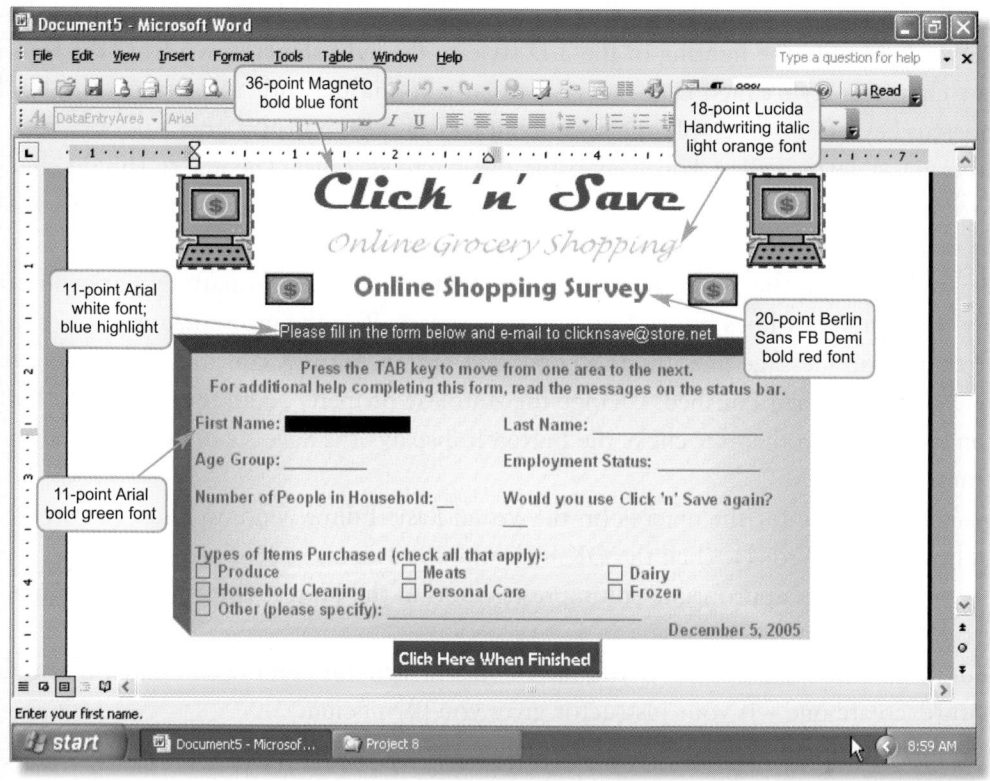

FIGURE 8-79

Instructions:

1. Open the template called Lab 7-3 Click N Save that you created in Lab 3 of Project 7 on page WD 548. If you did not complete this lab, see your instructor for a copy. Save the template with a new file name of Lab 8-3 Click N Save.
2. Modify the formats of the company name, form title, and user instructions as shown in Figure 8-79 (or similar fonts).

In the Lab

3. Remove the current clip art and insert the one of the computer shown in Figure 8-79 (or a similar clip). Format the image as floating with a square wrapping style. Crop the edge of the clip art so just the computer shows. Resize the graphic to 50 percent of its original size. Add a 1.5-point blue dashed border around the clip art. Copy and paste the clip to the right side of the form.

4. Crop one of the computer clip art images so just the dollar bill is on the image (as shown in Figure 8-79). Remove the border from this image. Copy the image and position both images as shown in Figure 8-79.

5. Change the fill effect in the rectangle drawing object to the preset Parchment color scheme. Add the 3-D effect called 3-D Style 2. Change the 3-D shadow color to red.

6. Create a new character style called DataEntryArea that is formatted with 11-point Arial bold green font. Assign a shortcut key of ALT+D. Apply the style to all text in the data entry area.

7. Create an automatic macro called AutoNew using the macro recorder. The macro should change the zoom percentage to page width and scroll down so the entire form fits in the document window. Run the macro to be sure it works.

8. Modify (edit) the macro in the Visual Basic Editor so that it also hides formatting marks and table gridlines. Also, modify the number of lines it scrolls down, if necessary. Run the macro again.

9. Create a macro that displays an error message when the user enters an out-of-range value in the number of people form field.

10. Remove the thank-you message line. Insert a command button ActiveX control. Change its caption property to the text, Click Here When Finished. Change the AutoSize property so the entire text fits on the button. Change its Font property to 12-point Berlin Sans FB Demi bold font. Change the background color of the button to blue and the foreground color to white. Add code to the button so that when the user clicks the button, it displays the Save As dialog box and displays a thank-you message.

11. Record a macro that prints the form data only. Add a toolbar button for this macro; use the image of a coffee cup for the button. Also, add a command to the Tools menu for this macro.

12. Print the form.

13. Copy the AutoNew macro to a macro called TestMacro. Rename the TestMacro name to the name, MacroTest.

14. Print the Visual Basic code for the macros (in the Visual Basic Editor window, click File on the menu bar, click Print, click Current Project, and then click the OK button).

15. Delete the macro called MacroTest.

16. Delete the coffee cup button from the toolbar. Delete the macro command from the Tools menu.

17. Protect the form by setting appropriate editing restrictions in the Protect Document task pane. Save the form. Print the blank form.

18. Access the template through Windows Explorer. Fill in the form. Print the filled-in form.

Cases and Places

The difficulty of these case studies varies:
■ are the least difficult and ■■ are more difficult. The last exercise is a group exercise.

1 ■ You created the online form for Happy Handyman Service that was defined in Cases and Places Assignment 1 in Project 7 on page WD 550. You decide to change its appearance; that is, change its fonts, font sizes, fill effects, colors, and clip art. You also decide that the form should include the following macros and VBA procedures:

1. When the form initially is displayed on the screen (as a blank document), Word zooms page width, scrolls down to display the entire form in the Word window, hides formatting marks, and hides gridlines.
2. If the user enters an invalid rating scale, an error message should be displayed.
3. The form should contain a Click Here When Finished button that, when clicked, does the following:
   a. If the user entered text in the Other text form field, then Word places an X in the Other check box (just in case the user left it blank).
   b. The Save As dialog box displays so the user can assign a file name to the filled-in form.
   c. A thank-you message appears on the screen that informs the user what file should be e-mailed back to the service.

Use the concepts and techniques presented in this project to modify the online form.

2 ■■ You created the survey for Fair Heart Fashions that was defined in Cases and Places Assignment 2 in Project 7 on page WD 550. The owner has asked you to change the survey's appearance (change all fonts, font sizes, colors, graphics, and fill effects), create a macro for the form so it is displayed properly on the screen when a user first opens it (as a blank form), and add a button that, when clicked, automatically displays the Save As dialog box for the user and then displays a thank-you message. Use the concepts and techniques presented in this project to modify the online form. Attach a digital signature to the document.

3 ■■ You created the survey for Royal Oaks Health Club that was defined in Cases and Places Assignment 3 in Project 7 on page WD 551. The director has asked you to change the survey's appearance (change all fonts, font sizes, colors, graphics, and fill effects), create a macro for the form so it is displayed properly on the screen when a user first opens it (as a blank form), and add a button that, when clicked, automatically displays the Save As dialog box for the user and then displays a thank-you message. Use the concepts and techniques presented in this project to modify the online form. Enter a password to protect the form and set editing restrictions. Be sure to use a different graphic from the Clip Organizer or from the Web.

Cases and Places

The difficulty of these case studies varies:
▦ are the least difficult and ▦▦ are more difficult. The last exercise is a group exercise.

4 ▦▦ You created the survey for Wheels on the Web that was defined in Cases and Places Assignment 4 in Project 7 on page WD 551. Your boss has asked you to change the survey's appearance (change all fonts, font sizes, colors, graphics, and fill effects), create a macro for the form so it is displayed properly on the screen when a user first opens it (as a blank form), and add a button that, when clicked, automatically displays the Save As dialog box for the user and then displays a thank-you message. Use the concepts and techniques presented in this project to modify the online form. Be sure to use a different graphic from the Clip Organizer or from the Web.

5 ▦▦ **Working Together** This team project expands on your knowledge of ActiveX controls and digital signatures. The owner of a local business would like to publish the a survey on the Web. One or more team members should design and create the form using only ActiveX controls; that is, do not use Word form fields; instead use ActiveX controls. Write a VBA procedure for every control, so it displays an error message if the user makes an invalid entry or leaves the entry blank. The form also should include a custom menu containing commands the team deems appropriate for the user. Other team members should search the Web for companies that certify digital signatures, such as VeriSign, Inc. Then, use Word to create a list of companies found, the kinds of information they require their customers to submit, and the cost. Search each certification company's Web site for customers they have certified in the past, and list two for each company. Team members should ask an IT professional at your school or place of employment if he or she can provide your team with an internal certificate. Write a report describing what you learned. Set appropriate formatting restrictions in the report. Attach a digital certificate to the form. E-mail your report and form with ActiveX controls to your instructor, if your instructor gives you permission to do so.

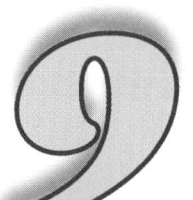

Office Word 2003

Working with a Master Document, an Index, a Table of Contents, and XML

PROJECT

9

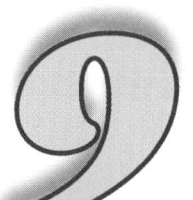

CASE PERSPECTIVE

As a service to students, the desktop publishing department at Westside Community College composes and distributes multipage pamphlets that contain information it deems appropriate to help the student population concerning a variety of academic, technical, and health-related issues. One of its series, titled *Computer Chronicles*, presents a brief discussion about various aspects of computers. Students can find current and previous editions of *Computer Chronicles* in the computer technology lab room.

Maria Lopez, director of computer technology, recently distributed a student opinion survey about *Computer Chronicles*. Feedback was very positive about the content of the pamphlets. She received suggestions that indicated the documents could be more useful if they included elements such as a table of contents and index.

Employees in the desktop publishing department compose the pamphlets with assistance from employees in other departments. For example, the computer technology staff writes the content for *Computer Chronicles*. The desktop publishing department then incorporates art, compiles the art and text content into a pamphlet, and publishes copies for the computer technology lab room. Maria Lopez has requested that the desktop publishing department incorporate student suggestions in future editions of *Computer Chronicles*. As a part-time specialist in the desktop publishing department, you have been assigned the task of redesigning the composition of these documents.

As you read through this project, you will learn how to use Word to work with long documents and create an index and table of contents.

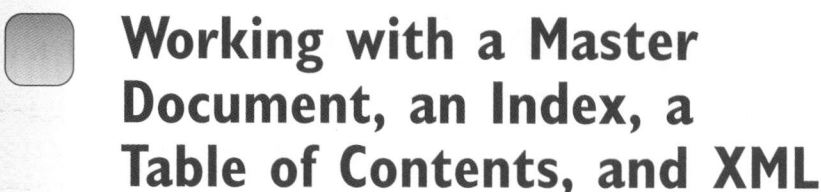
Working with a Master Document, an Index, a Table of Contents, and XML

P R O J E C T

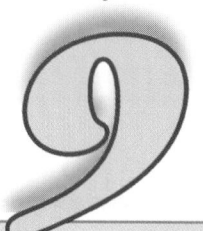

You will have mastered the material in this project when you can:

- Save versions of a document
- Add and modify a caption
- Create a cross-reference
- Hyphenate a document
- Work with a master document and subdocuments
- Create a table of figures
- Build and modify an index

- Create and modify a table of contents
- Work with bookmarks
- Create alternating headers
- Use the Document Map
- AutoSummarize a document
- Password-protect a document
- Work with XML

Introduction

During the course of your academic studies and professional endeavors, you may find it necessary to compose a document that is many pages in length or even one that is hundreds of pages. When composing a long document, you must ensure that the document is organized so a reader easily can locate material within the document. Sometimes a document of this nature is called a **reference document**.

By placing a table of contents at the beginning of the document and an index at the end, you help a reader navigate through a long document. If a document contains several illustrations, each illustration should have a caption. In addition, you could list the illustrations in a table, called a table of figures, that identifies the location of each figure in the document. For long documents that will be viewed online, you should incorporate hyperlinks so a user can click the link to jump from one portion of the document to another.

Project Nine — Reference Document

Project 9 uses Word to produce the reference document shown in Figure 9-1. The multipage document, titled *Computer Chronicles*, is a student information guide that is distributed by Westside Community College to the student population. Notice that the inner margin between facing pages has extra space to allow duplicated copies of the document to be bound — without the binding covering the words.

extra space for binding

table of figures

index

table of contents

title page

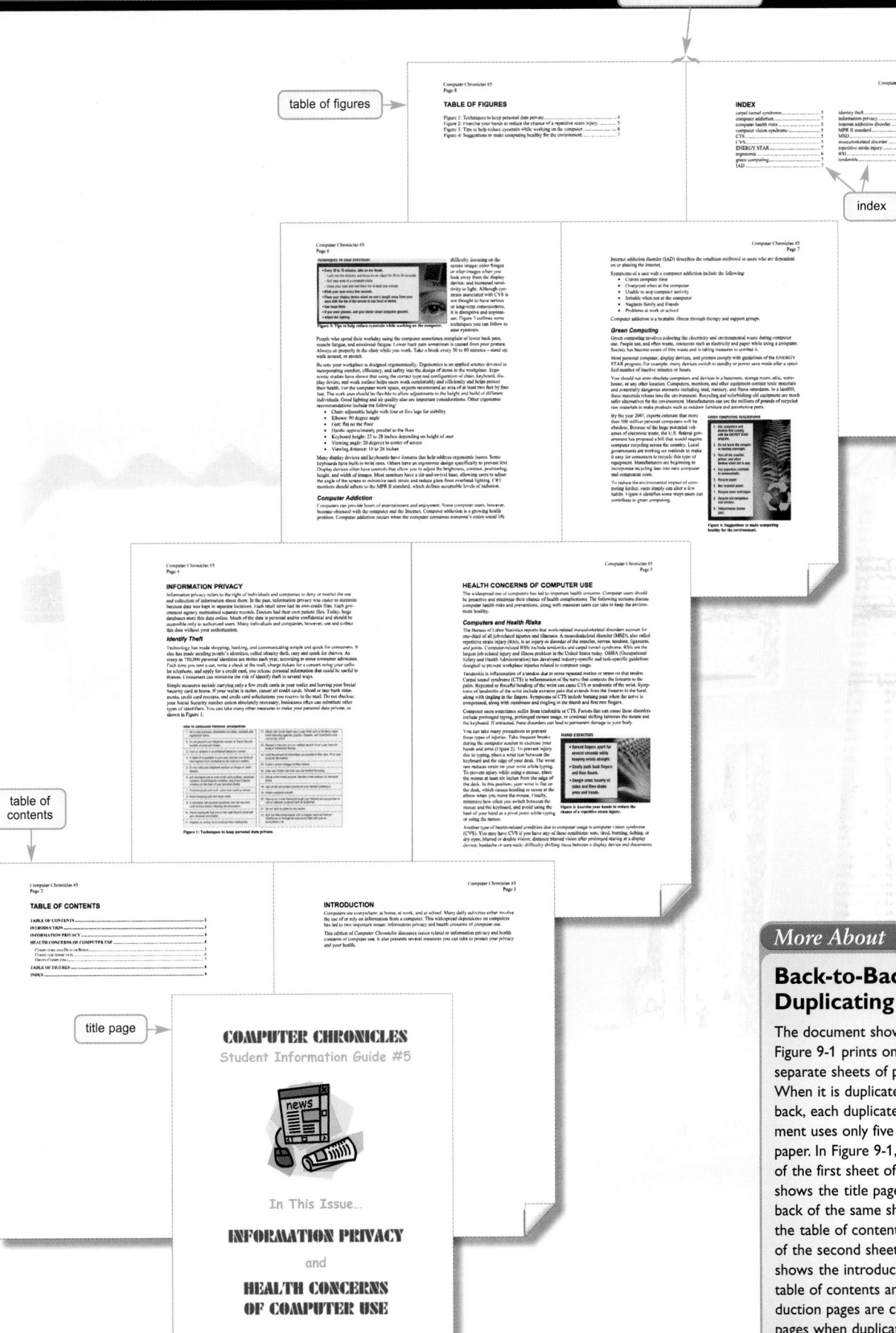

FIGURE 9-1

More About

Back-to-Back Duplicating

The document shown in Figure 9-1 prints on nine separate sheets of paper. When it is duplicated back to back, each duplicated document uses only five sheets of paper. In Figure 9-1, the top of the first sheet of paper shows the title page, and the back of the same sheet shows the table of contents; the top of the second sheet of paper shows the introduction. The table of contents and introduction pages are called facing pages when duplicated in this manner.

More About

Reference Documents

For a sample reference document on the Web that contains elements commonly found in long documents, visit the Word 2003 More About Web page (scsite.com/wd2003/more) and then click Sample Reference Document.

Computer Chronicles begins with a title page designed to entice the target audience to open the document and read it. Next is the table of contents, followed by an introduction. The document then discusses two topics: information privacy and health concerns of computer use. The end of the document has a table of figures and an index to assist readers in locating information. A miniature version of this *Computer Chronicles* student information guide document is shown in Figure 9-1 on the previous page; for a more readable view, visit scsite.com/wd2003/project9.

You have asked the computer technology staff to write the content for the information privacy and health concerns of computer use sections of the document and then e-mail the files to you for inclusion in the *Computer Chronicles* student information guide document. You have received the completed documents, which require a few modifications before you include them in this issue of *Computer Chronicles*. After modifying the two documents, you will incorporate them in a single file. Then, you will create a title page, table of contents, introduction, table of figures, and index to organize the document.

Drafts of the two documents, called Information Privacy Draft and Health Concerns of Computer Use Draft, are on the Data Disk that accompanies this book. If you did not download the Data Disk, see the inside back cover for instructions for downloading the Data Disk or see your instructor.

The following pages explain how to modify the drafts and how to assemble the final document. The end of the project explains how to use XML to modify a cover memo for the finished *Computer Chronicles* document.

Starting and Customizing Word

To start and customize Word, Windows must be running. If you are stepping through this project on a computer and you want your screen to match the figures in this book, then you should change your computer's resolution to 800 × 600 and reset the toolbars and menus. For information about changing the resolution and resetting toolbars and menus, read Appendix D.

The following steps describe how to start Word and customize the Word window. You may need to ask your instructor how to start Word for your system.

To Start and Customize Word

1 Click the Start button on the Windows taskbar, point to All Programs on the Start menu, point to Microsoft Office on the All Programs submenu, and then click Microsoft Office Word 2003 on the Microsoft Office submenu.

2 If the Word window is not maximized, double-click its title bar to maximize it.

3 If the Language bar appears, right-click it and then click Close the Language bar on the shortcut menu.

4 If the Getting Started task pane is displayed in the Word window, click its Close button.

5 If the Standard and Formatting toolbar buttons are displayed on one row, click the Toolbar Options button and then click Show Buttons on Two Rows in the Toolbar Options list.

6 Click View on the menu bar and then click Print Layout.

Word starts and, after a few moments, displays an empty document in the Word window.

Displaying Formatting Marks

It is helpful to display formatting marks that indicate where in the document you pressed the ENTER key, SPACEBAR, and other keys. The following step describes how to display formatting marks.

To Display Formatting Marks

1 If the Show/Hide ¶ button on the Standard toolbar is not selected already, click it.

Word displays formatting marks in the document window, and the Show/Hide ¶ button on the Standard toolbar is selected (shown in Figure 9-2 on the next page).

Zooming Page Width

When you zoom page width, Word displays the page on the screen as large as possible in print layout view. The following steps zoom page width.

To Zoom Page Width

1 Click the Zoom box arrow on the Standard toolbar.

2 Click Page Width in the Zoom list.

Word computes the zoom percentage and displays it in the Zoom box (shown in Figure 9-2). Your percentage may be different depending on your computer settings.

Opening a Document and Saving It with a New File Name

The first step in this project is to open the file called Information Privacy Draft on the Data Disk so that you can modify it. If you did not download the Data Disk, see the inside back cover for instructions for downloading the Data Disk or see your instructor. The following steps describe how to open the Information Privacy Draft file.

To Open a Document

1 With the disk containing the Information Privacy Draft file in drive A, click the Open button on the Standard toolbar.

2 When Word displays the Open dialog box, if necessary, click the Look in box arrow and then click 3½ Floppy (A:).

3 Double-click Information Privacy Draft.

Word displays the document titled, Information Privacy Draft, on the screen.

To preserve the contents of the original Information Privacy Draft file, save a copy of it with a new file name as described in the steps on the next page.

To Save a Document with a New File Name

1 With a floppy disk in drive A, click File on the menu bar and then click Save As.

2 When Word displays the Save As dialog box, type Information Privacy in the File name box. Do not press the ENTER key.

3 If necessary, click the Save in box arrow and then click 3½ Floppy (A:).

4 Click the Save button in the Save As dialog box.

Word saves the document on a floppy disk in drive A with the new file name, Information Privacy (shown in Figure 9-2).

Saving Multiple Versions of a Document

The previous steps described how to preserve a copy of a document by saving it with a new file name. An alternative is to save a separate version of the document. Each **version** represents the current state, or a snapshot, of the document at a specific time. Using the version feature saves disk space because Word saves only the changes among versions — as opposed to a complete copy of the file. The downside is that you cannot modify a version; you only can open and print versions. To modify a version, you must open it and save it with a new file name.

When saving a version of a document, you insert a description of the version so you can identify it at a later time. For illustration purposes, the following steps show how to save a version of the Information Privacy document.

To Save a Version of a Document

1

• **Click File on the menu bar (Figure 9-2).**

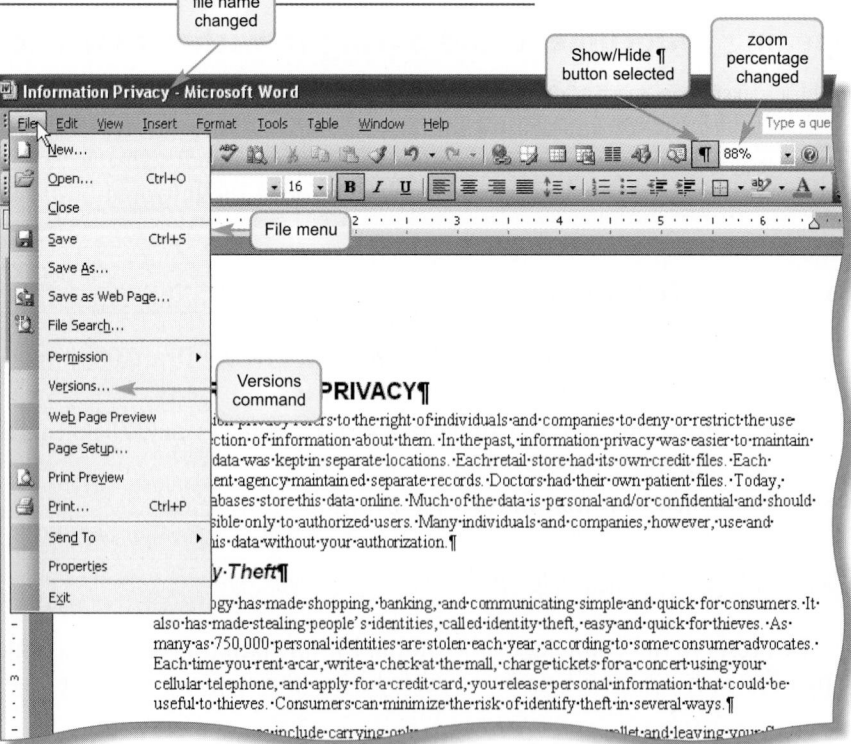

FIGURE 9-2

2

• **Click Versions on the File menu.**

Word displays the Versions in Information Privacy dialog box (Figure 9-3). Any previously saved versions are listed in the Existing versions area.

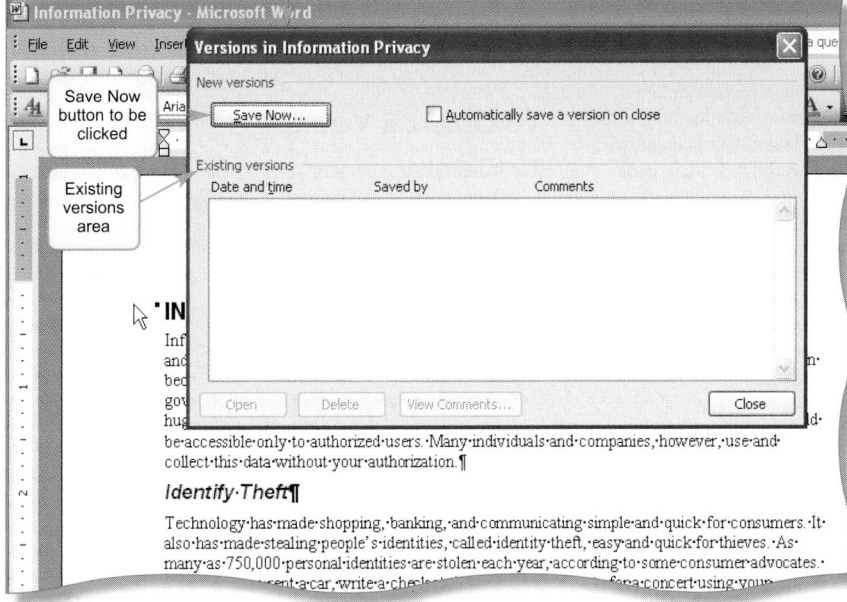

FIGURE 9-3

3

• **Click the Save Now button.**

• **When Word displays the Save Version dialog box, type** Original document before changes.

Word displays the comment associated with the version in the Save Version dialog box (Figure 9-4).

4

• **Click the OK button.**

Word saves the current state of the document along with the entered comment and closes the two open dialog boxes.

FIGURE 9-4

Other Ways

1. In Voice Command mode, say "File, Versions, Save Now, [type comment], OK"

When you open a document, Word displays the latest version in the document window. The following steps describe how to view a previous version of a document that is displayed on the screen.

TO VIEW A VERSION OF A DOCUMENT

1. Click File on the menu bar and then click Versions.
2. When Word displays the Versions in [file name] dialog box, click the version you wish to view.
3. Click the Open button in the Versions in [file name] dialog box.

If, for some reason, you wanted to edit a previous version of a document, you would view the version and then save it with a new file name.

The following steps describe how to delete a version.

TO DELETE A VERSION

1. Click File on the menu bar and then click Versions.
2. When Word displays the Versions in [file name] dialog box, click the version you wish to delete.
3. Click the Delete button.
4. When Word displays the Confirm Version Delete dialog box, click the Yes button.
5. Click the Close button in the Versions in [file name] dialog box.

To ensure you delete the correct version, be sure to read the comments for each version. If you cannot read the entire line of comments in the Versions in [file name] dialog box, select the appropriate version and then click the View Comments button.

Preparing a Document To Be Included in a Longer Document

After reviewing the Information Privacy and Health Concerns of Computer Use documents received from the computer technology staff, you notice they need several modifications.

In the Information Privacy document (Figure 9-5a), a figure is missing that identifies tips to keep data private. Once inserted, the graphic will need a caption because *Computer Chronicles* documents always have figure captions. Then, the text will need to reference the figure. Also, any words that should be listed in the index need to be marked as index entries. The document also should be hyphenated. Figure 9-5b shows the final copy of the Information Privacy document.

Finally, you will make one minor modification to the Health Concerns of Computer Use document, that is, sort paragraphs in a list.

The following pages outline the changes to be made to the Information Privacy and the Health Concerns of Computer Use documents.

Inserting and Formatting a Graphic

The graphic to be inserted in the Information Privacy document is located on the Data Disk that accompanies this book. If you did not download the Data Disk, see the inside back cover for instructions for downloading the Data Disk or see your instructor. The graphic shows a list of tips to keep data private. You will insert the graphic, resize it, and then change it from an inline graphic to a floating graphic.

The steps on page WD 642 show how to insert a graphic file from the Data Disk.

INFORMATION PRIVACY

Information privacy refers to the right of individuals and companies to deny or restrict the use and collection of information about them. In the past, information privacy was easier to maintain because data was kept in separate locations. Each retail store had its own credit files. Each government agency maintained separate records. Doctors had their own patient files. Today, huge databases store this data online. Much of the data is personal and/or confidential and should be accessible only to authorized users. Many individuals and companies, however, use and collect this data without your authorization.

Identify Theft

Technology has made shopping, banking, and communicating simple and quick for consumers. It also has made stealing people's identities, called identity theft, easy and quick for thieves. As many as 750,000 personal identities are stolen each year, according to some consumer advocates. Each time you rent a car, write a check at the mall, charge tickets for a concert using your cellular telephone, and apply for a credit card, you release personal information that could be useful to thieves. Consumers can minimize the risk of identify theft in several ways.

Simple measures include carrying only a few credit cards in your wallet and leaving your Social Security card at home. If your wallet is stolen, cancel all credit cards. Shred or tear bank statements, credit card receipts, and credit card solicitations you receive in the mail. Do not disclose your Social Security number unless absolutely necessary; businesses often can substitute other types of identifiers. You can take many other measures to make your personal data private, as shown below.

(a) Draft of Information Privacy Document

INFORMATION PRIVACY

Information privacy refers to the right of individuals and companies to deny or restrict the use and collection of information about them. In the past, information privacy was easier to maintain because data was kept in separate locations. Each retail store had its own credit files. Each government agency maintained separate records. Doctors had their own patient files. Today, huge databases store this data online. Much of the data is personal and/or confidential and should be accessible only to authorized users. Many individuals and companies, however, use and collect this data without your authorization.

Identify Theft

Technology has made shopping, banking, and communicating simple and quick for consumers. It also has made stealing people's identities, called identity theft, easy and quick for thieves. As many as 750,000 personal identities are stolen each year, according to some consumer advocates. Each time you rent a car, write a check at the mall, charge tickets for a concert using your cellular telephone, and apply for a credit card, you release personal information that could be useful to thieves. Consumers can minimize the risk of identify theft in several ways.

Simple measures include carrying only a few credit cards in your wallet and leaving your Social Security card at home. If your wallet is stolen, cancel all credit cards. Shred or tear bank statements, credit card receipts, and credit card solicitations you receive in the mail. Do not disclose your Social Security number unless absolutely necessary; businesses often can substitute other types of identifiers. You can take many other measures to make your personal data private, as shown in Figure 1.

HOW TO SAFEGUARD PERSONAL INFORMATION

1. Fill in only necessary information on rebate, warranty, and registration forms.	12. Obtain your credit report once a year from each of the three major credit reporting agencies (Equifax, Experian, and TransUnion) and correct any errors.
2. Do not preprint your telephone number or Social Security number on personal checks.	13. Request a free copy of your medical records once a year from the Medical Information Bureau.
3. Have an unlisted or unpublished telephone number.	14. Limit the amount of information you provide to Web sites. Fill in only required information.
4. If Caller ID is available in your area, find out how to block your number from displaying on the receiver's system.	15. Install a cookie manager to filter cookies.
5. Do not write your telephone number on charge or credit receipts.	16. Clear your history file when you are finished browsing.
6. Ask merchants not to write credit card numbers, telephone numbers, Social Security numbers, and driver's license numbers on the back of your personal checks.	17. Set up a free e-mail account. Use this e-mail address for merchant forms.
7. Purchase goods with cash, rather than credit or checks.	18. Turn off file and printer sharing on your Internet connection.
8. Avoid shopping club and buyer cards.	19. Install a personal firewall.
9. If merchants ask personal questions, find out why they want to know before releasing the information.	20. Sign-up for e-mail filtering through your Internet service provider or use an antispam program such as Brightmail.
10. Inform merchants that you do not want them to distribute your personal information.	21. Do not reply to spam for any reason.
11. Request, in writing, to be removed from mailing lists.	22. Surf the Web anonymously with a program such as Freedom WebSecure or through an anonymous Web site such as Anonymizer.com.

Figure 1: Techniques to keep personal data private.

(b) Final Copy of Information Privacy Document

FIGURE 9-5

To Insert a Graphic from a File

• **Scroll down to display the end of the Information Privacy document. Position the insertion point on the paragraph mark below the last paragraph of text (as shown in Figure 9-6).**

• **Click Insert on the menu bar and then point to Picture.**

FIGURE 9-6

• **Click From File on the Picture submenu.**

• **When Word displays the Insert Picture dialog box, if necessary, click the Look in box arrow and then click 3½ Floppy (A:).**

• **Click the file, Tips to Keep Data Private.**

The graphic to be inserted is selected (Figure 9-7).

• **Click the Insert button.**

Word inserts the graphic in the document (shown in Figure 9-8).

FIGURE 9-7

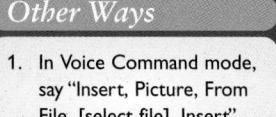

Other Ways

1. In Voice Command mode, say "Insert, Picture, From File, [select file], Insert"

You want the graphic to be smaller in the document. The following describes how to resize the graphic.

To Resize a Graphic

1 **Double-click the graphic.**

2 **When Word displays the Format Picture dialog box, if necessary, click the Size tab. Change the height and width values in the Scale area to 65%.**

3 **Click the OK button.**

Word reduces the size of the graphic to 65 percent of its original size (Figure 9-8).

graphic inserted and reduced to 65% of original size

FIGURE 9-8

Notice in Figure 9-8 that the graphic is inline, that is, part of the current paragraph. You want to move the graphic down and to the right. Thus, the graphic needs to be a floating graphic instead of an inline graphic. To do this, change the graphic's wrapping style to square, as described below.

To Format the Graphic as Floating

1 **If the Picture toolbar is not displayed, right-click the graphic, and then click Show Picture Toolbar on the shortcut menu. With the graphic still selected, click the Text Wrapping button on the Picture toolbar (Figure 9-9 on the next page).**

2 **Click Square in the list.**

3 **If necessary, scroll down to display the graphic.**

Word converts the graphic from inline to floating, which allows you to position it anywhere on the page.

Microsoft Office
Word 2003

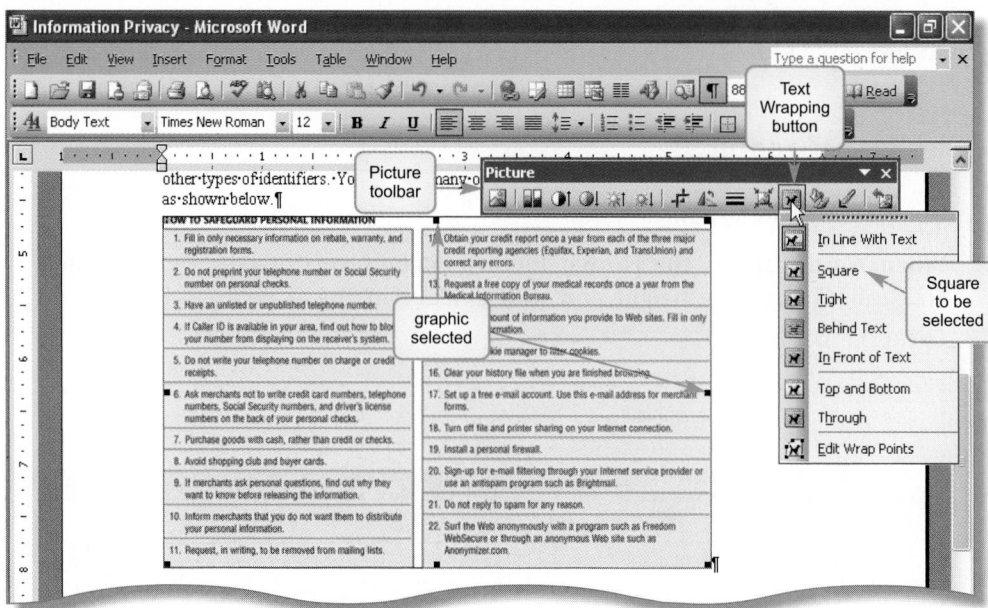

FIGURE 9-9

The next step is to center the graphic and move it down, as described below.

To Reposition a Graphic

1 Double-click the graphic. When Word displays the Format Picture dialog box, click the Layout tab. Click Center in the Horizontal alignment area. Click the OK button.

2 Drag the graphic downward slightly so all paragraph text is above the graphic, as shown in Figure 9-10.

FIGURE 9-10

Adding a Caption

At the end of the *Computer Chronicles* document is a table of figures, which lists all figures and their corresponding page numbers. Word generates this table of figures from the captions in the document. A **caption** is a numbered label, such as Figure 1, that you can add to a table, figure, equation, or other item. If you move, delete, or add captions in a document, Word renumbers remaining captions in the document automatically.

The following steps show how to add a caption to the graphic.

To Add a Caption

1

• **With the graphic still selected, click Insert on the menu bar and then point to Reference (Figure 9-11).**

FIGURE 9-11

2

• **Click Caption on the Reference submenu.**

• **When Word displays the Caption dialog box, if necessary, click the Caption text box to position the insertion point after the text, Figure 1.**

Word displays the Caption dialog box (Figure 9-12). Word will position the caption for this figure below the graphic.

FIGURE 9-12

3

• **Press the COLON (:) key and then press the SPACEBAR.**

• **Type** Techniques to keep personal data private.

Word enters the caption (Figure 9-13).

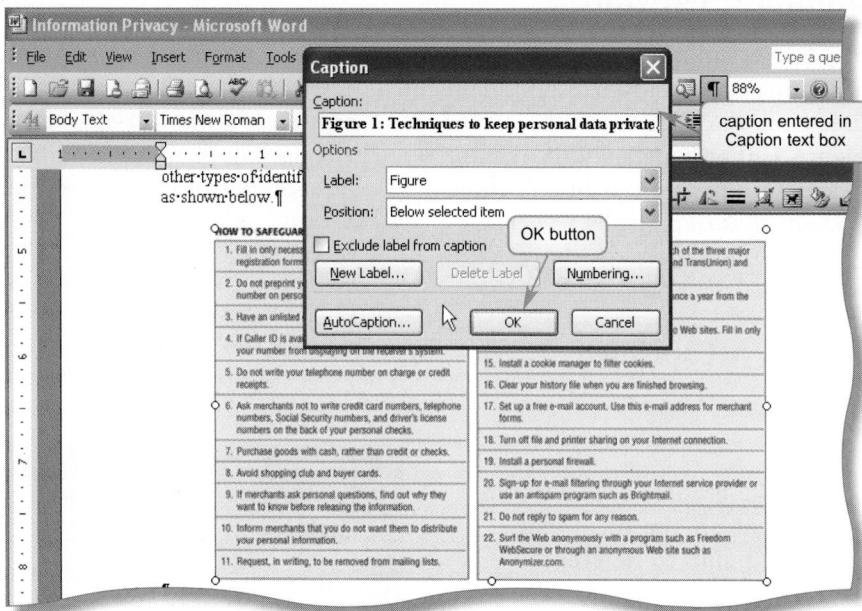

FIGURE 9-13

4

• **Click the OK button.**

Word inserts the caption in a text box below the selected graphic (Figure 9-14).

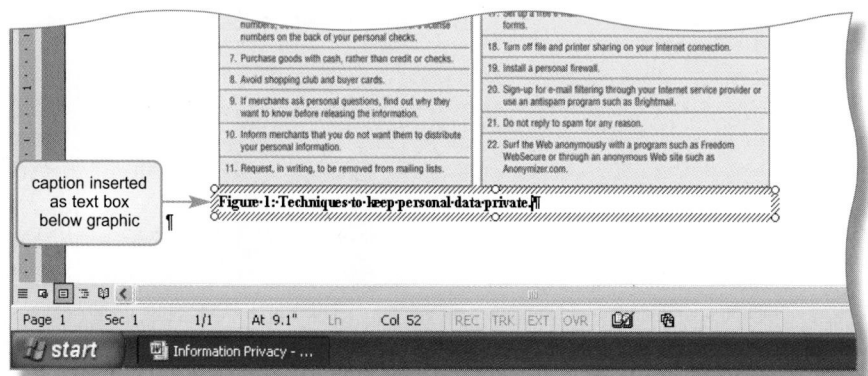

FIGURE 9-14

Other Ways

1. In Voice Command mode, say "Insert, Reference, Caption"

More About

Captions

If the caption appears with extra characters inside curly braces {}, Word is displaying field codes instead of field results. Press ALT+F9 to display the caption correctly as field results. If the caption prints field codes, click Tools on the menu bar, click Options, click the Print tab, remove the check mark from the Field codes check box, click the OK button, and then print the document again.

If, at a later time, you insert a new item with a caption, or move or delete items containing captions, Word automatically updates caption numbers throughout the document.

A caption contains a field. In Word, a **field** is a placeholder for data that might change in a document. Examples of fields you have used in previous projects are page numbers, merge fields, IF fields, form fields, and the current date. You update caption numbers using the same technique used to update any other field. That is, to update all caption numbers, select the entire document and then press the F9 key or right-click the selection and click Update Field on the shortcut menu. When you print a document, Word updates the caption numbers automatically, regardless of whether the document window displays the updated caption numbers.

When you add a caption to an inline graphic, the caption is not inserted in a text box. As just illustrated, however, the caption for a floating graphic is inserted in a text box. If you plan to generate a table of figures for a document, a caption cannot be in a text box. Instead, it must be in a frame.

The following steps show how to convert a text box to a frame.

To Convert a Text Box to a Frame

1

• **With the text box selected, click Format on the menu bar and then click Text Box.**

• **When Word displays the Format Text Box dialog box, if necessary, click the Text Box tab.**

Word displays the Format Text Box dialog box (Figure 9-15).

2

• **Click the Convert to Frame button.**

• **When Word displays a dialog box indicating some formatting may be lost, click the OK button.**

• **If Word displays a dialog box asking if you want a Frame command on the Insert menu, click the Cancel button.**

Word converts the text box to a frame.

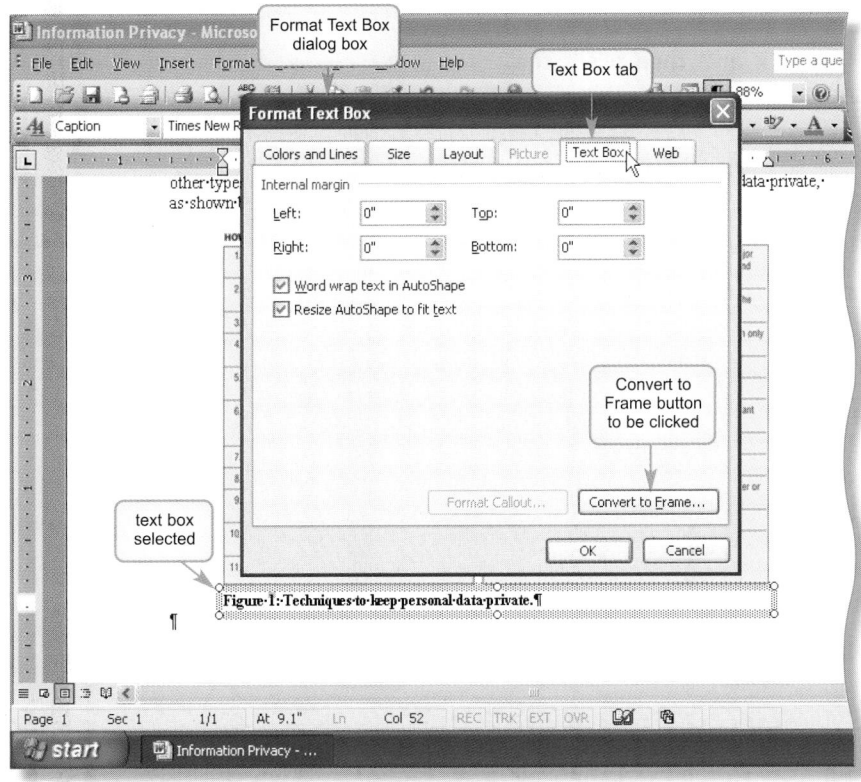

FIGURE 9-15

You did not format the text box; thus, you will not lose any formatting in the conversion from a text box to a frame.

Creating a Cross-Reference

In the *Computer Chronicles* documents, the text always makes a specific reference to a particular figure and explains the contents of the figure. Thus, you want to reference this figure in the text. Recall that the Information Privacy file will be inserted in a larger file. You do not know what the figure number of the graphic will be in the new document. In Word, you can create a **cross-reference**, which is a link to an item such as a heading, caption, or footnote in a document. By creating a cross-reference to the caption, the text that mentions the figure will update whenever the caption to the figure is updated.

The steps on the next page show how to create a cross-reference.

To Create a Cross-Reference

1

• **Delete the word, below, at the end of the last paragraph of text.**

• **Type** in **and then press the SPACEBAR.**

Word replaces the text (Figure 9-16).

FIGURE 9-16

2

• **Click Insert on the menu bar and then point to Reference (Figure 9-17).**

FIGURE 9-17

3

- **Click Cross-reference on the Reference submenu.**
- **When Word displays the Cross-reference dialog box, click the Reference type box arrow and then click Figure.**
- **Click the Insert reference to box arrow and then click Only label and number.**

Word displays the Cross-reference dialog box (Figure 9-18). You want the text to display only the label (which is the word, Figure) and the label number (which is the figure number).

FIGURE 9-18

4

- **Click the Insert button.**
- **Click the Close button in the Cross-reference dialog box.**

Word inserts the cross-reference to the figure in the document text (Figure 9-19). Because the figure number in the document is a field, Word may shade it gray — depending on your Word settings.

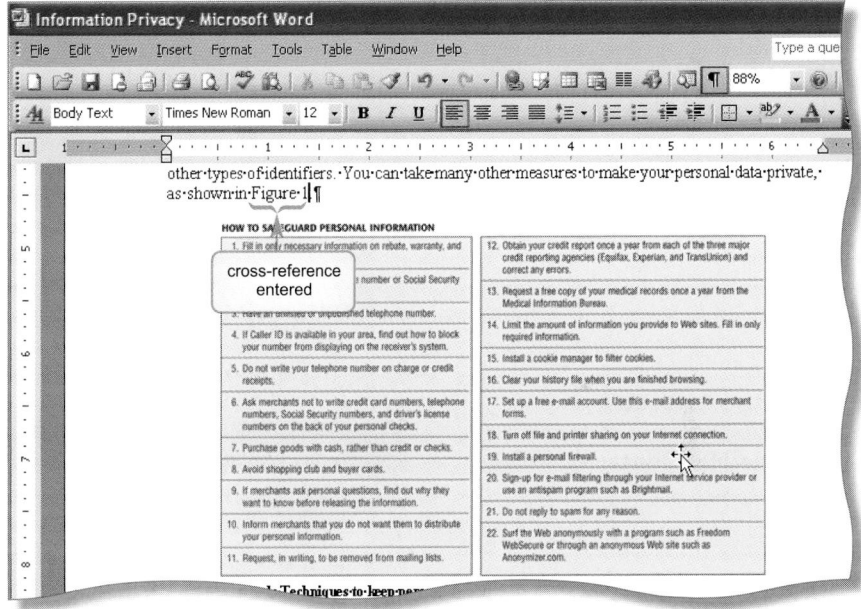

FIGURE 9-19

Other Ways

1. In Voice Command mode, say "Insert, Reference, Cross-reference"

As with a caption number, a cross-reference is a field. In many cases, Word automatically updates cross-references in a document if the item it refers to changes. To update a cross-reference manually, select the cross-reference and then press the F9 key, or right-click the selection and then click Update Field on the shortcut menu.

Marking Index Entries

The last page of the *Computer Chronicles* document is an index, which lists important terms discussed in the document along with each term's corresponding page number. For Word to generate the index, you first must mark any word or words you wish to appear in the index. When you mark an index entry, Word creates a field that is used to build the index. The fields are hidden and are displayed on the screen only when you show formatting marks, that is, when the Show/Hide ¶ button on the Standard toolbar is selected.

In this document, you want the words, information privacy, in the second sentence below the Information Privacy heading to be marked as an index entry. The following steps show how to mark this index entry.

To Mark an Index Entry

1

• **Press CTRL+HOME to position the insertion point at the beginning of the document.**

• **Select the text you wish to appear in the index (the words, information privacy, in this case).**

• **Press ALT+SHIFT+X.**

Word displays the Mark Index Entry dialog box (Figure 9-20).

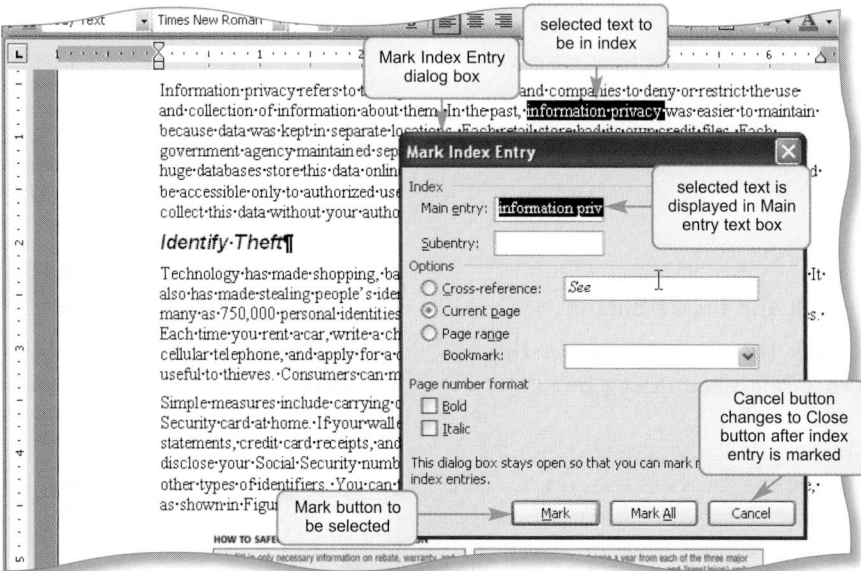

FIGURE 9-20

2

• **Click the Mark button.**

• **Click the Close button in the Mark Index Entry dialog box.**

Word inserts an index entry field in the document (Figure 9-21). These fields appear on the screen only when the Show/Hide ¶ button on the Standard toolbar is selected.

FIGURE 9-21

Word leaves the Mark Index Entry dialog box open until you close it, which allows you to mark multiple index entries without having to reopen the dialog box repeatedly. To mark multiple index entries; click in the document window; scroll to and select the next index entry; if necessary, click the Main entry text box in the Mark Index Entry dialog box (shown in Figure 9-20); and then click the Mark button.

The following steps describe how to mark one additional index entry.

To Mark Another Index Entry

1 Scroll to and then select the text, identity theft, in the second sentence below the Identity Theft heading.

2 Press ALT+SHIFT+X to display the Mark Index Entry dialog box (Figure 9-22).

3 Click the Mark button. Click the Close button in the Mark Index Entry dialog box.

Word inserts the index entry field in the document.

FIGURE 9-22

To remove the clutter of index entry fields from the document, you should hide formatting marks, as described next.

To Hide Formatting Marks

1 If the Show/Hide ¶ button on the Standard toolbar is selected, click it.

Word hides formatting marks (shown in Figure 9-23 on the next page).

If the index entries still appear, even with the Show/Hide ¶ button not selected, click Tools on the menu bar, click Options, click the View tab, remove the check mark from the Hidden text check box, and then click the OK button.

More About

Index Entries

Index entries may include a switch, which is a slash followed by a letter inserted after the field text. Switches include \b to apply bold formatting to the entry's page number, \f to define an entry type, \i to make the entry's page number italic, \r to insert a range of pages numbers, \t to insert specified text in place of a page number, and \y to specify that the subsequent text defines the pronunciation for the index entry. A colon in an index entry precedes a subentry keyword in the index.

Hyphenating a Document

Word, by default, does not hyphenate a word at the end of a line. Instead, it wraps long words to the beginning of the next line. To avoid gaps at the end of lines, you can instruct Word to use the hyphenation feature. Word can hyphenate an entire document, or you can select which words you want to be hyphenated.

The following steps show how to instruct Word to hyphenate an entire document automatically.

To Hyphenate a Document

1

• **Click Tools on the menu bar and then point to Language (Figure 9-23).**

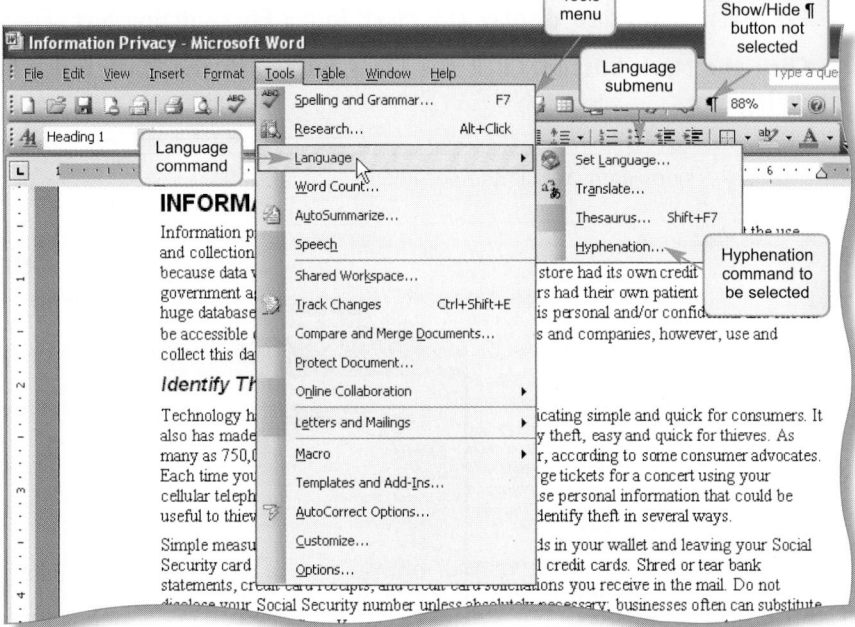

FIGURE 9-23

2

• **Click Hyphenation on the Language submenu.**

• **When Word displays the Hyphenation dialog box, place a check mark in the Automatically hyphenate document check box.**

Word displays the Hyphenation dialog box (Figure 9-24).

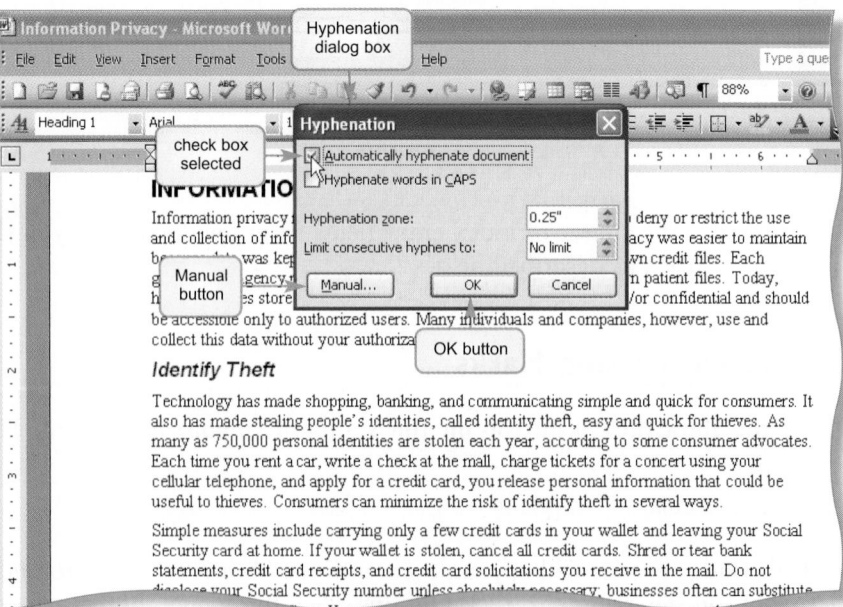

FIGURE 9-24

3

• **Click the OK button.**

Word hyphenates the entire document (Figure 9-25).

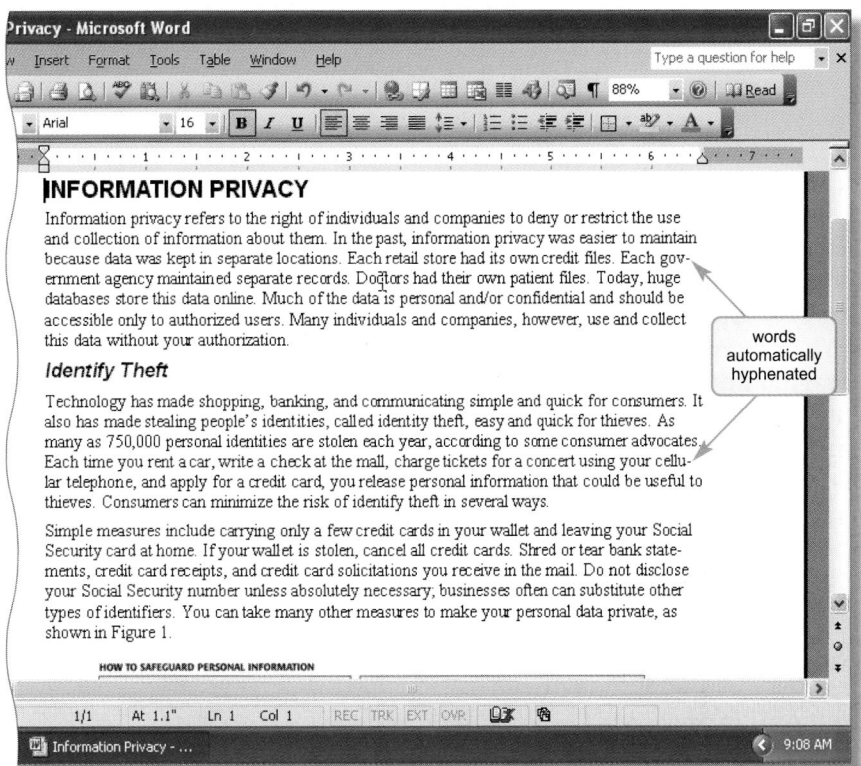

FIGURE 9-25

If you edit text in a document, Word automatically rehyphenates the document. To remove automatic hyphenation from a document, remove the check mark from the Automatically hyphenate document check box (Figure 9-24).

Instead of Word hyphenating a document automatically, you can hyphenate words manually. One technique of manual hyphens is through the Manual button in the Hyphenation dialog box (Figure 9-24). When you click the Manual button, Word asks you to confirm each proposed hyphen. As an alternative, you can press CTRL+HYPHEN to insert an optional hyphen. An **optional hyphen** is a hyphen that Word will use only if the word will not fit completely at the end of a line.

Controlling Widows and Orphans

A **widow** is created when the last line of a paragraph appears by itself at the top of a page. An **orphan** occurs when the first line of a paragraph appears by itself at the bottom of a page. Word, by default, prevents widows and orphans from occurring in a document.

Recall that the Information Privacy document will be incorporated in a larger document, the *Computer Chronicles* document. Although the Information Privacy document fits on a single page now, it may span multiple pages when inserted in a longer document. You can ensure that the first or last line of a paragraph does not appear by itself on any page. The steps on the next page show how to ensure that widows and orphans cannot occur.

To Verify the Widow and Orphan Setting

1

• **Press CTRL+A to select all the paragraphs in the document.**

• **Right-click the selection and then click Paragraph on the shortcut menu.**

• **When Word displays the Paragraph dialog box, click the Line and Page Breaks tab and then ensure that the Widow/Orphan control check box contains a check mark (Figure 9-26).**

2

• **Click the OK button. Click anywhere in the document to remove the selection.**

Word ensures that no widows or orphans can occur in this document.

FIGURE 9-26

The options in the Line and Page Breaks sheet in the Paragraph dialog box (Figure 9-26) are designed to provide you with options of how lines and paragraphs print. The Keep lines together check box can be used to ensure that a page break does not occur within a single paragraph, by positioning the insertion point in the appropriate paragraph and then selecting the check box. If you do not want a page break to occur between two paragraphs, click in the appropriate paragraph and then place a check mark in the Keep with next check box. Similarly, if you want a page break to occur immediately before a paragraph, place a check mark in the Page break before check box.

If, for some reason, you wanted to allow a widow or an orphan in a document, you would position the insertion point in the appropriate paragraph, display the Line and Page Breaks sheet in the Paragraph dialog box, and then remove the check mark from the Widow/Orphan control check box.

The Information Privacy file is complete. The following steps save and close the file.

To Save and Close a Document

1 **Click the Save button on the Standard toolbar.**

2 **Click File on the menu bar and then click Close.**

Word closes the Information Privacy file.

Sorting a List

When reviewing the Health Concerns of Computer Use Draft file, you notice the bulleted list on the second page should be sorted in alphabetical order. Thus, the next step is to open the file and sort the bulleted list.

To preserve the contents of the original file, save a copy of it with a new file name and sort the list in the new file. The following steps describe how to open the Health Concerns of Computer Use Draft file on the Data Disk and then save it with a new file name. If you did not download the Data Disk, see the inside back cover for instructions for downloading the Data Disk or see your instructor.

To Open a Document and Save It with a New File Name

1 **With the disk containing the Health Concerns of Computer Use Draft file in drive A, click the Open button on the Standard toolbar.**

2 **When Word displays the Open dialog box, if necessary, click the Look in box arrow and then click 3½ Floppy (A:).**

3 **Double-click Health Concerns of Computer Use Draft.**

4 **Click File on the menu bar and then click Save As.**

5 **When Word displays the Save As dialog box, type** Health Concerns of Computer Use **in the File name box. Do not press the ENTER key.**

6 **If necessary, click the Save in box arrow and then click 3½ Floppy (A:).**

7 **Click the Save button in the Save As dialog box.**

Word saves the document on a floppy disk in drive A with the new file name, Health Concerns of Computer Use (shown in Figure 9-27 on the next page).

The steps on the next page show how to sort the bulleted list on the second page of the document.

Q&A

Q: What sort order is used by Word?

A: If the items to be sorted begin with a mixture of characters, Word puts the lines that begin with punctuation marks or symbols at the top of the list, followed by items beginning with numbers, and then finally items beginning with letters.

To Sort a List

1

- **Scroll to the second page of the document to display the bulleted list.**
- **Drag through the bulleted list to select it.**
- **Click Table on the menu bar and then click Sort.**

Word displays the Sort Text dialog box (Figure 9-27). The list to be sorted is selected.

FIGURE 9-27

2

- **Click the OK button.**
- **Click anywhere in the document to remove the section.**

Word sorts the list alphabetically (Figure 9-28).

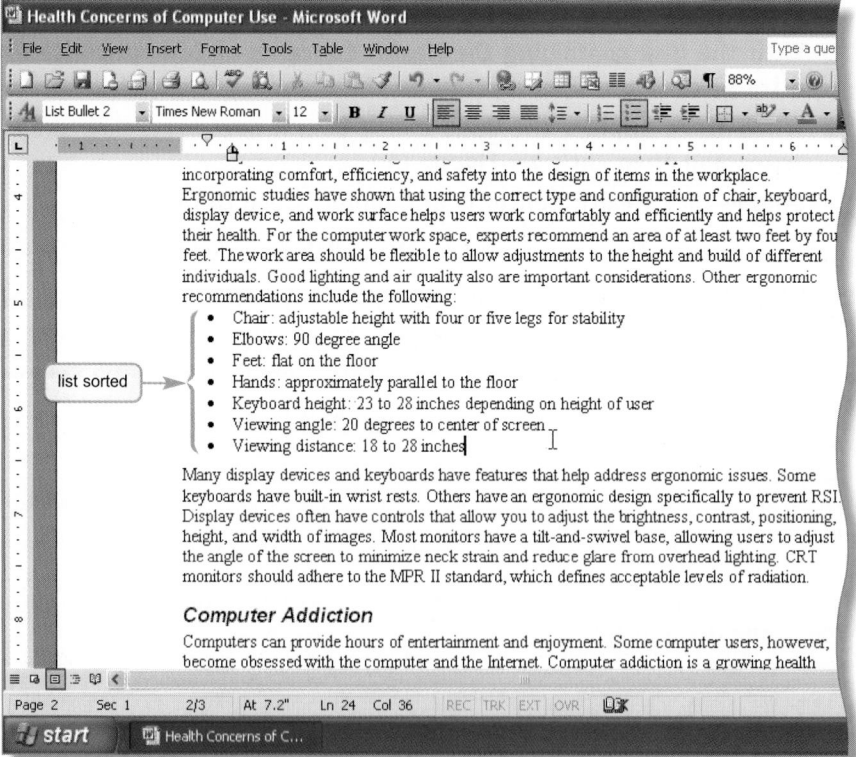

FIGURE 9-28

This is the only change to be made to the Health Concerns of Computer Use file. The next steps save and close the file.

To Save and Close a Document

1 **Click the Save button on the Standard toolbar.**

2 **Click File on the menu bar and then click Close.**

Word saves and closes the Health Concerns of Computer Use file.

Working with a Master Document

When you are creating a document from a series of other documents, you may want to create a master document to organize all the documents. A **master document** is simply a document that contains links to other documents, which are called the **subdocuments**. In addition to subdocuments, a master document can contain its own text and graphics.

In this project, the master document file is named COMPUTER CHRONICLES #5. The file, COMPUTER CHRONICLES #5, contains links to three subdocuments: an Introduction file, the Information Privacy file, and the Health Concerns of Computer Use file. The first has yet to be created, and the latter two (Information Privacy and Health Concerns of Computer Use) are finished. The master document also contains other items: a title page, a table of contents, a table of figures, and an index. The following pages illustrate how to create this master document and insert the necessary elements in the document to create the COMPUTER CHRONICLES #5 document.

Q&A

Q: When would I use a master document?

A: Master documents can be used when multiple people prepare different sections of a document or when a document contains separate elements such as the chapters in a book. If multiple people in a network need to work on the same document, divide the document into subdocuments and store the master document on the network server. Then, multiple users can work on different sections of the document simultaneously.

Creating an Outline

To create a master document, you must be in outline view. You then enter the headings of the document as an outline using Word's built-in heading styles. As discussed in previous projects, a style is a customized format that you can apply to text. Word has nine heading styles named Heading 1, Heading 2, and so on. Each contains different formatting that you can apply to headings in a document.

In an outline, the major heading is displayed at the left margin with each subordinate, or lower-level, heading indented. In Word, the built-in Heading 1 style is displayed at the left margin in outline view. Heading 2 style is indented below Heading Style 1, Heading 3 style is indented further, and so on.

You do not want to use a built-in heading style for the paragraphs of text within the document because when you create a table of contents, Word places all lines formatted using the built-in heading styles in the table of contents. Thus, the text below each heading is formatted using the Body Text style. By using styles in the document, all pages will be formatted similarly — even though various people create them.

The COMPUTER CHRONICLES #5 document contains the following seven major headings: Computer Chronicles, Table of Contents, Introduction, Information Privacy, Health Concerns of Computer Use, Table of Figures, and Index (shown in Figure 9-1 on page WD 635). Two of these headings (Information Privacy and Health Concerns of Computer Use) are not entered in the outline; instead, they are part of the subdocuments inserted in the master document.

Each heading is to print at the top of a new page. You might want to format the pages within a heading differently from those pages in other headings. Thus, you will insert next page section breaks between each heading.

The steps on the next page show how to create an outline that contains headings to be used in the master document.

To Create an Outline

1

• **Click the New Blank Document button on the Standard toolbar to display a blank document window.**

• **If it is not selected already, click the Show/Hide ¶ button on the Standard toolbar.**

• **Click the Outline View button on the horizontal scroll bar. If the Outlining toolbar is not displayed on your screen, click View on the menu bar, point to Toolbars, and then click Outlining.**

• **Be sure the Show Formatting and Master Document View buttons are selected on the Outlining toolbar.**

• **Type** COMPUTER CHRONICLES **and then press the ENTER key.**

In outline view, Word enters the first heading using the built-in Heading 1 style (Figure 9-29). An outline symbol appears to the left of each paragraph. You use outline symbols to rearrange text or display and hide text.

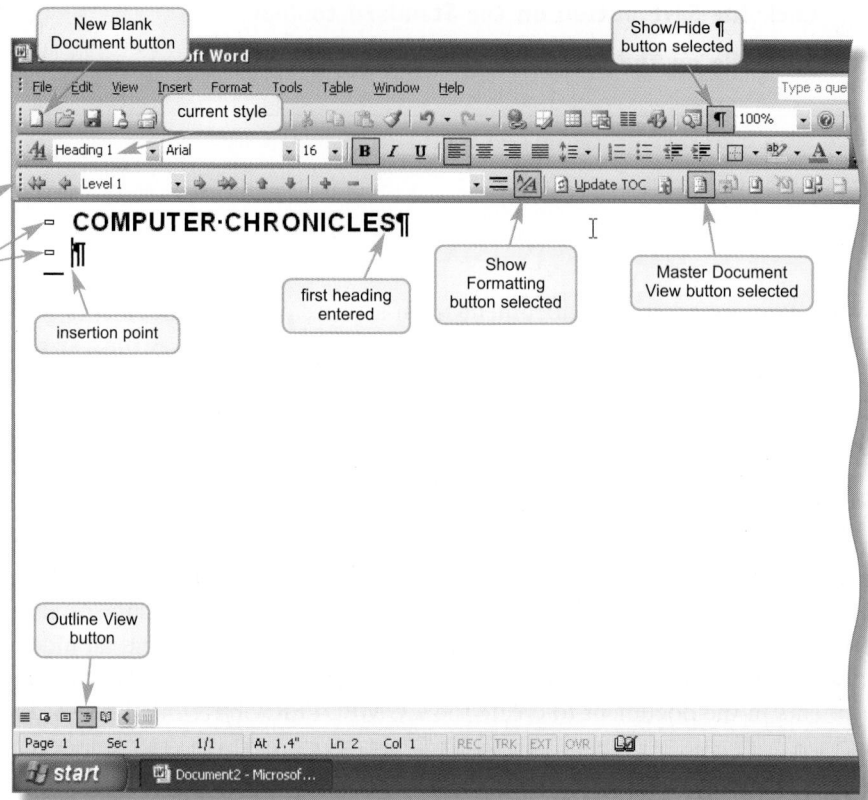

FIGURE 9-29

2

• **Click Insert on the menu bar and then click Break.**

• **When Word displays the Break dialog box, click Next page in the Section break types area.**

Word displays the Break dialog box (Figure 9-30).

FIGURE 9-30

3

- **Click the OK button.**
- **Type** TABLE OF CONTENTS **and then press the ENTER key.**

Word inserts a next page section break below the first heading (Figure 9-31). The next heading also is displayed.

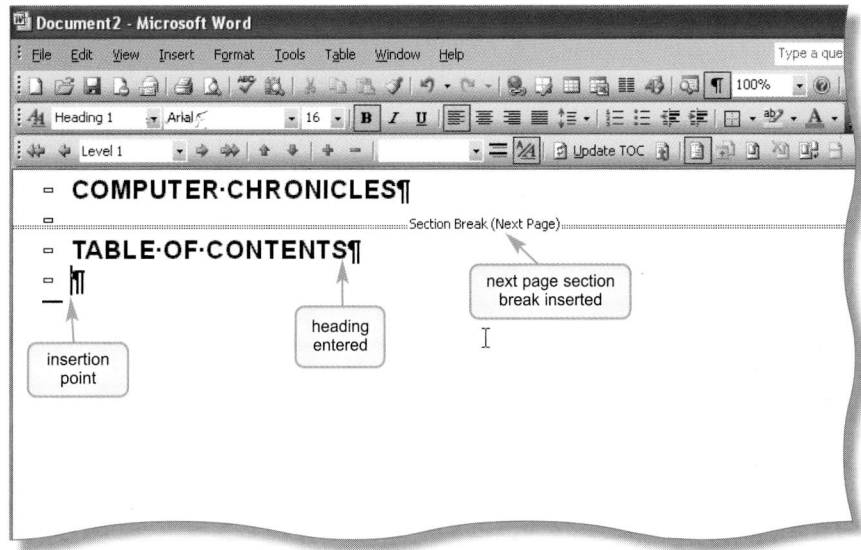

FIGURE 9-31

4

- **Click Insert on the menu bar and then click Break.**
- **When Word displays the Break dialog box, click Next page in the Section break types area and then click the OK button.**

5

- **Type** INTRODUCTION **and then press the ENTER key.**
- **Repeat Step 4.**
- **Type** TABLE OF FIGURES **and then press the ENTER key.**
- **Repeat Step 4.**
- **Type** INDEX **as the last entry.**

The headings in the master document are entered (Figure 9-32).

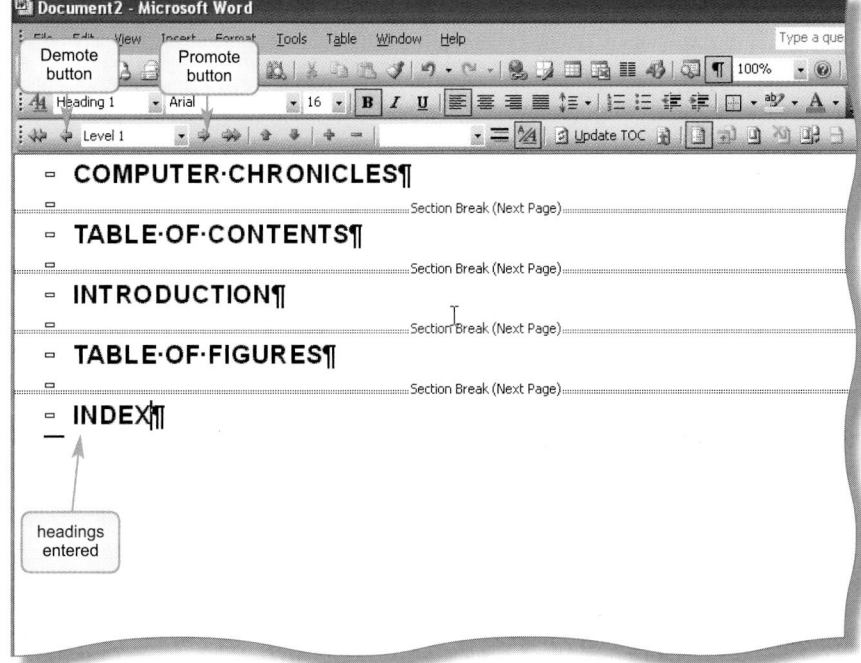

FIGURE 9-32

The Next Page section break between each heading will cause each heading to begin at the top of a new page. The two other major headings, Information Privacy and Health Concerns of Computer Use, will be inserted as subdocuments, as discussed in the following pages. When you insert these files as subdocuments, the headings will become part of the outline.

The Outlining toolbar contains buttons and boxes for promoting and demoting items in the outline, changing the outline level, as well as buttons to update and display the table of contents. Figure 9-33 on the next page identifies the buttons and boxes on the Outlining toolbar.

More About

Outlines

To rearrange the headings in an outline — for example, move an entry upward or downward — drag its outline symbol in the direction you want to move it.

FIGURE 9-33

Inserting a Subdocument in a Master Document

The next step is to insert one of the subdocuments in the master document. Word places the first line of text in the subdocument at the first heading level because it is defined using the Heading 1 style. Nonheading text uses the Body Text style. Figure 9-34 shows the subdocument and identifies the styles used in the document.

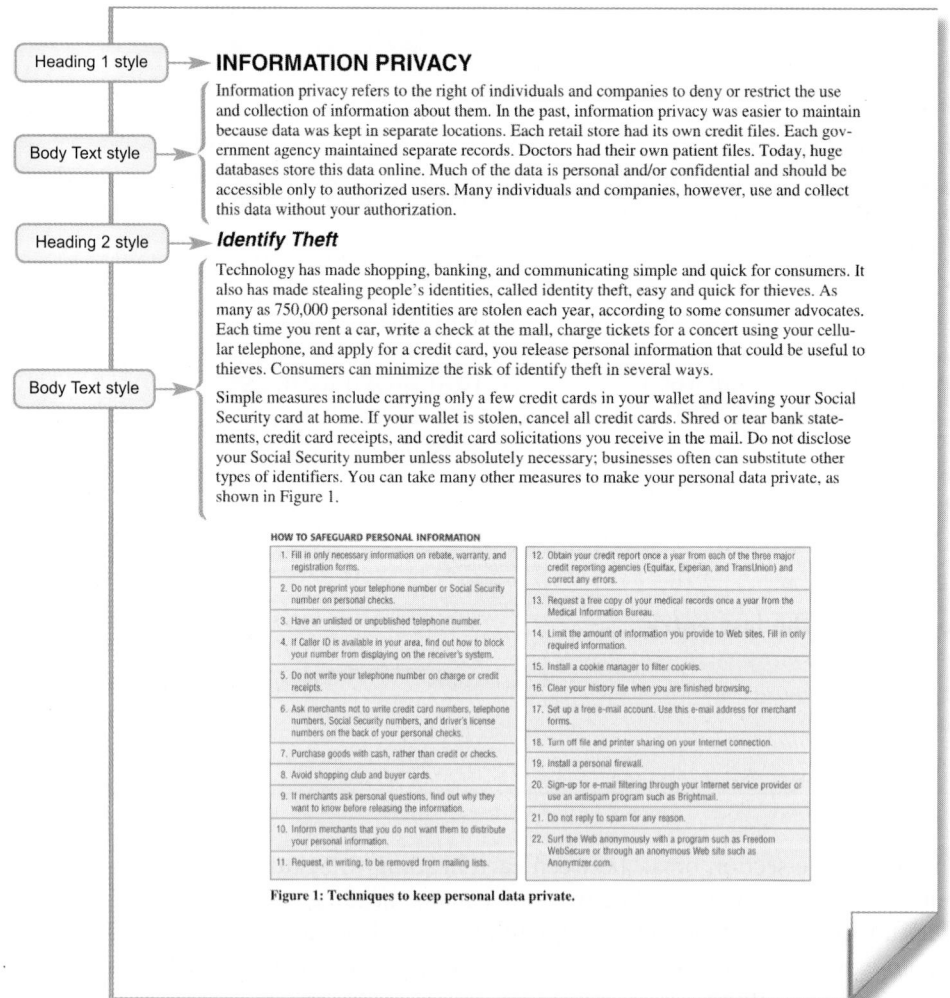

FIGURE 9-34

The subdocument to be inserted is the Information Privacy file modified earlier in this project. The next steps show how to insert a link to a subdocument in a master document.

To Insert a Subdocument

- **If necessary, insert in drive A the floppy disk containing the Information Privacy file.**

- **Position the insertion point where you want to insert the subdocument (on the section break between the INTRODUCTION and TABLE OF FIGURES headings).**

- **Click the Insert Subdocument button on the Outlining toolbar.**

- **When Word displays the Insert Subdocument dialog box, if necessary, click the Look in box arrow and then click 3½ Floppy (A:).**

- **Click the file name, Information Privacy.**

The subdocument will be inserted at the location of the insertion point (Figure 9-35).

FIGURE 9-35

2

- **Click the Open button in the dialog box.**

- **If Word displays a dialog box about styles, click the Yes to All button.**

Word inserts the Information Privacy file in the document (Figure 9-36). Notice the document contains marked index entries. The location of a caption in outline view does not necessarily reflect the location at which it will print. Your caption may appear in a different location.

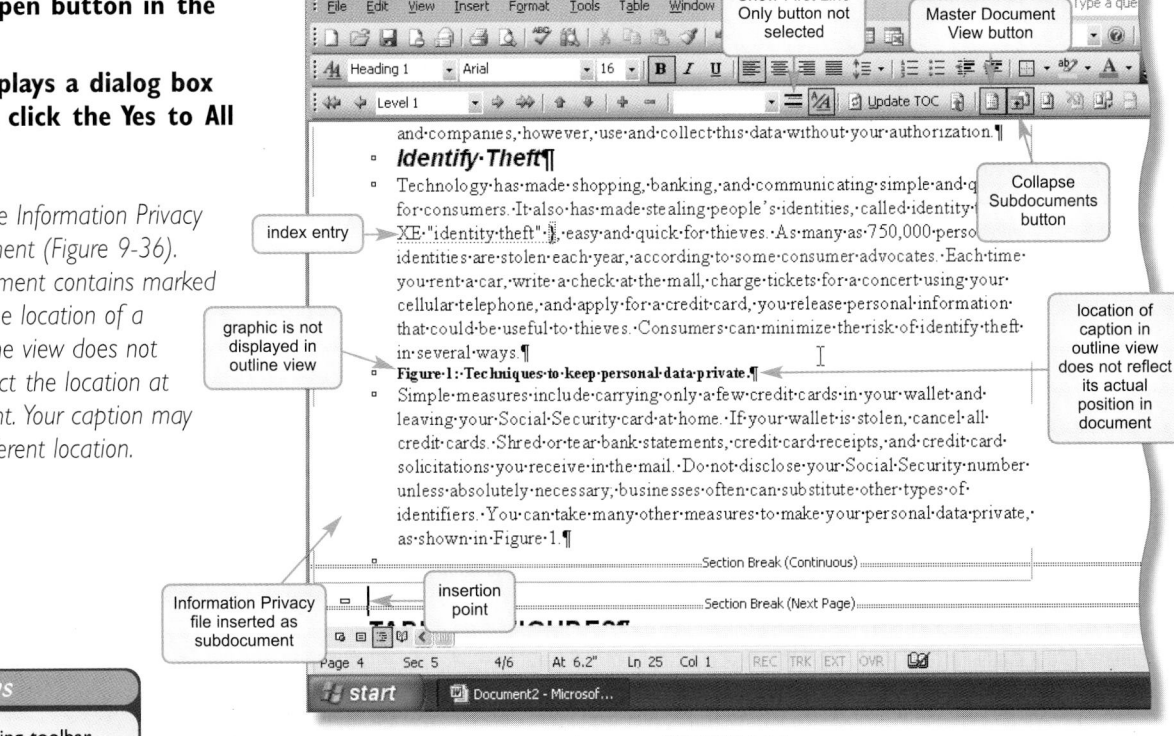

FIGURE 9-36

Other Ways

1. With Outlining toolbar displaying, in Voice Command mode, say "Insert Subdocument"

With the Show First Line only button not selected, the contents of each paragraph in the subdocument are displayed in outline view. To make the outline more readable, users often instruct Word to display just the first line of each paragraph, as shown next.

To Show First Line Only

1

• **If it is not selected already, click the Show First Line Only button on the Outlining toolbar.**

Word displays only the first line of each paragraph (Figure 9-37).

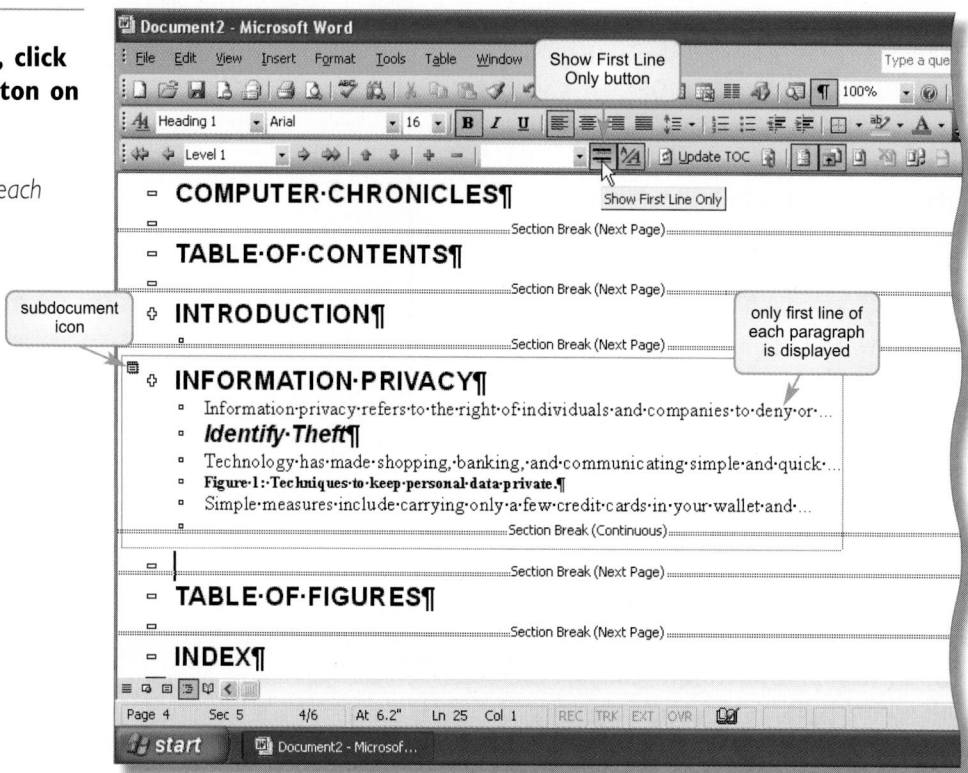

FIGURE 9-37

If you wanted to display all lines in all paragraphs again, you would click the Show First Line Only button so it is not selected.

The next step is to insert another subdocument below the Information Privacy subdocument. The next subdocument to be inserted is the Health Concerns of Computer Use file. The next steps describe how to insert another subdocument.

More About

The Lock Icon

If a lock icon is displayed next to a subdocument's name, either the master document is collapsed or the subdocument is locked. If the master document is collapsed, simply click the Expand Subdocuments button on the Outlining toolbar. If the subdocument is locked, you will be able to display the contents of the subdocument but will not be able to modify it.

To Insert Another Subdocument

1 If necessary, insert in drive A the disk that contains the Health Concerns of Computer Use file.

2 Scroll down and, if necessary, position the insertion point on the next page section break above the TABLE OF FIGURES heading.

3 Click the Insert Subdocument button on the Outlining toolbar.

4 When Word displays the Insert Subdocument dialog box, if necessary, click the Look in box arrow and then click 3½ Floppy (A:). Click the Health Concerns of Computer Use file in the Look in list and then click the Open button in the dialog box. If Word displays a dialog box about styles, click the Yes to All button.

5 Scroll up to display the top of the inserted subdocument.

Word inserts the Health Concerns of Computer Use file in the outline below the Information Privacy subdocument (Figure 9-38).

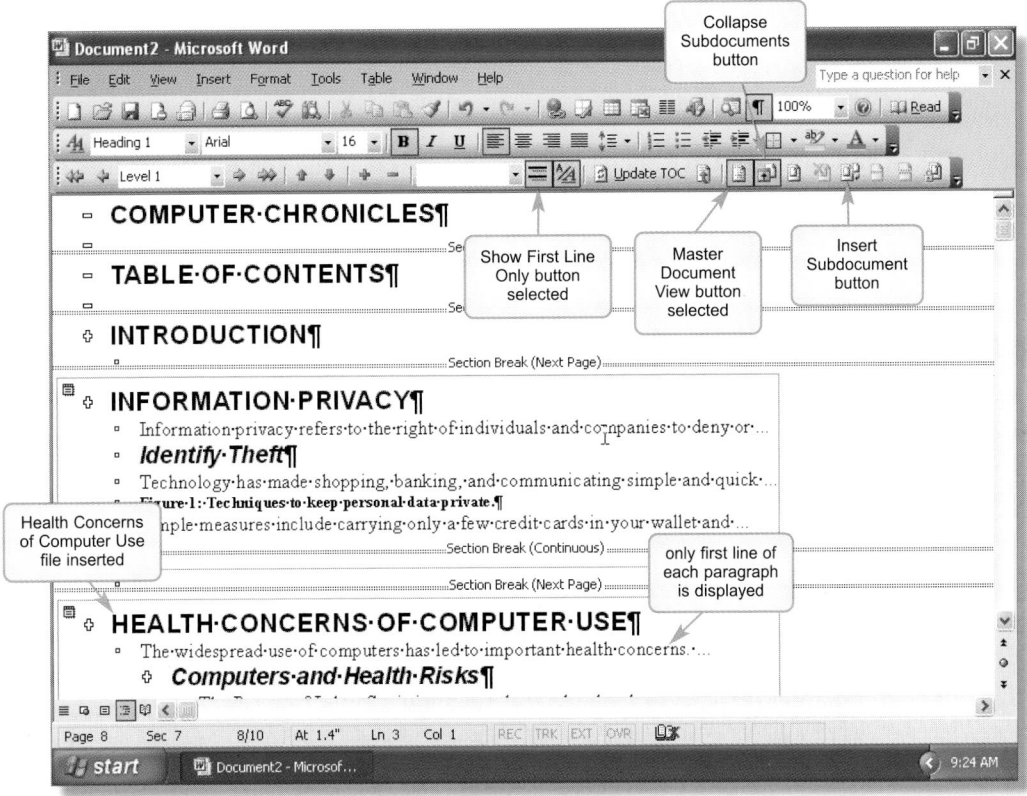

FIGURE 9-38

The inserted file shown in Figure 9-38 is the same document shown on pages 5, 6, and 7 in Figure 9-1 on page WD 635.

The master document shown in Figure 9-38 is expanded. When in outline view, an **expanded** document is one that shows the contents of its subdocuments. A **collapsed** document, by contrast, shows subdocuments as hyperlinks. That is, instead of displaying the contents of the subdocuments, Word displays the name of the subdocuments in blue and underlined. Later, this project shows how to work with a collapsed document.

To collapse an expanded document and display subdocuments as hyperlinks, click the Collapse Subdocuments button on the Outlining toolbar. To expand subdocuments, click the Expand Subdocuments button on the Outlining toolbar.

You can open a subdocument in a separate document window and modify it. To open a collapsed subdocument, click the hyperlink. To open an expanded subdocument, double-click the subdocument icon (shown in Figure 9-37 on page WD 662) to the left of the document heading. If the subdocument icon is not displayed on the screen, click the Master Document View button on the Outlining toolbar. When you are finished working on a subdocument, close it and return to the master document by clicking File on the menu bar and then clicking Close.

The following steps save the master document.

To Save a Document

1 With a floppy disk in drive A, click the Save button on the Standard toolbar.

2 Type COMPUTER CHRONICLES #5 in the File name box. Do not press the ENTER key after typing the file name.

3 If necessary, click the Save in box arrow and then click 3½ Floppy (A:). Click the Save button in the Save As dialog box. If a Microsoft Word dialog box is displayed, click the OK button.

Word saves the document on a floppy disk in drive A with the file name, COMPUTER CHRONICLES #5 (shown in Figure 9-39).

When you save a master document, Word also saves the subdocument files on the disk. Thus, the COMPUTER CHRONICLES #5 file, the Information Privacy file, and the Health Concerns of Computer Use file all are saved when you save the COMPUTER CHRONICLES #5 file.

Creating a Subdocument in a Master Document

The next step is to create a new subdocument for the INTRODUCTION section of the COMPUTER CHRONICLES #5 document. The following steps show how to create a subdocument.

To Create a Subdocument

1

• **Press CTRL+HOME.**

• **Position the mouse pointer on the plus outline symbol to the left of the heading, INTRODUCTION, and then click when the mouse pointer changes to a four-headed arrow.**

Word selects the INTRODUCTION heading (Figure 9-39).

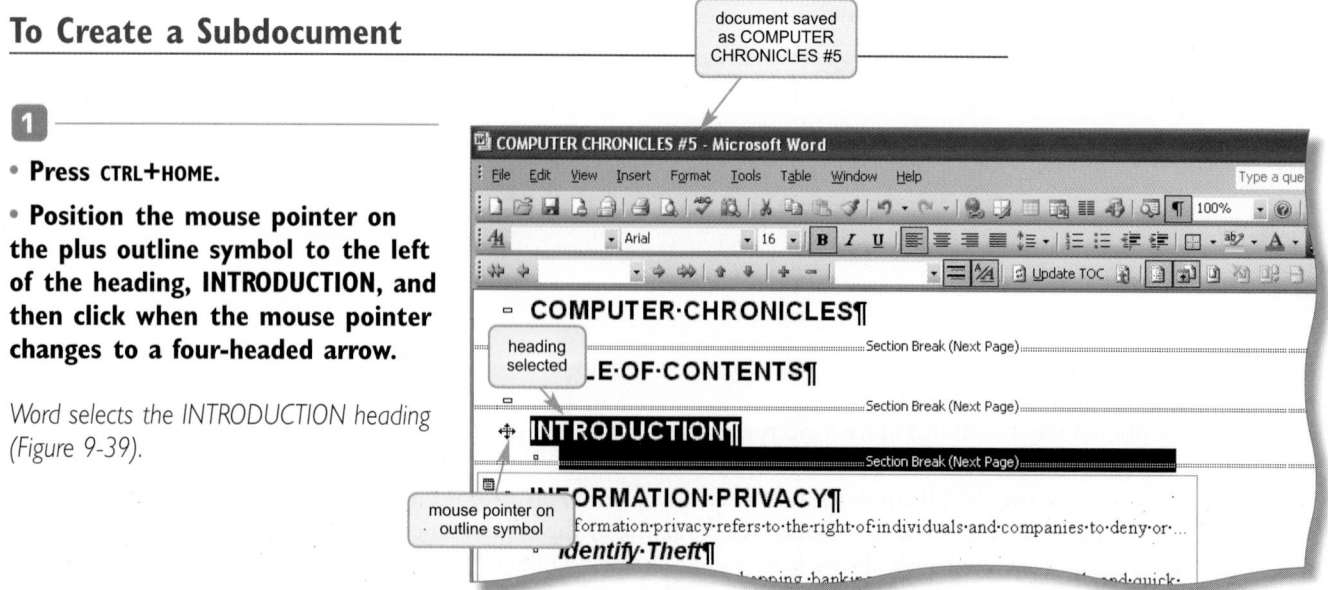

FIGURE 9-39

2

• **Click the Create Subdocument button on the Outlining toolbar.**

Word creates a subdocument for the INTRODUCTION heading (Figure 9-40). If Word places a continuous section break above or below the subdocument, do not remove this section break.

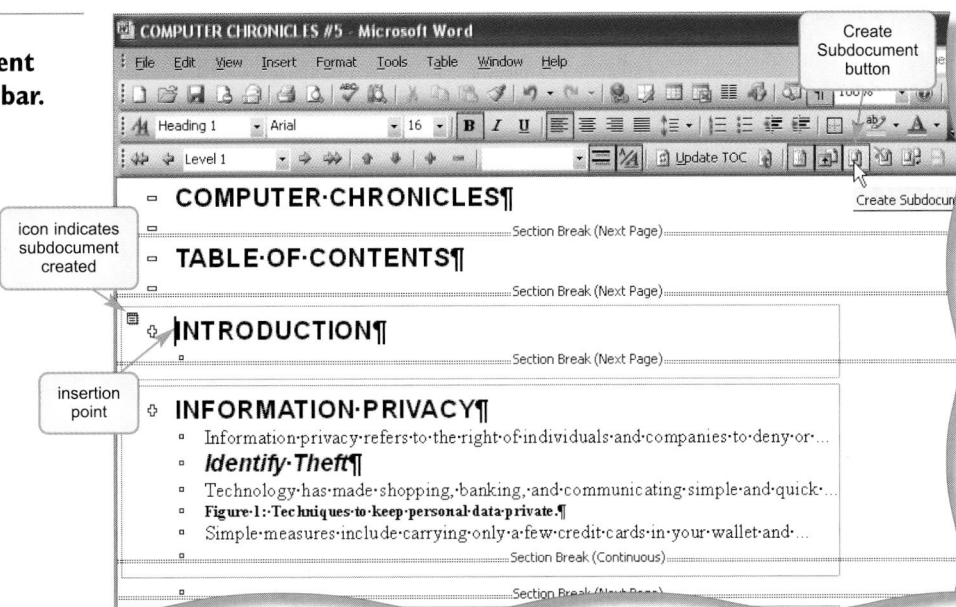

FIGURE 9-40

Other Ways

1. In Voice Command mode, say "Create Subdocument"

The next time you save the COMPUTER CHRONICLES #5 file, Word will create another document called INTRODUCTION on your disk.

You would like to enter the text for the INTRODUCTION section of the document. The paragraphs of text in the INTRODUCTION section should not use a built-in heading style; instead, they should be formatted using the Body Text style. You can enter the text in outline view, as shown in the following steps.

To Modify an Outline

1

• **With the insertion point positioned as shown in Figure 9-40, press the END key to position it after the N in INTRODUCTION.**

• **Press the ENTER key.**

Word positions the insertion point on a blank line at Level 1 in the outline (Figure 9-41).

FIGURE 9-41

2

• **Click the Demote to Body Text button on the Outlining toolbar.**

Word changes the level of the current line from Heading 1 to Body Text (Figure 9-42).

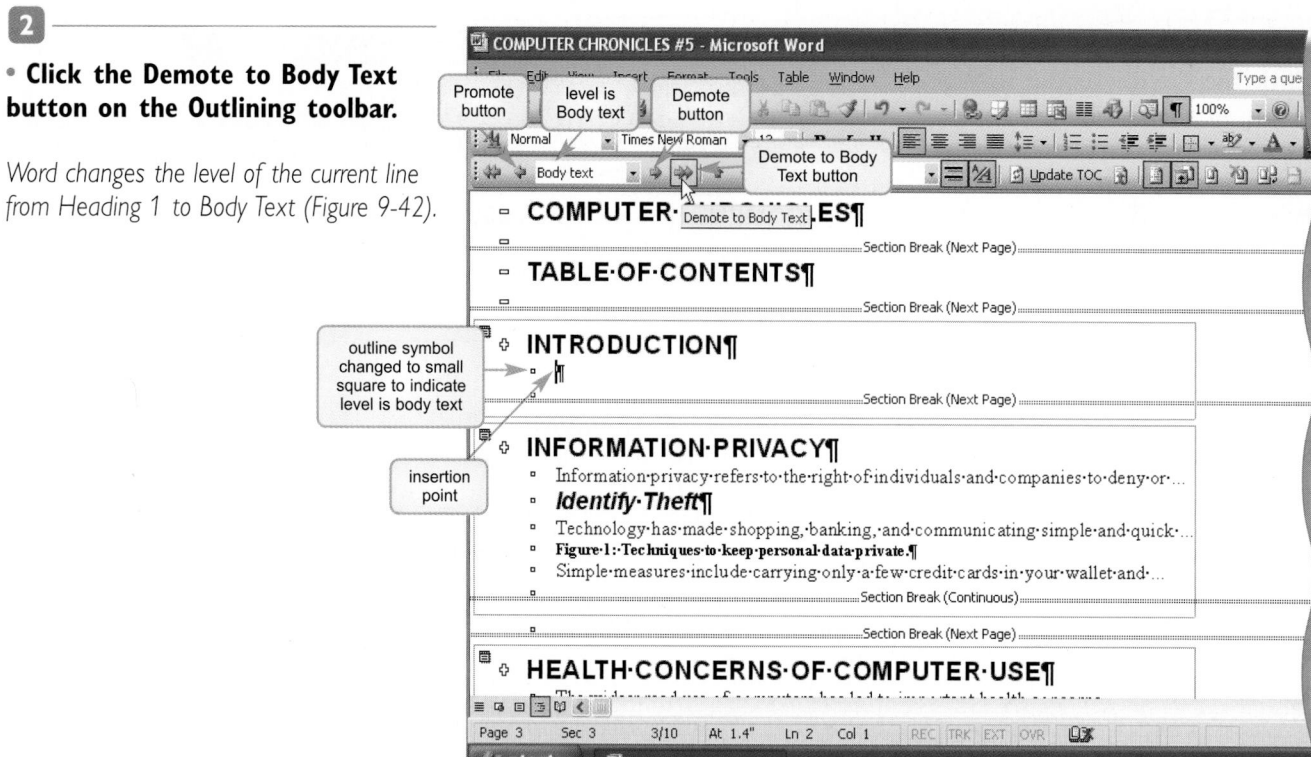

FIGURE 9-42

Notice in Figure 9-42 that the outline symbols changed. The outline symbol to the left of the INTRODUCTION heading changed from a minus sign to a plus sign, indicating the heading has subordinate text. The outline symbol below the heading changed from a minus sign to a small square, indicating it is at the Body Text level.

If you wanted to change a heading to a lower-level, or subordinate, level instead of to the Body Text level, such as for a subheading, you would press the TAB key or click the Demote button on the Outlining toolbar; or you can drag the outline symbol to the right. Likewise, to move a heading to a higher-level, you would press the SHIFT+TAB keys or click the Promote button on the Outlining toolbar; or you can drag the outline symbol to the left.

The next step is to enter the text of the introduction, as described below.

To Enter Body Text in an Outline

1 If the **Show First Line Only** button on the Outlining toolbar is selected, click it.

2 Click the **Style box arrow** on the **Formatting** toolbar, scroll to and then click **Body Text**.

3 With the insertion point on the line below the **INTRODUCTION** heading (shown in Figure 9-42), type the first paragraph shown in Figure 9-43. Press the **ENTER** key.

4 Type the second paragraph shown in Figure 9-43.

The INTRODUCTION section is complete (Figure 9-43).

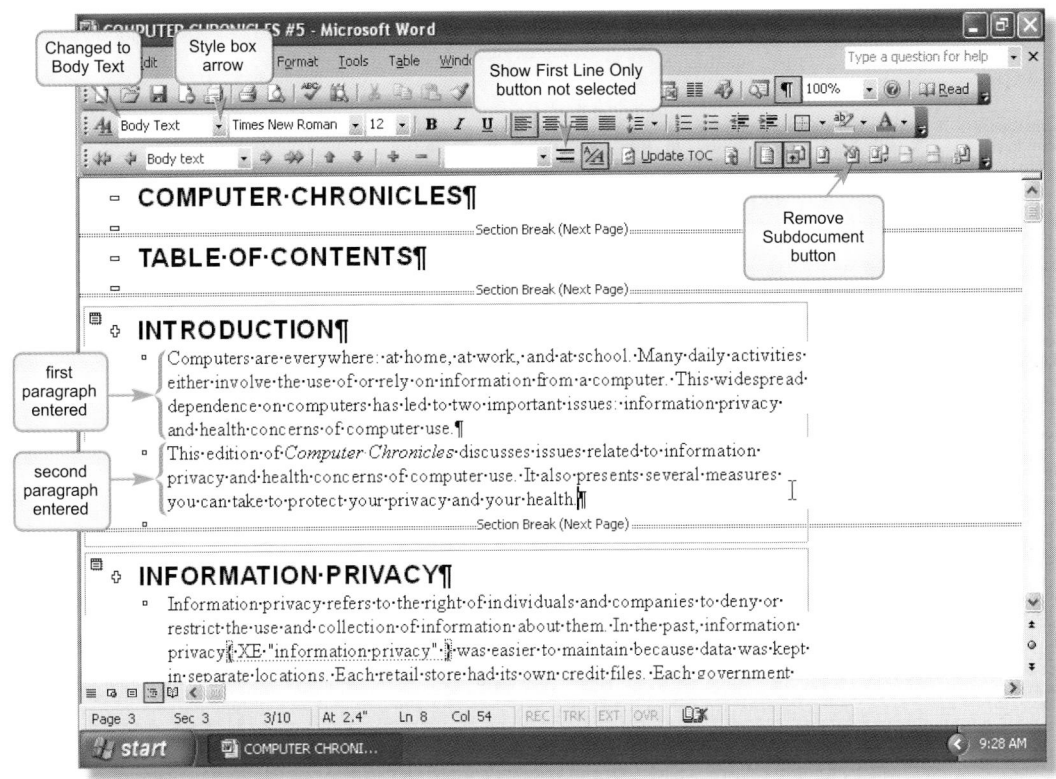

FIGURE 9-43

In outline view, text does not appear formatted. Instead, each subheading is indented below the previous heading. Text formatted using the Body Text style, such as that shown in Figure 9-43, also is displayed indented. To display text properly formatted, switch to print layout view.

If, for some reason, you wanted to remove a subdocument from a master document, you would expand the subdocuments, click the subdocument icon to the left of the subdocument's first heading, and then press the DELETE key. Although Word removes the subdocument from the master document, the subdocument file remains on disk.

Occasionally, you may want to convert a subdocument to part of the master document — breaking the connection between the text in the master document and the subdocument. To do this, expand the subdocuments, click the subdocument icon, and then click the Remove Subdocument button on the Outlining toolbar.

Entering Text and Graphics as Part of the Master Document

The next step is to create the title page for the *Computer Chronicles* document. The completed title page is shown in Figure 9-44 on the next page. On the title page, you do not want the first line of text (COMPUTER CHRONICLES) to show up in the table of contents. Thus, you will change it from the Heading 1 style to the Normal style. You decide not to create a subdocument for the title page; instead, you will enter the text as part of the master document. The title page contains graphics. Thus, you will work in print layout view as opposed to outline view.

More About

Outline View

When the Show First Line Only button on the Outline toolbar is selected, only the first line of each paragraph is displayed. When the button is not selected, all text associated with the paragraph is displayed.

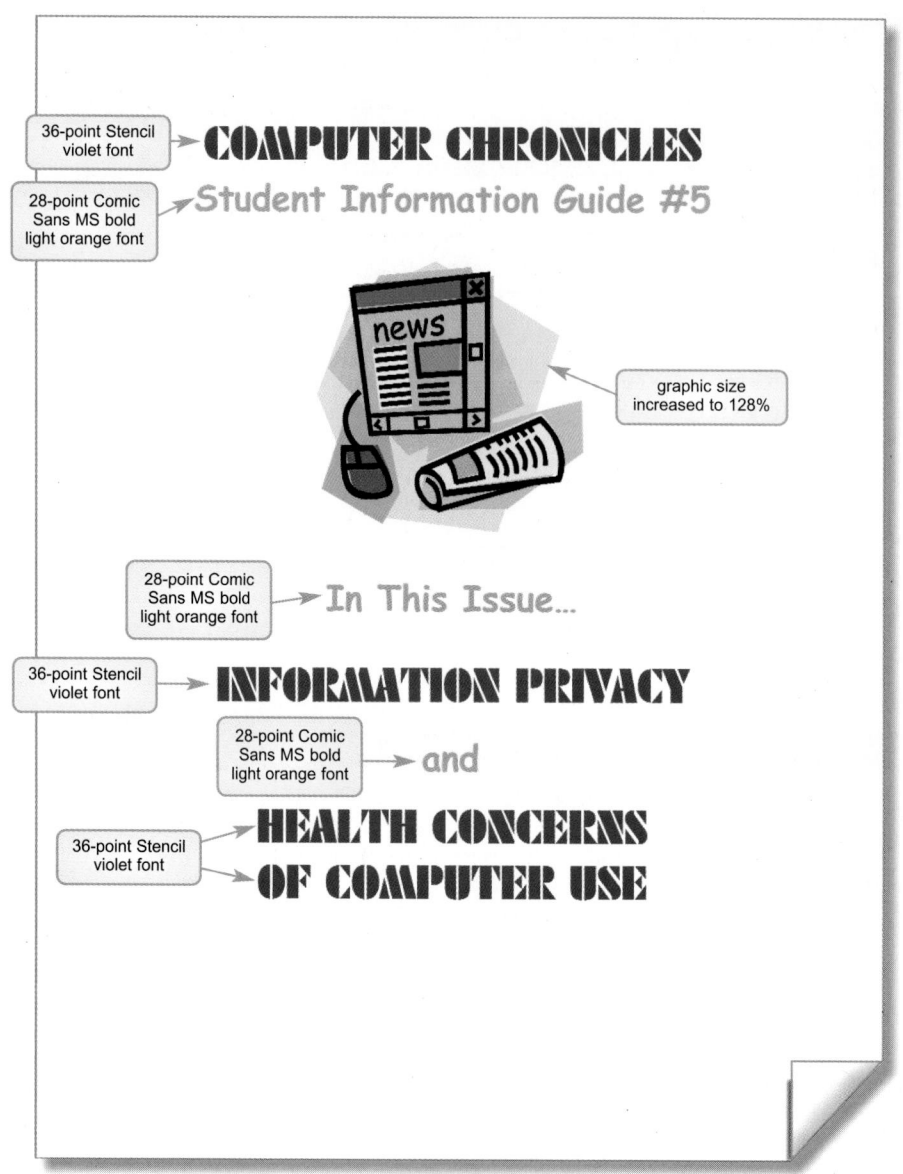

FIGURE 9-44

The next steps describe how to enter the text and graphics on the title page of the master document.

More About

**Publishing
and Graphic Arts**

For more information about terms used in publishing and graphic arts, visit the Word 2003 More About Web page (scsite.com/wd2003/more) and then click Publishing and Graphic Arts.

To Enter and Format the Title Page Text

1 Press CTRL+HOME to position the insertion point at the top of the document.

2 Click the Print Layout View button on the horizontal scroll bar to switch to print layout view.

3 Select the first line on the title page. Click the Style box arrow on the Formatting toolbar and then click Clear Formatting. Press the END key. Press the ENTER key twice. Press the UP ARROW key. **Type** Student Information Guide #5 and then press the ENTER key three times.

4 Click Insert on the menu bar, point to Picture, and then click Clip Art on the Picture submenu. In the Clip Art task pane, drag through any text in the Search for text box to select the text. **Type** computer newspaper and then press the ENTER key. Scroll to and then click the clip that matches the one shown in Figure 9-44 (or a similar clip). Click the Close button on the Clip Art task pane title bar.

5 Double-click the graphic to display the Format Picture dialog box and then, if necessary, click the Size tab. Change the height and width in the Scale area to 128%. Click the OK button.

6 Press the END key. Press the ENTER key three times. **Type** In This Issue... and then press the ENTER key three times. **Type** INFORMATION PRIVACY and then press the ENTER key twice. **Type** and and then press then ENTER key two times. If necessary, press CTRL+Z to undo an automatic capitalization of the word, and. **Type** HEALTH CONCERNS and then press the ENTER key. **Type** OF COMPUTER USE as the last line of text on the title page (Figure 9-45 on the next page).

7 Press CTRL+HOME. Select the COMPUTER CHRONICLES line.

8 Click the Font box arrow on the Formatting toolbar, scroll to and then click Stencil (or a similar font). Click the Font Size box arrow on the Formatting toolbar and then click 36 in the list. Click the Center button on the Formatting toolbar. Click the Font Color button arrow on the Formatting toolbar and then click Violet on the color palette.

9 Select the Student Information Guide #5 line.

10 Click the Font box arrow on the Formatting toolbar, scroll to and then click Comic Sans MS (or a similar font). Click the Font Size box arrow on the Formatting toolbar and then click 28 in the list. Click the Bold button and the Center button on the Formatting toolbar. Click the Font Color button arrow on the Formatting toolbar and then click Light Orange on the color palette.

11 Select the graphic and then click the Center button on the Formatting toolbar.

12 Select the In This Issue line and then repeat Step 10.

13 Select the INFORMATION PRIVACY line and then repeat Step 8.

14 Select the and line and then repeat Step 10.

15 Select the last two lines and then repeat Step 8.

The title page is complete (shown in Figure 9-44).

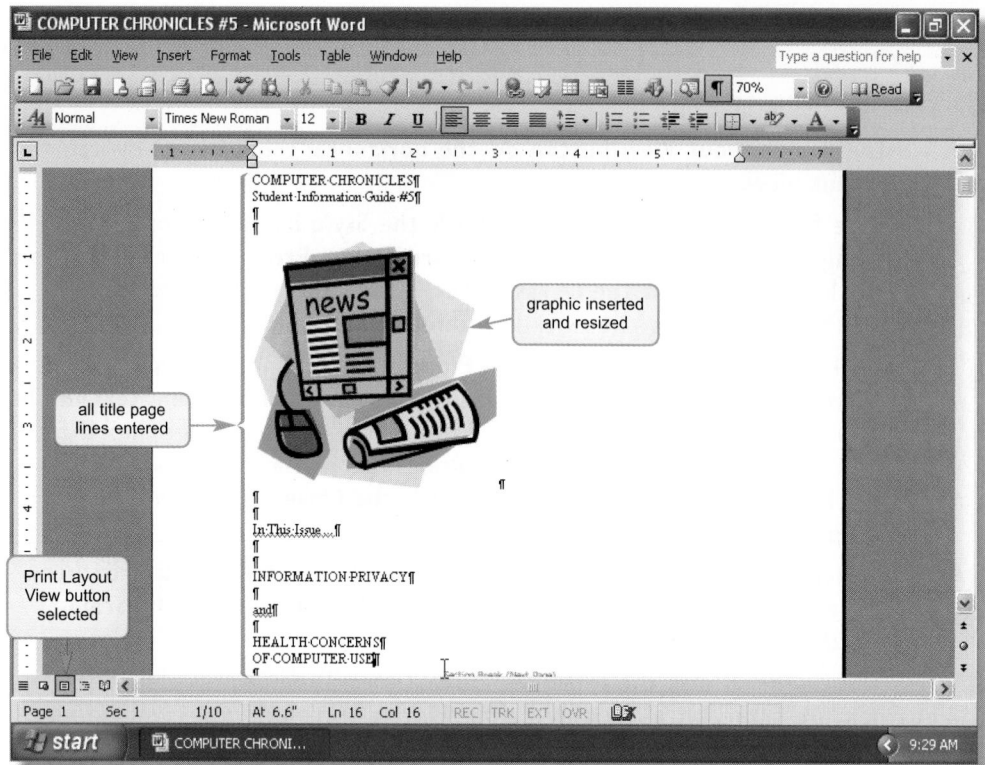

FIGURE 9-45

Creating a Table of Figures

The *Computer Chronicles* document has a table of figures following the text of the document. A **table of figures** is a list of all illustrations such as graphics, pictures, and tables in a document. Word creates the table of figures from the captions in the document.

Formatting marks, especially those for index entries, sometimes can cause wrapping to occur on the screen that will be different from how the printed document will wrap. These differences could cause a figure to move to the next page. To ensure that the page references in the table of figures will reflect the position of figures on printed pages, be sure that formatting marks are not displayed when you create a table of figures.

The next steps show how to create a table of figures.

To Create a Table of Figures

1

• If it is selected, click the **Show/Hide ¶** button on the Standard toolbar to hide formatting marks.

• Scroll down to display the **TABLE OF FIGURES** heading.

• Position the insertion point at the end of the heading and then press the **ENTER** key.

• Click **Insert** on the menu bar and then point to **Reference** (Figure 9-46).

FIGURE 9-46

2

• Click **Index and Tables** on the Reference submenu.

• If Word displays a dialog box asking you to open the subdocuments, click the **Yes** button.

• When Word displays the Index and Tables dialog box, if necessary, click the **Table of Figures** tab. Be sure that all check boxes in the dialog box contain check marks.

Word displays the Table of Figures sheet in the Index and Tables dialog box (Figure 9-47).

FIGURE 9-47

3

• **Click the OK button.**

Word creates a table of figures at the location of the insertion point (Figure 9-48).

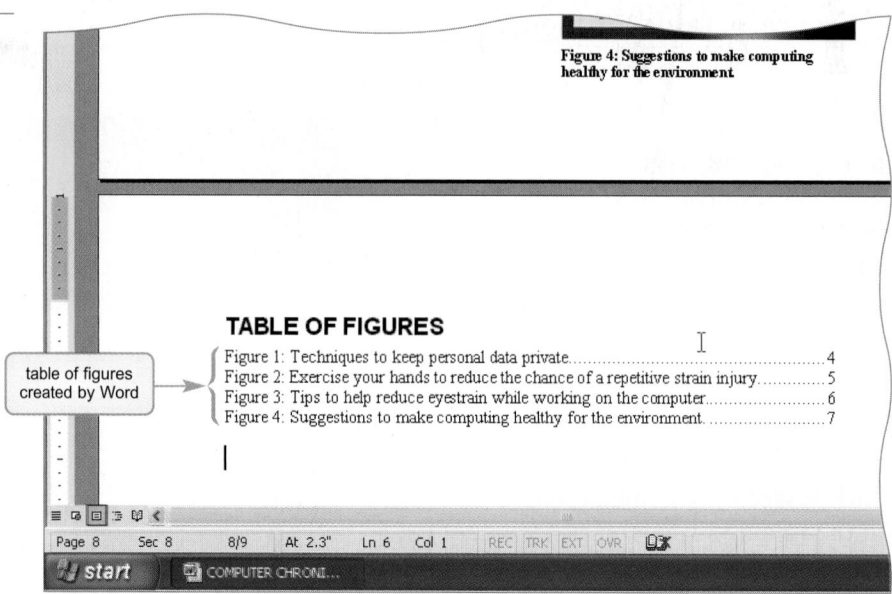

Figure 4: Suggestions to make computing healthy for the environment

TABLE OF FIGURES

table of figures created by Word

Figure 1: Techniques to keep personal data private................................4
Figure 2: Exercise your hands to reduce the chance of a repetitive strain injury.............5
Figure 3: Tips to help reduce eyestrain while working on the computer..................6
Figure 4: Suggestions to make computing healthy for the environment. 7

FIGURE 9-48

Other Ways

1. In Voice Command mode, say "Insert, Reference, Index and Tables, Table of Figures, OK"

When you modify captions in a document or move illustrations to a different location in the document, you will have to update the table of figures. To do this, click to the left of the table and then press the F9 key.

If you did not use captions to create labels for your illustrations in a document and would like Word to generate a table of figures, you can instruct Word to create the table using the built-in style you used for the captions. To do this, click the Options button in the Table of Figures sheet (Figure 9-47 on the previous page) to display the Table of Figures Options dialog box.

To change the format of the table of figures, click the Formats box arrow in the Table of Figures sheet and then click the desired format. If you want to modify the style used for the table of figures, click the Modify button in the Table of Figures sheet.

More About

Index Entries

Instead of marking index entries in a document, you can create a concordance file, which Word uses to mark index entries automatically. The concordance file contains two columns: (1) the first column identifies the text in the document you want Word to mark as an index entry, and (2) the second column lists the index entries to be generated from the text in the first column. To mark entries in the concordance file, click the AutoMark button in the Index and Tables dialog box.

Building an Index

As mentioned earlier in this project, *Computer Chronicles* documents end with an index. An **index** lists important terms discussed in a document along with each term's corresponding page number. For Word to generate the index, you first must mark any terms you wish to appear in the index. Earlier, this project showed how to mark index entries using the Information Privacy file. The Health Concerns of Computer Use file already has index entries marked.

Once all index entries are marked, Word can build the index from the index entry fields in the document. The index entry fields begin with XE and appear on the screen when formatting marks are displayed. When index entry fields show on the screen, the document's pagination probably will be altered because of the extra text in the index entries. Thus, you should hide formatting marks before building an index.

The next steps show how to build an index.

To Build an Index

1

• **Scroll down and click to the right of the INDEX heading and then press the ENTER key.**

• **If the Show/Hide ¶ button on the Standard toolbar is selected, click it to hide formatting marks.**

• **Click Insert on the menu bar, point to Reference, and then click Index and Tables on the Reference submenu.**

• **When Word displays the Index and Tables dialog box, if necessary, click the Index tab.**

Word displays the Index sheet in the Index and Tables dialog box (Figure 9-49).

FIGURE 9-49

2

• **Click the OK button.**

• **If necessary, click outside the index to remove the selection.**

Word creates an index at the location of the insertion point (Figure 9-50).

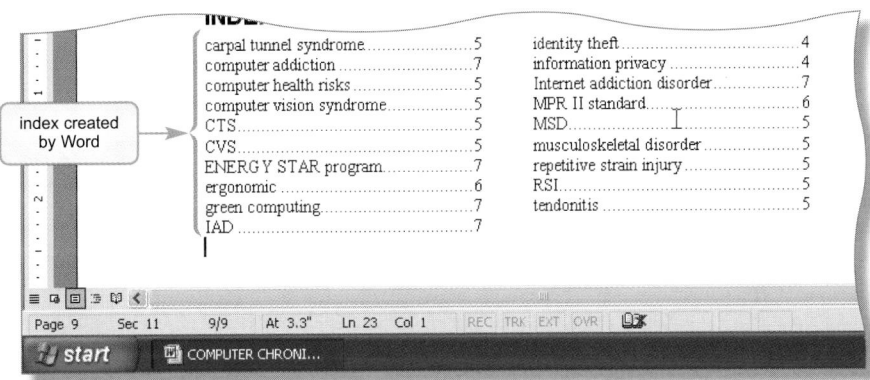

FIGURE 9-50

Other Ways

1. In Voice Command mode, say "Insert, Reference, Index and Tables, Index, OK"

To update an index, click to the left of the index to select it and then press the F9 key. To delete an index, click to the left of the index and then press SHIFT+F9 to display field codes. Drag through the entire field code, including the braces, and then press the DELETE key.

To change the format of the index, click the Formats box arrow in the Index sheet and then click the desired format. If you want to modify the style used for the index, click the Modify button in the Index sheet.

Creating a Table of Contents

A **table of contents** is a list of all headings in a document and their associated page numbers. When you use Word's built-in heading styles (for example, Heading 1), you can instruct Word to create a table of contents from these headings. In the

Computer Chronicles document, the heading of each section uses the Heading 1 style, and subheadings use the Heading 2 style.

The following steps show how to create a table of contents from Word heading styles.

To Create a Table of Contents

1

• Scroll up and click to the right of the TABLE OF CONTENTS heading and then press the ENTER key.

• Click Insert on the menu bar, point to Reference, and then click Index and Tables on the Reference submenu.

• When Word displays the Index and Tables dialog box, if necessary, click the Table of Contents tab.

• Click the Formats box arrow and then click Formal.

Word displays the Table of Contents sheet in the Index and Tables dialog box (Figure 9-51). The Formats list contains a variety of available table of contents styles.

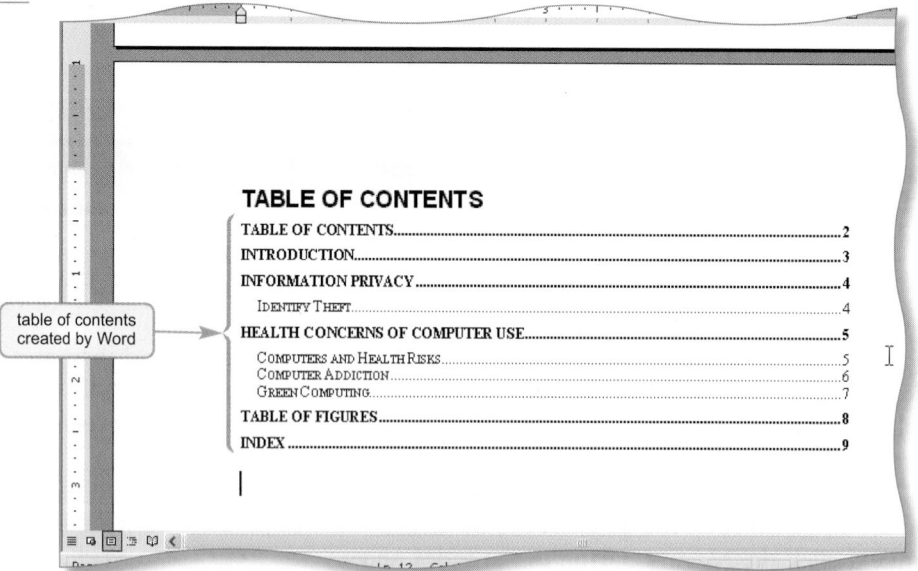

FIGURE 9-51

2

• Click the OK button.

Word creates a formal table of contents at the location of the insertion point (Figure 9-52).

TABLE OF CONTENTS

TABLE OF CONTENTS...2
INTRODUCTION..3
INFORMATION PRIVACY...4
   IDENTIFY THEFT...4
HEALTH CONCERNS OF COMPUTER USE.................................5
   COMPUTERS AND HEALTH RISKS..5
   COMPUTER ADDICTION..6
   GREEN COMPUTING...7
TABLE OF FIGURES..8
INDEX..9

table of contents created by Word

FIGURE 9-52

Other Ways

1. In Voice Command mode, say "Insert, Reference, Index and Tables, Table of Contents, OK"

When you change headings or text in a document, you should update its associated table of contents. To update a table of contents, click to the left of the table of contents to select it and then press the F9 key.

In a document that contains a table of contents or a table of figures, you can use these tables to navigate through a document. When you CTRL+click any of the entries in either table, Word displays the associated text or graphics in the document window. For example, if you CTRL+click Identity Theft in the table of contents, Word displays the page containing the Identity Theft section.

Adding Bookmarks

To further assist users in navigating through a document, you can add bookmarks. A **bookmark** is an item in a document that you name for future reference. For example, you could bookmark the two headings, Information Privacy and Health Concerns of Computer Use, so users easily could jump to these two areas of the document. The following steps show how to add these bookmarks.

To Add Bookmarks

1

- **Scroll to the INFORMATION PRIVACY heading in the document and then drag through the heading to select it.**

- **Click Insert on the menu bar (Figure 9-53).**

FIGURE 9-53

2

- **Click Bookmark on the Insert menu.**

- **When Word displays the Bookmark dialog box, type** `InformationPrivacy` **in the Bookmark name text box.**

Word displays the Bookmark dialog box (Figure 9-54). Bookmark names can contain only letters, numbers, and the underscore character (_). They also must begin with a letter and cannot contain spaces.

3

- **Click the Add button.**

Word adds the bookmark name to the list of existing bookmarks for the document.

FIGURE 9-54

The following steps describe how to add a second bookmark for the Health Concerns of Computer Use heading.

To Add Another Bookmark

1 Scroll to the **HEALTH CONCERNS OF COMPUTER USE** heading in the document and then drag through the heading to select it.

2 Click Insert on the menu bar and then click Bookmark.

3 When Word displays the Bookmark dialog box, type `HealthConcernsOfComputerUse` in the Bookmark name text box (Figure 9-55).

4 Click the Add button.

Word adds a second bookmark name.

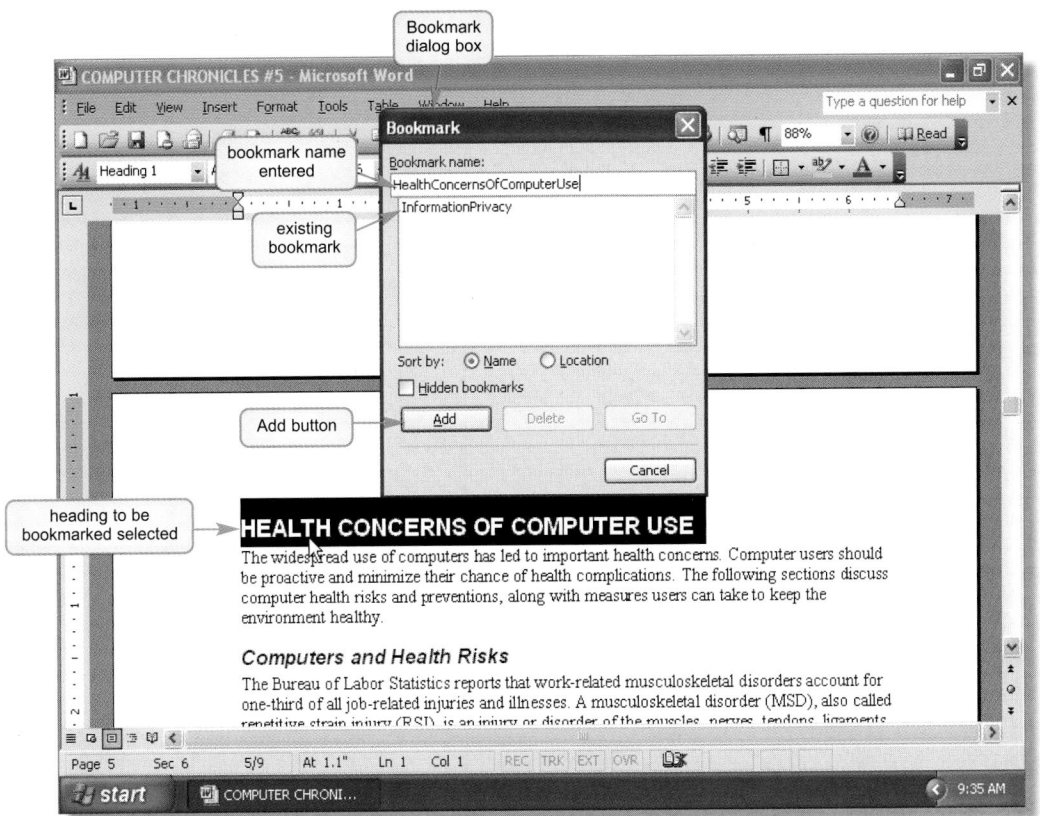

FIGURE 9-55

Once you have added bookmarks, you can jump to them by displaying the Bookmark dialog box (Figure 9-55), clicking the bookmark name in the list, and then clicking the Go To button; or by pressing the F5 key to display the Go To sheet in the Find and Replace dialog box, clicking bookmark in the list, selecting the bookmark name, and then clicking the Go To button.

Creating Alternating Headers and Footers

Computer Chronicles documents are designed so that they can be duplicated back-to-back. That is, the document prints on nine separate pages. When they are duplicated, however, pages one and two are printed on opposite sides of the same sheet of paper. Thus, the nine-page document when printed back-to-back uses only five sheets of paper.

In many books and documents that have facing pages, the page number is on the outside edges of the pages. In Word, you accomplish this task by specifying one type of header for even-numbered pages and another type of header for odd-numbered pages.

The steps on the next page show how to create alternating headers beginning with the second page of the document.

More About

Headers and Footers

If the Link to Previous button on the Header and Footer toolbar is dimmed (unavailable), the insertion point may be in the first section of the document or the document is not divided in sections. This button is available only if the document has more than one section.

To Create Alternating Headers

1

• **Position the insertion point in the Table of Contents heading (section 2 of the document).**

• **Click View on the menu bar and then click Header and Footer.**

• **Click the Page Setup button on the Header and Footer toolbar.**

• **When Word displays the Page Setup dialog box, if necessary, click the Layout tab.**

• **Click Different odd and even to place a check mark in the check box.**

• **Click the Apply to box arrow and then click This point forward.**

In the Layout sheet, you can specify header and footer settings (Figure 9-56).

FIGURE 9-56

2

• **Click the OK button.**

• **If the Link to Previous button on the Header and Footer toolbar is selected, click it.**

• **Type** Computer Chronicles #5 **and then press the ENTER key.**

• **Type** Page **and then press the SPACEBAR.**

• **Click the Insert Page Number button on the Header and Footer toolbar.**

Word displays the Even Page Header area (Figure 9-57). You want text on even page numbers to be left-aligned and text on odd page numbers to be right-aligned.

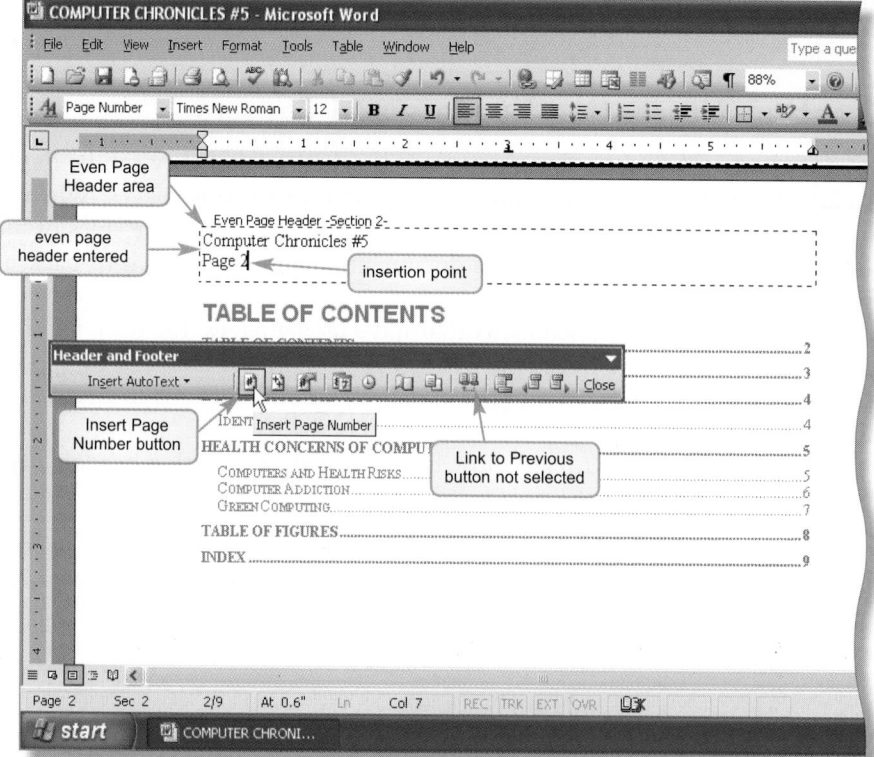

FIGURE 9-57

3

• **Click the Show Next button to display the Odd Page Header area.**

• **If the Link to Previous button on the Header and Footer toolbar is selected, click it.**

• **Click the Align Right button on the Formatting toolbar.**

• **Type** Computer Chronicles #5 **and then press the ENTER key.**

• **Type** Page **and then press the SPACEBAR.**

• **Click the Insert Page Number button on the Header and Footer toolbar.**

The odd page header is complete (Figure 9-58).

4

• **Click the Close button on the Header and Footer toolbar to remove the Header and Footer toolbar from the screen.**

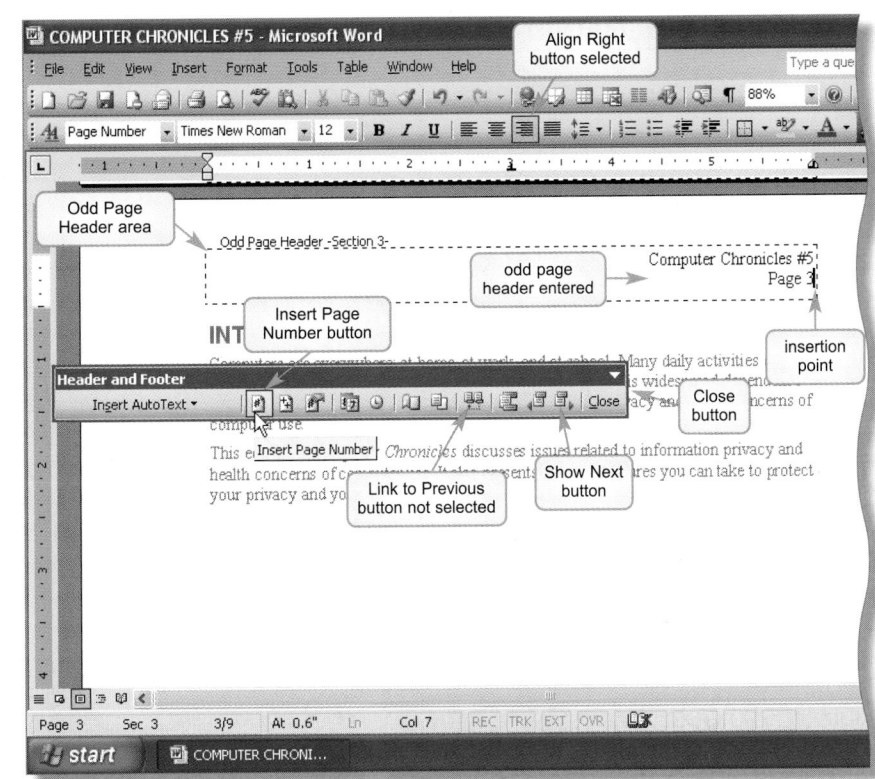

FIGURE 9-58

To create alternating footers, follow the same basic procedure as you would to create alternating headers, except enter text in the footer area instead of the header area.

Other Ways

1. In Voice Command mode, say "View, Header and Footer, Page Setup"

Setting a Gutter Margin

Computer Chronicles documents are designed so that the inner margin between facing pages has extra space to allow printed versions of the documents to be bound (such as stapled) — without the binding covering the words. This extra space in the inner margin is called the **gutter margin**.

The steps on the next page show how to set a three-quarter inch left and right margin and a one-half inch gutter margin.

To Set a Gutter Margin

1

- **Click File on the menu bar and then click Page Setup.**

- **When Word displays the Page Setup dialog box, if necessary, click the Margins tab.**

- **Type** .75 **in the Left box,** .75 **in the Right box, and** .5 **in the Gutter box.**

- **Click the Apply to box arrow and then click Whole document.**

The Preview area illustrates specified settings (Figure 9-59).

2

- **Click the OK button.**

Word sets the margins for the entire document.

FIGURE 9-59

To view the layout of all the pages in the document, display all the pages in print preview, as described in the following steps.

To Display Several Pages in Print Preview

1 Click the Print Preview button on the Standard toolbar.

2 Click the Multiple Pages button on the Print Preview toolbar. Click the right-bottom icon in the grid (when the description reads 2 x 6 pages) to display the pages in the *Computer Chronicles* document as shown in Figure 9-60.

3 Click the Close button on the Print Preview toolbar.

Q&A

Q: How do I save ink, print faster, or minimize printer overrun errors?

A: Print a draft. Click File on the menu bar, click Print, click the Options button, place a check mark in the Draft output check box, and then click the OK button in each dialog box.

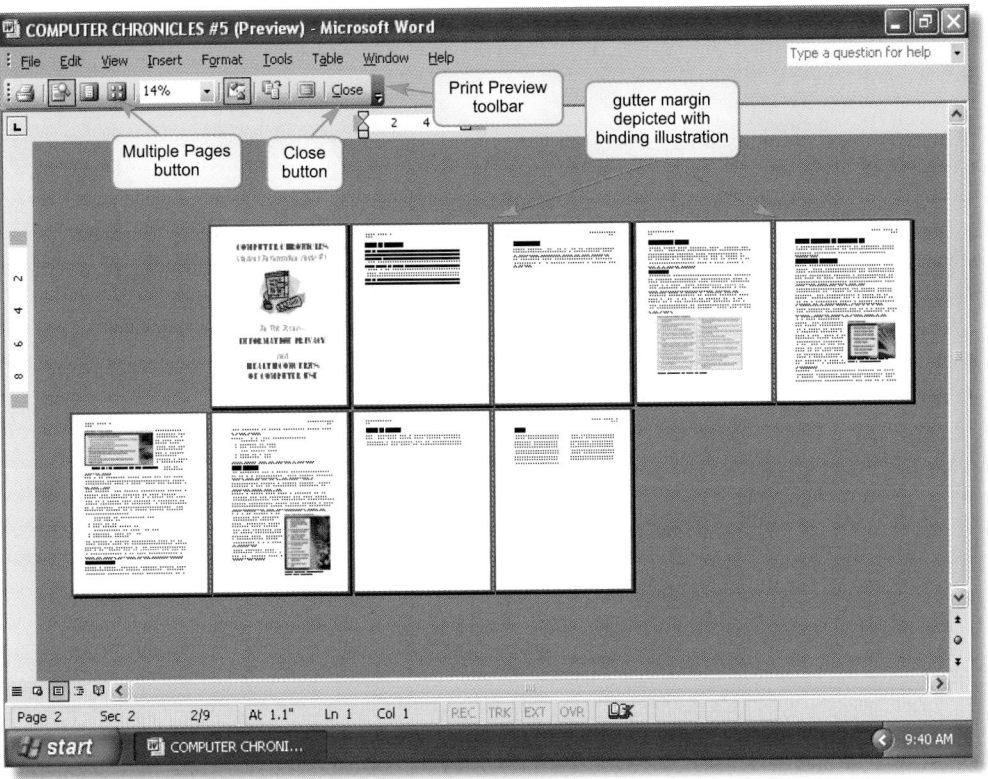

FIGURE 9-60

The reference master document for this project now is complete. The following steps save it again, print it, and then close the document.

To Save and Print a Document

1 Click the Save button on the Standard toolbar.

2 Click the Print button on the Standard toolbar.

Word saves the document with the same file name, COMPUTER CHRONICLES #5. The completed document prints each page shown in Figure 9-1 on page WD 635 on a separate piece of paper.

To Close a Document

1 Click File on the menu bar and then click Close.

Word closes the open document.

Opening a Master Document

You may need to open a master document at a later date to edit or print its contents. When you open the master document, the subdocuments are collapsed, that is, displayed as hyperlinks. Thus, to work with the contents of a master document, you switch to outline view and then expand the subdocuments. The steps on the next page show how to open a master document.

Q: What if errors are displayed for field codes (such as bookmarks and page numbers) when I open a master document?

A: Press CTRL+A to select the entire document and then press the F9 key to update all fields.

To Open a Master Document

1

• **Open the COMPUTER CHRONICLES #5 document.**

• **Click the Outline View button on the horizontal scroll bar.**

• **Scroll down to display the hyperlinks.**

Word displays the COMPUTER CHRONICLES #5 document in outline view (Figure 9-61). Notice the Show First Line Only button on the Outlining toolbar is selected and the Show/Hide ¶ button on the Standard toolbar is not selected.

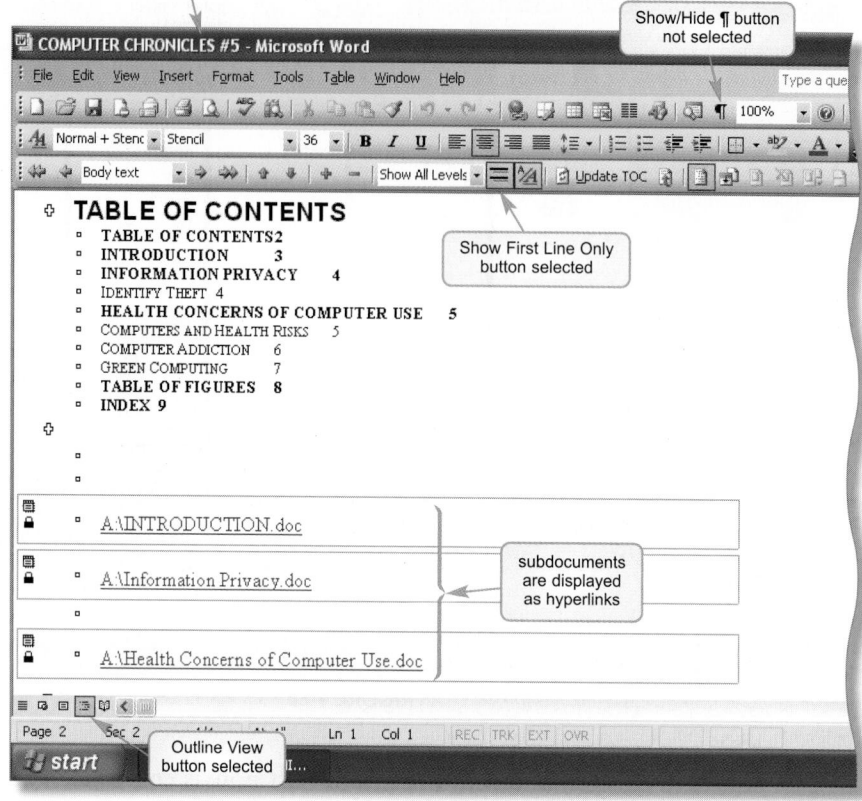

FIGURE 9-61

2

• **Click the Expand Subdocuments button on the Outlining toolbar.**

• **Scroll down to display the subdocuments.**

Word displays the contents of the subdocuments in the master document (Figure 9-62).

3

• **Click the Print Layout View button on the scroll bar.**

The master document is ready to be printed or modified.

Other Ways

1. In Voice Command mode, say "File, Open, [select file], OK, Outline View"

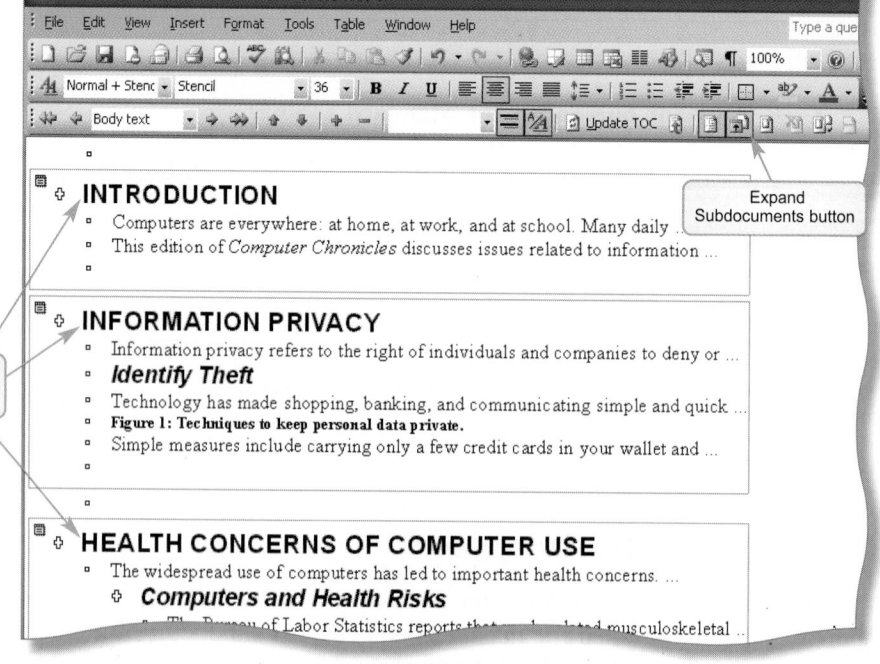

FIGURE 9-62

Using the Document Map

When you use Word's built-in heading styles in a document, you can use the Document Map to navigate quickly through the document. The **Document Map** is a pane at the left edge of the Word window that displays in an outline format the headings that are formatted using Word's heading styles. When you click a heading in the Document Map, Word displays the page associated with that heading in the document window.

The following steps show how to use the Document Map.

To Use the Document Map

1

• If the Show/Hide ¶ button on the Standard toolbar is selected, click it.

• Click the Document Map button on the Standard toolbar.

• Right-click the Document Map and then click All on the shortcut menu to ensure that all headings are displayed.

Word displays the Document Map in a separate pane at the left edge of the Word window (Figure 9-63). The Document Map lists all headings that are formatted using Word's built-in heading styles. The document map may show some blank lines between headings.

FIGURE 9-63

2

• Click INDEX in the Document Map.

Word displays the page containing the INDEX heading (Figure 9-64). The heading, INDEX, is displayed at the top of the document window.

FIGURE 9-64

Other Ways

1. On View menu click Document Map
2. In Voice Command mode, say "Document Map"

To display subheadings below a heading in the document pane, click the plus sign (+) to the left of the heading. Likewise, to hide subheadings, click the minus sign (–) to the left of the heading.

You can change the width of the Document Map pane by dragging the resize bar to the left or right. If a heading is too wide for the Document Map pane, you can point to the heading to display a ScreenTip that shows the complete title.

Updating an Index

Assume you wanted to change the index entry for ENERGY STAR program to delete the word, program. After making this change to the document, you must update the index, as shown in the following steps.

To Update an Index

1

• **Click the Green Computing heading in the Document Map pane.**

• **If it is not selected, click the Show/Hide ¶ button on the Standard toolbar to show formatting marks.**

• **Delete the word, program, so the index entry just reads ENERGY STAR.**

The document is modified (Figure 9-65). The index entries show only when formatting marks are showing on the screen.

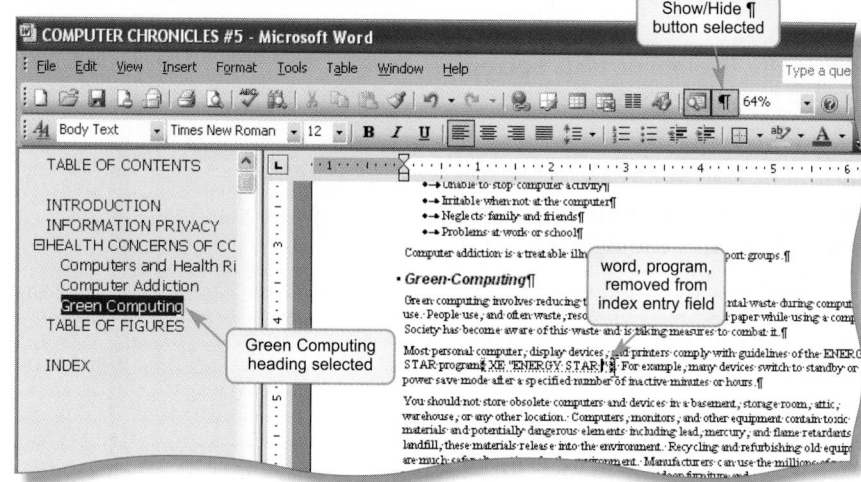

FIGURE 9-65

2

• **Click the Show/Hide ¶ button on the Standard toolbar to hide formatting marks.**

• **Click INDEX in the Document Map pane.**

• **Click to the left of the index to select the index in the document window.**

• **Press the F9 key.**

Word updates the index, changing the index entry from ENERGY STAR program to ENERGY STAR (Figure 9-66). The selected index may be shaded gray.

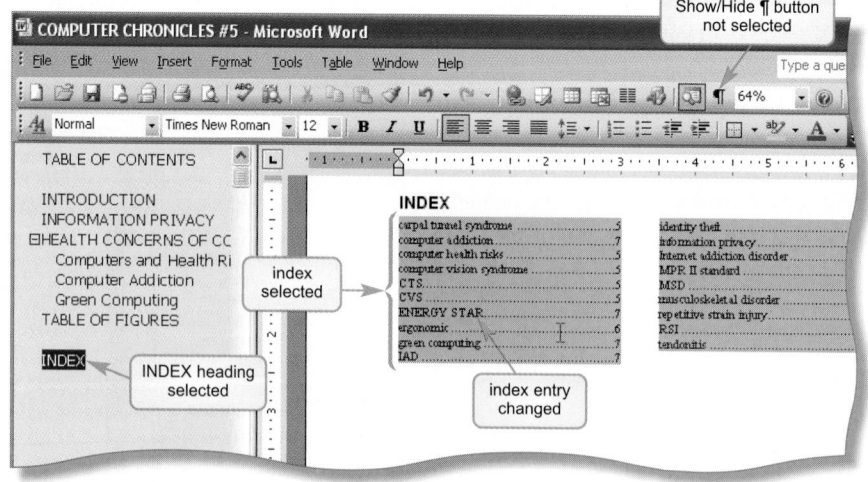

FIGURE 9-66

If you wanted to update all fields in the document, including an index, table of contents, and table of figures, select the entire document by pressing CTRL+A before pressing the F9 key. When you update a table of contents or table of figures, Word displays a dialog box asking if you want to update the page numbers only or update the entire table. Click whichever option you desire and then click the OK button in the dialog box.

The next step is to close the Document Map, as described in the following step.

To Close the Document Map

1 Click the Document Map button on the Standard toolbar.

Word removes the Document Map pane from the Word window.

You also can close the Document Map by double-clicking the resize bar to its right (shown in Figure 9-64 on page WD 683).

Summarize a Document

Word has an AutoSummarize feature that allows you to summarize key points in a document. You can instruct Word to place the summary on a separate page or document, highlight the summarized text in the current document, or hide all text in the current document except for the summary. Summarized text is useful if you want to review the main points in a document. The following steps show how to use the AutoSummarize feature.

To AutoSummarize a Document

1

• **Press CTRL+HOME to position the insertion point at the top of the document.**

• **Click Tools on the menu bar (Figure 9-67).**

More About

Modifying a Table of Contents

The table of contents that Word generates may contain a heading that you do not want in the table of contents. To remove a heading from the table of contents, change the style applied to the heading from a built-in heading to a non-heading style. Then, update the table of contents by selecting it and pressing the F9 key or clicking the Update TOC button on the Outlining toolbar.

FIGURE 9-67

2

• **Click AutoSummarize on the Tools menu.**

• **When Word displays the AutoSummarize dialog box, if necessary, click Highlight key points.**

In the AutoSummarize dialog box, you select how Word should summarize the document (Figure 9-68).

FIGURE 9-68

3

• **Click the OK button.**

• **Scroll down to display a page of text in the document window (e.g., page 5).**

Word highlights the key points in the document (Figure 9-69). The AutoSummarize toolbar appears in the Word window.

4

• **Click the Close button on the AutoSummarize toolbar to stop the AutoSummary.**

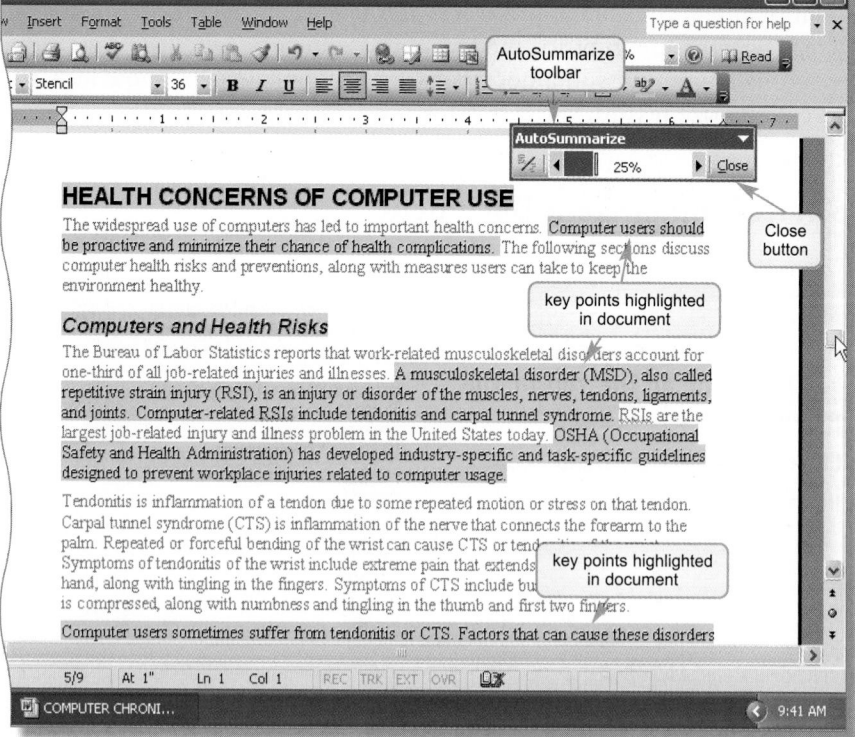

FIGURE 9-69

If you want more of the document in a summary, increase the percent of original in the AutoSummarize dialog box or on the AutoSummarize toolbar. To place the summary on a separate page or in a separate document, select the respective option in the AutoSummarize dialog box.

Using Readability Statistics

You can instruct Word to display readability statistics when it has finished a spelling and grammar check on a document. Three readability statistics presented are the percent of passive sentences, the Flesch Reading Ease score, and the Flesch-Kincaid Grade Level score. The **Flesch Reading Ease score** uses a 100-point scale to rate the ease with which a reader can understand the text in a document. A higher score means the document is easier to understand. The **Flesch-Kincaid Grade Level** score rates the text in a document on a U.S. school grade level. For example, a score of 10.0 indicates a student in the tenth grade can understand the material.

The following steps show how to instruct Word to display readability statistics when you check spelling and grammar in a document.

To Turn On Readability Statistics

1

• **Click Tools on the menu bar and then click Options.**

• **When Word displays the Options dialog box, if necessary, click the Spelling & Grammar tab.**

• **If necessary, place a check mark in the Show readability statistics check box.**

• **Be sure the Check grammar with spelling check box is selected.**

You instruct Word to show readability statistics through the Spelling & Grammar sheet in the Options dialog box (Figure 9-70).

2

• **Click the OK button.**

Word is set to display readability statistics the next time you check spelling and grammar in the document.

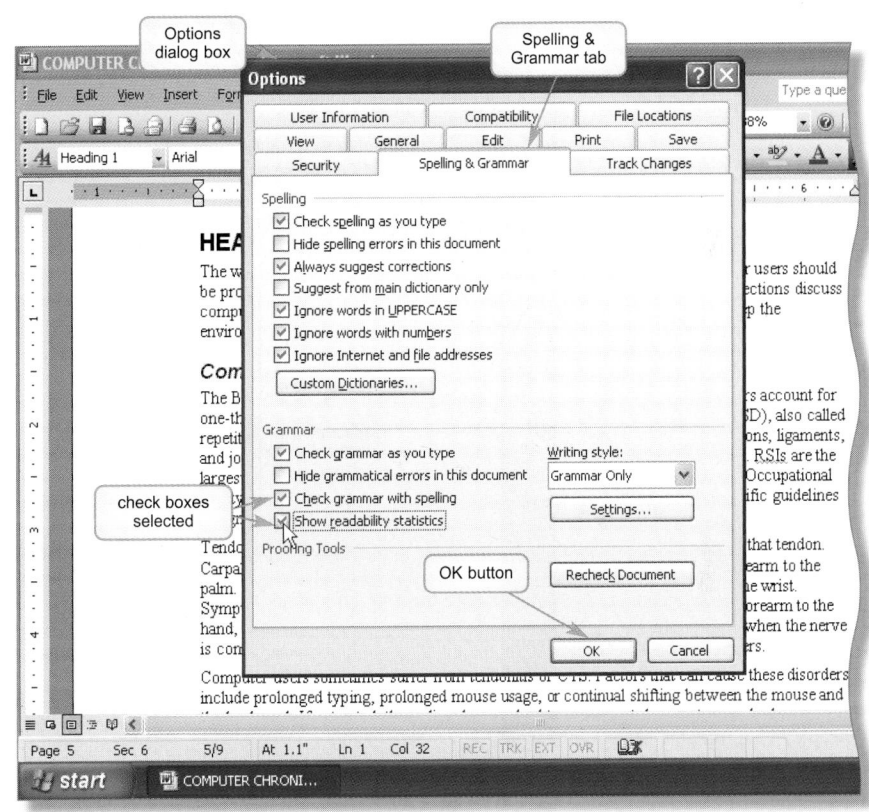

FIGURE 9-70

The steps on the next page show the readability statistics that are displayed when you check spelling and grammar.

Other Ways

1. In Voice Command mode, say "Tools, Options, Spelling & Grammar"

To Check Spelling and Display Readability Statistics

1 Click the Spelling and Grammar button on the Standard toolbar.

2 As Word displays dialog boxes, fix or ignore the spelling and/or grammar items it flags.

3 When Word displays a dialog box indicating the spelling and grammar check is complete, click the OK button.

4 When Word displays the Readability Statistics dialog box, review the readability statistics (Figure 9-71).

5 Click the OK button.

In addition to readability scores, Word presents a variety of other statistics about the document in the Readability Statistics dialog box.

FIGURE 9-71

Word may indicate that some text has been flagged as do not check spelling or grammar. For example, Word does not check entries such as the table of contents, index, and table of figures because these are generated from items in the document.

Go To a Bookmark

Earlier, this project showed how to bookmark the two headings, INFORMATION PRIVACY and HEALTH CONCERNS OF COMPUTER USE, so users easily could jump to these two areas of the document. The next steps describe how to jump to a bookmark.

To Go To a Bookmark

1 **Press the F5 key.**

2 **When Word displays the Go To sheet in the Find and Replace dialog box, click Bookmark in the Go to what list.**

3 **With HealthConcernsOfComputerUse shown in the Enter bookmark name box, click the Go To button (Figure 9-72).**

4 **Click the Close button.**

Word displays the page containing the bookmark in the document window.

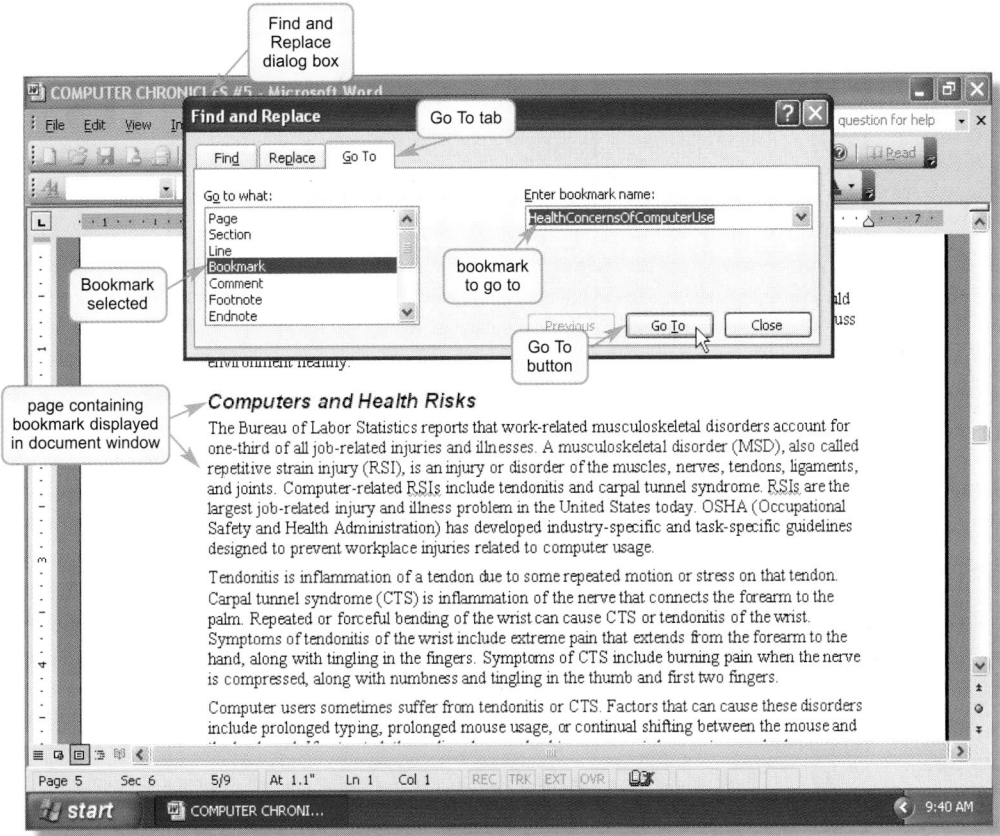

FIGURE 9-72

With Bookmark selected in the Go to what list, you can click the Enter bookmark name box arrow to display all previously marked bookmarks.

Customizing Document Properties

The document summary contains a standard set of properties about which you can enter data. For example, you can enter a title, subject, author, manager, company, category, keywords, and comments about a document in the Summary sheet in the Properties dialog box. Any value you enter is stored with the document. In Word, you also can create your own properties to store with a document. For example, you may want to store a Web address as a document property.

The following steps show how to enter a value for an existing custom property and add a new custom property.

To Work with Custom Properties

1

- **Press CTRL+HOME.**
- **Click File on the menu bar and then click Properties.**
- **When Word displays the COMPUTER CHRONICLES #5 Properties dialog box, if necessary, click the Custom tab.**
- **In the Name text box, type** Web address **as a new property.**
- **In the Value text box, type** www.scsite.com **as the value for the Web address property.**

In the Custom sheet, you enter values for custom properties or add new custom properties (Figure 9-73).

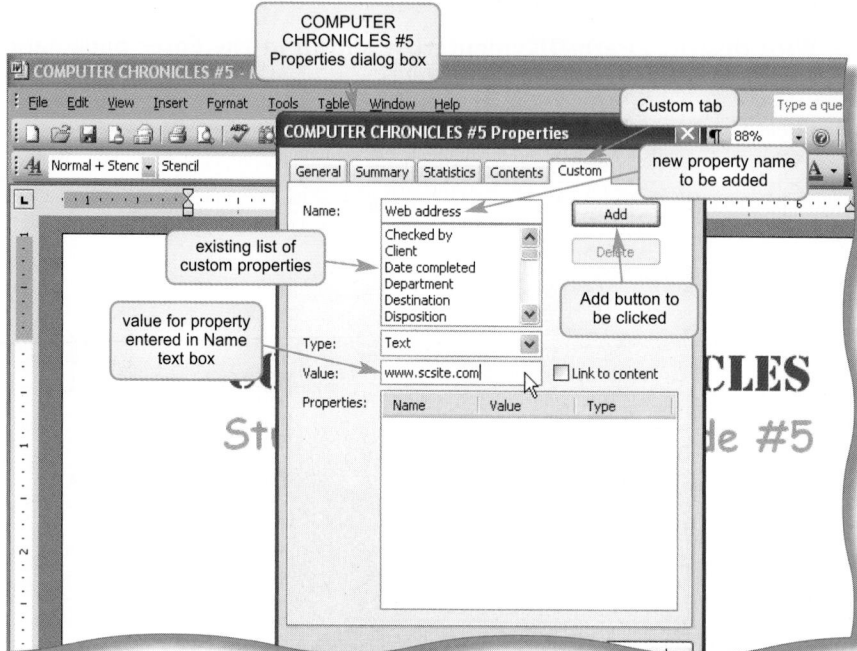

FIGURE 9-73

2

- **Click the Add button.**

Word adds the new property and its value to the Properties list.

3

- **In the list of existing properties, scroll to and then click the Document number property.**
- **In the Value text box, type** 5 **and then click the Add button.**

Word adds the property and its value to the properties list (Figure 9-74).

4

- **Click the OK button.**

FIGURE 9-74

Other Ways

1. In Voice Command mode, say "File, Properties, Custom"

If you wanted to delete a custom property, you would select the property name in the Custom sheet in the Properties dialog box and then click the Delete button.

Document properties are stored as fields. You can insert any field value in a document. For example, you may want to include the Web address on the document's title page. The following steps describe how you would insert the Web address field in a document.

To Insert a Document Property Field

1. Click Insert on the menu bar and then click Field.
2. When Word displays the Field dialog box, scroll through the Field names list and select the field name to be inserted (in this case, DocProperty).
3. In the Property list, click the desired property (in this case, Web address).
4. Click the OK button.

You can insert any field in a document by following the steps above. In some cases, you will omit Step 3 because the field does not have any properties.

Password-Protecting a File

A **password-protected document** is a document that requires a password to open or modify it. Password protecting a document helps to ensure that the document can be modified by only authorized individuals.

In Word, a password may be up to 15 characters in length and can include letters, numbers, spaces, and symbols. Passwords are **case-sensitive**, which means that the password always must be entered in the same case in which it was saved. That is, if you enter a password in all uppercase letters, it must be entered in uppercase letters when the file is opened or modified.

The password to be used for this file is the word, computer (in lowercase). The following steps show how to password-protect a file.

To Password-Protect a File

1

• **Click File on the menu bar and then click Save As.**

• **When Word displays the Save As dialog box, if necessary, click the Save in box arrow and then click 3½ Floppy (A:).**

• **Click the Tools button.**

Word displays the Save As dialog box (Figure 9-75).

FIGURE 9-75

2

• **Click Security Options on the Tools menu.**

• **When Word displays the Security dialog box, type** computer **in the Password to open text box.**

When you type the password, computer, in the Security dialog box, Word displays a series of dots (•) instead of the actual characters you type (Figure 9-76).

FIGURE 9-76

3

• **Click the OK button.**

• **When Word displays the Confirm Password dialog box, type** computer **in the Reenter password to open text box.**

Word displays the Confirm Password dialog box (Figure 9-77). Again, the password appears as a series of dots (•) instead of the actual characters you type.

4

• **Click the OK button.**

• **When the Save As dialog box is visible again, click its Save button.**

Word saves the document with the password, computer.

FIGURE 9-77

Other Ways

1. On Tools menu click Options, click Security tab, enter password, on File menu click Save As
2. In Voice Command mode, say "File, Save As, Tools, Security Options, [type password], [type password], OK, Save"

When someone attempts to open the document in the future, he or she will be prompted to enter the password.

You are finished modifying the document. The next step closes the document.

To Close a Document

1 **Click File on the menu bar and then click Close. If Word displays a dialog box asking if you wish to save changes, click the No button.**

Word closes the open document.

Working with XML

Assume you have written a memo to attach to the front of the *Computer Chronicles* document. After it is completed, you realize that you create many memos that are similar to one another. It would save time if you could reuse the content of the memo and, if necessary, share the data entered in the memo with other applications.

XML is a popular format for structuring data so the data can be reused and shared. **XML**, which stands for eXtensible Markup Language, is a language used to encapsulate data and a description of the data in a single text file, or **XML file**. XML files typically have an extension of xml. XML uses **tags** to describe data items. Each data item is called an **element**. Businesses often create standard XML file layouts and tags to describe commonly used types of data.

XML support is available only in the stand-alone version of Microsoft Office Word 2003 and in Microsoft Office Professional Edition 2003. If you are stepping through this project on a computer, you must have one of these versions of Word or Office to perform the steps.

To use the XML features of Word, you do not need to be an expert in XML. Word makes it easy to work with XML files. The following pages illustrate how to use XML while working with a memo. The first step is to open the memo file, which is on the Data Disk that accompanies this book. If you did not download the Data Disk, see the inside back cover for instructions for downloading the Data Disk or see your instructor.

To Open a Document

1 **With the Data Disk in drive A, click the Open button on the Standard toolbar.**

2 **When Word displays the Open dialog box, if necessary, click the Look in box arrow and then click 3½ Floppy (A:).**

3 **Double-click the Word document named Westside Memo.**

Word displays the document titled, Westside Memo, on the screen (shown in Figure 9-78 on the next page).

Working with an XML Schema

A Word **XML schema**, also called **WordML**, is a special type of XML file that describes the layout of elements in other XML files. Word users typically do not create Word XML schema files. Computer programmers or other technical personnel create a Word XML schema file and provide it to Word users. XML schema files, often simply called schema files, usually have an extension of xsd.

More About

Subdocuments

If you want to change the name of a subdocument, you cannot use Windows Explorer. Instead, display the document in outline view, click the Collapse Subdocuments button on the Outlining toolbar, and then click the hyperlink of the document to be renamed. When the subdocument is displayed in its own Word window, click File on the menu bar, click Save As, change the document name, and then click the Save button in the dialog box. Then, return to the master document by clicking File on the menu bar and then clicking Close.

The schema file to be used in this project is on the Data Disk that accompanies this book. If you did not download the Data Disk, see the inside back cover for instructions for downloading the Data Disk or see your instructor. The following steps show how to attach a schema to the Westside Memo file.

To Attach a Schema File

1

• **If it is not selected, click the Show/Hide ¶ button on the Standard toolbar to show formatting marks.**

• **Click Tools on the menu bar (Figure 9-78).**

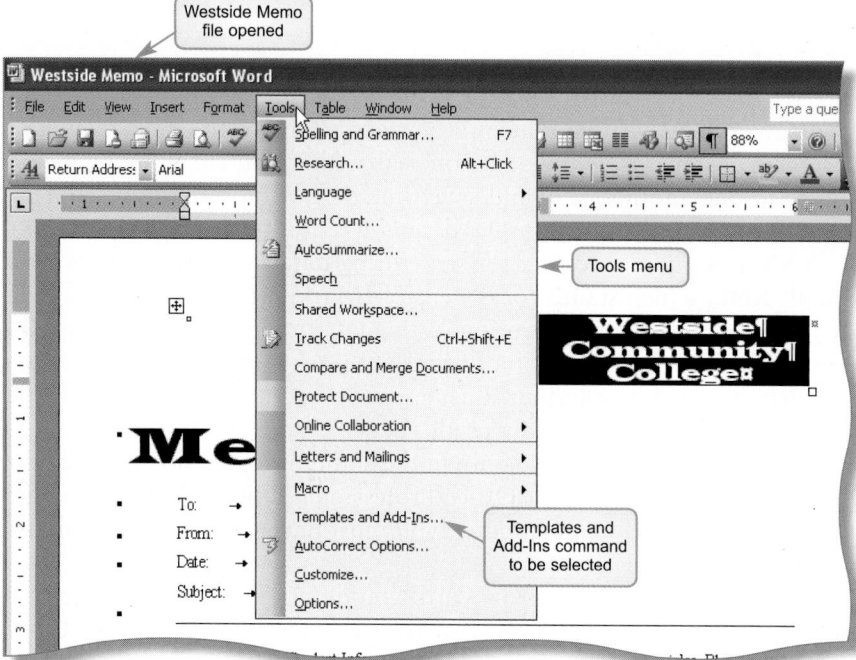

FIGURE 9-78

2

• **Click Templates and Add-Ins on the Tools menu.**

• **When Word displays the Templates and Add-ins dialog box, click the XML Schema tab.**

You can select from the list of available schemas in the XML Schema sheet or add a new schema to the list (Figure 9-79). Your list of available schemas may differ.

FIGURE 9-79

3

- **Click the Add Schema button.**
- **When Word displays the Add Schema dialog box, if necessary, click the Look in box arrow and then click 3½ Floppy (A:).**
- **Click Westside Memo in the Look in list.**

In the Add Schema dialog box, the file type is XML Schemas (Figure 9-80).

FIGURE 9-80

4

- **Click the Open button in the Add Schema dialog box.**
- **When Word displays the Schema Settings dialog box, type** urn:memo-schema-1 **in the URI text box and then type** Westside Memo **in the Alias text box.**

*Word uses the URI, or **namespace**, to refer to the schema. Because these names are difficult to remember, you can define a namespace alias (Figure 9-81). Your computer administrator will provide you with the appropriate namespace entry.*

FIGURE 9-81

5

• **Click the OK button.**

• **When the Templates and Add-ins dialog box is visible again, if necessary, place a check mark in the Westside Memo check box.**

Word adds the schema to the Schema Library and then adds the namespace alias to the list of available schemas in the XML schema sheet (Figure 9-82).

6

• **Click the OK button.**

Word attaches the selected schema to the open document and displays the XML Structure task pane in the Word window (shown in Figure 9-83).

FIGURE 9-82

Other Ways

1. In XML Structure task pane, click Templates and Add-Ins
2. In Voice Command mode, say "Tools, Templates and Add-Ins, XML Schema"

The previous steps first added the schema to the Schema Library and then added the schema to the document. To delete a schema from a document, you would remove the check mark from the schema name in the XML Schema sheet in the Templates and Add-ins dialog box (Figure 9-82). If, for some reason, you wanted to delete a schema altogether from the Schema Library, you would do the following.

TO DELETE A SCHEMA FROM THE SCHEMA LIBRARY

1. Click Tools on the menu bar and then click Templates and Add-Ins.
2. When Word displays the Templates and Add-ins dialog box, if necessary, click the XML Schema tab.
3. Click the Schema Library button.
4. When Word displays the Schema Library dialog box, click the schema to delete in the Select a schema list and then click the Delete Schema button.
5. When Word displays a dialog box asking if you are sure you wish to delete the schema, click the Yes button.
6. Click the OK button and then click the Cancel button.

The Schema Library dialog box also contains an Add Schema button that allows you to add a schema to the library. Clicking this button displays the Add Schema dialog box shown in Figure 9-80 on the previous page.

Through the Schema Library dialog box, you also can change a namespace alias by selecting the schema name, clicking the Schema Settings button, entering a new namespace alias, and then clicking the OK button in each dialog box.

Managing Elements in an XML Document

After a schema has been added to a document, the next step is to add XML elements to the document. XML elements are data items whose value often changes.

XML elements are similar to fields in a form. The memo in this project has six XML elements: the recipient of the memo, the sender of the memo, the date on the memo, the subject of the memo, the message on the memo, and the entire memo itself. The first step is to add the entire memo XML element, called the **parent element**, to the document and then add the elements subordinate to the parent, called the **child elements**.

The following steps show how to add XML elements to the document, which is called tagging the text. First, you select the item to be tagged and then you add the desired XML element to apply the tag.

To Add a Parent and Child XML Element

1

• **If the XML Structure task pane is not displayed, click View on the menu bar and then click Task Pane. If necessary, click the Other Task Panes button arrow and then click XML Structure in the list.**

• **Press CTRL+A to select the entire document.**

• **In the element list in the XML Structure task pane, click WestsideMemo.**

Word displays the Apply to entire document dialog box (Figure 9-83). WestsideMemo is the parent element in the XML file.

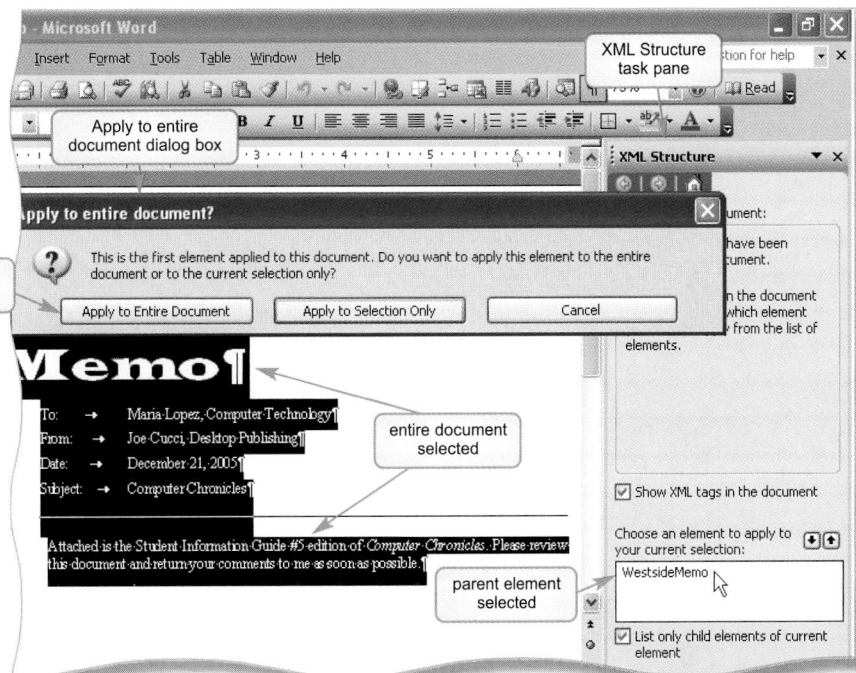

FIGURE 9-83

2

• **Click the Apply to Entire Document button.**

• **Be sure the Show XML tags in the document check box contains a check mark.**

Word places start and end tags on the text selected in the document (Figure 9-84). The parent element is displayed in the Elements in the document list, and the Choose an element to apply to your current selection list shows all child elements to the selected parent element. Depending on your XML Options settings, the namespace alias may be displayed next to the parent element name.

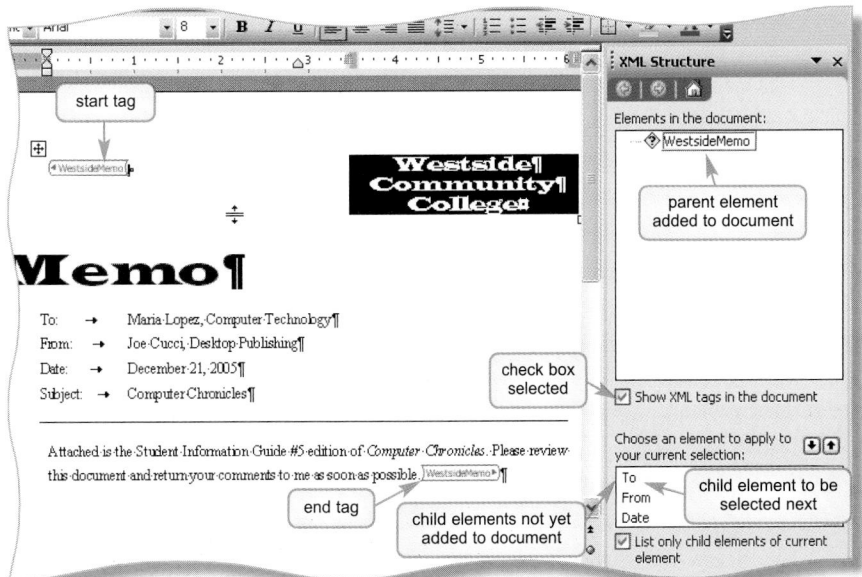

FIGURE 9-84

3

• **Drag through the recipient name and department in the document to select it.**

• **Click To in the Choose an element to apply to your current selection list.**

Word places start and end tags on the text selected in the document (Figure 9-85). The child element is displayed below the parent element in the Elements in the document list, called a **tree structure**. *The To XML element is removed from the Choose an element to apply to your current selection list.*

FIGURE 9-85

If the namespace alias is displayed to the right of the parent element in the XML Structure task pane, click the XML Options link, deselect the Hide namespace alias in XML Structure task pane check box, and then click the OK button. If necessary, redo the steps on the previous page.

The next step is to add the remaining child XML elements to the document, as described in the following steps.

To Add XML Elements

1 **Drag through the sender name and department in the document to select it. Click From in the Choose an element to apply to your current selection list.**

2 **Drag through the memo date in the document to select it. Click Date in the Choose an element to apply to your current selection list.**

3 **Drag through the memo subject in the document to select it. Scroll to and then click Subject in the Choose an element to apply to your current selection list.**

4 **Drag through the memo message in the document to select it. Scroll to and then click Message in the Choose an element to apply to your current selection list.**

5 **Click anywhere to remove the selection from the text.**

Word tags all XML elements in the document (Figure 9-86).

FIGURE 9-86

If you wanted to remove a tag that was added to a document, you would right-click the start or end tag and then click Remove tag on the shortcut menu – which instructs Word to remove both the start and end tag. You also can right-click the element name in the XML Structure task pane and then click Remove tag on the shortcut menu.

The next step is to save the XML Document.

To Save a Document as an XML File

1 With a floppy disk in drive A, click File on the menu bar and then click Save As.

2 When Word displays the Save As dialog box, if necessary, type `Westside Memo` in the File name box. Do not press the ENTER key.

3 If necessary, click the Save in box arrow and then click 3½ Floppy (A:).

4 If necessary, click the Save as type box arrow and then click XML Document.

5 Click the Save button in the Save As dialog box.

Word saves the document as an XML file on a floppy disk in drive A with the file name, Westside Memo.

This memo document is to be used by multiple people, where they fill in the recipient, sender, date, subject, and memo data whenever they wish to send a memo. Thus, you will create a template from the XML file. The next step is to delete the current data in the document (e.g., Maria Lopez, Computer Technology) and specify placeholder text for the XML elements. For example, the To XML element will say TYPE NAME AND DEPARTMENT HERE. This type of instruction in placeholder text makes a template user-friendly. The steps on the next page show how to select an XML element and modify its attributes to display placeholder text.

Microsoft Office
Word 2003

To Modify an Attribute of an XML Element

1

• **If the Show XML tags in the document check box is selected, click it to remove the check mark.**

• **Click the To XML element in the tree structure in the XML Structure task pane.**

Word selects the XML element data in the document window (Figure 9-87).

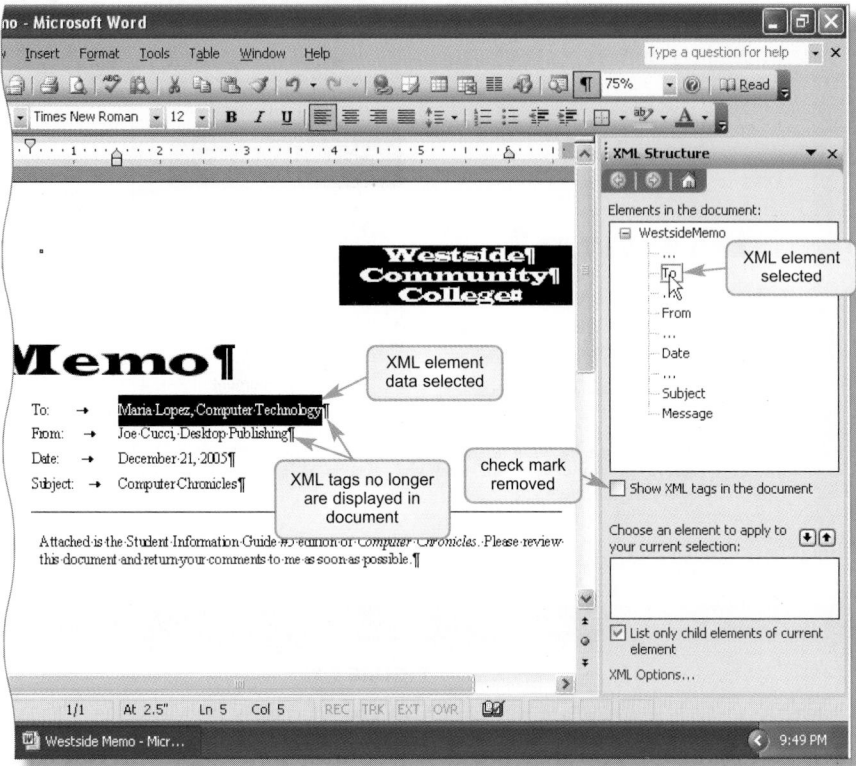

FIGURE 9-87

2

• **Press the DELETE key to delete the XML data in the document.**

• **Right-click the To XML element in the tree structure in the XML Structure task pane.**

Word displays a shortcut menu (Figure 9-88).

FIGURE 9-88

3

- **Click Attributes on the shortcut menu.**

- **When Word displays the Attributes for To dialog box, type** TYPE NAME AND DEPARTMENT HERE **in the Placeholder text text box.**

Word displays the Attributes for To dialog box (Figure 9-89).

FIGURE 9-89

4

- **Click the OK button.**

Word inserts placeholder text at the location of the XML element in the document (Figure 9-90).

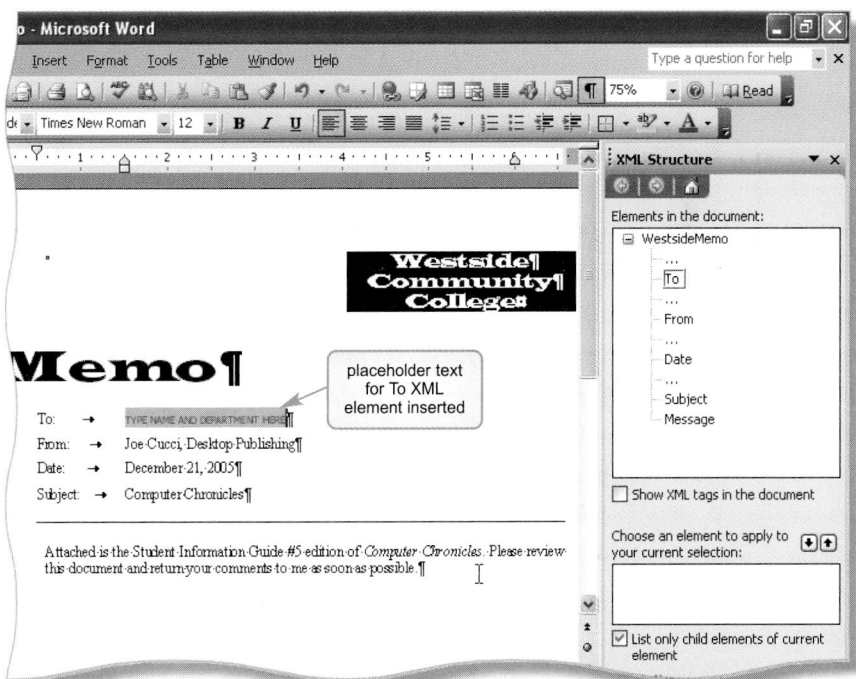

FIGURE 9-90

The next step is to add placeholder text for the remaining XML elements, as described on the next page.

To Modify More Attributes of XML elements

1 Click the From XML element in the tree structure in the XML Structure task pane. Press the DELETE key to delete the XML data in the document. Right-click the From XML element in the tree structure in the XML Structure task pane and then click Attributes on the shortcut menu. When Word displays the Attributes for From dialog box, type TYPE NAME AND DEPARTMENT HERE in the Placeholder text text box and then click the OK button.

2 Click the Date XML element in the tree structure in the XML Structure task pane. Press the DELETE key to delete the XML data in the document. Right-click the Date XML element in the tree structure in the XML Structure task pane and then click Attributes on the shortcut menu. When Word displays the Attributes for Date dialog box, type TYPE TODAY'S DATE HERE in the Placeholder text text box and then click the OK button.

3 Click the Subject XML element in the tree structure in the XML Structure task pane. Press the DELETE key to delete the XML data in the document. Right-click the Subject XML element in the tree structure in the XML Structure task pane and then click Attributes on the shortcut menu. When Word displays the Attributes for Subject dialog box, type TYPE SUBJECT HERE in the Placeholder text text box and then click the OK button.

4 Click the Message XML element in the tree structure in the XML Structure task pane. Press the DELETE key to delete the XML data in the document. Right-click the Message XML element in the tree structure in the XML Structure task pane and then click Attributes on the shortcut menu. When Word displays the Attributes for Message dialog box, type TYPE MESSAGE HERE in the Placeholder text text box and then click the OK button.

Word modifies the attributes of the XML elements to display placeholder text in the document (shown in Figure 9-91).

If you do not want specific text to be displayed in the placeholder text, you can instruct Word to show the name of the element as placeholder text. To do this, you set an XML option, as described below.

TO SET XML OPTIONS

1. Click the XML Options link in the XML Structure task pane.
2. When Word displays the XML Options dialog box, place check marks in the desired options (in this case, the last check box) and then click the OK button.

The XML Options dialog box contains a Schema Library button that displays the Schema Library dialog box, which allows you to add and delete schemas to and from the schema library. Instead of saving the document as an XML file, some users prefer to save the data only on the XML document by clicking the Save data only check box in the Save As dialog box. This check box appears when you change the file type to XML Document. When you save the data only, you can apply an XSL transformation file to the data. An **XSL transformation (XSLT) file** instructs Word how to display the data, formats it, and adds any additional text. With the memo, for example, you could have several different memo styles, each one saved in a separate XSLT file. The user would open the XML data file and then select the desired XSLT file using the following steps.

TO APPLY A TRANSFORMATION FILE TO AN XML DATA FILE

1. Open the XML data only file.
2. In the XML Document task pane, click the Browse link. When Word displays the Browse dialog box, locate the desired transformation file and then click the OK button.

As an alternative, you could save the XML file with a transform, as described below.

TO SAVE AN XML FILE WITH A TRANSFORM

1. With the XML file on the screen, click File on the menu bar and then click Save As. When Word displays the Save As dialog box, be sure the file type is XML Document.
2. Place a check mark in the Apply Transform check box and then click the Transform button.
3. When Word displays the Choose an XSL Transformation dialog box, locate the XSLT file and then click the Open button in the dialog box.
4. Click the Save button in the Save As dialog box.

Setting Editing Restrictions

When a user opens a memo, you want them to be able to edit only the placeholder text. You can use the Protect Document task pane to allow editing in just certain areas of the document, a procedure called adding users excepted from restrictions. The following steps show how to set exceptions to editing restrictions.

To Set Exceptions to Editing Restrictions

1

• **Click Tools on the menu bar and then click Protect Document.**

• **When Word displays the Protect Document task pane, place a check mark in the check box in the Editing restrictions area and be sure the associated text box displays No changes (Read only).**

• **Click the placeholder text for the To XML element to select it.**

• **Place a check mark in the Everyone check box in the Exceptions (optional) area in the Protect Document task pane.**

The selected placeholder text is the only item in the document that can be edited (Figure 9-91).

FIGURE 9-91

2

• **Click each of the remaining XML elements in the document (From, Date, Subject, and Message) to select them and place a check mark in the Everyone check box.**

• **Scroll to the bottom of the Protect Document task pane and then click the Yes, Start Enforcing Protection button.**

Word displays the Start Enforcing Protection dialog box (Figure 9-92). The To, From, Date, Subject, and Memo elements are the only items in the document that can be edited.

3

• **Click the OK button.**

• **Close the Protect Document task pane.**

Word sets exceptions for the XML elements.

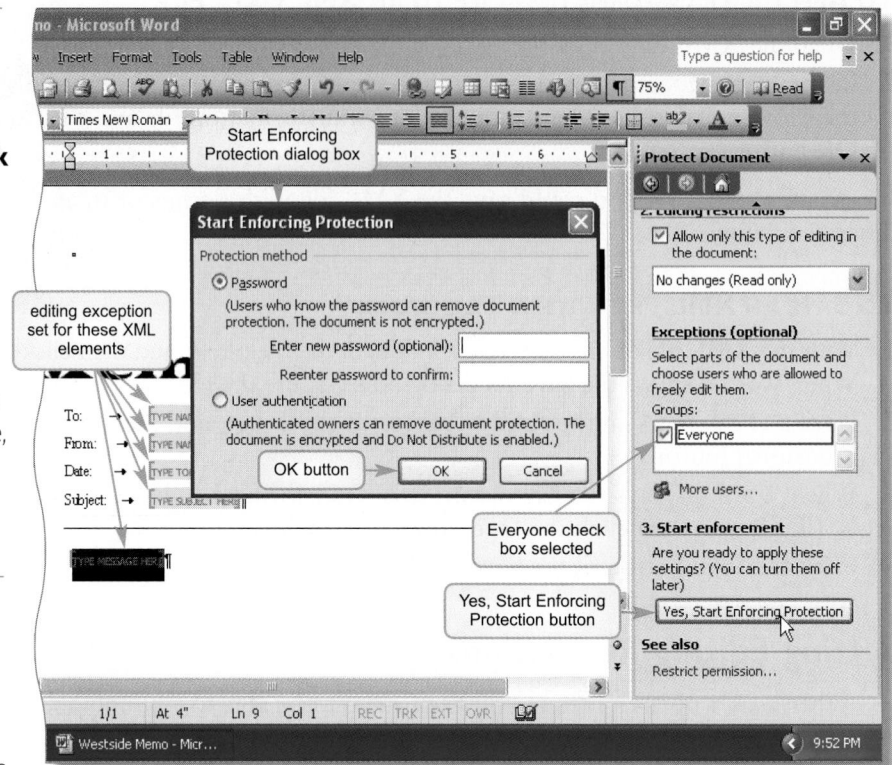

FIGURE 9-92

In addition to editing restrictions, Word allows you to place formatting restrictions on a document. To only allow certain types of formatting changes to be made to a document, you would perform the following steps.

To Set Formatting Restrictions

1. In the Protect Document task pane, place a check mark in the check box in the Formatting restrictions area.

2. In the Protect Document task pane, click the Settings link in the Formatting restrictions area.

3. When Word displays the Formatting Restrictions dialog box, place check marks in the check boxes that describe the types of formatting you want to allow. Click the OK button.

4. Click the Yes, Start Enforcing Protection button. When Word displays the Start Enforcing Protection dialog box, enter a password if desired, and then click the OK button.

5. Close the Protect Document task pane.

The next step is to save the document as a template so a user can open a new document window based on the template, as described next.

To Save an XML Document as a Template

1 **With a floppy disk in drive A, click File on the menu bar and then click Save As.**

2 **When Word displays the Save As dialog box, if necessary, type** Westside Memo **in the File name box. Do not press the ENTER key.**

3 **Click the Save as type box arrow and then click Document Template.**

4 **If necessary, click the Save in box arrow and then click 3½ Floppy (A:).**

5 **Click the Save button in the Save As dialog box.**

Word saves the template on a floppy disk in drive A with the file name, Westside Memo.

In environments other than an academic setting, you would not save the template on a floppy disk. Instead, you would save it in the Templates folder, which is the folder Word initially displays in the Save As dialog box for a document template file type. When you save a template in the Templates folder, Word places an icon for the template in the General sheet in the Templates dialog box. Thus, to open a new Word document that is based on a template that has been saved in the Templates folder, you click File on the menu bar, and then click New. When Word displays the New Document task pane, click On my computer, and then, in the General sheet, double-click the template icon.

For academic purposes, the template in this project was saved on a floppy disk in drive A. To open a new Word document that is based on a template saved on a floppy disk, you use Windows Explorer as described below.

To Access a Template Through Windows Explorer

1. Click the Start button on the Windows taskbar, right-click My Computer on the Start menu and then click Explore on the shortcut menu.
2. When the Explorer window opens, if necessary, double-click its title bar to maximize the window. In the Folders bar, click 3½ Floppy (A:).
3. Double-click the template in the Explorer window (in this case, Westside Memo).
   Word displays a new document window that is based on the contents of the Westside Memo.

Once opened, the user fills in the contents of the template using the same techniques as with any other Word template. If brackets surround entered text, they will not print.

This project is complete. The following step quits Word.

To Quit Word

1 **Click the Close button on the Word title bar.**

The Word window closes.

More About

Certification

The Microsoft Office Specialist Certification program provides an opportunity for you to obtain a valuable industry credential — proof that you have the Word 2003 skills required by employers. For more information, see Appendix E or visit the Word 2003 Certification Web page (scsite.com/wd2003/cert).

Project Summary

Project 9 introduced you to creating a long document with a table of contents, a table of figures, and an index. You learned how to save multiple versions of a document, add and modify a caption, create a cross-reference, mark index entries, hyphenate a document, add a bookmark, verify the widow/orphan setting, sort a list, create alternating headers, and set a gutter margin. You also worked with master documents and subdocuments. Next, you learned how to use the Document Map to navigate through a document, AutoSummarize a document, work with readability statistics, add custom properties, and password-protect a file.

You also learned how to work with XML. Specifically, the project showed how to attach and delete schema files, add and delete XML elements, save a document as an XML file, modify attributes of XML elements, set XML options, apply transformation files, and set exceptions to editing restrictions.

 If you have a SAM user profile, you may have access to hands-on instruction, practice, and assessment of the skills covered in this project. Log in to your SAM account and go to your assignments page to see what your instructor has assigned.

What You Should Know

Having completed this project, you should be able to perform the tasks below. The tasks are listed in the same order they were presented in the project. For a list of the buttons, menus, toolbars, and commands introduced in the project, see the Quick Reference Summary at the back of this book and refer to the Page Number column.

1. Start and Customize Word (WD 636)
2. Display Formatting Marks (WD 637)
3. Zoom Page Width (WD 637)
4. Open a Document (WD 637, WD 693)
5. Save a Document with a New File Name (WD 638)
6. Save a Version of a Document (WD 638)
7. View a Version of a Document (WD 639)
8. Delete a Version (WD 640)
9. Insert a Graphic from a File (WD 642)
10. Resize a Graphic (WD 643)
11. Format the Graphic as Floating (WD 643)
12. Reposition a Graphic (WD 644)
13. Add a Caption (WD 645)
14. Convert a Text Box to a Frame (WD 647)
15. Create a Cross-Reference (WD 648)
16. Mark an Index Entry (WD 650)
17. Mark Another Index Entry (WD 651)
18. Hide Formatting Marks (WD 651)
19. Hyphenate a Document (WD 652)
20. Verify the Widow and Orphan Setting (WD 654)
21. Save and Close a Document (WD 655, WD 657)

22. Open a Document and Save It with a New File Name (WD 655)
23. Sort a List (WD 656)
24. Create an Outline (WD 658)
25. Insert a Subdocument (WD 661)
26. Show First Line Only (WD 662)
27. Insert Another Subdocument (WD 663)
28. Save a Document (WD 664)
29. Create a Subdocument (WD 664)
30. Modify an Outline (WD 665)
31. Enter Body Text in an Outline (WD 666)
32. Enter and Format the Title Page Text (WD 669)
33. Create a Table of Figures (WD 671)
34. Build an Index (WD 673)
35. Create a Table of Contents (WD 674)
36. Add Bookmarks (WD 675)
37. Add Another Bookmark (WD 676)
38. Create Alternating Headers (WD 678)
39. Set a Gutter Margin (WD 680)
40. Display Several Pages in Print Preview (WD 680)
41. Save and Print a Document (WD 681)
42. Close a Document (WD 681, WD 693)

43. Open a Master Document (WD 682)

44. Use the Document Map (WD 683)

45. Update an Index (WD 684)

46. Close the Document Map (WD 685)

47. AutoSummarize a Document (WD 685)

48. Turn On Readability Statistics (WD 687)

49. Check Spelling and Display Readability Statistics (WD 688)

50. Go To a Bookmark (WD 689)

51. Work with Custom Properties (WD 690)

52. Insert a Document Property Field (WD 691)

53. Password-Protect a File (WD 691)

54. Attach a Schema File (WD 694)

55. Delete a Schema from the Schema Library (WD 696)

56. Add a Parent and Child XML Element (WD 697)

57. Add XML Elements (WD 698)

58. Save a Document as an XML File (WD 699)

59. Modify an Attribute of an XML Element (WD 700)

60. Modify More Attributes of XML Elements (WD 702)

61. Set XML Options (WD 702)

62. Apply a Transformation File to an XML Data File (WD 703)

63. Save an XML File with a Transform (WD 703)

64. Set Exceptions to Editing Restrictions (WD 703)

65. Set Formatting Restrictions (WD 704)

66. Save an XML Document as a Template (WD 705)

67. Access a Template through Windows Explorer (WD 705)

68. Quit Word (WD 705)

More About

Quick Reference

For a table that lists how to complete the tasks covered in this book using the mouse, menu, shortcut menu, and keyboard, see the Quick Reference Summary at the back of this book, or visit the Word 2003 Quick Reference Web page (scsite.com/wd2003/qr).

Learn It Online

Instructions: To complete the Learn It Online exercises, start your browser, click the Address bar, and then enter the Web address scsite.com/wd2003/learn. When the Office 2003 Learn It Online page is displayed, follow the instructions in the exercises below. Each exercise has instructions for printing your results, either for your own records or for submission to your instructor.

1 Project Reinforcement TF, MC, and SA

Below Word Project 9, click the Project Reinforcement link. Print the quiz by clicking Print on the File menu for each page. Answer each question.

2 Flash Cards

Below Word Project 9, click the Flash Cards link and read the instructions. Type 20 (or a number specified by your instructor) in the Number of playing cards text box, type your name in the Enter your Name text box, and then click the Flip Card button. When the flash card is displayed, read the question and then click the ANSWER box arrow to select an answer. Flip through Flash Cards. If your score is 15 (75%) correct or greater, click Print on the File menu to print your results. If your score is less than 15 (75%) correct, then redo this exercise by clicking the Replay button.

3 Practice Test

Below Word Project 9, click the Practice Test link. Answer each question, enter your first and last name at the bottom of the page, and then click the Grade Test button. When the graded practice test is displayed on your screen, click Print on the File menu to print a hard copy. Continue to take practice tests until you score 80% or better.

4 Who Wants To Be a Computer Genius?

Below Word Project 9, click the Computer Genius link. Read the instructions, enter your first and last name at the bottom of the page, and then click the PLAY button. When your score is displayed, click the PRINT RESULTS link to print a hard copy.

5 Wheel of Terms

Below Word Project 9, click the Wheel of Terms link. Read the instructions, and then enter your first and last name and your school name. Click the PLAY button. When your score is displayed, right-click the score and then click Print on the shortcut menu to print a hard copy.

6 Crossword Puzzle Challenge

Below Word Project 9, click the Crossword Puzzle Challenge link. Read the instructions, and then enter your first and last name. Click the SUBMIT button. Work the crossword puzzle. When you are finished, click the Submit button. When the crossword puzzle is redisplayed, click the Print Puzzle button to print a hard copy.

7 Tips and Tricks

Below Word Project 9, click the Tips and Tricks link. Click a topic that pertains to Project 9. Right-click the information and then click Print on the shortcut menu. Construct a brief example of what the information relates to in Word to confirm you understand how to use the tip or trick.

8 Newsgroups

Below Word Project 9, click the Newsgroups link. Click a topic that pertains to Project 9. Print three comments.

9 Expanding Your Horizons

Below Word Project 9, click the Expanding Your Horizons link. Click a topic that pertains to Project 9. Print the information. Construct a brief example of what the information relates to in Word to confirm you understand the contents of the article.

10 Search Sleuth

Below Word Project 9, click the Search Sleuth link. To search for a term that pertains to this project, select a term below the Project 9 title and then use the Google search engine at google.com (or any major search engine) to display and print two Web pages that present information on the term.

11 Word Online Training

Below Word Project 9, click the Word Online Training link. When your browser displays the Microsoft Office Online Web page, click the Word link. Click one of the Word courses that covers one or more of the objectives listed at the beginning of the project on page WD 634. Print the first page of the course before stepping through it.

12 Office Marketplace

Below Word Project 9, click the Office Marketplace link. When your browser displays the Microsoft Office Online Web page, click the Office Marketplace link. Click a topic that relates to Word. Print the first page.

Apply Your Knowledge

1 Using XML

Instructions: Start Word. Open the Word document, Westside Fax, on the Data Disk. If you did not download the Data Disk, see the inside back cover for instructions for downloading the Data Disk or see your instructor.

You are to attach an XML schema file, add XML elements to the fax document (Figure 9-93), save the Word document as an XML document, set exceptions to editing restrictions, and then save the XML document as a template.

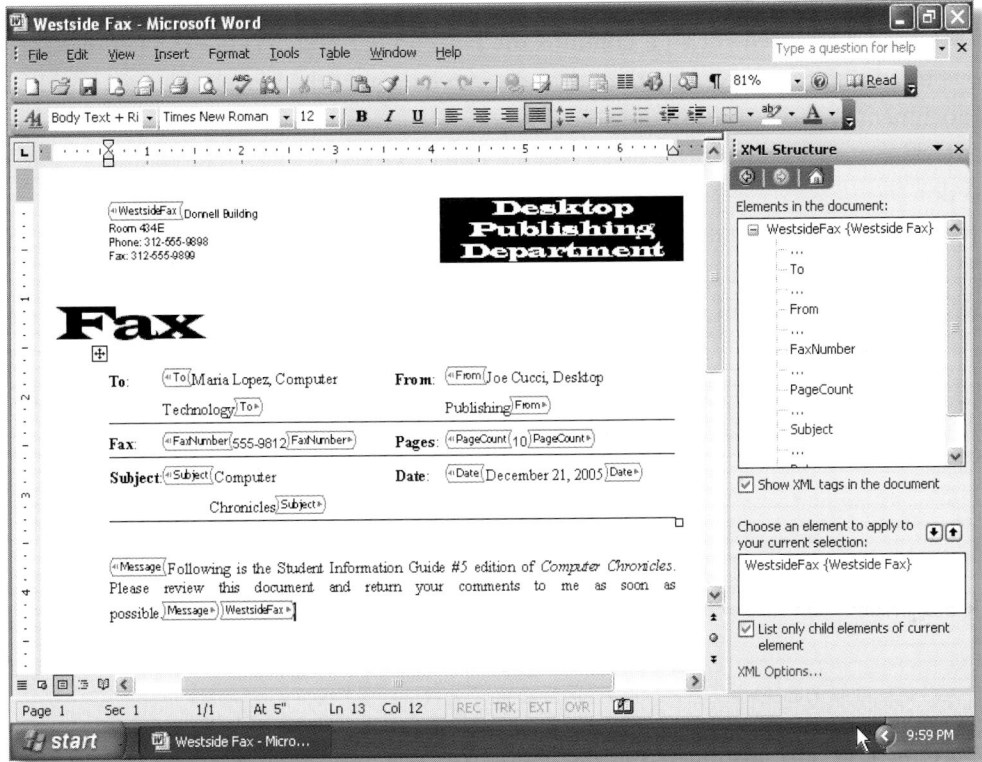

FIGURE 9-93

Perform the following tasks:

1. Attach the XML schema file called Westside Fax to the Westside Fax Word document (this file has an xsd extension). To attach the schema file, you will need to add this schema to the Schema Library. Use urn:fax-schema-1 as the URI and Westside Fax as the Alias. The schema file is on the Data Disk. If you did not download the Data Disk, see the inside back cover for instructions for downloading the Data Disk or see your instructor.
2. Add the parent element, WestSideFax, to the fax document.
3. Add all the child elements to the fax document: To, From, FaxNumber, PageCount, Subject, Date, and Message.
4. Save the document as an XML document using the file name, Westside Fax. (This file will have an xml extension.)
5. Print the XML document.

(continued)

Apply Your Knowledge

Using XML (continued)

6. Modify the To XML element so it contains the placeholder text: TYPE NAME AND DEPARTMENT HERE. (Be sure to hide XML tags in the document.)

7. Modify the From XML element so it contains the placeholder text: TYPE NAME AND DEPARTMENT HERE.

8. Modify the FaxNumber XML element so it contains the placeholder text: TYPE FAX NUMBER HERE.

9. Modify the PageCount XML element so it contains the placeholder text: TYPE NUMBER OF PAGES HERE.

10. Modify the Subject XML element so it contains the placeholder text: TYPE SUBJECT HERE.

11. Modify the Date XML element so it contains the placeholder text: TYPE TODAY'S DATE HERE.

12. Modify the Message XML element so it contains the placeholder text: TYPE MESSAGE HERE.

13. Set exceptions to editing restrictions so that all users can edit only the placeholder text in the document. Protect the document without a password.

14. Save the XML document as a template using the file name, Westside Fax. (The template will have an extension of dot.)

15. Access the template through Windows explorer to create a fax cover sheet. Fill in the fax with your personal information and print it. Do not save it.

16. Delete the XML schema file from the document. Then, delete the XML schema file from the Schema Library.

17. Turn on the following XML options: Save data only and Show placeholder text for all empty elements.

18. Exit Word and do not save changes to the file.

In the Lab

1 Working with a Table of Contents and an Index

Problem: You are the computer technician in the Computer Systems department at Cary Instructional Services. One of your responsibilities is to create a series of informational guides for laboratory users that explains various aspects of computers. The fourth one you create is titled, Database Management Systems and Web Databases. A miniature version of this document is shown in Figure 9-94; for a more readable view, visit scsite.com/wd2003/project9.

A draft of the body of the document is on the Data Disk. If you did not download the Data Disk, see the inside back cover for instructions for downloading the Data Disk or see your instructor.

In the Lab

FIGURE 9-94

Instructions:

1. Open the document, Lab 9-1 Database Draft, from the Data Disk. Save the document with a new file name, Lab 9-1 Computer Systems Overview #4.

2. If necessary, switch to print layout view. Add the following caption to the first figure: Popular database management systems. Add the following caption to the second figure: Sample data dictionary.

3. In the paragraph above the first graphic, insert a cross-reference to the figure caption inside the empty parentheses at the end of the first sentence in the paragraph.

(continued)

Working with a Table of Contents and an Index *(continued)*

4. In the sentence above the second graphic, begin the sentence with a cross-reference to the figure caption. Thus, replace the words, The figure below, with a cross-reference that shows only the word, Figure, and the figure number.

5. Mark the following items in the document as index entries: database, database approach, database management system (DBMS), database software, data dictionary, query, query by example (QBE), and query language.

6. Switch to outline view. At the top of the outline, create a new entry for the Table of Contents heading using the Heading 1 style. Insert a next page section break above and below the new heading. At the bottom of the outline, create a new entry for the Index using the Heading 1 style. Insert a next page section break above the new heading.

7. Switch to print layout view. On page 1 (the title page), enter the following heading using the Normal style: Computer Systems Overview. Format the heading using 48-point Freestyle Script orange font (or a similar font). Enter the next line of the heading: Information Guide #4. Format this line in 28-point Arial Narrow dark green font (or a similar font). Below that text, insert a clip art image of a person working at a computer. Below the graphic, enter these lines in 72-point Freestyle Script bold orange font (or a similar font): Database Management Systems and Web Databases. Center all text and graphics on the title page.

8. Build an index for the document. Remember to hide formatting marks prior to building the index.

9. Create a table of contents for the document. Use the Formal format.

10. Beginning on the second page (the table of contents), create a header as follows: Information Guide #4 - Page, followed by the page number at the right margin. The title page does not have a header. Note: Because you do not want facing pages in this document, do not create alternating headers.

11. Change all margins to 1" with a gutter margin of .5". Be sure to change the Apply to box to Whole document.

12. Verify that the following headings begin on a new page: Table of Contents, Database Management Systems, and Index. If any do not, insert a next page section break.

13. Because you modified the margins, update the table of contents and index.

14. Verify that widows and orphans cannot occur.

15. Save the document again. Print the document. Staple the document along the gutter margin.

2 Working with a Master Document and Subdocuments, Table of Contents, and an Index

Problem: As part of the Adventures in Logic class you are taking, your instructor has asked you to prepare a report about control structures. You create two documents: one that contains the introduction and one that contains the body of the report. These two documents are to be subdocuments in a master document that also contains a title page, a table of contents, and an index. A miniature version of the finished document Lab 9-2 Diagramming Logic is shown in Figure 9-95; for a more readable view, visit scsite.com/wd2003/project9.

The subdocuments are located on the Data Disk. If you did not download the Data Disk, see the inside back cover for instructions for downloading the Data Disk or see your instructor.

In the Lab

FIGURE 9-95

Instructions:

1. Open the document, Lab 9-2 Control Structures Draft, from the Data Disk. Save the document with a new file name, Lab 9-2 Control Structures.

2. Insert a cross-reference for each figure. Insert the cross-reference in the empty parentheses that end a sentence near each figure. Insert only the word, Figure, and the figure number as the cross-reference.

3. Mark these words/phrases as index entries: control structure, construct, sequence control structure, selection control structure, if-then-else control structure, case control structure, repetition control structure, loop, do-while control structure, and do-until control structure.

(continued)

Working with a Master Document and Subdocuments, Table of Contents, and an Index *(continued)*

4. Save the Lab 9-2 Control Structures file again and then close the file.

5. Start a new Word document. Switch to outline view. Enter the following Heading 1 headings on separate lines of the outline: Table of Contents and Index. Insert a next page section break above the Table of Contents heading and a next page section break between each heading.

6. Save the master document with the file name, Lab 9-2 Diagramming Logic.

7. Between the Table of Contents and Table of Figures headings, insert the Lab 9-2 Introduction file as a subdocument.

8. Just above the Table of Figures heading, insert the Lab 9-2 Control Structures file as a subdocument.

9. Switch to print layout view. On page 1 (the title page), enter the following heading using the Normal style: Adventures in Logic. Format the heading using 36-point Comic Sans MS bold brown font (or a similar font). Enter the next line of the heading: Assignment #2. Enter this line in 16-point Comic Sans MS bold teal font (or a similar font). Below that text, insert a diamond and a rectangle AutoShape on a drawing canvas. Insert the word, Control, in the diamond shape, and the word, Structures, in the rectangle shape. Format the text using 26-point Rockwell bold brown font. Fill the shapes with aqua and outline them in green. Fill the drawing canvas with a one-color gradient of tan. Outline the drawing canvas in brown. Draw an arrow shape connecting the two symbols together. Below the graphic, enter these lines in 24-point Comic Sans MS bold teal font (or a similar font): Understanding How to Diagram Sequence, Selection, and Repetition. Center all text and graphics on the title page.

10. Build an index for the document. In the Index sheet, use the From template format for the index, place a check mark in the Right align page numbers check box, and change the number of columns to 1. Remember to hide formatting marks prior to building the index.

11. Create a table of contents for the document. Use the Formal format.

12. Beginning on the second page (the table of contents), create a header as follows: Adventures in Logic #2 - Page, followed by the page number at the right margin. The title page does not have a header. Note: Because you do not want facing pages in this document, do not create alternating headers.

13. For the entire document, set the left and right margins to 1" and set a gutter margin of .5".

14. Verify that the following headings begin on a new page: Table of Contents, Introduction, Control Structures, and Index. If any do not, insert a next page section break.

15. Because you modified the margins, update the table of contents and index.

16. Verify that widows and orphans cannot occur.

17. Save the document again. Print the document. Staple the document along the gutter margin.

3 Working with a Master Document, an Index, and Tables of Figures and Contents

Problem: You are the computer technician at Software Solutions, Inc. Your boss has asked you to create a pamphlet outlining the features of popular business programs. A miniature version of the finished document is shown in Figure 9-96; for a more readable view, visit scsite.com/wd2003/project9.

Design the pamphlet as a master document with five subdocuments. Create one subdocument and insert four others. The existing subdocuments are on the Data Disk. If you did not download the Data Disk, see the inside back cover for instructions for downloading the Data Disk or see your instructor.

In the Lab

FIGURE 9-96

(continued)

In the Lab

Working with a Master Document, an Index, and Tables of Figures and Contents *(continued)*

Instructions:

1. Start a new Word document. Switch to outline view. Enter the following Heading 1 headings on separate lines of the outline: Table of Contents, Introduction, Table of Figures, and Index. Insert a next page section break between each heading and also above the Table of Contents.

2. Save the master document with the file name, Lab 9-3 Business Software. Between the Introduction and Table of Figures headings, insert these four subdocuments: Lab 9-3 Word Processing Software, Lab 9-3 Spreadsheet Software, Lab 9-3 Presentation Graphics Software, Lab 9-3 Database Software.

3. Create a subdocument using the Introduction heading. Using the Body Text style, enter the text for the paragraph shown in Figure 9-97 for the Introduction section.

> Business software is application software that assists people in becoming more effective and efficient while performing their daily business activities. Business software includes programs such as word processing, spreadsheet, presentation graphics, and database. This paper discusses the features of these popular business programs.

FIGURE 9-97

4. Switch to print layout view. On page 1 (the title page), enter the following heading on two separate lines using the Normal style: BUSINESS SOFTWARE. Format the heading using 48-point High Tower Text bold violet font (or a similar font) with a shadow. Below that text, insert a clip art image of business people. Below the graphic, enter these lines in 20-point High Tower Text bold violet font (or a similar font): Presented by Software Solutions, Inc. Center all text and graphics on the title page.

5. Build a table of contents for the document that does not include the headings on the title page or the table of contents page. *Hint*: To omit certain headings from the table of contents, change the style of the heading to a style other than a heading style.

6. Build an index for the document. In the Index sheet, use the Formal format for the index, place a check mark in the Right align page numbers check box, and change the number of columns to 2. Remember to hide formatting marks prior to building the index.

7. Create a table of figures for the document. Use the From template format.

8. Beginning on the second page (the table of contents), create alternating headings as follows: even-numbered pages should print at the left margin the words, Business Software, on the first line and the word, Page, followed by the page number on the second line. Odd-numbered pages should print the same text at the right margin. The title page does not have a header.

9. For the entire document, set the left and right margins to 1" and set a gutter margin of .5".

10. Verify that the following headings begin on a new page: Table of Contents, Introduction, Word Processing Software, Spreadsheet Software, Presentation Graphics Software, Database Software, Table of Figures, and Index. If any do not, insert a next page section break.

11. Read through the document and mark at least two more index entries.

12. Update the table of contents and index.

13. Instruct Word to automatically hyphenate the entire document.

14. Insert a bookmark to each heading in the document.

15. Verify that widows and orphans cannot occur.

16. Save the document again. Print the document. If you have access to a copy machine, duplicate the document back-to-back.

17. Turn on readability statistics. Check spelling and then display the readability statistics. On the last page of the paper, write down the percent of passive sentences, the Flesch Reading Ease score, and the Flesch-Kincaid Grade Level score.

18. Go to the SpreadsheetSoftware bookmark.

19. Display the Document Map. Use the Document Map to display the Index page in the document window. Use the Document Map to display the Presentation Graphics Software page in the document window.

20. AutoSummarize the document - highlighting key points. Close the AutoSummarize toolbar.

21. Print the document in reading layout view.

Cases and Places

The difficulty of these case studies varies:
■ are the least difficult and ■■ are more difficult. The last exercise is a group exercise.

1 ■ As a help desk assistant at your school, you have been asked to design a document that presents the features of Microsoft Office Word 2003. To compose the document, you can use any text in this textbook. The document should contain at least two screen shots. To capture a screen shot, display the screen on your computer and then press the PRINT SCREEN key. Use Paint or some other graphic program to save the screen shot and then insert the graphic file in the Word document. Add bubbles to the screens in the Word document using the callout AutoShape in Word. Add captions to the screen shots. The finished document should have a title page, an introduction, a table of contents, a table of figures, and an index. The entire document should be at least nine pages in length. Use the concepts and techniques presented in this project to format the document.

2 ■■ As a final project in your Technical Writing class, you are required to compose a document that discusses some aspect of the Internet or World Wide Web (e.g., history of the Internet, service providers, connection methods, Internet addresses, browsing, searching, types of Web pages, e-commerce, Web publishing, e-mail, FTP, newsgroups, instant messaging, chat rooms, etc.). The document is to be a master document that contains at least two subdocuments. It should contain at least two figures (tables, screen shots, charts, digital photographs, etc.). In addition, the finished document should have a title page, a table of contents, an introduction, and an index. Use the concepts and techniques presented in this project to format the document. On the last page of the paper, write down these readability statistics: percent of passive sentences, the Flesch Reading Ease score, and the Flesch-Kincaid Grade Level score.

3 ■■ As a course assistant, one of your responsibilities is to compose instructional pamphlets for students. Assume you are course assistant for one of the classes in which you are enrolled this semester. Compose an instructional or informational document that could be distributed to students in the course. The document is to be a master document that contains at least two subdocuments. It should contain at least two figures (tables, charts, screen shots, digital photographs, etc.). In addition, the finished document should have a title page, a table of contents, an introduction, and an index. Use the concepts and techniques presented in this project to format the document. AutoSummarize the finished document, placing the summary in a new document. Print the summary document (do not save it).

Cases and Places

4 ◼◼ You are the computer technician at Software Solutions, Inc. Your supervisor has asked you to create a series of informational pamphlets for customers that discuss various aspects of computers. The first informational pamphlet you prepared is shown in Figure 9-96 on page 715. Your boss has asked you to create another similar pamphlet outlining the features of another classification of programs: graphics, educational, home, communications, operating systems, etc. Write the informational pamphlet about software with which you are familiar and to which you have access. To capture a screen shot, display the screen on your computer and then press the PRINT SCREEN key. The document is to be a master document that contains at least two subdocuments. It should contain at least two figures. In addition, the finished document should have a title page, a table of contents, an introduction, and an index. Use the concepts and techniques presented in this project to format the document.

5 ◼◼ **Working Together** Your school provides several facilities and services such as registration, advising, cafeteria, day care, computer lab, career development, fitness center, library, bookstore, parking, and a tutoring center. Each team member is to select an item from this list, or another facility or service at your school, and write a two to three page report that describes the facility or service (e.g., features, costs, hours of operation, etc.). Each report should have at least two figures (e.g., tables, charts, digital photographs, etc.) and a sorted list. Each team member's report will be a subdocument in a master document. The finished document also should have at least three subdocuments and include a title page, a table of contents, an introduction, a table of figures, and an index. Use the concepts and techniques presented in this project to format the document. Be sure the document contains a gutter margin, alternating headers, and bookmarks. Add custom properties that contain the names of all team members. Modify the Date completed property to a value of today's date. Insert these custom fields (team member names and date completed) as elements on the title page. Save a version of the document with and without automatic hyphenation. View and print each version. Delete the version without hyphenation. Password-protect the final master document.

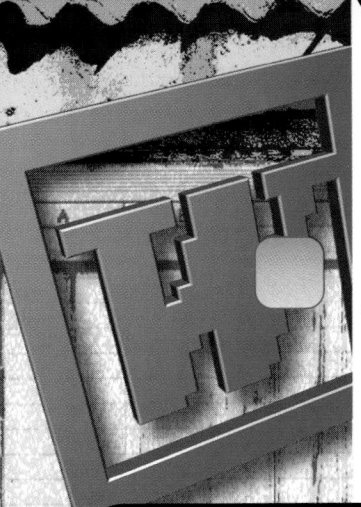

MICROSOFT
Office Word 2003

Linking an Excel Worksheet and Charting Its Data in Word

CASE PERSPECTIVE

WorldNet, a leading national Internet service provider, has more than seven million subscribers around the world that access the Internet via dial-up, cable, DSL, and satellite connections. At a recent meeting of managers at WorldNet, an agenda item led to a discussion about the marketing of its current services. After much debate, the meeting attendees had the following question: What is the breakdown of our current Internet access customer base?

Brittany Dugan, accounting manager, indicated she easily could obtain the answer to this question. In addition to the total number of dial-up, cable, DSL, and satellite customers, the managers asked Brittany if she could present the total revenue in each of these areas. She indicated she would distribute the results in memo form to all managers by next week.

As her assistant, Brittany has given you an Excel worksheet that summarizes the customer base at WorldNet. She has asked you to create a memo to all managers that includes the Excel worksheet. She also would like a chart of the worksheet to show graphically the customer breakdown.

As you read through this feature, you will learn how to use Word to link an Excel worksheet in a Word document and chart the Excel worksheet data in a Word document.

Objectives

You will have mastered the material in this project when you can:

● Link an Excel worksheet to a Word document
● Create a sample chart in Graph
● Chart Excel data in Word
● Edit a linked object

Introduction

With Microsoft Office products, you can insert part or all of a document, called an **object**, created in one program in a document created in another program. For example, you could insert an Excel worksheet in a Word document. In this case, the Excel worksheet (the object) is called the **source document** (inserted from) and the Word document is called the **destination document** (inserted in). You can use one of three techniques to insert objects from one program to another: copy and paste, embed, or link.

When you copy an object by clicking the Copy button on the Standard toolbar and then paste it by clicking the Paste button on the Standard toolbar, the source document becomes part of the destination document. You edit a **pasted object** using editing features of the destination program. For example, an Excel worksheet would become a Word table that you can edit in Word.

Similarly, an embedded object becomes part of a destination document. The difference between an embedded object and a pasted object is that you edit the contents of an **embedded object** using the editing features of the source program. For example, an embedded Excel worksheet remains as an Excel worksheet in the Word document. To edit the worksheet in the Word document, double-click the worksheet to display Excel menus and toolbars in the Word window. If you edit the Excel worksheet by opening the worksheet from within Excel, however, the embedded object will not be updated in the Word document.

A **linked object**, by contrast, does not become a part of the destination document even though it appears to be a part of it. Rather, a connection is established between the source and destination documents so that when you open the destination document, the linked object appears as part of it. When you edit a linked object, the source program starts and opens the source document that contains the linked object. For example, a linked Excel worksheet remains as an Excel worksheet. To edit the worksheet from the Word document, double-click the worksheet to start Excel and display the worksheet file in an Excel window. Unlike an embedded object, if you edit the Excel worksheet by opening it from Excel, the linked object will be updated in the Word document, too.

You would use the link method when the contents of an object are likely to change and you want to ensure that the most current version of the object appears in the source document. Another reason to link an object is if the object is large, such as a video clip or a sound clip.

As shown in Figure 1, this integration feature links an Excel worksheet to a Word document (a memo) and then links a Word chart to the Excel worksheet data.

(a) Draft of Word Document (without Links)

(b) Excel Worksheet in Excel Window

(c) Word Document with Links to Excel Worksheet

FIGURE 1

That is, the Excel worksheet is inserted in the Word document in the form of an Excel worksheet. Word also charts the data in the Excel worksheet. Because the data is inserted in the Word document as a link, anytime you open the memo in Word, the latest version of the Excel worksheet data is displayed in the memo. Figure 1a shows the memo draft (without any links to Excel); Figure 1b shows the Excel worksheet; and Figure 1c shows the final copy of the memo with links to the Excel worksheet and its data.

Starting Word and Opening a Document

The first step in this integration feature is to open the draft of the memo that is to include the linked worksheet data. The memo file, named Customer Breakdown Memo Draft, is located on the Data Disk. If you did not download the Data Disk, see the inside back cover for instructions for downloading the Data Disk or see your instructor.

The following steps describe how to start Word and open the memo.

To Start and Customize Word and Open a Document

1 Click the Start button on the Windows taskbar, point to All Programs on the Start menu, point to Microsoft Office on the All Programs submenu, and then click Microsoft Office Word 2003 on the Microsoft Office submenu.

2 If the Word window is not maximized, double-click its title bar to maximize it.

3 If the Language bar appears, right-click it and then click Close the Language bar on the shortcut menu.

4 If the Getting Started task pane is displayed in the Word window, click its Close button.

5 If the Standard and Formatting toolbar buttons are displayed on one row, click the Toolbar Options button and then click Show Buttons on Two Rows in the Toolbar Options list.

6 With the disk containing the Customer Breakdown Memo Draft file in drive A, click the Open button on the Standard toolbar.

7 When Word displays the Open dialog box, if necessary, click the Look in box arrow and then click 3½ Floppy (A:).

8 Double-click the file named Customer Breakdown Memo Draft.

9 Click View on the menu bar and then click Print Layout. If the Show/Hide ¶ button on the Standard toolbar is not selected, click it.

Word starts and opens the Customer Breakdown Memo Draft file.

Saving the Document with a New File Name

To preserve the contents of the original Customer Breakdown Memo Draft file, save a copy of it with a new file name, as described on the next page.

More About

Saving and Opening Linked Documents

When working with linked documents on floppy disks, both the source and destination documents must be saved on the same disk. If they reside on different disks, Word will display an error message indicating it cannot find the destination file when it attempts to save or open the source file. If Word cannot find a source file, right-click the object in the Word document, click Linked Worksheet Object on the shortcut menu, and then click Links. Select the appropriate source file in the Links dialog box, click the Change Source button, locate the source file, and then click the OK button.

To Save a Document with a New File Name

1 With the disk containing the Customer Breakdown Memo Draft file in drive A, click File on the menu bar and then click Save As.

2 Type Customer Breakdown Memo in the File name box. Do not press the ENTER key.

3 If necessary, click the Save in box arrow and then click 3½ Floppy (A:).

4 Click the Save button in the Save As dialog box.

Word saves the document on the disk in drive A with a new file name of Customer Breakdown Memo (shown in Figure 2).

More About

Linked Worksheets

If you link an Excel worksheet and the worksheet displays in the Word window with extra blank cells, use Crop button on Picture toolbar to remove the extra rows and columns of cells.

Linking an Excel Worksheet

The next step in this integration feature is to insert the Excel worksheet (source document) in the Customer Breakdown Memo (destination document) as a linked object. The Excel worksheet (Customer Base Breakdown) is located on the Data Disk. If you did not download the Data Disk, see the inside back cover for instructions for downloading the Data Disk or see your instructor.

The following steps show how to link the Excel worksheet to the Word document.

To Link an Excel Worksheet to a Word Document

1

• **Position the insertion point on the paragraph mark at the end of the memo (below the paragraph of text).**

• **Click Insert on the menu bar (Figure 2).**

FIGURE 2

2

• **Click Object on the Insert menu.**

• **When Word displays the Object dialog box, if necessary, click the Create from File tab.**

• **With the disk containing the Excel file named Customer Base Breakdown in drive A, click the Browse button.**

• **When Word displays the Browse dialog box, click the Excel file named Customer Base Breakdown.**

Word displays the Object dialog box and then the Browse dialog box (Figure 3).

FIGURE 3

3

• **Click the Insert button.**

• **When the Browse dialog box closes and the entire Object dialog box is visible again, place a check mark in the Link to file check box.**

The Object dialog box displays the name of the selected file in the File name text box (Figure 4). The xls following the file name, Customer Base Breakdown, identifies the file as an Excel worksheet.

FIGURE 4

4

- Click the **OK** button.

- Click the **Center** button on the Formatting toolbar.

- If necessary, scroll down so the Excel worksheet is displayed in the document window.

Word inserts the Excel worksheet as a linked object at the location of the insertion point (Figure 5). The object is centered between the document margins.

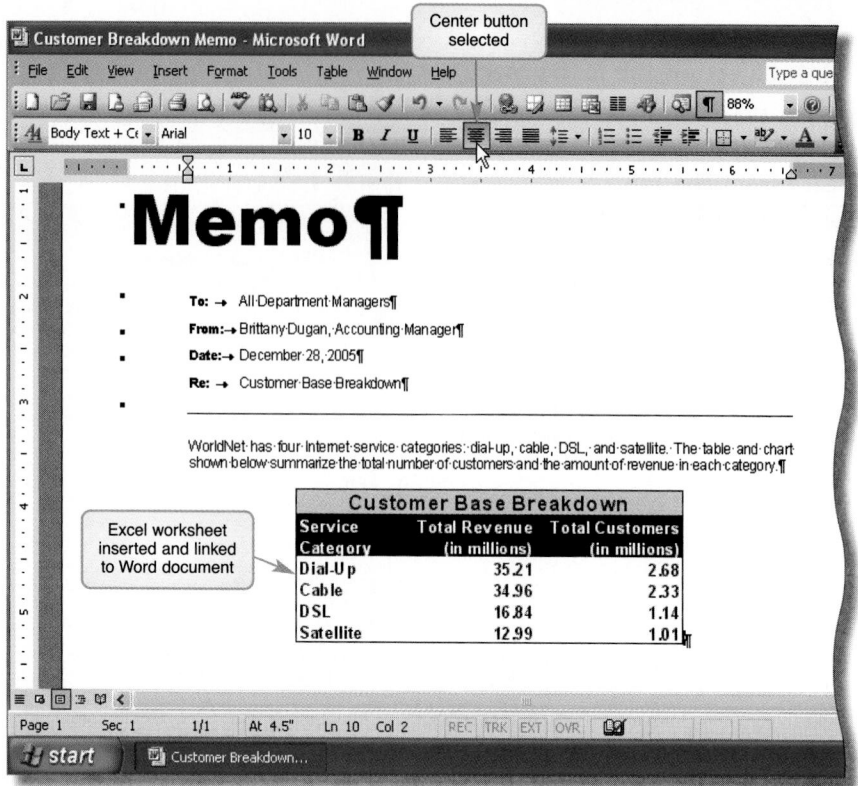

FIGURE 5

The Excel worksheet now is linked to the Word document. If you save the Word document and reopen it, the worksheet will be displayed just as it appears in Figure 5. If you wanted to delete the worksheet, you would select it and then press the DELETE key.

If you wanted to embed an Excel worksheet instead of link it, you would not place a check mark in the Link to file check box in the Object dialog box (shown in Figure 4 on the previous page).

Creating a Chart from an Excel Worksheet

You easily can use Word to chart data through **Microsoft Graph**, an embedded charting program. Because Graph is a program embedded in the Word program, Graph has its own menus and commands. With these commands, you can modify the appearance of the chart.

Graph can chart data in a Word table or it can chart data from another Office program, such as Excel. To chart data in a Word table, select the data to be charted prior to starting Graph; Graph then will chart the selected data automatically.

To chart data from another program, such as Excel, start Graph without selecting any data. This causes Graph to create a sample chart with sample data. Then, either copy and paste or link the data from another program to the sample chart.

The previous steps in this integration feature showed how to link the Excel worksheet data to the Word document. Thus, when you start Graph, it will create a sample chart. Then, you will link the Excel worksheet data to the chart.

The next steps show how to start Graph and create a sample chart.

To Create a Sample Chart in Graph

1

• **Position the insertion point on the paragraph mark to the right of the Excel worksheet in the Word document and then press the ENTER key.**

• **Click Insert on the menu bar and then point to Picture (Figure 6).**

FIGURE 6

2

• **Click Chart on the Picture submenu.**

• **If your screen does not display a Datasheet window, click the View Datasheet button on the Standard toolbar. (You can move the Datasheet window anywhere in the Word window by dragging its title bar.)**

Word starts the Microsoft Graph program (Figure 7). Graph creates a sample chart at the location of the insertion point and displays sample data in the Datasheet window.

FIGURE 7

Other Ways
1. In Voice Command mode, say "Insert, Picture, Chart"

The menus on the menu bar and buttons on the toolbars change to Graph menus and toolbars. That is, the Graph program is running inside the Word program.

You can copy and paste data from an Excel worksheet in the sample chart or you can link the Excel data to the sample chart. This integration feature shows how to link the data to the chart. To link the data, start Excel and display the workbook containing the worksheet data to be linked, copy the data in the worksheet to the Clipboard, and then use Graph's Paste Link command to link the data on the Clipboard to the Word document.

Thus, the first step in linking the data from the Excel worksheet to the Word chart is to open the Excel workbook that contains the worksheet data to be charted. The Excel workbook that contains the data to be linked to the chart is the Customer Base Breakdown workbook file, which is located on the Data Disk.

The following steps describe how to start Excel and open a workbook.

To Start and Customize Excel and Open an Excel Workbook

1 Click the Start button on the Windows taskbar, point to All Programs on the Start menu, point to Microsoft Office on the All Programs submenu, and then click Microsoft Office Excel 2003 on the Microsoft Office submenu.

2 If the Excel window is not maximized, double-click its title bar to maximize it.

3 If the Language bar appears, right-click it and then click Close the Language bar on the shortcut menu.

4 If the Getting Started task pane is displayed in the Excel window, click its Close button.

5 If the Standard and Formatting toolbar buttons are displayed on one row, click the Toolbar Options button and then click Show Buttons on Two Rows in the Toolbar Options list.

6 Reset Excel toolbars as described in Appendix D.

7 With the disk containing the Customer Base Breakdown file in drive A, click the Open button on the Standard toolbar.

8 When Excel displays the Open dialog box, if necessary, click the Look in box arrow and then click 3½ Floppy (A:). Double-click the Excel file named Customer Base Breakdown.

Excel starts and displays the Customer Base Breakdown file in the Excel window (shown in Figure 8).

With both Word and Excel open, you can switch between the two programs by clicking the appropriate program button on the taskbar.

The next step is to copy to the Clipboard the Excel data to be charted and then paste link it from the Clipboard to the chart in Word, as shown in the following steps.

More About

Starting Excel

If a Word document on the screen contains a linked Excel worksheet, you also can start Excel by double-clicking the Excel worksheet in the Word document. For example, if you double-click the Excel Customer Base Breakdown worksheet in the Word document, Excel starts and then displays the associated Excel workbook in an Excel window.

To Chart Excel Data in Word

1

- **In the Excel window, drag through cells in the range A4:B7 to select them.**
- **Click the Copy button on the Standard toolbar.**

The Excel window is active (Figure 8). A marquee appears around the range A4:B7, which has been copied to the Clipboard.

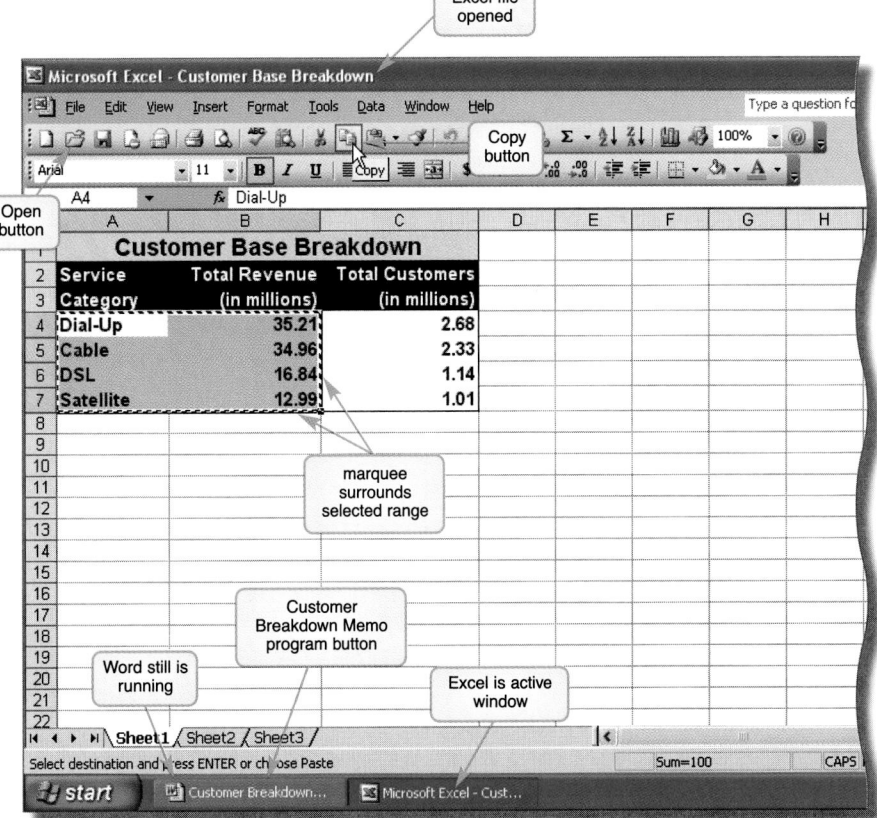

FIGURE 8

2

- **Click the Customer Breakdown Memo - Microsoft Word program button on the taskbar.**
- **Click anywhere in the Datasheet window. (If Graph is not active in the Word window, double-click the chart.)**
- **Click Edit on the menu bar.**

Graph still is active in Word (Figure 9).

FIGURE 9

3

• **Click Paste Link on the Edit menu.**

• **When Graph displays a dialog box indicating the linked data will replace existing data, click the OK button.**

Graph copies the data from the Clipboard in the Datasheet window, replacing the sample data currently in the Datasheet window (Figure 10). Graph then charts the contents of the Datasheet window. You can resize a Datasheet window by dragging any of its edges.

FIGURE 10

Graph charts the Excel data. The Excel data is linked to the chart. Thus, if you change any of the data in the Excel worksheet, it will be reflected in the chart.

If you wanted to copy and paste the chart data, instead of link it, you would not need to start Excel as described in the previous steps. Instead, you would perform the following steps.

TO COPY AND PASTE EXCEL DATA IN A CHART

1. Start Graph.
2. Click Edit on the Graph menu bar, click Import File, locate the file name in the Import File dialog box, click the Open button in the Import File dialog box, click Entire sheet or enter the range in the Import File Options dialog box, and then click the OK button.

When you use the Import File command to copy Excel worksheet data, the data in the chart will not be updated if the contents of the Excel worksheet change.

The next step is to format the chart. You want to make the size of the chart larger, as described next.

More About

Linking Excel Data

If you want to display a linked worksheet as an icon instead of as the worksheet itself, place a check mark in the Display as icon check box in the Object dialog box (shown in Figure 4 on page 725) when you link the worksheet to the Word document.

To Format the Chart in Graph

1 **Click the View Datasheet button on the Standard toolbar to remove the Datasheet window from the screen.**

2 **Position the mouse pointer on the bottom-right sizing handle on the selection rectangle that surrounds the chart and legend. When the mouse pointer changes to a two-headed arrow, drag the selection rectangle downward and rightward approximately one inch.**

Graph resizes the chart (shown in Figure 11).

You are finished modifying the chart. The next step is to exit Graph and return to Word.

To Exit Graph and Return to Word

1 **Click somewhere outside the chart.**

Word closes the Graph program (Figure 11). Word's menus and toolbars are redisplayed below the title bar.

FIGURE 11

If, for some reason, you wanted to modify an existing chart in a document, you would double-click the chart to restart the Microsoft Graph program. Then, you can make any necessary changes to the chart. When you are finished making changes to the chart, click anywhere outside the chart to return to Word.

You are finished with the memo. Save the document again, print it, and then quit Word as described in the steps on the next page.

To Save a Document

1 **With the disk containing the document in drive A, click the Save button on the Standard toolbar.**

Word saves the document on the disk in drive A.

To Quit Word

1 **Click the Close button on Word's title bar.**

The Word window closes.

Editing a Linked Worksheet

At a later time, you may find it necessary to change the data in the Excel worksheet. Any changes you make to the Excel worksheet while in Excel will be reflected in the Excel worksheet and chart in the Word document because the objects are linked.

The following steps show how to change the cable total revenue value and the total customers value in the Excel worksheet.

Q&A

Q: Can I break a link in a Word document?

A: Yes, if you want to break a link and make a linked object part of the Word document, right-click the object in the Word document, click Linked Worksheet Object on the shortcut menu, and then click Links. Select the appropriate source file in the Links dialog box, click the Break Link button, and then click the OK button.

To Edit a Linked Object

• **With the Excel worksheet displaying on the screen, if necessary, press the ESCAPE key to remove the marquee surrounding the previously selected cells.**

• **Click cell B5 to select it.**

• **Type** 37.96 **and then press the ENTER key.**

• **Click cell C5 to select it.**

• **Type** 2.93 **and then press the ENTER key.**

Excel displays the new cable total revenue and total customers values (Figure 12).

• **Click the Save button on the Standard toolbar.**

• **Click the Close button at the right edge of Excel's title bar.**

Excel saves the changes to the worksheet. The Excel window closes.

FIGURE 12

3

- **Start Word and then open the Customer Breakdown Memo document.**

- **If a dialog box is displayed about updating data from linked files, click the Yes button.**

- **Scroll to display the worksheet and chart in the document window.**

- **If the worksheet does not show the updated data, click the worksheet and then press the F9 key.**

- **If the chart does not display updated data, double-click the chart and then click outside the chart to exit Graph.**

The Word document displays the updates to the Excel worksheet object and chart object (Figure 13).

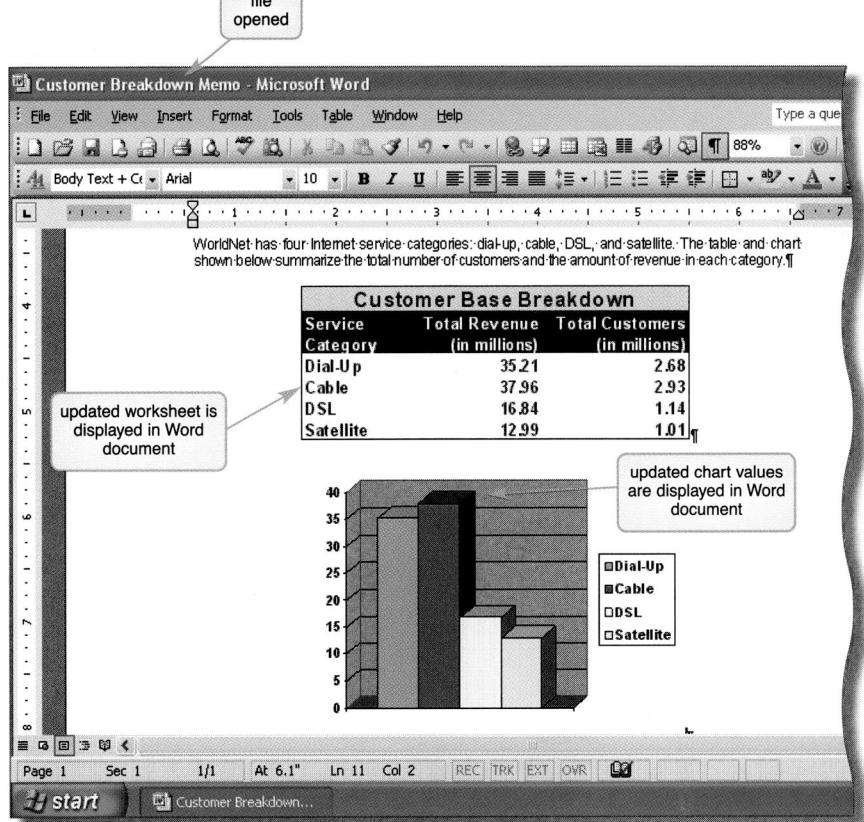

FIGURE 13

You also can edit any of the cells in the Excel worksheet (the object) while it is displayed as part of the Word document. To edit the worksheet, double-click it. If Excel is running already, the computer will switch to it and display the linked workbook in Excel. If Excel is not running, the computer will start Excel automatically and then display the linked workbook in Excel.

The following series of steps save and print the Word document and then quit Word.

To Save the Word Document Again

1 **Click the Save button on the Standard toolbar.**

Word saves the revised Customer Breakdown Memo on a floppy disk in drive A.

To Print a Document

1 **Click the Print button on the Standard toolbar.**

Word prints the memo as shown in Figure 1c on page WD 722.

To Quit Word

1 **Click the Close button at the right edge of Word's title bar.**

The Word window closes.

Integration Feature Summary

This Integration Feature introduced you to linking an Excel worksheet to a Word document. You also charted Excel data in Word using the embedded Microsoft Graph charting program. Then, you modified the linked worksheet to see the changes reflected in the Word document.

 If you have a SAM user profile, you may have access to hands-on instruction, practice, and assessment of the skills covered in this project. Log in to your SAM account and go to your assignments page to see what your instructor has assigned.

What You Should Know

Having completed this feature, you should be able to perform the tasks below. The tasks are listed in the same order as they were presented in the feature. For a list of the buttons, menus, toolbars, and commands introduced in the feature, see the Quick Reference Summary at the back of this book and refer to the Page Number column.

1. Start and Customize Word and Open a Document (WD 723)
2. Save a Document with a New File Name (WD 724)
3. Link an Excel Worksheet to a Word Document (WD 724)
4. Create a Sample Chart in Graph (WD 727)
5. Start and Customize Excel and Open an Excel Workbook (WD 728)
6. Chart Excel Data in Word (WD 729)
7. Copy and Paste Excel Data in a Chart (WD 730)
8. Format the Chart in Graph (WD 731)
9. Exit Graph and Return to Word (WD 731)
10. Save a Document (WD 732)
11. Quit Word (WD 732, WD 734)
12. Edit a Linked Object (WD 732)
13. Save the Word Document Again (WD 733)
14. Print a Document (WD 733)

In the Lab

1 Linking an Excel Worksheet to a Word Document

Problem: Jeremy Ogden, facilities manager at Royal Oaks Health Club, has created an Excel worksheet that lists the number of users in each of the club's facilities. He would like you to prepare a memo that includes the Excel worksheet.

Instructions:

1. Create a memo using a memo template. Save the memo using the file name, Lab IF-1 Royal Oaks Facility Usage Memo. The memo is to all staff, from Jeremy Ogden, and should have a subject of Facility Usage Study. In the memo, enter the following text: The facility usage study is complete. The results are summarized in the table below, which shows the number of members who used each facility in a 30-day period.
2. Link the Lab IF-1 Facility Usage Table Excel worksheet, which is on the Data Disk, to the Lab IF-1 Royal Oaks Facility Usage Memo file.
3. Save the Word memo file again.
4. Print the Word memo file.

2 Linking Data from an Excel Worksheet to a Word Chart

Problem: Jeremy Ogden, facilities manager at Royal Oaks Health Club, has created an Excel worksheet that lists the number of users in each of the club's facilities. He would like you to prepare a memo that includes a chart of the Excel worksheet data.

Instructions:

1. Create a memo using a memo template. Save the memo using the file name, Lab IF-2 Royal Oaks Facility Usage Memo with Chart. The memo is to all staff, from Jeremy Ogden, and should have a subject of Facility Usage Study. In the memo, enter the following text: The facility usage study is complete. The results are summarized in the chart below, which shows the number of members who used each facility in a 30-day period.
2. Link the Lab IF-1 Facility Usage Table Excel worksheet data, which is on the Data Disk, to a Word chart in the Lab IF-2 Royal Oaks Facility Usage Memo with Chart.
3. Save the Word memo file again.
4. Print the Word memo file.

3 Creating an Excel Worksheet and Linking It to a Word Document

Problem: As a part-time computer assistant at Fair Deal Realty Co., your boss has asked you to determine the number of homes sold in the last quarter and then create an Excel worksheet that lists the worksheet data. You are to prepare a memo that links the Excel worksheet to a memo and includes a chart of the Excel data.

(continued)

Creating an Excel Worksheet and Linking It to a Word Document *(continued)*

Instructions:

1. Create an Excel worksheet that has two columns (Price and Number of Homes Sold) and enough rows to list at least five different price ranges (e.g., $60,000 - $100,000 or > $200,000). Then, determine appropriate values for the Number of Homes Sold column for each price range you entered. Save the worksheet with the name Lab IF-3 Fair Deal Realty Sales Figures.

2. Create a memo to All Agents and Staff using a memo template. Save the memo using the file name, Lab IF-3 Fair Deal Realty Sales Memo. Explain the contents of the worksheet and chart in the memo. Link the Excel worksheet to the Word memo file. Link the Excel worksheet data to a Word chart.

3. Save the Word memo file again. Print the Word memo file. Close Word.

4. In Excel, change the number of homes sold for two of the price ranges. Open the Word memo file, be sure the linked table and chart data are updated, and then print the updated memo.

Appendix A

 # Microsoft Word Help System

Using the Word Help System

This appendix shows you how to use the Word Help system. At anytime while you are using Word, you can interact with its Help system and display information on any Word topic. It is a complete reference manual at your fingertips.

As shown in Figure A-1, five methods for accessing the Word Help system are available:

1. Microsoft Office Word Help button on the Standard toolbar
2. Microsoft Office Word Help command on the Help menu
3. Function key F1 on the keyboard
4. Type a question for help box on the menu bar
5. Office Assistant

TYPE A QUESTION FOR HELP BOX ON MENU BAR

OFFICE ASSISTANT

What would you like to do?

header

Options   Search

MICROSOFT OFFICE WORD HELP COMMAND ON HELP MENU

Help

Microsoft Office Word Help   F1
Show the Office Assistant
Microsoft Office Online
Contact Us
WordPerfect Help...
Check for Updates
Detect and Repair...
Activate Product...
Customer Feedback Options...
About Microsoft Office Word

FUNCTION KEY F1 ON KEYBOARD

F1

Esc   F1   F2

MICROSOFT OFFICE WORD HELP BUTTON ON STANDARD TOOLBAR

Word Help

Assistance

Search for:
header

Table of Contents

Office Online

- Connect to Microsoft Office Online
- Get the latest news about using Word
- Automatically update this list from the web

More...

Assistance
Training
Communities
Downloads

Search Results

30 results from Office Online

About headers and footers
Help > Headers and Footers

Headers and footers, simple to elaborate
Training > Word

Position headers and footers
Help > Headers and Footers

Change headers or footers
Help > Headers and Footers

Insert headers and footers
Help > Headers and Footers

Troubleshoot headers and footers
Help > Headers and Footers

Search

Microsoft Office Online

header

Can't find it?

Microsoft Office ...

About headers and footers

▶ Show All

Headers and footers are areas in the top and bottom margins of each page in a document.

Lorem

1

You can insert text or graphics in headers and footers—for example, page numbers, the date, a company logo, the document's title or file name, or the author's name—that are printed at the top or bottom of each page in a document.

You can work in the header and footer areas by clicking **Header and Footer** on the **View** menu.

▶ Headers and footers on a Web page

FIGURE A-1   **(a) Word Help Task Pane**   **(b) Search Results Task Pane**   **(c) Microsoft Office Word Help Window**

All five methods result in the Word Help system displaying a task pane on the right side of the Word window. The first three methods cause the **Word Help task pane** to display (Figure A-1a on the previous page). This task pane includes a Search text box in which you can enter a word or phrase on which you want help. Once you enter the word or phrase, the Word Help system displays the Search Results task pane (Figure A-1b on the previous page). With the Search Results task pane displayed, you can select specific Help topics.

As shown in Figure A-1, methods 4 and 5 bypass the Word Help task pane and display the **Search Results task pane** (Figure A-1b) with a list of links that pertain to the selected topic. Thus, any of the five methods for accessing the Word Help system results in displaying the Search Results task pane. Once the Word Help system displays this task pane, you can choose links that relate to the word or phrase on which you searched. In Figure A-1, for example, header was the searched topic (About headers and footers), which resulted in the Word Help system displaying the Microsoft Office Word Help window with information about headers and footers (Figure A-1c on the previous page).

Navigating the Word Help System

The quickest way to access the Word Help system is through the Type a question for help box on the right side of the menu bar at the top of the screen. Here you can type words, such as ruler, font, or column, or phrases, such as justify a paragraph, or how do I display formatting marks. The Word Help system responds by displaying a list of links in the Search Results task pane.

Here are two tips regarding the words or phrases you enter to initiate a search: (1) check the spelling of the word or phrase; and (2) keep your search very specific, with fewer than seven words, to return the most accurate results.

Assume for the following example that you want to know more about tables. The following steps show how to use the Type a question for help box to obtain useful information about tables by entering the keyword table. The steps also show you how to navigate the Word Help system.

To Obtain Help Using the Type a Question for Help Box

1

• **Click the Type a question for help box on the right side of the menu bar, type** table, **and then press the ENTER key (Figure A-2).**

The Word Help system displays the Search Results task pane on the right side of the window. The Search Results task pane contains a list of 30 links (Figure A-2). If you do not find what you are looking for, you can modify or refine the search in the Search area at the bottom of the task pane. The topics displayed in your Search Results task pane may be different.

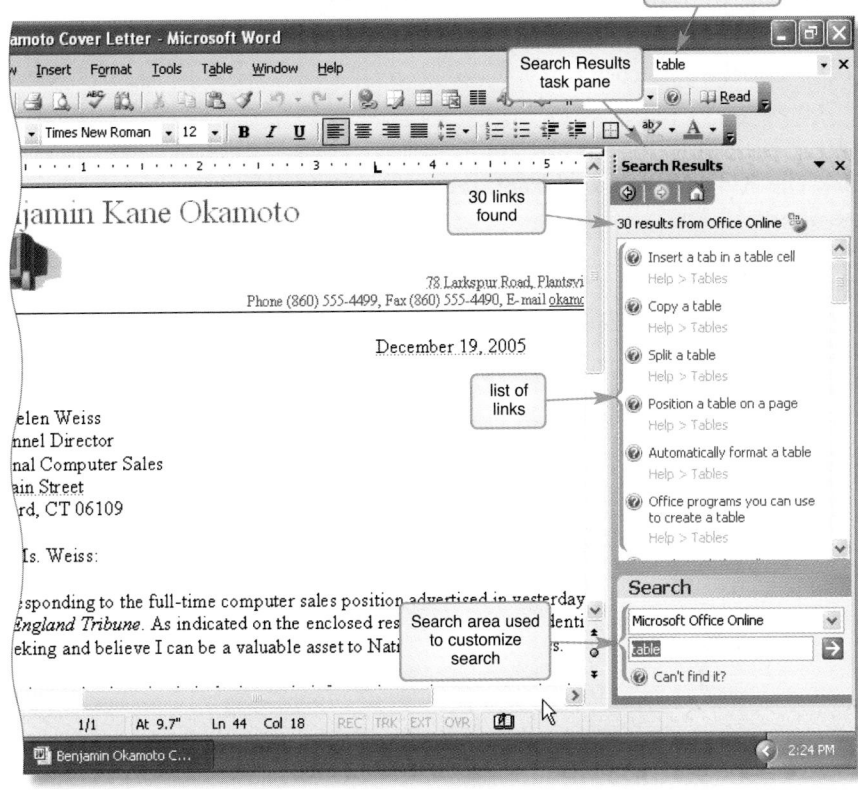

FIGURE A-2

2

• **Scroll down the list of links in the Search Results task pane and then click the About tables link.**

• **When Word displays the Microsoft Office Help Word window, click its Auto Tile button in the upper-left corner of the window (Figure A-4 on the next page), if necessary, to tile the windows.**

The Word Help system displays the Microsoft Office Word Help window with the desired information about tables (Figure A-3). With the Microsoft Office Word Help window and Microsoft Word 2003 window tiled, you can read the information in one window and complete the task in the other window.

FIGURE A-3

3

- **Double-click the Microsoft Office Word Help window title bar.**
- **Click the Show All link in the upper-right corner of the window.**
- **After reviewing the information, click the Hide All link that replaced the Show All link.**

The Microsoft Office Word Help window is maximized so it fills the entire screen (Figure A-4). If you are connected to the Internet, you can give Microsoft your opinion as to whether the information was helpful by clicking the Yes or No button at the bottom of the page. The Show All link expands the coverage of information and the Hide all link condenses the information displayed on the topic in the Microsoft Office Word Help window.

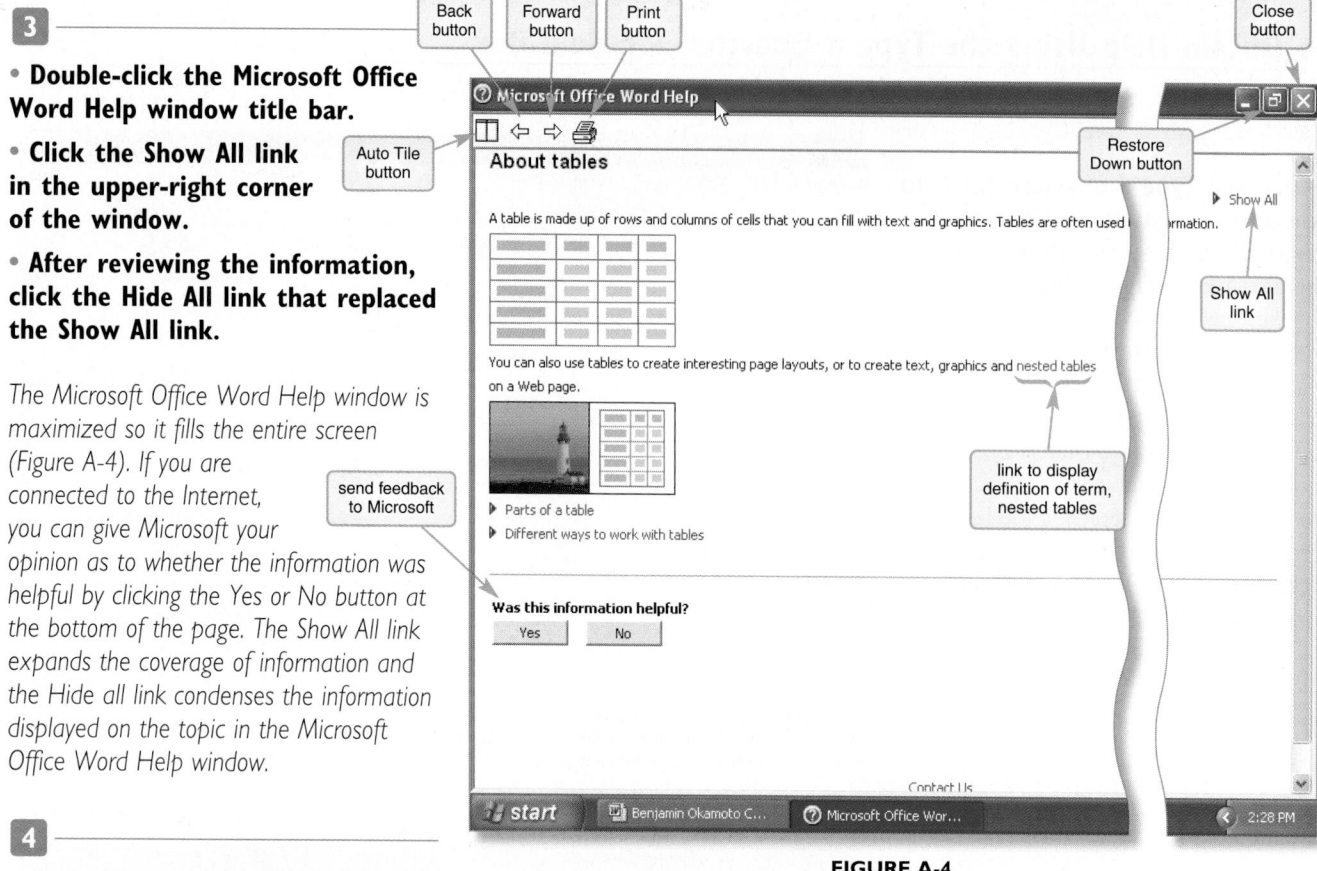

FIGURE A-4

4

- **Click the Restore Down button on the right side of the Microsoft Office Word Help window title bar to return to the tiled state shown in Figure A-3 on the previous page.**
- **Click the Close button on the Microsoft Office Word Help window title bar.**

The Microsoft Office Word Help window is closed and the Word document is active.

Use the four buttons in the upper-left corner of the Microsoft Office Word Help window (Figure A-4) to tile or untile, navigate through the Help system, or print the contents of the window. As you click links in the Search Results task pane, the Word Help system displays new pages of information. The Word Help System remembers the links you visited and allows you to redisplay the pages visited during a session by clicking the Back and Forward buttons (Figure A-4).

If none of the links presents the information you want, you can refine the search by entering another word or phrase in the Search text box in the Search Results task pane (Figure A-2 on the previous page). If you have access to the Web, then the scope is global for the initial search. **Global** means all of the categories listed in the Search box of the Search area in Figure A-2 are searched. For example, you can, restrict the scope to **Offline Help**, which results in a search of related links only on your hard disk.

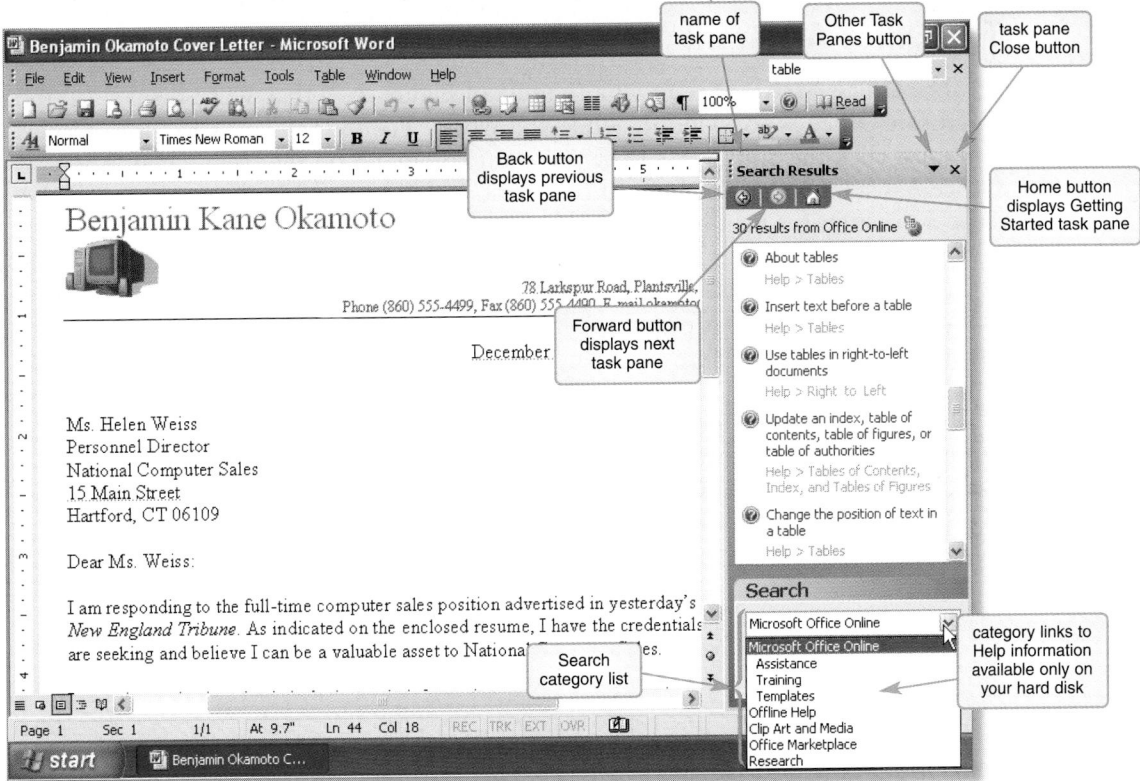

FIGURE A-5

Figure A-5 shows several additional features of the Search Results task pane. The Other Task Panes button and Close button on the Search Results task pane title bar allow you to display other task panes and close the Search Results task pane. The three buttons below the Search Results task pane title bar allow you to navigate between task panes (Back button and Forward button) and display the Getting Started task pane (Home button).

As you enter words and phrases in the Type a question for help box, the Word Help system adds them to the Type a question for help list. To display the list of previously typed words and phrases, click the Type a question for help box arrow (Figure A-6).

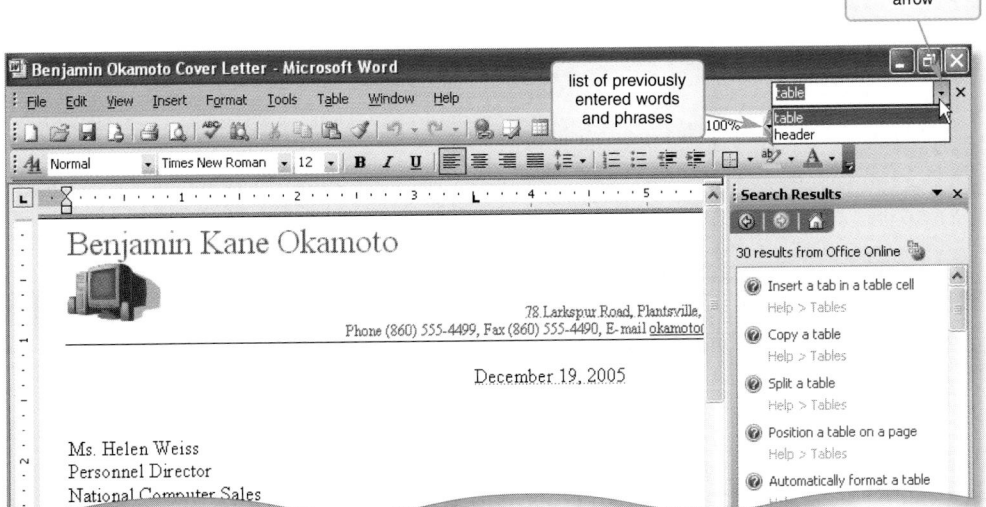

FIGURE A-6

The Office Assistant

The **Office Assistant** is an icon (middle of Figure A-7) that Word displays in the Microsoft Office Word window while you work. For the Office Assistant to display, you must click the Show the Office Assistant command on the Help menu. The Office Assistant has multiple functions. First, it will respond in the same way as the Type a question for help box with a list of topics that relate to the word or phrase you enter in the text box in the Office Assistant balloon. The entry can be in the form of a word or phrase as if you were talking to a person. For example, if you want to learn more about printing a file, in the balloon text box, you can type any of the following words or phrases: print, print a document, how do I print a file, or anything similar.

In the example in Figure A-7, the phrase, print a document, is entered into the Office Assistant balloon text box. The Office Assistant responds by displaying the Search Results task pane with a list of links from which you can choose. Once you click a link in the Search Results task pane, the Word Help system displays the information in the Microsoft Office Word Help window (Figure A-7).

FIGURE A-7

In addition, the Office Assistant monitors your work and accumulates tips during a session on how you might increase your productivity and efficiency. The accumulation of tips must be enabled. You enable the accumulation of tips by right-clicking the Office Assistant, clicking Options on the shortcut menu, and then selecting the types of tips you want accumulated. You can view the tips at anytime. The accumulated tips appear when you activate the Office Assistant balloon. Also, if at anytime you see a light bulb above the Office Assistant, click it to display the most recent tip. If the Office Assistant is hidden, then the light bulb shows on the Microsoft Office Word Help button on the Standard toolbar.

You hide the Office Assistant by invoking the Hide the Office Assistant command on the Help menu or by right-clicking the Office Assistant and then clicking Hide on the shortcut menu. The Hide the Office Assistant command shows on the Help menu only when the Office Assistant is active in the Word window. If the Office Assistant begins showing up on your screen without you instructing it to show, then right-click the Office Assistant, click Options on the shortcut menu, click the Use the Office Assistant check box to remove the check mark, and then click the OK button.

If the Office Assistant is active in the Word window, then Word displays all program and system messages in the Office Assistant balloon.

You may or may not want the Office Assistant to display on the screen at all times. As indicated earlier, you can hide it and then show it later through the Help menu. For more information about the Office Assistant, type office assistant in the Type a question for help box and then click the links in the Search Results task pane.

Question Mark Button in Dialog Boxes and Help Icon in Task Panes

You use the Question Mark button with dialog boxes. It is located in the upper-right corner on the title bar of the dialog boxes, next to the Close button. For example, in Figure A-8 on the next page, the Print dialog box appears on the screen. If you click the Question Mark button in the upper-right corner of the dialog box, the Microsoft Office Word Help window is displayed and provides information about the options in the Print dialog box.

Some task panes include a Help icon. It can be located in various places within the task pane. For example, in the Clip Art task pane shown in Figure A-8, the Help icon appears at the bottom of the task pane and the Tips for finding clips link appears to the right of the Help icon. When you click the link, the Microsoft Office Word Help window is displayed and provides tips for finding clip art.

Microsoft Office Word
Help window

Help icon in
task pane

Question
Mark button
in dialog box

FIGURE A-8

Other Help Commands on the Help Menu

Thus far, this appendix has discussed the first two commands on the Help menu:
(1) the Microsoft Office Word Help command (Figure A-1 on page APP 1) and
(2) the Show the Office Assistant command (Figure A-7 on page APP 6). Several
additional commands are available on the Help menu as shown in Figure A-9.
Table A-1 summarizes these commands.

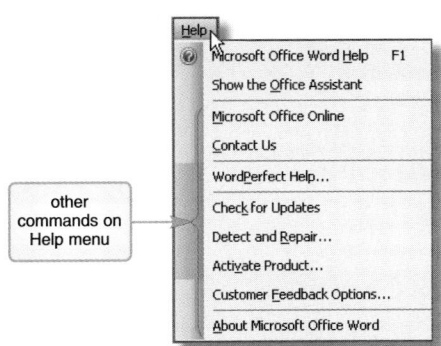

other commands on Help menu

FIGURE A-9

COMMAND ON HELP MENU	FUNCTION
Microsoft Office Online	Activates the browser, which displays the Microsoft Office Online Home page. The Microsoft Office Online Home page contains links that can improve Office productivity.
Contact Us	Activates the browser, which displays Microsoft contact information and a list of useful links.
WordPerfect Help	Displays the Help for WordPerfect Users dialog box, which includes information about carrying out commands in Word.
Check for Updates	Activates the browser, which displays a list of updates to Office 2003. These updates can be downloaded and installed to improve the efficiency of Office or to fix an error in one or more of the Office applications.
Detect and Repair	Detects and repairs errors in the Word program.
Activate Product	Activates Word if it has not already been activated.
Customer Feedback Options	Gives or denies Microsoft permission to collect anonymous information about the hardware.
About Microsoft Office Word	Displays the About Microsoft Word dialog box. The dialog box lists the owner of the software and the product identification. You need to know the product identification if you call Microsoft for assistance. The three buttons below the OK button are the System Info button, Tech Support button, and Disabled Items button. The System Info button displays system information, including hardware resources, components, software environment, and applications. The Tech Support button displays technical assistance information. The Disabled Items button displays a list of disabled items that prevents Word from functioning properly.

Table A-1   Summary of Other Help Commands on the Help Menu

Use Help

1 Using the Type a Question for Help Box

Instructions: Perform the following tasks using the Word Help system.

1. Use the Type a question for help box on the menu bar to get help on adding a bullet.
2. Click Add bullets or numbering in the list of links in the Search Results task pane. If necessary, tile the windows. Double-click the Microsoft Office Word Help window title bar to maximize it. Click the Show All link. Read and print the information. At the top of the printout, write down the number of links the Word Help system found.
3. Click the Restore Down button on the Microsoft Office Word Help title bar to restore the Microsoft Office Word Help window.
4. One at a time, click two additional links in the Search Results task pane and print the information. Hand in the printouts to your instructor. Use the Back and Forward buttons to return to the original page.
5. Use the Type a question for help box to search for information on adjusting line spacing. Click the Adjust line or paragraph spacing link in the Search Results task pane. Maximize the Microsoft Office Word Help window. Read and print the contents of the window. One at a time, click the links on the page and print the contents of the window. Close the Microsoft Office Word Help window.
6. For each of the following words and phrases, click one link in the Search Results task pane, click the Show All link, and then print the page: page zoom; date; print preview; office clipboard; word count; and themes.

2 Expanding on the Word Help System Basics

Instructions: Use the Word Help system to understand the topics better and answer the questions listed below. Answer the questions on your own paper, or hand in the printed Help information to your instructor.

1. Show the Office Assistant. Right-click the Office Assistant and then click Animate! on the shortcut menu. Repeat invoking the Animate! command to see various animations.
2. Right-click the Office Assistant, click Options on the shortcut menu, click the Reset my tips button, and then click the OK button. If necessary, repeatedly click the Office Assistant and then click off the Office Assistant until a light bulb appears above the Office Assistant. When you see the light bulb, it indicates that the Office Assistant has a tip to share with you.
3. Use the Office Assistant to find help on undoing. Click the Undo mistakes link and then print the contents of the Microsoft Office Word Help window. Close the window. Hand in the printouts to your instructor. Hide the Office Assistant.
4. Press the F1 key. Search for information on Help. Click the first two links in the Search Results task pane. Read and print the information for both links.
5. Display the Help menu. One at a time, click the Microsoft Office Online, Contact Us, and Check for Updates commands. Print the contents of each Internet Explorer window that displays and then close the window. Hand in the printouts to your instructor.
6. Click About Microsoft Office Word on the Help menu. Click the Tech Support button, print the contents of the Microsoft Office Word Help window, and then close the window. Click the System Info button. If necessary, click the plus sign to the left of Components in the System Summary list to display the Components category. Click CD-ROM and then print the information. Click Display and then print the information. Hand in the printouts to your instructor.

Appendix B

Speech and Handwriting Recognition and Speech Playback

Introduction

This appendix discusses the Office capability that allows users to create and modify worksheets using its alternative input technologies available through **text services**. Office provides a variety of text services, which enable you to speak commands and enter text in an application. The most common text service is the keyboard. Other text services include speech recognition and handwriting recognition.

The Language Bar

The **Language bar** allows you to use text services in the Office applications. You can utilize the Language bar in one of three states: (1) in a restored state as a floating toolbar in the Word window (Figure B-1a or Figure B-1b if Text Labels are enabled); (2) in a minimized state docked next to the notification area on the Windows taskbar (Figure B-1c); or (3) hidden (temporarily closed and out of the way). If the Language bar is hidden, you can activate it by right-clicking the Windows taskbar, pointing to Toolbars on the shortcut menu (Figure B-1d), and then clicking Language bar on the Toolbars submenu. If you want to close the Language bar, right-click the Language bar and then click Close the Language bar on the shortcut menu (Figure B-1e).

move handle Speech Tools Writing Pad Minimize

Microphone Handwriting Help Options

(a) Language Bar with Text Labels Disabled

Microphone 🎤 Tools Handwriting Writing Pad ❓

(b) Language Bar with Text Labels Enabled

2:01 PM

(c) Minimized Language Bar Docked on Windows Taskbar next to Notification Area

FIGURE B-1

Toolbars command

Language bar command

Toolbars
Cascade Windows
Tile Windows Horizontally
Tile Windows Vertically
Show the Desktop

Task Manager

✓ Lock the Taskbar
Properties

Address
Links
Language bar
Desktop
Quick Launch

New Toolbar...

Windows taskbar shortcut menu

Toolbars submenu

2:01 PM

(d) Windows Taskbar Shortcut Menu and Toolbars Submenu

Windows taskbar

Language bar shortcut menu

Close the Language bar command

Restore the Language bar
✓ Additional icons in taskbar
Adjust the Language band position
Settings...
Close the Language bar

2:01 PM

(e) Language Bar Shortcut Menu

When Windows was installed on your computer, the installer specified a default language. For example, most users in the United States select English (United States) as the default language. You can add more than 90 additional languages and varying dialects such as Basque, English (Zimbabwe), French (France), French (Canada), German (Germany), German (Austria), and Swahili. With multiple languages available, you can switch from one language to another while working in Word. If you change the language or dialect, then text services may change the functions of the keys on the keyboard, adjust speech recognition, and alter handwriting recognition. If a second language is activated, then a Language icon appears immediately to the right of the move handle on the Language bar and the language name is displayed on the Word status bar. This appendix assumes that English (United States) is the only language installed. Thus, the Language icon does not appear in the examples in Figure B-1 on the previous page.

Buttons on the Language Bar

The Language bar shown in Figure B-2a contains seven buttons. The number of buttons on your Language bar may be different. These buttons are used to select the language, customize the Language bar, control the microphone, control handwriting, and obtain help.

The first button on the left is the Microphone button, which enables and disables the microphone. When the microphone is enabled, text services adds two buttons and a balloon to the Language bar (Figure B-2b). These additional buttons and the balloon will be discussed shortly.

The second button from the left is the Speech Tools button. The Speech Tools button displays a menu of commands (Figure B-2c) that allow you to scan the current document looking for words to add to the speech recognition dictionary; hide or show the balloon on the Language bar; train the Speech Recognition service so that it can interpret your voice better; add and delete specific words to and from its dictionary, such as names and other words not understood easily; and change the user profile so more than one person can use the microphone on the same computer.

The third button from the left on the Language bar is the Handwriting button. The Handwriting button displays the Handwriting menu (Figure B-2d), which lets you choose the Writing Pad (Figure B-2e), Write Anywhere (Figure B-2f), or the on-screen keyboard (Figure B-2g). The On-Screen Symbol Keyboard command on the Handwriting menu displays an on-screen keyboard that allows you to enter special symbols that are not available on a standard keyboard. You can choose only one form of handwriting at a time.

The fourth button indicates which one of the handwriting forms is active. For example, in Figure B-2a, the Writing Pad is active. The handwriting recognition capabilities of text services will be discussed shortly.

The fifth button from the left on the Language bar is the Help button. The Help button displays the Help menu. If you click the Language Bar Help command on the Help menu, the Language Bar Help window appears (Figure B-2h). On the far right of the Language bar are two buttons stacked above and below each other. The top button is the Minimize button and the bottom button is the Options button. The Minimize button minimizes the Language bar so that it appears on the Windows taskbar. The next section discusses the Options button.

Customizing the Language Bar

The down arrow icon immediately below the Minimize button in Figure B-2a is called the Options button. The Options button displays a menu of text services options (Figure B-2i). You can use this menu to hide the Speech Tools, Handwriting, and Help buttons on the Language bar by clicking their names to remove the check mark to the left of each button. You also can show the Correction, Speak Text, and Pause Speaking buttons on the Language bar by clicking their names to place a check mark to the left of the respective command. When you select text and then click the Correction button, a list of correction alternatives is displayed in the Word window. You can use the Corrections button to correct both speech recognition and handwriting recognition errors. The Speak Text and Pause Speaking buttons are discussed at the end of this Appendix. The Settings command on the Options menu displays a dialog box that lets you customize the Language bar. This command will be discussed shortly. The Restore Defaults command redisplays hidden buttons on the Language bar.

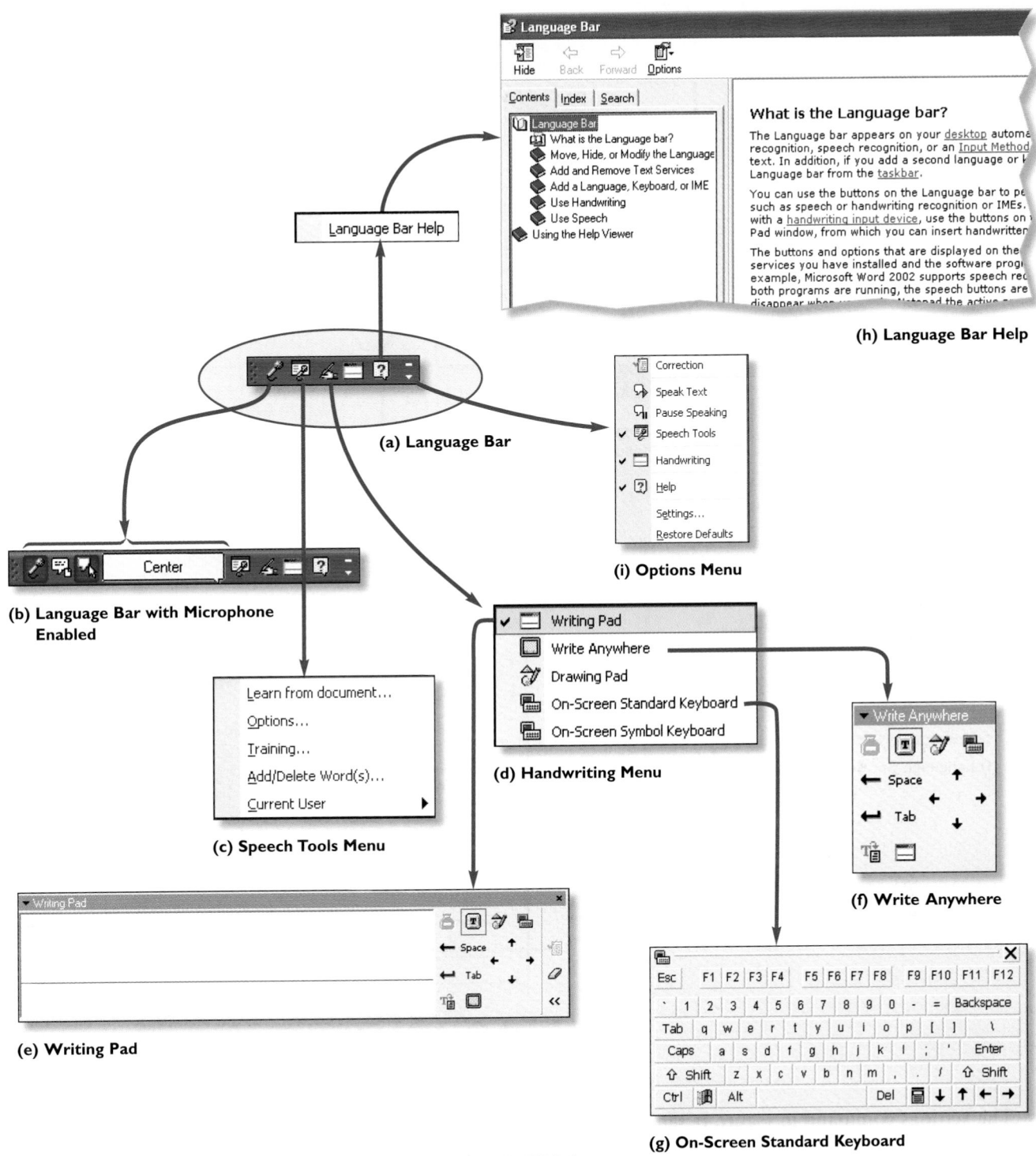

(a) Language Bar

(b) Language Bar with Microphone Enabled

(c) Speech Tools Menu

(d) Handwriting Menu

(e) Writing Pad

(f) Write Anywhere

(g) On-Screen Standard Keyboard

(h) Language Bar Help

(i) Options Menu

FIGURE B-2

If you right-click the Language bar, a shortcut menu appears (Figure B-3a on the next page). This shortcut menu lets you further customize the Language bar. The Minimize command on the shortcut menu docks the Language bar on the Windows taskbar. The Transparency command in Figure B-3a toggles the Language bar between being solid and transparent. You can see through a transparent Language bar (Figure B-3b). The Text Labels command toggles on text labels on the Language bar (Figure B-3c) and off (Figure B-3b). The Vertical command displays the Language bar vertically on the screen (Figure B-3d).

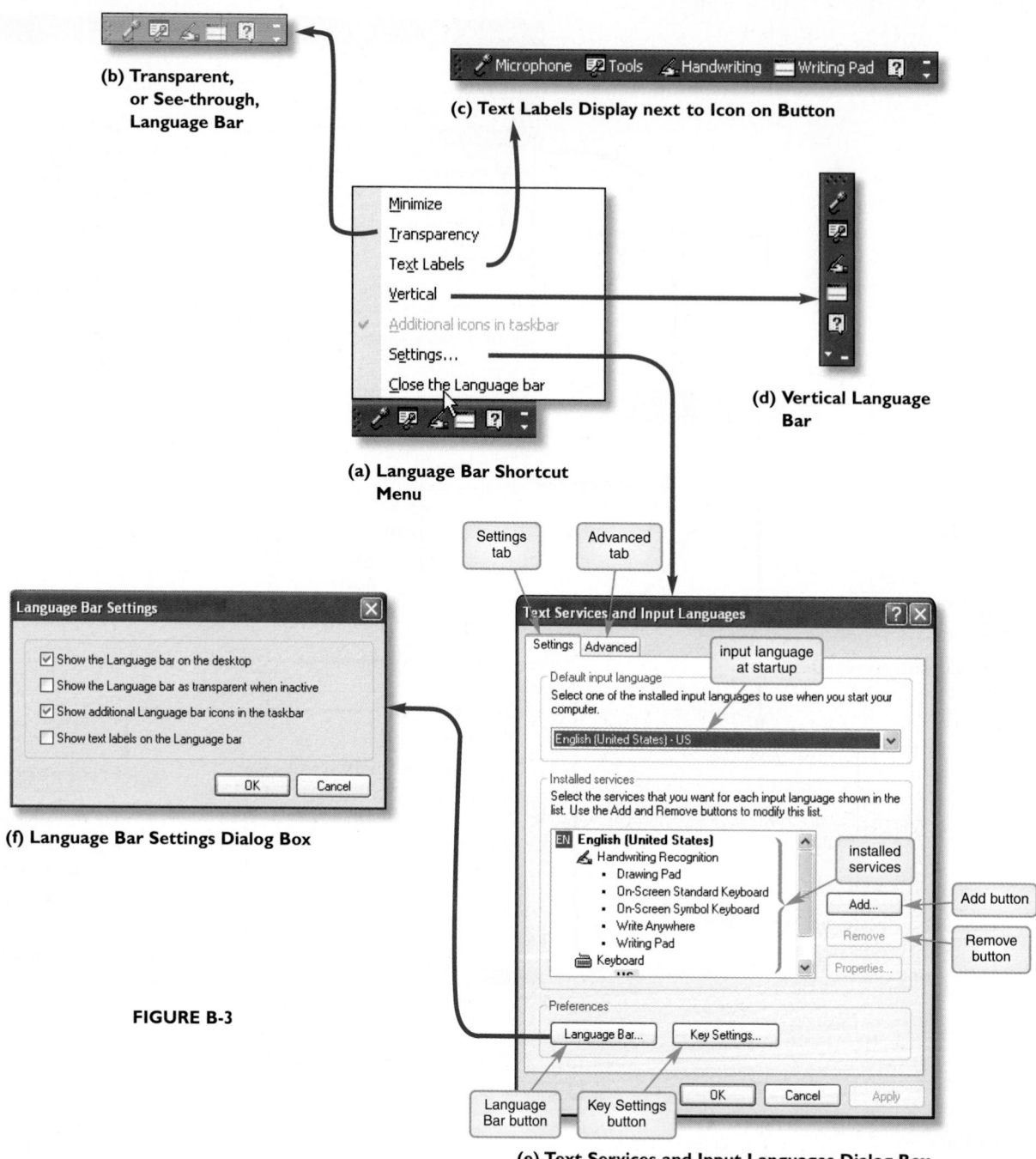

(b) Transparent,
or See-through,
Language Bar

(c) Text Labels Display next to Icon on Button

(a) Language Bar Shortcut
Menu

(d) Vertical Language
Bar

Settings tab

Advanced tab

input language at startup

installed services

Add button

Remove button

(f) Language Bar Settings Dialog Box

FIGURE B-3

Language Bar button

Key Settings button

(e) Text Services and Input Languages Dialog Box

The Settings command in Figure B-3a displays the Text Services and Input Languages dialog box (Figure B-3e). The Text Services and Input Languages dialog box allows you to add additonal languages, add and remove text services, modify keys on the keyboard, modify the Language bar, and extend support of advanced text services to all programs, including Notepad and other programs that normally do not support text services (through the Advanced tab). If you want to remove any one of the services in the Installed services list, select the service, and then click the Remove button. If you want to add a service, click the Add button. The Key Settings button allows you to modify the keyboard. If you click the Language Bar button in the Text Services and Input Languages dialog box, the Language Bar Settings dialog box appears (Figure B-3f). This dialog box contains Language bar options, some of which are the same as the commands on the Language bar shortcut menu shown in Figure B-3a.

The Close the Language bar command on the shortcut menu shown in Figure B-3a closes or hides the Language bar. If you close the Language bar and want to redisplay it, see Figure B-1d on page APP 11.

Speech Recognition

The **Speech Recognition service** available with Office enables your computer to recognize human speech through a microphone. The microphone has two modes: dictation and voice command (Figure B-4). You switch between the two modes by clicking the Dictation button and the Voice Command button on the Language bar. These buttons appear only when you turn on Speech Recognition by clicking the Microphone button on the Language bar (Figure B-5a on the next page). If you are using the Microphone button for the very first time in Word, it will require that you check your microphone settings and step through voice training before activating the Speech Recognition service.

The Dictation button places the microphone in Dictation mode. In **Dictation mode**, whatever you speak is entered as text at the location of the insertion point. The Voice Command button places the microphone in Voice Command mode. In **Voice Command mode**, whatever you speak is interpreted as a command. If you want to turn off the microphone, click the Microphone button on the Language bar or in Voice Command mode say, "Mic off" (pronounced mike off). It is important to remember that minimizing the Language bar does not turn off the microphone.

(a) Enter Text in Dictation Mode

(b) Enter Commands in Voice Command Mode

FIGURE B-4

The Language bar speech message balloon shown in Figure B-5b displays messages that may offer help or hints. In Voice Command mode, the name of the last recognized command you said appears. If you use the mouse or keyboard instead of the microphone, a message will appear in the Language bar speech message balloon indicating the word you could say. In Dictation mode, the message, Dictating, usually appears. The Speech Recognition service, however, will display messages to inform you that you are talking too soft, too loud, too fast, or to ask you to repeat what you said by displaying, What was that?

Getting Started with Speech Recognition

For the microphone to function properly, you should follow these steps:

1. Make sure your computer meets the minimum requirements.
2. Start Word. Activate Speech Recognition by clicking Tools on the menu bar and then clicking Speech.
3. Set up and position your microphone, preferably a close-talk headset with gain adjustment support.
4. Train Speech Recognition.

The following sections describe these steps in more detail.

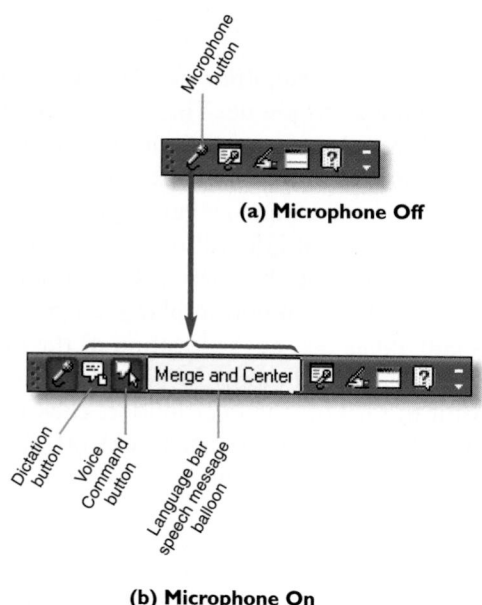

(a) Microphone Off

(b) Microphone On

FIGURE B-5

SPEECH RECOGNITION SYSTEM REQUIREMENTS   For Speech Recognition to work on your computer, it needs the following:

1. Microsoft Windows 98 or later or Microsoft Windows NT 4.0 or later
2. At least 128 MB RAM
3. 400 MHz or faster processor
4. Microphone and sound card

SETUP AND POSITION YOUR MICROPHONE   Set up your microphone as follows:

1. Connect your microphone to the sound card in the back of the computer.
2. Position the microphone approximately one inch out from and to the side of your mouth. Position it so you are not breathing into it.
3. On the Language bar, click the Speech Tools button and then click Options on the Speech Tools menu (Figure B-6a).
4. When text services displays the Speech input settings dialog box (Figure B-6b), click the Advanced Speech button. When text services displays the Speech Properties dialog box (Figure B-6c), click the Speech Recognition tab.
5. Click the Configure Microphone button. Follow the Microphone Wizard directions as shown in Figures B-6d, B-6e, and B-6f. The Next button will remain dimmed in Figure B-6e until the volume meter consistently stays in the green area.
6. If someone else installed Speech Recognition, click the New button in the Speech Properties dialog box and enter your name. Click the Train Profile button and step through the Voice Training dialog boxes. The Voice Training dialog boxes will require that you enter your gender and age group. It then will step you through voice training.

You can adjust the microphone further by clicking the Settings button in the Speech Properties dialog box (Figure B-6c). The Settings button displays the Recognition Profile Settings dialog box that allows you to adjust the pronunciation sensitivity and accuracy versus recognition response time.

(a) **Speech Tools Menu**

(d) **Adjust Microphone**

(b) **Speech Input Settings Dialog Box**

(c) **Speech Properties Dialog Box**

(e) **Adjust Volume**

(f) **Test Microphone**

FIGURE B-6

TRAIN THE SPEECH RECOGNITION SERVICE The Speech Recognition service will understand most commands and some dictation without any training at all. It will recognize much more of what you speak, however, if you take the time to train it. After one training session, it will recognize 85 to 90 percent of your words. As you do more training, accuracy will rise to 95 percent. If you feel that too many mistakes are being made, then continue to train the service. The more training you do, the more accurately it will work for you. Follow these steps to train the Speech Recognition service:

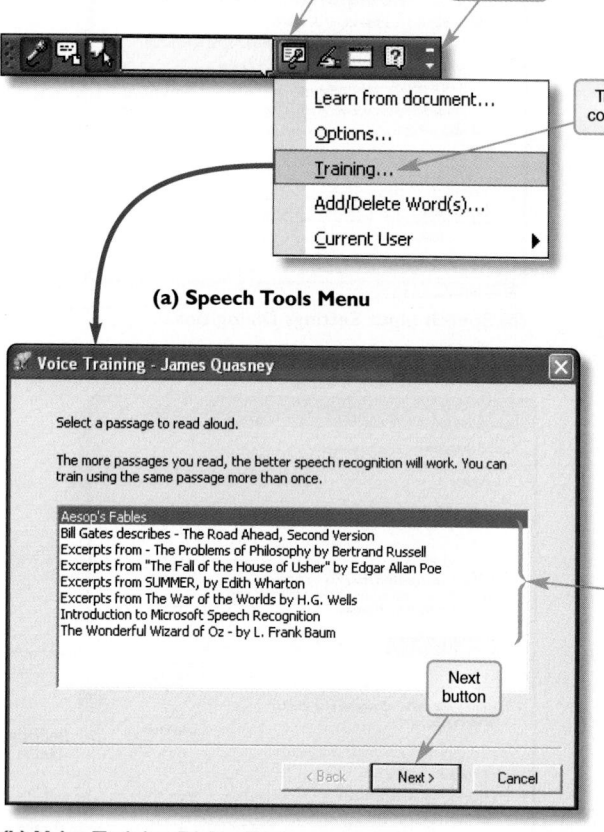

(a) Speech Tools Menu

(b) Voice Training Dialog Box

FIGURE B-7

1. Click the Speech Tools button on the Language bar and then click Training (Figure B-7a).
2. When the Voice Training dialog box appears (Figure B-7b), click one of the sessions and then click the Next button.
3. Complete the training session, which should take less than 15 minutes.

If you are serious about using a microphone to speak to your computer, you need to take the time to go through at least three of the eight training sessions listed in Figure B-7b.

Using Speech Recognition

Speech recognition lets you enter text into a document similarly to speaking into a tape recorder. Instead of typing, you can dictate text that you want to be displayed in the document, and you can issue voice commands. In Voice Command mode, you can speak menu names, commands on menus, toolbar button names, and dialog box option buttons, check boxes, list boxes, and button names. Speech recognition, however, is not a completely hands-free form of input. Speech recognition works best if you use a combination of your voice, the keyboard, and the mouse. You soon will discover that Dictation mode is far less accurate than Voice Command mode. Table B-1 lists some tips that will improve the Speech Recognition service's accuracy considerably.

Table B-1	Tips to Improve Speech Recognition
NUMBER	**TIP**
1	The microphone hears everything. Though the Speech Recognition service filters out background noise, it is recommended that you work in a quiet environment.
2	Try not to move the microphone around once it is adjusted.
3	Speak in a steady tone and speak clearly.
4	In Dictation mode, do not pause between words. A phrase is easier to interpret than a word. Sounding out syllables in a word will make it more difficult for the Speech Recognition service to interpret what you are saying.
5	If you speak too loudly or too softly, it makes it difficult for the Speech Recognition service to interpret what you said. Check the Language bar speech message balloon for an indication that you may be speaking too loudly or too softly.
6	If you experience problems after training, adjust the recognition options that control accuracy and rejection by clicking the Settings button shown in Figure B-6c on the previous page.
7	When you are finished using the microphone, turn it off by clicking the Microphone button on the Language bar or in Voice Command mode, say "Mic off." Leaving the microphone on is the same as leaning on the keyboard.
8	If the Speech Recognition service is having difficulty with unusual words, then add the words to its dictionary by using the Learn from document and Add/Delete Word(s) commands on the Speech Tools menu (Figure B-8a). The last names of individuals and the names of companies are good examples of the types of words you should add to the dictionary.
9	Training will improve accuracy; practice will improve confidence.

The last command on the Speech Tools menu is the Current User command (Figure B-8a). The Current User command is useful for multiple users who share a computer. It allows them to configure their own individual profiles, and then switch between users as they use the computer.

For additional information about the Speech Recognition service, enter speech recognition in the Type a question for help box on the menu bar.

Handwriting Recognition

Using the Office **Handwriting Recognition service**, you can enter text and numbers into Word by writing instead of typing. You can write using a special handwriting device that connects to your computer or you can write on the screen using your mouse. Four basic methods of handwriting are available by clicking the Handwriting button on the Language bar: Writing Pad; Write Anywhere; Drawing Pad; and On-Screen Keyboard. Although the on-screen keyboard does not involve handwriting recognition, it is part of the Handwriting menu and, therefore, will be discussed in this section.

If your Language bar does not include the Handwriting button, then for installation instructions, enter install handwriting recognition in the Type a question for help box on the menu bar.

Writing Pad

To display the Writing Pad, click the Handwriting button on the Language bar and then click Writing Pad (Figure B-9). The **Writing Pad** resembles a notepad with one or more lines on which you can use freehand to print or write in cursive. With the Text button enabled, you can form letters on the line by moving the mouse while holding down the mouse button. To the right of the notepad is a rectangular toolbar. Use the buttons on this toolbar to adjust the Writing Pad, select cells, and activate other handwriting applications.

FIGURE B-8

(a) Speech Tools Menu

(b) Add/Delete Word(s) Dialog Box

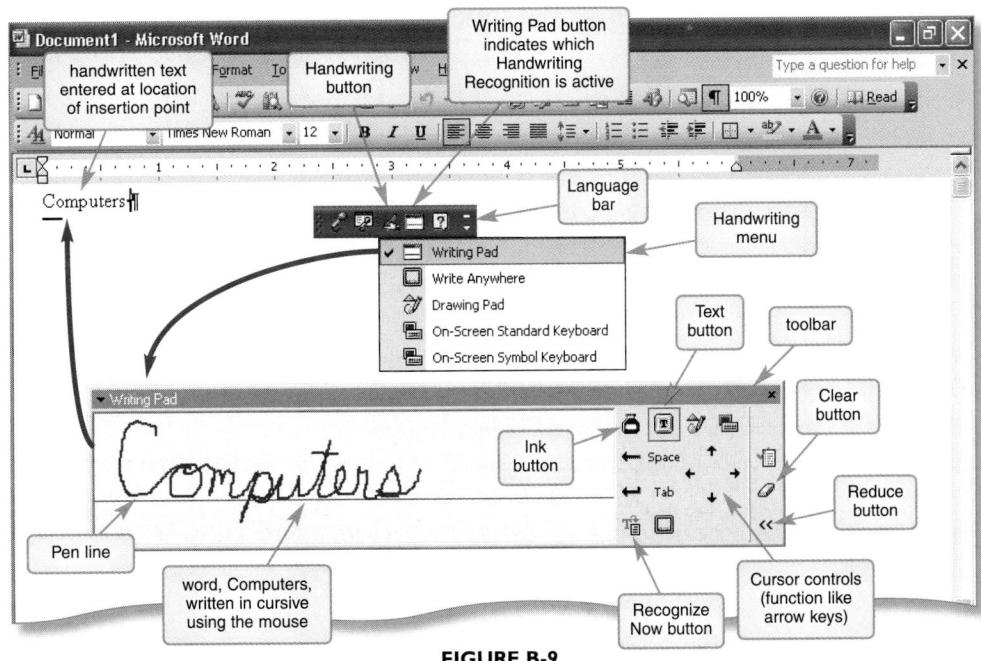

FIGURE B-9

Consider the example in Figure B-9 on the previous page. With the insertion point at the top of the document, the word, Computers, is written in cursive on the **Pen line** in the Writing Pad. As soon as the word is complete, the Handwriting Recognition service automatically converts the handwriting to typed characters and inserts the text at the location of the insertion point. With the Ink button enabled, instead of the Text button, the text is inserted in handwritten form in the document.

You can customize the Writing Pad by clicking the Options button on the left side of the Writing Pad title bar and then clicking the Options command (Figure B-10a). Invoking the Options command causes the Handwriting Options dialog box to be displayed. The Handwriting Options dialog box contains two sheets: Common and Writing Pad. The Common sheet lets you change the pen color and pen width, adjust recognition, and customize the toolbar area of the Writing Pad. The Writing Pad sheet allows you to change the background color and the number of lines that are displayed in the Writing Pad. Both sheets contain a Restore Default button to restore the settings to what they were when the software was installed initially.

(a) Writing Pad Options Menu

(b) Handwriting Options Dialog Box
with Common Sheet Active

(c) Handwriting Options Dialog Box
with Writing Pad Sheet Active

FIGURE B-10

When you first start using the Writing Pad, you may want to remove the check mark from the Automatic recognition check box in the Common sheet in the Handwriting Options dialog box (Figure B-10b). With the check mark removed, the Handwriting Recognition service will not interpret what you write in the Writing Pad until you click the Recognize Now button on the toolbar (Figure B-9 on the previous page). This allows you to pause and adjust your writing.

The best way to learn how to use the Writing Pad is to practice with it. Also, for more information, enter handwriting recognition in the Type a question for help box on the menu bar.

Write Anywhere

Rather than use Writing Pad, you can write anywhere on the screen by invoking the Write Anywhere command on the Handwriting menu (Figure B-11) that appears when you click the Handwriting button on the Language bar. In this case, the entire window is your writing pad.

In Figure B-11, the word, Report, is written in cursive using the mouse button. Shortly after the word is written, the Handwriting Recognition service interprets it, assigns it to the location of the insertion point, and erases what was written.

It is recommended that when you first start using the Write Anywhere service that you remove the check mark from the Automatic recognition check box in the Common sheet in the Handwriting Options dialog box (Figure B-10b). With the check mark removed, the Handwriting Recognition service will not interpret what you write on the screen until you click the Recognize Now button on the toolbar (Figure B-11).

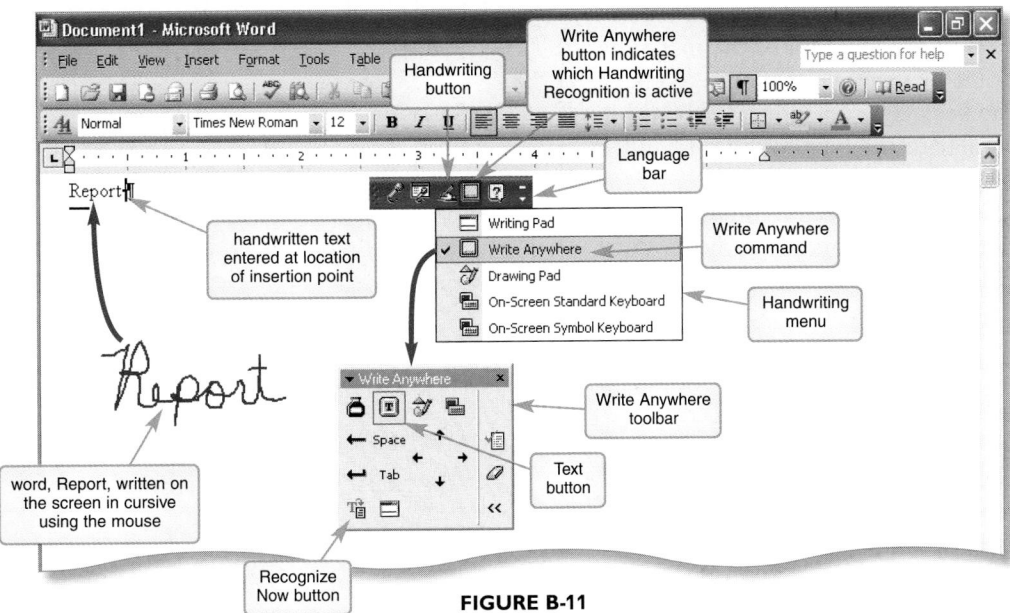

FIGURE B-11

Write Anywhere is more difficult to use than the Writing Pad, because when you click the mouse button, Word may interpret the action as moving the insertion point rather than starting to write. For this reason, it is recommended that you use the Writing Pad.

Drawing Pad

With the Drawing Pad, you can insert a freehand drawing or sketch in a Word document. To display the Drawing Pad, click the Handwriting button on the Language bar and then click Drawing Pad (Figure B-12). Create a drawing by dragging the mouse in the Drawing Pad. In Figure B-12, the mouse was used to draw a tic-tac-toe game. When you click the Insert Drawing button on the Drawing Pad toolbar, Word inserts the drawing in the document at the location of the insertion point. Other buttons on the toolbar allow you to erase a drawing, erase your last drawing stroke, copy the drawing to the Office Clipboard, or activate the Writing Pad.

FIGURE B-12

The best way to learn how to use the Drawing Pad is to practice with it. Also, for more information, enter drawing pad in the Type a question for help box on the menu bar.

On-Screen Keyboard

The On-Screen Standard Keyboard command on the Handwriting menu (Figure B-13) displays an on-screen keyboard. The **on-screen keyboard** lets you enter data at the location of the insertion point by using your mouse to click the keys. The on-screen keyboard is similar to the type found on hand-held computers or PDAs.

The On-Screen Symbol Keyboard command on the Handwriting menu (Figure B-13) displays a special on-screen key-board that allows you to enter symbols that are not on your key-board, as well as Unicode charac-ters. **Unicode characters** use a coding scheme capable of representing all the world's current languages.

FIGURE B-13

Speech Playback

Using **speech playback**, you can have your computer read back the text in a document. Word provides two buttons for speech playback: Speak Text and Pause Speaking. To show the Speak Text button on the Language bar, click the Options button on the Language bar (Figure B-14) and then click Speak Text on the Options menu. Similarly, click the Options button on the Language bar and then click Pause Speaking on the Options menu to show the Pause Speaking button on the Language bar.

To use speech playback, position the insertion point where you want the computer to start reading back the text in the document and then click the Speak Text button on the Language bar (Figure B-14). The computer reads from the location of the insertion point until the end of the document or until you click the Pause Speaking button on the Language bar. An alternative is to select the text you want the computer to read and then click the Speak Text button on the Language bar. After the computer reads back the selected text, it stops speech playback.

When you click the Speak Text button on the Language bar, it changes to a Stop Speaking button. Click the Stop Speaking button on the Language bar to stop the speech playback. If you click the Pause Speaking button on the Language bar to stop speech playback, the Pause Speaking button changes to a Resume Speaking button that you click when you want the computer to continue reading the document from the location at which it stopped reading.

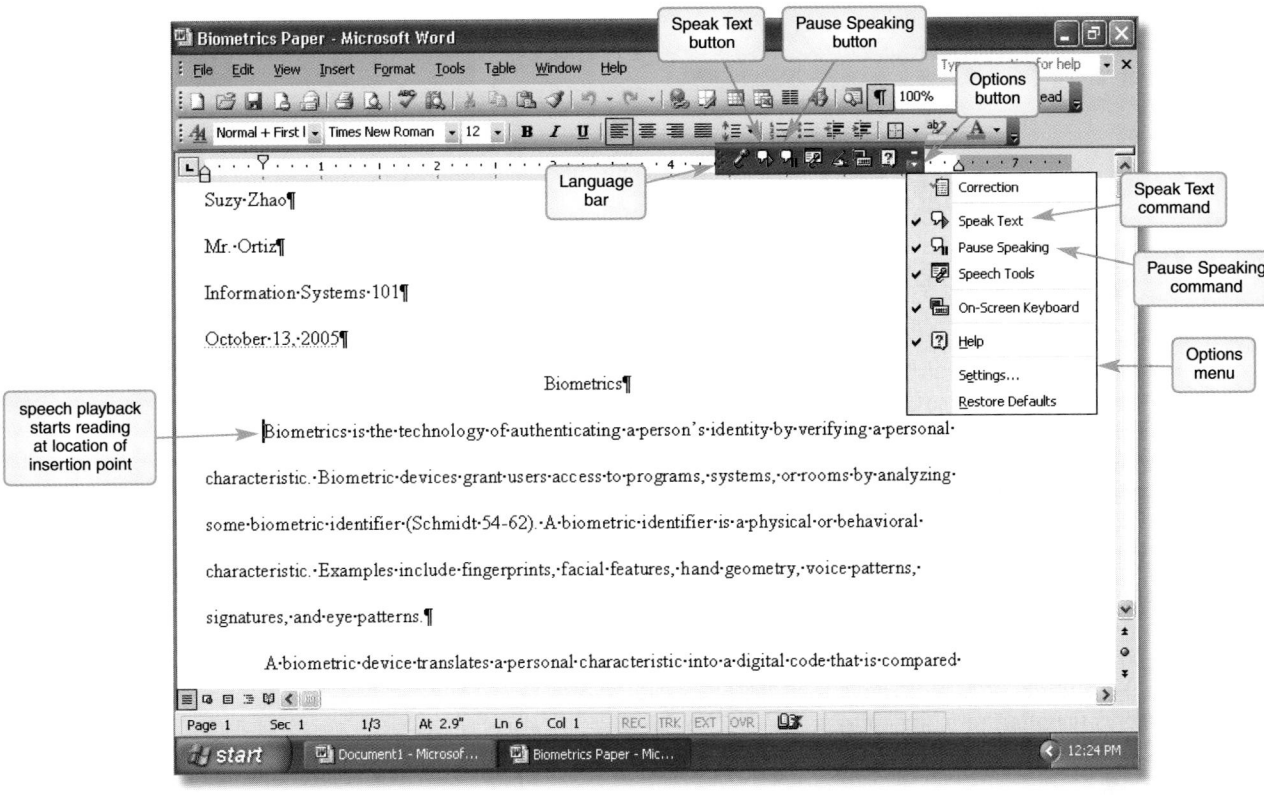

FIGURE B-14

Customizing Speech Playback

You can customize speech playback through the Speech Properties dialog box. Click the Speech Tools button on the Language bar and then click Options on the Speech Tools menu (Figure B-6a on page APP 17). When text services displays the Speech input settings dialog box (Figure B-6b), click the Advanced Speech button. When text services displays the Speech Properties dialog box, click the Text To Speech tab (Figure B-15). The Text To Speech sheet has two areas: Voice selection and Voice speed. The Voice selection area lets you choose between two male voices and one female voice. You can click the Preview Voice button to hear a sample of the voice. The Voice speed area contains a slider. Drag the slider to slow down or speed up the pace of the speaking voice.

FIGURE B-15

Appendix C

Publishing Office Web Pages to a Web Server

With the Office applications, you use the Save as Web Page command on the File menu to save the Web page to a Web server using one of two techniques: Web folders or File Transfer Protocol. A **Web folder** is an Office shortcut to a Web server. **File Transfer Protocol** (**FTP**) is an Internet standard that allows computers to exchange files with other computers on the Internet.

You should contact your network system administrator or technical support staff at your ISP to determine if their Web server supports Web folders, FTP, or both, and to obtain necessary permissions to access the Web server. If you decide to publish Web pages using a Web folder, you must have the Office Server Extensions (OSE) installed on your computer.

Using Web Folders to Publish Office Web Pages

When publishing to a Web folder, someone first must create the Web folder before you can save to it. If you are granted permission to create a Web folder, you must obtain the URL of the Web server, a user name, and possibly a password that allows you to access the Web server. You also must decide on a name for the Web folder. Table C-1 explains how to create a Web folder.

Office adds the name of the Web folder to the list of current Web folders. You can save to this folder, open files in the folder, rename the folder, or perform any operations you would to a folder on your hard disk. You can use your Office program or Windows Explorer to access this folder. Table C-2 explains how to save to a Web folder.

Using FTP to Publish Office Web Pages

When publishing a Web page using FTP, you first must add the FTP location to your computer before you can save to it. An FTP location, also called an **FTP site**, is a collection of files that reside on an FTP server. In this case, the FTP server is the Web server.

To add an FTP location, you must obtain the name of the FTP site, which usually is the address (URL) of the FTP server, and a user name and a password that allows you to access the FTP server. You save and open the Web pages on the FTP server using the name of the FTP site. Table C-3 explains how to add an FTP site.

Office adds the name of the FTP site to the FTP locations list in the Save As and Open dialog boxes. You can open and save files using this list. Table C-4 explains how to save to an FTP location.

Table C-1 Creating a Web Folder
1. Click File on the menu bar and then click Save As (or Open).
2. When the Save As dialog box (or Open dialog box) appears, click My Network Places on the My Places bar, and then click the Create New Folder button on the toolbar.
3. When the Add Network Place Wizard dialog box appears, click the Next button. If necessary, click Choose another network location. Click the Next button. Click the View some examples link, type the Internet or network address, and then click the Next button. Click Log on anonymously to deselect the check box, type your user name in the User name text box, and then click the Next button. Enter the name you want to call this network place and then click the Next button. Click the Finish button.

Table C-2 Saving to a Web Folder
1. Click File on the menu bar and then click Save As.
2. When the Save As dialog box appears, type the Web page file name in the File name text box. Do not press the ENTER key.
3. Click My Network Places on the My Places bar.
4. Double-click the Web folder name in the Save in list.
5. If the Enter Network Password dialog box appears, type the user name and password in the respective text boxes and then click the OK button.
6. Click the Save button in the Save As dialog box.

Table C-3 Adding an FTP Location
1. Click File on the menu bar and then click Save As (or Open).
2. In the Save As dialog box, click the Save in box arrow and then click Add/Modify FTP Locations in the Save in list; or in the Open dialog box, click the Look in box arrow and then click Add/Modify FTP Locations in the Look in list.
3. When the Add/Modify FTP Locations dialog box appears, type the name of the FTP site in the Name of FTP site text box. If the site allows anonymous logon, click Anonymous in the Log on as area; if you have a user name for the site, click User in the Log on as area and then enter the user name. Enter the password in the Password text box. Click the OK button.
4. Close the Save As or the Open dialog box.

Table C-4 Saving to an FTP Location
1. Click File on the menu bar and then click Save As.
2. When the Save As dialog box appears, type the Web page file name in the File name text box. Do not press the ENTER key.
3. Click the Save in box arrow and then click FTP Locations.
4. Double-click the name of the FTP site to which you wish to save.
5. When the FTP Log On dialog box appears, enter your user name and password and then click the OK button.
6. Click the Save button in the Save As dialog box.

Appendix D

Changing Screen Resolution and Resetting the Word Toolbars and Menus

This appendix explains how to change your screen resolution in Windows to the resolution used in this book. It also describes how to reset the Word toolbars and menus to their installation settings.

Changing Screen Resolution

The **screen resolution** indicates the number of pixels (dots) that your computer uses to display the letters, numbers, graphics, and background you see on your screen. The screen resolution usually is stated as the product of two numbers, such as 800 × 600 (pronounced 800 by 600). An 800 × 600 screen resolution results in a display of 800 distinct pixels on each of 600 lines, or about 480,000 pixels. The figures in this book were created using a screen resolution of 800 × 600.

The screen resolutions most commonly used today are 800 × 600 and 1024 × 768, although some Office specialists operate their computers at a much higher screen resolution, such as 2048 × 1536. The following steps show how to change the screen resolution from 1024 × 768 to 800 × 600.

To Change the Screen Resolution

1

• **If necessary, minimize all applications so that the Windows desktop appears.**

• **Right-click the Windows desktop.**

Windows displays the Windows desktop shortcut menu (Figure D-1).

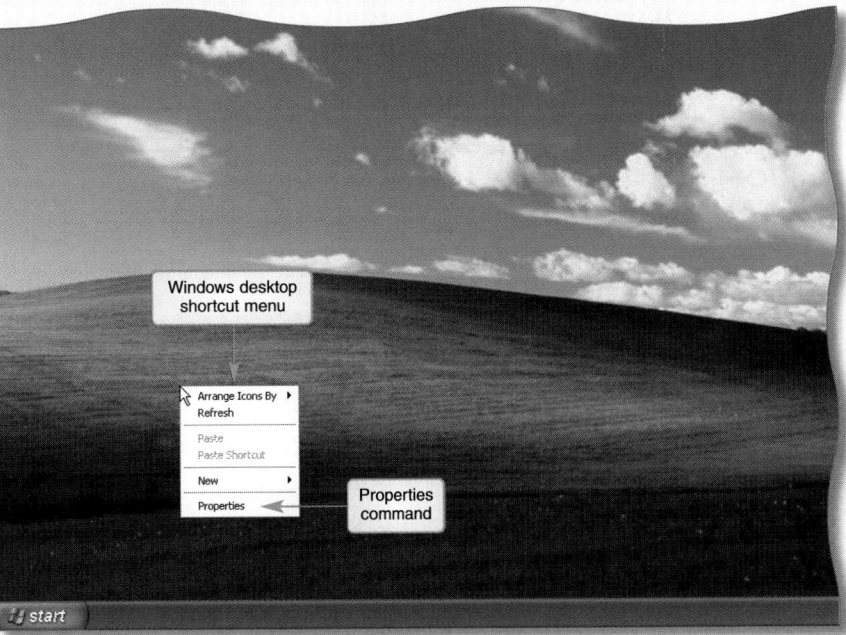

FIGURE D-1

2

• **Click Properties on the shortcut menu.**

• **When Windows displays the Display Properties dialog box, click the Settings tab.**

Windows displays the Settings sheet in the Display Properties dialog box (Figure D-2). The Settings sheet shows a preview of the Windows desktop using the current screen resolution (1024 x 768). The Settings sheet also shows the screen resolution and the color quality settings.

FIGURE D-2

3

• **Drag the slider in the Screen resolution area to the left so that the screen resolution changes to 800 x 600.**

The screen resolution in the Screen resolution area changes to 800 × 600 (Figure D-3). The Settings sheet shows a preview of the Windows desktop using the new screen resolution (800 × 600).

FIGURE D-3

4

• **Click the OK button.**

• **If Windows displays the Monitor Settings dialog box, click the Yes button.**

Windows changes the screen resolution from 1024 × 768 to 800 × 600 (Figure D-4).

800 × 600 screen resolution

start

FIGURE D-4

As shown in the previous steps, as you decrease the screen resolution, Windows displays less information on your screen, but the information increases in size. The reverse also is true: as you increase the screen resolution, Windows displays more information on your screen, but the information decreases in size.

Resetting the Word Toolbars and Menus

Word customization capabilities allow you to create custom toolbars by adding and deleting buttons and personalize menus based on their usage. Each time you start Word, the toolbars and menus are displayed using the same settings as the last time you used it. The figures in this book were created with the Word toolbars and menus set to the original, or installation, settings.

Resetting the Standard and Formatting Toolbars

The steps on the next page show how to reset the Standard and Formatting toolbars.

To Reset the Standard and Formatting Toolbars

1

• **Start Word.**

• **Click the Toolbar Options button on the Standard toolbar and then point to Add or Remove Buttons on the Toolbar Options menu.**

Word displays the Toolbar Options menu and the Add or Remove Buttons submenu (Figure D-5).

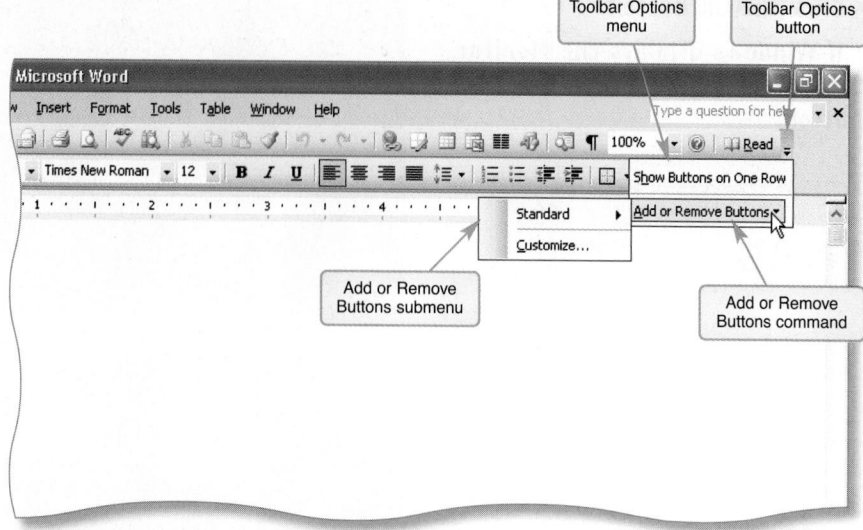

FIGURE D-5

2

• **Point to Standard on the Add or Remove Buttons submenu.**

• **When Word displays the Standard submenu, scroll down and then point to Reset Toolbar.**

The Standard submenu indicates the buttons and boxes that are displayed on the Standard toolbar (Figure D-6). To remove a button from the Standard toolbar, click a button name with a check mark to the left of the name to remove the check mark.

3

• **Click Reset Toolbar.**

• **If a Microsoft Word dialog box is displayed, click the Yes button.**

Word resets the Standard toolbar to its original settings.

4

• **Reset the Formatting toolbar by following Steps 1 through 3 and replacing any reference to the Standard toolbar with the Formatting toolbar.**

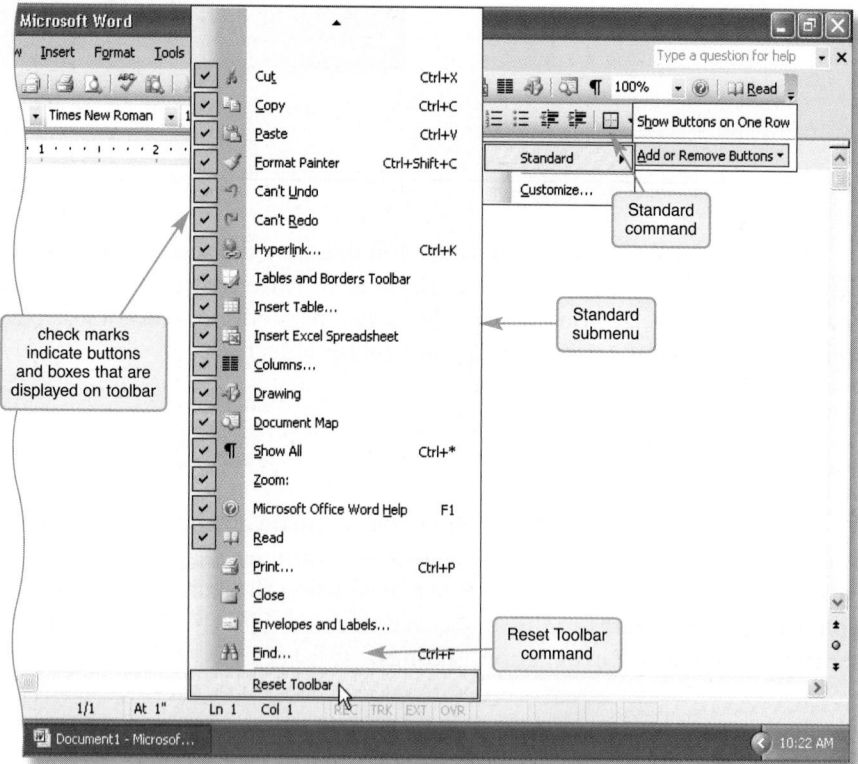

FIGURE D-6

Not only can you use the Standard submenu shown in Figure D-6 to reset the Standard toolbar to its original settings, but you also can use it to customize the Standard toolbar by adding and deleting buttons. To add or delete buttons, click the button name on the Standard submenu to add or remove the check mark. Buttons with a check mark to the left currently are displayed on the Standard toolbar; buttons without a check mark are not displayed on the Standard toolbar. You can complete the same tasks for the Formatting toolbar, using the Formatting submenu to add and delete buttons from the Formatting toolbar.

Resetting the Word Menus

The following steps show how to reset the Word menus to their original settings.

Other Ways

1. On View menu point to Toolbars, click Customize on Toolbars submenu, click Toolbars tab, click toolbar name, click Reset button, click OK button, click Close button
2. Right-click toolbar, click Customize on shortcut menu, click Toolbars tab, click toolbar name, click Reset button, click OK button, click Close button
3. In Voice Command mode, say "View, Toolbars, Customize, Toolbars, [desired toolbar name], Reset, OK, Close"

To Reset the Word Menus

1

• **Click the Toolbar Options button on the Standard toolbar and then point to Add or Remove Buttons on the Toolbar Options menu.**

Word displays the Toolbar Options menu and the Add or Remove Buttons submenu (Figure D-7).

FIGURE D-7

• **Click Customize on the Add or Remove Buttons submenu.**

• **When Word displays the Customize dialog box, click the Options tab.**

The Customize dialog box contains three sheets used for customizing the Word toolbars and menus (Figure D-8).

3

• **Click the Reset menu and toolbar usage data button.**

• **When Word displays the Microsoft Word dialog box, click the Yes button.**

• **Click the Close button in the Customize dialog box.**

Word resets the menus to the original settings.

FIGURE D-8

Other Ways

1. On View menu point to Toolbars, click Customize on Toolbars submenu, click Options tab, click Reset menu and toolbar usage data button, click Yes button, click Close button
2. Right-click toolbar, click Customize on shortcut menu, click Options tab, click Reset menu and toolbar usage data button, click Yes button, click Close button
3. In Voice Command mode, say "View, Toolbars, Customize, Options, Reset menu and toolbar usage data, Yes, Close"

Using the Options sheet in the Customize dialog box, as shown in Figure D-8 on the previous page, you can select options to personalize menus and toolbars. For example, you can select or deselect a check mark that instructs Word to display the Standard and Formatting toolbars on two rows. You also can select whether Word always displays full menus or displays short menus followed by full menus, after a short delay. Other options available on the Options sheet including settings to instruct Word to display toolbars with large icons; to use the appropriate font to display font names in the Font list; and to display a ScreenTip when a user points to a toolbar button. Clicking the Help button in the upper-right corner of the Customize dialog box displays Help topics that will assist you in customizing toolbars and menus.

Using the Commands sheet in the Customize dialog box, you can add buttons to toolbars and commands to menus. Recall that the menu bar at the top of the Word window is a special toolbar. To add buttons to a toolbar, click a category name in the Categories list and then drag the command name in the Commands list to a toolbar. To add commands to a menu, click a category name in the Categories list, drag the command name in the Commands list to a menu name on the menu bar, and then, when the menu is displayed, drag the command to the desired location in the list of menu commands.

Using the Toolbars sheet in the Customize dialog box, you can add new toolbars and reset existing toolbars and the menu. To add a new toolbar, click the New button, enter a toolbar name in the New Toolbar dialog box, and then click the OK button. Once the new toolbar is created, you can use the Commands sheet to add or remove buttons, as you would with any other toolbar. If you add one or more buttons to an existing toolbar and want to reset the toolbar to its original settings, click the toolbar name in the Toolbars list so a check mark is displayed to the left of the name and then click the Reset button. If you add commands to one or more menus and want to reset the menus to their default settings, click Menu Bar in the Toolbars list on the Toolbars sheet so a check mark is displayed to the left of the name and then click the Reset button. When you have finished, click the Close button to close the Customize dialog box.

Appendix E

Microsoft Office Specialist Certification

What Is Microsoft Office Specialist Certification?

Microsoft Office Specialist certification provides a framework for measuring your proficiency with the Microsoft Office 2003 applications, such as Microsoft Office Word 2003, Microsoft Office Excel 2003, Microsoft Office Access 2003, Microsoft Office PowerPoint 2003, and Microsoft Office Outlook 2003. The levels of certification are described in Table E-1.

Table E-1 Levels of Microsoft Office Specialist Certification			
LEVEL	DESCRIPTION	REQUIREMENTS	CREDENTIAL AWARDED
Microsoft Office Specialist	Indicates that you have an understanding of the basic features in a specific Microsoft Office 2003 application	Pass any ONE of the following: Microsoft Office Word 2003 Microsoft Office Excel 2003 Microsoft Office Access 2003 Microsoft Office PowerPoint 2003 Microsoft Office Outlook 2003	Candidates will be awarded one certificate for each of the Specialist-level exams they have passed: Microsoft Office Word 2003 Microsoft Office Excel 2003 Microsoft Office Access 2003 Microsoft Office PowerPoint 2003 Microsoft Office Outlook 2003
Microsoft Office Expert	Indicates that you have an understanding of the advanced features in a specific Microsoft Office 2003 application	Pass any ONE of the following: Microsoft Office Word 2003 Expert Microsoft Office Excel 2003 Expert	Candidates will be awarded one certificate for each of the Expert-level exams they have passed: Microsoft Office Word 2003 Expert Microsoft Office Excel 2003 Expert
Microsoft Office Master	Indicates that you have a comprehensive understanding of the features of four of the five primary Microsoft Office 2003 applications	Pass the following: Microsoft Office Word 2003 Expert Microsoft Office Excel 2003 Expert Microsoft Office PowerPoint 2003 And pass ONE of the following: Microsoft Office Access 2003 or Microsoft Office Outlook 2003	Candidates will be awarded the Microsoft Office Master certificate for fulfilling the requirements.

Why Should You Be Certified?

Being Microsoft Office certified provides a valuable industry credential — proof that you have the Office 2003 applications skills required by employers. By passing one or more Microsoft Office Specialist certification exams, you demonstrate your proficiency in a given Office 2003 application to employers. With more than 400 million people in 175 nations and 70 languages using Office applications, Microsoft is targeting Office 2003 certification to a wide variety of companies. These companies include temporary employment agencies that want to prove the expertise of their workers, large corporations looking for a way to measure the skill set of employees, and training companies and educational institutions seeking Microsoft Office 2003 teachers with appropriate credentials.

The Microsoft Office Specialist Certification Exams

You pay $50 to $100 each time you take an exam, whether you pass or fail. The fee varies among testing centers. The **Microsoft Office Expert** exams, which you can take up to 60 minutes to complete, consist of between 40 and 60 tasks that you perform on a personal computer in a simulated environment. The tasks require you to use the application just as you would in doing your job. The **Microsoft Office Specialist** exams contain fewer tasks, and you will have slightly less time to complete them. The tasks you will perform differ on the two types of exams. After passing designated Expert and Specialist exams, candidates are awarded the **Microsoft Office Master** certificate (see the requirements in Table E-1 on the previous page).

How to Prepare for the Microsoft Office Specialist Certification Exams

The Shelly Cashman Series offers several Microsoft-approved textbooks that cover the required objectives of the Microsoft Office Specialist certification exams. For a listing of the textbooks, visit the Shelly Cashman Series Microsoft Office Specialist Center at scsite.com/winoff2003/cert. Click the link Shelly Cashman Series Microsoft Office 2003-Approved Microsoft Office Textbooks (Figure E-1). After using any of the books listed in an instructor-led course, you should be prepared to take the indicated Microsoft Office Specialist certification exam.

How to Find an Authorized Testing Center

To locate a testing center, call 1-800-933-4493 in North America, or visit the Shelly Cashman Series Microsoft Office Specialist Center at scsite.com/winoff2003/cert. Click the link Locate an Authorized Testing Center Near You (Figure E-1). At this Web site, you can look for testing centers around the world.

Shelly Cashman Series Microsoft Office Specialist Center

The Shelly Cashman Series Microsoft Office Specialist Center (Figure E-1) lists more than 15 Web sites you can visit to obtain additional information about certification. The Web page (scsite.com/winoff2003/cert) includes links to general information about certification, choosing an application for certification, preparing for the certification exam, and taking and passing the certification exam.

FIGURE E-1

Microsoft Office Specialist Certification Maps for Microsoft Office Word 2003

This book has been approved by Microsoft as courseware for Microsoft Office Specialist certification. Table E-2 lists the skill sets and activities you should be familiar with if you plan to take the specialist-level examination for Microsoft Office Word 2003. Table E-3 on page APP 35 lists the skill sets and activities you should be familiar with if you plan to take the expert-level examination for Microsoft Office Word 2003.

Table E-2   Specialist-Level Skill Sets, Activities, and Locations in Book for Microsoft Office Word 2003

SKILL SET	SKILL BEING MEASURED	SKILL DEMONSTRATED IN BOOK	SKILL EXERCISE IN BOOK
I. Creating Content	A. Insert and edit text, symbols and special characters	WD 18-20, WD 22-25, WD 27, WD 57, WD 58-59, WD 83, WD 107, WD 112-114, WD 118-120, WD 125, WD 152, WD 154-157, WD 166-172, WD 180, WD 245, WD 360-361, WD 390-391, WD 418-419, WD 427-428	WD 65 (Apply Your Knowledge Steps 2-4), WD 67 (In the Lab 1 Step 3), WD 69 (In the Lab 2 Step 3), WD 70 (In the Lab 3 Step 1), WD 78 (Cases and Places 1-3), WD 129 (Apply Your Knowledge Steps 1, 7-8, 10), WD 131 (In the Lab 1 Steps 8-9), WD 133 (In the Lab 2 Part 1 Steps 3b, 4, Part 2 Step 1), WD 134 (In the Lab 3 Steps 2-3), WD 136 (Cases and Places 5), WD 199 (In the Lab 1 Steps 1-2), WD 202 (Cases and Places 5), WD 293 (In the Lab 3 Step 3a), WD 368 (In the Lab 1 Step 10), WD 371 (In the Lab 2 Step 11), WD 450-451 (In the Lab 1 Steps 2-6), WD 451-452 (In the Lab 2 Steps 2-6), WD 453 (In the Lab 3 Step 2)
	B. Insert frequently used pre-defined text	WD 84 (2nd paragraph), WD 89-90, WD 91-93, WD 177-179, WD 181-182	WD 129 (Apply Your Knowledge Step 10), WD 134 (In the Lab 3 Step 1), WD 135 (Cases and Places 1), WD 200 (In the Lab 2 Step 2)
	C. Navigate to specific content	WD 110-112, WD 116-117, WD 246	WD 129 (Apply Your Knowledge Step 6), WD 131 (In the Lab 1 Step 11), WD 133 (In the Lab 2 Part 2 Steps 2, 4), WD 456 (Cases and Places 5)
	D. Insert, position and size graphics	WD 46-50, WD 230-231, WD 304-311, WD 383-387, WD 393-396, WD 411-415	WD 60 (In the Lab 2 Steps 12-13), WD 65 (Apply Your Knowledge Step 15), WD 68 (In the Lab 1 Steps 13-14), WD 70 (In the Lab 3 Steps 6-7), WD 289 (In the Lab 1 Step 1), WD 291 (In the Lab 2 Step 1), WD 293 (In the Lab 3 Step 1), WD 367 (In the Lab 1 Step 2), WD 369 (In the Lab 2 Step 2), WD 374 (Cases and Places 1), WD 451 (In the Lab 2 Steps 2, 8), WD 454 (In the Lab 3 Step 6), WD 455-456 (Cases and Places 2-5)
	E. Create and modify diagrams and charts	WD 258-264, WD 421-431	WD 291 (In the Lab 2 Step 3b), WD 294 (In the Lab 3 Step 7), WD 295-296 (Cases and Places 2-5), WD 451 (In the Lab 2 Step 10), WD 455 (Cases and Places 4)
	F. Locate, select and insert supporting information	WD 118, WD 124, WD 125	WD 129 (Apply Your Knowledge Step 13), WD 134 (In the Lab 3 Step 3), WD 135 (Cases and Places 2-4)
II. Organizing Content	A. Insert and modify tables	WD 150-151, WD 182-187, WD 250-256, WD 272-280, WD 355, WD 357, WD 358	WD 198 (Apply Your Knowledge Steps 4-13), WD 200 (In the Lab 2 Step 2), WD 200 (In the Lab 3 Step 2), WD 287 (Apply Your Knowledge Steps 1-15), WD 290 (In the Lab 1 Step 3a), WD 291-292 (In the Lab 2 Step 3a), WD 293-294 (In the Lab 3 Steps 3c, 3e, 6), WD 295 (Cases and Places 1), WD 368 (In the Lab 1 Step 9), WD 370 (In the Lab 2 Step 10), WD 373 (In the Lab 3 Step 7)

Table E-2   Specialist-Level Skill Sets, Activities, and Locations in Book for Microsoft Office Word 2003 *(continued)*

SKILL SET	SKILL BEING MEASURED	SKILL DEMONSTRATED IN BOOK	SKILL EXERCISE IN BOOK
	B. Create bulleted lists, numbered lists and outlines	WD 153-154, WD 156, WD 187-189, WD 270-271, WD 329-331, WD 458-461	WD 70 (In the Lab 1 Step 5), WD 72 (Cases and Places 4), WD 199 (In the Lab 1), WD 200 (In the Lab 2), WD 200 (In the Lab 3 Step 2), WD 202 (Cases and Places 5), WD 290 (In the Lab 1 Step 3b), WD 291 (In the Lab 2 Step 3c), WD 293 (In the Lab 3 Step 3d), WD 295-296 (Cases and Places 2-5), WD 369-370 (In the Lab 2 Step 5), WD 374 (Cases and Places 1), WD 479 (In the Lab 1 Step 1)
	C. Insert and modify hyperlinks	WD 108, WD 122, WD 174, WD 207, WD 212-213	WD 131 (In the Lab 1 Step 8), WD 133 (In the Lab 2 Step 3b), WD 200 (In the Lab 2 Step 2), WD 216 (In the Lab 2 Steps 2, 4)
III. Formatting Content	A. Format text	WD 17, WD 34-36, WD 40-42, WD 44, WD 87, WD 117, WD 161, WD 173, WD 213, WD 221, WD 226-228, WD 265-269, WD 332, WD 403-404, WD 436-438, WD 459-460	WD 65 (Apply Your Knowledge Steps 5-6, 8-13), WD 67-68 (In the Lab 1 Steps 1, 5, 8-11), WD 68-69 (In the Lab 2 Steps 1, 5, 8-10), WD 70 (In the Lab 3 Steps 1, 3-4), WD 71 (Cases and Places 3), WD 72 (Cases and Places 4), WD 129 (Apply Your Knowledge Steps 2, 9), WD 198 (Apply Your Knowledge Steps 3, 9), WD 200 (In the Lab 2 Step 2), WD 288 (Apply Your Knowledge Step 19), WD 289 (In the Lab 1 Steps 1-2), WD 290 (In the Lab 1 Steps 2, 3c), WD 291 (In the Lab 2 Steps 1, 3c), WD 293 (In the Lab 3 Steps 1-2, 3e, 6e), WD 370 (In the Lab 2 Step 5), WD 449 (Apply Your Knowledge Steps 5-6), WD 455 (Cases and Places 1), WD 456 (Cases and Places 5), WD 479 (In the Lab 1 Step 1)
	B. Format paragraphs	WD 37-38, WD 79-80, WD 82-83, WD 86-89, WD 104-105, WD 163-165, WD 172-173, WD 176-177, WD 221-223, WD 223-225, WD 280, WD 312-313, WD 329-331, WD 388-390, WD 401, WD 409-410, WD 413	WD 65 (Apply Your Knowledge Steps 7, 14), WD 67 (In the Lab 1 Steps 6-7, 12), WD 69 (In the Lab 2 Steps 6-7, 11), WD 129 (Apply Your Knowledge Steps 3-4), WD 131 (In the Lab 1 Steps 3, 5-8), WD 133 (In the Lab 2 Part 1 Steps 1-3, Part 2 Step 2), WD 134 (In the Lab 3), WD 135-136 (Cases and Places 1-5), WD 198 (Apply Your Knowledge Steps 1-2), WD 199-200 (In the Lab 2 Step 2), WD 289 (In the Lab 1 Steps 1-2), WD 291 (In the Lab 2 Step 1-2), WD 293 (In the Lab Step 1), WD 368 (In the Lab 1 Step 3), WD 369-370 (In the Lab 2 Steps 3, 5), WD 449 (Apply Your Knowledge Step 1), WD 450-451 (In the Lab 1 Steps 2, 6, 8), WD 453-454 (In the Lab 3 Steps 2, 5, 9), WD 455 (Cases and Places 2-4)
	C. Apply and format columns	WD 398-400, WD 406, WD 409-410, WD 415-417, WD 420	WD 449 (Apply Your Knowledge Steps 2-4), WD 450-451 (In the Lab 1 Steps 3-4, 6-7), WD 451-452 (In the Lab 2 Steps 3-4, 6-7), WD 453-454 (In the Lab 3 Steps 3-5, 8-9), WD 455-456 (Cases and Places 1-5)
	D. Insert and modify content in headers and footers	WD 81-84, WD 246-249	WD 129 (Apply Your Knowledge Step 10), WD 131 (In the Lab 1 Step 4), WD 133 (In the Lab 2 Part 1 Step 1, Part 3 Step 2), WD 134 (In the Lab 3 Step 1), WD 135-136 (Cases and Places 1-5), WD 293-294 (In the Lab 3 Steps 8-9, 11), WD 295-296 (Cases and Places 2-5)
	E. Modify document layout and page setup	WD 77-79, WD 103, WD 235-237, WD 244, WD 356, WD 399, WD 404-405, WD 406	WD 131 (In the Lab 1 Steps 2, 7), WD 133 (In the Lab 2 Part 1 Steps 1-2, Part 3 Step 2), WD 134 (In the Lab 3), WD 135-136 (Cases and Places 1-5), WD 289 (In the Lab 1 Step 2), WD 291 (In the Lab 2 Step 2), WD 293-294 (In the Lab 3 Steps 2, 3b), WD 368 (In the Lab 1 Step 9), WD 370 (In the Lab 2 Step 10), WD 375-376 (Cases and Places 2-5), WD 449 (Apply Your Knowledge Steps 2-3), WD 451 (In the Lab 1 Steps 3, 7), WD 452 (In the Lab 2 Steps 3, 7), WD 453 (In the Lab 3 Steps 3, 8), WD 456-457 (Cases and Places 1-5)
IV. Collaborating	A. Circulate documents for review	WD 123, WD 461-462	WD 134 (In the Lab 3 Step 5), WD 479 (In the Lab 1 Step 3), WD 480 (In the Lab 2 Step 6)
	B. Compare and merge documents	WD 473-475	WD 480 (In the Lab 2 Steps 5-6), WD 480 (In the Lab 3)
	C. Insert, view and edit comments	WD 463-466	WD 480 (In the Lab 2 Steps 2-4), WD 480 (In the Lab 3)
	D. Track, accept and reject proposed changes	WD 466-471	WD 480 (In the Lab 2 Steps 3-6), WD 480 (In the Lab 3)
V. Formatting and Managing Documents	A. Create new documents using templates	WD 142-148, WD 175, WD 302-304	WD 199 (In the Lab 1 Steps 1-2), WD 201-202 (Cases and Places 1-5), WD 367 (In the Lab 1 Step 1), WD 369 (In the Lab 2 Step 1), WD 372 (In the Lab 3 Step 2)

Table E-2   Specialist-Level Skill Sets, Activities, and Locations in Book for Microsoft Office Word 2003

SKILL SET	SKILL BEING MEASURED	SKILL DEMONSTRATED IN BOOK	SKILL EXERCISE IN BOOK
	B. Review and modify document properties	WD 100-101, WD 102, WD 193-194	WD 131 (In the Lab 1 Step 12), WD 133 (In the Lab 2 Part 1 Step 7, Part 2 Step 6, Part 3 Step 5), WD 134 (In the Lab 3 Step 4), WD 200 (In the Lab 2 Steps 3, 6)
	C. Organize documents using file folders	WD 313, WD 344	WD 366 (Apply Your Knowledge Steps 3, 11), WD 368 (In the Lab 1 Steps 4-5, 8, 14), WD 370-371 (In the Lab 2 Steps 4-5, 8-9, 12, 15), WD 372-373 (In the Lab 3 Step 3), WD 374-376 (Cases and Places 1-5)
	D. Save documents in appropriate formats for different uses	WD 30, WD 205, WD 206, WD 240	WD 216 (In the Lab 1 Steps 2, 5-6), WD 216 (In the Lab 2 Step 2)
	E. Print documents, envelopes and labels	WD 53, WD 190-191, WD 241, WD 345-350, WD 350-351, WD 472	WD 65 (Apply Your Knowledge Step 17), WD 68 (In the Lab 1 Step 16), WD 69 (In the Lab 2, Step 15), WD 70 (In the Lab 3 Step 9), WD 131 (In the Lab 1 Step 12), WD 200 (In the Lab 2 Step 7), WD 200 (In the Lab 3 Step 3), WD 368 (In the Lab 1 Step 8), WD 370-371 (In the Lab 2 Steps 8-9), WD 479 (In the Lab 1 Step 1)
	F. Preview documents and Web pages	WD 52, WD 158-159, WD 208-209	WD 70 (In the Lab 3 Step 7), WD 199 (In the Lab 1 Step 5), WD 200 (In the Lab 2 Step 5), WD 216 (In the Lab 1 Step 3), WD 216 (In the Lab 2 Step 5), WD 290 (In the Lab 1 Step 4), WD 292 (In the Lab 2 Step 4), WD 294 (In the Lab 3 Step 14)
	G. Change and organize document views and windows	WD 9, WD 20-21, WD 77, WD 148-149, WD 169-170, WD 172, WD 220, WD 232, WD 282-284, WD 312, WD 361, WD 422, WD 426, WD 434-435, WD 441-444, WD 459, WD 472, WD 407-408	WD 67 (In the Lab 1 Step 2), WD 68 (In the Lab 2 Step 2), WD 71-72 (Cases and Places 1-5), WD 133 (In the Lab 2 Part 3 Step 1), WD 135-136 (Cases and Places 1-5), WD 199 (In the Lab 1 Step 2), WD 288 (Apply Your Knowledge Step 18), WD 289 (In the Lab 1), WD 294 (In the Lab 3 Step 15), WD 368 (In the Lab 1 Steps 3, 10), WD 369 (In the Lab 2 Step 3), WD 371 (In the Lab 2 Step 11), WD 449 (Apply Your Knowledge Steps 11-13), WD 450-451 (In the Lab 1), WD 451-452 (In the Lab 2), WD 452 (In the Lab 2 Step 13), WD 454 (In the Lab 3 Step 11), WD 455 (Cases and Places 1), WD 456 (Cases and Places 5), WD 479 (In the Lab 1 Step 1)

Table E-3   Expert-Level Skill Sets, Activities, and Locations in Book for Microsoft Office Word 2003

SKILL SET	SKILL BEING MEASURED	SKILL DEMONSTRATED IN BOOK	SKILL EXERCISE IN BOOK
I. Formatting Content	A. Create custom styles for text, tables and lists	WD 96-98, WD 267-269, WD 568-573	WD 133 (In the Lab 2 Part 1 Step 2, Part 2 Step 2), WD 135-136 (Cases and Places 2-5), WD 290 (In the Lab 1 Step 3c), WD 291 (In the Lab 2 Step 3c), WD 293-294 (In the Lab 3 Steps 3e and 6e), WD 625 (In the Lab 1 Steps 4 and 5), WD 627 (In the Lab 2 Step 5), WD 629 (In the Lab 3 Step 6)
	B. Control pagination	WD 103, WD 154-155, WD 236, WD 244, WD 653-654	WD 131 (In the Lab 1 Step 7), WD 133 (In the Lab 2 Part 1 Step 2, Part 3 Step 2), WD 134 (In the Lab 3 Step 1), WD 135-136 (Cases and Places 1-5), WD 199 (In the Lab 1 Step 2), WD 289 (In the Lab 1 Step 2), WD 291 (In the Lab 2 Step 2), WD 293 (In the Lab 3 Steps 2, 3b, and 5), WD 712 (In the Lab 1 Step 14), WD 714 (In the Lab 2 Step 16), WD 717 (In the Lab 3 Step 16)

Table E-3   Expert-Level Skill Sets, Activities, and Locations in Book for Microsoft Office Word 2003 *(continued)*

SKILL SET	SKILL BEING MEASURED	SKILL DEMONSTRATED IN BOOK	SKILL EXERCISE IN BOOK
	C. Format, position and resize graphics using advanced layout features	WD 49-51, WD 231, WD 310, WD 393-394, WD 396, WD 426, WD 427, WD 490-493, WD 563-567, WD 643-644	WD 69 (In the Lab 2 Step 13), WD 70 (In the Lab 3 Step 7), WD 199-200 (In the Lab 2 Step 1), WD 201 (Case 1), WD 289 (In the Lab 1 Step 1), WD 291 (In the Lab 2 Step 1), WD 293 (In the Lab 3 Step 1), WD 367 (In the Lab 1 Step 2), WD 369 (In the Lab 2 Step 2), WD 451-452 (In the Lab 2 Steps 2 and 10), WD 453-454 (In the Lab 3 Step 6), WD 455 (Cases and Places 2), WD 455 (Cases and Places 4), WD 544 (Apply Your Knowledge Step 15), WD 545 (In the Lab 1 Step 2), WD 546 (In the Lab 2 Step 2), WD 548 (In the Lab 3 Step 2), WD 550-551 (Cases and Places 1-4), WD 625 (In the Lab 1 Step 2), WD 627 (In the Lab 2 Step 2), WD 629 (In the Lab 3 Steps 2 and 3)
	D. Insert and modify objects	WD 304-311, WD 383-387, WD 411-415, WD 421-431, WD 518-527, WD 572-574, WD 642-644, WD 722-731	WD 367 (In the Lab 1 Step 2), WD 369 (In the Lab 2 Step 2), WD 450-451 (In the Lab 1 Steps 2 and 8), WD 451-452 (In the Lab 2 Steps 2 and 10), WD 453-454 (In the Lab 3 Steps 2 and 6), WD 455-456 (Cases and Places 2-5), WD 546 (In the Lab 1 Step 6), WD 547 (In the Lab 2 Steps 6 and 7), WD 549 (In the Lab 3 Step 6), WD 550-551 (Cases and Places 1-4), WD 625 (In the Lab 1 Step 3), WD 627 (In the Lab 2 Step 4), WD 629 (In the Lab 3 Step 5), WD 714 (In the Lab 2 Step 9), WD 718 (Cases and Places 1), WD 719 (Cases and Places 4), WD 732 (In the Lab 1 Step 2), WD 733 (In the Lab 2 Step 3), WD 733 (In the Lab 3 Steps 1, 2, and 4)
II. Organizing Content	A. Sort content in lists and tables	WD 109-110, WD 342, WD 359, WD 656	WD 133 (In the Lab 2 Part 1, Step 3), WD 134 (In the Lab 3 Step 1), WD 135-136 (Cases and Places 1-5), WD 366 (Apply Your Knowledge Step 6), WD 368 (In the Lab 1 Step 12), WD 371 (In the Lab 2 Step 13), WD 374 (Cases and Places 1), WD 719 (Cases and Places 5)
	B. Perform calculations in tables	WD 254	WD 198 (Apply Your Knowledge Step 7), WD 288 (Apply Your Knowledge Steps 9 and 10), WD 290 (In the Lab 1 Step 3a), WD 293 (In the Lab 3 Step 3c)
	C. Modify table formats	WD 177-178, WD 251-253, WD 274-275, WD 276-277, WD 279-280, WD 322-329, WD 358, WD 496-498, WD 500-511, WD 506, WD 514-516, WD 690-691	WD 200 (In the Lab 2 Step 2), WD 287-288 (Apply Your Knowledge Steps 4-7, 11-14), WD 289-290 (In the Lab 1 Step 3a), WD 291 (In the Lab 2 Step 3a), WD 293 (In the Lab 3 Step 3c), WD 366 (Apply Your Knowledge Step 2), WD 367-368 (In the Lab 1 Steps 4-5, 8, 9), WD 369-370 (In the Lab 2 Steps 4-5, 8-10), WD 372-373 (In the Lab 3 Steps 1, 3, 4, 7), WD 374-375 (Cases and Places 1-4), WD 544 (Apply Your Knowledge Step 14), WD 546 (In the Lab 1 Step 4), WD 546 (In the Lab 2 Step 4), WD 549 (In the Lab 3 Step 4), WD 719 (Cases and Places 5)
	D. Summarize document content using automated tools	WD 693-696	WD 717 (In the Lab 3 Steps 18 and 21), WD 718 (Cases and Places 2 and 3)
	E. Use automated tools for document navigation	WD 598-600, WD 612, WD 675-676, WD 683-385, WD 689	WD 629 (In the Lab 3 Step 9), WD 715 (In the Lab 3 Steps 15, 19, and 20), WD 718-719 (Cases and Places 1-5)
	F. Merge letters with other data sources	WD 301-304, WD 314-329, WD 335-345	WD 366 (Apply Your Knowledge Steps 4-8), WD 367-368 (In the Lab 1 Steps 1-7), WD 369-370 (In the Lab 2 Steps 1-7), WD 372-373 (In the Lab 3 Steps 1-6), WD 374-375 (Cases and Places 1-4)
	G. Merge labels with other data sources	WD 345-351	WD 368 (In the Lab 1 Step 8), WD 370 (In the Lab 2 Step 8), WD 374-375 (Cases and Places 1-4)
	H. Structure documents using XML	WD 694-703	WD 709-710 (Apply Your Knowledge Steps 1, 2, 3, 6-12, 16, and 17)
III. Formatting Documents	A. Create and modify forms	WD 486-529, WD 599-600, WD 604, WD 605-WD 616	WD 545-546 (In the Lab 1), WD 546-547 (In the Lab 2), WD 548-549 (In the Lab 3), WD 550-551 (Cases and Places 1-4), WD 627 (In the Lab 2 Step 8), WD 629 (In the Lab 3 Steps 9 and 10), WD 630-631 (Cases and Places 1-5)

Table E-3 Expert-Level Skill Sets, Activities, and Locations in Book for Microsoft Office Word 2003

SKILL SET	SKILL BEING MEASURED	SKILL DEMONSTRATED IN BOOK	SKILL EXERCISE IN BOOK
	B. Create and modify document background	WD 207-208, WD 280-281, WD 438-440, WD 522-523, WD 572-573	WD 216 (In the Lab 2 Steps 2 and 3), WD 294 (In the Lab 3 Step 10), WD 295-296 (Cases and Places 2-5), WD 449 (Apply Your Knowledge Steps 7-8), WD 456 (Cases and Places 5), WD 546 (In the Lab 1 Step 6), WD 547 (In the Lab 2 Step 6), WD 549 (In the Lab 3 Step 6), WD 550-551 (Cases and Places 1-4), WD 625 (In the Lab 1 Step 3), WD 627 (In the Lab 2 Step 4), WD 629 (In the Lab 3 Step 5), WD 630-631 (Cases and Places 2-4)
	C. Create and modify document indexes and tables	WD 645-646, WD 649-651, WD 670-675, WD 684-685	WD 719-720 (In the Lab 1 Steps 2, 5, 8, 9, 13), WD 713-714 (In the Lab 2 Steps 3, 10, 11, 15), WD 716-717 (In the Lab 3 Steps 5, 6, 7, 8, 13), WD 718-719 (Cases and Places 1-5)
	D. Insert and modify endnotes, footnotes, captions, and cross-references	WD 93-99, WD 647-649	WD 131 (In the Lab 1 Step 7), WD 133 (In the Lab 2 Part 1 Step 2, Part 2 Steps 3 and 4, Part 3 Steps 1-3), WD 134 (In the Lab 3 Step 1), WD 135-136 (Cases and Places 1-5), WD 711 (In the Lab 1 Step 3), WD 713 (In the Lab 2 Step 2)
	E. Create and manage master documents and subdocuments	WD 657-670, WD 681-682	WD 712-714 (In the Lab 2), WD 714-717 (In the Lab 3), WD 718-719 (Cases and Places 2-5)
IV. Collaborating	A. Modify track changes options	WD 471 (last paragraph on page), WD 472-473	WD 480 (In the Lab 3)
	B. Publish and edit Web documents	WD 205-215, Appendix C	WD 216 (In the Lab 1 Steps 2, 3, 4, 5), WD 216 (In the Lab 2 Steps 2-7)
	C. Manage document versions	WD 638-640	WD 719 (Cases and Places 5)
	D. Protect and restrict forms and documents	WD 528-529, WD 558-559, WD 614-615, WD 691-692, WD 703-704	WD 544 (Apply Your Knowledge Step 16), WD 546 (In the Lab 1 Step 8), WD 547 (In the Lab 2 Step 9), WD 549 (In the Lab 3 Step 8), WD 550-551 (Cases and Places 1-4), WD 626 (In the Lab 1 Step 9), WD 627 (In the Lab 2 Step 10), WD 629 (In the Lab 3 Step 17), WD 631 (Cases and Places 3 and 5), WD 710 (Apply Your Knowledge 13), WD 719 (Cases and Places 5)
	E. Attach digital signatures to documents	WD 617-620	WD 627 (In the Lab 2 Step 11), WD 630 (Cases and Places 2), WD 631 (Cases and Places 5)
	F. Customize document properties	WD 689-691	WD 719 (Cases and Places 5)
V. Customizing Word	A. Create, edit, and run macros	WD 576-581, WD 587-605	WD 624 (Apply Your Knowledge Steps 4-6), WD 626 (In the Lab 1 Steps 6 and 7), WD 627 (In the Lab 2 Steps 6, 7, and 8), WD 629 (In the Lab 3 Steps 7-10, 11, 13, 15), WD 630-631 (Cases and Places 1-4)
	B. Customize menus and toolbars	WD 582-586, Appendix D	WD 629 (In the Lab 3 Steps 11, 16), WD 630-631 (Cases and Places 1-5)
	C. Modify Word default settings	WD 121, WD 229, WD 538-540	WD 136 (Cases and Places 5), WD 296 (Cases and Places 5), WD 549 (In the Lab 3 Step 10), WD 550-551 (Cases and Places 1-4)

Index

Abbreviations, AutoCorrect entries for, WD 92
Accept All Changes in Document button (Reviewing toolbar), WD 471
Accept Change button (Reviewing toolbar), WD 470, WD 471
Access database file, data source saved as, WD 320
Active document, WD 160
ActiveX control, **WD 605**
  form field versus, WD 605
  inserting, WD 606-607
  procedure for, WD 610-613
  properties of, WD 608-610
Add a column, **WD 253**
Address
  envelopes, WD 350-352
  mailing labels, WD 345-350
  return, WD 333
AddressBlock merge field, **WD 323**
Adjustment handle, **WD 307**
Align button arrow (Tables and Borders toolbar), WD 279
Align Left button (Formatting toolbar), WD 37
Align Right button (Formatting toolbar), WD 37
Alignment
  cell, WD 279-280
  center, WD 38
  decimal point, WD 165
  of graphic, WD 644
  header, WD 247
  justified, WD 401, WD 408
  left, WD 36, WD 37
  paragraph using shortcut keys, WD 86
  right, WD 36-37
  section, WD 237
  tab stops and, WD 163, WD 389
  table, WD 186-187, WD 256
  text within cells, WD 183
  vertical, WD 232-234
All Programs submenu (Start menu), Microsoft Office, Microsoft Office Word 2003 command, WD 6
ALT+F9 (display format codes), **WD 335**
American Psychological Association (APA), **WD 74**, WD 75, WD 76
Animate text, WD 226, **WD 437-438**
Animation
  clip art, WD 229
  text, WD 226, WD 437-438
ANSI characters, **WD 391**
Antonym, **WD 119**
APA, see American Psychological Association
Applying style, WD 98, WD 267-269, WD 570
Arrange All command (Window menu), WD 443
Artistic border, WD 434
Ascending sort order, **WD 110**
ASK field, WD 328
Asterisk (*) wildcard character, WD 238
Attachment
  document for review as, WD 462
  research paper as, WD 123
AutoComplete tip, **WD 85, WD 182**
AutoCorrect, **WD 89-93**
AutoCorrect entries, WD 89, **WD 106**
  AutoFormat As You Type, WD 156
  creating, WD 90, WD 91-93
  smart tags, WD 115
  spell checking, WD 27
  symbols, WD 106
  turning off, WD 92
AutoCorrect Options button, **WD 90-91**
AutoCorrect Options command (Tools menu), WD 92
  AutoFormat As You Type, WD 156
  smart tags, WD 115
  spell checking, WD 27
AutoFit command (shortcut menu), columns, WD 185
AutoFit command (Table menu), columns, WD 185
AutoFormat As You Type, WD 155
  bulleted list, WD 187
  superscript, WD 156-157
Automatic macros, **WD 587-591**
Automatic page breaks, **WD 101-102**
AutoFormat diagram, WD 425
AutoNew macro, WD 588-592
  code, WD 592-594
AutoShape, **WD 305**
  adding formatted text to, WD 308-309
  adding in drawing canvas, WD 304-307
  banner, WD 305-309
  formatting, WD 307-308
  inserting, WD 306
  resizing, WD 308
AutoShape command (Format menu), WD 308
AutoShapes button (Drawing toolbar), WD 306

AutoShapes menu, Stars and Banners command, WD 306
AutoSum button (Tables and Borders toolbar), **WD 254**, WD 276
AutoSummarize command (Tools menu), WD 686
AutoSummarize feature, WD 685-686
AutoText command (Insert menu), WD 179, WD 181
AutoText entry, **WD 178-179**

Background color
  newsletter, WD 438-440
  pattern, WD 439-440
Background command (Format menu)
  newsletter, WD 438-439
  pattern, WD 439-440
  watermark, WD 281
Background repagination, **WD 101**
BACKSPACE key, erasing text using, WD 58
Back-to-back duplicating, WD 635
Backup copy, WD 30
Balloon Text style, WD 472-473
Banner
  adding AutoShape using drawing canvas, WD 304-309
  See also Nameplate
Base style, **WD 95**
Bibliographical references, WD 104
Biometrics research paper, WD 73-126
Blank line
  adding above paragraph, WD 280, WD 331
  between chart and table, WD 264
  entering using ENTER key, WD 20, WD 23
  removing above paragraph, WD 331
Block style, modified, WD 303
Body of newsletter
  first page of, WD 398-415
  second page of, WD 415-431
Body of research paper, WD 84
Body text, outline, WD 666
Body Text style, WD 328, WD 332
Bold, **WD 44**
  finding, WD 266
Bold button (Formatting toolbar), WD 44
Bookmark, WD 598, **WD 675-677**
  check box form field, WD 612
  drop-down form field, WD 599
  going to, WD 688-689
  text form field, WD 598-599, WD 612
Bookmark command (Insert menu), WD 675-676
Border, **WD 172**
  artistic, WD 434
  bottom, WD 172
  chart, WD 264
  color, WD 222
  deleting, WD 173
  form, WD 524
  graphic, WD 566
  line weight of, WD 222
  nameplate, WD 391
  newsletter, WD 433-434
  none, WD 495-496, WD 506
  paragraph, WD 221-223
  removing, WD 225
  ruling lines, WD 388
  table, WD 255, WD 273
Border button (Formatting toolbar)
  letterhead, WD 172
  most recently defined border and, WD 223
Border button arrow (Formatting toolbar), no border, WD 496
Border color, chart, WD 264
Border Color button (Tables and Borders toolbar), WD 222
Borderless table, WD 495-496, WD 506
Borders and Shading command (Format menu)
  page border, WD 433
  paragraph border, WD 223
  paragraph shading, WD 225
  pull-quote shading, WD 413
  vertical rule, WD 409-410
Borders and Shading dialog box, WD 223
Bottom border, WD 172, WD 391
Break command (Insert menu)
  continuous section break, WD 399, WD 416, WD 420
  next page section break, WD 658, WD 659
  page break, WD 103
Brightness, of graphic, WD 396, WD 491
Browsing document, WD 110-112
Bullet, **WD 154**, WD 187-189
  customizing, WD 270-271
Bulleted list, **WD 154**, WD 187-189, WD 269-271
  sorting, WD 655-656
Bullets and Numbering command (Format menu), outline numbered list, WD 330

Bullets and Numbering dialog box
  outline numbered list, WD 330
  picture bullets, WD 270-271
Business form letters, **WD 298-343**
  banner, WD 304-309
  body of, WD 324
  composing main document, WD 321-337
  data source, see Data source
  envelopes, WD 350-352
  mailing labels, WD 345-350
  main document, see Main document
  merging, see Merging
  merging documents, WD 338-342
  outline numbered list, WD 329-331
  printing, WD 326-327
Business letters
  components of, WD 175, WD 303
  form letters, see Business form letters
  salutation, WD 324
Button
  ActiveX control, WD 606-613
  adding to toolbar, WD 582-586
  assigning Web address to, WD 585
  deleting, WD 585-586
  images for, WD 584

Camera, inserting graphic from, WD 231
Canceling actions, WD 39
Cap
  drop, WD 403-404, WD 432
  stick-up, WD 404
Capital letter
  dropped, WD 403-404, WD 432
  stick-up, WD 404
  See also Capitalization
Capitalization
  CAPS LOCK key and, WD 22, WD 92
  errors, WD 92
CAPS LOCK key, WD 22, WD 92
Caption, **WD 645-647**
  ActiveX control, WD 608-609
  check box, WD 508
  cross-reference to, WD 647-649
  field, WD 497
Cascade down shape, WordArt and, WD 386-387
Case-sensitive, **WD 691**
Cell, WD 151, WD 183
  changing contents of, WD 184
  formatting text, WD 252
  line spacing in, WD 252
  margin at top of, WD 357-358
  merging, WD 252
  right-align contents of, WD 256
  shading, WD 277
  splitting, WD 253
  vertically displaying text in, WD 276-277
Center, **WD 38**
Center button (Formatting toolbar), WD 38, WD 45
Centering
  chart, WD 264
  insertion point, WD 230
  newsletter title, WD 387
  paragraph containing graphic, WD 48
  paragraph using Formatting toolbar, WD 38, WD 45
  paragraph using shortcut keys, WD 86
  table, WD 187, WD 256
  title of works cited page, WD 104
  vertically, WD 232-234
Certification authority, **WD 617**
Change Text Direction button (Tables and Borders toolbar), WD 277
Changed line, **WD 467**
Changes, tracking, WD 457, WD 466-472
Character formats, **WD 267**
Character formatting, **WD 31**, WD 267
  Grand Prix announcement document, WD 31-45
  sales proposal title page, WD 226-228
  shortcut keys for, WD 87
Character style, **WD 152, WD 568**
  applying, WD 267-269, WD 570
  creating, WD 267-269
Characters
  ANSI, WD 391
  drop cap, WD 403-404, WD 432
  formatting, see Character formatting
  formatting nonadjacent, WD 257-258
  merge field, WD 323
  nonprinting, WD 20
  special, see Special characters
  stick-up cap, WD 404
  superscript, WD 258
  Unicode, APP 22
  See also Text

Chart
  creating from Excel worksheet, WD 726-731
  Excel, WD 264
  formatting, WD 264
  legend, WD 260-261
  resizing, WD 262
  of table in sales proposal, WD 258-265
  types, WD 262-263
Chart Type command (shortcut menu), WD 263
Chart Type command (shortcut menu), WD 263
Check box, WD 484, WD 505-509
Check box form field, bookmark for, WD 612
Child elements, **WD 697**
Citations
  footnote, WD 93
  MLA style, WD 76
Clearing formatting, WD 173, WD 225-226, WD 235, WD 329, WD 388-389
Clever Clicks newsletter, WD 378-445
Click and Type, **WD 82-83**
Clip art, **WD 45, WD 229**
  animation, WD 229
  Clip Organizer and, WD 45
  on data disk, WD 231
  floating, WD 392-396
  inserting using Insert, Picture command, WD 46, WD 230, WD 392, WD 563
  online form, WD 490-494
  resizing, WD 231
  searching for, WD 47, WD 563
  on Web, WD 48, WD 229-232, WD 392
  See also Graphics
Clip Art task pane, WD 47-48, WD 229
Clip Organizer, **WD 45, WD 229**
Clipboard, **WD 112**, WD 245, WD 728-729
  Office, see Office Clipboard
  Windows, see Windows Clipboard
Clipboard task pane, WD 168-169
Close All command (File menu), WD 362
Close button (menu bar), WD 59
Close button (title bar), WD 54, WD 62
Close command (File menu), WD 59
Close the Language bar command (shortcut menu), WD 8
Closed (Language bar), **WD 16**
Closing
  all open documents, WD 362-363
  document and not saving, WD 59
  form letters, WD 362
  Getting Started task pane, WD 8
  Language bar, WD 8, WD 16
  note pane, WD 99
  window, WD 54, WD 62
Code, **WD 554**
  modifying, WD 596
  VBA, WD 592-596
Code statements, **WD 594**
  ActiveX control, WD 611, WD 612
  entering, WD 597
  executable, WD 594, WD 610, WD 611, WD 612
  object properties and, WD 614
  planning and writing, WD 601-603
Collaborate, **WD 457-478**
Collapsed
  document, **WD 663**
  heading, **WD 460**
Collect, **WD 165**
Colon, in salutation, WD 323
Color
  AutoShape, WD 307
  border, WD 222
  brightening, WD 396
  darkening, WD 396
  diagram segment, WD 422
  drawing object, WD 520
  drop cap, WD 432
  gradient, WD 384, WD 385
  highlight, WD 436
  reviewer ink, WD 472
  ruling lines, WD 388
  shading, WD 224-225
  text box, WD 412
  underline, WD 511-512
  WordArt drawing object, WD 385-386
Color scheme, preset, WD 572-573
Column boundary, **WD 186**
Column break, WD 404-406
Column number, displayed on status bar, WD 11
Columns, data source, WD 314
Columns, newsletter, WD 398-410
  balancing, WD 419-420
  continuous section break, WD 398-399, WD 415-416, WD 420
  formatting, WD 415-417
  multiple, WD 398-400
  number of, WD 400, WD 417
  snaking, WD 398-400, WD 415-416, WD 420

vertical rule between, WD 380, WD 409-410
width, WD 398, WD 400
Columns, table, WS 150, WD 182, WD 183
adding, WD 185, WD 253
boundary, WD 253
deleting, WD 250-251
distributing evenly, WD 275
drawing, WD 273-274
resizing, WD 185-186, WD 253
summing, WD 254, WD 276
width of, WD 279
Columns button (Standard toolbar), WD 400
Columns command (Format menu)
number of columns, WD 400
vertical rule, WD 409
Comma, in salutation, WD 323
Comma-delimited text file, **WD 533**
Command button, for ActiveX control, WD 606-613
Command Button button (Control Toolbox toolbar), WD 607
CommandButton1_Click procedure, WD 611
Commands
adding to menu, WD 586
deleting, WD 586
dimmed, WD 13
hidden, WD 13
macro, *see* Macro
menu, *see* Menu
name of, WD 586
procedure, WD 594-596
protected document, WD 615
redoing, WD 39
smart tag, WD 116
speaking, WD 7, WD 16
submenu, WD 13, WD 46
undoing, WD 39, WD 58
Comment, **WD 463**
editing, WD 464-465
ink, WD 465
inserting, WD 463-464, WD 465
locating, WD 466
reviewing, WD 468-472
voice, WD 464
Comment balloons, **WD 464,** WD 465, WD 469
Comment marks, **WD 463-464,** WD 465
Comment Text style, WD 473
Compare and Merge Documents command (Tools menu), WD 473-474
Compare Side by Side command (Window menu), WD 443
Compare Side by Side toolbar, **WD 443**
Complimentary close, **WD 175,** WD 189
Computer programming, WD 554
Computer virus, **WD 559**
Concordance file, WD 672
Condition, **WD 326**
merge, WD 340, WD 341
Context-sensitive menu, WD 12
Continuous section break, WD 398-399, WD 415-416, WD 420
Contrast, in graphics, WD 490-491
Control Toolbox toolbar, WD 606, WD 607
Convert command (Table menu), text to table, WD 355
Copy button (Standard toolbar), object, WD 721, WD 729
Copying
diagram, WD 429-430
Excel chart to Word document, WD 264
Excel data, WD 728-730
formatting, WD 428, WD 512
macro, WD 604
newsletter nameplate, WD 418-419
object, WD 721, WD 729
Office Clipboard and, WD 165-171
tables, WD 256
text across split window, WD 443
text from Research task pane, WD 125
Correcting errors, WD 18, WD 56-59
AutoCorrect and, WD 89-93
spelling, *see* Spell checking
Cover letter, **WD 138,** WD 139
components of, WD 140, WD 175
creating, WD 175-190
envelopes for, WD 190-191
letterhead for, WD 160-175
Create New Folder button (dialog boxes), WD 313
Create Subdocument button (Outlining toolbar), WD 665
Crop (graphics), **WD 564-567**
Crop button (Picture toolbar), WD 565
Cropping handle, **WD 565**
Cross-reference, **WD 647-649**
CTRL+0 (add or remove blank line), WD 331
CTRL+5 (cell line spacing), **WD 252**
CTRL+clicking, hyperlink and, **WD 107**
CTRL+ENTER, manual page break using, **WD 103**
CTRL+HOME, moving to beginning of document using, **WD 33**
Current date, WD 177
text form field that displays, WD 509-511
Current time, WD 511
Custom tab stop, **WD 164,** WD 176-177
Cut button (Standard toolbar), WD 114

Cut command (Edit menu), WD 59, WD 114, WD 244
Cutting, **WD 112**
using Cut command, WD 59, WD 115
using Standard toolbar, WD 114
Cylinder chart, WD 263

Darkening graphic, WD 396
Data Disk, clip art from, WD 231, WD 393
Data entry, online form for, *see* Online form
Data entry area, of online form, WD 498, WD 518-527
Data field, **WD 314**
Data record, **WD 314**
Data source, **WD 300**
creating, WD 314-321
editing records in, WD 321
location of, WD 351
mailing labels, WD 345-350
merging to directory, WD 352-353
merging with main document, WD 338-342
opening main document and, WD 335
organizing items in, WD 319
printing envelopes using, WD 350-352
saving, WD 320, WD 321
sorting, WD 342, WD 343
Database, data source saved as, WD 320
Datasheet, **WD 260**
Datasheet window, **WD 260**
Date
current, WD 177, WD 303
current, in text form field, WD 509-511
newsletter nameplate, WD 382
Date and Time command (Insert menu), WD 177, WD 341
Date field
formatting, WD 322
inserting, WD 341
Date line, **WD 175,** WD 176-177
Decimal point, alignment on, WD 165
Default (font), **WD 16**
Default text, **WD 498**
Delete a row, WD 251
Delete Columns command (shortcut menu), WD 251
Delete command (Table menu), columns or rows, WD 251
DELETE key, WD 58, WD 59
Delete Rows command (shortcut menu), WD 251
Deleting
AutoShape, WD 307
border, WD 173
button, WD 585-586
column, WD 250-251
command, WD 586
file, WD 240
linked object, WD 726
macro, WD 605
note, WD 99
page break, WD 244
schema, WD 696
section break, WD 238
style, WD 572
subdocument, WD 667
table contents, WD 256
text from document, WD 56, WD 58-59
watermark, WD 281
Demote to Body Text button (Outlining toolbar), WD 666
Demoted
heading level, WD 459, WD 460
list item, **WD 330,** WD 331
Descending sort order, **WD 110**
Design mode, **WD 605,** WD 607
Designing online form, WD 485-486
Desk checking, **WD 602-603,** WD 610
Desktop publishing terminology, WD 380
Destination document, **WD 721-722,** WD 724
Destination object, WD 418-419
Diagram, in newsletter, WD 421-431
copying and pasting, WD 429-430
formatting, WD 425, WD 427-428
moving, WD 431
resizing, WD 425-426
segments, WD 422-423
text in, WD 423-424, WD 426-427, WD 431
wrap text in, WD 426-427, WD 431
Diagram command (Insert menu), WD 421
Dialog boxes
Create New Folder button in, WD 313
Help buttons in, APP 7
resizing, WD 313
Dictating text, WD 7, WD 16, APP 15
Dictation mode, **APP 15**
Dictionary, spelling, WD 19, WD 25, WD 121
Digital camera, WD 45
Digital certificate, **WD 617**
Digital signature, **WD 617-620**
Dimension, of table, **WD 182**
Dimmed command, WD 13
Directory, merging records to, **WD 352-362**
Disabled macro, **WD 559-560**
Displaying
Clipboard task pane, WD 168-169
documents side by side, WD 443

field codes, WD 335
formatting marks, WD 20-21
Getting Started task pane, WD 10
header area, WD 81-82
menu, WD 12-13
smart tags, WD 115
toolbar buttons on two rows, WD 9, WD 14
Distribute Rows Evenly button (Tables and Borders toolbar), WD 274
.doc extension, **WD 28**
Dock, **WD 82**
Docked task pane title bar, WD 7
Docked toolbar, **WD 14,** WD 82, WD 223, WD 321
Document
active, WD 160
Biometrics research paper, WD 73-126
browsing, WD 110-112
changes made to, WD 56-59
chart, WD 726-731
clip art in, *see* Clip art
closing all open, WD 362-363
closing but not saving, WD 59
collaboration on, *see* Collaborate
collapsed, WD 663
comparing and merging, WD 473-475
destination, WD 721-722, WD 724
digitally signed, WD 617
displaying side by side, WD 443
e-mailing for review, WD 461-463
entering text, WD 16-27
expanded, WD 663, WD 682
formatting, *see* Formatting
going to specific location in, WD 110-112
Grand Prix announcement, WD 3-62
hyphenating, WD 652-653
long, WD 634
main, *see* Main document
master, *see* Master document
merging after reviewing, WD 473-475
merging for mail merge, WD 338-342
multiple open, WD 160
newsletter, WD 378-445
online form, *see* Online form
opening existing, WD 55-56
password-protected, WD 691-692
protected, WD 486, WD 528, WD 592, WD 614-615, WD 703
reviewing, WD 461-475
River Run Campground form letter, WD 298-343
saving existing, with new file name, WD 52
saving existing, with same file name, WD 51-52
saving new, WD 28-31
scrolling, WD 23-25, WD 43
section, *see* Section
source, WD 721-722, WD 724
statistics about, WD 101
sub-, *see* Subdocument
template, *see* Template
tracking changes, WD 457, WD 466-472
unprotecting, WD 486, WD 538, WD 558-559
versions of, WD 638-640
worksheet integration, WD 721-733
XML, WD 693-705
zooming, *see* Zooming
Document Map, **WD 683-684**
Document name, on title bar, WD 30
Document summary, **WD 193-194**
Document template, **WD 487**
macros saved in, WD 577
Document window, **WD 10-12**
merged document sent to, WD 339
scrolling, WD 23-25
template and, WD 487
Double-space, WD 79
footnote, WD 96, WD 97
text, WD 79-80
Draft, printing, WD 241, WD 336
Drag-and-drop editing, **WD 112-114**
Draw button (Drawing toolbar)
flipping graphic using, WD 394
moving graphic using, WD 395
Draw menu, Grid command, WD 564
Draw Table button (Tables and Borders toolbar), WD 223, **WD 272**
Draw Table command (Table menu), WD 273
Draw Table feature, WD 183, **WD 271-275**
Drawing canvas, **WD 304-307**
adding AutoShape in, WD 304-307
banner AutoShape, WD 305-309
formatting, WD 311
resizing, WD 309-310
transparent fill color, WD 310-311
Drawing Canvas command (Format menu), WD 311
Drawing Canvas toolbar, WD 305
Drawing grid, **WD 395,** WD 564
Drawing object, **WD 304, WD 382**
adding in drawing canvas, WD 304-307
color of, WD 520
filling with texture, WD 522-523
line color, WD 524-525
online form, WD 518-527
sending behind text, WD 521-522

shadow, WD 520, WD 526-527
stacking order, WD 520-522
3-D effect, WD 520, WD 574
See also WordArt drawing object
Drawing Pad, APP 21-22
Drawing table, WD 271-275
Drawing toolbar, WD 232, WD 518
Drop cap, **WD 403-404**
color, WD 432
Drop Cap command (Format menu), WD 403
Drop-down form field, WD 484, **WD 500-504**
bookmark for, WD 599

Edit menu
Cut command, WD 59, WD 114, page break, WD 244
Find command, formats, WD 267
Go To command, comments, WD 466
Go To command, page number, WD 429
Go To command, WD 111
Office Clipboard command, WD 166-167
Paste command, WD 114, WD 171
Paste Special command, linking text using, WD 418-419
Repeat command, WD 39
Replace command, WD 117
Undo command, WD 39
Edit mode, **WD 620**
Editing
cell contents, WD 184
comment, WD 464-465
data source records, WD 321
drag-and-drop, WD 112-114
field, WD 322
linked object, WD 722, WD 732, WD 733
macro, WD 592-598
note, WD 99
in reading layout view, WD 444
restrictions, WD 703
versions of document, WD 640
Electronic mail, *see* E-mail
Electronic signatures, WD 334
Elegant Merge Letter template, WD 302-303
Element, **WD 693**
in XML document, WD 696-698, WD 700
E-mail (electronic mail)
digital signature and, WD 617
document for review, WD 461-463
form, WD 540
research paper, WD 123
E-mail address, removing hyperlink, WD 174
E-mail button (Standard toolbar), WD 123
E-mail toolbar, **WD 462**
Embedded object, **WD 721,** WD 726
En dash, WD 158
Enabled macro, **WD 559-560**
End mark, **WD 11**
line spacing and, WD 80
End Sub statement, **WD 594**
Endnote, **WD 93,** WD 94
End-of-cell mark, **WD 151,** WD 183, WD 274, WD 497
End-of-row mark, WD 497
ENTER key
AutoComplete tip and, WD 85, WD 182
blank lines, WD 20, WD 23
bulleted list and, WD 154, WD 188
displaying formatting marks and, WD 20
hyperlink and, WD 108
new paragraph started using, WD 18, WD 21
paragraph formatting and, WD 89
paragraph in table cell using, WD 183
Entry-level resume, WD 144
Envelopes, WD 190-191
printing using mail merge, WD 350-352
Eraser button (Tables and Borders toolbar), **WD 274**
Event, **WD 554**
ActiveX control, WD 610-613
Excel chart, copying to Word document, WD 264
Excel workbook, opening, WD 728
Excel worksheet
copying to Word document, WD 264
creating chart from, WD 726-731
linking to Word document, WD 721-733
Executable code statement, **WD 594,** WD 610, WD 611, WD 612
Execute (code), **WD 554**
Execute the macro, **WD 576,** WD 581
Exit command (File menu), WD 54
Expanded
heading, **WD 460**
document, **WD 663,** WD 682
eXtensible Markup Language, *see* XML
Expression, in condition, WD 326

F1 key (Help), APP 1, WD 514
F3 key (AutoText entry), WD 181
F9 key (update field), **WD 322**
F12 (Save As dialog box), WD 240
False text, **WD 326**
Faxes, merged, WD 301
Field, **WD 322,** WD 485, **WD 646**
adding to data source, WD 316-317
current date or time as, WD 178

data, WD 314
document property, WD 691
form, *see* Form field
index entry, WD 650
inserting in main document, WD 323-324
locking, WD 334
merge, WD 323
merging to directory, WD 354
modifying, WD 322
shading, WD 517
updating, WD 322
Field caption, WD 497
Field codes, **WD 335**
displaying, WD 335, WD 646
printing, WD 336-337
turning off, WD 248, WD 326
Field command (Insert menu), WD 691
Field name, WD 314, WD 316-317
Field results, **WD 335**, WD 646
Field specification, **WD 485**
File, **WD 28**
comma-delimited text, WD 533
deleting, WD 240
digital signature, WD 617-620
graphic, *see* Graphic file
inserting in newsletter, WD 401-402, WD 406
password-protected, WD 691-692
previewing, WD 238-239, WD 240
source, WD 418
types, WD 30, WD 240
XML, WD 693
XSL transformation, WD 702
File attachment, *see* Attachment
File command (Insert menu), WD 239, WD 402, WD 407
File digital signature, **WD 617**
File extension, WD 487
worksheet, WD 725
File menu
Close All command, WD 362
Close command, WD 59
Exit command, WD 54
file names on, WD 55
New command, Resume Wizard, WD 142
New command, templates, WD 302, WD 487
Page Setup command, gutter margin, WD 680
Page Setup command, margins, WD 78, WD 381
Page Setup command, page orientation, WD 356
Page Setup command, vertical alignment, WD 237, WD 233
Print command, document, WD 13, WD 53
Print command, draft, WD 336
Print command, field codes, WD 336
Print command, page range, WD 241
Print Preview command, WD 159
Properties command, customizing, WD 690
Properties command, document summary, WD 193
Properties command, statistics, WD 101
Save All command, WD 363
Save As command, WD 30
Save As command, form data, WD 534
Save As command, passwords, WD 691
Send To command, document for review, WD 462
Send To command, form, WD 540
Send To command, outline to PowerPoint, WD 476
Send To command, research paper, WD 123
Versions command, WD 638-639
File name, **WD 28**
on File menu, WD 55
saving existing document with new, WD 52
saving existing document with same, WD 51-52
searching using wildcard, WD 238
File properties, **WD 193-194**
File Transfer Protocol, *see* FTP
Fill, **WD 522**
Fill color
diagram segment, WD 422
for drawing object, WD 522-523
transparent, WD 309-310
FILLIN field, WD 328
Find and Replace dialog box
formats, WD 265-266
go to text, WD 246
text, WD 116, WD 246
Finding
format, WD 265-266
text, WD 116, WD 246
First Line Indent marker, **WD 87**, WD 88
centering and, WD 104
First Record button (Mail Merge toolbar), **WD 343**
First-line indent, **WD 87**, WD 88
footnote, WD 96, WD 98
Flagged word, WD 26, WD 27, WD 119
Flipping graphic, WD 394-395

Floating graphic, WD 393-394, WD 563-564
changing from inline graphic to, WD 491, WD 643
caption, WD 645-646
Floating object, **WD 392**-397
changing inline object to, WD 393-394
text wrapping in, WD 426-427
Floating task pane title bar, WD 7
Floating toolbar, **WD 14**, WD 82
converting submenu to, WD 307
Folder, **WD 29**
creating in Word, WD 313
renaming, WD 344
for templates, WD 538
Web, APP 24
Font, **WD 16**
default, changing, WD 228-229
finding, WD 266
formatting marks, WD 41
variable character, WD 27
Font box arrow (Formatting toolbar), WD 36
Font color, for letterhead, WD 161
Font command (Format menu)
animated text effects, WD 226
bold, WD 44
font size, WD 17, WD 35
font style, WD 35
hidden text, WD 20, WD 360
italics, WD 41
superscript, WD 258
underline, WD 42
Font command (shortcut menu), underline color, WD 512
Font dialog box
accessing underline styles using, WD 42
animated text, WD 226
formatting sales proposal title page using, WD 226-228
Font size, **WD 16-17**
footnote, WD 96, WD 97
form letter, WD 334
Grand Prix announcement, WD 34-35
letterhead, WD 161, WD 162
Font Size box arrow (Formatting toolbar), WD 17, WD 34
Font style, Grand Prix announcement, WD 36
Footer, **WD 81**, **WD 246**
creating, WD 84
section, WD 249
Footnote, **WD 93-95**
deleting, WD 99
editing, WD 99
formatting, WD 95-99
Form
borders, WD 524
online, *see* Online form
printing data, WD 585
protected, WD 486, WD 528, WD 592, WD 614-615
unprotecting, WD 486, WD 538
Form design, **WD 485**
Form field
ActiveX control versus, WD 605
bookmark, WD 598-599, WD 612
check box, WD 484, WD 505-509
drop-down, WD 484, WD 500-504
formatting, WD 511-513
Help text, WD 514-517
modifying options, WD 598-599
moving to, WD 528, WD 532
running macro when user exits, WD 603-604
selecting, WD 512
shading, removing, WD 517
text, WD 497-500, WD 504-505
width of, WD 501
Form letters
business, *see* Business form letters
closing, WD 362
inserting merge fields in main document, WD 324-325
personal, WD 298
Format Legend command (shortcut menu), WD 261
Format menu
AutoShape command, WD 308
Background command, newsletter, WD 438-439
Background command, pattern, WD 439-440
Background command, watermark, WD 281
Borders and Shading command, page border, WD 433
Borders and Shading command, paragraph border, WD 223
Borders and Shading command, paragraph shading, WD 225
Borders and Shading command, pull-quote shading, WD 413
Borders and Shading command, vertical rule, WD 409-410
Bullets and Numbering command, outline numbered list, WD 530
Columns command, vertical rule, WD 409
Columns command, number of columns, WD 400
Drawing Canvas command, WD 311
Drop Cap command, WD 403

Font command, animated text effects, WD 226
Font command, bold, WD 44
Font command, default settings, WD 229
Font command, font size, WD 17, WD 35
Font command, font style, WD 35
Font command, hidden text, WD 20, WD 360
Font command, italics, WD 41
Font command, superscript, WD 258
Font command, underline, WD 42
Paragraph command, alignment, WD 37
Paragraph command, blank line, WD 280
Paragraph command, centering text, WD 38
Paragraph command, hanging indent, WD 105
Paragraph command, indents, WD 89, WD 224
Paragraph command, justified, WD 401
Paragraph command, line spacing, WD 80
Paragraph command, space before paragraph, WD 312
Picture command, brightness, WD 396
Reveal Formatting command, WD 283
Styles and Formatting command, style, WD 332, WD 268
Tabs command, WD 164, WD 176, WD 389
WordArt command, WD 386
Format Painter button (Standard toolbar), WD 427-428, WD 512-513
Format Picture button (Picture toolbar), WD 51
Format Picture dialog box, WD 162-163, WD 231-232, WD 491
Format WordArt button (WordArt toolbar), WD 385
Formatting
AutoFormat As You Type, WD 155-157
AutoShape, WD 307-308
Biometrics research paper, WD 77-89
cell, WD 252
characters, WD 31-45
chart, WD 264, WD 731
clearing, WD 173, WD 225-226, WD 235, WD 329, WD 388-389
copying, WD 512
date field, WD 322
diagram, WD 425, WD 427-428
drawing canvas, WD 311
finding, WD 265-266
first page of newsletter, WD 398-415
footnote, WD 95-99
form fields, WD 511-513
Grand Prix announcement document, WD 31-45
graphic as floating, WD 393-394
letterhead, WD 161
line, WD 40
master document, WD 667-669
merge fields, WD 326
modified block style, WD 303
multiple paragraphs, WD 33-35
nonadjacent characters, WD 257-258
online form, WD 489-494, WD 561-575
page number, WD 248
paragraph, WD 31-45
pull-quote, WD 412-413
restrictions, WD 704
revealing, WD 282-284
sales proposal title page, WD 221-229
searching for, WD 117
second page of newsletter, WD 415-431
section, WD 235, WD 238
shortcut keys for, WD 85-87
style, *see* Style
table, WD 186-187, WD 255-258, WD 276-280
text as hidden, WD 359-360
text box, WD 412
text form field, WD 498-500
user instructions, WD 494
WordArt drawing object, WD 384-386
Formatting mark, **WD 20**
displaying, WD 20-21
font, WD 41
hiding, WD 528
index entries and, WD 670
Formatting toolbar, **WD 14**, WD 34-45
resetting, APP 27-28
Formula, in table, WD 254
Formula command (Table menu), WD 254
Frame, **WD 404**
converting text box to, WD 646-647
FTP (File Transfer Protocol), APP 24
Full menu, WD 12-13
Full Screen command (View menu), WD 407-408
Full screen view, **WD 407-408**

Getting Started task pane
closing, WD 8
displaying, WD 10
hiding, WD 141
Global (search), **APP 3**
Go to bookmark, WD 688-689
Go To command (Edit menu)
comments, WD 466
page number, WD 429
text, WD 111

Go to Record text box (Mail Merge toolbar), **WD 343**
Go To sheet (Find and Replace dialog box), WD 246
Gradient, **WD 384**, WD 385
Grammar, salutation and, WD 324
Grammar checking, WD 19, WD 25, WD 119-120
Grand Prix announcement, WD 3-62
Graph, *see* Microsoft Graph
Graph menus, WD 260
Graphic file, inserting, WD 563, WD 640-642
Graphics, **WD 45**
alignment, WD 644
border, WD 566
brightness, WD 396, WD 491
caption, WD 645-647
centering paragraph containing, WD 48
contrast, WD 490-491
cropping, WD 564-567
darkening, WD 396
drawing object, *see* Drawing object
file types, WD 231
flipping, WD 394-395
floating, *see* Floating graphic
grouping, WD 397
inline, *see* Inline graphic
inserting in letterhead, WD 162
line spacing and, WD 80
master document, WD 667-669
moving, WD 395-396, WD 492-493, WD 567-568, WD 644
online form, WD 490-494
overlapping, WD 522
picture, *see* Picture
position of, WD 49
resizing using sizing handles, WD 49-50
resizing using Format Picture dialog box, WD 162-163, WD 231-232, WD 566, WD 643
restoring size, WD 51
rotating, WD 493-494
selecting, WD 49
types of, WD 232
wrapping style, WD 491, WD 563-564, WD 643
See also Clip art
GreetingLine merge field, **WD 323**
Grid command (Draw menu), WD 564
Gridlines, **WD 151**
hiding, WD 496
showing, WD 497
Group of words, selecting, WD 43-44
Grouping graphics, WD 397
Gutter margin, **WD 679-680**

Handwriting menu, Write Anywhere command, APP 21
Handwriting Recognition service, **APP 19-22**
Handwritten input, WD 4, APP 19-21
Hanging indent, **WD 104-105**
Hanging Indent marker, **WD 104-105**
Hard copy, **WD 53**
Hard page break, *see* Manual page break
Header, **WD 81**, **WD 246**
alternating, WD 677-679
creating from previous section header, WD 247
page number in, WD 81, WD 83-84
viewing, WD 102
Header and Footer command (View menu), WD 102
alternating headers, WD 678
page numbers, WD 81
section header, WD 247
Header and Footer toolbar, WD 82, WD 83-84
Header area, displaying, WD 81-82
Header record, **WD 314**
Headings
outline, WD 458, WD 459-460, WD 657-659
resume, WD 147
table of contents listing, WD 673
Height, of clip art, WD 231
Help dialog box (F1 key), WD 514
Help menu
commands on, APP 8
Microsoft Word Help command, APP 1
Help system, WD 14, **WD 60-62**, APP 1-8
accessing, APP 1
navigating, APP 2-5
Help text, in form fields, WD 514-517
Hidden (Language bar), **WD 16**, APP 11
Hidden command, **WD 13**
Hidden text, WD 20, **WD 228**, WD 359-360
Hidden toolbar buttons, WD 14
Hide White Space button, WD 149
Hiding
formatting marks, WD 528
Getting Started task pane, WD 141
gridlines, WD 496
Office Assistant, WD 9, APP 7
reviewer's changes, WD 471
spelling error underlines, WD 27
white space, WD 149
Highlight button (Formatting toolbar), WD 436, WD 494
Highlighting, **WD 436**-437, WD 494
Horizontal ruler, **WD 11**
amount displayed, WD 169

hanging indent and, WD 104-105
indent markers on, WD 87, WD 88
tab stops on, WD 163-164, WD 176-177
Horizontal scroll bar, Outline View button, WD 459
Hyperlink, WD 107-108
assigning to button, WD 585
automatic format, WD 109
converting to regular text, WD 174
creating while typing, WD 108
navigating to, WD 122-123
See also Link
Hyperlink button (Standard toolbar), WD 108
Hyphen
en dash, WD 158
nonbreaking, WD 180
Hyphenation, WD 652-653

IF field, WD 326
conditionally printing text using, WD 326-327
If...Then:, WD 326
If...Then...Else:, WD 326, WD 327
Images, for button, WD 584
In Front of Text wrapping style, WD 491
Increase Indent button (Formatting toolbar), WD 331
Indentation
changing using ruler, WD 223-224
first-line, see First-line indent
hanging, WD 104-105
left, WD 87
outline, WD 459-460, WD 465, WD 472
paragraphs in MLA style, WD 87-89
tab stops and, WD 163
Index, WD 672
building, WD 672-673
formatting marks and, WD 670
marking entries for, WD 649-651, WD 672
updating, WD 684-685
Ink comment, WD 465
Ink Comment command (Insert menu), WD 465
Ink input, WD 4
Inline graphic
caption, WD 646
changing to floating graphic, WD 393-394, WD 491, WD 643
Inline object, WD 392
Insert Columns button (Standard toolbar), WD 185, WD 253
Insert command (Table menu)
columns, WD 253
rows, WD 184
Insert Comment button (Reviewing toolbar), WD 463, WD 465
Insert Diagram or Organization Chart button (Drawing toolbar), WD 421
Insert menu
AutoText command, WD 179, WD 181
Bookmark command, WD 675-676
Break command, continuous section break, WD 399, WD 416, WD 420
Break command, next page section break, WD 236, WD 404, WD 658, WD 659
Break command, page break, WD 103
Date and Time command, WD 177, WD 341
Diagram command, WD 421
Field command, WD 691
File command, WD 239, WD 402
Ink Comment command, WD 465
Object command, chart, WD 260
Object command, worksheet, WD 724-725
Page Numbers command, WD 84, WD 248
Picture command, chart, WD 727
Picture command, charting table, WD 259-260
Picture command, clip art, WD 46, WD 230, WD 392
Picture command, drawing canvas, WD 305
Picture command, from file, WD 642
Picture command, WordArt, WD 384
Reference command, caption, WD 645
Reference command, cross-reference, WD 648
Reference command, footnote, WD 94, WD 99
Reference command, index, WD 673
Reference command, table of contents, WD 674
Reference command, table of figures, WD 671
Symbol command, issue information line, WD 390, WD 391
Symbol command, nonbreaking space, WD 107, WD 180
Text Box command, WD 412
Insert Merge Fields button (Mail Merge toolbar), WD 325
Insert mode, WD 57
Insert Page Number button (Header and Footer toolbar), WD 83
Insert Rows button (Standard toolbar), WD 184
Insert Rows command (shortcut menu), WD 251
Insert Shape button (Diagram toolbar), WD 423
Insert Subdocument button (Outlining toolbar), WD 661
Insert Table button (Forms toolbar), WD 495
Insert Table button (Standard toolbar), WD 182-183
Insert WordArt button (Drawing toolbar), WD 383

Inserting
ActiveX control, WD 606-607
AutoShape, WD 306
AutoText entry, WD 179, WD 181
chart, WD 259-260
check box, WD 505-509
clip art, WD 45-51, WD 229-232, WD 392, WD 563
column break, WD 404-406
columns, WD 185
comment, WD 463-464, WD 465
continuous section break, WD 398-399, WD 416, WD 420
current date, WD 177
diagram, WD 421-422
drawing canvas, WD 305
drop-down form field, WD 500-501
Excel worksheet in Word document, WD 724-733
existing document into open document, WD 235-240
file in newsletter, WD 401-402, WD 406
graphic file, WD 563, WD 640-642
graphic in letterhead, WD 162
merge fields in main document, WD 323-324, WD 325
nonbreaking space, WD 180
page number, WD 83-84
rows, WD 184, WD 251-252
section break, WD 235-236
special characters, WD 391
subdocument, WD 660-664
symbol, WD 390-391
table in letter, WD 182-183
table in online form, WD 495-497, WD 506
text box, WD 411-412
text form field, WD 497-498
text from Research task pane, WD 125
text in an existing document, WD 57
WordArt drawing object, WD 382-384
Insertion point, WD 11
bulleted list, WD 188
centering, WD 230
deleting text at, WD 58
fields and, WD 323
inserting clip art at, WD 46
inserting text at, WD 57
position displayed on status bar, WD 11
section break and, WD 236
status bar, WD 18
in table, WD 253
Inside address, WD 175, WD 178
Integration, of Excel worksheet and Word document, WD 721-733
Issue information line, WD 380, WD 389-391
Italic button (Formatting toolbar), WD 41
Italicized, WD 41

Jump lines, WD 405
Jumping, WD 107
Justified, WD 328, WD 401, WD 408
Justify, WD 328, WD 401, WD 408
Justify button (Formatting toolbar), WD 408

Keyboard
on-screen, APP 21-22
scrolling using, WD 25
shortcut keys, WD 85-87

Labels
chart, WD 258
mailing, see Mailing labels
Landscape orientation
setting in Page Setup dialog box, WD 79
table, WD 355-356
Language bar, WD 7, APP 11
buttons on, APP 12
closing, WD 8, APP 16
customizing, APP 12-14
states, APP 11
Language bar command (Toolbars submenu), WD 16
Language command (Tools menu)
hyphenation, WD 652
thesaurus, WD 118
Last Record button (Mail Merge toolbar), WD 343
Left Indent marker, WD 87
Left-aligned, WD 36, WD 37
paragraph using shortcut keys, WD 86
Legend, chart, WD 260-261
Less Brightness button (Picture toolbar), WD 396
Letter
business, WD 175
cover, see Cover letter
envelope for, WD 190-191
letterhead for, WD 160-175
Letterhead, WD 160-175
Letters, see Characters; Text
Letters and Mailings command (Tools menu)
data source, WD 315
mail merge, WD 303
mailing labels, WD 190-191, WD 345
Levels
outline, WD 458-461, WD 465
outline numbered list, WD 329-331

Line
blank, see Blank lines
border, see Border
changed, WD 467
drawing in table, WD 273
formatting, WD 40
issue information, see Issue information line
jump, WD 405
ruling, WD 380, WD 388
selecting, WD 40
vertical rule, WD 380, WD 409-410
Line break, WD 154
Line break character, WD 154
Line color, for drawing object, WD 524-525
Line number, displayed on status bar, WD 11
Line spacing, WD 79
Biometrics research paper, WD 79-80
cell, WD 252
double, see Double-space
table, WD 275
Line Spacing button arrow (Formatting toolbar), WD 80
Line Style box arrow (Tables and Borders toolbar), ruling line, WD 388
Line weight
border, WD 222
text box, WD 412
Link
mail merge, WD 315
master document and, WD 657, WD 660-664
text using Paste Special command, WD 418-419
updating, WD 419
See also Hyperlink
Linked document, saving and opening, WD 723
Linked object, WD 722-733
List
bulleted, see Bulleted list
numbered, WD 189
outline numbered, WD 329-331
sorting, WD 655-656
styles, WD 152
List boxes, drop-down, see Drop-down form fields
List styles, WD 152
Locking fields, WD 334

Macro, WD 555
automatic, WD 587-591
copying, WD 604
deleting, WD 605
digital certificate, WD 617
disabled, WD 559-560
editing, WD 592-598
enabled, WD 559-560
macro recorder used to create, WD 576-581, WD 588-590
renaming, WD 605
running, WD 581, WD 590-591, WD 603-604
saving, WD 577
security and, WD 559-561
shortcut key, WD 576-578
VBA code, WD 592-594
Macro command (Tools menu)
creating, WD 560
Macro command (Tools menu) viewing code, WD 592-593
Macro names, WD 576, WD 587-588
Macro recorder, WD 576-581, WD 588-590
Mail merge, WD 298-343
composing main document, WD 321-337
data source, WD 314-321
envelopes, WD 350-352
identifying main document, WD 301-303
inserting merge fields in main document, WD 324-325
mailing labels, WD 345-350
merging all records to directory, WD 352-362
merging documents, WD 338-342
Mail Merge Recipients button (Mail Merge toolbar), WD 339, WD 342
Mail Merge task pane, WD 301, WD 315
Mail Merge toolbar, WD 301, WD 321
Mailing labels
bar codes and, WD 350
for business form letters, WD 345-350
for resume, WD 190-191
Main document, WD 300
composing, WD 321-337
converting into regular Word document, WD 352
identifying, WD 301-303
IF field in, WD 327
inserting merge fields in, WD 323-324
merging data source with, WD 338-342
merging to directory, WD 352-353
opening, WD 335
template as, WD 302-303
types of, WD 301
Manual page break, WD 103
Margins
changing all, WD 381
changing in Page Setup dialog box, WD 78
changing in print layout view, WD 77, WD 79
gutter, WD 679-680
justified text, WD 401
MLA style, WD 77-79

top of cell, WD 357-358
See also Indentation
Mark Index Entry dialog box, WD 650-651
Markup, WD 466
Markup balloon, WD 467
Markup command (View menu), WD 471, WD 472
Master document, WD 657
creating subdocument in, WD 664-667
entering text and graphics, WD 667-669
inserting subdocument in, WD 660-664
opening, WD 681-682
outline, WD 657-659
saving, WD 664
Maximizing Help window, WD 61
Memory, document stored in, WD 28
Menu, WD 12
context-sensitive, WD 12
displaying, WD 12-13
full, WD 12-13
resetting, WD 15, APP 29-30
short, WD 12
sub-, WD 13, WD 46
Menu, adding command to, WD 586
Menu bar, WD 12-13
Merge Cells button (Tables and Borders toolbar), WD 252
Merge Cells command (shortcut menu), WD 252
Merge Cells command (Table menu), WD 252
Merge conditions, WD 340, WD 341
Merge field characters, WD 323
Merge fields, WD 323
formatting, WD 326
Merge to New Document button (Mail Merge toolbar), WD 339, WD 356
Merge to Printer button (Mail Merge toolbar), WD 338
Merged data, viewing, WD 343
Merging, WD 300. See also Mail merge
Message, business letter, WD 175, WD 180-189
Microphone, WD 7, WD 17, APP 15-17
setting up, APP 16
Microphone button, WD 7
Microsoft Graph, WD 258-260, WD 726-731
Microsoft Office Address List, WD 320
Microsoft Office Expert exams, APP 32
Microsoft Office Specialist Certification, WD 62, WD 121, WD 284, APP 3-7
Microsoft Office Specialist exams, APP 32
Microsoft Office submenu (All Programs submenu), Microsoft Office Word 2003 command, WD 6
Microsoft Office Word 2003 command (All Programs submenu), WD 6
Microsoft Word 2003, see Word 2003
Microsoft Word Help button (Standard toolbar), APP 1
Microsoft Word Help command (Help menu), APP 1
Minimized (Language bar), WD 16, APP 11
MLA, see Modern Language Association of America
Modern Language Association of America (MLA), WD 74
documentation style, WD 75, WD 76
Modified block style, WD 303
Modify Style dialog box, WD 96-98
More Brightness button (Picture toolbar), WD 396
Mouse
scrolling using, WD 24
selecting items using, WD 113
Mouse pointer, WD 11
drawing table and, WD 272
note reference mark and, WD 99
Move handle, WD 14
submenus and, WD 307
Moving
chart legend, WD 260-261
diagram, WD 431
docked toolbar, WD 321
graphic, WD 395-396, WD 492-493, WD 567-568, WD 644
shadow, WD 527
tab stops, WD 177
table, WD 252
task pane title bar, WD 7
text across split window, WD 443
text box, WD 415
text using drag-and-drop, WD 112-115
toolbars, WD 82, WD 223
Multiple paragraphs, formatting, WD 33-35

Name
automatic macros, WD 587-588
command, WD 586
document, on title bar, WD 30
file, see File name
macro, WD 576, WD 587-588
of reviewer, WD 466
Nameplate, WD 380
creating, WD 382-397
drawing object, WD 382-387
floating graphic, WD 392-396
inner page, WD 417-418
issue information line, WD 389-391
ruling lines, WD 388

Navigating to hyperlink, WD 122-123
Nested tables, WD 276
New Blank Document button (Standard toolbar), WD 59
New command (File menu)
  Resume Wizard, WD 142
  templates, WD 302, WD 487
New document window, merging to, WD 356-357
Newsletter, WD 378-445
  background color, WD 438-440
  diagram, WD 421-431
  drop cap color, WD 432
  first page of, WD 398-415
  issue information line, WD 380, WD 389-391
  nameplate, WD 380, WD 382-397, WD 417-418
  online viewing, WD 436-444
  pull-quote, WD 380, WD 410-415
  second page of, WD 415-431
  title, WD 382-397, WD 417
Next Page section break, WD 236, WD 404-406, WD 658
Next Record button (Mail Merge toolbar), WD 343
Nonadjacent characters, formatting, WD 257-258
Nonbreaking hyphen, WD 180
Nonbreaking space, WD 180
Noncontiguous text, WD 257
Nonprinting character, WD 20
Normal command (View menu), WD 77
Normal style, WD 95, WD 267
  returning paragraph to, WD 225
Normal template, macros saved in, WD 577
Normal view, WD 77
Note, comment, see Comment
Note pane, WD 95
  closing, WD 99
Note reference mark, WD 93, WD 95
  mouse pointer on, WD 99
Note text, WD 93
Null expression, WD 326
Number format, for footnotes, WD 99
Numbered list
  outline, WD 329-331
  resume, WD 189
Numbering button (Formatting toolbar), WD 331
Numbers
  alignment on decimal point, WD 165
  for captions, WD 645-646
Numeric entries, in text form field, WD 504

Object, WD 721
  adjustment handle, WD 307
  copying using Copy button (Standard toolbar), WD 721, WD 729
  destination, WD 418-419
  drawing, see Drawing object
  embedded, WD 721, WD 726
  floating, see Floating object
  inline, see Inline object
  linking, WD 418, WD 722-733
  pasted, WD 721
  rotate handle, WD 307
  source, WD 418-419
Object command (Insert menu)
  chart, WD 260
  worksheet, WD 724-725
Object menu, see Context-sensitive menu
Objective style, WD 151-152
Office Assistant, APP 1, APP 6-7
  hiding, WD 9
Office Clipboard, WD 165-171
Office Clipboard command (Edit menu), WD 166-167
Office Clipboard gallery, WD 171
Office Speech Recognition software, WD 7, WD 16
Office Web pages, publishing to Web server, APP 24
Offline Help, APP 3
Online form, WD 482-540
  ActiveX control, WD 605-613
  check boxes, WD 484, WD 505-509
  creating, WD 486-529
  data entry area, WD 518-527
  designing, WD 485-486
  drop-down list boxes, WD 484, WD 500-504
  e-mailing, WD 540
  entering data in, WD 532
  formatting, WD 489-494, WD 511-513, WD 561-575
  graphics, WD 490-494
  Help text, WD 514-517
  inserting table in, WD 495-497, WD 506
  modifying, WD 561-575
  protecting, WD 486, WD 528, WD 592, WD 614-615
  revised, WD 553-620
  saving data, WD 533-536
  template, WD 487-489
  testing, WD 615-616
  text boxes, WD 484, WD 497-500, WD 504-505, WD 509-511
  text form field, WD 497-500, WD 504-505

unprotecting, WD 538
user instructions, WD 494-495
uses of, WD 530
working with, WD 530-537
Online viewing, of newsletter, WD 436-444
On-screen keyboard, APP 22
Open dialog box
  file properties in, WD 194
  renaming folder using, WD 344
Open documents
  arranging all, WD 443
  as attachment, WD 462
  inserting existing document into, WD 235-240
  multiple, WD 160
  switching between, WD 166
Opening
  digitally signed document, WD 620
  Excel workbook, WD 728
  existing document, WD 55-56
  linked document, WD 723
  main document, WD 335
  master document, WD 681-682
  template, WD 557
  text file, WD 536
Optional hyphen, WD 653
Options command (Tools menu)
  dictionary, WD 121
  digital signature, WD 618
  printing field codes, WD 337
  readability statistics, WD 687
  showing formatting marks, WD 21
Order command (shortcut menu), WD 521, WD 522
Ordinal, making superscript, WD 156-157
Orphan, WD 653-654
Outline
  creating, WD 458-461
  master document and, WD 657-659
  modifying, WD 665-666
  printing, WD 465, WD 472
  sending to PowerPoint, WD 475-477
Outline command (View menu), WD 460
Outline numbered list, WD 329-331
Outline view, WD 458-459, WD 667
Outline View button (horizontal scroll bar), WD 459
Outlining toolbar, WD 459, WD 460
Outlook Calendar, smart tag to display, WD 192
Outside Border button (Tables and Borders toolbar), WD 223
Overtype mode, WD 12, WD 57
OVR indicator, WD 12, WD 57

Page
  facing, WD 677
  printing specific range, WD 240-241
  vertically centering on, WD 232-234
  zooming whole, WD 232
Page border, for newsletter, WD 433-434
Page breaks
  automatic, WD 101-102
  deleting, WD 244
  manual, WD 103
  in table, WD 275
Page number
  displayed on status bar, WD 11
  finding using Go To command, WD 429
  formatting, WD 248
  in header, WS 81, WD 83-84, WD 246-248
  table of contents listing, WD 673
Page Numbers command (Insert menu), WD 84, WD 248
Page Setup command (File menu)
  gutter margin, WD 680
  margins, WD 78, WD 381
  vertical alignment, WD 237
  vertical centering, WD 233
Page Setup dialog box
  margins, WD 78
  orientation, WD 79
Page totals, displayed on status bar, WD 11
Page width, zooming, WD 220-221, WD 301, WD 435
Panel names, WD 141
Paragraph
  adding or removing blank line above using CTRL+0, WD 331
  alignment, see Alignment
  blank line above, WD 280, WD 331
  bottom border, WD 172
  border, WD 172, WD 221-223
  centering, WD 38, WD 45
  demoting, WD 459, WD 460
  formatting, see Formatting; Paragraph formatting
  indenting, see Indentation
  justification, WD 328, WD 401
  new, pressing ENTER key to create, WD 18, WD 21
  orphan WD 653
  promoting, WD 459-460
  selecting multiple, WD 33-34
  shading, WD 224-225
  sorting, WD 109-110
  space before, WD 280, WD 312
  widow, WD 653
  wordwrap, WD 22-23

Paragraph command (Format menu)
  alignment, WD 37
  blank line, WD 280
  centering, WD 38
  indentation, WD 89, WD 224
  justified, WD 401
  line spacing, WD 80
  space before paragraph, WD 312
Paragraph dialog box, setting first-line indent using, WD 98
Paragraph formatting, WD 31
  copying, WD 512
  footnote, WD 96-98
  Grand Prix announcement document, WD 31-45
  sales proposal title page, WD 221-225
  shortcut keys for, WD 87
  using Reveal Formatting task pane, WD 311-312
Paragraph indent
  changing using ruler, WD 223-224
  See also Indentation
Paragraph mark (¶), displaying, WD 20-21
Paragraph style, WD 152, WD 568. See also Style
  applying, WD 570
Parent element, WD 697
Parenthetical citations, WD 76
Password, 30
Password-protected document, WD 691-692
Paste button (Standard toolbar), WD 114
Paste command (Edit menu), WD 114
  Clipboard task pane, WD 171
Paste Options button, WD 114-115, WD 170-171
Paste Options menu, WD 114-115
Paste Special command (Edit menu), linking text using, WD 418-419
Pasted object, WD 721, WD 728-730
Pasting, WD 112, WD 114, WD 165, WD 170
Pattern fill effect, for background, WD 439-440
Pen line (Writing Pad), APP 20
Percentage, zooming, WD 422, WD 426
Personal form letters, WD 298
Photographs, WD 45, WD 393
Phrase, deleting, WD 58
Picture, WD 304
Picture bullets, WD 270
Picture command (Format menu), brightness, WD 396
Picture command (Insert menu)
  chart, WD 727
  charting table, WD 259-260
  clip art, WD 46, WD 230, WD 392
  drawing canvas, WD 305
  from file, WD 642
Picture toolbar, WD 49, WD 51
Picture watermark, WD 280
Placeholder text, WD 152, WD 303
  merge letter, WD 303
  resume, WD 152-153
Plagiarism, WD 126
Planning proposal, WD 218
Point, WD 16
Portrait orientation, WD 79, WD 355-356
PowerPoint, sending outline to, WD 475-477
Preview, WD 238-239, WD 240
Previous Record button (Mail Merge toolbar), WD 343
Print button (Standard toolbar), WD 53
Print command (File menu), WD 13, WD 53
  draft, WD 336
  field codes, WD 336
  page range, WD 241
Print layout view, WD 82, WD 148
  changing margins in, WD 77, WD 79
  header in, WD 82
  sales proposal in, WD 222
  Text Width in, WD 170
Print preview, WD 158
  Grand Prix announcement document, WD 52
  resume, WD 158-159
  several pages in, WD 680
Print Preview button (Standard toolbar), WD 52, WD 158
Print Preview command (File menu), WD 159
Printer, merging form letters to, WD 338, WD 340
Printing
  conditionally using IF field, WD 326-327
  directory, WD 361
  document with accepted changes, WD 472
  draft, WD 241, WD 336
  envelope, WD 191
  field codes, WD 336-337
  form data, WD 585
  Grand Prix announcement, WD 53
  keyboard shortcuts, WD 87
  macro for, WD 576-581
  mailing labels, WD 191, WD 349
  merged document, WD 338-340, WD 342
  outline, WD 465, WD 472
  specific pages, WD 240-241
Printout, WD 53
Private procedure, WD 601
Procedure, WD 554
  ActiveX control, WD 610-613

code statements, WD 594, WD 597
comments, WD 594-596
desk checking, WD 602-603, WD 610
inserting, WD 600-601
modifying code in, WD 596
planning, WD 601-602, WD 610
private, WD 601
public, WD 601
writing, WD 601-603, WD 610-613
Program, WD 554
Promoted, WD 459-460
Proofreading, WD 110
  Biometrics research paper, WD 110
  proposal, WD 282
  resume, WD 189
Properties
  ActiveX control, WD 608-610
  changing using code statements, WD 614
  custom, WD 689-691
Properties button (Control Toolbox toolbar), WD 608
Properties command (File menu)
  customizing, WD 690
  document summary, WD 193
  statistics, WD 101
Proposal
  elements of, WD 235
  planning, WD 218
  proofreading, WD 282
  research, WD 218
  sales, see Sales proposal
Protect a form, WD 486, WD 528, WD 592, WD 614-615
Protect Document command (Tools menu), WD 614
Protect Document task pane, WD 614-615, WD 703
Protected form, WD 486, WD 528, WD 592, WD 614-615
Public procedure, WD 601
Publishing Office Web pages, to Web server, APP 24
Pull-quote, WD 380, WD 410-415
  formatting, WD 412
  text box for, WD 411-413
Punctuation, salutation and, WD 324

Question mark (?) wildcard character, WD 238
Quitting Word, WD 54, WD 62
Quote, pull-, see Pull-quote
Quoting source, WD 84

Radial diagram, in newsletter, WD 421-431
Read button (Standard toolbar), WD 443
Readability statistics, WD 687
Reading Layout toolbar, WD 444
Reading layout view, WD 443-444
Record, WD 314
  editing in data source, WD 321
  entering in data source, WD 318-319
  header, WD 314
  merging, WD 339-340, WD 342
  merging to directory, WD 352-362
  printing, WD 339-340, WD 342
  sorting, WD 342, WD 359
Recording macro, WD 576-580, WD 588-590
Rectangle, for online form, WD 518-527
Rectangle button (Drawing toolbar), WD 518-519
Redo button (Standard toolbar), WD 39
Reference command (Insert menu)
  caption, WD 645
  cross-reference, WD 648
  footnote, WD 94, WD 99
  index, WD 673
  table of contents, WD 674
  table of figures, WD 671
Reference document, WD 634
  bookmarks, WD 675-677
  caption, WD 645-646
  cross-reference, WD 647-649
  hyphenating, WD 652-653
  index entries, WD 649-651, WD 672
  properties, WD 689-691
  summarizing, WD 685-686
  table of contents, WD 673-675
  table of figures, WD 670-672
References
  footnotes, WD 94, WD 99
  MLA style, WD 76
  Research task pane and, WD 118, WD 124-126
  on resume, WD 157
Reject Change/Delete Comment button (Reviewing toolbar), WD 469, WD 470, WD 471
Removing
  borders, WD 225
  folder, WD 344
  form field shading, WD 517
  hyperlink, WD 174
  See also Deleting
Renaming macro, WD 605
Repeat command (Edit menu), WD 39
Replace command (Edit menu), WD 117
Replacing text, WD 116-117, WD 152
Reports, research, WD 73-126

Research command (Tools menu), WD 124
Research paper, WD 73-126
Research proposal, WD 218
Research task pane, WD 118, WD 119, WD 124-126
Resetting menus and toolbars, WD 15
Resize pointer, split window and, **WD 441**
Resizing
  AutoShape, WD 308
  button, WD 609
  chart, WD 262
  clip art, WD 231
  column, WD 253
  diagram, WD 425-426
  dialog boxes, WD 313
  drawing canvas, WD 309-310
  graphic using Format Picture dialog box, WD 162-163, WD 231-232, WD 566, WD 643
  graphic using sizing handles, **WD 49-50**
  table columns, WD 185-186
  text box, WD 309, WD 414
  WordArt drawing object, WD 384-385
Resolution, screen, APP 25-27
Restored (Language bar), **WD 16**, APP 11
Resume, WD 138-195
  cover letter for, WD 138, WD 139, WD 175-189
  envelopes for, WD 190-191
  letterhead for cover letter, WD 160-175
  personalizing, WD 150-159
  references on, WD 157
  wizard used to create, WD 141-148
Resume Wizard, WD 141-148
Return address, WD 333
Reveal Formatting command (Format menu), WD 283
Reveal Formatting task pane, **WD 282-284**
  paragraph formatting using, WD 311-312
Reviewer
  ink color, WD 472
  name of, WD 466
Reviewing document, WD 461-475
Reviewing pane, inserting comment in, WD 463-464
Reviewing toolbar, WD 444
Revision marks, **WD 468**
Right Indent marker (ruler), changing, WD 224
Right-aligned, **WD 36-37**
  cell contents, WD 256
  header, WD 247
  tab stop, WD 389
  text, WD 36
Right-click, shortcut menu and, WD 12
River Run Campground form letter, WD 298-343
Rivers, WD 408
Rotate handle, **WD 307**, WD 493-494
Rotating graphic, WD 493-494
Row, data source, WD 314
Row, table, WD 182, WD 183
  adding, WD 184, WD 251-252
  adding to end of table, WD 253
  deleting, WD 251
  distributing evenly, WD 274-275
  drawing, WD 273-274
  height of, WD 278
  summing, WD 254, WD 276
Row boundary, **WD 186**
Ruler, **WD 11**
  changing paragraph indent using, WD 223-224
  horizontal, *see* Horizontal ruler
  margins on, WD 79
  table and, WD 151, WD 253
  vertical, *see* Vertical ruler
Ruler command (View menu), WD 11, WD 87
Rules, **WD 380**
  vertical, WD 380, WD 409-410
Ruling lines, **WD 380**, WD 388
Run mode, **WD 605**
Run-around, **WD 380**
Running macro, WD 581, WD 590-591, WD 603-604

Sales proposal, **WD 218-285**
  bulleted list, WD 269-271
  chart, WD 258-265
  drawing table in, WD 271-275
  formats, WD 265-271
  formatting table, WD 276-280
  guidelines, WD 242
  header, WD 246-248
  inserting existing document into open document, WD 235-240
  page numbers, WD 246-248
  printing, WD 240-241
  revealing formatting, WD 282-284
  table for, WD 250-264
  title page, WD 221-234
  watermark in, WD 280-282
Salutation, WD 175
  business form letter, WD 323
  grammar and punctuation used in, WD 175
  resume letter, WD 175, WD 178, WD 180
Save All command (File menu), **WD 363**
Save As command (File menu), WD 30
  form data, WD 534
  passwords, WD 691

Save As dialog box, WD 28-30
  file type in, WD 240
  folder creation using, WD 313
  Tools button, WD 534
Save button (Formatting toolbar), WD 28
Save Options command (Tools submenu), WD 30
Saving
  backup copy, WD 30
  Biometrics research paper, WD 87
  data source, WD 320, WD 321
  digitally signed document, WD 620
  existing document with new file name, WD 52
  existing document with same file name, WD 51-52
  folder creation while, WD 313
  form data, WD 533-536
  linked documents, WD 723
  macro, WD 577
  mailing labels, WD 350
  master document, WD 664
  new document, WD 28-31
  passwords and, WD 691
  resume, WD 159
  as template, WD 175, WD 488
  version, WD 638-640
Scanned image, inserting, WD 231, WD 393
Scanner, WD 45
Screen
  resolution, APP 25-27
  size of text on, WD 444
ScreenTip, **WD 13**
Scroll bars, **WD 11**, WD 24, WD 43
Scroll box, **WD 11**, WD 24
Scrolls, **WD 23-25**, WD 43
  synchronous, WD 443
Search Results task pane, **APP 2-5**
Searching
  for clip art, WD 47, WD 230, WD 392, WD 563
  for comment, WD 466
  for file using wildcard, WD 238
  for formatting, WD 117
  Help system, WD 61, APP 2
  for special characters, WD 117
  for synonym, WD 118-119
  for text and replacing, WD 116-117
Section, **WD 235**, WD 415
  alignment, WD 237
  footer, WD 249
  formatting, WD 238
  go to, WD 246
  header, WD 246-247
Section break, **WD 235**
  continuous, WD 398-399, WD 415-416, WD 420
  deleting, WD 238
  inserting, WD 235-236
  next page, WD 236, WD 404-406, WD 658
  snaking columns, WD 398-399, WD 415-416, WD 420
Section number, displayed on status bar, WD 11
Security
  digital signature, WD 617-620
  macros and, WD 559-561
  passwords and, WD 691-692
  Segments, of diagram, WD 422-423
Select, **WD 33**. *See also* Selecting
Select Browse Object button (vertical scroll bar), WD 111, WD 117
Select Browse Object menu, WD 110
  Browse by Page icon, WD 111
  Find icon, WD 117
Selected text, **WD 33**
Selecting
  form field, WD 512
  graphic, WD 49
  group of words, WD 43-44
  items using mouse, WD 113
  line, WD 40
  multiple paragraphs, WD 33-34
  nonadjacent text, WD 113, WD 257
  resume text, WD 152
  sentence, WD 112
  table items, WD 186
  text to delete, WD 58
Selection, removing, WD 44
Selection rectangle, **WD 49**
Self-signed projects, **WD 617**
Send button (E-mail toolbar), WD 462
Send To command (File menu)
  document for review, WD 462
  form, WD 540
  outline to PowerPoint, WD 476
  research paper as attachment, WD 123
Sentence, selecting and moving, WD 112
Shading
  cells, WD 277
  form field, WD 517
  paragraph, WD 224-225
  pull-quote, WD 413
Shading Color button (Tables and Borders toolbar), WD 224
Shadow, **WD 226**
  drawing object, WD 520, WD 526-527
  sales proposal title page, WD 226-228
  settings, WD 527

Shadow Settings toolbar, WD 527
Shape, WordArt, WD 386-387
Shelly Cashman Series Microsoft Office Specialist Center, APP 32
SHIFT+F5, last editing location and, **WD 239**
Short menu, **WD 12**
Shortcut keys, **WD 85-87**, **WD 568**
  macro, WD 576-578
  style associated with, WD 568-570
Shortcut menu, WD 12
Show Buttons on Two Rows command (Toolbar Options list), WD 9
Show First Line Only button (Outlining toolbar), WD 662
Show/Hide ¶ button (Standard toolbar), WD 21, WD 228, WD 361, WD 497
Showing
  end-of-cell marks, WD 497
  gridlines, WD 497
Signature
  digital, WD 617-620
  electronic, WD 617
Signature block, **WD 175**, WD 189
Size
  font, *see* Font size
  graphic, WD 49-51
  of text on screen, WD 444
  zooming and, WD 21
  See also Resizing
Sizing handles, **WD 49**
  drawing canvas and, WD 310
  graphics and, WD 49-50
SKIP RECORD IF field, WD 328
Slide show, from Word outline, WD 475-477
Smart tag, WD 85, WD 91, **WD 115-116**, **WD 191-192**
Smart Tag Actions menu, WD 116
Smart tag indicator, **WD 116**, WD 191-192
Snaking columns, **WD 398-400**
Soft page breaks, *see* Automatic page breaks
Sort command (Table menu), WD 109, WD 359, WD 656
Sorting, **WD 109**
  list, WD 655-656
  records to merge and print, WD 342
  table, WD 109, WD 359
Sound clips, WD 45
Source document, **WD 721-722**, WD 724
Source object, **WD 418-419**
Space, nonbreaking, WD 180
SPACEBAR, displaying formatting marks and, WD 20, WD 21
Spacing
  before paragraph, WD 312
  character, WD 228
  line, *see* Line spacing
Speaking commands, WD 7, WD 16
Special characters
  finding, WD 265, WD 267
  inserting, WD 391
  searching for, WD 117
Speech command (Tools menu), APP 16
Speech playback, **APP 22-23**
Speech recognition, WD 7, WD 16, APP 15-19
Speech Recognition service, **APP 15**
Spell checking
  AutoCorrect and, WD 89-90
  automatically, WD 27
  dictionaries and, WD 19, WD 25, WD 121
  grammar checking with, WD 119-120
  using Spelling and Grammar Status icon, WD 19, WD 25-27
Spelling and Grammar button (Standard toolbar), WD 119
Spelling and Grammar command (Tools menu), WD 120
Spelling and Grammar Status icon, **WD 19**, WD 25-27
Split Cells button (Table and Borders toolbar), WD 253
Split Cells command (Table menu), WD 253
Split command (Window menu), WD 442
Splitting
  cells, WD 253
  window, WD 441-443
Square wrap text, WD 431
Stacking order, of drawing object, WD 520-522
Standard toolbar, **WD 14**
  customizing, WD 582-586
  resetting, APP 27-28
Stars and Banners command (AutoShapes menu), WD 306
Start button (Windows taskbar), All Programs, Microsoft Office, Microsoft Office Word 2003 command, WD 6
Start menu (Windows taskbar), All Programs, Microsoft Office, Microsoft Office Word 2003 command, WD 6
Starting Word, WD 6-7
Status bar, **WD 11-12**
  Help messages on, WD 514-517
  insertion point position, WD 18
Status indicators, **WD 12**
Stick-up cap, WD 404
Style, **WD 95, WD 151, WD 267, WD 568**
  applying, WD 98, WD 332, WD 570
  base, WD 95
  Body Text, WD 328, WD 332

business letter, WD 175
character, WD 152, WD 267-269, WD 568
deleting, WD 572
letter template, WD 303, WD 304
list, WD 152
modifying, WD 95-98, WD 571
new, WD 267
Normal, WD 95
paragraph, WD 152, WD 568
shortcut key associated with, WD 568-570
table, WD 152
Style box (Formatting toolbar)
  Body Text, WD 332
  clearing formatting using, WD 225-226
  insertion point and, WD 303
Style box arrow (Formatting toolbar), WD 95, WD 152
Styles and Formatting button (Formatting toolbar)
  clearing formatting, WD 173
  setting style, WD 98, WD 568
Styles and Formatting task pane, **WD 152**
Styles and Formatting command (Format menu)
  applying style, WD 332
  clearing formatting using, WD 225
  creating character style, WD 268
Sub statement, **WD 594**
Subdocuments, **WD 657**
  creating in master document, WD 664-667
  deleting, WD 667
  inserting in master document, WD 660-664
Subhead, **WD 380**
Subject, e-mail, WD 462
Submenu, **WD 13**, WD 46
  converting to floating toolbar, WD 307
  move handle, WD 307
Summarizing document, WD 685-686
Summing table contents, WD 254
Superscript, WD 93, WD 156-157, WD 258
Switch Between Header and Footer button (Header and Footer toolbar), WD 249
Symbol command (Insert menu), WD 107, WD 390
Symbols
  AutoCorrect entries, WD 106-107
  bullet, *see* Bullet
  inserting, WD 107
  issue information line, WD 390-391
  nonbreaking space, WD 180
  outline, WD 459, WD 460
Synchronous Scrolling button (Compare Side by Side toolbar), WD 443
Synonym, **WD 118-119**

Tab character, **WD 165**
TAB key
  adding rows to table using, WD 184
  creating tab stop using, WD 165
  demoting list item using, WD 330, WD 331
  demoting paragraph using, WD 460
  indent using, WD 89
  moving in table using, WD 183, WD 184
  moving to form field using, WD 532
Tab marker, WD 163-165
  moving, WD 177
Tab stop, **WD 163-165**
  cover letter, WD 176-177
  custom, WD 164, WD 176-177
  moving, WD 177
  right-aligned, WD 389
  on ruler, WD 163-164, WD 176-177
  setting using ruler, WD 176-177
  setting using Tabs dialog box, WD 163-165
Table, **WD 150**
  adding columns, WD 185, WD 253
  adding rows, WD 184, WD 251, WD 253
  alignment, WD 186-187, WD 256
  AutoFormat, WD 187, WD 255
  borderless, WD 495-496, WD 506
  borders, WD 255, WD 273
  centering, WD 187, WD 256
  charting, WD 258-265
  converting merge field text to, WD 354-355
  copying, WD 256
  creating with Insert Table button, WD 182-183
  data source, WD 314
  deleting column or row, WD 250-251
  deleting contents, WD 256
  drawing, WD 223, WD 271-275
  entering data in, WD 183-185
  formatting, WD 187, WD 255-258, WD 276-280
  formatting cell, WD 252
  formulas, WD 254
  gridlines, WD 496
  insertion point, WD 253
  line spacing, WD 275
  merging cells, WD 252
  moving, WD 252
  nested, WD 276
  online form, WD 495-497, WD 506
  orientation, WD 355-356
  page break in, WD 275
  resume, WD 150-151
  sales proposal, WD 250-264
  selecting items, WD 186
  shading cells, WD 277
  sorting, WD 359

summing contents, WD 254
tab settings versus, WD 495
Table AutoFormat command (Table menu),
  WD 255
Table AutoFormat feature, WD 255
Table menu
  AutoFit command, columns, WD 185
  Convert command, text to table, WD 355
  Delete command, columns or rows, WD 251
  Draw Table command, WD 273
  Formula command, WD 254
  Insert command, columns, WD 185
  Insert command, rows, WD 184
  Merge Cells command, WD 252
  Sort command, WD 109, WD 359, Sort
    command, WD 656
  Split Cells command, WD 253
  Table AutoFormat command, WD 255
Table move handle, WD 186
Table of authorities, WD 675
Table of contents, **WD 673-675**
Table of figures, WD 645, **WD 670-672**
Table resize handle, **WD 186**
Table styles, **WD 152**
Tables and Borders button (Standard toolbar),
  WD 183, **WD 221-222**
Tables and Borders toolbar, **WD 221-222**
  ruling lines, WD 388
Tabs, using table versus, WD 495
Tablet PC, **WD 4**
  ink comments using, WD 465
Tabs command (Format menu), WD 164,
  WD 176, WD 389
Tabs dialog box
  displaying, WD 177
  setting tab stops using, WD 163-165
Tags, **WD 693**
Task pane, **WD 7**
  Clip Art, WD 47-48
  moving title bar, WD 7
  switching among, WD 10
Task Pane command (View menu), WD 10
  Resume Wizard, WD 148
Template, **WD 138**, WD 141, **WD 302,
  WD 487-489**
  accessing through Windows Explorer,
    WD 530-531, WD 705
  form letter, WD 302-303
  macros saved in, WD 577
  modifying, WD 538-539
  opening, WD 557
  resume, WD 143
  saving as, WD 175
  workgroup, WD 539
Templates and Add-Ins command (Tools
  menu), XML schema, WD 694
Templates folder, WD 538
Testing
  online form, WD 615-616
  procedure, WD 602-603
Text
  animated effects, WD 226, WD 437-438
  AutoShape, WD 308-309
  Balloon, WD 472-473
  comment, WD 473
  cutting, WD 245
  default, WD 498
  deleting from document, WD 56, WD 58-59
  diagram, WD 423-424, WD 427-428
  dictating, WD 7, WD 16, APP 15
  entering using Click and Type, WD 82-83
  entering using keyboard, WD 16-27
  false, WD 326
  finding and replacing, WD 116-117
  Help, WD 514-517
  hidden, WD 20, WD 228, WD 359-360
  highlighting, WD 436-437, WD 494
  inserting in existing document, WD 57
  linking using Paste Special command,
    WD 418-419
  master document, WD 667-669
  moving using drag-and-drop, WD 112-115
  noncontiguous, formatting, WD 257
  note, WD 93
  online form, WD 489
  placeholder, see Placeholder text
  replacing, WD 116-117
  scrolling, WD 23-25, WD 43
  selecting, see Selecting
  sending drawing object behind, WD 521-522
  size on screen, WD 444
  true, WD 326
  WordArt, WD 383
  wordwrap, WD 22-23
  wrap-around, WD 380
Text box, **WD 411-413**
  converting to frame, WD 646-647

moving, WD 415
online form, WD 484, WD 497-500,
  WD 504-505, WD 509-511
resizing, WD 309, WD 414
Text Box button (Drawing toolbar), WD 412
Text Box command (Insert menu), WD 412
Text Effects sheet (Font dialog box),
  animation, WD 437
Text file
  comma-delimited, WD 533
  opening, WD 536
Text form field, **WD 497**
  any text, WD 497-500
  bookmark for, WD 598-599, WD 612
  current date in, WD 509-511
  formatting, WD 511-513
  Help text, WD 514-517
  modifying options, WD 598-599
  numeric entries, WD 504
  types, WD 504, WD 505
Text services, **APP 11**
Text watermark, WD 281
Text width, zooming, WD 169-170
Text Wrapping button (Picture toolbar),
  WD 393, WD 491, WD 563
Texture, filling drawing object with,
  WD 522-523
Thesaurus, WD 118
3-D effect, for drawing object, WD 520,
  WD 574
3-D Style button (Drawing toolbar), WD 574
Thumbnails, **WD 229**
Tight wrap text, WD 427, WD 431
Time, current, WD 511
Time field, inserting, WD 341
Title
  newsletter, WD 382-397, WD 417
  works cited, WD 76, WD 104
Title bar, document name on, WD 30
Title page
  master document, WD 667-669
  sales proposal, **WD 221-234**
Toggle Field Codes command (shortcut menu),
  WD 335
Toolbar, **WD 7**, WD 13
  customizing, WD 582-586
  docked, WD 14, WD 82, WD 223, WD 321
  floating, WD 14, WD 82
  Formatting, see Formatting toolbar
  hidden buttons, WD 14
  moving, WD 82, WD 223
  Picture, WD 49
  resetting, APP 27-29
  resetting, WD 15
  Standard, see Standard toolbar
  toggle buttons, WD 45
Toolbar buttons
  displaying on two rows, WD 9, WD 14
  size, WD 15
Toolbar Options list, WD 9, WD 14
Toolbars command (shortcut menu), Language
  bar command, WD 16
Toolbars command (View menu), APP 29
Tools menu
  AutoCorrect Options command, WD 92
  AutoCorrect Options command, AutoFormat
    As You Type, WD 156
  AutoCorrect Options command, smart tags,
    WD 115
  AutoCorrect Options command, spell
    checking, WD 27
  AutoSummarize command, WD 686
  Compare and Merge Documents command,
    WD 473-474
  Customize command, toolbars, WD 583
  Language command, hyphenation, WD 652
  Language command, thesaurus, WD 118
  Letters and Mailings command, data source,
    WD 315
  Letters and Mailings command, mail merge,
    WD 303
  Letters and Mailings command, mailing
    labels, WD 190-191, WD 345
  Macro command, security, WD 560
  Macro command, viewing code, WD 592-593
  Options command, dictionary, WD 121
  Options command, digital signature, WD 618
  Options command, printing field codes,
    WD 337
  Options command, readability statistics,
    WD 687
  Options command, reviewer name, WD 466
  Options command, showing formatting
    marks, WD 21
  Protect Document command, WD 614
  Research command, WD 124
  Speech command, APP 16

Spelling and Grammar command, WD 120
Templates and Add-Ins command, XML
  schema, WD 694
Track Changes command, WD 468
Unprotect Document command, WD 486,
  WD 538, WD 558-559
Word Count command, WD 100
Tools submenu, Save Options command,
  WD 30
Totals, in table, WD 254, WD 276
Track changes, WD 457, WD 466-472
  protected document and, WD 615
Track Changes button (Reviewing toolbar),
  WD 468
Track Changes command (Tools menu),
  WD 468
Transparent fill color, WD 309-310
TRK status indicator, WD 467
True text, **WD 326**
Two Page zoom, WD 434, WD 440
Type a question for help box (menu bar),
  WD 60, APP 1-5

Underline button (Formatting toolbar), WD 42
Underlined, **WD 42**
  color, WD 511-512
  text, WD 42
  titles of works, WD 76
Underscore characters, text form fields and,
  WD 498, WD 501, WD 502
Undo
  AutoCorrect, WD 90, WD 106
  sort, WD 110
Undo button (Standard toolbar), WD 39,
  WD 58
Undo command (Edit menu), WD 39
Unicode characters, **APP 22**
Unprotect Document command (Tools menu),
  WD 486, WD 538, WD 558-559
Unprotect the form, **WD 538**
Unprotecting document, WD 486, WD 538,
  WD 558-559
Updating
  date or time, WD 178
  field, WD 322
  link, WD 419
User instructions, in online form, WD 494-495

VBA, see Visual Basic for Applications
Version, **WD 638-640**
Versions command (File menu), WD 638-639
Vertical alignment, of section, WD 237
Vertical rule, **WD 380**, WD 409-410
Vertical ruler, **WD 11**
  print layout view, WD 148
Vertical scroll bar, WD 24, WD 43
  split box on, WD 441
Vertically centering on page, WD 232-234
Vertically displaying text, in cell, WD 276-277
Video clips, WD 45
View Code button (Control Toolbox toolbar),
  WD 612
View menu
  Full Screen command, WD 407-408
  Header and Footer command, WD 102
  Header and Footer command, alternating
    headers, WD 678
  Header and Footer command, page numbers
    in header, WD 81-82
  Header and Footer command, section header,
    WD 247
  Markup command, WD 471, WD 472
  Normal command, WD 77
  Outline command, WD 460
  Ruler command, WD 11, WD 87
  Task Pane command, WD 10
  Task Pane command, Resume Wizard,
    WD 148
  Toolbars command, APP 29
  Zoom command, header, WD 82
  Zoom command, text, WD 21
View Merged Data button (Mail Merge
  toolbar), **WD 343**
Virus, see Computer virus
Visual Basic Editor, WD 592-594, **WD 595,**
  WD 611
Visual Basic for Applications (VBA), **WD 554**
  macro created using, WD 598-604
Voice Command mode, **APP 15**
Voice comments, WD 464

Watermark, **WD 280-282**
Web, see World Wide Web
Web address
  assigning to button, WD 585
  removing hyperlink, WD 174
Web browser, WD 122

Web folder, **APP 24**
Web pages, publishing to Web server, APP 24
Web server, publishing Office pages to, APP 24
White space, hiding, WD 149
Whole page, zooming, WD 232
Widow, **WD 653-654**
Width
  form field, WD 501
  shadow, WD 527
Wildcard, searching for file using, WD 238
Window
  code, WD 593
  document, WD 10-12
  Help buttons in, APP 7
  splitting, WD 441-443
  Word, WD 8-15
Window menu
  Arrange All command, WD 443
  Compare Side by Side command, WD 443
  Split command, WD 442
Windows Clipboard, WD 165
Windows Explorer, accessing template
  through, WD 530-531, WD 705
Wizard, **WD 138**, WD 141
Word 2003, **WD 4**
  Help system, WD 14, **WD 60-62**, APP 1-8
  new features, WD 4
  quitting, WD 54, WD 62
  starting, WD 6-7
Word 2003 Help task pane, **APP 2**
Word Count command (Tools menu), WD 100
Word Count toolbar, WD 100-101
Word document, see Document
Word window
  customizing, WD 8-10
  elements of, WD 10-15
WordArt, **WD 382**
WordArt command (Format menu), WD 386
WordArt drawing object
  formatting, WD 384-386
  inserting, WD 382-384
  shape of, WD 386-387
WordArt Shape button (WordArt toolbar),
  WD 387
WordML, **WD 693**
Words
  antonyms for, WD 119
  deleting, WD 58
  flagged, WD 26, WD 27, WD 119
  hyphenating, WD 652
  rivers between, WD 408
  selecting group of, WD 43-44
  synonyms for, WD 118-119
Wordwrap, WD 22-15
Workgroup templates, **WD 539**
Works cited, **WD 76**
Worksheet, see Excel worksheet
World Wide Web
  clip art on, WD 48, WD 229-232, WD 392
  newsletter on, WD 436-444
  works cited from, WD 108
Wrap text
  in diagram, WD 426-427, WD 431
  in floating graphic, WD 426-427
  Square, WD 431
  in table, WD 273
  Tight, WD 427, WD 431
Wrap-around text, **WD 380**
Wrapping style, for graphic, WD 491,
  WD 563-564, WD 643
Wrist injury, WD 25
Write Anywhere command (Handwriting
  menu), APP 21
Writing Pad, **APP 19-21**

xls file extension, WD 725
XML (eXtensible Markup Language), WD 4,
  WD 693-705
XML file, **WD 693**
XML schema, **WD 693-696**
XSL transformation (XSLT) file, **WD 702**

Zoom box arrow (Standard toolbar), WD 221
Zoom page width, **WD 220-221, WD 301**
Zoom whole page, WD 232
Zoom command (View menu), WD 21, WD 82
Zooming
  document, WD 21
  header, WD 82
  page width, WD 220-221, WD 301, WD 435
  percentage, WD 82, WD 422, WD 426
  text width, WD 169-170
  two pages, WD 434, WD 440

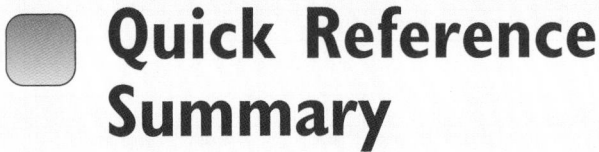

Quick Reference Summary

In Microsoft Office Word 2003, you can accomplish a task in a number of ways. The following table provides a quick reference to each task presented in this textbook. The first column identifies the task. The second column indicates the page number on which the task is discussed in the book. The subsequent four columns list the different ways the task in column one can be carried out. You can invoke the commands listed in the MOUSE, MENU BAR, and SHORTCUT MENU columns using Voice commands.

Microsoft Office Word 2003 Quick Reference Summary

TASK	PAGE NUMBER	MOUSE	MENU BAR	SHORTCUT MENU	KEYBOARD SHORTCUT
1.5 Line Spacing	WD 87	Line Spacing button arrow on Formatting toolbar	Format | Paragraph | Indents and Spacing tab	Paragraph | Indents and Spacing tab	CTRL+5
ActiveX Control, Insert	WD 606	Desired button on Control Toolbox toolbar			
ActiveX Control, Set Properties	WD 608	Properties button on Control Toolbox toolbar		Properties	
ActiveX Control, Write Code	WD 612	View Code button on Control Toolbox toolbar		View Code	
Animate Text	WD 437		Format | Font | Text Effects tab	Font | Text Effects tab	
Arrange All Open Documents	WD 443		Window | Arrange All		
AutoCorrect Entry, Create	WD 91		Tools | AutoCorrect Options | AutoCorrect tab		
AutoCorrect Options	WD 90	AutoCorrect Options button			
AutoShape, Add Text	WD 308			Add Text	
AutoShape, Format	WD 307	Double-click inside AutoShape	Format | AutoShape	Format AutoShape	
AutoShape, Insert	WD 306	AutoShapes button on Drawing toolbar	Insert | Picture | AutoShapes		
AutoSummarize Document	WD 685		Tools | AutoSummarize		
AutoText Entry, Create	WD 179		Insert | AutoText | New		ALT+F3
AutoText Entry, Insert	WD 181		Insert | AutoText		Type entry, then F3
Background Color, Change	WD 438		Format | Background		
Blank Line Above Paragraph	WD 87		Format | Paragraph | Indents and Spacing tab	Paragraph | Indents and Spacing tab	CTRL+0 (zero)
Bold	WD 44	Bold button on Formatting toolbar	Format | Font | Font tab	Font | Font tab	CTRL+B
Bookmark, Add	WD 675		Insert | Bookmark		
Bookmark, Go To	WD 689	Select Browse Object button on vertical scroll bar	Edit | Go To		CTRL+G
Border, Bottom	WD 172	Border button arrow on Formatting toolbar	Format | Borders and Shading | Borders tab		
Border, Page	WD 433		Format | Borders and Shading | Page Border tab	Borders and Shading | Page Border tab	
Bulleted List	WD 187	Bullets button on Formatting toolbar	Format | Bullets and Numbering | Bulleted tab	Bullets and Numbering | Bulleted tab	* and then space followed by text, then ENTER

Microsoft Office Word 2003 Quick Reference Summary *(continued)*

TASK	PAGE NUMBER	MOUSE	MENU BAR	SHORTCUT MENU	KEYBOARD SHORTCUT
Capitalize Letters	WD 87		Format | Font | Font tab	Font | Font tab	CTRL+SHIFT+A
Caption, Add	WD 645		Insert | Reference | Caption		
Caption, Update Caption Number	WD 646			Update Field	F9
Case of Letters	WD 87				SHIFT+F3
Center	WD 38	Center button on Formatting toolbar	Format | Paragraph | Indents and Spacing tab	Paragraph | Indents and Spacing tab	CTRL+E
Center Vertically	WD 233		File | Page Setup | Layout tab		
Character Formatting, Remove	WD 87		Format | Font | Font tab	Font | Font tab	CTRL+SPACEBAR
Character Spacing, Modify	WD 227		Format | Font | Character Spacing tab	Font | Character Spacing tab	
Character Style, Apply	WD 269	Style box arrow on Formatting toolbar	Format | Styles and Formatting		
Character Style, Create	WD 268	Styles and Formatting button on Formatting toolbar	Format | Styles and Formatting		
Chart, Change Chart Type	WD 262		Chart | Chart Type	Right-click chart, Chart Type	
Chart, Move Legend	WD 261		Select legend, Format | Selected Legend | Placement tab	Right-click legend, Format Legend | Placement tab	
Chart, Resize	WD 262	Drag sizing handles			
Chart Table	WD 259		Insert | Picture | Chart		
Clip Art, Insert	WD 46		Insert | Picture | Clip Art		
Clip Art, Insert from Web	WD 230		Insert | Picture | Clip Art		
Clipboard Task Pane, Display	WD 169	Double-click Office Clipboard icon in tray	Edit | Office Clipboard		
Close All Open Documents	WD 362		SHIFT+File | Close All		
Close Document	WD 59	Close button on menu bar	File | Close		CTRL+W
Color Characters	WD 161	Font Color button arrow on Formatting toolbar	Format | Font | Font tab	Font | Font tab	
Column Break, Insert	WD 406		Insert | Break		CTRL+SHIFT+ENTER
Column, Delete	WD 250		Table | Delete | Columns	Delete Columns	
Columns	WD 400	Columns button on Standard toolbar	Format | Columns		
Columns, Balance	WD 420		Insert | Break		
Columns, Format	WD 416		Format | Columns		
Comment, Insert	WD 463	New Comment button on Reviewing toolbar	Insert | Comment		
Compare and Merge Documents	WD 473		Tools | Compare and Merge Documents		
Contrast, Decrease	WD 491	Less Contrast button on Picture toolbar	Format | Picture | Picture tab	Format Picture | Picture tab	
Contrast, Increase	WD 490	More Contrast button on Picture toolbar	Format | Picture | Picture tab	Format Picture | Picture tab	
Copy (Collect Items)	WD 166	Copy button on Standard toolbar	Edit | Copy	Copy	CTRL+C
Count Words	WD 100	Recount button on Word Count toolbar	Tools | Word Count		
Cross-Reference, Create	WD 648		Insert | Reference | Cross-reference		
Custom Dictionary	WD 121		Tools | Options | Spelling and Grammar tab		
Cut Text	WD 245	Cut button on Standard toolbar	Select text, Edit | Cut	Select Text | Cut	Select text, CTRL+X
Data Source, Type New	WD 315	Mail Merge Recipients button on Mail Merge toolbar	Tools | Letters and Mailings | Mail Merge		
Date, Insert	WD 177		Insert | Date and Time		
Default Font Settings, Modify	WD 229		Format | Font	Font	
Delete (Cut) Text	WD 59	Cut button on Standard toolbar	Edit | Cut	Cut	CTRL+X or DELETE

Microsoft Office Word 2003 Quick Reference Summary

TASK	PAGE NUMBER	MOUSE	MENU BAR	SHORTCUT MENU	KEYBOARD SHORTCUT
Demote List Item	WD 189	Decrease Indent button on Formatting toolbar			
Diagram, Add Segments	WD 423	Insert Shape button on Diagram toolbar		Insert Shape	
Diagram, AutoFormat	WD 425	AutoFormat button on Diagram toolbar			
Diagram, Insert	WD 421	Insert Diagram or Organization Chart button on Drawing toolbar	Insert | Diagram		
Digitally Sign a File	WD 618		Tools | Options | Security tab		
Display Two Documents Side by Side	WD 443		Window | Compare Side by Side		
Distribute Columns Evenly	WD 275	Distribute Columns Evenly button on Tables and Borders toolbar	Table | AutoFit | Distribute Columns Evenly		
Distribute Rows Evenly	WD 274	Distribute Rows Evenly button on Tables and Borders toolbar	Table | AutoFit | Distribute Rows Evenly		
Document Map	WD 683	Document Map button on Standard toolbar			
Document Properties, Custom	WD 690		File | Properties | Custom tab		
Document Summary, Modify	WD 193		File | Properties | Summary tab		
Document Window, Open New	WD 160	New Blank document button on Standard toolbar		File | New | Blank document	CTRL+N
Double-Space Text	WD 80	Line Spacing button on Formatting toolbar	Format | Paragraph | Indents and Spacing tab	Paragraph | Indents and Spacing tab	CTRL+2
Double Strikethrough Characters	WD 229		Format | Font | Font tab	Font | Font tab	
Double-Underline	WD 87		Format | Font | Font tab	Font | Font tab	CTRL+SHIFT+D
Drawing Canvas, Format	WD 311	Double-click edge of drawing canvas	Format | Drawing Canvas	Format Drawing Canvas	
Drawing Canvas, Insert	WD 305		Insert | Picture | New Drawing		
Drawing Canvas, Resize	WD 310	Drag sizing handles	Format | Drawing Canvas | Size tab	Format Drawing Canvas | Size tab	
Drawing Grid	WD 395	Draw button on Drawing toolbar			
Drawing Object, 3-D Effect	WD 574	3-D Style button on Drawing toolbar			
Drawing Object, Fill	WD 522	Fill Color button arrow on Drawing toolbar	Format | AutoShape | Colors and Lines tab	Format AutoShape | Colors and Lines tab	
Drawing Object, Line Color	WD 524	Line Color button arrow on Drawing toolbar	Format | AutoShape | Colors and Lines tab	Format AutoShape | Colors and Lines tab	
Drawing Object, Order	WD 521	Draw button on Drawing toolbar, Order	Format | AutoShape | Layout tab	Order	
Drawing Object, Shadow	WD 526	Shadow Style button on Drawing toolbar			
Drop Cap	WD 403		Format | Drop Cap		
Edit Field	WD 322			Edit Field	
E-Mail Document	WD 123	E-mail button on Standard toolbar	File | Send To | Mail Recipient		
E-Mail Document, as Attachment	WD 123		File | Send To | Mail Recipient (as Attachment)		
E-mail Document, for Review	WD 462		File | Send To | Mail Recipient (for Review)		
Emboss, Characters	WD 229		Format | Font | Font tab	Font | Font tab	
Engrave, Characters	WD 229		Format | Font | Font tab	Font | Font tab	
Envelope, Address	WD 190		Tools | Letters and Mailings | Envelopes and Labels | Envelopes tab		
Exceptions, to Editing Restrictions	WD 703		Tools | Protect Document		
Field Code, Display	WD 335		Tools | Options | View tab	Toggle Field Codes	ALT+F9
Field Codes, Print	WD 336		Tools | Options | Print tab		
File Properties, Display	WD 194	Views button arrow in Open dialog box			

Microsoft Office Word 2003 Quick Reference Summary *(continued)*

TASK	PAGE NUMBER	MOUSE	MENU BAR	SHORTCUT MENU	KEYBOARD SHORTCUT
Find	WD 117	Select Browse Object button on vertical scroll bar	Edit | Find		CTRL+F
Find a Format	WD 266	Select Browse Object button on vertical scroll bar	Edit | Find | Format button		CTRL+F
Find and Replace	WD 116	Double-click status bar to left of status indicators	Edit | Replace		CTRL+H
First-Line Indent	WD 88	Drag First Line Indent marker on ruler	Format | Paragraph | Indents and Spacing tab	Paragraph | Indents and Spacing tab	
Folder, Create	WD 313		File | Save As | Create New Folder button		CTRL+F12 | Create New Folder button
Folder, Rename	WD 344			In Open dialog box, right-click folder | Rename	In Open dialog box, select folder, F2
Font	WD 36	Font box arrow on Formatting toolbar	Format | Font | Font tab	Font | Font tab	CTRL+SHIFT+F
Font Size	WD 17	Font Size box arrow on Formatting toolbar	Format | Font | Font tab	Font | Font tab	CTRL+SHIFT+P
Footer	WD 249	Switch Between Header and Footer button on Header and Footer toolbar	View | Header and Footer		
Footnote, Create	WD 94		Insert | Reference | Footnote		
Footnote, Delete	WD 99	Delete note reference mark in document window			
Footnote, Edit	WD 99	Double-click note reference mark in document window	View | Footnotes		
Footnotes to Endnotes, Convert	WD 99		Insert | Reference | Footnote		
Form, Add Help Text	WD 514	Double-click form field		Right-click form field, click Properties	
Form, Change Bookmark	WD 599	Double-click form field		Right-click form field, click Properties	
Form, Check Box Options	WD 508	Double-click check box form field		Right-click form field, click Properties	
Form, Drop-Down Form Field Options	WD 502	Double-click drop-down form field		Right-click form field, click Properties	
Form, Insert Check Box	WD 507	Check Box Form Field button on Forms toolbar			
Form, Insert Drop-Down Form Field	WD 501	Drop-Down Form Field button on Forms toolbar			
Form, Insert Table	WD 495	Insert Table button on Forms toolbar	Table | Insert | Table		
Form, Insert Text Form Field	WD 497	Text Form Field button on Forms toolbar			
Form, Protect	WD 528	Protect Form button on Forms toolbar	Tools | Protect Document		
Form, Remove Field Shading	WD 517	Form Field Shading button on Forms toolbar			
Form, Save Data Only	WD 534		File | Save As | Tools | Save Options		
Form, Text Form Field Options	WD 499	Double-click text form field		Right-click form field, click Properties	
Format Characters, Font Dialog Box	WD 227		Format | Font | Font tab	Font | Font tab	
Format Painter	WD 427	Format Painter button on Standard toolbar			
Formatting, Clear	WD 173	Styles and Formatting button on Formatting toolbar or Style box arrow on Formatting toolbar			CTRL+SPACEBAR; CTRL+Q
Formatting Marks	WD 21	Show/Hide ¶ button on Standard toolbar	Tools | Options | View tab		CTRL+SHIFT+*
Formatting Restrictions	WD 704		Tools | Protect Document		
Frame, New	WD 210	Click desired button on Frames toolbar			

Microsoft Office Word 2003 Quick Reference Summary

TASK	PAGE NUMBER	MOUSE	MENU BAR	SHORTCUT MENU	KEYBOARD SHORTCUT
Frame Properties, Modify	WD 214	Frame Properties button on Frames toolbar	Format | Frames | Frame Properties	Frame Properties	
Frames Page, Create	WD 210		Format | Frames | New Frames Page		
Full Menu	WD 13	Double-click menu name	Click menu name, wait few seconds		
Full Screen View	WD 407		View | Full Screen		
Go To	WD 111, WD 246	Select Browse Object button on vertical scroll bar	Edit | Go To		CTRL+G
Graph, Exit and Return to Word	WD 263	Click anywhere outside chart			
Graphic, Brighten	WD 396	More Brightness button on Picture toolbar	Format | Picture	Format Picture	
Graphic, Crop	WD 565	Crop button on Picture toolbar	Format | Picture | Picture tab		
Graphic, Darken	WD 396	Less Brightness button on Picture toolbar	Format | Picture	Format Picture	
Graphic, Flip	WD 394	Draw button on Drawing toolbar			
Graphic, Format as Floating	WD 393	Text Wrapping button on Picture toolbar	Format | Picture | Layout tab	Format Picture | Layout tab	
Graphic, Rotate	WD 492	Drag graphic's rotate handle	Format | Picture | Size tab	Format Picture | Size tab	
GreetingLine Merge Field, Edit	WD 323			Edit Greeting Line	
Gridlines, Show	WD 497		Table | Show Gridlines		
Gutter Margin	WD 680		File | Page Setup | Margins tab		
Hanging Indent, Create	WD 105	Drag Hanging Indent marker on ruler	Format | Paragraph | Indents and Spacing tab	Paragraph | Indents and Spacing tab	CTRL+T
Hanging Indent, Remove	WD 87	Drag Hanging Indent marker on ruler	Format | Paragraph | Indents and Spacing tab	Paragraph | Indents and Spacing tab	CTRL+SHIFT+T
Header, Different from Previous	WD 247		View | Header and Footer		
Header, Display	WD 81		View | Header and Footer		
Headers, Alternating	WD 678	Page Setup button on Header and Footer toolbar	File | Page Setup | Layout tab		
Help	WD 60 and Appendix A	Microsoft Office Word Help button on Standard toolbar	Help | Microsoft Office Word Help		F1
Hidden Text	WD 360		Format | Font | Font tab	Font | Font tab	
Hidden Text, Hide/Show	WD 361	Show/Hide ¶ button on Standard toolbar			CTRL+SHIFT+*
Highlight Text	WD 213, WD 436	Highlight button on Formatting toolbar			
HTML Source	WD 206		View | HTML Source		
Hyperlink, Convert to Regular Text	WD 174	AutoCorrect Options button | Undo Hyperlink		Remove Hyperlink	CTRL+Z
Hyperlink, Create	WD 108, WD 212	Insert Hyperlink button on Standard toolbar		Hyperlink	Web address then ENTER or SPACEBAR
Hyperlink, Edit	WD 207	Insert Hyperlink button on Standard toolbar		Hyperlink	CTRL+K
Hyphenate Document	WD 652		Tools | Language | Hyphenation		
IF Field, Insert	WD 327	Insert Word Field button on Mail Merge toolbar	Insert | Field		
Indent, Decrease	WD 87	Decrease Indent button on Formatting toolbar	Format | Paragraph | Indents and Spacing tab	Paragraph | Indents and Spacing tab	CTRL+SHIFT+M
Indent, Increase	WD 87	Increase Indent button on Formatting toolbar	Format | Paragraph | Indents and Spacing tab	Paragraph | Indents and Spacing tab	CTRL+M
Index, Build	WD 673		Insert | Reference | Index and Tables | Index tab		
Index Entry, Mark	WD 650		Insert | Reference | Index and Tables | Index tab		ALT+SHIFT+X
Index, Update	WD 684			Right-click selected index, click Update Field	Select index, F9

Microsoft Office Word 2003 Quick Reference Summary *(continued)*

TASK	PAGE NUMBER	MOUSE	MENU BAR	SHORTCUT MENU	KEYBOARD SHORTCUT
Insert File	WD 238		Insert | File		
Italicize	WD 41	Italic button on Formatting toolbar	Format | Font | Font tab	Font | Font tab	CTRL+I
Justify Paragraph	WD 401	Justify button on Formatting toolbar	Format | Paragraph | Indents and Spacing tab	Paragraph | Indents and Spacing tab	CTRL+J
Language Bar, Close	WD 16			Right-click Language bar, click Close the Language bar	
Last Editing Location	WD 239				SHIFT+F5
Leader Characters	WD 164		Format | Tabs		
Left-Align	WD 86	Align Left button on Formatting toolbar	Format | Paragraph | Indents and Spacing tab	Paragraph | Indents and Spacing tab	CTRL+L
Line Break, Enter	WD 154				SHIFT+ENTER
Link Copied Excel Data to Word Chart	WD 727		Edit | Paste Link		
Link Copied Item	WD 418		Edit | Paste Special		
Link Excel Worksheet	WD 722		Insert | Object | Create from File tab		
List Item, Demote	WD 331	Increase Indent button on Formatting toolbar			SHIFT+TAB
List Item, Promote	WD 331	Decrease Indent button on Formatting toolbar			TAB
Macro, Copy	WD 604	In Visual Basic Editor, Copy button on Standard toolbar, then Paste button on Standard toolbar	Tools | Macro | Macros	In Visual Basic Editor, Copy then Paste	In Visual Basic Editor, CTRL+C then CTRL+V
Macro, Delete	WD 605		Tools | Macro | Macros		
Macro, Record	WD 577	Double-click REC status indicator on status bar	Tools | Macro | Record New Macro		
Macro, Rename	WD 605		Tools | Macro | Macros		
Macro, Run	WD 581	Run Macro button on Standard toolbar in Visual Basic Editor	Tools | Macro | Macros		ALT+F8
Macro, Run on Exit	WD 604	Double-click form field		Right-click form field, click Properties	
Macro, View VBA Code	WD 592		Tools | Macro | Macros		ALT+F11
Mail Merge Fields, Insert	WD 325	Insert Merge Fields button on Mail Merge toolbar			
Mail Merge to New Document Window	WD 356	Merge to New Document button on Mail Merge toolbar			
Mail Merge, Directory	WD 353	Main document setup button on Mail Merge toolbar	Tools | Letters and Mailings | Mail Merge		
Mail Merge, Envelopes	WD 351	Main document setup button on Mail Merge toolbar	Tools | Letters and Mailings | Mail Merges		
Mail Merge, Mailing Labels	WD 345	Main document setup button on Mail Merge toolbar	Tools | Letters and Mailings | Mail Merge		
Mail Merge, Select Records	WD 339	Mail Merge Recipients button on Mail Merge toolbar			
Mail Merge, Sort Data Records	WD 342	Mail Merge Recipients button on Mail Merge toolbar			
Mail Merge to Printer	WD 338	Merge to Printer button on Mail Merge toolbar			
Mail Merged Data, View	WD 343	View Merged Data button on Mail Merge toolbar			
Mailing Label, Address	WD 191		Tools | Letters and Mailings | Envelopes and Labels | Labels tab		
Margins	WD 78	In print layout view, drag margin boundary on ruler	File | Page Setup | Margins tab		
Master Document, Open	WD 682	Open button on Standard toolbar, then Expand Subdocuments button on Outlining toolbar			
Menu, Add/Delete Commands	WD 586		Tools | Customize	Customize	
Menus and Toolbars, Reset	Appendix D	Toolbar Options button on toolbar | Add or Remove Buttons | Customize | Options tab	View | Toolbars | Customize | Options tab		

Microsoft Office Word 2003 Quick Reference Summary

TASK	PAGE NUMBER	MOUSE	MENU BAR	SHORTCUT MENU	KEYBOARD SHORTCUT
Move Selected Text	WD 113	Drag and drop	Edit | Cut; Edit | Paste	Cut; Paste	CTRL+X; CTRL+V
Nonbreaking Hyphen	WD 180		Insert | Symbol | Special Characters tab		CTRL+SHIFT+HYPHEN
Nonbreaking Space	WD 180		Insert | Symbol | Special Characters tab		CTRL+SHIFT+SPACEBAR
Note Pane, Close	WD 99	Close button in note pane			
Numbered List	WD 189	Numbering button on Formatting toolbar	Format | Bullets and Numbering | Numbered tab	Bullets and Numbering | Numbered tab	1. and then space followed by text, then ENTER
Open Document	WD 55	Open button on Standard toolbar	File | Open		CTRL+O
Outline, Create	WD 459	Outline View button on horizontal scroll bar	View | Outline		
Outline, Demote Heading	WD 666	Demote button on Outlining toolbar			TAB
Outline, Promote Heading	WD 666	Promote button on Outlining toolbar			SHIFT+TAB
Outline, Show First Line of Paragraphs	WD 662	Show First Line Only button on Outlining toolbar			
Outline Numbered List	WD 329		Format | Bullets and Numbering | Outline Numbered tab	Bullets and Numbering | Outline Numbered tab	
Outline, on Characters	WD 229		Format | Font | Font tab	Font | Font tab	
Page Alignment	WD 237		File | Page Setup | Layout tab		
Page Break	WD 103		Insert | Break		CTRL+ENTER
Page Break, Delete	WD 244	Cut button on Standard toolbar	Select page break, Edit | Cut	Select page break, Cut	Select page break, DELETE
Page Numbers, Insert	WD 83	Insert Page Number button on Header and Footer toolbar	Insert | Page Numbers		
Page Numbers, Modify	WD 248	Format Page Number button on Header and Footer toolbar	Insert | Page Numbers | Format button		
Page Orientation	WD 356		File | Page Setup | Margins tab		
Paragraph, Change Format	WD 312	Click link in Reveal Formatting task pane	Format | Paragraph | Indents and Spacing tab	Paragraph | Indents and Spacing tab	
Paragraph Formatting, Remove	WD 87		Format | Paragraph | Indents and Spacing tab	Paragraph | Indents and Spacing tab	CTRL+Q
Paragraph Style, Apply	WD 332	Style box arrow on Formatting toolbar	Format | Styles and Formatting		
Password-Protect File	WD 691		File | Save As | Tools | Security Options		
Paste	WD 170	Paste button on Standard toolbar or click icon in Office Clipboard gallery in Office Clipboard task pane	Edit | Paste	Paste	CTRL+V
Paste Options, Display Menu	WD 115	Paste Options button			
Pattern Fill Effect	WD 439		Format | Background | Fill Effects button		
Picture Bullets	WD 270		Format | Bullets and Numbering | Bulleted tab	Bullets and Numbering | Bulleted tab	
Print Document	WD 53	Print button on Standard toolbar	File | Print		CTRL+P
Print Preview	WD 158	Print Preview button on Standard toolbar	File | Print Preview		CTRL+F2
Print Specific Pages	WD 241		File | Print		CTRL+P
Promote List Item	WD 189	Increase Indent button on Formatting toolbar			
Propagate Labels	WD 350	Propagate Labels button on Mail Merge toolbar	Tools | Letters and Mailings | Mail Merge		
Quit Word	WD 54	Close button on title bar	File | Exit		ALT+F4
Readability Statistics, Turn On	WD 687		Tools | Options | Spelling & Grammar tab		
Reading Layout	WD 443	Read button on Standard toolbar	View | Reading Layout		ALT+R
Rectangle, Draw	WD 518	Rectangle button on Drawing toolbar			
Redo Action	WD 39	Redo button on Standard toolbar	Edit | Redo		

Microsoft Office Word 2003 Quick Reference Summary *(continued)*

TASK	PAGE NUMBER	MOUSE	MENU BAR	SHORTCUT MENU	KEYBOARD SHORTCUT
Research Task Pane, Display and Use	WD 124	ALT+click word in document	Tools | Research		
Research Task Pane, Insert text from	WD 125			Right-click selected text in task pane, click Copy; right-click location to paste in document, click Paste	Select text in task pane, CTRL+C; click location to paste in document, CTRL+V
Repeat Command	WD 39		Edit | Repeat		
Resize Graphic	WD 50	Drag sizing handle	Format | Picture | Size tab	Format Picture | Size tab	
Resize Graphic, Format Picture Dialog Box	WD 231	Double-click graphic	Format | Picture | Size tab	Format Picture | Size tab	
Restore Graphic	WD 51	Format Picture button on Picture toolbar	Format | Picture | Size tab	Format Picture | Size tab	
Resume Wizard	WD 142		File | New | General Templates | Other Documents tab		
Reveal Formatting	WD 283		Format | Reveal Formatting		SHIFT+F1
Reviewer Ink Colors, Change	WD 472		Tools | Options | Track Changes tab		
Right-Align	WD 37	Align Right button on Formatting toolbar	Format | Paragraph | Indents and Spacing tab	Paragraph | Indents and Spacing tab	CTRL+R
Ruler, Show or Hide	WD 11		View | Ruler		
Save, All Open Documents	WD 363		SHIFT + File | Save All		
Save as Web Page	WD 205		File | Save as Web Page		
Save Document - Different File Format	WD 206		File | Save As		
Save Document - New Name	WD 52		File | Save As		F12
Save Document - Same Name	WD 52	Save button on Standard toolbar	File | Save		CTRL+S
Save Document as XML File	WD 699		File | Save As		F12
Save New Document	WD 28	Save button on Standard toolbar	File | Save		CTRL+S
Schema, Delete	WD 696		Tools | Templates and Add-Ins | XML Schema tab		
Schema File, Attach	WD 694	Templates and Add-Ins in XML Structure task pane	Tools | Templates and Add-Ins | XML Schema tab		
Section Break, Continuous	WD 399		Insert | Break		
Section Break, Next Page	WD 236		Insert | Break		
Security Level	WD 560		Tools | Macro | Security | Security Level tab		
Select Document	WD 113	Point to left and triple-click	Edit | Select All		CTRL+A
Select Graphic	WD 49	Click graphic			
Select Group of Words	WD 43	Drag through words			CTRL+SHIFT+RIGHT ARROW
Select Line	WD 40	Point to left of line and click			SHIFT+DOWN ARROW
Select Multiple Paragraphs	WD 33	Point to left of first paragraph and drag down			CTRL+SHIFT+DOWN ARROW
Select Nonadjacent Text	WD 257				CTRL, while selecting additional text
Select Paragraph	WD 113	Triple-click paragraph			
Select Sentence	WD 112	CTRL+click sentence			CTRL+SHIFT+RIGHT ARROW
Select Word	WD 58	Double-click word			CTRL+SHIFT+RIGHT ARROW
Send Outline to PowerPoint	WD 476		File | Send To | Microsoft Office PowerPoint		

Microsoft Office Word 2003 Quick Reference Summary

TASK	PAGE NUMBER	MOUSE	MENU BAR	SHORTCUT MENU	KEYBOARD SHORTCUT
Shade Paragraph	WD 224, WD 413	Shading Color button on Tables and Borders toolbar	Format | Borders and Shading | Shading tab	Borders and Shading | Shading tab	
Shadow, on Characters	WD 229		Format | Font | Font tab	Font | Font tab	
Single-Space Text	WD 275	Line Spacing button arrow on Formatting toolbar	Format | Paragraph | Indents and Spacing tab	Paragraph | Indents and Spacing tab	CTRL+1
Small Uppercase Letters	WD 87		Format | Font | Font tab	Font | Font tab	CTRL+SHIFT+K
Smart Tag Actions, Display Menu	WD 192	Point to smart tag indicator, click Smart Tag Actions button			
Sort Paragraphs	WD 109		Table | Sort		
Spelling and Grammar Check At Once	WD 119	Spelling and Grammar button on Standard toolbar	Tools | Spelling and Grammar	Spelling	F7
Spelling Check as You Type	WD 26	Double-click Spelling and Grammar Status icon on status bar		Right-click flagged word, click correct word on shortcut menu	
Split Window	WD 441	Split box on vertical scroll bar	Window | Split		
Strikethrough, characters	WD 229		Format | Font | Font tab	Font | Font tab	
Style, Create	WD 568	Styles and Formatting button on Formatting toolbar	Format | Styles and Formatting		
Style, Modify	WD 96	Styles and Formatting button on Formatting toolbar	Format | Styles and Formatting		
Styles and Formatting Task Pane, Display	WD 152	Styles and Formatting button on Formatting toolbar	View | Task Pane		
Subdocument, Break Connection	WD 667	Remove Subdocument button on Outlining toolbar			
Subdocument, Create	WD 664	Create Subdocument button on Outlining toolbar			
Subdocument, Delete	WD 667	Click subdocument icon, press DELETE			
Subdocument, Insert	WD 661	Insert Subdocument button on Outlining toolbar			
Subdocuments, Collapse	WD 663	Collapse Subdocuments button on Outlining toolbar			
Subdocuments, Expand	WD 663	Expand Subdocuments button on Outlining toolbar			
Subscript	WD 87		Format | Font | Font tab	Font | Font tab	CTRL+=
Superscript	WD 87		Format | Font | Font tab	Font | Font tab	CTRL+SHIFT+PLUS SIGN
Switch to Open Document	WD 166	Program button on taskbar	Window | document name		ALT+TAB
Symbol, Insert	WD 390		Insert | Symbol		ALT+0 (zero) then ANSI code on numeric keypad
Synonym	WD 118		Tools | Language | Thesaurus	Synonyms | desired word	SHIFT+F7
Tab Stops, Set	WD 164	Click location on ruler	Format | Tabs		
Table, Align Cell Contents	WD 279	Align button arrow on Tables and Borders toolbar	Table | Table Properties | Cell tab	Table Properties | Cell tab	
Table, AutoFormat	WD 187, WD 255	Table AutoFormat button on Tables and Borders toolbar	Table | Table AutoFormat		
Table, Convert Text	WD 355		Table | Convert | Text to Table		
Table, Draw	WD 272	Draw Table button on Tables and Borders toolbar	Table | Draw Table		
Table, Erase Lines	WD 274	Eraser button on Tables and Borders toolbar			
Table, Fit Columns to Table Contents	WD 185	Double-click column boundary	Table | AutoFit | AutoFit to Contents	AutoFit | AutoFit to Contents	
Table, Insert Empty	WD 183	Insert Table button on Standard toolbar	Table | Insert | Table		
Table, Insert Row	WD 184		Table | Insert | Rows Above/Below	Right-click selected row; Insert Rows	TAB from lower-right cell
Table, Merge cells	WD 251	Merge Cells button on Tables and Borders toolbar	Select cells, Table | Merge Cells	Right-click selected cells, Merge Cells	

Microsoft Office Word 2003 Quick Reference Summary (continued)

TASK	PAGE NUMBER	MOUSE	MENU BAR	SHORTCUT MENU	KEYBOARD SHORTCUT
Table, Modify Properties	WD 258		Table | Table Properties	Table Properties	
Table, Resize Column	WD 186, WD 251	Drag column boundary	Table | Table Properties | Column tab	Table Properties | Column tab	
Table, Right-Align Cell Contents	WD 256	Align Right button on Formatting toolbar	Format | Paragraph | Indents and Spacing tab		CTRL+R
Table, Rotate Cell Text	WD 276	Change Text Direction button on Tables and Borders toolbar	Format | Text Direction	Text Direction	
Table, Row Height	WD 278	Drag row border	Table | Table Properties | Row tab	Table Properties | Row tab	
Table, Select	WD 186	Click table move handle	Table | Select | Table		ALT+5 (on numeric keypad)
Table, Select Cell	WD 186	Click left edge of cell			Press TAB
Table, Select Column	WD 186	Click top border of column			
Table, Select Multiple Cells	WD 186	Drag through cells			
Table, Select Row	WD 186	Click to left of row			
Table, Shade Cells	WD 277	Shading Color button arrow on Tables and Borders toolbar	Format | Borders and Shading | Shading tab	Borders and Shading | Shading tab	
Table, Sort	WD 359	Sort Ascending button on Tables and Borders toolbar	Table | Sort		
Table, Split Cells	WD 253	Split Cells button on Tables and Borders toolbar	Select cells, Table | Split Cells	Right-click selected cells, Split Cells	
Table, Sum a Column	WD 254	AutoSum button on Tables and Borders toolbar	Table | Formula		
Table of Contents, Create	WD 674		Insert | Reference | Index and Tables | Table of Contents tab		
Table of Contents, Update	WD 685	Update TOC button on Outlining toolbar		Right-click selected table of contents, click Update Field	Select table of contents, F9
Table of Figures, Create	WD 671		Insert | Reference | Index and Tables | Table of Figures tab		
Task Pane, Close	WD 10	Close button on task pane	View | Task Pane		
Task Pane, Display Different	WD 10	Other Task Panes button on task pane			
Template, Create	WD 487		File | New | On my computer		
Template, Open	WD 175		File | New | On my computer		
Template, Use	WD 302		File | New | On my computer		
Text Box, Convert to a Frame	WD 647	Double-click text box	Format | Text Box	Format Text Box	
Text Box, Format	WD 412	Double-click text box	Format | Text Box	Format Text Box	
Text Box, Insert	WD 411	Text Box button on Drawing toolbar	Insert | Text Box		
Theme, Apply	WD 208		Format | Theme		
Toolbar, Add Button	WD 582		Tools | Customize	Customize	
Toolbar, Delete Button	WD 586		Tools | Customize	Customize	
Toolbar, Dock	WD 82	Double-click toolbar title bar			
Toolbar, Float	WD 82	Drag toolbar move handle			
Toolbar, Show Entire	WD 14	Double-click move handle on toolbar	Tools | Customize | Options tab		
Track Changes	WD 467	Double-click TRK indicator on status bar	Tools | Track Changes		CTRL+SHIFT+E
Tracked Changes, Review	WD 469	Show button or Next button on Reviewing toolbar			
Underline	WD 42	Underline button on Formatting toolbar	Format | Font | Font tab	Font | Font tab	CTRL+U
Underline, in color	WD 511		Format | Font	Font	
Underline Words, not Spaces	WD 87		Format | Font | Font tab	Font | Font tab	CTRL+SHIFT+W
Undo Command or Action	WD 39	Undo button on Standard toolbar	Edit | Undo		CTRL+Z

Microsoft Office Word 2003 Quick Reference Summary

TASK	PAGE NUMBER	MOUSE	MENU BAR	SHORTCUT MENU	KEYBOARD SHORTCUT
Unprotect Document	WD 558	Protect Form button on Forms toolbar	Tools | Unprotect Document		
User Information, Change	WD 194		Tools | Options | User Information tab		
Version, Delete	WD 640		File | Versions		
Version, Save	WD 638		File | Versions		
Version, View	WD 639		File | Versions		
Vertical Rule	WD 409		Format | Borders and Shading | Borders tab		
Visual Basic Editor, Insert Procedure	WD 604	Insert UserForm button arrow on Standard toolbar	Insert | Procedure		
Visual Basic Editor, Quit	WD 598	Close button on title bar	File | Close and Return to Microsoft Word		ALT+Q
Watermark	WD 281		Format | Background | Printed Watermark		
Web Page Frame, Resize	WD 211	Drag frame border	Format | Frames | Frame Properties | Frame tab		
Web Page, Preview	WD 209		File | Web Page Preview		
White Space, Hide or Show	WD 149	Hide or Show White Space button	Tools | Options | View tab		
Widow/Orphan Setting	WD 654		Format | Paragraph	Paragraph	
WordArt Drawing Object, Format	WD 384	Format WordArt button on WordArt toolbar	Format | WordArt	Format WordArt	
WordArt Drawing Object, Insert	WD 383	Insert WordArt button on Drawing toolbar	Insert | Picture | WordArt		
WordArt Drawing Object, Shape	WD 387	WordArt Shape button on WordArt toolbar			
Workgroup Template, Modify	WD 539		Tools | Options | File Locations tab		
Wrap Text Around Graphic	WD 394, WD 427	Text Wrapping button Picture or Diagram toolbar	Format | Picture or Diagram | Layout tab	Format Picture or Format Diagram | Layout tab	
XML Element, Add	WD 697		Click element in XML Structure task pane		
XML Element, Modify Attribute	WD 700			Right-click element in XML Structure task pane	
XML Element, Set Options	WD 702	XML Options link in XML Structure task pane			
XML Transforms	WD 703	Apply Transform check box in Save As dialog box			
Zoom	WD 21	Zoom box arrow on Formatting toolbar	View | Zoom		
Zoom Text Width	WD 169	Zoom box arrow on Formatting toolbar	View | Zoom		
Zoom Two Pages	WD 435	Zoom box arrow on Formatting toolbar	View | Zoom		

SHELLY CASHMAN SERIES®

A few of the exercises in this book require that you begin
by opening a data file from a Data Disk. Choose one
of the following to obtain a copy of the Data Disk.

Instructors

☞ A copy of the Data Disk is on the Instructor Resources CD-ROM below the category Data Files for Students, which you can copy to your school's network for student use.

☞ Download the Data Disk via the World Wide Web by following the instructions below.

☞ Contact us via e-mail at reply@course.com.

☞ Call Thomson Course Technology's Customer Service department for fast and efficient delivery of the Data Disk.

Students

☞ Check with your instructor to determine the best way to obtain a copy of the Data Disk.

☞ Download the Data Disk via the World Wide Web by following the instructions below.

Instructions for Downloading the Data Disk from the World Wide Web

1 Insert your removable media (USB flash drive, floppy disk, or Zip disk) into your computer.
2 Start your browser. Enter the URL scsite.com in the Address box.
3 When the scsite.com Web page displays, scroll down to the Browse by Subject area and click the category to which your book belongs (for example, Office Suites).
4 When the category list expands, click the title of your textbook (for example, Microsoft Office 2003: Introductory Concepts and Techniques).
5 When the Textbook page displays, scroll down to the Data Files for Students area and click the appropriate link.
6 If Windows displays a File Download - Security Warning dialog box, click the Run button. If Windows displays an Internet Explorer - Security Warning dialog box, click the Run button.
7 When Windows displays the WinZip Self-Extractor dialog box, type in the Unzip to folder box the portable storage media drive letter followed a colon, backslash, and a sub-folder name of your choice (for example, f:/Office 2003).
8 Click the Unzip button.
9 When Windows displays the WinZip Self-Extractor dialog box, click the OK button.
10 Click the Close button on the right side of the title bar in the WinZip Self-Extractor dialog box.
11 Start Windows Explorer and display the contents of the folder to which you unzipped the Data Disk files in Step 7 to view the results.

Keep Your Skills Fresh with Quick Reference CourseCards!

Thomson Course Technology CourseCards allow you to easily learn the basics of new applications or quickly access tips and tricks long after your class is complete.

Each highly visual, four-color, six-sided CourseCard features:

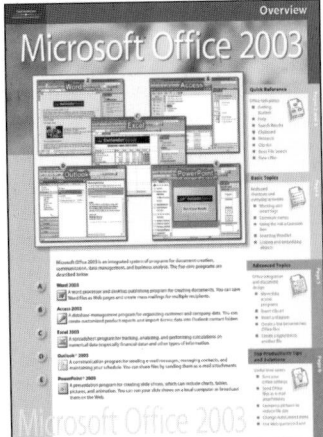

- **Basic Topics** enable users to effectively utilize key content.

- **Tips and Solutions** reinforce key subject matter and provide solutions to common situations.

- **Menu Quick References** help users navigate through the most important menu tools using a simple table of contents model.

- **Keyboard Shortcuts** improve productivity and save time.

- **Screen Shots** effectively show what users see on their monitors.

- **Advanced Topics** provide advanced users with a clear reference guide to more challenging content.

Over 75 CourseCards are available on a variety of topics! To order, please visit *www.courseilt.com/ilt_cards.cfm*